TEACHER'S EDITION

Hidden Treasures

VOLUME TWO

Signatures

Senior Authors

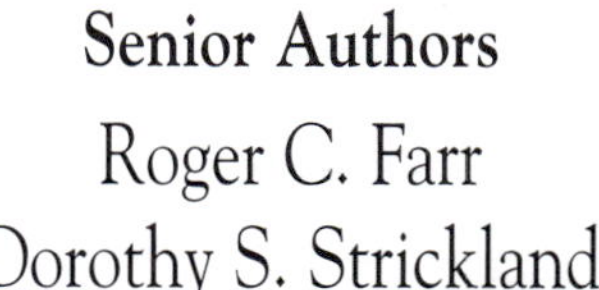

Roger C. Farr
Dorothy S. Strickland

Authors

Richard F. Abrahamson
Alma Flor Ada
Barbara Bowen Coulter
Bernice E. Cullinan
Margaret A. Gallego
W. Dorsey Hammond
Nancy Roser
Junko Yokota
Hallie Kay Yopp

Senior Consultant

Asa G. Hilliard III

Consultants

Lee Bennett Hopkins
David A. Monti
Rosalia Salinas

HARCOURT BRACE & COMPANY

Orlando Atlanta Austin Boston San Francisco
Chicago Dallas New York Toronto London

Acknowledgments appear in the back of this book.

Printed in the United States of America

ISBN 0-15-310128-8

1 2 3 4 5 6 7 8 9 10   059   00 99 98 97

Meet Our Authors!

SENIOR AUTHORS

Dr. Roger C. Farr

Chancellors' Professor of Education and Director of the Center for Reading and Language Studies, Indiana University, Bloomington

RESEARCH CONTRIBUTIONS: Assessment, Portfolios, Reading-Writing Strategies, Staff Development

Dr. Dorothy S. Strickland

The State of New Jersey Professor of Reading, Rutgers University

RESEARCH CONTRIBUTIONS: Emergent Literacy, Linguistic and Cultural Diversity, Intervention, Phonics in Literature-based Curriculum, Integrated Language Arts

AUTHORS

Dr. Richard F. Abrahamson

Professor of Literature for Children and Young Adults, University of Houston

RESEARCH CONTRIBUTIONS: Children's Literature, Strategic Reading, Reading Nonfiction

Dr. Alma Flor Ada

Director of Doctoral Studies in the International Multicultural Program, University of San Francisco

RESEARCH CONTRIBUTIONS: Bilingual Education, ESL, Family Involvement

Dr. Barbara Bowen Coulter

Director, Communication Arts, Detroit Public Schools

RESEARCH CONTRIBUTIONS: Multicultural Education, Spelling and Vocabulary, Staff Development

Dr. Bernice E. Cullinan

Professor of Reading, New York University

RESEARCH CONTRIBUTIONS: Children's Literature, Emergent Literacy, Intervention, Integrated Language Arts

Dr. Margaret A. Gallego

Visiting Researcher at Laboratory of Comparative Human Cognition, University of California, San Diego

RESEARCH CONTRIBUTIONS: ESL, Bilingual Education, Second Language Support, Culturally Relevant Curriculum

Dr. W. Dorsey Hammond

Professor of Education, Oakland University of Rochester, Michigan

RESEARCH CONTRIBUTIONS: Reading Comprehension, Reader Response, Staff Development, Critical Thinking, Classroom Management

Dr. Nancy Roser

Professor, Language and Literacy Studies, University of Texas, Austin

RESEARCH CONTRIBUTIONS: Beginning Reading, Book Discussions, Early Childhood, Emergent Literacy, Phonics in Literature-based Curriculum, Reading Comprehension

Dr. Junko Yokota

Associate Professor, Reading/Language Arts Department, National-Louis University, Evanston, Illinois

RESEARCH CONTRIBUTIONS: Multicultural Literature, Children's Literature

Dr. Hallie Kay Yopp

Professor, Department of Elementary Bilingual and Reading Education, California State University, Fullerton

RESEARCH CONTRIBUTIONS: Phonemic Awareness, Early Childhood

CONSULTANTS

Dr. David A. Monti

Professor, Reading and Language Arts Department, Central Connecticut State University, New Britain, Connecticut

RESEARCH CONTRIBUTIONS: During-learning Strategies, Flexible Grouping

Dr. Asa G. Hilliard III

Fuller E. Callaway Professor of Urban Education, Department of Educational Foundations, Georgia State University, Atlanta

RESEARCH CONTRIBUTIONS: Multicultural Education

Dr. Lee Bennett Hopkins

Poet, Author, Anthologist

RESEARCH CONTRIBUTIONS: Poetry, Children's Literature

Dr. Rosalia Salinas

Director of Bilingual Education, San Diego County Office of Education and Director of California Literature Project, Spanish

RESEARCH CONTRIBUTIONS: ESL, Bilingual Education

Dear Educator,

Signatures is a fully integrated reading and language arts program that will leave a lasting mark on your students' literacy—and also on their lives. The program is based on principles of effective reading and language arts instruction that emerge consistently from both research and practical experience:

High-quality trade-book literature should be accessible to *every* child in the classroom. The core of *Signatures* is its collection of high-quality, authentic children's literature, created by award-winning authors and illustrators and selected to represent not only a variety of genres and styles but also the pluralistic nature of our society. Meaningful thematic units encourage students to relate the selections to each other, to readings in other content areas, and to their own life experiences.

Skills and strategies are essential for success in school and in the real world. *Signatures* literature serves as the springboard for instruction in skills and strategies that will help students develop into fluent, lifelong readers and articulate, effective communicators. Cross-curricular content supports comprehensive development of reading, writing, listening, speaking and thinking skills presented in an easy-to-use yet flexible format.

Intervention strategies can help teachers meet the needs of *all* learners. The variety of materials and strategies available in *Signatures* will help teachers customize their teaching practices to meet the needs of all students in the broadest possible range of classroom environments.

Flexible grouping and classroom management are more important than ever in today's classrooms. *Signatures* is designed with abundant teacher-support for meeting the challenges of classroom management in the context of theme-based instruction.

Signatures will help you provide your students with the tools and strategies they need to make their imprint on the world around them.

Sincerely,
The *Signatures* Authors

Contents

Contents
Where the Red Fern Grows
by Wilson Rawls
Last Summer with Maizon
by Jacqueline Woodson
Art and Literature:
The Biglin Brothers Racing
by Thomas Eakins
Theme
Meeting
Challenges
The Challenge
by Gary Soto
The Inner Tube
by Gary Soto
Island of the Blue Dolphins
by Scott O'Dell
A Song of Greatness
transcribed by Mary Austin

Theme 2: Ancient Civilizations T217

Theme 3: Celebrating Differences T409

Theme 4: Turning Points T649

Reflecting on the Literature

INVITE STUDENTS TO THINK ABOUT WHAT THEY HAVE READ. Ask students to look at the Contents for Themes 1–3 on pages 4–9. Use questions such as the following to help them reflect on what they have read so far in *Hidden Treasures.*

- Which selection is your favorite so far? Why?
- Which author is your favorite so far? What makes his or her writing special to you?
- Which was your favorite *Signatures Library* or other Bookshelf book?

HELP STUDENTS PREVIEW THE REST OF THE BOOK. Ask students to preview the Contents for Themes 4–6 (pages 10–15). Have them examine the illustrations and read the theme and selection titles. Encourage them to use this information to make predictions about the remaining literature in the Student Anthology. Remind students that the Glossary and the Index of Titles and Authors can be found at the back of the book, and ask volunteers to tell how they can use each resource.

Thinking About Classroom Management

CONSIDER MANAGEMENT OPTIONS. At this point, you may find it useful to ask yourself the following questions. Use the answers as you think about classroom management options for the last three themes of *Hidden Treasures.*

- What kind of selections and which authors did my students find most enjoyable? How can I use this information to further "hook" my students on reading? (The numerous trade book suggestions in the lesson plans and Bookshelf in the Student Anthology will help you gather a list of titles that will appeal to your students.)
- What kinds of activities worked well with my students? How can I use this information to help me plan classroom management for the rest of the year? (Flexible Grouping charts, Tips for Classroom Management, and Intervention Strategies offer a variety of alternatives from which to choose.)

323

SIGNATURES

Senior Authors
Roger C. Farr
Dorothy S. Strickland

Authors
Richard F. Abrahamson • Alma Flor Ada • Barbara Bowen Coulter
Bernice E. Cullinan • Margaret A. Gallego
W. Dorsey Hammond
Nancy Roser • Junko Yokota • Hallie Kay Yopp

Senior Consultant
Asa G. Hilliard III

Consultants
Lee Bennett Hopkins • Stephen Krashen • David A. Monti • Rosalia Salinas

Harcourt Brace & Company
Orlando Atlanta Austin Boston San Francisco Chicago Dallas New York Toronto London

Requests for permission to make copies of any part of the work should be mailed to the following address: School Permissions, Harcourt Brace & Company, 6277 Sea Harbor Drive, Orlando, Florida 32887-6777

HARCOURT BRACE and Quill Design is a registered trademark of Harcourt Brace & Company.

Acknowledgments appear in the back of this book.

Printed in the United States of America

ISBN 0-15-310112-1

1 2 3 4 5 6 7 8 9 10 048 2000 99 98

SIGNATURES

Dear Reader,

When you open **Hidden Treasures**, you open doors to discovery. Behind one door you'll find the hidden treasures of ancient Egypt. Behind others you'll see how one ancient Roman city was built and how another was destroyed by the terrible force of a volcano.

During the year, you will learn how people lived in ancient Greece and how Arctic wolves survive at the top of the world. You will also come to understand how people find hidden strengths within themselves. You will read of Tuan Nguyen, a Vietnamese boy, who must learn to adapt to life in America and of Joan Benoit Samuelson, a long-distance runner who struggles to keep her Olympic dream alive.

So join us now in search of excitement, adventure, and hidden treasures.

Sincerely,

The Authors

The Authors

4

Contents

Meeting Challenges

5

Ancient Civilizations

CONTENTS

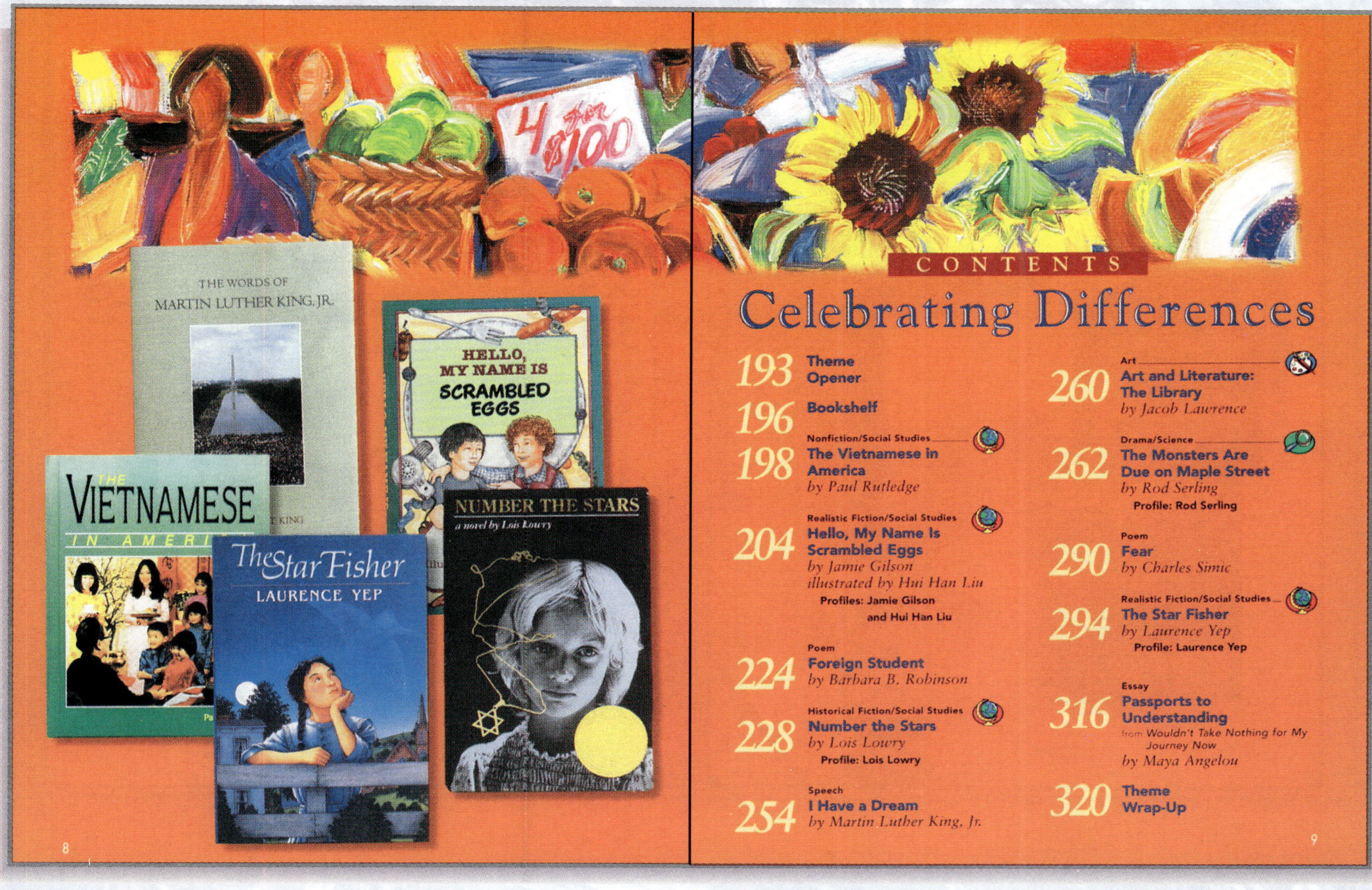

CONTENTS

Celebrating Differences

9

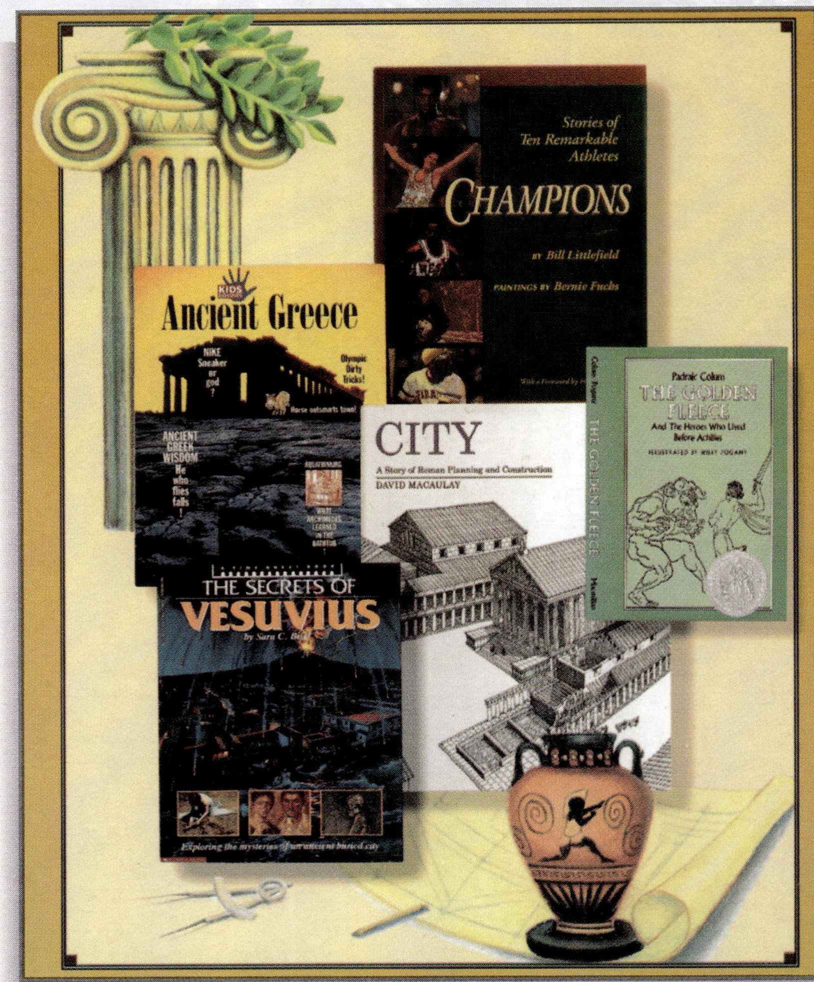

TURNING POINTS

CONTENTS

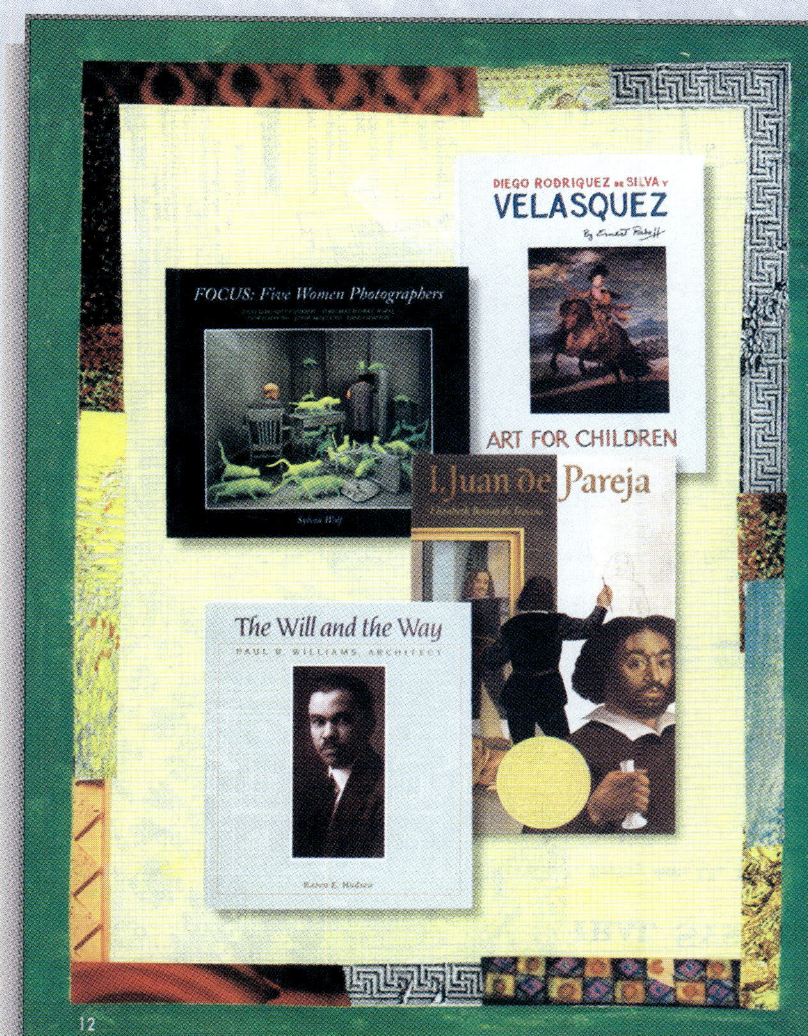

MASTERPIECES

CONTENTS

13

GARY PAULSEN
THE RIVER
JIM BRANDENBURG
To the Top of the World
ADVENTURES WITH ARCTIC WOLVES
JULIE OF THE WOLVES
by Jean Craighead George
CONFRONTING
NATURE
CONTENTS

14
15

Theme 4

Turning Points

CHANGES

Nowhere can change be shown more dramatically than in the turning points of people's lives, both ancient and modern.

Theme Overview

Turning Points

Changes

The selections in this theme will help students understand how and why change occurred in the past, making them more sensitive to change in their own lives.

Atalanta's Race by Padraic Colum T663–T696

"'He has won,' he heard her say, 'and I have not to hate myself for bringing a doom upon him. Gladly, gladly do I give up the race, and glad am I that it is this youth who has won the victory from me.'"

In this Greek myth, students will learn how Hippomenes alters the outcome of a race by introducing three golden apples.

Great Summer Olympic Moments by Nate Aaseng T697–T702

Students will learn about significant changes in the Olympic Games from ancient Greece to present times.

Joan Benoit Samuelson by Bill Littlefield T703–T740

"Now here was Joan Benoit on the brink of the glorious realization of that fantasy . . . But you don't get to run in the Olympics if you don't qualify in the trials. And you don't run in the trials on a knee that feels like somebody's working on it with pliers."

Students will read about an Olympic runner who overcomes physical injury to become a champion.

Ancient Greece T741–T752

Students will learn about ancient Greek civilization and how it changed over time.

ART AND LITERATURE: ***Autumn Leaves, Lake George, N.Y.*** by Georgia O'Keeffe T753–T754

The artist depicts a colorful turning point.

City: A Story of Roman Planning and Construction

by David Macaulay T755–T808

"By the time of Augustus' death in A.D. 14, the streets of Verbonia were lined with grocery shops, pastry shops, ceramic shops, furniture shops, clothing shops, drugstores, wine shops, and snack bars."

Students will learn about the step-by-step development and growth of a typical city in ancient Rome.

City by Langston Hughes T788–T789

A city changes magically from morning to night.

The Secrets of Vesuvius by Sara C. Bisel T809–T860

"This is where I came in. In the morning, I would help to dig up these bones and begin to study them. For the first time, we would know more about the Romans than what books and paintings and sculptures had shown us. We would be able to see the people themselves."

An archaeologist uncovers secrets buried by a volcano nearly two thousand years ago.

Volcano by Constance Levy T840–T841

The poet imagines what a volcano feels.

Flexible Grouping

ATALANTA'S RACE T663–T696

	BELOW-LEVEL READERS	ABOVE-LEVEL READERS	ESL	BILINGUAL
1 READING AND RESPONDING Build Concepts and Vocabulary Strategic Reading Response Corner	**BEFORE** reading the selection, use the Previewing the Literature pages of the *Intervention Strategies Manual* (pp. 74-75). **TEACHER-LED GROUP** **AFTER** the Vocabulary Strategies activities, model and guide completion of the *Practice Book* (p. 96). **TEACHER-LED GROUP**	**BEFORE** students read the selection, have them write story predictions in their personal journals. (p. T668) **INDEPENDENT** **WHILE** others complete the Strategic Reading, have students discuss the story together using Reader Response Card 9. **INDEPENDENT**	**WHILE** reading the selection, students may listen to Literature Cassette 3. **COOPERATIVE GROUPS** **BEFORE** students read the selection, use the Introducing the Literature pages of the *Sheltered English/ESL Manual* (pp. 50–52). **TEACHER-LED GROUP**	**WHILE** others are reading the selection in the anthology, students may read the translation in the appropriate *Anthology Translation Booklet.* **INDEPENDENT** **WHILE** others complete the Vocabulary Strategies, Spanish-speaking students may read poems from *Ríos de lava* in CIELO ABIERTO. **INDEPENDENT**
2 INTEGRATING LANGUAGE ARTS Idea Bank Writer's Workshop Grammar Spelling Vocabulary Workshop	**DURING** the Real-Life Resources activity, write a checklist on the board so students can be sure they have included the event, time, place, and cost in their announcements. (p. T683) **TEACHER-LED GROUP** **AFTER** the Grammar lesson, model and guide completion of the *Practice Book* (p. 98). **TEACHER-LED GROUP**	**INSTEAD OF** the Spelling activities, students who did well on the pretest may complete the *Practice Book* (p. 99). **INDEPENDENT** **WHILE** others work on Idea Bank activities, students may complete the *Writer's Magazine* (pp. 50–51). **INDEPENDENT**	**BEFORE** the Writer's Workshop, use the Responding to the Literature page of the *Sheltered English/ESL Manual* (p. 53). **TEACHER-LED GROUP** **AFTER** the Writer's Workshop assignment, students may use *The Amazing Writing Machine* to enter their descriptive paragraph, using the Spin mode. (p. T684) **PAIRS/INDEPENDENT**	**WHILE** others complete the Idea Bank activities, use one of the Activities for Responding to the Poem in the *Ríos de lava Teacher's Guide.* **INDEPENDENT/PAIRS** **INSTEAD OF** the Writer's Workshop, use the writing activity in the Activities for Responding to the Poem in the *Ríos de lava Teacher's Guide.* **PAIRS**
3 LEARNING THROUGH THE LITERATURE Direct Skills Instruction Integrated Curriculum Reading Trade Books Theme Project	**WHILE** others are working in groups, have students read the Take-Home book *Soccer Talk.* **INDEPENDENT** **AFTER** the Phonics lesson in the *Intervention Strategies Manual*, have students complete the reproducible Phonics page (p. 79). **INDEPENDENT**	**AFTER** the skills lessons, students may complete the *Practice Book* (pp. 100-101). **INDEPENDENT** **WHILE** others are in groups, have students learn about other Greek legends by reading a trade book such as *The Children's Homer.* **INDEPENDENT**	**WHILE** others are working in groups, have students read the Take-Home book *Soccer Talk.* **INDEPENDENT**	**WHILE** others are working in groups, have students choose and read a book from the *Multi-Language Library.* **INDEPENDENT** **WHILE** others are working in groups, complete the Minilesson for Structural Analysis, pages 42–43, in the CIELO ABIERTO *Teacher's Handbook.* **TEACHER-LED GROUP**

JOAN BENOIT SAMUELSON T703–T740

	BELOW-LEVEL READERS	ABOVE-LEVEL READERS	ESL	BILINGUAL
1 READING AND RESPONDING Build Concepts and Vocabulary Strategic Reading Response Corner	**BEFORE** students read the selection, have them write story predictions in their personal journals. (p. T708) **INDEPENDENT** **INSTEAD OF** having students read the selection with the whole class, use the Guiding the Reading page of the *Intervention Strategies Manual* (p. 82). **TEACHER-LED GROUP**	**AFTER** the Vocabulary Strategies, have students complete the *Practice Book* (p. 103). **INDEPENDENT** **AFTER** students have read the selection, challenge them to investigate another Olympic recordholder and create a time line of that person's life. (p. T722) **COOPERATIVE GROUPS**	**BEFORE** students read the selection, use the Introducing the Literature pages of the *Sheltered English/ESL Manual* (pp. 54–56). **TEACHER-LED GROUP**	**WHILE** others read the selection in the anthology, students may read the translation in the appropriate *Anthology Translation Booklet*. **INDEPENDENT** **WHILE** others are completing the Strategic Reading, Spanish-speaking students may read a section from *Sigue la palabra* in CIELO ABIERTO. Have Vietnamese students read *Eat the Starfruit, Pay in Gold* from the *Multi-Language Library*. **INDEPENDENT**
2 INTEGRATING LANGUAGE ARTS Idea Bank Writer's Workshop Grammar Spelling Vocabulary Workshop	**WHILE** others work on Idea Bank activities, pull out needs-based groups for a review of reading and writing directions. (p. T727) **TEACHER-LED GROUP** **AFTER** the Writer's Workshop, students may use the Spin mode of *The Amazing Writing Machine* to enter their poems. (p. T728) **PAIRS/INDEPENDENT**	**DURING** the Writer's Workshop, students familiar with the steps for writing a poem may skip the review and begin writing. (p. T728) **INDEPENDENT** **WHILE** groups review the Key Words, have students complete the Extending Vocabulary lesson in the *Practice Book* (p. 107). **INDEPENDENT**	**WHILE** others are completing Idea Bank activities, students can create a portfolio entry by answering the Self-Assessment questions about their poems. (p. T729) **COOPERATIVE GROUPS** **AFTER** the Spelling lesson, use the Students Acquiring English notes in the *Integrated Spelling* Teacher's Edition Lesson 20. **TEACHER-LED GROUP**	**INSTEAD OF** the Idea Bank activities, use the Responding Activities on page 7 of the *Sigue la palabra Teacher's Guide*. **PAIRS**
3 LEARNING THROUGH THE LITERATURE Direct Skills Instruction Integrated Curriculum Reading Trade Books Theme Project	**AFTER** the Phonics lesson in the *Intervention Strategies Manual*, have students complete the reproducible Phonics page (p. 85). **INDEPENDENT** **WHILE** others are working in groups, have students read the Take-Home book *A Real Winner*. **INDEPENDENT**	**AFTER** the skills lessons, challenge students to use comparisons and contrasts to write journal entries that Joan Benoit Samuelson might have written before and after the Olympic Trials. (p. T735) **INDEPENDENT**	**INSTEAD OF** creating a map of the Boston Marathon's course, students doing the Marathon Miles activity may want to plot a fictional race course by using *Imagination Express, Destination: Neighborhood* to write a story about a race. (p. T736) **PAIRS/COOPERATIVE GROUPS**	**WHILE** others are working in groups, have students choose and read a book from the *Multi-Language Library*. **INDEPENDENT** **WHILE** others are completing the Integrated Curriculum activites, have students work on the ongoing cross-curricular project on page 2 of the *Sigue la palabra Teacher's Guide*. **COOPERATIVE GROUPS**

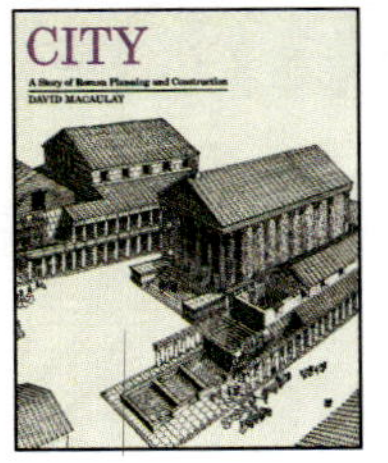

Flexible Grouping

CITY: A STORY OF ROMAN PLANNING AND CONSTRUCTION T755–T808

	BELOW-LEVEL READERS	ABOVE-LEVEL READERS	ESL	BILINGUAL
1 READING AND RESPONDING Build Concepts and Vocabulary Strategic Reading Response Corner	**INSTEAD OF** having students read the selection with the whole class, use the Guiding the Reading page of the *Intervention Strategies Manual* (p. 88). **TEACHER-LED GROUP** **DURING** the Strategic Reading, pair students with more-fluent readers and have partners pause after each page or two to discuss what they have read. (p. T760) **PAIRS**	**BEFORE** students read the selection, have them write story predictions in their personal journals. (p. T760) **INDEPENDENT** **AFTER** students read the selection, challenge them to identify each of the businesses or services shown in the cutaway illustrations. (p. T780) **COOPERATIVE GROUPS**	**BEFORE** students read the selection, use the Introducing the Literature pages of the *Sheltered English/ESL Manual* (pp. 58-60). **TEACHER-LED GROUP** **DURING** the Strategic Reading, help students understand the features of an atrium by guiding them to draw one and label its parts. (p. T777) **TEACHER-LED GROUP**	**WHILE** others are reading the selection in the anthology, students may read the translation in the appropriate *Anthology Translation Booklet.* **INDEPENDENT** **INSTEAD OF** completing the Vocabulary Strategies, Spanish-speaking students may read selections from *Así pasaron muchos años* in CIELO ABIERTO. Have Hmong students read *Tales of Marvel and Wonder* from the *Multi-Language Library.* **INDEPENDENT**
2 INTEGRATING LANGUAGE ARTS Idea Bank Writer's Workshop Grammar Spelling Vocabulary Workshop	**DURING** the Integrating Language Arts section, model and guide completion of the *Writer's Magazine* (pp. 56-57). **TEACHER-LED GROUP** **AFTER** the Writer's Workshop assignment, students may use *The Amazing Writing Machine* to enter their how-to articles, using the Spin mode. (p. T796) **PAIRS/ INDEPENDENT**	**INSTEAD OF** the Spelling activities, students who did well on the pretest may complete the *Practice Book* (p. 115). **INDEPENDENT** **INSTEAD OF** participating in the review of the steps involved in writing a how-to article, students familiar with the process may begin writing. (p. T796) **INDEPENDENT**	**BEFORE** the Writer's Workshop, use the Responding to the Literature page of the *Sheltered English/ESL Manual* (p. 61). **TEACHER-LED GROUP** **DURING** the Viewing activity, play the video for students more than once, pausing from time to time to check their understanding. (p. T795) **TEACHER-LED GROUP**	**WHILE** others complete the Writer's Workshop, use the Responding to the Writing section in the *Así pasaron muchos años Teacher's Guide.* **TEACHER-LED GROUP**
3 LEARNING THROUGH THE LITERATURE Direct Skills Instruction Integrated Curriculum Reading Trade Books Theme Project	**AFTER** the Phonics lesson in the *Intervention Strategies Manual*, students may complete the reproducible Phonics page (p. 91). **INDEPENDENT** **WHILE** others are working in groups, have students read *Hill of Fire* from the *ESL/Title I Library.* **INDEPENDENT**	**AFTER** the skills lessons, challenge students to classify by genre the selections they have read so far this year. (p. T803) **INDEPENDENT** **WHILE** students are working on the Theme Project, small groups may use Project Cards 19–24 to work at their own pace. **COOPERATIVE GROUPS**	**DURING** the Ruins of Ancient Rome activity, students can use the outlines provided in the Spin mode of *The Amazing Writing Machine* to help plan their reports. (p. T804) **COOPERATIVE GROUPS** **INSTEAD OF** reading the *Signatures Library* book *Detectives in Togas*, have students read the Take-Home book *Snack Attack.* (p. T807) **INDEPENDENT/PAIRS**	**WHILE** others are working in groups, have students choose and read a book from the *Multi-Language Library.* **INDEPENDENT**

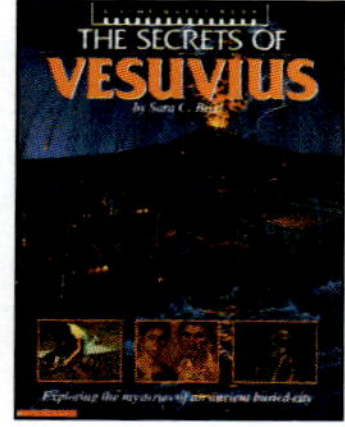

THE SECRETS OF VESUVIUS T809–T860

	BELOW-LEVEL READERS	ABOVE-LEVEL READERS	ESL	BILINGUAL
1 READING AND RESPONDING Build Concepts and Vocabulary Strategic Reading Response Corner	**BEFORE** students read the selection, use the Previewing the Literature pages of the *Intervention Strategies Manual* (pp. 92-93). **TEACHER-LED GROUP** **DURING** the Strategic Reading, help students keep track of information by directing them to list details. (p. T832) **TEACHER-LED GROUP**	**BEFORE** students read the selection, have them write story predictions in their personal journals. (p. T814) **INDEPENDENT** **AFTER** students have completed their safety diagrams in the Draw a Map activity, challenge them to conduct a mock safety drill that uses the diagrams they have made. (p. T842) **INDEPENDENT**	**DURING** the Strategic Reading, help students monitor their understanding by posing *who, why, when, where,* and *what* questions. (p. T826) **TEACHER-LED GROUP** **AFTER** introducing the selection, have students complete the reproducible page of the *Sheltered English/ESL Manual* (p. 63). **INDEPENDENT**	**WHILE** others are reading the selection in the anthology, students may read the translation in the appropriate *Anthology Translation Booklet.* **INDEPENDENT** **INSTEAD OF** completing the Strategic Reading, Spanish-speaking students may read *Ciudades en la arena* in CIELO ABIERTO and listen to the selection on the *Student Literature Cassette.* **COOPERATIVE GROUPS**
2 INTEGRATING LANGUAGE ARTS Idea Bank Writer's Workshop Grammar Spelling Vocabulary Workshop	**WHILE** others work on Idea Bank activities, pull out needs-based groups for a review of directions for performing a process. (p. T847) **TEACHER-LED GROUP** **AFTER** the Writer's Workshop assignment, students may use *The Amazing Writing Machine* to enter their research report (p. T848). **PAIRS/INDEPENDENT**	**WHILE** others are completing Idea Bank activities, have students create a portfolio entry by answering the Self-Assessment questions about their research report. (p. T849) **COOPERATIVE GROUPS** **WHILE** groups review the Key Words, students may complete the Extended Vocabulary lesson in the *Practice Book* (p. 124). **INDEPENDENT**	**DURING** the Grammar activities, have students match word cards of transitive verbs and objects and create sentences using them. (p. T851) **COOPERATIVE GROUPS** **INSTEAD OF** the Writer's Workshop, use the Responding to the Literature page of the *Sheltered English/ESL Manual* (p. 65). **COOPERATIVE GROUPS**	**WHILE** other students complete the Writer's Workshop, use CIELO ABIERTO *Teacher's Handbook* page 60 to have students write a research report. **INDEPENDENT** **INSTEAD OF** the Spelling lesson, refer to page 48 in the CIELO ABIERTO *Teacher's Handbook.* **TEACHER-LED GROUP**
3 LEARNING THROUGH THE LITERATURE Direct Skills Instruction Integrated Curriculum Reading Trade Books Theme Project	**BEFORE** the Skeleton Keys activity, students can use The Case of the Empty Fripple House from *Thinkin' Things: Collection 3* to help them develop their deductive reasoning. (p. T856) **TEACHER-LED GROUP** **WHILE** others work in groups, use the Phonics lesson in the *Intervention Strategies Manual* (pp. 96-97). **TEACHER-LED GROUP**	**AFTER** the skills lessons, challenge students to create a labeled diagram showing the steps in the process of buying lunch at school. (p. T855) **PAIRS/INDEPENDENT** **WHILE** others are working in groups, have students choose and read a trade book such as *Digging to the Past: Excavations in Ancient Lands.* **INDEPENDENT**	**AFTER** the skills lessons, model and guide completion of the *Practice Book* (p. 125). **TEACHER-LED GROUP** **WHILE** others are working in groups, have students read *Pompeii . . . Buried Alive!* from the *ESL/Title I Library.* Beginning-level ESL students should read along with the cassette tape. **INDEPENDENT**	**WHILE** others are working in groups, have students choose and read a book from the *Multi-Language Library.* **INDEPENDENT** **WHILE** others are working in groups, have students complete the Minilesson for Context Clues, pages 44–45, in the CIELO ABIERTO *Teacher's Handbook.* **TEACHER-LED GROUP**

Ongoing Assessment Strategies

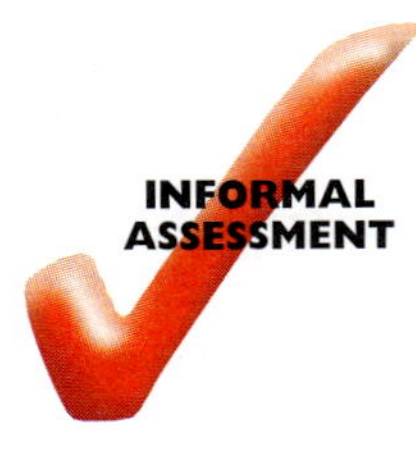

DO TELL!

Retellings are an assessment strategy in which readers tell what they remember about selections they have listened to or read. Conduct retellings to holistically assess the process of constructing meaning and to diagnose an individual's strengths and weaknesses in reading comprehension. From retellings you can gain insights into students' ability to construct meaning, identify important information, make inferences, and organize and summarize information.

Before conducting a retelling, tell students that when they finish reading, or listening, you are going to ask what they remember about the story. When conducting a retelling, ask the students to tell the story in their own words, and try not to interrupt. If a student needs prompting, first try using generic prompts such as "Tell me more," "Keep going," and "You're doing a nice job." If you need to elicit more detail and information, ask open-ended questions such as the following ones:

- What else do you remember about the story?
- Where did the story take place?
- What was your favorite part of the story?

Retellings can be used to assess whether the student

- comprehended fully, adequately, or partially.
- distinguished between relevant and irrelevant information.
- used clear and logical thinking.
- made inferences.
- related text to his or her own experiences.
- made connections to other pieces of literature.

THINKING ABOUT MY READING

Look for the student self-assessment opportunities in the selections in the next theme. These activities encourage students to monitor their reading strategies and to reflect on their attitudes and interests so that they can take responsibility for their own learning and development.

To encourage students' self-assessment of their reading, help them develop self-questioning strategies like the following:

Before reading	What do I already know about this topic? How can I use what I know to help me read this story?
During reading	Did I picture in my mind what I read? Is what I am reading making sense? If not, what can I do?
After reading	Did I achieve my purpose for reading this? If I needed help, did I ask the teacher or a friend? Did I reread? Did reading this piece seem easy? Hard? Why?

Students can also follow their reading development by recording in their reading logs—which are kept in their portfolios—reactions and comments about everything they read. Once students are given tools to assess their own reading development, they can then develop the reading strategies they need and thereby enhance their comprehension.

See the Thinking About My Reading Checklist on page T876.

End-of-Theme Formal Assessment Tools

SKILLS ASSESSMENT

Multiple-choice diagnostic tests that measure mastery of the following skills:

- Reading: vocabulary, structural analysis (prefixes, suffixes, roots) and compare and contrast
- Language: objects; comparing with adjectives; and action, main, helping, linking, transitive, and intransitive verbs

HOLISTIC READING ASSESSMENT

Fiction and/or nonfiction reading passages with multiple-choice and open-ended questions to assess students' application of literal, inferential, and critical thinking in a global and holistic manner

INTEGRATED PERFORMANCE ASSESSMENT

Performance tasks to gain a comprehensive view of a student's reading and writing progress. Students read and respond to SLJ Best Books of the Year Award, NCSS Notable Trade Book Award, and Notable Children's Trade Book for the Language Arts Award winner "Pompeii: Exploring a Roman Ghost Town" by Ron and Nancy Goor. Students demonstrate descriptive writing. One or both sections may be used.

THEME

TURNING

The following selections reveal something that is as true today as it was in ancient Greece and Rome: it may take many years to reach a goal, but a person's life or a community can be changed in an instant.

POINTS

321

THEME 4
Turning Points

DISCUSSING THE THEME

Have students offer their own definitions of a *turning point.* Then have them read about the theme on page 321. Encourage students to reflect on turning points in their own lives. Then have them discuss how a turning point in a story they have read compares with one in their own lives.

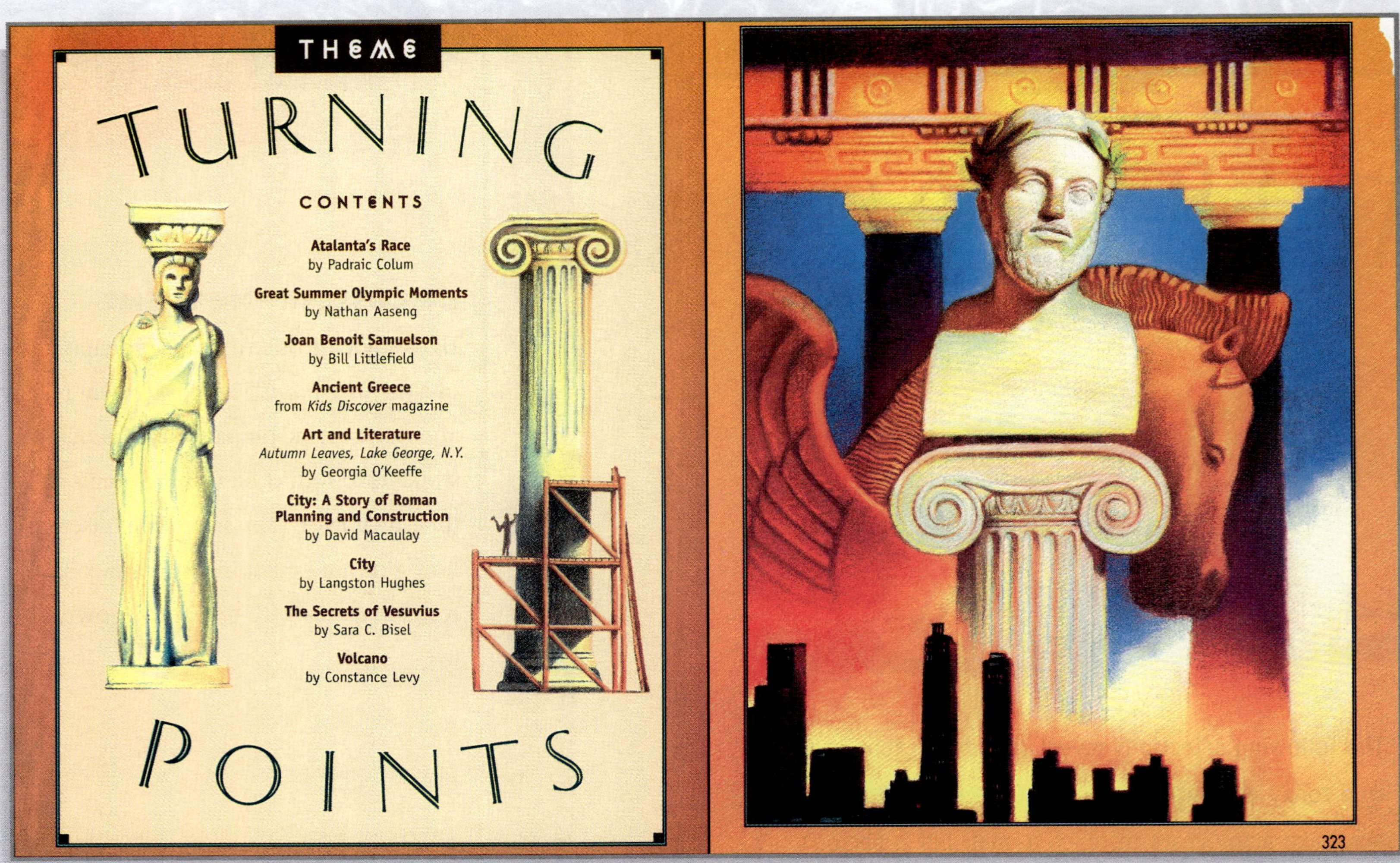
THEME

TURNING POINTS

CONTENTS

323

Previewing the Theme Literature

Invite students to read the theme table of contents on page 322. Encourage them to discuss the names of any authors, selection titles or subjects they recognize.

Ask students to brainstorm events in people's lives that might be considered turning points. Could a small incident be just as significant as a large one?

Suggest that students think about other selections they have read in which a story character, a real person, or a place reached a turning point. What significantly changed that person or place?

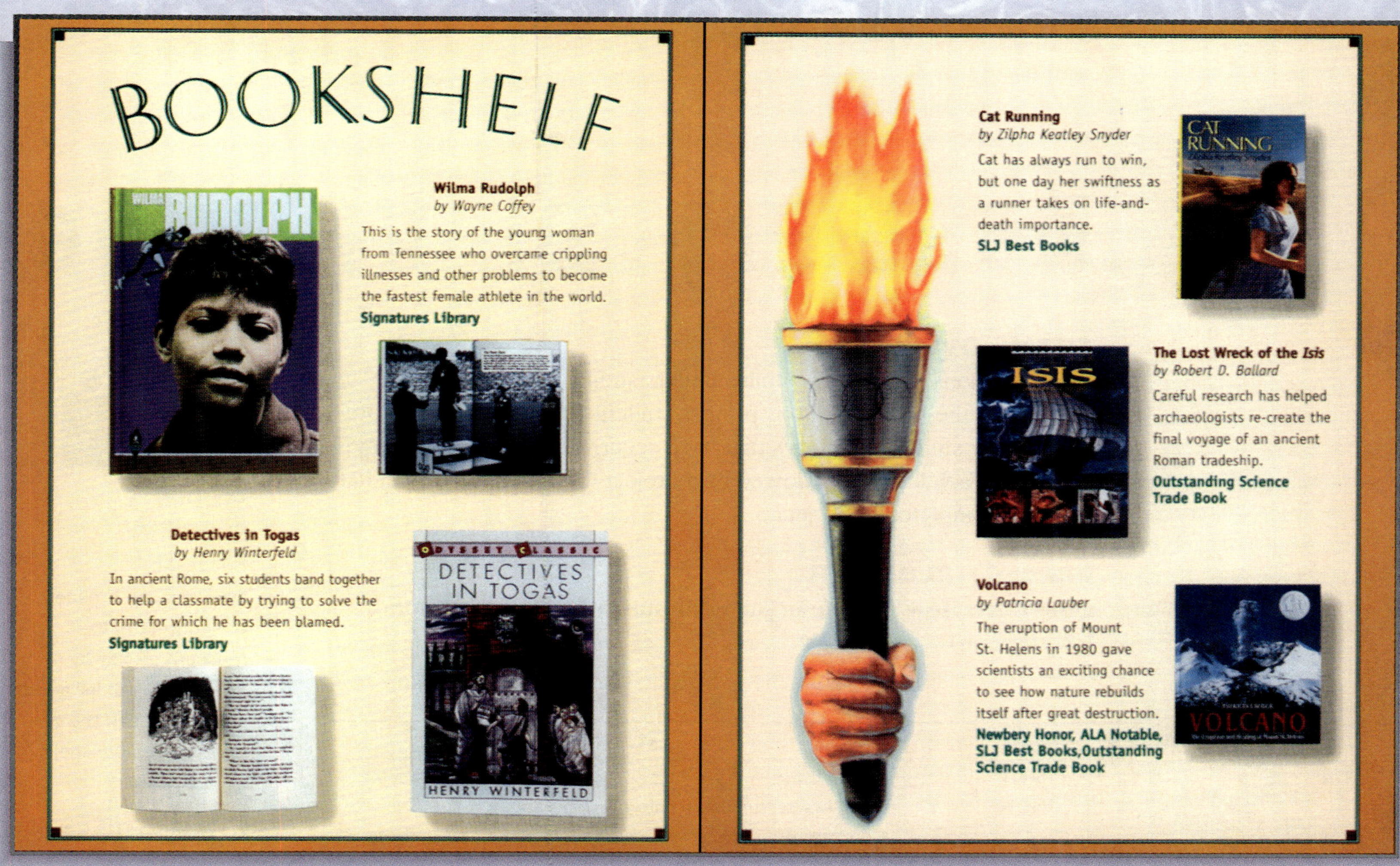

The Signatures Library

Wilma Rudolph by Wayne Coffey is the uplifting story of a woman who beat the odds to become the first American woman to capture three gold medals in the Olympics.

Detectives in Togas by Henry Winterfeld tells the story of Rufus, a student in ancient Rome who is accused of a crime he did not commit. His five friends band together to track down the real culprit in this humorous mystery.

Strategies for reading *Wilma Rudolph* appear with the "Joan Benoit Samuelson" lesson on page T738. Strategies for reading *Detectives in Togas* appear with the "City: A Story of Roman Planning and Construction" lesson on page T806.

Comprehensive lesson plans are available on pages T864–T875.

Related Reading

These trade books offer students further opportunities to work with the Turning Points theme.

ESL/Title I Library

These easy-to-read library books connect to the theme Turning Points: *Hill of Fire* by Thomas P. Lewis; *Pompeii . . . Buried Alive!* by Edith Kunhardt.

THEME PROJECT OVERVIEW

Historical Change

THEME OVERVIEW

Each selection in this theme builds understanding of changes, their causes, and their effects. In this project, students compare past and present as they study the changes that have occurred in their community over time. Each lesson is followed by a Project Checkpoint that will help students complete the project.

PROJECT PLANNER

QUESTION: How has life in my community changed? (Historical Investigation)

STAGES	GOALS
PROJECT LAUNCH (p.T661) 3-5 days	Create a list. • Discuss personal and cultural changes. • Form groups to discuss ways people and communities change.
CHECKPOINT 1 (p.T696) 4-6 days	Research change and take notes. • Interview community members about change. • Examine the resources of the local library and/or historical society for information about local history.
CHECKPOINT 2 (p.T740) 4-6 days	Design a chart. • Share research results. • Note conflicting stories or ideas about local changes. • Identify information to be included in the group's chart.
CHECKPOINT 3 (p.T808) 4-6 days	Revise findings and resolve contradictions. • Review the chart for conflicting ideas. • Do further interviews and research. • If possible, visit places that have changed.
CHECKPOINT 4 (p.T860) 4-6 days	Write group reports. • Assign responsibilities to group members. • Organize information.
PROJECT PRESENTATION (p.T862) 3-5 days	Share the results. • Write an oral history of the community. • Role-play interviews to share each group's work. • Design museum displays to present the information to other classes and the community.

STUDENTS ACQUIRING ENGLISH

Students can broaden the content of the museum display by interviewing older adults who also speak the students' first language.

MULTIPLE INTELLIGENCES

Students with visual/spatial intelligence can take a leadership role in designing the museum display and selecting visuals.

INQUIRY PROJECT IDEAS

Students may choose to investigate historical change by researching and sharing information on such topics as

- inventions that changed society.
- origins of holidays or cultural traditions.
- making a family tree.

PROJECT LAUNCH

LAUNCH OPTIONS

LIFE BEFORE TELEVISION (INDIVIDUAL)

Ask students to talk to older family members or friends who remember a time when there was no television in their home. Have students ask the adults to tell how television changed their lives and to name some activities that filled their time before television. Share information as a class.

SCIENCE FICTION—OR FACT? (SMALL GROUPS)

Science fiction authors often write about events that might happen in the future. Invite small groups of students to use their imagination to make a list of future inventions or events that would be considered science fiction today. Challenge them to predict the ones that might really happen someday.

WHOLE-GROUP DISCUSSION

In preparation, ask students to bring in baby pictures of themselves. Use the pictures to begin a discussion of how people and places change over time. Prompt discussion with questions such as *What fashions of clothing were popular when you were in third grade? What fashions are most popular now?*

FORM PROJECT GROUPS

Form groups that include students who have lived in the community all their lives and new residents.Have each group list things about individuals and communities that change. Suggest that each group

- brainstorm examples of the ways people change and how communities change.
- list ideas on a chart with the headings *People Change* and *Communities Change*.
- compare charts as a class.

Project Card 19 can be found as copying master on page R23.

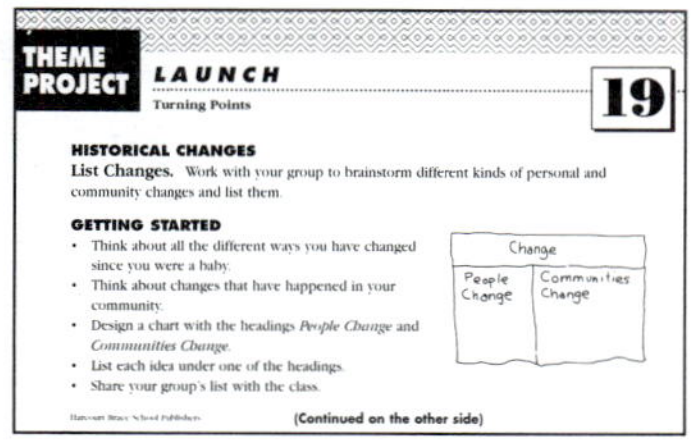

THEME PROJECT **LAUNCH** Turning Points **19**

HISTORICAL CHANGES

List Changes. Work with your group to brainstorm different kinds of personal and community changes and list them.

GETTING STARTED

- Think about all the different ways you have changed since you were a baby.
- Think about changes that have happened in your community.
- Design a chart with the headings *People Change* and *Communities Change*.
- List each idea under one of the headings.
- Share your group's list with the class.

Change	
People Change	Communities Change

Harcourt Brace School Publishers

(Continued on the other side)

Project Card 19

DID YOU KNOW?

Oral histories of community changes can be fascinating reading. Some enjoyable collections are *Tales of the Elders* by Carol Ann Bales (Follett, 1977), *My Folks Don't Want Me to Talk About Slavery*, edited by Belinda Hurmence (John F. Blair, 1984), or the *Foxfire* books.

PROJECT MANAGEMENT

ADDITIONAL RESOURCES

BOOKS

The Borning Room by Paul Fleischman. HarperCollins, 1991.

School Spirit by Johanna Hurwitz. William Morrow, 1994.

MAGAZINE

"It All Began in 1492," *Ranger Rick*, Oct. 1992, pp. 36–43.

AUDIO/VISUAL

Material World, Software, Star Press Multimedia, 1995.

FORMAL ASSESSMENT ✓

Prompts for self- and peer assessment and a rubric for teacher assessment that can be used at each checkpoint are provided on page T863.

Planning a Literacy Event

Museum Opening Get students excited about the Theme Project by beginning now to plan a Museum Opening. This event can serve as a culminating activity at which students can display their projects and share their knowledge of their community with family members and friends. Explain to students that they will write reports about community changes and display them at a special community gathering.

- Choose a date for the Museum Opening.
- Have student groups display their reports along with such items as photographs, artifacts, and tapes of interviews they conducted.
- Have student volunteers design and create invitations for family, friends, and other interested adults.
- Appoint a publicity committee to be in charge of posters or press releases. Another committee can plan for refreshments.
- Ask students who have experience with audiovisual equipment to set up an area in the museum where visitors can "contribute" to the museum by recording their own memories about the community.

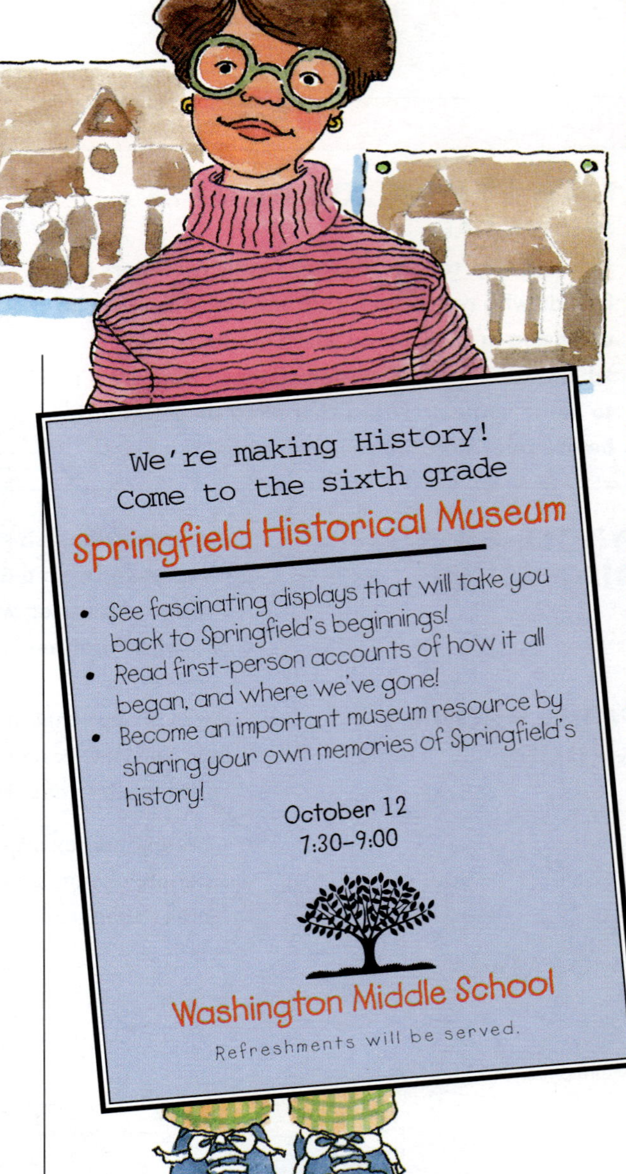

Enlisting Parents as Partners

What Is a Portfolio? Some family members who are used to a traditional grading system may be unfamiliar with student portfolios. Offer these tips about portfolios:

- ☑ A portfolio contains work your child is especially proud of. Several versions of the same project may be included to show progress.
- ☑ Teacher comments on the work in the portfolio let you know how your child's teacher views the work.
- ☑ Your child can take you on a "tour" of the portfolio. Tell him or her what you like best, and find out what your child wants to learn next.

TECHNOLOGY

The *At Home in Our Schools* videocassette contains numerous ideas for family involvement projects.

Surfing the Internet? See the *Issues & Ideas* on the Harcourt Brace Home Page: http://www.hbschool.com

***The Family Involvement Newsletter* for this theme contains furthur suggestions on this topic of interest to parents.**

ABOUT THE AUTHOR

PADRAIC COLUM (1881–1972) was a noted playwright, essayist, poet, and author of books for children. In 1922, his collection of ancient Greek mythology, *The Golden Fleece,* was named a Newbery Honor Book.

More information about Padraic Colum and his work appears on page T677.

THEME: CHANGES

Turning Points

The myth told in "Atalanta's Race" shows how cleverness and determination—and a little help from a goddess—can bring about a change.

SELECTION SUMMARY

Genre: Myth

Atalanta is so proud of her speed as a runner that she refuses to marry anyone who cannot outrun her. So many men come to race against Atalanta that her father, the king of Bœotia, creates a rule to discourage them: Anyone who races against Atalanta and loses, loses his life, too. But even that doesn't discourage everyone. One day a young man named Hippomenes decides to race Atalanta. He knows he cannot outrun her, but with the help of three golden apples given to him by Aphrodite, the goddess of beauty and love, he distracts Atalanta and succeeds in winning both the race and Atalanta's heart.

SUGGESTED LESSON PLANNER

Atalanta's Race

	DAY 1	DAY 2
PART 1 Reading, Listening, Speaking, Viewing **Key Words** immortal clamor imploring bestowed swerved	**BUILD BACKGROUND** T666 **VOCABULARY STRATEGIES** T667 *Transparency 32* *Practice Book* p. 96 **READING THE SELECTION** T668–T677 Options for Reading T668–T669 *Response Card 9* *Literature Cassette 3* **REVIEW PREDICTIONS/PURPOSE** T676 **APPRECIATING THE LITERATURE** T676 NOTE: Students may read the selection on Day 2.	**SUMMARIZE THE SELECTION** T677 *Practice Book* p. 97 ◆ **RESPONSE CORNER ACTIVITIES** T678 **CHECKING COMPREHENSION** T679 *End-of-Selection Test* 
PART 2 Writer's Workshop	**DESCRIPTIVE PARAGRAPH** Thinking as Writers T684 *Language Handbook* pp. 54–56 *Transparency 33*	Prewriting T684 *Language Handbook* p. 54
Grammar	✓**COMPARING WITH ADJECTIVES** Teach the Concept T686 Daily Language Practice (1–2) R14	Daily Language Practice (3–4) R14 Practice Activity T687
Spelling	**WORDS WITH MIXED SPELLING PATTERNS** *hero, stranger, spirit, further, escape, husband, chaos, honor, hotel, maiden, empty, crystal, victor, client, backward, figure* Pretest/Self-Check T688 *Integrated Spelling Teacher's Edition* pp. T129, T288	Open and Closed Sorts T688 *Integrated Spelling* p. 82 *Integrated Spelling Teacher's Edition* p. T130
PART 3 Skills and Strategies	◆ **INTEGRATED CURRICULUM** *Olympic Games* **Social Studies** T692 **Math/Art** T692 **Art** T693 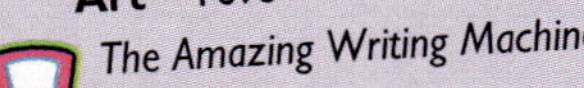 *The Amazing Writing Machine*	**VOCABULARY SKILL** T690–T691 ✓Structural Analysis (Introduce) *Transparency 34* *Practice Book* pp. 100–101
 	Use the Intervention Strategies on pages T680–T681 to help **below-level students** as they read.	To help students relate "Atalanta's Race" to modern Olympics, have students read "Great Summer Olympic Moments," pp. 338–341.

NOTE: An alternative lesson plan for **below-level students** appears on *Intervention Strategies Manual* pp. 74–79. A lesson for **students acquiring English** appears on *Sheltered English/ESL Manual* pp. 50–53.

DAY 3

◆ **IDEA BANK ACTIVITIES**
Retelling T682
Response Card 14
Oral Language T682
Rereading T683
Real-Life Resources: Reading an Announcement T683
Writer's Magazine pp. 50–51

School–Home Connection 13 R41

Drafting T684
Language Handbook p. 55
The Amazing Writing Machine

Daily Language Practice (5–6) R14
Practice Activity T687
Language Handbook pp. 142–145
The Amazing Writing Machine

Discuss the Generalization T688
Integrated Spelling p. 83
Integrated Spelling Teacher's Edition p. T131

LITERATURE MINILESSON T669
Myth (Review)

GRAMMAR MINILESSON T673
✓ Kinds of Adjectives (Review)

Above-level students may complete the Writer's Workshop independently at their own pace.

DAY 4

VOCABULARY WORKSHOP T689
Reviewing Key Words

READING TRADE BOOKS T694–T695

Take-Home Book

Responding and Revising T685
Language Handbook pp. 55, 138–145

Daily Language Practice (7–8) R14
Practice Activity T687
Grammar Practice Book pp. 34–35

Apply to Writing T688
Integrated Spelling pp. 84–85
Integrated Spelling Teacher's Edition pp. T132–133

VOCABULARY WORKSHOP T689
Neutral and Gender-Specific Words

Below-level students may read the *Take-Home Book: Soccer Talk* to help them review Key Words.

DAY 5

READING TRADE BOOKS T691, T693, T694–T695

Proofreading and Publishing T685
Language Handbook pp. 55–56

Daily Language Practice (9–12) R14
Practice Book p. 98

Posttest T688
Practice Book p. 99
Integrated Spelling Teacher's Edition p. T134

COMPREHENSION MINILESSON T675
Making Judgments (Review)
Practice Book p. 102

Theme Project Checkpoint 1 T696

Below-level and **ESL students** may read the *ESL/Title I Library* book *Archaeology: A New True Book.*

✓ = Tested Skill
◆ = Optional activities used to adjust pacing throughout the lesson
Titles in *italics* are optional materials.

BUILDING BACKGROUND AND CONCEPTS

PRIOR KNOWLEDGE

Relate to students' lives. Have students tell about important sports contests they have watched and what rewards were given to the winners. Then ask them to describe any contests they have read about in myths or folktales. Have them discuss how the rewards for winning or the penalties for losing in such stories are different from those in real life.

Create a web about Greek myths. Tell students that the next selection is a Greek myth. Invite them to brainstorm things they know about myths and to make predictions about what this myth might be. Create a web like the one shown to record students' ideas.

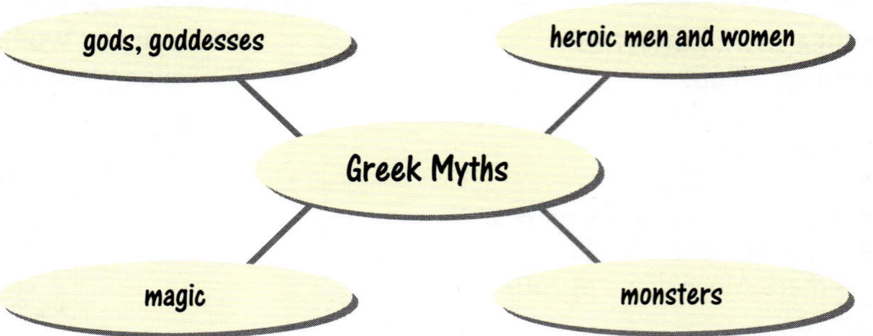

Encourage students to write a few sentences about one of the ideas in the word web. Suggest that students use prior knowledge from myths they have read to elaborate on the idea.

Intervention Strategies

For students who may have difficulty reading "Atalanta's Race," support is available in *Intervention Strategies Manual,* pages 74–79, and on pages T674, and T680–T681 in this lesson.

STUDENTS ACQUIRING ENGLISH

See *Sheltered English/ESL Manual,* pages 50–53.

FACT FINDER

SOCIAL STUDIES

Greek Mythology

The Greek myths are very familiar in Western culture because Western civilization has its roots in ancient Greek civilization. Stories like "Atalanta's Race" were told as early as the eighth or ninth century B.C. and probably even earlier. Although these myths were fantasy stories, some of them were set in real places. Bœotia, where Atalanta lived, for example, was located north of Athens. The Romans came into contact with the Greek culture in the 700s B.C. Though they had had their own mythology prior to that time, the Romans' gods and goddesses began to take on some of the attributes of those in Greek mythology. Despite having different names for the same divinities, there is a basic similarity between Roman and Greek mythology that can be traced to their common Indo-European heritage.

The Acropolis

VOCABULARY STRATEGIES

KEY WORDS DEFINED

immortal never dying; living forever

clamor loud, continuous noise

imploring begging; pleading

bestowed gave; presented as a gift

swerved turned aside suddenly

INTEGRATED SPELLING

Spelling Pretest: page T688

Spelling Generalization: Words with mixed spelling patterns

CONTEXT CLUES: MINI-STORY

Encourage students to use syntactic and semantic cues. Display the mini-story on Transparency 32. Have students read the sentences and use the context clues to figure out the meanings of the underlined words.

CHECK UNDERSTANDING

Have students make word associations. Organize students into five groups, and assign one of the Key Words to each group. Each group will use its Key Word as the starting point for a word association tree similar to the one shown below. Groups first think of two words or phrases they associate with the Key Word. Then they think of two words or phrases they associate with each of those words. When they have branched into three levels, a Reporter from each group can explain the group's word association tree to the other groups.

STRATEGY: CLASSIFYING

TRANSPARENCY 32

Key Words

Outside the stage door, a crowd of devoted fans waited to catch a glimpse of their favorite star, whose unfading beauty made her seem immortal. When she appeared, a clamor of voices rose, imploring her for an autograph. She waved a hand and bestowed her radiant smile on everyone present. Then, without warning, she swerved, ducked into a waiting car, and was driven away.

The driver of the car swerved to avoid the potholes in the road.

PRACTICE BOOK, page 96

Prereading Strategies

PREVIEW AND PREDICT

Encourage students to preview the myth by reading the title and introduction and looking at the illustration on pages 326–327.

You may want to have students begin a story map like the one shown. Students may use the map on *Practice Book* page 97 to record their ideas about the story.

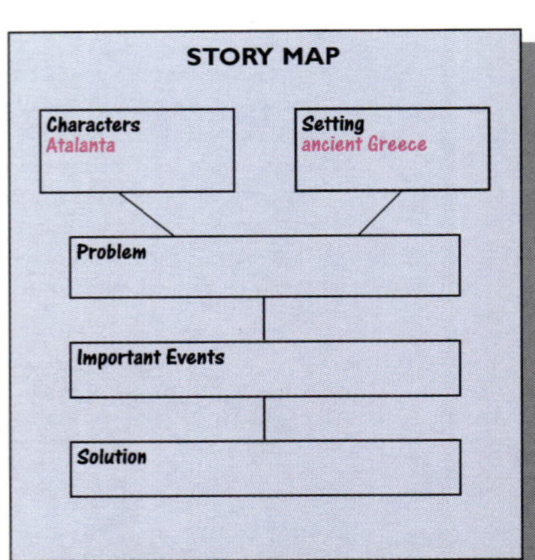

Students should write their predictions about the myth in their personal journals.

PURPOSE

You may want to model purpose-setting with a think-aloud:

MODEL **The story is called "Atalanta's Race." I'm going to read to find out who is racing against the young woman and whether she wins.**

SMALL GROUP

COOPERATIVE READING

READER RESPONSE GROUPS

Students who need a minimum of teacher support can organize themselves into **literature circles** and read and discuss the story, using Reader Response Card 9. It can be found at the back of this Teacher's Edition.

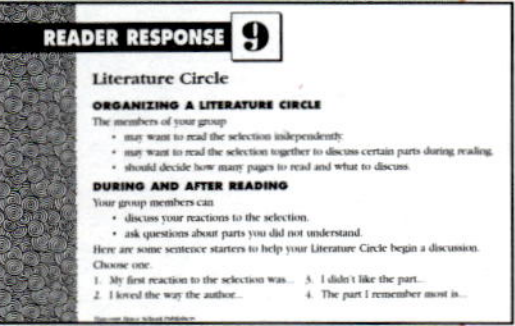

Response Card 9

PARTNER READING

Pair students who need extra support with more-fluent readers. Have partners read the story together, silently or aloud, pausing after each page or two to discuss what they have read. Encourage students to model strategies for each other.

MINILESSON

REVIEW: TYPES OF LITERATURE

Myth

INFORMAL ASSESSMENT

Ask students to tell what a myth is. (Possible response: a story from long ago that features heroes and gods and goddesses.)

TEACH/MODEL

Review with students any folktales they may have read. "Four Generals," for example, is a Chinese folktale. Explain that myths are like folktales in that they are tales from a particular culture from long ago. Many myths were told by people in early civilizations to explain elements in nature that they could not understand. For example, the origin of the universe, with its stars and planets, has been explained through various myths. Myths often feature gods, goddesses, strange animals, and people with superior strength.

PRACTICE/APPLY

After students have finished reading the selection, ask them to explain other things they learned about myths.

WHOLE CLASS

STRATEGIC READING

Use the suggestions on page T670 to model Strategic Reading. Encourage students to try the strategy of visualizing if they have trouble understanding the difficult passages.

READ ALOUD

Read aloud to students through page 329. Discuss the situation described in the story to this point, and have students confirm or revise their predictions. After students make new predictions, they can read the rest of the story independently or in small groups.

Strategic Reading

VISUALIZING

Invite students to talk about strategies they use when reading. Display the class-made strategy chart, and explain that the focus strategy for this selection is visualizing. Ask students how this strategy will help them as they read "Atalanta's Race." (Possible response: Visualizing will help me imagine the characters and their actions as I read the story.) **STRATEGY: VISUALIZING**

PAGES 326–334 Have students read through page 334 to find out what kind of race Atalanta is in.

There are two Atalantas, she said; she herself, the Huntress, and another who is noted for her speed of foot and her delight in the race—the daughter of Schœneus,[1] King of Bœotia,[2] Atalanta of the Swift Foot.

So proud was she of her swiftness that she made a vow to the gods that none would be her husband except the youth who won past her in the race. Youth after youth came and raced against her, but Atalanta, who grew fleeter and fleeter of foot, left each one of them far behind her. The youths who came to the race were so many and the clamor they made after defeat was so great, that her father made a law that, as he thought, would lessen their number. The law that he made was that the youth who came to race against Atalanta and who lost the race should lose his life into the bargain. After that the youths who had care for their lives stayed away from Bœotia.

Once there came a youth from a far part of Greece into the country that Atalanta's father ruled over. Hippomenes[3] was his name. He did not know of the race, but having come into the city and seeing the crowd of people, he went with them to the course. He looked upon the youths who were girded for the race, and he heard the folk say amongst themselves, "Poor youths, as mighty and as high-spirited as they look, by sunset the life will be out of each of them, for Atalanta will run past them as she ran past the others." Then Hippomenes spoke to the folk in wonder, and they told him of Atalanta's race and of what would befall the youths who were defeated in it. "Unlucky youths," cried Hippomenes, "how foolish they are to try to win a bride at the price of their lives."

Then, with pity in his heart, he watched the youths prepare for the race. Atalanta had not yet taken her place, and he was fearful of looking upon her. "She is a witch," he said to himself, "she must be a witch to draw so many youths to their deaths, and she, no doubt, will show in her face and figure the witch's spirit."

But even as he said this, Hippomenes saw Atalanta. She stood with the youths before they crouched for the first dart in the race. He saw that she was a girl of a light and a lovely form. Then they crouched for the race; then the trumpets rang out, and the youths and the maiden darted like swallows over the sand of the course.

[1] Schœneus (shō´nē·əs)
[2] Bœotia (bē·ō´shē·ə)
[3] Hippomenes (hip·om´ə·nēz)

328

LISTENING CENTER

"Atalanta's Race" is available on Literature Cassette 3. Students who have trouble comprehending the selection may want to listen to the story and then reread it.

On came Atalanta, far, far ahead of the youths who had started with her. Over her bare shoulders her hair streamed, blown backward by the wind that met her flight. Her fair neck shone, and her little feet were like flying doves. It seemed to Hippomenes as he watched her that there was fire in her lovely body. On and on she went as swift as the arrow that the Scythian shoots from his bow. And as he watched the race he was not sorry that the youths were being left behind. Rather would he have been enraged if one came near overtaking her, for now his heart was set upon winning her for his bride, and he cursed himself for not having entered the race.

She passed the last goal mark and she was given the victor's wreath of flowers. Hippomenes stood and watched her and he did not see the youths who had started with her—they had thrown themselves on the ground in their despair.

Then wild, as though he were one of the doomed youths, Hippomenes made his way through the throng and came before the black-bearded King of Bœotia. The king's brows were knit, for even then he was pronouncing doom upon the youths who had been left behind in the race. He looked upon Hippomenes, another youth who would make the trial, and the frown became heavier upon his face.

But Hippomenes saw only Atalanta. She came beside her father; the wreath was upon her head of gold, and her eyes were wide and tender. She turned her face to him, and then she knew by the wildness that was in his look that he had come to enter the race with her. Then the flush that was on her face died away, and she shook her head as if she were imploring him to go from that place.

329

Student Self-Assessment 

VISUALIZING

Encourage students to check their comprehension by visualizing.

- ☑ What do I picture after reading that *the youths and the maiden darted like swallows over the sand of the course?*
- ☑ How does visualizing the youths throwing themselves on the ground help me understand their despair?

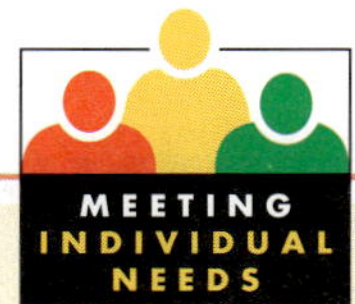

MEETING INDIVIDUAL NEEDS

STUDENTS ACQUIRING ENGLISH **Pair students acquiring English with fluent English speakers, and have them read the selection together. Encourage partners to take turns retelling parts of the story and to "translate" important dialogue into natural, everyday language as they go along.**

Critical Thinking Questions

1. **Why do the men come to race against Atalanta?** (Possible response: The men want to marry Atalanta, who is the daughter of a king, and she will marry only the man who can outrun her.) CRITICAL: SUMMARIZING

2. **What happens to the runners who lose a race against Atalanta? Why?** (Possible response: They lose their lives. Atalanta continually wins the races, and the young men complain so much that the King makes a law to discourage so many men from participating in the races.) CRITICAL: CAUSE-EFFECT

The dark-bearded king bent his brows upon him and said, "Speak, O youth, speak and tell us what brings you here."

Then cried Hippomenes as if his whole life were bursting out with his words: "Why does this maiden, your daughter, seek an easy renown by conquering weakly youths in the race? She has not striven yet. Here stand I, one of the blood of Poseidon, the god of the sea. Should I be defeated by her in the race, then, indeed, might Atalanta have something to boast of."

Atalanta stepped forward and said: "Do not speak of it, youth. Indeed I think that it is some god, envious of your beauty and your strength, who sent you here to strive with me and to meet your doom. Ah, think of the youths who have striven with me even now! Think of the hard doom that is about to fall upon them! You venture your life in the race, but indeed I am not worthy of the price. Go hence, O stranger youth, go hence and live happily, for indeed I think that there is some maiden who loves you well."

"Nay, maiden," said Hippomenes, "I will enter the race and I will venture my life on the chance of winning you for my bride. What good will my life and my spirit be to me if they cannot win this race for me?"

She drew away from him then and looked upon him no more, but bent down to fasten the sandals upon her feet. And the black-bearded king looked upon Hippomenes and said, "Face, then, this race tomorrow. You will be the only one who will enter it. But bethink thee of the doom that awaits thee at the end of it." The king said no more, and Hippomenes went from him and from Atalanta, and he came again to the place where the race had been run.

He looked across the sandy course with its goal marks, and in his mind he saw again Atalanta's swift race. He would not meet doom at the hands of the king's soldiers, he knew, for his spirit would leave him with the greatness of the effort he would make to reach the goal before her. And he thought it would be well to die in that effort and on that sandy place that was so far from his own land.

Even as he looked across the sandy course now deserted by the throng, he saw one move across it, coming toward him with feet that did not seem to touch the ground. She was a woman of wonderful presence. As Hippomenes looked upon her he knew that she was Aphrodite, the goddess of beauty and of love.

"Hippomenes," said the immortal goddess, "the gods are mindful of you who are sprung from one of the gods, and I am mindful of you because of your own worth.

330

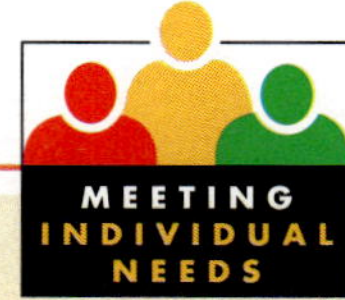

EXTRA SUPPORT Explain that in Greek mythology, as in other mythologies, the forces of nature or life were given human personalities and worshipped as divine beings. For example, in Greek mythology, Poseidon was god of the sea, and Aphrodite was the goddess of love and beauty.

EXPANDING VOCABULARY

The word *strive* has two meanings. Atalanta uses it to mean "to compete." When Hippomenes says of Atalanta *She has not striven yet,* he is using the meaning of *strive* that it has today— "to make great efforts; to try very hard."

I have come to help you in your race with Atalanta, for I would not have you slain, nor would I have that maiden go unwed. Give your greatest strength and your greatest swiftness to the race, and behold! Here are wonders that will prevent the fleet-footed Atalanta from putting all her spirit into the race."

And then the immortal goddess held out to Hippomenes a branch that had upon it three apples of shining gold.

"In Cyprus," said the goddess, "where I have come from, there is a tree on which these golden apples grow. Only I may pluck them. I have brought them to you, Hippomenes. Keep them in your girdle, and in the race you will find out what to do with them, I think."

So Aphrodite said, and then she vanished, leaving a fragrance in the air and the three shining apples in the hands of Hippomenes. Long he looked upon their brightness. They were beside him that night, and when he arose in the dawn he put them in his girdle. Then, before the throng, he went to the place of the race.

331

Tested Skill

MINILESSON

REVIEW: GRAMMAR

Kinds of Adjectives

INFORMAL ASSESSMENT

Display this sentence, and have students identify all the adjectives:

A Greek man named Hippomenes wanted to enter that race with Atalanta.

Ask students what different kinds of adjectives are included in the sentence. (article, *a*; proper, *Greek*; demonstrative, *that*)

TEACH/MODEL

Explain that adjectives help to define which person or thing is being talked about and describe that person or thing. Use the first sentence of the sixth paragraph on page 330 to model recognizing the function of adjectives: *He looked across the sandy course with its goal marks, and in his mind he saw again Atalanta's swift race.* If necessary, model the thinking:

MODEL

The article *the* tells me that it's a particular course, and *sandy* describes what it's like. The word *goal* functions as an adjective to tell what kind of marks. *Swift* describes how fast the race is.

PRACTICE/APPLY

Ask students to look for other examples of adjectives in the story and explain how they help the reader know what person or thing is being talked about.

MYTHOLOGY

Aphrodite, the goddess of love and beauty, was always eager to help lovers in distress. She had a magic sash that made everyone fall in love with the person wearing it. Her son, Eros, would make people fall in love by shooting them with golden arrows. In Roman mythology, Aphrodite is called Venus and her son is called Cupid.

Cupid

Cooperative Reading

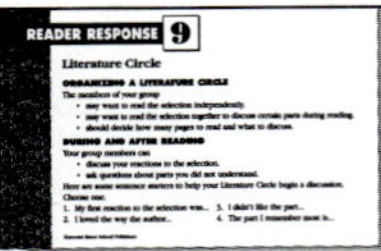
Response Card 9

Group members may want to discuss their reactions to the story. It may also be helpful to ask questions such as these:

- **Do you think Atalanta wants Hippomenes to win or lose the race?**
- **What do you think about King Schœneus? Is he a good king or a bad king?**
- **Do the characters seem like real people to you? Support your answer with details from the story.**

When he showed himself beside Atalanta all around the course were silent, for they all admired Hippomenes for his beauty and for the spirit that was in his face; they were silent out of compassion, for they knew the doom that befell the youths who raced with Atalanta.

And now Schœneus, the black-bearded king, stood up, and he spoke to the throng, saying: "Hear me all, both young and old: this youth, Hippomenes, seeks to win the race from my daughter, winning her for his bride. Now, if he be victorious and escape death I will give him my dear child, Atalanta, and many fleet horses besides as gifts from me, and in honor he shall go back to his native land. But if he fail in the race, then he will have to share the doom that has been meted out to the other youths who raced with Atalanta hoping to win her for a bride."

Then Hippomenes and Atalanta crouched for the start. The trumpets were sounded and they darted off.

Side by side with Atalanta Hippomenes went. Her flying hair touched his breast, and it seemed to him that they were skimming the sandy course as if they were swallows. But then Atalanta began to draw away from him. He saw her ahead of him, and then he began to hear the words of cheer that came from the throng — "Bend to the race, Hippomenes! Go on, go on! Use your strength to the utmost." He bent himself to the race, but further and further from him Atalanta drew.

Then it seemed to him that she checked her swiftness a little to look back at him. He gained on her a little. And then his hand touched the apples that were in his girdle. As it touched them it came into his mind what to do with the apples.

He was not far from her now, but already her swiftness was drawing her further and further away. He took one of the apples into his hand and tossed it into the air so that it fell on the track before her.

Atalanta saw the shining apple. She checked her speed and stooped in the race to pick it up. And as she stooped Hippomenes darted past her, and went flying toward the goal that now was within his sight.

But soon she was beside him again. He looked, and he saw that the goal marks were far, far ahead of him. Atalanta with the flying hair passed him, and drew away and away from him. He had not speed to gain upon her now, he thought, so he put his strength into his hand and he flung the second of the shining apples. The apple rolled before her and rolled off the course. Atalanta turned off the course, stooped and picked up the apple.

332

Intervention Strategies

PREDICTING **Ask students to repeat this sentence aloud or to themselves: *When I read, I make many predictions about what is going to happen next.* Have students tell how making predictions helps them understand the events in "Atalanta's Race."**

EXPANDING VOCABULARY

Have students reread the second paragraph, in which the king speaks to the throng, or crowd, of people gathered to watch the race. The king says that if Hippomenes wins the race, the king will allow him to marry Atalanta and give him many fleet horses. Point out that here, *fleet* is an adjective meaning "fast."

Then did Hippomenes draw all his spirit into his breast as he raced on. He was now nearer to the goal than she was. But he knew that she was behind him, going lightly where he went heavily. And then she was beside him, and then she went past him. She paused in her speed for a moment and she looked back on him.

As he raced on, his chest seemed weighted down and his throat was crackling dry. The goal marks were far away still, but Atalanta was nearing them. He took the last of the golden apples into his hand. Perhaps she was now so far that the strength of his throw would not be great enough to bring the apple before her.

But with all the strength he could put into his hand he flung the apple. It struck the course before her feet and then went bounding wide. Atalanta swerved in her race and followed where the apple went. Hippomenes marveled that he had been able to fling it so far. He saw Atalanta stoop to pick up the apple, and he bounded on. And then, although his strength was failing, he saw the goal marks near him. He set his feet between them and then fell down on the ground.

333

MINILESSON

REVIEW: COMPREHENSION

Making Judgments

INFORMAL ASSESSMENT

Ask students to make judgments about Hippomenes's method of slowing down Atalanta during the race. (Possible response: Hippomenes doesn't seem to be a faster runner than Atalanta. Using the apples to distract her doesn't seem fair, but it is a smart thing for him to do to slow her down.)

TEACH/MODEL

Explain that when you decide if a character's behavior is good or bad, appropriate or inappropriate, you are making a judgment. Remind students that sometimes it's important to make judgments about characters or other aspects of a selection to better comprehend what the author is saying. You may want to model the thinking:

MODEL **So many young men are losing their lives because of her, it's easy to think—as Hippomenes does at first—that Atalanta is evil. But there's no evidence of evil in her behavior. She just wants the man she marries to be faster than she is.**

PRACTICE/APPLY

Ask students to discuss whether it is appropriate or not for the king to pass a law sentencing all the losers to death.

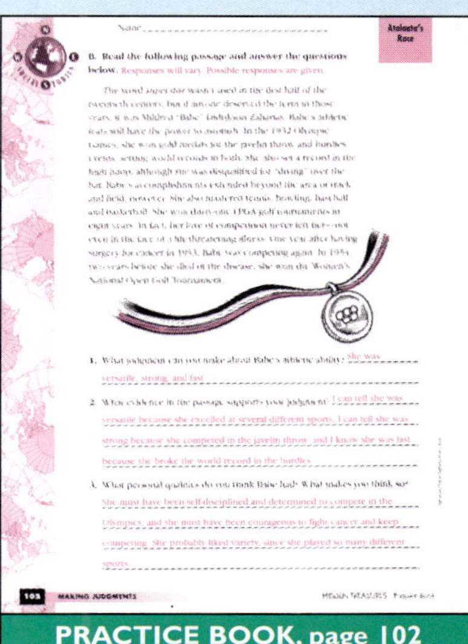

Name ______

Atalanta's Race

B. Read the following passage and answer the questions below. Responses will vary. Possible responses are given.

[illegible]

1. What judgment can you make about Babe's athletic ability? She was versatile, strong, and fast.
2. What evidence in the passage supports your judgment? I can tell she was versatile because she excelled at several different sports. I can tell she was strong because she competed in the javelin throw, and I know she was fast because she broke the world record in the hurdles.
3. What personal qualities do you think Babe had? What makes you think so? She must have been self-disciplined and determined to compete in the Olympics, and she must have been courageous to fight cancer and keep competing. She probably liked variety, since she played so many different sports.

102 MAKING JUDGMENTS

PRACTICE BOOK, page 102

STUDENTS ACQUIRING ENGLISH **Invite students learning English to retell the events of the race in their own words. Suggest that they use time-order words such as *first, next, then, after that,* and *finally* to help them track the events.**

Strategic Reading

PAGES 326–334 How does Hippomenes manage to win the race? (Possible response: When Atalanta gets ahead of him, he tosses a golden apple in front of her to distract her. In the time it takes her to pick it up, he manages to get ahead of her.) STRATEGIES: SUMMARIZING/ CONFIRMING PREDICTIONS

Why do you think Atalanta stops to pick up the golden apples? (Possible responses: The apples are rare and magical and come from Aphrodite. Also, Atalanta seems to like Hippomenes and may not mind if he wins the race.) CRITICAL: DETERMINING CHARACTERS' MOTIVES

Returning to the Predictions/Purpose

Did you find out what you wanted to know about Atalanta's race? Ask students whether their purposes for reading were met. STRATEGY: RETURNING TO THE PURPOSE

Appreciating the Literature

What did you like best about the story? Would you like to read other Greek myths? Why or why not? (Responses will vary.)

The attendants raised him up and put the victor's wreath upon his head. The concourse of people shouted with joy to see him victor. But he looked around for Atalanta and he saw her standing there with the golden apples in her hands. "He has won," he heard her say, "and I have not to hate myself for bringing a doom upon him. Gladly, gladly do I give up the race, and glad am I that it is this youth who has won the victory from me."

She took his hand and brought him before the king. Then Schœneus, in the sight of all the rejoicing people, gave Atalanta to Hippomenes for his bride, and he bestowed upon him also a great gift of horses. With his dear and hard-won bride, Hippomenes went to his own country, and the apples that she brought with her, the golden apples of Aphrodite, were reverenced by the people.

334

MULTICULTURAL CONNECTION

In ancient Greece, it was customary to crown the winner of an athletic contest with a wreath of flowers or leaves. In the earliest Olympic Games, the winners were crowned with wreaths from an olive tree that was considered sacred and that grew behind the temple of Zeus. According to tradition, this tree had been planted by Heracles, the founder of the Olympic Games.

Olive Tree

Padraic Colum

Padraic Colum was born in Ireland in 1881. He didn't begin writing stories for children until he moved to the United States in 1914. But he said his childhood friendship with Charlie MacGauran, a neighborhood storyteller, was what inspired him to become a writer. MacGauran taught Colum that "the storyteller must have respect for the child's mind and the child's conception of the world. . . . Strange words do not bewilder children if there is order in the action and the sentences." Colum kept this in mind when he retold the classic Greek myths in *The Golden Fleece*, which was named a Newbery Honor Book in 1922.

David Wilgus

David Wilgus worked for many years as an advertising art director before becoming a full-time illustrator. His highly detailed pencil drawings graced a series of books written by Jane Yolen, including *Here There Be Dragons* and *Here There Be Unicorns*. Wilgus prefers drawing to painting because he loves the feeling of working in pencil. He used colored pencils to illustrate "Atalanta's Race."

335

About the Author

After students read page 335, you may wish to discuss the following questions with them:

- **How did Charlie MacGauran influence Padraic Colum's writing?** (Possible response: He taught Colum that storytellers always have respect for the child's mind and ideas of the world.)
- **What do you think Charlie MacGauran meant when he told Padraic Colum that *strange words do not bewilder children if there is order in the action and the sentences?*** (Possible response: If the story is good and the events are well told, children will pay attention.)

Padraic Colum was the founder of the Irish National Theatre and the cofounder and editor for a time of the *Irish Review*. He also received many literary awards and honors—among them honorary doctorates from both the National University of Ireland and Columbia University as well as membership in the American Academy of Arts and Letters.

SUMMARIZING

Story Map

To help students summarize the story, have them complete the story map. Remind them that when they summarize the plot, they should include only the most important events. They can self-assess their story maps by asking themselves whether someone who had never read "Atalanta's Race" could use the story map to find out what the story is about. See *Practice Book* page 97.

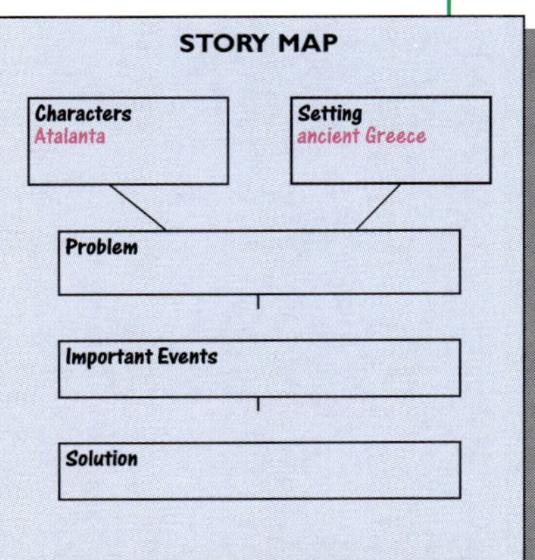

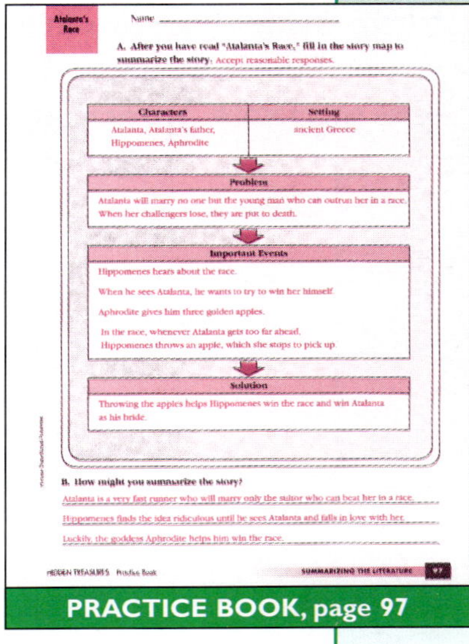

Atalanta's Race

Name ____________

A. After you have read "Atalanta's Race," fill in the story map to summarize the story. Accept reasonable responses.

Characters	Setting
Atalanta, Atalanta's father, Hippomenes, Aphrodite	ancient Greece

Problem

Atalanta will marry no one but the young man who can outrun her in a race. When her challengers lose, they are put to death.

Important Events

Hippomenes hears about the race.

When he sees Atalanta, he wants to try to win her himself.

Aphrodite gives him three golden apples.

In the race, whenever Atalanta gets too far ahead, Hippomenes throws an apple, which she stops to pick up.

Solution

Throwing the apples helps Hippomenes win the race and win Atalanta as his bride.

B. How might you summarize the story?

Atalanta is a very fast runner who will marry only the suitor who can beat her in a race.

Hippomenes finds the idea ridiculous until he sees Atalanta and falls in love with her.

Luckily, the goddess Aphrodite helps him win the race.

HIDDEN TREASURES Practice Book SUMMARIZING THE LITERATURE 97

PRACTICE BOOK, page 97

ACTIVITY CHOICES

TELL A MYTH

MYTH TELLING The minilesson on page T669 focuses on myths. If you haven't already done so, use the lesson to help students identify the characteristics of myths before they begin to create their own myths. **LISTENING AND SPEAKING**

MAKE A PLAN

A HEALTHFUL PLAN Discuss with students where they might find information about diet and exercise for runners. You might also suggest people they could interview to get ideas. Encourage students to share their finished plans with the rest of the group and get the group's reactions to their training regimens. **SCIENCE/WRITING**

ORGANIZE A RACE

LET THE GAMES BEGIN! Discuss the Olympic Games with the class before the teams begin working. Make a list of events they know are part of the Olympics, and have the entire class decide which events will be part of your games. Decide, too, whether you will invite other classes to take part in the games, either as contestants or as spectators. **PHYSICAL EDUCATION**

RESPONSE CORNER

TELL A MYTH

MYTH TELLING

Work with a small group to invent a myth. First, talk about the characteristics of myths. Then brainstorm the plot, characters, and setting for your myth. Be as creative as possible. Tell your myth to another group as though you were passing it down to another generation.

MAKE A PLAN

A HEALTHFUL PLAN

Healthy runners must follow a plan of exercise and nutrition. Look for information on rules for athletes in training. Write a one-week plan for meals and exercise that a runner could use.

336

CROSS-CULTURAL VIEWPOINT

Encourage students from different cultures to share myths from their cultures. Compare these myths with familiar myths of the Greek and Roman tradition to discover basic similarities and differences. What are the characteristics that seem to be shared by all the myths?

ORGANIZE A RACE

LET THE GAMES BEGIN!

Work with one of four teams in your class to organize a sixth-grade Olympic Race. Team One directs the opening ceremony. Team Two makes the rules for running the races and then times the runners. Team Three maps out the race course on the school grounds. Team Four designs the prizes and directs the awards ceremony. Anyone who wants to run in the race can do so.

- Do you think that the race between Atalanta and Hippomenes is fair? Explain your answer.
- If you could be one of the characters in this story, whom would you choose to be? Why?
- How would the story ending be different if Atalanta had won the race?

337

CHECKING COMPREHENSION

What Do You Think?

1. **Do you think that the race between Atalanta and Hippomenes is fair? Explain your answer.** (Possible response: No, it isn't fair. Hippomenes doesn't outrun Atalanta. He uses the golden apples to distract her.) DESCRIPTIVE RESPONSE
2. **If you could be one of the characters in this story, whom would you choose to be? Why?** (Responses will vary.) PERSONAL RESPONSE
3. **How would the story ending be different if Atalanta had won the race?** (Possible response: The king would have Hippomenes killed, and Atalanta would have to wait for someone else to beat her in a race before she could be married.) CRITICAL ANALYSIS/REFLECTING

VARYING THE ACTIVITY

Students needing **extra support** may benefit from a question-and-answer session with a guest speaker in the classroom for the A Healthful Plan activity. Write on the board the questions *Who? What? When? Where? Why?* and *How?* for students to refer to as they ask questions of the speaker.

Intervention Strategies

TIPS FOR CLASSROOM MANAGEMENT

IF second-language students need additional vocabulary and during-reading strategies to understand "Atalanta's Race," **THEN** use Sheltered English/ESL Manual, pages 50–53.

IF students had difficulty understanding "Atalanta's Race," **THEN** you may want them to read *Archaeology: A New True Book,* and complete the activity on page T681. See also *Intervention Strategies Manual,* pages 74–79.

REREADING

MAKING ASSOCIATIONS Point out that the goddess Aphrodite plays a very important role in the plot of this myth. Have students reread only the parts of the myth that are about Aphrodite. As they reread, students can add to a web like the one below to show objects and traits associated with Aphrodite.

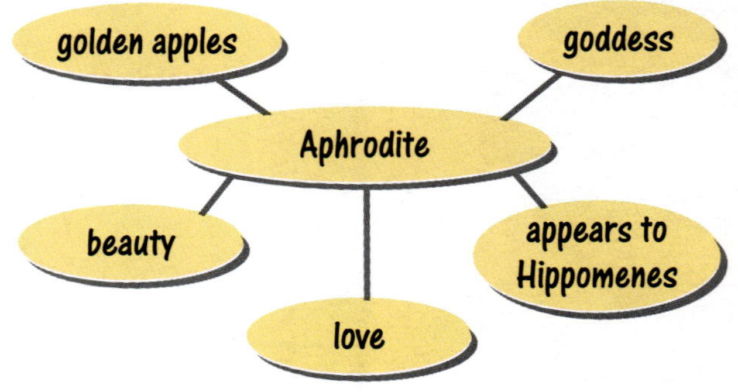

PERSONAL JOURNAL

How do students feel about the two leading characters of this myth? Was Atalanta too proud? Did Hippomenes cheat? Have students write two or three sentences in their journals that state their feelings.

STRUCTURAL ANALYSIS

SUFFIXES Point out that many adjectives are formed with certain suffixes, or endings. Choose a few examples from the opening pages of the myth, such as *fearful, envious,* and *sandy,* and show students how the suffix was added to a base word. Then write the following suffixes on the board:

Ask students to skim the selection to find other adjectives with these suffixes. (Possibilities include the following: *wonderful, unlucky, victorious.*) Work with students to find the base word in each of the adjectives, and have students tell what noun each adjective describes.

Call on volunteers to suggest some other examples of adjectives made with the suffixes on the board.

Writing to Summarize

Have students write a short summary of the selection. Suggest that they organize their summaries into three parts, using chronological order. The first part should tell about the race, and the third part should tell what happens after the race. Write a sample set of three sentence starters such as the following on the board:

Before the Race

Atalanta made a vow that no one would be her husband except ______.

Hippomenes made up his mind to run the race because ______.

Aphrodite helped Hippomenes by ______.

DECODING SUPPORT
Syllabication

***Intervention Strategies Manual* pp. 78–79**

ESL/Title I Reading

Reading Trade Books

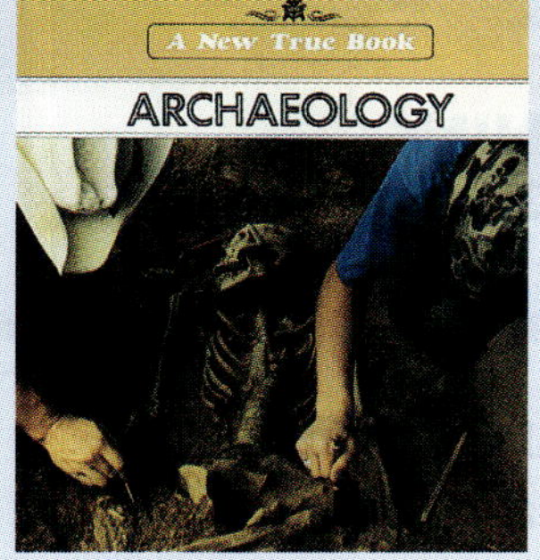

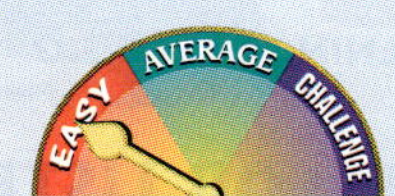

Archaeology: A New True Book

by Dennis B. Fradin

This entertaining work of nonfiction explores the field of archaeology through the use of lively text and colorful photographs. Have students use this diagram to contrast this book with the selection "Atalanta's Race."

I know that "Atalanta's Race" is fiction because
1. ______
2. ______

I know that *Archaeology: A New True Book* is nonfiction because
1. ______
2. ______

TAKE-HOME BOOK TO REINFORCE KEY WORDS

Students will enjoy reading this high-interest sports story. Students may wish to take the book home and read it to a family member.

PERSONAL JOURNAL

After students finish reading *Soccer Talk*, have them write their reactions to the book in their personal journals.

See also *Intervention Strategies Manual*, page 77.

WRITER'S WORKSHOP

Descriptive Paragraph

Thinking as Writers

WRITING FORM: Descriptive Paragraph
Remind students that many of the paragraphs in "Atalanta's Race" paint a vivid picture of the characters, the setting, and the events. Explain that descriptive writing appeals to a reader's senses of sight, hearing, smell, touch, and taste. Tell students that they are going to learn about descriptive writing and then write a descriptive paragraph of their own.

Display Transparency 33 and refer to the introduction and the side notes as you discuss with students the qualities of a descriptive paragraph.

TRANSPARENCY 33

Model: Descriptive Paragraph

*A **descriptive paragraph** appeals to the reader's senses of sight, hearing, smell, touch, and taste. In a few words, it paints a picture of a subject.*

topic sentence	Big Lake is prettiest just before sunset. The waves lap gently on the shoreline, and loons call eerily
vivid verbs	across the water. A breeze carries the spicy scent of pine trees. The
sensory details	sky fades at the edges, turning first light blue, then lilac, then pink, and then orange. Streaky clouds are reflected on the lake. Bass and pickerel dance just below the shimmering surface, sometimes rising up to capture a mosquito. Everything is calm.

WRITER'S CRAFT: Main Idea and Details
Explain that in a descriptive paragraph, one sentence may state the main idea, or who or what the paragraph is about. The other sentences contain details that support the main idea and are presented in logical order. The details often contain vivid verbs and words that appeal to the senses. Have students find sensory details and vivid verbs in the model. (hearing: *waves lap gently*; smell: *spicy scent*; sight: *sky fades, streaky clouds*)

PREWRITING AND DRAFTING

Remind students to select topics that can be described with rich sensory details. Refer to these strategies to help students begin their descriptions.

PREWRITING GRAPHIC ORGANIZER
Have students think about something they think is interesting or special. Suggest that students use a chart like the one below to make a list of words that relate to the different senses.

MAIN IDEA: A picnic in the park

Sight	Smell	Taste	Touch	Hearing
grass trees	food flowers	food	softball paper plates	ducks laughter wind

SUSTAINED SILENT WRITING Students who have a clear idea of what they want to write may begin writing without interruption.

DURING-WRITING GRAPHIC ORGANIZER
Some students may need to pause during writing to make an outline of the main idea and the supporting details.

TIPS FOR CLASSROOM MANAGEMENT

IF students are familiar with the steps for writing a descriptive paragraph, **THEN** have them begin writing, referring to the model on Transparency 33 as necessary.

IF you want a brief writing activity, **THEN** adapt this lesson by having students choose a topic and list sensory details that describe it.

TECHNOLOGY

THE AMAZING WRITING MACHINE **Have students enter their descriptive paragraphs. After they complete them, suggest that students work in pairs to check their writing and to underline details that contribute to the main idea.**

RESPONDING AND REVISING

Have students work in editing circles or with partners to help each other revise. Write this checklist on the board:

- Did you begin with a topic sentence that states the main idea?
- Did you include enough details to support the main idea?
- Does your paragraph contain vivid verbs and sensory details?

PROOFREADING

Offer the following tips as students proofread:

- Check for correct use of **adjectives.** (See the Grammar Minilesson on page T673.)
- Check for correct use of **commas** and **end punctuation.**
- Look for words you may have misspelled, and find out how to spell them correctly.

PUBLISHING

If you wish to have students publish their descriptive paragraphs, suggest the following options or have students choose their own.

ORAL Students may read their paragraphs aloud in small groups. Have groups comment on which phrases or sentences appeal to the senses and what adjectives the author uses to help portray the event.

WRITTEN Descriptive paragraphs may be displayed on a bulletin board under the title "Picture This!"

EVALUATION BENCHMARKS: DESCRIPTIVE PARAGRAPH		
A descriptive paragraph by a proficient student writer shows the following characteristics:		
FORM	**CRAFT**	**CONVENTIONS**
Demonstrates understanding of the form • clearly defined main idea • details support the main idea	**Uses clear and appropriate language** • vivid verbs and adjectives used • details described in words that appeal to the senses	**Follows conventions of grammar and usage** • adjectives used correctly • commas used correctly

Teacher Assessment As you assess students' writing, refer to the Evaluation Benchmarks chart. For additional information, including model papers, see *Integrated Performance Assessment* Teacher's Edition.

PORTFOLIO OPPORTUNITY

Have students answer the Student Self-Assessment questions and include both the answers and their descriptive paragraphs in their portfolios.

LANGUAGE HANDBOOK

Writing to Describe, pages 54–55; Descriptive Paragraph, page 56; Adding Details and Examples, page 27; Adjectives, pages 138–145

Student Self-Assessment ✓

Have students answer the following questions and include the answers in their portfolios:

- When you reread your paragraph, can you picture the scene?
- What might you do differently the next time you describe something in writing?

Tested Skill

GRAMMAR

Comparing with Adjectives

TECHNOLOGY

THE AMAZING WRITING MACHINE *Students can use the Journal feature in the program to write their accounts of the race.*

LANGUAGE HANDBOOK Comparing with Adjectives, pages 142–145

DAILY LANGUAGE PRACTICE See page R14 for oral language exercises.

Reading ↔ Writing Connection

Connect to the literature. Ask students to reread the first two paragraphs of "Atalanta's Race" and identify an example of a phrase that includes an adjective used to make a comparison. *(who grew fleeter and fleeter of foot)* Talk with students about what is being compared here.

Build oral language. Ask students to create sentences like the ones below about story characters and events that use adjectives to make comparisons. Write on the board the sentences students suggest, underlining the adjectives.

Atalanta refused to marry anyone who was not <u>fleeter</u> of foot than she was.

Was Hippomenes the <u>fastest</u> runner to challenge Atalanta?

Hippomenes was not <u>faster</u> than Atalanta, but his will to win was <u>stronger</u>.

Teach/Model

Use semantic and syntactic cues. Ask students to look at the sentences they created and decide who or what is being compared in each sentence. Help students conclude that when two people or things are being compared, an adjective with *-er* is used. This is the **comparative** form of an adjective. When three or more people or things are being compared, an adjective with *-est* is used. This is the **superlative** form of an adjective.

Discuss *more* and *most*. Explain to students that the words *more* and *most* are needed to form the comparative and superlative forms for some two-syllable adjectives and for adjectives with three or more syllables. Ask volunteers to make up sentences that use the comparative and superlative forms of these adjectives: *intelligent, wonderful,* and *imaginative*.

Practice/Apply

Check understanding. Write the following sentence frames on the board, and have students supply the appropriate comparative or superlative adjectives.

Hippomenes had never seen a (fair) or (lovely) young woman than Atalanta.

The golden apples were the (bright) Hippomenes had ever seen.

Hippomenes would have lost if his will to win had not been (strong) than Atalanta's.

Practice Activities

"I'm Thinking . . ."

ORAL APPLICATION Have students take turns making up clues about objects in the classroom or around the school. Each clue must include a comparative or superlative adjective. The rest of the class must guess what the adjective describes. Here are some examples: "I'm thinking of the highest thing in the room." (the ceiling) "I'm thinking of something that is taller than a person, shorter than a giraffe, and more fun than a ladder." (basketball hoop)
AUDITORY

Write About the Race

WRITING APPLICATION Ask students to write a brief account of Atalanta's race with Hippomenes. When they have finished, they can exchange papers with partners and count the number of comparative or superlative adjectives each other used in the summary. **VISUAL**

APPLY TO WRITING

You may want students to consider adding adjectives that compare to their descriptive paragraphs or other writing to make the writing clearer or more colorful.

USAGE TIP In a comparison, don't use both *more* and an adjective ending with *-er* or *most* and an adjective ending with *-est*.

STUDENTS ACQUIRING ENGLISH

Organize students and fluent English speakers into groups of three to practice comparing with adjectives. Have them take turns "best-ing" each other. The first student makes a statement such as "I am a fast runner." The second student tops that by saying, "I am a faster runner." Then the third tops that by saying "But I am the fastest runner of all."

RETEACH

See page R4 for lessons in multiple modalities.

GRAMMAR PRACTICE BOOK
pages 34–35

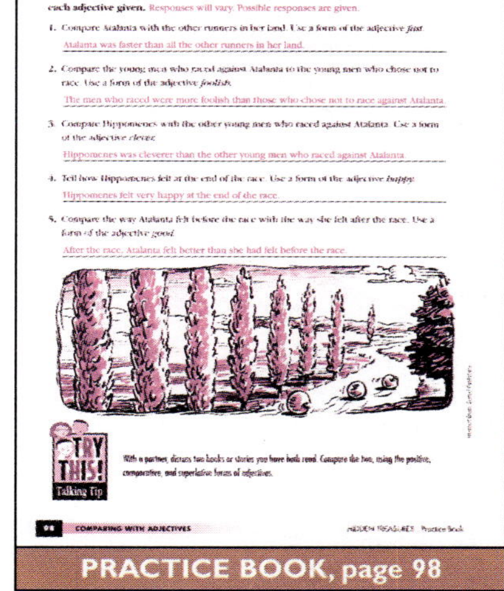

Name ______________

Atalanta's Race

Think about the story "Atalanta's Race," and write your own sentences. Use the positive, comparative, or superlative form of each adjective given. Responses will vary. Possible responses are given.

1. Compare Atalanta with the other runners in her land. Use a form of the adjective *fast*.
   Atalanta was faster than all the other runners in her land.
2. Compare the young men who raced against Atalanta to the young men who chose not to race. Use a form of the adjective *foolish*.
   The men who raced were more foolish than those who chose not to race against Atalanta.
3. Compare Hippomenes with the other young men who raced against Atalanta. Use a form of the adjective *clever*.
   Hippomenes was cleverer than the other young men who raced against Atalanta.
4. Tell how Hippomenes felt at the end of the race. Use a form of the adjective *happy*.
   Hippomenes felt very happy at the end of the race.
5. Compare the way Atalanta felt before the race with the way she felt after the race. Use a form of the adjective *good*.
   After the race, Atalanta felt better than she had felt before the race.

TRY THIS! Talking Tip

With a partner, discuss two books or stories you have both read. Compare the two, using the positive, comparative, and superlative forms of adjectives.

98 COMPARING WITH ADJECTIVES

PRACTICE BOOK, page 98

5-DAY PLAN

Use in conjunction with Daily Language Practice.

Day 1 Complete page T686.	**Day 4** Choose a Practice Activity or *Grammar Practice Book* pages 34–35.
Day 2 Complete a Practice Activity on page T687.	**Day 5** Complete *Practice Book* page 98.
Day 3 Choose a Practice Activity or *Language Handbook* pages 142–145.	

SPELLING

5-Day Plan

Integrated Spelling Lesson 19:
student book, pages 82–85;
Teacher's Edition, pages T129–T134.

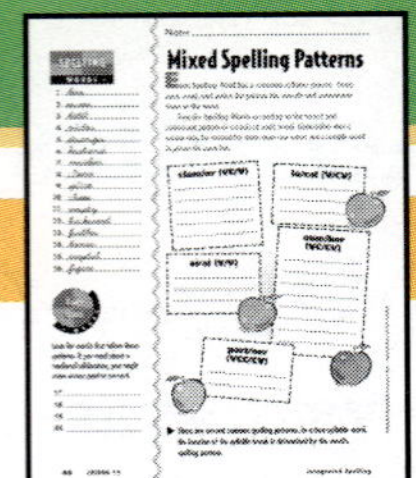
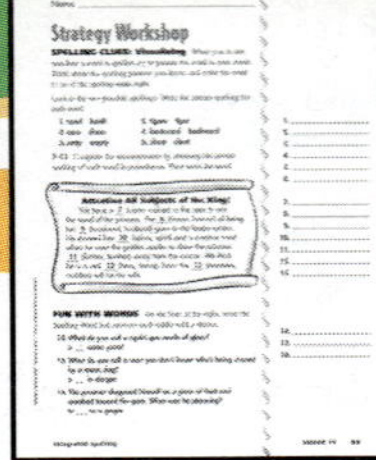
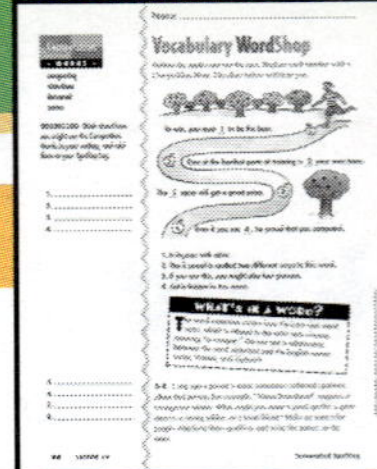
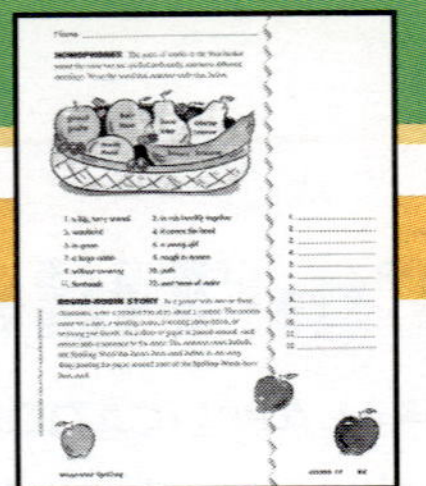

SPELLING WORDS

1. hero ★
2. escape ★
3. hotel
4. victor ★
5. stranger ★
6. husband ★
7. maiden ★
8. client
9. spirit ★
10. chaos
11. empty
12. backward ★
13. further ★
14. honor ★
15. crystal
16. figure ★

STUDENT'S PERSONAL WORDS

17. 19.
18. 20.

Additional story words are *perhaps, imploring,* and *delight.*

★ Words appearing in "Atalanta's Race"

Mixed Spelling Patterns

Pretest

DAY 1 **Administer the pretest.** Say each word, and then use it in the dictation sentence below. Help students self-check their pretests.

OPEN SORT

DAY 2 **Have students create categories.** Have students sort the Spelling Words into categories of their own choosing. Suggest these possibilities: part of speech, accented syllable, or short or long vowel sounds. Students may also invent their own categories.

CLOSED SORT

Sort by spelling pattern. Write on the board the headings from the chart below. Have volunteers write each Spelling Word under the appropriate heading. Then ask students to name other words that fit the categories. These words can be included on the student's personal words lists.

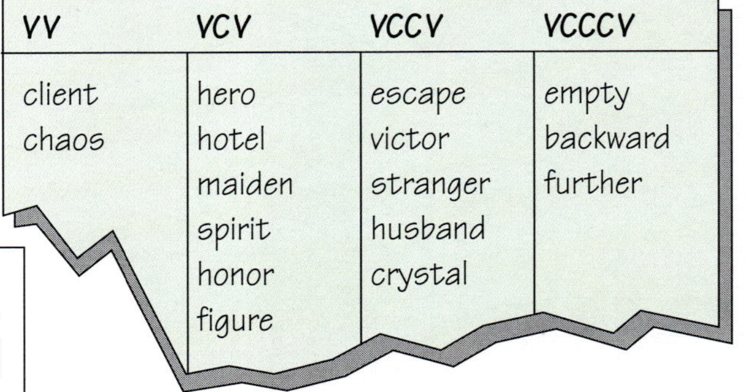

VV	VCV	VCCV	VCCCV
client	hero	escape	empty
chaos	hotel	victor	backward
	maiden	stranger	further
	spirit	husband	
	honor	crystal	
	figure		

Teach/Model

DAY 3 **Discuss the generalization.** All of the Spelling Words are two-syllable words. Remind students that every syllable contains a vowel sound. Then introduce the four spelling patterns represented by the words: VV (*chaos*), or no consonants between the two vowels; VCV (*honor*), or one consonant between the two vowels; VCCV (*victor*), or two consonants between the two vowels; and VCCCV (*empty*), or three consonants between the two vowels.

DAY 4 **Apply to writing.** Students should note the spelling patterns of words in their descriptions and see if they are spelled correctly.

Posttest

DAY 5 **Assess students' progress.** Use the sentences below to administer the posttest.

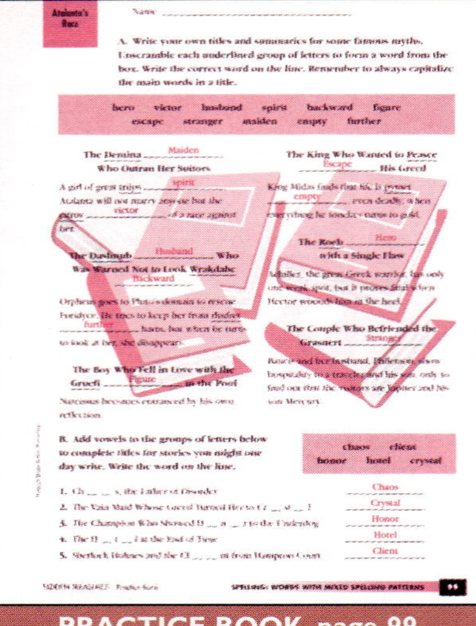

PRACTICE BOOK, page 99

DICTATION SENTENCES

1. The hero was praised for his bravery.
2. Close the door, or the dog might escape.
3. The tourists stayed at a small hotel.
4. This trophy will go to the victor.
5. A mysterious stranger came to town.
6. That woman and her husband are both teachers.
7. The dragon carried off the fair maiden.
8. The lawyer is having lunch with a client.
9. His energy and spirit cheered us up.
10. The disaster caused confusion and chaos.
11. Who put an empty milk carton back in the refrigerator?
12. The clown tumbled backward into the pool.
13. There is no reason to discuss the matter further.
14. Being asked to speak was a great honor.
15. The goblet was made of the finest crystal.
16. The little girl drew a stick figure.

VOCABULARY WORKSHOP

Reviewing Key Words

Display the Key Words. Then ask students to indicate the word that answers each question.

1. Which word would you use if you were describing your efforts to avoid running into something? *(swerved)*
2. Which word could be used to talk about a gift or an honor? *(bestowed)*
3. Which word has a similar meaning to the word *begging*? *(imploring)*
4. Which word shares a common root with *mortify*? *(immortal)*
5. Which word means "to cry out"? *(clamor)*

Extending Vocabulary

NEUTRAL AND GENDER-SPECIFIC WORDS

Explain that some words we use are gender-specific. They may refer to the masculine, the feminine, or neutral. The word *king* is masculine; *queen* is feminine. The word *ruler* is neutral.

Invite students to review "Atalanta's Race" to identify examples of gender-specific nouns. Make a list of the words they find. Then challenge students to name neutral nouns they know from their own experiences (for example, *news anchor, letter carrier, police officer*) and add those words to the list.

WRITE CAREER DESCRIPTIONS

Students should write brief career descriptions for some of the neutral nouns on their list. They should draw on prior experience and consult reference sources for additional information.

3 Learning Through the Literature

Tested Skill

Informal Assessment ✓

Are students able to

- ☑ identify prefixes and suffixes and tell their meanings?
- ☑ analyze words with Greek and Latin roots?

INTRODUCE: VOCABULARY STRATEGY

Structural Analysis

OBJECTIVE: To analyze words containing Greek and Latin roots, prefixes, and suffixes

Teach/Model

Return to the literature. Tell students that the Latin word *mors* means "death." Then ask them to identify a word in the story that is derived from the Latin word *mors*. If they have difficulty, offer the clue that it is one of the Key Words. (*immortal*)

Model analyzing word parts. Point out to students that looking at roots, prefixes, and suffixes can help them figure out the meanings of unfamiliar words such as *immortal*. Model analyzing the word *immortal*:

MODEL

I know the root of *immortal* is the Latin word *mors*, meaning "death." The prefix *im-* means "not," and the adjective-forming suffix *-al* adds the meaning "of" or "like." When I put the three parts together, I see that *immortal* must mean "not subject to death."

Practice/Apply

Have students demonstrate understanding. Work with students to analyze the meanings of these three story words that come from the Latin word *vincere*, meaning "to conquer." You may want to use Transparency 34 or create a different chart for another word.

TRANSPARENCY 34

Root: vincere ("to conquer")

Word	Prefix/ Suffix	Story Content	Meaning
victor	-or, "one who"	The attendants raised him up and put the victor's wreath upon his head.	the one who conquers; the winner
victory	-y, noun-forming suffix	...glad am I that it is this youth who has won the victory from me.	the fact of conquering or winning
victorious	-ious, "having or characterized by"	Now, if he be *victorious* and escape death I will give him my dear child.	adjective describing the person who conquers or wins

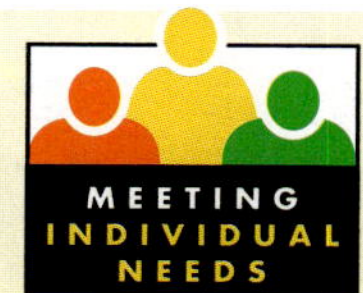

Practice Activities

EXPLORING WORD ORIGINS

COOPERATIVE LEARNING Have students work in small groups to use structural analysis and a dictionary to figure out the meanings of these words related to athletic events: *discus, pentathlon, decathlon*, and *stadium*. Have each group select a Recorder to write down the findings, a Checker to verify the information, and a Reporter to share the findings with the rest of the class. The groups may want to record their findings on a chart similar to Transparency 34 or create another kind of diagram to organize the facts. **VISUAL/AUDITORY**

Exploring Word Families

PERFORMANCE ASSESSMENT Challenge teams of three or four students to begin with the story word *attendant* and brainstorm other words that have the same Latin root *tendere*, meaning "to stretch," "to hold fast," or "to extend." Each team should appoint a Recorder to write down the words and a Checker to confirm that each word suggested has the Latin root *tendere*. When they have created their lists, teams should work together to create a word tree that shows clusters of closely related words. **AUDITORY/VISUAL**

STUDENTS ACQUIRING ENGLISH

To help students see relationships between words in English, invite them to collect words in which they see similarities—similarities that may or may not stem from Greek or Latin roots. Then together, explore the origins and meaning connections.

RETEACH

See page R5 for lessons in multiple modalities.

CHALLENGE

Have students dream up an athletic event and use Greek or Latin roots to create a suitable name for it.

D'Aulaires' Book of Greek Myths by Ingri and Edgar P. D'Aulaire. Doubleday, 1980. **EASY**

The Greeks and Troy by Deborah Tyler. Macmillan, 1993. **AVERAGE**

The Macmillan Book of Greek Gods and Heroes by Alice Low. Macmillan, 1985. **AVERAGE**

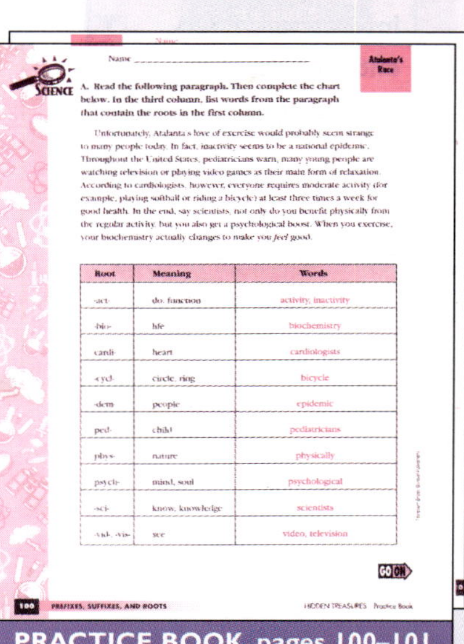

Name ______________________

Atalanta's Race

SCIENCE

A. Read the following paragraph. Then complete the chart below. In the third column, list words from the paragraph that contain the roots in the first column.

Unfortunately, Atalanta's love of exercise would probably seem strange to many people today. In fact, inactivity seems to be a national epidemic. Throughout the United States, pediatricians warn, many young people are watching television or playing video games as their main form of relaxation. According to cardiologists, however, everyone requires moderate activity (for example, playing softball or riding a bicycle) at least three times a week for good health. In the end, say scientists, not only do you benefit physically from the regular activity, but you also get a psychological boost. When you exercise, your biochemistry actually changes to make you *feel* good.

Root	Meaning	Words
-act-	do, function	activity, inactivity
-bio-	life	biochemistry
cardi-	heart	cardiologists
-cycl-	circle, ring	bicycle
-dem-	people	epidemic
ped-	child	pediatricians
phys-	nature	physically
psych-	mind, soul	psychological
-sci-	know, knowledge	scientists
-vid-, -vis-	see	video, television

GO ON

100 PREFIXES, SUFFIXES, AND ROOTS HIDDEN TREASURES Practice Book

PRACTICE BOOK, pages 100–101

PROJECT MANAGEMENT

Take Notes About Changes

SELECTION CONNECTION

"Atalanta's Race" shows how Hippomenes uses his wits to win a footrace against Atalanta, which changes forever the course of their lives. Encourage students to consider how all changes start with an idea.

PROJECT CHECKLIST

During this stage, students should

- ✔ interview community members about changes in the community.
- ✔ visit the library to examine sources of information about the community.
- ✔ contact the nearest historical society for information about printed, photographic, and recorded documents and records.
- ✔ take notes about what they learn.

Project Card 20 can be found as a copying master on page R24.

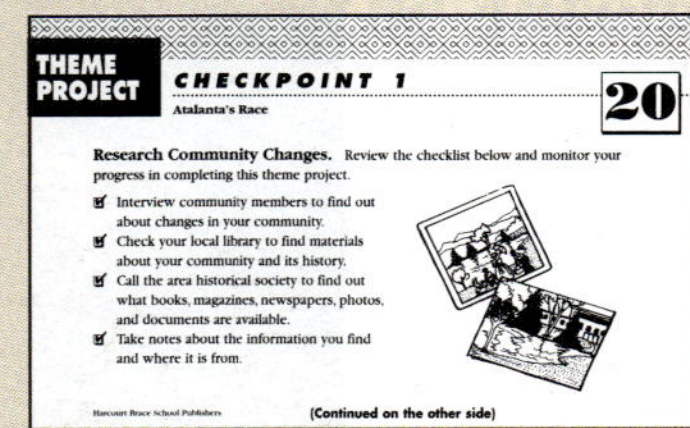

THEME PROJECT
CHECKPOINT 1
Atalanta's Race
20

Research Community Changes. Review the checklist below and monitor your progress in completing this theme project.

- ✔ Interview community members to find out about changes in your community.
- ✔ Check your local library to find materials about your community and its history.
- ✔ Call the area historical society to find out what books, magazines, newspapers, photos, and documents are available.
- ✔ Take notes about the information you find and where it is from.

Harcourt Brace School Publishers
(Continued on the other side)

Project Card 20

RESEARCH AND PLANNING TIPS

As students prepare to begin their research, suggest that they

- make a list of changes in their community they already know about.
- make a list of people who would be good interview subjects.
- prepare a list of questions for interviews and research.
- be ready to pursue a line of questioning different from the prepared questions if their research provides more interesting ideas.

Suggest that students write an entry in their project journals about new questions their research raises. Prompt students with questions such as *What would you like to know more about?*

Informal Assessment

At this checkpoint, students will use their research and note-taking skills to **synthesize** information about community changes and **evaluate** the importance of individual changes. Students are thinking critically if they

-  apply what they have learned to new situations.
- ✔ make decisions about the directions their research will take.

MEETING INDIVIDUAL NEEDS

STUDENTS ACQUIRING ENGLISH

Suggest that students work with a partner who speaks English fluently as they prepare for and conduct interviews. Encourage students to include interviews with subjects who speak the students' first language.

CLASSROOM MANAGEMENT

If possible, arrange for the class to conduct interviews at a Senior Citizens' center so all students will have access to interview subjects.

Great Summer Olympic Moments

by Nate Aaseng

SELECTION CONNECTION

Students have read "Atalanta's Race," an ancient Greek myth that celebrates the beauty and athletic gifts of a king's daughter, Atalanta. Now they will read an article about the origins and highlights of what one writer calls "the world's greatest showcase" of athletic talent—the Summer Olympics.

ABOUT THE AUTHOR

Nate Aaseng has written more than ninety books for young people on a great variety of subjects—everything from sports stars to the little-known creators of famous products such as Coca-Cola. His books have been recommended by such organizations as the National Council for Social Studies and the International Reading Association. He recalls being an avid reader as a child and says he took "the surfing approach" to reading: "You paddle around until you find an author you like and ride him or her until you reach dry land."

SUMMARY

GENRE: Nonfiction/Article

When the Olympic games were banned in A.D. 394, a thousand-year-old Greek tradition of honoring athletic prowess came to an end. Then, in the late nineteenth century, an archaeological dig near Olympia, Greece, revived interest in the games. But the first modern games, held in Athens in 1896, seemed unimpressive, especially to the medal-poor Greek athletes. Then Greek runner Spiridon Loues unexpectedly won a new, grueling event called the marathon, capturing a medal for Greece and rekindling enthusiasm for the games. That moment of national triumph was mirrored in Mexico in 1968, when Mexican swimmer Felipe Muñoz defeated the world champion to capture a gold medal for his country.

EXTRA SUPPORT

Encourage students to speculate about why people such as the ancient Greeks, who lived in a pre-industrial society, valued athletic competitions. Ask students why such skills as boxing, throwing a javelin, wrestling, and running would have been essential in time of war or emergency. To reinforce understanding, you might invite students to pantomime these activities and make judgments about the physical and mental challenges of each one.

Introducing the Article

PRIOR KNOWLEDGE

Have students discuss what they know about the history and events of the Summer Olympic games. On chart paper or on the board, begin a K-W-L chart like the one below. During the discussion, you may wish to check students' understanding of terms such as *trial heats, qualify*, and *finals*.

K	W	L
What I Know	What I Want to Know	What I Learned
Began in Greece Held every four years	How they were started What the events are	

Tell students that they are going to read an article about some memorable events in the Summer Olympics.

Reading an Article Remind students of "Atalanta's Race," a Greek myth about a runner. Now they will read an article about the games in which the world's best runners compete—the Summer Olympics. Ask them how reading a myth is different from reading an article. (The purpose for reading is different: A myth is generally read for entertainment; an article is read for factual information.) Then have students read pages 338–341 to find out more about the Summer Olympics.

GREAT SUMMER OLYMPIC MOMENTS

BY NATE AASENG

ILLUSTRATED BY DARRIN JOHNSTON

TIPS FOR CLASSROOM MANAGEMENT

SMALL GROUP

PARTNER READING

You may wish to have partners read the selection together. Encourage them to pause while reading to discuss anything new that they have learned about the Olympics.

WHOLE CLASS

SILENT READING/ DISCUSSION

Have students read the article silently. Suggest that as they read, they make notes about anything new that they have learned. When all students have finished reading, invite volunteers to complete the K-W-L chart.

For more than a thousand years, the ancient town of Olympia in western Greece was the gathering place for the greatest athletes of the world. Every four years, nations stopped their wars while men boxed, ran, jumped, and threw objects in the first Olympic stadium. First prize was a wreath of olive—and fame throughout the land. After the ancient Olympic games were banned by the Roman emperor in the year 394, the Olympian ideal of peaceful athletic competition among the nations became a distant memory. The stadium and temples of Olympia fell into ruin.

About 1,500 years later, in the 19th century, a group of German archaeologists began to dig in the area of Olympia. Many people around the world read about the ancient buildings that were being dug up. Scholars and students studied historical writings and learned how the ancient games had been organized. They even discovered the names of some of the great athletes who had competed in the games. Finally, in 1896, a group of sports fans set out to bring the games back to life.

Most of the pieces for this noble experiment had already been assembled. The games had a tireless organizer (Baron Pierre de Coubertin), a host country (Greece), financing (courtesy of a wealthy Greek architect), and competitors (more than 300, from 13 different nations).

At first, the games failed to inspire. The athletic performances of the 1896 Athens Olympics seemed very ordinary compared to the stories of legendary heroes who had battled for Olympic honors in ancient Greece. As the games progressed, the failure of the host country to win any track and field events

339

MINILESSON

REVIEW: STUDY SKILLS

Note-taking/ Outlining

INFORMAL ASSESSMENT

Have students reread and summarize the first paragraph. (Possible response: The Olympic games began in ancient Greece and featured the greatest athletes in the Greek world. The games were held every four years for more than a thousand years until a Roman emperor banned them in A.D. 394.)

TEACH/MODEL

Tell students that taking notes is similar to summarizing, except that notes do not need to be written in complete sentences. Notes should include only the most important information. Notes can then be organized into an outline. You may wish to model with a think-aloud:

MODEL **After reading the first paragraph, I know that the main topic is "The Ancient Olympic Games," so I'll write that down. Underneath I'll record these important details: *began in Olympia in ancient Greece; held every four years for more than 1,000 years; featured greatest athletes; banned in 394*. When I have finished reading and taking notes, I can arrange the notes to form an outline.**

PRACTICE/APPLY

Have students take notes on the rest of page 339.

CHALLENGE **Invite students to use the information in the article to estimate the date of the first Olympic games. Have students demonstrate how they arrived at their answer.** (The first recorded games were held in 776 B.C.)

Responding to the Article

Invite students to tell what information they found most interesting in the article. Encourage them to discuss the author's choice of the two incidents as illustrations of larger "great moments" in the Summer Olympics.

added to the disappointment of the fans. After lying dormant for 1,500 years, the Olympic games needed something extraordinary to bring them back to life.

Late in the competition, on April 10, 1896, a small group of men gathered at the Marathon Bridge. Marathon, a village north of Athens, was the site of an ancient Greek victory over Persian invaders in 490 B.C. According to a story passed down through the years, a Greek messenger had run all the way from the battlefield to Athens with news of the victory. After giving his report, the runner had collapsed and died from exhaustion. In honor of this legend, Baron de Coubertin had introduced a new event called the marathon. The runners would follow the road from Marathon to Athens, an incredible 40 kilometers (about 25 miles) away.

Nearly 100,000 spectators gathered at the stadium to witness the finish. All afternoon they anxiously awaited reports of the race's progress. Unfortunately, the early news was no more promising for Greece than the results of any of the other events had been. A French athlete named Lermusiaux had dominated the early portion of the race. Unable to maintain his own pace, Lermusiaux slowed, gave up the lead to Edwin Flack of Australia, and soon collapsed. A subdued Greek crowd passed along the latest information—Flack was just a few miles away and holding on to his lead.

Four kilometers from the finish line, Flack, a gold medalist in the 800 meters, faltered. Soon after, a Greek army major charged into the stadium on horseback to deliver the latest bulletin to the king and queen of Greece: A Greek was in the lead!

After running from Marathon, Greece, to Athens, the Greek runner Spiridon Loues closes in on the finish line amid the cheers of his homeland fans in the stadium.

SOCIAL STUDIES

FACT FINDER

The Olympics were held during a monthlong truce among the city-states to allow safe travel to Olympia, the site of the games. Only men and boys attended, either as contestants or as spectators. The first Olympic games featured a single event—a 200-yard footrace. Gradually other events were added, among them wrestling, the pentathlon (discus throw, javelin throw, long jump, a sprint, and wrestling), boxing, and the popular four-horse chariot race. An Olympic champion was rewarded only with a wild olive wreath at the games; on returning home, however, the athlete was often honored with special privileges, such as free meals for the rest of his life.

The news spread rapidly throughout the stadium. Sports fans, who had been mildly curious onlookers, became excited and tried to will the Greek along to the finish. A long, resounding roar from outside the stadium signaled that the first runner was nearing the finish. When the small form of Spiridon Loues appeared on the stadium track, the spectators leapt to their feet, shouting their delight. Loues crossed the finish line nearly seven minutes ahead of the next finisher and was practically drowned in a sea of congratulations.

This unexpected triumph by a poor man, who had finished no better than fifth in the Greek pre-Olympic trials, provided the spark that was needed to bring the Olympic games to life.

Years later, in 1968, the Olympic games in Mexico City followed a similar pattern. For 10 days of competition, the Mexican hosts politely applauded the victories of visiting athletes. In all that time, the Mexican athletes had faltered.

The host country's best prospect for a gold medal appeared to be in a swimming event, the 200-meter breaststroke. A 17-year-old named Felipe "Pepe" Muñoz had not only qualified for the finals but had also recorded the fastest time of the trial heats. Muñoz was still a long-shot to defeat Vladimir Kosinsky of the Soviet Union, who held the world record. But 8,000 Mexicans crowded the poolside bleachers to cheer his effort.

Halfway through the race, the Mexicans' hopes were evaporating. Muñoz, swimming in fourth place, appeared out of contention. Suddenly, the young swimmer surged forward. As he moved into third place, the hometown fans began cheering loudly. The inspired Muñoz continued to catch up to Kosinsky.

All spectators were on their feet as Muñoz touched the wall for the final turn just inches behind Kosinsky. Amid indescribable bedlam, the teenager caught the Soviet halfway down the final length and touched home half a second ahead of him to claim the gold medal.

In the celebration that followed, Muñoz was pulled out of the water and carried around the pool area. Spectators hugged and kissed each other. Television announcers wept openly. The Olympics had again provided hometown sports fans with an unforgettable experience.

Every four years, thousands of the world's greatest athletes gather to compete in the Olympic games. The grandeur and the massive scale of the Summer Olympics have made it the world's greatest showcase for what the human body and willpower can accomplish.

341

CHECKING COMPREHENSION

What Do You Think?

1. **How was the event in which Felipe Muñoz swam in 1968 like the one in which Spiridon Loues ran in 1896?** (Possible responses: Neither athlete was expected to win. Each athlete represented the host country, which had not won any medals. When Muñoz and Loues won their events, against the odds, the crowds were especially joyful.) **DESCRIPTIVE RESPONSE**

2. **Do you think that people's expectations for the games in 1896 were unrealistic? Explain your answer.** (Possible response: Yes. People in 1896 expected the athletes to be like the ancient Greek athletes, but the stories about those athletes may have been exaggerated. Also, those stories would have focused on the greatest moments of the games in over a thousand years.) **PERSONAL RESPONSE**

3. **What is the author's attitude toward his subject? How do you know?** (Possible response: He admires the Olympics and the athletes who compete in the games. He tells about the two races in an exciting way; he uses emotional words such as *unforgettable* and *grandeur* in writing about his subject.) **CRITICAL ANALYSIS/REFLECTING**

EXPANDING VOCABULARY

Have students find the word *bedlam* in the third-to-last paragraph on page 341. Explain that it means "a place or situation of noisy uproar and confusion." Ask students to tell what they think people in the crowd were doing to create bedlam.

Integrating Language Arts

TIPS FOR CLASSROOM MANAGEMENT

IF students show an interest in researching the Olympic games, **THEN** they should complete the Writing activity.

IF students need experience in using speaking strategies, **THEN** they should complete the Oral Language activity.

WRITING

Great Olympic Moments

Have students independently research other great summer or winter Olympic moments. Suggest that they first choose one sport, such as track and field, skating, or swimming. Encourage students to find information about the sport they have chosen in books or magazines at the library. You may wish to have them record information in the "lead paragraph" newspaper form below and then write a paragraph about their "great moment." Interested students could combine the paragraphs in a book for others to read. READING/WRITING

Lead Paragraph

Who? ______________________

What? ______________________

When? ______________________

Where? ______________________

Why? ______________________

How? ______________________

ORAL LANGUAGE

Create New Games

COOPERATIVE LEARNING Have small groups of students develop a new event for the Olympic games—either a summer or a winter sport, a men's or a women's event. A Recorder from each group can list rules group members have determined for their event. Have Reporters share their proposals with the rest of the class. LISTENING/SPEAKING/WRITING

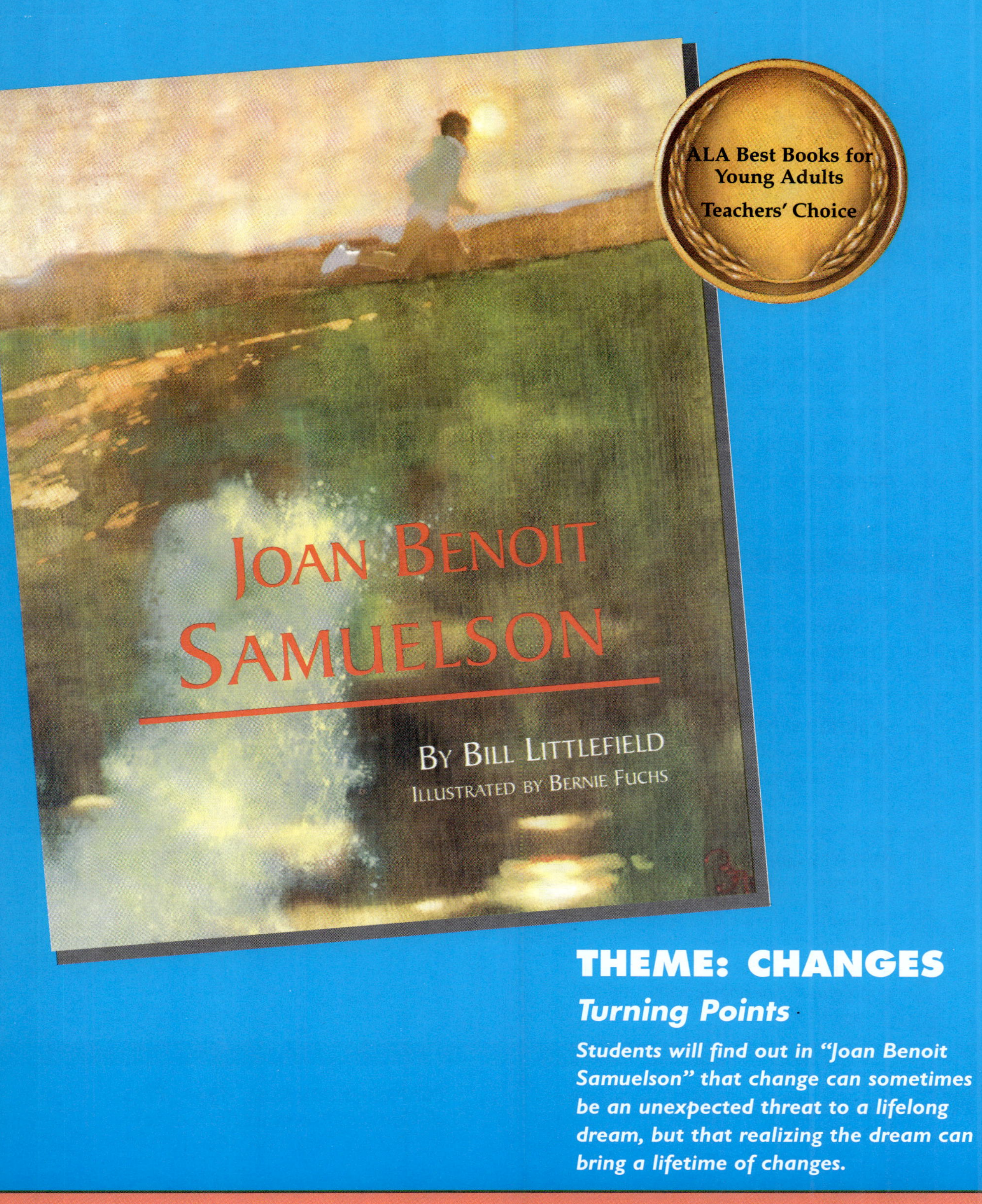

THEME: CHANGES

Turning Points

Students will find out in "Joan Benoit Samuelson" that change can sometimes be an unexpected threat to a lifelong dream, but that realizing the dream can bring a lifetime of changes.

SELECTION SUMMARY

Genre: Biography

In March of 1984, Joan Benoit, the country's best female distance runner, was looking forward to running in the 1984 Olympic Games in Los Angeles. But two months before the Olympic Trials, she suffered a knee injury that almost kept her from realizing her dream. Doctors recommended the one thing she couldn't do: rest. Then just three weeks before the Olympic Trials, she underwent arthroscopic surgery. Within a week, she was running again. At the trials, she finished first even though her knee began to hurt after twenty miles. She went on to win the marathon in the Olympic Games and set a new world record.

ABOUT THE AUTHOR AND THE ILLUSTRATOR

BILL LITTLEFIELD is a sports commentator for National Public Radio. He is the author of *Prospect,* a novel for adults, and currently lives in Needham, Massachusetts. In *Champions,* his first book for young people, Bill Littlefield says that reading stories about remarkable athletes teaches us "that imagination is essential, and that every champion was once a dreaming child."

BERNIE FUCHS is one of America's most highly regarded illustrators. In 1975, he was selected to join such artists as Norman Rockwell, Winslow Homer, and Frederick Remington in the Society of Illustrators Hall of Fame.

More information about Bernie Fuchs and his work appears on page T721.

SUGGESTED LESSON PLANNER

▶ *Joan Benoit Samuelson*

	DAY 1	DAY 2
PART 1 Reading, Listening, Speaking, Viewing **Key Words**: capable, rigors, incidental, brink, dominance	**BUILD BACKGROUND** T706 **VOCABULARY STRATEGIES** T707 *Transparency 35* *Practice Book* p. 103 **READING THE SELECTION** T708–T721 Options for Reading T708–T709 *Response Card 8* **REVIEW PREDICTIONS/PURPOSE** T718 **APPRECIATING THE LITERATURE** T718 NOTE: Students may read the selection on Day 2.	**SUMMARIZE THE SELECTION** T719 *Practice Book* p. 104 ◆ **RESPONSE CORNER ACTIVITIES** T722 **CHECKING COMPREHENSION** T723 *End-of-Selection Test* 
PART 2 Writer's Workshop	**POEM** Thinking as Writers T728 *Language Handbook* p. 51 *Transparency 36*	Prewriting T728 *Language Handbook* pp. 40, 51
Grammar	✓ **ACTION VERBS AND LINKING VERBS** Teach the Concept T730 Daily Language Practice (1–2) R15	Daily Language Practice (3–4) R15 Practice Activity T731
Spelling	**SUFFIXES *-ance/-ence*** *presence, entrance, audience, distance, difference, insurance, importance, conference, instance, allowance, experience, intelligence, independence, appearance, performance, ambulance* Pretest/Self-Check T732 *Integrated Spelling Teacher's Edition* pp. T135, T289	Open and Closed Sorts T732 *Integrated Spelling* p. 86 *Integrated Spelling Teacher's Edition* p. T136
PART 3 Skills and Strategies	◆ **INTEGRATED CURRICULUM** *Marathon Mania* **Social Studies** T736 **Health** T736 **Social Studies** T737 *Imagination Express, Destination: Neighborhood*	**COMPREHENSION SKILL** T734–T735 ✓ Compare/Contrast (Introduce) *Practice Book* pp. 108–109
	Use the Intervention Strategy note on page T713 to help **below-level** and **ESL students** as they read.	Have students read "Ancient Greece," pages 358–367, to connect Greek culture to the Olympic spirit.

NOTE: An alternative lesson plan for **below-level students** appears on *Intervention Strategies Manual* pp. 80–85. A lesson for **students acquiring English** appears on *Sheltered English/ESL Manual* pp. 54–57.

DAY 3	DAY 4	DAY 5
◆ **IDEA BANK ACTIVITIES** Retelling T726 Oral Language T726 Rereading T727 Real-Life Resources: Reading Directions for Performing a Process T727 *Writer's Magazine* pp. 52–53 School–Home Connection 14 R42 *Imagination Express, Destination: Neighborhood*	**VOCABULARY WORKSHOP** T733 Reviewing Key Words **READING TRADE BOOKS** T738–T739 *Signatures Library: Wilma Rudolph*  Signatures Library  Take-Home Book	**READING TRADE BOOKS** T735, T737, T738–T739 
Drafting T728 *Language Handbook* pp. 28, 41, 138 *The Amazing Writing Machine*	Responding and Revising T729 *Language Handbook* pp. 28, 41, 138	Proofreading and Publishing T729 *Language Handbook* p. 41
Daily Language Practice (5–6) R15 Practice Activity T731 *Language Handbook* pp. 146–147	Daily Language Practice (7–8) R15 Practice Activity T731 *Grammar Practice Book* pp. 36–37	Daily Language Practice (9–12) R15 *Practice Book* p. 105
Discuss the Generalization T732 *Integrated Spelling* p. 87 *Integrated Spelling Teacher's Edition* p. T137	Apply to Writing T732 *Integrated Spelling* pp. 88–89 *Integrated Spelling Teacher's Edition* pp. T138–T139	Posttest T732 *Practice Book* p. 106 *Integrated Spelling Teacher's Edition* p. T140
VOCABULARY MINILESSON T713 ✓Structural Analysis (Review) *Practice Book* p. 110 **COMPREHENSION MINILESSON** T715 Referents (Review) *Practice Book* p. 111	**VOCABULARY WORKSHOP** T733 Multiple-Meaning Words *Practice Book* p. 107	**GRAMMAR MINILESSON** T711 ✓ Comparing with Adjectives (Review) Theme Project Checkpoint 2 T740 *The Amazing Writing Machine*
Above-level students may choose and read a trade book independently.	**Below-level students** may read the *Take-Home Book: A Real Winner* to help them reinforce Key Words.	**Below-level** and **ESL students** may read the *ESL/Title I Library* book *Jesse Owens: Olympic Star.*

✓ = Tested Skill
◆ = Optional activities used to adjust pacing throughout the lesson
Titles in *italics* are optional materials.

1 Reading and Responding

BUILDING BACKGROUND AND CONCEPTS

PRIOR KNOWLEDGE

Relate to students' lives. Ask students to think about what they have to do to achieve a goal that is important to them. Discuss how studying hard might help them get good grades and how practice and good health habits might help them do well in sports.

Create a class web about marathons. "Joan Benoit Samuelson" is a nonfiction profile of a champion marathon runner. Have students show what they know about marathons by brainstorming facts about how and where marathons are run and about the history of marathons. Begin a web similar to the one at right. Have students tell what they know about marathons.

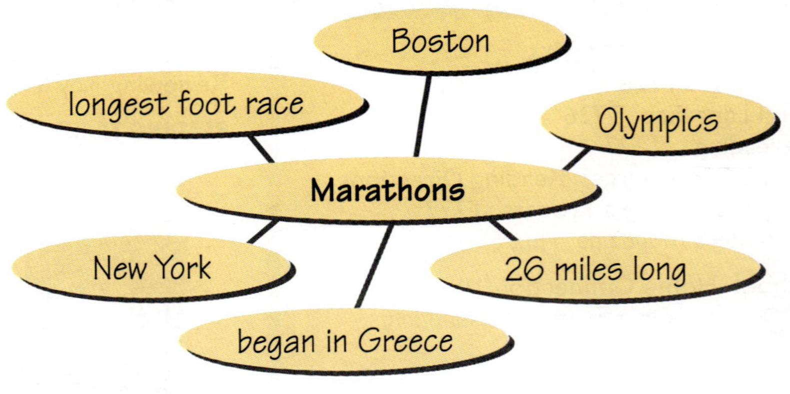

QUICKWRITE

Encourage students to write a few sentences about how they feel during and after a long run or brisk walk. Suggest that students consider how running affects their breathing and how their legs feel when they have finished running. Some students may want to describe what they look at as they run.

Intervention Strategies

For students who may have difficulty reading "Joan Benoit Samuelson," support is available in *Intervention Strategies Manual*, pages 80–85, and on pages T713 and T724–T725 in this lesson.

STUDENTS ACQUIRING ENGLISH

See *Sheltered English/ESL Manual*, pages 54–57.

FACT FINDER

SOCIAL STUDIES

Women at the Olympic Games

Women were forbidden to compete in any of the games in the original Olympics in ancient Greece. After the Romans conquered Greece, the games were ended; they were not held again for more than 1,500 years. The first modern Olympic Games were held in Athens, Greece, in 1896, but women were not allowed to participate until 1900 when the games were held in Paris, France. The first events in which women competed were lawn tennis and golf. Other games for women were gradually added, including some of the track and field events. Joan Benoit won the first Olympic marathon for women in Los Angeles in 1984. Before that year, women competed only in the shorter races.

VOCABULARY STRATEGIES

KEY WORDS DEFINED

capable having ability; able

rigors difficulties; harsh circumstances

incidental happening as a minor consequence

brink edge

dominance controlling power; importance

INTEGRATED SPELLING

Spelling Pretest: page T732

Spelling Generalization: Words with the suffixes *-ance* and *-ence*

CONTEXT CLUES: STATEMENTS ABOUT RUNNING

Encourage students to use syntactic and semantic cues. Display the statements about running on Transparency 35, and have a volunteer read them aloud. Model how to identify the context clues that can help determine the meaning of the word *capable*. (The words *but* and *not* help me realize that the word *capable* must have a similar meaning to the word *can*.) Have students continue to use context clues to figure out the meanings of the other Key Words.

CHECK UNDERSTANDING

Have students identify synonyms. Display the Key Words, and present the following word groups orally or write them on the board. Ask students to tell which Key Word belongs in each group and have an all-student vote on the choices. **STRATEGY: SYNONYMS**

Word Group	Key Word
control, power, mastery	(dominance)
minor, nonessential, unimportant	(incidental)
hardships, challenges, difficulties	(rigors)
verge, edge, brim	(brink)
competent, skilled, able	(capable)

TRANSPARENCY 35

Key Words

- Some people can run shorter races but are not capable of running marathons.
- Surviving the rigors of long-distance running can be a real challenge.
- For some people, simply being able to run fast is what's important, and winning is just incidental.
- Still, being on the brink of a championship and not winning can be heartbreaking.
- Only those who consistently succeed will have total dominance in the field of long-distance running.

PRACTICE BOOK, page 103

Prereading Strategies

PREVIEW AND PREDICT

Have students preview the selection by looking at the illustration on pages 342–343 and reading the introduction on page 344.

Begin a character chart on the board. Students may use the chart on *Practice Book* page 104 to record words that describe Joan Benoit Samuelson and to tell how they know.

CHARACTER CHART: Joan Benoit Samuelson

BEFORE READING
runner, champion, determined, delightful

HOW DO YOU KNOW?
The illustration shows her running, and the introduction says that people will remember her as a determined, delightful champion.

You may want to suggest that students write their predictions about the story in their personal journals.

PURPOSE

You may want to model setting a purpose:

MODEL **The author says, "There never was a more delightful champion." I'm going to read to find out what made her so special.**

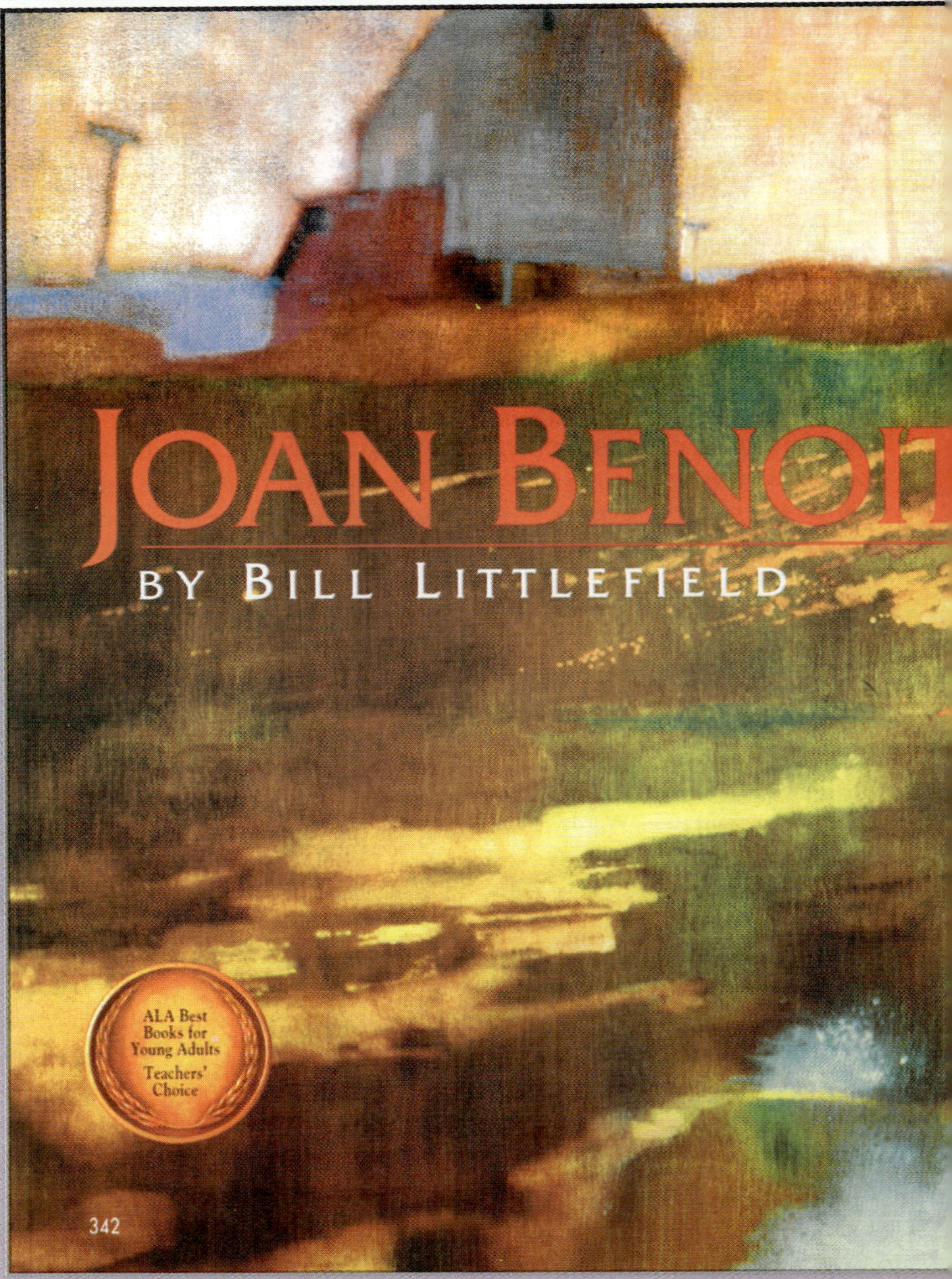

JOAN BENOIT

BY BILL LITTLEFIELD

ALA Best Books for Young Adults Teachers' Choice

342

SMALL GROUP

STRATEGIC READING

Use the suggestions on pages T710 and T714 to model Strategic Reading. Encourage students to try other strategies if **rereading** doesn't help them understand difficult passages.

COOPERATIVE READING

READER RESPONSE GROUPS

Have pairs of students pause during reading to talk about the story. Suggest they use Reader Response Card 8 to carry on a Written Conversation. Reader Response Card 8 can be found at the back of this Teacher's Edition.

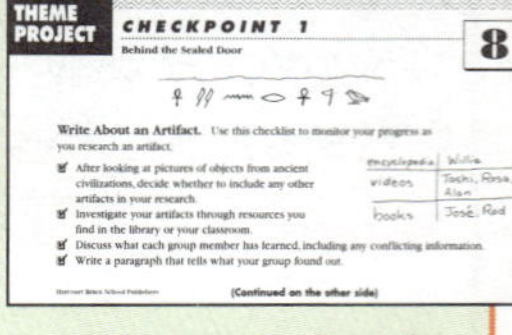

Response Card 8

SAMUELSON

ILLUSTRATED BY BERNIE FUCHS

from *CHAMPIONS*

Stories of Ten Remarkable Athletes

343

WHOLE CLASS

READ ALOUD

Read aloud the first two or three pages of the selection to familiarize students with the author's writing style. Then have students finish the selection on their own. Encourage them to make a list of words and phrases they think are difficult, interesting, or unusual.

INDEPENDENT READING

Students who don't need much teacher support should read the selection silently and answer the questions on page 357. Then encourage students to work with other classmates to complete one of the activities on pages 356 and 357.

Strategic Reading

REREADING

Invite students to talk about strategies they use while reading. Display the class-made strategy chart, and explain that the focus strategy for reading "Joan Benoit Samuelson" is rereading. Ask students how rereading might help them understand better what is happening in a selection. (Possible response: If I'm not sure of the sequence of events, I might reread to confirm what happened.) **STRATEGY: REREADING**

PAGES 342–349

Have students read to the middle of page 349 to find out more about Joan Benoit Samuelson and her goal of becoming a champion.

It is true that all records fall, and the ones Joan Benoit Samuelson set in the Boston Marathon in 1983 and the 1984 Olympic Marathon will be no exception. But long after her numbers have been eclipsed, people who saw her run will talk about her fierce and steady determination and her astonishing resilience. And then someone will remember that she wanted to call her autobiography *Out on a Limp,* and everybody will laugh. And somebody else will say, "You know, there never was a more delightful champion." And everyone will agree, because that will be true, too.

March is not Maine's best season. Spring never comes early to northern New England, and the wind off the ocean in March stings a runner's cheek. But that discomfort was nothing compared to the pleasure of running near home, and so Joan Benoit was training in Cape Elizabeth, minutes from her family, in the middle of the March preceding the 1984 Summer Olympics.

There were other advantages to Cape Elizabeth. Though the roads and paths there are not free of traffic, there is still farmland to see. The view of the sea is fine, if you don't mind the

344

SOCIAL STUDIES

Maine is the most northeasterly state in the country. Cape Elizabeth is a few miles southeast of Portland, Maine's largest city. The average temperature there ranges from 13°F to 31°F in the month of March.

solitude. And Joan Benoit knew all the routes up there so well that she was unlikely to be surprised or distracted from the business at hand. At one time she'd tried to keep to untraveled roads because running competitively had seemed so preposterous to her. As a schoolgirl she first discovered the joy running could bring her. It was all hers, and all she had to do to improve was run more. Her shyness was no handicap. Maybe it was even an advantage. She ran alone and loved it. But she was embarrassed about declaring herself a marathoner, saying it to the world by training seriously where anyone might notice. When cars would pass her in those days, she would sometimes stop running and pretend she was picking flowers. But now the solitude was simply one useful component to the concentration Joan Benoit had built to complement the joy. She'd acquired an iron sense of purpose that had been wearing down opponents for ten years, and that would drive Benoit through another decade of championship performances.

The run started off well. Why should it have been otherwise? Joan Benoit was the country's best female distance runner. She'd won the Boston Marathon twice, the second time the previous April (1983) in a world record time: 2 hours, 22 minutes, 43 seconds. She'd won major marathons in Eugene, Oregon, and in New Zealand as well, and too many shorter races to count. At least *she* hadn't counted them. And now, in the best shape of her career, she was pointing for the Olympic Trials, which were less than two months away. She'd picked the twenty-mile loop in Cape Elizabeth that day because it was a run that had always provided her with a sense of how well her training was going. She expected good news.

345

Tested Skill

MINILESSON

REVIEW: GRAMMAR

Comparing with Adjectives

INFORMAL ASSESSMENT

Ask students to locate an example on page 345 of an adjective used to make a comparison and tell what things are being compared. (Possible response: *Joan Benoit was the country's best female distance runner.* Joan Benoit is being compared with all the country's other female distance runners.)

TEACH/MODEL

Remind students of the three degrees of comparison: positive, comparative, and superlative. The superlative form is used to compare three or more things. In the sentence above, the word *best* is used to compare three or more runners. The comparative form is used to compare two items. For example, Tom ran a *better* race than Steve. The positive form of an adjective is used when no comparison is being made: Tom ran a *good* race. Explain that most regular comparative adjectives are formed by adding *-er* to the words and most superlatives are formed by adding *-est* to the words.

PRACTICE/APPLY

Ask students to look in the selection for other examples of adjectives that are used to make comparisons. Then have students write several sentences that contain comparative and superlative adjectives. Students should share their sentences with partners and identify each other's comparisons.

EXTRA SUPPORT **Explain to students that after the introduction to the selection the text refers to Joan Benoit Samuelson as Joan Benoit, omitting her married name. Joan Benoit married Scott Samuelson shortly after the 1984 Olympics.**

Critical Thinking Questions

1. **How might Joan Benoit's shyness have contributed to her strength as a runner?** (Possible response: Because of her shyness, Joan Benoit ran alone and was able to concentrate on what she wanted to accomplish as a runner.) **CRITICAL: DETERMINING CAUSE AND EFFECT**

2. **What details from the story show how determined Joan Benoit is as an athlete?** (Possible responses: She skied in the darkness of early evening when others may have quit. She drove herself harder than any coach would. She did not want to rest when doctors advised her to.) **CRITICAL: SUMMARIZING**

But with three miles to go, she felt an unfamiliar sensation in her knee. Later she would say it seemed as if "a spring were unraveling in the joint." She tried to run for another two miles, but the knee complained too loudly. When she could no longer stride, she hobbled. When she could no longer hobble, she walked.

"Injuries are part of the game." Maybe this is the most familiar cliché in all of sports. But each particular injury is new and ominous when it happens, and this one had picked a heck of a time to occur. Nearly every girl and boy who has ever run or jumped well enough to dream about excelling at it has entertained fantasies about the Olympics. Now here was Joan Benoit on the brink of the glorious realization of that fantasy. All she had to do was gradually bring her training to the peak she had learned to achieve for her biggest races and finish among the top three U.S. women in the marathon portion of the trials, which would be held in Washington State in May.

But you don't get to run in the Olympics if you don't qualify in the trials. And you don't run in the trials on a knee that feels like somebody's working on it with pliers.

"This was the most frightening moment of my life," Benoit said several years later in *Running Tide,* the autobiography she wrote with Sally Baker.

It was no exaggeration. Since childhood, Benoit had pushed herself to excel, first as a skier, then as a field hockey player, and finally as a runner. As a little girl, she had skied into the darkness of early evening rather than quit the slopes before she absolutely had to do it. A frostbitten fingertip was a small price to pay for the additional run or two that might make her more

346

EXPANDING VOCABULARY

WORD ORIGINS Point out that the word *ominous* in the second paragraph comes from the Latin base word *omen.* An omen is a prophetic sign that can signal something good or evil, but the adjective form *ominous* always has a negative connotation. Something that is *ominous* is threatening and is a sign of something bad to come.

competitive. Once she'd begun running seriously, she'd always driven herself harder than any coach would. "I liked pushing myself to keep going after exhaustion set in," she has said. "It was a game I played."

Always the point of the game was to be as good as she could possibly be at what she was doing, and always that goal seemed to be just beyond the next marathon, the next ten-kilometer run, the next workout. Setting that sort of goal is a private way of motivating oneself, a way that lots of people might not understand. Winning races, especially races as famous as the Boston Marathon, might seem to be achievement enough to the people lining the course and clapping as the runners rush by, but winning has been almost incidental to Benoit. Even as a freshman at Bowdoin College she was uncomfortable with the praise she gained as an outstanding field hockey player. "I would squirm under the compliments," she remembers, "not in false modesty, but because I had a voice inside that said, 'Watch it.' I knew I was capable of more, and that kept me honest."

Even Joan Benoit's closest friends—the ones who best understood her determination and her enormous capacity to endure the rigors of long-distance running—were worried in the spring of 1984. The fluky injury was followed by weeks of indecision. Some days the knee felt fine. On other days it hurt just to walk upstairs, and that was when participation in the Olympic Trials couldn't have seemed more impossible. The most frustrating part of the ordeal was that the doctors Benoit consulted kept advising rest, the one suggestion she couldn't take seriously. Who could rest? When in the past had rest ever helped her prepare for a race? She'd always said, "Mileage is my safety blanket. I feel

347

Tested Skill

MINILESSON

REVIEW: VOCABULARY

Structural Analysis

INFORMAL ASSESSMENT

Direct students' attention to this sentence in the second paragraph on page 346: *Now here was Joan Benoit on the brink of the glorious realization of that fantasy.* Have students use structural analysis to identify the base word and suffix of the word *realization.* *(realize, -ation)*

TEACH/MODEL

Explain that suffixes can change the way a word is used in a sentence. Lead students to see that the word *realization* is a noun formed by adding the suffix *-ation* to the verb *realize.* If necessary, model another example:

MODEL

In the sentence *It was no exaggeration,* I can tell that the word *exaggeration* is a noun, formed by replacing the final e in the verb *exaggerate* with the suffix *-ion.*

PRACTICE/APPLY

Help students locate other nouns in the selection that were created by adding suffixes to other words. *(exhaustion, achievement, modesty, determination, participation, suggestion)* Have students identify the base word and the suffix in each one.

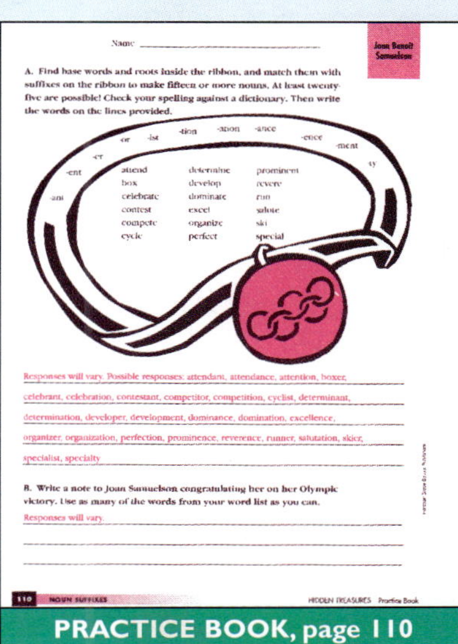

Name ______________________

Joan Benoit Samuelson

A. Find base words and roots inside the ribbon, and match them with suffixes on the ribbon to make fifteen or more nouns. At least twenty-five are possible! Check your spelling against a dictionary. Then write the words on the lines provided.

-ant -ent -er -or -ist -tion -ation -ance -ence -ment -ty

attend, box, celebrate, contest, compete, cycle, determine, develop, dominate, excel, organize, perfect, prominent, revere, run, salute, ski, special

Responses will vary. Possible responses: attendant, attendance, attention, boxer, celebrant, celebration, contestant, competitor, competition, cyclist, determinant, determination, developer, development, dominance, domination, excellence, organizer, organization, perfection, prominence, reverence, runner, salutation, skier, specialist, specialty

B. Write a note to Joan Samuelson congratulating her on her Olympic victory. Use as many of the words from your word list as you can.

Responses will vary.

110 NOUN SUFFIXES HIDDEN TREASURES Practice Book

PRACTICE BOOK, page 110

CONVENTIONS OF LANGUAGE

QUOTATION MARKS **Direct attention to the quotation at the end of the first paragraph on page 347. Point out the single quotation marks around the words *Watch it.* Explain that single quotes are used to set off a quotation within a quotation.**

Intervention Strategies

PREDICTING **Ask students to repeat this sentence aloud or to themselves: *When I read, I make many predictions about what is going to happen next.* Have students tell how making predictions helps them understand the events in "Joan Benoit Samuelson."**

Strategic Reading

PAGES 342–349 What does Joan Benoit describe as "the most frightening moment of my life"? Why? (Possible response: injuring a knee two months before the Olympic Trials because it might cost her something she'd worked toward her whole life)
STRATEGY: SUMMARIZING

Why do you think it is so important for Joan Benoit to compete in the 1984 Olympics? (Possible responses: She is in the best shape of her career and can perform in her own country since the games are in Los Angeles.) INFERENTIAL: NOTING IMPORTANT DETAILS

REREADING

You may want to use a think-aloud to model the strategy of rereading:

MODEL

I am confused when I read that "winning has been almost incidental to Benoit" because she is so competitive. So I reread the paragraph and see that Joan Benoit wants to be as good as possible, whether she wins or loses.

PAGES 349–353 Ask students to read to page 353 to find out how Joan Benoit copes with her knee injury.

I'm doing okay if I put in enough miles. And if I don't burn off my energy every day, I'm disoriented and grumpy." She was not likely to sit back and watch cartoons on T.V., even if that was what the doctor ordered. She was far more inclined to say, "When in doubt, run harder," and in her case "harder" meant more than the usual 100 to 120 miles each week.

March dragged into April, and the knee did not improve. In fact it seemed to be getting worse. Normally the doctors might have performed an arthroscopy, a procedure in which they insert a tiny scope into the knee and examine it to see if a ligament or cartilage has been torn. But with the Olympic Trials only weeks away, they were reluctant to do it. People recover from arthroscopy much more quickly than they do from more major knee surgery, but no surgery is truly minor. Even if they could diagnose and correct the problem with the arthroscope, the trauma of the surgery and the training time lost to it would certainly cost Benoit her shot at the Olympics.

To make matters even more improbably dramatic, the 1984 Olympics were particularly special for a number of reasons. The U.S. had boycotted the previous Games in 1980 to protest the presence of troops from the Soviet Union in Afghanistan. Hundreds of athletes, Joan Benoit included, had been denied the opportunity to participate in the spectacle by politics. Nobody, least of all Joan Benoit, wanted to be denied again. Beyond that, the 1984 Olympics were to be held in Los Angeles, so there would be an opportunity for U.S. athletes to perform before their countrymen and countrywomen. And finally the '84 Olympics would provide women with their first opportunity to run the marathon in the Games.

348

EXPANDING VOCABULARY

WORD ORIGINS The word *arthroscopy* is made up of two Greek combining forms: *arthro-* and *-scopy*. *Arthro-* means "joint." It's also part of the word *arthritis*, which names a disease that affects the joints. The other part, *-scopy*, indicates viewing, seeing, or observing.

SOCIAL STUDIES

When you *boycott*, you refuse to use, buy, or take part in something as a form of protest. Charles C. Boycott (1832–1897), an English land agent in Ireland, charged such unusually high rents that his tenants refused to have anything to do with him. This protesting became known as boycotting.

Under the curious assumption that females were somehow incapable of running twenty-six miles, the Olympic Committee had always limited them to shorter races. Even the growing popularity of marathoning among women and the triumphs of Benoit and other champions such as Ingrid Kristiansen, Rosa Mota, Grete Waitz, and Charlotte Teske hadn't earned female marathoners a chance to run in the Olympics until 1984. Now the opportunity was at hand, and there was serious doubt about whether the very best of all the American women runners would be able to compete.

Joan Benoit underwent arthroscopic surgery three weeks before the trials. Dr. Stan James found a fibrous mass called a plica that had become inflamed and was interfering with the normal movement of the knee joint. He removed it. Benoit awoke from the anesthetic and, still groggy, called a friend to ask if she could pick Joan up on her way home from work and take her running. It was a notion so goofy that even Benoit can't quite believe she ever had it.

Still, she was swimming and riding a stationary bicycle within days of her release from the hospital, and running again within a week. Drawing on her own determination and the support of her family and friends, she resumed her training, overcame a pulled hamstring muscle that resulted from favoring the knee, and appeared for the Olympic Trials as scheduled.

"Even as I was jogging to the starting line, I honestly didn't know if I could manage the race," she remembered afterward. She told her family not to come to the trials because she feared that she'd run badly if she ran at all. But when race day came, her brother and his wife were there. They claimed, transparently,

349

MINILESSON

REVIEW: COMPREHENSION

Referents

INFORMAL ASSESSMENT

Have students reread the first sentence of the first paragraph on page 349 and identify the pronoun in the sentence and what it refers to. (*them, females*)

TEACH/MODEL

Remind students that referents are the names of people, places, things, ideas, or actions that pronouns or other words replace. Read aloud the first sentence of the third paragraph on page 349. Explain to students that sometimes the name a pronoun refers to may not be in the same sentence as the pronoun. In this sentence, *she* and *her* refer to Joan Benoit. Encourage students to use context clues if they have trouble identifying what a pronoun refers to.

PRACTICE/APPLY

Ask students to locate other examples of pronouns and their referents on pages 348 and 349. Then have students tell what word or words the pronoun is taking the place of.

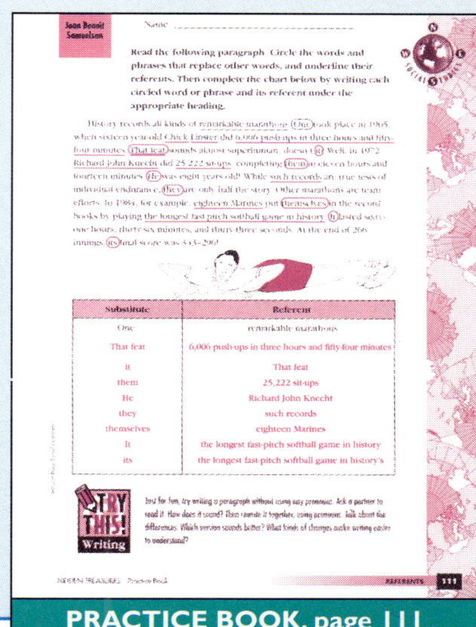

Joan Benoit Samuelson

Name ______________________

Read the following paragraph. Circle the words and phrases that replace other words, and underline their referents. Then complete the chart below by writing each circled word or phrase and its referent under the appropriate heading.

History records all kinds of remarkable marathons. One took place in 1965, when sixteen-year-old Chick Linster did 6,006 push-ups in three hours and fifty-four minutes. That feat sounds almost superhuman, doesn't it? Well, in 1972 Richard John Knecht did 25,222 sit-ups, completing them in eleven hours and fourteen minutes. He was eight years old! While such records are true tests of individual endurance, they are only half the story. Other marathons are team efforts. In 1984, for example, eighteen Marines put themselves in the record books by playing the longest fast-pitch softball game in history. It lasted sixty-one hours, thirty-six minutes, and thirty-three seconds. At the end of 266 innings, its final score was 343–296!

Substitute	Referent
One	remarkable marathons
That feat	6,006 push-ups in three hours and fifty-four minutes
it	That feat
them	25,222 sit-ups
He	Richard John Knecht
they	such records
themselves	eighteen Marines
It	the longest fast-pitch softball game in history
its	the longest fast-pitch softball game in history's

TRY THIS! Writing

Just for fun, try writing a paragraph without using any pronouns. Ask a partner to read it. How does it sound? Then rewrite it together, using pronouns. Talk about the differences. Which version sounds better? What kind of changes make writing easier to understand?

REFERENTS 111

PRACTICE BOOK, page 111

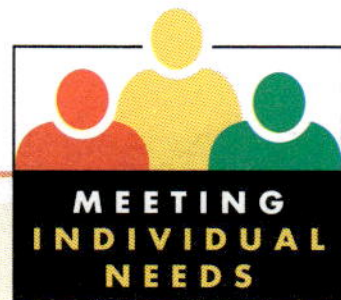

CHALLENGE **Have interested students investigate and report on topics in sports medicine, such as arthroscopic surgery. Encourage students to interview athletes and medical personnel for quotes to include in their reports.**

Cooperative Reading

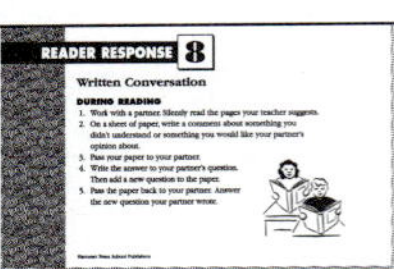
Response Card 8

Suggest that students work in pairs to discuss what they think about the photograph on page 351. Point out that the text on this page relates to the photograph. You may want to ask students the following questions before they share their opinions with partners:

- **How does the photograph help you understand the ways running is different from team sports?**
- **What does the photograph say to you about the nature of competition?**
- **How does the message of the photograph apply to your own life?**

that it was just one stop on a West Coast trip they'd been meaning to take anyway. Benoit admitted later that having them there had never been more important.

She ran conservatively that day and was surprised at the relative ease with which she covered the first twenty miles. The years of training and discipline seemed to carry her along automatically for a while. But with six miles to go, her legs suddenly remembered all the miles they'd missed over the past two months. The knee, only three weeks out from under the surgeon's scope, turned cranky. Benoit began concentrating on planting her feet with each stride to spare the joint unnecessary wobbling. She ran more and more slowly, more deliberately, less naturally, and although the commentators kept saying she was looking good, she knew otherwise. She kept sneaking peeks over her shoulder, wondering why some of the other runners were not moving up on her. That nobody did was a measure of her dominance of the U.S. marathoners.

Even as she crossed the finish line first, though, Joan Benoit was figuring that it would be different in the Olympics.

Perhaps it was partly doubt that drove her to train so effectively in the days between the trials and the Olympic Marathon itself. When that race finally came, it crushed other champions. The weather was so hot and miserably humid that Grete Waitz, one of the prerace favorites, later said, "I could have run faster, but I was afraid of dying." She was hardly overstating the case. Switzerland's Gabriela Anderson-Schiess was so dehydrated by the time she reached the finish line that she was disoriented and staggering.

Amid that drama, Joan Benoit was the picture of superb

350

HEALTH

DEHYDRATION Point out that running a long race in hot and humid weather might cause mild dehydration. Explain that dehydration is the loss of too much water from the body. Dryness in the mouth, nose, and throat are symptoms of dehydration. People with mild dehydration should drink plenty of fluids.

Joan Benoit Samuelson runs past a mural of herself on the way to Olympic gold.

efficiency. This time she never looked back. A photograph taken during the race says it all. It shows Benoit running past a building upon which there is a huge mural that depicts her victory a year earlier in the 1983 Boston Marathon. Also in the photograph is Bill Rodgers, the great marathoner whom Benoit had idolized as a young woman. He is perched on the back of the pace truck, providing television commentary for the race. The photograph is splendidly full of meaning. Joan Benoit is running alone, of course, since she ran most of the race alone. (She led it wire to wire.) But it also seems to symbolize the way in which she consistently ran beyond her own previous triumphs. The win in Boston depicted in the mural established a world

351

Student Self-Assessment

REREADING

Encourage students to use the rereading strategy to check their comprehension of the selection:

- How does rereading help me understand when the author has stopped writing about the events at the Olympic Trials and has begun describing Joan's experiences at the actual Olympic Games?
- How can rereading help me identify who is speaking?

MEETING INDIVIDUAL NEEDS

EXTRA SUPPORT **Point out that Bill Rodgers was a major runner in the late 1970s. By January 1981, he had won eighteen marathons and many shorter races.**

Bill Rodgers in New York City Marathon, 1979

Strategic Reading

PAGES 349–355 How does Joan Benoit cope with her injured knee? What happens during the trials? (Possible responses: She has surgery on her knee three weeks before the trials. During the trials, the pain in her knee flares up, but she still crosses the finish line first.) STRATEGY: SUMMARIZING

What does the author of this selection think about Joan Benoit? (Possible response: He thinks she is an exceptional athlete who tries to maintain a calm, quiet life despite all the attention she receives.) CRITICAL: RECOGNIZING AUTHOR'S VIEWPOINT

Returning to the Predictions/Purpose

Did you find out what you wanted to know about Joan Benoit Samuelson? Encourage students to discuss whether their purposes for reading were met. STRATEGY: RETURNING TO THE PURPOSE

Appreciating the Literature

Did you find this story inspirational? Why or why not? (Responses will vary.)

IDEA BANK

Invite students to make a collection of quotes about winning. They can begin with Joan Benoit's statement, "Winning is neither everything nor the only thing. It is one of many things." Encourage students to use reference sources such as *Bartlett's Familiar Quotations* to help them find quotes.

Three Australian runners at the finish.

record, but the central figure in this picture is not dreaming of a past victory; she is churning toward the next. And it is the man, Rodgers, who watches and talks about it, as the woman, Benoit, runs into history.

The Olympic course in Los Angeles ended in the Coliseum, an enormous stadium packed with fans from all over the world. In order to enter the stadium that day, Benoit ran through a tunnel. She was alone, and she knew she had won. She remembers thinking, "Once you leave this tunnel, your life will be changed forever," and she remembers that then she fastened her eyes on her shoes and turned her attention back to maintaining her pace. She concentrated on only that until she had crossed the finish line. Then she raised her arms over her head and ran a victory lap around the Coliseum, waving at the applauding crowd. Her smile was glorious, exalting, and grateful all at once.

Her life did change, as the lives of Olympic gold medal winners are likely to do. But it changed less than the lives of other winners who have not been so firmly grounded in values more substantial than winning. When she was asked where she could be found after the Games, Joan Benoit said, "Look for me in a berry patch in Maine." She was not entirely successful at keeping her distance from the clatter and clamor that inevitably follow a triumph as large and public as hers had been, but within a short while she had reestablished the calm that had always seemed to lie at the center of her running life and her life beyond running. Even under pressure from those who were competing for her attention, offering her endorsement opportunities, or merely calling to wish her well, she remained the quiet, somewhat shy young woman from Maine.

353

NOTES

Here's a place to list ideas or activities that you would like to use the next time you teach this lesson.

SUMMARIZING

Character Chart

If students have already completed the Before Reading section of the character chart, have them complete the After Reading section. Students can assess their charts by asking themselves whether the words and explanations they wrote in their charts show an accurate picture of Joan Benoit. See *Practice Book* page 104.

CHARACTER CHART: Joan Benoit Samuelson

BEFORE READING	AFTER READING
runner, champion, determined, delightful	

HOW DO YOU KNOW?	
The illustration shows her running, and the introduction says that people will remember her as a determined, delightful champion.	

Name ______________

Joan Benoit Samuelson

A. Fill in the character chart to summarize what you have learned about Joan Benoit Samuelson. Accept reasonable responses.

Character Chart: Joan Benoit Samuelson	
Before Reading runner, champion, determined, delightful	**After Reading** shy, self-motivated, focused, balanced, down-to-earth
How do you know?	
The illustration shows her running, and the introduction says that people will remember her as a determined, delightful champion.	When cars went by on her runs, Joan used to pretend she was picking flowers to avoid attracting attention as a marathoner. Her shyness was an advantage because she enjoyed the solitude of training. Joan would often stay on the slopes past sundown when she was skiing. Joan went running within a week of having surgery on her knee, and she competed in Olympic trials only three weeks later. She went on to win a gold medal. After winning the medal, Joan said she'd be "in a berry patch in Maine." She is able to balance a family life with her running career. She believes that winning is only "one of many things" in life.

B. Use the information in your character chart to write a summary of the selection.

Possible response: Joan Benoit Samuelson is a true champion, a determined person who strives to be the best she can be as an athlete. At the same time, she balances her career with a variety of other interests. She is shy and modest about her achievements.

104 SUMMARIZING THE LITERATURE HIDDEN TREASURES Practice Book

PRACTICE BOOK, page 104

ILLUSTRATOR'S CRAFT

Encourage students to compare the illustrations on pages 354 and 355. Have them discuss what makes Bernie Fuchs's illustrations so appealing. Ask volunteers to name athletes they think would make good subjects for Fuchs's art.

Satchel Paige, baseball pitcher

Nate "Tiny" Archibald, basketball player

Susan Butcher, dogsled race

355

About the Illustrator

Invite students to look at pages 354 and 355 and read about Bernie Fuchs, the artist who created the illustrations for "Joan Benoit Samuelson." You may wish to ask students the following questions:

- **What do Fuchs's illustrations on pages 342 and 343 and page 352 tell you about Joan Benoit, a professional athlete at the top of her form? Explain your answer.** (Responses will vary. Some students may say that the picture of Joan Benoit on page 352 shows her looking triumphant.)
- **Why do you think the impressionistic style of the illustrations of Joan Benoit and the paintings on pages 354 and 355 is appropriate to Bernie Fuchs's subject?** (Possible response: The impressionistic style seems to work well with pictures of athletes, who are almost always in motion.)

Bernie Fuchs says he is still unsure of the quality of his work even though he's won much acclaim. He describes how he decides to accept an illustration job:

> When I get a call to take on another assignment or commission, I just sort of automatically turn it down. Then I think about it for a while. And, sure enough, I usually find a solution—that's when I call back and accept.

ACTIVITY CHOICES

MAKE A TIME LINE

AND THE WINNER IS . . . Before students begin their research, inform them about the reference books they can use to find this kind of information. If necessary, remind them how a time line is structured. If students are particularly interested in marathons, you might suggest that they expand their time lines to include the winners of the Boston and New York Marathons each year since 1984 to trace the careers of champion marathoners. **LISTENING AND SPEAKING**

CALCULATE MILEAGE

GO FIGURE Encourage students to create additional math problems related to marathons or running. Then have them give their problems to a partner to solve. **MATH**

WRITE A POEM

THE DRIVE INSIDE Talk about Joan Benoit's quote and what she meant. Encourage students to brainstorm images about Joan Benoit and her life in Maine to put in their poems. Tell students that their poems should express feelings or create a mood. Explain to students that their poems do not have to rhyme. **CRITICAL THINKING/ WRITING**

STUDENTS ACQUIRING ENGLISH If necessary, have students work with English-proficient partners on these activities. Students with a limited English vocabulary should write their poems in their first language and then work with their partners to translate the poems into English.

Corner

WRITE A POEM

The Drive Inside

Reread the last two paragraphs of the selection. In the last paragraph, Joan Benoit says, "Look for me in a berry patch in Maine." What do you think she means by that? Write a short poem in which you explain what you think she means.

WHAT DO YOU THINK?

- What makes Joan Benoit different from other runners?
- What did you find out about athletes that you didn't know before?
- What are some things that people might learn about winning from Joan Benoit's story?

357

CHECKING COMPREHENSION

What Do You Think?

1. **What makes Joan Benoit different from other runners?** (Possible response: She is especially determined and has had to overcome special hardships.) DESCRIPTIVE RESPONSE
2. **What did you find out about athletes that you didn't know before?** (Responses will vary.) PERSONAL RESPONSE
3. **What are some things that people might learn about winning from Joan Benoit's story?** (Responses will vary.) CRITICAL ANALYSIS/REFLECTING

VARYING THE ACTIVITY

To challenge students, suggest they select a particularly interesting Olympic recordholder from their time line and find more information about that person. Students should then annotate their time line with biographical information.

Gail Devers, USA 100m
Barcelona Summer Olympics, 1992

Intervention Strategies

TIPS FOR CLASSROOM MANAGEMENT

IF second-language students need additional vocabulary and during-reading strategies to understand "Joan Benoit Samuelson," **THEN** use *Sheltered English/ESL Manual*, pages 54–57.

IF students had difficulty understanding "Joan Benoit Samuelson," **THEN** encourage them to read *Jesse Owens, Olympic Star* and complete the diagram. See also Intervention Strategies Manual, pages 80–85.

REREADING

IDENTIFYING MAIN IDEA Remind students that "Joan Benoit Samuelson" is an example of a biographical profile or article. Tell them that a biography—a true story of a person's life written by another person—is a type of nonfiction. As they reread portions of the selection, students can use the comprehension strategy of identifying the main idea of each paragraph.

Draw a web like the following on the board:

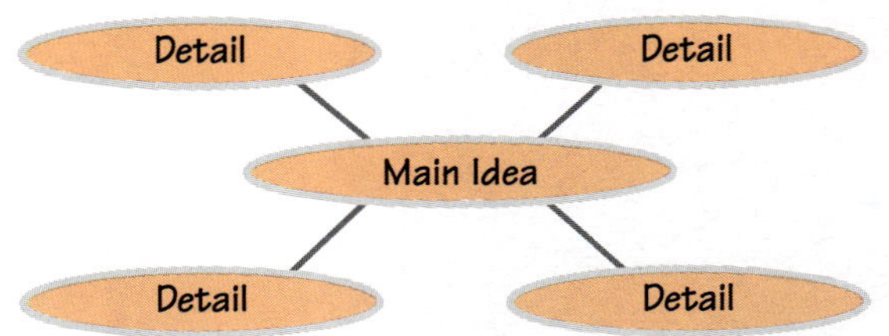

Choose paragraphs from the selection for students to reread. Suggestions may include the first full paragraph on page 346, the last paragraph that begins on page 346, and the last paragraph that begins on page 347. As each one is read, have a volunteer go to the board and fill in the web with suggestions from other students.

PERSONAL JOURNAL

Ask students if they agree or disagree with the statement of Joan Benoit Samuelson in her autobiography, "Winning is neither everything nor the only thing. It is one of many things." Have students write several sentences in their journals to explain their reactions.

STRUCTURAL ANALYSIS

VERB ENDINGS Remind students that certain endings are added to verbs to show the person and number of the subject (you run, she runs) and the time of the action (I look, I looked). On the board, write these endings that can be added to verbs:

Explain that adding such an ending sometimes involves a spelling change such as doubling a final consonant *(running)*, dropping a final *e (waving)*, or changing *y* to *i (tried)*. Ask students to skim the selection to find examples of verbs that show these spelling changes. (Some possibilities are: *provided, tried, excelling, motivating, worried, frustrating.*)

WRITING TO SUMMARIZE

Have students summarize the biographical profile by filling in a details chart like the following. Tell them to fill in the blanks with significant details that they recall from the selection.

Details List

Spring 1984: Training for the Olympic trials

____

____

Summer 1984: Olympic Marathon

____

____

DECODING SUPPORT
Syllabication and the Schwa

Intervention Strategies Manual **pp. 84–85**

ESL/TITLE I READING

Reading Trade Books

Jesse Owens: Olympic Star

by Patricia and Fredrick McKissack

Like Joan Benoit Samuelson, Jesse Owens trained hard and triumphed over setbacks to become a great Olympic champion. Have students use the following diagram to record similarities between the two biographies.

Joan Benoit Samuelson	Jesse Owens
Training/Challenges/ Setbacks:__________	__________
Olympic Games:__________	__________

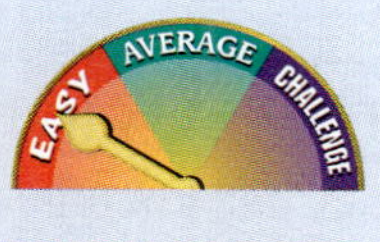

TAKE-HOME BOOK TO REINFORCE KEY WORDS

Students will read about a character who learns a lesson in this tale of competition that reinforces the Key Words in "Joan Benoit Samuelson." Students may wish to read the book independently in class or take it home to read.

PERSONAL JOURNAL

After students finish reading *A Real Winner*, have them write in their personal journals about a competition they have entered or watched.

See also *Intervention Strategies Manual*, page 83.

2 Integrating Language Arts

IDEA BANK

TIPS FOR CLASSROOM MANAGEMENT

IF students have trouble summarizing the selection, **THEN** they may want to be involved in the Retelling activity.

IF students need practice in writing directions, **THEN** they may participate in the Real-Life Resources activity.

TECHNOLOGY

IMAGINATION EXPRESS, DESTINATION: NEIGHBORHOOD Students can use the program to write directions for the Real Life Resources Activity.

RETELLING

Role-Play a Scene

Have volunteers work in groups to role-play scenes involving Joan Benoit's Olympic victory. Students should imagine that they are in the audience at the Los Angeles Coliseum when Joan Benoit wins the marathon. Encourage students to tell about Joan Benoit's determination and the hardships she overcame on the way to her victory.

LISTENING/SPEAKING

Informal Assessment

As students converse about Joan Benoit's victory, note whether they include details about her knee injury and her struggle during the trials.

ORAL LANGUAGE

Interviewing

Have students work with a partner to role-play interviewing a famous athlete. Suggest that they begin by working together to decide who will be the subject of the interview and what questions the interviewer will ask. Then one partner should take the role of the athlete and the other the part of the interviewer. Have them role-play the interview for other classmates.

LISTENING/SPEAKING

TIPS FOR LISTENING AND SPEAKING

Remind students that in an interview the participants should

- remember the audience and try to appeal to their interests.
- speak clearly.
- make eye contact with each other and with the audience.

Remind students who are the audience during the interview to listen critically

- to distinguish facts from opinions.
- to determine speakers' viewpoints.
- to identify speakers' tone and mood.

REREADING

Radio Commentary

Invite volunteers to read the selection or passages from the selection as if they were delivering a commentary on the radio. Share with students that the author, Bill Littlefield, delivers commentaries on National Public Radio. Encourage students to listen to a few radio commentaries first and then try to create their own delivery style. Ask other classmates who are the audience to critique each commentator, noting whether the delivery was clear, understandable, and lively. **LISTENING/ SPEAKING/READING**

REAL-LIFE RESOURCES

Directions for Performing a Process

READING DIRECTIONS Write these directions for a beginner's running program on the board. Discuss how these directions identify the steps in a process.

Week 1: Run 2 minutes, walk 4 minutes.
(5 times)
Week 2: Run 3 minutes, walk 3 minutes.
(5 times)
Week 3: Run 5 minutes, walk 2 ½ minutes.
(5 times)
Week 4: Run 7 minutes, walk 3 minutes.
(5 times)
Week 5: Run 8 minutes, walk 2 minutes.
(5 times)

ADDING TO DIRECTIONS Point out that the steps above do not present enough information for a true beginner to start a running program. General advice and tips should also be included. Ask students to work in teams to complete the directions. See *Writer's Magazine* pages 52 and 53.

REAL-LIFE CHALLENGE Have students write a ten-week plan for learning a new sport or fitness activity. Students might refer to books, magazines, or fitness experts before they write. **WRITING**

Budd Coates's running plan

Be a Runner in 10 Weeks!

Joan Benoit Samuelson discovered the joy of running when she was a schoolgirl. You can, too! Here's how to get started. Read the ten-week beginner plan below designed by Budd Coates of *Runner's World*, who teaches a beginners' running program.

To all Couch Potatoes: Start with 8 days of just walking (20 to 30 minutes a day) to get your legs ready for running.

DIRECTIONS
Pick 4 days (not in a row) to train and 3 days to rest.

Week 1	Run 2 minutes, walk 4 minutes. (5 times.)
Week 2	Run 3 minutes, walk 3 minutes. (5 times.)
Week 3	Run 5 minutes, walk 2 1/2 minutes. (4 times.)
Week 4	Run 7 minutes, walk 3 minutes. (3 times.)
Week 5	Run 8 minutes, walk 2 minutes. (3 times.)
Week 6	Run 9 minutes, walk 2 minutes. (2 times, then run 8 more minutes.)
Week 7	Run 9 minutes, walk 1 minute. (3 times.)
Week 8	Run 13 minutes, walk 2 minutes. (Repeat.)
Week 9	Run 14 minutes, walk 1 minute. (Repeat.)
Note	[illegible]
Week 10	Run 30 minutes.

52 Joan Benoit Samuelson • Writer's Magazine

WRITER'S MAGAZINE, pages 52–53

STUDENTS ACQUIRING ENGLISH

Encourage students who are fluent in English to converse with students in the early production phase during the Retelling activity. Fluent students should ask questions with "yes" and "no" answers about Joan Benoit.

WRITER'S WORKSHOP

Poem

TIPS FOR CLASSROOM MANAGEMENT

IF students are familiar with the steps for writing a poem, **THEN** have them begin writing, referring to the rhymed and unrhymed poem models on Transparency 36 as necessary.

IF you want a short writing activity, **THEN** adapt this lesson by having students focus on the Writer's Craft.

TECHNOLOGY

THE AMAZING WRITING MACHINE Have students use the poetry section of the program. They may use the Spin feature for ideas, and the Descriptive Words option to generate vivid adjectives.

Thinking as Writers

WRITING FORM: Poem Bill Littlefield writes that Joan Benoit's injured knee "complained" and "turned cranky." He also says that the conditions of the Olympic Marathon "crushed Joan's competitors." Many writers use vivid language such as this, but it is especially used by writers of poetry. Explain to students that writers use imagery, figurative language, and rhythm in poetry to express a mood or paint a picture in just a few words. Point out that poems can be rhymed or unrhymed. Ask students to name some poems they have read and liked and to share the images or moods the poems evoked. Tell students that they are going to learn about poetry and then write a poem of their own.

Display Transparency 36 and use the introductions and side notes to guide discussion of rhymed and unrhymed poems.

TRANSPARENCY 36

Model: Rhymed Poem

Poetry can express a mood or paint a picture with just a few words. Poetry is usually written in rhythmic lines rather than in sentences. In a rhymed poem, syllable sounds are repeated at the ends of paired lines. For example, the following poem follows a rhyme scheme, or pattern, of a/b/a/b: the first and third lines rhyme, and the second and fourth lines rhyme.

a pattern of rhythm and rhyme

A sleeping fawn,
A single crow—
Above, the dawn.
Still night below.

Model: Unrhymed Poem

In unrhymed poetry, rhythm, figurative language, and imagery express a mood.

imagery strengthened by rhythm

The quiet night
Gentle breathing of branches.
The sun creeps
Glinting edges of hilltops.
A crow calls
Shrill salute to the morning.

WRITER'S CRAFT: Emotional Words Explain that when people write poetry, they often use emotional words that create vivid images and strong feelings in their readers.

Have students look for emotional words in "Joan Benoit Samuelson" (*fierce and steady determination, delightful champion, glorious,* and *grateful*) or in the model. (*gentle breathing* and *shrill salute*)

PREWRITING AND DRAFTING

Suggest that students brainstorm poem ideas with a partner, as well as descriptive and emotional words that tell about that idea. Refer to these strategies to help students begin their poems.

PREWRITING GRAPHIC ORGANIZER Some students might construct a web like the one below to organize their ideas.

SUSTAINED SILENT WRITING Students who have a clear idea of what they want to write may begin writing without interruption.

DURING-WRITING GRAPHIC ORGANIZER Students may need to pause during writing to generate another web of emotional words related to their poem idea.

RESPONDING AND REVISING

Have students work in editing circles or with partners to help each other revise. Write this checklist on the board:

- Does your poem create a mood or an image?
- Does your poem contain appropriate descriptive or emotional words?
- Have you arranged the words to give the poem rhythm or a rhyming pattern?

PROOFREADING

Offer the following tips as students proofread:

- Check for correct use of **adjectives to compare**. (See Grammar Minilesson on page T711.)
- Check that the first letter of each new line is capitalized.
- Look for words you may have misspelled.

PUBLISHING

If you wish to have students publish their poems, suggest the following options or have students choose their own methods:

ORAL Students may read their poems aloud in poetry readings for the class. Have students comment on an image or mood the poem created and what adjectives the author used to help them visualize.

WRITTEN Suggest that students illustrate their poems and collect them in a class anthology titled "Poetry, Please." The poetry book may be displayed in the school library.

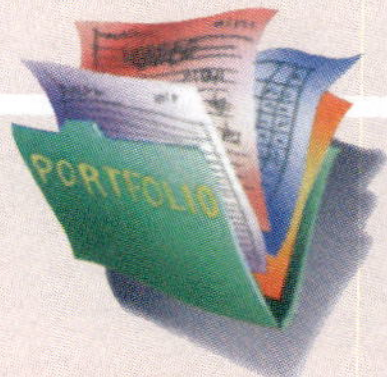

PORTFOLIO OPPORTUNITY

Have students answer the Student Self-Assessment questions and include both their answers and their poems in their portfolios.

LANGUAGE HANDBOOK

Writing to Entertain and Express, pages 40–41; Rhymed Poem/Unrhymed Poem, page 51; Using Figurative Language, page 28; Adjectives, pages 138–144

Student Self-Assessment ✓

Have students answer the following questions and include the answers in their portfolios:

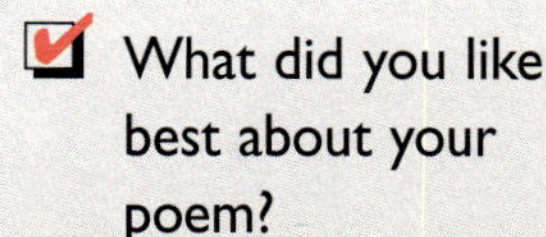

- What did you like best about your poem?

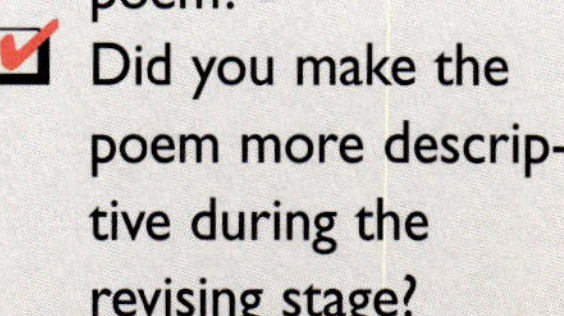

- Did you make the poem more descriptive during the revising stage?

EVALUATION BENCHMARKS: POEM

A poem by a proficient student writer shows the following characteristics:

FORM	CRAFT	CONVENTIONS
Demonstrates understanding of the form • creates a mood or image using few words • contains descriptive or emotional words • contains rhythm • contains a rhyming pattern (rhyming poems only)	**Uses clear and appropriate language** • adjectives are used effectively • language expresses image, mood, or feeling	**Follows conventions of grammar and usage** • adjectives used correctly in comparisons • capitalization used correctly

Teacher Assessment As you assess students' writing, refer to the Evaluation Benchmarks chart. For additional information, including model papers, see *Integrated Performance Assessment* Teacher's Edition.

Tested Skill

GRAMMAR

Action Verbs and Linking Verbs

Reading ↔ Writing Connection

Connect to the literature. Ask students to reread the first two sentences following the selection introduction on page 344. Break the second sentence into its two separate parts, and write all three sentences on the board:

March is not Maine's best season.

Spring never comes early to northern New England.

The wind off the ocean in March stings a runner's cheek.

Have a volunteer identify the verbs in each sentence. *(is, comes, stings)*

Build oral language. Ask students to make up new sentences using the verbs. Suggest that the sentences relate to the selection; for example:

- Joan Benoit *is* a fast runner.
- Her family *comes* from Maine.
- The hot road *stings* her heels as she runs.

Teach/Model

Discuss linking verbs. Explain that the verb *is* is a form of the linking verb *be*. A linking verb connects the subject to a noun or adjective that renames or describes it. Some of the forms of *be* are *am, are, is, were, has been*, and *have been*. Some other common linking verbs are *seem, appear, feel*, and *become*.

Discuss action verbs. *Comes* and *stings* are both action verbs. Action verbs tell what the subject of the sentence does or is doing. Point out that strong action verbs make a sentence more vivid. Some action verbs tell about action that cannot be seen. For example, Joan *dreams* about winning the marathon.

Practice/Apply

Check understanding. Write the following sentences on the board, and have students identify the verb in each sentence and tell whether the verb is an *action* verb or a *linking* verb:

- The runners *were* the best in the country. (linking)
- Joan *trained* for several months before the race. (action)
- She *ran* faster than anyone. (action)
- The spectators *seemed* proud of her. (linking)

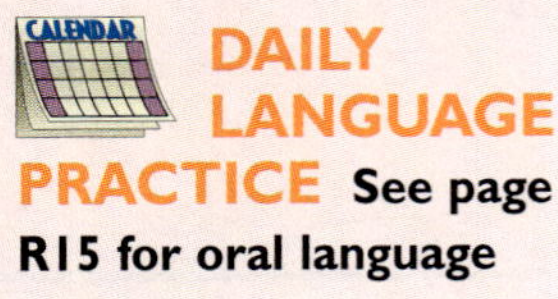

LANGUAGE HANDBOOK

Action Verbs and Linking Verbs, pages 146–147

DAILY LANGUAGE PRACTICE See page R15 for oral language exercises.

Practice Activities

TALK FAST

ORAL APPLICATION Have pairs of students play a word game with linking and action verbs. Students should take turns saying sentences. The listener should say whether the sentence contains an action verb or a linking verb. If students have trouble thinking of sentences, have them look around the classroom at objects and create sentences that feature them. **AUDITORY**

Write a Description

WRITING APPLICATION Have students work in pairs to write descriptive paragraphs about the same topic. One student should write sentences with only linking verbs. The other student should write sentences with only action verbs. When they're finished, partners should compare their work and use sentences from both paragraphs to create a new paragraph. **VISUAL**

APPLY TO WRITING

You may want to suggest that students look back at their poems or other writing to see if they can make any sentences stronger by rewriting them to include vivid action verbs instead of linking verbs.

USAGE TIP Check your writing to be sure the subjects and verbs agree.

MEETING INDIVIDUAL NEEDS

STUDENTS ACQUIRING ENGLISH

Pair students with fluent speakers and have them take turns reading aloud sentences from a selection they've already read. They should decide together if the sentences contain linking verbs or action verbs.

RETEACH

See page R6 for lessons in multiple modalities.

GRAMMAR PRACTICE BOOK
pages 36–37

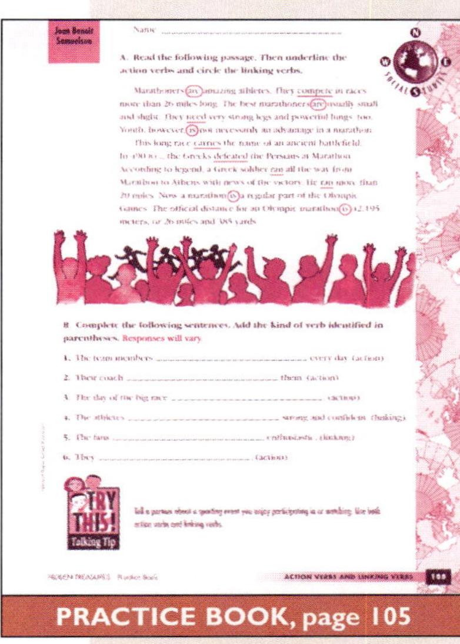
Joan Benoit Samuelson

Name ____________

A. Read the following passage. Then underline the action verbs and circle the linking verbs.

Marathoners are amazing athletes. They compete in races more than 26 miles long. The best marathoners are usually small and slight. They need very strong legs and powerful lungs, too. Youth, however, is not necessarily an advantage in a marathon.

This long race carries the name of an ancient battlefield. In 490 B.C., the Greeks defeated the Persians at Marathon. According to legend, a Greek soldier ran all the way from Marathon to Athens with news of the victory. He ran more than 20 miles. Now a marathon is a regular part of the Olympic Games. The official distance for an Olympic marathon is 42,195 meters, or 26 miles and 385 yards.

B. Complete the following sentences. Add the kind of verb identified in parentheses. Responses will vary.

1. The team members ____________ every day. (action)
2. Their coach ____________ them. (action)
3. The day of the big race ____________. (action)
4. The athletes ____________ strong and confident. (linking)
5. The fans ____________ enthusiastic. (linking)
6. They ____________. (action)

TRY THIS! Talking Tip

ACTION VERBS AND LINKING VERBS 105

PRACTICE BOOK, page 105

5-DAY PLAN

Use in conjunction with Daily Language Practice.

Day 1 Complete page T730.	**Day 4** Choose a Practice Activity or *Grammar Practice Book* pages 36–37.
Day 2 Complete a Practice Activity on page T731.	**Day 5** Complete *Practice Book* page 105.
Day 3 Choose a Practice Activity or *Language Handbook* pages 146–147.	

SPELLING

5-Day Plan

Integrated Spelling Lesson 20: student book, pages 86–89; Teacher's Edition, pages T135–T140.

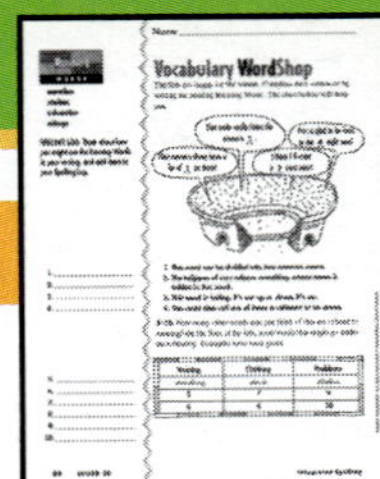
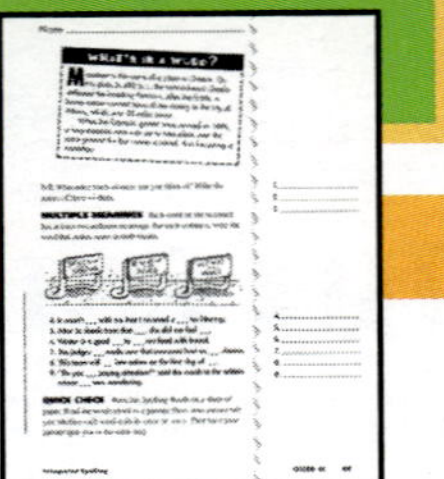

SPELLING WORDS

1. presence ★
2. entrance
3. audience
4. distance ★
5. difference
6. insurance
7. importance
8. conference
9. instance
10. allowance
11. experience
12. intelligence
13. independence
14. appearance
15. performance ★
16. ambulance

STUDENT'S PERSONAL WORDS

17.
18.
19.
20.

Additional story words are *dominance* and *resilience*.

★ Words appearing in "Joan Benoit Samuelson"

Suffix: *-ance/-ence*

Pretest

DAY 1 **Administer the pretest.** Say each word and then use it in the dictation sentence below. Help students self-check their pretests.

OPEN SORT

DAY 2 **Have students create categories.** Have students sort the Spelling Words into categories of their own choosing. For example, students can create lists of two-syllable words and lists of words with three or more syllables. Encourage students to come up with categories of their own.

CLOSED SORT

Sort by spelling pattern. Write on the board the headings from the chart below. Have volunteers write each Spelling Word under the appropriate heading. Encourage students to study the words in each category to see if they can discover a way to help themselves remember which words are spelled with *-ance* and which are spelled with *-ence*. Ask students to suggest other words that fit each category. Include these in the list as Student's Personal Words.

fragrance	excellence
importance	difference
entrance	independence
insurance	conference
performance	audience
ambulance	intelligence
instance	experience
allowance	presence
distance	
appearance	

Teach/Model

DAY 3 **Explain the generalization.** Explain that *-ance* and *-ence* are two versions of the same noun-forming suffix. When added to a verb like *perform*, the suffix turns the verb into a noun, *performance*. Point out that the suffix or final syllable in all the Spelling Words has an unstressed vowel sound /ə/, so you can't tell from the sound of the word if the word is spelled with *-ance* or *-ence*.

DAY 4 **Apply to writing.** Students should check their writing to be sure words with the suffixes *-ance* and *-ence* are spelled correctly.

Posttest

DAY 5 **Assess students' progress.** The sentences below should be used as the posttest.

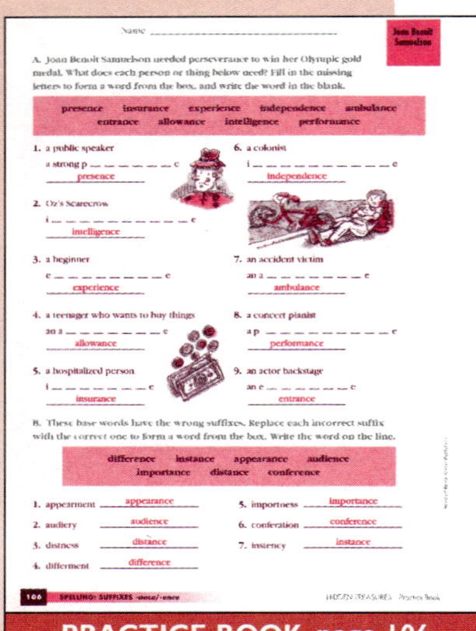

Name ______________________

Joan Benoit Samuelson

A. Joan Benoit Samuelson needed perseverance to win her Olympic gold medal. What does each person or thing below need? Fill in the missing letters to form a word from the box, and write the word in the blank.

presence insurance experience independence ambulance entrance allowance intelligence performance

1. a public speaker — a strong p _ _ _ _ _ _ e — presence
2. Oz's Scarecrow — i _ _ _ _ _ _ _ _ _ _ e — intelligence
3. a beginner — e _ _ _ _ _ _ _ _ e — experience
4. a teenager who wants to buy things — an a _ _ _ _ _ _ _ e — allowance
5. a hospitalized person — i _ _ _ _ _ _ _ e — insurance
6. a colonist — i _ _ _ _ _ _ _ _ _ _ e — independence
7. an accident victim — an a _ _ _ _ _ _ _ e — ambulance
8. a concert pianist — a p _ _ _ _ _ _ _ _ _ e — performance
9. an actor backstage — an e _ _ _ _ _ _ e — entrance

B. These base words have the wrong suffixes. Replace each incorrect suffix with the correct one to form a word from the box. Write the word on the line.

difference instance appearance audience importance distance conference

1. appearment — appearance
2. audiery — audience
3. distness — distance
4. differment — difference
5. importness — importance
6. conferation — conference
7. instency — instance

106 SPELLING: SUFFIXES -ance/-ence HIDDEN TREASURES Practice Book

PRACTICE BOOK, page 106

DICTATION SENTENCES

1. Your presence is requested at the party.
2. A guard met the guests at the front entrance.
3. The audience applauded wildly.
4. What is the distance between Maine and Los Angeles?
5. A good deed can make a difference.
6. In that state, auto insurance is a requirement.
7. Athletes understand the importance of training.
8. The students had a conference together.
9. Winning a race, for instance, can be very exciting.
10. Many children get an allowance.
11. Experience teaches us many things.
12. Rudeness is not a sign of intelligence.
13. Most teenagers want more independence.
14. Some people are too concerned about appearance.
15. That performance is sold out.
16. An ambulance took the injured player to the hospital.

VOCABULARY WORKSHOP

Reviewing Key Words

Draw a time line like the one below on the board. Then ask students to place the Key Words along the time line to indicate at what point they would most likely use each word if they were describing Joan Benoit's experience. Point out that, if necessary, students can place a word at more than one point.

Extending Vocabulary

MULTIPLE-MEANING WORDS

Point out the word *season* on page 344. In this sentence, the word *season* is a noun that means "a time of year." But *season* can also be a verb that means "to add spice." For example, *Mike was about to season the roast with salt and pepper*.

MAKE WORDS LIST

Challenge pairs of students to go through the selection to find and list other examples of words that have more than one meaning. For example, *spring* means "the season between winter and summer" or "to jump forward." When students have finished, invite them to share the multiple-meaning words they discovered and explain the different meanings.

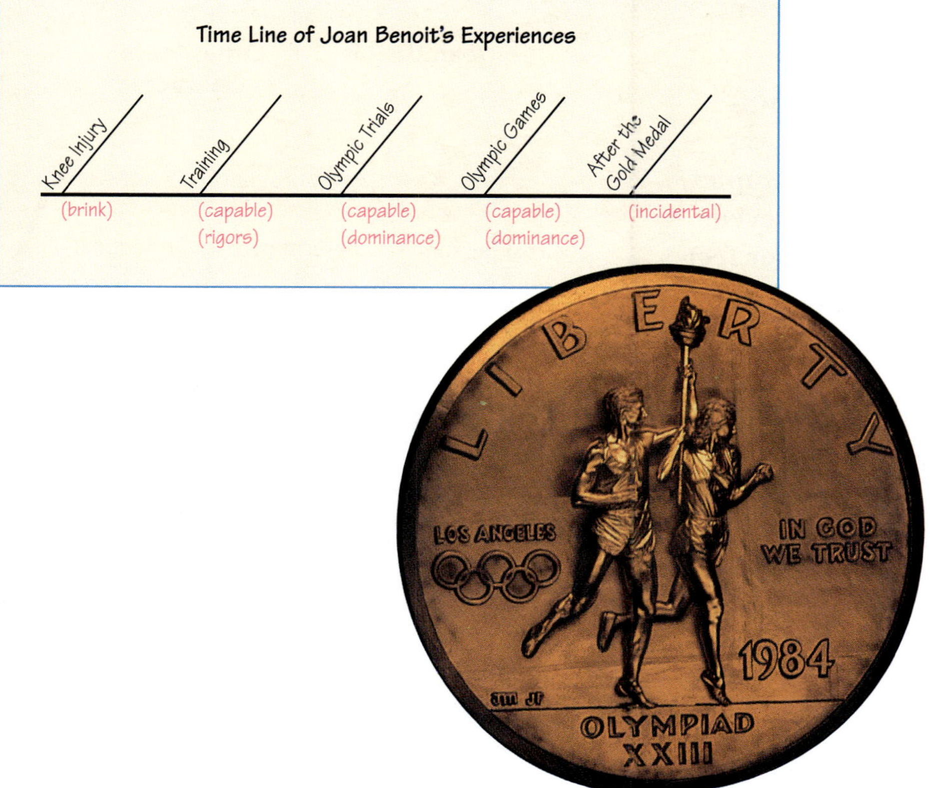

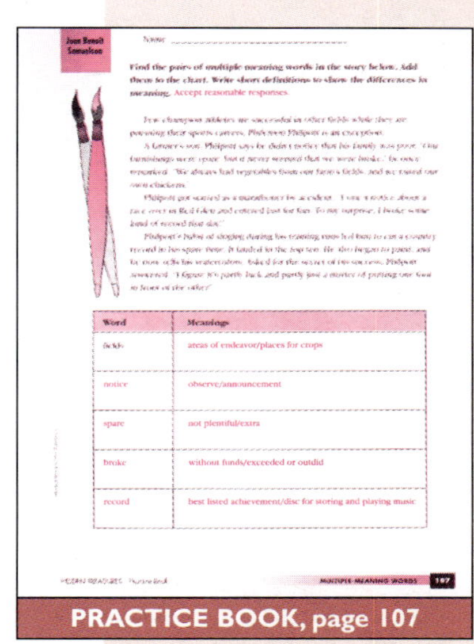
Joan Benoit Samuelson

Name

Find the pairs of multiple meaning words in the story below. Add them to the chart. Write short definitions to show the differences in meaning. Accept reasonable responses.

Word	Meanings
fields	areas of endeavor/places for crops
notice	observe/announcement
spare	not plentiful/extra
broke	without funds/exceeded or outdid
record	best listed achievement/disc for storing and playing music

MULTIPLE-MEANING WORDS 107

PRACTICE BOOK, page 107

INTRODUCE: COMPREHENSION STRATEGY

Tested Skill

Compare/Contrast

OBJECTIVE: To determine likenesses and differences

Teach/Model

Return to the literature. Have students explain how Joan Benoit Samuelson is like and unlike the character Atalanta or some other character or person they've read about. Encourage students to discuss these characters' personality traits and physical characteristics.

Model comparing and contrasting. Explain that comparing involves looking for similarities and contrasting involves looking for differences. Then model comparing and contrasting:

MODEL

Before the Olympic Trials, Joan was worried about her knee but she was determined to win. After the Olympics, she was joyful and probably relieved. By comparing and contrasting her feelings before and after the races, I can better understand how she felt about her triumph.

Practice/Apply

Have students demonstrate understanding. Draw a Venn diagram on the board. Ask students to compare and contrast Joan Benoit with another heroic character and to name similarities and differences between the two characters. Record their ideas on a diagram like the one below. When the diagram is complete, invite students to use it to assess the degree of similarity between Joan Benoit and the other heroic character.

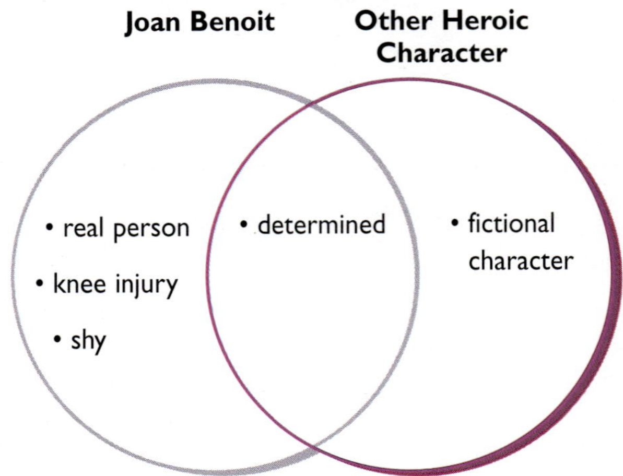

Informal Assessment ✓

Are students able to

- ☑ tell how Joan Benoit is similar to other heroes they've read about?
- ☑ see the differences between Joan Benoit and fictional heroes?

Practice Activities

Which Two?

COOPERATIVE LEARNING Have students work in small groups to think of two characters from previous selections who are alike in some way and to make up clues that show similarities and differences between them. For example, if students compared Estela from "The Challenge" with Atalanta from "Atalanta's Race," they might give these clues: "They both beat boys at a sport" or "One lived in ancient times; the other lives in modern times." A Recorder can list the clues. Groups can then take turns challenging each other. A Reporter from each group should offer compare-and-contrast clues until the members of another group can guess the identity of both characters. **AUDITORY**

My Marathon

PERFORMANCE ASSESSMENT The story of Joan Benoit and the 1984 Olympic Games is one of those amazing "against all odds" kinds of stories. She managed to win spectacularly in spite of a knee injury that required surgery just weeks before the Olympic Trials. Ask students to recall an experience in their lives when they have managed to do something in spite of an accident or circumstance that seemed to make it impossible. Have them create a chart or other graphic organizer to compare their experience with Joan Benoit's. **VISUAL/KINESTHETIC**

My Experience	Joan's Experience

EXTRA SUPPORT

If students have difficulty with the concept of comparing and contrasting, invite them to compare themselves with a character they've read about recently who they think is like them in some way.

RETEACH

See page R7 for lessons in multiple modalities.

CHALLENGE

Encourage students to write journal entries that Joan Benoit may have written before and after the Olympic Trials. Remind them to use comparisons and contrasts.

Reading Trade Books TO REINFORCE COMPARING AND CONTRASTING

***Bonnie Blair: Golden Streak* by Cathy Breitenbucher. Lerner, 1994. AVERAGE**

***The Summer Olympics* by Caroline Arnold. Franklin Watts, 1991. EASY**

***Winners and Losers* by Stephen Hoffius. Simon & Schuster, 1993. CHALLENGING**

PRACTICE BOOK, pages 108–109

PROJECT MANAGEMENT

STUDENTS ACQUIRING ENGLISH

Suggest that students read the information on the completed chart aloud before comparing, contrasting, and searching for contradictions.

MULTIPLE INTELLIGENCES

Choose students with a high level of interpersonal intelligence to be Facilitators. Ask these students to help the group resolve differences of opinion about the chart's format.

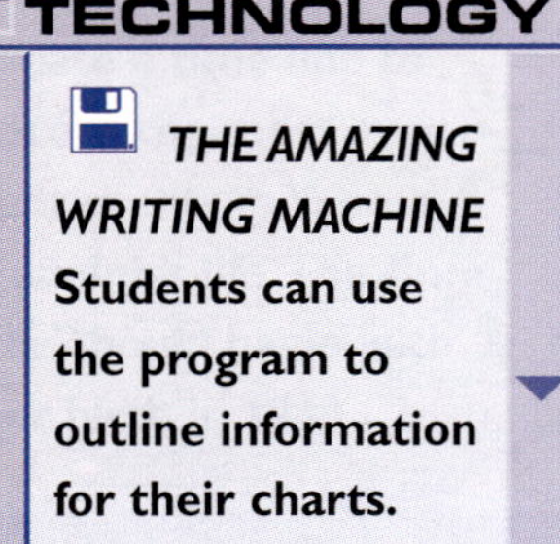

TECHNOLOGY

THE AMAZING WRITING MACHINE Students can use the program to outline information for their charts.

THEME PROJECT CHECKPOINT 2

Make a Comparison Chart

SELECTION CONNECTION

"Joan Benoit Samuelson" describes how the famous marathon runner overcame a career-threatening injury with the help of a new medical procedure called arthroscopic surgery. Ask students to give examples of how other recent technological advances have improved life.

PROJECT CHECKLIST

During this stage, students should

- ☑ share their research with the group.
- ☑ compare notes from different sources about a particular change or event.
- ☑ design a chart to help them compare and contrast information.
- ☑ highlight vague or contradictory information for further research.

Project Card 21 can be found as a copying master on page R25.

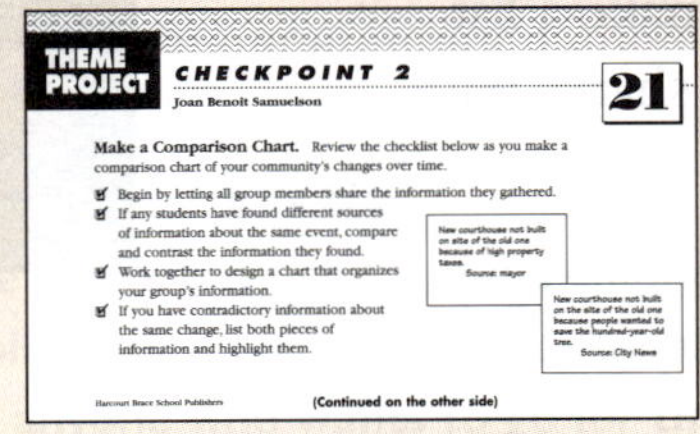

THEME PROJECT

CHECKPOINT 2

Joan Benoit Samuelson

21

Make a Comparison Chart. Review the checklist below as you make a comparison chart of your community's changes over time.

- ☑ Begin by letting all group members share the information they gathered.
- ☑ If any students have found different sources of information about the same event, compare and contrast the information they found.
- ☑ Work together to design a chart that organizes your group's information.
- ☑ If you have contradictory information about the same change, list both pieces of information and highlight them.

New courthouse not built on site of the old one because of high property taxes.
Source: mayor

New courthouse not built on the site of the old one because people wanted to save the hundred-year-old tree.
Source: City News

Harcourt Brace School Publishers

(Continued on the other side)

Project Card 21

RESEARCH AND PLANNING TIPS

As students organize their research, suggest that they

- start by holding a general discussion of their findings.
- choose broad categories and, where appropriate, subcategories for organizing their information.
- keep track of the source of each detail.
- plan a way to highlight facts or memories that seem to contradict each other.

Suggest that students write an entry in their project journal that describes a set of contradictory ideas in the research. Encourage students to respond to questions such as *How do you think historians resolve conflicts in their research?*

Informal Assessment

As students complete this checkpoint, each group will **organize, classify,** and **compare and contrast** information. Students are thinking critically if they

- ☑ can analyze information to locate apparent contradictions.
- ☑ can evaluate sources of information.

Ancient Greece

from Kids Discover *magazine*

SELECTION CONNECTION

Students have read selections about two runners—one mythical, and the other a modern Olympic champion. Now they will read a magazine article that presents an overview of the culture that celebrated great Olympic athletes.

SUMMARY

GENRE: Nonfiction/Magazine Article

Through descriptive text, illustrations, and detailed captions, this article offers a glimpse into the society of ancient Greece and its greatest achievements. The first part of the article discusses daily life, philosophy, medicine, science, democracy, and the arts. The second part discusses the methods used to gain knowledge about ancient Greece, including the study of pottery, shipwrecks, and the ruins of ancient buildings uncovered by archaeologists.

CHALLENGE

Gifted and talented students may want to find out more about Greek architecture, history, or another aspect of Greek culture explored in this article.

Introducing the Article

PRIOR KNOWLEDGE

Help students draw upon what they know about the ancient Greeks. Write each of the following phrases on a separate index card: *How the Ancient Greeks Lived, Great Achievements of the Ancient Greeks,* and *How We Know About the Ancient Greeks*. Organize students into three groups, and give a card to each group. Allow students a few minutes to brainstorm what they know about their topic, and then have a volunteer from each group present the information. If students have difficulty generating information, reassure them that they will find a lot of interesting facts about the ancient Greeks when they read the article from *Kids Discover* magazine.

THE PARTHENON, a temple to the Greek goddess Athena, was built nearly 2,500 years ago.

TIPS FOR CLASSROOM MANAGEMENT

SMALL GROUP

PARTNER READING

You may wish to have pairs of students read the article together. When they have finished, invite them to ask each other questions about the information it contains. Suggest that for each answered question, students tell their partners under what section of the article the answer is found.

ANCIENT GREECE

FROM *KIDS DISCOVER MAGAZINE*

Picture yourself in Athens in 500 B.C.—about 2,500 years ago. The days are hot and dry, so you wear a *chiton*, a loose-fitting tunic. If you are a girl, you stay at home and learn how to spin and weave from your mother. If you are a rich boy, you attend school from the age of seven, studying reading, writing, arithmetic, music, and debating. (Poor boys probably didn't go to school.) Instead of using pencils and paper, you use a stylus and a wax-covered wooden tablet. Pebbles or an abacus help you with your math. On lazy afternoons, you might enjoy knucklebones (a game similar to jacks). Perhaps you pick up a lyre and play your favorite tune. No doubt you participate in some sport, for sports honor the gods, and they help boys become excellent soldiers.

Most likely your house is made of sun-dried mud bricks and built around a central courtyard. Stairs lead to your upper-story bedroom. The servants' quarters are upstairs, too.

As you walk into the main entrance, a statue of the god Hermes greets you. It's there to prevent evil spirits from entering.

359

Reading an Article Remind students that the selections "Atalanta's Race" and "Joan Benoit Samuelson" represent an emphasis on physical fitness—which was one important aspect of ancient Greek civilization. Tell students that they will read an article that tells about other aspects of life in ancient Greece. Remind them that articles present factual information and often have design features, such as headings of different sizes, that help the reader quickly see how the information is organized. Have students preview the article and tell how the information is organized. (There are two large sections titled "Greek Folk" and "Digging Up the Past"; the first section is broken into smaller sections about lasting achievements; much of the information in the article is presented in captions.) Then have students read pages 358–367 to learn more about life in ancient Greece.

WHOLE CLASS

SILENT READING/ DISCUSSION

After students have read the selection once silently, invite volunteers to read aloud parts containing the information they found the most interesting. Encourage students to tell how reading the article changed their understanding of the ancient Greeks.

Critical Thinking Questions

1. **What do you think about the way the information in this section is presented? Explain your answer.** (Responses will vary, but students may express the opinion that many illustrations as well as specific examples—such as the menu—make a more interesting presentation of facts than just columns of text alone.) CRITICAL: EXPRESSING PERSONAL OPINIONS

2. **What do you think you would like best about being a citizen of ancient Greece?** (Responses will vary.) CRITICAL: EXPRESSING PERSONAL OPINIONS

GREEK FOLK

AS A CITIZEN, ONE of your duties was to defend the state as a hoplite (heavily equipped) warrior. Hoplites operated in a huge rectangular formation of many thousands of men. In this formation, all men were equal. No one was expected to be an individual hero. This is where the ancient Greeks' idea of fundamental political equality comes from.

FORGET ABOUT FAST FOOD!
Here's a typical Greek menu.

Breakfast:	Bread and figs
Lunch:	Bread with goat cheese or olives and figs
Dinner:	Barley porridge or bread or fish, with some vegetable, such as carrots, peas, or cabbage
Snacks:	Pomegranates, figs, apples, pears

BEES PROVIDED HONEY, the only sweetener available. Rich people ate more meat and fish than poor people, and they could afford bread made from wheat, not barley.

WEALTHY PEOPLE wore jewelry of gold, silver, and ivory. Poorer people might wear jewelry of bronze, lead, iron, bone, and glass.

360

MUSICAL INSTRUMENTS, such as cymbals, lyres, and kitharas (harplike instruments), kept Greeks entertained and entertaining. Popular wind instruments were the syrinx, or panpipes, which were made of reeds, and the *auloi* (single pipes) or *diauloi* (double pipes).

EVERY CITY-STATE had one or more gymnasia, where Greeks fine-tuned their bodies so they could successfully defend their city-state. Gymnasia were also important meeting places for exchanging ideas.

DRESSED FOR COMFORT
Rich and poor Greeks wore the same type of clothing. Richer people, however, might wear dyed clothes.

WHEN A BABY was born, it was shown to its father, who had the right to accept or reject it. If it was rejected, it was abandoned. People who wanted a child could adopt it.

EXPANDING VOCABULARY

Point out the word *gymnasia* in the middle of this page, and tell students that it is a plural form of a Latin word that was adopted from the Greek language. Ask students what the singular form of this word is. *(gymnasium)* Tell them that foreign words that have become common in English—like *gymnasium*—generally form a plural in the usual way, by adding *s*; the more common plural of this word in English is *gymnasiums*.

Critical Thinking Questions

1. **Do you think that using the Socratic method is a good way of teaching? Why?** (Possible responses: Yes, because it gives the student the chance to clear up anything that may be confusing. It allows different viewpoints or other information to be considered.) CRITICAL: MAKING CONNECTIONS

2. **What do you think would be an advantage to the Greek form of democracy? What would be a disadvantage?** (Possible response: One advantage might be that through a direct vote, citizens would feel that they could really influence what the government did. A disadvantage might be that the people who couldn't vote wouldn't have an interest in the government; those people could become restless and dissatisfied.) CRITICAL: SPECULATING

Lasting Achievements

The influence of ancient Greeks can be found in almost every area of our lives, from medicine to philosophy, from astronomy to drama. Here are some of the lasting achievements of these ingenious people, and the great Greeks whose legacies live on.

PHILOSOPHY

Early Greeks looked to the gods for explanations of life and of how the world worked. But by the sixth century B.C., people desired more practical explanations. Some started asking questions and making precise observations and calculations about the world. The Greeks called these people *philosophers*, which means "lovers of knowledge."

MEDICINE

HIPPOCRATES (460–377 B.C.) is known as the father of medicine. The Hippocratic oath, taken today by all doctors, requires physicians to act ethically and morally.

SCIENCE

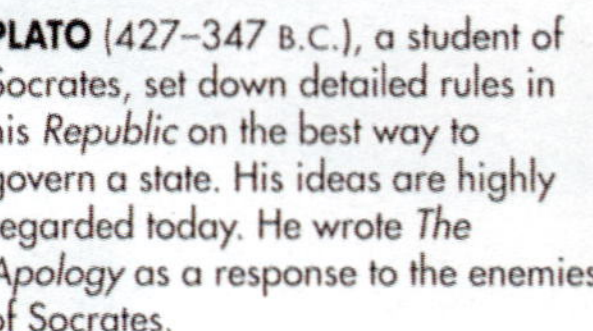

ANAXAGORAS (about 500–428 B.C.), an astronomer, explained that a solar eclipse is caused by the moon passing between the earth and the sun and blocking out the sun's light.

ARCHIMEDES (about 287–212 B.C.) is credited with having discovered a now widely accepted law of physics: a body displaces its own weight in water. Archimedes made his discovery in the bath. He also built a device that raised water from one level to another. Similar pumps are still used in parts of Africa today.

SOCRATES (469–399 B.C.) was one of the most famous philosophers of ancient Greece. His way of teaching, known as the Socratic method, incorporated questions and answers, not simply lecturing. When Socrates was old, the Athenians sentenced him to death by poison because he had criticized the government.

PLATO (427–347 B.C.), a student of Socrates, set down detailed rules in his *Republic* on the best way to govern a state. His ideas are highly regarded today. He wrote *The Apology* as a response to the enemies of Socrates.

ARISTOTLE (384–322 B.C.), a pupil of Plato, was a tutor to Alexander the Great, who ruled Greece in the fourth century B.C. Aristotle was probably the first person to promote the scientific method of observation, in which one first looks carefully and then comes up with a theory.

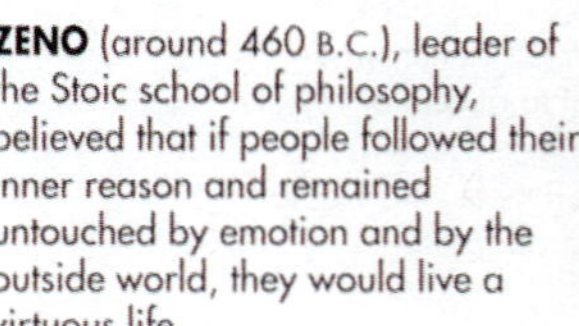

ZENO (around 460 B.C.), leader of the Stoic school of philosophy, believed that if people followed their inner reason and remained untouched by emotion and by the outside world, they would live a virtuous life.

362

EXPANDING VOCABULARY

Point out the word *Apology* in the Plato caption on page 362. Ask students what meaning they know for this word. (An apology is a statement that one is sorry for having done or said something.) Explain that another meaning is "a formal defense" and that the word *apology* comes from the Greek word meaning "speech." Guide students to see that Plato defended the teachings of Socrates in *The Apology*.

DEMOCRACY

Democracy in Ancient Greece was quite different from democracy as we know it. Today, we use the word *democracy* to describe a system of government in which everybody can vote. However, in the fifth century B.C. in Athens, many people—women, foreigners, and slaves—did not have the right to vote. Also, people in ancient Greece voted several times a year directly on the issues (direct democracy), whereas today, we vote once every several years to elect representatives who vote on issues (representational democracy).

There were no professional judges or lawyers, so citizens conducted their own cases in court. Over 200 men served on a jury to ensure that jurors were not bribed or intimidated. All citizens were expected to volunteer for jury duty.

JURORS' BALLOTS: The center token, above, with the hollow center, meant "guilty."

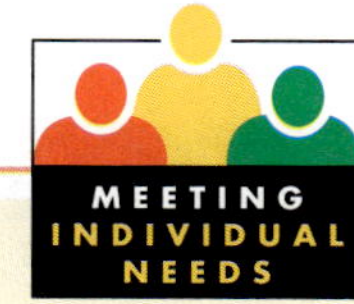

CHALLENGE **Encourage students to research how people vote today in the United States. Then have them create a chart that compares how people vote today with how people voted in ancient Greece.**

HISTORY

Herodotus (about 480–425 B.C.) is known as the father of history because he was the first person to gather facts about events and write them down. His history of the Persian Wars was the beginning of Western history writing.

LITERATURE

Greek myths, stories about gods and heroes, are still popular today. In one, Daedalus makes wings for himself and his son, Icarus, so they can fly out of the maze in which they are imprisoned. The wings are attached with wax. Icarus flies too close to the sun and the wax melts, causing him to fall into the Aegean Sea and drown.

ARCHITECTURE

The Parthenon, built between 447 and 432 B.C., is considered by some to be the most beautiful building in the world. Parts of it still stand today, almost 2,500 years later. Inside the Parthenon stood a huge gold and ivory statue of the goddess Athena, patron of Athens, appearing as the goddess of warfare. On her right hand was a small winged figure of Nike, the goddess of victory.

THE GREEKS CREATED THREE IMPORTANT ARCHITECTURAL STYLES.

THE DORIC STYLE is simple, with thick, sturdy columns and plain capitals (tops).

THE IONIC STYLE has thinner columns than the Doric, and its capitals are decorated with two volutes (swirls).

THE CORINTHIAN STYLE has elaborate capitals decorated with acanthus leaves. Corinthian columns were not often used by the Greeks but became popular in Roman times.

THE EARLIEST surviving examples of Greek literature are two epic poems, *The Iliad* and *The Odyssey*, credited to Homer, a blind poet who lived around the eighth century B.C. Little is known about him. His works give information about the Trojan War and about the hero Odysseus's return home from the war.

364

MULTICULTURAL CONNECTION

Tell students that people of ancient cultures throughout the world built great monuments like the Parthenon to honor their gods. In a jungle in western Cambodia, for instance, stands the Hindu temple of Angkor Wat, which was built in the 1100s to honor the god Vishnu. It is considered one of the architectural wonders of the world. In Mexico and Central America are ruins of the Mayan civilization, which was at its peak from A.D. 250 to A.D. 900. Still standing in Guatemala is the Temple of the Giant Jaguar. Allow students to share whatever knowledge they may have about the ancient architecture of their own cultures.

DRAMA

The origins of modern theater can be traced to ancient Greece. In its earliest form, Greek theater was songs and dances performed in the marketplace by a group of men called a chorus. Later, huge open-air theaters were built all over the Greek world.

TRAGEDY

COMEDY

SOPHOCLES

BY THE FIFTH century B.C., two types of plays emerged: tragedies and comedies. Tragedies were serious plays about past heroes who often came to tragic ends. Audiences today, as in ancient times, are spellbound by such tragedies as *Antigone* and *Oedipus Rex* (left), written by Sophocles (496–400 B.C.). Comedies were light-hearted plays that included a lot of clowning around, insults, rude jokes, and slapstick humor. Characters were everyday people who commented on politics and on famous people of the day.

THE 14,000-seat Epidaurus theater, cut into a hillside, was designed for excellent viewing and sound amplification.

LANGUAGE ARTS CONNECTION

DRAMA Tell students that in our culture we are exposed to new ideas and opinions in printed material. But the ancient Greeks lived long before the invention of the printing press. One way that writers and thinkers of that time made their ideas known to large numbers of people was through drama. Have students briefly discuss any experiences they have had with theater.

MINILESSON

REVIEW: STUDY SKILLS

Library

INFORMAL ASSESSMENT

Have students skim page 365 and imagine that they have been assigned a report about Greek theater. Ask them how they would go about finding more detailed information on this topic. (Possible responses: use a library catalog to look up books on the topic; use reference books such as encyclopedias; use the *Readers' Guide to Periodical Literature* for magazine articles about the topic)

TEACH/MODEL

Model how to use the library to locate information about Greek theater:

MODEL

I'll use the library's computerized catalog to find books on my topic. I'll enter a topic such as "Drama—Greek" or "Theater—Greece—history." Once I've found a book I want, I'll write down the call number and locate it on the shelf. If the library computer also has a magazine index, I can enter my topics to find articles in magazines that may have information I want. I can then locate the articles. I could also look in the *Readers' Guide to Periodical Literature* for listings of magazine articles.

PRACTICE/APPLY

Have students find other topics in this magazine article that they would like to investigate further. Have them write down research topics and tell how they would use library resources to find the information they want.

Responding to the Article

Have students share information from the article that they found particularly interesting. Encourage them to tell what additional questions they have about ancient Greece after reading this article.

DIGGING UP THE PAST

Eventually, ancient Greek civilization was destroyed by war. For 27 years, Athens and Sparta, a city-state in the south of Greece known for its devotion to warfare, battled fiercely in the Peloponnesian War (431–404 B.C.). When it was finally over, Sparta was victorious, but not for long. Within about 50 years, the Macedonians from northeastern Greece had conquered both Athens and Sparta, along with many other Greek states.

Over time, other conquests took place. New rulers, customs, buildings, and ideas replaced old ones. How, then, do we know as much as we do about a way of life that thrived more than 20 centuries ago? Read on to find out.

A GREAT DEAL OF our knowledge of ancient Greece comes from the detailed painting on pottery, much of it black on an orange background (black-figure technique), or vice versa (red-figure technique).

A MINOAN colony on the island of Santorini was buried over 3,000 years ago by an enormous volcanic explosion—one that spewed ash so high that it reached Greenland, more than 3,500 miles away! Parts of Santorini sat under 900 feet of ash, preserving wall paintings that vividly detail the Minoan way of life.

ONE WAY TO FIND out about the past is to examine shipwrecks. The oldest known shipwreck in the world dates from about 1200 B.C., during what is known as the Bronze Age. The wreck, discovered off the coast of Turkey in 1959, contained agricultural implements, weapons, bronze tools, amphorae (vases), and about six tons of copper—enough, when mixed with tin, to equip an army of over 300 men! From this and other findings, we know that extensive trade routes existed in the Mediterranean more than 3,000 years ago!

366

SOCIAL STUDIES CONNECTION

TRADE Provide students with copies of a map of Greece and other lands near the Aegean Sea. Then assist them in locating the places mentioned on pages 366 and 367. As they study the map, point out that most of the major cities could be reached easily by water, and remind them that this area of the world was known for trade as far back as 3,000 years ago. Ask students how trade among different cultures is beneficial. (Possible response: Through trade, people of various cultures can acquire knowledge and goods that they might not otherwise have.)

ANCIENT GREECE was at its height in the fifth century B.C., but the city of Knossos on the island of Crete thrived more than 2,000 years earlier. Archaeologist Sir Arthur Evans is credited with discovering the Knossos palace, which had more than 1,000 rooms! Excavations done in 1934 also revealed that the Minoans, who lived in Knossos during the Bronze Age, used at least two forms of writing. The Minoan civilization seems to have been thriving until it was struck by an earthquake and later overtaken by the Mycenaeans, early Greeks who lived on mainland Greece.

PEOPLE FIND OUT about the past by digging it up. In 1931, the enormous task of unearthing the ancient Athenian marketplace began. Houses that had been built over the agora were bought and torn down. Twenty-eight acres of soil were removed. Over 300,000 tons of earth were carted away before the ancient buildings were uncovered. Eventually, the stoa of Attalos was completely rebuilt and many other ancient monuments were brought to life.

HEINRICH SCHLIEMANN believed that the Trojan War was not simply a tale told by a blind bard named Homer but that it had actually taken place. Between 1870 and 1873, he began excavating where he felt Troy must have been. He unearthed many items (below), some going back 1,000 years earlier than Homer's poem: more than 8,000 gold rings, necklaces, bracelets, cups, and plates. Archaeologists today are fairly certain that Schliemann did, in fact, find the site of the Trojan War.

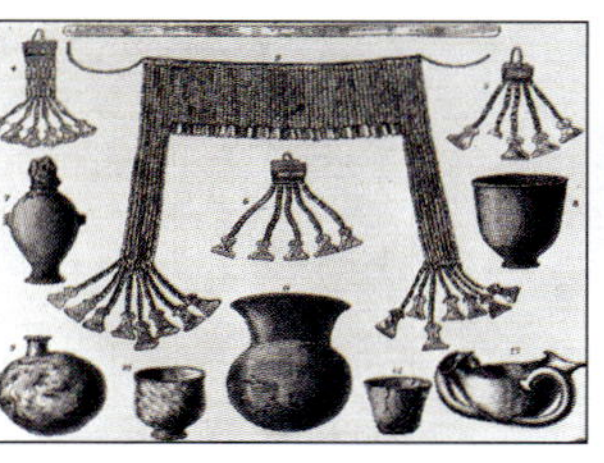

SOPHIA SCHLIEMANN wearing some of the jewelry discovered by her husband at Troy.

367

CHECKING COMPREHENSION

What Do You Think?

1. **In what ways have the ancient Greeks influenced our culture?** (Possible responses: Greek philosophers and scientists have influenced the way we acquire knowledge about ourselves and the world around us; we have a government that is based on Greek democracy; the Greek idea of equality is an important part of our culture; we still read Greek myths; Greek tragedies are still performed in our theaters.) **DESCRIPTIVE RESPONSE**

2. **If you could talk with one of the famous Greeks mentioned in this article, whom would you choose? Why?** (Responses will vary.) **PERSONAL RESPONSE**

3. **How does this article show that a study of Greek plays and epic poems can be a key to understanding the past?** (Possible responses: Plays such as the Greek tragedies tell us what people of that time thought was important; epic poems such as Homer's, which may be based on actual events, can give archaeologists and historians clues to help them figure out what happened in the past.) **CRITICAL ANALYSIS/REFLECTING**

Integrating Language Arts

TIPS FOR CLASSROOM MANAGEMENT

IF students show interest in learning about other ancient cultures, **THEN** they should complete the Writing activity.

IF students need experience in using speaking strategies, **THEN** they should complete the Oral Language activity.

WRITING

Create a Character

Through discoveries of clothing, jewelry, pottery, and other artifacts, archaeologists have learned a great deal about the way ancient people lived.

Have students work independently to research other ancient cultures such as those of the Egyptians, Vikings, Maya, and Romans. Have students look for information about daily life in the culture. They may want to record their information on a chart like the one below. When students have gathered enough information about a particular culture, have them create a character who could have lived in that ancient civilization. Students can write one or two paragraphs about that character's daily life. READING/WRITING

Ancient ______________
Food
Clothing
Government
Education
Entertainment

ORAL LANGUAGE

Digging Up the Present

COOPERATIVE LEARNING Have students imagine that they are archaeologists who live in the year A.D. 2300 and that they have just excavated a site in the United States. Have students form small groups to brainstorm a great discovery they have made, and then have a Reporter from each group tell why their discovery is important to understanding twentieth-century American culture. Suggest that students consider ordinary as well as extraordinary places and objects. LISTENING/SPEAKING

ART AND LITERATURE

Autumn Leaves, Lake George, N.Y. (1924)

Georgia O'Keeffe (1887–1986)

ABOUT THE ARTIST

Georgia O'Keeffe studied at the Art Institute of Chicago and at the Art Students League in New York City. She developed a painting style in which she flattened and simplified shapes while using colors boldly but harmoniously. Her first serious collection of works caught the attention of photographer and gallery owner Alfred Stieglitz. O'Keeffe and Stieglitz were later married. O'Keeffe decided to move to New Mexico, where she remained until her death in 1986. The influence of the natural forms and rich cultures of the Southwest are apparent in much of O'Keeffe's art.

ABOUT THE PAINTING

Georgia O'Keeffe painted *Autumn Leaves, Lake George, N.Y.* in the same year she married Alfred Stieglitz. She recognized that rare beauty is often overlooked because an object is small or common. In this painting, she enlarged and simplified the structure of autumn leaves while emphasizing the depth and variation of colors.

Autumn Leaves, Lake George, N.Y., by Georgia O'Keeffe, captures an image of nature's colorful change from one season to the next. In what ways is this painting similar to the selection you have read? In what ways is it different? If you could paint a picture of a turning point in your life, what would you show?

Autumn Leaves, Lake George, N.Y. (1924)
by Georgia O'Keeffe

Georgia O'Keeffe showed a talent for drawing when she was a child growing up in Wisconsin. She later studied art in Chicago and New York, and she taught school in Texas. Some of O'Keeffe's best-known works are of objects found in nature, such as flowers, rocks, and animal bones. When she then settled in New Mexico, she painted images of the canyons, mountains, bleached bones, and adobe buildings there.

LITERATURE

368

Columbus Museum of Art

Art and Literature

MAKING CONNECTIONS

Ask students to read the first paragraph on page 368, and encourage a discussion of the questions. Lead students to see that autumn leaves represent a turning point between the warm, sunny days of summer and the cold of winter. Like the painting, the reading selections contain examples of turning points. One main difference between the selections and the painting is that the selections include details about what happens before and after the turning point, while the painting captures only one moment in time. Encourage volunteers to describe what their painting of a turning point would look like.

EXTENDING FINE ART

Cross-Curricular Activity: Science Ask small groups of students to conduct research to determine what causes leaves to change color in autumn. Have them organize the information they find and then present it to the class. Encourage groups to create colored drawings on poster board to illustrate their presentations.

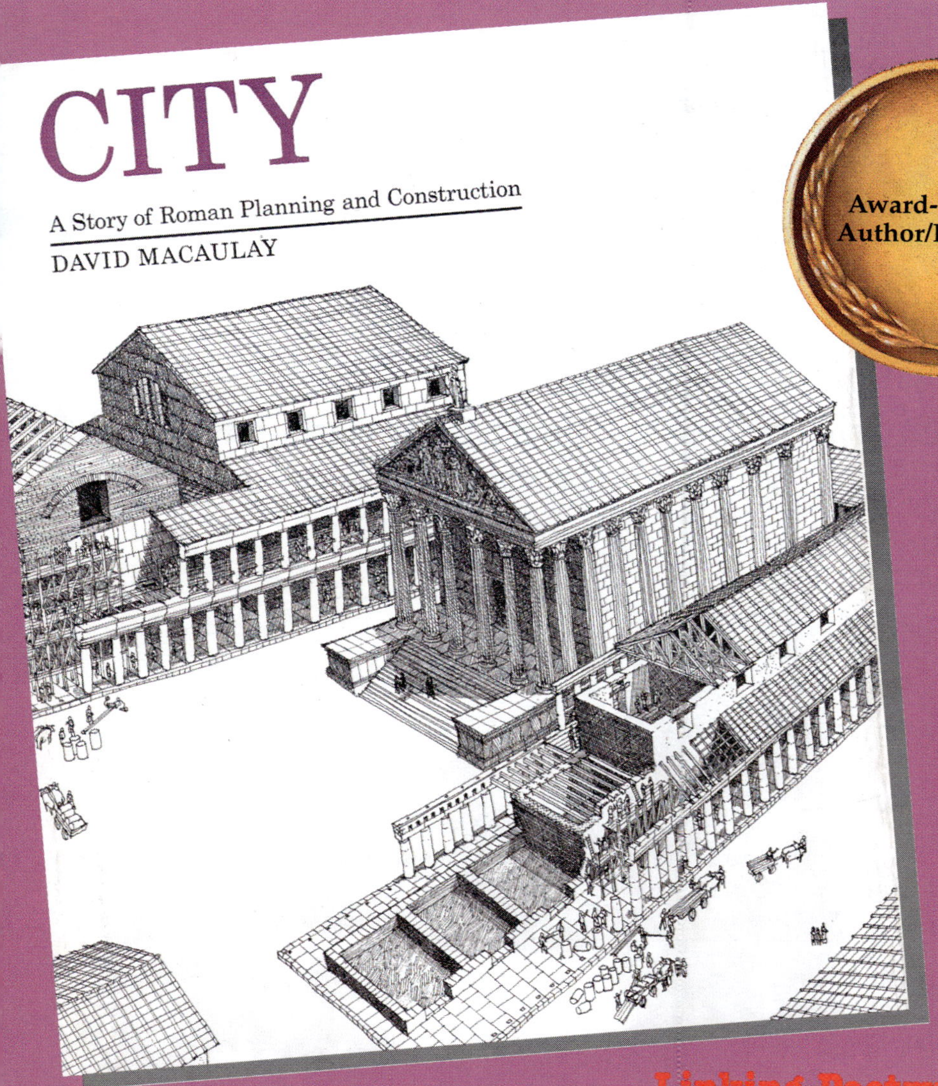

CITY: A STORY OF ROMAN PLANNING AND CONSTRUCTION (PP. 370–397) AND CITY (PP. 398–399)

CITY

A Story of Roman Planning and Construction

DAVID MACAULAY

Award-Winning Author/Illustrator

THEME: EXPLORATIONS

Turning Points

In "City: A Story of Roman Planning and Construction," students will discover that some changes in a community come about by chance, while others are carefully planned and executed.

Linking Poetry to Nonfiction

"City," a poem by Langston Hughes, speaks of a city in modern times.

David Macaulay

ABOUT THE AUTHOR/ ILLUSTRATOR

DAVID MACAULAY has a unique talent for being able to explain to young readers through finely detailed text and drawings how things are built, how gadgets work, and how abstract ideas become reality. His books have won numerous awards, including the 1991 Caldecott Medal for *Black and White,* and the 1989 *Boston Globe-Horn Book* Award for the best nonfiction book *The Way things Work.* His *City: A Story of Roman Planning and Construction* was a 1975 Children's Book Showcase.

More information about David Macaulay and his work appears on Page T786.

SELECTION SUMMARY

Genre: Nonfiction

Begun in 26 B.C., the fictional city of Verbonia is characteristic of Roman cities built at that time. In this nonfiction selection, the text and illustrations, including cutaway and three-dimensional views, provide information about the construction and function of various parts of a Roman city. Topics include roads, the city wall, the forum, the marketplace, private houses, and various small shops. Through text and drawings, the reader learns about cities, about Roman life, about the processes of building, and about the wisdom of planning for the future.

SUGGESTED LESSON PLANNER

▶ *City: A Story of Roman Planning and Construction*

	DAY 1	DAY 2
PART 1 Reading, Listening, Speaking, Viewing **Key Words** efficient consisted function residents	**BUILD BACKGROUND** T758 **VOCABULARY STRATEGIES** T759 *Transparency 37* *Practice Book* p. 112 **READING THE SELECTION** T760–T787 Options for Reading T760–T761 *Response Card 9* *Literature Cassette 3* **REVIEW PREDICTIONS/PURPOSE** T784 **APPRECIATING THE LITERATURE** T784 NOTE: Students may read the selection on Day 2.	**SUMMARIZE THE SELECTION** T785 *Practice Book* p. 113 **READ POETRY** T788–T789 "City" ◆ **RESPONSE CORNER ACTIVITIES** T790 **CHECKING COMPREHENSION** T791 *End-of-Selection Test*
PART 2 Writer's Workshop	**HOW-TO ARTICLE** Thinking as Writers T796 *Language Handbook* pp. 20, 66 *Transparency 38*	Prewriting T796 *Language Handbook* pp. 20, 60
Grammar	✓ **MAIN AND HELPING VERBS** Teach the Concept T798 Daily Language Practice (1–2) R16	Daily Language Practice (3–4) R16 Practice Activity T799
Spelling	**SUFFIXES: *-ship, -ment,* AND *-ity*** *statement, activity, development, argument, ability, government, majority, electricity, friendship, partnership, leadership, community, apartment, authority, security, championship* Pretest/Self-Check T800 *Integrated Spelling Teacher's Edition* pp. T141, T290	Open and Closed Sorts T800 *Integrated Spelling* p. 90 *Integrated Spelling Teacher's Edition* p. T142
PART 3 Skills and Strategies	◆ **INTEGRATED CURRICULUM** *Roman Empire* **Social Studies** T804 **Math** T804 **Science** T805 *The Amazing Writing Machine*	**COMPREHENSION SKILL** T802–T803 Classify/Categorize (Introduce) *Practice Book* pp. 116–117
MEETING INDIVIDUAL NEEDS	Use the Intervention Strategy note on page T781 with students throughout the reading of the selection.	Use the Intervention Strategies on page T792 to help **below-level** and **ESL students** with the vocabulary in the selection.

NOTE: An alternative lesson plan for **below-level students** appears on *Intervention Strategies Manual* pp. 86–91. A lesson for **students acquiring English** appears on *Sheltered English/ESL Manual* pp. 58–61.

DAY 3	DAY 4	DAY 5
◆ **IDEA BANK ACTIVITIES** Retelling T794 *Response Card 12* Oral Language T794 Viewing T795 Real-Life Resources: Reading a Menu T795 *Writer's Magazine* pp. 56–57 School–Home Connection 15 R43	**VOCABULARY WORKSHOP** T801 Reviewing Key Words **READING TRADE BOOKS** T806–T807 *Signatures Library: Detectives in Togas*  Signatures Library Take-Home Book	**READING TRADE BOOKS** T803, T805, T806–T807 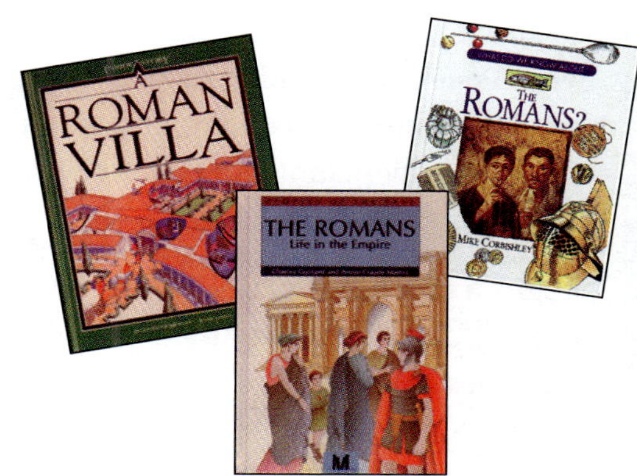
Drafting T796 *Language Handbook* p. 60 *The Amazing Writing Machine*	Responding and Revising T797 *Language Handbook* pp. 61, 146–147, 152–153	Proofreading and Publishing T797 *Language Handbook* p. 61
Daily Language Practice (5–6) R16 Practice Activity T799 *Language Handbook* pp. 148–149 *The Amazing Writing Machine*	Daily Language Practice (7–8) R16 Practice Activity T799 *Grammar Practice Book* pp. 38–39	Daily Language Practice (9–12) R16 *Practice Book* p. 114
Discuss the Generalization T800 *Integrated Spelling* p. 91 *Integrated Spelling Teacher's Edition* p. T143	Apply to Writing T800 *Integrated Spelling* pp. 92–93 *Integrated Spelling Teacher's Edition* pp. T144–T145	Posttest T800 *Practice Book* p. 115 *Integrated Spelling Teacher's Edition* p. T146
VOCABULARY MINILESSON T763 ✓ Structural Analysis—Greek and Latin Roots (Review) *Practice Book* p. 118 **GRAMMAR MINILESSON** T777 ✓ Action and Linking Verbs (Review)	**VOCABULARY WORKSHOP** T801 Dictionary/Glossary Use	**COMPREHENSION MINILESSON** T779 ✓ Compare/Contrast (Review) *Practice Book* p. 119 Theme Project Checkpoint 3 T808
Above-level students may complete the Writer's Workshop independently at their own pace.	**Below-level students** may read the *Take-Home Book: Snack Attack: A Story of a Boom Town* to reinforce Key Words.	**Below-level** and **ESL students** may read the *ESL/Title I Library* book *Hill of Fire*.

✓ = Tested Skill
◆ = Optional activities used to adjust pacing throughout the lesson
Titles in *italics* are optional materials.

1 Reading and Responding

BUILDING BACKGROUND AND CONCEPTS

PRIOR KNOWLEDGE

Relate to students' lives. Ask students how they would go about planning a city. Discuss what types of things they would need to consider, such as population, space, neighborhoods, commercial centers, and so on. Have students comment on how planning a city today would differ from planning a city in 26 B.C.

Begin a K-W-L chart. Discuss what students already know about life in the days of the Roman Empire. Have them record their ideas in the first column of a K-W-L chart. Explain that "City: A Story of Roman Planning and Construction" will describe part of the process of planning and building a Roman city.

K-W-L Chart

K	W	L
What I Know	What I Want to Know	What I Learned
Rome was ruled by an emperor. Many people of the Roman Empire lived by farming.		

QUICKWRITE

Encourage students to write a few sentences about whether they think it's possible to design and build a city that serves the needs of all the people who live within it.

Intervention Strategies

For students who may have difficulty reading "City: A Story of Roman Planning and Construction," support is available in *Intervention Strategies Manual,* pages 86–91, and on pages T767, T781, and T792–T793 in this lesson.

STUDENTS ACQUIRING ENGLISH

See *Sheltered English/ESL Manual,* pages 58–61.

FACT FINDER

SOCIAL STUDIES

Augustus Caesar

Although "City: A Story of Roman Planning and Construction" is a fictional account, it closely parallels the actual planning and construction of cities in the Roman Empire during the same period. David Macaulay names his fictional city Augusta Verbonia, in honor of Augustas Caesar. The name *Augustus* means "revered one." Augustus Caesar (*caesar* is the Roman word for "emperor") became the first emperor of Rome in 27 B.C. He was a legendary builder. He was often aided by his friend Agrippa, a man especially well known for the design and construction of aqueducts and sewers. Augustus is remembered for his love of marble, which he used on the faces of great public buildings. In fact, one of his favorite boasts was that he had found Rome a city of brick and had left it a city of marble.

VOCABULARY STRATEGIES

KEY WORDS DEFINED

efficient acting, performing, or doing without wasted cost or effort

consisted were made up of

function purpose; the role or action something is especially suited to perform or do

residents people who live in a certain place

INTEGRATED SPELLING

Spelling Pretest: page T800

Spelling Generalization: Suffixes *–ship*, *–ment*, and *–ity*

CONTEXT CLUES: INFORMATION

Encourage students to use semantic and visual cues. Display Transparency 37, and ask a volunteer to read the title and the first paragraph. Ask a second volunteer to read the other information on the transparency. Encourage students to use the information, including the heading, and the visual clues to help them understand the meanings of the underlined words. Remind students to use context clues, such as those surrounding the word *function*, to figure out the meanings of unfamiliar words.

CHECK UNDERSTANDING

Have students generate associations. Ask students to imagine that they are the residents of Schoolipius, an ancient city in an ancient civilization. Have them think of one thing they need to make life in their city more efficient, such as irrigation. Then ask students to tell what its function will be, what it will consist of, and why having it will make life in their city more efficient. STRATEGY: ASSOCIATIONS

TRANSPARENCY 37

Key Words

City Walls

In Roman times, because building a city wall cost less than some other methods, it was an efficient way to keep a city safe.

The walls consisted of many layers of stones.

The main function of the city wall was protection.

Residents stayed safe behind the walls.

The residents of the city came out for the parade.

Name ______________ City

Read the picture captions, using context clues to determine the meaning of each underlined word. Then write each word on the line next to its meaning.

Before he could complete a home's design, a Roman architect had to consider the residents who would live in the finished structure. What were their habits? Did they mainly like being outdoors or indoors? How large were their families?

A building was planned to suit its function. What would people do inside it? Was it for work or play? Was there a need for storage? Was beauty a consideration?

In Roman times, building materials consisted primarily of limestone, wood, clay, stones, stucco, and marble. For decoration, people used small tiles to make mosaics.

Technological advances make today's architects more efficient than ever. Designs can be input into a computer, and changes can be made quickly and effortlessly without redrawing.

1. purpose, proper use ___function___
2. producing results with the least effort or waste ___efficient___
3. were made up or composed ___consisted___
4. persons who live in a certain place ___residents___

TRY THIS! Writing

Using words and drawings, design a simple living space for someone living in the first moon colony. Think about the special needs someone who was adapting to the moon's environment would have. Your description should include three vocabulary words.

112 VOCABULARY HIDDEN TREASURES Practice Book

PRACTICE BOOK, page 112

Prereading Strategies

PREVIEW AND PREDICT

Ask students to read the title of the selection and look through the illustrations. Have them identify the section headings on pages 378, 382, and 386 and then read the first paragraph on page 373. Ask students what they would like to learn by reading this selection. Have them record their answers in the second column of their K-W-L charts or on *Practice Book* page 113.

K-W-L Chart

K	W	L
What I Know	What I Want to Know	What I Learned
Rome was ruled by an emperor. Many people of the Roman Empire lived by farming.	How long did it take to build the roads and walls? What kinds of structures did the Romans build?	

You may want to suggest that students write their predictions about the selection in their personal journals.

PURPOSE

You may want to model setting a purpose:

As I read, I'm going to focus on how this Roman city is the same as and different from our cities today.

CITY

A STORY OF ROMAN PLANNING AND CONSTRUCTION

by DAVID MACAULAY

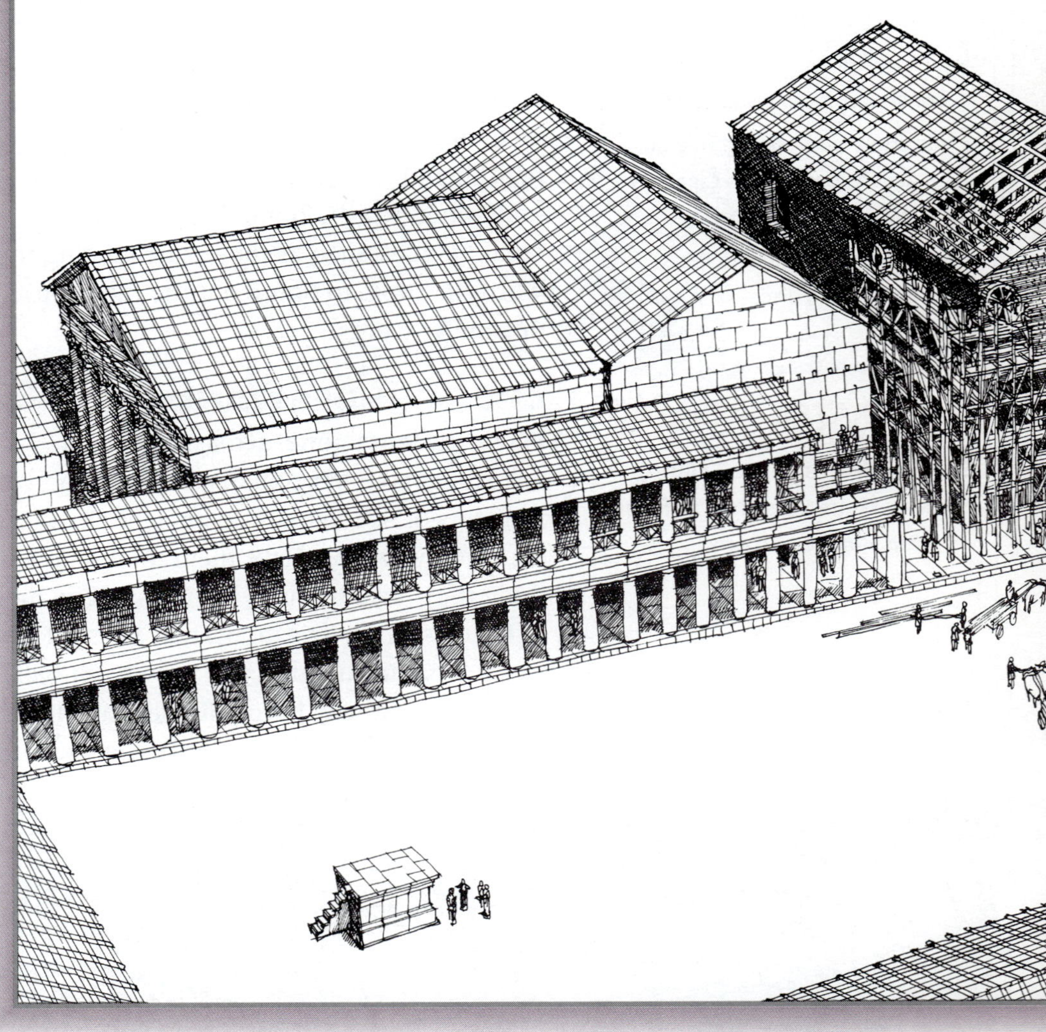

SMALL GROUP

PARTNER READING

Pair students who need extra support with more-fluent readers. Have students pause after each page or two to discuss what they have read and to comment on the illustrations. Encourage more-fluent readers to model strategies for their partners.

COOPERATIVE READING

READER RESPONSE GROUPS

Small groups may use Reader Response Card 9, **Literature Circle,** to discuss the selection. Reader Response Card 9 can be found at the back of this Teacher's Edition.

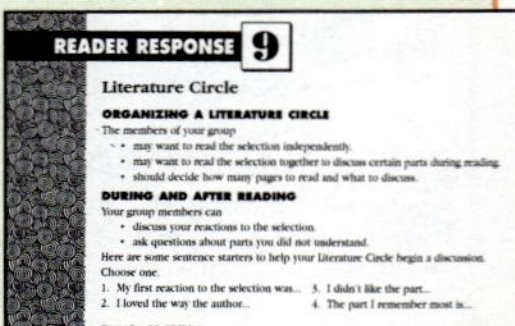

Response Card 9

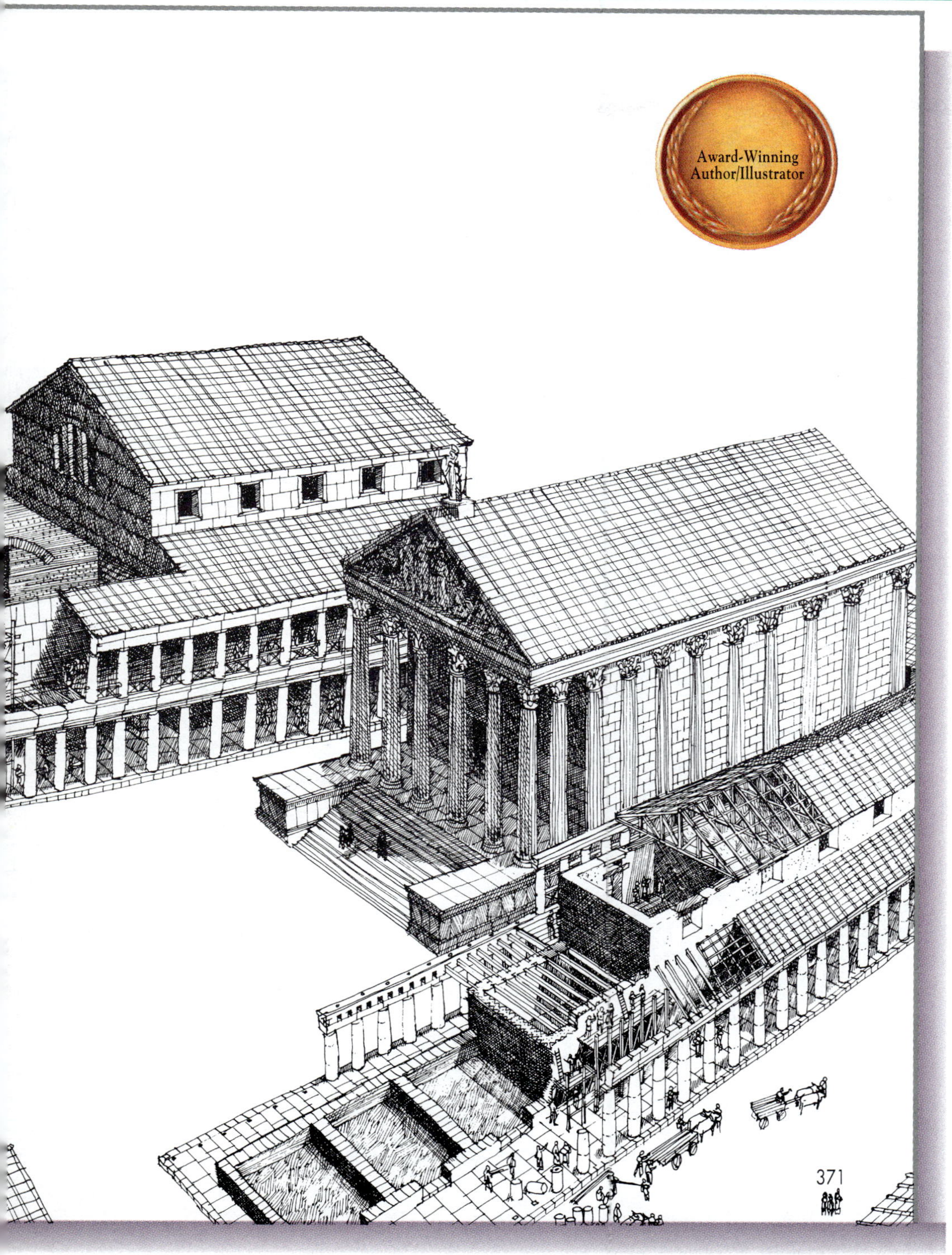

Award-Winning
Author/Illustrator

371

WHOLE CLASS

STRATEGIC READING

To help students understand difficult concepts and unfamiliar words, reinforce the focus strategy of **adjusting reading rate.** Pages T762, T766 and T774 are excellent places to have students model adjusting their reading rate to help them gain meaning as they read.

INDEPENDENT READING/DISCUSSION

Successful readers can read the entire selection on their own. Suggest that, after they finish, they meet with other independent readers and use their completed K-W-L charts to discuss what they learned from the selection.

Strategic Reading

ADJUSTING READING RATE

Using the class-made strategy chart, invite students to talk about some of the strategies they use when reading. Then tell students that they will focus on **adjusting reading rate** as they read this selection. Explain that reading rate is the speed at which a person reads something. For example, when the text is easy or words are familiar, a reader is likely to read quickly; however, when new ideas are introduced, when vocabulary is unfamiliar, or when sentences are long and complicated, good readers slow down. Ask students how adjusting their reading rate might help them better understand a selection. (Possible response: It will cause me to slow down and think about difficult ideas or concepts.) STRATEGY: ADJUSTING READING RATE

PAGES 370–377 Have students read through page 377 to confirm their predictions.

MATH

Point out to students the date 26 B.C. on page 373. Draw a simple timeline on the board to illustrate that dates B.C. run backward and dates A.D. run forward.

26 B.C. — 19 B.C. — 0 — A.D. 14

Explain that larger numbers in dates B.C. indicate dates further in the past and larger numbers in dates A.D. indicate dates further in the future.

ILLUSTRATOR'S CRAFT

This illustration depicts a scene from the time during which Verbonia was planned and built. The emperor's clothing is long and loose, people wear sandals, the setting is opulent and dramatic and made of marble.

For almost two hundred years the wheat and grapes of northern Italy's fertile Po Valley had been collected in small trading villages and shipped to Rome. In 26 B.C. a disastrous spring flood destroyed the villages along the Po riverbanks as well as an important bridge. When news reached the Emperor Augustus he immediately dispatched to the stricken area forty-five military engineers, including planners, architects, surveyors, and construction specialists. They were to supervise the building of a new bridge and new roads and to lay plans for a new city. The city was named Verbonia, and—in honor of the Emperor—Augusta Verbonia.

Augustus hoped to combine all the remaining trading villages into one secure and efficient trading center and so increase the amount of produce coming into Rome. To speed up development of the new city, he retired to the area two thousand soldiers, who would not only help build Verbonia but also become its first citizens.

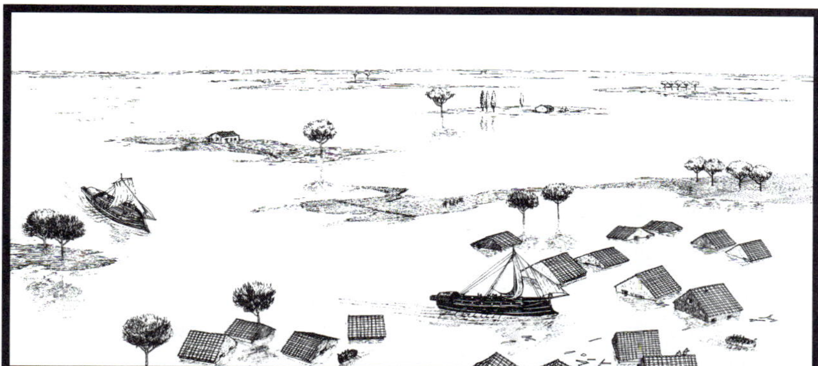

373

Tested Skill

MINILESSON

REVIEW: VOCABULARY

Structural Analysis—Greek and Latin Roots

INFORMAL ASSESSMENT

Ask students to find the word *architects* in the first paragraph on page 373 and tell what it means. (Possible response: A person who designs a building.) Tell students that *architect* comes from the Greek word *architektōn; archi-* meaning "principal" "chief," and *-tektōn*, meaning "builder."

TEACH/MODEL

Have students find the word *supervise* in the same paragraph. Explain that the word *supervise* contains two Latin word parts: the prefix *super-*, which means "over" or "above," and *vise*, which comes from a Latin root that means "to see." If necessary, model the thinking:

MODEL

When I'm not sure of the meaning of a word, sometimes I can use what I know about the meanings of Greek and Latin roots to help me figure it out. When I put together the meanings of *super-* and *vise*, I figure out that *supervise* means "to oversee or direct."

PRACTICE/APPLY

Have students tell how the meanings of *super-* and *vise* help them understand the meanings of the following English words: *visual, invisible, vista, revision, superior, superintendent, superb.*

SOCIAL STUDIES

The Po River is the largest waterway in Italy. It begins near Mount Viso and flows east approximately 405 miles to the Adriatic Sea. Nearly every river in northern Italy is a branch of the Po.

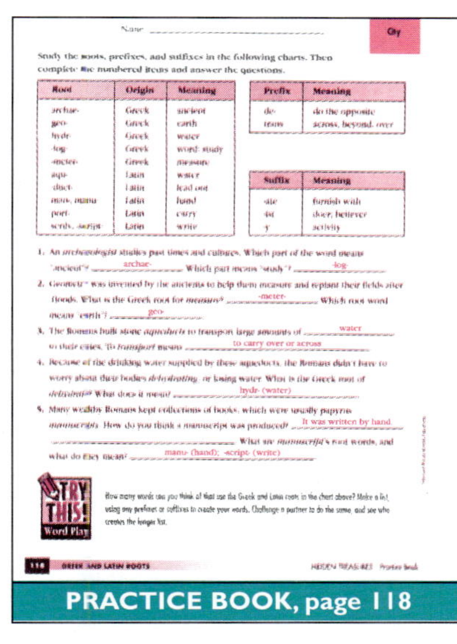

Name ____________________ City

Study the roots, prefixes, and suffixes in the following charts. Then complete the numbered items and answer the questions.

Root	Origin	Meaning
archae-	Greek	ancient
geo-	Greek	earth
hydr-	Greek	water
-log-	Greek	word; study
-meter-	Greek	measure
aqu-	Latin	water
duct-	Latin	lead out
man-, manu-	Latin	hand
port-	Latin	carry
scrib-, script-	Latin	write

Prefix	Meaning
de-	do the opposite
trans	across, beyond, over

Suffix	Meaning
-ate	furnish with
-ist	doer, believer
-y	activity

1. An *archaeologist* studies past times and cultures. Which part of the word means "ancient"? archae- Which part means "study"? -log-
2. Geometry was invented by the ancients to help them measure and replant their fields after floods. What is the Greek root for *measure*? -meter- Which root word means "earth"? geo-
3. The Romans built stone *aqueducts* to transport large amounts of water to their cities. To *transport* means to carry over or across
4. Because of the drinking water supplied by these aqueducts, the Romans didn't have to worry about their bodies *dehydrating*, or losing water. What is the Greek root of *dehydrate*? What does it mean? hydr- (water)
5. Many wealthy Romans kept collections of books, which were usually papyrus *manuscripts*. How do you think a manuscript was produced? It was written by hand. What are *manuscript's* root words, and what do they mean? manu- (hand); -script- (write)

TRY THIS! Word Play

How many words can you think of that use the Greek and Latin roots in the chart above? Make a list, using any prefixes or suffixes to create your words. Challenge a partner to do the same, and see who creates the longer list.

118 GREEK AND LATIN ROOTS HIDDEN TREASURES Practice Book

PRACTICE BOOK, page 118

Critical Thinking Questions

1. **What is the main idea of this page?** (how Roman roads were built) CRITICAL: DETERMINING MAIN IDEA

2. **How much time and effort and how many people do you think might have been involved in building a road?** (Possible response: Considerable time would have been spent planning and marking out the road; even more time, and a whole army of workers, would have been needed to deliver the stones and scrap iron to the site, to dig the ditches, and to fill them. To build a road of several miles probably took years.) CRITICAL: SPECULATING

The new roads and bridge were completed before work began on the city itself. Once the surveyors had marked out a road with stakes, a ditch was dug on each side into which a row of curbstones was set. A deeper ditch was then dug between the two rows of curbstones which was filled with layers of stones of varying size. The top layer formed the pavement of the road and rose slightly in the center to force the rainwater into the side ditches. The pavement was constructed of flat stones that were carefully fitted together. Any spaces left between them were filled with smaller stones or pieces of scrap iron.

374

STUDENTS ACQUIRING ENGLISH To help students understand the steps in the process of road making, provide and read aloud a numbered list like this: (1) Mark the road. (2) Dig a ditch. (3) Set curbstones. . . .

SOCIAL STUDIES

The Romans have been called the first true road-builders. They created 53,000 miles of roads across their empire. With all those roads, the Romans had their own traffic problems. Therefore, they also had stop signs, one-way streets, two-lane highways, lanes for slower and faster vehicles, and even alternate-side-of-the-street parking.

SCIENCE

FACT FINDER **Present-day roads still have four Roman features: multilayered paving (to provide additional support); slightly curved surfaces (to drain water); elevation (to decrease the amount of stress at work on the road); and adjacent ditches (to provide for drainage).**

Strategic Reading

PAGES 370–377 What have you learned so far about Roman cities? Is this what you thought you would learn? (Possible response: So far, how roads and city walls were built have been described.) STRATEGIES: SUMMARIZING/CONFIRMING PREDICTIONS

What were some of the most important features of the Roman city walls? (Possible response: Important features included the depth of the base of the wall, so no one could tunnel under it; the crenelations that protected the soldiers defending the city; and the fact that there were two walls, with the inner wall being several feet higher than the outer wall.) LITERAL: NOTING IMPORTANT DETAILS

STRATEGY FOCUS

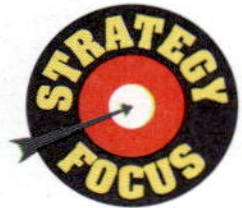

ADJUSTING READING RATE

If necessary, model the strategy of adjusting reading rate:

MODEL **I came to the word *furrow* in the second sentence, and I wasn't sure what it referred to. I knew that I needed to slow down and concentrate on all the facts I was reading to be sure I understood what the walls were like and what was so special about them.**

PAGES 378–385
Students should read to page 385 to find out what else the Romans designed and built.

STRATEGIES WE USE DURING READING
- ✓ Summarize/Paraphrase
- ✓ Visualize
- ✓ Reread
- ✓ Adjust Reading Rate

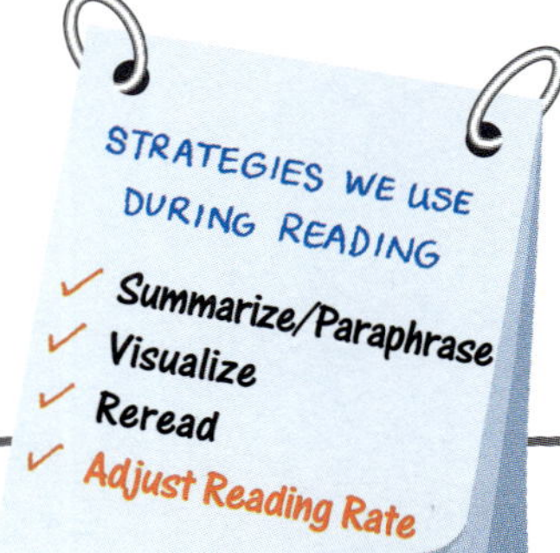

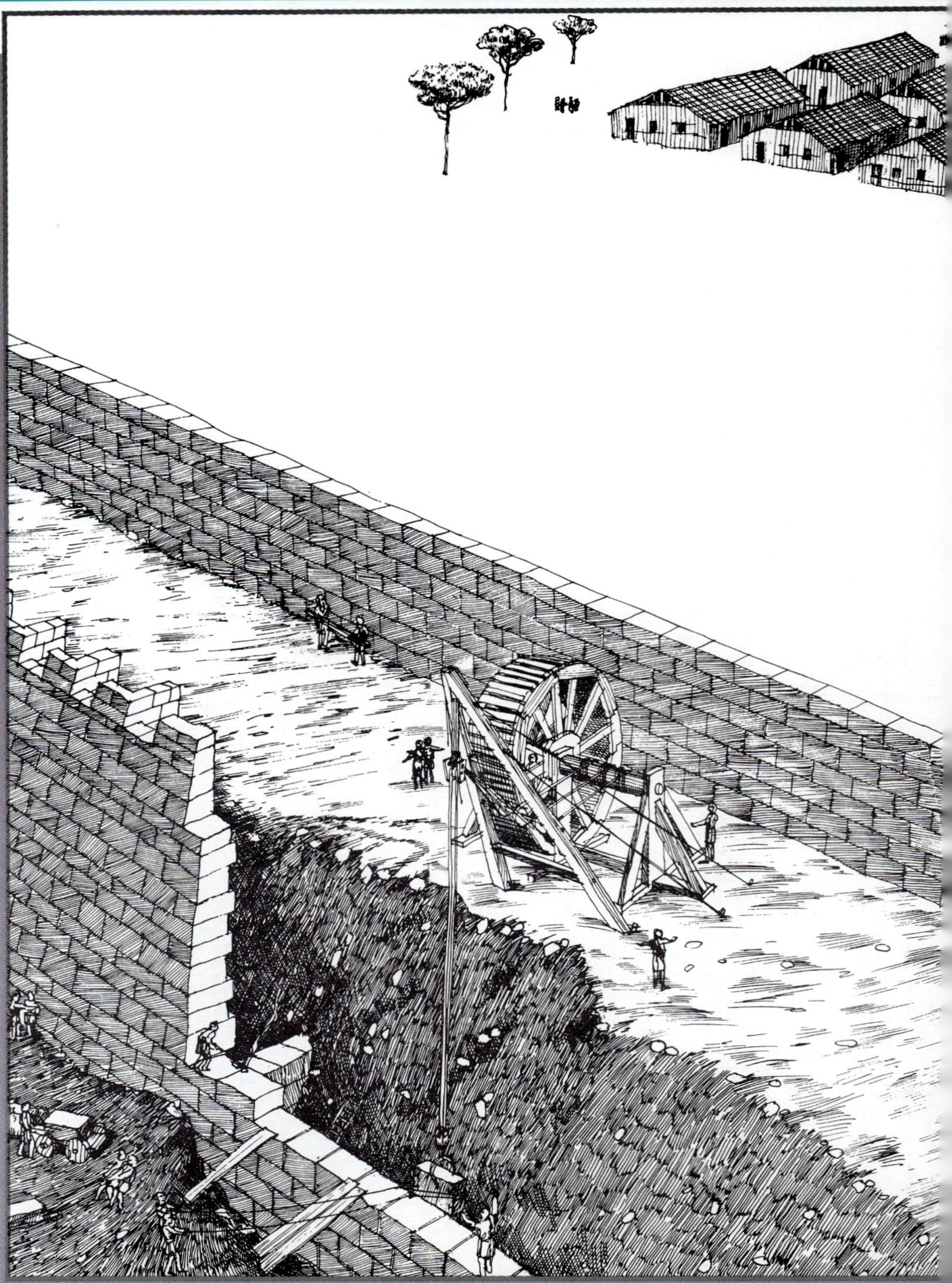

FROM THE AUTHOR

"For me the point is to leave a picture in somebody's mind—not necessarily a sentence or a paragraph—but if you can leave a picture in someone's mind, the chances they'll remember the idea are that much greater."

—David Macaulay

The city wall was built next. Two large ditches were dug along the furrow and the dirt was heaped into a high mound between them. A stone wall was built against each side for additional strength. The base of the outer wall went down thirty feet below ground level, making it almost impossible for anyone to tunnel under. On top of the outer wall alternating high and low sections called crenelations were built. The soldiers were protected behind the high sections while firing their weapons over the low sections. The inner wall was several feet higher than the outer wall to block the path of rocks and arrows that might be fired into the city.

Cranes on top of the mound lowered the stones into place. Four men standing inside a wooden wheel at the base of the crane provided the power. As they walked forward the wheel turned, rotating an axle which wound the rope. The engineers constantly checked to make sure each course of stones was level.

377

Student Self-Assessment

ADJUSTING READING RATE

Remind students that, as they read, they may wish to adjust their reading rate.

- Did I understand the meaning of the unfamiliar word *crenelations?*
- Did I read slowly enough to be able to explain how the city wall was built?

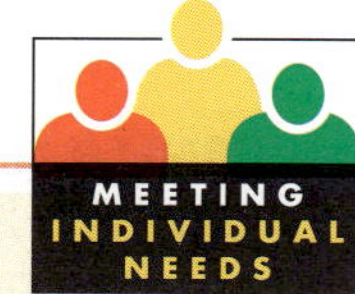

Intervention Strategies

READING AHEAD Ask students to repeat this sentence aloud or to themselves: *When I read, I sometimes read ahead if things aren't making sense.* Students should tell when and how reading ahead helped clarify any parts of the story.

THE FORUM

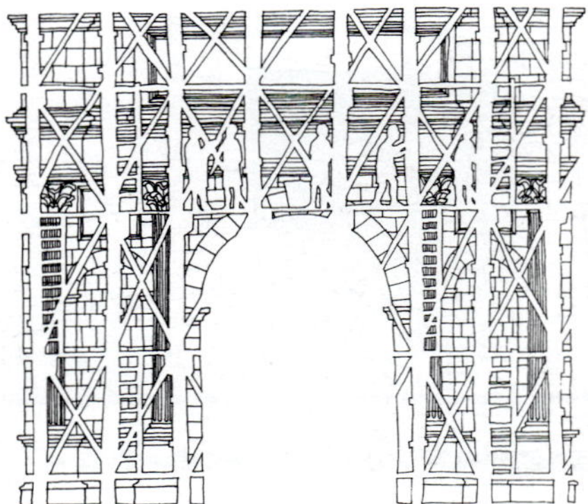

By 19 B.C. the city walls were finished and work began on the first and most important public areas of the city—the forum and the market.

The forum was paved and covered two entire blocks. At one end the temple of Jupiter, Juno, and Minerva was built. Of all the temples to be built in the forum this was the most important. At the opposite end, facing the temple, was the rostrum. This was a raised platform from which speeches were made and decrees were read to the residents of the city. Along one side of the forum stood the Curia—the building in which the elected senators of the city met. Next to the Curia was the Basilica, the court of justice. The temple was constructed of polished limestone, while the other two buildings were brick-faced concrete covered with sheets of limestone. All the roofs were made of triangular wooden frames called trusses, covered by rows of clay tiles.

378

SOCIAL STUDIES

Jupiter was king of the gods and ruler of the universe in Roman mythology. Juno was the wife and sister of Jupiter, and Minerva was his favorite child. The temple, which had shrines to Jupiter, Juno, and Minerva, was the religious center of the city.

EXPANDING VOCABULARY

The word *decrees* in the second paragraph means "orders" or "judgments." In Roman times, laws were announced by reading them in a public place to the assembled townspeople.

ILLUSTRATOR'S CRAFT

The illustrator emphasizes the building process by presenting partial views and showing construction in progress. The viewer can imagine what the inside of the building as well as the outside looked like.

Cooperative Reading

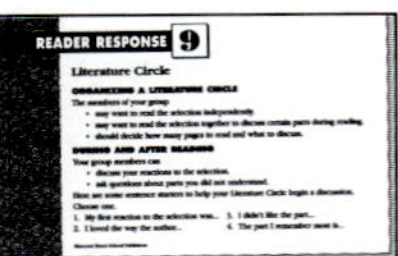

Response Card 9

Provide an opportunity for students who are reading cooperatively to share their questions and reactions with group members. You can prompt ideas for a discussion with questions like the following:

- **What kinds of things did Roman city planners consider important?**
- **So far, what do you think is the smartest thing the planners decided to do? Why?**

The buildings and the forum were surrounded by rows of columns called colonnades. The columns were either built of cylindrical stone blocks set on top of each other or they were constructed of brick and mortar covered by cement. A long two-story structure enclosed on both

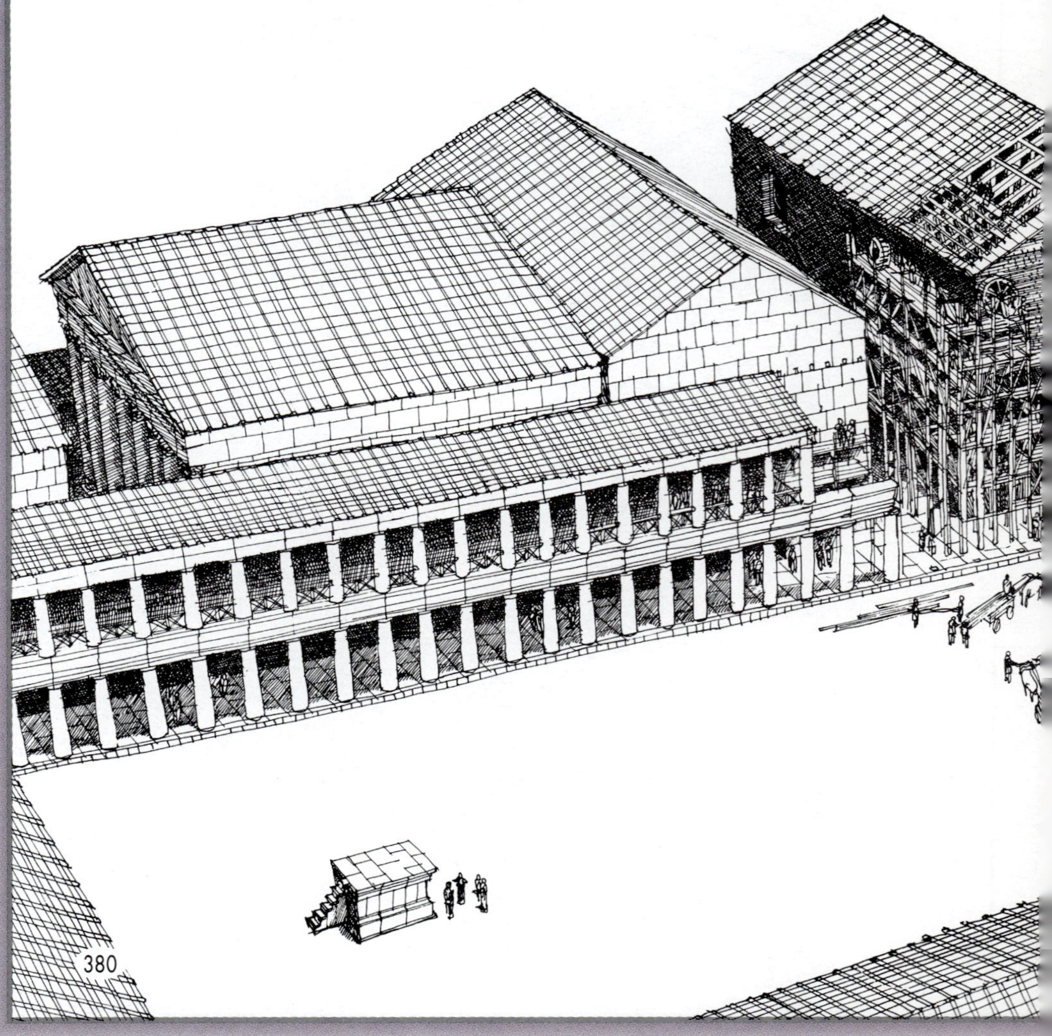

380

MATH CONNECTION

Discuss with students various geometric shapes found in the selection, such as the cylindrical stone columns. Students might list other geometric shapes they notice in the illustrations.

sides by colonnades was built to separate the forum from the busy streets. On the lower level were little shops which faced the street. On the second level were offices and schoolrooms which faced the forum.

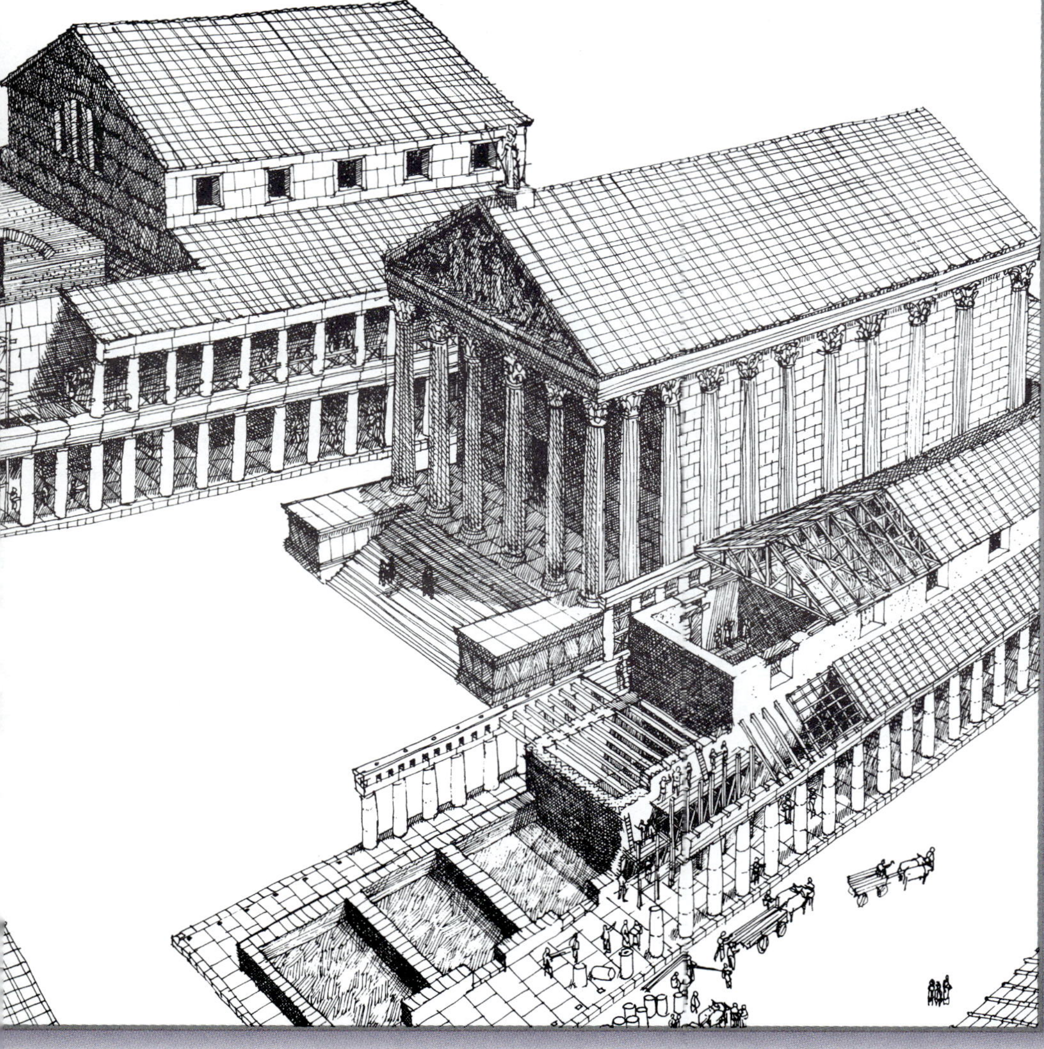

Informal Assessment

CLASSIFY/CATEGORIZE

To determine whether students can classify and categorize, ask them questions such as the following:

- What kind of work was done by Verbonia's soldiers?
- What kind of work was done by Emperor Augustus's military engineers?

QUICKWRITE

The forum was located at the heart of a Roman city. Ask students to write a few sentences in their personal journals telling what kind of building or monument they would plan at the center of a model city.

Critical Thinking Questions

1. **Why do you think the central market was finished in less than five years?** (Possible responses: Verbonia's main function was to be a trading center; part of the marketplace consisted only of a central courtyard with awnings which were easy to put up and remove.) CRITICAL: DRAWING CONCLUSIONS

2. **Why do you think bread was one of the most important foods?** (Possible response: The Romans grew wheat, so bread was probably easier to get, make, and store than some other foods.) CRITICAL: MAKING CONNECTIONS

THE CENTRAL MARKET

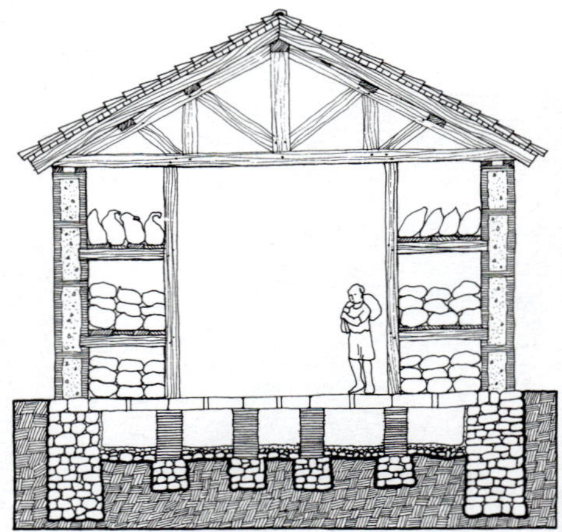

Because new temples were always being enlarged or replaced the forum really wasn't finished for two hundred years. But the central market across the street was finished in less than five. This was not surprising since Verbonia's main function was that of a trading center.

Along the streets that connected the markets, shops and workshops were built side by side. On one street Marcus Licinius, who came from Rome, built a bakery. Bread was one of the most important foods for the people of Verbonia and many bakeries were built throughout the city.

382

CROSS-CULTURAL VIEWPOINT

Bread takes many different forms and is a basic food in many cultures. Invite students to share the types of bread they and their families enjoy.

VIEWING

Ask students to decide what the round, gazebo-like structure in the upper left–hand corner of the illustration is and to give a reason why it is in the marketplace. (Possible response: It is a fountain or well; people at the market would need fresh water.)

CROSS-CULTURAL VIEWPOINT

Open-air markets like the one shown on page 383 are found in virtually every country. Invite students from various cultural backgrounds to tell about central markets they have seen. Encourage students to mention whether the markets are open every day, what time the markets open and close, what kinds of things are sold there, and so on.

Strategic Reading

PAGES 378–385 **What have you learned so far about Roman cities? Is that what you predicted you would learn?** (Possible response: So far, the selection has provided information about roads, city walls, the forum, and the marketplace.) STRATEGIES: SUMMARIZING/CONFIRMING PREDICTIONS

How did the Romans make their bread? (Possible response: They made flour by grinding grain in stone mills. They mixed the flour with water to make dough and added salt and leaven. Then they kneaded the dough, formed it into loaves, and baked it.) INFERENTIAL: RECOGNIZING STEPS IN A PROCESS

ADJUSTING READING RATE

If necessary, model adjusting reading rate:

MODEL **As I read page 385, I have trouble understanding the main idea. I reread the page slowly so that I understand unfamiliar words and difficult concepts.**

PAGES 386–395 Ask students to finish reading the selection and revise their predictions if necessary.

STUDENTS ACQUIRING ENGLISH Have pre- and early production students write the following steps on self-stick notes and label the illustration on page 384:

1. Grind the grain.
2. Make the dough.
3. Bake the bread.

The main ingredient in the bread was flour, which was obtained by grinding grain in stone mills. Each mill consisted of two main pieces. The outer piece was rotated around the inner piece by pushing on the projecting arms. The grain was crushed or milled as it passed through the narrow space between the two. The flour that came out at the bottom of the mill was mixed with water and made into dough. Salt and leaven were then added. The dough was kneaded and formed into flat circular loaves and baked in a large brick oven.

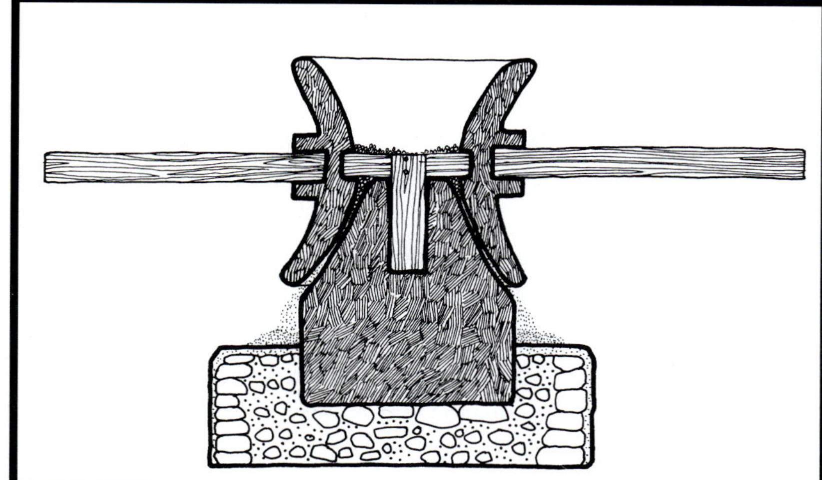

385

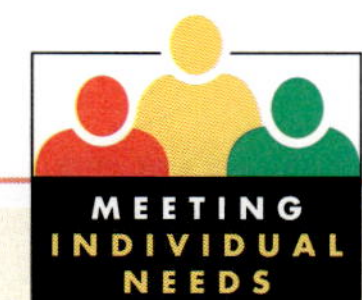

EXTRA SUPPORT Pair students with fluent readers to review how flour was ground by paraphrasing the process or by drawing and explaining a diagram or a sequence of sketches.

REAL-LIFE CONNECTION

PERSONAL EXPERIENCES Let students who have made bread share their experiences. If necessary, explain that leaven is yeast or anything used to make bread rise.

THE HOUSE OF MARCUS LICINIUS

The contractor who built Marcus' bakery also built his house. Like those of his neighbors, Marcus' house was quite large. The exterior walls were brick-faced concrete. Some of the interior walls were the same, while others were vertical wooden frames filled with small stones and mortar. All the walls were covered with a thick coat of plaster called stucco and painted.

There were many areas shown on the plan but two were much larger than the others. The first, at the front of the house, was called the atrium and was connected to the sidewalk by a narrow passage. The second, in the rear of the house, was a garden surrounded by a colonnade. This area was called the peristyle. The dining room, library, kitchen, and storerooms were located around the atrium, while the bedrooms and servants' quarters were on a second level.

386

EXPANDING VOCABULARY

Students can keep a list of words that name building materials, and then talk about their meanings. Words mentioned on this page include *brick, concrete, mortar, plaster,* and *stucco*. Students can also add words from other parts of the text, such as *marble*.

brick
plaster
concrete
stucco
marble

Most of the activities took place in the atrium because of its size and the light that came through a square opening in the roof. Under the opening, called a compluvium, a shallow pool, called an impluvium, was sunk into the floor. Rain which fell into the impluvium ran through a small hole and into an underground tank. When water was needed the cover was taken off the tank and a clay jug lowered into it.

Marcus' favorite part of the house was the peristyle. It was quiet and private and very relaxing after a few hours in the bakery. It contained a fountain which could be turned off and on by a faucet. It also contained a shrine to the Lares—the gods who protected Marcus' house.

The floors of the atrium and peristyle were covered with mosaic—small black and white marble tiles that were pressed into wet cement in a variety of geometric patterns.

387

STUDENTS ACQUIRING ENGLISH **Help students understand the features of the atrium by guiding them to draw and label the square opening in the roof (compluvium), the shallow pool sunk into the floor (impluvium), and the underground tank.**

Tested Skill

MINILESSON

REVIEW: GRAMMAR

Action and Linking Verbs

INFORMAL ASSESSMENT

Ask students to identify one linking verb and one action verb in the second paragraph on page 387. (*was*—linking; *contained*—action) Then ask a volunteer to tell the difference between a linking verb and an action verb. (Possible response: A linking verb connects the subject to a noun that renames the subject or to an adjective that describes it. An action verb tells what the subject does, did, or will do.)

TEACH/MODEL

Explain that the most common linking verb is *be*. Some forms of *be* are *am, is, are, was, were, has been*, and *have been*. You may wish to model the thinking:

MODEL **In the first sentence of the second paragraph, the linking verb *was* connects the subject *part* to a noun that renames the subject (*peristyle*). In the second sentence, the linking verb *was* connects the subject *It* to adjectives that describe it (*quiet, private, relaxing*). In the third sentence, the action verb *contained* tells what the subject *It* did.**

PRACTICE/APPLY

Ask students to find other examples of action and linking verbs in the selection. (Possible response: page 386, first two sentences: *built*—action; *was*—linking) For each example, ask students to explain why the verb is a linking verb or an action verb. (Possible response: The verb *built* tells what the subject did; *was* connects the subject to the adjective *large*, which tells about it.)

By the time of Augustus' death in A.D. 14, the streets of Verbonia were lined with grocery shops, pastry shops, ceramic shops, furniture shops, clothing shops, drugstores, wine shops, and snack bars.

390

CHALLENGE Invite students to identify the types of businesses or services shown in each of the cut-away illustrations and to give reasons for their answers. Students might also use the illustrations to compare and contrast a Roman city with a present-day city.

Many of the craftsmen on a particular street often specialized in the same or related crafts. Most of the shops along a small quiet street near the forum were owned by highly skilled gold workers and the street eventually became known as "the street of gold." The craftsmen and their families lived in rooms behind or above their shops. As neighborhoods developed, families often got together to build shrines on their streets dedicated to the Lares.

391

CONVENTIONS OF LANGUAGE

QUOTATION MARKS Call attention to the quotation marks enclosing the words *the street of gold* on page 391. Explain that quotation marks are sometimes used to set off words that name or rename something.

Intervention Strategies

SUMMARIZING Ask students to repeat this sentence aloud or to themselves: *While I'm reading, I stop to think about the main points to see if I'm understanding what has happened.* Students should tell how using this strategy might help them understand the planning of the city of Verbonia.

Critical Thinking Question

How has Verbonia changed since 26 B.C.? (Possible response: In 26 B.C. Verbonia was little more than an area of destroyed villages. By 14 B.C. it was a fully functioning city with a wide variety of shops, different types of housing and roads, a central market, a forum, and a city wall.) CRITICAL: MAKING COMPARISONS

ILLUSTRATOR'S CRAFT

To encourage students to look critically at the illustration, ask them to compare and contrast a Roman snack bar with a modern snack bar or fast-food counter. (Possible responses: Similarities—both food and drink are served; Differences—There is a dog behind the counter in the Roman snack bar, which would be against public health laws in a modern snack bar; the mood at the snack bar seems relaxed, rather than hurried.)

Most of the snack bars were owned by Servius Vitellius, who also owned a chain of snack bars in Ariminum. The snack bars opened onto the sidewalk and each contained a concrete serving counter decorated with pieces of colored marble. Clay jugs embedded in the counter contained hot and cold drinks to be sold. A row of clay drinking cups marked with Servius' name stood on a marble shelf next to the counter.

At night and during the hot afternoons all the shops could be closed by fitting wooden panels into grooves on the tops and bottoms of the doorways. A lock was used to secure them in place. At night the city provided torch-carrying watchmen who patrolled the streets checking the locks and doors of all the buildings.

One hundred and twenty-five years after its founding, Verbonia had reached its limit. With the empire stronger than ever the walls once constructed to keep the enemy out were now serving a more important function—that of keeping the city in.

393

NOTES

Here's a place to list ideas or activities that you would like to use the next time you teach this lesson.

SOCIAL STUDIES

FACT FINDER

CRIME With the great differences that existed between rich and poor, owner and slave, crime was common in Roman cities. This is one reason why there were locks and night watchmen and houses had so few windows and doors.

Strategic Reading

PAGES 386–395 Why do you think the author, David Macaulay, wrote an entire book about building a Roman city? (Possible response: He wanted to show how an ancient city was planned and how it grew, and to make the point that all cities are better when people plan carefully for the needs of the residents.) STRATEGIES: SUMMARIZING/DETERMINING AUTHOR'S PURPOSE

Returning to the Predictions/Purpose

Did you find out what you wanted to know about the planning and building of a Roman city? Encourage students to discuss whether their purposes for reading were met. STRATEGY: RETURNING TO THE PURPOSE

Appreciating the Literature

How did the illustrations in this story help you better understand the text? Give some examples. (Responses will vary.)

Although Verbonia is imaginary, its planning and construction are based on those of the hundreds of Roman cities founded between 300 B.C. and A.D. 150. No matter what brought about their creation, they were designed and built to serve the needs of all the people who lived within them. This kind of planning is the basis of any truly successful city. The need for it today is greater than ever.

MATH CONNECTION

Invite students to use the data on this page to speculate about the rate at which Roman cities were built during the period mentioned. For example, if hundreds of Roman cities were built in a 450-year period, then cities could have been built at the staggering rate of about one every year or eighteen months.

SUMMARIZING

K-W-L Chart

Have students complete the K-W-L charts they began at the beginning of the selection. Then ask them to use their charts to summarize what happened in "City: A Story of Roman Planning and Construction." See also *Practice Book* page 113.

K-W-L Chart

K What I Know	W What I Want to Know	L What I Learned
Rome was ruled by an emperor. Many people of the Roman empire lived by farming.	How long did it take to build the roads and walls? What kinds of structures did the Romans build?	It took roughly seven years to build the roads and walls of the city. The Romans built forums, markets, temples, shops, workshops, bakeries, and houses.

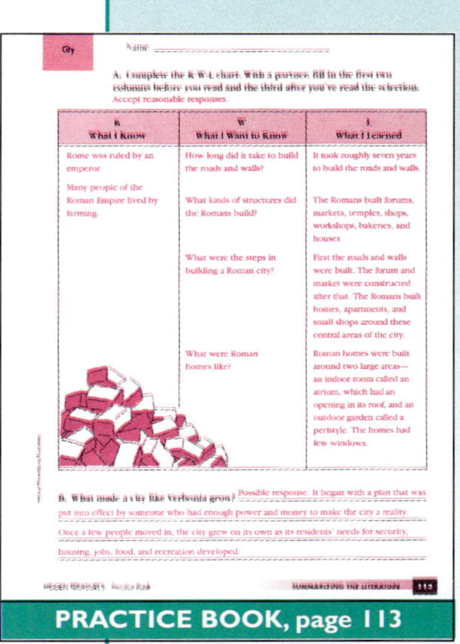
City Name

A. Complete the K-W-L chart. With a partner, fill in the first two columns before you read and the third after you've read the selection. Accept reasonable responses.

K What I Know	W What I Want to Know	L What I Learned
Rome was ruled by an emperor. Many people of the Roman Empire lived by farming.	How long did it take to build the roads and walls?	It took roughly seven years to build the roads and walls.
	What kinds of structures did the Romans build?	The Romans built forums, markets, temples, shops, workshops, bakeries, and houses.
	What were the steps in building a Roman city?	First the roads and walls were built. The forum and market were constructed after that. The Romans built homes, apartments, and small shops around these central areas of the city.
	What were Roman homes like?	Roman homes were built around two large areas—an indoor room called an atrium, which had an opening in its roof, and an outdoor garden called a peristyle. The homes had few windows.

B. What made a city like Verbonia grow? Possible response: It began with a plan that was put into effect by someone who had enough power and money to make the city a reality. Once a few people moved in, the city grew on its own as its residents' needs for security, housing, jobs, food, and recreation developed.

SUMMARIZING THE LITERATURE 113

PRACTICE BOOK, page 113

About the Author/Illustrator

After students read pages 396–397, you may wish to discuss the following questions with them:

- **In your opinion, what is the secret behind David Macaulay's distinguished success as an author and illustrator of nonfiction books?** (Possible responses: He draws things so that you feel like you are right there; he makes complicated buildings easier to understand; he knows how things work and is good at explaining how buildings are constructed; he has an active imagination.)
- **Imagine being David Macaulay's assistant. What might be the most interesting part of your job?** (Possible responses: It would be great to travel with him to exotic places and to see different kinds of architecture; it would be great to learn how to draw in pen and ink.)
- **What topic or structure would you like to see David Macaulay illustrate and write about next? Tell why.** (Answers will vary.)

DAVID MACAULAY

Making the complicated understandable is David Macaulay's great gift. He has done it in his many books that look at structures, from the pyramids to cathedrals. He has shown audiences how buildings are built and how they are unbuilt—in *Unbuilding,* he takes apart the Empire State Building. He has looked beneath the earth in *Underground.* He's been called "a born teacher with an interest in things nobody before had the skill or the courage to try to explain." Macaulay himself has said, "I consider myself first and foremost an illustrator, in the broadest sense, someone who makes things clear through pictures and teaches through pictures."

IDEA BANK

VIEWING Invite students to display a world map on a bulletin board and use pushpins to identify all the places and settings to which they have traveled this year between the covers of their Student Anthology.

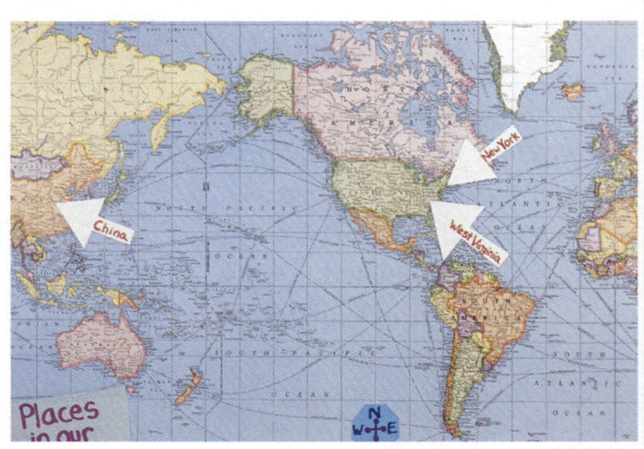

David Macaulay was born in England, and he remembers his early years there very happily. He liked to take his time getting to school and let his mind wander. "Whenever the opportunity to daydream presented itself, I did." At age 11, Macaulay moved to America with his family.

Although Macaulay had always enjoyed watching his mother draw scenes from family tales, it wasn't until he was a teenager that he discovered his own talent. He began drawing portraits of the Beatles, much to his classmates' delight. But when it was time to go to college, he thought it would be more practical to study architecture. That helped Macaulay learn a way of thinking that allowed him to understand how things worked.

After a year of teaching and working in an interior design studio, Macaulay became interested in book illustration. He also began writing stories. Although they weren't very good, as he admits, the illustrations that accompanied the stories were good enough to interest a publisher. There was a gargoyle in one of his stories, and it was that creature that made an editor suggest he write a book about cathedrals.

Since then, Macaulay has traveled to exotic places to research his books. He's been to France, visited Rome, climbed the Great Pyramid, all the while making sketches for his books. Macaulay is most interested in making his books realistic. He says, "One of the things I always try to do in a picture is to make the reader more of a participant than a spectator. I want him up on the roof of the building, and I want him to feel slightly sick because it's a long way up. If a reader can share that experience of being involved in a process, he will remember it. If I have any expertise at all, it is in that kind of communication."

397

David Macaulay was born in England and moved to the United States at age eleven. He especially remembers his family being involved in arts and crafts at the kitchen table during his childhood. "We were blatantly encouraged to make things, to understand how things went together and how they came apart. . . . By the time we got out of that kitchen, we actually believed that creativity and craftsmanship were desirable—even normal."

After graduating from high school, David Macaulay entered the Rhode Island School of Design to study architecture. Although he had some talent for drawing, it was not until several years later that he became interested in book illustration. Today, Macaulay's books are popular with children and adults and have even found their way into college classrooms as texts for design and architecture classes. Macaulay says that, above all, he wants young readers not to be intimidated by technology. He says, "You can figure it out. Follow this through and you'll understand how it works."

POETRY

City

by Langston Hughes

INTRODUCING THE POEM Have students recall "City" by David Macaulay, and point out that, just as it was in Roman times, a city is a center of much activity. Ask students why a poet might compare a city to a living thing. (Possible response: A city has movement and a "voice," such as people talking and shouting, dogs barking, children playing, and car horns honking.) Then tell students they will find out how one famous poet described a city.

APPRECIATING THE POEM Read the poem aloud to students as they follow along. Then ask questions such as the following:

How does Langston Hughes make the city seem alive? (Possible responses: He compares it to a bird that spreads its wings and sings; he compares it to a person in that it goes to bed and has a head.)

Do you think Hughes likes the city? How do you know? (Possible response: Yes. The images he uses to describe the city are beautiful.)

Organize students into two groups, and either have them alternate reading two lines at a time or have each group read a verse.

CITY

BY LANGSTON HUGHES

LISTENING CENTER

"City" is available on Literature Cassette 3. To help students who have difficulty reading the text, have them listen to the poem before they read it silently.

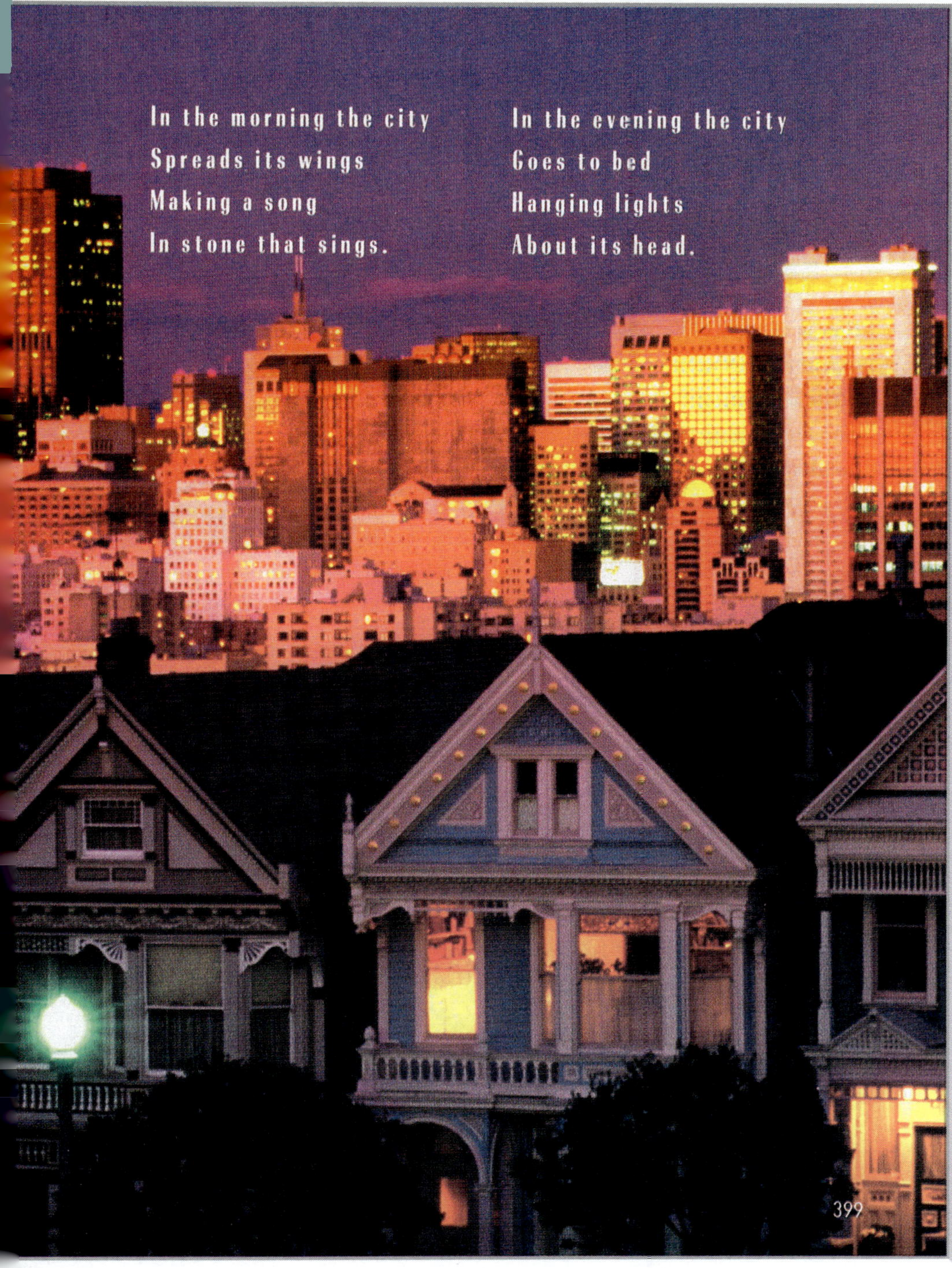

In the morning the city
Spreads its wings
Making a song
In stone that sings.

In the evening the city
Goes to bed
Hanging lights
About its head.

About the Poet

Langston Hughes, born in Joplin, Missouri, in 1902, is probably the best-known literary artist of the Harlem Renaissance of the 1920s. His poetry celebrates the experiences and culture of African Americans and is distinguished by the use of musical rhythms. Much of his childhood was shaped by his grandmother, Mary Langston, with whom he lived in Lawrence, Kansas. From her he heard "long, beautiful stories" about the effort to free enslaved blacks, and he learned to defend himself against discrimination. Hughes once reassured students that good writers find their material within their own experience, regardless of where they live: "You will find the whole world just outside your doorstep even if, seemingly, there is nothing there but the concrete sidewalk and a water plug."

POET'S CRAFT Tell students that although the poems of Langston Hughes are often about common things and seem to be written very simply, the images he uses often affect the reader deeply. Encourage students to explore Hughes's imagery of an awakening and sleeping city, asking them to visualize and describe a city scene as the sun rises and then again as it sets.

MORE POETRY

The Best of Simple **by Langston Hughes. Farrar, Straus & Giroux, 1990.**

The Dream Keeper: And Other Poems **by Langston Hughes, illustrated by Brian Pinkney. Alfred A. Knopf, 1994.**

Langston Hughes

ACTIVITY CHOICES

COMPARE AND CONTRAST

SHOPPING SPREE Encourage students to reread the parts of the selection that tell about the shops and marketplace in Verbonia. You might also suggest that students use a Venn diagram for prewriting. CRITICAL THINKING/WRITING

DESIGN A MOSAIC

FLOOR ART Remind students that they will need many small pieces of paper. To prepare, students might first decide on a color scheme, make judgments about the relative amounts of each color that they will need, and then cut or tear small squares. Then students can begin the job of arranging and gluing. ART

WRITE A PARAGRAPH

CITY SIDEWALKS Model how to prewrite by choosing one word or phrase from the poem, writing it down, and then making notes or listing associations and ideas about how this word or phrase does or does not refer to Verbonia. Encourage students to prewrite in a similar way. CRITICAL THINKING/WRITING

RESPONSE

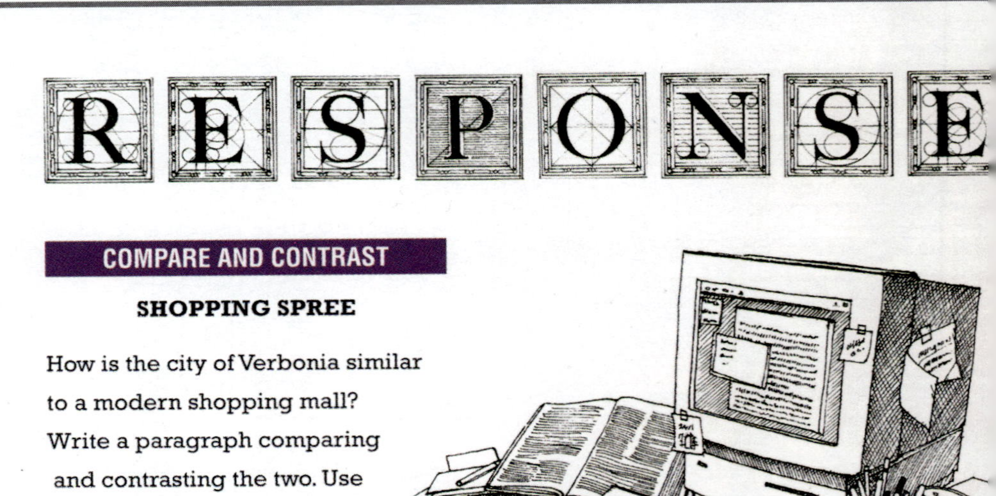

COMPARE AND CONTRAST

SHOPPING SPREE

How is the city of Verbonia similar to a modern shopping mall? Write a paragraph comparing and contrasting the two. Use details from the selection.

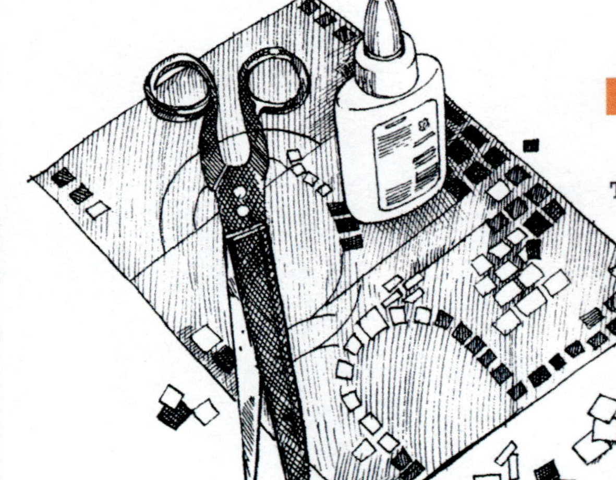

DESIGN A MOSAIC

FLOOR ART

The floors in Marcus Licinius' house were covered with mosaics. Work with a small group to design and make a mosaic using small pieces of colored paper. Display your mosaic in the classroom.

400

MEETING INDIVIDUAL NEEDS

STUDENTS ACQUIRING ENGLISH Some students may prefer to tape-record their paragraphs in their first language and work with English-proficient partners to record their paragraphs in English. The recording can be played back for the student, for you, or for a larger audience if the student is comfortable with the result.

WRITE A PARAGRAPH

CITY SIDEWALKS

Could the city in the poem be Verbonia? Write a paragraph stating your thoughts. Use details from both the story and the poem in your paragraph.

What Do You Think?

- What are the most important ideas that you learned about the planning and construction of a Roman city?
- What else would you like to learn about Roman cities?
- How were Roman cities similar to modern cities? How were they different?

401

CHECKING COMPREHENSION

What Do You Think?

1. **What are the most important ideas that you learned about the planning and construction of a Roman city?** (Possible response: The planning covered many parts of life, including roads, shops, houses, and city walls. The construction involved many steps.) DESCRIPTIVE RESPONSE
2. **What else would you like to learn about Roman cities?** (Responses will vary.) PERSONAL RESPONSE
3. **How were Roman cities similar to modern cities? How were they different?** (Possible response: Roman and modern cities both contain roads, marketplaces, places to be entertained, public gathering places, places to live, and water and sewer systems. Modern cities have electrical, gas, and telecommunications systems that Roman cities didn't have. Modern cities are not walled as Roman cities were.) CRITICAL ANALYSIS/REFLECTING

VARYING THE ACTIVITY

To **challenge** students, suggest that they read aloud their paragraphs from the City Sidewalks activity as if they were a Roman reading a decree at the forum.

Intervention Strategies

TIPS FOR CLASSROOM MANAGEMENT

IF second-language students need additional vocabulary and during-reading strategies to understand "City: A Story of Roman Planning and Construction," **THEN** use *Sheltered English/ESL Manual*, pages 58–61.

IF students had difficulty understanding "City: A Story of Roman Planning and Construction," **THEN** have students read *Hill of Fire* and complete the diagram. See also *Intervention Strategies Manual*, pages 86–91.

REREADING

SPECIALIZED VOCABULARY This nonfiction selection contains many unfamiliar terms that may pose stumbling blocks for even the most proficient readers. Remind students that the author is careful to define all the technical terms he uses in context. Give students some examples, such as *forum, rostrum, curia*, and *basilica*.

Assign small groups each a different section of "City: A Story of Roman Planning and Construction." For example, one group can be responsible for the section dealing with the forum, another with the section on Marcus's house, and so on. Each group should compile a chart of specialized vocabulary such as the following. When students have finished rereading, have each group share its chart with the rest of the class.

Chart of Technical Terms	
atrium	interior courtyard at front
peristyle	rear garden surrounded by colonnade
compluvium	________
________	________
________	________

PERSONAL JOURNAL

At the end of this selection, the author claims that the need today for city planning is greater than ever. Do students agree or disagree? Have them write a few sentences in their journals giving reasons for their opinions.

WORDS AND MEANINGS

CONTEXT CLUES Tell students that they can often use context clues to figure out the meanings of unfamiliar words. Model the strategy by reading the first paragraph of the selection. Draw students' attention to the verb *dispatched*. What clues in the context hint that this verb means *sent at once*? (Clues include the adverb *immediately*, the adverb phrase *to the stricken area,* and the description in the next sentence of the experts' duties.)

Choose other words from the selection to give students practice in using context clues; for example, *rotating* (page 377), *cylindrical* (page 380), *ingredient* (page 385), *kneaded* (page 385), *contractor* (page 386), *exotic* (page 389), and *embedded* (page 393). Call on volunteers to identify context clues to the words' meanings. If necessary, have students verify the definition of each word in a dictionary.

WRITING DETAILS

Work with students to summarize the main facts and ideas of "City: A Story of Roman Planning and Construction" by completing the following details chart. For each topic in the left-hand column, have students write in the right-hand column a significant detail or two that they recall from the selection.

Details Chart

Roads ______

City Wall ______

Forum ______

Bakery ______

Private Houses ______

Snack Bar ______

Other Shops ______

DECODING SUPPORT
Contractions, Possessives, and the Apostrophe

Intervention Strategies Manual pp. 90–91

ESL/TITLE I READING

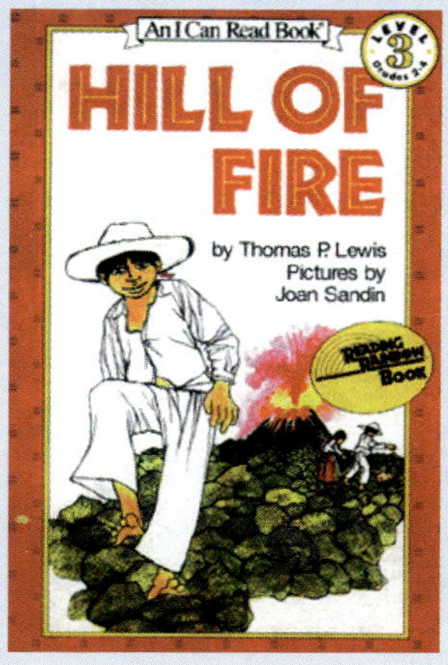

ESL/Title I Library

Hill of Fire
by Thomas P. Lewis

Like the ancient Romans, the inhabitants of Pablo's village have to rebuild after a natural disaster destroys their home. The settings for the two selections, however, are very different. Have students use the diagram below to contrast these selections.

	"City"	*Hill of Fire*
Cause of Disaster	______	______
People's Occupations	______	______
Structures Rebuilt	______	______

TAKE-HOME BOOK TO REINFORCE KEY WORDS

Students will enjoy reading this humorous historical tale. Encourage students to take the book home to read.

PERSONAL JOURNAL

After students finish reading *Snack Attack: A Story of a Boom Town*, have them write their reactions to the book in their personal journals.

See also *Intervention Strategies Manual,* page 89.

IDEA BANK

TIPS FOR CLASSROOM MANAGEMENT

IF students would benefit from being given additional visual clues, **THEN** have them complete the Viewing activity.

IF students need to focus on listening strategies, **THEN** have them complete the Oral Language activity.

RETELLING

Text Sets

Divide the class into small groups, and have them find one other text about cities—perhaps a magazine or newspaper article, an encyclopedia article, or a book. Then distribute Response Card 12 (Text Sets). Have students follow the directions on the card to compare and contrast "City: A Story of Roman Planning and Construction," the poem "City," by Langston Hughes, and the student-chosen text. LISTENING/SPEAKING/READING

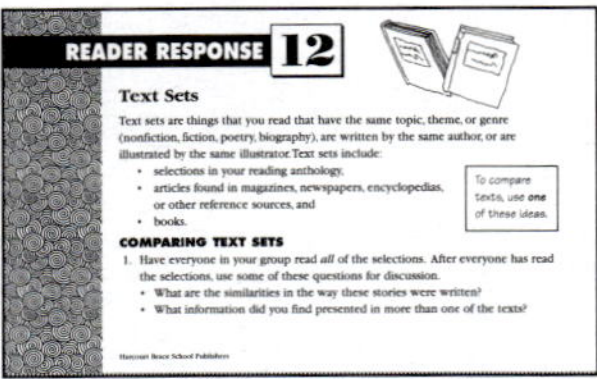
READER RESPONSE 12

Text Sets

Text sets are things that you read that have the same topic, theme, or genre (nonfiction, fiction, poetry, biography), are written by the same author, or are illustrated by the same illustrator. Text sets include:

- selections in your reading anthology,
- articles found in magazines, newspapers, encyclopedias, or other reference sources, and
- books.

To compare texts, use **one** of these ideas.

COMPARING TEXT SETS

1. Have everyone in your group read *all* of the selections. After everyone has read the selections, use some of these questions for discussion.
   - What are the similarities in the way these stories were written?
   - What information did you find presented in more than one of the texts?

Harcourt Brace School Publishers

Response Card 12

ORAL LANGUAGE

Giving Directions

Suggest that students work in small groups to prepare a set of directions for planning a Roman city. Invite students to practice giving their directions, using visual aids such as illustrations from the text. Then have groups decide whether to share the task of performing or to choose one member to give the directions to another group. LISTENING/SPEAKING/WRITING

TIPS FOR LISTENING AND SPEAKING

Remind **speakers** who are giving directions to

- ☑ use and emphasize transitional words such as *first*, *next*, and *then*.
- ☑ use formal language.
- ☑ be sure listeners can clearly see any illustrations used.

Remind **listeners** to

- ☑ note each step in the process by listening for transitional words such as *first*, *next*, and *then*.
- ☑ focus on the speaker by maintaining eye contact and appropriate posture.

VIEWING

Video/Documentary

Have students watch an audiovisual presentation about ancient Rome. One possibility is *World of Ancient Rome* (United Learning Inc.), a ten-minute videotape that shows how Rome became the cultural, economic, and political center of the world under Augustus Caesar. Students can then compare and contrast this information with what they have learned from "City: A Story of Roman Planning and Construction." Encourage students to work individually or in pairs to complete a Venn diagram like the one below. When they are finished, invite students to summarize what the diagram shows. WRITING/VIEWING

What I Learned About Ancient Rome

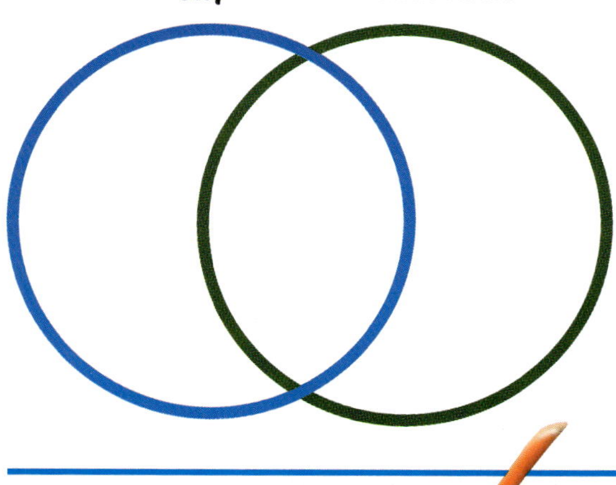

Informal Assessment

Note whether students' summaries include the main ideas and not just extraneous details.

REAL-LIFE RESOURCES

Menu

ELEMENTS OF A MENU Discuss the parts of a menu, including food categories such as appetizers, main courses, and beverages, and descriptions and prices. Students might compare how menus vary among different types of restaurants, from fast food to full service.

READING A MENU Write this portion of an ancient Roman menu on the board.

GUSTATIO (APPETIZERS)

OYSTERS AND EGGS
DOLPHIN STEAKS STUFFED WITH ONIONS
SALTED SEA-URCHIN WITH SPICES, HONEY, AND OIL
STUFFED DORMICE SPICED WITH PEPPERS

PRIMAE MENSAE (MAIN COURSE)

FINE SELECTION OF ROASTED OR BOILED MEATS AND POULTRY
STEWED OSTRICH WITH SWEET SAUCE
BAKED HAM WITH NUT AND HONEY SAUCE
VENISON [DEER] BOILED WITH GARLIC
VEGETABLE STEW
PEACOCK STEWED WITH VEGETABLES AND SPICES
PARROT BAKED WITH LEEKS AND SERVED WITH PLUM SAUCE

SECUNDAE MENSAE (DESSERTS)

FRUIT TRAY— APPLES, GRAPES, FIGS, AND DATES
PASTRY OF ROSE PETALS
SWEET CAKES

Discuss what additional information students would like to see included on this menu, such as descriptions and prices. Students can also compare their diets with the Roman menu and consider how medical discoveries have affected the way we eat. See *Writer's Magazine,* pages 56 and 57.

REAL-LIFE CHALLENGE Have students write a menu for a restaurant they would like to open in your community. WRITING

A ROMAN MEAL

DO THE DINNERS ON THE MENU SOUND APPETIZING? SOME DISHES MAY SOUND MORE APPETIZING THAN OTHERS. BUT IF YOU WERE A ROMAN LIVING AROUND A.D. 100, ALL OF THEM MIGHT MAKE YOUR MOUTH WATER.

Real-Life Skills MENU

TITUS'S TABERNA

All dinners include wheat bread or honey bread.

GUSTATIO *(appetizers)*

Oysters and eggs
Dolphin steaks stuffed with onions
Salted sea urchin with spices, honey, and oil
Boiled calf brains cooked with milk and honey
Stuffed dormice spiced with pepper

PRIMAE MENSAE *(main course)*

Fine selection of roasted or boiled meats and poultry
Stewed ostrich with sweet sauce
Baked ham with nut and honey sauce
Flamingo roasted in honey and spices
Veniso deer boiled with garlic
Vegetable stew
Peacock stewed with vegetables and spices
Parrot baked with leeks and served with plum sauce

SECUNDAE MENSAE *(desserts)*

Fruit tray—apples, grapes, figs, and dates
Dates stuffed with nuts and rolled in honey
Pastry of rose petals
Sweet cake

56 City • Writer's Magazine

As you can see by the menu on page 56, wealthy Romans did not have a simple diet. They had a variety of foods to choose from. The meals of the poor were

WRITER'S MAGAZINE, pages 56–57

STUDENTS ACQUIRING ENGLISH

Allow students to watch the videotape more than once. You might pause the videotape from time to time to check their understanding.

WRITER'S WORKSHOP

How-to Article

TIPS FOR CLASSROOM MANAGEMENT

IF students are familiar with the steps for writing a how-to article, **THEN** have them refer to the model on Transparency 38 as necessary.

IF you want a short writing activity, **THEN** adapt this lesson by having students use what they learn about the Writer's Craft to revise a how-to article they have written earlier.

TECHNOLOGY

THE AMAZING WRITING MACHINE Have students write directions using the program and create illustrations using the Wacky Pencil.

Thinking as Writers

WRITING FORM: How-to Article Remind students that "City: A Story of Roman Planning and Construction" contains information about how roads and structures were built. Explain that how-to articles describe how to do or make something. Ask students to give examples of other types of how-to articles. (recipes, assembly instructions, and so on)

Display Transparency 38, and discuss the main parts of a how-to article, which include an introduction that clearly states the topic and the materials needed, a body that gives step-by-step directions, and a conclusion that describes the finished product.

TRANSPARENCY 38

Scale-Model Drawing

introduction	Your assignment is to draw a scale model of your classroom. You will need a yardstick, white paper, a pencil, an eraser, a ruler, a calculator, and scrap paper.
body	First, measure your classroom with the yardstick. Next, determine a scale for your drawing, such as 1 inch = 1 foot.
	Next, calculate the scale measurements of the room and write them down on the scrap paper. Then, sketch the room on the white paper. Don't forget to include the scale you used.
conclusion	Finally, add drawings of furniture and other objects to your scale model. Someone who has never been in your classroom should be able to tell what it looks like from your drawing.

WRITER'S CRAFT: Time-Order Words
Explain that in a how-to article, time-order words help the reader understand the order in which each step must be completed. Students may find time-order words in "City: A Story of Roman Planning and Construction" (page 374: *before, once, then*) or on the transparency (*First, Next, Finally*).

PREWRITING AND DRAFTING

Remind students to choose a topic related to the theme. Refer to these strategies to help students begin their how-to articles.

PREWRITING GRAPHIC ORGANIZER Some students may benefit by making a how-to chart that organizes steps in time order.

Step 1:
Step 2:
Step 3:

SUSTAINED SILENT WRITING Students who have a clear idea of what they want to write may begin by writing without interruption.

DURING-WRITING GRAPHIC ORGANIZER Some students may need to pause during writing to reorganize, combine, or delete steps in their how-to charts.

RESPONDING AND REVISING

Have students work in editing circles or with partners to help each other revise. Write this checklist on the board:

- Does your article begin with an introduction that includes a topic sentence?
- Did you list all the materials needed?
- Does your article describe each step clearly and present steps in a logical sequence?
- Did you conclude your article by describing the finished product?

PROOFREADING

Offer the following tips as students proofread:

- Check for correct use of **action verbs** and **linking verbs**. (See Grammar Minilesson on page T777.)
- Check for subject-verb agreement. Remember that the subject of an imperative sentence is (*you*) understood.

PUBLISHING

- Look for words you may have misspelled.

If you wish to have students publish their how-to articles, suggest the following options or have students choose their own method:

ORAL Students may wish to use their how-to articles as a basis for demonstrations for the class. Class members should comment on whether the demonstration presented information in a clear, logical way.

WRITTEN Suggest that students write and illustrate their how-to articles on large index cards, arrange the cards in a file box according to subject matter, and then title the box *Helpful How-To's*.

EVALUATION BENCHMARKS: HOW-TO ARTICLE		
A how-to article by a proficient student writer shows the following characteristics:		
FORM	CRAFT	CONVENTIONS
Demonstrates understanding of the form • clearly stated topic sentence • all needed materials listed • steps presented in a logical sequence	**Uses clear and appropriate language** • precise words used to describe each step clearly • time-order words used effectively	**Follows conventions of grammar and usage** • action and linking verbs used correctly • contains subject-verb agreement

Teacher Assessment As you assess students' writing, refer to the Evaluation Benchmarks chart. For additional information, including model papers, see *Integrated Performance Assessment* Teacher's Edition.

PORTFOLIO OPPORTUNITY

Have students answer the Student Self-Assessment questions and include both their answers and their articles in their portfolios.

LANGUAGE HANDBOOK

Writing to Inform, pages 60–61; Directions, page 66; How-To Chart, page 20; Action and Linking Verbs, pages 146–147, 152–153

Student Self-Assessment ✓

Have students answer the following questions and include the answers in their portfolios:

- ☑ What did you learn from writing your how-to article?
- ☑ What other process could you explain in a how-to article?

2

SPELLING

5-Day Plan

Integrated Spelling Lesson 21: student book, pages 90–93; Teacher's Edition, pages T141–T146.

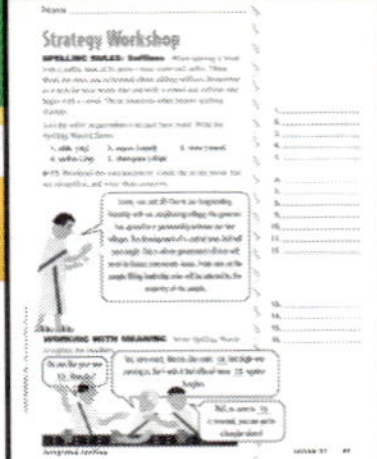

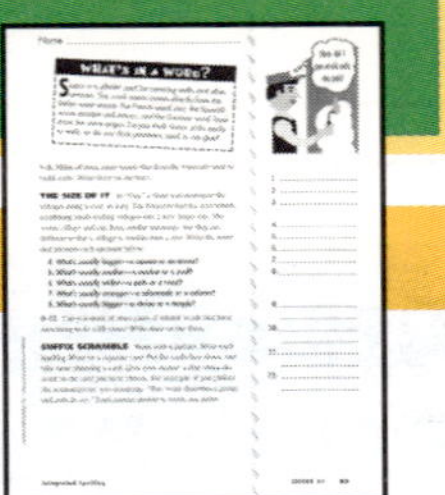

SPELLING WORDS

1. statement
2. ability
3. friendship
4. apartment ★
5. activity
6. government ★
7. partnership
8. authority
9. development ★
10. majority
11. leadership
12. security ★
13. argument
14. electricity
15. community
16. championship

STUDENT'S PERSONAL WORDS

17. 19.
18. 20.

An additional story word is *pavement*.

★ Words appearing in "City: A Story of Roman Planning and Construction"

Suffixes: *-ship*, *-ment*, and *-ity*

Pretest

DAY 1 **Administer the pretest.** Say each word, and then use it in the dictation sentence below. Help students self-check their pretests.

OPEN SORT

DAY 2 **Have students classify words.** Invite students to sort the spelling words according to their own criteria. You might suggest sorting according to number of syllables or by whether a final vowel is dropped when the suffix is added to the base word.

CLOSED SORT

Sort by suffixes. Write the headings from the following chart on the board, leaving the third column heading blank. Ask volunteers to write the Spelling Words under the correct heading, and to suggest a heading for the remaining words. Then invite students to name other words with the suffixes *-ship, -ment,* and *-ity*, and have them add these words to their personal words list.

-ship	-ment	-ity
friendship	statement	electricity
leadership	argument	activity
partnership	government	ability
championship	apartment	community
	development	majority
		security
		authority

Teach/Model

DAY 3 **Discuss the generalization.** Some suffixes are added to base words to create nouns. These suffixes include *-ship, -ment,* and *-ity*. Words that end in silent *e* drop the *e* when the suffix *-ity* is attached, but keep the *e* when the suffix *-ship* or *-ment* is attached. (You may want to point out that the word *argument* is an exception to the general rule. The *e* in *argue* is dropped before the suffix *-ment* is added.)

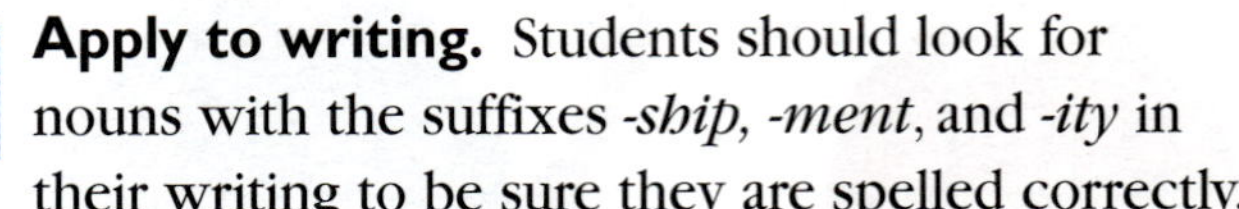

DAY 4 **Apply to writing.** Students should look for nouns with the suffixes *-ship, -ment,* and *-ity* in their writing to be sure they are spelled correctly.

Posttest

DAY 5 **Assess students' progress.** The sentences below should be used as the posttest.

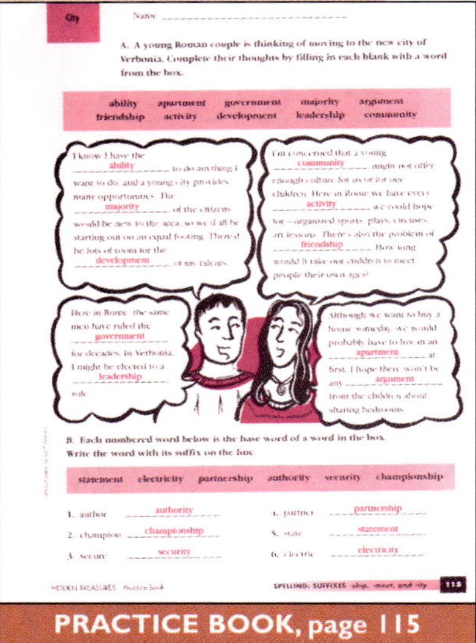

City

Name ______

A. A young Roman couple is thinking of moving to the new city of Verbonia. Complete their thoughts by filling in each blank with a word from the box.

ability apartment government majority argument friendship activity development leadership community

I know I have the ability to do anything I want to do, and a young city provides many opportunities. The majority of the citizens would be new to the area, so we'd all be starting out on an equal footing. There'd be lots of room for the development of my talents.

I'm concerned that a young community might not offer enough culture for us or for our children. Here in Rome we have every activity we could hope for—organized sports, plays, circuses, art lessons. There's also the problem of friendship. How long would it take our children to meet people their own ages?

Here in Rome the same men have ruled the government for decades. In Verbonia, I might be elected to a leadership role.

Although we want to buy a house someday, we would probably have to live in an apartment at first. I hope there won't be any argument from the children about sharing bedrooms.

B. Each numbered word below is the base word of a word in the box. Write the word with its suffix on the line.

statement electricity partnership authority security championship

1. author authority
2. champion championship
3. secure security
4. partner partnership
5. state statement
6. electric electricity

HIDDEN TREASURES Practice Book SPELLING: SUFFIXES -ship, -ment, and -ity 115

PRACTICE BOOK, page 115

DICTATION SENTENCES

1. Jackie made a statement to the press.
2. Jason has the ability to be a football star.
3. Your friendship means a great deal to me.
4. That apartment has seven rooms.
5. The activity was assigned as homework.
6. Our government leaders meet in Washington, D.C.
7. The partnership between Luigi and Juan didn't last long.
8. Mrs. Woo has the authority to enter the vault.
9. The development of this city took hundreds of years.
10. The majority of the students prefer math to science.
11. We need new leadership on the city's recreation committee.
12. Do you have a security system in your home?
13. His argument for lower taxes is a good one.
14. The electricity bill increases during colder, darker months.
15. Our community is made up of 425 people.
16. We won the championship game against Jefferson High.

VOCABULARY WORKSHOP

Reviewing Key Words

Write the Key Words on the board, and have students replace the underscored word or words in each sentence below with the Key Word that is the synonym. **STRATEGY: SYNONYMS**

1. **The people who built Verbonia were also its first inhabitants.** *(residents)*
2. **The purpose of the inner wall was to block the path of rocks and arrows being fired into the city.** *(function)*
3. **Having an impluvium, or shallow pool, was an effective way to collect rainwater.** *(efficient)*
4. **Each stone mill was made up of two pieces.** *(consisted)*

Extending Vocabulary

DICTIONARY/GLOSSARY USE

Resources for learning new words include dictionaries and glossaries. Invite small groups of students to complete a Venn diagram like the one below to tell how dictionaries and glossaries are alike and different:

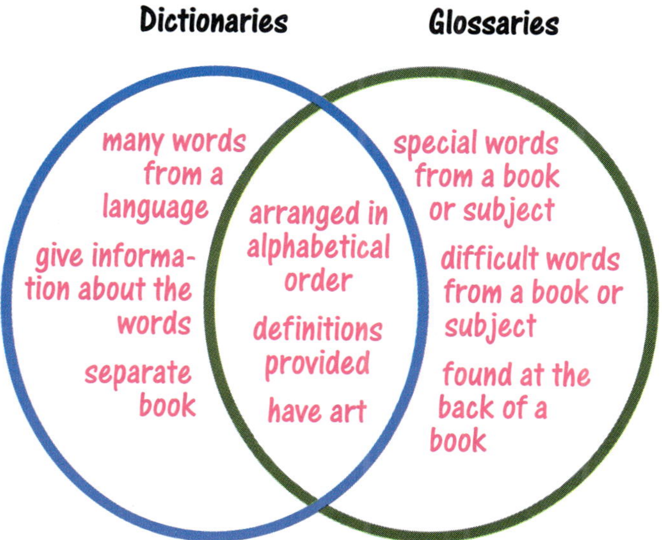

Challenge groups of students to work together to create a glossary for "City: A Story of Roman Planning and Construction."

INTRODUCE: COMPREHENSION STRATEGY

Classify/Categorize

OBJECTIVE: To create, organize, and label categories

Informal Assessment ✓

Are students able to

- ☑ classify objects, words, or ideas?
- ☑ label categories?

Teach/Model

Return to the literature. Have students reread the first paragraph on page 373. Then ask them what the following words found in that paragraph have in common: *engineers, planners, architects, surveyors, construction specialists*. (They all name professions.) Point out to students that they have just classified, or categorized, the words.

Model classifying. Explain to students that classifying involves deciding which objects, words, or ideas go together, putting them in groups, and then listing them under a common heading. Model classifying:

MODEL

As I read the first paragraph on page 373, I see the words *bridge, roads,* and *trading center*. If I were to classify these words, I would put them under the category *Parts of a City*.

Have students look at page 373 and name other categories they could create for words from that page. (Accept reasonable responses: *Numbers, Proper Nouns, Words Ending with Y*.)

Practice/Apply

Have students demonstrate understanding. On the board, draw a three-column chart with the headings *Words That Name Household Decorations*, *Words That Name Building Materials*, and *Words That Name Things That Connect Places in a City*.

Words That Name Household Decorations	Words That Name Building Materials	Words That Name Things That Connect Places in a City
mosaics	concrete	sidewalks

Have students work in small groups to complete the chart, using words from the selection. Have groups compare their completed charts.

Practice Activities

Word Sort

COOPERATIVE LEARNING Using index cards, students can create twenty or more word cards, each with one word from a single subject area (such as ancient Rome) or a current unit of study in your classroom (such as systems of the human body). Challenge groups of students to exchange cards and sort the word cards into piles, creating category headings for each. When students are through, ask them to explain which headings they created, and why they placed the words in them. VISUAL/AUDITORY/KINESTHETIC

The Forum, Rome

Category Chart

PERFORMANCE ASSESSMENT Provide pairs of students with a list of words or terms from a nonfiction selection, such as "The Great Wall of China." Have students categorize the words by creating and completing a chart with headings. Provide time for each pair to explain the completed chart. VISUAL/AUDITORY/KINESTHETIC

The Great Wall of China

MEETING INDIVIDUAL NEEDS

STUDENTS ACQUIRING ENGLISH

Have students classify by using picture cards or illustrations to reinforce vocabulary.

RETEACH

See page R9 for lessons in multiple modalities.

CHALLENGE

Ask students to categorize by genre the selections they have read so far this year.

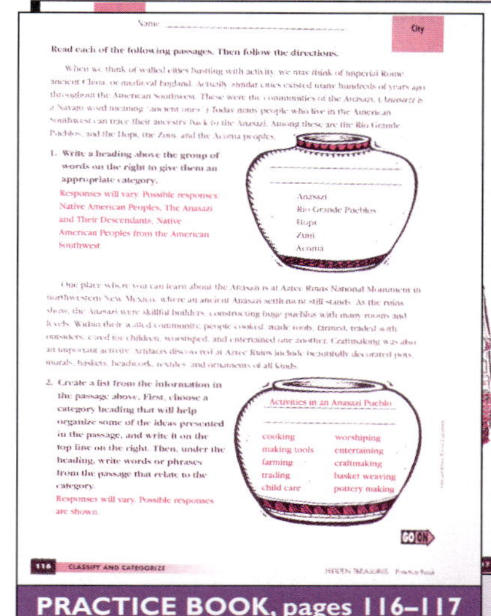

Name ______ City

Read each of the following passages. Then follow the directions.

When we think of walled cities bustling with activity, we may think of imperial Rome, ancient China, or medieval England. Actually, similar cities existed many hundreds of years ago throughout the American Southwest. These were the communities of the Anasazi. (*Anasazi* is a Navajo word meaning "ancient ones.") Today many people who live in the American Southwest can trace their ancestry back to the Anasazi. Among these are the Rio Grande Pueblos, and the Hopi, the Zuni, and the Acoma peoples.

1. Write a heading above the group of words on the right to give them an appropriate category.
Responses will vary. Possible responses: Native American Peoples, The Anasazi and Their Descendants, Native American Peoples from the American Southwest

Anasazi
Rio Grande Pueblos
Hopi
Zuni
Acoma

One place where you can learn about the Anasazi is at Aztec Ruins National Monument in northwestern New Mexico, where an ancient Anasazi settlement still stands. As the ruins show, the Anasazi were skillful builders, constructing huge pueblos with many rooms and levels. Within their walled community, people cooked, made tools, farmed, traded with outsiders, cared for children, worshiped, and entertained one another. Craftmaking was also an important activity. Artifacts discovered at Aztec Ruins include beautifully decorated pots, murals, baskets, beadwork, textiles, and ornaments of all kinds.

2. Create a list from the information in the passage above. First, choose a category heading that will help organize some of the ideas presented in the passage, and write it on the top line on the right. Then, under the heading, write words or phrases from the passage that relate to the category.
Responses will vary. Possible responses are shown.

Activities in an Anasazi Pueblo

cooking	worshiping
making tools	entertaining
farming	craftmaking
trading	basket weaving
child care	pottery making

GO ON

116 CLASSIFY AND CATEGORIZE

HIDDEN TREASURES Practice Book

PRACTICE BOOK, pages 116–117

Digging Up the Past: The Story of an Archaeological Adventure by Carollyn James. Franklin Watts, 1990. CHALLENGING

Digging Up Tyrannosaurus Rex by John R. Horner and Don Lessem. Crown, 1992. EASY

The Kingfisher Book of the Ancient World: From the Ice Age to the Fall of Rome by Hazel Mary Martell. Kingfisher, 1995. AVERAGE

Integrated Curriculum

SOCIAL STUDIES

Roman Empire

TIPS FOR CLASSROOM MANAGEMENT

IF students are mathematically inclined, **THEN** they may want to participate in the Roman Numerals activity.

TECHNOLOGY

THE AMAZING WRITING MACHINE Students can write their reports using the program. They may want to examine some of the outlines in the Spin mode before they begin planning their reports.

Explain to students that ancient Rome was one of the great civilizations in human history. The following activities provide students with an insight into the many achievements of ancient Rome.

SOCIAL STUDIES/ART

Ruins of Ancient Rome

The remains of ancient architecture and engineering still exist in Rome today, including such landmarks as the Colosseum, the Baths of Caracalla, the Catacombs, and the Pantheon. Have students work in small groups to research each of these structures and prepare written reports accompanied by scale models or drawings. Then have students use the visual aids to present their findings to the class. Following the presentations, have the class vote on the ruins they would most like to visit.
LISTENING/SPEAKING/READING/WRITING

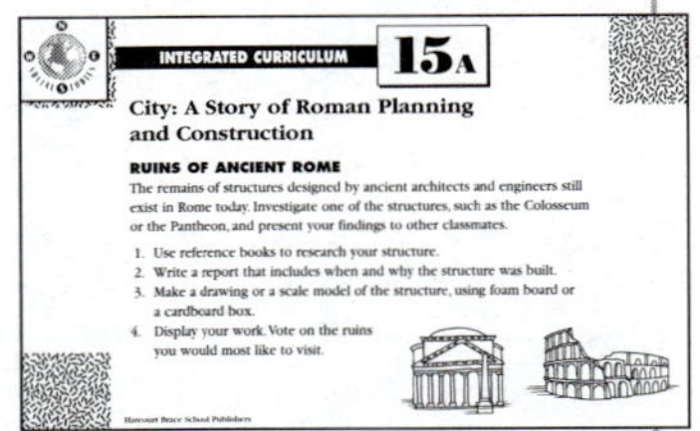
INTEGRATED CURRICULUM 15A

City: A Story of Roman Planning and Construction

RUINS OF ANCIENT ROME

The remains of structures designed by ancient architects and engineers still exist in Rome today. Investigate one of the structures, such as the Colosseum or the Pantheon, and present your findings to other classmates.

1. Use reference books to research your structure.
2. Write a report that includes when and why the structure was built.
3. Make a drawing or a scale model of the structure, using foam board or a cardboard box.
4. Display your work. Vote on the ruins you would most like to visit.

Harcourt Brace School Publishers

Curriculum Card 15A

The Colosseum The Pantheon

MATH

Roman Numerals

COOPERATIVE LEARNING Arrange students in groups of three with the following roles: Researcher, Recorder, and Checker. The Researcher finds out what Roman numerals are and briefly explains how they are used. The Recorder makes a chart of the Roman numerals for 1, 5, 10, 50, 100, 500, and 1,000. The Recorder should also include tricky constructions such as 4, 9, and 49. Then the entire group chooses numbers to write as Roman numerals, such as the current year, dates of birth, and telephone numbers. The Checker verifies the accuracy of each written numeral. Groups can exchange their numerals with other groups to "decode."
LISTENING/SPEAKING

SCIENCE

Rise to the Occasion

COOPERATIVE LEARNING Remind students that bread was one of the most important foods for the residents of Verbonia. Explain to students that baker's yeast is used as a leaven, a substance that makes dough rise. Have students work with a partner to do an experiment with yeast. Display the following steps on chart paper:

Curriculum Card 15B

Step 1: Pour 1 cup of warm water into a plastic bag.

Step 2: Add one package of yeast and two teaspoons of sugar to the bag of water. Seal the bag.

Step 3: Mix the yeast, sugar, and water by kneading the bag.

Step 4: Wait for 30 to 40 minutes, and observe what happens.

Invite students to write in their personal journals what they predict will happen and their observations of what actually happens. (The yeast breaks down the sugar, producing the carbon dioxide gas bubbles that make bread dough rise.) LISTENING/SPEAKING/READING/WRITING

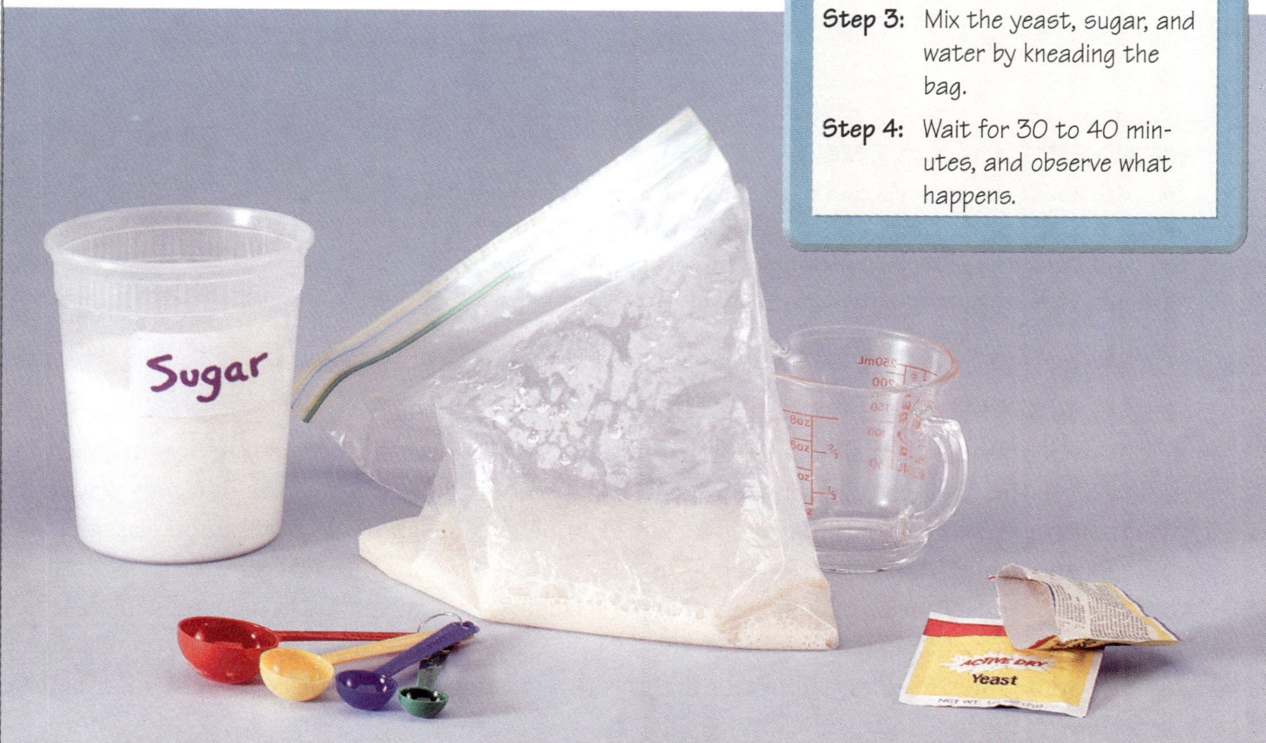

Reading Trade Books

CROSS-CURRICULAR READING

Ancient Rome by Simon James. Dorling Kindersley, 1990. AVERAGE

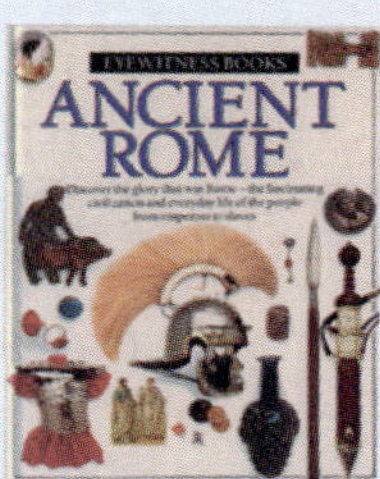

The Roman Empire and the Dark Ages by Giovanni Casilli. Peter Bedrick, 1985. CHALLENGING

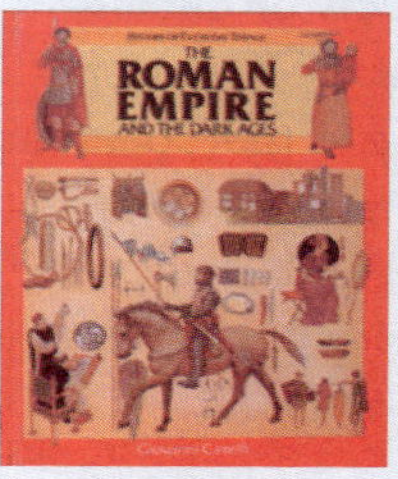

MULTI-AGE CLASSROOMS

Have older students work with younger students to carry out the steps in the Science activity.

Reading Trade Books

TIPS FOR CLASSROOM MANAGEMENT

INDEPENDENT READING Suggest that students who want to read this novel independently list interesting facts or details about life in ancient Rome in their personal journals. Encourage readers to share their favorite facts or details with the class.

For a comprehensive lesson plan, refer to the complete lesson for *Detectives in Togas* on pages T870–T875.

EXTRA SUPPORT To become familiar with the Roman names in the novel, students may wish to keep a list of characters' names and a detail about each character to refer to as they read.

Detectives in Togas

by Henry Winterfeld

Signatures Library

READER'S CHALLENGE

You read about the construction of the ancient Roman city Verbonia in "City: A Story of Roman Planning and Construction." When you read *Detectives in Togas*, notice how the settings are similar to Verbonia. How many similarities can you find? Keep a list as you read.

READING STRATEGY: CLASSIFICATION

Before students read *Detectives in Togas*, remind them that classification can be useful when they analyze the characters in a novel. Suggest that readers keep track of the different ways in which each character might be classified. For example, Lucius and Antonius can be classified as students and also as detectives. Students can use charts to record their classifications as they read. Additional categories may include teachers, villains, gods, suspicious characters, major characters, and minor characters. Emphasize that many characters belong in more than one category and that sometimes readers will need to reclassify a character as they discover new information about him or her.

LINK TO THE THEME

After reading *Detectives in Togas*, encourage students to work together to discuss the novel. Suggest these topics for discussion:

- **How does the mystery novel *Detectives in Togas* fit into the theme Turning Points?**
- **How can you learn historical facts by reading a novel set in the past? How can you separate facts from fictional events?**

Other Trade Books

A Roman Villa

by Jacqueline Morley
illustrated by John James

This colorful nonfiction selection offers readers many fascinating details about Roman life, buildings, and culture. Suggest that students create a web or chart about ancient Rome based on "City: A Story of Roman Planning and Construction" and then add to their web as they read *A Roman Villa*.

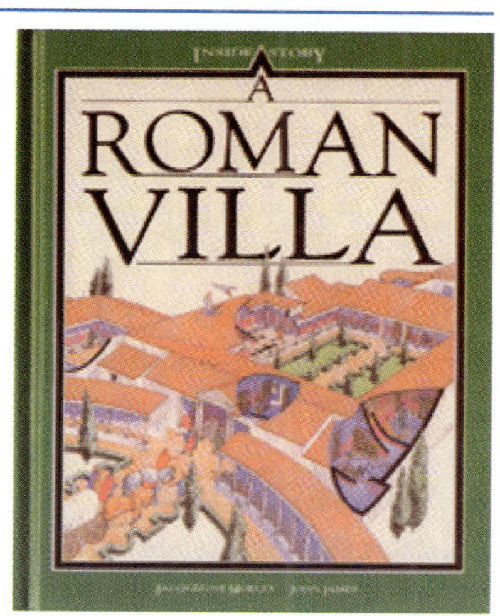

The Romans

by Charles Guittard and Annie-Claude Martin

Readers can continue their exploration of life in ancient Rome through this detailed and well-organized account. After reading, students might use information from this source and from "City: A Story of Roman Planning and Construction" to write two or three entries from the journal of a fictional student living in ancient Rome.

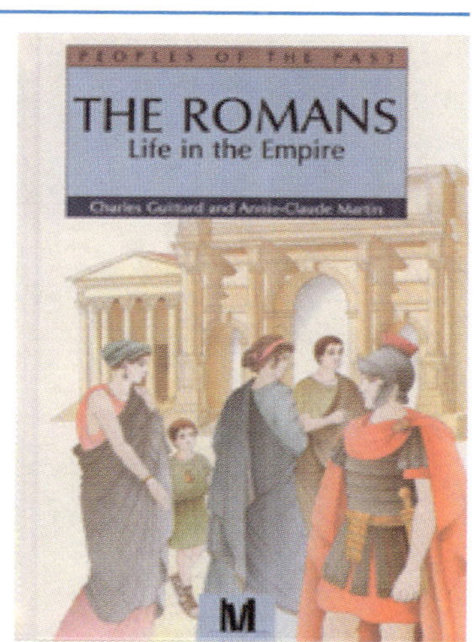

What Do We Know About the Romans?

by Mike Corbishley

Students can use this source to gain a good overview of Roman culture. Encourage readers to make a list of ten important facts from this book. After evaluating these facts, readers can state their main idea and compare it with the main idea in "City: A Story of Roman Planning and Construction."

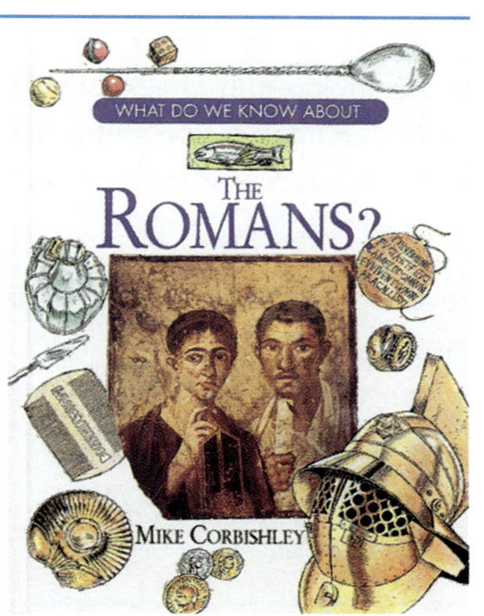

STUDENTS ACQUIRING ENGLISH

Suggest that students at the intermediate fluency level read *What Do We Know About the Romans?* independently.

CHALLENGE

Have students select one specific topic about ancient Rome, research it, and prepare posters, newspaper articles, brochures, or other projects to share the information with the class.

Trade Books

THEME PROJECT CHECKPOINT 3

Revise the Chart and Resolve Contradictions

SELECTION CONNECTION

In "City: A Story of Roman Planning and Construction," Emperor Augustus builds a new, well-planned city in the Po Valley. Encourage students to talk about how cities have changed since that time, and how they remain the same.

PROJECT CHECKLIST

During this stage, students should

- ☑ check their charts for contradictions.
- ☑ interview more people and do extra research to resolve any contradictions.
- ☑ visit places in the community that have changed.
- ☑ revise their charts.

Project Card 22 can be found as a copying master on page R26.

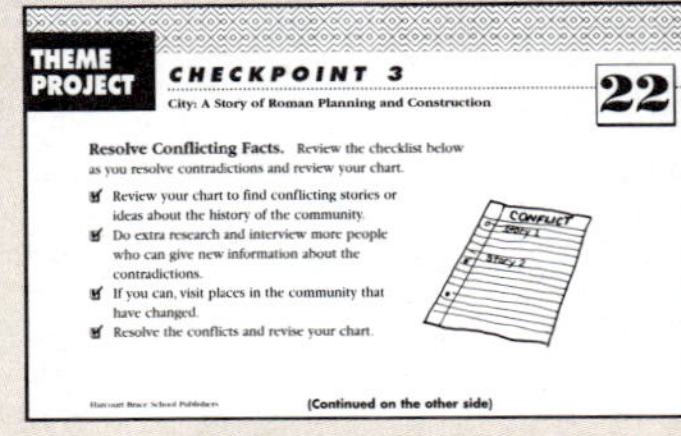

THEME PROJECT

CHECKPOINT 3

City: A Story of Roman Planning and Construction

22

Resolve Conflicting Facts. Review the checklist below as you resolve contradictions and review your chart.

- ☑ Review your chart to find conflicting stories or ideas about the history of the community.
- ☑ Do extra research and interview more people who can give new information about the contradictions.
- ☑ If you can, visit places in the community that have changed.
- ☑ Resolve the conflicts and revise your chart.

Harcourt Brace School Publishers

(Continued on the other side)

Project Card 22

RESEARCH AND PLANNING TIPS

As students resolve contradictions about an event, suggest that they

- collect all the contradictory information about the idea or event.
- organize the information according to which story it supports.
- evaluate the quantity of evidence on each side.
- evaluate the sources of information on each side.

Students may want to use their project journals to tell how they were able to resolve one of the contradictions. Encourage students to respond to questions such as *How do you think the conflicting stories began?*

Informal Assessment

As students complete this checkpoint, group members will **analyze** information and **make judgments** about its validity. Students are thinking critically if they

 can evaluate information for relevance and validity.

 can distinguish between fact and opinion.

 can use information to solve problems.

MEETING INDIVIDUAL NEEDS

STUDENTS ACQUIRING ENGLISH

As students organize their chart information, encourage them to discuss any contradictions in the information with you or with a group member.

MULTIPLE INTELLIGENCES

Students with high verbal/linguistic intelligence may enjoy organizing a debate or a panel discussion to resolve the contradictions.

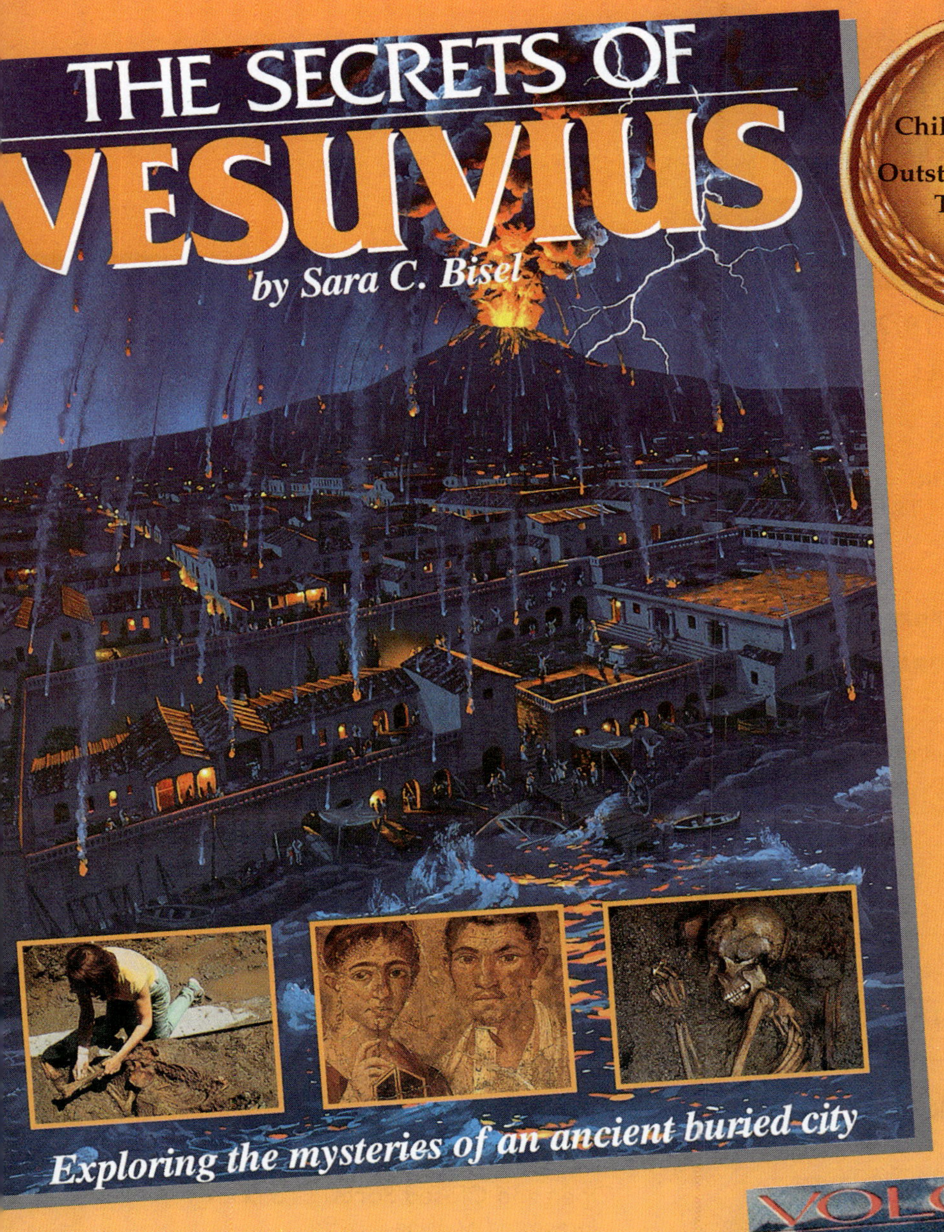

Children's Choice

Outstanding Science Trade Book

THEME: CHANGES

Turning Points

In "The Secrets of Vesuvius," students will see how an unexpected discovery explains secrets from the past.

Linking Poetry to Nonfiction

"Volcano," a poem by Constance Levy, asks readers to imagine themselves as a fiery mountain.

SELECTION SUMMARY

Genre: Nonfiction

When bones buried since the eruption of Mount Vesuvius were discovered in modern-day Herculaneum, Dr. Sara Bisel, an archaeologist and anthropologist, was called to examine them. In a personal narrative, Bisel recounts her thrill at the opportunity, her horror at the thought of the fiery rage that was Vesuvius, and her wonder at what she found. Through Bisel's narrative, the reader learns about the eruption that blanketed and preserved the cities of both Herculaneum and Pompeii, as well as about the process of uncovering and examining bones. These bones speak: they tell a person's gender, age, and state of health; they give clues to a person's facial features and overall appearance; and, collectively, they provide clues to human life as it was lived almost two thousand years ago.

ABOUT THE AUTHOR

SARA CLARK BISEL was a housewife in Rochester, Minnesota, in the early 1970s when she began studying Greek archaeology at the University of Minnesota. She'd earned a degree in nutrition nearly 20 years before with which she hoped to do research, "not just cook for people." After working with Bisel on skeletons in Greece and Turkey, Larry Angel, curator of physical anthropology at the Smithsonian, and Bisel's mentor, said of her: "Sara was exceptional. Only people with a special sense that allows them to imagine in 3-D can see the human form in a broken skeleton."

More information about Sara Bisel and her work appears on page T839.

SUGGESTED LESSON PLANNER

▶ ***The Secrets of Vesuvius***

	DAY 1	DAY 2
PART 1 **Reading** **Listening** **Speaking** **Viewing** **Key Words** extinct collapsed awe intricate	**BUILD BACKGROUND** T812 **VOCABULARY STRATEGIES** T813 *Transparency 39* *Practice Book* p. 120 **READING THE SELECTION** T814–T839 Options for Reading T814–T815 *Response Card 9* *Literature Cassette 3* **REVIEW PREDICTIONS/PURPOSE** T838 **APPRECIATING THE LITERATURE** T838 NOTE: Students may read the selection on Day 2.	**SUMMARIZE THE SELECTION** T838 *Practice Book* p. 121 **READ POETRY** T840–T841 "Volcano" ◆ **RESPONSE CORNER ACTIVITIES** T842 **CHECKING COMPREHENSION** T843 *End-of-Selection Test* 
PART 2 **Writer's Workshop**	**RESEARCH REPORT** Thinking as Writers T848 *Language Handbook* pp. 15, 72, 76–77 *Transparency 40*	Prewriting T848 *Language Handbook* pp. 60, 72
Grammar	✓ **TRANSITIVE AND INTRANSITIVE VERBS; OBJECTS** Teach the Concept T850 Daily Language Practice (1–2) R17	Daily Language Practice (3–4) R17 Practice Activity T851
Spelling	**PREFIX:** ***com- (con-)*** *contact, comfort, comment, contain, connected, complete, continued, commercial, consider, constantly, commander, construction, constitution, conclusion, communicate, committee* Pretest/Self-Check T852 *Integrated Spelling Teacher's Edition* pp. T147, T291	Open and Closed Sorts T852 *Integrated Spelling* p. 94 *Integrated Spelling Teacher's Edition* p. T148
PART 3 **Skills and Strategies**	◆ **INTEGRATED CURRICULUM** *Archaeology* **Social Studies/Art** T856 **Social Studies** T856 **Science** T857 *Thinkin' Things: Collection 3*	**STUDY SKILLS** T854–T855 Graphic Aids (Introduce) *Practice Book* p. 125
 	Use the Intervention Strategies notes on pages 829 and 832 to help **below-level students** as they read.	Use the Students Acquiring English note on page T851 to help **below-level** and **ESL students** while they write.

NOTE: An alternative lesson plan for **below-level students** appears on *Intervention Strategies Manual* pp. 92–97. A lesson for **students acquiring English** appears on *Sheltered English/ESL Manual* pp. 62–65.

DAY 3	DAY 4	DAY 5
◆ **IDEA BANK ACTIVITIES** Retelling T846 Oral Language T846 Viewing T847 Real-Life Resources: Reading Directions for Performing a Process T847 *Writer's Magazine* pp. 60–61 School–Home Connection 16 R44	**VOCABULARY WORKSHOP** T853 Reviewing Key Words **READING TRADE BOOKS** T858–T859  Take-Home Book	**READING TRADE BOOKS** T855, T857, T858–T859 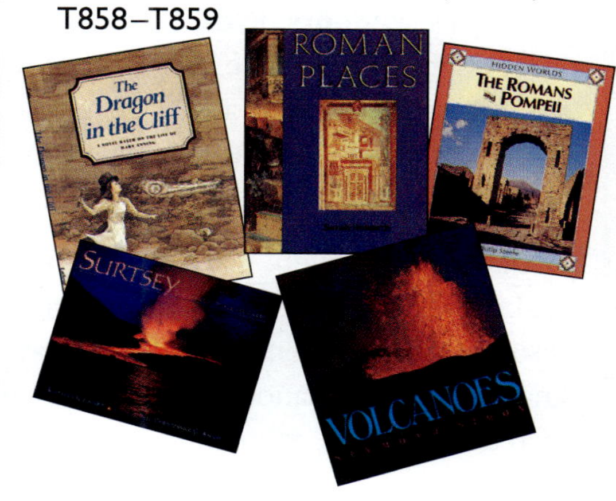
Drafting T848 *Language Handbook* pp. 60, 76–77 *The Amazing Writing Machine*	Responding and Revising T849 *Language Handbook* p. 61	Proofreading and Publishing T849 *Language Handbook* p. 61
Daily Language Practice (5–6) R17 Practice Activity T851 *Language Handbook* pp. 150–151 *The Amazing Writing Machine*	Daily Language Practice (7–8) R17 Practice Activity T851 *Grammar Practice Book* pp. 40–41	Daily Language Practice (9–12) R17 *Practice Book* p. 122
Discuss the Generalization T852 *Integrated Spelling* p. 95 *Integrated Spelling Teacher's Edition* p. T149	Apply to Writing T852 *Integrated Spelling* pp. 96–97 *Integrated Spelling Teacher's Edition* pp. T150–T151	Posttest T852 *Practice Book* p. 123 *Integrated Spelling Teacher's Edition* p. T152
COMPREHENSION MINILESSON T829 Expository Elements (Review) *Practice Book* p. 126 **GRAMMAR MINILESSON** T831 ✓ Main and Helping Verbs (Review)	**VOCABULARY WORKSHOP** T853 Specialized Vocabulary: Social Studies Words *Practice Book* p. 124	**COMPREHENSION MINILESSON** T837 ✓ Compare/Contrast (Review) *Practice Book* p. 127 Theme Project Checkpoint 4 T860 *The Amazing Writing Machine*
Above-level students may read a trade book independently.	**Below-level students** may read the *Take-Home Book: The Unwelcome Uncle* to help them review Key Words.	**Below-level** and **ESL students** may read the *ESL/Title I Library* book *Pompeii . . . Buried Alive!*

✓ = Tested Skill
◆ = Optional activities used to adjust pacing throughout the lesson
Titles in *italics* are optional materials.

BUILDING BACKGROUND AND CONCEPTS

PRIOR KNOWLEDGE

Relate to students' lives. Ask students what they would do if they suddenly became aware that a natural disaster was about to occur in their area. Discuss natural disasters such as floods, hurricanes, and earthquakes, and have students talk about the preparations they would make if time permitted.

Create a word web. Explain that "The Secrets of Vesuvius" is about a Roman city that was buried in ash and mud as a result of the eruption of a volcano. Have students pool their knowledge of volcanoes, and guide them in completing a web similar to the following.

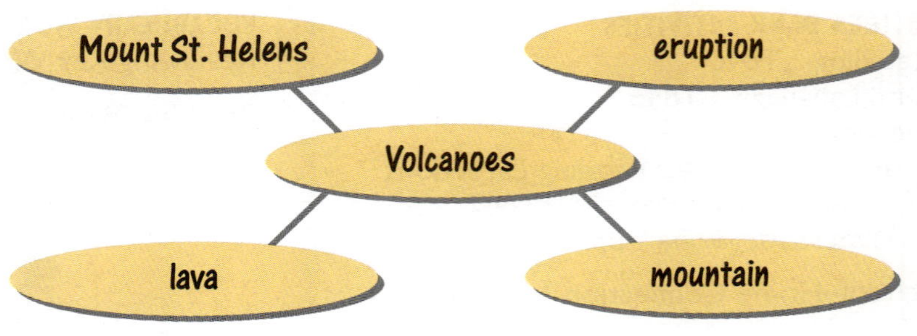

QUICKWRITE

Encourage students to write a few sentences about why they would like to explore an ancient buried city.

Intervention Strategies

For students who may have difficulty reading "The Secrets of Vesuvius," support is available in *Intervention Strategies Manual,* pages 92–97, and on pages T829 and T844–T845 in this lesson.

STUDENTS ACQUIRING ENGLISH

See *Sheltered English/ESL Manual,* pages 62–65.

FACT FINDER

SCIENCE

Mount Vesuvius

Mount Vesuvius is the only active volcano on the mainland of Europe. It is located on the Bay of Naples, about 7 miles (11 km) southeast of Naples, Italy. Because it is easy to reach and erupts frequently, Vesuvius has been studied more than any other volcano. Many people live on the lower slopes of the mountain and farm the fertile volcanic soil nearby.

The first recorded eruption of Vesuvius, in A.D. 79, blanketed the cities of Herculaneum, Pompeii, and Stabiae with lava and ash. Other destructive eruptions occurred in 1631, 1794, 1822, 1855, 1872, 1906, and 1944.

Naples, Italy

VOCABULARY STRATEGIES

KEY WORDS DEFINED

extinct no longer active or in existence

collapsed caved in

awe feeling of wonder, surprise, and respect

intricate complicated or involved

INTEGRATED SPELLING

Spelling Pretest: page T852

Spelling Generalization: Words with the prefix *com- (con-)*

CONTEXT CLUES: NARRATIVE

Encourage students to use syntactic and semantic cues. Display Transparency 39, and ask a volunteer to read the narrative aloud. Have students identify context clues that can help them determine the meaning of *extinct*. *(one of the rarest birds, I was lucky enough to spot one)* Prompt students to use similar strategies to figure out the meanings of the other Key Words.

CHECK UNDERSTANDING

Have students identify synonyms and antonyms. Display the Key Words, and have students complete a chart like the one below:

Word	Synonym	Antonym
collapsed	fell down	rose up
extinct	inactive	active
awe	wonder	boredom
intricate	fancy	plain

Once students have generated synonyms and antonyms, invite them to create for each word sentences that contain strong context clues.

STRATEGY: SYNONYMS/ANTONYMS

The dodo, which is now extinct, was a large, pigeonlike bird that could not fly.

TRANSPARENCY 39

Key Words

The whooping crane, already one of the rarest birds in North America, is in danger of becoming extinct. I was lucky enough to see one once when I was in Canada. The crane looked much smaller after it landed in a marshy area and collapsed its wings. It stood almost five feet tall and was all white except for its black-tipped wings and a patch of bare, red skin on its head. My eyes were wide as I watched in awe as it gathered grasses, weeds, and other plants to carefully shape its intricate nest.

PRACTICE BOOK, page 120

Prereading Strategies

PREVIEW AND PREDICT

As students preview the selection, ask whether it is fiction or nonfiction, and how they know. The selection details the true experiences of an anthropologist as she attempts to understand events in the past. Have students begin the SQR chart on *Practice Book* page 121 by filling in the first column of the chart with section headings from the selection. Have them write questions generated by those headings in the second column.

S—Survey	Q—Question
A New Assignment	What kind of assignment does the author get?
Why Did Vesuvius Erupt?	Why were people living so close to an active volcano?
The People on the Beach	Who were the people on the beach?

You may want to suggest that students write their predictions about the selection in their personal journals.

PURPOSE

You may want to model setting a purpose:

I want to find out what happened to the people and town of Herculaneum when Mount Vesuvius erupted. I predict that clues will be found in the ruins.

THE SECRETS OF

by Sara C. Bisel

with Jane Bisel *and* Shelley Tanaka

SMALL GROUP

PARTNER READING

Students who need little support with the selection may benefit from working with a partner. Encourage them to pause after every few pages to comment on what they have read and to discuss any strategies they used while reading. Students may share their predictions and revise them, if necessary.

COOPERATIVE READING

READER RESPONSE GROUPS

Small groups may use Reader Response Card 9 to organize a **literature circle** to discuss the selection. Reader Response Card 9 can be found at the back of this Teacher's Edition.

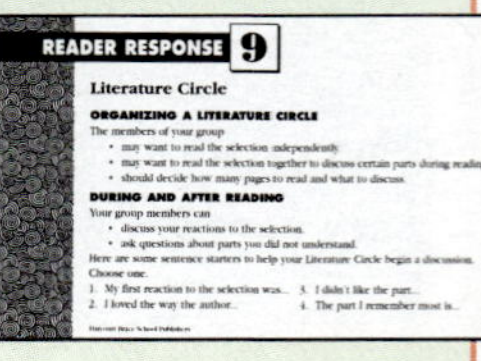

Response Card 9

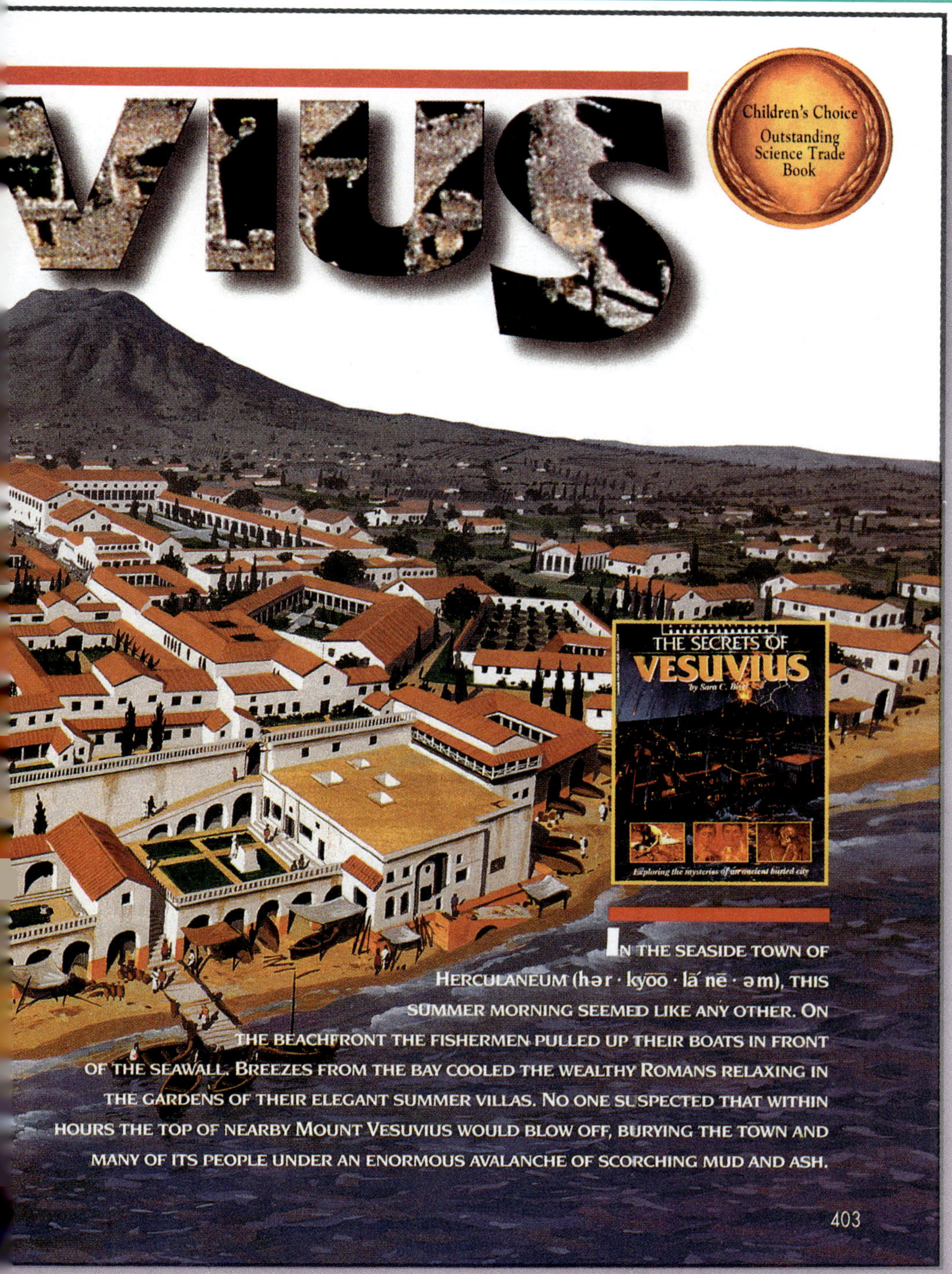

VIUS

Children's Choice
Outstanding Science Trade Book

THE SECRETS OF VESUVIUS

IN THE SEASIDE TOWN OF HERCULANEUM (hər · kyo͞o · lā´ nē · əm), THIS SUMMER MORNING SEEMED LIKE ANY OTHER. ON THE BEACHFRONT THE FISHERMEN PULLED UP THEIR BOATS IN FRONT OF THE SEAWALL. BREEZES FROM THE BAY COOLED THE WEALTHY ROMANS RELAXING IN THE GARDENS OF THEIR ELEGANT SUMMER VILLAS. NO ONE SUSPECTED THAT WITHIN HOURS THE TOP OF NEARBY MOUNT VESUVIUS WOULD BLOW OFF, BURYING THE TOWN AND MANY OF ITS PEOPLE UNDER AN ENORMOUS AVALANCHE OF SCORCHING MUD AND ASH.

403

WHOLE CLASS

STRATEGIC READING

Read the entire selection as a class, stopping on pages T816, T822, T826, and T832 to discuss how **using graphic aids** can help students gain meaning as they read. Ask volunteers to discuss other strategies they have been using as they read.

TEACHER READ-ALOUD

Read the entire selection to students. Then provide an opportunity for students to reread the selection independently or in pairs. As students reread, they can record in their journals any interesting information or any questions they may have.

Strategic Reading

USING GRAPHIC AIDS

Encourage students to discuss some strategies good readers use and why they are useful. Then tell students that as they read this selection, they will focus on **using graphic aids**, such as maps, charts, and diagrams. Ask students how using graphic aids might help them better understand a selection. (Possible responses: Graphic aids can help readers obtain and organize new information. Graphic aids make it easier to understand some information.) STRATEGY: USING GRAPHIC AIDS

PAGES 402–411

Have students read through page 411, keeping their purposes for reading in mind.

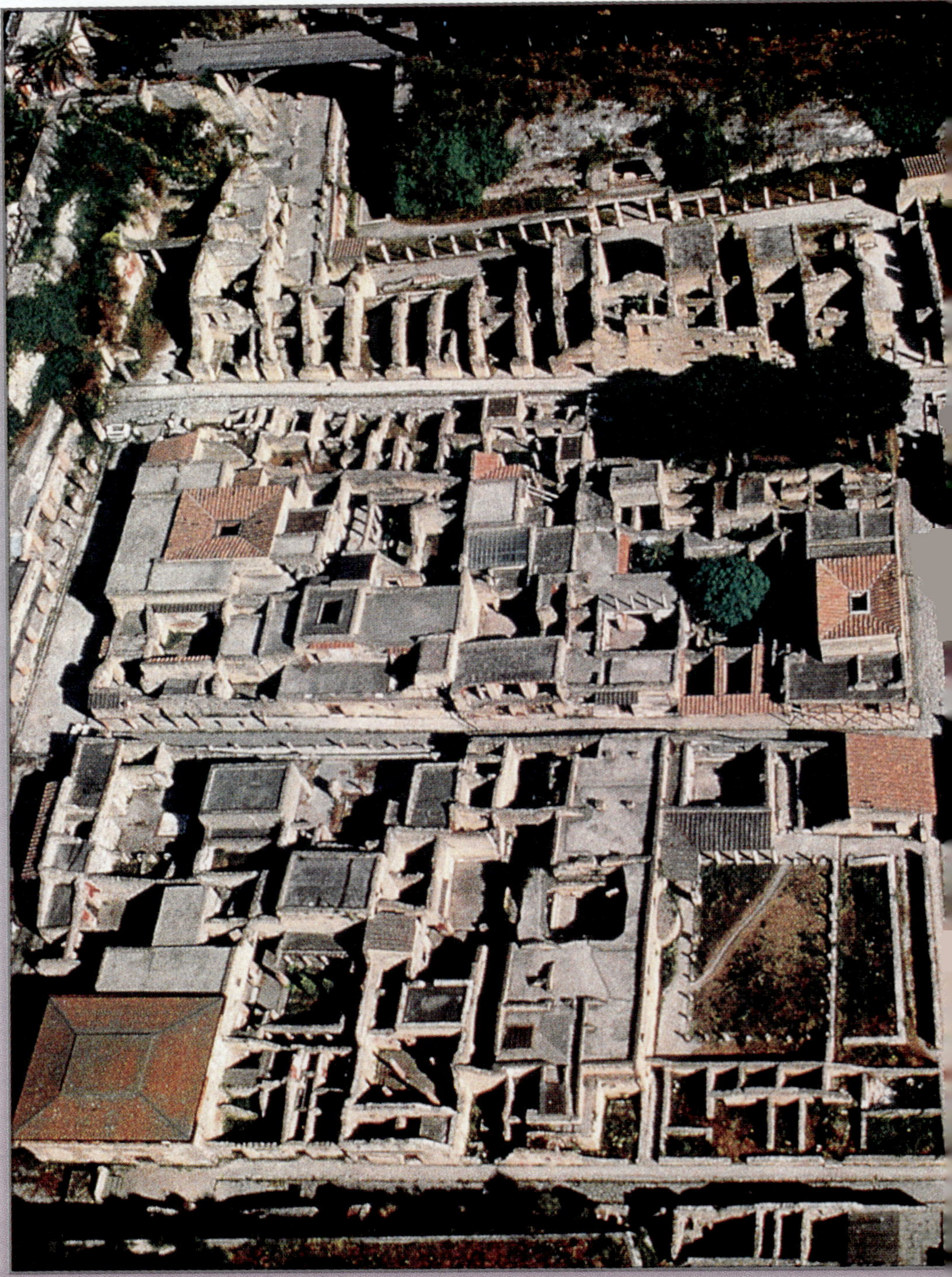

VIEWING

The photograph shows the town of Herculaneum as it is today. Ask students who have read "City: A Story of Roman Planning and Construction" to point out the features that identify Herculaneum as a Roman town. (Possible responses: city walls; tiled roofs with center holes; impluvia; colonnades; and houses built right up against one another)

Today the town of Herculaneum sits silently under the cone of the volcano that killed it. On the walls of its ruined villas, ghostly paintings and mosaics remind us of the thousands of people who once lived here. But what were these ancient Herculaneans really like and what happened to them on that fateful day in August, A.D. 79? Did most of them escape? One day an astonishing new discovery brought anthropologist Sara Bisel face to face with the actual victims of the fiery rage of Vesuvius.

405

AUTHOR'S CRAFT

Point out how the eruption of Vesuvius is personified with a description of the Herculaneans as *the actual victims of the fiery rage*. Ask students what human characteristics they might use to describe an erupting volcano.

EXPANDING VOCABULARY

Explain that a *villa* is the home of a wealthy person. A Roman villa was likely to have many rooms, pools, marble statues, fountains, grand gardens, fine mosaics, and luxurious furnishings.

Critical Thinking Question

Why do you think the author spends so much time describing how she learns about her new assignment? (Possible response: The job is a very special and exciting one, so the author builds excitement about what it will entail. As she does so, she tells more about herself.) CRITICAL: DETERMINING AUTHOR'S PURPOSE

A NEW ASSIGNMENT

Athens, Greece, June 1982

The telegram lying at my door was marked 'Urgent." As I bent down to pick it up, I hoped that it wasn't bad news. After spending a long hot day on my knees in the dusty ruins of an ancient Greek town, I was in no mood for surprises. When I ripped open the envelope I saw that it was from the National Geographic Society in Washington, D.C. They wanted me to telephone them immediately about a special project.

Why are they in such a hurry, I asked myself. As an archaeologist and anthropologist I have been involved in many expeditions. But my jobs are almost never emergencies. If something has been lying in the ground for a few thousand years, another week or two usually doesn't make much difference.

As I shut the door to my tiny apartment, I calculated the time difference between Athens, Greece, and Washington, D.C., and then dialed the long-distance number. My contact at the National Geographic Society wondered if I could spare a few days to examine some human skeletons that had just been found at the town of Herculaneum in Italy. Skeletons in Herculaneum, I thought to myself. Now *that* would be interesting!

Human bones are my specialty. In fact, I'm often called "the bone lady" because most of my work involves examining and reconstructing old skeletons. Believe it or not, bones are fascinating. They can tell you a great deal about someone, even if the person has been dead for thousands of years.

I can examine a skeleton and find out whether a person was male or female. If she was female, for example, I can tell you about how old she was when she died, whether she had children, what kind of work she might have done and what kind of food she ate. I can even glue dozens of small pieces of a skull back together like a jigsaw puzzle and show you what that person looked like.

The editor at *National Geographic* explained that workmen digging a drainage ditch near the ruins of Herculaneum had accidentally discovered some skeletons lying on what had once been the town's beachfront. Nearby, archaeologists had later uncovered some

406

MATH/SOCIAL STUDIES CONNECTION

TIME ZONES Invite students to calculate the time difference between Washington, D.C., and Athens, Greece, by supplying them with a map marked with meridians and providing the following facts: The earth is divided into twenty-four time zones; on a globe, each of these is approximately 15° (360° ÷ 24). Going west, the traveler gains one hour at each new zone; going east, the traveler loses one hour at each new zone. (It is six hours later in Athens.)

boat storage chambers in the ancient seawall. Much to their surprise, there were more skeletons inside these cave-like rooms. Here people had found shelter from the terrifying eruption of Mount Vesuvius in A.D. 79. As they lay huddled together in the dark, they were smothered by an enormous surge of scorching gas and ash from the volcano. Flowing hot ash, rock and pumice then buried them. Today, almost two thousand years later, the tangled remains of these ancient Romans lie as they fell, preserved in the wet volcanic earth.

This was an amazing discovery. Although archaeologists have been digging out Herculaneum for centuries, very few bodies had ever been found. As a result, experts had decided that almost all of the Herculaneans must have escaped before the disaster. We now knew that this was not true.

But even more exciting for me was the chance to study the actual skeletons of real ancient Romans. Because the Romans cremated their dead, they left behind plenty of urns full of human ashes but very few complete remains. So these Herculaneans represented the first large group of Roman skeletons ever found.

My job is to excavate and study the bones of people who lived and died many centuries ago.

SCIENCE

FACT FINDER **The type of eruption that occurred at Vesuvius in A.D. 79 tends to be among the most violent of volcanic eruptions. Although these eruptions do not produce a lava flow, red-hot clouds of ash and pumice blanket the surrounding area at hurricane speeds, suffocating and burying everything in their path.**

Marianas, Micronesia

Cooperative Reading

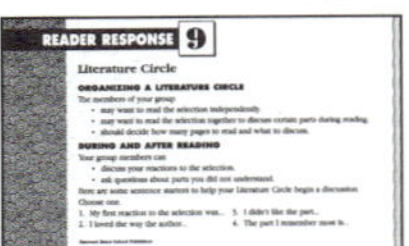
Response Card 9

Students who are reading cooperatively can expand their reactions to the literature. Use questions such as these:

- **Do you think the author has done a good job so far of explaining who she is and what she is doing in Herculaneum? Why or why not?**
- **What part of the selection have you found most interesting so far? Why?**
- **Are there any parts of the selection you have read so far that you do not understand? If so, discuss them with your group members.**

When Vesuvius erupted, ash and gas came spewing out of the summit, forced straight up into the air by the pressure and heat of the blast. Eventually, this cloud cooled, and some of it collapsed, sending ash and hot gas racing down the slopes at speeds of up to seventy miles (110 kilometers) per hour, ripping the roofs off houses and overturning ships in the bay. These surges were followed by thick and glowing avalanches of fiery ash, rock and pumice—hot magma that has cooled so quickly that it is still full of volcanic gases, like a hard foamy sponge.

Vesuvius had not actually erupted for hundreds of years before A.D. 79, and the people of the area believed the volcano was extinct. But they could remember an earthquake seventeen years earlier that had caused much damage to the town. And in the days before the volcano erupted, occasional rumblings and ground tremors were felt, creating the odd crack in a wall, or causing a statue to tumble off its stand. And other strange things happened: wells and springs mysteriously dried up, flocks of birds flew away, and animals were exceptionally restless.

408

SCIENCE

Scientific research supports the theory of animal instincts. We now know that birds have inborn magnetic-field detectors and that some animals are sensitive to extremely small sound waves and vibrations.

CONVENTIONS OF LANGUAGE

PARENTHESES Point out the use of parentheses in the first paragraph. Parentheses are often used to enclose some form of restatement, such as metric equivalents of customary measures.

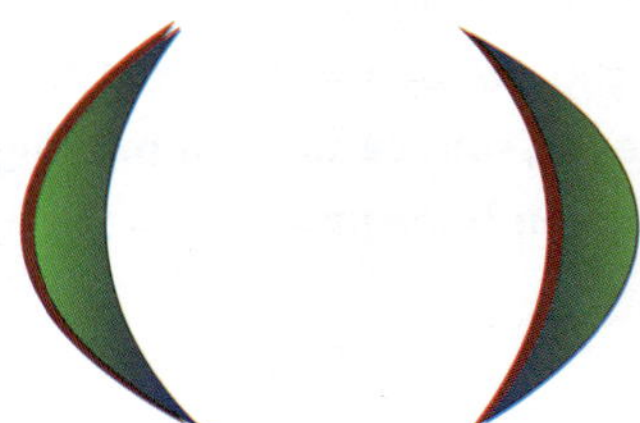

ILLUSTRATOR'S CRAFT

This illustration shows the type of eruption that occurred. It shows the cloud that rose 12 miles (19 km) into the air and then collapsed, sending a rain of fire and ash over Herculaneum.

Strategic Reading

PAGES 402–411 What have you learned so far about Vesuvius? (Possible response: Sara Bisel goes to Herculaneum to study skeletons buried there. She pieces together information about what she discovers.) STRATEGIES: SUMMARIZING

Why did so much of Herculaneum remain intact? (Possible response: Herculaneum was covered by 65 feet of debris, which hardened and sealed the town underneath, protecting it from the weather and human activities.) INFERENTIAL: DETERMINING CAUSE-EFFECT

USING GRAPHIC AIDS

If necessary, model the strategy of using graphic aids:

MODEL

When I read, I look for information in charts, graphs, maps, and diagrams. The diagram on page 411 makes it easy to understand how Herculaneum was covered in layers.

PAGES 412–415

Ask students to revise their predictions as necessary. Then ask them to read through page 414.

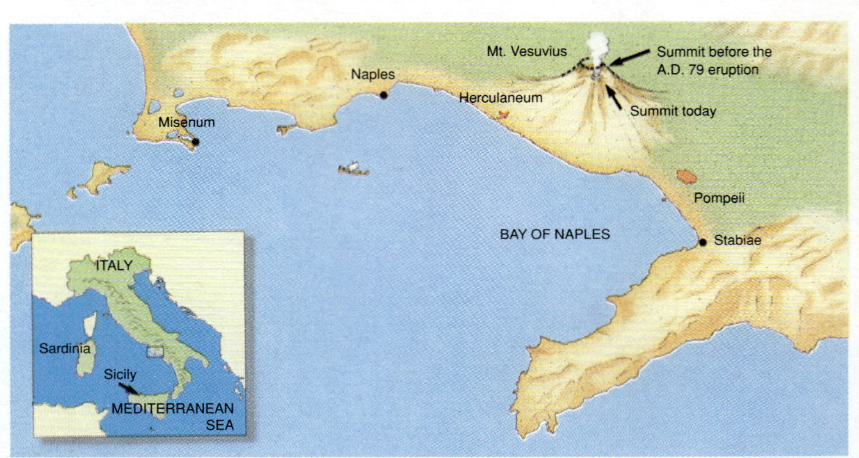

WHY DID VESUVIUS ERUPT?
Far below the earth's surface, gigantic plates of the earth's crust are constantly moving. Where these plates meet, one piece may rub against another, causing an earthquake. But if one plate pushes itself under another, it will melt and become liquid rock, or magma. The super-hot liquid rock creates gas and steam, building pressure until it blasts through weak places in the earth's surface. These weak spots are the world's volcanoes.

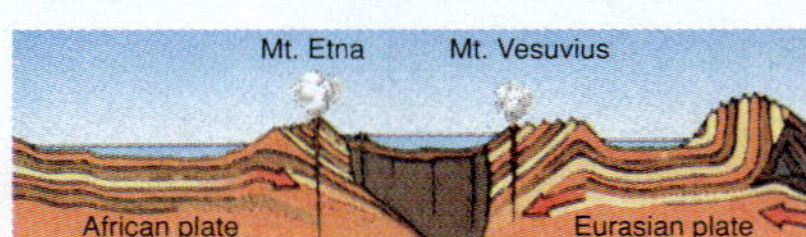

Above: Vesuvius is located in an area of the world where two plates of the earth's crust meet.

We know now that the dry wells were caused by the increasing heat and pressure that were building deep in the earth, and that animals are always more sensitive than humans to changes in the earth and the atmosphere. But, I wondered, were the people in Herculaneum aware that something was about to happen? Before the mountain actually erupted, did it occur to anyone that it might be a good idea to leave town? How many waited until the streets were so crowded that escape was almost impossible? Were they spooked by the tremors, their suddenly dry wells, or the nervous actions of their animals? Did they think the gods were showing their anger?

We will probably never know exactly what the volcano's victims were thinking in those days before the eruption. We do know that the glowing avalanches that buried Herculaneum and the nearby city of Pompeii created two time capsules of ancient Roman life that have not

410

VIEWING

Call students' attention to the two maps at the top of page 410. Explain that the larger map shows how close Vesuvius is to the sea and where nearby cities are located. Point out the small white box on the inset map, and lead students to see that it shows the area pictured in the larger map.

changed in almost two thousand years.

Sealed by volcanic ash and rock, the buried buildings have been protected from the wind and rain that would have worn down the columns and statues over the centuries. Wooden doors, shutters, stairs, cupboards and tables have not been exposed to the air to rot away, or been destroyed by fire. And unlike other ancient towns, the roads and buildings have not been repaired, or torn down and replaced by something more modern.

Instead, Herculaneum and Pompeii look the way they did so many years ago. The roofs of the houses may be gone, the mosaic floors cracked and the wall paintings faded. But we can still walk down the streets over the same stones that the ancient Romans walked on. We can see a 2,000-year-old loaf of bread, now turned to stone, or eggs still in their shells waiting to be served for lunch.

Herculaneum, which was less than three miles (five kilometers) from Vesuvius, was upwind of the volcano. Most of the falling ash blew in the opposite direction, leaving less than an inch lying over the town by the end of the day. Instead, at about 1:15 early the next morning, a violent surge of ash and hot gas poured over the town. By the time the waves of hot mud followed, everyone was dead. In a few hours, Herculaneum was completely buried under sixty-five feet (twenty meters) of hot volcanic matter, which, when it cooled, covered the town like a cement shield.

And so the town lay tightly sealed, for about 1,500 years.

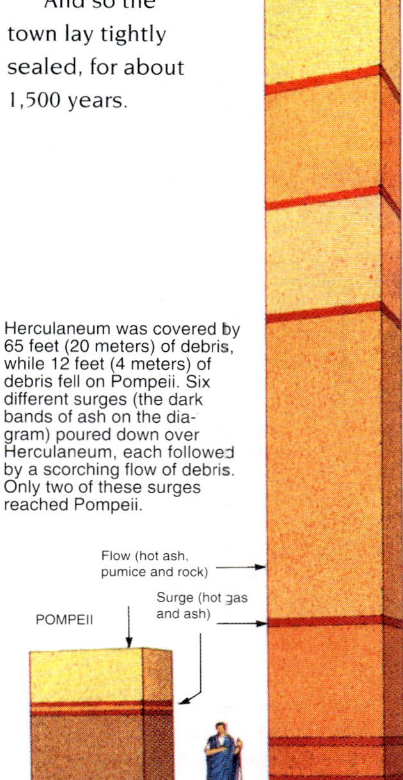

Herculaneum was covered by 65 feet (20 meters) of debris, while 12 feet (4 meters) of debris fell on Pompeii. Six different surges (the dark bands of ash on the diagram) poured down over Herculaneum, each followed by a scorching flow of debris. Only two of these surges reached Pompeii.

411

Informal Assessment

GRAPHIC AIDS

To determine whether students are paying attention to graphic aids as they read, ask them a question like the following:

 How does the graphic aid on page 410 help you understand how Vesuvius erupted?

EXPANDING VOCABULARY

WORDS FROM OTHER LANGUAGES

Students may notice the unusual spelling and silent final *s* in the word *debris*. Explain that *debris*, like many other words, came into English from another language. *Debris* is a French word meaning "remains" or "remains of a wreck."

Then in 1709, a well-digger accidentally struck fine polished marble beneath the ground. An Austrian prince who was building a villa in the area realized that the marble was likely just the beginning of a major buried treasure, and he started to dig into the site.

Luckily for the prince, and unhappily for modern archaeologists and historians, the well-digger had found Herculaneum's ancient theater, one

1. *At midday on August 24, A.D. 79, Vesuvius erupts, sending a cloud of ash and pumice 12 miles (20 kilometers) into the air.*

2. *After midnight, the cloud collapses, sending a surge of ash and hot gas down the mountain, killing the Herculaneans. A flow of hot ash, rock and pumice eventually buries the town.*

412

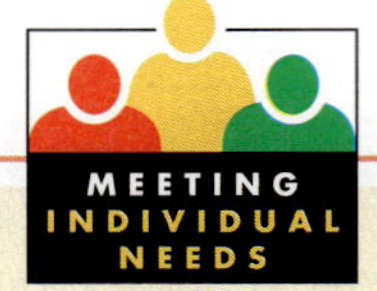

STUDENTS ACQUIRING ENGLISH Use the diagram to help students understand what happened when Vesuvius erupted. If necessary, help students break down captions into shorter sentences.

of the most luxurious and treasure-filled buildings in the town. The prince wanted art and fine building materials for his villa, so he hired diggers who bored tunnels through the theater, not knowing what it was, and not caring in the least about the damage they were doing to the structure itself.

The prince plundered the building of its bronze and stone statues and vases. Marble was ripped off the walls and pillars, and the treasures were carted off to the prince's own house or those of his rich friends. Before long these valuable artifacts were scattered in museums and private collections all over Europe.

The prince's raiders, burrowing through the site like greedy moles sniffing out treasure, did more damage to Herculaneum than the volcano itself.

More raiding expeditions followed, and it was only in 1860 that serious archaeological work began. But even with many of the most precious objects gone, the excavated town itself told historians a great

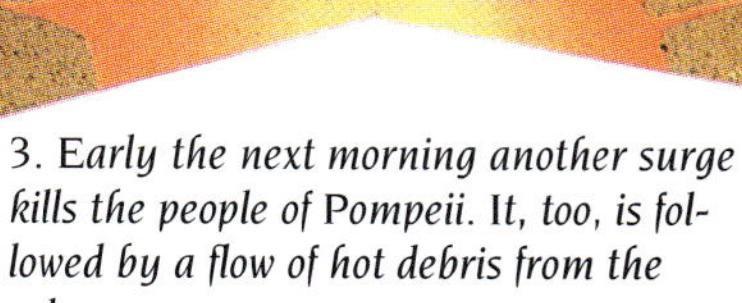

3. *Early the next morning another surge kills the people of Pompeii. It, too, is followed by a flow of hot debris from the volcano.*

413

Student Self-Assessment

FIX-UP STRATEGY: REREADING

Ask students what they can do if they don't understand the captions that accompany the diagram on these pages. (Possible response: I can reread to clarify meaning.)

If necessary, model using rereading as a fix-up strategy:

MODEL **I'm confused about the events of August 24, A.D. 79. I'm going to reread the captions on pages 412 and 413 and refer to the diagram as I do so.**

AUTHOR'S CRAFT

Call students' attention to the second complete paragraph on this page. Point out how the author expresses her opinion of the people who damaged the remains of Herculaneum by using words such as *raiders, burrowing, greedy moles,* and *sniffing out.*

SCIENCE

At least one volcano erupts every day on Earth. We don't notice most of these eruptions because many are small and take place on the ocean floor. Even with so many eruptions, Earth is not the most volcanically active place in the solar system. That distinction belongs to Jupiter's moon Io, shown here.

Io

Strategic Reading

PAGES 412–415 What new information have you learned about Vesuvius and Herculaneum? (Possible response: Damage was done to the ancient city when an Austrian prince discovered the site and had treasures taken from it.) **STRATEGIES: SUMMARIZING**

Why was Herculaneum covered in more layers of ash and debris than Pompeii was? (Possible response: The first surge of gas and ash, which traveled toward Herculaneum, must have been greater than the second surge, which traveled toward Pompeii. Also, Herculaneum is much closer to Vesuvius than Pompeii is.) **INFERENTIAL: SYNTHESIZING**

USING GRAPHIC AIDS

If necessary, model the strategy of using graphic aids:

MODEL **I look at the inset diagram on page 415 and read its caption to find out additional information related to the photograph.**

PAGES 416–421 Ask students to record or revise questions that are still unanswered. Then ask them to read through page 421.

deal about the ancient Romans and how they lived. Because the ruin had been snugly covered by a wet and heavy layer of earth, Herculaneum was even better preserved than Pompeii (which had suffered more damage under its airy blanket of ash and pumice).

Then just a few years ago came the most amazing discovery of all, when ditch-diggers accidentally found the group of skeletons on the ancient beachfront.

By the time these beach skeletons were found, scientists had discovered that we could learn a great deal about people by examining their bones. We could do much more than make plaster casts. Now we can analyze the bones themselves and reconstruct the skulls to see what the people looked like.

This is where I came in. In the morning, I would help to dig up these bones and begin to study them. For the first time, we would know more about the Romans than what books and paintings and sculptures had shown us. We would be able to see the people themselves.

I would be one of the first modern people to look an ancient Roman in the face.

When I got to the site, Dr. Maggi, the director of the excavation, was nowhere to be seen. Workmen sat around in small groups, drinking coffee out of thermoses. They eyed me curiously, then went back to their chat. I took a deep breath and decided to be patient. Later I would discover that waiting for Dr. Maggi's permission to begin work every morning was part of the routine. He made sure that excavation at the site was always closely supervised.

He arrived a few minutes later and introduced me to Ciro Formuola, the foreman of the work crew that was going to help me dig out the skeletons. These men were highly trained in doing delicate excavation work, and I knew I was lucky to have such experienced co-workers. In this business, a false move with a spade or trowel can do damage beyond repair.

A wall painting showing a villa by the sea.

414

STUDENTS ACQUIRING ENGLISH Here and elsewhere, you may want to help students monitor their understanding by posing *who, why, when, where,* and *what* questions. As needed, follow up by paraphrasing, summarizing, or using another method to clarify the text.

When volcanic rock was chipped away from this room in the Suburban Baths, a beautiful statue of Apollo was discovered.

Volcanic flow burst through a window in the Suburban Baths throwing a heavy marble basin like this one *(above)* across the room. You can still see pieces of window glass in the bottom of the basin.

CHALLENGE **Invite students to make conjectures on what the Suburban Baths were and who used them. Students might also research Apollo and give reasons his statue was found among Roman ruins. (Apollo was a major god in Greek and Roman mythology and was regarded as the ideal young man.)**

Apollo, from Temple of Apollo, Pompeii

THE PEOPLE ON THE BEACH

Herculaneum, June 1982

It was quiet on Herculaneum's ancient beach. Above my head, drying sheets and underwear fluttered from the apartment balconies that now overlook the ruins.

Today this beach is just a narrow dirt corridor that lies several feet below sea level. But thousands of years ago, the waves of the Mediterranean would have lapped where I now stood, and my ears would have been filled with the gentle sound of the surf, rather than the dull roar of Ercolano's midday traffic.

To one side of me stood the arched entryways of the boat chambers, most of them still plugged by volcanic rock, their secrets locked inside. Only one chamber had been opened so far, and its contents were now hidden behind a padlocked plywood door.

I eyed the wooden door longingly, wishing for a sudden gift of X-ray vision. Dr. Maggi, the keeper of the key, had been called away to a meeting with some government officials, and would not be back until sometime in the afternoon.

"*Dottoressa!*"[1]

Ciro was calling me from farther down the old beach. He was waving me toward a roped-off area

[1]Dottoressa (dō·tō·re′ sä): Italian title for a woman who is a doctor or scholar

416

MULTICULTURAL CONNECTION

Different titles of respect are used in different cultures. Draw students' attention to the footnote explaining *Dottoressa,* which in Italian is the feminine form of *doctor* or *scholar*. Ask students to volunteer titles of respect from English and other languages and to tell to whom they apply, when they are used, and who uses them.

Professor Ma'am Sir Doctor

The beachfront, the ruins of Herculaneum and Vesuvius as they look today.

It didn't look like much at first—just a heap of dirt with bits of bone poking out. I knelt down and gently scraped earth off the skeleton, exposing it to the light for the first time in two thousand years. It almost looked as if the bones had been carelessly tossed there, they were so broken and tangled.

I looked up. Above me was the open terrace where Herculaneans had held sacred ceremonies. Above that was the wall of the town itself, most of the surrounding balustrade[2] now missing.

surrounding three ordinary-looking piles of dirt.

I have examined thousands of skeletons in my life, but seeing each one for the first time still fills me with a kind of awe. As I walked over to the mound that Ciro was pointing at, I knew I was about to meet my first Herculanean.

[2] balustrade (bal´ə·strād): a handrail supported by posts

417

MINILESSON

REVIEW: COMPREHENSION

Expository Elements

INFORMAL ASSESSMENT

Ask students to identify the subject of this selection. (finding information about life in ancient Herculaneum by examining skeletal remains) Ask students to name different structures or patterns that writers of nonfiction use to organize their ideas. (sequence, main ideas and supporting details, cause and effect)

TEACH/MODEL

Have students reread page 417. Ask them how they can tell that the author uses sequence to structure this part of the text. (The author tells what she did in time order.) If necessary, model the thinking:

MODEL

The author is using a sequence structure because she is telling what she did in the order in which the events happened. First, she walked over to the mound. Then, she knelt down.

PRACTICE/APPLY

Have students look through the selection to identify more examples of sequence and other text structures.

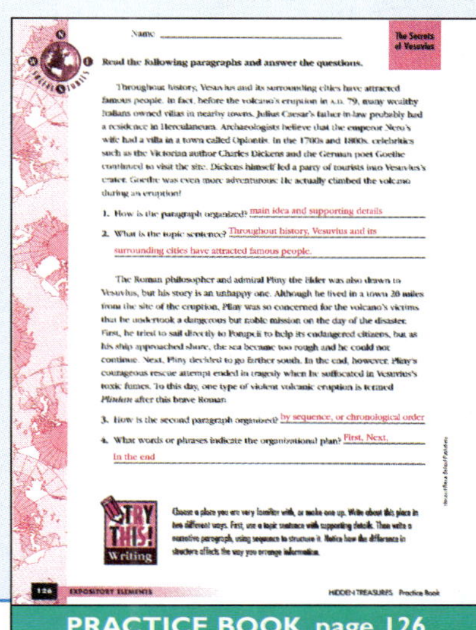

Name: ______

The Secrets of Vesuvius

Read the following paragraphs and answer the questions.

Throughout history, Vesuvius and its surrounding cities have attracted famous people. In fact, before the volcano's eruption in A.D. 79, many wealthy Italians owned villas in nearby towns. Julius Caesar's father-in-law probably had a residence in Herculaneum. Archaeologists believe that the emperor Nero's wife had a villa in a town called Oplontis. In the 1700s and 1800s, celebrities such as the Victorian author Charles Dickens and the German poet Goethe continued to visit the site. Dickens himself led a party of tourists into Vesuvius's crater. Goethe was even more adventurous: He actually climbed the volcano during an eruption!

1. How is the paragraph organized? main idea and supporting details
2. What is the topic sentence? Throughout history, Vesuvius and its surrounding cities have attracted famous people.

The Roman philosopher and admiral Pliny the Elder was also drawn to Vesuvius, but his story is an unhappy one. Although he lived in a town 20 miles from the site of the eruption, Pliny was so concerned for the volcano's victims that he undertook a dangerous but noble mission on the day of the disaster. First, he tried to sail directly to Pompeii to help its endangered citizens, but as his ship approached shore, the sea became too rough and he could not continue. Next, Pliny decided to go farther south. In the end, however, Pliny's courageous rescue attempt ended in tragedy when he suffocated in Vesuvius's toxic fumes. To this day, one type of violent volcanic eruption is termed *Plinian* after this brave Roman.

3. How is the second paragraph organized? by sequence, or chronological order
4. What words or phrases indicate the organizational plan? First, Next, In the end

TRY THIS! Writing

Choose a place you are very familiar with, or make one up. Write about this place in two different ways. First, use a topic sentence with supporting details. Then write a narrative paragraph, using sequence to structure it. Notice how the difference in structure affects the way you arrange information.

126 EXPOSITORY ELEMENTS HIDDEN TREASURES Practice Book

PRACTICE BOOK, page 126

Intervention Strategies

SELF-QUESTIONING **Say this sentence aloud to students: *While I'm reading, I try to answer the questions I asked myself before reading.* Have students share any questions they had and tell how answering their questions helps them keep track of what Sara Bisel learns about the people on the beach.**

Critical Thinking Questions

1. **Page 418 is a series of questions. Why do you think Bisel asks one question after another?** (Possible response: This technique emphasizes how many unanswered questions there are when bones and a few objects are the only evidence.) CRITICAL: CHALLENGING THE TEXT

2. **What does this illustration show about the author?** (Possible response: The author knows how to find evidence or information from a bone, whereas other people might look at the bone and think it has nothing to tell.) INFERENTIAL: REFLECTING/MAKING CONNECTIONS

I closely examine each bone of a skeleton as I lift it from the wet volcanic earth.

Had this woman fallen from the wall above? Had some huge force propelled her from the town, perhaps a piece of flying debris, or the blast from the volcano itself, so that she smashed face down onto the ground? What had she been doing on the wall in the first place? Calling down to the people on the beach for help?

418

STUDENTS ACQUIRING ENGLISH Students may be confused by the past perfect tense on this page. You might want to simplify by restating each question in the simple past tense: *Did this woman fall from the wall above?* and so on.

I picked up one of the bones and felt its cool smoothness in my hands. Because this was the first Herculanean I got to know, this skeleton was extra special to me. I named her Portia.

By measuring the bones, I could tell that Portia was about 5 feet 1 inch (155 centimeters) tall. She was about forty-eight when she died—an old woman by Roman standards—and had buck teeth.

Later, after a chemical analysis, we learned that Portia also had very high levels of lead in her bones. Lead is a poison, but in Roman times it was a common substance. It was used in makeup, medicines, paint pigment, pottery glazes, and to line drinking cups and plates.

On either side of Portia was a skeleton. One was another female. She lay on her side, almost looking as if she had died in her sleep. As I brushed dirt from her left hand, something shiny caught my eye as it glinted in the sunlight. It was a gold ring.

When we uncovered the rest of the hand, we found a second ring. And in a clump on her hip we found two intricate snakes' head bracelets made of pure gold, a pair of earrings that may have held pearls, and some coins (the cloth purse that had probably once held these valuables had long since rotted away).

We ended up calling her the Ring Lady. She was about forty-five when she died. She was not terribly good-looking; her jaw was large and protruding. There were no cavities in her teeth, but she did have gum disease, which left tiny pits in the bone along her gum line. If she had lived today, her dentist probably would have advised her to floss more often!

In fact, most of the Herculaneans I examined had very good teeth, with only about three cavities each. Today, many of us have about sixteen cavities each, in spite of all our fluoride treatments, regular dental checkups and constant nagging to floss and brush! But the Romans had no sugar in their diet. They used honey, but not much, because it was expensive. Instead, the Herculaneans ate a well-balanced diet, including much seafood, which is rich in fluoride. Not only that, but they had strong jaws from chewing and tearing food without using knives and forks. And they did clean their teeth, scrubbing them with the stringy end of a stick rather than using a brush and toothpaste.

419

Tested Skill

MINILESSON

REVIEW: GRAMMAR

Main and Helping Verbs

INFORMAL ASSESSMENT

Ask students to identify one main verb and one helping verb on this page. (Accept reasonable responses.) Then ask a volunteer to explain why some verbs have helping verbs. (to help the main verb express action or being)

TEACH/MODEL

Draw students' attention to the sixth paragraph on page 419, and model identifying main and helping verbs:

MODEL

When I read *There were no cavities in her teeth, but she did have gum disease*, I see the helping verb *did*. It is followed by the main verb, *have*.

PRACTICE/APPLY

Have students find two other phrases in the sixth paragraph and identify the main and helping verbs. (*had* [helping], *lived* [main]; *would* [helping], *have* [main])

SOCIAL STUDIES

The Romans had such high regard for candy makers that their status was equal to that of master road builders and architects. The pots, pans, strainers, and measuring cups of a Roman candy maker were discovered at one archaeological dig in Herculaneum.

Cooking pots on hearth, Pompeii, Italy

Strategic Reading

PAGES 416–421 What kinds of observations was Bisel able to make after examining the skeletons? (Possible response: She could speculate as to the person's age, physical features, and conditions of health.) STRATEGIES: SUMMARIZING

How is Bisel able to draw conclusions about what the various people looked like? (Possible response: She studies the bones and compares them with what she already knows. Then she imagines flesh on the bones. Finally, she makes a judgment about what a person might have looked like.) INFERENTIAL: DETERMINING SEQUENCE/SUMMARIZING

USING GRAPHIC AIDS

To model using graphic aids, use a think-aloud like this one:

MODEL **I use the diagram on page 420 to understand what steps Sara Bisel takes to imagine what the soldier's face might have looked like.**

PAGES 422–426
Ask students to read the conclusion of the selection.

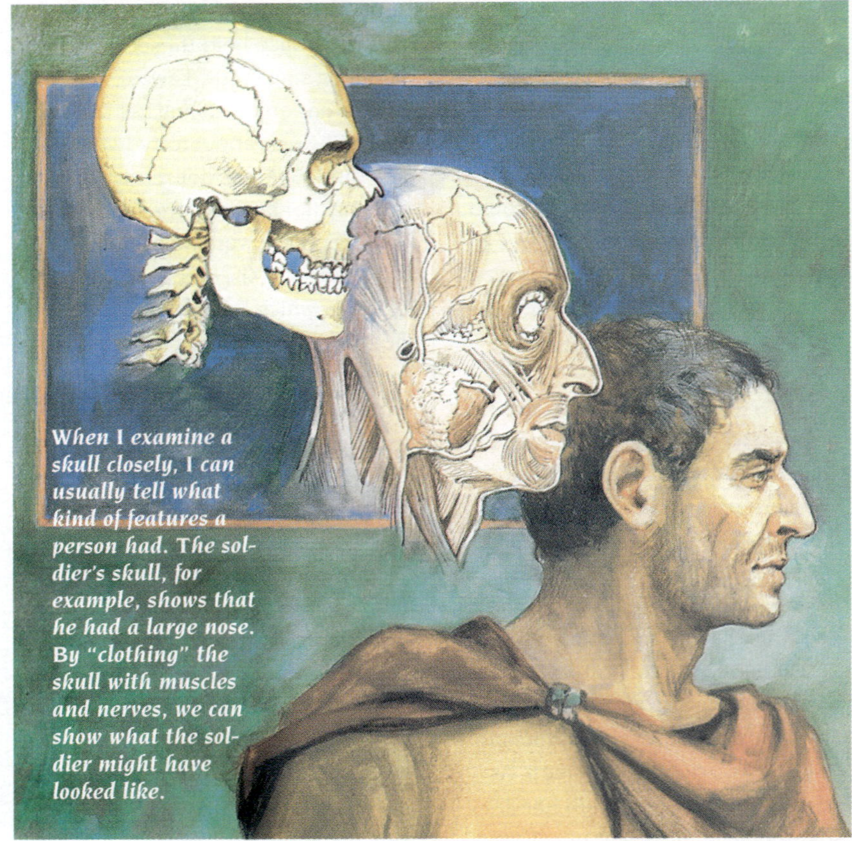

When I examine a skull closely, I can usually tell what kind of features a person had. The soldier's skull, for example, shows that he had a large nose. By "clothing" the skull with muscles and nerves, we can show what the soldier might have looked like.

On the other side of Portia we dug up the skeleton we called the Soldier. He was found lying face down, his hands outstretched, his sword still in his belt. We found carpenter's tools with him, which had perhaps been slung over his back. (Roman soldiers often worked on building projects when they were between wars.) He also had a money belt containing three gold coins. He was quite tall for a Roman, about 5 feet 8 inches (173 centimeters).

When I examined the man's skull, I could see that he was missing six teeth, including three at the front,

420

EXTRA SUPPORT One way for students to keep track of information is by listing details. Here students might list the things found with the soldier (tools, money, sword) as well as physical facts about him. (tall, missing six teeth)

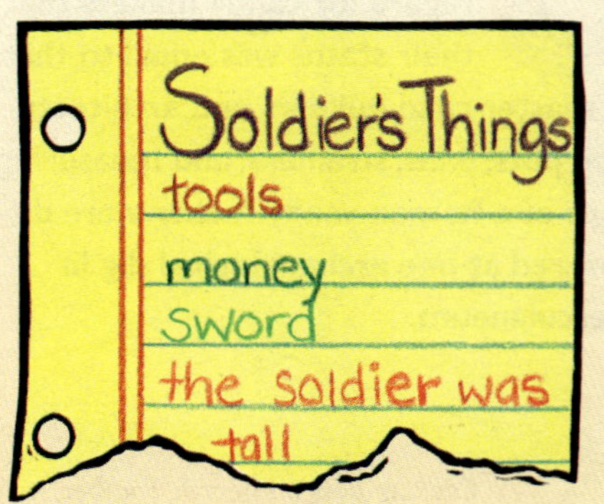

We found these coins in the soldier's money belt.

and that he'd had a huge nose. And when I examined the bone of his left thigh, I could see a lump where a wound had penetrated the bone and caused a blood clot that eventually had hardened. Near the knee, where the muscle would have been attached, the bone was enlarged slightly. This indicated that he would have had well-developed thighs, possibly due to gripping the sides of a horse with the knees while riding (Romans didn't use saddles).

Had the soldier lost those front teeth in a fight, I wondered. Had he been wounded in the leg during the same fight or another one? His life must have been fairly rough and tumble.

While members of the excavation team poured buckets of water on the three skeletons to loosen the debris, I continued to scrape off the dirt and volcanic matter with a trowel. Later, in the laboratory, each bone and tooth would be washed with a soft brush. Then they would be left to dry before being dipped in an acrylic solution to preserve them. Finally, each bone would be measured, then measured again to prevent errors, and the figures would be carefully recorded.

By late afternoon my back and knees were stiff from crouching, and the back of my neck was tight with the beginning of a sunburn.

I stood up and stretched. There was still much to do before the three skeletons would be free of their volcanic straitjackets. I started to think about heading back to the hotel for a shower and bite to eat. But a flurry of activity down the beach caught my eye, and suddenly I no longer felt tired.

To my right, Dr. Maggi stood outside the locked wooden door I had seen earlier. He was unbolting the padlock. When he saw me, he waved. I put down my trowel, wiped my hands on my jeans and hurried over. Inside, I knew, was the only group of Roman skeletons that had ever been found—the twelve people who had huddled in the shelter and died together when the volcanic avalanches poured down the mountainside into the sea.

Student Self-Assessment

FIX-UP STRATEGY: SELF-QUESTIONING

Remind students that as they read, they should monitor their own comprehension by using self-questioning.

If necessary, model self-questioning as a fix-up strategy:

I wonder if Sara Bisel will find anything besides skeletons behind the wooden door.

AUTHOR'S CRAFT

Call students' attention to the way the author builds excitement about the unlocking of the padlocked door. She begins by underscoring how tired she was—and how willing she was to call it a day. Nevertheless, when she saw activity on the beach, she was immediately ready for action.

Critical Thinking Questions

1. **Why is everyone quiet as Dr. Maggi opens the door?** (Possible response: They are full of excitement and eager to see what's inside the chamber. Everyone's attention is on the opening of the door.) INFERENTIAL: DETERMINING CAUSE-EFFECT

2. **What kind of mood does the author create? How does she create this mood?** (Possible response: She makes the scene seem mysterious and spooky. She talks about the *dank smell of damp earth*, the *cave-like* chamber, and the *greenish shadows*. She calls attention to *an oddly shaped, lumpy mound halfway back*.) CRITICAL: AUTHOR'S CRAFT/ APPRECIATING IMAGERY

This surviving loaf of bread is now as hard as rock.

I could hear an odd echo from inside the chamber as Dr. Maggi clicked the padlock open. Behind me, a number of the crew members had gathered. We were all very quiet.

The plywood door seemed flimsy as Dr. Maggi pulled it open. From inside the chamber came the dank smell of damp earth.

A shiver crept up my neck. We were opening a 2,000-year-old grave. What would we find?

As I entered the cave-like boat chamber, I could barely see, even though the sun flooded through the door. Someone handed me a flashlight, but its light cast greenish shadows, making it feel even more spooky.

The light played over the back of the shelter, no bigger than a single garage and still crusted over with volcanic rock. I saw an oddly shaped,

Richard Steffy, a specialist in ancient boat construction, examines the fragile boat found on the beachfront.

422

MEETING INDIVIDUAL NEEDS

STUDENTS ACQUIRING ENGLISH Students may be unfamiliar with the use of the verb *played* in the last sentence on this page. Explain to students that here, *played* means "darted about in quick movements."

lumpy mound halfway back. I took several steps into the chamber and pointed the light at the mound.

The narrow beam found a skull, the pale face a grimace of death. As my eyes grew accustomed to the dim light, I soon realized there were bones and skulls everywhere. They were all tangled together—clinging to each other for comfort in their final moments—and it was hard to distinguish one from another. But I knew that twelve skeletons had been found in all—three men, four women and five children. One child had an iron house key near him. Did he think he would be going back home?

I took another step into the cave. At my feet was a skeleton that was almost entirely uncovered. From the pelvis I could see it was a female, a girl, lying face down. Beneath her, we could just see the top of another small skull.

It was a baby.

I knelt down and gently touched the tiny skull. My throat felt tight as I thought about this girl, this baby, and what it must have been like for them in this dark cave in the moments before they died.

"Allora, è la sorella?"

I frowned, pulled my Italian-English dictionary out of the back

This wall painting from Pompeii shows what the boat from Herculaneum might have looked like under full sail.

pocket of my jeans and flipped through it. I realized Ciro thought these two skeletons belonged to a baby and its older sister.

"We'll see," I murmured. I knew it was important not to jump to conclusions. You have to question everything about bones, especially ones that have been lying around for two thousand years.

I struggled to free a bronze cupid pin and two little bells from the baby's bones. Whoever the child was, it had been rich enough to wear expensive ornaments. But I knew it would take many more hours of careful study before we knew the real story behind these two skeletons.

Later, in the laboratory, I gained enough information to put together a more likely background for the skeleton of the young girl.

423

NOTES

Here's a place to list ideas or activities that you would like to use the next time you teach this lesson.

CHALLENGE **Invite students to investigate different kinds of wall decorations, such as mosaics, fresco paintings, and secco paintings, and the artists who have created them.**

Unlike the baby, she had not come from a wealthy family. She had been about fourteen, and from the shape of her skull I knew she had probably been pretty. When I examined her teeth I could tell that she had been starved or quite ill for a time when she was a baby. She had also had two teeth removed about one or two weeks before she died, probably giving her a fair bit of pain. And her life had been very hard. She had done a lot of running up and down stairs or hills, as well as having to lift objects too heavy for her delicate frame.

This girl could not have been the child of a wealthy family, like the baby. She had probably been a slave who died trying to protect the baby of the family she worked for.

And there were many others.

Excavators have nearly cleared one of these boat chambers, but the one next to it is still blocked by hard volcanic rock.

424

SCIENCE

FACT FINDER

SKELETAL AGE Doctors evaluate growth on the basis of the growth of the bones of the skeleton and often assign a developmental rather than a chronological age. A six-year-old child who is developing slowly might only have reached the bone structure of a five-year-old. A person's skeletal age could run below his actual age until he becomes an adult. Most humans stop growing some time between the ages of eighteen and thirty. After people stop growing in height, they begin to shrink. This is due to the thinning of the pads of cartilage between the bones of the spine.

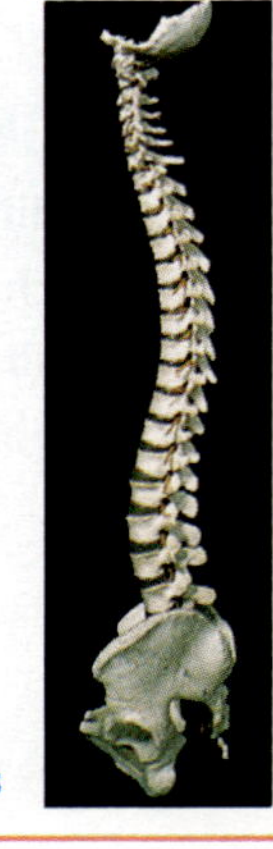

The human spine and pelvis

Near the slave girl lay the skeleton of a seven-year-old girl whose bones also showed that she had done work far too heavy for a child so young.

We found a sixteen-year-old fisherman, his upper body well developed from rowing boats, his teeth worn from holding cord while he repaired his fishing nets.

Though it is fascinating to reconstruct the life of a single person by examining his or her bones, for anthropologists and historians the most useful information comes from examining all of the skeletons of one population. This is one reason why Herculaneum is so important.

During the next few months we opened two more boat chambers. In one we discovered forty tangled human skeletons and one of a horse; in another we found twenty-six skeletons creepily lined up like a row of dominoes, as if heading in single file for the back of the chamber.

The skeletons represented a cross-section of the population of a whole town—old people, children and babies, slaves, rich and poor, men and women, the sick and the healthy. By examining all these skeletons, we can get some ideas about how the townspeople lived and what they were like physically.

We found out, for example, that the average Herculanean man was 5 feet 5 inches (165 centimeters) tall, the average woman about 5 feet 1 inch (155 centimeters). In general, they were well nourished. And we have examined enough people to know that although the rich people had easy lives, the slaves often worked so hard that they were in pain much of the time.

Tested Skill

MINILESSON

REVIEW: COMPREHENSION

Compare/Contrast

INFORMAL ASSESSMENT

Ask students to compare and contrast the fourteen-year-old girl with the baby. (The baby had come from a wealthy family, whereas the girl had had a difficult life as a slave.)

TEACH/MODEL

Remind students that comparing involves looking for similarities and that contrasting involves looking for differences. Explain that comparing and contrasting while reading can help students draw conclusions.

MODEL **By comparing and contrasting the details about the girl and the baby, I can see how different the lives of the rich and the poor were in Herculaneum. By age fourteen, the slave girl had already had a very difficult life, whereas the baby probably would have continued to live a life of great ease.**

PRACTICE/APPLY

Have students compare and contrast what some of the other skeletons reveal. Ask them to use that information to draw a conclusion about the residents of Herculaneum or about life there.

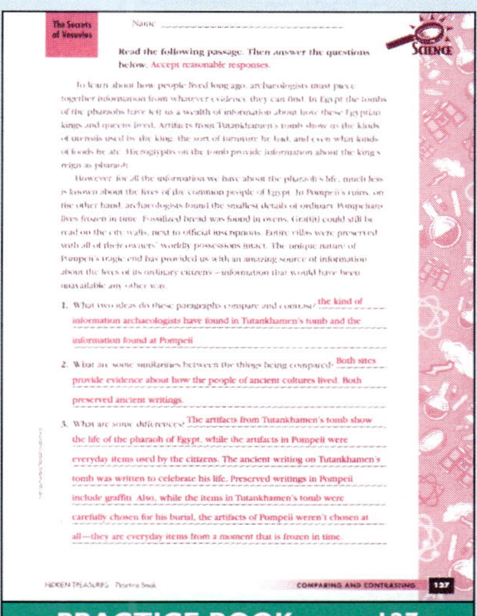
The Secrets of Vesuvius

Name ____________

SCIENCE

Read the following passage. Then answer the questions below. Accept reasonable responses.

To learn about how people lived long ago, archaeologists must piece together information from whatever evidence they can find. In Egypt the tombs of the pharaohs have left us a wealth of information about how these Egyptian kings and queens lived. Artifacts from Tutankhamen's tomb show us the kinds of utensils used by the king, the sort of furniture he had, and even what kinds of foods he ate. Hieroglyphs on the tomb provide information about the king's reign as pharaoh.

However, for all the information we have about the pharaoh's life, much less is known about the lives of the common people of Egypt. In Pompeii's ruins, on the other hand, archaeologists found the smallest details of ordinary Pompeians' lives frozen in time. Fossilized bread was found in ovens. Graffiti could still be read on the city walls, next to official inscriptions. Entire villas were preserved with all of their owners' worldly possessions intact. The unique nature of Pompeii's tragic end has provided us with an amazing source of information about the lives of its ordinary citizens—information that would have been unavailable any other way.

1. What two ideas do these paragraphs compare and contrast? the kind of information archaeologists have found in Tutankhamen's tomb and the information found at Pompeii
2. What are some similarities between the things being compared? Both sites provide evidence about how the people of ancient cultures lived. Both preserved ancient writings.
3. What are some differences? The artifacts from Tutankhamen's tomb show the life of the pharaoh of Egypt, while the artifacts in Pompeii were everyday items used by the citizens. The ancient writing on Tutankhamen's tomb was written to celebrate his life. Preserved writings in Pompeii include graffiti. Also, while the items in Tutankhamen's tomb were carefully chosen for his burial, the artifacts of Pompeii weren't chosen at all—they are everyday items from a moment that is frozen in time.

HIDDEN TREASURES Practice Book COMPARING AND CONTRASTING 127

PRACTICE BOOK, page 127

REAL-LIFE CONNECTION

Ask students to use what they know from experience and from what they have read and seen in the selection so far to tell why they think people were found in the beachfront caves. (Possible response: They may have run toward the sea to escape the heat. Maybe they planned to escape in boats. They might have believed that the caves would protect them.)

Strategic Reading

PAGES 422–426 What secrets do bones reveal, and which do they keep? (Possible response: Bones tell about people's height, age, and diet, the diseases they have had, and the work they have done. Bones do not tell about peoples' personalities, thoughts, or feelings.)
STRATEGY: SUMMARIZING

Returning to the Predictions/Purpose

Did you find out what you wanted to know about "The Secrets of Vesuvius"? Why or why not? Encourage students to discuss whether their purposes for reading were met. **STRATEGY: RETURNING TO THE PURPOSE**

Appreciating the Literature

Would you encourage a friend to read this selection? Explain your answer. (Responses will vary.)

A coin box found on the beach.

Studying these skeletons closely can also help medical researchers and doctors. In ancient times, many diseases could not be cured by surgery or drugs. Instead, people kept getting sicker, until they eventually died. By examining the bones of these people, we can learn a great deal about how certain diseases progress.

By the end of my stay in Herculaneum, I had examined 139 skeletons. Their bones were sorted into yellow plastic vegetable crates that lined the shelves in my laboratory. And each box of bones has a different story to tell.

Even though I can't tell the good guys from the bad, and I can't tell you whether they were happy or not, I know a great deal about these people. I can see each person plainly. I even imagine them dressed as they might have been, lounging on their terraces or in the baths if they were wealthy, toiling in a mine or in a galley if they were the most unfortunate slaves.

Most of all, I feel that these people have become my friends, and that I have been very lucky to have had a part in bringing their stories to the rest of the world.

Among the ruins, archaeologists found these unusual glass beads with tiny faces on them.

426

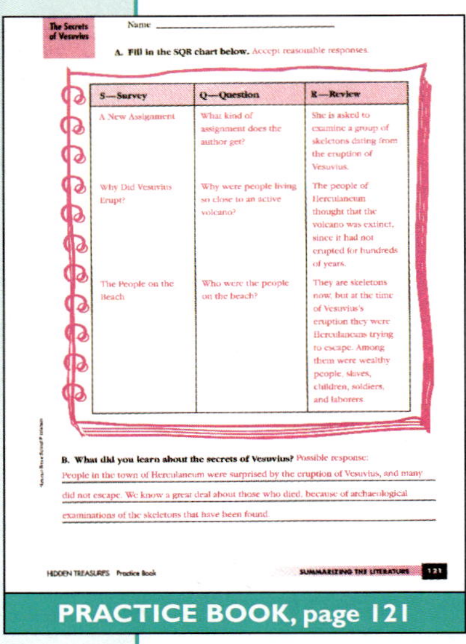

The Secrets of Vesuvius

Name ______

A. Fill in the SQR chart below. Accept reasonable responses.

S—Survey	Q—Question	R—Review
A New Assignment	What kind of assignment does the author get?	She is asked to examine a group of skeletons dating from the eruption of Vesuvius.
Why Did Vesuvius Erupt?	Why were people living so close to an active volcano?	The people of Herculaneum thought that the volcano was extinct, since it had not erupted for hundreds of years.
The People on the Beach	Who were the people on the beach?	They are skeletons now, but at the time of Vesuvius's eruption they were Herculaneans trying to escape. Among them were wealthy people, slaves, children, soldiers, and laborers.

B. What did you learn about the secrets of Vesuvius? Possible response: People in the town of Herculaneum were surprised by the eruption of Vesuvius, and many did not escape. We know a great deal about those who died, because of archaeological examinations of the skeletons that have been found.

HIDDEN TREASURES Practice Book SUMMARIZING THE LITERATURE 121

PRACTICE BOOK, page 121

SUMMARIZING

SQR Chart

Have students complete the third column of their SQR chart. Invite them to use their charts to talk with a partner about what they learned. Students might also use their charts to self-assess their understanding of the selection. See also *Practice Book* page 121.

S—Survey	Q—Question	R—Review
A New Assignment	What kind of assignment does the author get?	
Why Did Vesuvius Erupt?	Why were people living so close to an active volcano?	
The People on the Beach	Who were the people on the beach?	

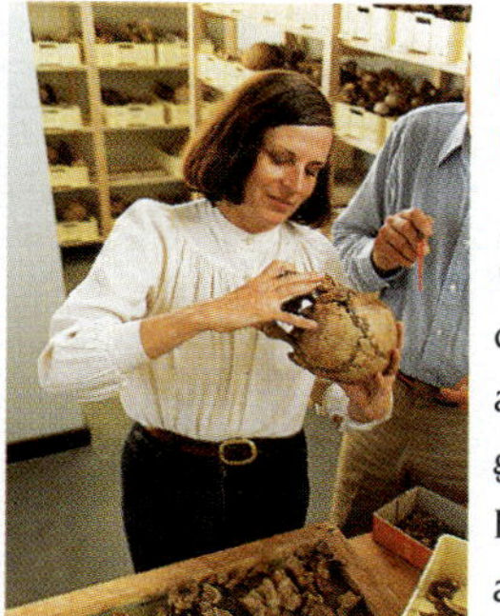

Sara C. Bisel

Sara Bisel is one of the world's top experts when it comes to digging up facts about old bones. She is an archaeologist and physical anthropologist who graduated from the University of Minnesota in 1980. Bisel has studied ancient skeletons uncovered at archaeological sites in Greece, Turkey, and Israel. The National Geographic Society asked her to visit the ruins of the old Roman towns of Herculaneum and Pompeii and study the many well-preserved skeletons there. The results of her investigation of these buried cities were published in *Discover* magazine and *National Geographic*. The investigation was also recorded on film and shown on television by the National Geographic Society.

427

About the Author

After students read page 427, you may wish to discuss these questions with them:

- **Why do you think Sara Bisel decided to study archaeology and anthropology?** (Responses will vary.)
- **Why do you think Sara Bisel is considered one of the world's top experts on ancient bones?** (Possible response: because she has proven her skills on numerous digs and was invited by the National Geographic Society to study the remains at Herculaneum and Pompeii)

Sara Bisel, known in archaeological circles as the Bone Lady, has been in charge of preserving skeletons at Herculaneum. "They like to be fussed over, and they tell me their histories," she says.

IDEA BANK

Students can learn about careers by reading fiction and nonfiction selections that portray people at work. Invite students to begin a book of careers, devoting one page to each career. Suggest that students list facts they learn and questions they think of, based on their reading. Students can then compile their pages into a book to keep in the classroom.

POETRY

Volcano

by Constance Levy

INTRODUCING THE POEM Have students recall reading about the eruption of Mount Vesuvius in "The Secrets of Vesuvius," and ask them what the ancient Herculaneans probably thought was happening. (Possible response: They thought that the volcano was extinct, so they were probably confused by the strange rumblings and ground tremors.) Then tell students they will read about a volcano in a poem that an ancient Roman would probably appreciate.

APPRECIATING THE POEM Read the poem aloud to students as they follow along. Then ask questions such as the following:

To what does the poet compare an erupting volcano? (Possible response: an angry person waking from a long sleep)

Do you think the comparison is a good one? Explain your answer. (Possible response: Yes. Sometimes anger builds inside you like the pressure inside a volcano and makes you feel like you'll explode.)

After discussing the poem, organize the class into two groups and have them perform a choral reading of the poem, with each group reading six lines.

VOLC

LISTENING CENTER

"Volcano" is available on Literature Cassette 3. You may wish to have students listen to the recording of the poem as they read along.

Poet's Craft

Remind students that poets sometimes use personification, a figure of speech in which inanimate objects are given human characteristics. Have volunteers find words in the poem that attribute human actions or feelings to the volcano. (Possible responses: *asleep, anger, awake, screaming, spitting, throwing, not caring*) Then reread the last six lines for students, and have them listen for the strong accents that punctuate the lines. Ask students how they might describe the rhythm of these lines. (Responses will vary.) Point out that the poet has chosen words for both meaning and sound to contribute to the image of an angry volcano.

MORE POETRY

More of Constance Levy's poetry may be found in *A Tree Place and Other Poems*, M.K. McElderry Books, 1994; and *I'm Going to Pet a Worm Today: And Other Poems*, M.K. McElderry Books, 1991.

ACTIVITY CHOICES

DRAW A MAP

SAFETY FIRST This is a good time to review the skills of drawing, labeling, and reading a diagram. If possible, show students a familiar diagram, such as one you have just studied in a social studies or science textbook, and point out how the drawings, arrows, and labels combine to give information quickly. When each student has completed a diagram, provide time for students to tell a partner what it shows.
ART/LISTENING AND SPEAKING

RECORD YOUR DIET

SWEET TOOTH Show students a food label, and explain that sugars are listed under carbohydrates. Remind students that sugar can also be listed as *brown sugar, sucrose, corn syrup*, and *dextrose*.
HEALTH/LISTENING AND SPEAKING

WRITE A POEM

LOOK OUT BELOW! Students can share their poems by contributing them to a class book of poems, by taking part in a class or small-group reading of their poems, by publishing their poems on a class or school bulletin board, or by displaying them in a creative-writing corner of the classroom.
CRITICAL THINKING/WRITING

STUDENTS ACQUIRING ENGLISH

Invite students who are proficient in other languages to create diagrams and labels that will ensure the safety of students who are acquiring English.

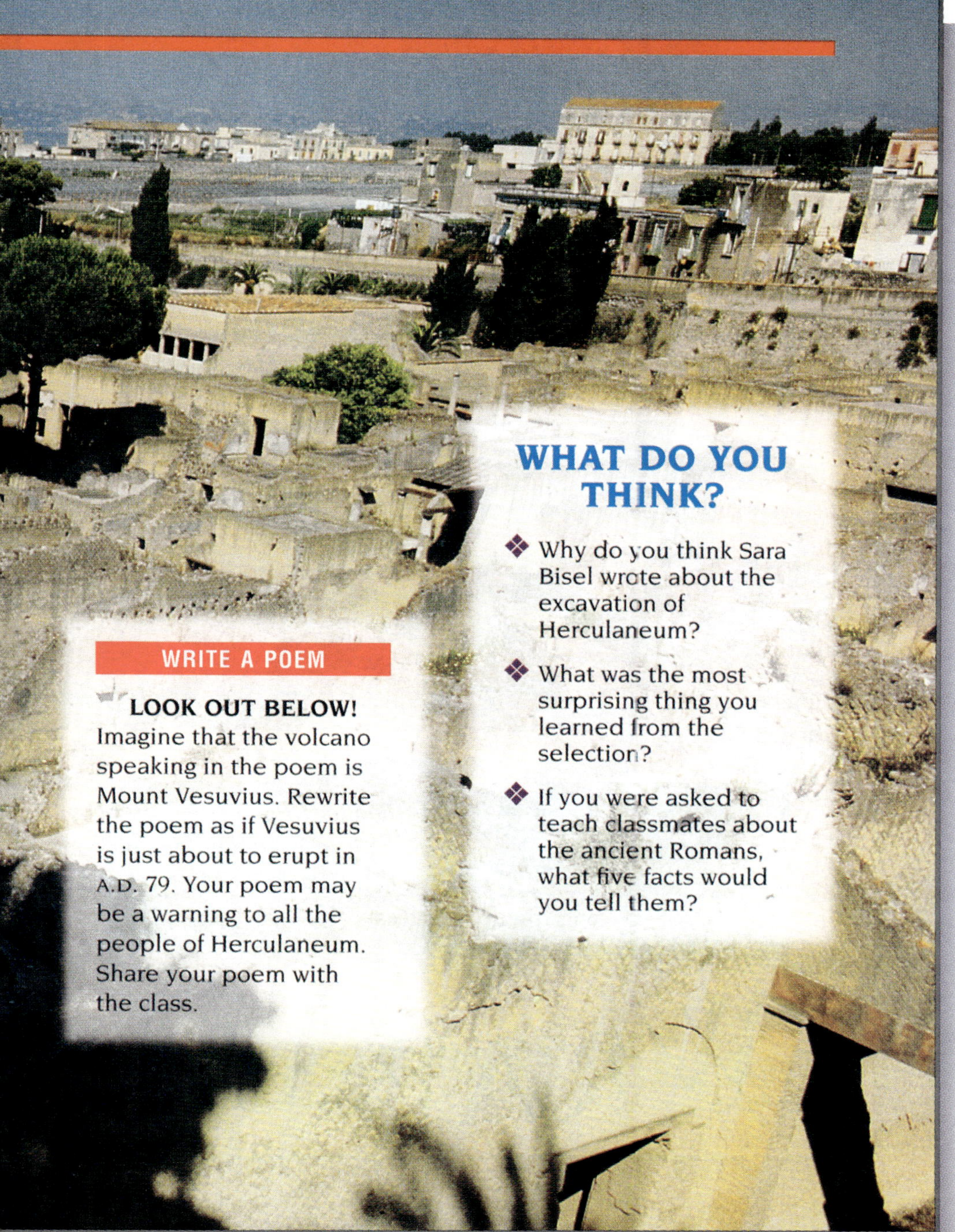

CHECKING COMPREHENSION

What Do You Think?

1. **Why do you think Sara Bisel wrote about the excavation of Herculaneum?** (Possible response: She wanted readers to know what the excavation tells about life in Herculaneum at the time of the eruption, and why it is important to treat places like Herculaneum carefully so that we can learn as much as possible from them.) DESCRIPTIVE RESPONSE

2. **What was the most surprising thing you learned from the selection?** (Responses will vary.) PERSONAL RESPONSE

3. **If you were asked to teach classmates about the ancient Romans, what five facts would you tell them?** (Possible responses: Some Romans were rich and had an easy life. Others were slaves and worked very hard. Some Romans who were wealthy lived in big houses called villas. Romans held sacred ceremonies, often wore jewelry, cleaned their teeth using a stick, and had few sweets in their diet.) CRITICAL ANALYSIS/REFLECTING

VARYING THE ACTIVITY

To **challenge** students who have completed their safety diagrams, encourage them to conduct a mock safety drill to demonstrate how they would use the diagrams during an emergency.

Intervention Strategies

TIPS FOR CLASSROOM MANAGEMENT

IF second-language students need additional vocabulary and during-reading strategies to understand "The Secrets of Vesuvius," **THEN** use *Sheltered English/ESL Manual,* pages 62–65.

IF students had difficulty understanding "The Secrets of Vesuvius," **THEN** complete the Rereading and Decoding Strategies. See also *Intervention Strategies Manual,* pages 92–97.

REREADING

DETERMINING CHRONOLOGICAL ORDER
"The Secrets of Vesuvius" is a nonfiction story that tells about important events in the town of Herculaneum. Have students reread the selection and fill out a chart like the following with the important events in choronological order.

After students have finished rereading, ask volunteers to summarize the author's principal findings about the people of Herculaneum.

DATE	IMPORTANT EVENT
August, A.D. 79	(Vesuvius erupted and buried Herculaneum.)
1709	(A well-digger discovered Herculaneum's buried theatre.)
1860	(Serious archaeological work began.)
June 1982	(Sara Bisel studied the skeletons on Herculaneum's beach.)

PERSONAL JOURNAL Have students write a few sentences in their journals comparing and contrasting life in ancient Herculaneum with their own lives.

DECODING LONG WORDS

VCV WORDS Explain to students that they can use their knowledge of sounds and letters to figure out words with a single consonant between vowels.

Present the following words from the story: *pumice, tremors, humans.* Have students divide each word into syllables before the consonant and pronounce the first syllable using a long vowel sound. Ask students if they've said a recognizable word. If not, have them divide the word into syllables after the consonant and pronounce the first syllable using a short vowel sound.

Have students complete the chart by dividing the story words into syllables and then indicating whether the first syllable has a long or a short vowel sound.

	In Syllables	Vowel Sound
humans		
pumice		
tremors		
private		
second		
shiver		

Then have students divide other story words into syllables.

Write a Diary Entry

Help students write a diary entry about a time when they made an exciting discovery such as what a lunar eclipse looks like. Encourage them to follow these steps:

1. Describe a time when you were very curious about something.
2. Tell the circumstances of your discovery: what happened, when it happened, and how it happened.
3. Tell how you felt about your discovery.

DECODING SUPPORT
r*-Controlled Vowels: /ôr/ *or, oar, oor, ore;* /ûr/ *er, ir, ur

Intervention Strategies Manual pp. 96–97

ESL/Title I Reading

Reading Trade Books

ESL/Title I Library

Pompeii . . . Buried Alive!

by Edith Kunhardt

Like "The Secrets of Vesuvius," this short book offers readers an intriguing, detailed picture of the discoveries that archaeologists have made about everyday life in ancient Rome. Have students use a diagram like the one below to list specific facts that they have learned from the selections.

Everyday Life in Ancient Rome
Facts I Learned from "The Secrets of Vesuvius" 1. 2. Facts I Learned from *Pompeii . . . Buried Alive!* 1. 2. 3.

TAKE-HOME BOOK TO REINFORCE KEY WORDS

Students may relate to the boy in this story. They may want to read it when they have independent reading time in class, or they might want to take it home to read.

PERSONAL JOURNAL

After students finish reading *The Unwelcome Uncle*, have them write in their personal journals about a time when they learned something surprising.

See also *Intervention Strategies Manual,* page 95.

IDEA BANK

TIPS FOR CLASSROOM MANAGEMENT

IF students need to focus on speaking and listening strategies, **THEN** they should complete the Oral Language activity.

IF students need practice reading and writing directions, **THEN** they should complete the Real-Life Resources activity.

RETELLING

Text Experts

Arrange students in small groups, and ask one student in each group to become an expert on a different part of the text. For example, in a group of five, one student could take responsibility for everything up through "A New Assignment," a second could take responsibility for pages 406–411; a third for pages 412–414; a fourth for pages 415–421; and a fifth for page 422 through the end. Then have each individual share his or her expertise with the group. LISTENING/SPEAKING

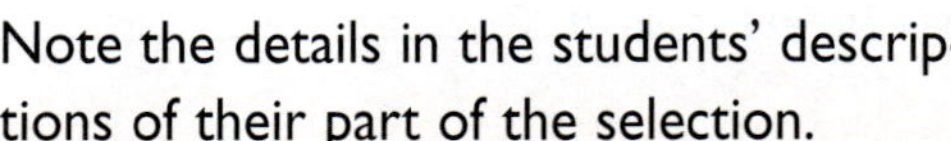

Informal Assessment

Note the details in the students' descriptions of their part of the selection.

ORAL LANGUAGE

Talk Show

Suggest that students work in small groups to present a talk show. Students can choose the roles of host, Sara Bisel, Dr. Maggi, and so on. Ask students to rely on the information they read in the selection to carry out an interview about the disaster at Herculaneum and the experts who studied the remains of its inhabitants. Allow students time to rehearse before making their presentation to the class. Classmates in the "audience" should be encouraged to participate by asking their own questions of the experts. LISTENING/SPEAKING

TIPS FOR LISTENING AND SPEAKING

Remind talk show participants that during their presentation they should

- ask appropriate questions and give appropriate answers.
- speak clearly and concisely.
- use accurate information from the selection in their questions and answers.

As they **listen**, audience members should

- recognize facts from the selection.
- formulate questions of their own to ask.

VIEWING

Video/Documentary

Have students watch an audiovisual presentation about Mount Vesuvius. One excellent choice is *Rome and Pompeii*, in which the devastation of Pompeii by fiery lava is dramatically recreated. Another choice is *In the Shadow of Vesuvius* (National Geographic, 1989), which describes how the volcano affects the lives of the approximately two million people who live in its shadow today. Before students view the video you select, invite them to complete the first column of a two-column chart such as the one shown. When they finish viewing the video, have them complete the second column. Invite students to discuss in small groups what they learned.

LISTENING/SPEAKING/WRITING/VIEWING

Prior Knowledge About Vesuvius	New Knowledge About Vesuvius

REAL-LIFE RESOURCES

Directions for Performing a Process

READING DIRECTIONS Write the directions below on the board. Discuss how following each step helps you complete the process accurately. Talk about what might happen if you do the steps out of order or skip a step.

How to Make a Mosaic Tray

1. Sketch a design on a wooden breadboard.
2. Glue tiny square ceramic tiles to the board. Use permanent adhesive.
3. Fill in the spaces between the tiles with a thin mixture of mosaic cement and water.
4. Wipe off excess cement with a sponge.

WRITING DIRECTIONS Students can work in teams to write directions for completing an art project. Suggest that they begin by listing all of the necessary materials and then describe the steps in the process. See *Writer's Magazine* pages 60 and 61.

REAL-LIFE CHALLENGE Have students try to follow another team's directions. As they work, they should note unclear or missing steps. **READING/ART**

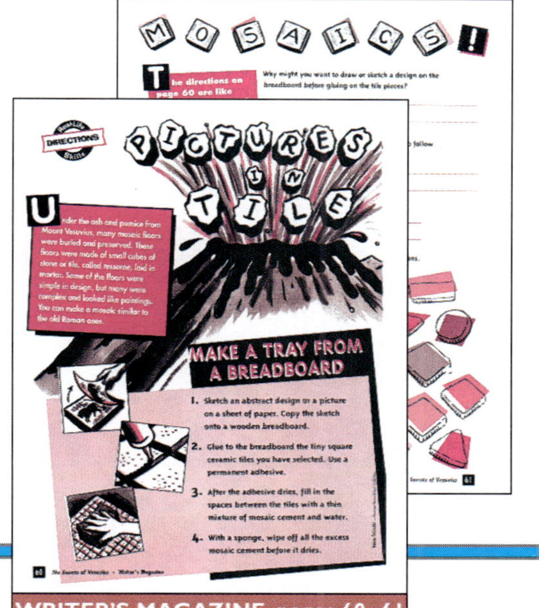
MOSAICS!

The directions on page 60 are like

Why might you want to draw or sketch a design on the breadboard *before* gluing on the tile pieces?

DIRECTIONS

PICTURES IN TILE

Under the ash and pumice from Mount Vesuvius, many mosaic floors were buried and preserved. These floors were made of small cubes of stone or tile, called *tesserae*, laid in mortar. Some of the floors were simple in design, but many were complex and looked like paintings. You can make a mosaic similar to the old Roman ones.

MAKE A TRAY FROM A BREADBOARD

1. Sketch an abstract design or a picture on a sheet of paper. Copy the sketch onto a wooden breadboard.
2. Glue to the breadboard the tiny square ceramic tiles you have selected. Use a permanent adhesive.
3. After the adhesive dries, fill in the spaces between the tiles with a thin mixture of mosaic cement and water.
4. With a sponge, wipe off all the excess mosaic cement before it dries.

WRITER'S MAGAZINE, pages 60–61

STUDENTS ACQUIRING ENGLISH

Students participating in the Retelling activity may wish to become the expert on the first of the text assignments.

EXTRA SUPPORT

Write the Tips for Listening and Speaking on chart paper, and display them in the classroom. Remind students to refer to the tips while they participate in the talk show.

WRITER'S WORKSHOP

Research Report

Thinking as Writers

WRITING FORM: Research Report Remind students that the author of "The Secrets of Vesuvius" presented factual information. Explain to students that in informational writing, such as a research report, a writer gathers information from a variety of sources, takes detailed notes, and then prepares an outline from those notes. Tell students that they are going to learn about a research report and then write one.

Display Transparency 40 and discuss the main parts of an outline. Explain to students that an outline is helpful in organizing a writer's thoughts. Ideas can be organized by main topics, subtopics, and supporting details.

TRANSPARENCY 40

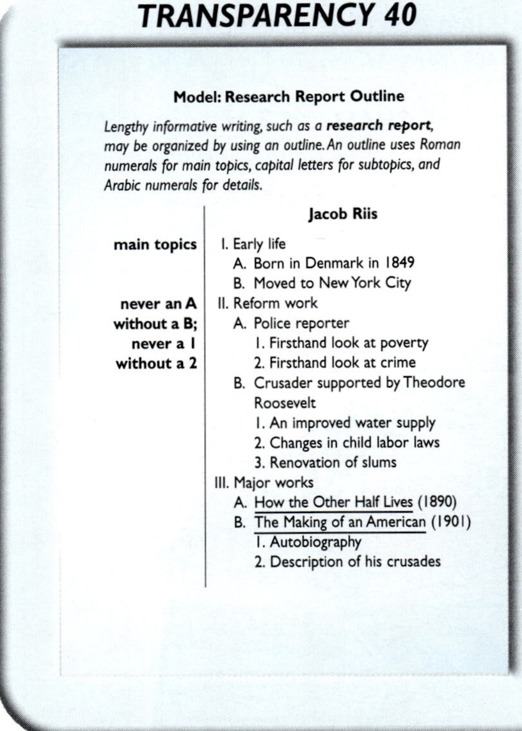

Model: Research Report Outline

Lengthy informative writing, such as a ***research report****, may be organized by using an outline. An outline uses Roman numerals for main topics, capital letters for subtopics, and Arabic numerals for details.*

Jacob Riis

main topics

I. Early life
- A. Born in Denmark in 1849
- B. Moved to New York City

never an A without a B; never a 1 without a 2

II. Reform work
- A. Police reporter
  - 1. Firsthand look at poverty
  - 2. Firsthand look at crime
- B. Crusader supported by Theodore Roosevelt
  - 1. An improved water supply
  - 2. Changes in child labor laws
  - 3. Renovation of slums

III. Major works
- A. How the Other Half Lives (1890)
- B. The Making of an American (1901)
  - 1. Autobiography
  - 2. Description of his crusades

WRITER'S CRAFT: Logical Order Explain that the details included in a research report should be presented in a logical order. Students may notice the logical retelling of events in time order in "The Secrets of Vesuvius" (first paragraph, page 408—Vesuvius erupted, gas and ash spewed out and formed a cloud, the cloud cooled and collapsed, and so on).

PREWRITING AND DRAFTING

Suggest students pick a topic having to do with an exploration of some kind. Remind them to introduce the topic in the first paragraph and to end the research report with a summarizing statement. Refer to these strategies to help students begin their research reports.

PREWRITING STRATEGIES Students who do not have a clear idea for a research report may brainstorm a list of topics that interest them. Once they have chosen a topic, they may use an inverted pyramid to narrow the focus.

PREWRITING GRAPHIC ORGANIZER Some students may benefit from taking notes on a separate index card for each main idea.

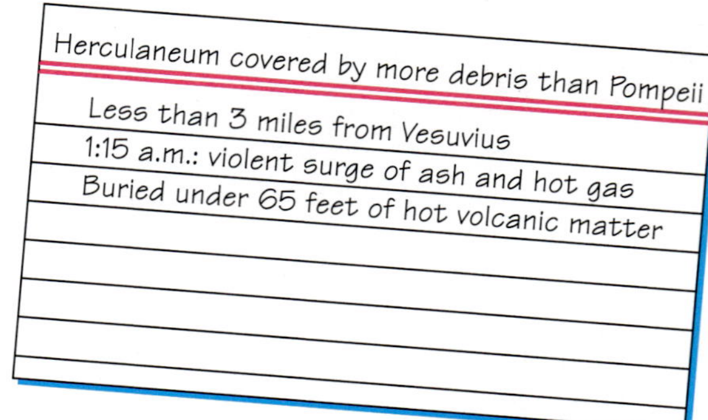

DURING-WRITING GRAPHIC ORGANIZER Students who need to organize their research reports by sequence of events may pause during writing to create a time line of events.

TIPS FOR CLASSROOM MANAGEMENT

IF students are familiar with the steps for writing a research report, **THEN** have them begin writing, referring to the model on Transparency 40 as necessary.

IF you want a short writing activity, **THEN** adapt this lesson by having students focus on the Writer's Craft.

TECHNOLOGY

THE AMAZING WRITING MACHINE Have students enter their research reports.

RESPONDING AND REVISING

Have students work in editing circles or with partners to help one another revise. Write this checklist on the board:

- Does your research report begin with an introductory paragraph?
- Do the paragraphs present ideas that support the main topic?
- Do details in each paragraph support the subtopics?
- Are details presented in a logical order?
- Did you conclude your research report with a summarizing statement?

PROOFREADING

Offer the following tips as students proofread:

- Check for correct use of **main** and **helping verbs**. (See Grammar Minilesson on page T831.)
- Check for correct use of parentheses and other punctuation.
- Look for words you may have misspelled.

PUBLISHING

If you wish to have students publish their research reports, suggest the following options, or have students choose their own methods:

ORAL Students may hold a lecture series for the class based on the information they researched. Have students who chose similar topics form small groups. Group members can read their reports to one another and identify the information their lecture will include.

WRITTEN Display completed reports on the bulletin board under the heading *FYI*.

PORTFOLIO OPPORTUNITY

Have students answer the Self-Assessment questions and include both their answers and their research reports in their portfolios.

LANGUAGE HANDBOOK

Gathering Ideas and Information, page 15; Writing to Inform, pages 60–61; Research Report, pages 72–77; Main and Helping Verbs, pages 148–149

Student Self-Assessment ✓

Have students answer the following questions and include the answers in their portfolios:

- ☑ What did you learn from writing your research report?
- ☑ What will you do differently the next time you write a research report?

EVALUATION BENCHMARKS: RESEARCH REPORT

A research report by a proficient student writer shows the following characteristics:

FORM	CRAFT	CONVENTIONS
Demonstrates understanding of the form • clearly defined topic • supporting details • details presented in logical order • clear summarizing statement	**Uses clear and appropriate language** • time-order words used effectively	**Follows conventions of grammar and usage** • main and helping verbs used correctly • parentheses used correctly

Teacher Assessment As you assess students' writing, refer to the Evaluation Benchmarks chart. For additional information, including model papers, see *Integrated Performance Assessment* Teacher's Edition.

2

SPELLING

5-Day Plan

Integrated Spelling Lesson 22:
student book, pages 94–97;
Teacher's Edition, pages T147–T152.

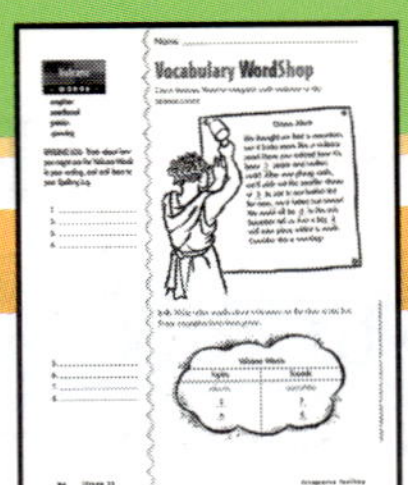
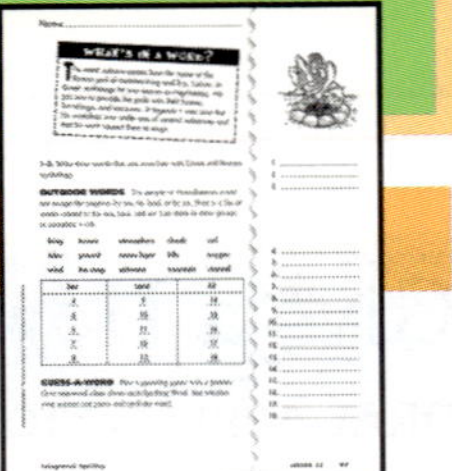

SPELLING WORDS

1. contact ★
2. comfort ★
3. comment
4. contain ★
5. connected
6. complete ★
7. continued ★
8. commercial
9. consider
10. constantly ★
11. commander
12. construction ★
13. constitution
14. conclusion ★
15. communicate
16. committee

STUDENT'S PERSONAL WORDS

17.
18.
19.
20.

Additional story words are *completely, common, contents, constant, containing,* and *conclusions.*

★ Words appearing in "The Secrets of Vesuvius"

Prefix: *com-* (*con-*)

Pretest

DAY 1 **Administer the pretest.** Say each word, and then use it in the dictation sentence below. Help students self-check their pretests.

OPEN SORT

DAY 2 **Have students classify words.** Invite students to think of ways to sort the Spelling Words. For example, students might sort according to the number of syllables or according to the presence or absence of a suffix.

CLOSED SORT

Sort by prefix. Write the headings from the following chart on the board, and have volunteers write each Spelling Word under the correct heading. Then invite students to name other words that might be placed under each heading.

compare	**control**
comfort	contact
comment	contain
complete	connected
commercial	continued
commander	consider
communicate	constantly
committee	construction
	constitution
	conclusion

Teach/Model

DAY 3 **Discuss the generalization.** Explain that many words contain the prefix *com-* or *con-*. Write these words on the board, and underline the prefix in each:

<u>con</u>tact <u>com</u>plete

Tell students that these two prefixes have the same meaning but that the prefix *con-* is used when the second syllable begins with a hard *c* or *g* sound, *n, s,* or *t*. The prefix *com-* is used when the second syllable begins with *m, p,* or *f*.

DAY 4 **Apply to writing.** Students should look for words with the prefix *com- (con-)* in their research reports to see if they are spelled correctly.

Posttest

DAY 5 **Assess students' progress.** The sentences below should be used as the posttest.

PRACTICE BOOK, page 123

DICTATION SENTENCES

1. Mr. Kunkelman is our <u>contact</u> in Berlin.
2. The child ran to his dad for <u>comfort</u>.
3. Mrs. Chin would not <u>comment</u> on her recipe.
4. Those books <u>contain</u> information about frogs.
5. Are you <u>connected</u> to an on-line service?
6. Do you have a <u>complete</u> set of dominoes?
7. Keiko <u>continued</u> to practice every day.
8. That <u>commercial</u> advertises facial tissues.
9. I will <u>consider</u> your offer carefully.
10. The shoreline is <u>constantly</u> changing.
11. I wrote to the <u>commander</u> of the armed forces.
12. The new highway <u>construction</u> is moving along slowly.
13. Not every country has a <u>constitution</u>.
14. The police drew a logical <u>conclusion</u> from the evidence.
15. We <u>communicate</u> by telephone and fax.
16. That <u>committee</u> raises money for the library.

VOCABULARY WORKSHOP

Reviewing Key Words

Display a chart like the one below. Ask students to explore who or what might fit each category:

Who or What . . .
might collapse?
might be intricate?
might feel awe?
might be extinct?

Extending Vocabulary

SPECIALIZED VOCABULARY: SOCIAL STUDIES WORDS

Write on the board the words *archaeologist, excavates, artifact*, and *trowel*. Ask students how these words are all related. (They all relate to archaeology, or the study of past times and cultures.) Invite students to help you complete the following sequence chain. Provide definitions and clues as needed.

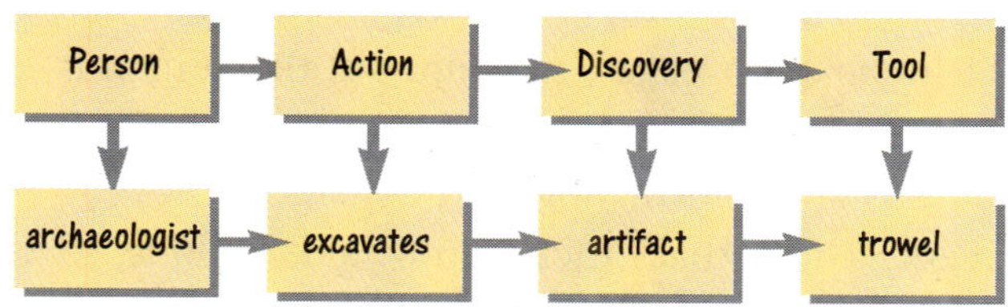

Invite students to work in pairs to make a web showing the relationship between these words and suggest they add other words.

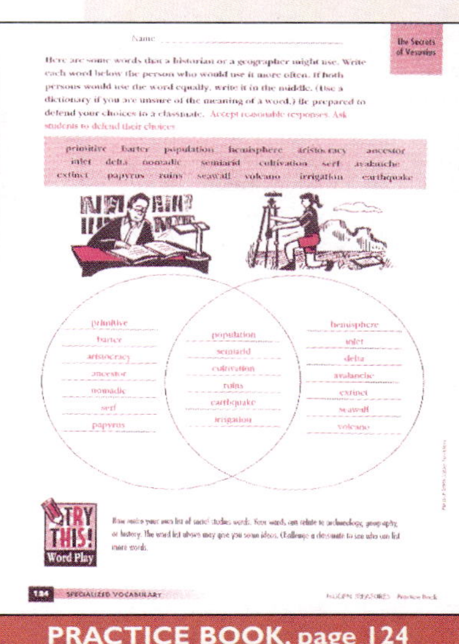

PRACTICE BOOK, page 124

3 Learning Through the Literature

Informal Assessment ✓

Are students able to

- ☑ interpret maps, charts, diagrams, and other graphic aids?
- ☑ create a graphic aid, such as a time line?

INTRODUCE: STUDY SKILLS

Graphic Aids

OBJECTIVE: To interpret information from a graphic aid

Teach/Model

Return to the literature. Have students look at the map on page 410. Point out that a map is one kind of **graphic aid** that can help readers understand information in the material they read. Explain that other graphic aids include graphs, diagrams, charts, tables, schedules, and time lines.

Model interpreting a graphic aid. Explain to students that graphic aids can show many things, such as how something works, how things are connected, important dates and events, and comparisons and contrasts. Model using the information shown on the map on page 410:

MODEL **The map on page 410 helps me visualize where Mount Vesuvius is in relation to Herculaneum and Pompeii. The smaller inset map shows me where Mount Vesuvius is in relation to the rest of Italy. This helps me as I read the selection.**

Have students look through the selection and explain how the various graphic aids helped them gain understanding as they read. (Accept reasonable responses.)

Practice/Apply

Have students demonstrate understanding. Draw on the board a time line like the one below.

Have students look through "The Secrets of Vesuvius" to fill in an important event in the history of Herculaneum for each date listed. Invite students to research other events to add to the time line.

Time Line of Herculaneum

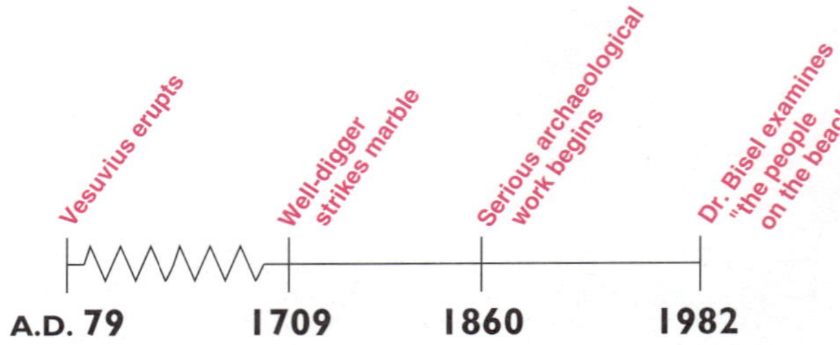

Practice Activities

Map Makers

COOPERATIVE LEARNING Divide the class into cooperative groups of five or more students. Challenge each group to draw to scale a map of the playground, classroom, gym, auditorium, or other part of the school. Encourage students to include a key or legend, scale bar, and compass rose with their maps. Students may want to use their social studies textbooks or atlases as reference sources for types of maps. Have groups exchange their finished maps and interpret them. VISUAL/AUDITORY/KINESTHETIC

Tell Me About It

PERFORMANCE ASSESSMENT Ask students to find a chart, map, or diagram in a literature selection, textbook, or other source they have read recently and interpret it orally. VISUAL/AUDITORY

STUDENTS ACQUIRING ENGLISH

As needed, point out and make concrete connections between the places and objects on group maps and the labels that represent them.

RETEACH

See page R11 for lessons in multiple modalities.

CHALLENGE

Encourage students to create a labeled diagram showing the steps in the process of buying lunch at the cafeteria.

Pompeii by Peter Connolly. Oxford University Press, 1990. AVERAGE

The Romans by Pamela Odijk. Macmillan, 1989. AVERAGE

Volcano & Earthquake by Susanna Van Rose. Knopf, 1992. EASY

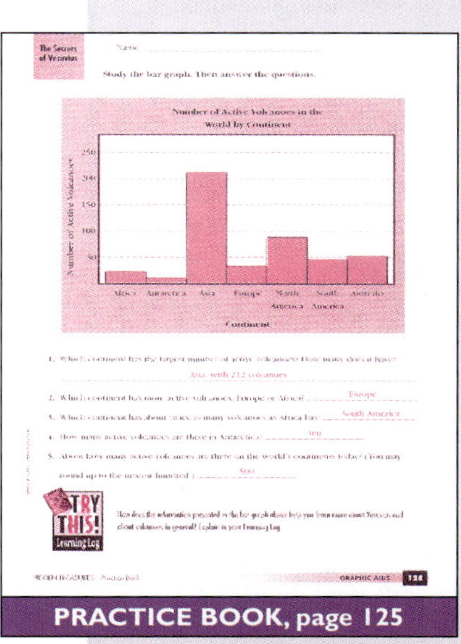

The Secrets of Vesuvius

Name

Study the bar graph. Then answer the questions.

1. Which continent has the largest number of active volcanoes? How many does it have? Asia, with 212 volcanoes
2. Which continent has more active volcanoes, Europe or Africa? Europe
3. Which continent has about twice as many volcanoes as Africa has? South America
4. How many active volcanoes are there in Antarctica? 10
5. About how many active volcanoes are there on the world's continents today? (You may round up to the nearest hundred.) 500

TRY THIS! Learning Log

How does the information presented in the bar graph above help you learn more about Vesuvius and about volcanoes in general? Explain in your Learning Log.

HIDDEN TREASURES Practice Book GRAPHIC AIDS 125

PRACTICE BOOK, page 125

Integrated Curriculum

SOCIAL STUDIES

Archaeology

TIPS FOR CLASSROOM MANAGEMENT

IF students are artistically inclined, **THEN** have them complete the Diorama activity.

TECHNOLOGY

THINKIN' THINGS COLLECTION 3
Students can use The Case of the Empty Fripple House program to help them practice deductive reasoning before they complete the Skeleton Keys activity.

Remind students that Sara Bisel is an anthropologist and archaeologist who studies the remains of people who lived long ago and deduces information from those remains. The following activities lead students to understand the lives people lived in places like Herculaneum.

SOCIAL STUDIES/ART

Make a Diorama

Ask students to work in pairs or groups to create a diorama of a Roman villa. To begin, students can find pictures of and information about villas in this selection and in "City: A Story of Roman Planning and Construction." Ask students to consider the floor plan of such a home, the number and position of windows, the relative sizes of rooms, and other architectural details. Students might also include decorative features such as mosaics and fountains. Provide an opportunity for pairs or groups to share their dioramas and explain what they show.

LISTENING/SPEAKING

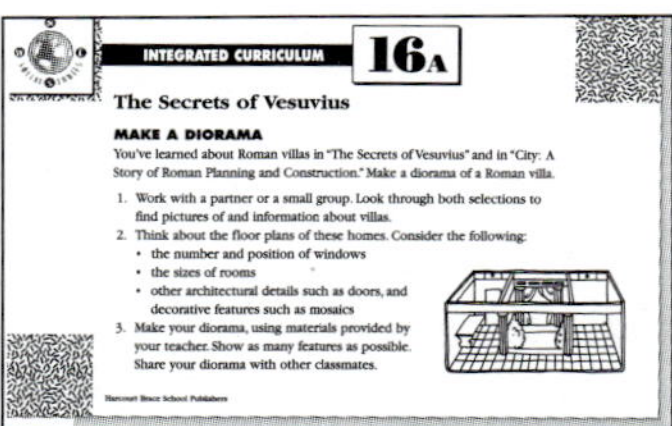
INTEGRATED CURRICULUM 16A

The Secrets of Vesuvius

MAKE A DIORAMA

You've learned about Roman villas in "The Secrets of Vesuvius" and in "City: A Story of Roman Planning and Construction." Make a diorama of a Roman villa.

1. Work with a partner or a small group. Look through both selections to find pictures of and information about villas.
2. Think about the floor plans of these homes. Consider the following:
   - the number and position of windows
   - the sizes of rooms
   - other architectural details such as doors, and decorative features such as mosaics
3. Make your diorama, using materials provided by your teacher. Show as many features as possible. Share your diorama with other classmates.

Harcourt Brace School Publishers

Curriculum Card 16A

SOCIAL STUDIES

Ancient Civilizations

COOPERATIVE LEARNING Divide the class into six groups, and assign one of these early civilizations to each: Maya (Central America), Inca (Peru), Nile Valley, Lower Mesopotamia, Indus, and Shang. Have two Researchers in each group locate books, encyclopedias, or other research materials about the civilization. Assign two Readers in each group to use book parts such as table of contents, index, glossary, captions, maps, and illustrations to find out what was unique about each civilization, where and when the civilization flourished, what caused its downfall, and what the roles of various members in the society were. Have a Summarizer in each group combine the information into a short report. Then invite a Reporter from each group to share the knowledge with the rest of the class.

LISTENING/SPEAKING

Photo far right: Mayan observatory, Chichén Itzá, Mexico.
Near right: Incan stone wall, Peru.

Reading Trade Books

CROSS-CURRICULAR READING

Digging to the Past: Excavations in Ancient Lands by W. John Hackwell. Charles Scribner's Sons, 1986.
CHALLENGING

SUNK! *Exploring Underwater Archaeology*. Runestone, 1994.
AVERAGE

SCIENCE

Skeleton Keys

Bones tell archaeologists a great deal. Invite the class to work together to plan and organize a chart, collage, or diagram that tells how bones unlock secrets for archaeologists. Students can begin gathering information about what bones tell by rereading or skimming "The Secrets of Vesuvius." They might also use additional resources from the school or local library. When students finish their display, they should work together to create a title for it.

LISTENING/ SPEAKING/ WRITING

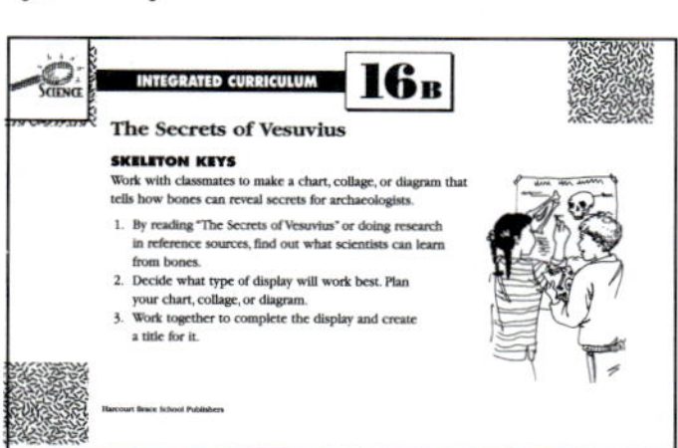
SCIENCE INTEGRATED CURRICULUM 16B

The Secrets of Vesuvius

SKELETON KEYS

Work with classmates to make a chart, collage, or diagram that tells how bones can reveal secrets for archaeologists.

1. By reading "The Secrets of Vesuvius" or doing research in reference sources, find out what scientists can learn from bones.
2. Decide what type of display will work best. Plan your chart, collage, or diagram.
3. Work together to complete the display and create a title for it.

Harcourt Brace School Publishers

Curriculum Card 16B

Above: Egyptian archaeology
Right: Dinosaur National Park, Utah

MULTI-AGE CLASSROOMS

Older students acquiring English may not be as fluent as younger students who speak the same home language. Grouping these students to work on various activities may aid in increasing communication.

Reading Trade Books

Other Trade Books That Connect to "The Secrets of Vesuvius"

TIPS FOR CLASSROOM MANAGEMENT

SMALL-GROUP READING Students might work together to read and take notes on one of the nonfiction books. Group roles might include Reader, Summarizer, and Recorder. Students might take turns looking up unfamiliar words.

The Dragon in the Cliff

by Sheila Cole

Readers can compare the archaeological methods presented in this book about nineteenth-century paleontology with those used by Sara Bisel in "The Secrets of Vesuvius." Suggest that students create a chart to show similarities and differences.

Roman Places

by Sarah Howarth

Students may want to write their thoughts about what it might have been like to live in ancient Rome. How would their daily lives be different?

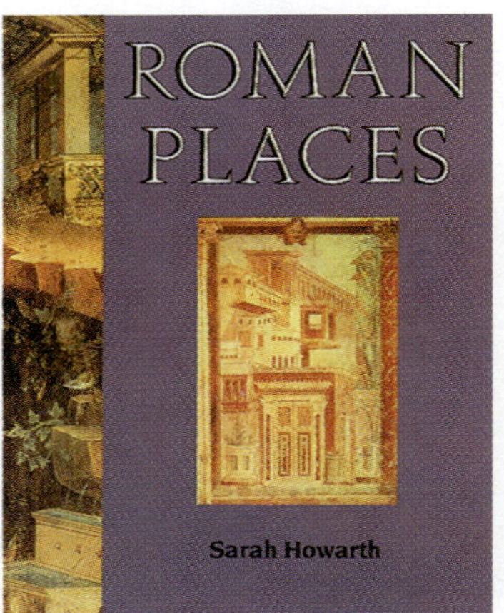

STUDENTS ACQUIRING ENGLISH

Suggest that students work with a partner to read *Volcanoes*. Encourage readers to watch for social studies and science words that appear in both this book and in "The Secrets of Vesuvius."

The Romans and Pompeii

by Philip Steele

After reading this introduction to Roman life and the destruction of Pompeii, students might want to discuss the methods scientists and historians use to gather information about ancient cultures. Students might debate a statement such as "We can never know what it was like to live in ancient Rome."

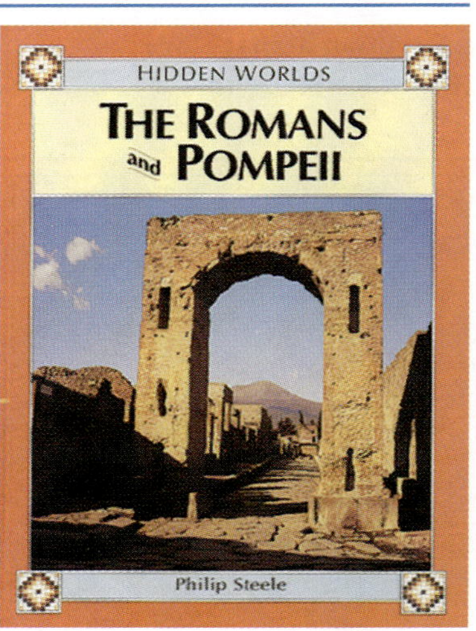

The Shark Callers

by Eric Campbell

This adventure novel tells about the events surrounding a volcanic eruption near Papua, New Guinea. After reading this fictional account, students might be inspired to write their own stories set during the eruption of Mount Vesuvius. Remind them to use facts and details from "The Secrets of Vesuvius."

Surtsey: The Newest Place on Earth

by Kathryn Lasky
photographs by Christopher G. Knight

Dramatic photos help to tell this story of the birth of an island near Iceland in 1963. Encourage students to draw diagrams to compare the effects of Surtsey's fiery beginning with Mount Vesuvius's violent eruption.

Volcanoes

by Seymour Simon

This nonfiction book provides a clear description of what makes volcanoes erupt. After reading, suggest that students create a chain-of-events chart that shows each stage of the eruption of Mount Vesuvius.

CHALLENGE

Have students locate another book or reference source about volcanoes or their aftermath. Ask each student to share the findings with the class. Then discuss how these books and sources tie to the theme Turning Points.

THEME PROJECT CHECKPOINT 4

Write Group Reports

SELECTION CONNECTION

In "The Secrets of Vesuvius," archaeologist Sara Bisel learns about Roman history by examining skeletons and artifacts that are almost two thousand years old. Invite students to tell what they have learned about their community from its historical artifacts.

PROJECT CHECKLIST

During this stage, students should

- ☑ assign roles to individual members for the group's cooperative work.
- ☑ decide together how to organize the report.
- ☑ assign responsibilities for parts of the report to individual members.
- ☑ write a final group report about changes in their community.

Project Card 23 can be found as a copying master on page R27.

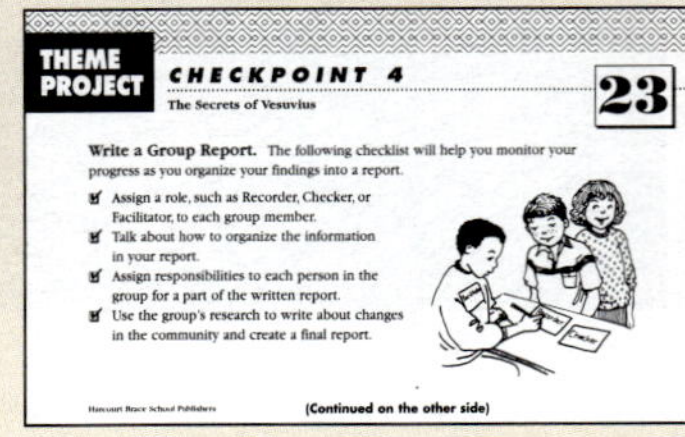

THEME PROJECT

CHECKPOINT 4

The Secrets of Vesuvius

23

Write a Group Report. The following checklist will help you monitor your progress as you organize your findings into a report.

- ☑ Assign a role, such as Recorder, Checker, or Facilitator, to each group member.
- ☑ Talk about how to organize the information in your report.
- ☑ Assign responsibilities to each person in the group for a part of the written report.
- ☑ Use the group's research to write about changes in the community and create a final report.

Harcourt Brace School Publishers

(Continued on the other side)

Project Card 23

RESEARCH AND PLANNING TIPS

As groups prepare to write the report, suggest that students

- use their charts to help them organize report information.
- assign Checkers to proofread the final report and to check facts against research notes.
- assign a Facilitator to make sure the group keeps working and to settle disputes.

Suggest that as the group writes its report students use their project journals to plan how they will complete their task. Encourage students to respond to questions such as *What is my most important job?*

Informal Assessment

At this checkpoint, groups will **synthesize** information they have gathered and write their final report. Students are thinking critically if they

- ☑ can make valid decisions about what information to include in the report.
- ☑ can synthesize information from different sources.
- ☑ can write clearly and logically about changes in the community.

PROJECT MANAGEMENT

STUDENTS ACQUIRING ENGLISH

Students can design a cover and illustrations for their group's report with pictures showing one or more community changes.

EXTRA SUPPORT

Make sure students understand that a first draft's purpose is to get ideas down on paper. Encourage them to rely on the Checkers to help edit the revised draft.

TECHNOLOGY

THE AMAZING WRITING MACHINE

Suggest that students use the Essay feature to write their reports so they will be able to revise, edit, and spell-check them easily.

THEME

The people and communities in this theme are going through changes. Which of the people reach a turning point in their lives, and how does it come about? How do the communities change? What is the result of each change?

What kinds of things would Dr. Sara Bisel have uncovered if the site of her dig had been the city in "City: A Story of Roman Planning and Construction?"

ACTIVITY CORNER

Imagine that an archaeologist in the distant future is excavating a site that was once your neighborhood. What interesting objects will he or she find? Make a diorama showing a futuristic museum display of the archaeologist's most unusual finds.

WRAP-UP

THEME 4
Wrap-Up

1. **The people and communities in this theme are going through changes. Which of the people reach turning points in their lives and how does each come about? How do the communities change? What is the result of each change?** (Possible responses: Atalanta's life changes when she meets Hippomenes in a race. A disastrous flood in northern Italy changed the structure of community life when the emperor ordered a city built to replace the villages. The eruption of Mt. Vesuvius completely buried the town of Herculaneum, killing many of its citizens.) CRITICAL: SUMMARIZING

2. **What kinds of things would Dr. Sara Bisel have uncovered if the site of her dig had been the city in "City: A Story of Roman Planning and Construction"?** (Possible response: She would find a walled Roman city with a central forum and market, side streets with shops and workshops, and neighborhoods of houses and shrines.) CRITICAL: SPECULATING

ACTIVITY CORNER Suggest that students work together to plan their dioramas. Students should begin by roughly sketching a map of their neighborhood, noting significant features and objects likely to be around in the distant future.

THEME PROJECT PRESENTATIONS

Options

ORAL HISTORY

- Suggest that students write an oral history of their community, using the words of their interview subjects.
- Students can use information from their library research to write background material for the interviews.
- Help students bind pages into a booklet.
- If possible, make a copy for each student, the school library, the local historical society, and each person whose interview is in the book.

ROLE-PLAY

- Invite students to improvise a role-play based on their interviews.
- Suggest that students make up an imaginary interview subject who has the combined knowledge of all the interview subjects as well as knowledge from research sources.
- Have students prepare questions about a range of community changes.
- Students can rehearse their role-plays and then visit other classrooms to perform them.

Community Connections

By sharing their work with the community, students will have an opportunity to see that they themselves are valuable members of the community, while creating an avenue of communication between the generations. These suggestions will help students share their projects:

- Have students turn their reports into museum displays by mounting the pages of their reports on large sheets of poster board.
- Encourage them to add drawings, photographs, or charts to illustrate their reports. If they taped interviews, they can make the tapes available.
- Suggest that students invite community members to visit their museum.
- Afterward, students can lend their museum exhibits to the public library.

SCHOOL↔HOME CONNECTION

Students can plan a Museum Opening to share their projects with family members and friends. Have students create invitations to the Museum Opening, and suggest that they write their invitations in their first language. Family members who cannot attend may wish to contribute old photographs.

To extend their project, students may wish to equip a corner of the classroom with an audio or video recorder and invite visitors to record their memories of community changes.

THEME PROJECT ***PRESENTATION*** **24**

Turning Points

HISTORICAL CHANGES

Community Connections Now that you know how your community has changed over the years, it's time to share your information. Your projects may unite community members and encourage others to share their own memories.

- Turn your reports into museum displays by mounting the pages on poster boards. Illustrate report pages with drawings or photographs.
- If you can borrow historical objects or clothing, add them to your display.
- Invite community members to your museum opening.

(Continued on the other side)

Project Card 24

Project Card 24 can be found as a copying master on page R28.

THEME PROJECT ASSESSMENT

SELF-ASSESSMENT

To assess students' perception of their own performance during this project, ask them to respond to the following questions orally or in writing:

- What did you contribute to the group project?
- Did you finish your tasks on time? If not, explain why.
- What was the most interesting thing you learned? How did you learn it?

Students may also complete the Student Self-Assessment Checklist on page T216 in the Teacher's Edition, Volume 1.

PEER ASSESSMENT

To assess their group's efficiency in working cooperatively during this project, ask students to respond to the following questions orally or in writing:

- Did each person in your group contribute to the theme project? Explain.
- What did you learn from other members of your group?

Students may also complete the Peer-Assessment Checklist on page T408 in the Teacher's Edition, Volume 1.

RUBRIC

Performance Goals	Observable Characteristics 3	2	1
LAUNCH List of things that change	• contributes many examples of personal and community changes	• may have difficulty generating community changes	• tries to avoid offering ideas for the chart
CHECKPOINT 1 Research on community changes	• takes notes that are concise, to the point, and well organized	• notes are appropriate, but lengthy or copied directly from source	• takes notes which are not appropriate for the research question
CHECKPOINT 2 Comparison chart	• takes the lead in designing a chart to organize information	• helps organize information after chart has been designed	• is unable to help the group organize information
CHECKPOINT 3 Resolving contradictions and revising chart	• takes the lead in assessing sources and resolving contradictions	• may not understand how to resolve contradictions, but helps revise chart	• does not offer suggestions for revising chart
CHECKPOINT 4 Group report	• leads discussion of chart and notes • completes tasks appropriate to assigned role	• joins in discussion of chart and notes • completes appropriate tasks after discussion of tasks	• does not contribute to discussion of chart and notes • is unable to complete assigned tasks
PRESENTATIONS Overall project	• is willing to offer ideas or act as leader • completes entire task on time	• cooperates but does not show leadership • finishes on time, but parts of task are incomplete	• lets attention wander or focuses on one idea • does not finish or finishes only parts of assigned tasks

Reading Trade Books
Signatures Library

Wilma Rudolph

by Wayne Coffey

THEME: CHANGES

Turning Points

Wilma Rudolph's metamorphosis from a physically challenged young girl to America's best-loved and most successful Olympic athlete is a story of courage, determination, and the refusal to fail.

SUMMARY **Genre: Biography**

This biography traces Wilma's path to stardom, beginning with her roots in a segregated Southern town, where she was the twentieth of twenty-two children. Polio struck Wilma when she was very young, leaving her severely crippled—she wore a brace for a decade. In a remarkable scene, the biographer tells of the reception at Wilma's church when she walked without her brace for the first time—a true turning point in her life.

She joined the basketball team in seventh grade and in three years became a star. It was through basketball that she was discovered by the man who would coach her to track-and-field victory.

Sixteen-year-old Wilma entered the 1956 Olympic Games in Australia. She failed to place in her event, but never gave up. In the 1960 Olympic Games, no female runner could catch her. She ran away with three gold medals.

ABOUT THE AUTHOR

Wayne Coffey is the author of several nonfiction books for children. His interest in sports, evident in this biography, inspired him to write other sports-themed books.

Building Background and Concepts

Discuss overcoming challenges. Initiate a conversation about personal goals and the obstacles that must be overcome before those goals can be reached. Have students talk about their own ambitions and challenges and then have them suggest some heroes from history, sports, music, or other areas who overcame obstacles to achieve their goals. Use a diagram like this one to map people's achievements.

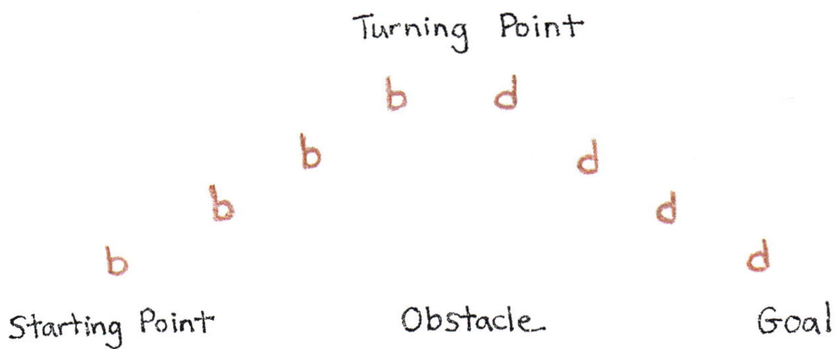

STUDENTS ACQUIRING ENGLISH

Pair students with native English speakers to discuss the captions for the photographs in the center of the book. Have native speakers define any unfamiliar words for their partners, using the pictures as a guide.

Developing Concept Vocabulary

Have students use this vocabulary from the book to generate sentences like the ones below about overcoming obstacles and reaching success.

Overcoming Challenges

overcame	With hard work, we overcame our problems.
effort	All of our effort paid off in the long run.
discipline	It takes discipline to be a success.
faith	You must have faith in your ability.
idols	All of my idols have overcome hardships.

Prefixes that tell position
Integrated Spelling Lesson 23

OTHER VOCABULARY IDEAS

MULTIPLE MEANINGS

Have students look up these multiple-meaning words in the dictionary and record the various definitions they find, circling the ones that have to do with running.

anchor dash relay track

Re•lay (rē′ lā) the act of passing something along from one person, group or station to another.

CHARACTER ACRONYMS

Ask students to write the letters of Wilma's name vertically and use each one as the first letter of an adjective that describes her personality.

Willing
Independent
Loyal
Magnificent
Active

OPTIONS FOR

FLEXIBLE GROUPING

	SMALL GROUPS	WHOLE CLASS	INDEPENDENT
PREVIEW AND PREDICT	Have students use the pictures in the book to answer these **character questions.** • Who is the main character? • Why is she famous? Students can use Reader Response Card 9, Literature Circles, to help them conduct group discussions.	Have students read the title aloud and skim the pictures. Work together to complete a set of **prediction questions** to be answered while reading.	Have students skim the pictures and **quickwrite** their predictions about the story genre and content. QUICKWRITE
CHAPTER 1	Have groups **explain** the way Wilma Rudolph exemplifies the title of this chapter: "Courage and Determination."	Explain that this first chapter is a summary of Wilma's life. Have volunteers **retell** the chapter events in time order. Discuss the fact that the chapter does not follow time order, but skips back and forth.	Have students create a **time line** and plug specific details from the chapter into their correct locations. WILMA'S LIFE childhood teenage years adulthood
CHAPTERS 2-3	Assign students in each group a subtitled section of each chapter for which to be responsible. As you call out each subtitle, one student should **summarize** the facts given in the section.	Make a **before-and-after diagram** that shows some important turning points in Wilma's life. Before / After Wilma could not walk. / She could run and play. Wilma watched kids play basketball. / Wilma started to play herself. Basketball season ended. / Wilma took up running.	PERSONAL JOURNAL Have students record adjectives in their **personal journals** that describe Wilma's character.

TIPS FOR CLASSROOM MANAGEMENT

IF students are reading at different levels, **THEN** you may want to begin with whole-class activities and move into small groups.

IF some students need to expand their social skills, **THEN** you might choose group activities in which they are encouraged to participate with others.

READING

FLEXIBLE GROUPING

	SMALL GROUPS	WHOLE CLASS	INDEPENDENT
CHAPTERS 4-5	Ask students to choose one subsection from these two chapters and write about it in a **news article**. One member of each group could draw a picture and caption it, one could write the headline, and the others could work together to write the article. Share the results with the class. Students can use Reader Response Card 9, Literature Circles, to help them conduct group discussions.	Have students work together to write in their own words an **interpretation** of the statement: "...truly successful people are the ones who learn how to lose." Have them explain it from Wilma's point of view and from their own experiences.	Have students **write a letter** home from Wilma's point of view on her first trip north, to Philadelphia.

PERSONAL RESPONSE 

- **What personal characteristics make Wilma Rudolph a good subject for a biography?**
- **What other facts about Wilma Rudolph's life would you like to know? How could you find out?**

RESPONSE

Celebrating: *Wilma Rudolph*

INTRODUCING WILMA RUDOLPH

LANGUAGE ARTS Have students pretend that they have been selected to introduce Wilma Rudolph as a speaker at a banquet. On note cards, have them outline the introductory speech they might give. Provide class time for students to present their speeches aloud. **WRITING/SPEAKING**

Taking Words Apart

STRUCTURAL ANALYSIS: PREFIXES/SUFFIXES/ROOTS Give students these three words from the story:

prematurely   unattractive   international

Discuss the meaning of each word. Show students how to reduce the first word to prefix + root word + suffix: *pre* + *mature* + *ly.* Have them do the same with the other two words. Then challenge them to write three more words that contain both a prefix and a suffix. **READING/WRITING**

un + attract + ive   inter + national

HOW FAST IS FAST?

MATH Have students refer to an almanac to find Olympic or world records in various years for women in track and field. Ask them to display the information in the form of a graph, choosing one sport to feature and showing changes over time. **READING/WRITING/VIEWING**

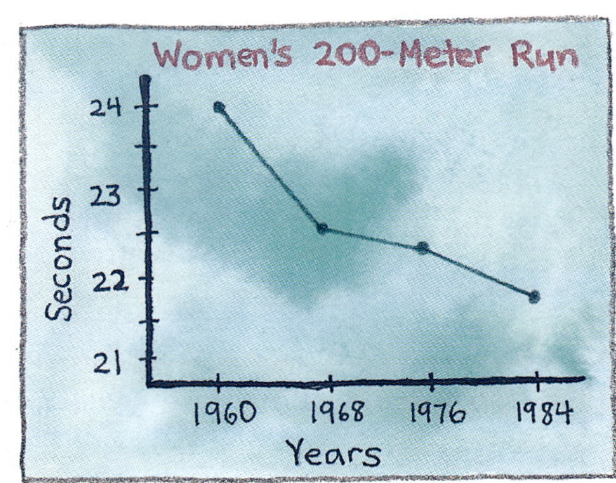

ACTIVITIES

Family Heroes

HOME-SCHOOL CONNECTION Discuss the qualities that make Wilma Rudolph a hero. Ask students to interview family members to find out who their heroes are and why. Students should take notes on their findings and use them to write a brief report on family heroes.

LISTENING/ SPEAKING/WRITING

Dear Olympic Committee

SOCIAL STUDIES Have students look up the Olympics in an almanac or encyclopedia to find out where it has been held in the past. Then have them choose a city anywhere in the world where the Olympics has never been held and write a letter to the Olympic Committee proposing that they hold the Olympics there sometime in the future. Students can use guide books and reference books to learn more about the city they chose in order to write a convincing letter.

READING/WRITING

Dear Olympic Committee:
I would like to propose that you hold a future Winter Games in Spokane, Washington...

My Key Events

ART Review the photo insert in *Wilma Rudolph*. Ask students to decide what photographs they would include if they were writing about their own lives. What important events would they portray? Why? Have them design a "photo spread" containing six photos or illustrations with captions explaining the event pictured and its importance in their lives.

WRITING/VIEWING

When I was nine, I talked at a Board of Education meeting about our school recycling plan. It was the first time I ever had to speak in front of a crowd.

Reading Trade Books
Signatures Library

Detectives in Togas

by Henry Winterfeld

THEME: CHANGES

Turning Points

The sudden calamity that is the focus of *Detectives in Togas* proves to be a turning point for all the characters. The schoolboys learn to value each other's skills and accommodate each other's weaknesses, and even their teacher learns the value of a hearty laugh.

SUMMARY Genre: Historical Fiction

When their classmate Rufus is accused of a crime, it is up to Mucius, Flavius, Antonius, Julius, and Publius to find the real criminal before Rufus is put aboard a galley ship and sent away forever. Despite his denial of the crime, Rufus *had been* out all night when the desecration occurred, and he will not tell where he was. Strangest of all, someone reported the crime to the newspaper—before it happened!

As the boys work together to solve the mystery, they are faced with a number of challenges from powerful men and a dangerous political climate. Using their personal skills, the classmates race against time to save their friend, uncovering a terrible plot by a desperate man.

ABOUT THE AUTHOR

Henry Winterfeld was born and raised in Germany but moved to the United States in 1940. Many of his books for children, including *Detectives in Togas*, were written in German and later translated.

Winterfeld wrote his first book for children, *Trouble at Timpetill*, to entertain his young son. He says, "Since then I have written only children's books. It's painful but I do it because I love children so much. Most of my best friends are children."

Building Background and Concepts

Contrast childhood in the past with childhood today. Talk to students about the changes that occur between childhood and adulthood in the present culture. In their opinion, when does the turning point between childhood and adulthood occur? How is it different today than it was in ancient times? Students might use a diagram like this one to contrast the times.

	Now	Long Ago	Turning Point
Children	go to school	go to school if rich work if poor	around college age
Adults	go to work	soldiers or rulers work if poor	early teenage

Developing Concept Vocabulary

Students can connect vocabulary from the story to the theme by matching words to synonyms and then using the words in sentences of their own about the change from childhood to adulthood.

Entering Adulthood	
1. citizen (e)	a. trained
2. educated (a)	b. manner
3. character (b)	c. self
4. identity (c)	d. behavior
5. conduct (d)	e. resident

(Sentences will vary.)

STUDENTS ACQUIRING ENGLISH

Students from other countries may have a good sense of what it means to be a citizen. Have them share their experiences with the class as classmates share the meanings of the other concept words with them.

SPELLING GENERALIZATION

Prefixes that tell position

Integrated Spelling Lesson 23

OTHER VOCABULARY IDEAS

THE SIGHTS OF ROME

Have students record words that name specific sights of ancient Rome—from *forum* to *arcade*. They can look up the meanings of these words and then draw a picture of ancient Rome labeled with the words they discovered.

ROMAN PYRAMIDS

Students can use story vocabulary to build word pyramids so they can better understand the roots of related words. Encourage them to use a dictionary. They might start with the words *consul* and *senate*.

consul
consulate
consult
consultant
consultation

OPTIONS FOR

FLEXIBLE GROUPING

TIPS FOR CLASSROOM MANAGEMENT

IF some students need extra support, **THEN** you may want to begin by working with small groups before allowing students to read independently.

IF some students are highly proficient readers, **THEN** you might have them read ahead and return to activities when they have completed their reading.

	SMALL GROUPS	WHOLE CLASS	INDEPENDENT
PREVIEW AND PREDICT	Have students skim the artwork in the story and use it to **predict** when the story takes place and who will be involved. Students can use Reader Response Card 9, Literature Circle, to help them conduct group discussions.	Have students read the title aloud. Discuss the kinds of **problems** they expect to find in a detective story. How is it different from other kinds of stories? They might put their thoughts in chart form. (chart) Columns: Detective Stories; Other Stories. Rows: characters; plot	Explain that the title of the book gives significant information about the type of story it is. Have students **quickwrite** a list of word associations to the words *detectives* and *togas*. QUICKWRITE
CHAPTERS 1-4	Have groups discuss the **problem** that faces the boys at the end of this cluster of chapters and suggest ways that this connects to the title of the book.	Begin an **attribute list** for each of the characters. Have students add adjectives to the list that qualify each character. (chart) Caius: slow, mean. Antonius: violent, imaginative	Have students choose one character to follow through the chapters. Ask them to record that **character's feelings** about the action throughout the section. Mucius's feelings: surprise, concern, scorn, horror
CHAPTERS 5-10	Ask students to tell **how they would feel** if one of their best friends were in Rufus's situation. Would they believe their friend unconditionally? Would they doubt him or her? What would they do to help?	Make a **cause-and-effect diagram** that explains why Rufus is in trouble. (chart) Cause: Someone painted the wall. The writing looked like Rufus's. Scribonus found that the writing was Rufus's. Effect: Rufus is in trouble.	 Students can record in their **personal journals** the clues that lead to Rufus and the clues that lead away from him. 

READING

FLEXIBLE GROUPING

	SMALL GROUPS	WHOLE CLASS	INDEPENDENT
CHAPTERS 11-15	Students can work in small groups to **act out** the scene in which the boys confront Lukos.	**Discuss** as a class the things about Lukos the Soothsayer that seem suspicious. Record students' suggestions. He has Rufus's cloak. He won't tell the boys anything. He walks oddly.	Have students pretend to be Mucius and **write a letter** from his point of view to tell a faraway friend about his dreadful adventure in Lukos's home and in the baths. Dear Cassius, The most terrible thing happened to me as I was trying to solve a mystery...
CHAPTERS 16-18	Have groups work together to **summarize** what the boys learn in each scene. Discuss how the information helps them or confuses the issue.	To aid in discussion of these long chapters, make a chart in which students can record **settings, characters,** and **main plot events.** Setting / Who Is Involved / What Happens 1. Censor's office 2. Tenement	Remind students that Rufus is still in prison during these scenes. Have them imagine that they could communicate with Rufus and tell him what his friends are doing to help him. Ask them to write the **dialogue** they might have with Rufus.
CHAPTERS 19-22	Discuss what has happened to the **characters** during the course of the novel. How have the characters grown and changed? Who has changed the most? Who has changed the least? Students can use Reader Response Card 9, Literature Circle, to help them conduct group discussions.	Make a **problem-solution chart** to record how the boys solved the mystery. Problem / Actions / Solution Rufus is wrongly accused.	Have students **illustrate** a scene from the final three chapters.

PERSONAL RESPONSE

"Which character would you rather be? Why?
Are you satisfied by the ending of this mystery? Would you have preferred a different ending?"

RESPONSE

Celebrating *Detectives in Togas*

MADE-FOR-TV MOVIE

ART/LANGUAGE ARTS Have students work in small groups to turn a scene into a television script. Students can list settings, characters, and main plot events for the scene and use their lists to create illustrations of the set and write dialogue and stage directions for the script itself. Provide time for students to present a formal reading of their scripts to the class. **SPEAKING/ READING/WRITING/VIEWING**

School Days

COMPARE/CONTRAST Ask students to write a four-paragraph essay comparing and contrasting the school in *Detectives in Togas* with their own school. They should begin by skimming the book and developing a list of details about the school the boys attended—its size and location, the boys' course of study and time of attendance, and so on. Have students use this outline to develop their essays.

I. Introduction
II. How the Schools Are Alike
III. How the Schools Differ
IV. Conclusion

READING/WRITING

MAP IT OUT

SOCIAL STUDIES Send students to the library to locate a map of ancient Rome that shows sites mentioned in the story—Greece, Gaul, and Germany. Have them copy the map and caption it with information from the story that refers to each site. **READING/WRITING/VIEWING**

ACTIVITIES

SCHOOL↔HOME CONNECTION

Freedom of Speech

Remind students that the boys in the story were afraid to speak negatively about the emperor. Point out that today we have freedom of speech in this country—we can say almost anything we wish to say about people in power without fear of being put in jail. Ask students to bring up freedom of speech with adults at home and to ask parents or guardians why they feel this freedom is important. Discuss students' findings. LISTENING/SPEAKING

Teamwork Works!

HEALTH Discuss the fact that each of the boys in the story contributed his own special expertise and talent to help solve the mystery. Divide the class into groups of four or five and have students pretend that they need to solve a similar mystery. Have them brainstorm a list of special talents and skills each of them has that might contribute to a successful solution. LISTENING/SPEAKING/WRITING

My Life in Ancient Rome

SOCIAL STUDIES Ask students to use what they learned about the typical life of a boy of a certain social class in Rome to write their own diary entries from the point of view of a child in that place and time. Have them begin with a schedule that runs from morning to night, filling in activities that might be typical. Then have them use the schedule to write a diary entry for one day. READING/WRITING

5:30 AM	wake up
6:30 AM	buy rolls at the baker
7 AM.	arrive at school

End-of-Theme Assessment Tools

IF you want to measure a student's mastery of reading and language skills and strategies, **THEN** administer the multiple-choice diagnostic **Skills Assessment.**	**IF** you want information about a student's ability to apply thinking skills in a global and holistic manner, **THEN** administer the **Holistic Reading Assessment.**	**IF** you want a comprehensive view of a student's reading and writing development skills, **THEN** administer the **Integrated Performance Assessment.**

Name ____________________ Date __________

Teacher ____________________ Grade __________

The topics I like to read about most are:
The kinds of things I like to read most are:
I use my imagination when I read by:
I guess what is going to happen next when I read by:
I like to read books and stories that:
I don't enjoy reading books and stories that:
I (do/do not) talk with my friends about things I read because:
I think I would be a better reader if:
I would like to read more about:

Thinking About My Reading Checklist

Theme 5

Masterpieces

CREATIVITY

This theme reveals that a masterpiece is no accident; it is the result of talent, inspiration, and careful planning.

Theme Overview

Masterpieces

Creativity

Artistic expression takes many forms, including painting, photography, and architecture. The selections in this theme will help students understand and appreciate the process and power of creativity.

The Art of Velázquez by Ernest Raboff T891–T924

"His paintings showed both the reality and the dreams of his times. This dedication to truth in art brought him fame in his lifetime."

Students will examine some of the masterpieces of classical Spanish painter Diego Velázquez.

I, Juan de Pareja by Elizabeth Borton de Treviño T925–T966

"He stood hesitating a moment, and then turned a canvas toward him. It was mine. In the late light, the faithful hounds shone out from the dark background, sunlight on their glistening hides, light in their big, loving, dark eyes. His Majesty stood transfixed."

Students will share the moment when a slave's artistic talent is great enough to win him his freedom.

The Paint Box by E. V. Rieu T946–T947

A talented artist is asked to create a picture that is utterly new.

ART AND LITERATURE: ***Women Playing Koto, Samisen and Kokyu***
by Katsushika Oi T967–T968

This hanging silk scroll celebrates one form of creativity.

Two Women Photographers by Sylvia Wolf T969–T1010

"She became a legendary figure in photography and paved the way for future photojournalists, men and women alike."

Students will learn about the lives and photographic techniques of Margaret Bourke-White and Flor Garduño and examine each woman's work.

Photograph by Cynthia Rylant T990–T991

A boy's thoughts are revealed as he poses for a photograph.

The Will and the Way by Karen E. Hudson T1011–T1052

"'Building styles change with time and fashion, but I measure my worth as an architect by my ability to please my client. Each home I design has something special and different from anyone else's home. . . .'"

Students will gain insight into the works and philosophies of Paul R. Williams, a prominent African American architect.

On Watching the Construction of a Skyscraper by Burton Raffel T1032–T1033

The poet celebrates the sights and sounds of a construction site.

Flexible Grouping

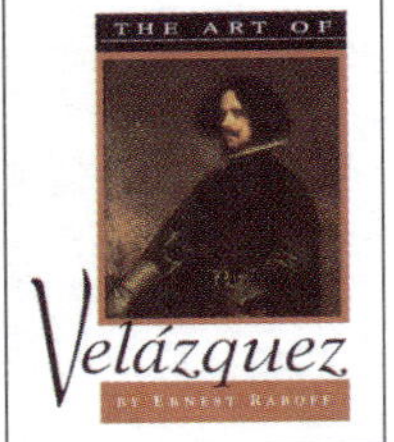

THE ART OF VELÁZQUEZ T891–T924

	BELOW-LEVEL READERS	ABOVE-LEVEL READERS	ESL	BILINGUAL
1 READING AND RESPONDING Build Concepts and Vocabulary Strategic Reading Response Corner	**BEFORE** students read the selection, use the *Intervention Strategies Manual.* (pp. 98–100) **TEACHER-LED GROUP** **DURING** the Write a Description activity, encourage students to think about describing the painting without rereading the author's description. (p. T906) **INDEPENDENT/PAIRS**	**AFTER** students read the selection, challenge them to learn more about their favorite painting from the selection and present a report to the class. (p. T907) **COOPERATIVE GROUPS** **INSTEAD OF** doing the Vocabulary Strategies activities, students who know the Key Words may do the *Practice Book* activity (p. 128). **INDEPENDENT**	**BEFORE** students read the selection, do a picture walk through the book. **TEACHER-LED GROUP** **BEFORE** students read the selection, use the Introducing the Literature pages of the *Sheltered English/ESL Manual* (pp. 66–68). **TEACHER-LED GROUP**	**WHILE** others read the selection in the anthology, students may read the translation in the appropriate *Anthology Translation Booklet.* **INDEPENDENT** **WHILE** others complete the Vocabulary Strategies, Spanish-speaking students may read a play from *Acto final* in CIELO ABIERTO. Have Vietnamese students read *Beyond the East Wind* from the *Multi-Language Library.* **INDEPENDENT**
2 INTEGRATING LANGUAGE ARTS Idea Bank Writer's Workshop Grammar Spelling Vocabulary Workshop	**AFTER** the Writer's Workshop assignment, students may use the Spin mode of *The Amazing Writing Machine* to enter their descriptive essays. (p. T912) **PAIRS/INDEPENDENT** **DURING** the Spelling lesson, use the extra support pages of the *Integrated Spelling* Teacher's Edition Lesson 25. **TEACHER-LED GROUP**	**DURING** the Integrating the Language Arts section, have students complete the *Writer's Magazine* (pp. 66-67). **INDEPENDENT/PAIRS** **WHILE** other groups review the Key Words, have students complete the Extended Vocabulary lesson in the *Practice Book* (p. 132). **INDEPENDENT**	**BEFORE** the Writer's Workshop, use the Responding to the Literature page of the *Sheltered English/ESL Manual* (p. 69). **TEACHER-LED GROUP** **AFTER** the Grammar lesson, model and guide completion of the *Practice Book* (p. 130). **TEACHER-LED GROUP**	**INSTEAD OF** the Idea Bank, use one of the Responding to the Script activities in the *Acto final Teacher's Guide.* **TEACHER-LED GROUP**
3 LEARNING THROUGH THE LITERATURE Direct Skills Instruction Integrated Curriculum Reading Trade Books Theme Project	**WHILE** others work in groups, use the Phonics lesson in the *Intervention Strategies Manual* (pp. 102-103). **TEACHER-LED GROUP** **WHILE** others work in groups, have students read the Take-Home book with a partner, describing the illustrations in their own words. (p. T923) **PAIRS**	**WHILE** others are working on the Theme Project, students may use *Imagination Express, Destination: Castle* to write a story set in the past. (p. T920) **COOPERATIVE GROUPS** **WHILE** others are in groups, have students read a trade book such as *Don Quixote and Sancho Panza* and do the response activities. (p. T922) **INDEPENDENT**	**DURING** the Create a Scene activity, have students work with English-fluent partners to write scenes based on their sentence strips. (p. T919) **PAIRS** **WHILE** others are working in groups, have students read *Diego Rivera* from the *ESL/Title I Library.* Beginning-level ESL students should read along with the cassette tape. **INDEPENDENT/PAIRS**	**WHILE** others are working in groups, have students choose and read a book from the *Multi-Language Library.* **INDEPENDENT** **WHILE** others are working in groups, have students complete the Minilesson for Main Idea and Details, pages 24–25, in the CIELO ABIERTO *Teacher's Handbook.* **TEACHER-LED GROUP**

I, JUAN DE PAREJA T925–T966

	BELOW-LEVEL READERS	ABOVE-LEVEL READERS	ESL	BILINGUAL
1 READING AND RESPONDING Build Concepts and Vocabulary Strategic Reading Response Corner	**BEFORE** students read the selection, use the Previewing the Literature page in the *Intervention Strategies Manual* (p. 104). **TEACHER-LED GROUP** **WHILE** others complete the Strategic Reading, work with a needs-based group to review footnotes. (p. T942) **TEACHER-LED GROUP**	**AFTER** students complete the Write a Persuasive Paragraph activity, challenge them to stage a debate using ideas from their paragraphs. (p. T949) **COOPERATIVE GROUPS**	**BEFORE** students read the selection, use the Introducing the Literature pages of the *Sheltered English/ESL Manual* (pp. 70-73) **TEACHER-LED GROUP** **INSTEAD OF** writing a report, students doing the Create a Class Book activity may want to create a series of captioned drawings. (p. T948) **COOPERATIVE GROUPS**	**WHILE** others are reading the selection in the anthology, students may read the translation in the appropriate *Anthology Translation Booklet*. **INDEPENDENT** **WHILE** others complete the Strategic Reading, Spanish-speaking students may read a selection from *Sigue la palabra* in CIELO ABIERTO. **INDEPENDENT**
2 INTEGRATING LANGUAGE ARTS Idea Bank Writer's Workshop Grammar Spelling Vocabulary Workshop	**WHILE** others work on Idea Bank activities, review the Tips for Listening and Speaking (p. T952) **TEACHER-LED GROUP** **AFTER** the Writer's Workshop, students may use *The Amazing Writing Machine* to enter their historical fiction stories (p. T954). **PAIRS/INDEPENDENT**	**WHILE** others are completing Idea Bank Activities, have students do the *Writer's Magazine* (pp. 68-69). **INDEPENDENT** **AFTER** the Writer's Workshop, students may create a portfolio entry by answering the Self-Assessment questions. (p. T955) **COOPERATIVE GROUPS**	**DURING** the Grammar Practice activities, have students look at pictures or photographs of busy scenes and describe them using the past tense. (p. T957) **COOPERATIVE GROUPS**	**INSTEAD OF** the Vocabulary Workshop activities, use the Responding Activities on page 7 of the *Sigue la palabra Teacher's Guide*. **PAIRS**
3 LEARNING THROUGH THE LITERATURE Direct Skills Instruction Integrated Curriculum Reading Trade Books Theme Project	**AFTER** the skills lessons, model and guide completion of the *Practice Book* (pp. 141-142). **TEACHER-LED GROUP** **WHILE** others are working in groups, have students read *I Am an Artist* from the *ESL/Title I Library*. **INDEPENDENT**	**WHILE** others are doing the Practice Activities, challenge students to create a crossword puzzle using multiple-meaning words. (p. T961) **COOPERATIVE GROUPS** **WHILE** others are working in groups, have students choose and read a trade book such as *Leonardo da Vinci: Artist, Inventor, and Scientist of the Renaissance*. **INDEPENDENT**	**WHILE** other groups are working in centers, have students choose and read a book from the *ESL/Title I Library*. **INDEPENDENT/PAIRS** **WHILE** others read trade books, have students work with fluent English-speakers to determine the meanings of multiple-meaning words. (p. T961) **COOPERATIVE GROUPS**	**WHILE** others are working in groups, have students choose and read a book from the *Multi-Language Library*. **INDEPENDENT** **WHILE** others are completing the Integrated Curriculum activities, have students work on the ongoing cross-curricular project on page 2 of the *Sigue la palabra Teacher's Guide*. **COOPERATIVE GROUPS**

Flexible Grouping

TWO WOMEN PHOTOGRAPHERS T969-T1010

	BELOW-LEVEL READERS	ABOVE-LEVEL READERS	ESL	BILINGUAL
1 READING AND RESPONDING Build Concepts and Vocabulary Strategic Reading Response Corner	**BEFORE** students read the selection, use the Previewing the Literature pages of the *Intervention Strategies Manual* (pp. 110-111). **TEACHER-LED GROUP** **AFTER** the Vocabulary Strategies activities, model and guide completion of the *Practice Book* (p. 144). **TEACHER-LED GROUP**	**BEFORE** students read the selection, have them write story predictions in their personal journals. (p.T974) **INDEPENDENT** **AFTER** students have read the selection, have them invite a photographer to speak to the class and prepare interview questions for the visit. (p.T993) **COOPERATIVE GROUPS**	**BEFORE** students read the selection, use the Introducing the Literature pages of the *Sheltered English/ESL Manual* (pp. 74–76). **TEACHER-LED GROUP** **BEFORE** students do the Discuss Ideas activity, have them do a Quickwrite of their photographic ideas in their first language and refer to these notes during the discussion. (p.T992) **COOPERATIVE GROUPS**	**WHILE** others are reading the selection in the anthology, students may read the translation in the appropriate *Anthology Translation Booklet*. **INDEPENDENT** **WHILE** others complete the Vocabulary Strategies, Spanish-speaking students may read poems from *Ríos de lava* in CIELO ABIERTO. Have Chinese students read *The Fairy Cloak* from the *Multi-Language Library*. **INDEPENDENT**
2 INTEGRATING LANGUAGE ARTS Idea Bank Writer's Workshop Grammar Spelling Vocabulary Workshop	**WHILE** others are completing Idea Bank activities, students may create a portfolio entry by answering the Self-Assessment questions about their comparison and contrast articles. (p.T999) **COOPERATIVE GROUPS** **DURING** the Spelling lesson, use the *Integrated Spelling* Teacher's Edition Lesson 27. **TEACHER-LED GROUP**	**WHILE** others are completing Idea Bank Activities, students may do the *Writer's Magazine* (pp. 72-75). **INDEPENDENT** **INSTEAD OF** participating in the review of comparison and contrast articles, students familiar with the process may begin writing. (p.T998) **INDEPENDENT**	**WHILE** others work on Idea Bank activities, pull out a needs-based group for a review of the Tips for Listening and Speaking (p.T997). **TEACHER-LED GROUP** **DURING** the Grammar lesson, use the *Language Handbook* to help students better understand perfect tenses (p. 156). **TEACHER-LED GROUP**	**INSTEAD OF** using the Writer's Workshop, use the writing activity in the Activities for Responding to the Poem in the *Ríos de lava Teacher's Guide*. **PAIRS** **WHILE** others complete the Spelling activity, use one of the Activities for Responding to the Poem in the *Ríos de lava Teacher's Guide*. **INDEPENDENT/PAIRS**
3 LEARNING THROUGH THE LITERATURE Direct Skills Instruction Integrated Curriculum Reading Trade Books Theme Project	**WHILE** others are working in groups, have students complete the reproducible Phonics page of the *Intervention Strategies Manual* (p. 115). **INDEPENDENT** **WHILE** others are working in groups, students can read the Take-Home book. **INDEPENDENT**	**AFTER** the skills lessons, students may complete the *Practice Book* (p. 148). **INDEPENDENT** **WHILE** others are working in groups, challenge students to analyze the information they synthesized for a recent decision they made. (p.T1005) **INDEPENDENT**	**WHILE** others are working in groups, have students read the Take-Home book *Beauty Surrounds Us*. **INDEPENDENT/PAIRS**	**WHILE** others are working in groups, have students choose and read a book from the *Multi-Language Library*. **INDEPENDENT**

THE WILL AND THE WAY T1011–T1052

	BELOW-LEVEL READERS	ABOVE-LEVEL READERS	ESL	BILINGUAL
1 READING AND RESPONDING Build Concepts and Vocabulary Strategic Reading Response Corner	**INSTEAD OF** having students read the selection with the whole class, use the Guiding the Reading page of the *Intervention Strategies Manual* (p. 118). **TEACHER-LED GROUP** **AFTER** students read the selection, use the Intervention Strategies activities. (pp.T1036–T1037) **TEACHER-LED GROUP**	**BEFORE** students read the selection, have them write story predictions in their personal journals. (p.T1016) **INDEPENDENT** **AFTER** the Vocabulary Strategies, students may complete the *Practice Book* (p. 151). **INDEPENDENT**	**BEFORE** reading the selection, use the Introducing the Literature pages of the *Sheltered English/ESL Manual* (pp. 78-80). **TEACHER-LED GROUP** **DURING** the Write a Letter activity, have students write their letters in their first language and then work with English-proficient partners to translate the letters into English. (p.T1034) **PAIRS**	**WHILE** others read the selection in the anthology, students may read the translation in the appropriate *Anthology Translation Booklet.* **INDEPENDENT** **WHILE** others are completing the Strategic Reading, Spanish-speaking students may read a selection from *Así pasaron muchos años* in CIELO ABIERTO. **INDEPENDENT**
2 INTEGRATING LANGUAGE ARTS Idea Bank Writer's Workshop Grammar Spelling Vocabulary Workshop	**DURING** the Grammar lesson, students may use *Imagination Express, Destination: Neighborhood* to write and illustrate their sentences. (p.T1042) **PAIRS** **DURING** the Spelling lesson, use *Integrated Spelling* Teacher's Edition Lesson 28. **TEACHER-LED GROUP**	**WHILE** others are completing Idea Bank activities, have students do the *Writer's Magazine* (pp. 76-79). **INDEPENDENT** **INSTEAD OF** participating in the review of business letters, students familiar with the process may begin writing. (p.T1040) **INDEPENDENT**	**DURING** the Writer's Workshop assignment, students may use the Spin business letter in *The Amazing Writing Machine* as a frame for their own letters. (p.T1040) **PAIRS** **DURING** the Grammar Practice activities, pair students with English-proficient partners and have them list common irregular verbs and use them in sentences. (p.T1043) **PAIRS**	**INSTEAD OF** the Writer's Workshop, use the Personal Writing Profile on page 16 of the *Así pasaron muchos años Teacher's Guide.* **TEACHER-LED GROUP**
3 LEARNING THROUGH THE LITERATURE Direct Skills Instruction Integrated Curriculum Reading Trade Books Theme Project	**WHILE** others are working independently, use the Phonics lesson in the *Intervention Strategies Manual* (pp. 120-121). **TEACHER-LED GROUP** **WHILE** others are working in groups, students may read the Take-Home book as homework. **INDEPENDENT**	**WHILE** others are in groups, have students read *The Wright Brothers* from the *Signatures Library.* **INDEPENDENT** **WHILE** students are working on the Theme Project, small groups may use Project Cards 25–30 to work at their own pace. **COOPERATIVE GROUPS**	**INSTEAD OF** having students read *The Wright Brothers* independently, have them work in groups to read each chapter. (p.T1050) **PAIRS** **WHILE** others are working in groups, have students read the Take-Home book *Better Late Than Never.* **INDEPENDENT/PAIRS**	**WHILE** others are working in groups, have students choose and read a book from the *Multi-Language Library.* **INDEPENDENT**

Ongoing Assessment Strategies

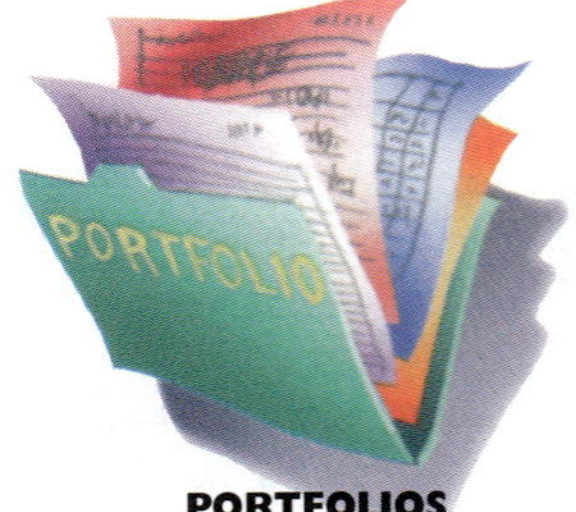

KIDS SHARING WITH PARENTS

Encourage students to share their portfolios with their family members because

- family involvement will often generate more student involvement.
- parents and guardians can learn more from their child's portfolio than from homework assignments or test results.

Here are some tips for having students share their portfolios with family members:

- Explain, through a letter or in person, the purpose of a portfolio and the student's role.
- Make portfolios available on open house nights.
- Consider holding more formal student-parent portfolio conferences, similar to your student-teacher portfolio conferences, at school.
- Advise family members on how to respond to their child while reviewing the portfolios. Tell them they should
  — praise the child's efforts.
  — encourage the child to talk about the reading and writing activities by asking open-ended questions; that is, avoid yes or no questions.
  — ask the child to choose a favorite piece of writing to read aloud.
  — encourage the child to make a school-home connection by adding materials written at home to the portfolio at school.

See the SIGNATURES *Portfolio Assessment Teacher's Guide.*

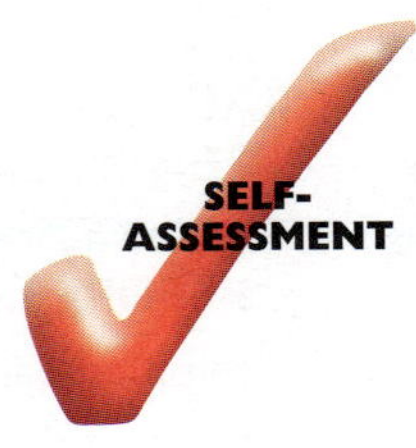

THINKING ABOUT MY WRITING

Look for the student self-assessment opportunities in the Writer's Workshops in the next theme. These activities encourage students to monitor and reflect on their writing so that they can become more involved in their learning and their progress as writers.

Helping students develop strategies for reflecting on their writing encourages them to become independent learners. Encourage students to ask themselves questions such as the following ones:

- Who will be reading what I write?
- What is my reason for writing?
- Where did I get my ideas for writing?
- Did I read over my writing after I finished? How did I make it better?
- How do I feel about what I wrote? What are some parts I especially like?
- How can I make my writing better the next time?

Also, encourage students to reflect on their writing regularly in their personal journals. Questions they might ask themselves include *Did this piece of writing seem easy? Hard? Why?*

See the Thinking About My Writing Checklist on page T1068.

End-Of-Theme Formal Assessment Tools

SKILLS ASSESSMENT

Multiple-choice diagnostic tests that measure mastery of the following skills:

- Reading: vocabulary, context clues, and main idea and details
- Language: predicate nominatives and adjectives, simple and perfect tenses, and regular and irregular verbs

HOLISTIC READING ASSESSMENT

Fiction and/or nonfiction reading passages with multiple-choice and open-ended questions to assess students' application of literal, inferential, and critical thinking in a global and holistic manner

INTEGRATED PERFORMANCE ASSESSMENT

Performance tasks to gain a comprehensive view of a student's reading and writing progress. Students read and respond to "Paul Revere, Metalworker" by Karen E. Hong. Students demonstrate expressive writing in a compare/contrast essay. One or both sections may be used.

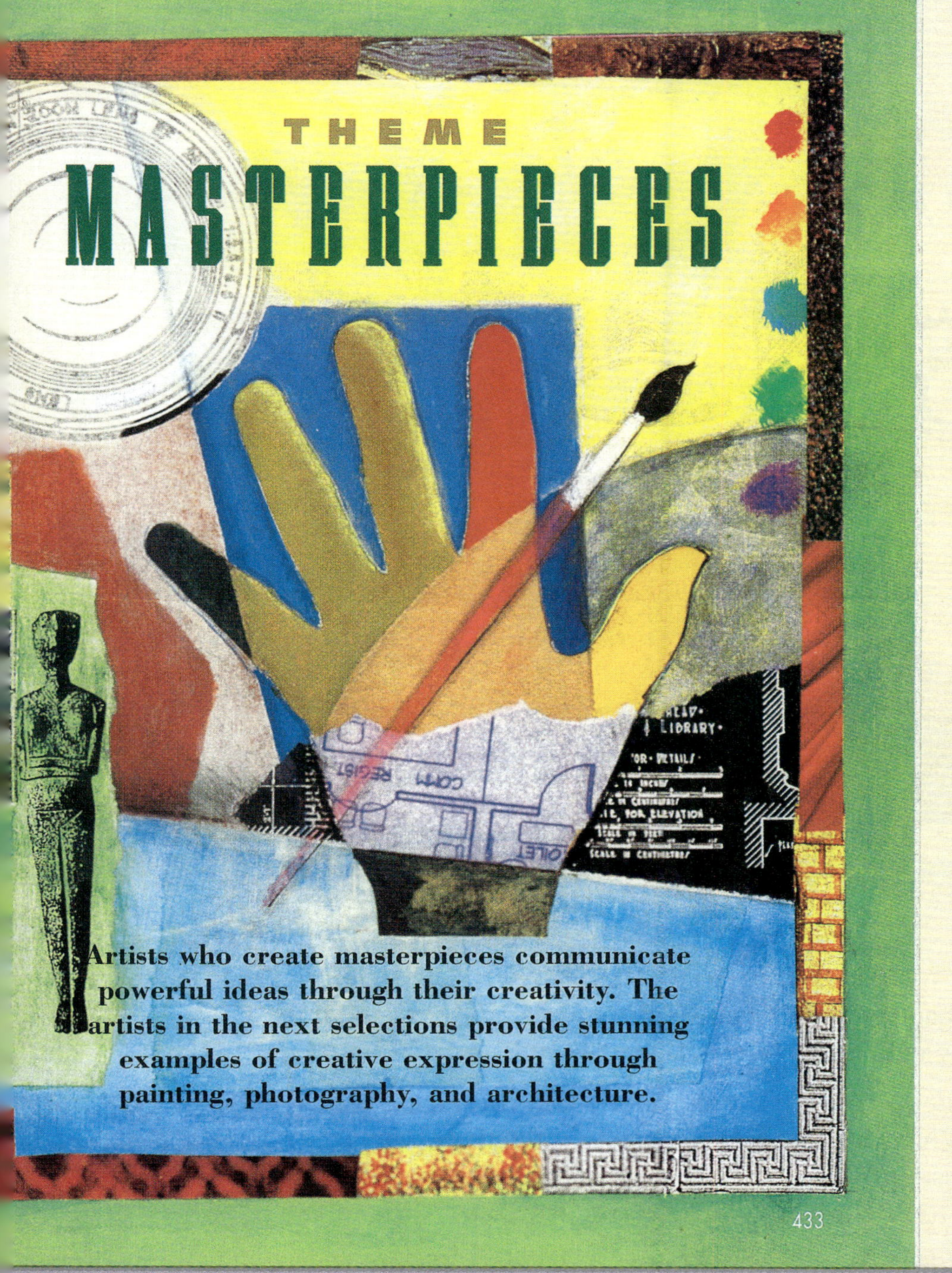

THEME 5

Masterpieces

DISCUSSING THE THEME

Invite students to read about the theme on page 433. Discuss how paintings, photographs, and buildings can be used as a means of communication. Ask students about drawings, paintings, or posters they have created that make a statement about an important idea. If they used one of these mediums to make a statement about nonviolence, for instance, what might they show?

Previewing the Theme Literature

Have students read the table of contents on page 435. Ask them if they are familiar with any of the authors or subjects.

Suggest that students think for a moment about the theme title *Masterpieces.* What kinds of art are considered masterpieces? How does a message or story told through a painting or a photograph compare to one told through speech or print?

Have students think of paintings, photographs, or buildings that are considered masterpieces. What message do these works seem to convey? What makes these works masterpieces?

The Signatures Library

Journal of a Teenage Genius by Helen V. Griffith is about Zack who discovers that his dream girl may have a time machine in her basement. Despite humorous interferences from family and friends, Zack is determined to find out the truth in this science-fiction story.

The Wright Brothers: How They Invented the Airplane by Russell Freedman tells the story of Wilbur and Orville Wright, two bicycle mechanics, and their invention of the airplane. Vivid photographs illustrate the brothers' frustration, excitement, and triumph.

Strategies for reading *Journal of a Teenage Genius* appear with the "I, Juan de Pareja" lesson on page T964. Strategies for reading *The Wright Brothers: How They Invented the Airplane* appear with the "The Will and the Way" lesson on page T1050.

Comprehensive lesson plans are available on pages T1056–T1067.

Related Reading

These trade books offer students further opportunities to work with the Masterpieces theme.

ESL/Title I Library

These easy-to-read library books connect to the theme Masterpieces: *Diego Rivera* by Mike Venezia; *I Am an Artist* by Pat Lowery Collins.

THEME PROJECT OVERVIEW

Art in the Community

THEME OVERVIEW

Each selection in this theme contributes to students' understanding of how people overcome obstacles or take risks to fulfill a deep need to express themselves creatively. In this project, students look closely at the creative process and discover the works of artists who live in their own community. Each lesson is followed by a Project Checkpoint that will help students complete the Theme Project.

PROJECT PLANNER

QUESTION: How can we experience art events in school and in the larger community? *(Creativity)*

STAGES	GOALS
PROJECT LAUNCH (p.T889) 3–5 days	Make a list of different art forms. • Brainstorm categories of art. • Discuss various works of art (in all genres) that students enjoy.
CHECKPOINT 1 (p.T924) 4–6 days	Research community art events. • Research information about exhibits, galleries, museums, performances, and artists in the community. • Arrange art experiences such as field trips to view art, guest speakers, or classroom art displays.
CHECKPOINT 2 (p.T966) 4–6 days	Write reviews of art experiences. • Take field trips, listen to guest speakers, or examine art. • Discuss strengths and weaknesses of the art and share information about the experience.
CHECKPOINT 3 (p.T1010) 4–6 days	Produce works of art. • Decide on a type of art to produce. • Discuss materials needed to produce the art. • Form interest groups to produce art.
CHECKPOINT 4 (p.T1052) 4–6 days	Make an art directory. • Organize and illustrate a guide to local art events. • Design a map showing locations of art opportunities in the area and make a calendar of upcoming events.
PROJECT PRESENTATION (p.T1054) 3–5 days	Share the directory with the community. • Make presentations of the directory to other students. • Distribute the directory to interested organizations. • Arrange publicity by calling radio and television stations.

STUDENTS ACQUIRING ENGLISH

As the class discusses works of art they enjoy, encourage students acquiring English to share their thoughts about the artists and art of their native country.

MULTIPLE INTELLIGENCES

Encourage students with visual/spatial intelligence to make a chart for the class that illustrates the different categories of the visual arts.

INQUIRY PROJECT IDEAS

Students may want to examine the creative process in other times or geographical areas. They may research and share information on topics such as

- biographies of famous artists in history.
- artists and art in their native countries.
- art education opportunities within the community.

PROJECT LAUNCH

LAUNCH OPTIONS

TIME CAPSULE (SMALL GROUPS)

Ask groups to imagine they are a committee whose purpose is to choose this decade's ten best works of art, in any genre and without limitation of size or materials, to go into a time capsule. Have a Reporter from each group share the group's list with the class and explain the group's criteria for "best works of art."

ART IS EVERYWHERE (WHOLE GROUP)

Invite students to look around their house, their block, and their community for "found art"—things that weren't necessarily meant to be art, but may look like art to the viewer. Some examples of found art might be window displays, discarded objects, or clothing accessories. Have students share what they found, using notes, sketches or photographs and, if possible, the object itself.

WHOLE-GROUP DISCUSSION

Begin by asking what works of art are most popular among the students and why. Then discuss categories of art that students seem to neglect. Prompt discussion with questions such as *If only one form of art could remain in the world, which would you keep? Why would you choose this medium over others?*

FORM PROJECT GROUPS

Arrange the class in groups, combining students who may be knowledgeable about art with those who may know very little. Have groups brainstorm as many genres of art as they can, and ask them to think of specific examples they know and like in each. Students should

- draw on personal experiences, launch activities, and literature selections to create their list.
- share information about the items on the list.

DID YOU KNOW?

The very first cameras dated from antiquity and were actually rooms big enough for people to enter. In these early cameras, light entered the darkened room through a small pinhole and formed an inverted picture on the opposite wall of whatever lay outside.

Project Card 25 can be found as a copying master on page R74.

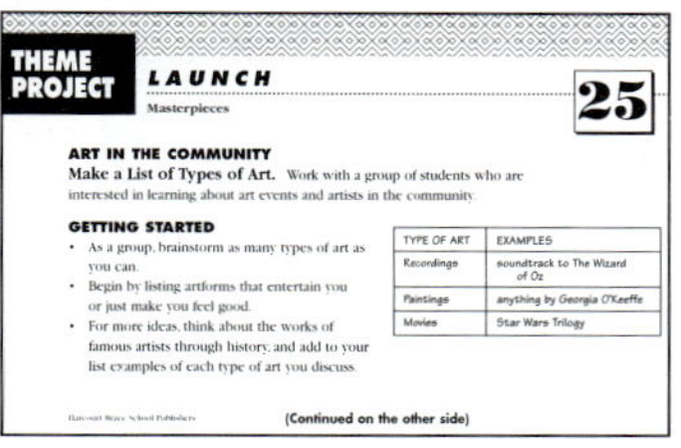

THEME PROJECT **LAUNCH** 25

Masterpieces

ART IN THE COMMUNITY

Make a List of Types of Art. Work with a group of students who are interested in learning about art events and artists in the community.

GETTING STARTED

- As a group, brainstorm as many types of art as you can.
- Begin by listing artforms that entertain you or just make you feel good.
- For more ideas, think about the works of famous artists through history, and add to your list examples of each type of art you discuss.

TYPE OF ART	EXAMPLES
Recordings	soundtrack to The Wizard of Oz
Paintings	anything by *Georgia O'Keeffe*
Movies	Star Wars Trilogy

(Continued on the other side)

Project Card 25

ADDITIONAL RESOURCES

BOOKS

Think Like an Eagle by Kathryn Lasky. Little, Brown, 1992.

History of Art for Young People by H.W. Janson and Anthony F. Janson. Harry N. Abrams, 1992.

MAGAZINES

"Meet the Artist, Elisa Kleven," by Lisa Keating. *Crayola Kids,* Feb.–Mar. 1995, p. 18.

"The Town of Magical Murals," *World,* Aug. 1995, pp. 7–10.

FORMAL ASSESSMENT ✓

Prompts for self- and peer assessment and a rubric for teacher assessment that can be used at each checkpoint are provided on page T1055.

Planning a Literacy Event

Art Show Plan an Art Show as the culminating activity of the theme. Students who complete the Theme Project can showcase their individual artwork and their group's Community Art Directory at the event. To increase family participation, invite family members to contribute artwork to the event, which may include collaborations with the students. Students can also invite local artists to display their work at the Art Show.

- Identify a date for the Art Show.
- Ask students to pre-plan space to display their own artwork and the artwork family members and local artists will contribute to the event.
- Have groups of students design invitations for family members and interested adults.
- If possible, arrange to have refreshments at the event.
- Appoint a publicity committee to generate interest for the event.

Enlisting Parents as Partners

Artful Living During conferences parents may ask for ways to develop their own children's interest in creative expression. Offer these suggestions:

- ☑ Visit museums and galleries and attend artistic performances together. Notice the kinds of artistic media that most appeal to your child.
- ☑ Plan an at-home project together that involves creativity. You might build and creatively decorate something practical, such as a birdhouse, or experiment with techniques such as clay modeling or watercolor painting.
- ☑ Visit the library with your child, and help him or her select books to share with you about artists or works of art.

TECHNOLOGY

The *At Home in Our Schools* videocassette contains numerous ideas for family involvement projects.

Surfing the Internet? See *Issues & Ideas* on the Harcourt Brace Home Page:

http://www.hbschool.com

***The Family Involvement Newsletter* for this theme contains further suggestions on this topic and other topics of interest to parents.**

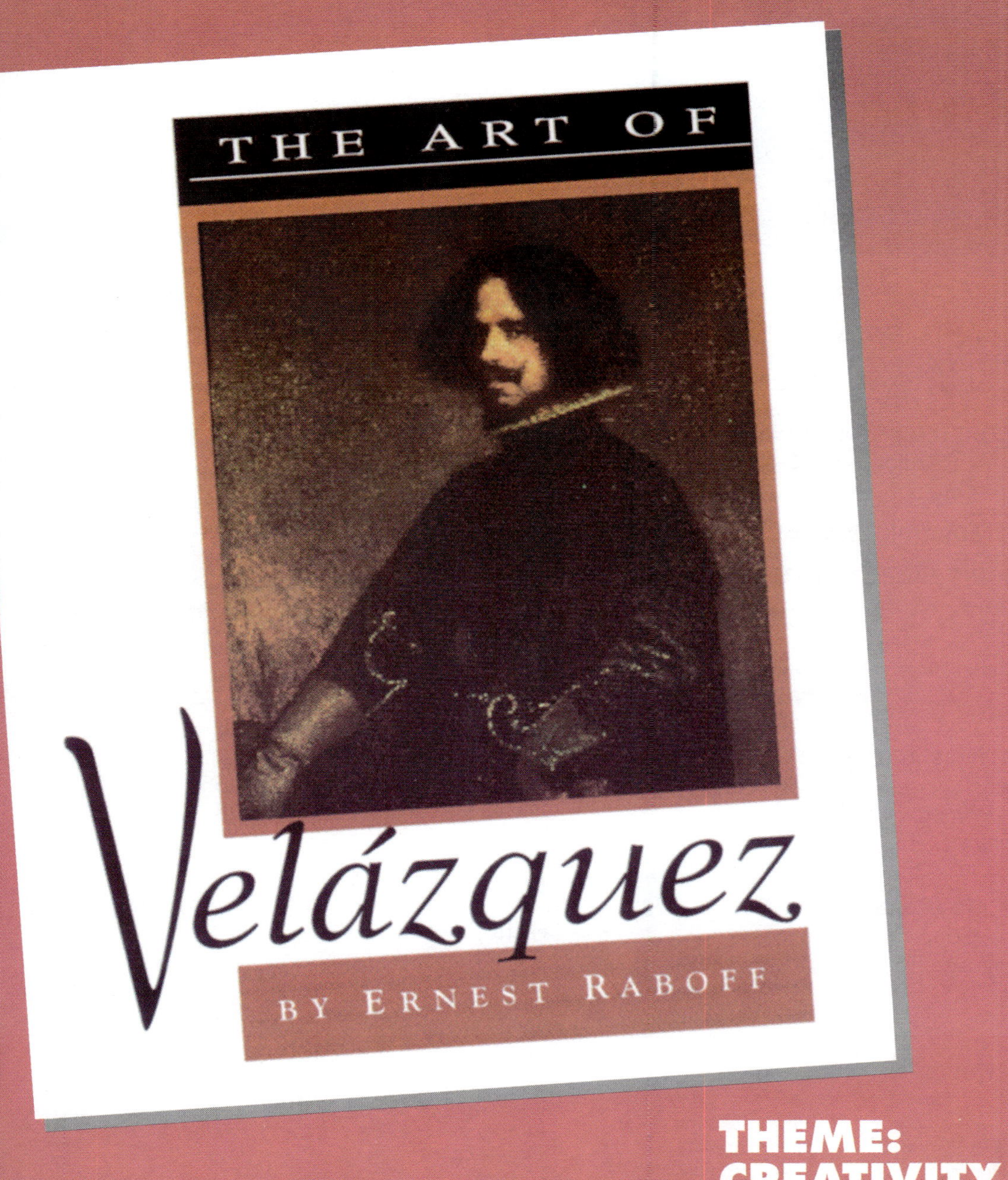

ABOUT THE AUTHOR

ERNEST RABOFF was the author of fifteen books in the "Art for Children" series. Each book in the series provides a brief biography of the artist and a discussion of the artist's major works, which are included as color reproductions.

More information about Ernest Raboff and his work appears on page T905.

THEME: CREATIVITY

Masterpieces

In "The Art of Velázquez," students will learn about Diego Velázquez's training as an artist and about five of his masterpieces.

SELECTION SUMMARY

Genre: Nonfiction

Diego Velázquez, a Spanish painter who was born in 1599, showed an unusual talent for drawing as a young child. He studied the fine art of painting for several years and at the age of twenty-five was appointed the king's painter. He strived to paint exactly what he saw, and after his death at the age of sixty-one, Velázquez was recognized as a great realistic painter. In a discussion of five of Velázquez's masterpieces, the author describes the painter's use of specific details and provides some historical background for the paintings.

SUGGESTED LESSON PLANNER

▶ *The Art of Velázquez*

	DAY 1	DAY 2
PART 1 **Reading** **Listening** **Speaking** **Viewing** **Key Words** appointed devotion striving precisely bond	**BUILD BACKGROUND** T894 **VOCABULARY STRATEGIES** T895 *Transparency 41* *Practice Book* p. 128 **READING THE SELECTION** T896–T905 Options for Reading T896–T897 *Response Card 5* **REVIEW PREDICTIONS/PURPOSE** T904 **APPRECIATING THE LITERATURE** T904 NOTE: Students may read the selection on Day 2.	**SUMMARIZE THE SELECTION** T905 *Practice Book* p. 129 ◆ **RESPONSE CORNER ACTIVITIES** T906 **CHECKING COMPREHENSION** T907 *End-of-Selection Test* 
PART 2 **Writer's Workshop**	**DESCRIPTIVE ESSAY** Thinking as Writers T912 *Language Handbook* pp. 58–59 *Transparencies 42A, 42B*	Prewriting T912 *Language Handbook* pp. 54–55
Grammar	✓ **PREDICATE NOMINATIVES AND ADJECTIVES** Teach the Concept T914 Daily Language Practice (1–2) R64	Daily Language Practice (3–4) R64 Practice Activity T915
Spelling	**RELATED WORDS** *artist, equal, companion, comparison, familiar, history, fantastic, precise, artistic, fantasy, company, precision, family, historic, equality, compare* Pretest/Self-Check T916 *Integrated Spelling Teacher's Edition* pp. T165, T294	Open and Closed Sorts T916 *Integrated Spelling* p. 106 *Integrated Spelling Teacher's Edition* p. T166
PART 3 **Skills and Strategies**	◆ **INTEGRATED CURRICULUM** *Reflecting the Times* **Social Studies/Art** T920 **Art** T920 **Music** T921 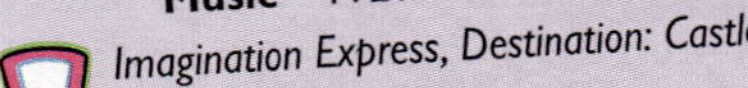 *Imagination Express, Destination: Castle*	**COMPREHENSION SKILL** T918–T919 ✓ Main Idea and Details (Introduce) *Practice Book* p. 133
 	Use the Intervention Strategies on pages T908–T909 with **below-level students** after they have read the selection.	Use the Extra Support note on page T915 to help **below-level** and **ESL students** while they are writing.

NOTE: An alternative lesson plan for **below-level students** appears on *Intervention Strategies Manual* pp. 98–103. A lesson for **students acquiring English** appears on *Sheltered English/ESL Manual* pp. 66–69.

DAY 3	DAY 4	DAY 5
◆ **IDEA BANK ACTIVITIES** Retelling T910 *Response Card 13* Oral Language T910 Viewing T911 Real-Life Resources: Viewing Commercials T911 *Writer's Magazine* pp. 66–67 School–Home Connection 17 R94	**VOCABULARY WORKSHOP** T917 Reviewing Key Words **READING TRADE BOOKS** T922–T923  Take-Home Book	**READING TRADE BOOKS** T919, T921 T922–T923 
Drafting T913 *Language Handbook* pp. 54–55 *The Amazing Writing Machine*	Responding and Revising T913 *Language Handbook* pp. 28, 54–55	Proofreading and Publishing T913 *Language Handbook* pp. 54–55
Daily Language Practice (5–6) R64 Practice Activity T915 *Language Handbook* pp. 152–153 *The Amazing Writing Machine*	Daily Language Practice (7–8) R64 Practice Activity T915 *Grammar Practice Book* pp. 42–43	Daily Language Practice (9–12) R64 *Practice Book* p. 130
Discuss the Generalization T916 *Integrated Spelling* p. 107 *Integrated Spelling Teacher's Edition* p. T167	Apply to Writing T916 *Integrated Spelling* pp. 108–109 *Integrated Spelling Teacher's Edition* pp. T168–T169	Posttest T916 *Practice Book* p. 131 *Integrated Spelling Teacher's Edition* p. T170
STUDY SKILLS MINILESSON T897 Graphic Aids (Review) *Practice Book* p. 134 **COMPREHENSION MINILESSON** T901 Referents (Review) *Practice Book* p. 135	**VOCABULARY WORKSHOP** T917 Figurative Language *Practice Book* p. 132	**GRAMMAR MINILESSON** T903 ✓ Transitive and Intransitive Verbs, Objects (Review) Theme Project Checkpoint 1 T924 *The Amazing Writing Machine*
Above-level students may complete the Writer's Workshop independently.	**Below-level students** may read the *Take-Home Book: Charlie Spots a Fake* to help them reinforce Key Words.	**Below-level** and **ESL students** may read the *ESL/Title I Library* book *Diego Rivera.*

✓ = Tested Skill
◆ = Optional activities used to adjust pacing throughout the lesson
Titles in *italics* are optional materials.

BUILDING BACKGROUND AND CONCEPTS

PRIOR KNOWLEDGE

Relate to students' lives. Ask students to think about how old photographs, television shows, and paintings show how people lived in the past. Discuss how photographs or painted portraits show clothing styles and other details of the time period.

Create a web about portraits. Explain to students that "The Art of Velázquez" features portraits of people the artist knew, including his assistant, Juan de Pareja, and King Philip IV. Have students discuss what an artist might include in a portrait. Record students' responses in a web like the following:

QUICKWRITE

Have students write a few sentences telling about times they have drawn or painted. Encourage them to tell whether the experience was difficult or enjoyable, and if they showed anyone their efforts.

Intervention Strategies

For students who may have difficulty reading "The Art of Velázquez," support is available in *Intervention Strategies Manual,* pages 98–103, and on pages T903 and T908–T909 in this lesson.

STUDENTS ACQUIRING ENGLISH

See *Sheltered English/ESL Manual,* pages 66–69.

FACT FINDER — ART

Patronage

In Velázquez's time, many artists made a living by working for a patron, a wealthy person who would pay the artists to create art. The wealthiest patrons, such as monarchs and religious leaders, might support more than one artist. Philip IV of Spain, who made Velázquez his court painter, was also the patron of Francisco de Zurbarán and the Flemish painter Peter Paul Rubens. Under the patronage system, artists produced works commissioned specifically by their patrons or designed to appeal to the patron's taste. In the seventeenth century painters in Holland first began to produce works to be sold in the marketplace or at auction.

Philip IV

VOCABULARY STRATEGIES

KEY WORDS DEFINED

appointed selected for a position or duty

devotion dedication

striving making a strong effort

precisely exactly; accurately

bond a uniting force or influence

INTEGRATED SPELLING

Spelling Pretest: page T916

Spelling Generalization: Related Words

CONTEXT CLUES: EXPOSITORY PARAGRAPH

Encourage students to use syntactic and semantic cues. Display the passage on Transparency 41, and have students read the paragraph silently. Prompt students to use context clues along with phonetic and structural analysis to decode and figure out the meanings of the underlined words. Guide them, for example, to recognize that *chose an artist for this position* is a context clue to the meaning of *appointed*.

CHECK UNDERSTANDING

Have students identify synonyms. Write the words below on the board, or read the words in each row aloud. Ask students to identify the word in each group that does not belong. Correct responses are underlined.

STRATEGY: SYNONYMS/ANTONYMS

striving	**failing**	trying
disloyalty	dedication	devotion
accurately	precisely	**incorrectly**
designated	appointed	**rejected**
bond	**separation**	tie

TRANSPARENCY 41

Key Words

Many kings appointed artists as court painters. A king chose an artist for this position because of the artist's style and talent. Court painters often showed great devotion to their art and spent most days painting. An artist might paint and repaint a portrait, striving to make it perfect. If the result of his efforts pleased the king, the artist could become very wealthy. Some artists did not paint portraits that looked precisely like the subjects. They made their subjects look better and nobler on the canvas. Others painted accurate portraits of their subjects. Over the years a bond of friendship might develop between a painter and the king.

Jackie mixed her paints to precisely the right color.

PRACTICE BOOK, page 128

Prereading Strategies

PREVIEW AND PREDICT

Invite students to preview the selection by reading the first paragraph on page 439 and viewing the illustrations.

Have students begin a K-W-L chart. Have them write in the first column what they know about Velázquez and his work. They may use *Practice Book* page 129.

K	W	L
What I Know	What I Want to Know	What I Learned
Velázquez was a Spanish painter who was born in 1599.	Who are the people in his paintings? What was his painting style? What did he want to say through his artwork?	

You may want students to write their predictions about the selection in their personal journals.

PURPOSE

You may want to model setting a purpose:

I know that Diego Velázquez was a Spanish painter who lived a long time ago. I'm going to read to find out more about Velázquez and his paintings.

THE ART OF

VELÁZQUEZ: SELF-PORTRAIT

438

TIPS FOR CLASSROOM MANAGEMENT

SMALL GROUP

STRATEGIC READING

Reinforce the focus strategy of **using picture clues** to help students understand what they are reading. Page T898 is an appropriate place to invite students to discuss and model how using picture clues can help them gain meaning.

COOPERATIVE READING

READER RESPONSE GROUPS Small groups might use Reader Response Card 5 to focus on the **author's viewpoint.** Reader Response Card 5 can be found at the back of this Teacher's Edition.

Response Card 5

Diego Velázquez (dē·ā′gō bä·läs′kās) was born in Seville, Spain, on June 6, 1599, one hundred and seven years after Christopher Columbus left that city to sail to the Americas.

As a small child, Diego's drawings were so good that his parents sent him to study with Master Painter Francisco Herrera (frän·sēs′kō ā·rā′rä). But Diego soon wanted a greater freedom so he joined the studio of Francisco Pacheco (frän·sēs′kō pä·chā′kō), a teacher who allowed him creative artistic freedom. From this great teacher he learned the fine art of painting as well as literature and philosophy. Five years later, at the age of twenty, Diego married Juana, his teacher's daughter.

After rendering three portraits of King Philip IV, young Velázquez, at the age of twenty-five, was appointed the king's painter. With his wife and two daughters, he lived a happy life at court with plenty of time to fulfill his occupation as artist to the royal household.

Velázquez painted 121 outstanding canvases and became advisor and friend to his king. He died at the age of sixty-one, recognized as a great artist.

His paintings showed both the reality and the dreams of his times. This dedication to truth in art brought him fame in his lifetime.

From his devotion to art came the compassion and understanding that made him popular with both kings and commoners.

BY ERNEST RABOFF

MINILESSON

REVIEW: STUDY SKILLS

Graphic Aids

INFORMAL ASSESSMENT

Display a large wall map of Europe. Ask students to name some features on the map that help them interpret information. (mileage scale or distance bar, compass rose, lines of latitude and longitude, key or legend)

TEACH/MODEL

Remind students that a key, or legend, shows what the symbols on a map mean; a scale bar gives the distance on the map in relation to real distances; and a compass rose shows directions on the map. Point out that latitude lines run east and west and longitude lines run north and south.

PRACTICE/APPLY

Guide students in locating Spain on the map. Ask volunteers to carry out the following instructions:

- Point out the key or legend, the mileage scale bar, and the compass rose.
- Point out Seville, the city where Diego Velázquez was born.
- Find the approximate distance in miles between Madrid and Seville.

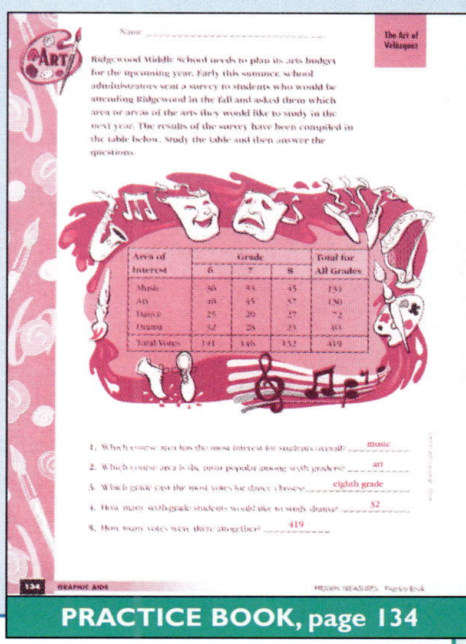

PRACTICE BOOK, page 134

WHOLE CLASS

INDEPENDENT READING

Have students read the entire selection silently. When students have finished, check their comprehension by having them answer the questions on page 449. Then encourage students to work with other classmates to complete one of the activities on pages 448–449.

READ ALOUD

Read the entire selection to students, directing their attention to one painting at a time as you read the accompanying description. Then have students reread the selection independently or in small groups.

Strategic Reading

USING PICTURE CLUES

Invite volunteers to discuss reading strategies they might use to help them understand the selection. Display the class-made strategy chart, and explain that another strategy they can use for "The Art of Velázquez" is using picture clues. Recall with students that pictures often add to or explain information provided in the text. **STRATEGY: USING PICTURE CLUES**

PAGES 438–447
Direct students to read through page 447 to learn about Velázquez and his paintings.

PHILIP IV ON HORSEBACK PRADO, MADRID

440

ART

Explain to students that the National Museum of the Prado, in Madrid, Spain, owns almost all Velázquez's important works, including the one pictured above and those shown on pages 443 and 446.

The Prado, Madrid

"Philip IV on Horseback" shows us the vast knowledge Velázquez had of men and of horses. Both figures are powerful and alive with action yet are masterfully balanced by the artist so one does not overshadow the other.

Study the two heads. Study the posture of the rider and the position of the horse. Notice how Velázquez compares the sparkling armor of the king to the glistening brown coat of his mount.

This great portrait artist urges us to use our eyes to learn of men, horses, and all of life.

441

Informal Assessment 

MAIN IDEA AND DETAILS

To determine whether students can recognize the main idea of a passage and the details that support the main idea, ask them questions like the following:

- ☑ What does the artist want to say about men and horses?
- ☑ What details does the author include about them?

CONVENTIONS OF LANGUAGE

ROMAN NUMERALS Call students' attention to the Roman numerals in the king's name: Philip IV. Kings, queens, emperors, and popes with the same names are differentiated by Roman numerals. The Roman numeral IV—four—shows that Philip was the fourth king of Spain to bear that name.

Critical Thinking Questions

1. **Why do you think Velázquez was asked to paint a portrait of Queen Isabella that matched her husband's and son's portraits?** (Possible responses: The paintings of the king and his son may have been displayed in one room. Perhaps the king wanted portraits of the entire family to be displayed together.) CRITICAL: DRAWING CONCLUSIONS

2. **The author states that Velázquez was dedicated to reality. Do you think the paintings of the king and queen show how they might have looked in real life? Explain your answer.** (Possible response: Yes, the king and queen look real; it's almost as if the paintings were photographs.) CRITICAL: MAKING JUDGMENTS

"Queen Isabella on Horseback" was painted to match the portraits of her husband, King Philip IV, and her son, Baltasar Carlos, both of whom were shown on horseback. By looking carefully at the horse's head and the raised hoof, you can see the artist's first painted outlines. He often repainted details in his constant striving for perfection.

Queen Isabella was the mother of Princess Maria Teresa, who became Queen of France.

In this graceful picture, the Queen's riding skirt, her arms, the horse's neck and prancing leg—even the clouds and the sloping hills—curve softly.

Velázquez was dedicated to reality and disciplined himself to painting precisely what he saw. He saw the world as it was and loved it. His joy in nature and human beings illuminates every painting and brightens those moments each of us spends in studying them.

442

SOCIAL STUDIES

HISTORICAL NOTE Queen Isabella, who is pictured on page 443, died in 1644. King Philip's second wife, Queen Mariana, is pictured and referred to on pages 446–447.

QUEEN ISABELLA ON HORSEBACK PRADO, MADRID

443

MINILESSON

REVIEW: COMPREHENSION

Referents

INFORMAL ASSESSMENT

Have students reread the first sentence on page 442 and tell to whom the word *her* refers. (Queen Isabella)

TEACH/MODEL

Remind students that writers often use pronouns and other words to substitute for a preceding word or group of words in order to avoid repetition. Model how to identify referents, using the first and second paragraphs on page 439:

MODEL

In the first paragraph the words *that city* refer to Seville. In the third sentence of the second paragraph I see the phrase *this great teacher* and the pronoun *he*. I see that the phrase refers to Francisco Pacheco and the antecedent of *he* is Velázquez.

PRACTICE/APPLY

Ask students to find examples of pronouns or other words and their referents in this selection.

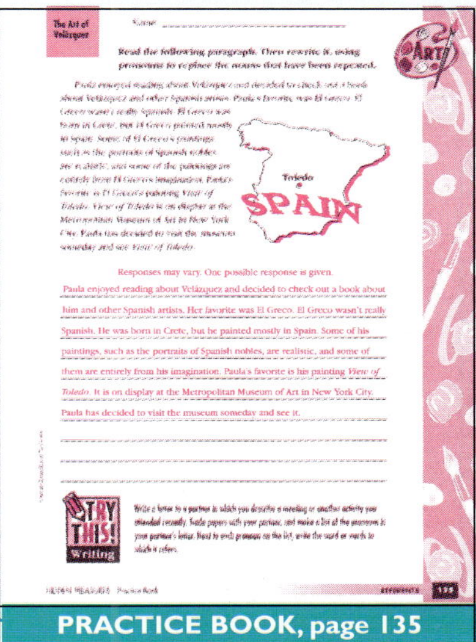

The Art of Velázquez

Name ______________

Read the following paragraph. Then rewrite it, using pronouns to replace the nouns that have been repeated.

Paula enjoyed reading about Velázquez and decided to check out a book about Velázquez and other Spanish artists. Paula's favorite was El Greco. El Greco wasn't really Spanish. El Greco was born in Crete, but El Greco painted mostly in Spain. Some of El Greco's paintings, such as the portraits of Spanish nobles, are realistic, and some of the paintings are entirely from El Greco's imagination. Paula's favorite is El Greco's painting View of Toledo. View of Toledo is on display at the Metropolitan Museum of Art in New York City. Paula has decided to visit the museum someday and see View of Toledo.

Responses may vary. One possible response is given.

Paula enjoyed reading about Velázquez and decided to check out a book about him and other Spanish artists. Her favorite was El Greco. El Greco wasn't really Spanish. He was born in Crete, but he painted mostly in Spain. Some of his paintings, such as the portraits of Spanish nobles, are realistic, and some of them are entirely from his imagination. Paula's favorite is his painting *View of Toledo*. It is on display at the Metropolitan Museum of Art in New York City. Paula has decided to visit the museum someday and see it.

TRY THIS! Writing

Write a letter to a partner in which you describe a meeting or another activity you attended recently. Trade papers with your partner, and make a list of the pronouns in your partner's letter. Next to each pronoun on the list, write the word or words to which it refers.

PRACTICE BOOK, page 135

SOCIAL STUDIES

Point out that the queen is using a special type of saddle called a sidesaddle. Until wearing pants became acceptable for women, they used a sidesaddle and sat with both legs on the same side of the horse.

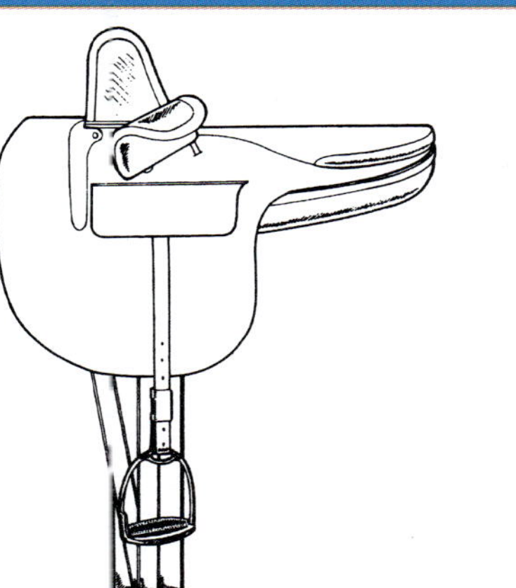

Cooperative Reading

Response Card 5

You may want to ask students who are working together the following questions about the author's viewpoint:

- **Does the author draw conclusions about the subjects of the paintings he discusses? How do you know?**
- **What biographical information does the author include in his discussions of the paintings?**

THREE MUSICIANS STAATLICHE MUSEUM, BERLIN

"Three Musicians" is one of the paintings that Velázquez painted between the ages of eighteen and twenty-one. These youthful paintings tell a story. In this one we can learn about some of the instruments people played at the beginning of the seventeenth century. We can study the clothing, the hair styles, and the shapes of the drinking glasses of the time when the artist lived.

Velázquez warms the happy scene with glowing yellow colors. The boy, with his pet monkey looking over his shoulder, seems almost to invite us to join the fun and to share the food and drink.

444

MULTICULTURAL CONNECTION

SEVENTEENTH-CENTURY CLOTHING Initiate a discussion of the clothing worn by seventeenth-century Spaniards, as shown in Velázquez's paintings. Encourage students to use reference sources to find out about the clothing worn during the seventeenth century in various parts of the world, such as China, Japan, India, Africa, and the British colonies in North America. Students might use their findings to create an illustrated world map.

JUAN DE PAREJA PRIVATE COLLECTION

"Juan de Pareja" is a portrait of Velázquez's servant and pupil. He assisted the artist by grinding paints, cleaning brushes, and when necessary was a welcome traveling companion. At the age of forty-five, Pareja greatly surprised Velázquez by turning out his own fine paintings.

By carefully studying Pareja's shining eyes in this painting, we can get an idea of the bond of friendship and respect between these two men. This portrait inspires us with its quiet strength. The bronzed glow of Pareja's open, intelligent face is highlighted by the snow-white collar and the sensitively painted folds of the rich brown tunic and cape.

445

Tested Skill

MINILESSON

REVIEW: GRAMMAR

Transitive and Intransitive Verbs; Objects

INFORMAL ASSESSMENT

Have students look at the second sentence on page 445. Ask them to find a transitive verb and to explain how they identified it. (*Assisted*; it has a direct object, *artist*.) Next, ask students to find an intransitive verb in the same paragraph and to tell how they identified it. (Possible response: *Is* is a linking verb; all linking verbs are intransitive.)

TEACH/MODEL

Review the following points with students, using examples from the selection:

- A transitive verb is an action verb that is followed by a noun or a pronoun that receives the action.
- An intransitive verb is a linking verb or an action verb that does not take an object.
- The noun or pronoun that receives the action of the verb is the direct object. A direct object tells who or what receives the action.
- An indirect object tells to whom or for whom the action of the verb is done.
- Use object pronouns as direct or indirect objects.

PRACTICE/APPLY

Ask students to find examples of intransitive verbs in the selection and to identify them as either linking verbs or action verbs that do not take an object. Then have students look for transitive verbs and identify whether the object of the verb is direct or indirect. You may want to have students create a chart like the one below:

Transitive Verb	Object	Direct/Indirect
tell	story	direct
inspires	us	direct

Intervention Strategies

USING BACKGROUND KNOWLEDGE **Ask students to repeat this sentence aloud or to themselves: *While I'm reading, I keep thinking about what I already know about painting to help me understand the descriptions in the selection.* Have students share experiences they may have had painting in school or at home.**

Strategic Reading

PAGES 438–447 What are the most important characteristics of Velázquez as a painter? (Possible responses: dedication to the truth, knowledge of his subjects, ability to capture a moment in time) STRATEGY: SUMMARIZING

How can you tell that Velázquez respected the people he painted? (Possible responses: He painted them realistically and depicted them as noble and graceful people.) METACOGNITIVE: MAKING INFERENCES

Returning to the Predictions/Purpose

Did you find out what you wanted to know about the life and work of Velázquez? Encourage students to discuss whether their purposes for reading were met. STRATEGY: RETURNING TO THE PURPOSE

Appreciating the Literature

Which of the paintings do you like best? Tell why you like it. (Responses will vary.)

THE MAIDS OF HONOR PRADO, MADRID

446

IDEA BANK

Encourage students to help you plan a visit to an art museum in or near your community. Before the field trip, they should find out what artists, periods, and so on are represented in the museum's collections. Suggest that during the field trip students take notes on works that especially interest them. Following the trip, encourage a discussion of what students learned from the visit or most enjoyed about it.

In "The Maids of Honor," called "Las Meninas" (läs mā·nē′ näs) in Spanish, Velázquez has painted a tender story of the Spanish Court. The artist shows himself with his brush and palette at work on a life-size portrait of King Philip and Queen Mariana. You can see them reflected in the mirror hanging on the back wall of the studio.

The little Princess Margarita does not want to pose, even though her attendant is offering her a bribe. No one in the scene—her maids of honor, the two dwarfs, nor her teachers—can persuade her. Velázquez understood this moment, and by painting the scene just as it happened, he has recorded an intimate glimpse into family life at the royal court.

This is one of the most famous paintings in the world. Velázquez has vividly captured this moment of childhood and made it live eternally.

ERNEST RABOFF

Ernest Raboff was uniquely qualified to write about artists, since he himself studied art in two of the world's most influential art centers, Rome and Paris. Throughout his life, in fact, Raboff maintained his connection to the art world in a variety of ways, working not only as an artist, but as an art critic, collector, and gallery owner. By writing his "Art for Children" series, Raboff was able to share his lifelong passion for great art with younger readers. In each book of this series, Raboff provides a striking introduction to the work of a different artist, including full-color reproductions of some of the world's most famous masterpieces. His subjects range from Old Masters, such as Velázquez and Michelangelo, to revolutionary talents like Pablo Picasso and Paul Klee.

447

About the Author

After students read about the author, you may wish to discuss the following questions with them:

- **Why do you think Ernest Raboff decided to write an "Art for Children" series?** (Possible response: He wrote the series for young people because he wanted them to learn at an early age to appreciate the world of art.)
- **Ernest Raboff had several successful careers that grew out of his love of art. Think of something you are interested in. How many related careers can you think of?** (Responses will vary.)
- **Why do you think Ernest Raboff included Old Masters and revolutionary talents in his series?** (Possible response: to share his knowledge of artists from different time periods)

Ernest Raboff was involved in the world of art for more than thirty years. In addition to being an art critic and gallery owner, he was also a lecturer in American art at the United States Embassy in Sweden. His popular "Art for Children" series has been described by *Publisher's Weekly* as "a satisfying reading and visual experience."

SUMMARIZING

K-W-L Chart

Encourage students to complete the third column of their K-W-L charts independently. Students might use their charts to write a brief summary statement. See *Practice Book* page 129.

K	W	L
What I Know	**What I Want to Know**	**What I Learned**
Velázquez was a Spanish painter who was born in 1599.	Who are the people in his paintings? What was his painting style? What did he want to say through his artwork?	Velázquez painted the king and queen, members of the court, his assistant, and other people.

PRACTICE BOOK, page 129

ACTIVITY CHOICES

DRAW A PICTURE

MASTERFUL MOMENTS Students may want to discuss important childhood memories with a partner before coming to a decision. Suggest that students create titles for their pictures that convey the scene's significance. **CRITICAL THINKING/ART**

WRITE A DESCRIPTION

DIFFERENT STROKES Remind students to use details from the selection as needed to support or illustrate their ideas. Students may write their descriptions in their personal journals. **WRITING**

SHARE YOUR AMBITION

BE ALL THAT YOU CAN BE Small groups may want to share their ambitions orally. Encourage groups to agree on a few tips for achieving a goal that they can pass on to other people. **LISTENING/SPEAKING**

Response Corner

DRAW A PICTURE

MASTERFUL MOMENTS

The author states that in the painting "The Maids of Honor," Velázquez seemed to capture a moment of childhood and make it eternal. What is a memory that you wish to preserve forever? Draw a picture of this memory, and share it with a partner.

448

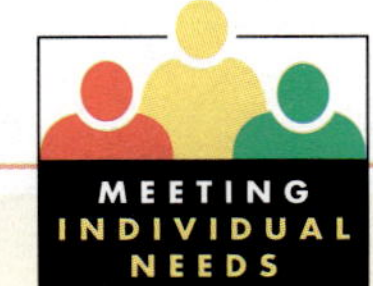

EXTRA SUPPORT Encourage students working on the Different Strokes activity to think about how to describe the painting without rereading the author's description.

WRITE A DESCRIPTION

DIFFERENT STROKES

Which of the paintings featured in the selection do you like best? Write a brief description of the painting. Tell what you like most about this work and why.

SHARE YOUR AMBITION

BE ALL THAT YOU CAN BE

Velázquez had an ambition—to be a great painter. He was dedicated to his goal and disciplined in his work. What is one of your lifelong ambitions? Share with a small group your goal and how you plan to pursue it.

What Do You Think?

- What do you think the author wanted you to learn about Velázquez?
- Has this selection changed the way you feel about art? Explain your answer.
- How would you describe this selection to someone who has not read it?

449

CHECKING COMPREHENSION

What Do You Think?

1. **What do you think the author wanted you to learn about Velázquez?** (Possible response: He wanted readers to learn that Velázquez was a realistic painter who captured his subjects' personalities in his work.) DESCRIPTIVE RESPONSE
2. **Has this selection changed the way you feel about art? Explain your answer.** (Responses will vary.) PERSONAL RESPONSE
3. **How would you describe this selection to someone who has not read it?** (Possible response: By studying an artist's work, a viewer can learn a great deal about both the artist and the time period in which the artist lived.) CRITICAL ANALYSIS/REFLECTING

VARYING THE ACTIVITY

To challenge interested students, suggest that they learn more about their favorite painting from the selection. Encourage them to research the painting and report to the class on its subject matter, composition, color, and any other information they learn.

Intervention Strategies

TIPS FOR CLASSROOM MANAGEMENT

IF second-language students need additional vocabulary and during-reading strategies to understand "The Art of Velázquez," **THEN** use *Sheltered English/ESL Manual,* pages 66–69.

IF students had difficulty understanding "The Art of Velázquez," **THEN** complete the Rereading Strategy. See also *Intervention Strategies Manual,* pages 98–103.

REREADING

EXPRESSING OPINIONS Point out to students that "The Art of Velázquez" is a nonfiction selection in the form of a picture essay. The text accompanying each picture tells about the subjects of the paintings and discusses details Velázquez included to bring the paintings to life. Have each student choose a favorite painting from the selection and reread the text about it. Then have students fill in a chart like the one shown with a summary of the text and a statement of their own thoughts and feelings. Allow students to compare and discuss the ideas in their charts.

What the Author Tells About the Painting	What I Think About the Painting

PERSONAL JOURNAL

Ask students to skim through their Student Anthologies to find particular pictures they like or think are interesting. Have students write about the pictures in their personal journals.

WORDS AND MEANINGS

SYNONYMS Tell students that synonyms, or words with the same or approximately the same meaning, are often used by writers to avoid awkward repetition; and that understanding synonyms can help them read more efficiently.

Write the following synonym pairs from page 439 on the board:

court	canvases	dedication
royal household	paintings	devotion

Call on volunteers to read the sentences in which these words occur. Discuss with students the meanings of the words. Then ask students to skim the selection and point out where the author uses other synonym pairs. (Possibilities include the following: *sparkling/glistening* and *illuminates/brightens*.)

WRITING TO DESCRIBE

Help students write a memory record about a painting or another work of art they may have seen on a visit to a museum, at a crafts fair, or in a magazine. Encourage students to use the following steps as a guide.

1. **Tell where and when you saw the work of art.**
2. **Tell what the work of art looked like.**
3. **Tell how the work of art made you feel.**

DECODING SUPPORT
Clusters with *s*

Intervention Strategies Manual **pp. 102–103**

ESL/TITLE I READING

Reading Trade Books

ESL/Title I Library

EASY AVERAGE CHALLENGE

Diego Rivera

by Mike Venezia

Like "The Art of Velázquez," *Diego Rivera* is the story of a famous artist.

Have students use a diagram like the one below to chart some of the differences between the two painters.

	Velázquez	Diego Rivera
Type of Paintings		
Beliefs About Art		
Career		
Personality		

EASY AVERAGE CHALLENGE

TAKE-HOME BOOK TO REINFORCE KEY WORDS

Students will enjoy reading about a girl who uncovers the truth in this realistic story. Students may want to read the book when they have independent reading time in class, or they may want to take it home to read.

PERSONAL JOURNAL

After students have finished reading *Charlie Spots a Fake,* have them write their reactions to the book in their personal journals.

See also *Intervention Strategies Manual,* page 101.

WRITER'S WORKSHOP

Descriptive Essay

TIPS FOR CLASSROOM MANAGEMENT

IF students are familiar with the steps for writing a descriptive essay, **THEN** have them begin writing, referring to the model on Transparencies 42A–42B as necessary.

IF you want a short writing activity, **THEN** adapt this lesson by having students use what they learn about the Writer's Craft to revise a description they have written earlier.

TECHNOLOGY

THE AMAZING WRITING MACHINE Students can use the drawing tools in the program to illustrate their descriptive essays.

Thinking as Writers

WRITING FORM: Descriptive Essay Remind students that the author of "The Art of Velázquez" used sensory language and vivid words to describe the artist's paintings. Tell students that they are going to learn more about descriptive writing and then write a descriptive essay.

Display Transparencies 42A–42B, and discuss the parts of a descriptive essay. (The complete model appears at the back of this Teacher's Edition.)

Explain that like a descriptive paragraph, a descriptive essay paints a vivid picture of a subject. Use the introduction and the side notes to guide discussion of the descriptive essay in the model.

TRANSPARENCY 42A, 42B

Model: Descriptive Essay

*A **descriptive essay** is longer and more complete than a descriptive paragraph. Like a descriptive paragraph, however, it uses sensory details to paint a picture.*

Morning in Barbados

introduction	When I am visiting my grandmother and aunt in Barbados, I find that I get up very early. I want to spend every possible moment outdoors. That is because mornings in Barbados are not like mornings anywhere else.
sensory details in time order	Morning in Barbados begins with the crow of a dozen roosters. Moments later, the clop-clop of hooves tells me that our neighbor is leaving for work. Wagon wheels whir and crunch over the rocky dirt road outside.
figurative language / **vivid verbs**	I run to the doorway and look out. To the east, the sun is a ball of fire over the ocean. The waves glisten as though they were brand-new today. Seagulls wheel on the air currents over the cliffs.

WRITER'S CRAFT: Sensory Language The details in the essay should appeal to the reader's senses of sight, hearing, smell, touch, and taste. Read aloud the last sentence on page 445 of "The Art of Velázquez," and have students identify precise nouns and vivid adjectives that help them visualize the artist's subject. *(bronzed glow, snow-white collar, rich brown tunic and cape)*

PREWRITING AND DRAFTING

Remind students to pick a topic that interests them, perhaps one involving art or a creative experience. Refer to these strategies to help students begin their descriptive essays.

PREWRITING GRAPHIC ORGANIZER Some students may benefit from using a web like the one below to organize sensory details.

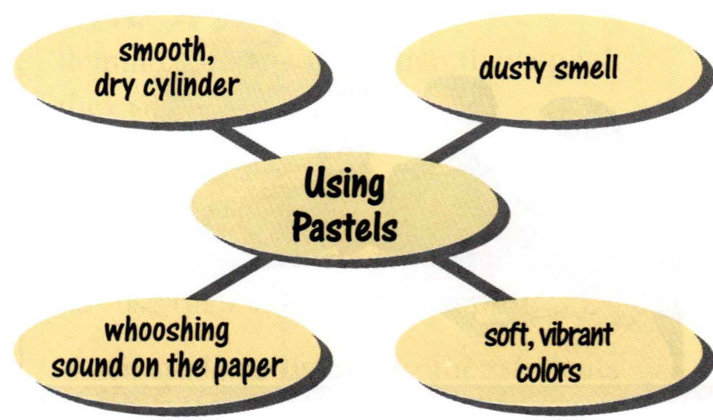

SUSTAINED SILENT WRITING Students who readily decide on a topic may begin writing without interruption.

DURING-WRITING GRAPHIC ORGANIZER Students who need to organize their thoughts may benefit from making a time line if their essay is to describe something across time or a sketch showing relative positions if their essay is to describe something in space order.

RESPONDING AND REVISING

Suggest that students work in editing circles or with partners to help each other revise their writing. Write this checklist on the board:

- Did you begin with an introduction?
- Have you used words that appeal to the senses?
- Is your essay organized logically?

PROOFREADING

Offer the following tips as students proofread:

- Check for errors in capitalization and punctuation.
- Circle any words you think are misspelled, and find out how to spell them correctly.
- Check for correct use of **object pronouns** as **direct** or **indirect objects**. (See Grammar Minilesson on page T903.)

PUBLISHING

If you want to have students publish their descriptive essays, suggest these options, or have students choose their own methods:

ORAL Students might deliver their descriptions to classmates orally by role-playing the narrator of an educational television program.

WRITTEN Encourage students to illustrate their essays and display them on a classroom bulletin board. After the display has been disassembled, have students save their writing in their portfolios.

PORTFOLIO OPPORTUNITY

Have students answer the Student Self-Assessment questions and include both their answers and their descriptive essays in their portfolios.

LANGUAGE HANDBOOK

Using Exact Words, page 28; Writing to Describe, pages 54–55; Descriptive Essay, pages 58–59

Student Self-Assessment ✓

Have students answer the following questions and include the answers in their portfolios:

- ☑ What did you like best about your descriptive essay?
- ☑ Did you make the essay more descriptive in the revising stage? Tell how.

EVALUATION BENCHMARKS: DESCRIPTIVE ESSAY

A descriptive essay by a proficient student writer shows the following characteristics:

FORM	CRAFT	CONVENTIONS
Demonstrates understanding of the form • clear introduction • details in logical order	**Uses clear and appropriate language** • vivid verbs and adjectives • language that appeals to the reader's senses	**Follows conventions of grammar and usage** • correct use of pronouns as direct or indirect objects • correct capitalization and punctuation

Teacher Assessment As you assess students' writing, refer to the Evaluation Benchmarks chart. For additional information, including model papers, see *Integrated Performance Assessment* Teacher's Edition.

Tested Skill

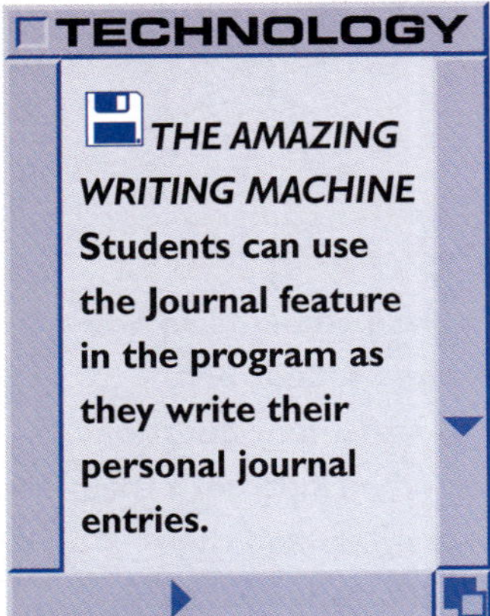

LANGUAGE HANDBOOK Predicate Nominatives and Predicate Adjectives, pages 152–153

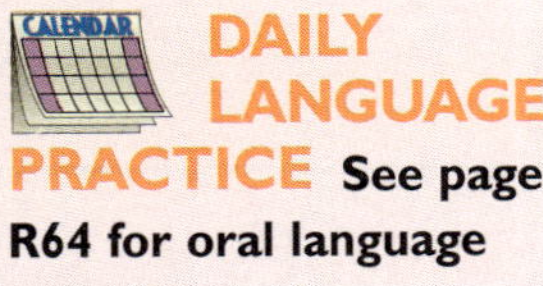

DAILY LANGUAGE PRACTICE See page R64 for oral language exercises.

GRAMMAR

Predicate Nominatives and Adjectives

Reading ↔ Writing Connection

Connect to the literature. On the board, write the following sentences:

Queen Isabella was the mother of Princess Maria Teresa.

Velázquez was dedicated to reality.

Call on a volunteer to read aloud the first sentence. Ask what noun tells who Queen Isabella was. (*mother*) Underline *was* and circle *mother*. Then have the second sentence read aloud, and ask what adjective describes the subject, *Velázquez*. (*dedicated*) Underline *was* and circle *dedicated*.

Build oral language. Point out that in the first sentence a noun follows the linking verb *was*, and in the second sentence an adjective follows the linking verb. Encourage students to offer oral sentences in which a noun or an adjective that tells about the subject follows a linking verb.

Portrait of Francesco I by Velázquez

Teach/Model

Discuss predicate nominatives and predicate adjectives. Explain the following points to students:

- **A noun or pronoun that follows a linking verb and renames the subject is called a predicate nominative.**
- **An adjective that follows a linking verb and describes the subject is called a predicate adjective.**

Practice/Apply

Check understanding. Write the following sentences on the board, and have students tell whether the underlined word or group of words is a predicate nominative or a predicate adjective:

Velázquez became famous for his portraits. (predicate adjective)

King Philip IV was the painter's sponsor. (predicate nominative)

Princess Margarita was reluctant to pose. (predicate adjective)

Velázquez seemed compassionate and understanding. (predicate adjectives)

Practice Activities

Rename or Describe

ORAL APPLICATION Have pairs of students take turns creating oral sentences that contain predicate nominatives and predicate adjectives. If the first student uses a predicate nominative, the second student must use the same subject in a sentence that contains a predicate adjective; for example:

FIRST STUDENT: Philip was the king of Spain.

SECOND STUDENT: Philip seemed noble and powerful.

Encourage students to use a variety of linking verbs in their sentences. **AUDITORY**

Write Sentences

WRITING APPLICATION Have each student write four or five sentences that include a subject, a linking verb, and a blank where a predicate nominative or a predicate adjective might go. Then have students exchange papers and complete each other's sentences. Ask students to return the completed sentences and discuss how the sentences turned out. **VISUAL/AUDITORY**

Write a Description

WRITING APPLICATION Display one or more prints of famous paintings or reproductions of paintings in art books. Have groups of four or five students choose one painting and brainstorm adjectives that might be used to describe elements in the painting or the painting as a whole. Have each group choose one member to act as Recorder and write down the group's adjectives. Students should then work together to write a description of the painting, using the adjectives in complete sentences. The group's Recorder can write the final copy, and a student-chosen Reporter can read the finished piece to the class. **VISUAL/AUDITORY**

APPLY TO WRITING

You may want to suggest to students that they check their descriptions to be sure they did not overuse the linking verb *be*.

USAGE TIP Pronouns used as predicate nominatives must be subject pronouns. Example: The first people to arrive were Sharon and I.

EXTRA SUPPORT

Remind students that forms of *be* are the most common linking verbs. Other linking verbs include forms of *appear, become, feel, look, seem, smell,* and *taste.* You may want to post a chart of linking verbs on a bulletin board. Be sure to point out that some linking verbs can also be action verbs.

RETEACH

See page R54 for lessons in multiple modalities.

GRAMMAR PRACTICE BOOK
pages 42–43

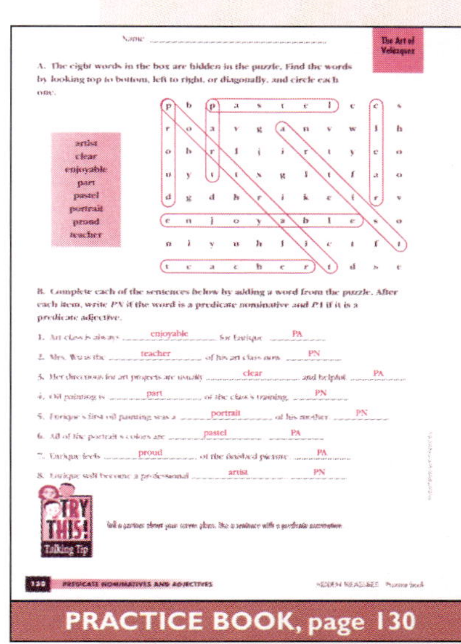

Name ______________________

The Art of Velázquez

A. The eight words in the box are hidden in the puzzle. Find the words by looking top to bottom, left to right, or diagonally, and circle each one.

artist
clear
enjoyable
part
pastel
portrait
proud
teacher

p	b	p	a	s	t	e	l	c	c	s
r	o	a	v	g	a	n	v	w	l	h
o	h	r	l	j	i	r	t	y	e	o
u	y	t	t	s	g	l	t	f	a	o
d	g	d	h	r	i	k	e	i	r	v
e	n	j	o	y	a	b	l	e	s	o
n	i	y	u	h	f	i	e	t	f	t
t	e	a	c	h	e	r	t	d	s	e

B. Complete each of the sentences below by adding a word from the puzzle. After each item, write *PN* if the word is a predicate nominative and *PA* if it is a predicate adjective.

1. Art class is always ___enjoyable___ for Enrique. ___PA___
2. Mrs. Wu is the ___teacher___ of his art class now. ___PN___
3. Her directions for art projects are usually ___clear___ and helpful. ___PA___
4. Oil painting is ___part___ of the class's training. ___PN___
5. Enrique's first oil painting was a ___portrait___ of his mother. ___PN___
6. All of the portrait's colors are ___pastel___. ___PA___
7. Enrique feels ___proud___ of the finished picture. ___PA___
8. Enrique will become a professional ___artist___. ___PN___

TRY THIS! Talking Tip

130 PREDICATE NOMINATIVES AND ADJECTIVES

PRACTICE BOOK, page 130

5-DAY PLAN	
Day 1 Complete page T914.	**Day 4** Choose a Practice Activity or *Grammar Practice Book* pages 42–43.
Day 2 Complete a Practice Activity on page T915.	**Day 5** Complete *Practice Book* page 130.
Day 3 Choose a Practice Activity or *Language Handbook* pages 152–153.	

Use in conjunction with Daily Language Practice.

2

SPELLING

5-Day Plan

Integrated Spelling Lesson 25: student book, pages 106–109; Teacher's Edition, pages T165–T170.

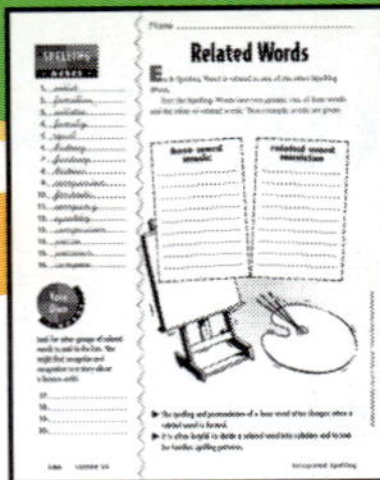

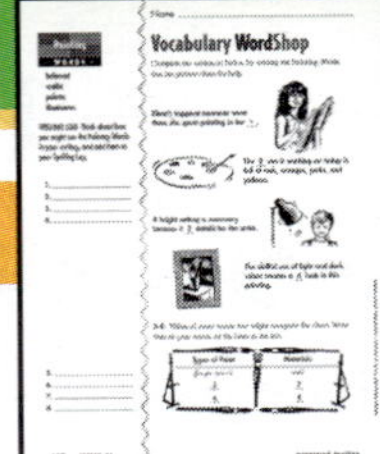
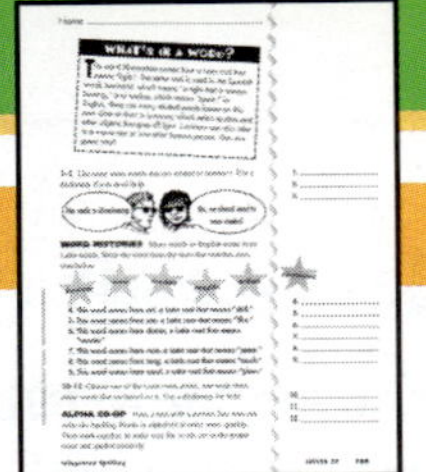

SPELLING WORDS

1. artist ★
2. familiar
3. artistic ★
4. family ★
5. equal
6. history
7. fantasy
8. historic
9. companion ★
10. fantastic
11. company
12. equality
13. comparison
14. precise ★
15. precision
16. compare ★

STUDENT'S PERSONAL WORDS

17. 19.
18. 20.

★ Words appearing in "The Art of Velázquez"

Related Words

Pretest

DAY 1 **Administer the pretest.** Say each word, and then use it in the dictation sentence below. Help students self-check their pretests.

OPEN SORT

DAY 2 **Have students classify words.** Have groups of students study the list of Spelling Words and decide how the words could be sorted into categories. For example, they might sort the words according to part of speech. Encourage groups to compare their lists and explain their categories.

CLOSED SORT

Sort by common root. On the board, write the first word in each pair below. Then call on volunteers to write on the board the Spelling Word that goes with each of the words.

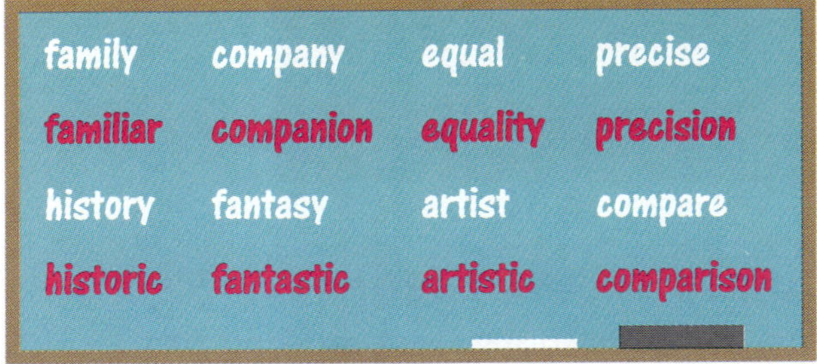

Teach/Model

DAY 3 **Discuss the generalization.** Invite students to tell what they notice about each pair of words. Guide students to recognize that the two words share a common root.

DAY 4 **Apply to writing.** Encourage students to look for related words in their descriptions to make sure they are spelled correctly.

Posttest

DAY 5 **Assess students' progress.** Use the sentences below to administer the posttest.

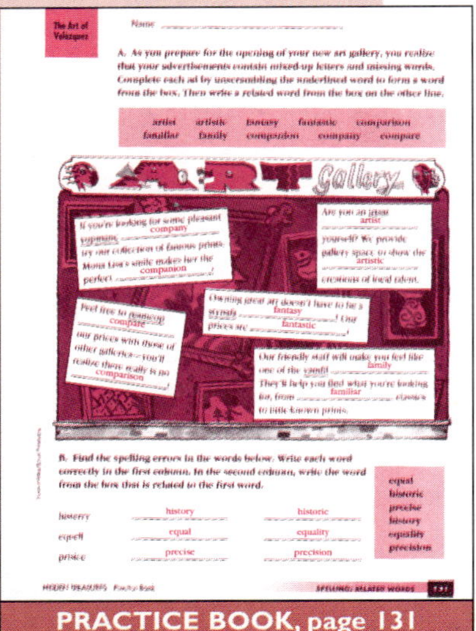

PRACTICE BOOK, page 131

DICTATION SENTENCES

1. An artist drew a picture of me.
2. We are studying the history of Europe.
3. My dog is my favorite companion.
4. Sarah is artistic and paints pictures.
5. All people should have equal rights.
6. We made a comparison of two paintings.
7. Are you familiar with this artist's work?
8. The signing of the Declaration of Independence was a historic event.
9. The map shows the precise location of the treasure.
10. Equality under the law is important.
11. There are three children in my family.
12. I have a fantasy about becoming famous.
13. A draftsperson draws with precision.
14. Compare the governments of Canada and the United States.
15. I saw a fantastic movie last night.
16. Jerry is very good company.

VOCABULARY WORKSHOP

Reviewing Key Words

Have students answer the following questions orally or in writing:

1. To what position was Velázquez *appointed*? (court painter)
2. What did Velázquez show great *devotion* to? (his art)
3. What was Velázquez *striving* for in his work? (perfection)
4. What quality in his work shows that Velázquez *precisely* painted his subjects? (He painted them as accurately as possible.)
5. How would you describe the *bond* between Velázquez and King Philip? (Velázquez worked for the king and was his friend.)

King Philip IV

Extending Vocabulary

FIGURATIVE LANGUAGE

Explain to students that authors often use figurative language to make their writing more interesting and to help paint pictures in the reader's mind. Share the following sentence with students:

Velázquez's paintings are like mirrors of the world.

Help students recognize that this sentence compares paintings with mirrors. Remind students that a comparison that uses the word *like* or *as* is called a **simile**, and that a comparison that does not use the word *like* or *as* is called a **metaphor**.

Discuss other types of figurative language:

- **Hyperbole:** an exaggeration that goes beyond reality to emphasize a point
- **Personification:** figures of speech that give human qualities to nonhuman objects
- **Idioms:** expressions with figurative meanings different from their literal meanings

Encourage students to write their own examples of figurative language, using Velázquez's paintings in the selection for inspiration.

Name

The Art of Velázquez

These art critics are describing one of the museum's newest paintings. Help them out by completing their comments with similes, metaphors, or other figures of speech. Responses will vary.

The artist is painting her impression of a storm at sea. Notice how the clouds loom overhead like menacing birds of prey

How muted all of the colors are—except for the captain's uniform! It's as red as a warning flare

The sea is tossing the ship like an angry child with a toy

Yes, it's a terrifying scene. It's a nightmare of wind and rain

Look! Even the captain is cowering, as if he were a dog being scolded

Yet the first mate clings to the tiller like ivy on a tree trunk

You can feel his courage! In the middle of the driving rain, he's as immovable as a mountain

This is the best work I've seen by this artist. After some years struggling uphill, she has finally reached the peak of her creativity

TRY THIS! Talking Tip

Find examples of artwork that you like. Share your favorites with a classmate. Tell what you like about them, using figurative language whenever possible.

132 FIGURATIVE LANGUAGE

HIDDEN TREASURES Practice Book

PRACTICE BOOK, page 132

Tested Skill

INTRODUCE: COMPREHENSION STRATEGY

Main Idea and Details

OBJECTIVE: To identify a main idea and supporting details

Informal Assessment ✓

Are students able to

- ☑ identify the stated main idea of a passage?
- ☑ use details to infer an unstated main idea?
- ☑ identify details that support the main idea?

Teach/Model

Return to the literature. Ask students to reread the text on page 445. Point out that the main idea, that Juan de Pareja was Velázquez's servant and pupil, is clearly stated. The other sentences give details that support this main idea. For example, one sentence states that Juan assisted the artist by grinding paints and cleaning brushes.

Model identifying the unstated main idea. Explain that sometimes an author infers the main idea of a passage instead of stating it directly. Have students reread page 444 and review the painting that goes with it. Point out that the main idea is not clearly stated, but must be inferred. You may wish to model the thinking:

MODEL **I read in the text that Velázquez's paintings tell a story. I look in the painting "Three Musicians" for details that tell a story. The painting shows a happy scene of people who lived in the seventeenth century. I can infer from the text and picture that this is the most important idea on this page.**

Explain that recognizing the stated or unstated main idea of a selection, passage, or paragraph, with the supporting details, enables students to understand the information they are reading.

Practice/Apply

Have students demonstrate understanding. Have small groups of students create a chart like the one below for other passages in the selection. Have students share their results and explain how the details support the main idea. Ask students to explain how they used details to infer main ideas not stated directly.

Main Idea	Juan de Pareja was Velázquez's servant and pupil.
Supporting Detail	Pareja ground paint and cleaned brushes.
Supporting Detail	Pareja turned out his own fine paintings.

Practice Activities

Create a Scene

COOPERATIVE LEARNING Have each student write on a strip of paper a main-idea sentence about a particular scene from real life or their imaginations. For example, *My family had fun at the beach*. Put the sentence strips into a container and mix them up. Have each student draw one sentence strip from the container and write three details that support it. Some students may want to illustrate their own or another classmate's scene. **VISUAL/KINESTHETIC**

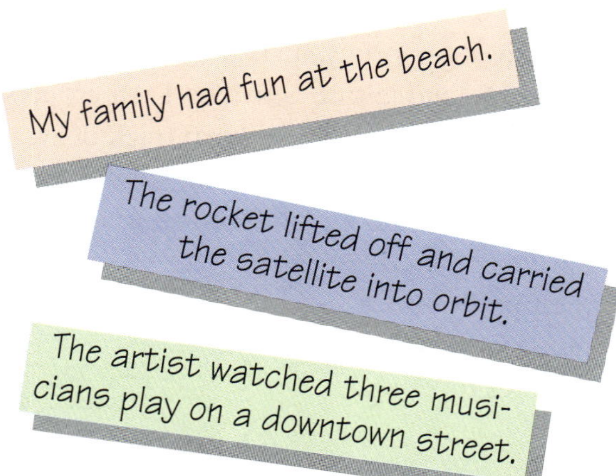

Ask and Answer Questions

PERFORMANCE ASSESSMENT Have students find the main idea and supporting details of a passage or chapter in their social studies textbook. Suggest that they ask themselves questions such as these: What is the stated or unstated main idea? What do the details that support the main idea tell about it? Students may want to use a chart like the one below to organize their ideas. Have students share their results and explain how the details support the main idea. **VISUAL**

Main Idea	
Supporting Detail	
Supporting Detail	

STUDENTS ACQUIRING ENGLISH

Have students work with fluent English-speakers to write scenes based on the sentence strips.

RETEACH

See page R55 for lessons in multiple modalities.

CHALLENGE

Have students research the life of another important person in the seventeenth century, such as a composer or an architect, and write a passage about this person. To plan their passages, students should note their main idea and the details they will include to support it.

The American Eye: Eleven Artists of the Twentieth Century **by Jan Greenberg and Sandra Jordan. Delacorte, 1995.** **AVERAGE**

Boy of the Painted Cave **by Justin Denzel. G. P. Putnam's Sons, 1988.** **EASY**

Take a Look: An Introduction to the Experience of Art **by Rosemary Davidson. Viking, 1993.** **CHALLENGING**

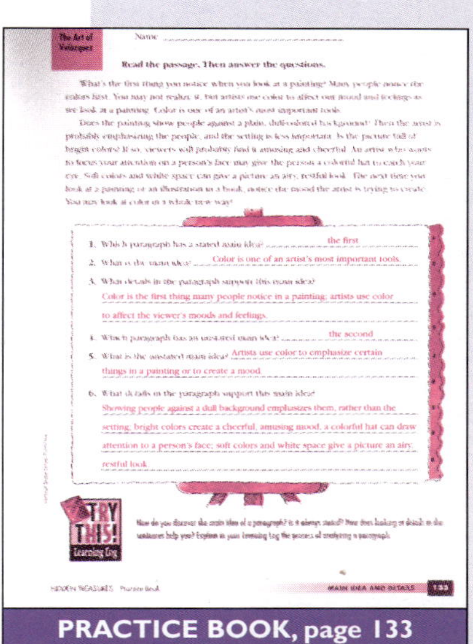

PRACTICE BOOK, page 133

Integrated Curriculum

ART/SOCIAL STUDIES

Reflecting the Times

Point out to students that "The Art of Velázquez" shows the musical instruments, clothing, hairstyles, and everyday activities that were common in the seventeenth century. In the following activities, students will investigate how art might reflect life.

TIPS FOR CLASSROOM MANAGEMENT

IF students are artistically inclined, **THEN** they may want to participate in the Our Life and Times activity.

SOCIAL STUDIES/ART

Lives of the Artists

Use reference sources. Assign students to small groups, and have group members choose an artist such as Mary Cassatt, Rembrandt, Edgar Degas, Norman Rockwell, or an artist of their choice to profile. Students should use reference sources, such as art books and encyclopedias, to create a profile of the artist. Encourage students to present an oral report accompanied by examples of the chosen artist's work. LISTENING/SPEAKING/READING/WRITING

Rembrandt Self-Portrait

ART

Our Life and Times

COOPERATIVE LEARNING Have students form groups of four or five. Explain that each group will work on one part of a mural that will show their own life and times. Groups should choose different aspects of their lives to portray, such as school life, home life, and leisure activities. Each group's Materials Manager should keep track of art supplies. The group's Facilitator should organize work on the mural. When all groups have completed their part of the mural, display the pictures together. Each group's Reporter can describe that group's section of the mural. LISTENING/SPEAKING/WRITING

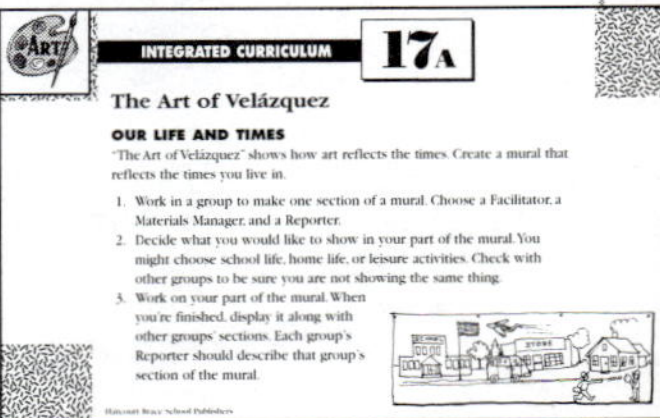

INTEGRATED CURRICULUM 17A

The Art of Velázquez

OUR LIFE AND TIMES

"The Art of Velázquez" shows how art reflects the times. Create a mural that reflects the times you live in.

1. Work in a group to make one section of a mural. Choose a Facilitator, a Materials Manager, and a Reporter.
2. Decide what you would like to show in your part of the mural. You might choose school life, home life, or leisure activities. Check with other groups to be sure you are not showing the same thing.
3. Work on your part of the mural. When you're finished, display it along with other groups' sections. Each group's Reporter should describe that group's section of the mural.

Curriculum Card 17A

TECHNOLOGY

IMAGINATION EXPRESS, DESTINATION: CASTLE Students can write a story set in the past and use details appropriate to an old-world setting.

MUSIC

Back to Bach

Set aside a time for students to listen to music of the Baroque period (the seventeenth and eighteenth centuries), such as works by Johann Sebastian Bach and Antonio Vivaldi. Have students compare the music of this period with present-day music. Students may want to take notes about the music they listen to using a chart like the one shown.

LISTENING/SPEAKING

Curriculum Card 17B

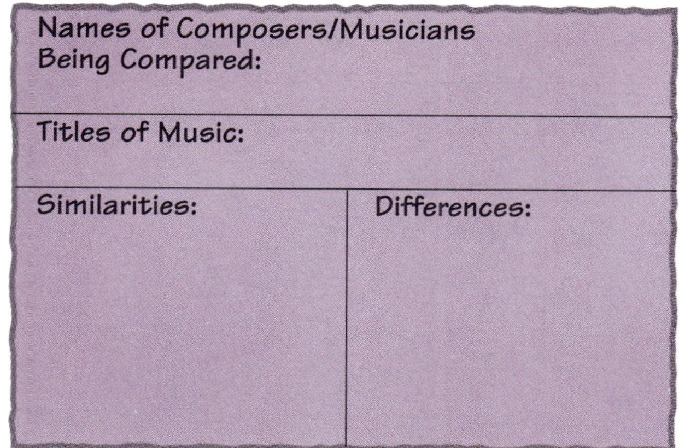

CROSS-CURRICULAR READING

Mary Cassatt by Robyn Montana Turner. Little, Brown, 1992. AVERAGE

Monet by Antony Mason. Barron's, 1994. AVERAGE

MULTI-AGE CLASSROOMS

Have older students participating in the mural activity act as Facilitators and help decide how the mural should be displayed.

Reading Trade Books

Trade Books That Connect to "The Art of Velázquez"

Don Quixote and Sancho Panza

by Miguel de Cervantes
adapted by Margaret Hodges

Students can explore the work of another Spanish master, author Miguel de Cervantes, by reading this vivid adaptation of his classic tale. After reading, encourage students to make a list of traits shared by Don Quixote and Velázquez's subjects.

Roy Lichtenstein: The Artist at Work

by Lou Ann Walker

Students can compare this in-depth portrait of a contemporary painter with what they learned in "The Art of Velázquez." Encourage students to choose one painting by each artist and write a description in which they compare the artists' subjects and styles.

Walking the Log: Memories of a Southern Childhood

by Bessie Nickens

This imaginative autobiography combines written descriptions with colorful paintings to create a vivid impression of the artist's past. Challenge students to describe how Diego Velázquez might have written a similar autobiography.

TIPS FOR CLASSROOM MANAGEMENT

SMALL-GROUP READING You might have small groups work together to preview one of the books by looking through the illustrations. Then readers can take turns reading and summarizing sections.

MEETING INDIVIDUAL NEEDS

STUDENTS ACQUIRING ENGLISH
Suggest that students at the intermediate fluency level read *Walking the Log: Memories of a Southern Childhood* independently.

A Weekend with Velázquez

by Florian Rodari
translated by Ann K. Beneduce

Velázquez acts as a tour guide in this illustrated introduction to his art. Encourage readers to use a web to collect information from both this book and from "The Art of Velázquez."

Western Art: 1600–1800

by Christopher McHugh

Readers can use this chronological overview to gain a larger perspective on the period during which Velázquez painted. After reading, encourage students to write their ideas about how Velázquez is similar to and different from other artists who painted during the 17th century.

The Young Artist

by Thomas Locker

This illustrated book tells the fictional story of Adrian Van der Weld, who is torn between his desire to paint landscapes and his job to paint portraits. Suggest that students use a cause-and-effect chart to compare Van der Weld's goals with those of Velázquez.

EXTRA SUPPORT

Suggest that students read *A Weekend with Velázquez* with a partner. Ask students to begin reading by describing each illustration in their own words. After partners take turns reading the text aloud, ask them to discuss how the text may have changed their ideas about the art.

Books

PROJECT MANAGEMENT

- PROJECT LAUNCH
- CHECKPOINT 1
- CHECKPOINT 2
- CHECKPOINT 3
- CHECKPOINT 4
- PRESENTATIONS
- ASSESSMENT

STUDENTS ACQUIRING ENGLISH

As students do their research, help them understand abstract art terms by showing examples that illustrate each term.

CLASSROOM MANAGEMENT

To spark student interest during the project, display art books, magazines, journals, and catalogs around the room for students to browse through.

TECHNOLOGY

THE AMAZING WRITING MACHINE
Students can use the Journal feature to express their thoughts about the range of art opportunities in their community.

THEME PROJECT CHECKPOINT 1

Research Community Art Events

SELECTION CONNECTION

In "The Art of Velázquez," students learn that Velázquez's teacher, Pacheco, taught his student literature and philosophy as well as the art of painting. Ask students why they think Velázquez's teacher included more areas in his instruction than painting alone.

PROJECT CHECKLIST

During this stage, students should

- ☑ use the library to identify upcoming art exhibits in the community.
- ☑ contact the Chamber of Commerce, museums, art schools, local colleges, and galleries for further information.
- ☑ decide who will visit each artistic event and schedule visits.
- ☑ if trips are not possible, invite speakers (artists, museum curators, or art teachers) to visit the class or arrange for in-school art exhibits.

Project Card 26 can be found as a copying master on page R75.

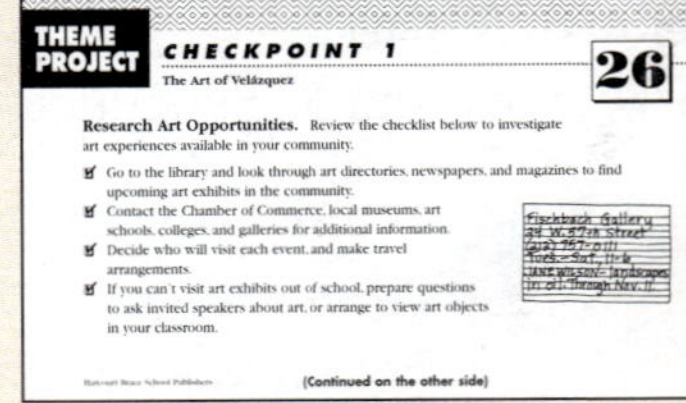
THEME PROJECT
CHECKPOINT 1
The Art of Velázquez
26

Research Art Opportunities. Review the checklist below to investigate art experiences available in your community.

- ☑ Go to the library and look through art directories, newspapers, and magazines to find upcoming art exhibits in the community.
- ☑ Contact the Chamber of Commerce, local museums, art schools, colleges, and galleries for additional information.
- ☑ Decide who will visit each event, and make travel arrangements.
- ☑ If you can't visit art exhibits out of school, prepare questions to ask invited speakers about art, or arrange to view art objects in your classroom.

(Continued on the other side)

Project Card 26

RESEARCH AND PLANNING TIPS

As students gather information, suggest that they

- record the name of each organization on a separate index card, along with its address, phone number, hours of operation, and schedule of exhibits or performances.
- use library resources to find information about the artists whose work they will see.
- feel free to split into subgroups or join with students from other groups to plan visits to art exhibits or performances in the community.

When students have completed the checkpoint, have them think about their experiences and write their thoughts in their project journal. Prompt them with questions such as *Which art events are you most eager to see? Why?*

Informal Assessment

As students complete this checkpoint, each group will research and **evaluate** information and **make decisions** about which exhibits and performances to see. Students are thinking critically if they

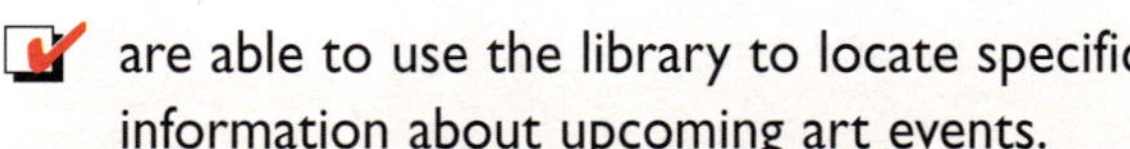

- ☑ are able to use the library to locate specific information about upcoming art events.
- ☑ work cooperatively to find ways for group members to attend art events.

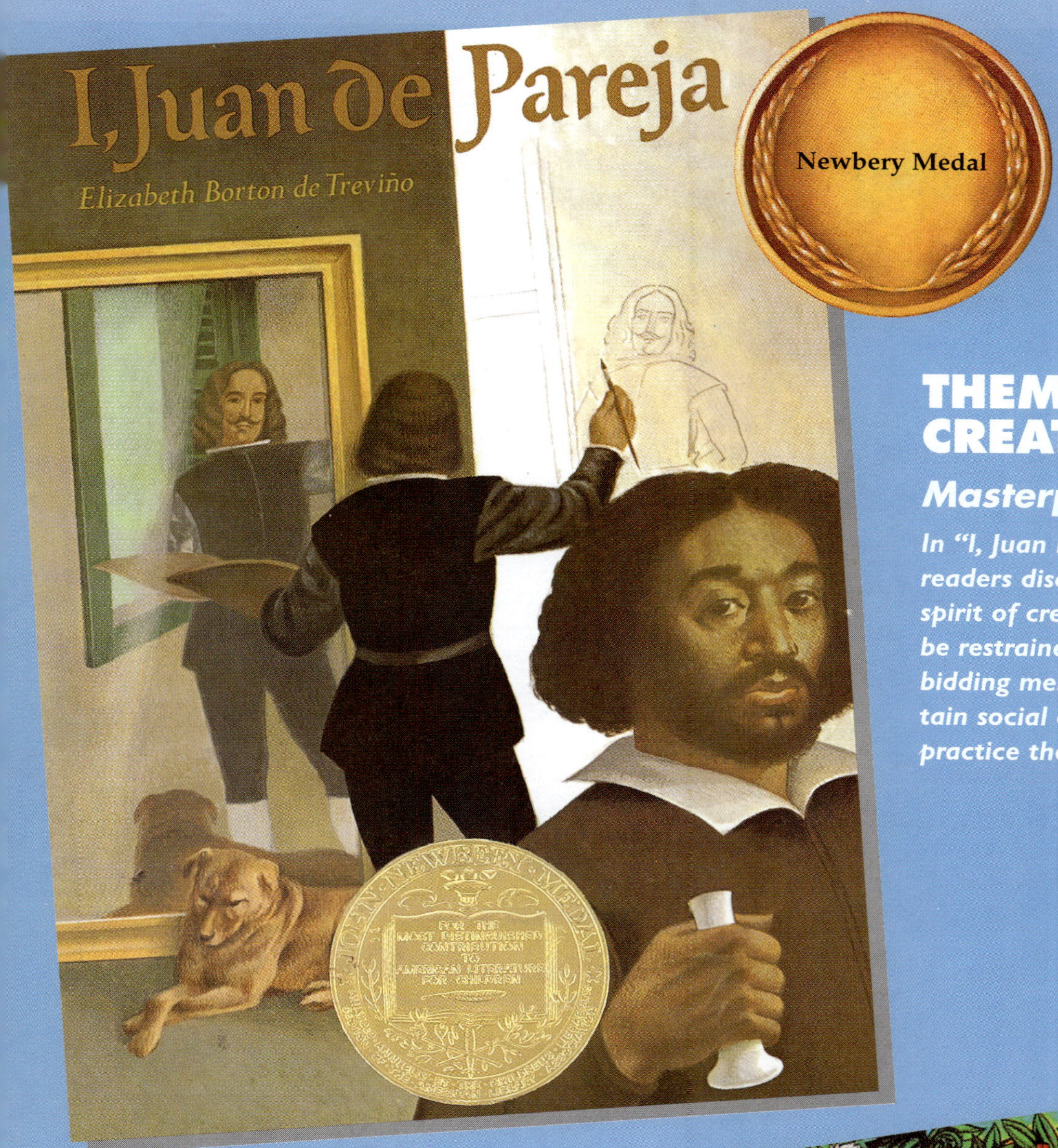

I, Juan de Pareja

Elizabeth Borton de Treviño

Newbery Medal

THEME: CREATIVITY

Masterpieces

In "I, Juan De Pareja," readers discover that the spirit of creativity cannot be restrained by laws forbidding members of certain social classes to practice the arts.

Elizabeth Borton de Treviño

ABOUT THE AUTHOR AND THE ILLUSTRATOR

ELIZABETH BORTON de TREVIÑO is a successful journalist and writer whose literary works focus on stories of interest to young people. In 1966, she won the Newbery Medal for excellence in children's literature for *I, Juan de Pareja.*

RICK FARRELL lives in Tacoma, Washington. He studied many books on Velázquez before he began illustrating "I, Juan de Pareja." "It was painless research," Farrell says. "Velázquez's work is so strongly drawn. I particularly like his portrait of Juan de Pareja, which is so rich and realistic that de Pareja seems to be alive."

More information about Elizabeth Borton de Treviño and her work appears on page T965.

Linking Poetry to Fiction

"The Paint Box" is a poem by E.V. Rieu that describes the relationship a painter has with colors.

SELECTION SUMMARY

Genre: Historical Fiction

Juan de Pareja, the slave of Diego Velázquez, court painter to King Philip IV of Spain, has secretly begun painting on his own—an activity forbidden to slaves. De Pareja has placed one of his paintings among those of his master, hoping, fearing, that the King will see it. When it happens, de Pareja confesses the painting is his and begs the King's forgiveness. Velázquez, to remedy the situation, which he sees as his own fault, frees de Pareja instantly. When de Pareja later admits that he loves Lolis, a female household slave, Velázquez gives them permission to marry. Surprisingly, Lolis refuses de Pareja, saying that she will not rear children in slavery. Velázquez's wife responds by freeing Lolis, and Lolis and de Pareja look forward to a time when not only their own children, but all people, will be born free.

SUGGESTED LESSON PLANNER

▶ *I, Juan de Pareja*

	DAY 1	DAY 2
PART 1 Reading / Listening / Speaking / Viewing **Key Words**: intention, radiantly, virtues, indisposed	**BUILD BACKGROUND** T928 **VOCABULARY STRATEGIES** T929 *Transparency 43* *Practice Book* p. 136 **READING THE SELECTION** T930–T945 Options for Reading T930–T931 *Response Card 6* *Literature Cassette 3* **REVIEW PREDICTIONS/PURPOSE** T944 **APPRECIATING THE LITERATURE** T944 NOTE: Students may read the selection on Day 2.	**SUMMARIZE THE SELECTION** T945 *Practice Book* p. 137 **READ POETRY** T946–T947 "The Paint Box" ◆ **RESPONSE CORNER ACTIVITIES** T948 **CHECKING COMPREHENSION** T949 *End-of-Selection Test*
PART 2 Writer's Workshop	**HISTORICAL FICTION STORY** Thinking as Writers T954 *Language Handbook* pp. 44–45 *Transparencies 44A, 44B*	Prewriting T954 *Language Handbook* p. 40
Grammar	✓ **SIMPLE TENSES** Teach the Concept T956 Daily Language Practice (1–2) R65	Daily Language Practice (3–4) R65 Practice Activity T957
Spelling	**PREFIX:** ***ad- (ac-, af-, ap-, as-)*** *accounts, applause, assigned, accused, accurate, affection, assistant, apparent, affair, appointed, approach, assembly, accident, association, appreciate, accustomed* Pretest/Self-Check T958 *Integrated Spelling Teacher's Edition* pp. T171, T295	Open and Closed Sorts T958 *Integrated Spelling* p. 110 *Integrated Spelling Teacher's Edition* p. T172
PART 3 Skills and Strategies	◆ **INTEGRATED CURRICULUM** *The Science of Art* **Science/Art** T962 **Art/Social Studies** T962 **Art/Math** T963 *Thinkin' Things Collection 2: Snake Blox*	**COMPREHENSION SKILLS** T960–T961 ✓ Context Clues/Multiple Meaning Words (Introduce) *Practice Book* pp. 141–142
MEETING INDIVIDUAL NEEDS	Use the Extra Support note on page T942 to help **below-level** and **ESL students** while they are reading.	Use the Extra Support note on page T957 to help **below-level students** in forming verb tenses.

NOTE: An alternative lesson plan for **below-level students** appears on *Intervention Strategies Manual* pp. 104–109. A lesson for **students acquiring English** appears on *Sheltered English/ESL Manual* pp. 70–73.

DAY 3	DAY 4	DAY 5
◆ **IDEA BANK ACTIVITIES** Retelling T952 *Response Card 11* Oral Language T952 Rereading T953 Real-Life Resources: Making Book Jackets T953 *Writer's Magazine* pp. 68–69 School–Home Connection 18 R95	**VOCABULARY WORKSHOP** T959 Reviewing Key Words **READING TRADE BOOKS** T964–T965 *Signatures Library: Journal of a Teenage Genius*  Signatures Library  Take-Home Book	**READING TRADE BOOKS** T961, T963, T964–T965 
Drafting T954 *Language Handbook* p. 41 *The Amazing Writing Machine*	Responding and Revising T955 *Language Handbook* p. 41	Proofreading and Publishing T955 *Language Handbook* p. 41
Daily Language Practice (5–6) R65 Practice Activity T957 *Language Handbook* pp. 154–155 *The Amazing Writing Machine*	Daily Language Practice (7–8) R65 Practice Activity T957 *Grammar Practice Book* pp. 44–45	Daily Language Practice (9–12) R65 *Practice Book* p. 138
Discuss the Generalization T958 *Integrated Spelling* p. 111 *Integrated Spelling Teacher's Edition* p. T173	Apply to Writing T958 *Integrated Spelling* pp. 112–113 *Integrated Spelling Teacher's Edition* pp. T174–175	Posttest T958 *Practice Book* p. 139 *Integrated Spelling Teacher's Edition* p. T176
COMPREHENSION MINILESSON T937 ✓ Main Idea and Details (Review) **COMPREHENSION MINILESSON** T939 ✓ Fact-Opinion/Author's Purpose and Viewpoint (Maintain)	**VOCABULARY WORKSHOP** T959 Denotation/Connotation *Practice Book* p. 140	**GRAMMAR MINILESSON** T943 ✓ Predicate Nominatives and Adjectives (Review) Theme Project Checkpoint 2 T966
Above-level students may read the selection independently.	**Below-level students** can read the *Take-Home Book: The Kids of Survival* to help them reinforce Key Words.	**Below-level** and **ESL students** may read the *ESL/Title I Library* book *I Am an Artist*.

✓ = Tested Skill
◆ = Optional activities used to adjust pacing throughout the lesson
Titles in *italics* are optional materials.

1 Reading and Responding

BUILDING BACKGROUND AND CONCEPTS

PRIOR KNOWLEDGE

Relate to students' lives. Ask students how they would feel and what they would do if they were forbidden to take part in an activity because of some personal characteristic. Discuss the feelings such prohibitions might evoke not only in the banned group, but in other people as well. Invite volunteers to tell what actions they might take because of such prohibitions.

Create a class chart about exclusion from activities. Remind students that in the previous selection, "The Art of Velázquez," they saw a portrait of the artist's servant, Juan de Pareja. Explain that in the selection they are about to read, Juan de Pareja's life changes when he breaks a law forbidding him to do something he desperately wants to do. With students, create a class chart, such as the following, about feelings and actions related to exclusion from activities.

Exclusion from Activities	
Feelings	
Of Excluded Persons	**Of Others**
determination to change laws resentment sadness helplessness	pity determination to change laws
Actions	
Of Excluded Persons	**Of Others**
do activity secretly give up try to change laws	try to change laws help people somehow

QUICKWRITE

Encourage students to write a few sentences stating their opinions about whether it is fair or unfair to prohibit people from performing an activity because of particular personal characteristics.

Intervention Strategies

For students who may have difficulty reading "I, Juan de Pareja," support is available in *Intervention Strategies Manual*, pages 104–109, and on pages T938 and T950–T951 in this lesson.

STUDENTS ACQUIRING ENGLISH

See *Sheltered English/ESL Manual* pages 70–73.

FACT FINDER

SOCIAL STUDIES

Slavery

Slavery existed in many past societies throughout the world. Slave-owning societies included Athenian Greece and Rome between the second century B.C. and the fourth century A.D. Slavery was practiced in various forms throughout Europe and in England, and throughout the United States until after the Civil War. Slaves usually had few rights, always fewer than their owners. In some societies, slaves were denied education. In seventeenth-century Spain, slaves were not allowed to practice the arts, such as painting.

Frederick Douglass, an American born into slavery, became a leading speaker against slavery.

VOCABULARY STRATEGIES

KEY WORDS DEFINED

intention plan; purpose

radiantly brilliantly, in a bright or glowing way

virtues good qualities or features

indisposed ill; unwell

INTEGRATED SPELLING

Spelling Pretest: page T958

Spelling Generalization: Prefix: *ad-* (*ac-*, *af-*, *ap-*, *as-*)

CONTEXT CLUES: EXPOSITORY PARAGRAPHS

Encourage students to use syntactic and semantic cues. Display the paragraphs on Transparency 43, and direct students to read them silently. Remind students to use both context clues and syntactic cues to help them determine the meanings of the underlined words. For instance, students should note that *or purpose* is used to show the meaning of *intention*.

CHECK UNDERSTANDING

Have students identify related words. Display the Key Words. Guide students in creating a chart similar to the one below by adding words and phrases that are related in some way to the Key Words. STRATEGY: CATEGORIZING

Key Words	Related Words
intention	(purpose; plan)
radiantly	(brightly; luminously)
virtues	(good qualities; fine traits)
indisposed	(ill; sick; unwell)

TRANSPARENCY 43

Key Words

Diego Velázquez and Peter Paul Rubens lived and painted during the same time. It was not Velázquez's intention, or purpose, to copy the style of Rubens. However, he did adopt the richer colors used by Rubens. Some of his later paintings seemed to glow radiantly, with the colors of life.

Velázquez possessed many virtues. Chief among his good qualities were kindness and consideration. He cared about the feelings of everyone, including those of his slave, Juan de Pareja. When Velázquez's wife was indisposed, he spent a great deal of time comforting her in her illness.

Jessica smiled radiantly when she received the award for making the honor roll.

Name ____________

I, Juan de Pareja

Read the boldface words and their definitions. Then complete the story in the picture frame by filling in each blank with the best word for each sentence.

intention: purpose; goal
indisposed: feeling somewhat ill
virtues: positive qualities or traits
radiantly: in a bright or glowing way

1. It was always Marisa's ___intention___ to study portrait painting.
2. Even her early portraits glowed ___radiantly___ with the rich colors of her unique style.
3. Finally, though, she heard of a teacher whose ___virtues___ as a portrait painter were said to rival those of the Old Masters.
4. The famous artist was ___indisposed___ on the day Marisa was to have met him, but when she sent him samples of her work, he instantly agreed to be her teacher.

TRY THIS! Writing

What art or skill would you like to study? Write a short paragraph about your interest, using as many of the vocabulary words as possible. In your paragraph, give clues to the words' meanings.

136 VOCABULARY HIDDEN TREASURES Practice Book

PRACTICE BOOK, page 136

Prereading Strategies

PREVIEW AND PREDICT

Direct students to preview the selection by reading the title and the introduction on page 451. Ask students what they know about Juan de Pareja's problem from their preview.

Begin a story map on the board. Students may use *Practice Book* page 137. Call on volunteers to fill in the characters, setting, and problem.

Story Map

Characters	Setting
Juan de Pareja Diego Velázquez King Philip IV	Spain seventeenth century

Problem

Juan de Pareja, a slave, wants to be a painter, but a law forbids slaves from practicing the arts.

You may want to suggest that students write their predictions about the selection in their personal journals.

PURPOSE

You may want to model setting a purpose:

I want to read to find out how Juan lets the King know about his desire to paint and what happens when he does.

450

TIPS FOR CLASSROOM MANAGEMENT

SMALL GROUP

STRATEGIC READING

Have students who need guidance with reading strategies, especially the focus strategy of **summarizing/paraphrasing**, read silently, pausing at pages T932 and T936 to discuss the strategies they are using. Remind students to refer to the class-made strategy chart for ideas.

COOPERATIVE READING

READER RESPONSE GROUPS

Suggest that small groups of students use Reader Response Card 6 to focus on the **author's craft**. Encourage students to record interesting words or phrases in their personal journals.

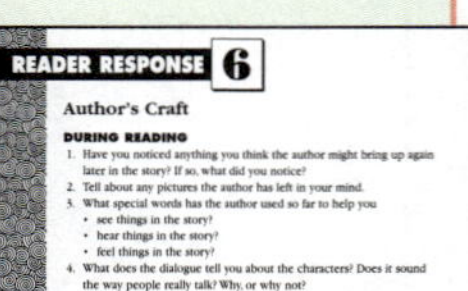

Response Card 6

I, JUAN DE PAREJA

SINCE HIS YOUTH, JUAN DE PAREJA (wän dāpä·rā′hä) HAS BEEN THE PERSONAL SLAVE OF THE GREAT SPANISH PAINTER DIEGO VELÁZQUEZ. WATCHING HIS MASTER AT WORK, JUAN HAS DEVELOPED A GREAT LOVE FOR THE ART OF PAINTING. SADLY, HE HAS HAD TO KEEP HIS OWN ARTISTIC TALENT A SECRET, FOR A LAW IN SEVENTEENTH-CENTURY SPAIN FORBIDS SLAVES FROM PRACTICING THE ARTS. THE TWO MEN ARE NOW IN THE EMPLOY OF KING PHILIP IV, AND JUAN HAS CHOSEN TO ENTRUST THE KING WITH HIS SECRET PASSION.

BY ELIZABETH BORTON DE TREVIÑO
ILLUSTRATED BY RICK FARRELL

451

WHOLE CLASS

READ ALOUD

After students have read the selection silently, invite volunteers to read aloud parts of the dialogue. Encourage students to use tone and inflection to convey the characters' moods and personalities.

SILENT READING/ DISCUSSION

Have students read the entire selection silently. After students have finished reading, have them discuss in pairs the predictions they made and whether they were confirmed. Encourage them to choose an activity at the end of the story and to work individually or in small groups to complete it.

Strategic Reading

SUMMARIZING/PARAPHRASING

Call on volunteers to discuss strategies they use during reading. Then display the class-made strategy chart, and explain that the focus strategy for reading "I, Juan de Pareja" is summarizing/paraphrasing. Remind students that summarizing involves briefly retelling the main points of a passage and that paraphrasing is restating an author's ideas in your own words. **STRATEGIES: SUMMARIZING/PARAPHRASING**

PAGES 450–457 Have students read through page 457 to find out what happens when Juan lets the King know about his desire to paint.

The King was in the habit of coming often, at odd hours, to pass a short while in the studio.

"You have only to see me as your sovereign when I speak," he told Master. "I wish to be able to slip in and out, quietly, without any formality, to sit and enjoy a painting of my choosing, and feel at peace." He had given me orders that I was not to "see" him either unless he spoke, whenever he came unaccompanied. "I wish to spend a little time in complete invisibility," he told us, smiling.

So cakes were always waiting for him in the studio, and one of his own easy chairs. His accustomed hour to drop in was late afternoon, before he had to dress for some court function.

Long ago I had heard some of the courtiers in Rubens' train say that the Spanish court was the stiffest and most boring in Europe. I am sure His Majesty found it so, but did not know what to do about it.

So he escaped, and sat gazing at some picture of Master's, which he had turned round from where they were stacked, and set up, at some distance from his chair.

I had secretly painted a large canvas, for Master was frequently in attendance on Mistress in her bedroom, where she rested many hours, and to which she called him to chat with her. She often felt lonely and needed him near.

452

STUDENTS ACQUIRING ENGLISH Remind students that many words in English have multiple meanings. Guide students in using context clues to determine the meanings of such words as *odd, slip, function, train*, and *round* on this page.

CONVENTIONS OF LANGUAGE

PROPER NOUNS Call students' attention to the use of capital letters in *King, Corso, Master, Communion, Our Lady, His Majesty*, and *Flanders*. Remind students that the names of specific people, places, things, and ideas are proper nouns and are capitalized.

My subject was the King's favorite hounds. All were dead, and they had not been contemporaries, but they had been favorites of his, and I knew that he would recognize them.

The three hounds (one of them was Corso) lay in a forest glade; a shaft of golden light came through the branches of the trees and lay warmly on them. One dog was turned toward me, tongue drooping from his mouth, the black doggy lips turned up in a smile; one looked away into the distance with pricked ears; and one dozed, nose on paws. I had taken their likenesses carefully from many paintings of Master, and I had worked out the setting with all the art of which I was capable.

Having received Communion and commended myself to Our Lady, I took that canvas and put it amongst those of Master turned against the wall, to await the King's pleasure. Then, trembling and already frightened, I awaited the hour when I would have to confess.

Several days went by. His Majesty was indisposed and remained in his apartments.

Master was painting another mirror arrangement, fussily moving his mirrors about, checking lights and reflections; he paid no attention to me and did not notice that I was nervous.

Then my hour struck.

It was late in the afternoon. Master was not painting, but sitting at his desk making out some accounts and writing to order special pigments from Flanders. The door of the studio opened quietly and His Majesty stepped in, looking around in his uncertain, apologetic way. He was dressed for some court ceremony: black velvet shoes and long black silk stockings, black velvet trousers, but instead of a doublet he wore

453

Student Self-Assessment 

FIX-UP STRATEGY: REREADING

Ask students what they could do if they do not understand why de Pareja has painted his canvas in secrecy and is so nervous about confessing that it is his. If students are unsure, model rereading as a fix-up strategy:

MODEL **I don't understand why Juan has to paint secretly. I'll reread the introduction to the story to find out why Juan is so nervous.**

ART CONNECTION

ART TERMS Point out to students that because de Pareja worked for a painter, the author uses terms related to painting, such as *canvas* and *pigments*. Invite students to identify other words that are related to art. Suggest that they create an illustrated glossary of art terms.

Critical Thinking Questions

1. **Why do you think Juan de Pareja decides to entrust his secret to the King rather than to his master, Velázquez?** (Possible response: He may be afraid that his master will disapprove.) CRITICAL: DETERMINING CHARACTERS' MOTIVATIONS

2. **As the subject of his painting, Juan chooses the King's favorite dogs. In your opinion, is this a good choice of subject or not? Explain your answer.** (Possible response: It is a good choice, because it will probably please the King.) CRITICAL: MAKING JUDGMENTS

454

SCIENCE

FACT FINDER

Hounds are among the most ancient breeds of dogs. Coursing hounds appear in ancient Egyptian drawings and may have existed in the area of the Black and Caspian seas more than 6,000 years ago. In every age, hounds have been the hunting dogs and companions of kings and members of the nobility. Ownership of these breeds was often forbidden by law to anyone but members of the aristocracy.

QUICKWRITE

Ask students to imagine that they are King Philip IV, and that they are seeing this painting for the first time. Encourage them to write a few sentences telling their reactions to the painting.

Student Self-Assessment

SUMMARIZING/PARAPHRASING

Remind students that they can check their comprehension of the story by summarizing and paraphrasing.

- ☑ How does summarizing the important events in the story so far help me understand why Juan wants the King to see his painting?
- ☑ What information would I give if I had to paraphrase the story for someone who had never read it?

VIEWING

Although the King's dogs are dead by the time Juan paints them, the story mentions how Juan has managed to use the dogs as a subject. He has studied various paintings of the dogs by Velázquez and has created new poses for them. Have students imagine how difficult it would be to paint a portrait from memory.

Detail of a portrait by Diego Velázquez

Strategic Reading

PAGES 450–457 **How does the King react to Juan's confession?** (Possible response: The King seems hesitant, calls Juan a "disobedient slave," and asks Velázquez what should be done with him.) STRATEGIES: SUMMARIZING/ CONFIRMING PREDICTIONS

What do you think Velázquez has written in his letter? (Responses will vary.) STRATEGY: MAKING PREDICTIONS

SUMMARIZING/ PARAPHRASING

If necessary, model the strategy of summarizing/paraphrasing:

MODEL **In order to remember the events on these pages, I can summarize them: When the King sees the painting of the hounds, Juan de Pareja confesses that it is his. The King asks Velázquez what to do. Velázquez asks the King's permission to write a letter.**

PAGES 458–464 Have students finish reading the story to find out how Juan de Pareja's problem is solved.

only a white shirt of thin cotton, and a dressing gown of dark silk brocade. I supposed that after contemplating a picture he meant to return to his rooms, put on his doublet, call the barber to shave him and curl his hair and mustache, and then attach his big white starched ruff at the last moment.

He pulled out his chair, sat, and stretched his long legs with a deep sigh. He smiled amiably at Master, who smiled back warmly, affectionately, and then went on with his accounts.

After a short time the King rose and went toward the wall. He stood hesitating a moment, and then turned a canvas toward him. It was mine.

In the late light, the faithful hounds shone out from the dark background, sunlight on their glistening hides, light in their big, loving, dark eyes. His Majesty stood transfixed; he had never seen that canvas before. I could watch his always-slow mind adjusting to the fact that this was a portrait of his own favorite hounds.

I threw myself on my knees before him.

"I beg mercy, Sire," I pleaded. "The painting is mine. I have been working secretly all these years, with bits of canvas and color, copying the works of Master, to

SOCIAL STUDIES CONNECTION

FABRICS **Point out to students the references to various fabrics and materials: cotton, silk brocade, velvet, Cordovan leather, and silk. Explain that, in the past, only natural materials were available. Invite interested students to investigate the types of fabrics and materials used in the seventeenth century, their origins, and their manufacture and to present an oral report to the class.**

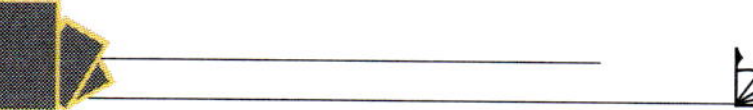

learn from them, and trying some original subjects by myself. I know very well that this is against the law. Master has never even suspected and has had nothing to do with my treachery. I am willing to endure whatever punishment you mete out to me."

I remained on my knees, begging the Virgin to remember my promise, praying and asking her forgiveness and her help. Opening my eyes, I saw the feet of His Majesty moving nervously about. Evidently he did not know what to reply. Then he cleared his throat and took a deep breath. The feet in the velvet shoes remained quiet.

"What . . . what shall we do . . . with this . . . this . . . disobedient slave?" I heard his voice lisping and stuttering, as he turned toward Master.

Still on my knees, I saw Master's neat small feet, in their shoes of Cordovan leather, approach and place themselves in front of my picture. He studied it some time in silence, and the King waited.

Then Master spoke. "Have I Your Majesty's leave to write an urgent letter before I answer?"

"You have it."

Master returned to his desk and I heard his quill scratching against the paper. His Majesty returned to his chair and threw himself into it. I remained where I was, praying with all my might.

Master rose, and his feet moved toward me.

"Get up, Juan," he said. He put a hand under my elbow and helped me to my feet. He was looking at me with the gentle affection he had always shown me.

He took my hand and put a letter into it. I have worn that letter sewed into a silk envelope and pinned inside my shirt ever since.

457

Tested Skill

MINILESSON

REVIEW: COMPREHENSION

Main Idea and Details

INFORMAL ASSESSMENT

Ask students to identify the most important thing that happens on page 456. (Possible response: The King discovers Juan de Pareja's painting.) Have students identify details that tell more about this important event.

TEACH/MODEL

Remind students that in fictional stories, other elements, such as plot, setting, and characters are used by the author to tell the story. Because of this, the main idea may not be stated directly. If it is not, the reader must infer the main idea by looking at the important details. Model determining the main idea of the last paragraph on page 456, which ends on page 457:

MODEL **Most of the details tell how Juan de Pareja works in secret to learn how to paint and that Velázquez does not know what Juan is doing. The main idea must be that Juan secretly teaches himself to paint, even though he knows it is against the law.**

PRACTICE/APPLY

Ask students to determine the main idea and supporting details of another passage in the story. Have them list several details from the passage and then write above the list what they infer the main idea to be.

EXTRA SUPPORT **Point out to students that although the characters in this selection—Juan de Pareja, King Philip IV, and Velázquez—were actual people, "I, Juan de Pareja" is an example of historical fiction. The author has made up the characters' dialogue and actions.**

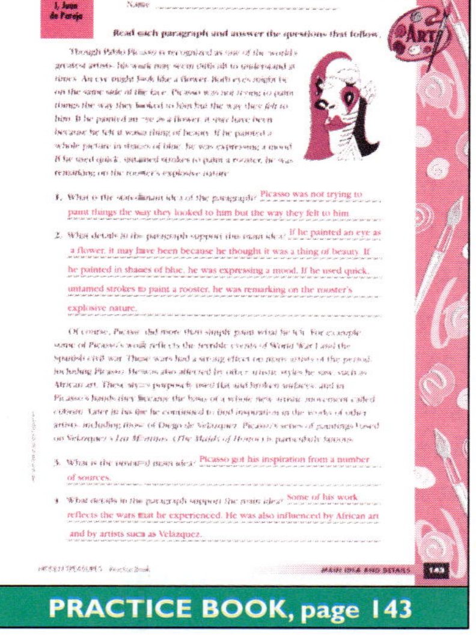
I, Juan de Pareja

Name

Read each paragraph and answer the questions that follow.

Though Pablo Picasso is recognized as one of the world's greatest artists, his work may seem difficult to understand at times. An eye might look like a flower. Both eyes might be on the same side of the face. Picasso was not trying to paint things the way they looked to him but the way they *felt* to him. If he painted an eye as a flower, it may have been because he felt it was a thing of beauty. If he painted a whole picture in shades of blue, he was expressing a mood. If he used quick, untamed strokes to paint a rooster, he was remarking on the rooster's explosive nature.

1. What is the unstated main idea of the paragraph? Picasso was not trying to paint things the way they looked to him but the way they felt to him.
2. What details in the paragraph support this main idea? If he painted an eye as a flower, it may have been because he thought it was a thing of beauty. If he painted in shades of blue, he was expressing a mood. If he used quick, untamed strokes to paint a rooster, he was remarking on the rooster's explosive nature.

Of course, Picasso did more than simply paint what he felt. For example, some of Picasso's work reflects the terrible events of World War I and the Spanish civil war. These wars had a strong effect on many artists of the period, including Picasso. He was also affected by other artistic styles he saw, such as African art. These styles purposely used flat and broken surfaces, and in Picasso's hands they became the basis of a whole new artistic movement called cubism. Later in his life he continued to find inspiration in the works of other artists, including those of Diego de Velázquez. Picasso's series of paintings based on Velázquez's *Las Meninas* (*The Maids of Honor*) is particularly famous.

3. What is the unstated main idea? Picasso got his inspiration from a number of sources.
4. What details in the paragraph support the main idea? Some of his work reflects the wars that he experienced. He was also influenced by African art and by artists such as Velázquez.

MAIN IDEA AND DETAILS 143

PRACTICE BOOK, page 143

Cooperative Reading

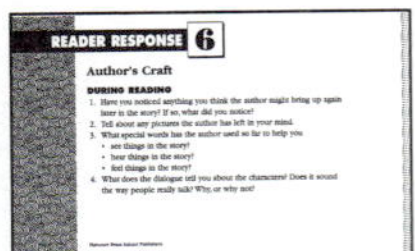
Response Card 6

As you circulate among cooperative reading groups, you may want to prompt discussion by asking questions such as these about the author's craft:

- **What details has the author included to show that this story is set in the past?**
- **What special words has the author used so far to help you see, hear, or feel things in the story?**
- **What does the dialogue tell you about the characters? How is the King's dialogue different from Juan's?**

The letter said:

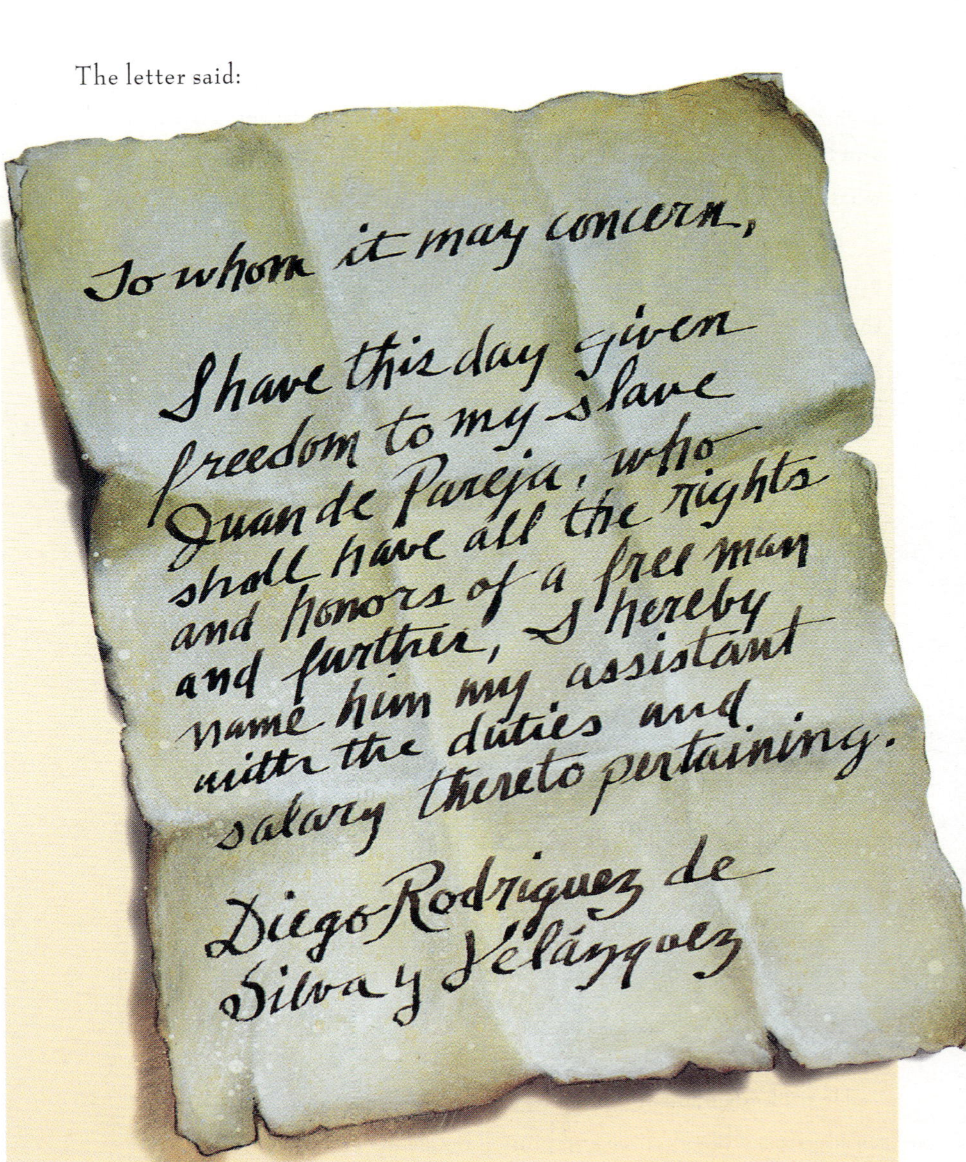
To whom it may concern,

I have this day given freedom to my slave Juan de Pareja, who shall have all the rights and honors of a free man and further, I hereby name him my assistant with the duties and salary thereto pertaining.

Diego Rodriguez de Silva y Velázquez

458

AUTHOR'S CRAFT

The incident related on these pages is an example of poetic license: the alteration of facts for dramatic effect. Having Velázquez write a letter of manumission, or formal emancipation from slavery, at the time his slave admits to the King that he has performed an illegal act is a dramatic and highly effective event in the story. In reality, however, Velázquez granted Juan de Pareja his freedom during a trip to Italy in 1650.

Intervention Strategies

SUMMARIZING Ask students to repeat this sentence aloud or to themselves: *When I read, it helps me to think about what's happened so far.* Have students tell how using this strategy might help them understand why the characters act as they do in "I, Juan de Pareja."

Master took the letter gently from my hand, after I had read it, and took it to the King who, reading, smiled radiantly. It was the first time in all those years that I had seen His Majesty smile. His teeth were small and uneven, but that smile seemed to me as beautiful as any I had ever seen.

The letter was given back to me, and I stood there, tears of joy streaming from my eyes.

"You were saying, Sire, something about a slave?" inquired Master softly. "I have no slave."

I seized his hand, to carry it to my lips.

"No, no," cried Master, snatching his hand back. "You owe me no gratitude, my good friend. The contrary. I am ashamed that in my selfish preoccupations I did not long ago give you what you have earned so well and what I know you will grace with your many virtues. You are to be my assistant if you wish, as you are my friend always."

"I am pleased," said His Majesty, and rose to his feet. At the door, before he left, he turned and said again, "I am pleased."

We waited, Master and I, side by side, bowing, as the King sailed down the corridor, his dressing gown billowing out behind him.

"Let us pack up our things, Juan," (he never again called me Juanico) "and go home. Mistress is fretful when I am not more often at her side. And I am tired."

"As your assistant, Master . . ."

"Now, do not call me Master anymore. Call me Diego."

"I cannot. You are still Master. My Master, as you were Master to the apprentices, and to other painters. Master means teacher, does it not?"

459

CHALLENGE **Guide students to recognize that the phrase *sailed down the corridor* is an example of figurative language: the author compares the King's movement, with his dressing gown billowing out like a sail, with the movement of a ship. Encourage students to think of other ways to describe the way the King moved.**

Tested Skill

MINILESSON

MAINTAIN: COMPREHENSION

Fact-Opinion/ Author's Purpose and Viewpoint

INFORMAL ASSESSMENT

Ask students what they think Elizabeth Borton de Treviño's opinion of King Philip IV is. (Possible response: The King is weak and indecisive but kind.) Call on volunteers to point out facts and opinions in the story that led them to determine the author's viewpoint. Then ask students to identify the author's purpose for writing the story. (to inform and to entertain)

TEACH/MODEL

Recall with students that recognizing the way an author uses facts and opinions can provide clues to an author's viewpoint—his or her opinion, attitude, or feeling—about a subject. If necessary, model the thinking:

MODEL **I know that the author's purpose in writing "I, Juan de Pareja" is not just to entertain but also to inform readers about this man's life. I can tell that the author disapproves of slavery because she tells her story from Juan's point of view. She also has Velázquez say that he is ashamed that he didn't free Juan before. I can tell that she approves of Velázquez freeing his slave because she uses emotional words, such as *smiled radiantly* and *tears of joy*.**

PRACTICE/APPLY

Have students create lists of facts and opinions from different passages in the selection. Students should use these lists to determine the author's purpose and viewpoint.

Critical Thinking Questions

1. **In what ways has being given his freedom changed Juan de Pareja? How can you tell?** (Possible responses: He has become more assertive; he tells Velázquez that he was in error when he said he had no slave, and he asks to marry Lolis. He is happier than he was before; everything seems new to him; and he says he has a new joy in his heart.) CRITICAL: COMPARING AND CONTRASTING

2. **What other changes do you think Juan's new freedom will make in his life?** (Possible responses: He will be able to paint openly rather than secretly. As a free man, he no longer has to serve Velázquez. He can own his own property and home.) CRITICAL: SPECULATING

"Yes."

"I was never ashamed to call you my Master, and I am not ashamed now. I shall always give you the respect of that title."

"As you wish."

We were walking through the streets of Madrid toward our home. I took each step with a new spring in my knees, a new joy in my heart, for I walked as a free man, beside my Teacher.

"But, Master," I said, as we crossed the Plaza Mayor, "you were in error when you said that you had no slave. There is Lolis."

"Lolis belongs to my wife," he told me.

I determined to make this a day radiant in my memory in every way.

"Master, when we were in Italy, you told me that I could ask anything of this hand" (and I took his right hand lightly in my own) "and you would give it to me. Now I know what to ask for."

He stopped in the square where the last rays of the sun struck level against us. "You want Lolis," he said, smiling.

"I wish to marry her. If she will have me."

"I will speak to my wife about it. I see no reason why you should not marry if you both wish it," he answered, and we continued to stroll in silence.

Inside our house—that house where I had lived so many years in peace of mind and spirit, even though I had not been free—everything now seemed new to me. The corridors, so much a part of my daily existence, the dark heavy carved furniture, the life-sized crucifix with its small glow and flicker of light always in a glass bowl at the feet of the Christ,

460

REAL-LIFE CONNECTION

Point out that now that Juan de Pareja is a free man, many new privileges and courses of action are open to him that were closed before, such as becoming a painter in his own right. Focus the discussion on gaining new privileges at certain points in one's life. Invite students to share their experiences, such as the first time they were allowed to go somewhere on their own or do something without a parent's assistance.

the dark red velvet curtains now drawn against the declining day to keep out the humors[1] and evils of night—all were dear and known to me, but somehow fresh and new.

We had no sooner entered than Lolis came running toward us, finger to lip.

"The Mistress has been in much pain today," she whispered, "and I have just now been able to get her to sleep."

"I will not go up then," answered Master.

We went into the dining room. Very often Paquita[2] came, with her little daughter, but today the house was quiet and still. I could see that Master was worried, and I knew why. Mistress was more and more often ill and weak, and sometimes she lay and cried.

When I went into the kitchen later Lolis came and laid her head on my shoulder. She was not weeping—I have always been quick to tears, but I have never seen one glittering on her lashes—but she sighed deeply.

"My poor lady," she grieved. "I have come to be fond of her, Juan. And soon we will have to give her some opium to stop the awful paroxysms of coughing. The King could get it for Master. It will be a sad time now, Juan, until God calls her."

Actually, as sometimes happens, Mistress rallied and seemed much better a few days later. She got up and was dressed and began to eat some of the dainties Lolis had prepared for her. On the second evening she came to the supper table and smiled and seemed very happy, sitting at Master's side. She ate quite a bit of supper and did not cough once.

[1] humors: air currents that people once believed could affect the way a person feels
[2] Paquita (pä·kē′tä): the daughter of the Mistress and the Master

461

Informal Assessment ✓

CONTEXT CLUES/MULTIPLE-MEANING WORDS

To assess whether students are using context clues to determine the meanings of multiple-meaning words, ask them questions like these:

- ☑ The word *square*, on page 460, has several different meanings. What could you do if you were not certain which meaning of the word is being used?
- ☑ What context clues help you recognize the correct meaning of the word *drawn* in the first line on page 461?

SOCIAL STUDIES

Point out to students that the author includes religious references to Christianity throughout the story. For example, earlier in the story, Juan receives Communion, and on page 460, Juan mentions a crucifix that is in a corridor he walks through. Christianity was introduced into Spain during the time of the Roman Empire. Today, 99 percent of the people of Spain are Roman Catholic.

Cooperative Reading

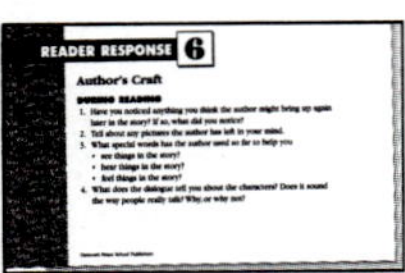
Response Card 6

Cooperative reading groups may want to discuss their reactions to the last few pages of the story.

- **What is your reaction to Juan's statement to Velázquez that he was never ashamed to call him master?**
- **Did your feelings about the characters change as you continued reading the story?**
- **What do you think about the conversation Juan and Velázquez have about Lolis?**

Master looked up at me suddenly and I could read his intention in his eyes. Turning to her, he said, "*Mi vida,*[3] I have given our good friend Juan his freedom and he is now my honored assistant. He will take many duties off my shoulders and I will rest more and be more often with you. I know you have been lonely with our daughter married and gone from the house."

"Ah yes!" cried Mistress, her thin face lighting up. "That is why I have been ailing. I have been lonely."

"And Juan wishes to marry. He has given his heart to you, Lolis. What do you say?"

Mistress clasped her hands. "Lolis!" she cried. "What is your answer?"

I remember that Lolis was wearing a dress of pale almond green, and she had bound back her hair with a rose-colored scarf.

"I can answer as I wish?" asked Lolis.

"Of course."

"My answer is No."

I felt as if my heart had been pierced with a dagger. Lolis saw the hurt in my face.

"It is not that I do not like him," she said, in her deep soft voice. "He is a good kind man, but I do not wish to bear any children into slavery."

Master's quiet voice was heard. "You are right, Lolis. Juan is now a free man. And I am sure my wife would like to give you your freedom, as a wedding gift. Isn't it so, my love?"

Mistress took her cue and answered at once, for she was always eager to please Master in every way she knew, and now that she was

[3] Mi vida (mē bē´ dä): love of my life

462

EXTRA SUPPORT Call attention to the numeral 3 after *vida*, and remind students that this directs them to look at a footnote with the same number at the bottom of the page. Ask students what information this footnote provides. (It translates the Spanish phrase *mi vida* into English.) Ask students to look back at the previous page and tell what information the first footnote there provides. (It tells the meaning of the word *humors*.) Explain that footnotes may also explain or add to information given in the text or provide the source of information.

ill, more than ever, it seemed.

"It is so indeed. If you will hand me the paper and pen and inkpot, I will write the letter of manumission now."

Mistress wrote the letter and put it into Lolis' hand.

"My dear Lolis," she said, "you are as free now, as you have always been in your spirit, I think. But I would ask a favor of you. Please stay on as my nurse. Do not leave me . . . just yet."

Lolis put the letter in her bosom, and she looked with tenderness at Mistress.

"I am glad to be free," she said. "More than you can know. I never dreamed that it would come to pass so soon, though I had seen in the future that it would be so, one day. Just as I have seen that I would marry Juan. Yes, I shall stay with you, Mistress, as long as you want me. And I thank you."

Quietly she gathered up some dishes and left the room softly.

Master gave me permission with his eyes, and I followed Lolis out into the kitchen. She was in a corner, on her knees, praying.

Tested Skill

MINILESSON

REVIEW: GRAMMAR

Predicate Nominatives and Adjectives

INFORMAL ASSESSMENT

Ask students to reread the first paragraph on page 462. Have them identify an example of a predicate nominative *(assistant)* and a predicate adjective *(lonely)*.

TEACH/MODEL

Review the following points with students, using examples from the selection:

- A predicate nominative is a noun or a subject pronoun that follows a linking verb and renames the subject: *Juan is now a free* man.
- A predicate adjective is an adjective that follows a linking verb and describes the subject: *I have been* lonely.

PRACTICE/APPLY

Ask pairs of students to find other examples of predicate nominatives and predicate adjectives in the selection. Call on volunteers to read aloud the sentences they find, and have other students name the predicate nominatives or adjectives in the examples.

CONVENTIONS OF LANGUAGE

DIVIDED QUOTATIONS Direct students' attention to the third paragraph. Explain that when a quotation is divided into two parts by explanatory words or a speaker tag such as *she said*, each part of the quotation is enclosed by quotation marks. If the divided quotation is a single sentence, as it is here, the first part of the quotation is followed by a comma placed within the quotation marks, and the second part begins with a lowercase letter.

Strategic Reading

PAGES 458–464 Why is it important that Lolis's mistress free her? (Possible response: Although Lolis loves Juan, she does not want to bring children into the world as slaves. She refuses to marry Juan because she is not free herself.) STRATEGY: SUMMARIZING

How is Lolis's attitude toward being a slave different from Juan's attitude? (Juan loves his master and is grateful for his kindness. Lolis cannot feel grateful for kindness because she deeply resents being owned.) INFERENTIAL: COMPARING AND CONTRASTING

Returning to the Predictions/Purpose

Did you find out what happened to Juan after he showed his painting to the King? Encourage students to discuss whether their purposes for reading were met. STRATEGY: RETURNING TO THE PURPOSE

Appreciating the Literature

Did you feel sympathy for any of the characters in this story? Explain your answer. (Responses will vary.)

"I was thanking God," she told me. "I have prayed for this every day of my life."

"And you will marry me, Lolis?"

"Yes. But you could have found a better woman, Juan. I am proud and haughty and sometimes I have a sharp tongue."

"It is you I want, just as you are."

She came into my arms then, and let me caress her hair, her cheek and her forehead.

"I have resented being a slave," she said. "I could not feel grateful in my heart, for deep inside me I resented being bound. I know that God made us all free and that no man should own another. I hated serving people because I was a slave and had to do their will. Only here in this house I had some peace because you are all kind and Mistress is sweet and affectionate. I will do my best to make her last days comfortable. But I am not like you, Juan, grateful and loving. I *hated* being owned! It was all I could do, some days, to keep the hot words inside my mouth and the resentment out of my voice."

"Never mind. Everything is different now. And if we have children, they will be born free."

"Yes. But many of our race are not, Juan. My heart aches for them."

"Some day," I assured her, "some day, I know that all men will be free."

464

SOCIAL STUDIES

FREEING SLAVES Manumission—the granting of freedom to slaves—varied greatly between societies and over time. Many Islamic societies required slave owners to free their slaves after a certain number of years. Most other societies allowed owners to free their slaves whenever they wished. Many societies, such as those in Athens and Rome, had laws requiring manumission after three generations. The ancient Israelites granted freedom after a specified number of years. The Aztecs freed all children born into slavery. In the American South, on the other hand, manumission was extremely rare, especially after laws prohibited the importation of new slaves.

ELIZABETH BORTON DE TREVIÑO

Elizabeth Borton de Treviño was born on September 2, 1904, in Bakersfield, California. In 1934, while on a newspaper assignment in Mexico, she met Luis Treviño Gomez, whom she married a year later, and settled in Mexico, where she still lives.

I generally get story ideas from some true event or moment in history that fires my imagination. All of my books contain a little kernel of truth, something that really happened. Each of my stories tries to show some phase of love, that powerful emotion that makes the world go round.

It was my son, Luis, who, while studying painting, learned the true story of Juan de Pareja and told it to me. I loved the story, and when I saw a reproduction of the portrait Velázquez painted of Juan, I was determined to write about him, for his face seemed to be that of a dignified, noble, and proud person whose story should be told.

465

About the Author

After students read page 465, you may wish to discuss the following questions with them:

- **What inspired Elizabeth Borton de Treviño to tell the story of Juan de Pareja?** (Possible responses: She loved the story and thought it should be told; she saw the portrait of Juan de Pareja painted by Velázquez and thought she would like to write about him.)
- **Why do you think the author's books contain only a "kernel of truth"?** (Possible response: Although the characters may be real people, they are placed in fictional stories.)

Elizabeth Borton de Treviño says that her beloved family instilled in her a love of literature. She recalls, "My father and mother peppered their conversation with quotations from Shakespeare, the Bible, Byron, and Bobbie Burns. My maternal grandmother loved poetry and could recite it, pages and pages of it, by heart. . . ."

SUMMARIZING

Story Map

If students began the story map before they read the selection, they should now complete it by summarizing important story events and writing the solution to the story problem. See *Practice Book* page 137.

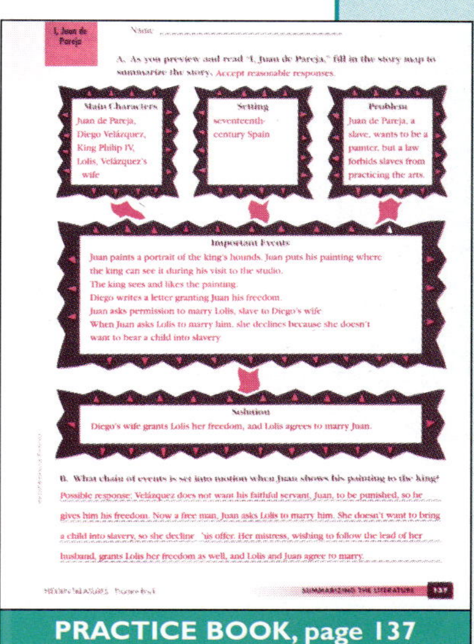

I, Juan de Pareja

Name ______

A. As you preview and read "I, Juan de Pareja," fill in the story map to summarize the story. Accept reasonable responses.

Main Characters	Setting	Problem
Juan de Pareja, Diego Velázquez, King Philip IV, Lolis, Velázquez's wife	seventeenth-century Spain	Juan de Pareja, a slave, wants to be a painter, but a law forbids slaves from practicing the arts.

Important Events

Juan paints a portrait of the king's hounds. Juan puts his painting where the king can see it during his visit to the studio.
The king sees and likes the painting.
Diego writes a letter granting Juan his freedom.
Juan asks permission to marry Lolis, slave to Diego's wife
When Juan asks Lolis to marry him, she declines because she doesn't want to bear a child into slavery

Solution

Diego's wife grants Lolis her freedom, and Lolis agrees to marry Juan.

B. What chain of events is set into motion when Juan shows his painting to the king?

Possible response: Velázquez does not want his faithful servant, Juan, to be punished, so he gives him his freedom. Now a free man, Juan asks Lolis to marry him. She doesn't want to bring a child into slavery, so she decline[illegible] his offer. Her mistress, wishing to follow the lead of her husband, grants Lolis her freedom as well, and Lolis and Juan agree to marry.

SUMMARIZING THE LITERATURE 137

PRACTICE BOOK, page 137

POETRY

The Paint Box

by E.V. Rieu

INTRODUCING THE POEM Ask students if they can remember how they felt as young children when they got a new box of crayons or paints and a sheet of clean white paper. Tell them that in this poem a painter with a box of rich colors considers an unusual request for a painting.

APPRECIATING THE POEM Read the poem aloud to students as they follow along. Then ask questions such as the following:

What do you think the second speaker in the poem means by "You painted them true"? (Possible response: The speaker finds the fact that the painter has painted a camel blue and a panther purple true to what he or she has in mind, although the colors are not realistic.)

Great art is the result of talent, training, and imagination. Which of these do you think this poem is mostly about? Why do you think that? (Possible responses: The poem is mostly about an artist's imagination—the painter has painted the subjects in an imaginative way, not realistically; the second speaker asks for something completely imaginary.)

After discussing the poem, organize students into three groups for a choral reading, with each group reading a stanza.

LISTENING CENTER

"The Paint Box" is available on *Literature Cassette 3*.

ILLUSTRATOR'S CRAFT

David Diaz won the Caldecott Award for *Smoky Night*, a picture book written by Eve Bunting. His striking illustrations in that book, and here for "The Paint Box," show subjects in vivid color. One technique Diaz uses is to capture the faces and animals within thick black lines, making the colors stand out even more.

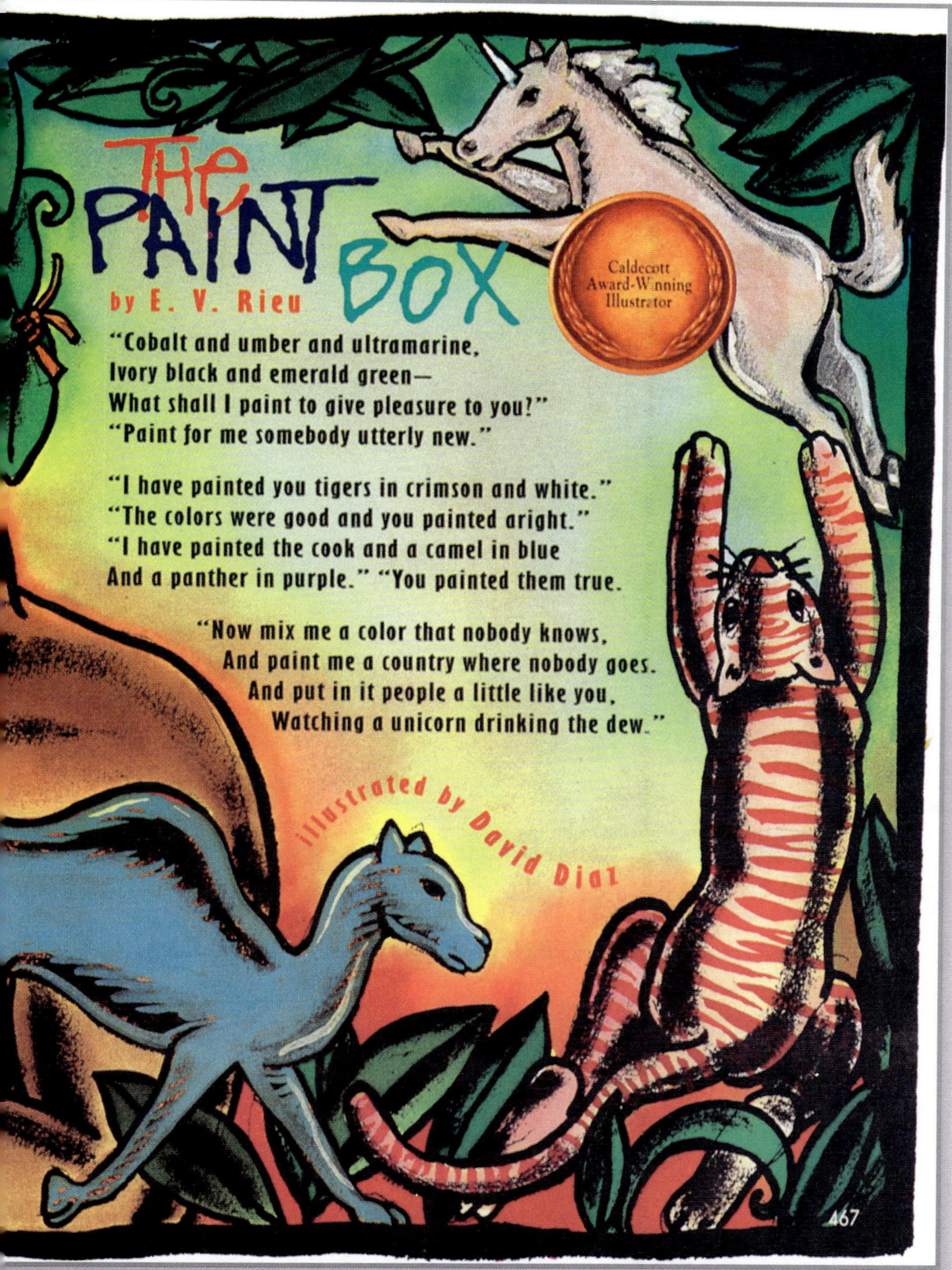

The Paint Box

by E. V. Rieu

Caldecott Award-Winning Illustrator

"Cobalt and umber and ultramarine,
Ivory black and emerald green—
What shall I paint to give pleasure to you?"
"Paint for me somebody utterly new."

"I have painted you tigers in crimson and white."
"The colors were good and you painted aright."
"I have painted the cook and a camel in blue
And a panther in purple." "You painted them true.

"Now mix me a color that nobody knows,
And paint me a country where nobody goes.
And put in it people a little like you,
Watching a unicorn drinking the dew."

illustrated by David Diaz

467

About the Poet

Emile Victor Rieu [rōō] (1887-1972) worked as a publishing executive, an editor, a translator, and an author. He established and managed the Oxford University Press in Bombay, India, early in his career, but he was best known as an editor and a translator of the paperback Penguin Classics series. Rieu's favorite method for writing was to take an ordinary situation, turn it this way and that, and then find in it some absurdity to illuminate its ordinariness.

POET'S CRAFT Reread the poem for students, having them notice that the poet's choice and placement of words creates a regular rhythm that is repeated from line to line. Students may also observe that the poet has chosen words for their repeated sounds, such as the vowel sounds in the first line or the beginning consonant sounds in phrases such as *panther in purple*. Have students select favorite lines or phrases to share with the class.

STUDENTS ACQUIRING ENGLISH Students may benefit from a brief discussion of the following colors. If possible, provide a sample of each.

cobalt a deep blue

umber one of various shades of brown

ultramarine a vivid blue

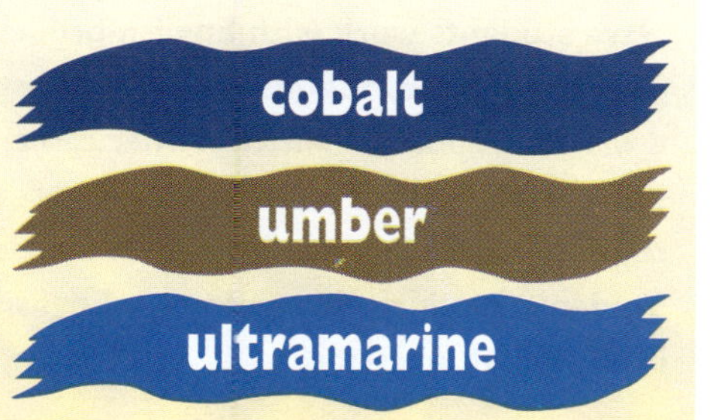

ACTIVITY CHOICES

WRITE A PERSUASIVE PARAGRAPH

NO ART ALLOWED Remind students to state their opinions near the beginning of their paragraphs. Students may write their paragraphs in their personal journals. **CRITICAL THINKING/WRITING**

WRITE A NOTE

¡MUCHAS GRACIAS! Remind students that a thank-you note—like all friendly letters—has five parts: heading, greeting, body, closing, and signature. Suggest that they look at the model of a friendly letter in the *Language Handbook* before they begin to write. **WRITING**

CREATE A CLASS BOOK

KEEPING THE DREAM ALIVE You may want to have a class brainstorming session to generate names of African Americans in the arts. Then encourage individual students to choose one person and to use reference sources, such as encyclopedias and nonfiction books, to aid their research. **SOCIAL STUDIES/WRITING**

RESPONSE CORNER

WRITE A PERSUASIVE PARAGRAPH

NO ART ALLOWED

Think about Juan de Pareja's talent as described in the story. Do you think the law barring slaves in seventeenth-century Spain from practicing the arts was fair? Write a persuasive paragraph stating your opinion.

WRITE A NOTE

¡MUCHAS GRACIAS!

Velázquez writes a letter declaring Juan's freedom. Imagine that you are Juan. Write a note of response to Master Velázquez. Use the appropriate format for a thank-you note.

To whom it may concern,
I have this day given
freedom to my slave
Juan de Pareja, who
shall have all the rights
and honors of a free man
and further, I hereby
name him my assistant
with the duties and
salary thereto pertaining.
Diego Rodriguez de
Silva y Velázquez

468

STUDENTS ACQUIRING ENGLISH

Have students work with English-proficient partners for the response activities. Instead of a written report on African American artists, some students may want to create a series of captioned drawings to illustrate the artist's life. Students can include captions in English and in their first language.

CREATE A CLASS BOOK

KEEPING THE DREAM ALIVE

The poem and the selection are about freedom of expression. Many African Americans expressed their longing for freedom and equality through the arts—painting, drama, music, and dance. Research an African American artist and write a report about that person's life. Bind your report together with those of your classmates in a book titled "Dream Keepers."

WHAT DO YOU THINK?

- What two problems does Juan de Pareja have to face in the story? How are these problems solved?
- How did you feel at the end of the story? Explain your answer.
- If the poet of "The Paint Box" were to describe Juan de Pareja's portrait of the hounds, what might he say?

CHECKING COMPREHENSION

What Do You Think?

1. **What two problems does Juan de Pareja have to face in the story? How are these problems solved?** (Juan wants to paint, but slaves are forbidden to practice the arts. He wants to marry Lolis, but she refuses to marry him because she doesn't want to have children who would be born slaves. Both problems are solved when first Velázquez gives Juan his freedom and then Velázquez's wife frees Lolis.) DESCRIPTIVE RESPONSE
2. **How did you feel at the end of the story? Explain your answer.** (Responses will vary.) PERSONAL RESPONSE
3. **If the poet of "The Paint Box" were to describe Juan de Pareja's portrait of the hounds, what might he say?** (Responses will vary.) CRITICAL ANALYSIS/SPECULATING

VARYING THE ACTIVITY

To **challenge** students participating in the No Art Allowed activity, encourage them to stage a debate using the ideas in their persuasive paragraphs.

Intervention Strategies

TIPS FOR CLASSROOM MANAGEMENT

IF second-language students need additional vocabulary and during-reading strategies to understand "I, Juan de Pareja," **THEN** use *Sheltered English/ESL Manual,* pages 70–73.

IF students had difficulty understanding "I, Juan de Pareja," **THEN** complete the Rereading and Structural Analysis Strategies. See also *Intervention Strategies Manual,* pages 104–109.

REREADING

MAKING PREDICTIONS Point out that the author has included a considerable amount of suspense or tension in the story.

Have students use a "stop and question" strategy as they reread the story. Assign four places in the reading where students should stop and question themselves about what will happen next.

STOP	QUESTION
Juan confesses.	Will the King punish him?
Velázquez writes a letter.	What will the letter say?
Lolis refuses to marry Juan.	How will Juan react?
Velázquez asks his wife to free Lolis.	Will she agree to do so?

PERSONAL JOURNAL Why do students think that Juan de Pareja chose to confess his secret to the King, rather than to his master, the painter Velázquez? Have students write a few sentences in their journals about Juan's possible reasons.

STRUCTURAL ANALYSIS

PLURAL NOUNS Remind students that plural nouns are formed in a variety of ways. Display the chart below on the board, and ask students to study each pattern.

-s	-es	y→i+es	f→v+es
hour	likeness	contemporary	leaf
hours	likenesses	contemporaries	leaves

Also explain that the plural form of certain nouns is irregular: for example, *foot/feet, sheep/sheep, and child/children*.

Ask students to skim two or three pages of the selection to find examples of plural nouns. Have them classify the nouns by pattern, grouping together the forms that follow the rules shown in the chart. (Possibilities include: *days, lashes, duties*.)

WRITING A SUMMARY

Help students summarize the action in "I, Juan de Pareja" by rewriting the following statements in chronological order.

Velázquez promises to speak to his wife about Lolis. (3)

Lolis agrees to marry Juan. (5)

Mistress tells Lolis she is free and puts a letter into her hand. (4)

Velázquez writes a letter and shows it to the King. (2)

Juan confesses to the King that he is an artist. (1)

Juan assures Lolis that their children will be born free. (6)

DECODING SUPPORT
Digraphs *ch, sh, th*

Intervention Strategies Manual pp. 108–109

ESL/TITLE I READING

Reading Trade Books

ESL/Title I Library

I Am an Artist

by Pat Lowery Collins

In this brief, illustrated book, the narrator focuses on answering the question, "What is an artist?" We are artists when we use our senses and our imaginations to appreciate the everyday world. Have students use the chart below to list some comparisons with "I, Juan de Pareja."

According to "I, Juan de Pareja," an artist needs:	According to *I Am an Artist*, an artist needs:
1.	1.
2.	2.
3.	3.

TAKE-HOME BOOK TO REINFORCE KEY WORDS

Students will enjoy reading about a special project in this engrossing nonfiction book. Have students read during independent reading time in class or take the book home to read.

PERSONAL JOURNAL

After students finish reading *The Kids of Survival*, have them write in their personal journals any ideas they may have for art projects.

See also *Intervention Strategies Manual*, page 107.

2 Integrating Language Arts

IDEA BANK

TIPS FOR CLASSROOM MANAGEMENT

IF students had difficulty answering the Strategic Reading questions on page T936, **THEN** they should complete the Retelling activity.

IF students need to focus on speaking strategies, **THEN** they should complete the Oral Language activity.

RETELLING

Critics Circle

COOPERATIVE LEARNING Arrange students in small groups, and distribute Reader Response Card 11 (Critics Circle). Ask students who have also read "The Art of Velázquez" to compare that selection to "I, Juan de Pareja." Students should talk about the important scenes or information in both selections and about how the selections are alike and how they are different.

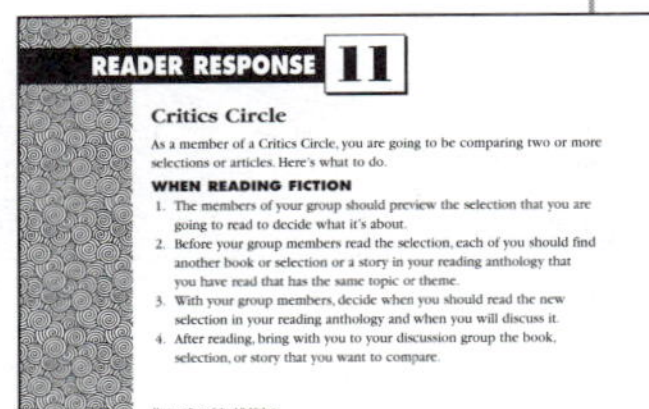

READER RESPONSE 11

Critics Circle

As a member of a Critics Circle, you are going to be comparing two or more selections or articles. Here's what to do.

WHEN READING FICTION

1. The members of your group should preview the selection that you are going to read to decide what it's about.
2. Before your group members read the selection, each of you should find another book or selection or a story in your reading anthology that you have read that has the same topic or theme.
3. With your group members, decide when you should read the new selection in your reading anthology and when you will discuss it.
4. After reading, bring with you to your discussion group the book, selection, or story that you want to compare.

Harcourt Brace School Publishers

Response Card 11

LISTENING/SPEAKING

Informal Assessment

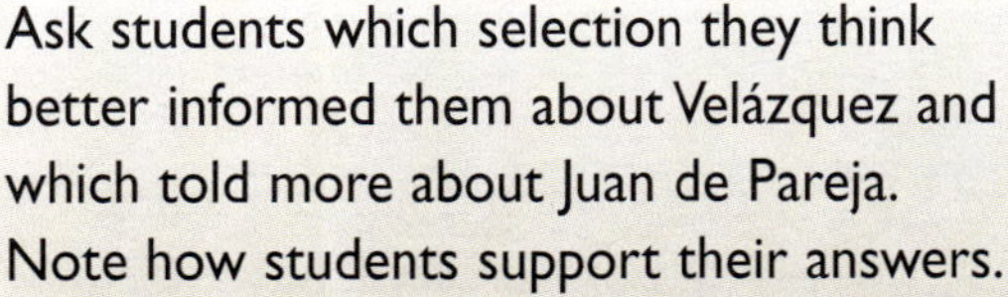

Ask students which selection they think better informed them about Velázquez and which told more about Juan de Pareja. Note how students support their answers.

ORAL LANGUAGE

Persuasive Speech

Point out to students that Lolis's speech to Juan on page 464 about her hatred of slavery is extremely persuasive. Explain that in a persuasive speech, the speaker expresses a particular viewpoint and tries to convince listeners to agree. Have students choose a subject on which they have strong opinions and about which they can develop persuasive speeches. Have students research facts and expert opinions about the subject to add support to their viewpoints. Students can present their speeches in small groups.

LISTENING/SPEAKING

TIPS FOR LISTENING AND SPEAKING

When students **listen** to other people's opinions, they should

- listen attentively and politely.
- wait until the speaker has finished before responding.

Remind students that when they **speak**, they should

- speak clearly.
- make eye contact with their listeners.
- support their opinions with reasons.

REREADING

Dramatic Reading

Have groups of students read part of the story aloud. For example, three students might take the roles of King Philip IV, Juan, and Velázquez and read pages 456–459. Or four students might choose the roles of Velázquez, his wife, Juan, and Lolis and read the scene on pages 462–463. Model reading expressively to demonstrate using your voice to convey the characters' feelings. Suggest that students reread the chosen passages silently first. Allow time for students to rehearse before they present their readings. **LISTENING/SPEAKING/READING**

REAL-LIFE RESOURCES

Making Book Jackets

USING BOOK JACKETS TO PREDICT Have students discuss what the cover of *I, Juan de Pareja* suggests the book will be about. Write the following titles on the board and have students predict what each book might be about. Then ask students to evaluate the jackets of books they have not read. Remind them to consider pictures as well as the writing on each book jacket.

PARTS OF A BOOK JACKET Discuss what kinds of information publishers put on book jackets, including the title, the author, the illustrator, an eye-catching picture, an exciting "teaser" or summary, the author's biography and photo, and favorable reviews. See *Writer's Magazine* pages 68 and 69.

REAL-LIFE CHALLENGE Ask students to choose and talk about a group of poems, stories, or other writing composed by classmates. Then have students brainstorm ideas for a title for the collection. Students can work in groups to create effective book jackets. **SPEAKING**

Real-Life Book Jackets Skills

COVER STORY

Can you judge a book by its cover? Sometimes. In the case of "I, Juan de Pareja," the cover picture suggests that the story will be about seventeenth-century painters. Look at the three book jackets below. Write the word *fiction* or *nonfiction* next to each book. Circle the book you'd most like to read. Cross out the book that looks the least interesting to you. What's your reason for each choice?

68 I, Juan de Pareja • Writer's Magazine

I might read book # ______ because ______

I wouldn't read book # ______ because ______

Juan de Pareja 69

WRITER'S MAGAZINE, pages 68–69

STUDENTS ACQUIRING ENGLISH

Students might plan their speeches by making notes in their first language. They can refer to these notes as they present their speeches.

EXTRA SUPPORT

On chart paper, write the Tips for Listening and Speaking, and display them prominently. Suggest that students refer to the tips while they participate in the Oral Language activity.

WRITER'S WORKSHOP

Historical Fiction Story

TIPS FOR CLASSROOM MANAGEMENT

IF students are familiar with the elements of historical fiction, **THEN** have them begin writing, referring to the model on Transparencies 44A and 44B as necessary.

IF you want a brief writing activity, **THEN** adapt this lesson by having students use what they learn about the Writer's Craft to revise a story they have written previously.

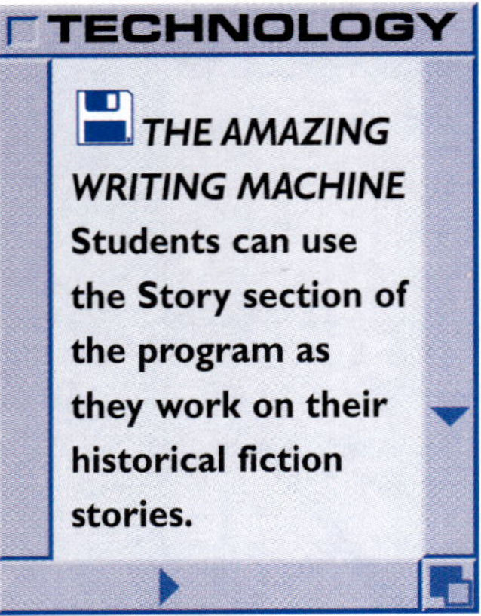

Assessment Workshop ✓

Scoring Student Writing, Intermediate Level

Thinking as Writers

WRITING FORM: Historical Fiction Remind students that "I, Juan de Pareja" is an example of historical fiction. Point out that historical fiction is realistic fiction that takes place at a specific time in the past. Tell students that they are going to learn about historical fiction and then write their own historical fiction stories.

Display Transparencies 44A–44B. (The complete model appears in the back of this Teacher's Edition.) Discuss the elements that historical fiction should include:

- a description of setting
- cultural details from a specific time and place
- accurate historical details
- dialogue to move the story forward

TRANSPARENCIES 44A/44B

Model: Historical Fiction

Historical fiction *is realistic fiction that takes place at a specific time in the past. Historical fiction relies on details of time and place to paint a picture of an earlier world.*

Alicia Troy, Minutegirl

setting The year was 1775. All over Massachusetts, men were forming militias for the fight they feared would come. Benjamin Troy and his son Daniel joined the **cultural details from a specific time and place** Minutemen in their town, Lexington. Every few days, they were called to drill. As the women of the town gathered in the square, they often saw the men marching up the main street.

Alicia Troy watched this with growing excitement. She was never content to sit home by the fire, **accurate historical details** darning her brother's socks or embroidering her sampler. She wished that she could drill with her father and brother.

One evening Alicia was left at home as the men went off to drill. As she sat glumly by the window spinning wool, she saw something frightening. A column of men in red coats was marching up the long road toward Lexington. If these British soldiers saw the Minutemen drilling, there might be trouble.

Alicia ran out the back door and saddled her horse. She rode through the woods until she reached the clearing where the Minutemen drilled. She jumped off her horse and marched up to Colonel Adams.

WRITER'S CRAFT: Point of View Explain that point of view is the angle from which a story is told. "I, Juan de Pareja" is told from the first-person point of view—one of the characters tells the story. In the third-person point of view, a narrator tells the story. Discuss with students the different effects of each type of narration—for example, that a first-person narration can make a story seem more immediate and real. Have students decide on the narrative point of view they will use in their own stories.

PREWRITING AND DRAFTING

Remind students to choose historical time periods they are interested in researching. To help students begin their stories, refer to these strategies.

PREWRITING GRAPHIC ORGANIZER Encourage students to organize the notes from their research on a chart like the following to detail place, time, characters, and events:

Setting	Characters	Events
San Francisco April 18–22, 1906	grandparents mother father sister brother	house starts shaking huddle under table

SUSTAINED SILENT WRITING Some students may come up with story ideas right away. Allow them to begin writing without interruption and then to research the topic to confirm their ideas.

DURING-WRITING GRAPHIC ORGANIZER Students who have trouble organizing their thoughts may need to pause during writing to create a sequence chart of story events.

RESPONDING AND REVISING

Have students work in editing circles or with partners to help one another revise their stories. Encourage students to offer positive feedback and suggestions for improvement. You may want to write the following checklist on the board:

- Have you included historical details?
- Have you used the same point of view—first person or third person—throughout the story?
- Does the order of events make sense?
- Have you used vivid language to help readers visualize the characters and events?

PROOFREADING

Offer the following tips as students proofread:

- Check **capitalization**, especially of proper nouns, and **punctuation**, especially with dialogue.
- Check for correct use of pronouns in **predicate nominatives**. (See Grammar Minilesson on page T943.)
- Look for words you may have misspelled, and correct any errors.

PUBLISHING

If you wish to have students publish their stories, offer these options or allow students to choose their own methods:

ORAL Students might form groups to present their stories as a Readers Theatre. Allow time for groups to rehearse, and encourage students to read with dramatic expression.

WRITTEN Have students illustrate their stories, bind them separately, and create book covers. Set the stories up as a minilibrary.

EVALUATION BENCHMARKS: HISTORICAL FICTION

A story by a proficient student writer shows the following characteristics:

FORM	CRAFT	CONVENTIONS
Demonstrates understanding of the form • set in a specific time and place • accurate historical details • dialogue to move the story forward • satisfying ending	**Uses clear and appropriate language** • many vivid verbs, adverbs, and adjectives	**Follows conventions of grammar and usage** • proper nouns capitalized • punctuation marks with dialogue used correctly • correct use of pronouns in predicate nominatives

Teacher Assessment As you assess students' writing, refer to the Evaluation Benchmarks chart. For additional information, including model papers, see *Integrated Performance Assessment* Teacher's Edition.

PORTFOLIO OPPORTUNITY

Have students answer the Student Self-Assessment questions and include both their answers and their stories in their portfolios.

LANGUAGE HANDBOOK

Writing to Entertain and Express, pages 40–41; Historical Fiction, pages 44–45

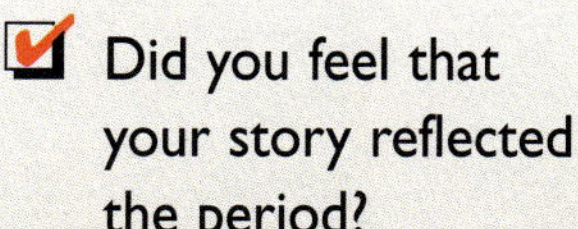

Student Self-Assessment ✓

Have students answer the following questions and include the answers in their portfolios:

- ☑ Did you feel that your story reflected the period?
- ☑ Which did you develop most successfully—the setting, the characters, or the plot? Why?

Tested Skill

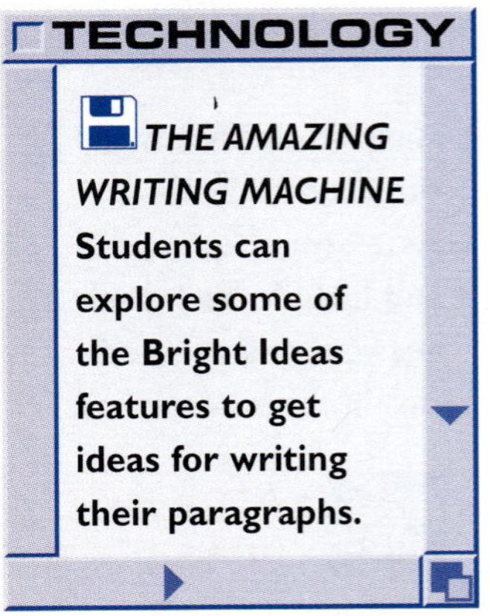

LANGUAGE HANDBOOK Present, Past, and Future Tenses, pages 154–155

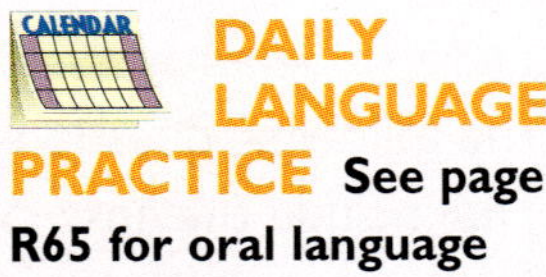

DAILY LANGUAGE PRACTICE See page R65 for oral language exercises.

GRAMMAR

Simple Tenses

Reading ⟷ Writing Connection

Connect to the literature. Display the following passages from "I, Juan de Pareja":

I remained on my knees. (past)

"You have it." (present)

"I will speak to my wife about it." (future)

Call on volunteers to read aloud each sentence and tell whether it expresses an action that is happening now, that happened in the past, or will happen in the future.

Build oral language. Ask volunteers to change the verb in each sentence so that it tells about actions happening at different times. For example, if the sentence tells about a past action, students should revise it to tell about present and future actions. Record students' sentences on the board.

I spoke to my wife about it.

I speak to my wife about it.

Teach/Model

Discuss present-tense verbs. Tell students that a verb that shows an action happening now or an action that happens over and over is called a present-tense verb. Present the following sentence frames:

I ________. He ________.

You ________. She ________.

Ask a volunteer to complete the first pair of sentences with the present-tense form of *paint*. (I paint. He paints.) Ask another student to complete the second pair of sentences with the present-tense form of *wish*. (You wish. She wishes.) Point out that when the subject of the sentence is *he, she, it*, or a singular noun, the present tense of most verbs is formed by adding *-s* or *-es*.

Discuss past- and future-tense verbs. Tell students that when a verb shows action in the past, we say that the verb is in the past tense. Explain that for most verbs, the past tense is formed by adding *-ed* or *-d*. Verbs that show action that will happen in the future are formed by adding the helping verb *will* to the main verb.

Practice/Apply

Check understanding. On the board, begin the following chart, and have students fill in the past- and future-tense forms of each verb:

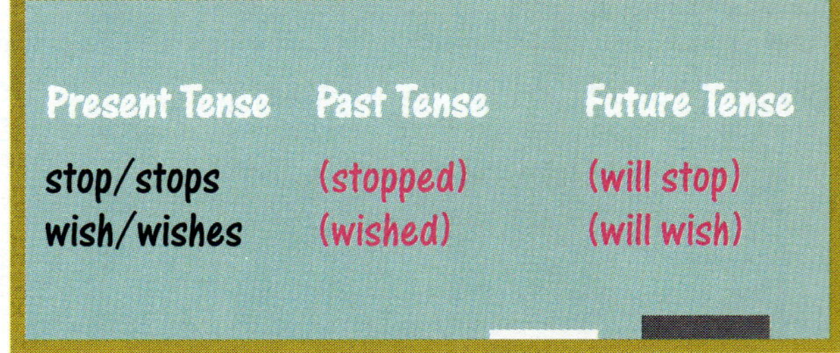

Present Tense	Past Tense	Future Tense
stop/stops	(stopped)	(will stop)
wish/wishes	(wished)	(will wish)

Practice Activities

DESCRIBE ACTIONS

ORAL APPLICATION Provide word cards with actions students can perform in the classroom, such as sharpening a pencil, stacking books, or handing out paper. Then have volunteers take turns drawing a card and performing the action for the class. Ask the onlookers to say two sentences telling what each volunteer did, one with a present-tense verb and the other with a past-tense verb. Students' sentences might resemble these:

Tyler sharpens his pencil.

Tyler sharpened his pencil.

Ask students to write the sentences and underline the verbs. VISUAL/AUDITORY/ KINESTHETIC

Write Paragraphs

WRITING APPLICATION Have students form groups of three to write paragraphs, using the past, present, and future tenses. Each group should brainstorm three main-idea sentences, one using each tense. Students' sentences may be similar to these:

- The hot-air balloon rose from the fairgrounds and sailed into the sky.
- I will swim in my neighbor's pool.
- My dog catches the ball in its teeth.

After students have their main-idea sentences, they should write a paragraph for each one that tells more about the topic, using only verbs with the same tense that is used in the main-idea sentence. Then students can share their paragraphs with other groups. VISUAL/AUDITORY

APPLY TO WRITING

You may want to have students check the stories they wrote or other writing to be sure they have maintained the correct verb tenses throughout.

USAGE TIP Check your writing to be sure you have used the correct present-tense form of verbs with singular and plural subjects.

5-DAY PLAN

Use in conjunction with Daily Language Practice.

Day 1 Complete page T956.	**Day 4** Choose a Practice Activity or *Grammar Practice Book* pages 44–45.
Day 2 Complete a Practice Activity on page T957.	**Day 5** Complete *Practice Book* page 138.
Day 3 Choose a Practice Activity or *Language Handbook* pages 154–155.	

STUDENTS ACQUIRING ENGLISH

Some students may have difficulty making the correct sounds at the end of past-tense verbs. To give them practice, ask them to look at magazine or book pictures of busy scenes. Encourage them to describe each scene, using the past tense.

EXTRA SUPPORT

Have students make a chart with the columns *Yesterday, Today,* and *Tomorrow.* Work with them to fill in examples of verbs in past, present, and future tense.

RETEACH

See R56 for lessons in multiple modalities.

GRAMMAR PRACTICE BOOK
pages 44–45

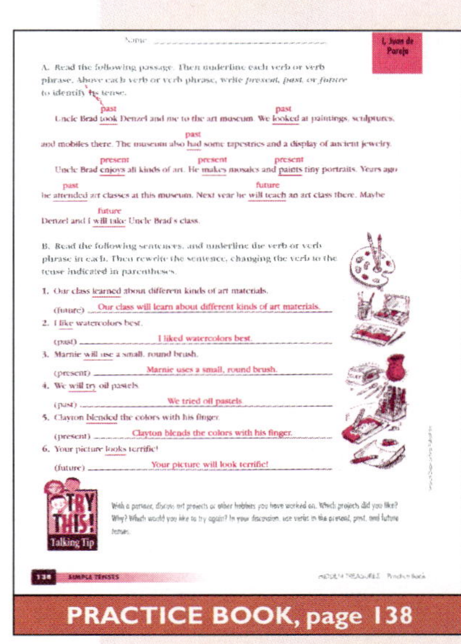

Name ____________

I, Juan de Pareja

A. Read the following passage. Then underline each verb or verb phrase. Above each verb or verb phrase, write *present, past,* or *future* to identify the tense.

Uncle Brad took (past) Denzel and me to the art museum. We looked (past) at paintings, sculptures, and mobiles there. The museum also had (past) some tapestries and a display of ancient jewelry.

Uncle Brad enjoys (present) all kinds of art. He makes (present) mosaics and paints (present) tiny portraits. Years ago he attended (past) art classes at this museum. Next year he will teach (future) an art class there. Maybe Denzel and I will take (future) Uncle Brad's class.

B. Read the following sentences, and underline the verb or verb phrase in each. Then rewrite the sentence, changing the verb to the tense indicated in parentheses.

1. Our class learned about different kinds of art materials.
   (future) Our class will learn about different kinds of art materials.
2. I like watercolors best.
   (past) I liked watercolors best.
3. Marnie will use a small, round brush.
   (present) Marnie uses a small, round brush.
4. We will try oil pastels.
   (past) We tried oil pastels.
5. Clayton blended the colors with his finger.
   (present) Clayton blends the colors with his finger.
6. Your picture looks terrific!
   (future) Your picture will look terrific!

TRY THIS! Talking Tip

With a partner, discuss art projects or other hobbies you have worked on. Which projects did you like? Why? Which would you like to try again? In your discussion, use verbs in the present, past, and future tenses.

138 SIMPLE TENSES

PRACTICE BOOK, page 138

SPELLING

5-Day Plan

Integrated Spelling Lesson 26:
student book, pages 110–113;
Teacher's Edition, pages T171–T176.

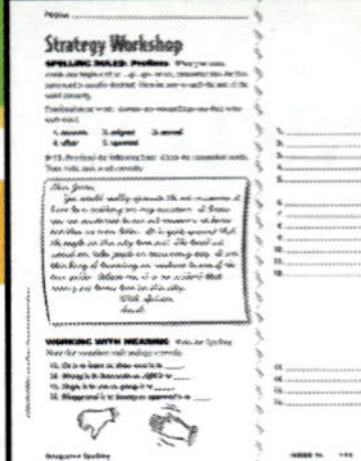
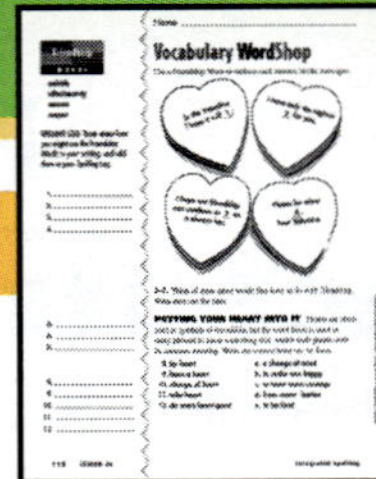
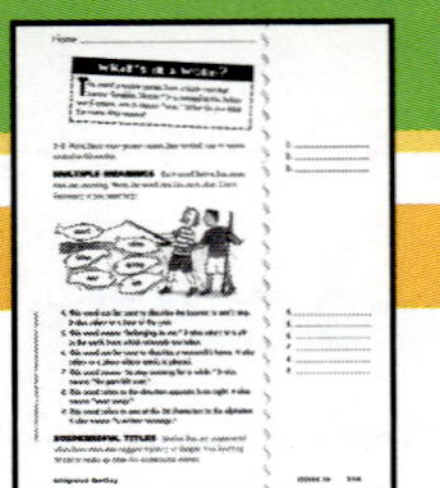

SPELLING WORDS

1. accounts ★
2. applause
3. assigned
4. accused
5. accurate
6. affection ★
7. assistant ★
8. apparent
9. affair
10. appointed
11. approach ★
12. assembly
13. accident
14. association
15. appreciate
16. accustomed ★

STUDENT'S PERSONAL WORDS

17.
18.
19.
20.

Additional story words are *affectionately, affect, apprentices,* and *assured.*

★ Words appearing in "I, Juan de Pareja"

Prefix: *ad-* (*ac-*, *af-*, *ap-*, *as-*)

Pretest

DAY 1 **Administer the pretest.** Say each word, and then use it in the dictation sentence below. Help students self-check their pretests.

OPEN SORT

DAY 2 **Have students classify words.** Have groups of students classify the Spelling Words according to categories they choose themselves. For instance, groups might sort by number of syllables, by part of speech, or by some other criterion. Invite groups to compare their lists.

CLOSED SORT

Sort by prefix. On the board, write the headings from the chart below, and ask volunteers to write each Spelling Word where it belongs.

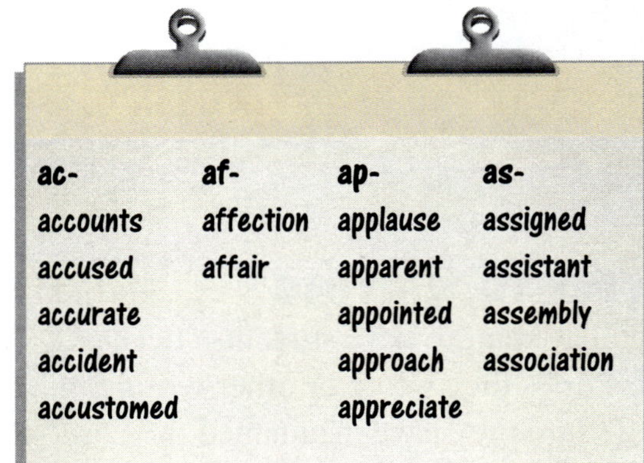

ac-	af-	ap-	as-
accounts	affection	applause	assigned
accused	affair	apparent	assistant
accurate		appointed	assembly
accident		approach	association
accustomed		appreciate	

Teach/Model

DAY 3 **Discuss the generalization.** Ask students what all the words have in common. (They all begin with *a*.) Ask how the words in the four columns are different from each other. (The letter *a* is followed by different consonants.) Explain that *ac-*, *af-*, *ap-*, and *as-* are all forms of the prefix *ad-*, which means "to; toward." Guide students to arrive at the following generalization:

The prefix *ad-* changes to *ac-* before *c*, to *af-* before *f*, to *ap-* before *p*, and to *as-* before *s*.

DAY 4 **Apply to writing.** Suggest that students look in the stories they wrote or in other writing for words beginning with *ac-*, *ad-*, *af-*, *ap-*, and *as-* to see whether they are spelled correctly.

Posttest

DAY 5 **Assess students' progress.** Use the sentences below to administer the posttest.

PRACTICE BOOK, page 139

DICTATION SENTENCES

1. Our accounts showed we owed taxes.
2. The audience greeted the singer with applause.
3. Our teacher assigned four pages of homework.
4. The clerk accused the man of stealing.
5. This clock keeps accurate time.
6. Grandma hugged Lisa with affection.
7. Juan enjoyed being the artist's assistant.
8. Her scowl made her anger apparent.
9. The prom will be a grand affair.
10. The king appointed a new court painter.
11. The judge told us to approach the bench.
12. There will be an all-school assembly today.
13. Kim was hurt in a bike accident.
14. Mom gives money to an association that protects animals.
15. I appreciate the help you gave me.
16. Our accustomed time for gym is before lunch.

VOCABULARY WORKSHOP

Reviewing Key Words

Display the Key Words. Have students answer the following questions, orally or in writing. (Possible responses are given.)

1. **What might you do if you were *indisposed*?** (stay home from school, see a doctor, stay in bed)
2. **Name three *virtues*.** (kindness, unselfishness, helpfulness)
3. **If you have an *intention*, what do you have?** (a plan or purpose)
4. **What might shine *radiantly*?** (a lamp, a happy face, a hot toaster)

Extending Vocabulary

DENOTATION/CONNOTATION

Point out that words have two types of meanings: denotation and connotation. Explain to students that a dictionary definition, or a word's exact meaning, is its denotation. Then explain that the word's connotation is what it suggests to the reader. Connotations can be positive or negative.

COMPLETE A CHART

Display the following chart, omitting the words in the second and third columns. Invite students to work in small groups to define each of the story words in the first column. Then have them decide whether each word has a positive or negative connotation.

Story Word	Denotation	Connotation
affectionately	(in a fond or loving way)	(positive)
grieved	(felt sorrow)	(negative)
respect	(honor, high regard)	(positive)

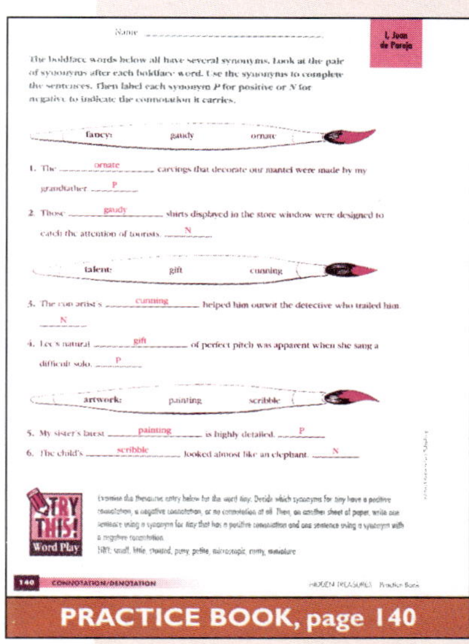

Name ____________

I, Juan de Pareja

The boldface words below all have several synonyms. Look at the pair of synonyms after each boldface word. Use the synonyms to complete the sentences. Then label each synonym *P* for positive or *N* for negative to indicate the connotation it carries.

fancy: gaudy ornate

1. The ___ornate___ carvings that decorate our mantel were made by my grandfather. ___P___
2. Those ___gaudy___ shirts displayed in the store window were designed to catch the attention of tourists. ___N___

talent: gift cunning

3. The con artist's ___cunning___ helped him outwit the detective who trailed him. ___N___
4. Lee's natural ___gift___ of perfect pitch was apparent when she sang a difficult solo. ___P___

artwork: painting scribble

5. My sister's latest ___painting___ is highly detailed. ___P___
6. The child's ___scribble___ looked almost like an elephant. ___N___

TRY THIS! Word Play

Examine the thesaurus entry below for the word *tiny*. Decide which synonyms for *tiny* have a positive connotation, a negative connotation, or no connotation at all. Then, on another sheet of paper, write one sentence using a synonym for *tiny* that has a positive connotation and one sentence using a synonym with a negative connotation.

TINY: small, little, stunted, puny, petite, microscopic, runty, miniature

140 CONNOTATION/DENOTATION HIDDEN TREASURES Practice Book

PRACTICE BOOK, page 140

Tested Skill

INTRODUCE: COMPREHENSION STRATEGY

Context Clues/ Multiple-Meaning Words

OBJECTIVE: To use context clues to determine the meanings of multiple-meaning words

Informal Assessment ✓

Are students able to

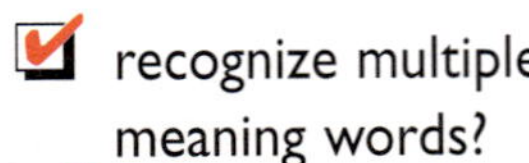
recognize multiple-meaning words?

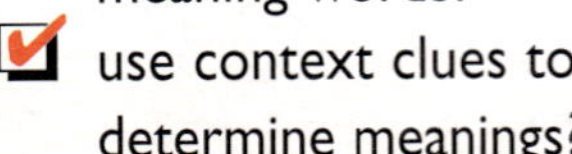
use context clues to determine meanings?

Teach/Model

Return to the literature. Have students reread the sentence on page 452 that begins with the words *Long ago*. Point out to students that they may be confused by the word *train* in this sentence because it has more than one meaning. Point out clues in the passage, such as *courtiers*, that show that the correct meaning of *train* here is "a group of attendants," not "a line of railway cars coupled together."

Model using context clues to determine word meaning. Explain that when students come to a word that has more than one meaning, they can use context clues in the surrounding text to figure out which meaning of the word is intended. Write the following sentences on the board. Model using context clues to determine which meaning of the word *leave* is used in each sentence.

Have I Your Majesty's leave to write an urgent letter?

The King got up to leave, said "Certainly," and then walked down the corridor.

MODEL

In the first sentence, the word *leave* is used as a noun; and the subject of the sentence, *I*, is asking for leave. The word seems to mean "permission." In the second sentence, the King gets up and walks down the corridor. The meaning of *leave*, which is used as a verb, is the one I'm more familiar with —"go away."

Practice/Apply

Have students demonstrate understanding. Have students use context clues to determine the appropriate meanings of the words from the story in the chart below:

Word	Appropriate Meaning
function (page 452)	(a social occasion)
might (page 457)	(force or strength)
rose (page 459)	(stood)

Practice Activities

JUST FOR THE PUN OF IT

Motivate students with a few puns and riddles based on multiple-meaning words, such as these:

"I get the *point!*" he cried when he sat on a tack.

How do you stop a lion from *charging*? Take away his credit card.

Encourage students to create their own multiple-meaning-word puns and riddles or to collect puns from joke books. Invite students to share their puns and explain the jokes, if necessary.
AUDITORY

Multiple-Meaning Charts

PERFORMANCE ASSESSMENT Encourage students to find and list on a chart like the one below other multiple-meaning words from the selection or from previously read selections. Students should provide two meanings for each word: the story meaning and another meaning.

Multiple-Meaning Word	Story Meaning	Additional Meaning
struck (page 453)	"happened suddenly; came to be"	"hit"
order (page 453)	"to request to buy something"	"to give a command to"

Ask students to display their charts. Call on volunteers to tell whether they agree with the information and to give reasons for their opinions.
VISUAL

STUDENTS ACQUIRING ENGLISH

Have intermediate-fluency students make lists of multiple-meaning words they have trouble understanding and work with fluent English-speakers to determine the meanings of the words.

RETEACH

See page R57 for lessons in multiple modalities.

CHALLENGE

Encourage students to create crossword puzzles using multiple-meaning words. Have them use dictionary definitions to develop clues.

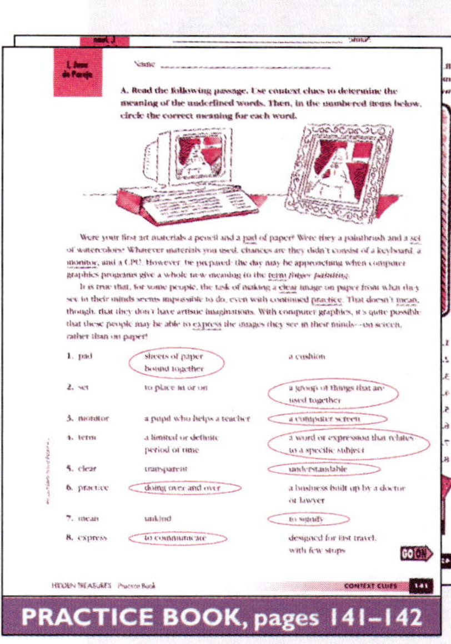

I, Juan de Pareja

Name ______________________

A. Read the following passage. Use context clues to determine the meaning of the underlined words. Then, in the numbered items below, circle the correct meaning for each word.

Were your first art materials a pencil and a pad of paper? Were they a paintbrush and a set of watercolors? Whatever materials you used, chances are they didn't consist of a keyboard, a monitor, and a CPU. However, be prepared: the day may be approaching when computer graphics programs give a whole new meaning to the term *finger painting*.

It is true that, for some people, the task of making a clear image on paper from what they see in their minds seems impossible to do, even with continued practice. That doesn't mean, though, that they don't have artistic imaginations. With computer graphics, it's quite possible that these people may be able to express the images they see in their minds—on screen, rather than on paper!

1. pad	sheets of paper bound together	a cushion
2. set	to place in or on	a group of things that are used together
3. monitor	a pupil who helps a teacher	a computer screen
4. term	a limited or definite period of time	a word or expression that relates to a specific subject
5. clear	transparent	understandable
6. practice	doing over and over	a business built up by a doctor or lawyer
7. mean	unkind	to signify
8. express	to communicate	designed for fast travel, with few stops

GO ON

HIDDEN TREASURES Practice Book CONTEXT CLUES 141

PRACTICE BOOK, pages 141–142

Reading Trade Books TO REINFORCE CONTEXT CLUES / MULTIPLE-MEANING WORDS

Looking at Paintings: Dogs by Peggy Roalf. Hyperion, 1993. AVERAGE

The Cuckoo Clock by Mary Stolz. Godine, 1986. EASY

Georgia O'Keeffe by Robyn Montana Turner. Little, Brown, 1991. AVERAGE

Integrated Curriculum

ART/SCIENCE

The Science of Art

Point out that as an art student, Juan de Pareja had to learn the scientific principles of perspective and color mixing. Through the following activities, students investigate the science behind art.

TIPS FOR CLASSROOM MANAGEMENT

IF students are mathematically inclined, **THEN** they may want to participate in the Keep It in Perspective activity.

IF students are artistically inclined, **THEN** they may want to participate in the Creating Colors activity.

TECHNOLOGY

THINKIN' THINGS COLLECTION 2: SNAKE BLOX

Students may wish to explore depth and perspective by using this program.

SCIENCE/ART

Creating Colors

Explain to students that pigments—colors used to tint other materials—give paints their colors. Have students form small groups, and assign Materials Managers who will provide the groups with small amounts of different colors of paint. Encourage students to mix different colors of paint to see what happens. For example, students may mix red paint with yellow paint to produce orange. Ask students to work together to create a chart showing the results. LISTENING/VIEWING

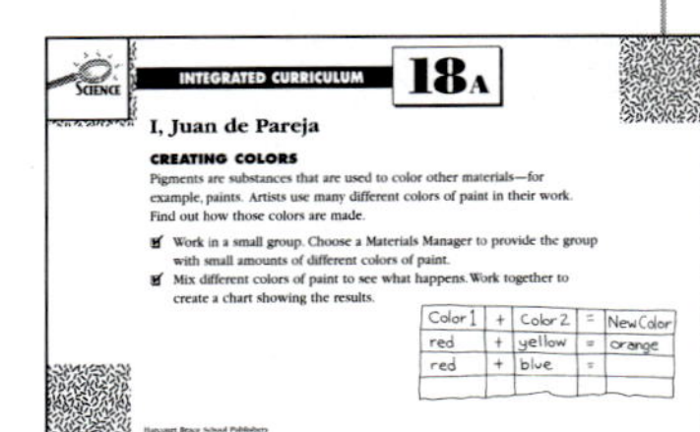

SCIENCE INTEGRATED CURRICULUM 18A

I, Juan de Pareja

CREATING COLORS

Pigments are substances that are used to color other materials—for example, paints. Artists use many different colors of paint in their work. Find out how those colors are made.

- Work in a small group. Choose a Materials Manager to provide the group with small amounts of different colors of paint.
- Mix different colors of paint to see what happens. Work together to create a chart showing the results.

Color 1	+	Color 2	=	New Color
red	+	yellow	=	orange
red	+	blue	=	

Harcourt Brace School Publishers

Curriculum Card 18A

ART/SOCIAL STUDIES

Historical Perspective

Use reference sources. Tell students that perspective is a technique used by artists to give paintings the illusion of depth and distance. Artists working during the height of the Greek and Roman civilizations were the first to use perspective. Encourage students to consult reference sources, such as encyclopedias and art books, to find examples of paintings from different periods both before and after the development of the principles of perspective. Students might look up these periods and styles: European cave paintings, ancient Egypt, ancient Rome, ancient Mexico (Mixtec, Maya), and European paintings from the sixteenth through the nineteenth centuries. Invite students to display and discuss examples of the work they find. LISTENING/SPEAKING/READING/VIEWING

ART/MATH

Keep It in Perspective

Explain that the fifteenth-century Italian architect Brunelleschi developed mathematical principles for perspective. These involved a horizontal line that represented the viewer's eye level and a vanishing point at which all lines and planes in the picture meet. Illustrate this on the board as shown here:

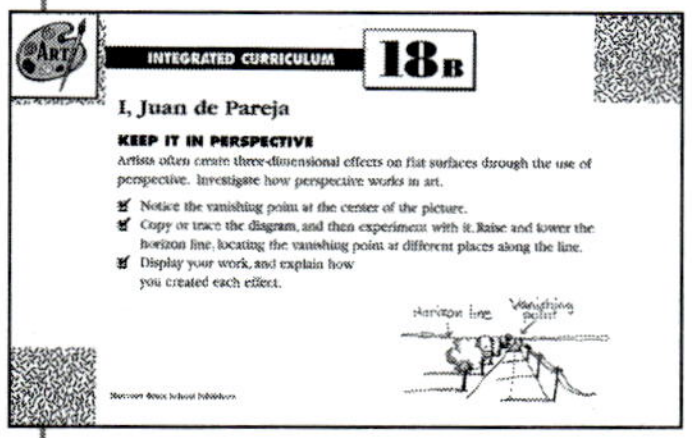

Curriculum Card 18B

Invite interested students to experiment with effects created by raising and lowering the horizon line, locating the vanishing point at different places along the line, and using more than one vanishing point. Suggest that students display their finished work and explain how they created particular effects.

LISTENING/SPEAKING/VIEWING

The lines of perspective (light blue) converge at the vanishing point on the horizon line (red). Equidistant parallel lines appear to be closer together as they near the horizon.

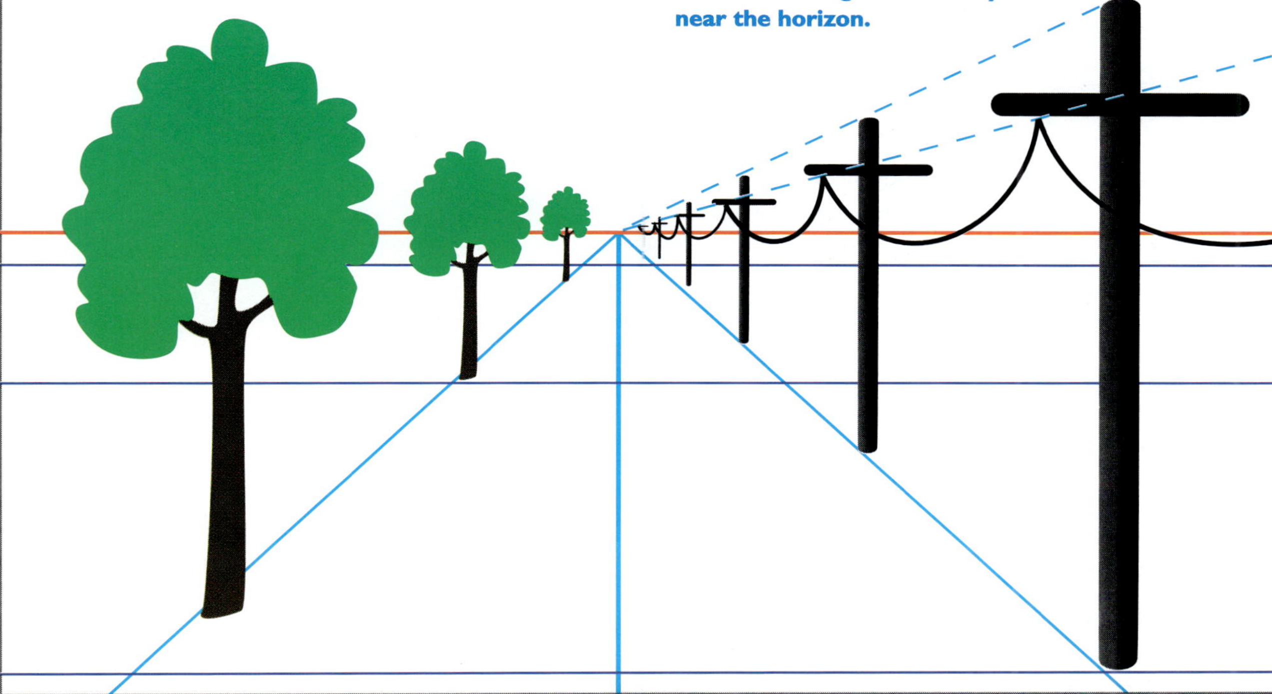

Reading Trade Books

CROSS-CURRICULAR READING

Painting: Behind the Scenes **by Andrew Pekarik. Hyperion, 1992.** EASY

Perspective **by Alison Cole. Dorling Kindersley, 1992.** AVERAGE

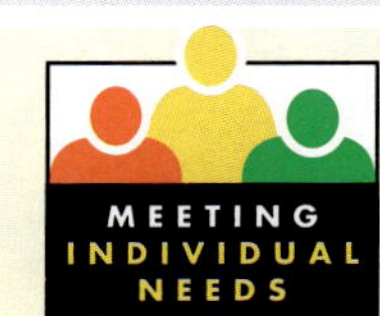

MULTI-AGE CLASSROOMS

Encourage younger students to ask older ones who may have a more advanced science or math background to help them with these activities.

Reading Trade Books

TIPS FOR CLASSROOM MANAGEMENT

INDEPENDENT READING Suggest that students who want to read *Journal of a Teenage Genius* independently create a story map as they read to note the main events in the novel.

For a comprehensive lesson plan, refer to the complete lesson for *Journal of a Teenage Genius* on pages T1056–T1061.

STUDENTS ACQUIRING ENGLISH

Have students read with English-proficient partners, stopping after each journal entry to discuss any questions they may have.

Journal of a Teenage Genius

by Helen V. Griffith

Signatures Library

READER'S CHALLENGE

Juan de Pareja was forced to hide his artistic talent. In *Journal of a Teenage Genius,* Zack shows an unusual talent for science. Do you think science and art are unrelated? Or do they have something in common? Write your ideas after you've read about Zack's surprising experiments.

READING STRATEGY: CONTEXT CLUES

Before students read *Journal of a Teenage Genius*, remind them that readers often come across words they do not know. Encourage students to discuss their strategies for determining meanings of unknown words. Suggest that students write unfamiliar words in a journal as they read. Then they should reread and use context clues before and after each unfamiliar word to determine its meaning. For example, students might not know the italicized words in the following sentences:

- **In another fifteen minutes the liquid bubbling in a beaker over my Bunsen burner should reach *sufficient* heat for the necessary chemical change to occur, and I will have invented the formula for the *transmutation* of matter! (page 1)**
- **But as long as there is a *discrepancy* in our heights, our relationship will remain static. (page 15)**

Have volunteers show how they can use context clues to figure out each meaning. At the end of each chapter, suggest that students use a dictionary to check their definitions.

LINK TO THE THEME

After students have read *Journal of a Teenage Genius*, suggest that they work in small groups to discuss the novel. Suggest these points for discussion:

- **What happens when people are not allowed to express their creativity?**
- **What traits do you need to be an inventor? In what other careers might these traits help you succeed?**

Other Trade Books

The Apprentice

by Pilar Molina Llorente
translated by Robin Longshaw
illustrated by Juan Ramón Alonso

This historical novel tells how Arduino works as an apprentice in order to fulfill his dream of becoming a painter. Suggest that students use a Venn diagram to compare Arduino with Juan de Pareja.

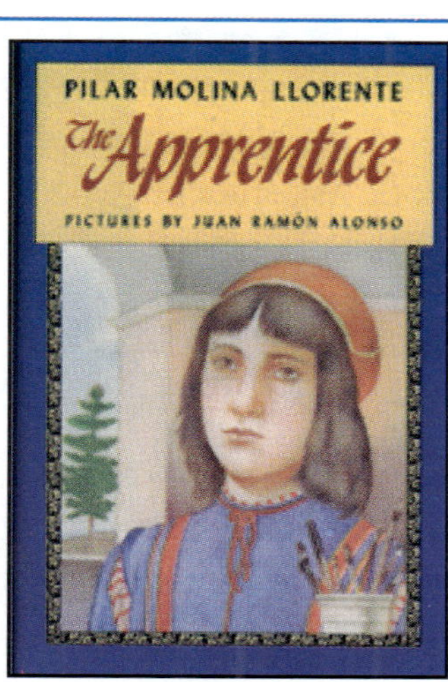

Leonardo da Vinci: Artist, Inventor, and Scientist of the Renaissance

by Francesca Romei

This vividly illustrated volume introduces readers to the famous Renaissance artist. After reading, encourage students to make their own generalizations about what was required for an artist to succeed during this period.

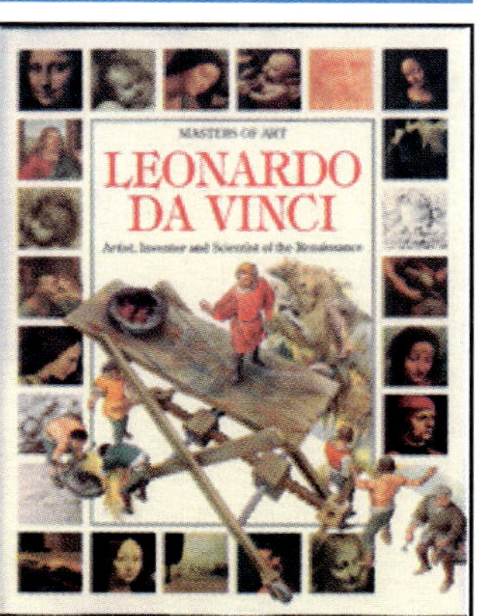

Paint and Painting

This colorful guide describes painting techniques of famous painters in basic terms. Suggest that readers write a step-by-step plan describing how Juan de Pareja might have created a painting.

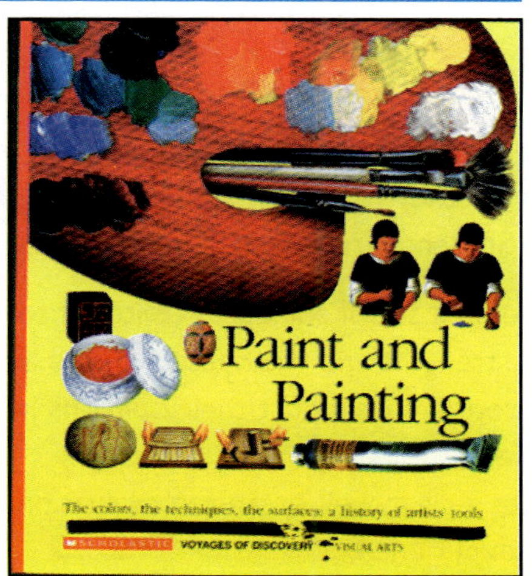

EXTRA SUPPORT

Students might read *Paint and Painting* in a small group. Encourage students to create an "artists' glossary" as they read, including any art terms they discover.

CHALLENGE

Have students work in groups to create a display of student artwork and short biographies of famous artists.

Trade Books

PROJECT MANAGEMENT

- PROJECT LAUNCH
- CHECKPOINT 1
- CHECKPOINT 2
- CHECKPOINT 3
- CHECKPOINT 4
- PRESENTATIONS
- ASSESSMENT

STUDENTS ACQUIRING ENGLISH

Work with students in a group and encourage them to describe how they felt when they saw the art. Focusing on their feelings may help them start on their reviews.

CHALLENGE

After students have completed their own reviews, invite them to use library resources to find published reviews of the work they saw and to compare their own opinions to those of professional art critics.

Write Reviews of Art Experiences

SELECTION CONNECTION

In "I, Juan de Pareja," Juan shows one of his paintings to the king, who is pleased with Juan's work. Ask students what they think people respond to in a work of art they like.

PROJECT CHECKLIST

During this stage, students should

- ☑ visit art shows and exhibits, listen to speakers, or view art in the classroom.
- ☑ take notes about sketches of selected works in an art journal.
- ☑ discuss their experiences in class, comparing responses to different media.
- ☑ write art reviews, focusing on one show or artist.

Project Card 27 can be found as a copying master on page R76.

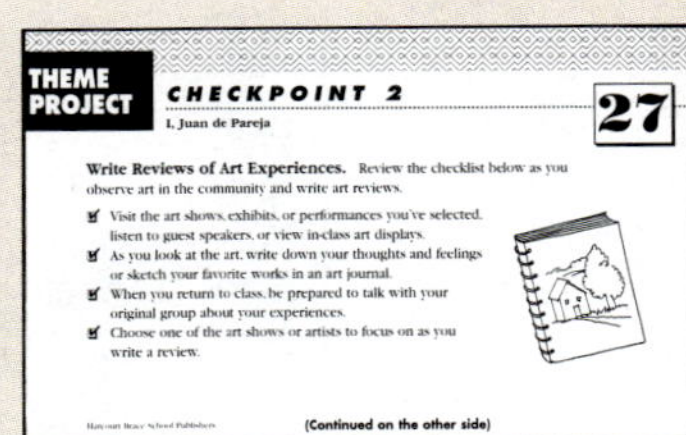
THEME PROJECT

CHECKPOINT 2 — 27

I, Juan de Pareja

Write Reviews of Art Experiences. Review the checklist below as you observe art in the community and write art reviews.

- ☑ Visit the art shows, exhibits, or performances you've selected, listen to guest speakers, or view in-class art displays.
- ☑ As you look at the art, write down your thoughts and feelings or sketch your favorite works in an art journal.
- ☑ When you return to class, be prepared to talk with your original group about your experiences.
- ☑ Choose one of the art shows or artists to focus on as you write a review.

Harcourt Brace School Publishers — (Continued on the other side)

Project Card 27

RESEARCH AND PLANNING TIPS

As students organize their notes to write an art review, suggest that they

- discuss the art with a partner who saw the same art and compare notes.
- read art reviews in newspapers and magazines for ideas about format and content.
- use handouts from exhibits and library resources to provide information and background about the artist.
- support their opinions about the artwork with concrete examples.

When students have completed the checkpoint, encourage them to write about their art experiences in their project journals. You may wish to provide a prompt such as *How did your opinions differ from those of other students who saw the same art?*

Informal Assessment

As students complete this checkpoint, they will describe art they have seen and **make judgments** about it. Students are thinking critically if they

- ☑ develop a set of standards (criteria) to evaluate the strengths and weaknesses of the art.
- ☑ appropriately support their opinions in the review.
- ☑ write a clear, well-organized evaluation of their art experience.

ART AND LITERATURE

Women Playing Koto, Samisen and Kokyu (date unknown)

by Katsushika Oi (active 1818–1854)

ABOUT THE ARTIST

The dates of Katsushika Oi's birth and death are not known exactly but she is thought to have produced artworks between the years 1818 and 1854. During this period, it was unusual for a woman to achieve any stature as an artist. Oi had the dual advantages of being free-thinking and being born the daughter of a successful artist. After a failed marriage, Oi moved back in with her father. The two worked well together, enjoyed each other's company, and shared a disregard for material wealth and household cleanliness. In spite of her free-spirited lifestyle, Oi produced a collection of artworks that reflect a disciplined skill and talent.

ABOUT THE PRINT

Women Playing Koto, Samisen and Kokyu is a hanging silk scroll that depicts three kneeling women, each playing a stringed instrument. The rich colors of the costumes create a stark contrast with the women's white faces and hands, drawing the viewer's attention to those features. The soft folds and elegant fabric design of the costumes, as well as the circular placement of the women, suggest a gentle rhythm, similar perhaps to the one the women are creating in their performance.

ART & LITERATURE

Artists create masterpieces in a variety of ways. What are the artists in this painting creating? Can you think of ways in which making a painting and playing an instrument are similar? How is this painting like the paintings you have seen by Velázquez? How is it different?

Women Playing Koto, Samisen and Kokyu
by Katsushika Oi

Katsushika Oi, a 19th-century Japanese artist, was one of the few well-known female painters of her time. As a child, Oi showed a talent for painting. Later, she and her father—who was also a successful artist—shared a studio. They worked well together and enjoyed each other's company. *Women Playing Koto, Samisen and Kokyu* is one of Oi's best-known artworks. Like music, this painting includes rhythm and pattern. Can you find examples of these?

470

The Museum of Fine Arts, Boston

471

Art and Literature

MAKING CONNECTIONS

Have students read and discuss the first paragraph on page 470. Name several art forms (painting, sculpture, music composition, music performance, many forms of writing, dance, drama performance, and so forth), and encourage students to discuss the value of each. You may want to organize a discussion, comparing and contrasting this silk scroll with the paintings of Velázquez by drawing a Venn diagram on the board and filling it in as students list similarities and differences. Accept all reasonable suggestions.

EXTENDING FINE ART

Across the Curriculum: Social Studies Have pairs of students research nineteenth-century Japan, focusing particularly on one aspect of life depicted in *Women Playing Koto, Samisen and Kokyu* (forms of entertainment, musical instruments, ways of dressing, accepted roles for women). Then have them present their findings to the class.

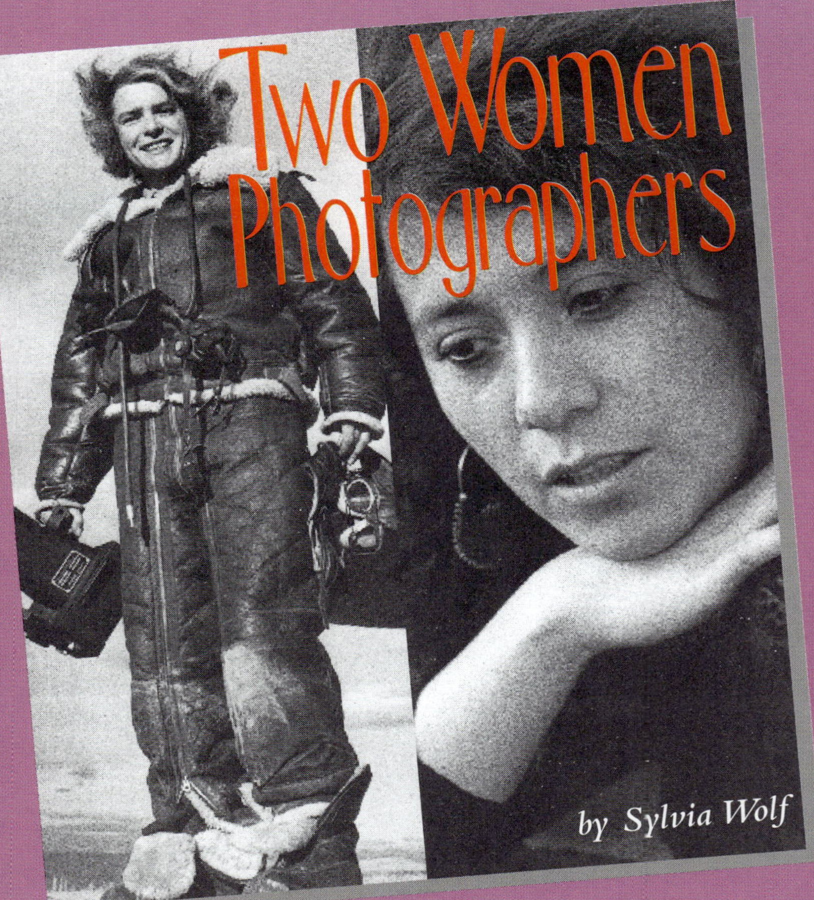

Sylvia Wolf

ABOUT THE AUTHOR

As an educator and a photographer, **SYLVIA WOLF** has taught age groups ranging from second-graders to doctoral candidates. She is currently Associate Curator of Photography at The Art Institute of Chicago. This is her first work of children's literature.

More information about Sylvia Wolf and her work appears on page T989.

Linking Poetry to Nonfiction

The visions of photographer Walker Evans and writer Cynthia Rylant unite in the poem "Photograph."

THEME: CREATIVITY

Masterpieces

In "Two Women Photographers," students will learn that creative expression is an expression of the human spirit.

SELECTION SUMMARY

Genre: Nonfiction

"Two Women Photographers" describes the work of Margaret Bourke-White and Flor Garduño [gär·do͞o′nyō]. Margaret Bourke-White was born in 1904 and grew up in the Bronx section of New York City. After several years in Cleveland, Ohio, she returned to New York, first as a staff photographer for *Fortune* magazine, and then as one of the first photographers for *Life.* Her career at *Life* took her through Europe at the end of World War II, to India, and into the gold mines of South Africa. When she retired from *Life* in 1959, Margaret Bourke-White was one of its most famous photographers.

Growing up on a farm in Mexico, Flor Garduño knew she would become an artist. While she was studying drawing and painting, Flor turned to photography during a teacher's strike and found that she could produce art as fine as painting or sculpture. She has traveled throughout Latin America, photographing animals and documenting how native Indians keep their traditional cultures alive.

SUGGESTED LESSON PLANNER

▶ ***Two Women Photographers***

	DAY 1	DAY 2
PART 1 — Reading, Listening, Speaking, Viewing **Key Words** legendary monumental avid spontaneously pose	**BUILD BACKGROUND** T972 **VOCABULARY STRATEGIES** T973 *Transparency 45* *Practice Book* p.144 **READING THE SELECTION** T974–T989 Options for Reading T974–T975 *Response Card 7* *Literature Cassette 3* **REVIEW PREDICTIONS/PURPOSE** T988 **APPRECIATING THE LITERATURE** T988 NOTE: Students may read the selection on Day 2.	**SUMMARIZE THE SELECTION** T988 *Practice Book* p. 145 **READ POETRY** T990–T991 "Photograph" ◆ **RESPONSE CORNER ACTIVITIES** T992 **CHECKING COMPREHENSION** T993 *End-of-Selection Test* 
PART 2 — Writer's Workshop	**COMPARISON AND CONTRAST ARTICLE** Thinking as Writers T998 *Language Handbook* pp. 15, 67 *Transparency 46*	Prewriting T998 *Language Handbook* pp. 15, 67
Grammar	✓ **PERFECT TENSES** Teach the Concept T1000 Daily Language Practice (1–2) R66	Daily Language Practice (3–4) R66 Practice Activity T1001
Spelling	**PREFIX:** ***in- (im-, il-, ir-)*** *invisible, inability, indefinite, independent, incorrect, incomplete, informal, inexpensive, impossible, impolite, illegal, indigestion, injustice, irregular, impatient, incredible* Pretest/Self-Check T1002 *Integrated Spelling Teacher's Edition* pp. T177, T296	Open and Closed Sorts T1002 *Integrated Spelling* p. 114 *Integrated Spelling Teacher's Edition* p. T178
PART 3 — Skills and Strategies	◆ **INTEGRATED CURRICULUM** *Learning from Images* **Science** T1006 **Health** T1006 **Art** T1007 *Thinkin' Things Collection 2: Snake Blox, 2-3D Blox*	**COMPREHENSION SKILL** T1004–T1005 Synthesizing Information (Introduce) *Transparency 47* *Practice Book* p. 148 *Thinkin' Things: 3: Fripple Place*
 	Use the Intervention Strategies note on page T985 to help **below-level students** as they read.	Use the Challenge note on T1005 to give **above-level students** practice in synthesizing information.

NOTE: An alternative lesson plan for **below-level students** appears on *Intervention Strategies Manual* pp. 110–115. A lesson for **students acquiring English** appears on *Sheltered English/ESL Manual* pp. 74–77.

DAY 3	DAY 4	DAY 5
◆ **IDEA BANK ACTIVITIES** Retelling T996 *Response Card 7* Oral Language T996 Viewing T997 Real-Life Resources: Reading Photo Essays T997 *Writer's Magazine* pp. 72–73 School–Home Connection 19 R96	**VOCABULARY WORKSHOP** T1003 Reviewing Key Words **READING TRADE BOOKS** T1008–T1009  Take-Home Book	**READING TRADE BOOKS** T1005, T1007, T1008–T1009 
Drafting T998 *Language Handbook* pp. 26–28 *The Amazing Writing Machine*	Responding and Revising T999 *Language Handbook* pp. 26–28	Proofreading and Publishing T999 *Language Handbook* pp. 26–28
Daily Language Practice (5–6) R66 Practice Activity T1001 *Language Handbook* pp. 156–157 *The Amazing Writing Machine*	Daily Language Practice (7–8) R66 Practice Activity T1001 *Grammar Practice Book* pp. 46–47	Daily Language Practice (9–12) R66 *Practice Book* p. 146
Discuss the Generalization T1002 *Integrated Spelling* p. 115 *Integrated Spelling Teacher's Edition* p. T179	Apply to Writing T1002 *Integrated Spelling* pp. 116–117 *Integrated Spelling Teacher's Edition* pp. T180–T181	Posttest T1002 *Practice Book* p. 147 *Integrated Spelling Teacher's Edition* p. T182
COMPREHENSION MINILESSON T977 ✓ Main Idea and Details (Review) *Practice Book* p. 150 **COMPREHENSION MINILESSON** T983 ✓ Context Clues (Review) *Practice Book* p. 149	**VOCABULARY WORKSHOP** T1003 Synonyms	**GRAMMAR MINILESSON** T985 ✓ Simple Tenses (Review) Theme Project Checkpoint 3 T1010
Use the Students Aquiring English notes on pages T997 and T1005 with **ESL students** as they complete the activities.	**Below-level students** can use the *Take-Home Book: Beauty Surrounds Us* to help them review Key Words.	**Below-level** and **ESL students** can read the *ESL/Title I Library* book *The Jade Stone.*

✓ = Tested Skill
◆ = Optional activities used to adjust pacing throughout the lesson
Titles in *italics* are optional materials.

BUILDING BACKGROUND AND CONCEPTS

PRIOR KNOWLEDGE

Relate to students' lives. Ask students about their experiences taking photographs and having their photographs taken. Discuss what kinds of things they like to take pictures of. Ask students whether they prefer having their picture taken or taking pictures.

Create a web about the photographs. Explain to students that "Two Women Photographers" is about Margaret Bourke-White and Flor Garduño, two photographers whose work has documented people's lives. Point out that photographs serve many purposes. Have students create a web about the uses of photographs, and discuss how each is important.

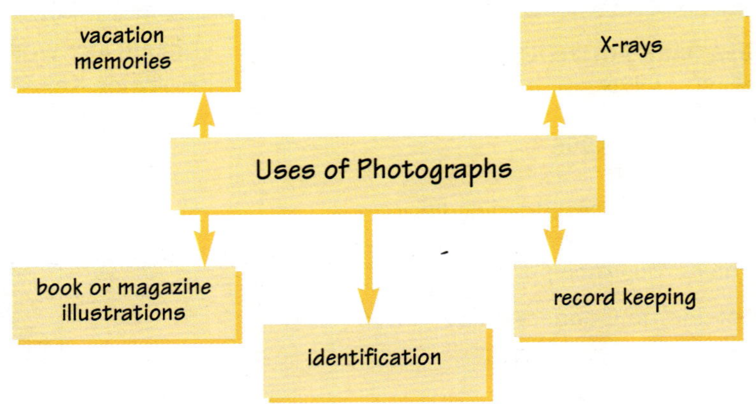

QUICKWRITE

Encourage students to write a few sentences in their journals about what they think it would be like to earn their living taking pictures.

Intervention Strategies

For students who may have difficulty reading "Two Women Photographers," support is available in *Intervention Strategies Manual,* pages 110–115, and on pages T985, and T994–T995 in this lesson.

STUDENTS ACQUIRING ENGLISH

See *Sheltered English/ESL Manual,* pages 74–77.

FACT FINDER

SCIENCE

Taking Fast Shots

Besides electronic flashes and automatic film winding, the greatest differences between the cameras Margaret Bourke-White used and those used by today's photographers are size, weight, and shutter speed. (There have been enormous technological developments in film, as well.) The shutter speed controls the amount of light that enters the camera through the lens. Shutter speeds can range from one second to one thousandth of a second.

Light entering a camera is also controlled by the aperture, the little hole at the front of the camera. The aperture adjustments are called f-stop numbers. A higher f-stop number indicates a smaller aperture opening, which allows less light to enter the camera.

Taking a picture in bright light of something in motion would require a high shutter speed and a high f-stop in order to "freeze" the action; otherwise, the picture would appear blurred or dark.

VOCABULARY STRATEGIES

KEY WORDS DEFINED

legendary like a legend; remembered, admired, and much talked about

monumental like a monument; large and important

avid very eager

pose to hold oneself in a position for a photograph

spontaneously acting quickly and naturally without planning

INTEGRATED SPELLING

Spelling Pretest: page T1002

Spelling Generalization: Words with the prefix *in-* (*im-*, *il-*, *ir-*)

CONTEXT CLUES: STORY

Encourage students to use syntactic and semantic cues. Display Transparency 45, and have a volunteer read the story aloud. Explain to students how you know that *pose* is a verb. (It names an action; it is an infinitive.) Then have students identify the context clues that tell what *pose* means. *(hardly make a move without being asked to stop)* Help students use similar strategies to figure out the meanings of the other Key Words.

CHECK UNDERSTANDING

Have students make associations. As you say each word aloud, have students brainstorm associations — synonyms, examples, or anything they think of that the word reminds them of. Some students may pantomime the word *spontaneously*, for example, by reaching for something that is about to fall, while others may think of synonyms *(quickly, automatically)*

STRATEGY: ASSOCIATIONS

TRANSPARENCY 45

Key Words

My friend Mike's hero is Walker Coles, the legendary news photographer from *The Journal*. Mike used to spend hours looking at the public library's monumental collection of Coles's works. Now he spends hours with his new birthday present—a fancy camera. Mike has become such an avid photographer that nothing escapes his lens. We can hardly make a move without being asked to stop and pose for a picture. We can't wait until Mike figures out how to use all the gadgets on his camera so he can just point and shoot spontaneously without ever telling us what he's doing.

A sports photographer must respond spontaneously to the action.

PRACTICE BOOK, page 144

Prereading Strategies

PREVIEW AND PREDICT

Have students preview "Two Women Photographers" by reading the title and looking at the opening photographs and reading the captions in the rest of the selection. Ask students who the two photographers are and what types of subjects they have photographed.

Ask students to begin a Venn diagram like the one below. They will return to it after reading.

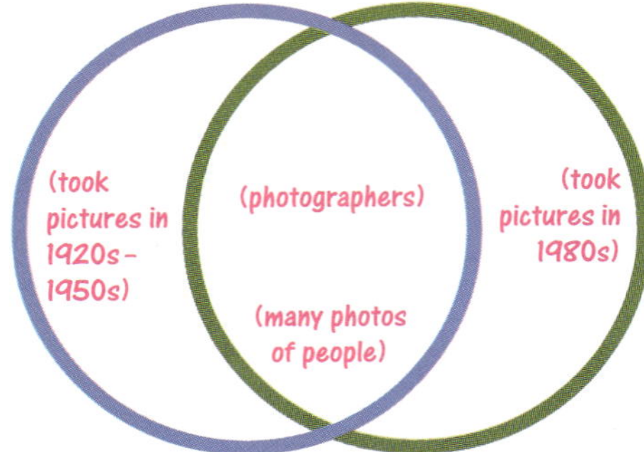

Students may write their predictions about "Two Women Photographers" in their personal journals.

PURPOSE

You may want to model setting a purpose:

I want to find out how and why these women became photographers.

Margaret Bourke-White in High-Altitude Flying Suit, 1943

Flor Garduño in 1986

472

SMALL GROUP

PARTNER READING

Pair students who need extra support with partners who are more-proficient readers. Encourage them to stop after every page or two to talk about the photographer's life and the photographs shown on that page.

COOPERATIVE READING

READER RESPONSE GROUPS

Small groups may use Reader Response Card 7 to **respond freely** to the selection. Reader Response Card 7 can be found at the back of this Teacher's Edition.

Response Card 7

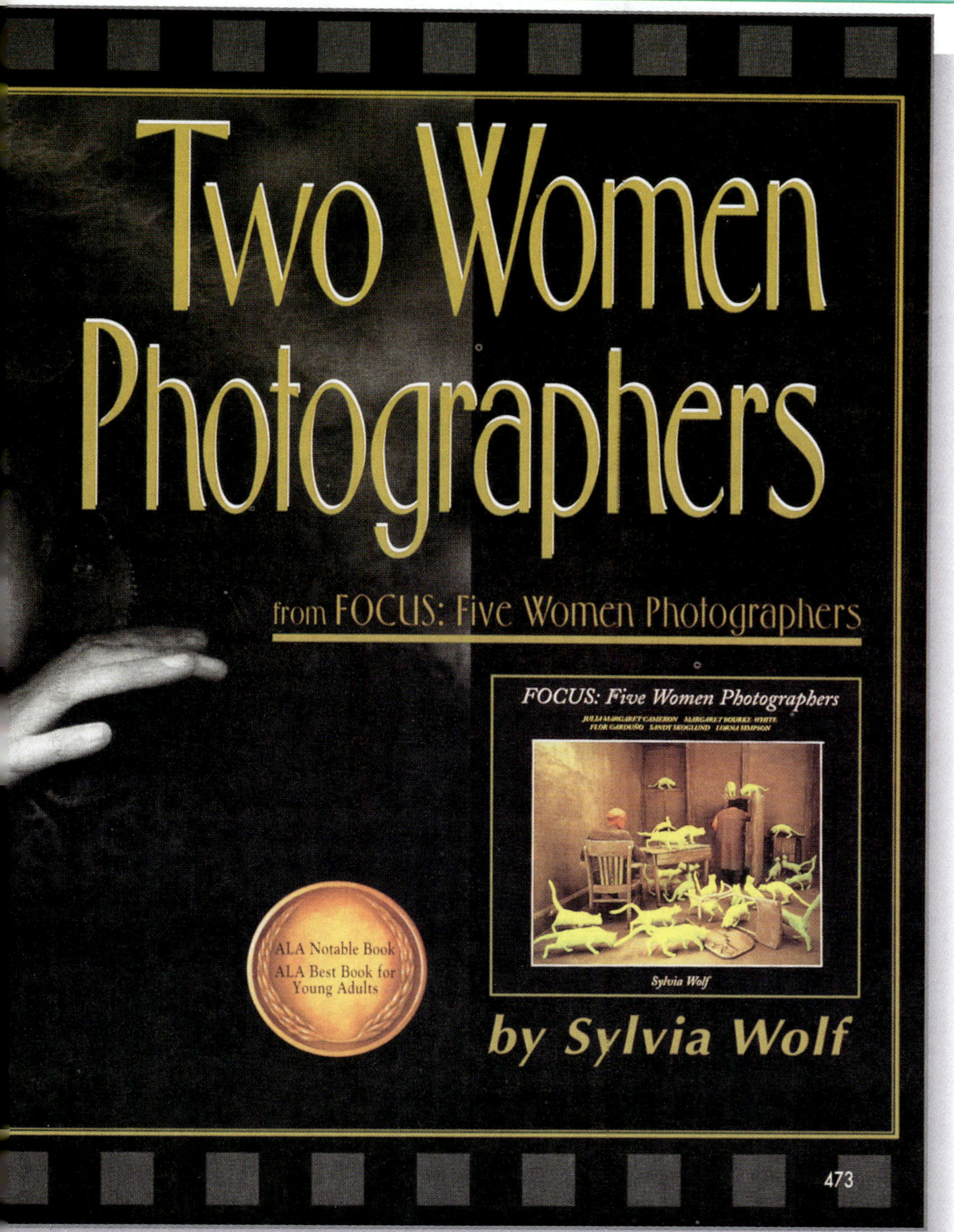

Two Women Photographers

from FOCUS: Five Women Photographers

FOCUS: Five Women Photographers

Sylvia Wolf

ALA Notable Book
ALA Best Book for Young Adults

by Sylvia Wolf

473

WHOLE CLASS

STRATEGIC READING

To help students clarify anything they don't understand, reinforce the focus strategy of **rereading**. Use the questions on pages T976 and T982 to help students practice reading strategically.

SILENT READING/ DISCUSSION

Have students read the entire selection silently. When they finish, have them complete their Venn diagrams, and invite them to discuss any questions or comments they have about the selection.

Strategic Reading

REREADING

Ask students to recall what reading strategies they have used. Then display the class-made strategy chart, and explain that the focus strategy for "Two Women Photographers" is rereading. Remind students that when they don't understand a particular passage the first time, or when they have a question about something they read in the selection, rereading can be an effective strategy. **STRATEGY: REREADING**

PAGES 472–480

Have students read through page 480 to confirm their predictions.

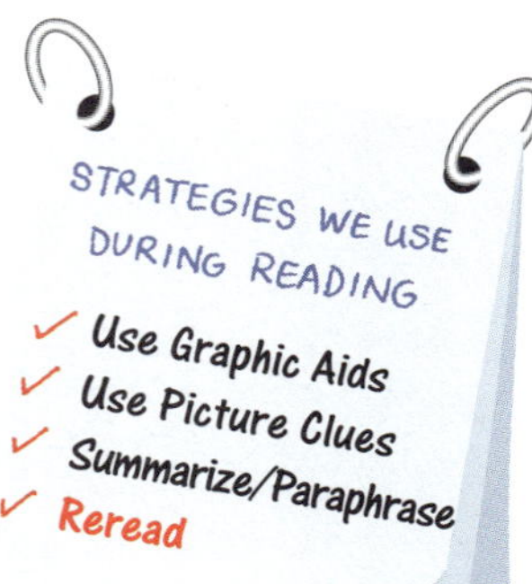

MARGARET BOURKE-WHITE

When she was young, Margaret Bourke-White's best friends were the garter snakes she caught in the woods near her house. Margaret was a quiet girl—too serious to be popular with other children. But when she took her snakes to school, her classmates thought she was wonderfully strange. Margaret liked being different. She once wrote in her diary that she pictured herself "doing all the things that women never do."

Margaret Bourke-White was born to Minnie and Joseph White in the Bronx, New York, on June 14, 1904. (Margaret added Minnie's maiden name, Bourke, when she started her career in photography.) Margaret's mother was an avid reader with an adventurous spirit. She taught Margaret and her younger brother and sister to be curious, determined, and fearless. Her father was a mechanical engineer and inventor who worked for a printing company. He felt that hard work and striving for perfection were the highest human virtues. When Margaret was faced with a tough task, he would urge her to keep trying. "*You can,*" he would say.

When Margaret was eight years old, her father took her on a tour of a foundry, a place where iron and other materials are melted at very high temperatures to make steel. (The steel is then shaped into machine parts.) Margaret watched with fascination as flames jumped from the bubbling vats of molten steel. In the heat, noise, and fiery light of the foundry, she saw beauty and power. When Margaret became a photographer, her first and favorite subjects were factories and machines.

Margaret was introduced to photography by her father, an amateur photographer. As a young girl, she often helped him in his darkroom. When her father died during her first year in college, Margaret decided to pursue photography on her own. Apart from her science courses at

474

VIEWING

A silhouette is an outline that has been filled in with a solid color, usually black. In this photograph, a silhouette was created by placing the light source behind the object being photographed.

EXPANDING VOCABULARY

Explain that a *maiden name* is the surname a woman had before she was married; that is, if she took her husband's surname once they were married. When Margaret added her mother's maiden name to her father's surname, it gave her a double surname. Relate the use of the hyphen in Bourke-White's name to the hyphen in some compound words.

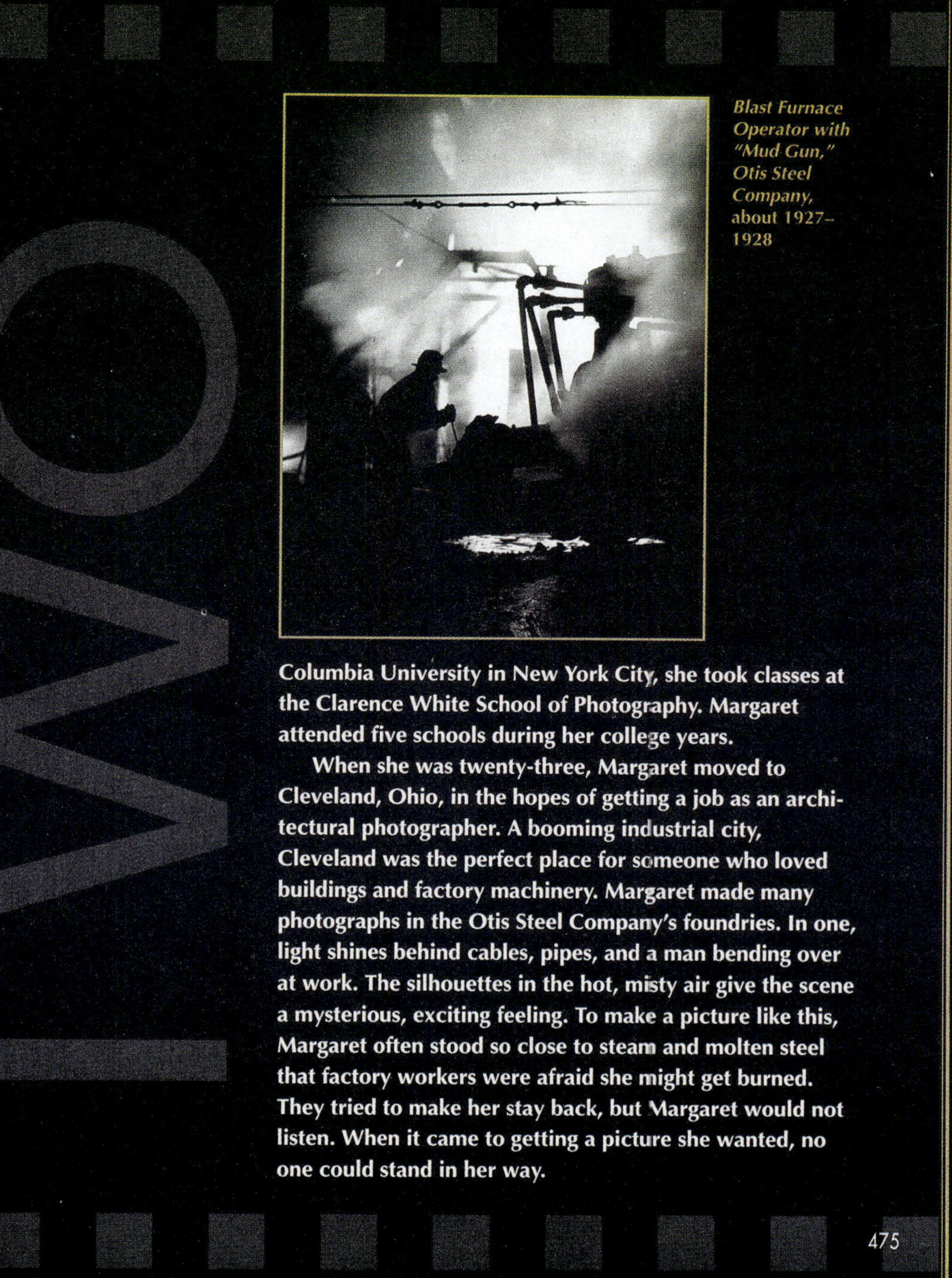

Blast Furnace Operator with "Mud Gun," Otis Steel Company, about 1927–1928

Columbia University in New York City, she took classes at the Clarence White School of Photography. Margaret attended five schools during her college years.

When she was twenty-three, Margaret moved to Cleveland, Ohio, in the hopes of getting a job as an architectural photographer. A booming industrial city, Cleveland was the perfect place for someone who loved buildings and factory machinery. Margaret made many photographs in the Otis Steel Company's foundries. In one, light shines behind cables, pipes, and a man bending over at work. The silhouettes in the hot, misty air give the scene a mysterious, exciting feeling. To make a picture like this, Margaret often stood so close to steam and molten steel that factory workers were afraid she might get burned. They tried to make her stay back, but Margaret would not listen. When it came to getting a picture she wanted, no one could stand in her way.

475

Tested Skill

MINILESSON

REVIEW: COMPREHENSION

Main Idea and Details

INFORMAL ASSESSMENT

Ask students to reread the full paragraph on page 475 and identify its main idea. (When it came to getting a picture she wanted, no one could stand in Margaret's way.)

TEACH/MODEL

Remind students that the main idea of a paragraph, passage, or whole selection may be stated or unstated. If the main idea is unstated, readers need to infer the main idea from the details. If necessary, model identifying the main idea:

MODEL

As I read the paragraph, I notice that all the sentences tell something about Margaret's determination to get the pictures she wants: She moves to Cleveland to take architectural pictures; she goes to the factories; she gets up close to the men working. The last sentence of the paragraph ties the other sentences together and states the main idea.

PRACTICE/APPLY

Have students identify the main idea and supporting details of the paragraphs on page 474.

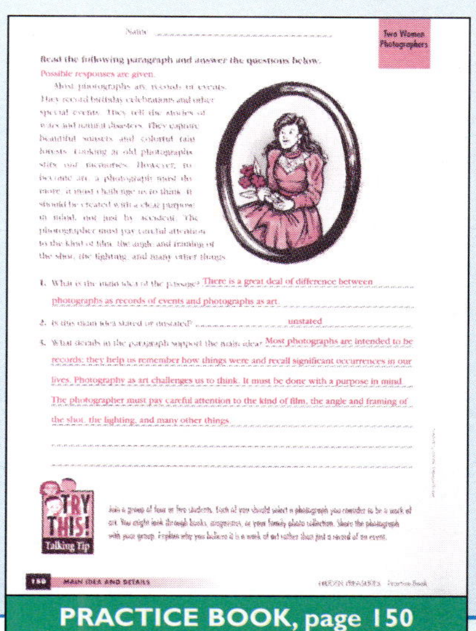

PRACTICE BOOK, page 150

SOCIAL STUDIES

NEW YORK BOROUGHS

The Bronx (1), where Margaret Bourke-White was born, is one of five boroughs, or political divisions, in New York City. The other four boroughs are Brooklyn (2), Manhattan (3), Queens (4), and Staten Island (5). A borough is an incorporated town.

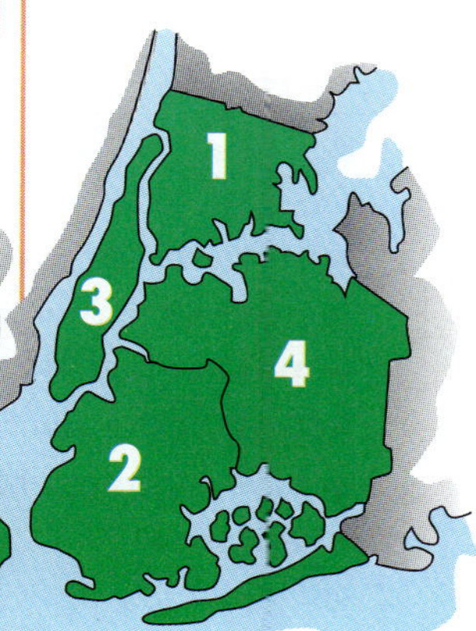

Critical Thinking Questions

1. Margaret inherited her father's interests in photography and factories. What trait did she seem to inherit from her mother that made her successful in her work? (Possible response: her mother's adventurous spirit) CRITICAL: MAKING CONNECTIONS/DETERMINING CHARACTER'S TRAITS

2. Were you surprised that Henry Luce asked Margaret to be one of *Life*'s first photographers? What clues lead up to that information? (Possible response: He had asked her to take pictures for his new magazine *Fortune*. They were so successful that he decided to start another magazine.) INFERENTIAL: DRAWING CONCLUSIONS

Henry Luce, publisher of *Time* magazine, saw Margaret's Otis Steel photographs and thought they were terrific. Luce was founding a new magazine, called *Fortune*. It would be the first to use photographs to bring industry and big business to life. Luce offered Margaret a job photographing for *Fortune* magazine, and she accepted.

Margaret quickly became known for taking pictures no woman—and few men—had taken before. During the winter months of 1929–30, she photographed construction work at the top of New York City's Chrysler Building as the skyscraper was being built. Eight hundred feet up, in cold wind, she teetered on a scaffold with her camera and tripod as the building swayed.

When the Chrysler Building was finished, Margaret rented a studio behind the stainless steel gargoyles that decorated the top of the building. She liked to climb out on the gargoyles and photograph the city below. Amazed by Margaret's fearlessness, newspaper and magazine reporters wrote about her daring. The stories were not just about her photographs—they were about *her*. Margaret Bourke-White was becoming a celebrity.

The photographs published in *Fortune* were so popular that its founders decided to start another magazine—one with even more photographs. The magazine, named *Life*, contained very little writing. Instead, in a new format called the "photographic essay," it let the pictures tell the story. Margaret joined *Life* when the magazine was formed in 1936 and was the only woman among the magazine's first four staff photographers. Except for a short time working for a daily newspaper in 1940, she stayed with *Life* until she retired twenty-one years later.

Early in 1945, Margaret photographed a famous American, Gen. George S. Patton, in Germany. Then she followed his troops as they pursued retreating German forces. On April 11 of that year, Patton's regiment arrived

476

SOCIAL STUDIES

The cover photograph of the first issue of *Life*, November 23, 1936, and the opening photo essay of construction of the Fort Peck Dam in Montana were Margaret's. In the introduction to the new magazine, the editors wrote, "What the Editors expected—for use in some later issue—were construction pictures as only Bourke-White can take them. What the Editors got was a human document of frontier life which, to them at least, was a revelation."

Buchenwald, Germany, the Day after Liberation, April 1945

at Buchenwald, one of many concentration camps built by the Nazis. In these camps alone, the Germans killed over four million Jews, along with gypsies and political prisoners.

At first, it was difficult for Margaret to take pictures of the dead and starving prisoners, but she knew that without photographs, people would not believe reports of the horror at Buchenwald. One image is of inmates lined up behind a barbed wire fence, staring blankly at the camera. These men have seen so much death and brutality that they have little spirit left. Although physically they are alive, they seem emotionally dead. Photographs like these shocked the American public. Few who saw them will ever forget them.

477

Student Self-Assessment

REREADING

Remind students to reread passages they don't understand or any information from earlier in the selection that they may have forgotten.

- Do I remember how Margaret was inspired to be a photographer?
- Do I know why Margaret would be taking photographs at Buchenwald?

For example, if they don't remember why Margaret was at Buchenwald, they could reread the previous page to rediscover that she was a staff photographer for *Life* magazine, which published photo-essays of newsworthy events.

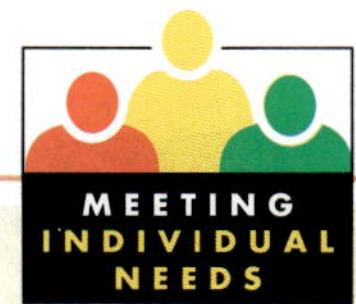

STUDENTS ACQUIRING ENGLISH Students may be familiar with the word *photo*. Explain that *photo* is an abbreviated form of *photograph*. Mention other synonyms for *photograph*, such as *picture* and *snapshot*.

DESIGNER'S CRAFT

Point out that the design of this selection, with white type on a black background, mimics the negative of a black-and-white photograph. The selection designer emphasized this with the squares along the top and bottom edges of the pages representing the feed holes on the edges of a roll of film.

Gandhi, India, 1946

A year later, with the war ended, Margaret was sent to document India's struggle for independence from Great Britain. India's great peace leader, Mahatma Gandhi, agreed to pose for her. First, though, Gandhi's secretary insisted Margaret take a lesson in spinning cotton so that she could understand the Mahatma's philosophy. To Gandhi, the spinning wheel represented India's break from Britain. He believed that cotton grown in India should be spun there, not in British textile mills, as was done at the time. When Margaret photographed Gandhi, she positioned his spinning wheel in the foreground of the portrait. It fills almost half the frame. By giving it so much space and importance, she reminds us of Gandhi's desire for India to be free from British rule.

In late 1949, Margaret was sent to do a photographic essay on racial injustice in South Africa, where whites, who were in the minority, brutally mistreated native Africans. She traveled two miles underground into a gold mine to photograph men who did hard and dangerous work for little pay. These men were known not by their names, but by numbers tattooed on their arms. In Margaret's photograph, #1139 and #5122 stand facing the camera. Their sweat shimmers in the artificial light of Margaret's flash. She positioned the camera to fill the frame with their torsos. In spite of miserable conditions and racial oppression, the workers appear noble and monumental.

478

SOCIAL STUDIES CONNECTION

TITLES OF RESPECT *Mahatma* is a title of respect given to people of great knowledge and love for humankind. It comes from Sanskrit and means "Great Soul" or "Great Spirit." Mahatma Gandhi's given name was Mohandas Karamchand Gandhi. Students could compile a directory of titles, defining those for civil, military, religious, and professional offices, as well as for nobility.

Civil	Military	Religious/ Spiritual	Professional	Nobility
president	general	reverend	president	duchess
senator	admiral	pastor	doctor	queen
		mahatma		

Gold Miners, Johannesburg, South Africa, 1950

479

Informal Assessment

SYNTHESIZING

To determine whether students are synthesizing information from the selection, ask them questions like the following:

- How did Margaret use what she learned about spinning to plan and compose the photograph?
- What do you know about the miners through the information in the text and Margaret's photograph?

MULTICULTURAL CONNECTION

Cotton was first spun and woven into cloth in India. Spinning cotton involves three jobs: (1) drafting the cotton, or reducing it to smaller and smaller structures; (2) straightening the fibers; and (3) twisting the fibers into yarn.

VIEWING

In the photograph of the miners, students may note the helmet lights that illuminate the mine tunnel, and the whistle for signaling or calling for help. Suggest that students consider what the author meant by stating that the workers appear *noble and monumental*.

Strategic Reading

PAGES 472–480 **What kinds of photographs did Margaret Bourke-White take?** (Possible response: Her photographs recorded historical events and people at work in factories.)
STRATEGIES: SUMMARIZING/CONFIRMING PREDICTIONS

How do you think Margaret's work helped pave the way for other photojournalists? (Possible answer: Since her adventurous spirit gave her courage to go to difficult places, like the gold mine in South Africa and Buchenwald, others probably found it easier to take similar risks.)
INFERENTIAL: RECOGNIZING CHARACTERS' MOTIVES/MAKING CONNECTIONS

REREADING If necessary, model the strategy of rereading:

MODEL

I review parts of the text and look again at the photographs and their captions. I wonder about the courage it took for someone to go where Margaret did. I think that if she had the courage to go there, I might, too.

PAGES 481–486 Students should continue reading to find out about Flor Garduño and her work.

This picture and ones Margaret made during the Korean War in the early fifties are among the last of her career. In 1954, when she was forty-nine, Margaret was diagnosed with Parkinson's disease, an illness that attacks the nervous system. She continued to work for *Life* until 1957. Then, for fourteen years, she fought Parkinson's disease with the same bravery and determination that had made her a great photographer. In 1971, at age sixty-six, Margaret died of her illness.

During her years with *Life,* Margaret Bourke-White's photographs were seen by over one hundred million viewers each year. Today, they are admired both as historical documents and as works of art; they can be found in history textbooks and in museum collections around the world. She became a legendary figure in photography and paved the way for future photojournalists, men and women alike. Margaret succeeded many times over in fulfilling her childhood dream of doing things women of her time did not do. She never forgot her mother's lessons in curiosity and fearlessness and her father's words "*You can.*"

Dam at Fort Peck, Montana, 1936. (First cover of Life.)

480

STUDENTS ACQUIRING ENGLISH To help students understand Bourke-White's long-lasting contribution to the development of photojournalism, explain that the idiom *paved the way* means "made easier, prepared."

FLOR GARDUÑO

FLOR GARDUÑO (flôr gär • do͞on′ yō) was born the youngest of three children in Mexico City, Mexico, on March 21, 1957. Her mother, Estela, was a merchant, and her father, Gregorio, was a civil engineer. When Flor was five years old, her family moved to a farm outside of Mexico City. Flor's father had a strong love for animals and for life in the country. He often took the children on walks and pointed out animals, beautiful flowers, and fruit. It was from him that Flor developed her appreciation of nature.

From the time Flor was a girl, she knew she wanted to be an artist. At age eighteen, she left home to enter the San Carlos School of Fine Arts in Mexico City. For three years, she studied painting and drawing and read poetry, literature, and philosophy. She went to see films, sometimes two in one day. Then the teachers went on strike. Flor was anxious to keep learning, so she signed up to study with the only teacher who was not on strike, a photographer named Kati Horna.

Before then, Flor had not been interested in photography. She had watched photographers on the streets of Mexico City who took portraits of people for a few pesos. But their work looked boring to Flor. It was not until she studied with Kati Horna that Flor discovered how wonderful photography could be.

Horna was a Hungarian photographer who had moved to Mexico City during the Second World War. In Europe, she had been friends with many important artists who were pioneers of modern art. Horna considered photography to be a fine art equal to painting and sculpture.

481

Tested Skill

MINILESSON

REVIEW: COMPREHENSION

Context Clues

INFORMAL ASSESSMENT

Ask students what the word *strike* means. (Possible responses: "to hit," "to remove," "to stop working," "a pitch that a batter misses in baseball," "knocking down all the pins in bowling") Then have students reread the second paragraph on page 481. Ask them what *strike* means in the next-to-last sentence. ("to stop working")

TEACH/MODEL

Remind students that when they read, they will come across new words or words that are used in a new way. If they're not sure of the meaning of such a word, they can look at the context, or surrounding text, for clues to the words' meaning. To model, use the following think-aloud:

MODEL **I know that the word *strike* has several meanings. I use the context clues *the teachers went on strike* and *Flor was anxious to keep learning* to figure out that here, *strike* means "to stop working."**

PRACTICE/APPLY

Have students use context clues to figure out the meaning of the word *pioneers* in the last paragraph.

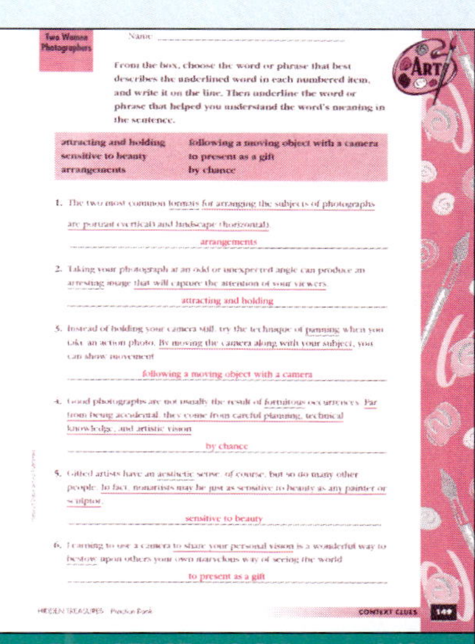
Two Women Photographers

Name ______

From the box, choose the word or phrase that best describes the underlined word in each numbered item, and write it on the line. Then underline the word or phrase that helped you understand the word's meaning in the sentence.

attracting and holding	following a moving object with a camera
sensitive to beauty	to present as a gift
arrangements	by chance

1. The two most common formats for arranging the subjects of photographs are portrait (vertical) and landscape (horizontal).
arrangements

2. Taking your photograph at an odd or unexpected angle can produce an arresting image that will capture the attention of your viewers.
attracting and holding

3. Instead of holding your camera still, try the technique of panning when you take an action photo. By moving the camera along with your subject, you can show movement.
following a moving object with a camera

4. Good photographs are not usually the result of fortuitous occurrences. Far from being accidental, they come from careful planning, technical knowledge, and artistic vision.
by chance

5. Gifted artists have an aesthetic sense, of course, but so do many other people. In fact, nonartists may be just as sensitive to beauty as any painter or sculptor.
sensitive to beauty

6. Learning to use a camera to share your personal vision is a wonderful way to bestow upon others your own marvelous way of seeing the world.
to present as a gift

HIDDEN TREASURES Practice Book CONTEXT CLUES 149

PRACTICE BOOK, page 149

MULTICULTURAL CONNECTION

The *peso* is the monetary unit of Bolivia, Chile, Colombia, Cuba, the Dominican Republic, and Mexico. Originally, it was the name of the old Spanish dollar.

SOCIAL STUDIES

Mexico City is the capital of Mexico and the largest city in the world. With over 20 million residents, it is Mexico's center of higher education, transportation, and tourism. In 1325 the Aztec Indians built the city of Tenochtitlán where Mexico City now stands. Aztec ruins still remain in some parts of the city, and most of its inhabitants have both Indian and Spanish ancestry.

Cooperative Reading

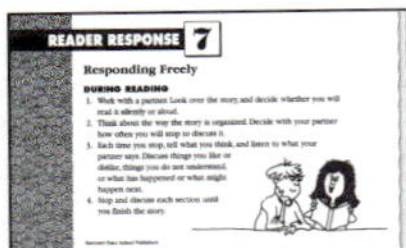
Response Card 7

Encourage cooperative reading groups to discuss the section on Margaret Bourke-White. Students might respond to questions such as these:

- **What do you admire most about Margaret Bourke-White?**
- **Which of her photographs do you like the most? Why?**
- **If she were alive today, what subjects do you think Margaret Bourke-White would photograph?**

When Flor was twenty-two, she left school to work as a photographer. Flor's first job was with the Mexican secretary of public education. Her assignment was to visit and photograph in remote villages throughout Mexico where native Indians lived. Before the sixteenth century, when Spanish conquerors arrived in Latin America (Mexico, Central America, and South America), this area was inhabited by native Indians. From region to region, they had different languages and cultures. Today, over forty million Indians occupy villages all over Latin America. They still speak native languages, and they maintain many of their old customs. Other customs are mixed with the Christian practices brought by the Spaniards.

In these Indian communities, Flor's task was to take pictures of everyday activities. Later, the photographs appeared in children's schoolbooks written in native languages as well as Mexico's national language, Spanish. The images were used to illustrate words and help children learn how to read and write.

One of these early pictures is of two brothers walking home from the fields in Tulancingo, Mexico. Each one carries a huge squash over his shoulder like a baseball bat.

Kings of Canes, Tulancingo, Mexico, 1981

482

CROSS-CULTURAL VIEWPOINT

Encourage students from various cultural backgrounds to share examples of their customs. They might discuss things such as holidays, dress, table manners, weddings, and so on.

The squash has been dried and hollowed out to be used as a tool for getting sap out of the agave plant. The sap is then used to make *pulque* (pōōl´kā), once the sacred drink of the Aztec people, who ruled an empire in Mexico in the fifteenth and early sixteenth centuries. In the photograph, the boys look one way, and the squashes tilt the other. The bold but simple composition makes this a dynamic picture.

Flor worked for the secretary of education for two years. After that, she photographed sculptures and paintings for art books. Then an exciting thing happened. Francisco Toledo, one of Mexico's famous painters and a friend of Flor's, offered to publish a book of her photographs. He liked her pictures and thought other people would like them, too. This was a great honor.

Flor selected her favorite photographs for the book. One is of a dense cloud of hundreds of birds flying above a country farm. Flor had seen them from a distance as they landed in the trees. They were so beautiful that she drove closer and loaded her film as quickly as she could. She hoped to photograph the birds as they flew away. Just as she was ready, they took flight. Flor had barely enough time to take one quick picture before they were gone.

Cloud, Jocotitlán, Mexico, 1982

483

Tested Skill

MINILESSON

REVIEW: GRAMMAR

Simple Tenses

INFORMAL ASSESSMENT

Have students reread the first sentence of the first full paragraph on page 483. Ask them when the action is happening. (in the past) Then ask them how they know that. (The *-ed* ending indicates that the verb *worked* is in the past tense.)

TEACH/MODEL

Remind students that the tense of a verb shows when the action in a sentence happens. Ask volunteers to name the three basic verb tenses. (past, present, future) Explain that these are called the simple verb tenses. Knowing when the action happens helps readers keep track of the sequence of events. You may want to model the thinking:

MODEL **When I see the past tense verbs in that paragraph, I know that these experiences have already happened. The past tense also gives me a clue that Flor is doing something else now.**

PRACTICE/APPLY

Have students locate and identify the tenses of other verbs in the selection or in an earlier selection in their anthologies.

VIEWING

Encourage students to compare how the author describes the photographs on these pages with what they themselves see in the photographs. Students might also consider why Flor named the photographs as she did and whether they would name them differently.

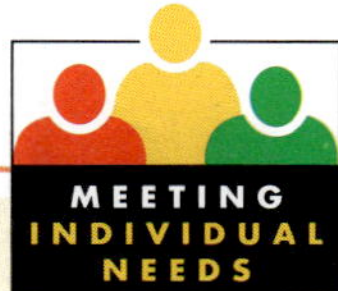

Intervention Strategies

SELF-QUESTIONING **Say this sentence aloud to students: *While I'm reading, I try to answer the questions I asked myself before reading.* Have students share any questions they had, and tell how answering their questions, helps them keep track of story details.**

Critical Thinking Questions

1. What do you think Flor means by "it is one of the best feelings in the world" at the end of the first paragraph? What things have you done that have given you that feeling? (Responses will vary.) INFERENTIAL: RECOGNIZING CHARACTER'S EMOTIONS/MAKING CONNECTIONS

2. Flor's photography teacher, Kati Horna, thought photography was as fine an art as painting or sculpture. When you look at *Basket of Light*, do you agree with her? Why or why not? (Responses will vary.) CRITICAL: MAKING JUDGMENTS

Flor's equipment made it possible for her to act spontaneously in taking this picture. Her cameras are small and light. Also, her film speed is fast. This allowed her to stop the birds' motion as they flew. Even so, she knew she was lucky. It is difficult to be in the right place at the right time. When that happens and Flor takes a picture she is happy with, she says it is one of the best feelings in the world.

When Flor's book, *Magic of the Eternal Game,* was published in 1985, she took it to the international book fair in Frankfurt, Germany. One company there liked her work so much that they asked her to publish a book with them. She proposed one on animals. (Flor has loved animals since her childhood days on the farm.) The company liked the idea and she got started.

While working on her book *Bestiarium* (the Latin word for collection of animals), Flor traveled with Adriano Heitmann, a Swiss journalist and photographer. Like Flor, he was interested in the Indian cultures of Latin America, and he had helped her plan the book. Over time, Flor and Adriano fell in love.

During the next few years, they visited Guatemala, Ecuador, Bolivia, Peru, and tiny villages throughout Mexico. One picture she took in Guatemala celebrates the beauty of nature and light. Flor was driving along a small country road when she saw a girl, about ten or twelve years old, walking with a basket of lilies balanced on her head. The girl wore the traditional dress of the area. Flor followed the girl to her house, then asked if she could take a picture. By positioning the girl half in shadow, half in light, she made a striking composition. The lilies shine in the sunlight like a floral crown.

484

STUDENTS ACQUIRING ENGLISH Help students use context clues to identify the meaning of *dress* in the last paragraph. Lead them to see that it means a style of clothing, not the specific article that girls and women wear. Point out the difference between *traditional dress* and *costume.*

IDEA BANK

You may wish to make disposable cameras available in the classroom. Students could use the cameras to create a photographic display or album to document school activities. An album could be cumulative, with the pictures from each roll of film added to the album with appropriate captions.

Basket of Light, Sumpango, Guatemala, 1989

NOTES

Here's a place to list ideas or activities that you would like to use the next time you teach this lesson.

SCIENCE CONNECTION

LIGHT AND SHADOW The play of light and shadow makes *Basket of Light* "a striking composition." On their own, interested students could use a flashlight to experiment with how light from different angles and in different degrees changes the appearance of things.

Strategic Reading

PAGES 481–486 What kind of photographs does Flor Garduño take? (Possible response: She takes pictures showing how the Indian cultures in Latin America have survived.)
STRATEGIES: SUMMARIZING/CONFIRMING PREDICTIONS

The author says Flor Garduño's photographs are "documents of timeless traditions." What do you think she means? (Possible response: The photographs are documents that give important information.) CRITICAL: CHALLENGING THE TEXT

Returning to the Predictions/Purpose

Did you find out what you wanted to know about Margaret Bourke-White and Flor Garduño? Encourage students to discuss how their purposes for reading were met.
STRATEGY: RETURNING TO THE PURPOSE

Appreciating the Literature

Which photograph from the selection do you like the most? Why? (Responses will vary.)

In 1992, Flor published her third book, *Witnesses of Time.* The book became an instant hit. It won a Kodak award as one of the best photography books of 1992 and was translated from Spanish into five languages. That same year, an exhibition of photographs from the book began a tour of museums in Europe and the United States.

Flor's photographs are popular because they are stunning pictures as well as documents of timeless traditions. Though modern technology has come to many villages, native Indians have maintained their heritage. With the camera, Flor shows us the survival of Indian cultures in Latin America.

A year after *Witnesses of Time* was published, Flor gave birth to her first child, a baby girl named Azul. Today, Flor, her husband, Adriano, and Azul divide their time between two homes. For part of the year, they live in a small white house in the foothills of the Swiss Alps. For the rest, they live in the Mexican village of Tepoztlán. Flor will continue making pictures, and she may even return to painting someday. In the meantime, however, she is enjoying the success of her most recent book and her days and nights with Azul.

The Woman, Juchitán, Mexico, 1987

486

PRACTICE BOOK, page 145

SUMMARIZING

Venn Diagram

Students can complete their diagrams by summarizing the important events in each photographer's career and writing what they have in common. See *Practice Book* page 145.

Margaret Bourke-White	Both	Flor Garduño
(took pictures in 1920s–1950s)	(photographers)	(took pictures in 1980s)
(born in Bronx, NY)	(many memorable photos of people)	(born in Mexico City)
(worked for *Life* magazine)	(accomplished, hard-working, talented, outstanding)	(photographed native Indians in Latin America)
(photographed people and events in Europe, India, South Africa)	(documented history of the time)	(won award for *Witnesses of Time*)

About the Author

After students read page 487, you may wish to discuss these questions with them:

- **What does Sylvia Wolf mean when she talks about creating art with a camera?** (Possible responses: She means that almost anyone can learn how to work a camera, but not everyone can turn photographs into things of beauty; she means that photography, when it's done well, can show emotion about the world.)
- **If you were a talented photographer, what subject matter would you focus on in your pictures in order to show deep feelings about the world?** (Responses will vary.)

Sylvia Wolf has written and lectured considerably on photography since receiving her master's degree in fine arts from Rhode Island School of Design. She produces her own photographic work and is a member of the faculty and advisory board of *SPEOS*, an American-accredited photography school in Paris. In addition, she is on the advisory board of *Picture This*, a nonprofit inner-city program that teaches photography to children in the Chicago area. She published *Focus: Five Women Photographers* in 1994.

POETRY

Photograph

by Cynthia Rylant

INTRODUCING THE POEM Have students recall from reading "Two Women Photographers" how many of Flor Garduño's extraordinary photographs focus on otherwise uneventful moments in people's lives. Ask students to imagine how they would feel if a famous photographer stopped them in the street to take a photograph. Then tell students they will read a poem about a young boy who is the subject of such a photograph.

APPRECIATING THE POEM Read the poem aloud to students as they follow along. Then ask questions such as the following:

What can you tell about the boy in the photo on page 489? (Responses may vary, but among other things, students may observe from clues such as furnishings and hairstyles that the picture was taken a long time ago and that the boy's surroundings are humble.)

If the boy had spoken aloud to the photographer, what do you think he might have said? (Responses will vary.) **How would you have felt in his situation?** (Responses will vary.)

What do you think the last four lines mean? (Possible responses: The boy feels, for a moment, that he is worthy of having his photograph taken; the photograph makes him feel good about himself.)

After discussing the poem, invite students to read it aloud with you.

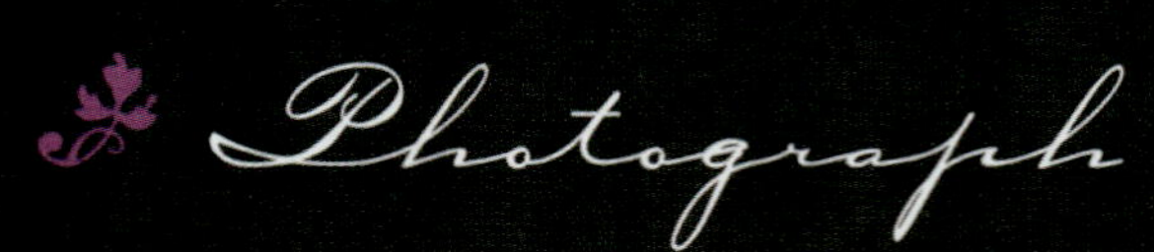

He washed his feet for the picture,
even his knees,
and wondered about that man
who cared enough to want him to sit there
for a photograph
even though he didn't have
nothing good to hold in his hands,
nor even a dog to sit by his chair.
It gave him, briefly,
some sort of feeling
of just being
enough.

BY CYNTHIA RYLANT

488

LISTENING CENTER

"Photograph" is available on Literature Cassette 3. Be sure students look at the photograph on page 489 as they listen to the poem.

PHOTOGRAPH BY WALKER EVANS

489

About the Poet

Cynthia Rylant spent four years of her childhood in rural Cool Ridge, West Virginia, with her grandparents, whom she describes as soft-spoken, gentle, capable people who were "accustomed to poverty." Many of the details in her books are drawn from those childhood memories. Unlike many other authors, Cynthia Rylant recalls reading very little, mainly because the community had no library and no bookstores. Yet, she says there were hints that she would someday be a writer: "The clues . . . had something to do with the way I grieved over stray animals, the heroes I chose, and the love I had of solitude. It is called sensitivity, this quality which sets creative people apart." The author of over thirty books for young people, Cynthia Rylant was the 1993 Newbery Medal winner for her book *Missing May.*

You may wish to share more of Cynthia Rylant's poetry with students. Her collection *Waiting to Waltz: A Childhood,* Macmillan, 1984, features poems about her childhood in Appalachia.

POET'S CRAFT Point out to students how simple the words are in this poem, and ask them why they think the poet might have written the poem this way. (Possible response: to show the simplicity of the boy's life) Have students reread the poem silently, focusing on the boy's feelings, and ask them how they might describe the tone, or feeling, of this poem. (Possible responses: a little hopeful; quiet; maybe a little sad)

PHOTOGRAPHER'S CRAFT

Point out the caption beneath the photo on page 489. Tell students that Walker Evans was famous for his black-and-white photographs of Southern sharecroppers, taken during the Great Depression in the 1930s. Have students look at the photograph on page 489 again, and ask them why they think Evans composed the photo with the boy to one side. (Possible responses: to show the boy's home; to get a sense of how his family lived)

ACTIVITY CHOICES

DEBATE AN ISSUE

GENDER DEBATE Students should discuss possible topics and agree on a single topic. At the end of their debate, they could consider if and how "the things that women never do" are the same today as they were for Margaret Bourke-White seventy-five years ago. CRITICAL THINKING/LISTENING AND SPEAKING

COMPARE TWO STYLES

BEHIND THE LENS Remind students to look at Margaret Bourke-White's and Flor Garduño's photographs, as well as the author's words describing the pictures, for details to use when they compare and contrast. WRITING

DISCUSS IDEAS

SIMPLE SUBJECT Students should be prepared with ideas to back up their choice before the group discussion. They could think about such questions as these: *How did you become interested in the subject? What do you like most about it? What aspect of the subject seems most interesting?* CRITICAL THINKING/LISTENING AND SPEAKING

Margaret Bourke-White

Response

DEBATE AN ISSUE

GENDER DEBATE

Margaret Bourke-White wished that she could do "all the things that women never do." Debate with a partner about something women normally don't do but could. Each of you should take one side of the issue. Allow equal time for each point of view to be expressed.

COMPARE TWO STYLES

BEHIND THE LENS

Compare and contrast the life and work of Margaret Bourke-White and Flor Garduño. Using details from the selection, tell what is different about each woman's style of photography. Include a statement about which woman's photographs you prefer, and why.

490

STUDENTS ACQUIRING ENGLISH Suggest that students do a Quickwrite of their photographic ideas in their first language, and then refer to their Quickwrite during the group discussion.

Corner

Flor Garduño

DISCUSS IDEAS

SIMPLE SUBJECT

If you were a photographer, what subject would you shoot for a book or magazine? Why would you choose that subject? Discuss your ideas with a small group of your classmates.

What Do You Think?

- How did the early experiences of the two women prepare them for a career in photography?
- What did you learn from the selection that you thought was especially interesting or important?
- What do you think that poet Cynthia Rylant would say about Flor Garduño's photograph "Basket of Light"?

491

CHECKING COMPREHENSION

What Do You Think?

1. **How did the early experiences of the two women prepare them for a career in photography?** (Possible responses: Margaret Bourke-White was introduced to photography by her father and helped him in his darkroom; she learned to be curious, determined, and fearless from her mother. Flor Garduño grew up on a farm and learned to appreciate nature from her father.) DESCRIPTIVE RESPONSE
2. **What did you learn from the selection that you thought was especially interesting or important?** (Possible response: Photographs can be works of art and important historical documents.) PERSONAL RESPONSE
3. **What do you think that poet Cynthia Rylant would say about Flor Garduño's photograph *Basket of Light*?** (Responses will vary.) CRITICAL ANALYSIS/REFLECTING

VARYING THE ACTIVITY

To **challenge** students, have them invite a photographer to speak to the class. Students should prepare interview questions to ask.

Intervention Strategies

TIPS FOR CLASSROOM MANAGEMENT

IF second-language students need additional vocabulary and during-reading strategies to understand "Two Women Photographers," **THEN** use *Sheltered English/ESL Manual*, pages 74–77.

IF students had difficulty understanding "Two Women Photographers," **THEN** complete the Rereading and Words and Meanings Strategies. See also *Intervention Strategies Manual*, pages 110–115.

REREADNG

NOTING MAIN IDEAS Remind students that "Two Women Photographers" is nonfiction. To read nonfiction effectively, students can use the strategy of looking for the main idea of each paragraph. By rereading paragraphs and identifying main ideas, students may better understand the selection as a whole. Draw on the board a web like the one below:

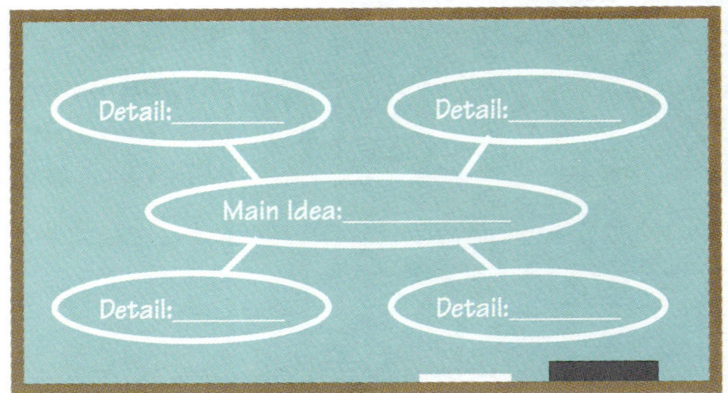

Choose paragraphs from the selection for students to reread. As each one is read aloud, have volunteers go to the board and fill in the web with suggestions from other members of the group.

PERSONAL JOURNAL

Ask students whether they think, after reading this selection, that photographers and other artists can make a difference to society as a whole. If so, how? Have students write a few sentences to give their thoughts and reactions.

WORDS AND MEANINGS

CONTEXT CLUES Remind students that context clues often hint at the meanings of unfamiliar words. Model the strategy of using context clues by asking students how they would make an intelligent guess at the meaning of the word *striving* in the second paragraph on page 474. (The phrases *hard work* and *for perfection*, as well as the quotation in the next sentence, serve as clues to the meaning.)

Choose other words from the selection to give students additional practice in using context clues. You may wish to use the following:

teetered (page 476)

dynamic (page 483)

shimmers (page 478)

floral (page 484)

WRITING TO SUMMARIZE

Help students summarize the information in the selection by filling out the following fact sheet.

Fact Sheet		
	Margaret Bourke-White	Flor Garduño
Year of Birth Native Country First Important Photographs Favorite Subjects for Photography		

DECODING SUPPORT
Hard *g* and Soft *g*

Intervention Strategies Manual pp. 114–115

ESL/TITLE I READING

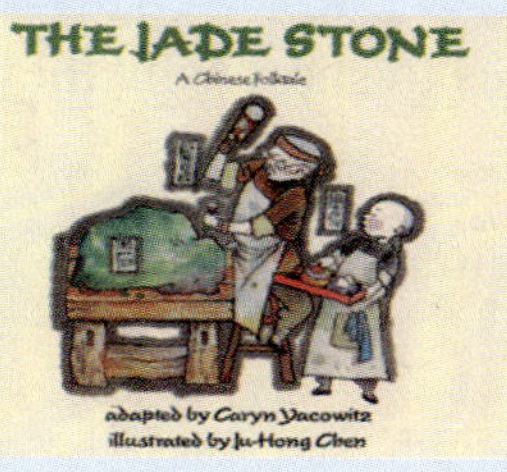

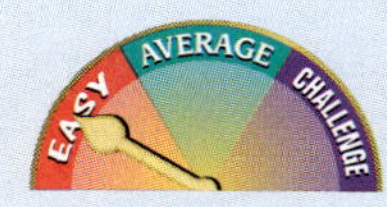

The Jade Stone

by Caryn Yacowitz

In *The Jade Stone,* a master carver in ancient China remains true to his artistic calling, despite the threats of the all-powerful emperor. Have students use the diagram below to contrast this folktale with the nonfiction selection "Two Women Photographers."

I know that "Two Women Photographers" is nonfiction because
1. ______________________
2. ______________________
3. ______________________

I know that *The Jade Stone* is fiction because
1. ______________________
2. ______________________
3. ______________________

EASY AVERAGE CHALLENGE

TAKE-HOME BOOK TO REINFORCE KEY WORDS

Students will enjoy reading about a class photography project. You may wish to have students read the book during independent reading time in class or they may wish to take the book home to read.

PERSONAL JOURNAL

After students have finished reading *Beauty Surrounds Us,* have them write in their personal journals about their favorite part of the book.

See also *Intervention Strategies Manual,* page 113.

IDEA BANK

TIPS FOR CLASSROOM MANAGEMENT

IF students had difficulty answering the Strategic Reading questions on page T988, **THEN** they should complete the Retelling activity.

IF students need support or practice in noting details, **THEN** have them complete the Viewing activity.

RETELLING

Conversation

Invite groups to speculate on what a conversation between Margaret Bourke-White and Flor Garduño would be like. Have students discuss what the two photographers might talk about. Then choose two volunteers to role-play the photographers engaging in an informal discussion about their lives, their work, and the places their work has taken them. Other group members could prompt occasionally with questions, or, at the end of the discussion, "Margaret" and "Flor" could field questions from the listeners. LISTENING/SPEAKING

Informal Assessment 

Note how students use information from the text and the photographs in their conversation.

ORAL LANGUAGE

Responding Freely

COOPERATIVE LEARNING Distribute Reader Response Card 7 (Responding Freely). Instruct partners to follow the suggestions on the card to discuss their favorite parts of the selection, including which photographs they enjoyed the most.
LISTENING/SPEAKING/VIEWING

TIPS FOR LISTENING AND SPEAKING

When students **listen** to their partner's opinions, they should

- ☑ wait until the speaker has finished before responding.
- ☑ draw on story details to show why they agree or disagree.

Remind students that when they **speak**, they should

- ☑ speak clearly.
- ☑ use details from the story to support their opinions.
- ☑ ask interesting questions that their partners might answer.

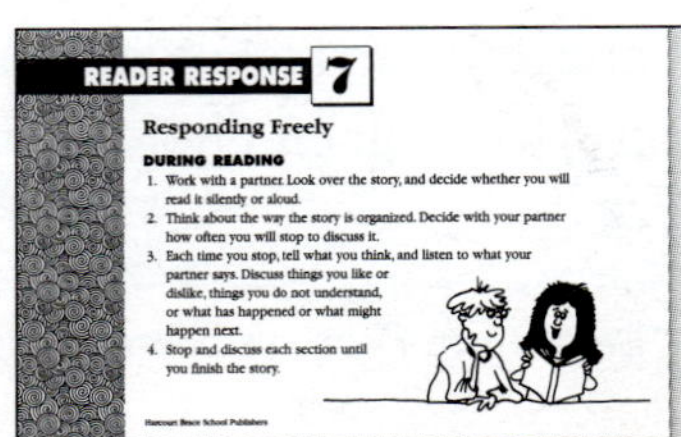
READER RESPONSE 7

Responding Freely

DURING READING

1. Work with a partner. Look over the story, and decide whether you will read it silently or aloud.
2. Think about the way the story is organized. Decide with your partner how often you will stop to discuss it.
3. Each time you stop, tell what you think, and listen to what your partner says. Discuss things you like or dislike, things you do not understand, or what has happened or what might happen next.
4. Stop and discuss each section until you finish the story.

Harcourt Brace School Publishers

Response Card 7

VIEWING

Photographs

Most libraries have collections of well-known photographers' works to borrow. Have several collections available for students to look at. Start a whole-group discussion by showing examples of each photographer's works and having students note similarities and differences among them, using the works of Margaret Bourke-White and Flor Garduño as points of reference. Then make the collections available for students to look at individually or in small groups. Encourage them to choose two or three photographs to look at more closely, noting details of who or what the subject is and whether it's important historically, what the picture's "message" is, how the picture is lit, and how they evaluate the picture overall. Have them complete a chart like the one below with their comments.

WRITING/VIEWING

Looking at Photographs		
Name of Photograph	**Photographer**	**Comments**

REAL-LIFE RESOURCES

Photo Essays

PHOTO ESSAYS Remind students that Margaret Bourke-White contributed many photos to early issues of *Life* magazine. This magazine helped to popularize the photo essay, in which photographs and captions work together to tell a story. Have students look for examples of photo essays in current magazines.

EVALUATING A PHOTO ESSAY Point out that the words and photos in a successful photo essay work together. Students can evaluate photo essays by covering up the captions to decide if they contain interesting or necessary information. They can also read only the captions to decide if the photographs add additional information. See *Writer's Magazine* pages 72 and 73.

REAL-LIFE CHALLENGE Have students plan a photo essay. They can take new photos or use existing snapshots. For example, they might find several photos of themselves at different ages. Encourage them to use a chart such as the following to plan their essay.

WRITING/ART

Photograph	Caption

Look again at the photo-essay on page 72. Then write four different titles for the essay. Each should emphasize the elements listed.

(characters)

PHOTO-ESSAY

SMILE FOR THE CAMERA!

1936 Margaret Bourke-White and three other staff photographers were hired to shoot pictures for a new magazine called *Life*. The magazine was different from other magazines of the time because it used a new format called the photo-essay. A photo-essay can be one or more pictures that tell a story. The photo-essay on this page was taken by the famous photographer Alfred Eisenstaedt.

WRITER'S MAGAZINE, pages 72–73

STUDENTS ACQUIRING ENGLISH

Since the Viewing activity involves many visual clues, you might suggest that students complete it. Allow them to write their comments in their first language if they feel more comfortable doing so.

EXTRA SUPPORT

Write the Tips for Listening and Speaking on chart paper, and display them in the classroom. Remind students to refer to the tips while they participate in the Oral Language and Retelling activities.

WRITER'S WORKSHOP

Comparison and Contrast Article

Thinking as Writers

WRITING FORM: Comparison and Contrast Article Tell students that the author of "Two Women Photographers" compared the lives and work of Margaret Bourke-White and Flor Garduño by writing two articles. Sometimes when writers want to write about two things that are similar, they write an article that discusses how the subjects are alike (comparing) and how they are different (contrasting). Ask students where they see written comparisons and contrasts. *(writing that informs; nonfiction selections)* Tell them that they are going to learn about articles that compare and contrast, and then write one.

Display Transparency 46 and discuss the parts of a comparison and contrast article.

TRANSPARENCY 46

Model: Comparison and Contrast

A ***comparison*** *shows how two subjects are alike. A* ***contrast*** *shows how they differ. Sometimes comparison and contrast are used in a single piece of writing.*

topic sentence	Because they have a lot in common, bald eagles and ospreys are often mistaken for each other.
points of comparison	Both are extremely large birds of prey. They often live in the same territory, and you may see either one soaring gracefully above the earth. Both hunt mostly fish.
topic sentence	If you know what to look for, however, you can tell these birds apart.
points of contrast	Seen from below, the bald eagle is mostly dark, while the osprey is mostly light. The bald eagle soars with flat wings, but the osprey has a crook in its wings. Bald eagles prefer their fish dead or on the verge of dying. Ospreys, on the other hand, are the only large birds of prey that dive feet-first into the water after live fish.

WRITER'S CRAFT: Clue or Signal Words Explain that clue words such as *too, both, either,* and *neither* help writers make comparisons. Words like *however, but,* and *instead* are useful when making contrasts. Ask students to find signal words of comparison and contrast in Transparency 46. *(both, same, either, however, apart, while, but, on the other hand)*

PREWRITING AND DRAFTING

Remind students to choose two subjects, such as painting and photography, that they can compare and contrast. Refer to these strategies to help students begin their articles.

PREWRITING GRAPHIC ORGANIZER Suggest that students make a Venn diagram to note how their subjects are alike and different.

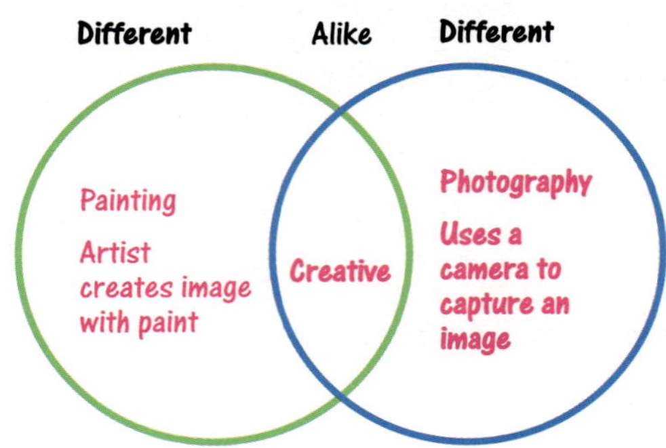

SUSTAINED SILENT WRITING Some students may be able to begin writing without interruption.

DURING-WRITING GRAPHIC ORGANIZER Students who need to vary clue or signal words in their articles may need to pause during writing to keep a running list of such words.

TIPS FOR CLASSROOM MANAGEMENT

IF students are familiar with the steps for writing an informative article that compares and contrasts, **THEN** have them begin writing, referring to the model on Transparency 46 as necessary.

IF you want a short writing activity, **THEN** adapt this lesson by having students focus on the Writer's Craft.

TECHNOLOGY

THE AMAZING WRITING MACHINE **Have students enter their comparison and contrast articles.**

RESPONDING AND REVISING

Have students work with partners or in editing circles for support while revising their articles. Write this checklist on the board:

- Does your topic sentence or introduction make clear what two things you are comparing and contrasting?
- Does your article include at least three details about how your subjects are alike or different?
- Have you used signal words that make your comparisons clear?

PROOFREADING

As students proofread, suggest they

- look for misspelled words.
- check to be sure they used the correct **verb tenses**. (See Grammar Minilesson on page T985.)
- check for capitalization at the beginning of sentences and correct end punctuation.

PUBLISHING

If you want to have students publish their articles, let them choose their own method or use one of the following:

ORAL Have students read their articles to the class and explain how they decided to write about that topic.

WRITTEN Students could save their articles on a shared computer disk for others to read.

EVALUATION BENCHMARKS: COMPARISON AND CONTRAST ARTICLE

A comparison and contrast article by a proficient student writer shows the following characteristics:

FORM	CRAFT	CONVENTIONS
Demonstrates understanding of the form • topic sentence or introduction • points of comparison • points of contrast	**Uses clear and appropriate language** • sufficient clue words	**Follows conventions of grammar and usage** • appropriate and consistent verb tenses • correct end punctuation of sentences

Teacher Assessment As you assess students' writing, refer to the Evaluation Benchmarks chart. For additional information, including model papers, see *Integrated Performance Assessment* Teacher's Edition.

PORTFOLIO OPPORTUNITY

Have students answer the Student Self-Assessment questions and include both their answers and their articles in their portfolios.

LANGUAGE HANDBOOK

Gathering Ideas and Information, page 15; Comparison and Contrast, page 67; Expanding Your Writing, pages 26–28

Student Self-Assessment ✓

Have students answer the following questions and include the answers in their portfolios:

- ☑ What did you like best about your comparison and contrast article?
- ☑ What other topics would you like to write about in a comparison and contrast article?

Tested Skill

GRAMMAR

Perfect Tenses

LANGUAGE HANDBOOK
Perfect Tense, pages 156–157

DAILY LANGUAGE PRACTICE See page R66 for oral language exercises.

Reading ↔ Writing Connection

Connect to the literature. Display the following sentences:

The Indians maintain many of their old customs.

Flor took photographs of them.

Many people will see the pictures.

Have volunteers read the sentences aloud and identify the main verb or verb phrase in each. *(maintain, took, will see)* Then ask students when the action of each verb occurs. (present, past, future)

Build oral language. Ask volunteers to add a different form of the helping verb *have* to each sentence, making other changes to the verb as necessary. (The Indians have maintained many of their old customs. Flor had taken photographs of them. Many people will have seen the pictures.)

Teach/Model

Discuss perfect tense verbs. Display the following sentences:

The Indians have maintained many of their old customs.

Flor had taken photographs of them for years before she published a book.

Many people will have seen her pictures in magazines before they see her book.

Ask volunteers to underline the helping verb and the main verb in each sentence and identify the tense of the helping verb. (*have maintained, have*—present; *had taken, had*—past; *will have seen, will have*—future) Point out that the tense of the helping verb tells whether the verb phrase is in the **present perfect tense**, the **past perfect tense**, or the **future perfect tense**. Use the example sentences to help students understand the use of each tense to make the sequence of events clear. The present perfect shows action that started in the past and which may be continuing; the past perfect shows action that happened before a specific time in the past; the future perfect shows action that will be completed before a specific time in the future, and includes the helping verb *will*.

Practice/Apply

Check understanding. Display the following sentences. Have students label each sentence as either present perfect, past perfect, or future perfect.

The birds had flown off before we came. (past perfect)

The birds have flown off, and the nest is empty. (present perfect)

The birds will have flown off by winter. (future perfect)

Ask volunteers to read the sentences aloud and explain why they labeled them as they did.

Practice Activities

BEE PERFECT

ORAL APPLICATION Have small groups sit in a circle. One member of each group should say an original sentence using simple verb tense. The next student to the right should repeat the sentence, changing the verb to the present perfect tense. Continuing clockwise, students say the sentence in the past perfect tense and the future perfect tense. Students should continue until each member of the group has supplied an original sentence and has used each of the three perfect tenses. **AUDITORY**

Write Perfect Tense Verbs

WRITING APPLICATION Have small groups create three sets of "time" cards for each of the following words: *yesterday, today,* and *tomorrow.* Then have one member of the group state a subject and a verb and then select a "time" card. The student should then form a sentence with that subject and the correct perfect tense verb. Have other group members decide whether the sentence is correct and makes sense. **VISUAL/KINESTHETIC**

APPLY TO WRITING

Suggest that students look at their comparison and contrast articles to see if using the perfect tense would make the sequence of events clearer.

USAGE TIP When you use the perfect tenses in your writing, be sure to check subject-verb agreement.

STUDENTS ACQUIRING ENGLISH

When participating in the oral application activity, students could be given one chance to supply the past participle of a regular verb and two chances to supply the past participle of an irregular verb.

RETEACH

See page R58 for lessons in multiple modalities.

GRAMMAR PRACTICE BOOK
pages 46–47

Name ______________

Two Women Photographers

Complete each person's comment below by adding a verb phrase. Use the verb and the tense indicated in parentheses. Then write one more sentence that someone at the exhibit might say. Use a verb in one of the perfect tenses. Original sentences will vary.

How ___have___ you ___enjoyed___ the exhibit so far? (*enjoy* — present perfect)

It ___has made___ me interested in photography. (*make* — present perfect)

___Had___ you ___seen___ this particular photo before? (*see* — past perfect)

We ___have recommended___ this exhibit to all our friends. (*recommend* — present perfect)

By the end of the year, I ___will have taken___ hundreds of photos. (*take* — future perfect)

I ___have asked___ for a camera as a birthday present. (*ask* — present perfect)

We ___had___ never ___toured___ such a great exhibit before. (*tour* — past perfect)

TRY THIS! Talking Tip

PRACTICE BOOK, page 146

5-DAY PLAN

Use in conjunction with Daily Language Practice.

Day 1 Complete page T1000.	**Day 4** Choose a Practice Activity or *Grammar Practice Book* pages 46–47.
Day 2 Complete a Practice Activity on page T1001.	**Day 5** Complete *Practice Book* page 146.
Day 3 Choose a Practice Activity or *Language Handbook* pages 156–157.	

2

SPELLING

5-Day Plan

Integrated Spelling **Lesson 27: student book, pages 114–117; Teacher's Edition, pages T177–T182.**

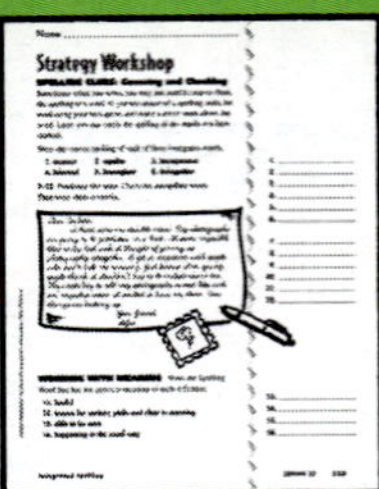
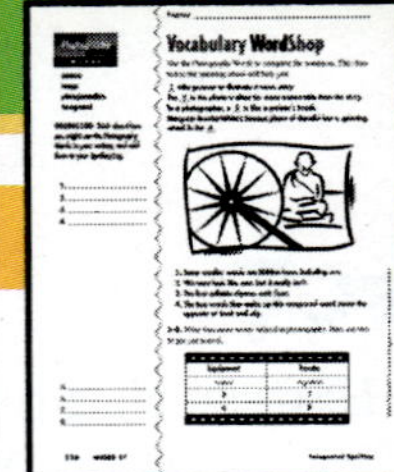

SPELLING WORDS

1. invisible
2. incorrect
3. impossible
4. injustice ★
5. inability
6. incomplete
7. impolite
8. irregular
9. indefinite
10. informal
11. illegal
12. impatient
13. independent ★
14. inexpensive
15. indigestion
16. incredible

STUDENT'S PERSONAL WORDS

17. 19.
18. 20.

Additional story words are *inventor, industrial,* and *important.*

★ Words appearing in "Two Women Photographers"

PRACTICE BOOK, page 147

Prefix: *in- (im-, il-, ir-)*

Pretest

DAY 1 **Administer the pretest.** Say each word, and then use it in the dictation sentence below. Help students self-check their pretests.

OPEN SORT

DAY 2 **Have students classify words.** Students can work in groups to classify the Spelling Words according to some similarity—spelling or syllabication. Groups might, for instance, make lists of three-, four-, and five-syllable words. Have groups compare their lists.

CLOSED SORT

Sort by spelling pattern. Write the headings from the chart below on the board and ask volunteers to write each Spelling Word in the appropriate column.

in-	im-	other spellings
invisible incorrect injustice inability incomplete indefinite informal independent inexpensive indigestion incredible	impossible impolite impatient	irregular illegal

Teach/Model

DAY 3 **Discuss the generalization.** Have students look at the words in the chart. Explain that the prefix *in-*, meaning "not," is sometimes spelled *im-, il-,* or *ir-*. Help students figure out that when the prefix *in-* is added to words that begin with *p*, the spelling of the prefix changes to *im-*. When the prefix is added to words beginning with *l* and *r*, the *n* is dropped and the initial letter of the base word is doubled.

- **in- → im- + patient = impatient**
- **in- → il- + legal = illegal**
- **in- → ir + regular = irregular**

Explain that these spelling changes make the words easier to say.

DAY 4 **Apply to writing.** Encourage students to check their comparison and contrast articles to be sure that any words containing the prefix *in-* (or *im-, il-, ir-*) are spelled correctly.

Posttest

DAY 5 **Assess students' progress.** The sentences below should be used as the posttest.

DICTATION SENTENCES

1. The fog made everything seem invisible.
2. He had only one incorrect word on his spelling test.
3. This jigsaw puzzle is impossible to do!
4. A court of law must prevent injustice.
5. I can't join the chorus because of my inability to sing.
6. A circus seems incomplete without the clowns.
7. Were you impolite or merely in a hurry?
8. Unfortunately, his study habits are irregular.
9. My science project plans are still indefinite.
10. Wear casual clothes because the party is informal.
11. In many towns it is illegal to jaywalk.
12. I was ready to leave and became impatient.
13. Margaret was an independent woman.
14. The sweaters at the sale were inexpensive.
15. The pizza was so spicy that it gave me indigestion.
16. A perfect rainbow is an incredible thing to see!

VOCABULARY WORKSHOP

Reviewing Key Words

Write the Key Words on the board. Ask volunteers to define each one in their own words. Then have students write sentences using the words. Suggest that if they have trouble thinking of a strong context for a word, they can try to remember how the word might have been used to describe the life and work of Margaret Bourke-White or Flor Garduño. When students have finished writing, ask volunteers to share their sentences with the class or have students trade papers with a partner for checking.

Extending Vocabulary

SYNONYMS

Tell students that Sylvia Wolf described Margaret's mother as an *avid* reader; that is, she was *eager* to read. Point out that *avid* and *eager* are synonyms, words that mean nearly the same thing. Remind students that authors choose their words carefully. If two or more words are synonyms, they choose the word that describes exactly what they want to say.

MAKE CROSSWORD PUZZLES

Challenge pairs of students to brainstorm synonyms for several words and then use the synonym pairs to make a crossword puzzle. One word of the pair is the clue, and the other is the word in the puzzle. Completed puzzle blanks could be copied and stapled together to make puzzle books for the class, or they could be entered into an open computer file.

Across
3. useful
5. eager
6. rot

Down
1. whole
2. throw
3. cure
4. also

INTRODUCE: COMPREHENSION STRATEGY

Synthesizing Information

OBJECTIVE: To gather and combine information to form an original product or conclusion

Informal Assessment ✓

Are students able to

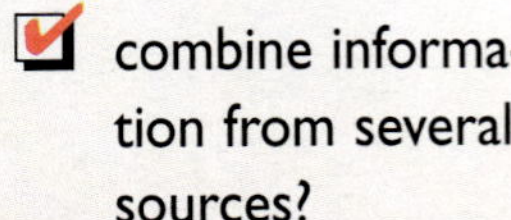
combine information from several sources?

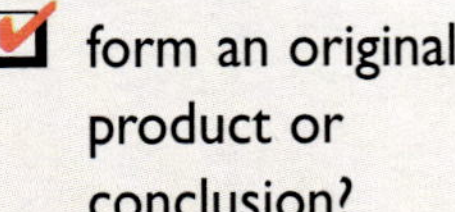
form an original product or conclusion?

TECHNOLOGY

THINKIN' THINGS 3 **Students can use The Case of the Empty Fripple House program to synthesize information.**

Teach/Model

Return to the literature. Have students reread the first paragraph on page 478. Point out that to prepare to photograph Gandhi, Margaret had to gather and combine information from different sources — including her own experience. That combining is called synthesizing information.

Model synthesizing information. Explain that, as we gather information to make decisions, we combine individual ideas and facts. Model the thinking:

MODEL

Before she photographed Gandhi, Margaret learned how to spin cotton to understand his philosophy. She combined that knowledge with what she knew about the history of India and Great Britain, as well as with her own knowledge and experience taking pictures. She synthesized all of that information to create something new.

Practice/Apply

Have students demonstrate understanding. Draw on the board the following frame, or display Transparency 47.

Discuss with students the steps involved in synthesizing information. Then use Transparency 47 as a model to talk about synthesizing information for an actual report students might be writing about photography, for instance, or for a science or social studies project.

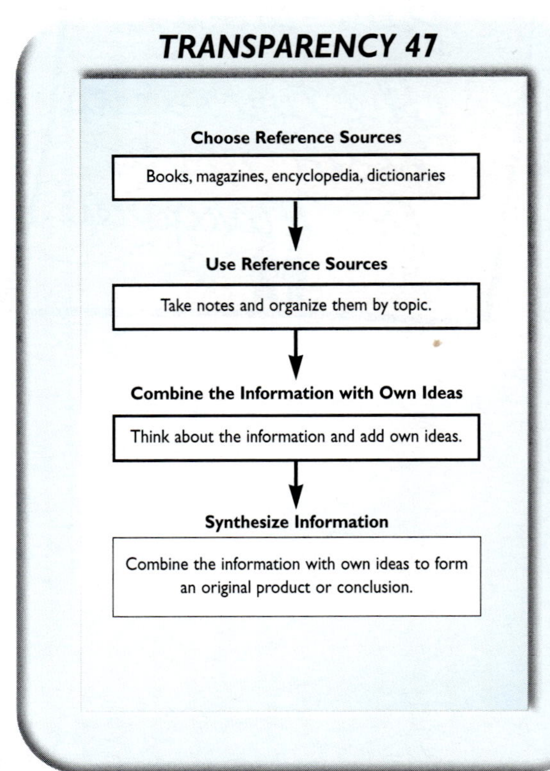

Practice Activities

Planning a Photograph

COOPERATIVE LEARNING Have students work in pairs or groups of three to plan a photograph that will represent a typical day in their classroom. This composite should include the students and the activities they do on a typical day. The group should work together to gather and combine information to create a sketch (or an actual photo shoot setup) of their photograph. **VISUAL/AUDITORY/KINESTHETIC**

Research Plans

PERFORMANCE ASSESSMENT Students can use the basic synthesizing steps to plan future research projects. Encourage them to decide on a topic of interest. Students should consider the sources they might use to find out about the topic as well as experiences they have had or might have and/or information they already know. Students should then write a short statement of what they expect to learn. **VISUAL/AUDITORY**

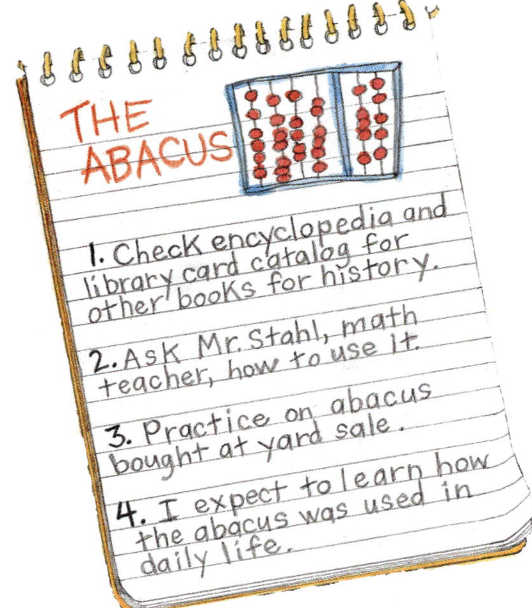

STUDENTS ACQUIRING ENGLISH

Have students make notes about their research projects in their first language and then explain their plans orally in English.

RETEACH

See page R59 for lessons in multiple modalities.

CHALLENGE

Have students analyze the information they synthesized for a recent decision they made.

TO REINFORCE SYNTHESIZING INFORMATION

Kids at Work: Lewis Hine and the Crusade Against Child Labor **by Russell Freedman. Clarion, 1994. AVERAGE**

Starting Home: The Story of Horace Pippin, Painter **by Mary E. Lyons. Scribner's, 1993. AVERAGE**

Talking with Artists **by Pat Cummings. Bradbury, 1992. CHALLENGING**

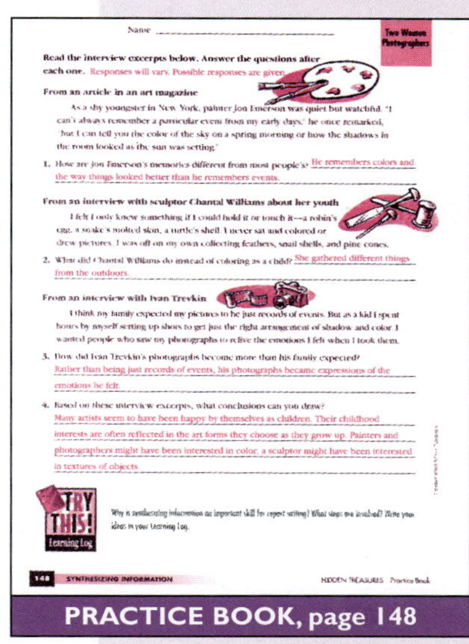

Name ______________________ Two Women Photographers

Read the interview excerpts below. Answer the questions after each one. Responses will vary. Possible responses are given.

From an article in an art magazine

As a shy youngster in New York, painter Jon Emerson was quiet but watchful. "I can't always remember a particular event from my early days," he once remarked, "but I can tell you the color of the sky on a spring morning or how the shadows in the room looked as the sun was setting."

1. How are Jon Emerson's memories different from most people's? He remembers colors and the way things looked better than he remembers events.

From an interview with sculptor Chantal Williams about her youth

I felt I only knew something if I could hold it or touch it—a robin's egg, a snake's molted skin, a turtle's shell. I never sat and colored or drew pictures. I was off on my own collecting feathers, snail shells, and pine cones.

2. What did Chantal Williams do instead of coloring as a child? She gathered different things from the outdoors.

From an interview with Ivan Trevkin

I think my family expected my pictures to be just records of events. But as a kid I spent hours by myself setting up shots to get just the right arrangement of shadow and color. I wanted people who saw my photographs to relive the emotions I felt when I took them.

3. How did Ivan Trevkin's photographs become more than his family expected? Rather than being just records of events, his photographs became expressions of the emotions he felt.

4. Based on these interview excerpts, what conclusions can you draw? Many artists seem to have been happy by themselves as children. Their childhood interests are often reflected in the art forms they choose as they grow up. Painters and photographers might have been interested in color; a sculptor might have been interested in textures of objects.

TRY THIS! Learning Log: Why is synthesizing information an important skill for report writing? What steps are involved? Write your ideas in your Learning Log.

148 SYNTHESIZING INFORMATION HIDDEN TREASURES Practice Book

PRACTICE BOOK, page 148

Integrated Curriculum

ART

Learning from Images

TIPS FOR CLASSROOM MANAGEMENT

IF students are artistically oriented, **THEN** they might want to combine their talents to produce a Mixed Media show.

TECHNOLOGY

THINKIN' THINGS 2
Students can use the Snake Blox and 2–3D Blox programs as they prepare their mixed media show.

Point out that "Two Women Photographers" describes the work of two highly skilled photojournalists. Through the following activities, students can investigate the scientific and artistic aspects of photography.

SCIENCE

The Camera's Eye and Our Own

Use reference sources. Suggest that students find out how their eyes work and how they perceive light and form images. Encourage them to compare their findings with the way a camera lens works, how it gathers light and focuses on film: creating a picture of what the photographer's eyes see. Students can use the information to make diagrams—one of the human eye and one of the camera lens. If an instant camera is available for students' use, they could photograph specific objects and compare and contrast the camera's picture with what they see with the naked eye. **LISTENING/SPEAKING/READING/WRITING**

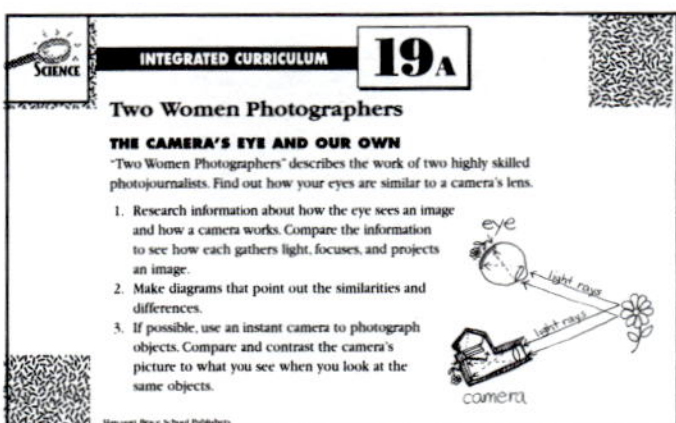
SCIENCE INTEGRATED CURRICULUM 19A

Two Women Photographers

THE CAMERA'S EYE AND OUR OWN

"Two Women Photographers" describes the work of two highly skilled photojournalists. Find out how your eyes are similar to a camera's lens.

1. Research information about how the eye sees an image and how a camera works. Compare the information to see how each gathers light, focuses, and projects an image.
2. Make diagrams that point out the similarities and differences.
3. If possible, use an instant camera to photograph objects. Compare and contrast the camera's picture to what you see when you look at the same objects.

Harcourt Brace School Publishers

Curriculum Card 19A

HEALTH

Images at Work

Making photographic images of what we see is interesting, enlightening, and fun. Making images of what we cannot see is helpful and sometimes lifesaving. Individual students or pairs could find out about how images—photographs, X-rays, computer scans—are used in the medical world. When are different kinds of images used? How are they made? What do medical people learn from the images? Although most of students' research will be done with reference sources, suggest that they interview classmates, friends, or family members who have had X-rays or CAT scans for their point of view. Students can then present an oral report to share their findings with the class. **LISTENING/SPEAKING/READING/WRITING**

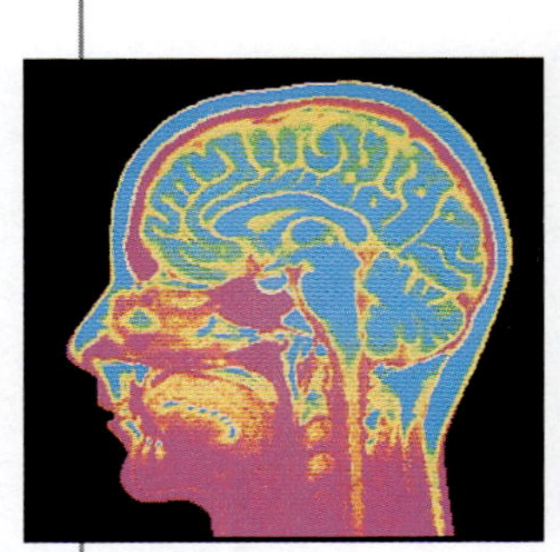

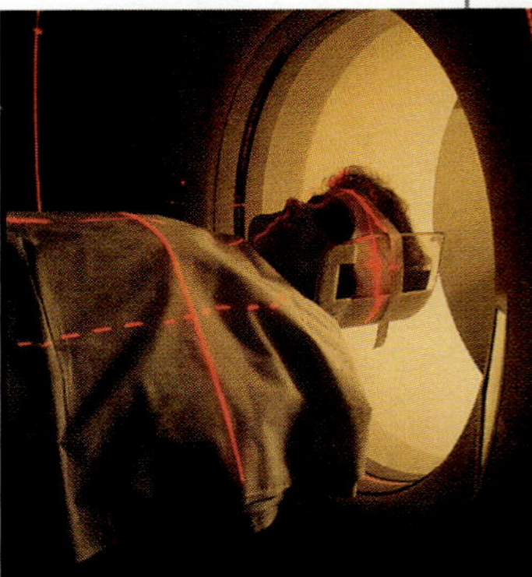

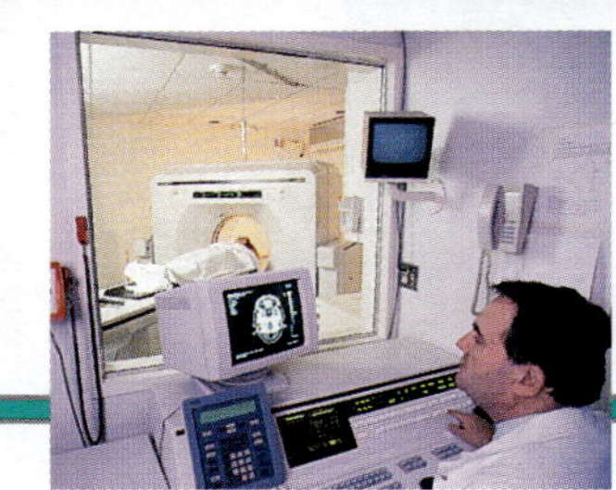

ART

Mixed Media Shows

COOPERATIVE LEARNING Small groups of students could put together a mixed media show illustrating how different artists view the same thing. The group should choose a single topic—for example, a snowstorm, a cornfield, a river, a historical event, a dancer. Then individual students can make an image of the subject using different art forms, such as photography, collage, sculpture, paints or markers, computer images, and so on. When the group presents their show to the class, a Reporter should introduce and explain the theme, but the "artists" should talk about their individual work.

LISTENING/SPEAKING/WRITING

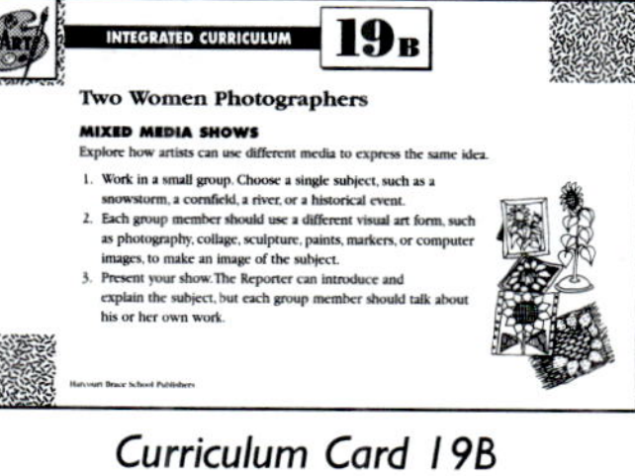

ART

INTEGRATED CURRICULUM **19B**

Two Women Photographers

MIXED MEDIA SHOWS

Explore how artists can use different media to express the same idea.

1. Work in a small group. Choose a single subject, such as a snowstorm, a cornfield, a river, or a historical event.
2. Each group member should use a different visual art form, such as photography, collage, sculpture, paints, markers, or computer images, to make an image of the subject.
3. Present your show. The Reporter can introduce and explain the subject, but each group member should talk about his or her own work.

Harcourt Brace School Publishers

Curriculum Card 19B

Reading Trade Books

CROSS-CURRICULAR READING

Cameras **by Ian Graham. Franklin Watts, 1991.** **AVERAGE**

Natural Wonders: Stories Science Photos Tell **by Vicki Cobb. Lothrop, 1990.** **AVERAGE**

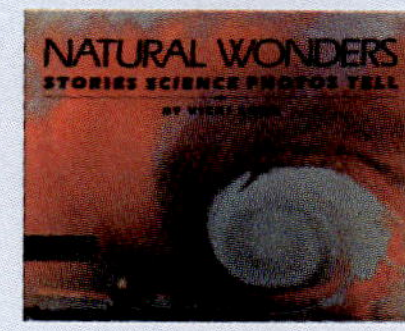

MULTI-AGE CLASSROOMS

Students have different learning styles and preferences. If a student always works with a group, encourage him or her to occasionally work independently on a project.

Reading Trade Books

TIPS FOR CLASSROOM MANAGEMENT

SMALL-GROUP READING Allow students who need assistance to read *Jace the Ace* in small groups.

Trade Books That Connect to "Two Women Photographers"

Dorothea Lange

by Robyn Montana Turner

After students read this informative biography of photographer Dorothea Lange, encourage them to create a chart to compare Lange with Margaret Bourke-White and Flor Garduño.

Hold Fast to Dreams

by Andrea Davis Pinkney

In this novel, Deirdre tries to improve her photography skills while adjusting to her new life in Connecticut. After reading, students might want to describe how Deirdre might feel about Flor Garduño's photographs.

MEETING INDIVIDUAL NEEDS

STUDENTS ACQUIRING ENGLISH

Suggest that students look for words about photography that are used in both *Dorothea Lange* and "Two Women Photographers." Encourage students to use these words in sentences of their own.

Jace the Ace

by Joanne Rocklin

Jace dreams of becoming a photojournalist. Remind students that Margaret Bourke-White followed this career. Ask readers to make a list of five things Jace might do to help him train for his dream profession.

Jacques-Henri Lartigue: Boy with a Camera

by John Cech

This surprising collection includes photographs taken by Lartigue in his youth, starting with his first camera, which he received at the age of seven in 1902. Suggest that students select one of the photographs and tell how Margaret Bourke-White or Flor Garduño might have taken a picture of the same subject.

Looking at Photographs: People

by Jacques Lowe

This varied collection of portraits provides readers with a method of analysis that they can apply to any photograph. After reading, encourage students to return to the photographs in "Two Women Photographers" and see if they can look at them from a new perspective.

My First Photography Book

by Dave King

After reading this how-to guide, students might want to make a list of ways that photography is different from other arts, such as painting or drawing. Groups might discuss why artists are drawn to each medium.

STUDENTS ACQUIRING ENGLISH

Encourage partners to describe to each other the photographs in *Looking at Photographs: People* before they read the text. Suggest that partners take turns to write down a list of five words that describe the photos and then read to see if any of these words are used by the author.

Produce Works of Art

SELECTION CONNECTION

"Two Women Photographers" discusses the careers of Margaret Bourke-White and Flor Garduño, photographers who captured startling images of people, technology, and nature. Ask students what qualities they think a good photographer has.

PROJECT CHECKLIST

During this stage, students should

- make a list of necessary art supplies.
- form temporary groups based on interest.
- produce a work of art inspired by the work they saw.
- discuss their experiences with their original groups.

Project Card 28 can be found as a copying master on page R77.

THEME PROJECT

CHECKPOINT 3 — 28

Two Women Photographers

Produce a Work of Art. Review the checklist below as you choose a type of artwork that you've seen in the community and produce your own work of art in that medium.

- Form a new, temporary group with others who are interested in making the same kind of artwork that you are.
- With your new group, make a list of materials you'll need for the art project.
- Produce a work of art inspired by a type of art you saw in the community.
- Show and discuss your work of art in your original group.

Harcourt Brace School Publishers (Continued on the other side)

Project Card 28

RESEARCH AND PLANNING TIPS

As students prepare to work on art, suggest that they

- appoint a Recorder to list the materials their art project will need.
- make preliminary sketches of ideas to share with interest-group members for feedback.
- discuss technical problems and share solutions with interest-group members as they work.

Students may want to write about the art projects in their project journals. You may want to provide prompts such as *What problems did you have in producing your art, and how did you try to solve them?*

Informal Assessment

As students complete this checkpoint, they will **analyze** the steps involved in creating a work of art and apply **problem-solving** skills. Students are thinking critically if they

- discern the distinguishing features of a genre of artwork and incorporate them in their own work.
- solve technical and creative problems.

STUDENTS ACQUIRING ENGLISH

Allow students to title their art in their first language, while encouraging them to add an English translation for their classmates.

CLASSROOM MANAGEMENT

As students work on their art, you may want to invite an art teacher to provide technical advice or give feedback on the works in progress.

The Will and the Way
PAUL R. WILLIAMS, ARCHITECT
Karen E. Hudson
RIZZOLI

Notable Trade Book in Social Studies

THEME: CREATIVITY

Masterpieces

In "The Will and the Way," students explore the life and ideas of Paul R. Williams, an African American architect who designed more than 3000 projects during his lifetime.

Linking Poetry to Nonfiction

Burton Raffel speaks of the harsh machinery used to create beautiful structures in his poem "On Watching the Construction of a Skyscraper."

ON WATCHING THE CONSTRUCTION OF A SKYSCRAPER

SELECTION SUMMARY

Genre: Biography

Told in the form of a journal written for his grandson, this selection provides a look at architect Paul R. Williams (1894-1980), the first African American to become a member—and Fellow—of the American Institute of Architects. Williams's interest in drawing dates from his early childhood in Los Angeles, and by the time he entered high school he had decided to become an architect. Undiscouraged by others' attempts to dissuade him from a field in which few African Americans had practiced, Williams went to art school after graduating from high school, took a job as an architect's helper, and later began working for a landscape architecture firm. When he found that architecture involved more than drawing, he enrolled in an engineering program at the University of Southern California, where he learned both the technical and the business aspects of architecture. As a person determined to succeed, Williams adhered to the motto "You can be whatever you want to be—as long as you have the will and the way."

Karen Hudson

ABOUT THE AUTHOR

KAREN HUDSON, one of Paul R. Williams's four grandchildren, decided that her gift to her grandfather would be to tell his story. But in a letter to her grandfather, Karen says, "How could I have ever thought that this was my gift to you? Remembering your smile and gentle touch, you were always with me guiding the search. . . . And it was through the search that I realized that what I had naively believed was my gift to you had become nothing less than your gift to me. For all of your gifts, I will be forever grateful."

More information about Karen Hudson can be found on page T1031.

SUGGESTED LESSON PLANNER

▶ *The Will and the Way*

	DAY 1	DAY 2
PART 1 Reading, Listening, Speaking, Viewing **Key Words**: prestigious, intensive, trendy, restraint	**BUILD BACKGROUND** T1014 **VOCABULARY STRATEGIES** T1015 *Transparency 48* *Practice Book* p. 151 **READING THE SELECTION** T1016–1031 Options for Reading T1016–T1017 *Response Card 11* *Literature Cassette 3* **REVIEW PREDICTIONS/PURPOSE** T1030 **APPRECIATING THE LITERATURE** T1030 NOTE: Students may read the selection on Day 2.	**SUMMARIZE THE SELECTION** T1030 *Practice Book* p. 152 **READ POETRY** T1032–T1033 "On Watching the Construction of a Skyscraper" ◆ **RESPONSE CORNER ACTIVITIES** T1034 **CHECKING COMPREHENSION** T1035 *End-of-Selection Test*
PART 2 Writer's Workshop	**BUSINESS LETTER** Thinking as Writers T1040–T1041 *Language Handbook* p. 93 *Transparency 49*	Prewriting T1040 *Language Handbook* pp. 86, 93
Grammar	✓ **REGULAR AND IRREGULAR VERBS** Teach the Concept T1042 Daily Language Practice (1–2) R67	Daily Language Practice (3–4) R67 Practice Activity T1043
Spelling	**LATIN ROOTS: *-vis-, -sign-*** *advise, revised, sign, visit, signing, vision, assign, signal, televised, signature, designed, visitors, designated, visual, assignment, supervise* Pretest/Self-Check T1044 *Integrated Spelling Teacher's Edition* pp. T183, T297	Open and Closed Sorts T1044 *Integrated Spelling* p. 118 *Integrated Spelling Teacher's Edition* p. T184
PART 3 Skills and Strategies	◆ **INTEGRATED CURRICULUM** *The Wonderful World of Architecture* **Social Studies/Art** T1048 **Art** T1048 **Science** T1049 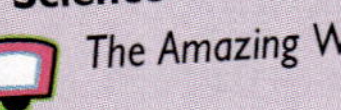 *The Amazing Writing Machine*	**LITERARY APPRECIATION SKILL** T1046–T1047 Figurative Language (Introduce) *Transparency 50* *Practice Book* pp. 155–156

Use the Intervention Strategies note on page T1024 to help **below-level students** as they read.

Use the Challenge note on page T1047 to encourage **above-level students** to write figurative language.

NOTE: An alternative lesson plan for **below-level students** appears on *Intervention Strategies Manual* pp. 116–121. A lesson for **students acquiring English** appears on *Sheltered English/ESL Manual* pp. 78–81.

DAY 3	DAY 4	DAY 5
◆ **IDEA BANK ACTIVITIES** Retelling T1038 Oral Language T1038 Rereading T1039 Real-Life Resources: Reading Diagrams T1039 *Writer's Magazine* pp. 76–77 School–Home Connection 20 R97  	**VOCABULARY WORKSHOP** T1045 Reviewing Key Words **READING TRADE BOOKS** T1050–T1051 *Signatures Library: The Wright Brothers: How They Invented the Airplane*  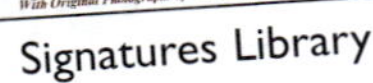 Signatures Library  Take-Home Book	**READING TRADE BOOKS** T1047, T1049, T1050–T1051 
Drafting T1040 *Language Handbook* pp. 87, 93 *The Amazing Writing Machine*	Responding and Revising T1041 *Language Handbook* pp. 87, 93	Proofreading and Publishing T1041 *Language Handbook* pp. 87, 93, 156
Daily Language Practice (5–6) R67 Practice Activity T1043 *Language Handbook* pp. 158–159 *Imagination Express, Destination: Neighborhood*	Daily Language Practice (7–8) R67 Practice Activity T1043 *Grammar Practice Book* pp. 48–49	Daily Language Practice (9–12) R67 *Practice Book* p. 153
Discuss the Generalization T1044 *Integrated Spelling* p. 119 *Integrated Spelling Teacher's Edition* p. T185	Apply to Writing T1044 *Integrated Spelling* pp. 120–121 *Integrated Spelling Teacher's Edition* pp. T186–T187	Posttest T1044 *Practice Book* p. 154 *Integrated Spelling Teacher's Edition* p. T188
GRAMMAR MINILESSON T1019 ✓ Perfect Tenses (Review) **VOCABULARY MINILESSON** T1023 ✓ Context Clues/Multiple-Meaning Words (Review) *Practice Book* p. 157	**VOCABULARY WORKSHOP** T1045 Compound Words	**COMPREHENSION MINILESSON** T1027 Synthesizing Information (Review) *Practice Book* p. 158 Theme Project Checkpoint 4 T1052
Use Intervention Strategies on pages T1036–T1037 with **below-level** and **ESL students**.	**Below-level students** may read the *Take-Home Book: Better Late Than Never* to help them reinforce Key Words.	**Below-level** and **ESL students** may read the *ESL/Title I Library* book *The Wonderful Towers of Watts*.

✓ = Tested Skill
◆ = Optional activities used to adjust pacing throughout the lesson
Titles in *italics* are optional materials.

BUILDING BACKGROUND AND CONCEPTS

PRIOR KNOWLEDGE

Relate to students' lives. Ask students to explain what they think is meant by the word *talent*. Discuss with them whether they think a person is born with a certain talent or talents or if a talent can be learned or acquired. Encourage students to talk about talents they possess.

Create a word web about architecture. Explain that "The Will and the Way" is a biography of Paul R. Williams, a man whose talent for architecture was recognized around the world. Have students discuss what they know about the field of architecture. Record students' responses in a word web like the following:

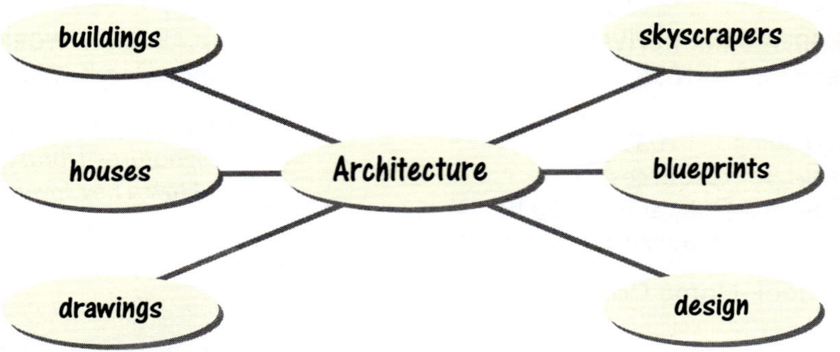

QUICKWRITE

Encourage students to write a few sentences about whether they would or would not want to become architects. Suggest that students supply reasons for their answers.

Intervention Strategies

For students who may have difficulty reading "The Will and the Way," support is available in *Intervention Strategies Manual,* pages 116–121, and on pages T1024 and T1036–T1037 in this lesson.

STUDENTS ACQUIRING ENGLISH

See *Sheltered English/ESL Manual,* pages 78–81.

FACT FINDER — SOCIAL STUDIES

African American Architects

Paul R. Williams and his predecessor, William S. Pittman, were pioneers as African Americans in the field of architecture. However, their example was not followed by many other African Americans. As recently as the 1950s only about one hundred African American architects were practicing in the United States. The first African American woman architect, Norma Sklarek, became licensed to practice in 1954.

Norma Sklarek

To address this problem, in 1969 the American Institute of Architects (AIA) established the Task Force on Equal Opportunity. This task force set up a scholarship program for minorities and accredited architecture programs in historically black colleges and universities. The National Organization of Black Architects—which later changed its name to the National Organization of Minority Architects—was created in 1971. Its purpose is to encourage young minority group members to become architects. Today there are more than 3,800 African American architects in the United States.

VOCABULARY STRATEGIES

KEY WORDS DEFINED

prestigious honored; esteemed

intensive thorough and complete

trendy in keeping with the latest fashions

restraint the act of holding back

INTEGRATED SPELLING

Spelling Pretest: page T1044

Spelling Generalization: Latin Roots *-vis-*, *-sign-*

CONTEXT CLUES: JOURNAL ENTRY

Encourage students to use syntactic and semantic cues. Display Transparency 48. Have students read the passage silently, using context clues with phonetic and structural analysis to figure out the meanings of the underlined words. For example, if students do not know what *trendy* means, they can use the context—"what's new"—to gain meaning.

CHECK UNDERSTANDING

Have students classify Key Words. Display the Key Words and the pairs of related words below. Ask students to read the related words and tell which Key Word belongs with each pair. Encourage students to explain their choices. **STRATEGY: CLASSIFYING**

Related Words		Key Words
complete	thorough	(intensive)
stylish	fashionable	(trendy)
reserve	restriction	(restraint)
honored	esteemed	(prestigious)

TRANSPARENCY 48

Key Words

I really admire my Aunt Zora. She works with other important fashion designers at a prestigious design firm in New York City. Her assistant does intensive preparation for Aunt Zora's hectic travel schedule. She flies back and forth to Paris, London, and Milan every few months to view what's new and trendy abroad. Although she sees some wild and bizarre clothes at the fashion shows, Aunt Zora likes to use a bit more restraint with her creations.

The swimmer from the United States won the prestigious Olympic gold medal.

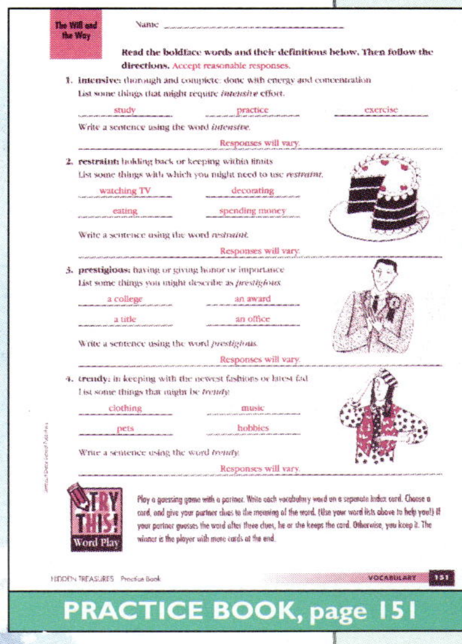

The Will and the Way

Name ____________

Read the boldface words and their definitions below. Then follow the directions. Accept reasonable responses.

1. **intensive:** thorough and complete; done with energy and concentration
   List some things that might require *intensive* effort.
   study — practice — exercise
   Write a sentence using the word *intensive*.
   Responses will vary.
2. **restraint:** holding back or keeping within limits
   List some things with which you might need to use *restraint*.
   watching TV — decorating
   eating — spending money
   Write a sentence using the word *restraint*.
   Responses will vary.
3. **prestigious:** having or giving honor or importance
   List some things you might describe as *prestigious*.
   a college — an award
   a title — an office
   Write a sentence using the word *prestigious*.
   Responses will vary.
4. **trendy:** in keeping with the newest fashions or latest fad
   List some things that might be *trendy*.
   clothing — music
   pets — hobbies
   Write a sentence using the word *trendy*.
   Responses will vary.

TRY THIS! Word Play

Play a guessing game with a partner. Write each vocabulary word on a separate index card. Choose a card, and give your partner clues to the meaning of the word. (Use your word lists above to help you!) If your partner guesses the word after three clues, he or she keeps the card. Otherwise, you keep it. The winner is the player with more cards at the end.

HIDDEN TREASURES Practice Book — VOCABULARY 151

PRACTICE BOOK, page 151

Prereading Strategies

PREVIEW AND PREDICT

Have students read the title and the first two paragraphs of the selection and then look at several of the photographs. Ask students what they think they might find out about Paul R. Williams as they read the selection.

Begin a K-W-L chart like the one below. Students may use *Practice Book* page 152. Encourage students to fill in the first two columns of the chart.

K What I Know	W What I Want to Know	L What I Learned
(Williams studied architecture in college.) (He designed buildings.)	(How did Paul R. Williams get interested in architecture?) (What steps did Paul Williams take to become an architect?)	

You may want to suggest that students write their predictions about the selection in their personal journals.

PURPOSE

You may want to model setting a purpose:

I want to read to find out how Paul R. Williams became such an honored and respected architect.

Notable Trade Book in Social Studies

492

Litton Industries, Beverly Hil California, 1968

SMALL GROUP

PARTNER READING

Have pairs of students share the questions they wrote on their K-W-L charts. Then have partners read the selection silently, pausing periodically to discuss what they have learned and to add new questions to their charts as needed. Remind partners to consult the class-made strategy chart for strategies to use while reading.

COOPERATIVE READING

READER RESPONSE GROUPS

Small groups may read the selection silently, stopping at page 499 for a brief discussion of the way information is presented in the selection. Reader Response Card 11, **Critics Circle,** can be found at the back of this Teacher's Edition.

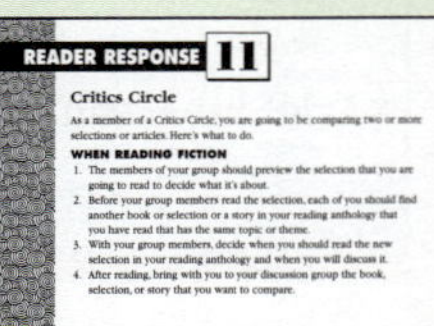

Response Card 11

The Will and the Way

PAUL R. WILLIAMS, ARCHITECT

BY KAREN E. HUDSON

The Will and the Way

PAUL R. WILLIAMS, ARCHITECT

Karen E. Hudson

WHOLE CLASS

STRATEGIC READING

To help students gain meaning as they read, reinforce the focus strategy of **adjusting reading rate**. Pages T1018 and T1022 are good points at which to have students model how adjusting their reading rate can be used to help them better understand what they are reading.

SILENT READING/ DISCUSSION

Have students read the entire selection silently. As individuals finish, have them complete their K-W-L charts. When all students have finished reading, use the chart to stimulate discussion. Encourage students to complete one or more of the activities on pages 510 and 511.

Strategic Reading

ADJUSTING READING RATE

Call on volunteers to tell about strategies they use when they are reading. Display the class-made strategy chart, and remind students that another strategy they can use is adjusting reading rate. Explain that when they come to difficult passages, they should read more slowly than when they are reading easier material. **STRATEGY: ADJUSTING READING RATE**

PAGES 494–499
Ask students to read through page 499 to find answers to the questions they wrote in their K-W-L charts.

Has anyone ever asked you what you want to be when you grow up? Maybe someone has suggested a road for you to follow. But what if you discovered that the road to your dreams hadn't been built yet?

This is the story of Paul Revere Williams, architect. Paul Williams didn't start out as an architect; he began as a kid, just like the rest of us. As a high school student, he made a commitment to himself to become an architect, and, in 1923, he became the first African-American member of the American Institute of Architects—later the AIA named him a Fellow, a prestigious honor. During a career that spanned nearly sixty years, he designed more than three thousand projects throughout the world—from Canada to Jamaica, Hawaii to Liberia, New York to Colombia, and, of course, in Los Angeles, his hometown. His vision and interests led him to build everything from houses to churches, schools, hospitals, office buildings, and public-housing projects.

Probably the only thing he loved more than architecture was his family. He was a loving husband, father, and—ultimately—a grandfather. That's where I come in. As his granddaughter I learned to wonder about the world around me. And when I grew up I became curious about him, too. I knew Paul Williams—my grandfather—but I knew little about Paul R. Williams, architect. As I uncovered this side of him, I realized his life was a story that was meant to be shared.

Williams with grandchildren, Karen and Paul

First of all, no biography about Paul Williams would be complete without looking at his childhood, where the roots of the courage and fierce determination he exhibited throughout his life first took hold.

Paul was born on February 18, 1894, in downtown Los Angeles, at Eighth and Santee Streets. His father, Chester; mother, Lila; and brother, Chester, Jr.; had just moved there from Memphis, where his father had been a waiter at the Peabody Hotel. Los Angeles was full of opportunities. Chester, Sr., opened his own fruit stand at the Plaza, which is now known as Olvera Street. When Paul was a toddler, he and his mother would walk three blocks to the horsecar to take their daily ride to visit his father's stand. Sadly, Paul's mother and father both died by the time he was four. Orphaned, Paul was raised by loving foster parents, Mr. and Mrs.

494

CALIFORNIA
Vallejo
San Francisco
Palo Alto
Modesto
Fresno
Tulare
Los Angeles
La Jolla
San Diego

SOCIAL STUDIES CONNECTION

PLACE NAMES Point out that Los Angeles ("the angels") is just one of many Spanish place names in California, which was settled by Spaniards. Explain that in many parts of the United States, place names reflect the early history of the area. Students may research the origins of place names in their region.

CONVENTIONS OF LANGUAGE

SEMICOLONS IN A SERIES Point out the commas and semicolons in the second sentence of the last paragraph. Remind students that commas are used to separate the items in a series. Explain that when the items in a series contain commas—as in *His father, Chester*—semicolons are used to separate the items.

Clarkson, while Chester, Jr., went to live with another foster family. Even though the brothers weren't able to see each other often, Chester was five years older and made an effort to keep in touch with his little brother.

The Clarksons lived in the neighborhood where Paul was born, so he continued to attend First African Methodist Episcopal Church (First A.M.E.), which is the oldest African-American church in Los Angeles. He was the only African-American in his class at Sentuous Avenue School on Pico Boulevard, where he was known as the class artist; otherwise his childhood experiences were like those of most people in early downtown Los Angeles. He lived in an integrated neighborhood. After school he and his playmates explored their surroundings. Sometimes they used wheat to catch the wild quail that roamed their street. At other times they visited their neighbors. The vegetable man taught them how to conserve natural resources, particularly water. They learned Chinese and German from the new kids who moved to the neighborhood.

His foster father worked as a janitor in a bank at First and Spring Streets. When he was still in elementary school, Paul began selling newspapers on the corner outside the bank to help support the family. Paul sold *The Record* and *The Express,* one for three cents or two for a nickel. U.S. Senator Frank Flint was a regular customer.

Although Paul traveled the world over, Los Angeles remained his home all of his life. Drawing was his lifelong love, too. By holding fast to his dreams and becoming an architect, Paul carved his own road and made it a little easier for more African-American architects to follow. (By 1993, there were 595 African-American members, including forty-two Fellows, in the AIA.)

In 1948, Paul became a grandfather for the first time. It was no small coincidence that his grandson, my brother, was named after him. Paul left us a legacy through his personal notes. Although the following notes are addressed to his grandson, we know he would be happy that we are sharing them with you. Maybe you'll want to take the road to an architectural career—or perhaps you'll decide that you, too, can blaze a new trail. Whatever you choose, remember to celebrate your creativity, learn from the accomplishments of others, and share your knowledge with those who follow.

Karen Elyse Hudson
Director
The Paul R. Williams Collection

495

MULTICULTURAL CONNECTION

Note the reference to neighborhood children learning Chinese and German from new children who moved into the neighborhood. Guide students to recognize that our lives are enriched by cultural diversity. Encourage students to find out and list the different languages that are spoken in their classroom, school, or neighborhood.

Tested Skill

MINILESSON

REVIEW: GRAMMAR

Perfect Tenses

INFORMAL ASSESSMENT

Ask students to look at the first paragraph on page 494 and find an example of a perfect tense verb. *(has asked, has suggested, hadn't been built)* Ask students how they identified the perfect tense. (The perfect tense is made up of a form of the helping verb *have* and the past participle.)

TEACH/MODEL

Remind students that there are three perfect tenses—present perfect, past perfect, and future perfect—and that each is made up of the past participle and a form of the helping verb *have*. Review the following points:

- A verb in the present perfect tense shows action that started to happen sometime before now and that may still be happening.
- A verb in the past perfect tense shows action that happened before a specific time in the past.
- A verb in the future perfect tense shows action that will happen before a specific time in the future.

PRACTICE/APPLY

Ask pairs of students to find examples of verbs in the present perfect and past perfect tenses in the selection and to add them to a chart like the one below. Have students write their own examples of future perfect tense verbs in the third column. Possible responses are provided.

Present Perfect	Past Perfect	Future Perfect
(has suggested)	(had been)	(will have planned)
(has asked)	(had moved)	(will have worked)

Critical Thinking Questions

1. In the last sentence on page 497, Paul R. Williams says, *You can be whatever you want to be—as long as you have the will and the way.* Do you agree with this statement? Explain your answer. (Possible response: Yes, because if you are determined to be something and can figure out the way to achieve this, you will succeed.) CRITICAL: CHALLENGING THE TEXT

2. What other real-life person have you read about who achieved success by having "the will and the way"? Describe that person's experiences. (Responses will vary but students may mention Juan de Pareja, who had the will to become a painter and found the way to do so.) CRITICAL: MAKING CONNECTIONS

Williams and his grandson, Paul Claude

496

VIEWING

Point out the black triangles on the corners of the photograph, and ask students why they think the designer placed them there. If necessary, explain that in old photograph albums, triangular pockets with glue on one side were used to secure photographs onto the pages. The designer has incorporated this element to give the impression that this is a page from an old album.

"How can you, as an individual, fit into this pattern of tomorrow? First, we must be a part of the community in which we live and not apart from it."

To my grandson:

I thought you'd never get here—but finally you've arrived! You should have seen the commotion at the hospital as Claude, your other grandfather, and I anxiously awaited your arrival. You're the first grandchild on both sides of the family. Your parents didn't get a chance to name you, because as soon as Claude and I found out you were a boy, we announced your name to be Paul Claude.

From the moment we heard you were due to join the family, I've kept a special notebook just for you. There's so much I want to tell you, so many experiences I want to share with you. I want you to know I love being an architect. . . . Perhaps you'll be an architect one day yourself. Don't let anyone keep you from achieving your dreams, Paul. You can be whatever you want to be—as long as you have the will and the way.

497

Student Self-Assessment

ADJUSTING READING RATE

Remind students that from time to time, they should monitor their own understanding of the selection by asking themselves whether they need to adjust their reading rate.

 Am I reading slowly and carefully enough to understand any unfamiliar words or ideas?

 Are there any parts of the selection in which I can increase my reading rate?

GENRE

Help students note the change in point of view between pages 494–495 and the rest of the selection. Guide them to recognize that the first two pages of the selection are a biographical sketch of Paul Williams written by his granddaughter and that the remainder of the selection is in the form of an autobiography written by Paul Williams himself.

DESIGNER'S CRAFT

Point out and discuss the separate design elements on this page: the quotation in the box at the top, the heading in boldface italic type, and the symbol and large *I* at the beginning of the first paragraph. Encourage students to consider how these elements add interest to the page. Ask why the designer placed the quotation in a box. (to signal its importance)

Strategic Reading

PAGES 494–499 What made Paul R. Williams decide to become an architect? (Possible responses: He was excited by the idea that what an architect drew could become a real building. He wanted to prove to himself and to other people that an African American could be a good architect.) STRATEGY: SUMMARIZING

ADJUSTING READING RATE

If necessary, model the strategy of adjusting reading rate:

MODEL **The boxed quotation at the top of the page is probably important or it wouldn't be set off by itself this way. I'll read this material slowly and carefully to be sure I understand it.**

PAGES 500–506 Have students finish reading the selection to confirm their predictions about Paul R. Williams and to answer the questions on their K-W-L charts.

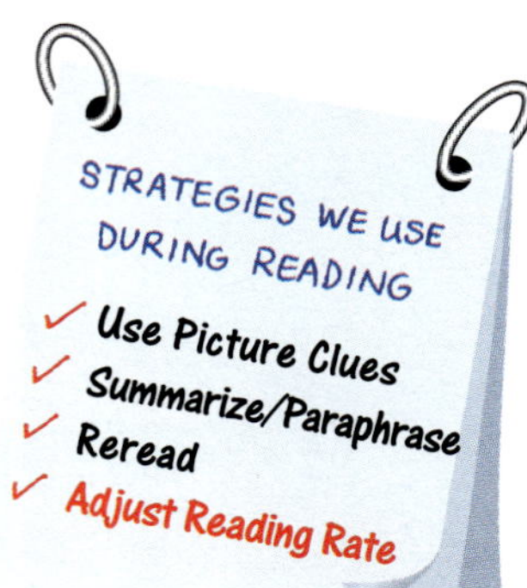

> ***"To be sincere in my work, I must design homes, not houses. I must take into consideration each family's mode of living, its present economic problems, and its probable economic future."***

❖ When I was very young I drew pictures of animals. Soon I found myself drawing each building on my route to school. One day a family friend, who was a local builder, said I should become an architect. At the time I wasn't sure what it meant to be one, but I soon found out. I felt like a detective in a dime-store novel, questioning everyone I could about architecture. When I discovered that architects design homes, schools, churches, office buildings—and just about everything imaginable to live and work in—I decided this was the profession for me. Architects also draw the plans of how buildings should be built and supervise their construction. To think that something I drew on a piece of paper would become a building of bricks and boards was nothing less than magical!

When I entered high school the first question the counselor asked me was, "Why do you want to be an architect?" I told him I had heard of only one Negro architect in America, and I was sure this country could use at least one or two more. (The architect I knew of was Booker T. Washington's son-in-law, William S. Pittman. Of course, there were a few others, but they were back East and I wasn't aware of them.)

My career plans were not well accepted by everyone. Although my family encouraged me at every step, my guidance counselor continued to give me reasons why I would fail. I took architecture courses at Polytechnic High School, but when I told my adviser that I wanted to continue my studies at the university, he stared at me with as much astonishment as he would have had I proposed a rocket flight to Mars!

I suppose it was about 1912 when I made the commitment to become an architect. This was the turning point in my life because I realized I would forever question my right to be all that I could be if I allowed others to discourage me because of the color of my skin. I developed a fierce desire to prove to myself that I could become one of the best architects ever.

I knew I had the will. All I had to do was find the way.

498

MULTICULTURAL CONNECTION

The first American architects were Native Americans, who created houses that perfectly fit their various environments and lifestyles. From the wood-and-bark longhouses of the Iroquois to the portable tepees of the Plains tribes to the multistory dwellings of the Pueblos, these creations exemplified the guiding principle of architect Louis Henri Sullivan: "Form ever follows function."

Pool house and pool, Jay Paley residence, Bel Air, California, 1934

499

Tested Skill

MINILESSON

REVIEW: VOCABULARY

Context Clues/Multiple-Meaning Words

INFORMAL ASSESSMENT

Ask students how they can figure out which meaning of the word *fierce* is intended in the last sentence of the fourth paragraph on page 498. (by using context clues) Have students identify the intended meaning and the context clues they used. ("intense"; clues may include *prove to myself* and *become one of the best*)

TEACH/MODEL

Remind students that when they come across a word that has more than one meaning, they can use context clues in the surrounding text to figure out which meaning of that word is intended. You may want to model the strategy:

MODEL

I see that the word *plans* is used in both the first and third paragraphs. In the first paragraph, the words *draw* and *of how buildings should be built* are context clues that tell me that *plans* means "drawings showing how the parts of something are arranged."

PRACTICE/APPLY

Have students use context clues to determine the intended meaning of *plans* in the third paragraph. (designs for attaining a goal) Then have students determine the meanings of other multiple-meaning words in the selection, such as *vision* in the second paragraph and *stand* in the last paragraph on page 494.

SCIENCE

THE ZODIAC **The design at the bottom of the pool is of the zodiac. Ancient Babylonian astronomers divided the sky into twelve sections for the twelve constellations the sun passes through: Aquarius, Capricorn, Sagittarius, Scorpio, Libra, Virgo, Leo, Cancer, Gemini, Taurus, Aries, and Pisces. This led to the modern division of the year into twelve months.**

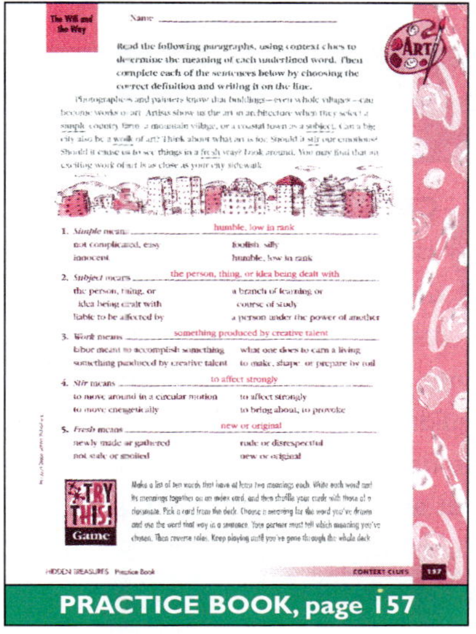

The Will and the Way

Name ______________________

Read the following paragraphs, using context clues to determine the meaning of each underlined word. Then complete each of the sentences below by choosing the correct definition and writing it on the line.

Photographers and painters know that buildings—even whole villages—can become works of art. Artists show us the art in architecture when they select a simple country farm, a mountain village, or a coastal town as a subject. Can a big city also be a work of art? Think about what art is for. Should it stir our emotions? Should it cause us to see things in a fresh way? Look around. You may find that an exciting work of art is as close as your city sidewalk.

1. *Simple* means humble, low in rank
   not complicated, easy / foolish, silly / innocent / humble, low in rank
2. *Subject* means the person, thing, or idea being dealt with
   the person, thing, or idea being dealt with / a branch of learning or course of study / liable to be affected by / a person under the power of another
3. *Work* means something produced by creative talent
   labor meant to accomplish something / what one does to earn a living / something produced by creative talent / to make, shape, or prepare by toil
4. *Stir* means to affect strongly
   to move around in a circular motion / to affect strongly / to move energetically / to bring about, to provoke
5. *Fresh* means new or original
   newly made or gathered / rude or disrespectful / not stale or spoiled / new or original

TRY THIS! Game

Make a list of ten words that have at least two meanings each. Write each word and its meanings together on an index card, and then shuffle your cards with those of a classmate. Pick a card from the deck. Choose a meaning for the word you've drawn and use the word that way in a sentence. Your partner must tell which meaning you've chosen. Then reverse roles. Keep playing until you've gone through the whole deck.

HIDDEN TREASURES Practice Book — CONTEXT CLUES 157

PRACTICE BOOK, page 157

Cooperative Reading

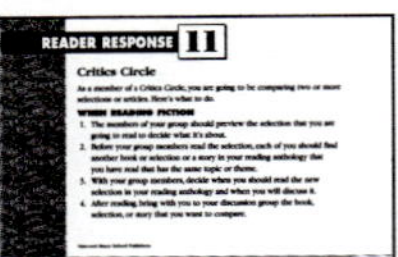
Response Card 11

Cooperative reading groups may expand their discussions by sharing their reactions to the selection and comparing aspects of it with the other selection(s) they have chosen. Use questions such as these:

- **What is the same about the selections you have chosen to compare? What is different?**
- **What qualities do the people in the selections have in common?**
- **Which selection do you like better so far? Why?**

❖ After graduating from high school I enrolled in the Los Angeles Art School and took a job as an architect's helper. The Beaux Arts Institute of Design of New York had a workshop in Los Angeles that accepted me as a student. After three years of study I won the coveted Beaux Arts Medal for excellence in design. Winning this competition reinforced my belief that I would succeed. I realized that the only chance I had of being accepted in the elite world of architecture was to compete on individual merit.

To find a job I went through the yellow pages and copied the addresses of all the architects listed. I arranged them in geographical order, put on my best suit of clothes, and called on each office. I asked if they were hiring or not. Next to each name I wrote down whether the answer was "no" or "maybe next week," and whether it was said with a smile or a frown. The following week I put my sketches in a smart portfolio and went back to each office where someone had smiled. Finally I was offered three positions. Three dollars per week was the highest salary, and one office paid nothing but gave me the chance to work in one of the most prestigious architectural firms in the city. I knew that this firm would give me invaluable experience, so I took the job. To my surprise they broke their contract and paid me three dollars beginning my very first week.

Shortly thereafter I began working for Wilbur D. Cook, a landscape architect and town planner. My first day in the office I informed the chief draftsman that I was a working-drawing man, meaning that I prepared drawings to be used on the job by construction workers. I bluffed my way through the day; then, at night, I took his drawings home and worked until daybreak. I went into the office early the next morning, laid out the drawings on my drafting table, and waited for the chief draftsman to drop by. He was astonished at how quickly I had completed the assignment. Thereafter, he considered me the fastest working-drawing man in the office. That's when I decided that I would do things faster, more efficiently, and better than others in order to be judged for my abilities rather than simply dismissed because of the color of my face.

In 1914, when I was twenty, my design for a neighborhood civic center in Pasadena, California, won the first prize of two hundred dollars,

500

SOCIAL STUDIES CONNECTION

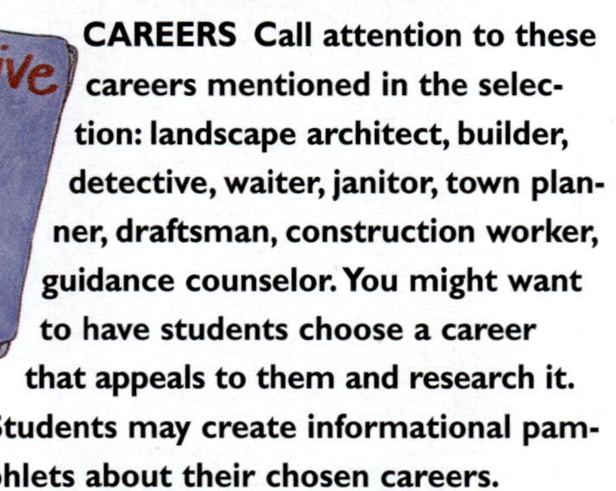

CAREERS Call attention to these careers mentioned in the selection: landscape architect, builder, detective, waiter, janitor, town planner, draftsman, construction worker, guidance counselor. You might want to have students choose a career that appeals to them and research it. Students may create informational pamphlets about their chosen careers.

Intervention Strategies

PICTURE CLUES Say this sentence aloud to students: *While I'm reading, I look at the photographs to gain a better understanding of Paul R. Williams's work.* Have students tell how looking at the photographs helps them understand the type of buildings Paul R. Williams designed.

Ambassador Hotel coffee shop, California, 1949

501

Informal Assessment

FIGURATIVE LANGUAGE

To determine whether students are able to understand the use of figurative language, ask them questions such as the following:

- What does the author mean when she says on page 495 that Paul "carved his own road"?
- What effect does Paul achieve on page 498 by stating that his counselor would have been just as astonished if Paul had proposed a rocket flight to Mars?

MEETING INDIVIDUAL NEEDS

STUDENTS ACQUIRING ENGLISH Some students may not be familiar with the *Yellow Pages* mentioned in the second paragraph. If possible, bring in a current edition of the Yellow Pages and point out some of its features, such as community information, ZIP code and area maps, coupons, and directory listings.

Critical Thinking Questions

1. **How do you know that Paul was talented as an architect?** (Possible responses: He was hired by prominent firms. He won prizes in national competitions.) METACOGNITIVE: SUMMARIZING

2. **What did Paul's enrollment in the engineering program show about him?** (Possible responses: He felt the need to keep improving his knowledge and skill. He wasn't content merely to be talented at drawing. He wanted to be the best he could be.) CRITICAL: DETERMINING CHARACTERS' TRAITS

beating older and more experienced contestants. I won first honorable mention in architecture at the Chicago Emancipation Celebration in 1915 and the following year placed third for the Sperling Prize, an All-American competition held in New York. It was especially exciting to compete with other architects from across the country, because it's easy to be the best in your town and forget that there's a whole world of competition out there.

I thought drawing ability was all I needed to become an architect, but my boss told me how wrong I was. Even though I had some promising ideas, he explained that I'd never succeed if I only cared about the artistic part. That accounted for only about one quarter of an architect's job. I had not considered how architects obtain commissions to design buildings, only about how thrilling it was to work on them at my drafting board. Once again, my will wasn't enough. I had to find the way.

At the University of Southern California, I enrolled in an engineering program that included business classes. The degree required many math courses, and I was certainly glad I took them. The math helped me make the correct measurements on floor plans and gave me a foundation for the business side of architecture.

Meanwhile, I worked my way through college by making brass U's, S's, and C's for men's watch fobs and women's handbags. At one point

County Courthouse, Los Angeles, California

502

CONVENTIONS OF LANGUAGE

PROPER NOUNS Remind students that proper nouns—the names of particular persons, places, things, or ideas—are capitalized. If a proper noun consists of more than one word, the important words are capitalized and unimportant words, such as *of*, are lowercased. Call on volunteers to name proper nouns they find on this page. (Chicago Emancipation Celebration; Sperling Prize; All-American; University of Southern California; County Courthouse, Los Angeles, California)

"Building styles change with time and fashion, but I measure my worth as an architect by my ability to please my client. Each home I design has something special and different from anyone else's home, but I've never made a house so trendy that, when the owners wanted to move, no one else would be interested in buying it."

The interior of the residence of E.L. Cord, an auto manufacturer. The drawing details how to build the staircase, which is shown in its final form.

503

MINILESSON

REVIEW: COMPREHENSION

Synthesizing Information

INFORMAL ASSESSMENT

Ask students what synthesizing information involves. (gathering information from different sources, combining it, and using it in an original way)

TEACH/MODEL

Point out to students that after they gather information about a single topic from several different sources, they can then synthesize—or combine—the information in new ways to form an original product or conclusion. You may want to model the way Paul Williams synthesized information to become a successful architect:

MODEL

Paul Williams took architecture courses in high school, went to art school, worked for architects, and enrolled in a university engineering program. He synthesized all the knowledge he gained from these different sources to form the philosophy he followed when he designed buildings.

PRACTICE/APPLY

Ask students to develop plans for a research project on the history of a significant building in your city or town. Direct them to list the possible information sources they could use.

MATH CONNECTION

METRIC SYSTEM Tell students that measurements can be made by using more than one system, such as the English system and the metric system. Have students take measurements of parts of your classroom, first using inches and feet and then using centimeters and meters. You may want to discuss the merits of each system.

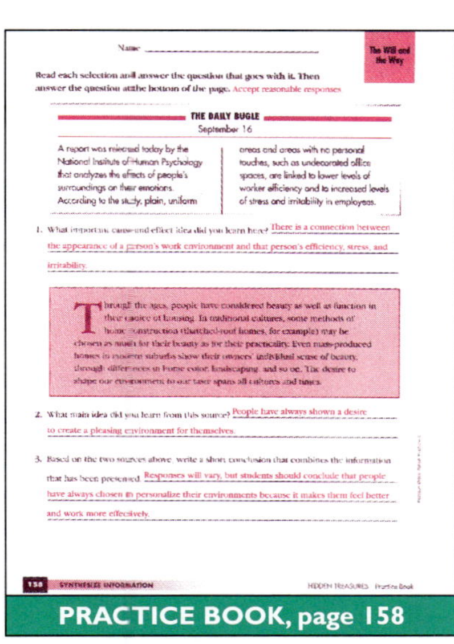

Name ______________________

The Will and the Way

Read each selection and answer the question that goes with it. Then answer the question at the bottom of the page. Accept reasonable responses.

THE DAILY BUGLE
September 16

A report was released today by the National Institute of Human Psychology that analyzes the effects of people's surroundings on their emotions. According to the study, plain, uniform areas and areas with no personal touches, such as undecorated office spaces, are linked to lower levels of worker efficiency and to increased levels of stress and irritability in employees.

1. What important cause-and-effect idea did you learn here? There is a connection between the appearance of a person's work environment and that person's efficiency, stress, and irritability.

Through the ages, people have considered beauty as well as function in their choice of housing. In traditional cultures, some methods of home construction (thatched-roof homes, for example) may be chosen as much for their beauty as for their practicality. Even mass-produced homes in modern suburbs show their owners' individual sense of beauty, through differences in home color, landscaping, and so on. The desire to shape our environments to our taste spans all cultures and times.

2. What main idea did you learn from this source? People have always shown a desire to create a pleasing environment for themselves.

3. Based on the two sources above, write a short conclusion that combines the information that has been presented. Responses will vary, but students should conclude that people have always chosen to personalize their environments because it makes them feel better and work more effectively.

158 SYNTHESIZE INFORMATION HIDDEN TREASURES Practice Book

PRACTICE BOOK, page 158

Cooperative Reading

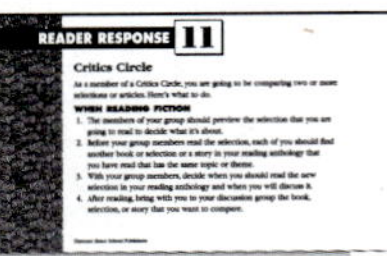
Response Card 11

After cooperative reading groups have finished reading the selection, group members should discuss the selection(s) they decided to compare. Encourage students to discuss questions such as these:

- **How are the experiences of the main characters in each selection alike? How are they different?**
- **Did one of the selections offer more or better information? Which one? Give examples.**
- **Now that you have read several selections about creativity, what is your viewpoint on it?**

five other students worked for me, and I made so much money that I considered changing my mind about school and architecture. Deep down inside, however, I knew the money was temporary and I'd grow bored. Becoming an architect would be a lot of work, but my future depended on staying in school. I took a hard look at my experience (or lack of it) and decided to attend three different art schools for intensive study in interior design, color harmony, and rendering.

With additional education and experience in landscaping under my belt, it was time to find a job that would give me experience in fine home design. I couldn't have asked for a better training ground than working in the offices of Reginald Johnson. Would you believe my first assignment was to design a $150,000 home? Up until then I'd never even been in a home that cost more than $10,000! I couldn't imagine how you could spend so much on a home, but then my employer sent me to look at homes in Santa Barbara, and I soon found out. That trip taught me more than where money was spent; it also taught me how it was spent. The most important lesson I learned was restraint. A room should have a single focal point, regardless of how much money goes into it. If not arranged well, a magnificent collection of furnishings can look like an expensive junk shop. Restraint, then, is a matter of choosing and carefully planning for the total effect.

Frederick Douglass, as shown in facade of the Twenty-eighth Street YMCA, Los Angeles

504

ART

RELIEF SCULPTURE The image of Frederick Douglass and the surrounding design on the facade of the building shown in the photograph are an example of relief, a type of sculpture in which the modeled form is projected above the surface and undercut to create a three-dimensional effect.

Paul Williams in front of the Los Angeles International Airport theme building

> ***"Planning is thinking beforehand how something is to be made or done, and mixing imagination with the product—which in the broad sense makes all of us planners. The only difference is that some people get a license to get paid for thinking and the rest of us just contribute our good thoughts to our fellow man."***

505

NOTES

Here's a place to list ideas or activities that you would like to use the next time you teach this lesson.

SOCIAL STUDIES

FACT FINDER

FREDERICK DOUGLASS (1817–1895) was an escaped slave who became a prominent abolitionist and social reformer. Following his escape, he went north and became a lecturer for the Massachusetts Anti-Slavery Society. After purchasing his freedom to avoid being returned south as a fugitive slave, he founded and edited an abolitionist paper, the *North Star*, and helped recruit black soldiers during the Civil War. After the war, Douglass held several government posts, including that of U.S. consul general to Haiti.

Strategic Reading

PAGES 500–506 How did having both the will and the way help Paul R. Williams succeed in achieving his dream of becoming an architect? (Possible response: Because of his will—his determination to become an architect—he kept trying to find ways to achieve this goal. He succeeded by means of his own talent and his constant attempts to improve his skill and knowledge.) STRATEGY: SUMMARIZING

Returning to the Predictions/Purpose

Did you find out what you wanted to know about Paul R. Williams or architecture as a profession? Encourage students to tell whether their purposes for reading were met. STRATEGY: RETURNING TO THE PURPOSE

Appreciating the Literature

What was the most important thing you learned from the selection? Why did this interest you? (Responses will vary.)

From that day on my motto became: "Good design is the pleasing assemblage of parts, not the assemblage of pleasing parts." I remember this whenever creative vision is involved. The same idea holds true whether you're getting dressed and putting an outfit together, redecorating your room, or setting the table. It even holds true when selecting people for a committee—it's important to choose people who work well together.

Satellite City, Paul Williams's vision of a city of the future

> ***"Remember, imagination can be a tool in creative problem solving. Use your imagination, and you'll never give up on finding solutions to problems, whatever they are."***

506

Name ______________________

The Will and the Way

A. Fill in the K-W-L chart for "The Will and the Way."
Accept reasonable responses.

K What I Know	W What I Want to Know	L What I Learned
Williams studied architecture in college.	How did Paul Williams get interested in architecture?	He drew buildings as a child; a local builder said he should become an architect; he researched what architects do.
He designed buildings.	What steps did Paul Williams take to become an architect?	He studied architecture in high school, went to art school, worked for architects, took engineering courses in college, and enrolled in art classes.
	What buildings did Paul Williams design?	Litton Industries headquarters, the Ambassador Hotel coffee shop, the Los Angeles County Courthouse, the Los Angeles International Airport's theme building, and others

B. Summarize what you learned about Paul Williams from reading the selection. Possible response:
Williams was interested in buildings even as a child. He worked hard studying architecture, art, and engineering. He designed a number of important buildings, including the Los Angeles County Courthouse.

152 SUMMARIZING THE LITERATURE HIDDEN TREASURES Practice Book

PRACTICE BOOK, page 152

SUMMARIZING

K-W-L Chart

Guide students in completing the third column of their K-W-L charts. Encourage them to summarize the selection by recalling the important facts they learned about architecture and Paul R. Williams's life. See *Practice Book* page 152.

K What I Know	W What I Want to Know	L What I Learned
(Williams studied architecture in college.) (He designed buildings.)	(How did Paul R. Williams get interested in architecture?) (What steps did Paul Williams take to become an architect?)	(He drew buildings as a child; local builder said he should become an architect; he researched what architects do.)

❖ Karen Hudson ❖

Karen Hudson says Paul Williams, her grandfather, could make a sketch come alive right before his clients' eyes. He would sit across the table from his clients and draw his sketches upside down. "A sparkle still comes to their eyes when they start talking about it," Ms. Hudson says.

Ms. Hudson talked to many of her grandfather's clients as part of her research for *The Will and the Way*. She realized that there were many remarkable things about her grandfather that few people knew. That's why she decided to write her book.

But putting the book together took a great deal of imagination and creativity. Ms. Hudson says one thing her grandfather always wanted her to do was use her imagination. She knew he would be proud if she tried to help others use imagination and creativity in their lives.

"It wasn't just important for him to inspire us to be architects," Ms. Hudson says. "It was important to him that we use imagination in our everyday lives, as a way to solve problems."

Ms. Hudson had problems finding information about her grandfather for the book. There weren't many public records about him, but Della Williams, her grandmother, had saved newspaper clippings about him since 1917.

As part of her research, Ms. Hudson also sent a questionnaire to the owners of the buildings her grandfather designed. The owners were eager to give her the information she needed. "I received most of the information through the generosity of others," Ms. Hudson says.

When her research was complete, Ms. Hudson realized that her grandfather's story could be inspirational to everyone, not only to kids who want to be architects.

"What you need to be is a person who contributes to your community," Ms. Hudson says. "That may or may not be as an architect. But if you listen, read, think, and use your imagination, you can apply that to anything," she says.

507

About the Author

After students read page 507, you may wish to discuss these questions with them:

- **How do you know that it is important to Karen Hudson to tell her grandfather's story?** (Possible responses: She wants to preserve his legacy and share things about her grandfather that few people know; she went to great lengths to gather information about her grandfather.)
- **Do you agree with Karen Hudson when she says, "If you listen, read, think, and use your imagination, you can apply that to anything"?** (Responses will vary.)
- **One of the reasons that Karen Hudson wrote "The Will and the Way" was because she felt that there were many remarkable things about her grandfather that she wanted to share. Is there someone in your family who has achieved something that you would like to share? Explain.** (Responses will vary.)

Karen Hudson lives in Los Angeles where she chronicles the African American experience through writing and photographs. In a letter to her grandfather, she expresses her gratitude for his pride:

> "Again, by example, you have shown us the value of following our hearts and making decisions true to our own convictions, and no one else's."

IDEA BANK

Paul R. Williams is an example of someone who achieved a dream. Suggest that students brainstorm a list of other people—in any field or endeavor—who have achieved their dreams. Have each student choose a person to research. Students may use their findings to create an illustrated bulletin board display.

POETRY

On Watching the Construction of a Skyscraper

by Burton Raffel

INTRODUCING THE POEM Ask students if they have ever watched a building being built, and have them briefly describe the sights and sounds of a construction site. Ask students to think about what they can see and hear as they read this poem about the building of a skyscraper.

APPRECIATING THE POEM Read the poem aloud to students as they follow along. Then ask questions such as the following:

To what does the poet compare the construction cranes? (He compares them to trees.)

How does the poet continue the metaphor through the poem? (Possible responses: All the images are of things associated with trees. The steel is compared to the smooth bark of a sapling; the crane's wheezing sound to the singing of a bird; the rivets to bees that enter flowers for nectar.)

After discussing the poem, organize students into two groups for a choral reading. Have the groups read alternating lines.

LISTENING CENTER

"On Watching the Construction of a Skyscraper" is available on Literature Cassette 3. Have students listen to the poem once or twice to help them answer the Appreciating the Poem questions.

Nothing sings from these orange trees,
Rindless steel as smooth as sapling skin,
Except a crane's brief wheeze
And all the muffled, clanking din
Of rivets nosing in like bees.

509

About the Poet

Burton Raffel has been a college teacher, an attorney, an editor, and a translator. Although best known as a translator, Mr. Raffel says that the pull of poetry is stronger than anything else: "My principal concern is and has always been poetry. . . . I prefer to create. All attempts to sidetrack that impulse have failed."

POET'S CRAFT Remind students that poets choose words for their sounds as much as for their meanings. Have students identify rhyming words at the end of lines *(trees/wheeze/bees; skin/din)*; the repetition of a beginning consonant (initial *s* in the second line); and words that imitate a sound *(wheeze, clanking)*. Allow students to briefly explore the poet's imagery by asking them whether they found the poet's comparison an interesting one and, if so, why.

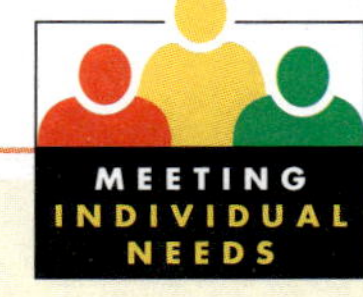

EXTRA SUPPORT Discuss the meanings of the following words:

rindless: without the tough, outer covering or layer that some kinds of fruit have, such as oranges
sapling: a young tree
rivets: metal bolts used to join two or more pieces

ACTIVITY CHOICES

WRITE A LETTER

A FINE EXAMPLE Review with students the format of a friendly letter, or refer them to *The Amazing Writing Machine* floppy disk. The program contains a model for a letter. CRITICAL THINKING/WRITING

WRITE A POEM

WHERE THERE'S A WILL, THERE'S A WAY Before students write their poems, they may wish to discuss in small groups the saying "Where there's a will, there's a way." Remind them that poems may be rhymed or unrhymed. WRITING

DESIGN A ROOM

ARCHITECTS IN TRAINING Point out to students that architects' plans, like maps, are drawn to scale. Explain that before students begin their drawings, they will have to decide on an appropriate scale. Suggest that they experiment with different scales. MATH/ART

Response

WRITE A LETTER

A FINE EXAMPLE

Suppose you are Paul R. Williams's grandson. You have just read your grandfather's journal, which he wrote for you. Write a thank-you letter. Tell your grandfather how his journal has inspired you to reach your goals in life.

DESIGN A ROOM

ARCHITECTS IN TRAINING

Work with a partner to take measurements of your classroom. Draw a design of the room, indicating the measurements of each wall, window, doorway, and chalkboard. In your drawing, rearrange the items in the room in a way that is both functional and pleasing. With your classmates, vote on the design you like best.

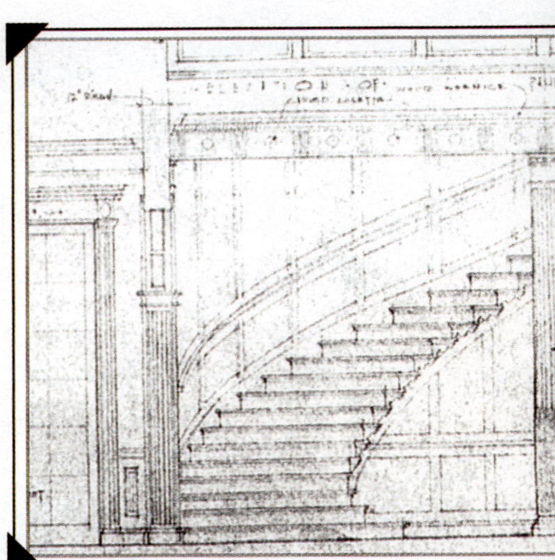

510

STUDENTS ACQUIRING ENGLISH

Have students work with English-proficient partners and in integrated groups for the response activities. Some students may wish to write their letters in their first language and then translate them into English.

WRITE A POEM

WHERE THERE'S A WILL, THERE'S A WAY

Write the word *WILL* vertically on a sheet of paper. Using each letter as the first letter of a line, write a poem about the importance of having the will to accomplish a goal. Share your poem with your classmates.

WHAT DO YOU THINK?

- Do you think that the title of the selection appropriately describes the life of Paul R. Williams? Explain your answer.
- Which one of Paul R. Williams's designs was your favorite? Why?
- What do you think Paul R. Williams would say about the poem "On Watching the Construction of a Skyscraper"?

511

CHECKING COMPREHENSION

What Do You Think?

1. **Do you think that the title of the selection appropriately describes the life of the architect Paul R. Williams? Explain your answer.** (Possible response: Paul believed that if you had the will to do something and could find the way, you could accomplish whatever you wanted. He practiced this philosophy throughout his life.) DESCRIPTIVE RESPONSE
2. **Which one of Paul R. Williams's designs was your favorite? Why?** (Responses will vary.) PERSONAL RESPONSE
3. **What do you think Paul R. Williams would say about the poem "On Watching the Construction of a Skyscraper"?** (Responses will vary.) SYNTHESIS

VARYING THE ACTIVITY

For **extra support,** work with students to calculate the scale and then encourage them to cut from construction paper shapes approximating the furniture and other objects in the classroom. Students may use these shapes to arrange and rearrange the room until they decide on a final design. Then students may wish to glue the pieces onto a sheet of paper.

Intervention Strategies

TIPS FOR CLASSROOM MANAGEMENT

IF second-language students need additional vocabulary and during-reading strategies to understand "The Will and the Way," **THEN** use *Sheltered English/ESL Manual*, pages 78–81.

IF students had difficulty understanding "The Will and the Way," **THEN** complete the Rereading and Decoding Strategies. See also *Intervention Strategies Manual*, pages 116–121.

REREADNG

UNDERSTANDING SEQUENCE Have students reread the selection to understand the sequence, keeping these questions in mind:

What did Paul do when . . .

- he was very young?
- he was in high school?
- he was an architect's helper?
- he worked for Wilbur Cook?
- he attended college?
- he worked in Reginald Johnson's office?

Point out that students should skim the selection for key phrases and then read more slowly the passages where the key phrases appear.

PERSONAL JOURNAL

Paul R. Williams's motto was "Good design is the pleasing assemblage of parts, not the assemblage of pleasing parts." Explain the meaning of the word *assemblage*, and have students write in their journals what they think Williams meant by this statement.

DECODING LONG WORDS

REVIEW Present the following story words:

rocket	local	dollars	hometown	complete
little	nearly	drawing	honor	husband

Review with students which strategy they would use to decode each word.

- Look for compound words: *home-town*.
- Look for familiar prefixes, suffixes, and endings: *com-plete, near-ly, draw-ing*.
- Look for two consonants between vowels. If the two consonants form a cluster or digraph, divide the word after the two consonants: *rock-et*. Otherwise divide between the two consonants: *dol-lars, hus-band*.
- Look for three consonants between vowels. If the word ends in the consonant *-le* pattern, divide before the consonant preceding the *le*: *lit-tle*.
- Look for a single consonant between vowels. Try dividing in front of the consonant and pronouncing the first syllable with a long vowel sound: *lo-cal*. If you don't get a recognizable word, divide after the consonant and pronounce the first syllable with a short vowel sound: *hon-or*.

Have students list an additional story word under each heading.

Compounds	Prefixes	Suffixes/Endings
Consonants Between Vowels		
One	Two	Three
Three or More Syllables		

WRITING A DIARY ENTRY

Paul R. Williams says that his family supported him in his ambition to become an architect. He also says that his guidance counselor in school tried to make him change his mind. Ask students to write a diary entry about what they think they would like to do when they grow up. Suggest that they think about whose support they would need to achieve this goal and how they would deal with any opposition.

ESL/TITLE I READING

DECODING SUPPORT
Hard *c* and Soft *c*

Intervention Strategies Manual pp. 120–121

Reading Trade Books

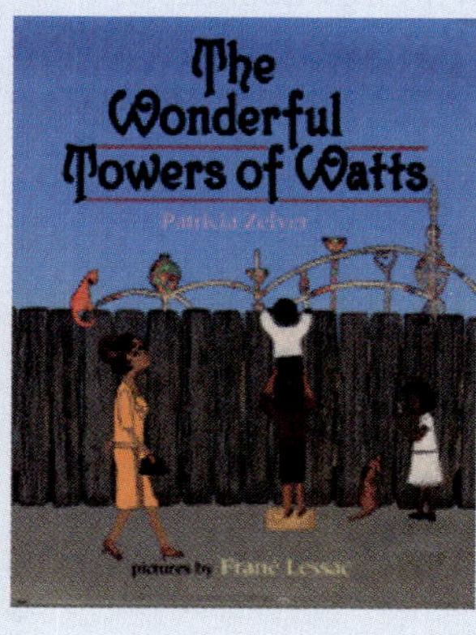

The Wonderful Towers of Watts

by Patricia Zelver

Like Paul R. Williams, Old Sam Rodia remains true to his artistic calling. Have students complete the sentences below to compare the two selections.

1. Because both Paul R. Williams and Old Sam wanted to create beauty in the world around them, we might call both men _____.
2. Despite some people's negative opinions, both Paul R. Williams and Old Sam were _____.
3. One personality trait that both men shared was _____.

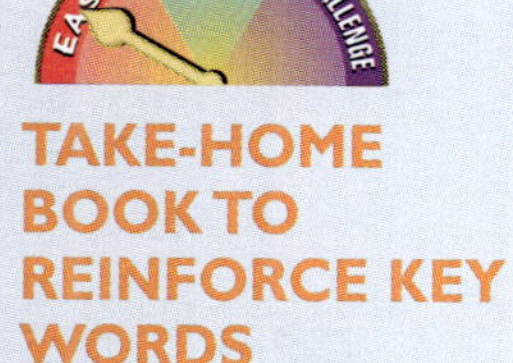

TAKE-HOME BOOK TO REINFORCE KEY WORDS

Students will enjoy reading this story about a mysterious discovery. They may want to read it when they have independent reading time in class, or they might want to take it home to read.

PERSONAL JOURNAL

After students finish reading *Better Late Than Never*, have them write their reactions to the book in their personal journals.

See also *Intervention Strategies Manual,* page 119.

2 Integrating Language Arts

IDEA BANK

TIPS FOR CLASSROOM MANAGEMENT

IF students had difficulty completing their K-W-L charts, **THEN** they should complete the Retelling activity.

IF students need to focus on speaking or listening strategies, **THEN** they should complete the Oral Language activity.

RETELLING

Role-Playing

Have pairs of students take turns role-playing Paul R. Williams telling his grandson, Paul Claude, about his life and ideas. After one partner retells part of the selection, partners should switch roles. Have students continue doing this until they have retold the entire selection. LISTENING/SPEAKING

Informal Assessment

Note whether students include the most important details of the selection as they retell it.

ORAL LANGUAGE

Making a Speech with Visuals

Recall with students that Paul R. Williams received many awards during his career as an architect. Explain that the persons who presented the awards probably delivered speeches explaining why the awards were being given, and they may have accompanied their speeches with visual aids, such as slides of buildings Williams designed. Have students choose people to honor. Then have them prepare brief speeches, accompanied by visual aids, such as they might make when presenting an award to someone. Have students take turns presenting their speeches in small groups. LISTENING/SPEAKING/WRITING

TIPS FOR LISTENING AND SPEAKING

When students **listen** to one another's speeches, they should

- listen attentively and appreciatively.
- refrain from making distracting noises or actions.

Remind students that when they **speak**, they should

- speak clearly.
- adjust their pitch, volume, and stress appropriately.
- direct listeners' attention to the visual aids.
- make eye contact with the audience.

REREADING

Key Passages

Have individual students take turns rereading key passages from the selection aloud. You may want to direct them to reread the first and second paragraphs on page 502, for example, or another passage of their choice. After students reread the passage silently, model reading a few lines of the text aloud. Give students an opportunity to rehearse before they present their readings. **LISTENING/SPEAKING/READING**

Renderings by Paul R. Williams

REAL-LIFE RESOURCES

Diagrams

USING DIAGRAMS Discuss how architects describe their ideas before building a new house. Have students compare writing a description with creating a diagram, or blueprints, of the house. Talk about how diagrams can present visual information effectively. Students can find examples of blueprints in reference sources and books on homes and architecture.

READING A DIAGRAM Explain that many diagrams use symbols to show information effectively. Draw these symbols on the board and label them. Discuss why each might be useful when drawing a blueprint of a house or building:

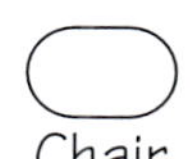

Have students make a chart of symbols used on the blueprints they find. See *Writer's Magazine* pages 76 and 77.

REAL-LIFE CHALLENGE Have students create a diagram showing the floor plan of their dream house. Encourage them to review the symbols and styles used in blueprints they have found. **WRITING/MATH CONNECTION**

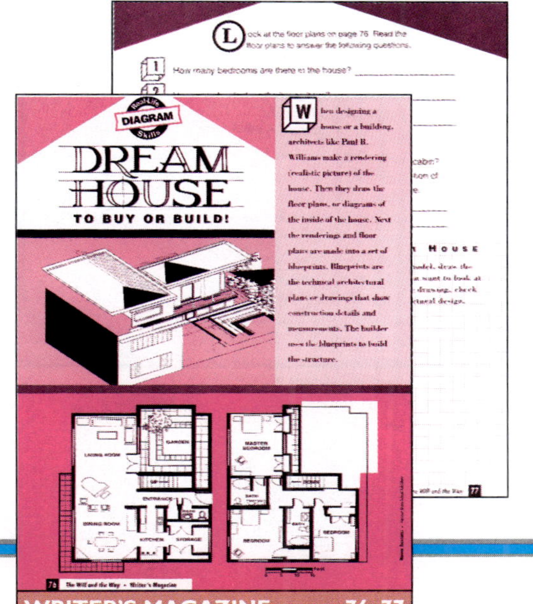

WRITER'S MAGAZINE, pages 76–77

STUDENTS ACQUIRING ENGLISH

Have students work with English-proficient partners for the Retelling activity.

EXTRA SUPPORT

On the board or on chart paper, write the Tips for Listening and Speaking. Suggest that students refer to the tips before they present their speeches.

WRITER'S WORKSHOP

Business Letter

TIPS FOR CLASSROOM MANAGEMENT

IF students are familiar with the format and style of a business letter, **THEN** have them begin writing, referring to the model on Transparency 49 as necessary.

IF you want a short writing activity, **THEN** adapt this lesson by having students focus on the Writer's Craft.

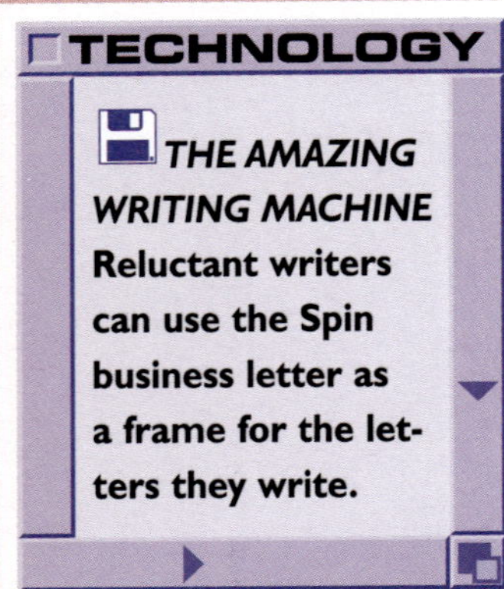

Thinking as Writers

WRITING FORM: Business Letter Point out to students that as an architect, Paul R. Williams probably wrote many business letters to clients, other professionals, and organizations. Explain that a business letter may be sent to inform, to persuade, or to request information. Tell students that they are going to learn about business letters and then write one.

Display Transparency 49, and discuss the parts of a business letter. Point out that the body of the letter should begin with a sentence that states its purpose.

TRANSPARENCY 49

Model: Business Letter

*A **business letter** is more formal than a friendly letter. It may be sent to inform, to persuade, or to request information.*

heading	40 Terrace Rd. Fremont, CA 94539 May 28, 199–
inside address	Mr. Peter Decker Decker Industries 717 Decker Court Carmel, IN 46032
greeting	Dear Mr. Decker:
body	We are studying environmental issues at school, and I have learned that your company is on the cutting edge of recycling technology. Please send a catalog or a brochure about your recycled products to the address above. Thank you.
closing	Sincerely,
signature	Cal Ventura
return address	Cal Ventura 40 Terrace Rd. Fremont, CA 94539
mailing address	Mr. Peter Decker Decker Industries 717 Decker Court Carmel, IN 46032

WRITER'S CRAFT: Formal Language Tell students that a business letter is more formal than a friendly letter. Discuss the difference between formal and informal language. Have students suggest circumstances in which each kind of language is appropriate. Point out that a business letter is usually written to a stranger for a particular reason; therefore, formal language is more appropriate for this purpose. Help students recognize the importance of using clear, concise sentences and formal language when writing a business letter.

PREWRITING AND DRAFTING

Remind students to choose an audience and a strong reason for writing their letters. Refer to these strategies to help students begin their business letters.

PREWRITING GRAPHIC ORGANIZER If students need help in stating a purpose for their business letters or choosing an audience, provide a variety of sentence starters such as the following to which they can refer.

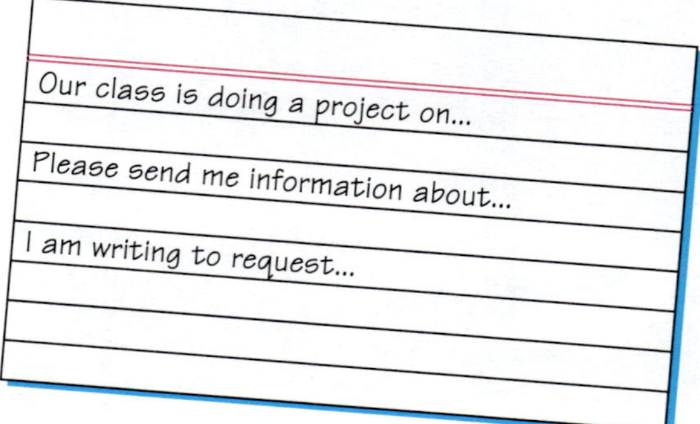

SUSTAINED SILENT WRITING Students who have strong ideas for business letters may begin writing without interruption.

DURING-WRITING GRAPHIC ORGANIZER Students who need guidance in following the format of a business letter may use the sideheads of the model as a frame.

RESPONDING AND REVISING

Have students work in editing circles or with partners to help one another revise their letters. Display the following checklist on the board:

- Are all the parts of the letter arranged properly?
- Does the body of the letter begin with a sentence that states the purpose?
- Is the language used in the letter formal enough for the audience and purpose?

PROOFREADING

Offer the following tips to help students proofread their work and make changes:

- ☑ Check capitalization, punctuation, and paragraph indentation.
- ☑ Check for correct use of **perfect tense verbs**. (See Grammar Minilesson on page T1019.)
- ☑ Look for words you may have misspelled.

PUBLISHING

If you wish to have students publish their business letters, suggest these options or let students choose their own methods:

ORAL Students may deliver their business letters to classmates who are role-playing a panel of experts. Encourage students to practice, and remind them to use good speaking techniques during delivery.

WRITTEN Students may type or print out their letters so that they look businesslike and display them on a bulletin board titled "Ask the Experts."

PORTFOLIO OPPORTUNITY

Have students answer the Student Self-Assessment questions and include both their answers and their letters in their portfolios.

LANGUAGE HANDBOOK

Everyday Writing, pages 86–87; Business Letter and Envelope, page 93; Perfect Tenses, pages 156–157

EVALUATION BENCHMARKS: BUSINESS LETTER

A business letter by a proficient student writer shows the following characteristics:

FORM	CRAFT	CONVENTIONS
Demonstrates understanding of the form • all letter parts arranged properly • clearly stated purpose and audience	**Uses clear and appropriate language** • sentences clear and concise • formal language used	**Follows conventions of grammar and usage** • proper nouns capitalized • paragraphs indented • correct use of perfect tense verbs

Teacher Assessment As you assess students' writing, refer to the Evaluation Benchmarks chart. For additional information, including model papers, see *Integrated Performance Assessment* Teacher's Edition.

Student Self-Assessment ✓

Have students answer the following questions and include the answers in their portfolios:

- ☑ What did you learn as you wrote your business letter?
- ☑ What will you do differently the next time you write a business letter?

Tested Skill

GRAMMAR

Regular and Irregular Verbs

TECHNOLOGY

IMAGINATION EXPRESS, DESTINATION: NEIGHBORHOOD **CD-ROM** Students can use the program to write and illustrate their sentences.

LANGUAGE HANDBOOK

Principal Parts of Regular and Irregular Verbs, pages 158–159

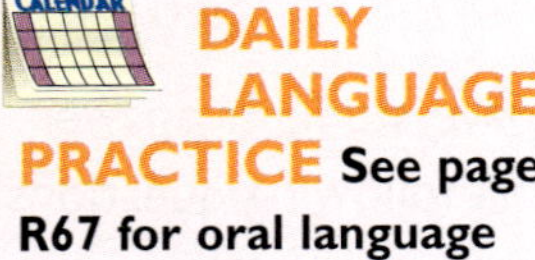

DAILY LANGUAGE PRACTICE See page R67 for oral language exercises.

Reading ↔ Writing Connection

Connect to the literature. Display the following sentence from "The Will and the Way":

Probably the only thing he loved more than architecture was his family.

Have a volunteer read the sentence aloud. Then ask students to identify the verbs in the sentence. *(loved, was)*

Build oral language. Guide students to see that *loved* and *was* are past-tense verbs. Ask students to name the present tense of the verbs. *(love, is)* Ask students to describe how each verb changes from the present tense to the past tense. Then ask students to name the present perfect tense of each verb. *(has loved, has been)* Have students make up sentences with each tense of the verb.

Teach/Model

Discuss regular verbs. Display the following sentences:

Paul hopes to be an architect.

Paul is hoping to be an architect.

Paul hoped to be an architect.

Paul has hoped to be an architect.

Ask a volunteer to underline the verbs. *(hopes, is hoping, hoped, has hoped)* Explain that every verb has four principal parts, and display the following chart:

Principal Parts			
Infinitive	Present Participle	Past	Past Participle
(to) hope	(is) hoping	hoped	(has) hoped

Point out that participles are forms used with helping verbs. Most verbs are regular verbs; the past and past participles of regular verbs are formed by adding *-ed* or *-d*.

Discuss irregular verbs. Explain that while most verbs are regular, some are irregular. Present the following sentences:

Paul flies to San Diego.

Paul is flying to San Diego.

Paul flew to San Diego.

Paul has flown to San Diego.

Ask a volunteer to underline the verbs. *(flies, is flying, flew, has flown)* Point out that the past tense of the irregular verb *fly* is formed by changing the word's spelling, not just by adding the ending *-ed* or *-d*.

Practice/Apply

Check understanding. Write the following chart on the board, and have students fill in the forms of the verbs and tell whether each verb is regular or irregular.

Infinitive	Past	Present Participle	Past Participle
(to) walk (regular)	(walked)	(is) (walking)	(has) (walked)
(to) see (irregular)	(saw)	(is) (seeing)	(has) (seen)
(to) wear (irregular)	(wore)	(is) (wearing)	(has) (worn)

Practice Activities

Add Sentence Parts

ORAL APPLICATION Prepare a set of sentence strips for sentence subjects—for example, *The architect*—and another set for sentence predicates, using the past-tense and perfect tense forms of irregular verbs such as *built*. Have students take turns choosing a subject and a predicate to make a sentence and then reading it aloud. Classmates should listen, identify the verb, and then name its infinitive form—for example, *built, build*. VISUAL/AUDITORY

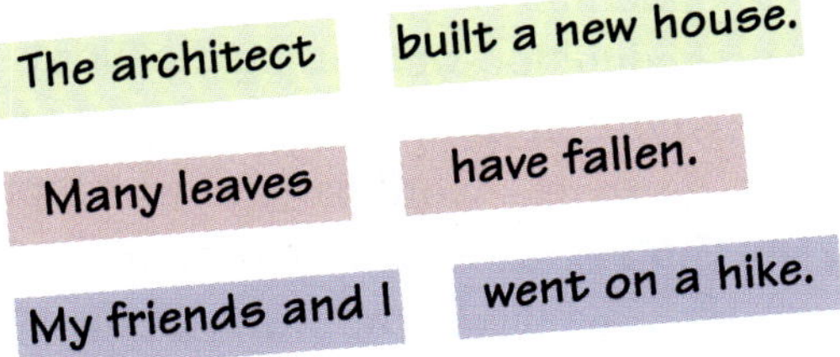

Find Irregular Verbs

WRITING APPLICATION Have groups of three students look for examples of irregular verbs in "The Will and the Way." Assign the roles of Recorder, Checker, and Reporter. Ask group members to list the examples they find on a chart of principal parts. Encourage groups to share and compare their findings. You may want to maintain a class list of irregular verbs that begins with students' findings. VISUAL/AUDITORY

Write Cloze Sentences

WRITING APPLICATION Using irregular verbs from the selection, small groups should write the infinitive of a verb and then create Cloze sentences for both regular and irregular verbs such as these:

(to) build The workers (built) a skyscraper.

(to) plan The designer (planned) a swimming pool.

Have groups exchange sentences and complete the sentences they receive. VISUAL/AUDITORY

APPLY TO WRITING

Suggest that students look in their business letters or other writing for regular and irregular verbs to be sure they have formed them correctly.

USAGE TIP Pay special attention to *lie* and *lay* and *sit* and *set*, two pairs of easily confused irregular verbs. *Lie* means "rest" or "recline." *Lay* means "place something in a reclining position." *Sit* means "rest, as in a chair." *Set* means "put something in a certain place."

Principal Parts			
Infinitive	**Present Participle**	**Past**	**Past Participle**
lie	(is) lying	lay	(has) lain
lay	(is) laying	laid	(has) laid
sit	(is) sitting	sat	(has) sat
set	(is) setting	set	(has) set

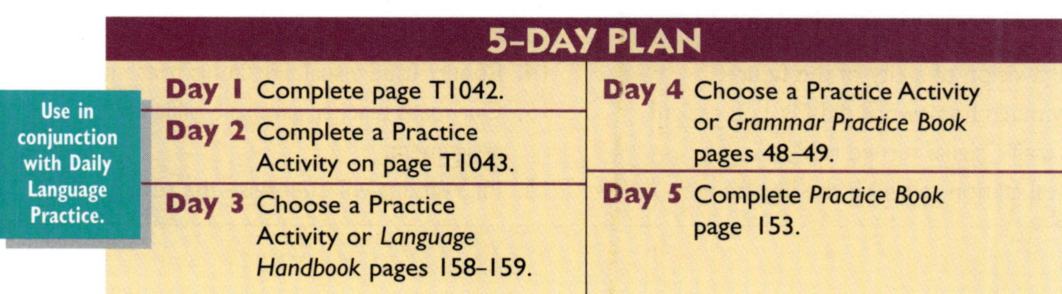

5-DAY PLAN

Use in conjunction with Daily Language Practice.

Day 1 Complete page T1042.

Day 2 Complete a Practice Activity on page T1043.

Day 3 Choose a Practice Activity or *Language Handbook* pages 158–159.

Day 4 Choose a Practice Activity or *Grammar Practice Book* pages 48–49.

Day 5 Complete *Practice Book* page 153.

STUDENTS ACQUIRING ENGLISH

Pair students with English-proficient peers to develop lists of common irregular verbs. Partners should then practice using the verbs in sentences. Be sure the following irregular verbs are included: *be, say, see, do, have, come,* and *go*.

RETEACH

See page R60 for lessons in multiple modalities.

GRAMMAR PRACTICE BOOK
pages 48–49

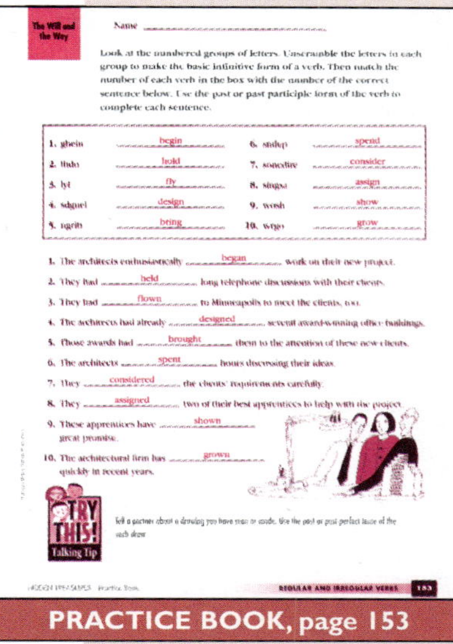

The Will and the Way

Name ____________

Look at the numbered groups of letters. Unscramble the letters in each group to make the basic infinitive form of a verb. Then match the number of each verb in the box with the number of the correct sentence below. Use the past or past participle form of the verb to complete each sentence.

1. begin
2. hold
3. fly
4. design
5. bring
6. spend
7. consider
8. assign
9. show
10. grow

1. The architects enthusiastically began work on their new project.
2. They had held long telephone discussions with their clients.
3. They had flown to Minneapolis to meet the clients, too.
4. The architects had already designed several award-winning office buildings.
5. Those awards had brought them to the attention of these new clients.
6. The architects spent hours discussing their ideas.
7. They considered the clients' requirements carefully.
8. They assigned two of their best apprentices to help with the project.
9. These apprentices have shown great promise.
10. The architectural firm has grown quickly in recent years.

TRY THIS! Talking Tip

REGULAR AND IRREGULAR VERBS 153

PRACTICE BOOK, page 153

SPELLING

5-Day Plan

Integrated Spelling Lesson 28:
student book, pages 118–121;
Teacher's Edition, pages T183–T188.

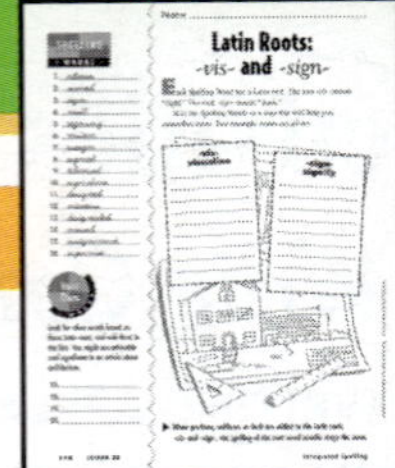
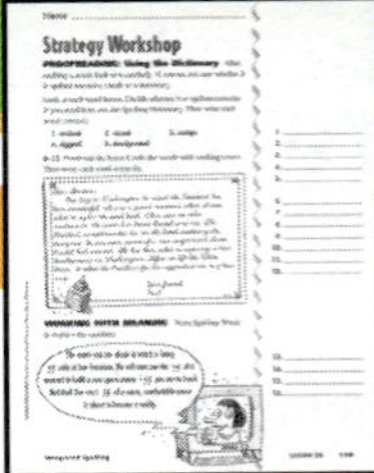
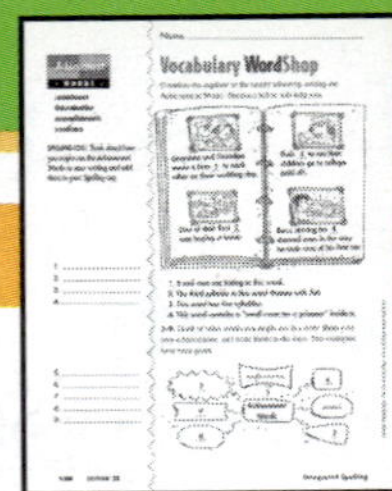
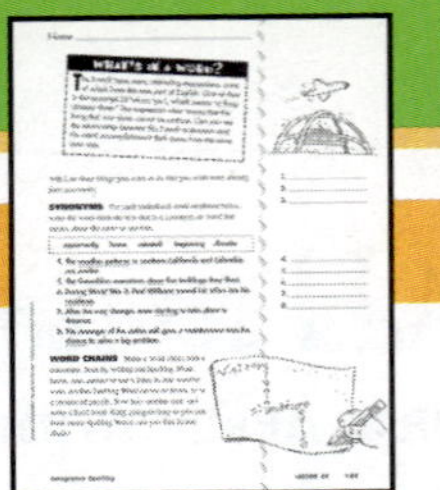

SPELLING WORDS

1. advise ★
2. revised
3. sign
4. visit ★
5. signing
6. vision ★
7. assign
8. signal
9. televised
10. signature
11. designed ★
12. visitors
13. designated
14. visual
15. assignment ★
16. supervise ★

STUDENT'S PERSONAL WORDS

17.
18.
19.
20.

★ Words appearing in "The Will and the Way"

Latin Roots: *-vis-* and *-sign-*

Pretest

DAY 1 **Administer the pretest.** Say each word, and then use it in the dictation sentence below. Help students self-check their pretests.

OPEN SORT

DAY 2 **Have students classify words.** Have groups of students classify the Spelling Words according to their similarities. For instance, groups might sort words according to the part of speech, number of syllables, or some other criterion. Have groups compare their lists and discuss their methods.

CLOSED SORT

Sort by Latin root. On the board, write the headings *-vis-* and *-sign-*, and ask pairs of students to copy the headings and write each Spelling Word in the correct column.

-vis-		-sign-	
advise	televised	sign	signature
revised	visitors	signing	designed
visit	visual	assign	designated
vision	supervise	signal	assignment

Teach/Model

DAY 3 **Discuss the generalization.** Write the words *visit* and *advise* on the board. Ask what word part is the same in both words. (*-vis-*) Ask a volunteer to underline *vis* in each word. Follow a similar procedure for *-sign-*, using the words *signal* and *assign*. Explain that some English words contain Latin roots—word parts to which prefixes and suffixes are added to form new words. Discuss the meanings of the words in the two lists, and help students form generalizations about the Latin roots *-vis-* and *-sign-*:

- The Latin root *-sign-* means "mark."
- The Latin root *-vis-* means "see."

DAY 4 **Apply to writing.** Encourage students to look in their business letters for words with the Latin roots *-vis-* and *-sign-* to see whether they are spelled correctly.

Posttest

DAY 5 **Assess students' progress.** The sentences below should be used as the posttest.

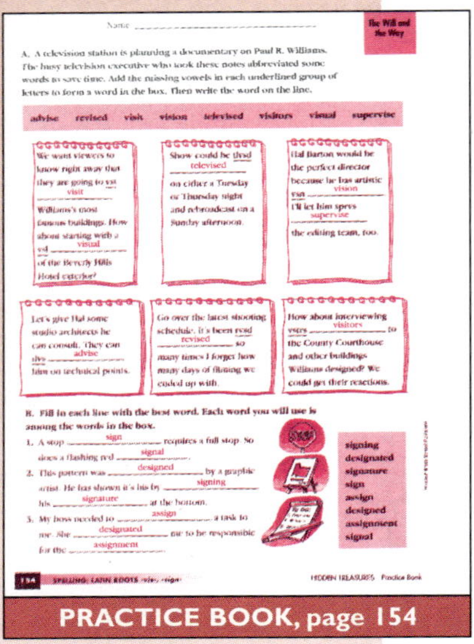
PRACTICE BOOK, page 154

DICTATION SENTENCES

1. What do you advise me to do?
2. Lucy revised her poem three times.
3. Please sign your name on the line.
4. I will visit my aunt in New York.
5. The rock star is signing his name on albums.
6. I had a vision of a city of the future.
7. How much homework did Ms. Loft assign?
8. The traffic signal turned red.
9. A local station televised the big game.
10. The signature on the letter was not legible.
11. Some buildings are designed to withstand earthquakes.
12. Visitors must check in at the office.
13. Ms. Grand designated Juan as leader of our group.
14. Robert used visual aids in his presentation.
15. Our math teacher gave us a difficult assignment.
16. Mr. Watkins will supervise the test.

VOCABULARY WORKSHOP

Reviewing Key Words

Display the Key Words, and draw a report form on the board similar to the one below. Ask students to imagine that they are supervising the construction of a major building. Then have volunteers read aloud the questions on the report. As students discuss each question, have them define each Key Word before indicating the answer.

Extending Vocabulary

COMPOUND WORDS

On the board, write *hometown, high school*, and *good-bye*, and ask students what these words have in common. (They are all compound words.) Point out that *hometown* is a closed compound, that *high school* is an open compound, and that *good-bye* is a hyphenated compound.

Have students work with partners or in small groups to go on a "treasure hunt" through the selection to find and list as many compound words of each type as possible. Students should add words of their own when they are unable to find any more in the story. Sample lists are provided below.

Closed Compounds	Open Compounds	Hyphenated Compounds
anyone	high school	good-bye
hometown	three thousand	son-in-law
grandfather	no one	
downtown		
horsecar		

CREATE NEW COMPOUND WORDS

Point out that people develop compound words to describe new things in familiar terms. For example, the word *spacewalk*, which came into use in recent times, combines two familiar words: *space* and *walk*. Ask students to imagine that they are living a hundred years from now. Encourage them to create descriptive compound words to name inventions and activities of the future.

INTRODUCE: LITERARY APPRECIATION

Figurative Language

OBJECTIVE: To understand the use of figurative language in a selection

Informal Assessment ✓

Are students able to

- ☑ identify examples of figurative language in a selection?
- ☑ explain the meaning of each example?

Teach/Model

Return to the literature. Ask students how the author helps them form a vivid mental picture of the guidance counselor by saying that he showed "as much astonishment as he would have had I proposed a rocket flight to Mars!" (The author's language helps you picture the guidance counselor as being extremely surprised.) Explain that this is an example of figurative language—words or phrases that mean something other than their literal definitions. Authors use figurative language to add color and humor to their writing and to help readers picture in their minds what is being described.

Model recognizing figurative language. Display Transparency 50, and ask volunteers to read each definition and the examples that follow. As each example is read, have students compare it to the definition and discuss how the figurative language adds to the meaning of the sentence. You may want to model the thinking:

MODEL **In the first simile, the word *like* tells me that the writer is comparing the road to a snake. The road seems to wind around in the way a snake moves. The comparison helps me visualize how winding the road was.**

TRANSPARENCY 50

Figurative Language

Simile: A comparison of two different things that uses the word *like* or *as*.

Examples: The road wound through the hills *like* a snake. The workers were *as* busy *as* bees.

Metaphor: A comparison of two different things that says one thing is another thing.

Example: The river *is* a long blue ribbon.

Personification: Giving an inanimate or a nonhuman object human characteristics.

Example: *Chilly fingers of wind* tried to pry the door open.

Hyperbole: An exaggeration that goes beyond reality to emphasize a point.

Example: He carried the *weight of the world* on his shoulders.

Practice/Apply

Have students demonstrate understanding. Have students identify the figure of speech used in each sentence below and discuss how it helps them visualize each scene. Students may refer to the Transparency as needed.

The air was so clear that I could see next year. (hyperbole)

The sun sulked behind a cloud. (personification)

The icy hill was a wall of glass. (metaphor)

The butterflies were like fluttering flowers. (simile)

Practice Activities

Figuratively Speaking

COOPERATIVE LEARNING Have each small group choose a topic, such as the moon, a city, or rain. Students should then write examples of different kinds of figurative language about the chosen topic. Assign an Encourager to keep up members' spirits, a Recorder to write down the group's sentences, and a Reader to read the examples to the class. **VISUAL/AUDITORY**

Raining cats and dogs

Identify Figurative Language

PERFORMANCE ASSESSMENT Have students find examples of figurative language in other selections they have read. Invite them to share and explain the examples they find and to restate each example in literal language. **VISUAL**

Fit as a fiddle

STUDENTS ACQUIRING ENGLISH

Choose one example of figurative language students find, and ask students to generate other sentences that could be used in the same comparison. For example, "What else can wind like a snake?"

RETEACH

See page R61 for lessons in multiple modalities.

CHALLENGE

Have students create pairs of similes, metaphors, personifications, and hyperboles. The items in a pair should show contrasting moods. Encourage students to share their examples of figurative language with classmates.

Reading Trade Books TO REINFORCE FIGURATIVE LANGUAGE

AS: A Surfeit of Similes by Norton Juster. Morrow, 1989. **EASY**

Children of Promise: African-American Literature and Art for Young People edited by Charles Sullivan. Harry N. Abrams, 1991. **CHALLENGING**

Home edited by Michael J. Rosen. HarperCollins, 1992. **AVERAGE**

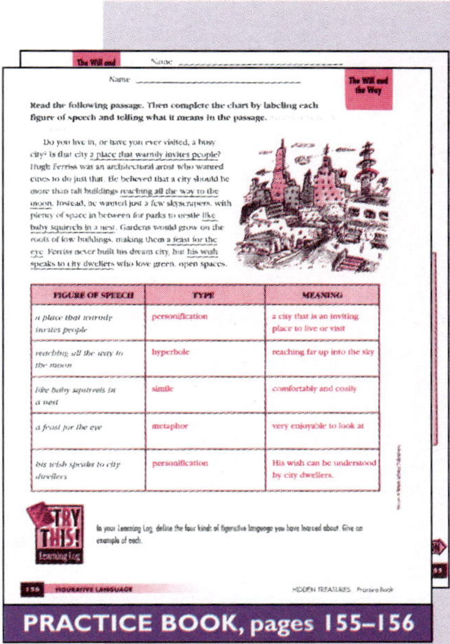

Name ____________ The Will and the Way

Read the following passage. Then complete the chart by labeling each figure of speech and telling what it means in the passage.

Do you live in, or have you ever visited, a busy city? Is that city a place that warmly invites people? Hugh Ferriss was an architectural artist who wanted cities to do just that. He believed that a city should be more than tall buildings reaching all the way to the moon. Instead, he wanted just a few skyscrapers, with plenty of space in between for parks to nestle like baby squirrels in a nest. Gardens would grow on the roofs of low buildings, making them a feast for the eye. Ferriss never built his dream city, but his wish speaks to city dwellers who love green, open spaces.

FIGURE OF SPEECH	TYPE	MEANING
a place that warmly invites people	personification	a city that is an inviting place to live or visit
reaching all the way to the moon	hyperbole	reaching far up into the sky
like baby squirrels in a nest	simile	comfortably and cozily
a feast for the eye	metaphor	very enjoyable to look at
his wish speaks to city dwellers	personification	His wish can be understood by city dwellers.

TRY THIS! Learning Log — In your Learning Log, define the four kinds of figurative language you have learned about. Give an example of each.

156 FIGURATIVE LANGUAGE HIDDEN TREASURES Practice Book

PRACTICE BOOK, pages 155–156

Integrated Curriculum

ART

The Wonderful World of Architecture

Architecture is influenced by many factors, including location, environment, purpose, and time. The activities that follow guide students in investigating architecture as a link to the past and a symbol of the present.

TIPS FOR CLASSROOM MANAGEMENT

IF students enjoy doing research, **THEN** they may want to participate in the Architecture Around the World activity.

TECHNOLOGY

THE AMAZING WRITING MACHINE Students can use the Paintbrush tool to create illustrations for their posters.

SOCIAL STUDIES/ART

Architecture Around the World

COOPERATIVE LEARNING Divide students into cooperative learning groups to research styles of architecture found in different countries or regions, such as northern Europe, Japan, or the American Southwest. Have students use encyclopedias, travel books, and books on architecture to aid in their research. You might assign roles such as Reader, Recorder, and Reporter within each group or allow students to assign their own roles. Encourage groups to create posters showing buildings typical of the region. When students present their posters to the class, they should explain the factors that influenced that particular building style, such as climate and the availability of building materials. LISTENING/SPEAKING/READING/WRITING

INTEGRATED CURRICULUM 20A

The Will and the Way

ARCHITECTURE AROUND THE WORLD

As an architect, Paul Williams had to consider location, environment, and purpose. Investigate different styles of architecture around the world.

1. Work in a small group. Assign such roles as Reader, Recorder, and Reporter.
2. Choose a country, or a region of the United States. Use reference sources, such as encyclopedias, travel books, and books on architecture, to find out what factors affect the building styles found in that area.
3. Create posters showing typical buildings of the region.
4. Present your posters to the class. Explain how factors such as climate and availability of building materials have influenced the architecture.

Harcourt Brace School Publishers

Curriculum Card 20A

ART

Architect for a Day

Remind students that architects and urban planners consider the surroundings—other buildings, natural setting, and so on—before planning new structures. Invite students to become architects for a day and design a new building to be constructed somewhere in their area, such as in a downtown shopping area, a suburban office park, or in the country. Students should illustrate their design in the setting it will have. Encourage students to display and discuss their buildings. LISTENING/SPEAKING/WRITING

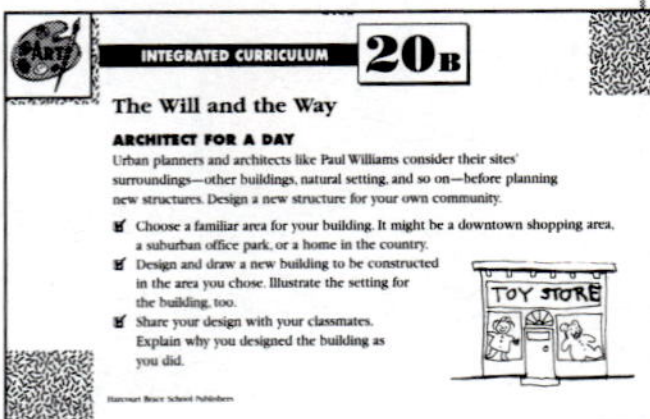

INTEGRATED CURRICULUM 20B

The Will and the Way

ARCHITECT FOR A DAY

Urban planners and architects like Paul Williams consider their sites' surroundings—other buildings, natural setting, and so on—before planning new structures. Design a new structure for your own community.

- Choose a familiar area for your building. It might be a downtown shopping area, a suburban office park, or a home in the country.
- Design and draw a new building to be constructed in the area you chose. Illustrate the setting for the building, too.
- Share your design with your classmates. Explain why you designed the building as you did.

TOY STORE

Harcourt Brace School Publishers

Curriculum Card 20B

Falling Water, by Frank Lloyd Wright, is considered a masterpiece in uniting a building to its site

SCIENCE

The Triumph of Technology

Use reference sources. Discuss with students developments that have made possible the construction of skyscrapers and other large structures such as the Gateway Arch in St. Louis, Missouri. With students, make a list of questions that stem from the discussion, such as these:

- What special equipment do construction workers use to assemble tall buildings?
- How are building materials raised to great heights?
- How does an elevator work?
- What keeps a skyscraper from falling over or collapsing under its own weight?

Encourage students to choose one or more questions and to research the answers. Students might consult encyclopedias and other reference books or interview experts, such as engineers or construction workers. Invite students to share the results of their research with classmates. LISTENING/SPEAKING/READING

Above: Empire State Building, New York City
Left: Gateway Arch, St. Louis, Missouri

Reading Trade Books

CROSS-CURRICULAR READING

Amazing Buildings by Philip Wilkinson. Dorling Kindersley, 1993. EASY

A Short Walk Around the Pyramids and Through the World of Art by Philip M. Isaacson. Knopf, 1993. CHALLENGING

MULTI-AGE CLASSROOMS

Have students with different experiences and varying skill levels work together to complete one of the activities.

Reading Trade Books

TIPS FOR CLASSROOM MANAGEMENT

INDEPENDENT READING Encourage students who want to read *The Wright Brothers* independently to keep a time line on which to record major events in the brothers' lives.

For a comprehensive lesson plan, refer to the complete lesson for *The Wright Brothers*, on pages T1062–T1067.

STUDENTS ACQUIRING ENGLISH
Suggest that students work in groups to read each chapter. Before students begin, suggest that they look up these terms in a dictionary: *flight, propellers, glider, lift, propel, control, balance,* and *angle*.

The Wright Brothers

by Russell Freedman

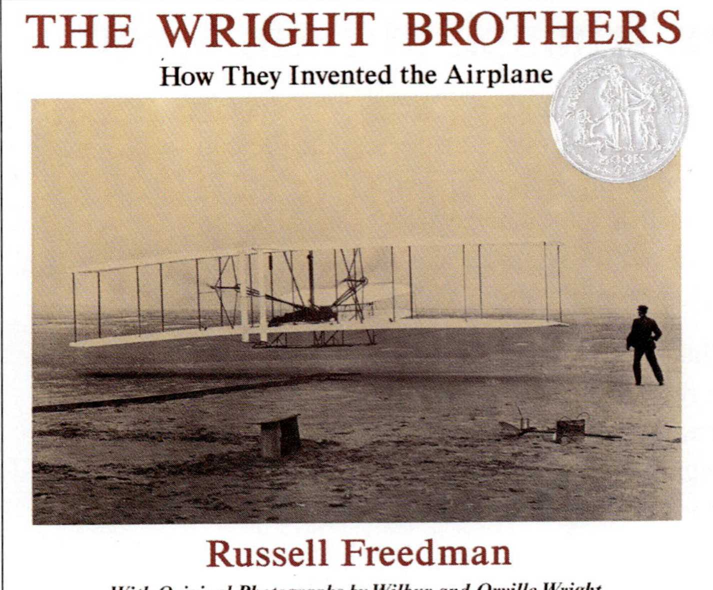

Signatures Library

READER'S CHALLENGE

You have read about the challenges that Paul R. Williams overcame to become an architect. What challenges do you think the Wright brothers faced when they tried to invent a flying machine? After you've read this biography, create a Venn diagram to compare and contrast the careers of these men.

READING STRATEGY: FIGURATIVE LANGUAGE

Before students read *The Wright Brothers*, remind them that nonfiction writers often use figurative language to create clear and vivid images. Ask students to use a three-column chart to keep track of examples of similes, metaphors, and personification in this book. Encourage readers to share examples they find, such as the following:

- **metaphor:** Imagine a locomotive without any wheels, we will say, but with white wings instead...coming right toward you with a tremendous flap of its propellers... (p. 2)
- **simile:** People often remarked that Wilbur and Orville were as inseparable as twins. (p. 3)
- **personification:** The machine refused to act like our machine last year and at times seemed to be entirely beyond control. (p. 40)

LINK TO THE THEME

After students have finished reading *The Wright Brothers*, encourage them to work in small groups to discuss the biography. Suggest these topics for discussion:

- **What is the difference between something that is very difficult and something that is impossible? Can you always tell whether or not something is possible?**
- **What different goals can motivate people to build new machines or buildings?**

Other Trade Books

Cutters, Carvers & the Cathedral

by George Ancona

This photographic essay describes a neighborhood apprenticeship program in which young people from many different backgrounds learned to carve stones to renovate a cathedral. Encourage readers to compare the work done by these apprentices with Paul R. Williams's architecture.

Julia Morgan: Architect of Dreams

by Ginger Wadsworth

After reading this biography of Morgan's remarkable accomplishments as an architect, readers might use a web or chart to compare the careers of Morgan and Williams. Encourage groups to discuss the steps each architect followed to achieve success.

Maya Lin: Architect and Artist

by Mary Malone

This biography provides an overview of Lin's career, highlighting her work as designer of the Vietnam Veterans Memorial in Washington, D.C. After reading, suggest that students imagine that Paul R. Williams and Maya Lin were able to meet. Ask students to role-play or write about this imaginary encounter.

STUDENTS ACQUIRING ENGLISH

Students at the intermediate fluency level may read *Cutters, Carvers, & the Cathedral* independently.

CHALLENGE

Have students locate a book that relates to the Masterpieces theme and to "The Will and the Way." Ask students to share what they read with the class.

Make an Art Directory

SELECTION CONNECTION

In "The Will and the Way," students learn that Paul Williams studied art as part of his training to be an architect. Ask students why they think it is important to make art opportunities available to all people, whatever their path in life.

PROJECT CHECKLIST

During this stage, students should

- ☑ volunteer as illustrators, researchers, and writers for an art directory.
- ☑ include in the directory their reviews of current arts events.
- ☑ design a map of community art opportunities and a calendar of future events.
- ☑ organize materials into an art directory.

Project Card 29 can be found as a copying master on page R78.

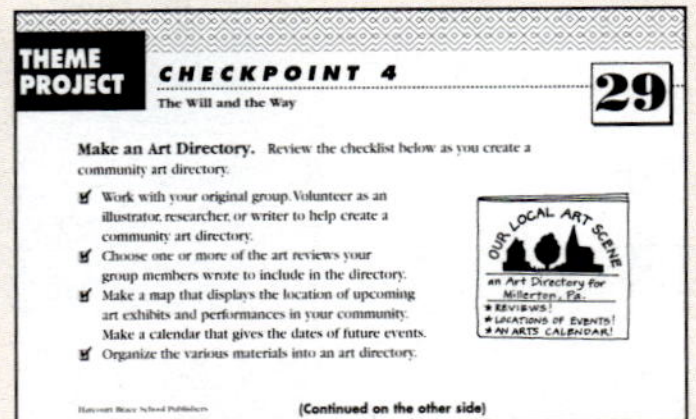

THEME PROJECT

CHECKPOINT 4

The Will and the Way

29

Make an Art Directory. Review the checklist below as you create a community art directory.

- ☑ Work with your original group. Volunteer as an illustrator, researcher, or writer to help create a community art directory.
- ☑ Choose one or more of the art reviews your group members wrote to include in the directory.
- ☑ Make a map that displays the location of upcoming art exhibits and performances in your community. Make a calendar that gives the dates of future events.
- ☑ Organize the various materials into an art directory.

(Continued on the other side)

Project Card 29

RESEARCH AND PLANNING TIPS

As students put together the directory, suggest that they

- consider the kind of information they want to include in each entry on the map and the calendar.
- look at different community maps to find the best model.
- have a computer-proficient student prepare possible layouts for the map and the calendar.
- share responsibility for the directory so that everyone has a clearly defined task.

Suggest that students write about their experience in their project journals. As a prompt, you might ask *What effect do you want your art directory to have on the community?*

STUDENTS ACQUIRING ENGLISH

If there is a significant population in your community of non-English speakers, encourage groups of students to translate the directory into other languages and distribute the directory to churches and other appropriate outlets.

TECHNOLOGY

THE AMAZING WRITING MACHINE Suggest that students use the program's drawing tools to create symbols for museums, galleries, and other exhibition spaces to display on the map and the calendar.

Informal Assessment

As students complete this checkpoint, each group will work cooperatively to **synthesize** information about community arts into the written and graphic format of a directory. Students are thinking critically if they

- ☑ are able to work cooperatively and are clear about the objectives for the directory.
- ☑ are able to distill what they have learned about art in their community into a clear and well-organized directory format.

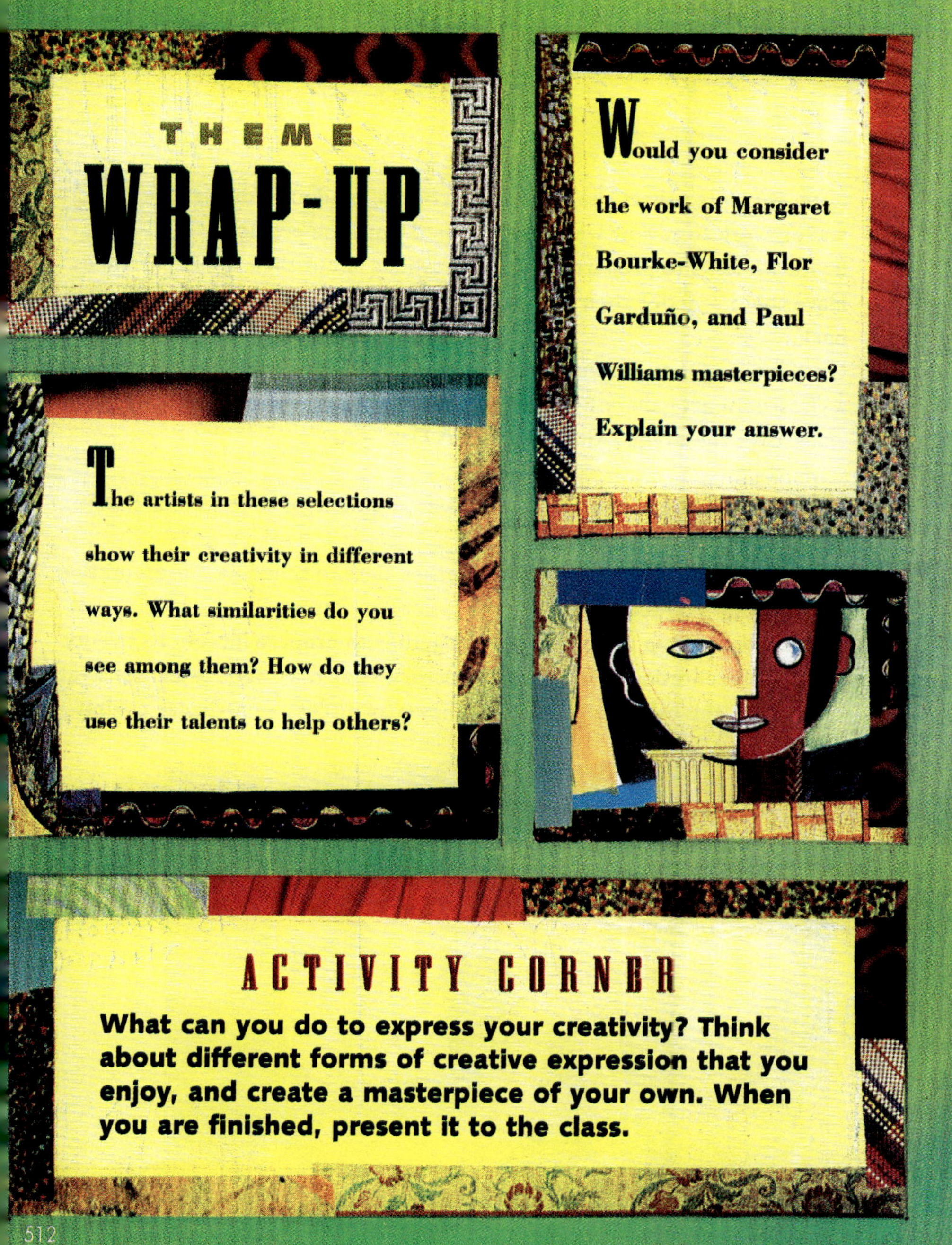

THEME 5

Wrap-Up

1. **The artists in these selections show their creativity in different ways. What similarities do you see among them? How do they use their talents to help others?** (Possible response: They are all creative, determined individuals. Their works show and help preserve the reality and dreams of the people of their time.) CRITICAL: SYNTHESIZING
2. **Would you consider the work of Margaret Bourke-White, Flor Garduño, and Paul Williams masterpieces? Explain your answer.** (Possible responses: Yes, because they make strong statements and are highly regarded by many. Only their best photographs or buildings should be considered masterpieces. No, it is too soon to regard them as masterpieces; they haven't stood the test of time.) CRITICAL: EXPRESSING PERSONAL OPINIONS

ACTIVITY CORNER Encourage students to look again at the masterpieces in this theme. Encourage them to think about how the artist used his or her medium to convey a message. Students might work in pairs or small groups to create artwork conveying the same message.

THEME PROJECT PRESENTATIONS

Options

TALK ABOUT ART

- Have students collect their notes, brochures, handouts, journals, reviews, and artwork to review what they learned from the project.
- Invite students to prepare oral presentations about their art experiences. Have them practice their presentations in their original groups for feedback.
- On the day of the presentations to the class, encourage students to create a classroom art gallery by displaying their artwork and photography on the walls. Give the event a title, such as "A Day of Art."

DIRECTORY PRESENTATION

- Have students design and create a cover and table of contents for their group's art directory.
- Encourage each group to contact another class to schedule a presentation of the group's directory and to take orders for copies.
- Suggest that group members work together to prepare fifteen- to twenty-minute presentations of their art directory. They may want to demonstrate how to use the calendar or map, or they may discuss a particular exhibit.

SCHOOL↔HOME CONNECTION

Have students plan an Art Show to celebrate the publication of their community art directory. They can plan to display their own work, the work of family members, work that is a collaboration between a student and a family member, or work lent by local artists for the occasion.

Have students prepare invitations and write a news release about the event for the school or community newspaper.

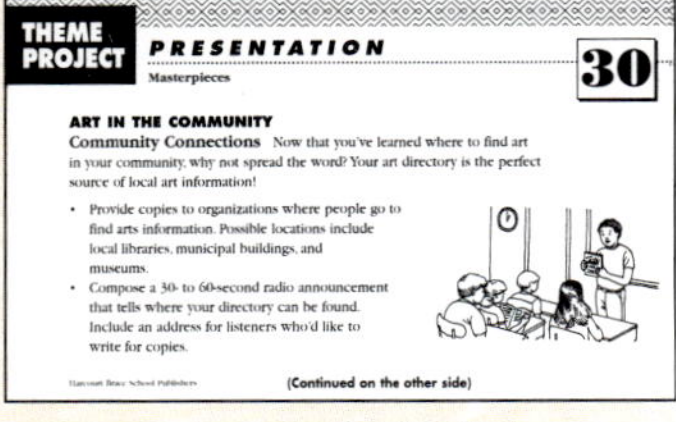

THEME PROJECT **PRESENTATION** 30

Masterpieces

ART IN THE COMMUNITY

Community Connections Now that you've learned where to find art in your community, why not spread the word? Your art directory is the perfect source of local art information!

- Provide copies to organizations where people go to find arts information. Possible locations include local libraries, municipal buildings, and museums.
- Compose a 30- to 60-second radio announcement that tells where your directory can be found. Include an address for listeners who'd like to write for copies.

Harcourt Brace School Publishers

(Continued on the other side)

Project Card 30

Project Card 30 can be found as a copying master on page R79.

Community Connections

Now that students are excited about the art opportunities that are available locally, suggest these ways to share the directories with the community:

- Ask students which populations in the community they want to target, and then determine the number of photocopies to make.
- Have students compile a mailing list of appropriate places to send the directory, such as elementary school libraries, the community library, town hall, and other municipal buildings.
- Encourage student groups to develop a thirty- to sixty-second radio or television ad to publicize the directory, and have them contact the appropriate media organizations.

THEME PROJECT ASSESSMENT

PROJECT MANAGEMENT
PROJECT SET-UP
CHECKPOINT 1
CHECKPOINT 2
CHECKPOINT 3
CHECKPOINT 4
PRESENTATIONS
ASSESSMENT

SELF-ASSESSMENT

To assess students' perception of their own performance during this project, ask them to respond to the following questions orally or in writing:

- Did you actively participate in your group? Explain.
- Did you complete your responsibilities? Describe the work you did.
- What did you learn from working on this project? How did you learn this?

Students may also complete the Self-Assessment Checklist on page T216 in the Teacher's Edition, Volume 1.

PEER ASSESSMENT

To assess their group's effectiveness in working together cooperatively during this project, ask students to respond to the following questions orally or in writing:

- Did each person in your group contribute to the theme project?
- What did you learn from other members of your group?

Students may also complete the Peer-Assessment Checklist on page T408 in the Teacher's Edition, Volume 1.

RUBRIC

Performance Goals	Observable Characteristics		
	3	2	1
LAUNCH List categories of art	• uses personal experience to contribute a number of items to the list	• uses personal experience to contribute some items to the list	• contributes few or no items to the list
CHECKPOINT 1 Research and attend art events	• locates information about a number of upcoming community art events • works cooperatively to enable group members to attend art events	• locates information about one or two upcoming community art events • finds a way to attend an art event but does not help with group's arrangements	• does not locate information about upcoming art events • takes no interest in attending art events
CHECKPOINT 2 Write reviews of art experiences	• develops thoughtful evaluation and supports it with details	• develops some standards for evaluation and offers some supporting details	• develops no standards for evaluation and gives unsupported opinions
CHECKPOINT 3 Produce a work of art	• imaginatively solves technical problems during execution of artwork	• needs help to solve technical problems during execution of artwork	• cannot solve technical problems and does not bother to seek help
CHECKPOINT 4 Create a community art directory	• cooperates with and helps lead group effort • offers much information	• cooperates with group effort but does not lead • offers some information	• shows no interest in group effort • offers no information
PRESENTATIONS Overall project	• creative and well organized • strongly focused and cooperative	• somewhat creative and reasonably organized • somewhat focused and reasonably cooperative	• fails to show creativity and may be disorganized • unfocused and uncooperative

Reading Trade Books
Signatures Library

Journal of a Teenage Genius

by Helen V. Griffith

THEME: CREATIVITY

Masterpieces

This novel takes a tongue-in-cheek look at how a young genius struggles to express his talents. Through the humor, readers come to understand that the challenges an artist and a scientist face are similar: they share the goal of self-expression. Zack's adventures also highlight the way that one change can quickly lead to another.

SUMMARY Genre: Fantasy

This humorous journal describes three months in the life of self-confessed genius, Zack. His wild experiments always have unpredictable results. He changes his family's poodle, Toodles, into a young boy and causes a pet mouse to shrink.

Zack's spirits soar when he meets Loretta. Not only does she believe in him—she also has a time machine in her basement! He finally gets permission to use the time machine when he helps Loretta's grandfather fix another odd contraption.

Unfortunately, Zack travels back only one year instead of one hundred years. To make matters worse, he brings Toodles back with him. In the end, Toodles is a dog again, and Zack discovers that the odd contraption is a spaceship in which Loretta's grandfather will return home—to the planet Qerbik.

ABOUT THE AUTHOR

Helen V. Griffith has written many books for young readers, including *Alex Remembers, Grandaddy's Place,* and *Georgia Music,* which was an ALA Notable Book. *Alex and the Cat* was chosen as an *SLJ* Best Book in 1982. Griffith began writing as a child some "funny sketches which still make me laugh—interviews with our dog, Wooly, about current events and little skits about school life that were very unflattering (and unfair) to our teachers."

Building Background and Concepts

PRIOR KNOWLEDGE

Scientific Vocabulary Have students imagine that they are in a science lab. Use a chart to help them brainstorm words that might be used to describe the events that take place in a lab.

- Nouns can include any items or people they might see there.
- Verbs can include any actions that might take place there.
- Adjectives might describe a lab item or action.

Developing Concept Vocabulary

Help students develop concepts by connecting the following words to the theme. Students can create word webs for each word which include the part of speech, a definition, an example sentence, and related words.

formula consequences chemistry dosage experiment

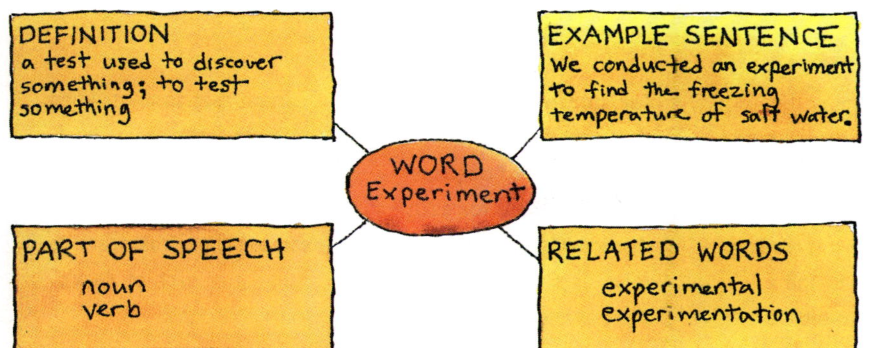

STUDENTS ACQUIRING ENGLISH

Suggest that students use photographs in a science textbook or magazine to help them remember content vocabulary. Have partners try to use content vocabulary as they describe photographs to each other.

Clipped words

Integrated Spelling Lesson 29

OTHER VOCABULARY IDEAS

WORD TREE

Suggest that students choose an important theme or concept word and begin a word tree. For example, write *genius* in the trunk of the tree and have students build branches and leaves with related words.

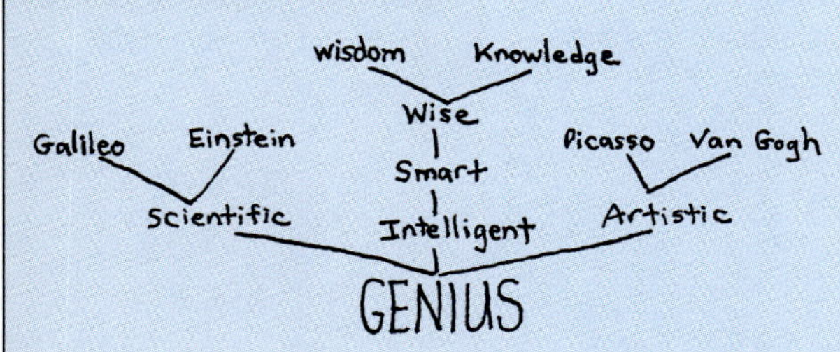

GLOSSARY

Have students put together a glossary of terms that might be included at the end of this book. Students might collect terms in their journals or on bookmarks as they read. After reading, groups can collect words and write definitions for each.

paraphernalia: stuff
potential: possible
rudimentary: basic, simple

OPTIONS FOR

FLEXIBLE GROUPING

	SMALL GROUPS	WHOLE CLASS	INDEPENDENT
PREVIEW AND PREDICT	Have students read aloud the first journal entry and then **quickwrite predictions** by completing these sentence starters: • I think that Zack will . . . • By the end of the book, Zack will learn that . . . Students can use Reader Response Card 9, Literature Circle, to help them conduct group discussions. QUICKWRITE	Have students **make a list** of people they think are geniuses. Then have them make a second list that identifies traits or characteristics that these people share.	 Suggest that students use their personal journals to record **three focus questions** that they hope will be answered as they read the book.
PAGES 1-34	Groups can discuss the tone of the journal by reading aloud several entries. Encourage them to experiment with different reading styles. When they find a style that suits the tone, they might make an **audio recording**. 	Ask students to create a **character chart** in which they can record descriptions and details for each character in the book. Allow volunteers to add to the chart as they read. (Description: Zack, Loretta, Toodles, Maynard, Mrs. Bringhurst)	Suggest that students keep track of story events by drawing a **calendar** for August and September. They can use these calendars to summarize each of Zack's journal entries. 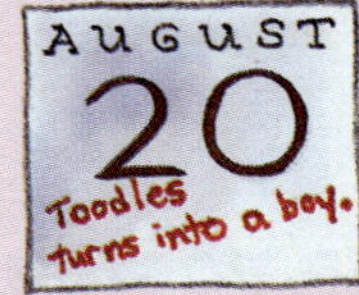
PAGES 35-54	Students can prepare a **lab report** that shows the hypothesis, steps, and results of Zack's Growth Encourager experiment. 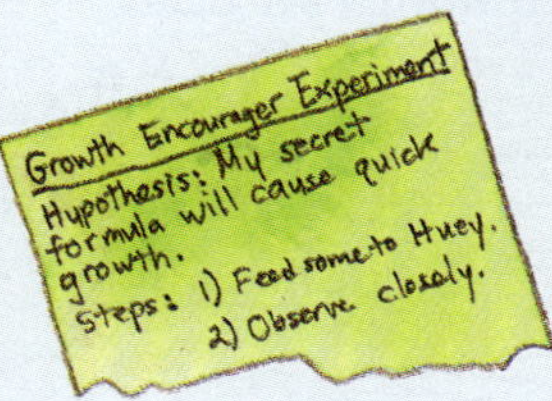	Ask the class to work together to create a **chain of events chart** for this section. Encourage them to identify the main events and then place them in chronological order.	Readers can draw a **sketch** showing the time machine in Loretta's basement. Encourage them to add captions that describe what has happened or what might happen next. 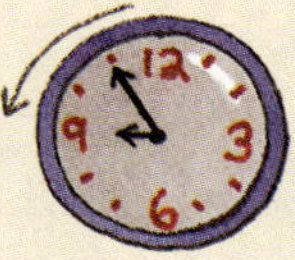

TIPS FOR CLASSROOM MANAGEMENT

IF students are reading at various levels, **THEN** you may want to begin with whole-class activities and then organize students of different abilities into small groups.

IF some students are visual or physical learners, **THEN** you may want to have them work in small groups to act out each major episode after they have read about it.

READING

FLEXIBLE GROUPING

	SMALL GROUPS	WHOLE CLASS	INDEPENDENT
PAGES 55-77	Suggest that students **role-play** the events Zack describes on September 25 and September 27. Encourage them to switch roles as they begin to dramatize the second day's events.	Have students complete a **web** to analyze how the author presents each character's personality. Begin by having volunteers create a web for Zack; then follow-up with other major characters. His Words / His Actions / ZACK / What Other Characters Say About Him	PERSONAL JOURNAL Readers can **make generalizations** about Zack's talents and personality in their journals. Encourage them to answer these questions: • Do you think Zack is really a genius? • How would you describe Zack to someone who has never read this book?
PAGES 78-98	Zack is a multi-dimensional character. Some of his traits are exact opposites. Encourage students to think of different ways to **complete this sentence:** • Zack is very _____, but can also be very _____.	Students can work together to create a **rating scale** to discuss the elements of fantasy in this novel. totally realistic — totally fantastic Ask volunteers to describe events from the novel and place them on the scale.	If students recorded focus questions in their journals, suggest that they **look back** to see if they can answer each question. If they can, encourage students to write new questions that could be answered in the final section of the book. ???
PAGES 99-121	Have students **check their predictions**. Encourage them to order their original predictions from least to most accurate. Students can use Reader Response Card 9, Literature Circle, to help them conduct group discussions.	Have students identify the climax and resolution of the novel in a **story map**. Volunteers might suggest alternative endings that describe other possible resolutions. Climax → Resolution	Have students **find three quotations** from the book that they think reflect the style and feeling of the book. After students write their quotations, encourage them to share their choices with the class.
PERSONAL RESPONSE	**• Would you like to read another book by Helen Griffith?** **• Do you think these characters could be used in a television program? Explain your opinion.**		

RESPONSE

Celebrating *Journal of a Teenage Genius*

THIS TIME

DRAMATIC PLAY Have students work together to write a time travel story. They might begin their story by having a character discover Loretta's time machine in the basement. Suggest that teams work together to research the year to which their character or characters will travel. After sharing their research, students use improvisation to help them think of events for their story.

Suggest that students write a first draft of their play and then revise it by reading it aloud and listening for parts that need reworking. Allow teams to present their work for the class as a dramatic reading or staged production.

READING/WRITING/SPEAKING

Name That Band

BRAINSTORMING AND POLLING Zack comes up with the name Rock Chompers for Maynard's band. Students might enjoy brainstorming a list of names for a new band. After creating a list of several choices, have students design and conduct a poll to determine which name is most popular. Encourage students to create a graph showing the poll results. Some students might try to form their own band as well.

WRITING/LISTENING/SPEAKING

OUT OF CONTEXT

VOCABULARY: CONTEXT CLUES Students can make word puzzles for each other to solve by following these steps.

- Find an unusual or difficult word in the novel.
- Write the sentence it is in on an index card. Leave a blank in place of the word.
- Have other students guess what the word is. Encourage them to use context clues to guess what part of speech is missing and what the meaning of the word is.

Students can write their guesses on the back of each card. Then they should return the cards to their creators and have them announce the actual word and its definition. Suggest that they circle any correct guesses. READING

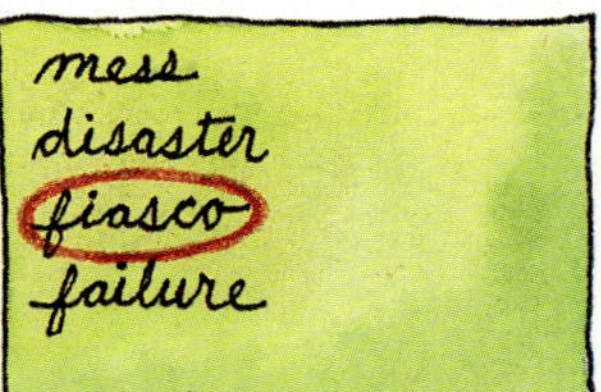

ACTIVITIES

Not the Normal Form

FICTION *Journal of a Teenage Genius* tells a story by using a series of fictional journal entries. Suggest that students write a story by creating another series of fictional documents. For example, they might write a story made up of fictional

- phone messages on answering machines.
- pages from a date book.
- letters and postcards.
- newspaper or magazine articles.

Students can study real models to get an idea of format and content. Then encourage them to think about the fictional character who is creating each item. Students can collect their stories and create a class book. **READING/WRITING**

More to Explore

SCIENCE Encourage students to design and conduct their own experiments about science topics of interest. Before they begin, review basic safety procedures, reminding students not to use any products or chemicals that are poisonous or hazardous. Encourage them to follow experiments described in nonfiction science books for young readers. Have students keep a moment-by-moment journal of the experiment, using Zack's entries as models. **READING/WRITING/VIEWING**

Three Times

SCHOOL-HOME CONNECTION Zack often writes more than one journal entry a day. Encourage students to try writing three journal entries in one evening. In each entry, they might write about the same topic, but tell how their perspective has changed since the last entry. Students might repeat the experiment by writing at five different times on a Saturday. In class, have students reflect on their writing and discuss how their ideas changed over time. **WRITING**

5:30 PM Tomorrow is going to be great. I can't wait to give my book report.
7:30 PM Uh oh. I dripped glue all over my book report poster. It's going to be a disaster.
9:30 PM The glue dried clear. It actually makes a nice shiny effect. I guess tomorrow might be OK after all.

Reading Trade Books Signatures Library

The Wright Brothers

by Russell Freedman

THEME: CREATIVITY

Masterpieces

The airplane is a masterpiece of engineering that reflects the problem-solving abilities of the Wright brothers. Their dedication and persistence eventually paid off as they achieved a goal that many people thought was impossible. Their invention changed the world of transportation forever, bringing people from around the globe closer together.

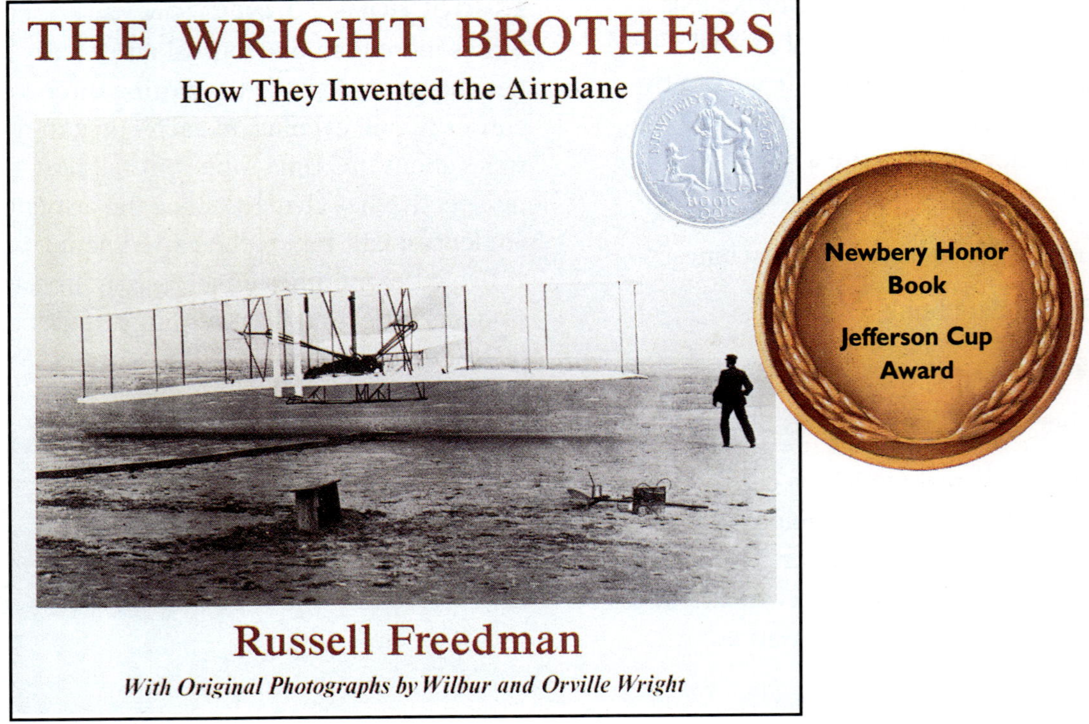

Newbery Honor Book

Jefferson Cup Award

SUMMARY Genre: Photobiography

This vivid biography uses photographs by the Wright brothers themselves to bring to life the story of the creation of the airplane. Freedman's text describes how two self-taught bicycle mechanics invented a machine that could fly.

The Wright brothers grew up together in Dayton, Ohio. Although very close, they had very different personalities. Orville was very neat and enthusiastic; Wilbur was calm and more private. Freedman describes how the Wright brothers succeeded in solving the problems of flight by breaking the problem into steps and solving them one at a time. New ideas, such as the flexible wing, help them in flying a plane at Kitty Hawk in 1903. Wilbur died of typhoid fever in 1912. Orville lived until 1948, long enough to see airplanes transform the world.

ABOUT THE AUTHOR

Russell Freedman has written many celebrated nonfiction works for young readers. Since writing his first book, *Teenagers Who Made History*, he has written many fascinating biographies, often including well-selected historical photographs. *Lincoln: A Photobiography* was the first nonfiction book to win the Newbery Medal. He has also written biographies of Franklin and Eleanor Roosevelt. He says that "one of the great joys of writing nonfiction for youngsters is the opportunity to explore almost any subject that excites your interest."

Building Background and Concepts

PRIOR KNOWLEDGE

DISCUSSING AIRPLANES Have students use a web to collect ideas and facts that they already know about airplanes. Encourage volunteers to add words to each section of the web and define any words that are unfamiliar to classmates.

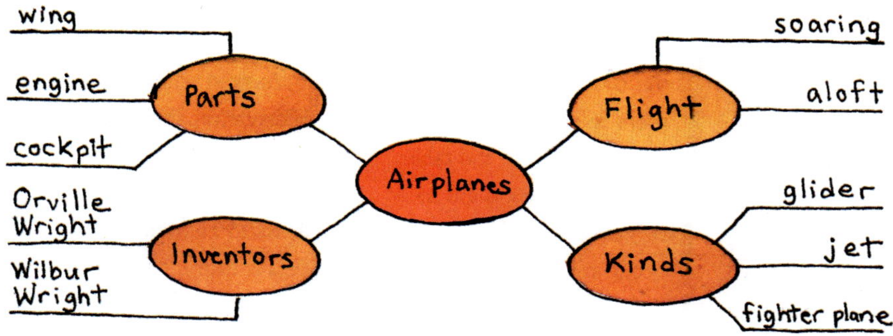

Developing Concept Vocabulary

Point out that every artist or inventor uses a special vocabulary to describe his or her work. Have students begin to create their own glossary of flight terms by looking up these five words:

aeronautics
aircraft
airfoil
equilibrium
glider

To create their glossary, students can write each word on an index card and then add a definition, example sentence, and illustration if helpful. Students can then arrange the terms in alphabetical order. Encourage them to add new words to their file cards as they read *The Wright Brothers.*

STUDENTS ACQUIRING ENGLISH

Encourage students to create sketches to illustrate each new term. Photographs and diagrams from the biography can also be used to identify specific airplane parts. Suggest that partners read aloud sentences from the book that contain technical terms.

SPELLING GENERALIZATION

Clipped words
Integrated Spelling Lesson 29

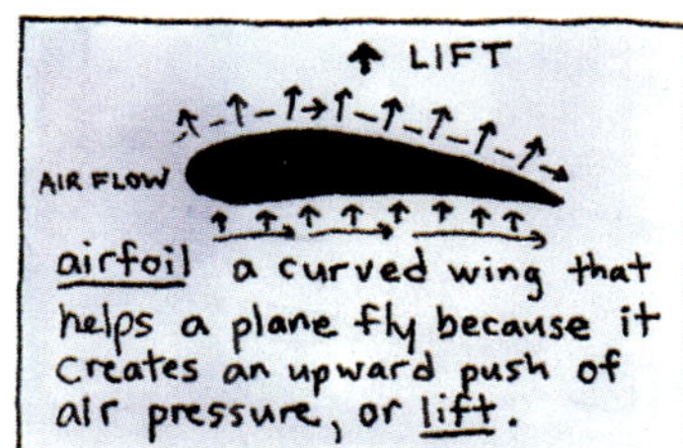

OTHER VOCABULARY IDEAS

ADJECTIVE ANALYSIS

Have students begin to use specific adjectives to describe the photographs in this book by asking them to look at the cover and write a list of adjectives that describe the photo or its subject. Allow students to compare lists.

barren fragile delicate
windy vast

WORD MOBILE

Have students create a mobile showing interesting words from *The Wright Brothers.* Suggest that students select specific nouns, sketch the objects on cardboard and cut them out, writing the word inside. Then use thread to hang each word from a support such as a cut-out airplane. Definitions might also be included.

OPTIONS FOR

FLEXIBLE GROUPING

	SMALL GROUPS	WHOLE CLASS	INDEPENDENT
PREVIEW AND PREDICT	Have students complete the first two columns of a **K-W-L chart** about the Wright brothers. Encourage them to underline any ideas that they think might be inaccurate or incomplete.	**Preview the book** with the class by asking volunteers to read the chapter titles aloud from the table of contents. Ask them to suggest events that might occur in each chapter.	Suggest that readers create a **chart** in which to collect information about the Wright brothers and early airplanes. Encourage students to add one or two details to the chart after reading each chapter.   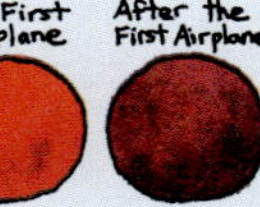
CHAPTERS 1-2	Suggest that groups work together to create a **comic strip** showing events described in this section. Encourage team members to share tasks such as illustrating, drawing, and lettering.	Have the class create a **Venn diagram** to compare and contrast Orville and Wilbur Wright. Remind them to write qualities that the brothers shared in the overlapping region.  	Would you rather meet Orville or Wilbur Wright? Ask readers to **quickwrite** their response, explaining the reasons for their choice. 
CHAPTERS 3-4	Students can work together to create **how-to plans** for building a model airplane based on photographs in this book. Encourage group members to work together to analyze information in each photo and then write step-by-step instructions including materials to be used. 	Develop **critical thinking** skills by focusing class discussion on these questions: • What qualities does an inventor need to be successful? • In 1901, Wilbur predicted that "man would sometime fly" but that it would not be in his lifetime. Why do you think he made this prediction? 	Suggest that students imagine they are one of the Wright brothers and create a **journal entry** for one of the flight experiments described in this section. 

TIPS FOR CLASSROOM MANAGEMENT

IF some students are ready to read independently, **THEN** have them join whole class activities and then work on their own to complete independent assignments.

IF some students have experience with building or flying model planes, **THEN** encourage them to work as peer tutors to help others complete individual and small group activities that promote an understanding of flight.

READING

FLEXIBLE GROUPING

	SMALL GROUPS	WHOLE CLASS	INDEPENDENT
CHAPTERS 5-6	Have students work together to create a **radio broadcast** that might have been broadcast from Kitty Hawk on December 17, 1903. If possible, students can tape-record the broadcast and play it for the class.	Have students create a **time line** showing the events described in this section that led up to the famous flight at Kitty Hawk. Time lines should begin in 1901. Orville and Wilbur test new wing designs. 1901	Encourage readers to **list the obstacles** that the Wright brothers overcame as they invented the first airplane.
CHAPTERS 7-8	Have students reread this section, looking for **first-person quotations.** Ask students to read each quotation aloud and think about why Freedman chose to include this person's exact words.	Ask the class to **analyze the photographs** in this section. Discuss: • who took each photo • what the photo details communicate • what information you can't get from the photo alone • why Freedman selected each photo	PERSONAL JOURNAL Suggest that readers use their **personal journals** to describe what surprised them most about the Wright brothers' lives after their first successful flight.
CHAPTERS 9-10	If students created a K-W-L chart, encourage them to **complete their charts** using facts and ideas from their reading. Students can use Reader Response Card 13, Grand Conversation, to help them conduct group discussions.	Have students discuss these **end-of-book features:** • About the Photographs • Places to Visit • For Further Reading • Index Ask them to describe the type of information found in each feature, and to say which one they think is most helpful.	Readers can create **advertisements** for the Wright brothers' early airplanes. Encourage them to include factual details from their reading in each ad. Fly higher in a WRIGHT FLYER

PERSONAL RESPONSE 

- **Do you think that photobiographies are better sources of information than biographies with only a few photographs? Why or why not?**
- **If you met Russell Freedman, what would you like to say to him about this book?**

End-of-Theme Assessment Tools

IF you want to measure a student's mastery of reading and language skills and strategies, **THEN** administer the multiple-choice diagnostic **Skills Assessment.**	**IF** you want information about a student's ability to apply thinking skills in a global and holistic manner, **THEN** administer the **Holistic Reading Assessment.**	**IF** you want a comprehensive view of a student's reading and writing development skills, **THEN** administer the **Integrated Performance Assessment.**

Name ______________________ Date ______________

Teacher ______________________ School ______________

I like these things about my writing.
I can improve my writing by
I (do, do not) like writing when
I get most of my ideas for writing from
I think other people (like, dislike) my writing because
I'd like to write more about

This is what I will be looking for in my writing:

Thinking About My Writing Checklist

Theme 6

Confronting Nature

NATURE

Nature is beautiful and terrifying by turns. In this theme, nature poses obstacles for various individuals who confront the elements in order to survive.

Theme Overview

Confronting Nature

Nature

The forces of nature are uncontrollable. But some courageous individuals choose to confront nature and survive in spite of it. The selections in this theme will show students the power of nature and the courage of those who successfully withstand its challenges.

FREEDOM RIDE

By Liz Fordred with Susie Blackmun

Freedom Ride by Liz Fordred with Susie Blackmun T1085–T1126
"The wind and seas kicked up. The self-steering vane invariably quit, so we had to steer by hand, and the motion was so bad that we couldn't sleep."

Students will learn the true story of a husband and wife, paraplegics, who overcame physical and emotional obstacles not only to build a boat but also to sail it across the Atlantic Ocean.

Until I Saw the Sea by Lilian Moore T1106–T1107
The poet is amazed by the effects of nature on the sea.

Flexible Grouping

FREEDOM RIDE T1085–T1126

	BELOW-LEVEL READERS	ABOVE-LEVEL READERS	ESL	BILINGUAL
1 READING AND RESPONDING Build Concepts and Vocabulary Strategic Reading Response Corner	**INSTEAD OF** having students read the selection with the whole class, use the Guiding the Reading page of the *Intervention Strategies Manual* (p. 124). **TEACHER-LED GROUP** **BEFORE** students read the selection, have them write story predictions in their personal journals. (p.T1090) **INDEPENDENT**	**INSTEAD OF** the Vocabulary Strategies activities, students who know the Key Words may do the *Practice Book* (p. 159). **AFTER** the Have a Discussion activity, challenge students to interview a participant in the discussion and then present the interview in a talk-show format. (p.T1109) **COOPERATIVE GROUPS**	**BEFORE** students read the selection, use the Introducing the Literature pages of the *Sheltered English/ESL Manual* (pp. 82–84). **TEACHER-LED GROUP** **WHILE** students read the selection, guide them by using the Students Acquiring English notes. (pp.T1088–T1111) **TEACHER-LED GROUP**	**WHILE** others read the selection in the anthology, students may read the translation in the appropriate *Anthology Translation Booklet.* **INDEPENDENT** **WHILE** others complete the Vocabulary Strategies, Spanish-speaking students may read a play from *Acto final* in CIELO ABIERTO. Have Vietnamese students read *The Call of the Wild* from the *Multi-Language Library.* **INDEPENDENT**
2 INTEGRATING LANGUAGE ARTS Idea Bank Writer's Workshop Grammar Spelling Vocabulary Workshop	**WHILE** others work on Idea Bank activities, pull out needs-based groups for a review of reading maps. (p.T1112) **TEACHER-LED GROUP** **AFTER** the Grammar lesson, model and guide completion of the *Practice Book* (p. 161). **TEACHER-LED GROUP**	**DURING** the Integrating the Language Arts section, have students complete the *Writer's Magazine* (pp. 82-83). **INDEPENDENT/PAIRS** **AFTER** the Writer's Workshop, students may use the Spin mode of *The Amazing Writing Machine* to enter their news stories. (p.T1114) **PAIRS**	**WHILE** others are completing Idea Bank activities, have students create a portfolio entry by answering the Self-Assessment questions. (p.T1115) **COOPERATIVE GROUPS** **DURING** the Write a Journal Entry activity, students may use the Journal feature of *The Amazing Writing Machine.* (p.T1117) **PAIRS**	**INSTEAD OF** the Idea Bank, use one of the Responding to the Script activities in the *Acto final Teacher's Guide.* **TEACHER-LED GROUP**
3 LEARNING THROUGH THE LITERATURE Direct Skills Instruction Integrated Curriculum Reading Trade Books Theme Project	**AFTER** the Phonics lesson in the *Intervention Strategies Manual*, students may complete the reproducible Phonics page (p. 127). **INDEPENDENT** **INSTEAD OF** *Life in the Oceans,* have students read the Take-Home book *A Vacation to Remember.* **INDEPENDENT**	**AFTER** the skills lessons, students may complete the *Practice Book* (pp. 164-165). **INDEPENDENT** **WHILE** others are in groups, have students read *Life in the Oceans* from the *Signatures Library.* **INDEPENDENT**	**WHILE** others read trade books, students can use *Imagination Express, Destination: Ocean* to learn more about marine life. (p.T1122) **COOPERATIVE GROUPS** **WHILE** others are working in groups, have students read *Sailing with the Wind* from the *ESL/Title I Library.* Beginning-level ESL students should read along with the cassette tape. **INDEPENDENT/PAIRS**	**WHILE** others are working in groups, have students choose and read a book from the *Multi-Language Library.* **INDEPENDENT**

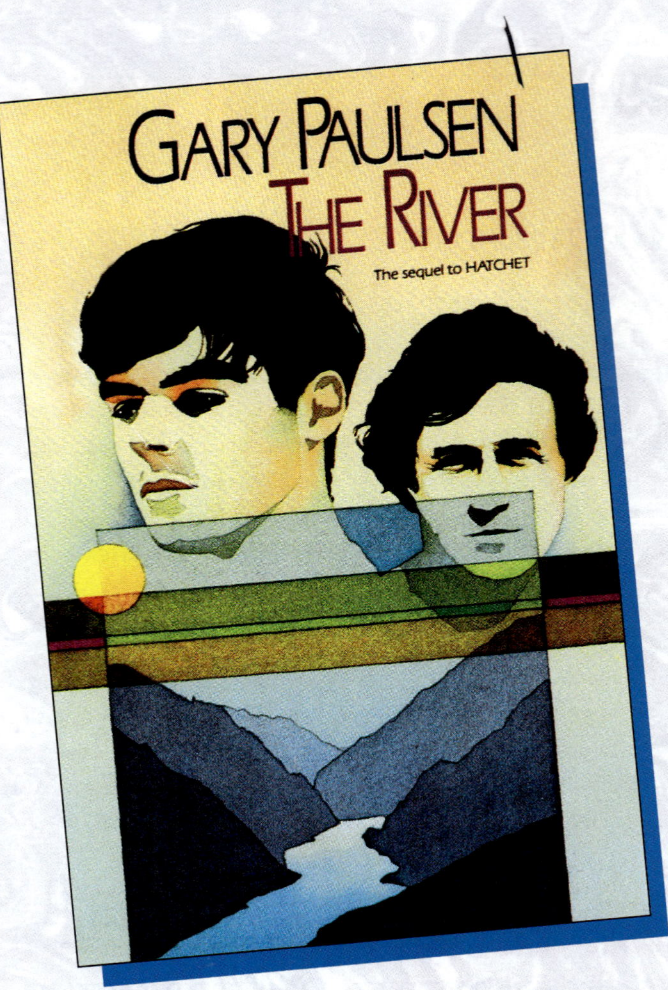

The River by Gary Paulsen T1127–T1172

"The raft bucked and tore at the water, slammed sideways. Brian tried to steer, using the paddle to swing the stern to the left and right, trying to avoid the boulders, but it was no use. The water owned the raft, owned Derek, owned him."

A teenage boy struggles to guide a raft along a treacherous river in order to save the life of a friend onboard.

ART AND LITERATURE: ***The Gulf Stream*** by Winslow Homer T1173–T1174

This dramatic painting captures a confrontation with nature.

Flexible Grouping

THE RIVER T1127–T1172

	BELOW-LEVEL READERS	ABOVE-LEVEL READERS	ESL	BILINGUAL
1 READING AND RESPONDING Build Concepts and Vocabulary Strategic Reading Response Corner	**DURING** the Vocabulary Strategies lesson, model and guide completion of the *Practice Book* (p. 167). **TEACHER-LED GROUP** **WHILE** others are reading the selection, use the Guiding the Reading page of the *Intervention Strategies Manual* (p. 130). **TEACHER-LED GROUP**	**INSTEAD OF** the Vocabulary Strategies activities, students who know the Key Words may do the *Practice Book* (p. 167). **INDEPENDENT** **AFTER** students have read the selection, have them make a list of other challenges a hero might face and then write a scene about one of them. (p.T1151) **INDEPENDENT**	**BEFORE** students read the selection, use the Introducing the Literature pages of the *Sheltered English/ESL Manual* (pp. 86–88). **TEACHER-LED GROUP** **WHILE** reading the selection, students may listen to Literature Cassette 3. **COOPERATIVE GROUPS**	**WHILE** others read the selection in the anthology, students may read the translation in the appropriate *Anthology Translation Booklet.* **INDEPENDENT** **INSTEAD OF** completing the Strategic Reading, Spanish-speaking students may read poems from *Ríos de lava* in CIELO ABIERTO. Have Chinese students read *Tiger Nanny* from the *Multi-Language Library.* **INDEPENDENT**
2 INTEGRATING LANGUAGE ARTS Idea Bank Writer's Workshop Grammar Spelling Vocabulary Workshop	**DURING** the Oral Language activity, encourage some students to write reviews focusing on the author's style, and others to focus on story events. (p.T1159) **INDEPENDENT** **DURING** the Writer's Workshop activities, review the *Language Handbook* (pp. 42-43). **TEACHER-LED GROUP**	**INSTEAD OF** the Real-Life Resources, have students complete the *Writer's Magazine* (pp. 84-85). **INDEPENDENT** **WHILE** others are completing Idea Bank activities, have students create a portfolio entry by answering the Self-Assessment questions about their adventure stories. (p.T1161) **COOPERATIVE GROUPS**	**BEFORE** the Writer's Workshop, use the Responding to the Literature page of the *Sheltered English/ESL Manual* (p. 89). **COOPERATIVE GROUPS** **DURING** the Retelling activity, have students tell the sequence of events in their first language before they develop their maps. (p.T1159) **TEACHER-LED GROUP**	**WHILE** other students complete the Writer's Workshop, use the writing activity in the Activities for Responding to the Poem in the *Ríos de lava Teacher's Guide.* **PAIRS** **INSTEAD OF** using the Grammar activities, use one of the Activities for Responding to the Poem in the *Ríos de lava Teacher's Guide.* **INDEPENDENT/PAIRS**
3 LEARNING THROUGH THE LITERATURE Direct Skills Instruction Integrated Curriculum Reading Trade Books Theme Project	**WHILE** others work in groups, have students read the Take-Home book *Jordan Waiting.* **INDEPENDENT** **WHILE** others work in groups, use the Phonics lesson in the *Intervention Strategies Manual* (p. 132). **TEACHER-LED GROUP**	**WHILE** others are working on the Theme Project, students can use the Fact Book option of *Imagination Express, Destination: Time Trip, USA* to find information for their time lines. (p.T1168) **COOPERATIVE GROUP** **WHILE** others are in groups, have students read a trade book such as *Swift Rivers.* **INDEPENDENT**	**AFTER** the skills lessons, model and guide completion of the *Practice Book* (p. 171). **TEACHER-LED GROUP** **WHILE** other groups are working in centers, have students read the Take-Home book *Jordan Waiting.* **INDEPENDENT/PAIRS**	**WHILE** others are working in groups, have students choose and read a book from the *Multi-Language Library.* **INDEPENDENT** **WHILE** others are working in groups, complete the Minilesson for Summarizing, pages 30–31, in the CIELO ABIERTO *Teacher's Handbook.* **TEACHER-LED GROUP**

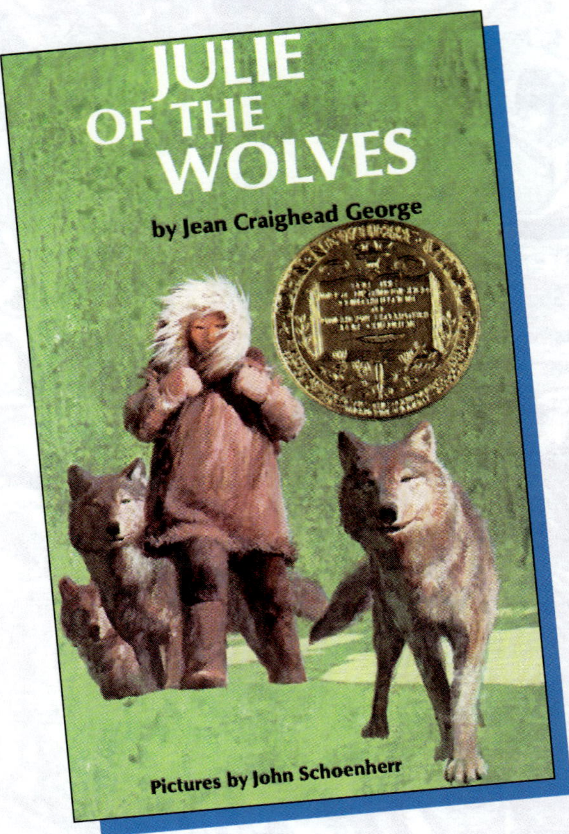

Julie of the Wolves by Jean Craighead George T1175–T1212

"Any fear Miyax had of the wolves was dispelled by their affection for each other. They were friendly animals and so devoted to Amaroq that she needed only to be accepted by him to be accepted by all. She even knew how to achieve this—bite him under the chin. But how was she going to do that?"

Students will learn how a thirteen-year-old Eskimo girl uses her wits and instincts to survive hunger and danger in the Alaskan wilderness.

Flexible Grouping

JULIE OF THE WOLVES T1175–T1212

	BELOW-LEVEL READERS	ABOVE-LEVEL READERS	ESL	BILINGUAL
1 READING AND RESPONDING Build Concepts and Vocabulary Strategic Reading Response Corner	**BEFORE** students read the selection, use the Previewing the Literature pages of the *Intervention Strategies Manual* (pp. 134-135). **TEACHER-LED GROUP** **AFTER** the Vocabulary Strategies activities, model and guide completion of the *Practice Book* (p. 173). **TEACHER-LED GROUP**	**WHILE** students read the selection, have them form groups to use Reader Response Card 2. (p.T1180) **COOPERATIVE GROUPS** **AFTER** students read the selection, use the response activities (pp.T1194-T1195). **COOPERATIVE GROUPS**	**BEFORE** students read the selection, use the Introducing the Literature pages of the *Sheltered English/ESL Manual* (pp. 90–92). **TEACHER-LED GROUP** **WHILE** students read the selection, guide them by using the Students Acquiring English notes. (pp.T1178–T1197) **TEACHER-LED GROUP**	**WHILE** others are reading the selection in the anthology, students may read the translation in the appropriate *Anthology Translation Booklet.* **INDEPENDENT** **WHILE** others complete the Vocabulary Strategies, Spanish-speaking students may read *Aydin* in CIELO ABIERTO and listen to the selection on the *Student Literature Cassette.* **COOPERATIVE GROUPS**
2 INTEGRATING LANGUAGE ARTS Idea Bank Writer's Workshop Grammar Spelling Vocabulary Workshop	**WHILE** others are completing Idea Bank activities, have students create a portfolio entry by answering the Self-Assessment questions. (p.T1201) **COOPERATIVE GROUPS** **AFTER** the Grammar lesson, use the Reteach lesson on p. R108. (p.T1203) **TEACHER-LED GROUP**	**DURING** the Integrating Language Arts section, have students complete the *Writer's Magazine* (pp. 88-91). **INDEPENDENT/PAIRS** **AFTER** the Grammar lesson, have students complete the *Practice Book* (p. 175). **INDEPENDENT**	**BEFORE** the Writer's Workshop, use the Responding to the Literature page of the *Sheltered English/ESL Manual* (p. 93). **TEACHER-LED GROUP** **DURING** the Grammar lesson, pull out needs-based groups for a review of prepositions. (p.T1203) **TEACHER-LED GROUP**	**WHILE** other students complete the Writer's Workshop, use CIELO ABIERTO *Teacher's Handbook* page 55 to have students write an explanatory paragraph. **INDEPENDENT** **INSTEAD OF** having students complete the Spelling lesson, refer to page 51 in the CIELO ABIERTO *Teacher's Handbook.* **TEACHER-LED GROUP**
3 LEARNING THROUGH THE LITERATURE Direct Skills Instruction Integrated Curriculum Reading Trade Books Theme Project	**AFTER** the skills lessons, model and guide completion of the *Practice Book* (pp. 177-178). **TEACHER-LED GROUP** **WHILE** others are working in groups, have students read the Take-Home Book. **INDEPENDENT**	**WHILE** others are working on the Theme Project, have students retell a story event from their reading using all three points of view. (p.T1207) **COOPERATIVE GROUPS** **WHILE** others are working in groups, have students choose and read a trade book such as *Lost in the Barrens.* **INDEPENDENT**	**DURING** the skills lessons, have students use their first language to describe a scene by using each point of view. (p.T1207) **COOPERATIVE GROUPS** **WHILE** others are working in groups, have students read the Take-Home book *The Intruder.* **INDEPENDENT/PAIRS**	**WHILE** others are working in groups, have students choose and read a book from the *Multi-Language Library.* **INDEPENDENT** **WHILE** others are working in groups, have students complete the ongoing cross-curricular project. See *Aydin Teacher's Guide* page 2. **COOPERATIVE GROUPS**

To the Top of the World by Jim Brandenburg T1213–T1262

"A pair of binoculars allowed me to keep track of the pack's activities. My presence did not seem to affect the wolves in a negative way. They made regular trips to the camp, apparently to satisfy their curiosity. My goal was to blend in, to lie low without trying to hide or trick the wolves."

Students will join wildlife photographer Jim Brandenburg as he tracks and films a pack of Arctic wolves over several months.

Flexible Grouping

TO THE TOP OF THE WORLD T1213–T1262

	BELOW-LEVEL READERS	ABOVE-LEVEL READERS	ESL	BILINGUAL
1 READING AND RESPONDING Build Concepts and Vocabulary Strategic Reading Response Corner	**INSTEAD OF** having students read the selection with the whole class, use the *Guiding the Reading* page of the *Intervention Strategies Manual* (p. 142). **TEACHER-LED GROUP** **AFTER** students read the selection, use the Intervention Strategies activities. (pp. T1246–T1247) **TEACHER-LED GROUP**	**AFTER** the Vocabulary Strategies, students may complete the *Practice Book* (p. 181). **INDEPENDENT** **AFTER** students read the selection, use the response activities. (pp. T1244-T1245) **COOPERATIVE GROUPS**	**BEFORE** students read the selection, have them write story predictions in their personal journals. (p. T1218) **INDEPENDENT** **BEFORE** students read the selection, use the Introducing the Literature pages of the *Sheltered English/ESL Manual* (pp. 94-96). **TEACHER-LED GROUP**	**WHILE** others read the selection in the anthology, students may read the translation in the appropriate *Anthology Translation Booklet*. **INDEPENDENT** **WHILE** others complete the Strategic Reading, Spanish-speaking students may read *Guía para los niños que quieren salvar el planeta* in CIELO ABIERTO. **INDEPENDENT**
2 INTEGRATING LANGUAGE ARTS Idea Bank Writer's Workshop Grammar Spelling Vocabulary Workshop	**DURING** the Writer's Workshop activities, review the *Language Handbook* (pp. 74-75). **TEACHER-LED GROUP** **AFTER** the Writer's Workshop, students may use the Spin mode of *The Amazing Writing Machine* to enter their research reports. (p. T1250) **PAIRS/INDEPENDENT**	**INSTEAD OF** participating in the review of report writing, students familiar with the process may begin writing. (p. T1250) **INDEPENDENT** **WHILE** others review Key Words, have students complete the Extended Vocabulary lesson in the *Practice Book* (p. 185). **INDEPENDENT**	**DURING** the Spelling lesson, use the Students Acquiring English notes from *Integrated Spelling* Teacher's Edition Lesson 34. **TEACHER-LED GROUP** **INSTEAD OF** the Writer's Workshop, use the Responding to the Literature page of the *Sheltered English/ESL Manual* (p. 97). **COOPERATIVE GROUPS**	**INSTEAD OF** the Writer's Workshop, use CIELO ABIERTO *Teacher's Handbook* page 59 to have students write a persuasive paragraph. **INDEPENDENT** **WHILE** other students complete the Spelling lesson, refer to page 46 in the CIELO ABIERTO *Teacher's Handbook*. **TEACHER-LED GROUP**
3 LEARNING THROUGH THE LITERATURE Direct Skills Instruction Integrated Curriculum Reading Trade Books Theme Project	**AFTER** the Phonics lesson in the *Intervention Strategies Manual*, have students complete the reproducible Phonics page (p. 145). **INDEPENDENT** **WHILE** others are working in groups, have students read *Long Claws* from the *ESL/Title I Library*. **INDEPENDENT**	**WHILE** others are working in groups, have students choose and read a trade book such as *Making the Grades*. **INDEPENDENT** **WHILE** others are in groups, have students use *Imagination Express, Destination: Ocean* to create weather-related graphs or charts for the Integrated Curriculum activities. (p. T1258) **INDEPENDENT/PAIRS**	**WHILE** others are working in groups, have partners read the Take-Home book *Susan Butcher and the Iditarod*. **PAIRS**	**WHILE** others are working in groups, have students choose and read a book from the *Multi-Language Library*. **INDEPENDENT** **WHILE** others are working in groups, complete the Minilessons for Cause and Effect, pages 26–27, and Fact/Opinion, pages 32–33, in the CIELO ABIERTO *Teacher's Handbook*. **TEACHER-LED GROUP**

Ongoing Assessment Strategies

REPORTING PORTFOLIO ACHIEVEMENTS

Use the student's portfolio to report the child's achievement and progress in a parent-teacher conference. While reviewing portfolio contents with family members, you can share information about, and examples of, their child's authentic literacy development. Before the scheduled conference, ask the student to select five reading or writing activities he or she thinks are the best or most interesting, were the hardest to do, or show the most effort or greatest improvement.

Here are some tips for successful portfolio conferences with family members:

- Emphasize the things the student can do.
- Talk about successes and progress the student has been making.
- Show the student's growth and development by comparing earlier pieces of writing with more recent ones.
- Encourage family members to talk about the student's reading and writing activities outside of school.
- Plan literary activities for home that build on the student's language strengths. These might include visiting the library, setting a specific time in the evening for journal writing, or talking about favorite authors, stories, or characters.

People judging the accountability of schools—principals, administrators, school board members, state legislators, the public, and the media—need easily interpreted test scores that reveal the effectiveness of schools, curriculum, materials, and teachers. When a teacher thinks standardized test scores do not accurately represent students' ability, portfolios can become a key source of information.

See the SIGNATURES *Portfolio Assessment Teacher's Guide.*

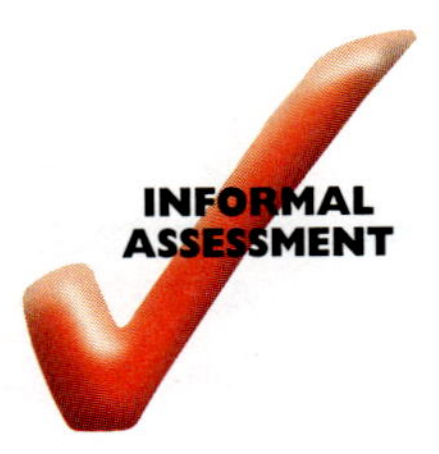

"CRITICAL FRIENDS"

Peer assessment, or peer conferences between students, provides an opportunity to teach students how to ask questions of others so that they will then ask these questions of themselves. A peer conference also

- increases the capacity for open-mindedness and the opportunity for new possibilities.
- helps students internalize high standards and develop criteria for judging their own work.
- gives students a chance to see the task from different perspectives.
- builds constructive thinking and speech.
- provides an opportunity for students to ask for and count on the help of classmates.

When teaching students to be a good "critical friend," tell them that a "critical friend" is a non-judgmental critic who is also a supportive friend. Teach students that during peer conferences a "critical friend" is supposed to

- encourage and praise.
- share opinions, but also listen and respond to others' opinions and reasoning.
- provide critical and supportive feedback.
- raise questions.

See the "Critical Friends" Checklist on page T1284.

End-of-Theme Formal Assessment Tools

SKILLS ASSESSMENT

Multiple-choice diagnostic tests that measure mastery of the following skills:

- Reading: vocabulary, summarize/paraphrase, and reference sources
- Language: adverbs, negatives, adjective and adverb phrases, prepositions, and prepositional phrases

HOLISTIC READING ASSESSMENT

Fiction and/or nonfiction reading passages with multiple-choice and open-ended questions to assess students' application of literal, inferential, and critical thinking in a global and holistic manner

INTEGRATED PERFORMANCE ASSESSMENT

Performance tasks to gain a comprehensive view of a student's reading and writing progress. Students read and respond to award-winning "Arctic Explorer: The Story of Matthew Henson" by Jeri Ferris. Students demonstrate expressive writing in news story form. One or both sections may be used.

THEME

CONFRONTING NATURE

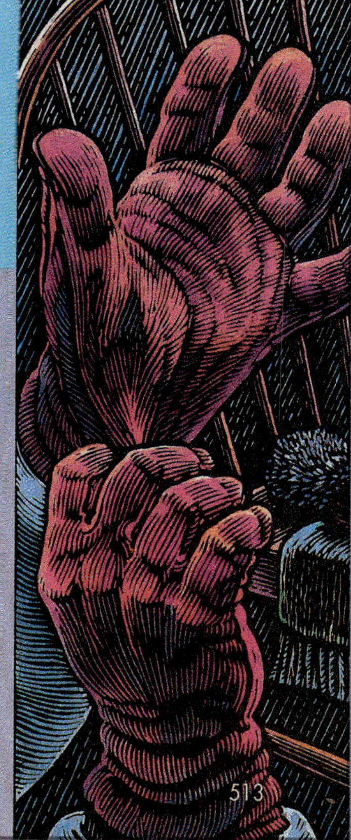

What would it take to overcome a disability and sail across the vast Atlantic Ocean? To battle a raging river? To survive in the frozen Arctic wilderness? The characters in the next selections rely on courage, strength, instinct, and common sense to survive.

513

THEME 6

Confronting Nature

DISCUSSING THE THEME

Ask students to read about the theme on page 513. Have them consider what a confrontation is. Then encourage students to discuss their own experiences with nature, such as swimming in a river or ocean or walking in a severe rain- or snowstorm.

Previewing the Theme Literature

Have students preview the theme by reading the table of contents on page 515. If they recognize any of the authors or selection titles, provide time to discuss previously-read selections or other selections by familiar authors.

Ask students how they would describe a wilderness. What personal resources might help someone survive in the wilderness? What kinds of hardships might someone face?

Encourage students to recall selections they have read about wilderness adventures. Where did the story or article take place? How did the story character or person react to the situations that arose? How did these characters or people confront nature?

BOOKSHELF

Life in the Oceans
by Norbert Wu

A photojournalist explores the many forms of life in the coral reefs, the kelp forest, the open sea, and the deep ocean.
Outstanding Science Trade Book
Signatures Library

Bearstone
by Will Hobbs

Cloyd finds strength in himself and in his Native American heritage when he must begin a new life in the mountains of Colorado.
ALA Notable Book, Children's Choice
Signatures Library

516

Stranded
by Ben Mikaelsen

Koby's physical disability has made her feel like an outsider. She finds a new sense of purpose, though, as she struggles to save two stranded whales.

Climb or Die
by Edward Myers

After a serious automobile accident, Jake and his sister must climb a mountain with improvised climbing gear to save their parents' lives.

Making Sense:
Animal Perception and Communication
by Bruce Brooks

Are five senses enough in the animal kingdom? Learn about the wonderful ways in which animals are able to make sense of their world.
Orbis Pictus Award

517

The Signatures Library

Life in the Oceans **by photojournalist Norbert Wu explores life beneath the sea. From a school of blue rockfish in a forest of kelp to an ancient shipwreck off Grand Caymen Island, Wu's vivid photographs take us deep into this mystifying world.**

Bearstone **by Will Hobbs is the story of Cloyd, a Native American boy who has grown up without his parents. One summer, Cloyd goes to work for an old rancher in the nearby mountains, where he goes on a journey of self-discovery that involves both physical danger and emotional growth.**

Strategies for reading *Life in the Oceans* appear with the "Freedom Ride" lesson on page T1124. Strategies for reading *Bearstone* appear with the "Julie of the Wolves" lesson on page T1210.

Comprehensive lesson plans are available on pages T1268–T1279.

Related Reading

These trade books offer students further opportunities to work with the Confronting Nature theme.

ESL/Title I Library

These easy-to-read library books connect to the theme Confronting Nature: *Sailing with the Wind* by Thomas Locker; *Long Claws* by James Houston.

THEME PROJECT OVERVIEW

THEME OVERVIEW

The selections in this theme contribute to students' understanding of how people overcome nature's most unpredictable challenges. This project offers students the opportunity to consider the difficulties of venturing into nature's more untamed areas. Each lesson is followed by a Project Checkpoint that will help students complete the project.

PROJECT PLANNER

QUESTION: How can people plan for a trip into the wilderness? (Problem Solving)

STAGES		GOALS
	PROJECT LAUNCH (p.T1083) 3-5 days	**Choose an expedition destination.** • Discuss trips students have taken in the wilderness. • Solve a survival quiz.
	CHECKPOINT 1 (p.T1126) 4-6 days	**Write nature journal entries.** • Go on a nature walk. • As an alternative, view nature walks on film. • Discuss sights and sounds of nature.
	CHECKPOINT 2 (p.T1172) 4-6 days	**Write a mission statement about a fantasy expedition.** • As a group, assume the role of a wilderness team. • Brainstorm a possible setting for a trip. • Use reference sources to find information.
	CHECKPOINT 3 (p.T1212) 4-6 days	**Write a group story about a fantasy expedition.** • Brainstorm supplies to take. • Narrow supplies to the ten most important. • Think about problems that might arise. • Develop a plot that includes challenging situations and the team's responses to them.
	CHECKPOINT 4 (p.T1262) 4-6 days	**Tape-record "travelogues" of fantasy expeditions.** • Assign roles. • Brainstorm sound effects. • Create two endings.
	PROJECT PRESENTATIONS (p.T1264) 3-5 days	**Share the journeys.** • Play the tape for the class in an Adventurer's Forum. • Play the tapes on the school PA system as a serial. • Offer tapes to hospital audio libraries for patients to enjoy.

STUDENTS ACQUIRING ENGLISH

Encourage students to share their thoughts about the natural wonders of their native communities.

MULTIPLE INTELLIGENCES

Encourage students with different intelligences to assume leadership roles at various points. For example, students with logical/mathematical intelligence can offer leadership in making a list of supplies.

INQUIRY PROJECT IDEAS

Students may wish to experience nature in other ways. They may want to investigate

- biographies of people who faced nature's greatest challenges.
- wilderness areas in their native country.
- overlooked natural areas in or near the community.

PROJECT LAUNCH

LAUNCH OPTIONS

DISCOVERERS (SMALL GROUPS)

Ask groups to imagine that they have sailed to an island and discovered an animal no one has ever seen before. Have them describe the animal, name it, make a sketch, and share their discovery with the class. Discuss how past explorers must have felt when they arrived in new lands.

MEET PEOPLE WHO KNOW (WHOLE GROUP)

Invite to class someone who spends a lot of time outdoors. A good choice would be a naturalist or a Sierra Club member. Have students prepare questions in advance.

WHOLE-GROUP DISCUSSION

Refer to student experiences and to information presented in the launch activities in the discussion of wilderness travel. Students who have not gone on such trips can discuss movies, documentaries, or books they have read about wilderness trips. Prompt a discussion of adventure travel with questions such as *What areas in the world would you like to explore?*

FORM PROJECT GROUPS

Arrange the class in groups, and ask group members to decide where to go on their fantasy expedition. Have groups list wilderness locations they would like to explore before they agree on a destination. One member should take notes as the group

- brainstorms to list ideas.
- discusses the pros and cons of each location.
- comes to a consensus about the final destination.

Project Card 31 can be found as a copying master on page R122.

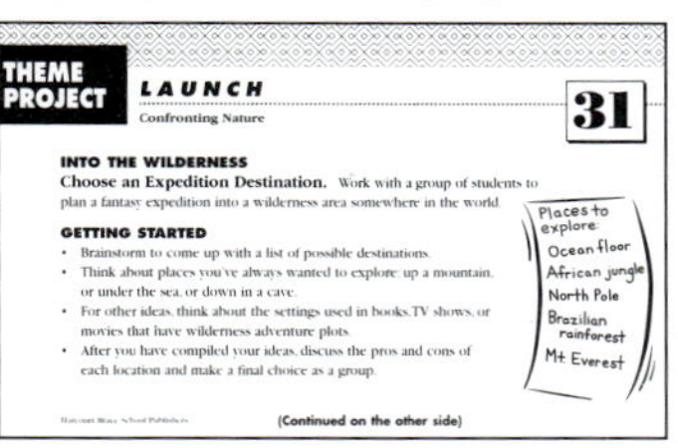

THEME PROJECT **LAUNCH** 31

Confronting Nature

INTO THE WILDERNESS

Choose an Expedition Destination. Work with a group of students to plan a fantasy expedition into a wilderness area somewhere in the world.

GETTING STARTED

- Brainstorm to come up with a list of possible destinations.
- Think about places you've always wanted to explore: up a mountain, or under the sea, or down in a cave.
- For other ideas, think about the settings used in books, TV shows, or movies that have wilderness adventure plots.
- After you have compiled your ideas, discuss the pros and cons of each location and make a final choice as a group.

Places to explore:
Ocean floor
African jungle
North Pole
Brazilian rainforest
Mt Everest

(Continued on the other side)

Project Card 31

DID YOU KNOW?

- Sacajawea, a Shoshone Indian, led the Lewis and Clark expedition (1804–1806) across the Rockies.
- French oceanographer Jacques-Yves Cousteau co-invented the self-contained underwater breathing apparatus we call scuba.

PROJECT MANAGEMENT

ADDITIONAL RESOURCES

MAGAZINES

"Get Out! Enjoy the Great Outdoors," "Are You a Camping Champ . . . or Chump?," "Don't Leave Home Without It," *Kid City*, June 1995, pp. 6–7, 8–9, 26–27.

"Three Weeks on the Trail," *Boy's Life*, June 1995, pp. 14–17.

AUDIO/VISUAL

National Parks of America. CD-ROM, Muliticom Publishing, 1995.

FORMAL ASSESSMENT

Prompts for self- and peer assessment and a rubric for teacher assessment that can be used at each checkpoint are provided on page T1265.

Planning a Literacy Event

Wilderness Party Plan a Wilderness Party as a culminating activity of the theme. Students who complete the Theme Project can showcase their wilderness travelogue recordings at the event. To set the mood for family participation, invite guests to wear clothes appropriate for a wilderness expedition. In addition, use the opportunity to have students explain the steps they took to create their travelogues.

- Set a date for the Wilderness Party.
- Have students plan an agenda for the event, including opportunities for guests to hear their recordings.
- Ask students to design posters showing animals, maps, and scenery from their "expeditions."
- If possible, arrange to have refreshments at the event and a door prize for the most creative wilderness costume.
- Appoint a publicity committee to generate interest for the event.

Enlisting Parents as Partners

Nature Exploration During conferences parents may ask for ideas for sharing their children's interest in wilderness adventures. Offer these suggestions:

- ☑ Investigate local campgrounds. Many offer complete facilities on-site while providing easy access to wilderness trails.
- ☑ Check out the locations of the nearest national parks and plan a day trip together.
- ☑ Set aside time to view wilderness shows or adventure films together. Many real-life nature adventures, such as the voyages of Jacques Cousteau, are readily available on video and can spark discussions about exploring nature.

TECHNOLOGY

The *At Home in Our Schools* videocassette contains numerous ideas for family involvement projects.

Surfing the Internet? See *Issues & Ideas* on the Harcourt Brace Home Page:

http://www.hbschool.com

***The Family Involvement Newsletter* for this theme contains further suggestions on this topic and other topics of interest to parents.**

FREEDOM RIDE

by Liz Fordred with Susie Blackmun

ABOUT THE AUTHORS

LIZ FORDRED and **SUSIE BLACKMUN** are working together on a book-length version of "Freedom Ride." They wrote "Freedom Ride" for *Florida* magazine, a section of the *Orlando Sentinel.*

More information about Liz and Pete Fordred appears on page T1090.

HEME: NATURE

onfronting Nature

or humans, whose natural habitat is land, ne sea has long been a place of challenge nd danger. Sailing across a vast expanse of ater in a small boat requires unusual ourage for an able-bodied person and xtraordinary courage for those who have hysical disabilities.

Linking Poetry to Nonfiction

"Until I Saw the Sea" is a poem by Lillian Moore that describes what it is like to see the ocean for the first time.

SELECTION SUMMARY

Genre: Nonfiction/Magazine Article

Liz and Pete Fordred had always wanted to travel, but traveling was difficult for them because they are both paraplegics, paralyzed from the chest down. One day, Pete had a great idea: he and Liz would build a boat and sail across the Atlantic Ocean. Liz discovered a shipyard that could fabricate the hull; the rest of the boat they designed and built themselves, customizing it so they could live in it and sail it on their own. Before the boat was completely finished, Liz and Pete moved it to Durban, South Africa, where they could launch it and learn how to sail it. After four years of hard work, the Fordreds were ready to set out across the Atlantic. Less than six weeks later, they arrived in Fortaleza, Brazil, having accomplished what most people thought was nearly impossible.

SUGGESTED LESSON PLANNER

▶ ***Freedom Ride***

	DAY 1	DAY 2
PART  **Key Words** turmoil restrictions lapse incompetent **Reading** **Listening** **Speaking** **Viewing**	**BUILD BACKGROUND** T1088 **VOCABULARY STRATEGIES** T1089 *Transparency 51* *Practice Book* p. 159 **READING THE SELECTION** T1090–T1105 Options for Reading T1090–T1091 *Response Card 7* *Literature Cassette 3* **REVIEW PREDICTIONS/PURPOSE** T1104 **APPRECIATING THE LITERATURE** T1104 NOTE: Students may read the selection on Day 2.	**SUMMARIZE THE SELECTION** T1104 *Practice Book* p. 160 **READ POETRY** T1106–T1107 "Until I Saw the Sea" ◆ **RESPONSE CORNER ACTIVITIES** T1108 **CHECKING COMPREHENSION** T1109 *End-of-Selection Test* Visit our Web site http://www.hbschool.com
PART 2 **Writer's Workshop**	**NEWS STORY** Thinking as Writers T1114 *Language Handbook* pp. 70–71 *Transparency 52*	Prewriting T1114 *Language Handbook* p. 60
Grammar	✓ **ADVERBS** Teach the Concept T1116 Daily Language Practice (1–2) R114	Daily Language Practice (3–4) R114 Practice Activity T1117
Spelling	**PREFIXES: *ex-* and *re-*** *remain, reduced, explain, exchange* *expand, regain, explore, express* *represent, refused, experts, expected* *exhausted, resolve, relationship, excitement* Pretest/Self-Check T1118 *Integrated Spelling Teacher's Edition* pp. T201, T300	Open and Closed Sorts T1118 *Integrated Spelling* p. 130 *Integrated Spelling Teacher's Edition* p. T202
PART 3 **Skills and Strategies**	◆ **INTEGRATED CURRICULUM** *The Changing Map of Africa* **Social Studies** T1122 **Art** T1122 **Social Studies** T1123 *Imagination Express, Destination: Ocean*	**STUDY SKILLS** T1120–T1121 ✓ Reference Sources (Introduce) *Transparency 53* *Practice Book* pp. 164–165
 MEETING INDIVIDUAL NEEDS	Use the notes on pages T1092 and T1101 to help **below-level** and **ESL students** understand the selection.	Allow **below-level students** to work in pairs while they use reference sources.

NOTE: An alternative lesson plan for **below-level students** appears on *Intervention Strategies Manual* pp. 122–127. A lesson for **students acquiring English** appears on *Sheltered English/ESL Manual* pp. 82–85.

DAY 3	DAY 4	DAY 5
◆ **IDEA BANK ACTIVITIES** Retelling T1112 Oral Language T1112 Viewing T1113 Real-Life Resources: Reading Warning Labels/Signs T1113 *Writer's Magazine* pp. 82–83 School–Home Connection 21 R141	**VOCABULARY WORKSHOP** T1119 Reviewing Key Words **READING TRADE BOOKS** T1124–T1125 *Signatures Library: Life in the Oceans*  Signatures Library  Take-Home Book	**READING TRADE BOOKS** T1121, T1123, T1124–T1125 
Drafting T1114 *Language Handbook* pp. 61 *The Amazing Writing Machine*	Responding and Revising T1115 *Language Handbook* p. 61	Proofreading and Publishing T1115 *Language Handbook* p. 61
Daily Language Practice (5–6) R114 Practice Activity T1117 *Language Handbook* pp. 160, 162–163, 220–222 *The Amazing Writing Machine*	Daily Language Practice (7–8) R114 Practice Activity T1117 *Grammar Practice Book* pp. 50–51	Daily Language Practice (9–12) R114 *Practice Book* p. 161
Discuss the Generalization T1118 *Integrated Spelling* p. 131 *Integrated Spelling Teacher's Edition* p. T203	Apply to Writing T1118 *Integrated Spelling* pp. 131–132 *Integrated Spelling Teacher's Edition* pp. T204–T205	Posttest T1118 *Practice Book* p. 163 *Integrated Spelling Teacher's Edition* p. T206
GRAMMAR MINILESSON T1097 ✓ Regular and Irregular Verbs (Review) **COMPREHENSION MINILESSON** T1103 ✓ Sequence/Cause-Effect (Maintain)	**VOCABULARY WORKSHOP** T1119 Context Clues *Practice Book* p. 163	**STUDY SKILLS MINILESSON** T1105 Graphic Aids (Review) *Practice Book* p. 166 Theme Project Checkpoint 1 T1126
Above-level students may read a trade book independently.	**Below-level students** may read the *Take-Home Book: A Vacation to Remember* to help them review Key Words.	**Below-level** and **ESL students** may read the *ESL/Title I Library* book *Sailing with the Wind.*

✓ = Tested Skill
◆ = Optional activities used to adjust pacing throughout the lesson
Titles in *italics* are optional materials.

1 Reading and Responding

BUILDING BACKGROUND AND CONCEPTS

PRIOR KNOWLEDGE

Relate to students' lives. Talk with students about any traveling they may have done. Discuss what was fun and what was difficult about going places. Ask students who may not have been on trips to talk about places they'd like to visit and how they might get there.

Create a web about traveling with disabilities. Explain that "Freedom Ride" is about a couple with disabilities who want to travel. Discuss with students how traveling might be difficult for such people. Have students talk about different modes of transportation (walking, driving, flying, or sailing) and what challenges persons with disabilities might face with each. Record students' responses in a web like the following:

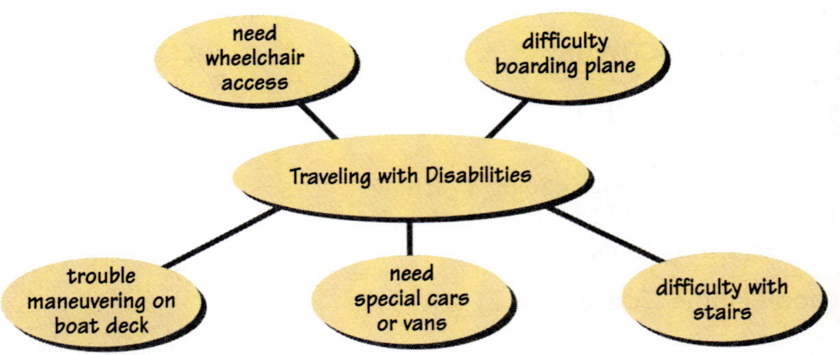

QUICKWRITE

Encourage students to write a few sentences about why traveling is important to some people. Suggest to students that they think about why someone might try to travel despite seemingly insurmountable obstacles.

Intervention Strategies

For students who may have difficulty reading "Freedom Ride," support is available in *Intervention Strategies Manual*, pages 122–127, and on page T1099 and T1110–T1111 in this lesson.

STUDENTS ACQUIRING ENGLISH

See *Sheltered English/ESL Manual* pages 82–85.

FACT FINDER

HEALTH

Paraplegia

Paraplegia is paralysis of the lower body, commonly affecting both legs and often the internal organs below the waist. Paraplegia can be caused by diseases that damage the spinal cord, but it is more often caused by an injury that completely severs the spinal cord or damages the nerve tissue in the cord. Automobile and horseback-riding accidents are among the most common causes of this injury. Modern methods of treatment and therapy have greatly increased the ability of people with paraplegia to live full and productive lives.

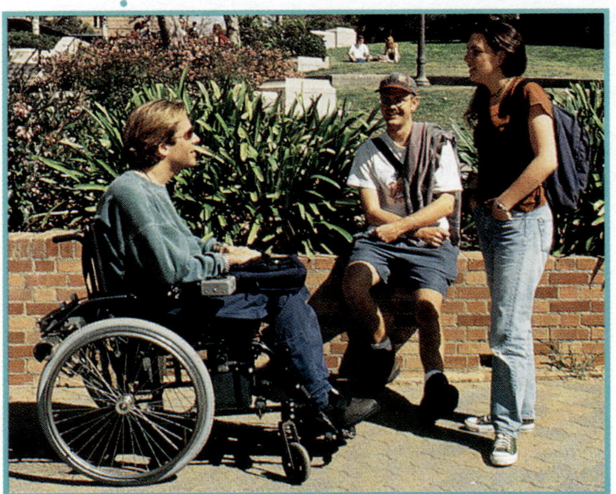

VOCABULARY STRATEGIES

KEY WORDS DEFINED

turmoil state of unrest or uncertainty

restrictions things that restrict or limit

lapse falling or slipping into a worse condition

incompetent incapable; without adequate ability or knowledge

INTEGRATED SPELLING

Spelling Pretest: page T1118

Spelling Generalization: Prefixes: *ex-, re-*

CONTEXT CLUES: PERSONAL NARRATIVE

Encourage students to use syntactic and semantic cues. Display the paragraph on Transparency 51, and ask a volunteer to read the passage aloud. Model identifying the context clue that reveals the meaning of *turmoil (power changes hands so often)*. Prompt students to use similar strategies to figure out the meanings of the other Key Words.

CHECK UNDERSTANDING

Have students make word associations. Read aloud each group of words or phrases below, or write them on the board. Have students tell which Key Word they would associate with each set of words.

Word Groups			Key Words
unrest	disturbance	confusion	(turmoil)
incapable	unqualified	unskilled	(incompetent)
backslide	slip	weaken	(lapse)
rules	regulations	limitations	(restrictions)

TRANSPARENCY 51

Key Words

I work for a major newspaper, and last month, my editor sent me to the island of Jabberwock to report on the most recent government changes there. Because power changes hands so often, the country is in a constant state of political turmoil. Traditionally, Jabberwock's officials have imposed harsh restrictions, making it very difficult for foreigners to enter the country. I took advantage of the chaos, confusion, and a lapse in security to get through immigration. I was thankful that the immigration officer I encountered was either new at his job or totally incompetent; he didn't even bother to check my passport.

Upon entering the park, we immediately saw the signs announcing restrictions on skateboarding and biking.

PRACTICE BOOK, page 159

Prereading Strategies

PREVIEW AND PREDICT

As students preview the selection, ask them to identify its genre and explain how they know.

Explain that "Freedom Ride" is about Liz Fordred and her husband, Pete, both paraplegics, who build a boat and sail it across the Atlantic Ocean. Begin a summary chart like the one below. Students can use *Practice Book* page 160 to record details and events under each subheading from the story.

SUMMARY CHART

INTRODUCTION: (Liz thinks back to what it was like sailing on the boat that she and her husband—both paraplegics—built ten years before.)

LET'S BUILD A BOAT:

You may want students to record their predictions about the selection in their personal journals.

PURPOSE

This think-aloud can help you model setting a purpose:

MODEL **I want to find out how the Fordreds build a boat and sail across the Atlantic Ocean.**

TIPS FOR CLASSROOM MANAGEMENT

SMALL GROUP

STRATEGIC READING

To help students gain meaning as they read, reinforce the focus strategy of **using picture clues.** Pages T1092 and T1098 are excellent places to model how students can use picture clues to understand what they are reading.

COOPERATIVE READING

PARTNER READING Partners can use Reader Response Card 7 to help them **respond freely** to the selection and share their responses as they read. Response Card 7 can be found at the back of this Teacher's Edition.

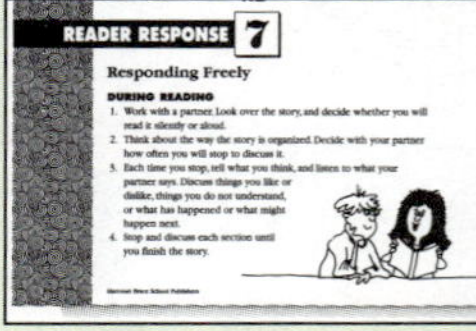

Response Card 7

WHOLE CLASS

READ ALOUD

Read aloud to students through the middle of the second column on page 520. Discuss what they learned about Liz and Pete Fordred from these opening paragraphs. Then have students continue reading on their own.

SILENT READING/ DISCUSSION

Have students read the entire selection silently. When everyone has finished reading, encourage students to talk about the selection and what impressed them most about the Fordreds. To check students' comprehension, have them complete one of the activities on pages 536 and 537.

Strategic Reading

USING PICTURE CLUES

Ask volunteers to name some strategies they use while reading. Encourage them to predict which strategies will be important in helping them understand this selection. Display the class-made strategy chart, and (if students haven't already suggested it) point out that using picture clues will be a useful strategy in understanding the selection. **STRATEGY: USING PICTURE CLUES**

PAGES 520–526 Have students read to the "Bon Voyage" section on page 526 to learn how Liz and Pete built their boat and learned to sail it.

I sometimes sit and ponder what we have done. Now that Pete and I own a house and a business in Fort Lauderdale and are busy being parents, our sailing trip seems like more than a mere decade ago. At times it doesn't even seem real. But if I close my eyes and allow myself to drift back in time, I can see Pete heading for the foredeck, clipped onto a lifeline as he scoots along on his bottom. . . .

Every time our boat climbs up a wave, he holds on with all the strength in his massive arms and waits for the plunge. When it comes, and the deck of Usikusiku (yōō•sē´kōō•sē´kōō) drops out from under him, he uses the momentary loss of gravity to slide farther down the deck.

After each plunge we hit bottom, and for a few seconds the sea spray blocks my view of him, but once I see the 18-foot running poles slowly rising into place I can relax.

I'm never comfortable when he's on the foredeck. What if he should go overboard? But that is a lapse into the negative, a state I refuse to enter. And, of course, we have planned and practiced a man-overboard procedure.

When Pete heaves himself back into the cockpit, he is exhausted by the enormous physical effort of moving around the boat and hoisting the poles. Without back or stomach muscles, he must do everything with his arms. At least our bodies are strong now, a far cry from their condition back in Rhodesia, in hospital beds. Wheelchairs might be permanent fixtures in our lives, but our quality of life is good.

Let's Build a Boat

During the first two years of our marriage, Pete and I were busy. He was in charge of an instrument workshop and I worked full time at the rehab center, where I'd been promoted to administrative assistant. Three times we represented Rhodesia in the South African Championships for the Disabled, which meant a lot of training. We organized sports activities for young disabled kids, and I was secretary for the Paraplegic Club. We went on two hilarious camping expeditions.

Somehow, all of that wasn't enough. We'd accepted our disabilities, but we weren't going to accept their restrictions. We wanted a challenge.

520

EXTRA SUPPORT Point out that the introduction to the selection on page 518 is told from the third-person point of view. Explain that the point of view changes on page 520 to first person, Liz Fordred's point of view. The pronoun *I* in the first sentence is a clue that Liz Fordred is telling her own story.

Both Pete and I had always wanted to travel. Now that we were paraplegics, though, traveling was tough. Going on an aircraft was practically impossible. You had to be carried up the steps because in Rhodesia passengers still went out on the tarmac to board, and once on the plane you couldn't use the bathroom. You couldn't get onto a train or bus, nor could you rent a car with hand controls. We liked camping so we tried to get a VW van, but the government wouldn't let us purchase the foreign currency to buy it. And with much of Africa in turmoil, South Africa was practically the only place to go. It was pretty frustrating.

One Saturday we were driving along a country road when Pete said, absolutely out of the blue, "Why don't we build a boat?"

I suppose it's hard to believe that two paraplegics could even dream of physically building a boat, let alone sailing it across an ocean. Why would we want to create more obstacles than we already had? The only answer I can come up with is that we weren't conventional people, even before our accidents.

The restrictions of being a paraplegic had made me want to scream at times. When Pete suggested building a boat, I felt suddenly free. It was almost like being on a horse again, galloping toward a difficult jump that others might think twice about but that I knew I could manage. It was a challenge, and I had always responded well to a challenge.

The goal would be regaining our independence. It never occurred to us that being in wheelchairs and building a boat was an unheard-of combination.

The closest either of us had been to a sailboat was looking at pictures, but you can't go through life doing only the things you know how to do, can you? We talked

Liz works on the unfinished cabin in her mother's backyard in Salisbury, Rhodesia (now Harare, Zimbabwe).

521

Student Self-Assessment

FIX-UP STRATEGY: REREADING

Ask students what they can do if they are confused by the time frame of this story and the difference between when the events happened and when the selection is being written. (Possible response: I can reread to clarify the sequence of events.)

If necessary, model using rereading as a fix-up strategy:

MODEL **I was confused by all the present-tense verbs in the first section. I had to go back and reread the first paragraph, which made it clear the author was thinking back to events that happened ten years earlier.**

SOCIAL STUDIES CONNECTION

OCEAN VOYAGES Point out to students that even for people who don't use wheelchairs, crossing an ocean in a small boat is extremely difficult. Have interested students research other difficult ocean voyages, such as the Kon-Tiki expedition, as well as modern ocean crossings. Students can make oral presentations of their findings.

The raft used on Thor Heyerdahl's Kon-Tiki expedition, 1947

Cooperative Reading

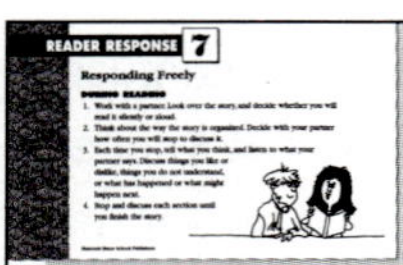
Response Card 7

Cooperative reading partners can share their reactions to what they have read thus far. Use questions such as these to stimulate discussion:

- **What is your impression of Liz and Pete after reading just a little bit about them?**
- **What is it about the way they approach the task of building a boat that makes it clear they will probably succeed?**

about all the wonderful things future yachtsmen dream of. We envisioned sunny blue lagoons, palms and islands, white sand (sand and wheelchairs—we didn't think that one through very well).

In my normal fashion I went at the idea like a bull at a flag and found out as much as possible about buying or building a hull. Right in the middle of the countryside, hundreds of miles from the sea, I discovered a shipyard that fabricated hulls. A hull, though, represented only 10 percent to 15 percent of the work. The rest we would have to do ourselves.

During the four months it took for our hull to be built we saved like mad, read all we could lay our hands on and started planning the interior to suit our wheelchairs. We taped an outline of the cabin floor on Mom's veranda, so we could see where our chairs would fit and where everything would go. We knew there was nothing more frustrating than a wheelchair jamming and bashing into something at every turn.

When the 43-foot hull arrived, we put it into a huge hole we had had dug in Mom's backyard, so that the deck was brought down to ground level and we could just wheel right across in our chairs. Now our priority jobs were getting railings on the deck, so that we wouldn't roll off, and building a hydraulic lift to lower us inside.

As our commitment to building our boat grew, so did our realization that we could help other disabled people see that just because their bodies had been damaged didn't mean all their hopes and dreams were over. We also wanted to help able-bodied people understand that just because a person is physically disabled doesn't mean he or she is mentally incompetent as well.

Having a challenge and a goal were the most important steps we had taken since our accidents.

From Hull to Yacht

"I want to build something," I insisted after several evenings of passing tools to Pete while he had all the fun of doing the work. I wanted to do something constructive, even though I knew dangerously little about a T-square and tape measure.

Pete suggested that I start on the clothes cupboards on either side of the forward lift. He explained how

522

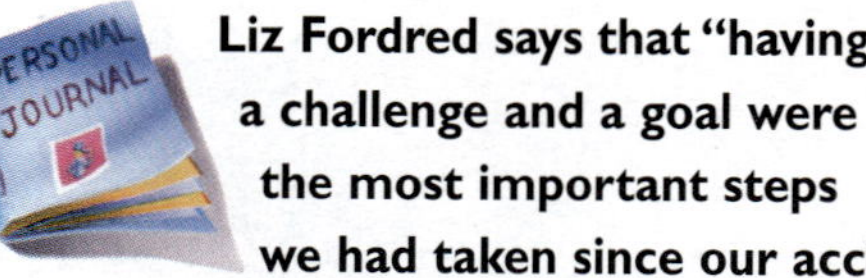

QUICKWRITE

Liz Fordred says that "having a challenge and a goal were the most important steps we had taken since our accidents." Ask students to write a few sentences about a challenge they have faced or how having a goal in life can be important.

STUDENTS ACQUIRING ENGLISH Help students understand the meaning of the expression *like a bull at a flag*. Bulls will charge something that is bright-colored and moving, like a flag, so to say that you "went at the idea like a bull at a flag" suggests that you charged ahead without hesitation.

Liz and Pete with their boat in Durban, South Africa.

Student Self-Assessment

USING PICTURE CLUES

Remind students that when they read nonfiction, they should monitor their understanding of the selection by using picture clues.

- ☑ How does looking at the photographs in the selection help me imagine the actions and setting?
- ☑ How have the pictures of the Fordreds shown me some of the challenges they faced while building their boat?

CROSS-CULTURAL VIEWPOINT

PERSONS WITH DISABILITIES Liz and Pete Fordred and other people with disabilities had a difficult time getting around in Rhodesia. Discuss with students whether the Fordreds, now living in Fort Lauderdale, Florida, might still experience the restrictions they did a decade ago in Africa. Students with disabilities or those acquainted with someone with a disability may want to tell about the difficulties involved in traveling.

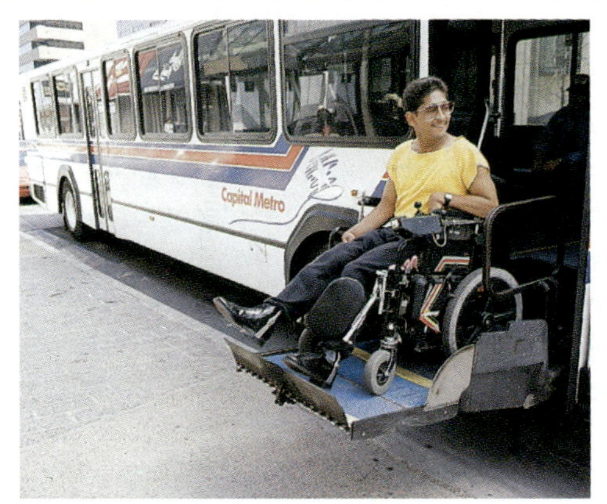

Critical Thinking Questions

1. **Liz and Pete both enjoyed the challenge of building the boat. In what ways are they different from one another?** (Possible response: Pete seems more patient and methodical. Liz comes across as a real person of action.) INFERENTIAL: DETERMINING CHARACTERS' TRAITS/MAKING COMPARISONS

2. **Why do you think Liz and Pete chose a word that can mean "dawn" or "dusk" as the name for their boat?** (Responses will vary but may suggest that because dawn signals a beginning and dusk signals an ending, the name *Usikusiku* was appropriate because the boat could lead them to either disaster or victory.) CRITICAL: SPECULATING

to go about it. I began with great enthusiasm, got absolutely tangled up with curves and angles, and let out what soon became a familiar cry for help. Pete would explain once again. Sometimes I would hurl the board as far away as possible and yell, "If you're so smart, *you* can do it!"

"Oh?" he'd say innocently. "I thought you wanted to learn."

Frustrations were plentiful. Things would continually fall off my lap. I'd pick them up and something else would fall. I'd back up and find I couldn't move because something was in the way of a wheel, or an electrical wire from the drilling machine or jigsaw had caught in the chair. It was worse when we first started to build, since the floor was the only place to put anything. Pete swore he would get a box and put everything that gave him trouble into it, and once we were sailing he would hurl it over the side. Humor was one way of coping with the frustration, so we often ended up laughing at each other.

I invented a way of getting up the sloping hull—up five feet and across two feet—by collecting bricks and stacking them against the side of the hull. Then I'd lay a plank from the bricks across to my armrest and drag my body across. We always found a way of doing a job. Sure, it might take an hour, whereas if we were able-bodied it would have taken five minutes, but it was best not to think of it like that; rather we should feel the satisfaction of trying and succeeding.

Slowly I learned new skills. I finally finished the first cupboard and got it all screwed into place. "Right," said Pete. "Now take it apart and glue it." I was rapidly losing patience with the cupboard and with Pete. I took it apart and glued it, although it did not fit as well the second time. Pete, who is a perfectionist, must have had to swallow hard to accept my cupboard.

In their spare time Pete and his dad were inventing a way for us to get down into the boat. This involved a lot of thinking, which taxed my patience. Whenever I saw Pete sitting there daydreaming, I would explode: "We have work to do!" He finally came up with an ingenious idea for a lift, all worked out to the last detail. I asked when he had done it. "While I was daydreaming," he said quietly.

We worked on the boat every second that we weren't occupied with our regular jobs; we could get in an average of six hours every

524

EXPANDING VOCABULARY

Draw students' attention to the use of the word *cupboards.* In American usage, the word is rarely used to describe anything outside the kitchen, and even in that sense it is rapidly being replaced by the word *cabinet.* The British, on the other hand, tend to use the word *cupboard* for all kinds of storage areas—closets, cabinets, and cupboards.

MATH CONNECTION

Have students calculate how many hours Liz and Pete spent each week working on their boat. When they have done that, ask students if there is anything, besides sleeping, that they spend that many hours doing every week.

night and 36 hours over a weekend. Making the wooden parts of the boat, such as the cabin and interior, are a normal part of boat building, but because we had little money for ready-made equipment—and because Rhodesia was under worldwide sanctions preventing us from importing much—we had to make nearly everything else as well. We made our own bolts out of brass rod. Pete and his dad fabricated the railings, wheelchair lift, steel rudder, self-tailing halyard winches and roller furling drums. Pete bought a reconditioned Mercedes engine and "marinized" it himself.

All of the physical activity made us more fit and agile and improved our balance, and the enormous feeling of satisfaction we got from even the smallest physical achievements made us soar. Life in wheelchairs had taken on some sort of meaning.

South Africa

We had been searching for a name for our boat. We finally settled on Usikusiku, an African word describing the hour between day and night, both dusk and dawn.

We hired a couple of workmen to trowel on epoxy to smooth out the hull. Then they rubbed it down and began to brush on paint. Suddenly it appeared we'd made major progress. Usikusiku looked like a yacht.

In order to properly finish the boat, and avoid making dangerous mistakes out of ignorance, we had to get her out of Rhodesia. We had to get to the sea so we could be around other yachtsmen and learn from them.

We hired a truck to make the 1,200-mile trip from Salisbury, Rhodesia (now Harare, Zimbabwe), to Durban, South Africa. After three months in dry dock, we were ready to launch. Usikusiku actually floated the first night in port. As we lay in our bunks, we were gently rocked to sleep by the lapping of water against the hull and the crackling of barnacles on the jetty walls. Already we were in a different world.

But during the time we were in Durban, nearly every member of every committee from the Durban Yacht Club came to inspect us. They told us we were attempting the impossible. The harbor authorities weren't impressed with us either. One continually came to visit us, telling us of all the horrors

525

Tested Skill

MINILESSON

REVIEW: GRAMMAR

Regular and Irregular Verbs

INFORMAL ASSESSMENT

Have students scan page 525 to locate an example of the past form of a regular verb *(improved, settled)* and the past form of an irregular verb. *(made, got, were)*

TEACH/MODEL

Explain that the past and the past participle of regular verbs are both formed by adding *-ed* or *-d*. The past and past participle of irregular verbs are formed differently. Display the following examples to show the present, past, and past participle forms of these verbs:

Regular Verb	bloom	bloomed	(has) bloomed
Irregular Verb	do	did	(has) done

Explain that some irregular verbs follow a certain pattern in their principal parts. For example, for one group of irregular verbs, the past participle is formed by adding *-n* or *-en* to the present form. Display the following examples:

take	took	(has) taken
see	saw	(has) seen
give	gave	(has) given

PRACTICE/APPLY

Have students make a short list of regular and irregular verbs from the selection and create a chart showing the present, past, and past participle forms of each verb.

CONVENTIONS OF LANGUAGE

CAPITAL LETTERS It's customary to name boats, and the names are capitalized just as the names of people and places are. The Fordreds' boat is named *Usikusiku,* which, as the selection reveals, is an African word that describes the hour between day and night.

Strategic Reading

PAGES 520–526 Why do Liz and Pete decide to build a boat and sail across the Atlantic Ocean? (Possible response: They want to travel. They want to regain their independence, which they'd lost after their accidents.) CRITICAL: SUMMARIZING

How do the Fordreds build their boat? (Possible response: While a hull is being built, the Fordreds plan the interior. Then in their spare time, they complete the boat and move it to Durban, South Africa.) STRATEGY: SUMMARIZING

USING PICTURE CLUES

STRATEGY FOCUS

You may want to have students glance at the photographs on pages 523 and 528 before you model the strategy of using picture clues. Use a think-aloud like this:

MODEL **On pages 523 and 528, I see Liz and Pete on the boat. I can tell that maneuvering on the boat must be difficult, but the photographs also show me how much the Fordreds accomplished.**

PAGES 526–533
Students should read to page 533 to find out what happened when Liz and Pete set sail from Cape Town.

we were going to face, then kicking our cabin and telling us it would come off with the first wave. We accepted these opinions as only to be expected. What really mattered was what we thought. We knew we were ignorant about sailing, but we weren't stupid and could learn.

Even nonsailors, more often than not, looked at us with disbelief. "You'll never make it," they told us bluntly.

Others wanted to know how we would sail the boat. "How will you go up the mast?" was a favorite question.

"We'll do it the same as everybody else does," I'd answer. "I'll winch Pete up in a bosun's chair."

"What happens if the engine stops?"

"Well, seeing as Pete is good with engines, that shouldn't be a problem. Besides, we're a sailboat."

"What will you do if the boat is sinking?"

"Having legs in a life raft is not absolutely necessary."

Sometimes I could have screamed.

Most of the world is unaware of the capabilities of wheelchair-bound paraplegics. I wanted my independence as much as anyone. I wanted to do as I liked, when I liked, but more often than not I had to fight to keep my independence. It was a constant battle when strangers made judgments without bothering to get to know us.

Fortunately, our supporters more than made up for the critics. A wealthy Greek businessman loaded us down with food, gear and advice. Several people we'd never even met sent us money. Many of the other yachtsmen pitched in by helping with the rigging, by teaching us to sail and navigate and by skippering the boat during our sea trials and the trip to Cape Town. In all we spent four years building our boat, and we couldn't have done it without the wonderful people who believed in us.

When the time came to sail, we were tense as we waved to the friends who'd followed us out of the bay. Once their shouts had faded, we were left with only the sounds of wind and water.

Bon Voyage

Looking back over the waves I could see Table Mountain looming over Cape Town in her grandeur. It was strange to be sailing alone with Pete for the first time, with

526

REAL-LIFE CONNECTION

MAKING JUDGMENTS Encourage students to talk about times when they may have made a judgment about someone before getting to know that person or when someone made a judgment like that about them. Help them see that people underestimate one another for all sorts of reasons, not just because of physical disabilities.

1,700 miles of the South Atlantic between us and St. Helena Island, our first stop.

As the wind increased, Usikusiku heeled toward the water, slowly picking up speed. The main sheet block should have zipped across the traveler, as it had on all our other sails, but it twisted and stuck.

"Let the sheet out a little," Pete said, but the traveler still didn't budge. What a good start!

On a regular sailboat the problem would have been simple because the traveler, which holds the end of the boom down, is usually at deck level. But we'd had to build ours so that it didn't block our wheelchairs when we were in port, and that meant putting it 4 1/2 feet above the deck. At sea, out of our chairs, the "roll bar," as we called it, loomed even higher over our heads. How could we get up there to untangle the snag?

While I pondered, Pete jumped (so to speak) into action. With his incredibly strong upper body, he grabbed hold of one of the traveler's vertical supports and pulled himself up, hand over hand, to the horizontal bar. Hanging from one arm, his body swinging with the motion of the boat, he stretched the other up and freed the block. The boom swung over with a crash.

Then Pete worked his way back across the bar and dropped safely onto his bottom into the cushioned cockpit.

We *could* do anything. Some things might require more thought and time, but we always got there in the end.

Around 5 p.m. the wind began to strengthen, so we furled the No. 1 jib and set the smaller No. 2. Pete connected the self-steering vane, though we ended up having to steer by hand since the seas were confused. I went below to fix our dinner, a stew I'd made the day before that I only had to heat up and ladle into deep dishes with lids that I could move in front of me without anything slopping over. We didn't eat much, out of excitement I suppose, with a bit of seasickness thrown in. My stomach was starting to churn—little did I know it wouldn't ever stop.

Because of my queasiness I suggested that Pete take the first watch while I tried to sleep. I tucked myself into the berth down below and set the leeboard to keep myself from rolling out.

Pete called me at midnight. When I finally got to the cockpit to relieve him, he announced that sleeping below was not going to work because it took too long to

527

NOTES

Here's a place to list ideas or activities that you would like to use the next time you teach this lesson.

Intervention Strategies

REREADING **Students should repeat this sentence aloud or to themselves: *While I'm reading, I reread some parts of the story to see if I can figure out what is happening.* Have students tell if rereading has helped them understand parts of "Freedom Ride."**

Critical Thinking Question

What kinds of difficulties do the Fordreds have eating their meals? (Possible response: As paraplegics, it is important for them to drink lots of fluids, but drinking and eating soup is difficult for them with the boat rocking all the time.) CRITICAL: DETERMINING CAUSE AND EFFECT

Liz lowers Pete into the water in port so he can work on the propeller shaft.

SCIENCE

FACT FINDER

SEASICKNESS The Fordreds' seasickness is caused by the unusual motion they experience on the boat. People suffering from this form of motion sickness can become pale, sleepy, and extremely nauseous. The boat's motion affects a person's sense of balance, which causes these symptoms.

get up on deck—in an emergency we could end up in a real pickle. He grabbed a blanket and stretched out in the cockpit.

That first night watch was tough as I struggled to stay awake. Once I fell asleep and the mainsail slammed from one side of the boat to the other. Pete didn't sleep well at all, and when he did get to sleep I had to wake him so I could visit the head. That made me feel sicker than ever and was exhausting because I had to hand crank the broken lift to get myself up on deck again. Halfway up I dropped the handle and had to go back down to fetch it. This happened twice!

Pete relieved me at 6 a.m. I slept until 9, then plotted our course, which made me feel awful. Pete was feeling sick too, so he went back to sleep. The porpoises, though, were enjoying it. Six of them showed off for us, moving incredibly fast and making fun of our five knots. They made us feel better and took the gloom out of our seasickness.

Later in the afternoon I made some soup and put it in a flask to keep our fluids up. Paraplegics are supposed to drink great quantities of fluids to flush the kidneys, so we kept pushing each other to drink. The pump flask I'd bought in Cape Town was a real life-saver. At night, when it was cold, we could have hot chocolate or soup. The only problem was getting it to the cockpit from below because, with the rolling of the boat, we could not keep it upright. It often fell, inevitably landing on its pump handle and spraying hot stuff everywhere, including on us. It became a matter of getting it to the cockpit as quickly as possible. It was not an ideal type of flask for the sailing environment, but it was best for us because we didn't have the abdominal and back muscles to hold a cup and pour from the usual kind, all the while balancing on a rocking boat.

We forced ourselves to wash and to change clothes daily, in order to keep sores away from our bottoms and legs, and we wore socks and high-top sneakers to protect our ankles and feet. One of the most important things we had to do if we were to succeed was avoid sickness and sores.

That second night the weather got worse, so we reduced sail again. The waves seemed to loom all around us—better not to look at them or listen to the water washing through the cockpit and swishing through the spare gas bottles. I tried to sleep, telling myself it was

529

Informal Assessment

REFERENCE SOURCES

To find out whether students can determine which reference sources to use, ask them questions like the following:

- Where would you look to find the meaning of the word *inevitably*?
- What source would you use to find out more about porpoises?

STUDENTS ACQUIRING ENGLISH Help students understand the meaning of *pickle* and *head* as they are used in this context. As used here, *pickle* means "difficult situation or predicament" and *head* is the lavatory or toilet on a boat.

Cooperative Reading

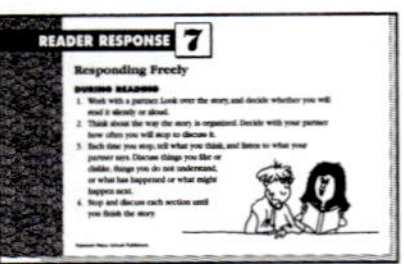
Response Card 7

Suggest that cooperative reading partners stop at this point to share their responses to Liz and Pete's sailing experience. You may want to initiate discussion by asking questions like these:

- **Is the trip turning out to be what you imagined it would be like?**
- **Why do you think Liz chose the particular incidents she did to tell about in detail?**

no good being tired. It took me ages to get to sleep, unless I was on watch—then it was everything I could do to stay awake.

By the fifth day out we were getting used to the motion of the boat and didn't keep falling all over the place. Learning to live at sea was, in a way, like being a paraplegic for the first time because we had to relearn each task. Getting dressed was complicated for us at the best of times, but now we had to do it on a rolling boat while holding on. To put on my sneakers I had to lift my foot up with one hand and put the shoe on with the other. My foot would curl up with a spasm and refuse to go all the way in, then the boat would lurch and I'd end up lying on my back with my foot in the air, still trying to get the shoe on. Eventually we learned to use the motion of the boat to help us. It was hilarious watching each other slide about. When the cockpit cushions were wet we could move really quickly—we just had to make sure we ended up where we wanted to go.

Emotionally, sailing was the same for us as for other sailors. The first few days were more or less miserable. It was a chore to do everything. We felt sick, and sleep was hard to come by. Then we'd get a stretch of pleasant weather with reasonable winds and gentle seas—real picture-book sailing. We read, listened to BBC World Service and relaxed. We marveled at the flying fish and the porpoises and the miracle of this experience. We turned brown as nuts. One day Pete got into the wash basin on the aft deck, where he whistled and sang and sloshed about, while the basin, with him in it, slid around.

Then, just when we began enjoying the good, the unpleasant would rear its head. The wind and seas kicked up. The self-steering vane invariably quit, so we had to steer by hand, and the motion was so bad that we couldn't sleep. We were plagued by merciless seasickness and wondered what we were doing here. For four years we had worked for this? Feeling sick and having to hold on all the time?

"Sir Francis Drake must have been nuts to do this all his life," Pete would moan.

Then the weather would brighten again.

Sailing was a blend of extremes, and we reacted no differently than anyone else. Some practical matters required more ingenuity, but so had they when women began sailing, especially alone: They learned to use their intellect and

530

SOCIAL STUDIES

Sir Francis Drake was the first Englishman to sail around the world, and it took him nearly three years to do it, from 1577 to 1580. Drake spent almost his whole life at sea. He worked as a sailor while he was still a boy and went on his first expedition to Africa when he was twenty. Before his great voyage around the world, he had already made three trips to the New World. Drake became ill and died on board his ship in 1596, while on an expedition to the West Indies.

Sir Francis Drake

the motion of the boat to compensate for their lack of brute strength.

We did the same to compensate for the parts of our bodies we couldn't use. We developed tricky ways of docking, of going for a swim, of getting in and out of the dinghy. For a long time we'd debated about sailing in our chairs (we could attach them to tracks) or out of them. Our sea trials had made it clear that *out* was the only way, so on deck we scooted about on our bottoms and down below we had false floors for use at sea. They raised us to a height where we could reach things in the saloon and galley and get in and out of our bunks, while Pete had access to his workbench.

Instead of letting our handicaps serve as obstacles, we simply found ways to work around them.

A porpoise entertains us.

531

Tested Skill

MINILESSON

MAINTAIN : COMPREHENSION

Sequence/ Cause-Effect

INFORMAL ASSESSMENT

Write the following sentences on the board:

The first few days were more or less miserable. It was quite a chore to do everything.

Then we'd get a stretch of pleasant weather with reasonable winds and gentle seas.

Ask students what the weather was like first *(more or less miserable)* and next. *(pleasant)* Ask which words helped them decide this. *(first and then)* Then have a volunteer tell why it was a chore to do everything. (because the weather was miserable)

TEACH/MODEL

Explain that the events in "Freedom Ride" happen in a logical sequence and that they are often linked together in causal chains. Explain that a causal chain is a sequence of events that cause other events to happen. You may want to model identifying a causal chain:

MODEL

The Fordreds' steering vane breaks causing them to steer by hand, which causes the boat to rock more and the Fordreds to experience sleeplessness and seasickness.

PRACTICE/APPLY

Have students find other causal chains in the selection and create diagrams like the one below that show the sequence of events.

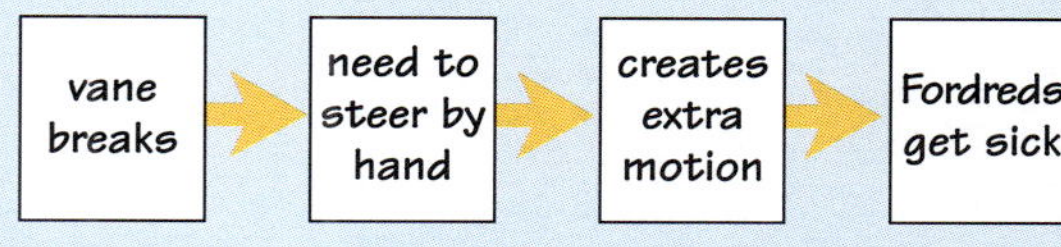

SCIENCE

FACT FINDER

PORPOISES AND DOLPHINS

Porpoises are small, toothed whales that are classified by most zoologists as being in the same family as dolphins. Most porpoises have rounded snouts; dolphins have beaklike snouts. Both are mammals and are considered very intelligent.

Strategic Reading

PAGES 526–533 What are some of the problems the Fordreds faced as they sailed across the Atlantic Ocean? (Possible responses: They struggled with seasickness and sleeplessness. They had trouble moving around the boat quickly. The weather caused problems with the sails and with steering.) **STRATEGY: SUMMARIZING**

How do the Fordreds manage to sail across the ocean in spite of their disabilities? (Possible response: They develop ways of moving about the boat and reaching objects they need.) **CRITICAL: DETERMINING CHARACTERS' TRAITS**

Returning to the Predictions/Purpose

Did you find out how the Fordreds build a boat and sail across the Atlantic Ocean? Encourage students to discuss whether their purposes for reading were met. **STRATEGY: RETURNING TO THE PURPOSE**

Appreciating the Literature

What part of the selection did you find most exciting? Why? (Responses will vary.)

Land Ho!

Being a new navigator, I grew increasingly apprehensive as we approached our first landfall. What if we were there and the island of St. Helena wasn't?

But one magical morning, 17 days after we'd left Cape Town, Pete woke me and told me to get the anchor ready. Was he being funny? No, there was St. Helena amongst the clouds, dead ahead. We hugged each other. My navigation worked! It really worked! Yahoo! Seventeen days at sea and out of the clouds loomed the blue outline of a mountain. Oh, how we wanted to dance for joy on the deck!

After another week at sea I found Ascension Island, too, which was memorable for the welcome we received. We'd been told that it would be difficult for us to get ashore on Ascension, but the islanders obviously had been warned by the St. Helenians that we were coming. As soon as we anchored, a boat came out to Usikusiku to fetch us. It motored straight to a crane, which lifted our boat and put it into a cradle on land.

"How are we going to get

down?" I whispered to Pete, but within minutes a forklift roared alongside and lowered us to our waiting chairs, while at least a hundred islanders looked on. I felt like a nit, but how wonderful it was that the islanders had thought of everything. Meeting people like these was another reward for all our hard work.

Our third and final leg across the Atlantic took two weeks and ended

532

SUMMARIZING

Summary Chart

Ask students to complete the summary chart by writing notes under each subhead to summarize the information in that section. Some students may have written their notes immediately after reading each section. See *Practice Book* page 160.

SUMMARY CHART

INTRODUCTION: (Liz thinks back to what it was like sailing on the boat that she and her husband—both paraplegics—built ten years before.)

LET'S BUILD A BOAT:

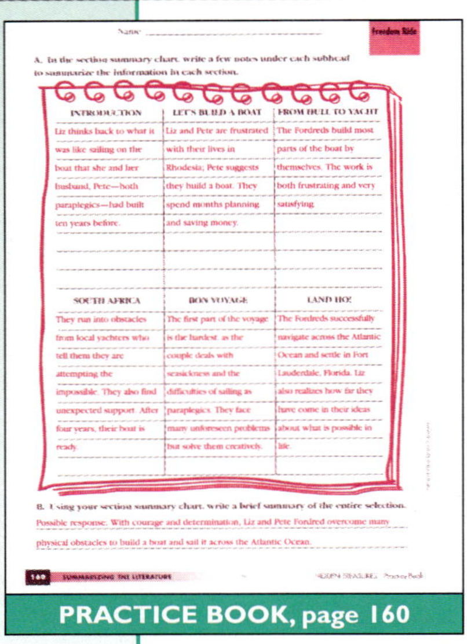

Name ______________ Freedom Ride

A. In the section summary chart, write a few notes under each subhead to summarize the information in each section.

INTRODUCTION	LET'S BUILD A BOAT	FROM HULL TO YACHT
Liz thinks back to what it was like sailing on the boat that she and her husband, Pete—both paraplegics—had built ten years before.	Liz and Pete are frustrated with their lives in Rhodesia; Pete suggests they build a boat. They spend months planning and saving money.	The Fordreds build most parts of the boat by themselves. The work is both frustrating and very satisfying.
SOUTH AFRICA	**BON VOYAGE**	**LAND HO!**
They run into obstacles from local yachters who tell them they are attempting the impossible. They also find unexpected support. After four years, their boat is ready.	The first part of the voyage is the hardest, as the couple deals with seasickness and the difficulties of sailing as paraplegics. They face many unforeseen problems but solve them creatively.	The Fordreds successfully navigate across the Atlantic Ocean and settle in Fort Lauderdale, Florida. Liz also realizes how far they have come in their ideas about what is possible in life.

B. Using your section summary chart, write a brief summary of the entire selection.

Possible response: With courage and determination, Liz and Pete Fordred overcome many physical obstacles to build a boat and sail it across the Atlantic Ocean.

160 SUMMARIZING THE LITERATURE HIDDEN TREASURES Practice Book

PRACTICE BOOK, page 160

with the most wonderful smell of wet earth and vegetation a full day before we saw land; I just couldn't stop breathing it in deeply. A few pretty butterflies flitted about Usikusiku, another indication that land must be close. With the following day's sunrise we could see Brazil ahead and the city of Fortaleza on our port bow. Yahoo! We were here! We had crossed the Atlantic!

"Well, we made it," Pete said that night after we'd cleaned up and settled in.

"Of course, my love. There was never any doubt, was there?"

Pete got a job in Fortaleza, I began writing, and we settled in for the remainder of hurricane season. Then we made our way up the South American coast and entered the Northern Hemisphere for the first time in our lives. We cruised Caribbean islands in the manner we'd dreamed of, went aground in Puerto Rico and were rescued by the U.S. Coast Guard. We finally wound up in Fort Lauderdale, which we have made our home.

I can look back now and see how we have grown—mentally and physically. At the beginning of our rehabilitation, simple tasks like changing clothes were a real physical challenge that could bring tears of frustration. Pushing half a mile to the grocery store was unthinkable. Now all that seems like nothing, because we have overcome far bigger obstacles.

I might not be able to run wild with my dog through a field until I'm tired or jump on a horse and feel that exhilarating freedom under me, but there are plenty of other satisfying things to do in life. You just have to look for them.

533

MINILESSON

REVIEW: STUDY SKILLS

Graphic Aids

INFORMAL ASSESSMENT

Have students look at the map on pages 532 and 533. Ask them about how far it is between Harare and Durban. (about 850 miles) What feature on the map helped them figure this out? (the distance scale)

TEACH/MODEL

Discuss the map and the information it provides. Remind students that a distance scale gives the distance on the map in relation to real distances, and a compass rose shows directions on the map. Point out the other labels on the map. Explain that the line going across the map shows the route the Fordreds traveled. Ask students what direction the Fordreds were going when they went from Harare to Durban. (south)

PRACTICE/APPLY

Ask students the following questions:

- **Which distance is longer—Cape Town to St. Helena Island or Durban to Cape Town?** (Cape Town to St. Helena Island)
- **What direction did the Fordreds travel when they went from Cape Town to St. Helena Island?** (northwest)

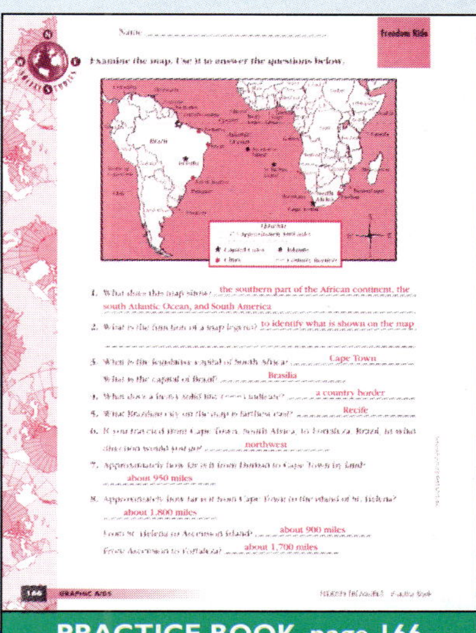
Freedom Ride

Examine the map. Use it to answer the questions below.

1. What does this map show? the southern part of the African continent, the south Atlantic Ocean, and South America
2. What is the function of a map legend? to identify what is shown on the map
3. What is the legislative capital of South Africa? Cape Town
   What is the capital of Brazil? Brasilia
4. a country border
5. What Brazilian city on the map is farthest east? Recife
6. If you traveled from Cape Town, South Africa, to Fortaleza, Brazil, in what direction would you go? northwest
7. Approximately how far is it from Durban to Cape Town by land? about 950 miles
8. Approximately how far is it from Cape Town to the island of St. Helena? about 1,800 miles
   From St. Helena to Ascension Island? about 900 miles
   From Ascension to Fortaleza? about 1,700 miles

GRAPHIC AIDS

PRACTICE BOOK, page 166

POETRY

Until I Saw the Sea

by Lilian Moore

INTRODUCING THE POEM Remind students that the Fordreds' experience on the ocean was both exhilarating and frightening. Ask students to give their impressions of the ocean—either from actual experience or from having read about it in selections like "Freedom Ride." Tell students that they will read a famous poet's impression of the sea.

APPRECIATING THE POEM Read the poem aloud as students follow along. Point out that a good poem often allows the reader to experience something familiar in a new way. Then have students close their eyes, and tell them to inhale and exhale very slowly to evaluate the poet's use of this image in describing the sound of the sea washing in and out on the shore. Ask students to share any other images in the poem that they especially liked.

After discussing the poem, allow three volunteers to each read a section of the poem aloud.

LISTENING CENTER

"Until I Saw the Sea" is available on *Literature Cassette 3.*

Until I Saw the Sea

Until I saw the sea
I did not know
that wind
could wrinkle water so.

I never knew
that sun
could splinter a whole sea of blue.

Nor
did I know before,
a sea breathes in and out
upon a shore.

Lilian Moore

A Holiday, 1915
Edward Potthast

535

About the Poet

Lilian Moore has written a wide variety of poetry collections for children. She focuses on the universal experiences and feelings of childhood and enables her audience to find beauty in familiar and unexpected places. Moore says, "Poems should be like fireworks, packed carefully and artfully, ready to explode with unpredictable effects." Moore received the National Council of Teachers of English Award for excellence in poetry for children in 1985.

POET'S CRAFT Remind students that there are subtle ways a poet can link sounds in a line or verse. Slowly reread the first verse for students, and ask them what consonant sound they hear repeated. (*w* in *wind* and *water*) Ask volunteers to find other repeated sounds in the poem. (Students may point out the end rhymes in *know/so, knew/blue,* and *nor/before/shore*; the initial consonants in *saw/sea, not/know, never/knew,* and *sun/splinter/sea*; and vowel sounds in *sea/breathes.*) If you wish, have the whole class read the poem chorally, listening for the poet's use of repeated sounds.

STUDENTS ACQUIRING ENGLISH **Remind students that homophones are words that are pronounced alike but have different meanings and spellings, such as *sea* and *see*.**

ACTIVITY CHOICES

MAKE A DIAGRAM

SEAWORTHY SKETCH You may want to display a copy of the diagram in the Vocabulary Workshop on page T1119. Encourage students to compare their diagram with the photographs of the Fordreds' boat. ART

HAVE A DISCUSSION

GOING FOR GLORY You may want to remind students of something that Bill Littlefield said about Joan Benoit—that for her the point of the game was always "to be as good as she could possibly be at what she was doing." It might be interesting for students to compare that attitude, held by an athlete involved in competition, with the attitude Liz and Pete Fordred have toward their lives. CRITICAL THINKING/LISTENING AND SPEAKING

CALCULATE TIME

TIME FLIES Encourage students to compare their answers and their methods of calculating the total number of hours Liz and Pete spent building the boat. MATH

RESPONSE CORNER

MAKE A DIAGRAM

SEAWORTHY SKETCH

Make a diagram of a sailboat. Label your diagram by adding the names of the boat parts mentioned in the selection. For more information, check an encyclopedia or books about sailing.

HAVE A DISCUSSION

GOING FOR GLORY

Why do you think Pete and Liz were so determined to build the boat and sail it? Discuss your thoughts with a small group. Talk about a time when you showed determination in spite of obstacles.

536

STUDENTS ACQUIRING ENGLISH Ask students to work with peers who are fluent in English to prepare their discussions. Have students working on the diagram label the parts of their sailboat both in English and in their first language.

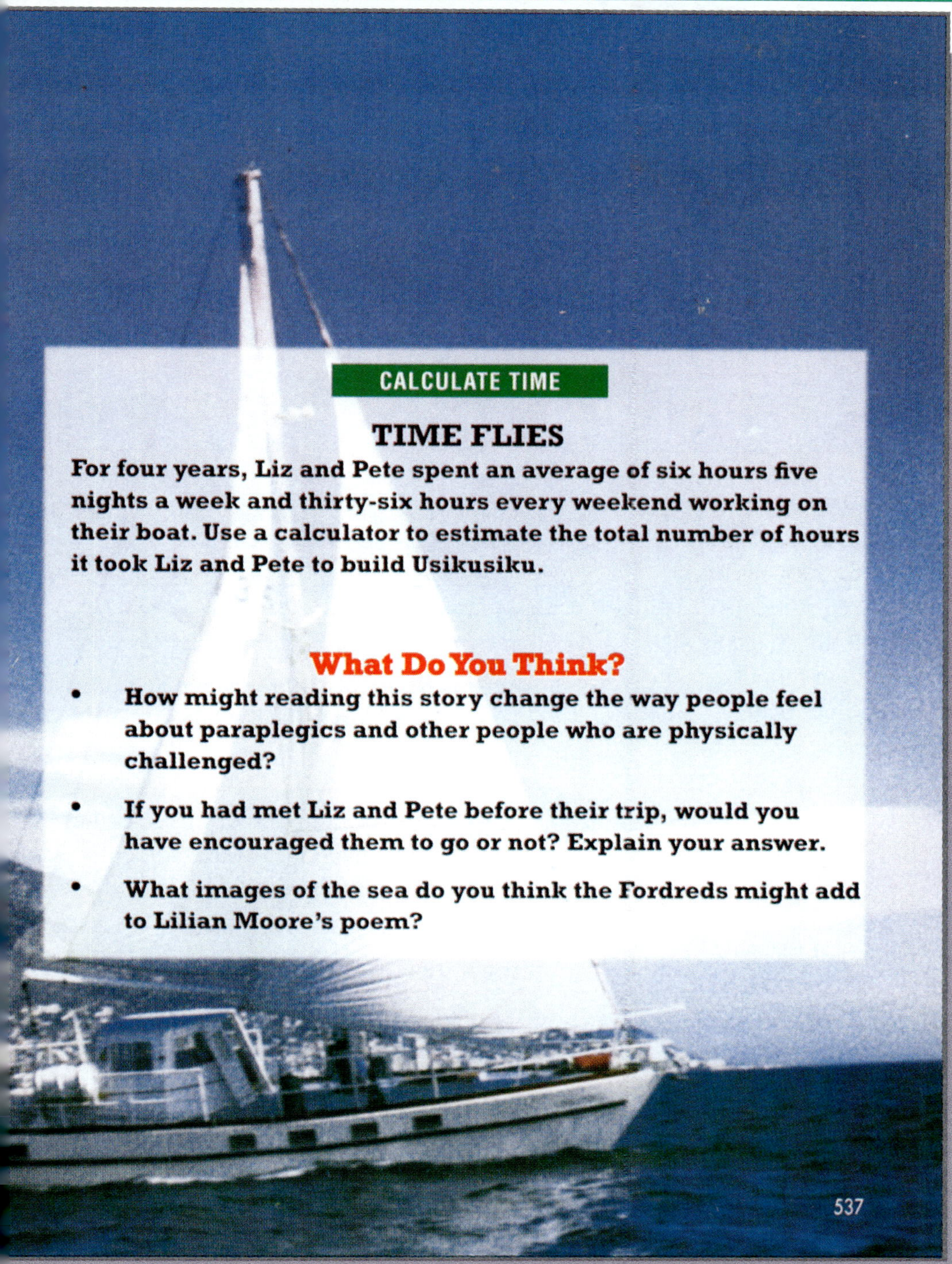

CALCULATE TIME

TIME FLIES

For four years, Liz and Pete spent an average of six hours five nights a week and thirty-six hours every weekend working on their boat. Use a calculator to estimate the total number of hours it took Liz and Pete to build Usikusiku.

What Do You Think?

- **How might reading this story change the way people feel about paraplegics and other people who are physically challenged?**
- **If you had met Liz and Pete before their trip, would you have encouraged them to go or not? Explain your answer.**
- **What images of the sea do you think the Fordreds might add to Lilian Moore's poem?**

537

CHECKING COMPREHENSION

What Do You Think?

1. **How might this story change the way people feel about paraplegics and other people who are physically challenged?** (Possible responses: Through this story readers can realize that determined people with physical disabilities can fulfill their dreams.) CRITICAL ANALYSIS/REFLECTING
2. **If you had met Liz and Pete before their trip, would you have encouraged them to go or not? Explain your answer.** (Responses will vary.) PERSONAL RESPONSE
3. **What images of the sea do you think the Fordreds might add to Lilian Moore's poem?** (Possible responses: storms, seasickness, overcoming obstacles) CRITICAL ANALYSIS/CREATIVE

VARYING THE ACTIVITY

To **challenge** students, have them interview a classmate participating in the discussion and present the interview in a talk-show format or radio broadcast.

Intervention Strategies

TIPS FOR CLASSROOM MANAGEMENT

IF second-language students need additional vocabulary and during-reading strategies to understand "Freedom Ride," **THEN** use *Sheltered English/ESL Manual*, pages 82–85.

IF students had difficulty understanding "Freedom Ride," **THEN** complete the Rereading and Decoding Strategies. See also *Intervention Strategies Manual*, pages 122–127.

REREADING

CHALLENGE CARDS Organize students into small groups and give each group an index card. Assign groups a section of the story for rereading, such as "Let's Build a Boat." Tell students that as they reread, they should recall the challenges the Fordreds faced. Then have them fill out a Challenge Card for each section they read.

In this part of the story, Liz and Pete faced and overcame the following challenge(s): ______________________
____
____
____

When students have finished rereading, have the groups share and discuss their Challenge Cards.

PERSONAL JOURNAL

How does the title of this selection tell its main idea? Have students write a few sentences.

DECODING LONG WORDS

REVIEW Present the following words from the story:

ankles	basketball	skippering	sickness
sailboat	problem	perfectionist	humor
aircraft	invented	yachtsmen	rudder
weather	relearn	battle	travel
refuse	plentiful	cabin	commitment

Have volunteers help you complete the chart with the words as you review each strategy that students can use for decoding longer words.

Compounds	Prefixes	Suffixes/Endings
Consonants Between Vowels:		
One	Two	Three
Three or More Syllables		

- Look for compound words: *air-craft*.
- Look for familiar prefixes, suffixes, and endings: *re-learn, sick-ness, in-vent-ed*.
- Look for two consonants between vowels. If they form a cluster or digraph, divide after the two consonants: *weath-er*. Otherwise, divide between the two consonants: *rud-der.*
- Look for three consonants between vowels. If the third consonant is the letter *l*, divide before the consonant preceding the *le: an-kles*.
- Look for a single consonant letter between vowels. Divide in front of the consonant: *hu-mor*, or after it: *cab-in,* until you pronounce a recognizable word.

Have students work with a partner to describe a strategy for other story words.

WRITING TO SUMMARIZE

Provide students with strips of paper labeled with the following geographical reference points:

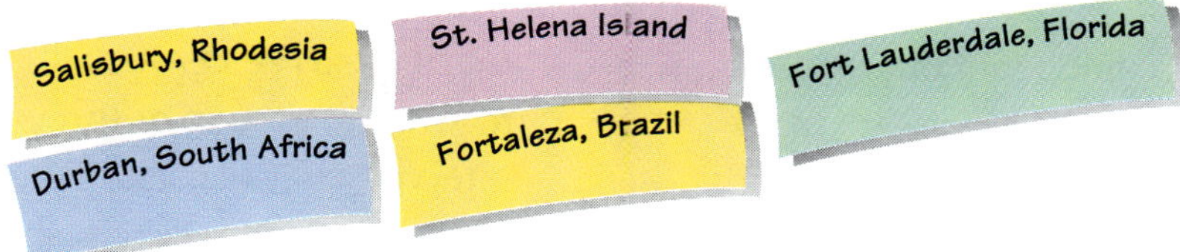

Then have students write a sentence or two on each strip to sum up the major events that happened to Liz and Pete at each location.

DECODING SUPPORT
y with endings -s, -es

Intervention Strategies Manual pp. 126–127

ESL/TITLE I READING

Reading Trade Books

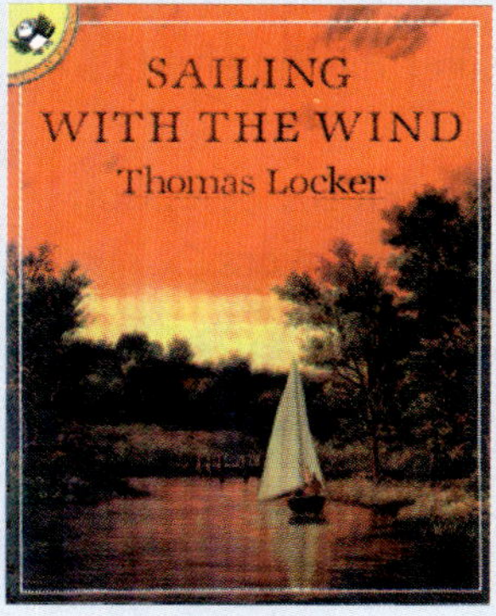

ESL/Title I Library

Sailing with the Wind

by Thomas Locker

This story about Elizabeth's sailing excursion downriver with her Uncle Jack is a delightful account of a young person's discovery of nature and a wider world. Have students use the diagram below to compare "Freedom Ride" with *Sailing with the Wind*.

	"Freedom Ride"	*Sailing with the Wind*
Characters		
Challenges		

EASY AVERAGE CHALLENGE

TAKE-HOME BOOK TO REINFORCE KEY WORDS

Students will enjoy reading about a hurricane that left a special gift. Have students read the book in class during independent reading time or take it home to read.

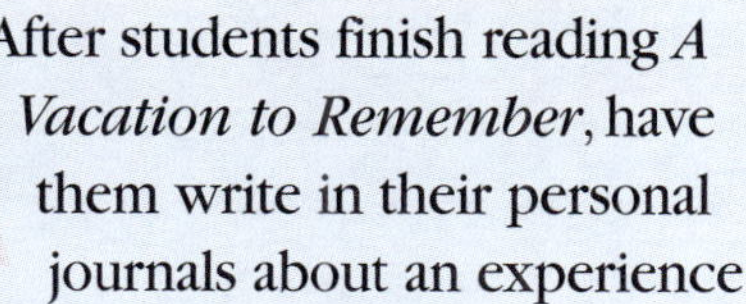

PERSONAL JOURNAL

After students finish reading *A Vacation to Remember*, have them write in their personal journals about an experience they may have had with a storm.

See also *Intervention Strategies Manual*, page 125.

IDEA BANK

TIPS FOR CLASSROOM MANAGEMENT

IF students need practice reading maps, **THEN** they should work on the Retelling activity.

IF students have a special interest in ocean stories, **THEN** they should participate in the Viewing activity.

RETELLING

Annotated Map

Have students work independently, with partners, or in small groups to create maps that include Africa, the South Atlantic, South America, and Florida. On their maps they should trace the Fordreds' progress, beginning in Salisbury, Rhodesia (now Harare, Zimbabwe), and ending in Fort Lauderdale, Florida. Using captions or illustrations, they should describe what happened at each important point along the way.
LISTENING/SPEAKING/VIEWING

Informal Assessment

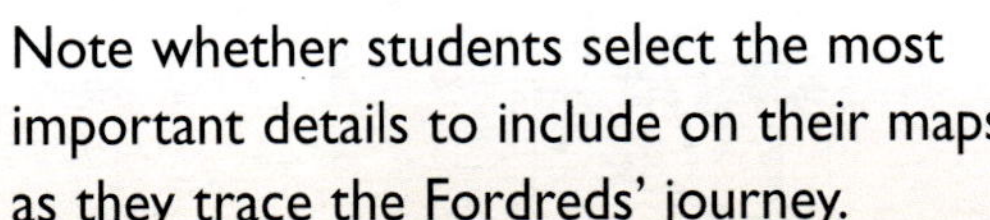

Note whether students select the most important details to include on their maps as they trace the Fordreds' journey.

ORAL LANGUAGE

Interview

COOPERATIVE LEARNING Invite students to work in groups of three to role-play an interview with Liz and Pete Fordred. The members of each group should collaborate on the questions for the interview. Then, taking the roles of the Interviewer, Liz, and Pete, each group of three will conduct their interview before an audience of their classmates. LISTENING/SPEAKING/WRITING

TIPS FOR LISTENING AND SPEAKING

Students involved in the interview should remember to

- wait until the speaker has finished before responding.
- incorporate details from the selection in their questions and answers.

Students in the audience should listen to

- distinguish between facts from the selection and inferences made by interview participants.
- respond appropriately to what is said.
- judge the success of the interview.

VIEWING

Video/Documentary

Have students watch the documentary about the seafaring expedition of Thor Heyerdahl—*Kon-Tiki*. Before, during, and after students view the documentary, have them think about how this voyage was similar to Liz and Pete Fordred's. After viewing, encourage students to compare and contrast the journeys. LISTENING/SPEAKING/VIEWING

REAL-LIFE RESOURCES

Warning Labels/Signs

READING WARNING SIGNS Explain that international signs have been created for world travelers like Liz and Peter Fordred. Display these signs and discuss how they communicate a message:

Ask students to identify other nonverbal signs that are important in daily life.

READING WARNING LABELS Students may find examples of warning labels on cleaning products, art supplies, or medicines. Talk about the standard elements included in any warning label. Emphasize the importance of reading warning labels carefully before using a product. See *Writer's Magazine* pages 82 and 83.

REAL-LIFE CHALLENGE Students can hold a class contest to see who can create the longest list of products that include warning labels. Each entry should name the product and describe the warning. READING/WRITING

STUDENTS ACQUIRING ENGLISH

Students can collaborate with English-proficient students to create maps that include illustrations as well as labels and captions.

EXTRA SUPPORT

Help students tap their prior knowledge of interviewing by making the connection between television talk shows and interviews. Help students see that popular talk-show hosts are interviewers and the conversations they have with their guests are interviews.

A number of organizations are working on more signs.
Try making up your own signs in the space below.
Begin with signs for familiar people and things, such as doctor, poison, and various animals. Then see whether

Real-Life INTERNATIONAL ROAD SIGNS Skills

WARNING! WATCH OUT!

International road signs were created for world travelers such as Liz and Pete Fordred. Because there are so many languages spoken in the world, the United Nations designed nonverbal signs that everyone could understand. Words aren't needed because the pictures say it all. Look at some of the international warning signs here. Which ones have you seen before?

Falling Rocks — Pedestrian Crossing — Children
Cyclists — Animal Crossing — Other Dangers

Now look at the following signs. Draw lines to match the signs with their meanings in the second column.

STOP

Stop
No Entry
No Motorcycles
No Cycles
No Mopeds
No Pedestrians

TAMPER PROOF

82 Freedom Ride • Writer's Magazine
Freedom Ride 83

WRITER'S MAGAZINE, pages 82–83

WRITER'S WORKSHOP

News Story

TIPS FOR CLASSROOM MANAGEMENT

IF students are familiar with the steps for writing a news story, THEN have them begin writing, referring to the model on Transparency 52 as necessary.

IF you want a short writing activity, THEN adapt this lesson by having students focus on the Writer's Craft.

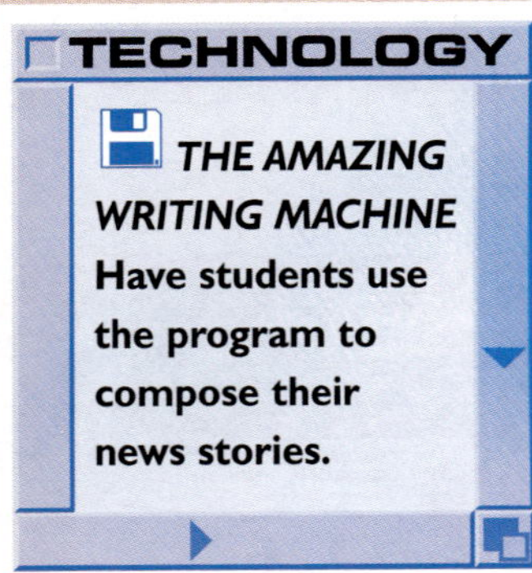

Thinking as Writers

WRITING FORM: News Story Distribute copies of a local newspaper. Have students read the news stories and headlines critically, discussing the kinds of events and issues being reported. Tell students that they will learn about news stories and then write one.

Display Transparency 52, and use the introduction and the side notes to discuss the main parts of a news story.

TRANSPARENCY 52

Model: News Story

*A **news story** contains a headline, a lead, and a body. It gives information about a current event, an issue, or a person.*

headline	**Sanchez Seeks Presidency of School Board**
lead telling *who, what, where, when,* and *why*	Maria Sanchez, a local business executive, is running for president of the school board in Duane County this year because she wants to make the board more responsive to the needs of students and their taxpaying parents.
body telling *how*	Sanchez, who grew up in Duane County and attended its public schools, says she wants to help students realize their full potential. She wants the board to focus on keeping potential dropouts in school and on spending tax dollars where they can do the most good. "Head Start and Students in Business are examples of two successful programs I would continue to support," Sanchez says. "Let's fund programs that work." Sanchez would like to change the way board meetings are run. If elected, she would encourage students to participate as nonvoting members of the board. Sanchez believes she can accomplish most of these changes within the first six months if she is elected.

WRITER'S CRAFT: Who, What, Where, When, Why, and How Explain that a news story presents the facts about something in a straightforward manner. The story should tell

- who was involved.
- what happened to those involved.
- where, when, why, and how it happened.

Have students find that information in the model. Point out that in a news story a writer gives only facts and not his or her opinion of those facts.

PREWRITING AND DRAFTING

As students choose a topic and work on their news stories, remind them to keep in mind who will read it. Refer to these strategies to help students begin their news stories.

PREWRITING GRAPHIC ORGANIZER Students may want to use the chart below to organize their ideas.

Subject:
Who:
What:
Where and when:
Why and how:

SUSTAINED SILENT WRITING Students who have a good sense of how they want to write their news story can begin writing without interruption.

DURING-WRITING STRATEGY Students can keep a checklist of the questions a news story should answer beside them as they write to be certain they have answered each one.

RESPONDING AND REVISING

Have students work with partners to help each other revise. Display this checklist:

- Does my headline tell readers what the story is about and catch their interest?
- Does my lead tell who, what, where, when, and why?
- Does the body of my story tell how?
- Have I included only facts and not my opinion?

PROOFREADING

Offer the following tips for students when they proofread:

- Check **capitalization** of proper nouns.
- In direct quotes, check **punctuation** to be sure that periods, commas, and question marks appear inside the quotation marks.
- Check for correct forms of verbs, particularly **irregular verbs**. (See Grammar Minilesson on page T1097.)
- Look for misspelled words.

PUBLISHING

If students are going to publish their news stories, suggest these options or let students choose their own method:

ORAL Students can present their news stories as a news broadcast with stories on similar topics grouped together.

WRITTEN Use a computer to organize the stories by subject and print them together in a class paper you might call "News of the Day."

EVALUATION BENCHMARKS: NEWS STORY		
A news story by a proficient student writer shows the following characteristics:		
FORM	CRAFT	CONVENTIONS
Demonstrates understanding of the form • effective headline • strong lead • answers the questions *who, what, where, when, why*, and *how* in a logical order	**Uses clear and appropriate language** • direct quotes used effectively • uses straightforward language that doesn't give opinion	**Follows conventions of grammar and usage** • quotation marks used correctly with other punctuation • correct forms of regular and irregular verbs used • proper nouns capitalized

Teacher Assessment As you assess students' writing, refer to the Evaluation Benchmarks chart. For additional information, including model papers, see *Integrated Performance Assessment* Teacher's Edition.

PORTFOLIO OPPORTUNITY

Have students answer the Student Self-Assessment questions and include both their answers and their news stories in their portfolios.

LANGUAGE HANDBOOK

Planning Tips, pages 14–17; Writing to Inform, pages 60–61; News Story, pages 70–71; Punctuation, pages 174–175

Student Self-Assessment

Have students answer the following questions and include the answers in their portfolio:

 Did you find it difficult to include only facts and not your opinion? Do you think that is important in a news story?

 What was the most interesting part of your news story?

Tested Skill

GRAMMAR

Adverbs

TECHNOLOGY

THE AMAZING WRITING MACHINE Students can use the Journal feature in the program to write their journal entries.

LANGUAGE HANDBOOK

Adverbs, pages 160, 162–163, 220–222

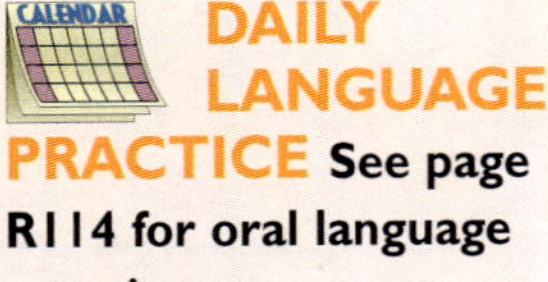

DAILY LANGUAGE PRACTICE See page R114 for oral language exercises.

Reading ↔ Writing Connection

Connect to the literature. With students, reread the following sentences from page 524 of the selection:

Slowly I learned new skills. I finally finished the first cupboard and got it all screwed into place. "Right," said Pete. "Now take it apart and glue it." I was rapidly losing patience with the cupboard and with Pete. In their spare time Pete and his dad were inventing a way for us to get down into the boat.

Tell students that this passage contains many **adverbs**. Explain to students that an adverb can describe *how, when, where*, or *to what extent*, and that many adverbs end in *-ly*. On the board, write *How, When, Where*, and *To What Extent* as headings. Then have students list the adverbs from the sentences above under each of these headings.

How	When	Where	To What Extent
(slowly)	(finally)	(down)	(all)
(apart)	(now)		
(rapidly)			

Build oral language. Have students use the words in the list in sentences of their own. Encourage them to add more words to the list and use them in sentences as well.

Teach/Model

Discuss adverbs. Explain that adverbs tell how, when, where, and to what extent. Adverbs may modify, or describe, verbs, adjectives, or other adverbs. Words that end with the suffix *-ly* are usually adverbs, but not all adverbs end with *-ly*. Write these sentences on the board and ask students to underline the adverb and circle the word or words it modifies.

The whole world was amazingly (peaceful.)

The stars (twinkled) overhead.

The lapping water (rocked) the boat gently.

Sleep (would come) soon.

Practice/Apply

Check understanding. Have students draw a simple sketch of a sailboat. Around the sketch, students should use adverbs to write phrases that describe how the boat moves and sounds, where it goes, and so on. For example, students might write phrases like these: *sails smoothly, cuts through the water quickly, turns slowly*.

Practice Activities

Anything You Can Say. . .

ORAL APPLICATION Have students form pairs for this game of "one-upmanship." The first student says a very simple sentence—for example, "She walked." The other student must repeat the sentence, adding an adverb—"She walked quickly." Then the first student repeats the sentence adding a second adverb—"She walked upstairs quickly." When students can no longer add adverbs, one of the players makes up a new sentence. **AUDITORY**

How Did You Do That?

WRITTEN APPLICATION Have students form small groups and take turns moving in a particular way or pantomiming an action. Each time someone makes a move, each of the other group members must write a sentence that includes an adverb describing what the person did. Students should read their sentences aloud so the group can decide which sentence best describes the action. **VISUAL/KINESTHETIC**

Write a Journal Entry

WRITTEN APPLICATION Have each student write a journal entry that describes an exciting or challenging personal experience. Encourage students to use adverbs in their writing. When the journal entries are completed, students can exchange their work with partners. They should discuss the content and then identify the adverbs in the entry. **VISUAL**

APPLY TO WRITING

The placement of some adverbs, such as *only*, can affect the meaning of a sentence. You may want students to look for adverbs in their news stories or other writing and decide whether they are in the right place to give the intended meaning.

USAGE TIP You can turn most adjectives into adverbs by adding *-ly: happy, happily; quiet, quietly; weary, wearily*.

STUDENTS ACQUIRING ENGLISH

Emphasize that although the ending *-ly* often signals an adverb, the true test is whether or not a word tells something about a verb, an adjective, or another adverb.

RETEACH

See page R104 for lessons in multiple modalities.

GRAMMAR PRACTICE BOOK
pages 50–51

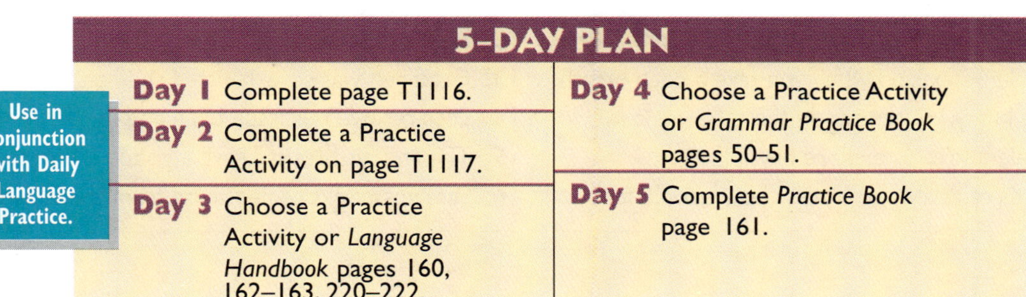

Use in conjunction with Daily Language Practice.

5-DAY PLAN	
Day 1 Complete page T1116.	**Day 4** Choose a Practice Activity or *Grammar Practice Book* pages 50–51.
Day 2 Complete a Practice Activity on page T1117.	**Day 5** Complete *Practice Book* page 161.
Day 3 Choose a Practice Activity or *Language Handbook* pages 160, 162–163, 220–222.	

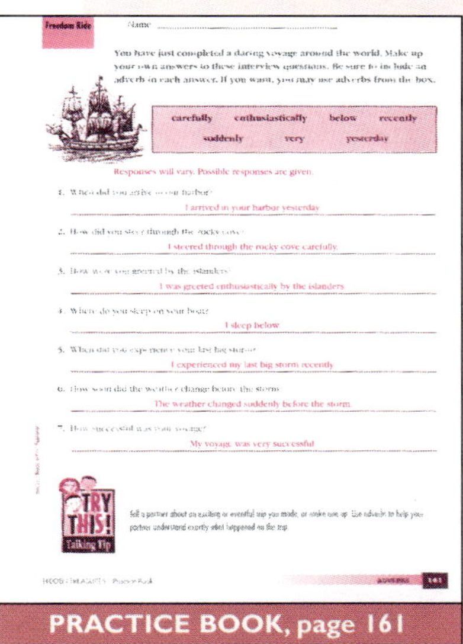

Freedom Ride

Name

You have just completed a daring voyage around the world. Make up your own answers to these interview questions. Be sure to include an adverb in each answer. If you want, you may use adverbs from the box.

carefully	enthusiastically	below	recently
suddenly	very	yesterday	

Responses will vary. Possible responses are given.

1. When did you arrive in our harbor?
   I arrived in your harbor yesterday.
2. How did you steer through the rocky cove?
   I steered through the rocky cove carefully.
3. How were you greeted by the islanders?
   I was greeted enthusiastically by the islanders.
4. Where do you sleep on your boat?
   I sleep below.
5. When did you experience your last big storm?
   I experienced my last big storm recently.
6. How soon did the weather change before the storm?
   The weather changed suddenly before the storm.
7. How successful was your voyage?
   My voyage was very successful.

TRY THIS! Talking Tip

Tell a partner about an exciting or eventful trip you made, or make one up. Use adverbs to help your partner understand exactly what happened on the trip.

ADVERBS 161

PRACTICE BOOK, page 161

2

SPELLING

5-Day Plan

Integrated Spelling Lesson 31: student book, pages 130–133; Teacher's Edition, pages T201–206.

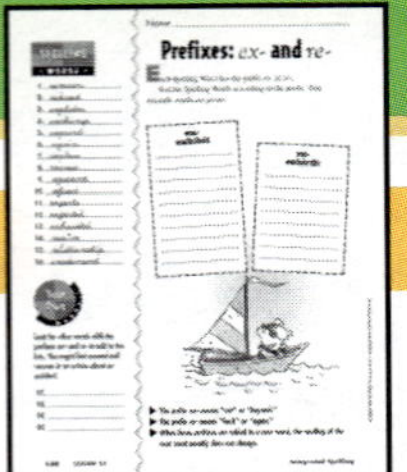

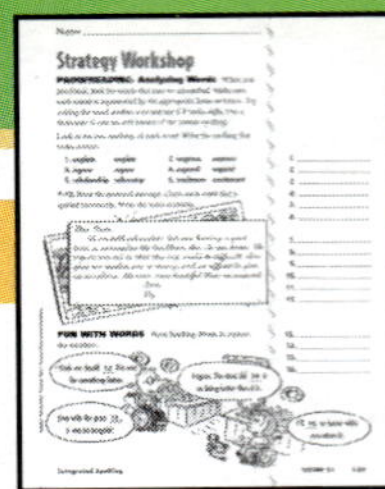

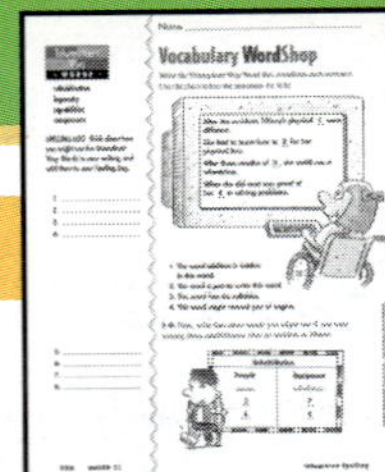

SPELLING WORDS

1. remain ★
2. reduced ★
3. explain ★
4. exchange
5. expand
6. regain ★
7. explore
8. express
9. represent ★
10. refused ★
11. experts
12. expected ★
13. exhausted ★
14. resolve
15. relationship
16. excitement ★

STUDENT'S PERSONAL WORDS

17. 19.
18. 20.

Additional story words are *relax, expedition, responded, explode, extreme,* and *relearn.*

★ Words appearing in "Freedom Ride"

Prefix: *ex-* and *re-*

Pretest

DAY 1 **Administer the pretest.** Say each word, and then use it in the dictation sentence below. Help students self-check their pretests.

OPEN SORT

DAY 2 **Have students classify words.** Have groups sort the Spelling Words according to part of speech, categorizing them as verbs, nouns, or words that could be either. Invite the groups to compare their lists.

CLOSED SORT

Sort by spelling pattern. Duplicate the chart below on the board or on chart paper. Ask students to work with a partner to copy the chart and write each Spelling Word in the appropriate column.

exhibit		rebirth	
exchange	expand	refused	resolve
excitement	explore	remain	represent
expected	express	relationship	regain
explain	experts	reduced	
exhausted			

Teach/Model

DAY 3 **Discuss the generalization.** Explain that *ex-* and *re-* are both prefixes, and prefixes change the meanings of base words. The prefix *ex-* sometimes means "out of" or "from," as in *expand* and *express*. It can also mean "completely; thoroughly," as in *exhausted* and *experts*. The prefix *re-* usually means "again" or "back," as in *reduced* and *regain*.

DAY 4 **Apply to writing.** Have students look for words with the prefixes *ex-* and *re-* in their news stories or in other writing to be sure they are spelled correctly.

Posttest

DAY 5 **Assess students' progress.** The sentences below should be used to administer the posttest.

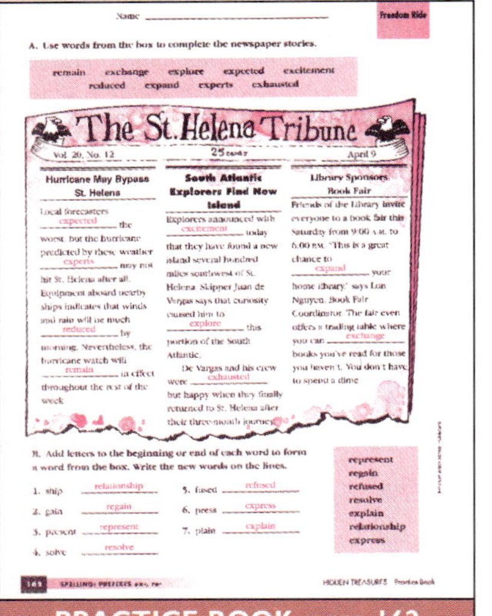

Name ______________ Freedom Ride

A. Use words from the box to complete the newspaper stories.

remain exchange explore expected excitement reduced expand experts exhausted

The St. Helena Tribune

Vol. 20, No. 12 25 cents April 9

Hurricane May Bypass St. Helens

Local forecasters expected the worst, but the hurricane predicted by these weather experts may not hit St. Helena after all. Equipment aboard nearby ships indicates that winds and rain will be much reduced by morning. Nevertheless, the hurricane watch will remain in effect throughout the rest of the week.

South Atlantic Explorers Find New Island

Explorers announced with excitement today that they have found a new island several hundred miles southwest of St. Helena. Skipper Juan de Vargas says that curiosity caused him to explore this portion of the South Atlantic.

De Vargas and his crew were exhausted but happy when they finally returned to St. Helena after their three-month journey.

Library Sponsors Book Fair

Friends of the Library invite everyone to a book fair this Saturday from 9:00 A.M. to 6:00 P.M. "This is a great chance to expand your home library," says Lon Nguyen, Book Fair Coordinator. The fair even offers a trading table where you can exchange books you've read for those you haven't. You don't have to spend a dime.

B. Add letters to the beginning or end of each word to form a word from the box. Write the new words on the lines.

represent regain refused resolve explain relationship express

1. ship relationship
2. gain regain
3. present represent
4. solve resolve
5. fused refused
6. press express
7. plain explain

162 SPELLING: PREFIXES *ex-, re-* HIDDEN TREASURES Practice Book

PRACTICE BOOK, page 162

DICTATION SENTENCES

1. Please remain seated.
2. All the prices have been reduced.
3. He didn't explain why he left.
4. *Swap* and exchange have similar meanings.
5. Your lungs expand when you take a deep breath.
6. If we hurry, we can regain the time we lost.
7. Travelers love to explore new places.
8. Words can't always express how people feel.
9. Jamal will represent our class in the finals.
10. He refused to answer the reporter's question.
11. All the experts agree.
12. She worked hard and expected to do well.
13. Gretchen was so exhausted she had to sleep.
14. Let's resolve this issue once and for all.
15. Tim and his brother have a good relationship.
16. Screams of excitement rose from the crowd.

VOCABULARY WORKSHOP

Reviewing Key Words

Write the Key Words on the board. Then present each of these situations. Have students choose a Key Word they think relates to the situation and use the word in a sentence they might say if they were in that situation.

Situation 1: You forgot your best friend's birthday. *(lapse)*

Situation 2: You find out you can't hold a dog show in the school gymnasium. *(restrictions)*

Situation 3: A mail-order company sends you the wrong stuff. *(incompetent)*

Situation 4: You're trying to study while your family is rearranging the furniture in the living room. *(turmoil)*

Extending Vocabulary

CONTEXT CLUES

Explain to students that some of the words used to describe the Fordreds' experiences have different meanings from their usual ones. Write the following sentences from the selection on the board, and ask students to use picture clues and context clues to identify the nautical meaning of each word.

Liz works on the unfinished *cabin* in her mother's backyard . . . (page 521 caption)

Six of (the porpoises) showed off for us, moving incredibly fast and making fun of our five *knots*. (page 529)

If necessary, help students see that in the second sentence *moving incredibly fast* provides the clue that tells that *knots* is a measure of speed or distance.

WRITE SENTENCES

Have students reread page 527 to find more nautical terms that also have everyday meanings. Students should write sentences using each word and provide enough context clues to help another person figure out its meaning.

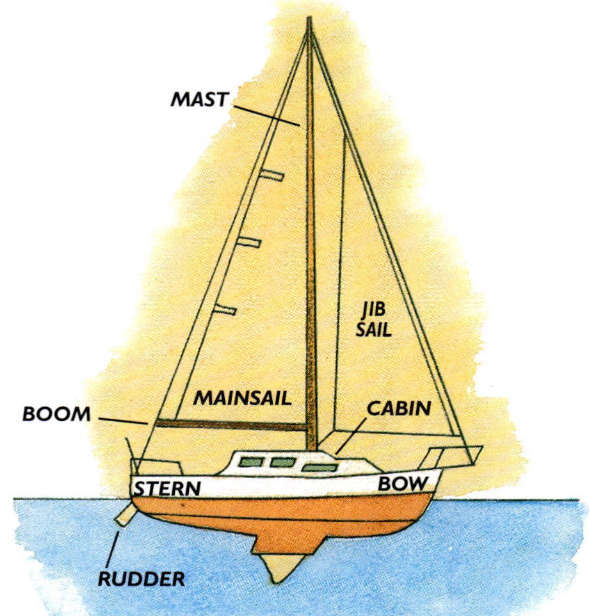

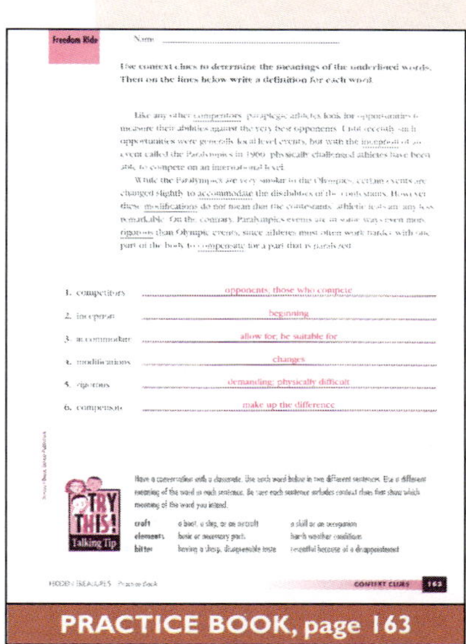

Freedom Ride

Name

Use context clues to determine the meanings of the underlined words. Then on the lines below write a definition for each word.

1. competitors — opponents, those who compete
2. inception — beginning
3. accommodate — allow for, be suitable for
4. modifications — changes
5. rigorous — demanding; physically difficult
6. compensate — make up the difference

TRY THIS! Talking Tip

craft	a boat, a ship, or an aircraft	a skill or an occupation
elements	basic or necessary parts	harsh weather conditions
bitter	having a sharp, disagreeable taste	resentful because of a disappointment

CONTEXT CLUES 163

PRACTICE BOOK, page 163

Tested Skill

INTRODUCE: STUDY SKILLS

Reference Sources

OBJECTIVE: To identify and use reference sources

Informal Assessment ✓

Are students able to

- ☑ identify the information needed?
- ☑ predict where the information will be found?
- ☑ explain their choices?

Teach/Model

Return to the literature. Recall with students that the Fordreds landed in Fortaleza, Brazil, and settled there for the remainder of the hurricane season. Ask students what references they would use to find out where Fortaleza, Brazil, is. (atlas, encyclopedia) Point out that by knowing what reference source to use and how to use it, readers can locate the information they want quickly and easily.

Model how to use the reference sources. Display Transparency 53 or the material on it.

Model choosing a reference source.

MODEL **If I wanted to check the spelling of the word *hurricane*, I'd probably look up the word in the dictionary. If I wanted to know when the hurricane season was, however, I might look in an almanac or an encyclopedia.**

TRANSPARENCY 53

Reference Sources

dictionary	word definitions, histories, and pronunciations
specialized dictionary	definitions of words related to a specific topic
thesaurus	synonyms for words
encyclopedia	information about important people, places, and other topics
almanac	up-to-date information and statistics about various topics
atlas	different kinds of maps
Readers' Guide to Periodical Literature	list of magazine articles, arranged according to topic
Books in Print	titles, authors, and publishers of books

Practice/Apply

Have students demonstrate understanding. Have students work in groups to name the reference sources in which the following information can be found:

- the publisher of *The Voyage of the Frog* by Gary Paulsen (*Books in Print*)
- a synonym for *obstacle* (thesaurus)
- the point at which you enter the Northern Hemisphere when sailing around South America (atlas)
- the names of all of last year's major hurricanes (almanac)

Practice Activities

Look It Up

PERFORMANCE ASSESSMENT Remind students that while the hull of their boat was being built, Liz and Pete read "all we could lay our hands on" about boats and sailing. Some of what they read might have been articles in magazines and other periodicals. Ask students to work with a partner to choose a subject they want to learn more about. Then have them look up that subject in the *Readers' Guide to Periodical Literature* and make a list of the articles about the subject that appeared in magazines in the last year.
VISUAL/AUDITORY/KINESTHETIC

A Guide to Finding Out

COOPERATIVE LEARNING Have students work together to design a poster that will educate people about reference sources. Have two or three students work on the text that will appear on the poster describing each reference source.

A Designer can plan out what the poster will look like, and an Illustrator can create or cut out pictures for the poster. Give the groups ample time and access to materials. You may want to ask the school librarian for permission to display the finished posters in the library. **VISUAL/KINESTHETIC**

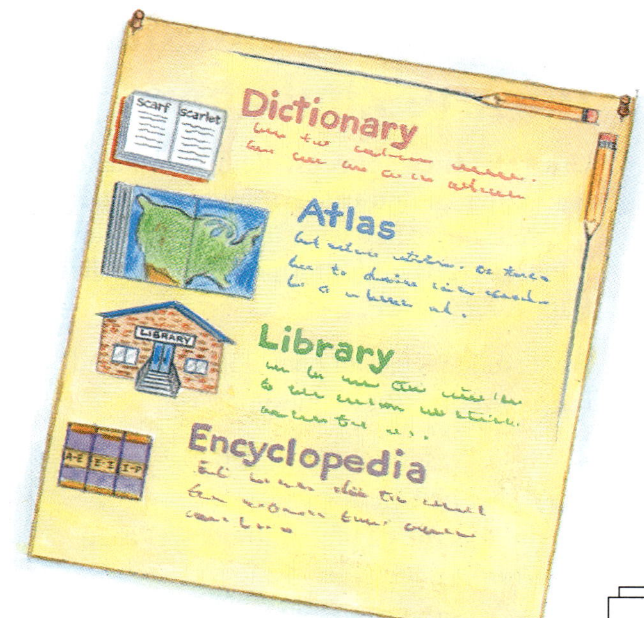

MEETING INDIVIDUAL NEEDS

STUDENTS ACQUIRING ENGLISH

Have students work in pairs to quiz one another on which reference source to use to find a map of your community, more information about sailing, and the definition of a sailing term.

RETEACH

See page R105 for lessons in multiple modalities.

CHALLENGE

Have students research Fortaleza, Brazil, and the surrounding area to find out why Liz and Pete could smell wet earth and vegetation for a day before they could even see land. Have students report their findings to the class orally and with pictures.

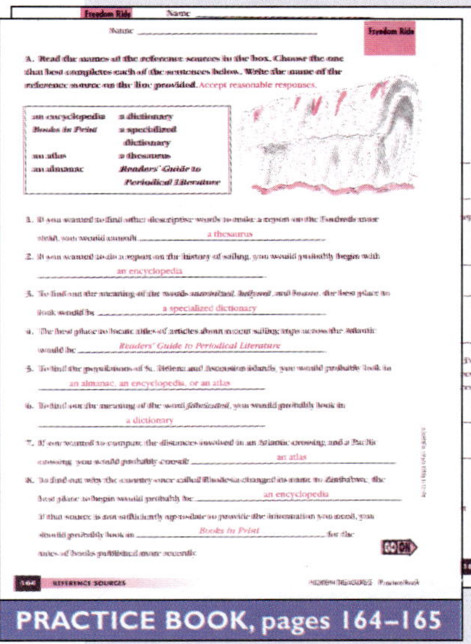
Freedom Ride

Name ______________

A. Read the names of the reference sources in the box. Choose the one that best completes each of the sentences below. Write the name of the reference source on the line provided. Accept reasonable responses.

an encyclopedia	a dictionary
Books in Print	a specialized dictionary
an atlas	a thesaurus
an almanac	*Readers' Guide to Periodical Literature*

1. a thesaurus
2. an encyclopedia
3. a specialized dictionary
4. *Readers' Guide to Periodical Literature*
5. an almanac, an encyclopedia, or an atlas
6. a dictionary
7. an atlas
8. an encyclopedia; *Books in Print*

164 REFERENCE SOURCES

PRACTICE BOOK, pages 164–165

TO REINFORCE REFERENCE SOURCES

How to Write a Great School Report by Elizabeth James and Carol Barkin. Morrow, 1993. **EASY**

Everyday Things and How They Work by Steve Parker. Kingfisher Books, 1991. **AVERAGE**

Research to Write by Maity Schrecengost. Highsmith, 1994. **AVERAGE**

SOCIAL STUDIES

The Changing Map of Africa

There are more than fifty independent countries in Africa. The following activities have students investigate more about the continent where Liz and Pete Fordred lived and built their boat.

TIPS FOR CLASSROOM MANAGEMENT

IF students are artistically inclined, **THEN** they may enjoy making travel posters and brochures for the Visit Africa activity.

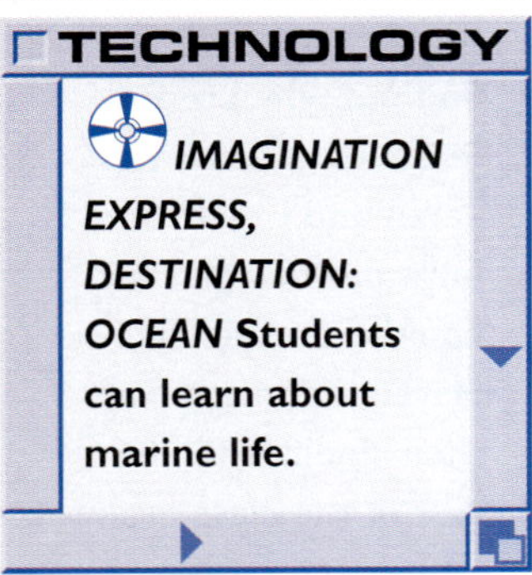

SOCIAL STUDIES

Salisbury, Rhodesia—Harare, Zimbabwe

Use reference sources. Remind students that when Liz and Pete Fordred were building their boat, they were living in Salisbury, Rhodesia. Today, their former home is called Harare, Zimbabwe.

Have students use an encyclopedia to find the answers to these questions:

- Whom was Rhodesia named for? What did that person do?
- Why was the capital of Rhodesia called *Salisbury*?
- Why was the name of the country changed? When did this happen?
- Why was the name *Zimbabwe* chosen for the country?
- Why was the name *Harare* chosen for the capital city?

Encourage researchers to get together afterward to confirm their findings and to discuss other interesting facts about Zimbabwe they have learned. LISTENING/READING/SPEAKING

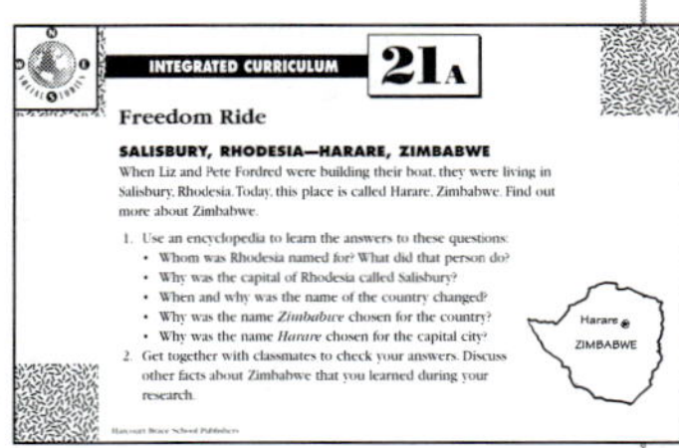
INTEGRATED CURRICULUM 21A

Freedom Ride

SALISBURY, RHODESIA—HARARE, ZIMBABWE

When Liz and Pete Fordred were building their boat, they were living in Salisbury, Rhodesia. Today, this place is called Harare, Zimbabwe. Find out more about Zimbabwe.

1. Use an encyclopedia to learn the answers to these questions:
   - Whom was Rhodesia named for? What did that person do?
   - Why was the capital of Rhodesia called Salisbury?
   - When and why was the name of the country changed?
   - Why was the name *Zimbabwe* chosen for the country?
   - Why was the name *Harare* chosen for the capital city?
2. Get together with classmates to check your answers. Discuss other facts about Zimbabwe that you learned during your research.

Curriculum Card 21A

ART

Visit Africa

Part of the reason the Fordreds built their boat was that they loved to travel, but for various reasons the only place they could go was South Africa. There are many wonderful places to go in Africa and many amazing things to see. Ask students to name some places in Africa they know about or have heard about that they'd like to visit. Encourage students to spend some time in the library browsing through magazines such as *Smithsonian, Natural History, Travel & Leisure*, and *National Geographic* to learn more about Africa and places to visit there. Then have students select a place in Africa that most appeals to them and create a travel poster to advertise that place. LISTENING/SPEAKING/READING/VIEWING

CROSS-CURRICULAR READING

African Landscapes by Warren J. Halliburton. Macmillan, 1993. EASY

Zimbabwe: A Treasure of Africa by Al Stark. Macmillan, 1986. AVERAGE

SOCIAL STUDIES

Discovering Colonial Africa

COOPERATIVE LEARNING Remind students that what is now the eastern United States was once controlled by Great Britain. Point out that Zimbabwe was also a British colony. At the beginning of the twentieth century, almost every country in Africa was a colony of some European country.

Have students work together to use a modern map of Africa to trace and create an overlay that shows the name of each country, the name of its colonial power, and the date it gained independence.

Help students think of methods to make their map and overlay large enough so that it can be displayed in the classroom for all to see. A Reporter can present the two maps to other classmates. LISTENING/SPEAKING/WRITING/VIEWING

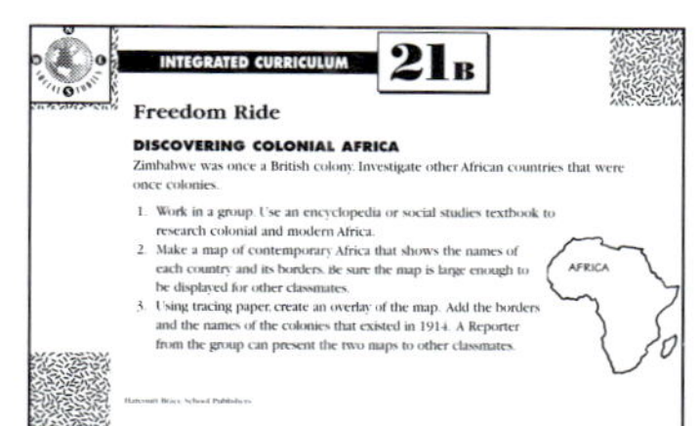

INTEGRATED CURRICULUM **21B**

Freedom Ride

DISCOVERING COLONIAL AFRICA

Zimbabwe was once a British colony. Investigate other African countries that were once colonies.

1. Work in a group. Use an encyclopedia or social studies textbook to research colonial and modern Africa.
2. Make a map of contemporary Africa that shows the names of each country and its borders. Be sure the map is large enough to be displayed for other classmates.
3. Using tracing paper, create an overlay of the map. Add the borders and the names of the colonies that existed in 1914. A Reporter from the group can present the two maps to other classmates.

AFRICA

Curriculum Card 21B

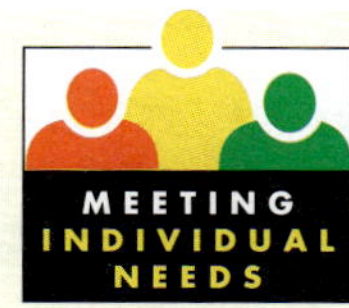

MULTI-AGE CLASSROOMS

Some students may not read at an advanced level, but may be good artists. These students may want to work on the colonial map or travel poster.

Reading Trade Books

TIPS FOR CLASSROOM MANAGEMENT

WHOLE-CLASS READING The vivid, oversized photographs in *Life in the Oceans* can be shared with the class in a whole-class reading. Encourage volunteers to scan the book, select a photograph, and describe it to the class. Then ask them to read the accompanying text.

For a comprehensive lesson plan, refer to the complete lesson for *Life in the Oceans* on pages T1268–T1273.

EXTRA SUPPORT

Suggest that students work in pairs to preview one chapter from *Life in the Oceans*. Partners can take notes as they read, using the subheads in the chapter as guides.

Life in the Oceans

by Norbert Wu

Signatures Library

READER'S CHALLENGE

You have read about Liz and Pete Fordred's exciting journey across the Atlantic Ocean. But what kinds of life did they sail over? Write down three things you know about ocean life. Then expand your list after you've read *Life in the Oceans*.

READING STRATEGY: REFERENCE SOURCES

After students have read *Life in the Oceans*, ask them to identify a specific topic from the book that they would like to know more about, such as starfish, ocean conservation, or the author, Norbert Wu. Discuss with students what reference sources they might use to locate such information. Students might name encyclopedias, periodical guides, dictionaries, computer information banks, and subject pages on the World Wide Web. Encourage students to create a library plan that includes at least three different types of reference sources they could consult. If possible, allow students to carry out their plans and share their results with the class.

LINK TO THE THEME

After students have read *Life in the Oceans*, suggest that they work in small groups to discuss the book. Encourage groups to answer these questions:

- **Do you think you can find out more about the ocean by observing it from above or below the water line? Why?**
- **How do you think Liz and Pete Fordred might describe the ocean? Would Norbert Wu describe it differently?**

Other Trade Books

Jodie's Journey

by Colin Thiele

This powerful novel describes how Jodie courageously adapts to her new life when she is faced with a disabling illness. Readers can use a chart to compare Jodie with Liz and Pete Fordred.

Second Ascent: The Story of Hugh Herr

by Alison Osius

This book tells the true story of a young rock climber who loses both legs to frostbite, but has the persistence to return to his sport. Encourage readers to create time lines to compare the events in Hugh Herr's life with those in Liz and Pete Fordred's lives.

The Voyage of the Frog

by Gary Paulsen

When a freak storm blows David's sailboat 350 miles from his home harbor, he needs to use all of his knowledge and skill to stay alive. After reading, students might discuss the difference between fictional and real-life adventure stories. Encourage them to compare this book with "Freedom Ride" by looking at the people, events, problems, and solutions.

CHALLENGE

Have students locate information about rock climbing programs, as well as parks, bodies of water, or other recreational facilities in their area. Encourage students to share information they find.

Trade Books

PROJECT MANAGEMENT

- PROJECT LAUNCH
- CHECKPOINT 1
- CHECKPOINT 2
- CHECKPOINT 3
- CHECKPOINT 4
- PRESENTATIONS
- ASSESSMENT

Write Nature Journal Entries

SELECTION CONNECTION

In "Freedom Ride," Liz Fordred writes about the challenges she and her husband faced as they built a boat and sailed it across the Atlantic. Ask students what makes personal narratives about wilderness experiences interesting to read.

PROJECT CHECKLIST

During this stage, students should

- ☑ take a nature walk in a local area or view nature treks on film or video.
- ☑ take notes and draw sketches of plants and wildlife they observe.
- ☑ discuss with their group the sights and sounds of nature they observe on their walk.
- ☑ write entries in their nature journals.

Project Card 32 can be found as a copying master on page R123.

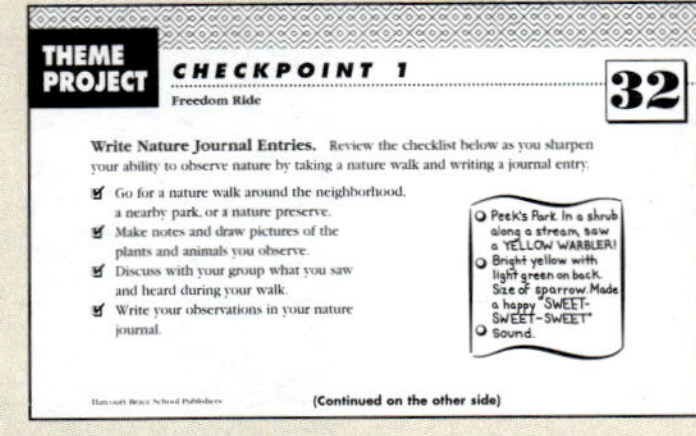
THEME PROJECT
CHECKPOINT 1
Freedom Ride
32

Write Nature Journal Entries. Review the checklist below as you sharpen your ability to observe nature by taking a nature walk and writing a journal entry.

- ☑ Go for a nature walk around the neighborhood, a nearby park, or a nature preserve.
- ☑ Make notes and draw pictures of the plants and animals you observe.
- ☑ Discuss with your group what you saw and heard during your walk.
- ☑ Write your observations in your nature journal.

(Continued on the other side)

Project Card 32

RESEARCH AND PLANNING TIPS

As students prepare for their walk, suggest that they

- look through nature guides (bird, tree, wildflower) to note plants and wildlife that are native to the area.
- bring a pair of binoculars or a camera, if possible.
- plan to have some moments of silence so they can listen carefully to natural sounds.

As students write entries about the nature walk in their journals, prompt them with questions such as *What did you see or hear on the walk that surprised you?*

STUDENTS ACQUIRING ENGLISH

During the nature walk, pair students with English proficient partners who can take notes, allowing the students acquiring English to focus on sketching their observations.

CLASSROOM MANAGEMENT

You may want to invite an adult family member or guest on the walk who is knowledgeable about the plants and animals in the area to help answer students' questions.

Informal Assessment

As students complete this checkpoint, they will **make inferences** about wildlife by using clues in their surroundings and will record their observations in a journal entry. Students are thinking critically if they

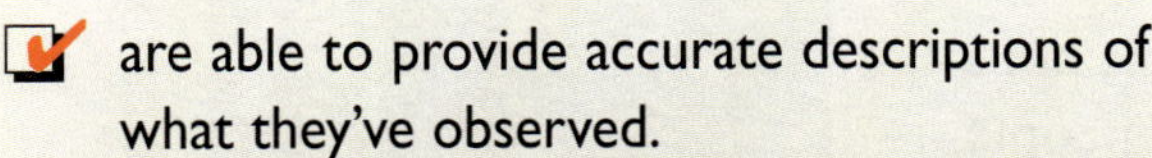
☑ are able to provide accurate descriptions of what they've observed.

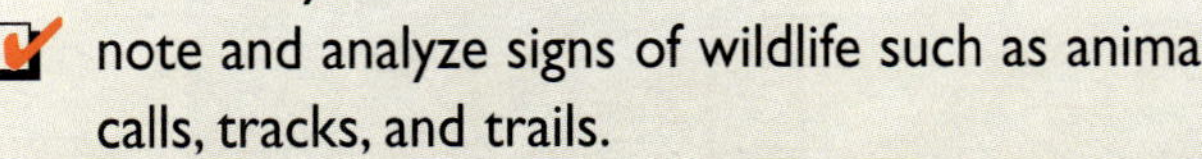
☑ note and analyze signs of wildlife such as animal calls, tracks, and trails.

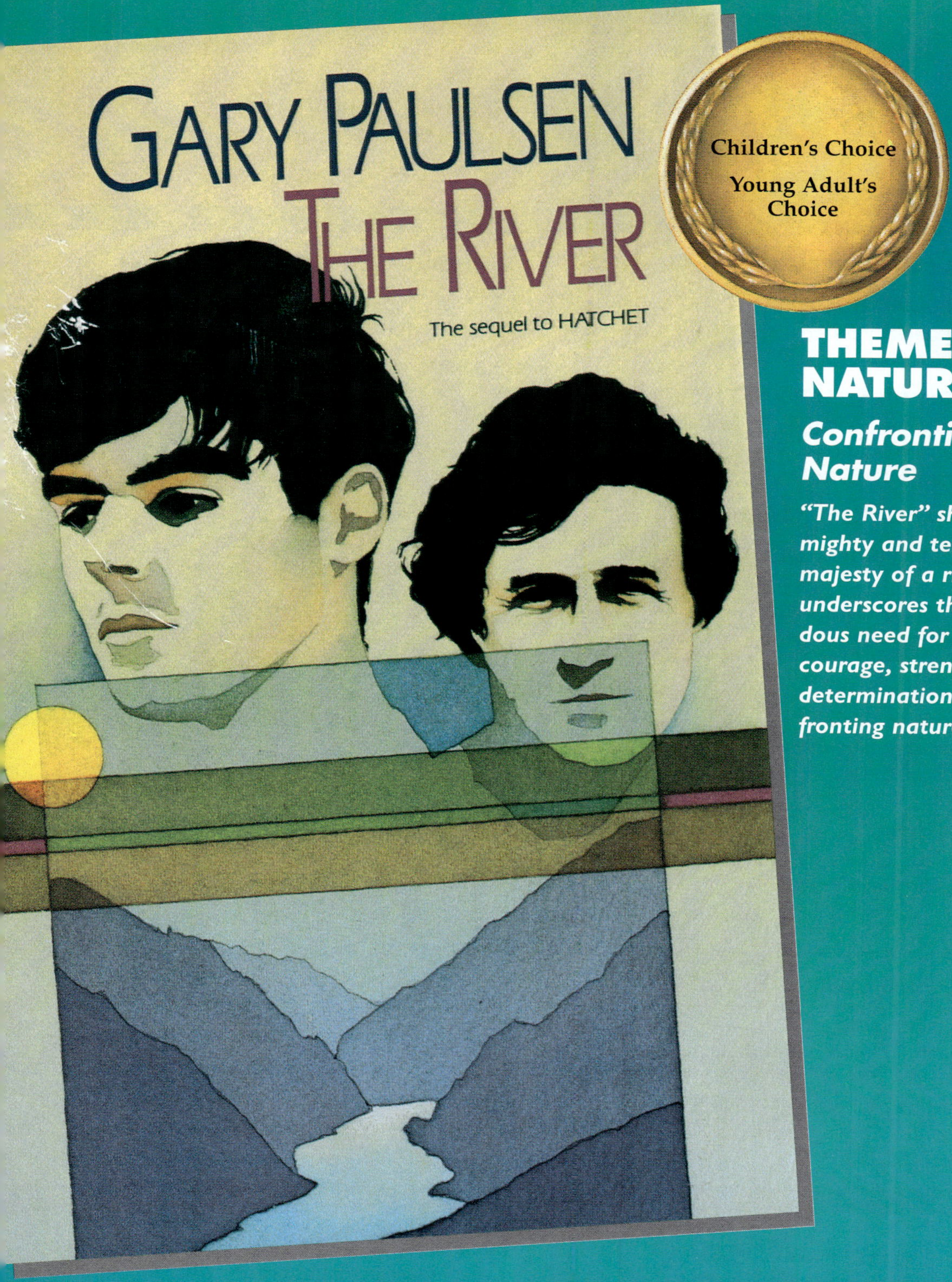

GARY PAULSEN
THE RIVER
The sequel to HATCHET

Children's Choice
Young Adult's Choice

THEME: NATURE

Confronting Nature

"The River" showcases the mighty and terrible majesty of a river and underscores the tremendous need for intelligence, courage, strength, and determination when confronting nature.

Gary Paulsen

ABOUT THE AUTHOR

GARY PAULSEN is a prolific writer of both fiction and nonfiction books. He has received wide acclaim for his young adult fiction, which is usually set in wilderness areas and features teenagers who face the challenge of day-to-day survival. He has been awarded a Newbery Honor Book citation for excellence in children's literature for three of his books, *Hatchet, Dogsong,* and *The Winter Room.*

More information about Gary Paulsen and his work appears on page T1153.

SELECTION SUMMARY

Genre: Realistic Fiction

Brian Robeson is stranded in the wilderness with a man named Derek, a government psychologist. During a freak storm, Derek is struck by lightning and falls into a coma. Brian ties Derek to a raft, determined to get him downstream to a trading post as fast as possible. Brian fails to make sense of a map of the area, and then disaster strikes when the raft hits a boulder and Brian is thrown into the rapids. After barely surviving this mishap, Brian has to swim downriver searching for Derek and the raft. Eventually Brian finds the raft with Derek miraculously still on it. Then the frantic and exhausting push to the trading post begins. Thanks in part to Brian's efforts, Derek recovers and sends Brian a canoe as a thank-you gift.

SUGGESTED LESSON PLANNER

▶ *The River*

	DAY 1	DAY 2
PART 1 Reading, Listening, Speaking, Viewing **Key Words** hallucinations relented coma infected	**BUILD BACKGROUND** T1130 **VOCABULARY STRATEGIES** T1131 *Transparency 54* *Practice Book* p. 167 **READING THE SELECTION** T1132–T1153 Options for Reading T1132–T1133 *Response Card 6* *Literature Cassette 3* **REVIEW PREDICTIONS/PURPOSE** T1152 **APPRECIATING THE LITERATURE** T1152 NOTE: Students may read the selection on Day 2.	**SUMMARIZE THE SELECTION** T1153 *Practice Book* p. 168 ◆ **RESPONSE CORNER ACTIVITIES** T1154 **CHECKING COMPREHENSION** T1155 *End-of-Selection Test* 
PART 2 Writer's Workshop	**ADVENTURE STORY** Thinking as Writers T1160 *Language Handbook* pp. 42–43 *Transparency 55*	Prewriting T1160 *Language Handbook* p. 40
Grammar	✓ **NEGATIVES** Teach the Concept T1162 Daily Language Practice (1–2) R115	Daily Language Practice (3–4) R115 Practice Activity T1163
Spelling	**UNSTRESSED ENDINGS: *-ant* AND *-ent*** *absent, current, president, instant, elephant, element, servant, excellent, important, constant, permanent, different, significant, innocent, opponent, incident* Pretest/Self-Check T1164 *Integrated Spelling Teacher's Edition* pp. T207, T301	Open and Closed Sorts T1164 *Integrated Spelling* p. 134 *Integrated Spelling Teacher's Edition* p. 208
PART 3 Skills and Strategies	◆ **INTEGRATED CURRICULUM** Rivers **Science/Art** T1168 **Social Studies** T1168 **Music** T1169 *Imagination Express, Destination: Time Trip, USA*	**COMPREHENSION SKILL** T1166–T1167 ✓ Summarizing/Paraphrasing (Introduce) *Practice Book* p. 171

Use the Extra Support notes on pages T1134, T1137, and T1149 to help **below-level students** as they read.

Use the Students Aquiring English note on T1154 with **ESL students** to help them complete the Response Corner activities.

NOTE: An alternative lesson plan for **below-level students** appears on *Intervention Strategies Manual* pp. 128–133. A lesson for **students acquiring English** appears on *Sheltered English/ESL Manual* pp. 86–89.

DAY 3	DAY 4	DAY 5
◆ **IDEA BANK ACTIVITIES** Retelling T1158 Oral Language T1158 Viewing T1159 Real-Life Resources: Reading a Magazine Interview T1159 *Writer's Magazine* pp. 84–85 School–Home Connection 22 R142	**VOCABULARY WORKSHOP** T1165 Reviewing Key Words **READING TRADE BOOKS** T1170–T1171  Take-Home Book	**READING TRADE BOOKS** T1167, T1168, T1170–T1171 
Drafting T1161 *Language Handbook* pp. 27, 41	Responding and Revising T1161 *Language Handbook* pp. 27, 41	Proofreading and Publishing T1161 *Language Handbook* p. 41
Daily Language Practice (5–6) R115 Practice Activity T1163 *Language Handbook* pp. 163, 223	Daily Language Practice (7–8) R115 Practice Activity T1163 *Grammar Practice Book* pp. 52–53	Daily Language Practice (9–12) R115 *Practice Book* p. 169
Discuss the Generalization T1164 *Integrated Spelling* p. 135 *Integrated Spelling Teacher's Edition* p. T209	Apply to Writing T1164 *Integrated Spelling* pp.136–137 *Integrated Spelling Teacher's Edition* pp. T210–T211	Posttest T1164 *Practice Book* p. 170 *Integrated Spelling Teacher's Edition* p. T212
GRAMMAR MINILESSON T1137 ✓ Adverbs (Review) **LITERARY APPRECIATION MINILESSON** T1145 Figurative Language	**VOCABULARY WORKSHOP** T1165 Figurative Language	**COMPREHENSION MINILESSON** T1149 Making Judgments *Practice Book* p. 172 Theme Project Checkpoint 2 T1172
Above-level students may read a trade book independently.	**Below-level students** may read the *Take-Home Book: Jordan Waiting* to help them review Key Words.	**Below-level** and **ESL students** may read the *ESL/Title I Library* book *The Wreck of the Zephyr*.

✓ = Tested Skill
◆ = Optional activities used to adjust pacing throughout the lesson
Titles in *italics* are optional materials.

1 Reading and Responding

BUILDING BACKGROUND AND CONCEPTS

PRIOR KNOWLEDGE

Relate to students' lives. Ask students what they would do if someone they were with were injured and immediate medical attention was not available. You may want to briefly discuss emergency phone procedures and some first aid basics.

Create a concept web about confronting a river. Explain that "The River" is an adventure story about a boy who must confront the natural power of a river in order to save someone's life. Discuss dangers that might arise when someone needs to travel down a swift-moving river. Record students' responses on a web like the following:

QUICKWRITE

Encourage students to write a few sentences about experiences they've had either boating or swimming in rivers or other bodies of water. Suggest that students use sensory words in their writing.

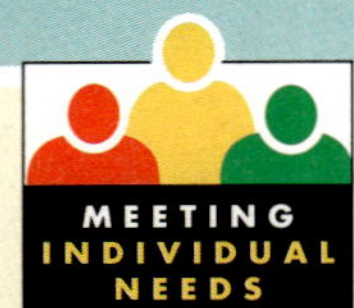

Intervention Strategies

For students who may have difficulty reading "The River," support is available in *Intervention Strategies Manual*, pages 128–133, and on pages T1143 and T1156–T1157 in this lesson.

STUDENTS ACQUIRING ENGLISH

See *Sheltered English/ESL Manual*, pages 86–89.

FACT FINDER

SCIENCE

Rivers

A river is formed when water flows between clearly defined banks. The water comes from springs, rain, or snow. Most rivers characteristically have an upper course where the river begins, a middle course where it flows through a relatively flat area of land, and a lower course where it empties into a larger body of water. The upper course of a river is at a high elevation and flows fast. The river might spill over waterfalls and churn over large boulders or rock ledges to form dangerous rapids. At the middle course, the river flows more slowly over gently sloping land. Small stones and gravel carried by the river drop to the riverbed where they form sandbars and islands. The river slows when it reaches the gentle slopes of its lower course. When the river reaches the sea, a lake, or another large body of water, it deposits sand, gravel, and silt at the mouth of the river and forms a triangular-shaped area called a delta.

VOCABULARY STRATEGIES

KEY WORDS DEFINED

hallucinations impressions of sights or sounds that aren't actually there

relented gave in or softened

coma state of deep unconsciousness caused by injury, disease, or poisoning

infected diseased with bacteria, viruses, or other organisms

INTEGRATED SPELLING

Spelling Pretest: page T1164
Spelling Generalization:
Unstressed endings *-ant*/*-ent*

CONTEXT CLUES: NARRATIVE

Encourage students to use semantic and syntactic cues. Display Transparency 54. Ask a volunteer to read the dialogue. (You may wish to help with the pronunciation of *hallucinations.*) Ask students to use context clues and clues about the function of the words to figure out the meaning of each underlined word. For example, point out the context clue *seeing things that aren't there* to help students figure out the meaning of *hallucinations*.

CHECK UNDERSTANDING

Have students complete sentence frames. Display the following sentence frames on the board, and have students complete them by providing a Key Word for each one. **STRATEGY: ANTONYMS**

1. His finger was (infected) last week, but today it is healthy.
2. She is conscious now, but yesterday she was in a (coma).
3. This morning I refused, but later I (relented).
4. We thought he was having (hallucinations), but he insisted he wasn't imagining things.

TRANSPARENCY 54

Key Words

Dr. Tobias: Here's a list of patients who were just brought in.

Dr. Chan: This patient claims he's seeing things that aren't there. He says he's been having these hallucinations for days.

Dr. Tobias: I just heard that at first he refused to take any medication to calm him down. He's okay now though, because he finally relented.

Dr. Chan: Good! This patient was in a car accident and lost consciousness hours ago. She is still in a coma.

Dr. Tobias: Here's a little boy who cut his hand on broken glass and then exposed it to bacteria by playing in a mud puddle. Now the cut is infected. He hasn't stopped crying since he arrived.

Dr. Chan: Well, let's get busy!

Dirt entering a cut can cause it to become infected.

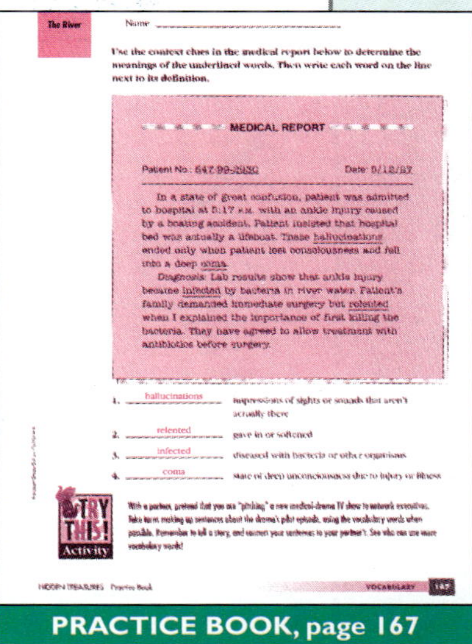

The River

Name ______________

Use the context clues in the medical report below to determine the meanings of the underlined words. Then write each word on the line next to its definition.

MEDICAL REPORT

Patient No.:

Date:

In a state of great confusion, patient was admitted to hospital at 5:17 A.M. with an ankle injury caused by a boating accident. Patient insisted that hospital bed was actually a lifeboat. These hallucinations ended only when patient lost consciousness and fell into a deep coma.

Diagnosis: Lab results show that ankle injury became infected by bacteria in river water. Patient's family demanded immediate surgery but relented when I explained the importance of first killing the bacteria. They have agreed to allow treatment with antibiotics before surgery.

1. hallucinations — impressions of sights or sounds that aren't actually there
2. relented — gave in or softened
3. infected — diseased with bacteria or other organisms
4. coma — state of deep unconsciousness due to injury or illness

TRY THIS! Activity

With a partner, pretend that you are "pitching" a new medical-drama TV show to network executives. Take turns making up sentences about the drama's pilot episode, using the vocabulary words when possible. Remember to tell a story, and connect your sentences to your partner's. See who can use more vocabulary words!

HIDDEN TREASURES Practice Book — VOCABULARY 167

PRACTICE BOOK, page 167

Prereading Strategies

PREVIEW AND PREDICT

Have students preview "The River" by reading the introduction and looking at the illustration on pages 538–539. Have students make predictions by asking questions such as, *What do you think will happen on the river? Will Brian and Derek make it to the trading post?*

Begin a story map on the board. Students may use *Practice Book* page 168. Ask volunteers to fill in the characters, setting, and problem.

Story Map

Characters	Setting
Brian Derek	the river

Problem
Brian must get help for Derek, who is in a coma.

You may want to suggest that students write their predictions about the selection in their personal journals.

PURPOSE

You may want to model setting a purpose:

MODEL **I want to read to find out what happens to Brian and Derek on the river and to see if they both make it safely to the trading post.**

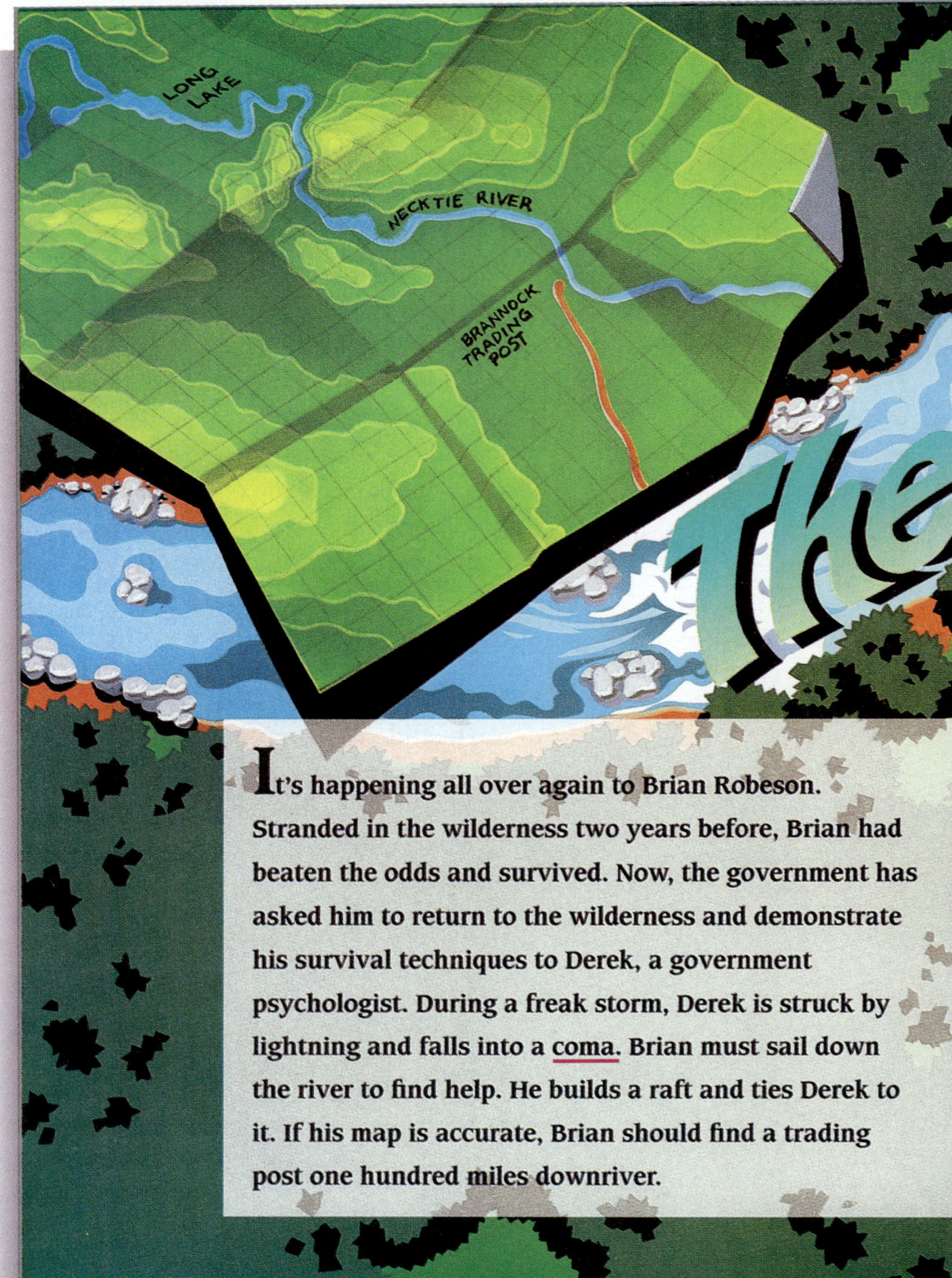

It's happening all over again to Brian Robeson. Stranded in the wilderness two years before, Brian had beaten the odds and survived. Now, the government has asked him to return to the wilderness and demonstrate his survival techniques to Derek, a government psychologist. During a freak storm, Derek is struck by lightning and falls into a coma. Brian must sail down the river to find help. He builds a raft and ties Derek to it. If his map is accurate, Brian should find a trading post one hundred miles downriver.

SMALL GROUP

STRATEGIC READING

Those students who need help with **visualizing** or other reading strategies will benefit by reading silently and stopping at pages T1134, T1138, and T1144 to discuss their reading strategies.

COOPERATIVE READING

READER RESPONSE GROUPS Small groups may use Reader Response Card 6 to focus on the **author's craft.** Reader Response Card 6 can be found at the back of this Teacher's Edition.

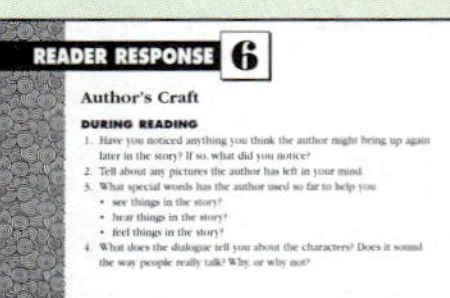

Response Card 6

WHOLE CLASS

READ ALOUD

After students have had a chance to read the entire selection silently, allow volunteers to read aloud different parts of the story. Encourage them to convey the various emotions Brian feels on his trip down the river.

SILENT READING/ DISCUSSION

Ask students to record their reactions and questions in their personal journals while they are reading. When they are finished, students might like to discuss some of their responses with others who have read the selection independently.

Strategic Reading

VISUALIZING

Remind students of some of the strategies they have recently focused on, such as using picture clues. Then tell students that, as they read this selection, they will focus on visualizing. Ask a volunteer to explain what visualizing is and how it might help readers better understand a selection. (Possible response: Visualizing is picturing in your mind what is happening in the story. If you visualize story characters and events, they seem more real.) **STRATEGY: VISUALIZING**

PAGES 538–545 Have students read through page 545 to confirm their predictions.

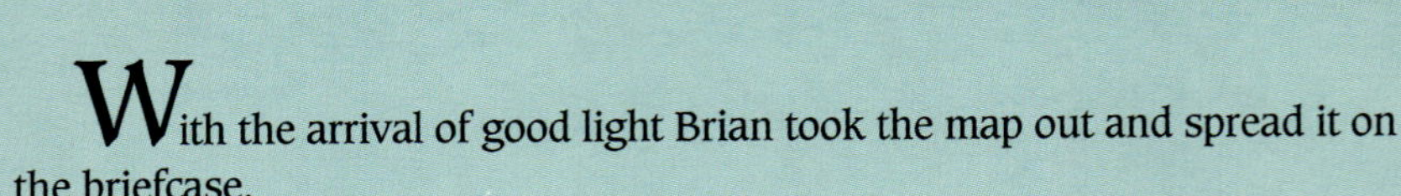

With the arrival of good light Brian took the map out and spread it on the briefcase.

The lake he had crossed did not show. He was positive. There were lakes, some large and small, but he was not moving fast enough to have reached any of them yet and that meant the map was not accurate.

It showed clean river with narrow banks where he guessed the lake to be and if it was inaccurate about this one thing then it might be wrong about all things.

Say the distance to the trading post. If the map had been made many years before and not updated, then the river might have changed direction, might not even go by the trading post any longer.

The trading post might not even be there.

The thought stunned him and he realized how foolish it had been to leave the lake and trust the map. There were so many variables, so many ways to go wrong.

He studied the map again and took some heart from it. It was so . . . so definite. It must be basically right. Close. Things could change, but not that much. The river was probably up a bit and the lake he had come through in the night was a low place that filled when the river ran high and not really a permanent lake that would be on the map.

Sure. There was logic there. All right. All he had to do was test the map, find some way to ensure that it was mostly right.

He put his finger on the river and followed it, tracing the path as the blue line cut through the green, followed it to where he thought he must be.

There.

If the map was right and he was guessing right, he should be about where his finger had stopped. It showed a long straight stretch and the contour lines were spread far apart, which would indicate a large low or flat area where there might be a lake.

540

LISTENING CENTER

"The River" is available on Literature Cassette 3. Students may want to listen to the selection and then read it silently.

EXTRA SUPPORT **Show students a contour map. Explain that a blue line on a contour map is a river. Explain that green lines show changes in elevation.**

VIEWING

Encourage students to look critically at the illustration by asking questions such as the following: *Who is on the raft?* (Brian, who is reading the map, and Derek, who is tied down) *Does the raft seem sturdy? Why or why not?* (Possible response: The raft actually looks fairly large and sturdy. Its logs are of uniform size, they seem fairly evenly tied together, and the raft is large enough to accommodate Brian and Derek with room to spare.)

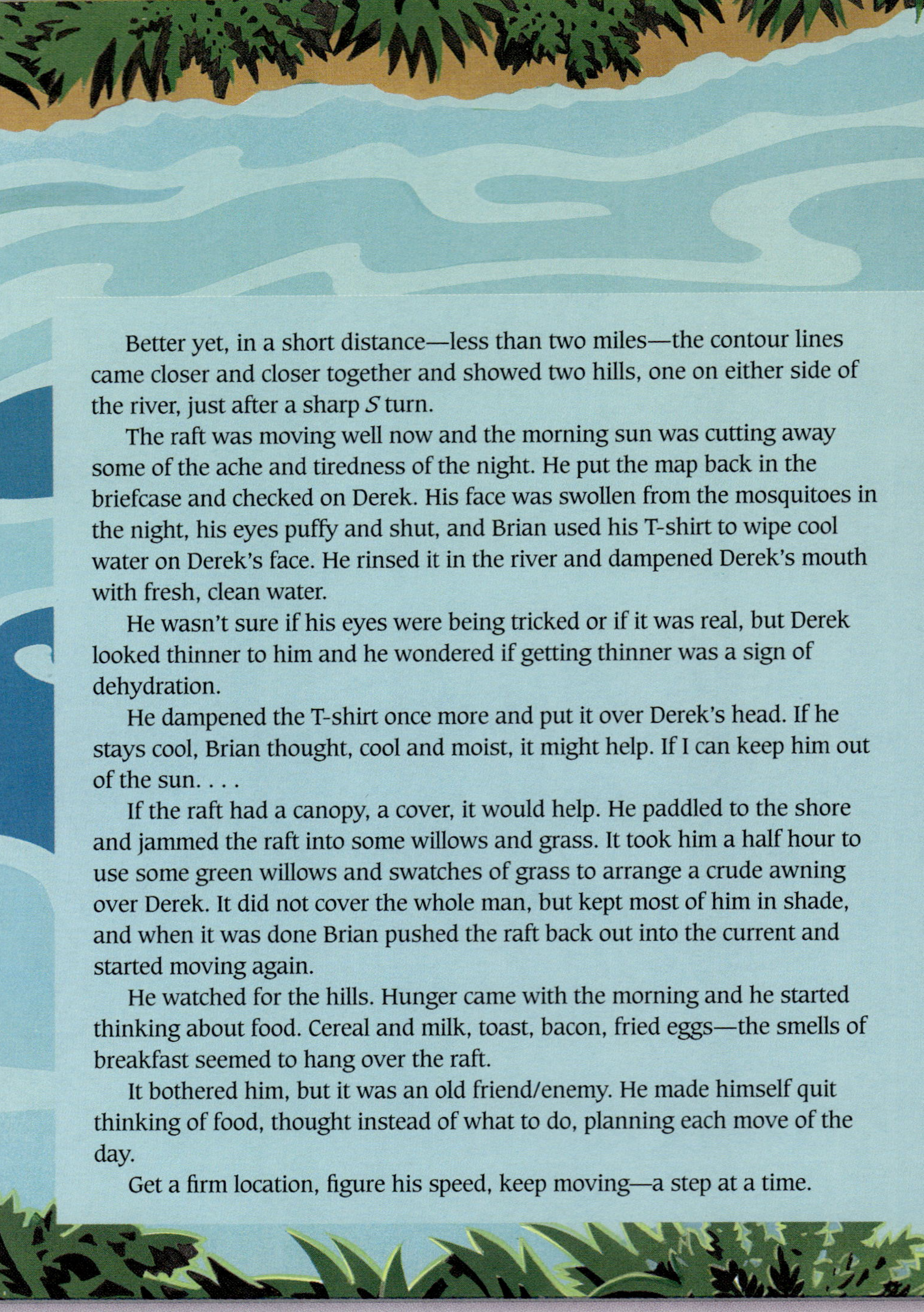

Better yet, in a short distance—less than two miles—the contour lines came closer and closer together and showed two hills, one on either side of the river, just after a sharp *S* turn.

The raft was moving well now and the morning sun was cutting away some of the ache and tiredness of the night. He put the map back in the briefcase and checked on Derek. His face was swollen from the mosquitoes in the night, his eyes puffy and shut, and Brian used his T-shirt to wipe cool water on Derek's face. He rinsed it in the river and dampened Derek's mouth with fresh, clean water.

He wasn't sure if his eyes were being tricked or if it was real, but Derek looked thinner to him and he wondered if getting thinner was a sign of dehydration.

He dampened the T-shirt once more and put it over Derek's head. If he stays cool, Brian thought, cool and moist, it might help. If I can keep him out of the sun. . . .

If the raft had a canopy, a cover, it would help. He paddled to the shore and jammed the raft into some willows and grass. It took him a half hour to use some green willows and swatches of grass to arrange a crude awning over Derek. It did not cover the whole man, but kept most of him in shade, and when it was done Brian pushed the raft back out into the current and started moving again.

He watched for the hills. Hunger came with the morning and he started thinking about food. Cereal and milk, toast, bacon, fried eggs—the smells of breakfast seemed to hang over the raft.

It bothered him, but it was an old friend/enemy. He made himself quit thinking of food, thought instead of what to do, planning each move of the day.

Get a firm location, figure his speed, keep moving—a step at a time.

HEALTH

DEHYDRATION Define *dehydration* as "an extreme loss of water from the body." Also explain that, in serious cases of dehydration, the body loses so much water that it may not be able to function properly, and life is threatened. Invite students to add this word to their Personal Words lists.

Time.

Time was so strange. It didn't mean anything, then it meant everything. It was like food. When he didn't have it he wanted it, when there was plenty of it he didn't care about it.

He stretched, sighed. "You know, if we were in a canoe and had a lunch and a cooler full of pop, we'd think this was the most beautiful place in the world."

And it was, he thought, truly beautiful. The trees, pines and spruce and cedars, towered so high they made the river seem to become narrow and in places where the bank was cut away by the moving water the trees had actually leaned out over the river until they were almost touching. They made the river seem like a soft, green tunnel.

The character of the river had changed. It happened almost suddenly, but with such a natural flow that Brian didn't notice it for a short time. The trees grew closer, the brush thicker and the banks higher.

Where they had been grassy and sloping away gradually, the banks were steeper and cut away, exposing the dirt and mud. The trees were so close and high that Brian would not be able to see the hills on the map when he came to them. He could see nothing but a wall of green.

He wiped Derek's face several times. All this time the raft had kept moving, and when his break was over he saw that they were coming into another bend.

He put the T-shirt back on, wet, and picked up the paddle and started to work, swinging the stern of the raft, keeping it in the middle of the current.

It would get hot soon and cook him, but he thought that it wouldn't matter. His hands were raw from the rough wood of the paddle and he thought that it wouldn't matter either.

All that mattered now was to keep moving.

543

Tested Skill

MINILESSON

REVIEW: GRAMMAR

Adverbs

INFORMAL ASSESSMENT

Ask students to find some adverbs in the paragraph beginning *The character of the river had changed.* (*almost, suddenly, closer, thicker, higher*) Then ask them what words the adverbs modify or describe. (*Almost* modifies *suddenly*; *suddenly* modifies *happened*; and *closer, thicker*, and *higher* modify *grew*.)

TEACH/MODEL

Ask a volunteer to explain what adverbs tell. (They tell *how, when, where*, and *to what extent*.) You may want to model the thinking:

MODEL

***Suddenly* tells how. It is an adverb that describes the verb *happened*. *Almost* tells to what extent. It is an adverb that modifies another adverb, *suddenly*. Adverbs can modify verbs, adjectives, or other adverbs.**

PRACTICE/APPLY

Have students find the adverbs *actually, away*, and *gradually* on this page. Ask students what words each adverb modifies or describes, and what it tells. (*Actually* modifies *leaned*: it tells how; *away* modifies *had been sloping*: it tells where; *gradually* modifies *had been sloping*: it tells how.)

Begin a discussion focusing on students' experiences camping with friends or their family members. Ask students to compare their experiences to Brian's.

EXTRA SUPPORT **Point out that the *stern* of the raft is the rear part.**

Strategic Reading

PAGES 538–545 How does Brian's view of the river change the farther he goes? (At first, Brian thinks the river and the area around it are beautiful. Suddenly, however, the character of the river changes. It narrows and begins moving faster, and the water begins to roar.)
STRATEGIES: SUMMARIZING/CONFIRMING PREDICTIONS

How does the author build suspense in the story? (Possible response: The author describes the river as Brian sees it. We don't know what is happening until Brian does.)
CRITICAL: RECOGNIZING AUTHOR'S CRAFT

VISUALIZING

You may want to use a think-aloud to model the visualizing strategy:

MODEL **The author's descriptions help me visualize Brian and the raft on the river. I can picture the sun beating down on the raft as it moves calmly down the river. Then the river's speed increases so dramatically that Brian doesn't have time to paddle to shore.**

PAGES 546–551
Students should read to page 551 to find out what happens to Brian, Derek, and the raft.

He saw the hills from the map sooner than he thought he should see them.

But they were the right ones. He was sure of it. They rose steeply ahead and on either side, rounded but high, covered with trees.

It was just about noon and the sun was beating down on him. He reached under the shelter and used the damp T-shirt to cool Derek again.

"We're moving," he said, his voice thick with exhaustion, not believing it. "We're moving along now. . . ."

And when he said it he knew it was true. The raft was increasing in speed. Even as he watched, the speed seemed to pick up.

"We're hauling. . . ." He started, then trailed off as it dawned on him.

The contour lines being close together on the map meant that the banks steepened between the hills.

If there were hills and steep banks, the river might drop, fall a bit.

He reached for the briefcase to take another look at the map, but stopped with his hand halfway out.

A sound.

Some sound was there that at first he could not place. It was so soft, he could almost not hear it at all over the sounds of the birds.

But there it was again. A hissing? Was that it?

No.

It was lower than that. Not to be heard, but felt.

A *whooshing*—water.

A water sound.

A rumbling sound. The sound of water moving fast, dropping, falling.

Falling water.

A waterfall.

They were heading for a waterfall!

There was no time left. The river had narrowed slightly, but now there was more of a drop and the speed had increased dramatically.

They were dead in the middle of the river and Brian knew he had to get to shore, had to stop, but there was no time.

CONVENTIONS OF LANGUAGE

ONOMATOPOEIA Point out the word *whooshing*, and explain that this is an example of onomatopoeia, or a word whose sound imitates its meaning. *Hissing* is another example on this page.

Twice as fast as he could walk, the raft was fairly careening now.

The sound was louder.

If he tried to paddle for shore, he would succeed only in turning the raft sideways. He was not sure how he could get over a waterfall—if indeed he could at all—but he was fairly certain he did not want to try it with the raft sideways. If it went the long way over the waterfall, it would be harder to roll over. Sideways and it would roll easily.

The sound was a definite rumble now, and in seconds they wheeled around a bend and Brian could see it.

"God . . ."

It was a whisper.

It was not a waterfall, but it might as well have been.

The river moved between two large stone bluffs that formed the sides of the two hills Brian had seen on the map.

The bluffs forced the river to a narrower width, deeper, and at the same time aimed it through some boulders that had split off either side and dropped in the middle.

All of this had the effect of making a monstrous chute where the water fought and roared to get through, smashing around the rocks in huge sprays of white water.

And the raft was aimed right down the middle of the chute.

Things happened so fast after that, there was not a way he could prepare for it.

The raft seemed to come alive, turn into a wild, crazy animal.

The front end took the river, swung down and into the current, grabbed the madness of the water and ran with it.

Brian had just time to look down at Derek, just time to see that he was still tied to the raft securely, and they were into it.

The raft bucked and tore at the water, slammed sideways. Brian tried to steer, using the paddle to swing the stern to the left and right, trying to avoid the boulders, but it was no use.

The water owned the raft, owned Derek, owned him. In the roaring, piling thunder of the river he had no control.

545

NOTES

Here's a place to list ideas or activities that you would like to use the next time you teach this lesson.

EXPANDING VOCABULARY

Draw students' attention to the words *bluff* and *chute*. Explain that a bluff is a broad, steep bank or cliff. Brian's raft moves between two large stone bluffs into a chute, which is a fast-moving section of the river that has a steep drop in the riverbed.

Cooperative Reading

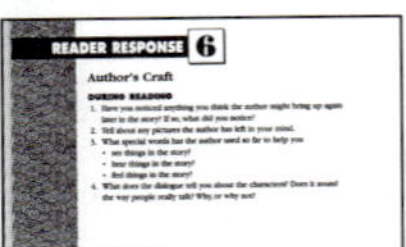
READER RESPONSE 6

Author's Craft

Response Card 6

Encourage students reading in cooperative groups to respond to the literature through questions such as the following:

- **What pictures has the author left in your mind?**
- **How does the author give you information about Brian without using dialogue?**
- **Can you "hear" things in the story as well as see things? Why or why not?**

They were flying, the logs of the raft rearing out of the water on pressure ridges, slamming back down so hard it rattled his teeth.

In the middle of the chute was a boulder—huge, gray, wet with waves and spray—and the raft aimed directly at the center of it.

He had time to scream—sound lost in the roar of water—and throw himself on Derek. The raft wheeled slightly to the left and struck the boulder.

Brian thought for part of a second that they had made it.

Derek's body lurched beneath him and dropped back, the raft took the blow, flexed, gave, but held together; and Brian started one clear thought: we made it.

Then it hit. There was an underwater boulder next to the giant in the middle of the river. Hidden by a pressure wave, it lay sideways out and to the left, halfway to the left wall.

The nose of the raft made it, carried over by the pressure ridge, hung for a second, then dropped, plummeted down.

As it tipped forward the rear of the raft cut down into the water and came against the submerged ledge.

"Whunk!"

Brian heard it hit, felt the impact and the sound through his whole body. He grabbed, tried to hold on to the logs beneath Derek, but it was no use.

The stern kicked off the ledge, slapped him up and away, clear of the raft, completely in the air.

He hung for a split instant in midair, looking down on the raft, on Derek—then he plunged down, down into the boiling, ripping water.

Everything was madness—frothy green bubbles, hissing, roiling water.

He came up for a moment, saw the raft shooting away downstream carrying Derek, then he was down again, mashed down and tumbled by the pressure wave, smashed into the rocks on the bottom, and all he could think was that he had to stay alive, had to get up, get air, get back to the raft.

But the wave was a great weight on him, a house on him; the world was on him and he could not move up against it.

AUTHOR'S CRAFT

Point out things that the reader can see *(frothy green bubbles)*, feel *(boiling, ripping water)*, and hear *(hissing . . . water)*. Call attention to the metaphor *a house on him*, and note how well this comparison expresses the difficulty of Brian's fight against the river.

547

Student Self-Assessment

VISUALIZING

Encourage students to monitor their comprehension by using the visualizing strategy.

- What do I picture to help me understand what's happening in this scene?
- How does visualizing Brian hanging "for a split instant in midair, looking down on the raft, on Derek" help me understand how Brian experiences hitting the boulder?

ILLUSTRATOR'S CRAFT

Point out how the illustration shows only a small image of Brian in the frothy water. Most of the illustration is devoted to the downward flow of the water, the boulders, and the white bubbles, emphasizing the river's sheer force and energy and Brian's helplessness.

Critical Thinking Questions

1. **Earlier in the story, Brian thought, "Time was so strange. It didn't mean anything, then it meant everything." What do you think time means to Brian after he discovers that the raft is gone?** (Possible response: Time is an enemy. Brian must quickly search for Derek.) CRITICAL: CHALLENGING THE TEXT

2. **Why do you think Brian says, "I have to figure he's still alive"?** (Possible response: Brian doesn't know what happened to Derek, but Derek's only chance of survival is for Brian to assume he's still alive.) CRITICAL: DRAWING CONCLUSIONS

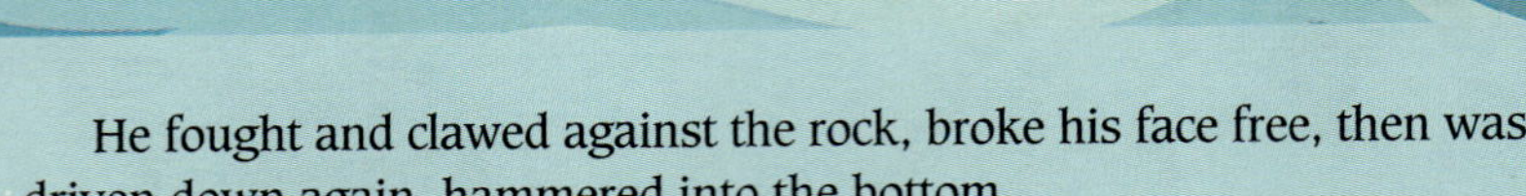

He fought and clawed against the rock, broke his face free, then was driven down again, hammered into the bottom.

Sideways.

He'd have to work sideways. Smashed, buffeted, he dragged himself to the side beneath the pressure wave.

It became stronger. He could not rise, could not get air, and his lungs seemed about to burst, demanded that he breathe, even if it was water. He willed the urge away, down, but it grew worse, and just when he knew it was over, when he would have to let the water in—when he would die—just then he made the edge of the pressure wave at the side of the boulder.

The current roared past the rock and took him like a chip, sucking him downstream.

He brought his head clear for one tearing breath, opened and shook water out of his eyes long enough to see that the raft was gone, out of sight—then he was driven back under, down to the bottom, smashing into boulders in a roaring green thunder, end over end until he knew nothing but the screaming need to breathe, to live, and then his head smashed into something explosively hard and he thought nothing at all.

Bright light flashed inside Brian's eyes—red and glaring—and he opened them to find that he was on his back, staring directly at the sun.

"Ecchh!" He rolled onto his stomach and spit and nearly choked on water.

He was in the shallows below the rapids, caught up in a small alcove in the shoreline.

The water was six or seven inches deep, with a gravel bottom. His senses returned and with them came the realization that he was all right. He was bruised, but nothing was broken; he had taken a little water, but apparently had coughed it out.

He was all right.

Derek.

CONVENTIONS OF LANGUAGE

DASHES Call attention to the dashes in the middle of this page. Read aloud the sentence in which they appear: *Bright light flashed inside Brian's eyes—red and glaring—and he opened them to find that he was on his back, staring directly at the sun.* Point out that the dashes not only set off the phrase *red and glaring* but also emphasize it.

The word slammed into him. Somehow, he had forgotten. . . .

He stood—his legs were a bit wobbly, but they held—and looked down the river.

It stretched away for half a mile, becoming more calm and peaceful as it dropped, nestled in trees and thick brush, a blue line in a green background. Birds flew across the water, ducks swam. . . .

There was no raft.

Brian turned, stood dripping, looking upriver into the rapids.

From below they did not look as bad. The pressure waves appeared smaller—even the boulder didn't seem as large. There was still the sound of the water—although that, too, was muted.

But there was no raft.

No Derek.

"Derek!"

He yelled, knowing it was futile.

He looked downriver again. There was no way the raft would have stopped in the rapids. It had to have come down, floated on downstream.

What had he seen? He frowned, trying to remember what had happened.

Oh, yes—the wave. The big submerged rock and the wave, the great wave had taken the raft and he had seen that—the raft moving off downriver. He did not think it had tipped; he seemed to remember that it was upright.

But Derek—was he still on the raft? He couldn't remember for certain, but it seemed that he was—everything was so confused. Tumbling in the rapids seemed to have shaken his brain loose.

He fought panic.

Things were—were what they were. If the raft rolled or if Derek fell off the raft, then . . . well then, that was it.

If not, Derek might still be all right.

"I have to figure he's still alive."

And if Derek was still on the raft, still alive, he was downriver.

Brian had to catch him, catch the raft.

549

Intervention Strategies

SELF-QUESTIONING Say this sentence aloud to students: ***While I'm reading, I try to answer the questions I asked myself before reading.*** **Have students share any questions they had, and tell how answering their questions helps them keep track of story details.**

QUICKWRITE

Have students write a few sentences in their personal journals telling what they think Brian is feeling when he first realizes that Derek is gone.

Strategic Reading

PAGES 546–551 What happens to Brian and the raft? (Possible response: The raft enters a chute and hits a boulder. Brian recovers, but the raft and Derek disappear down the river.) STRATEGIES: SUMMARIZING/CONFIRMING PREDICTIONS

How can you tell that Brian is determined to find Derek and the raft? (Possible response: He yells for Derek even though it is futile, and he tries to run through the brush on the bank. Then he decides to swim, no matter how far he has to go.) CRITICAL: NOTING IMPORTANT DETAILS

VISUALIZING

Help students visualize what is happening by modeling with a think-aloud:

MODEL **I know what it's like to step into mud, so I can see how the mud easily stopped Brian. I can picture Brian trying to walk in the thick mud, and the mud pulling his right shoe off.**

PAGES 552–558 Ask students to read the rest of the story to find out if Brian finds Derek and the raft.

He started to move along the bank, and did well for fifty or so yards. The bottom was gravel—spilled out by the rapids—but then it ended.

The river moved rapidly back into flatter country, swamps, lakes, and the first thing that happened was the bottom turned to mud.

Brian tried to move to the bank and run, but the brush was so thick and wild that it was like a jungle—grass, willows, and thick vines grabbed at him, holding him.

550

SCHOOL↔HOME CONNECTION

Brian is determined to find the raft and bring Derek to safety. You might want to suggest that students have a discussion about taking responsibility for sick or injured family members.

He moved back into the river—where the mud stopped him. If he tried to walk, when his weight came down, his feet sunk and just kept on going—two, three feet. The mud was so thick it pulled his right tennis shoe off, and when he groped to find it the mud held his arm, seemed to pull at him, tried to take him down.

He lost the shoe, clawed back to the bank and knew there was only one way to chase the raft.

"I'll have to swim."

But how far?

It didn't matter, he thought—Derek was down there somewhere. Brian had to catch him.

He shook his head, took off his remaining shoe, and left it on the bank.

He kept his pants on—they were not so heavy—and entered the river, pushed away from the bank until he was far enough out to start floating a bit.

551

MINILESSON

REVIEW: LITERARY APPRECIATION

Figurative Language

INFORMAL ASSESSMENT

Have students reread the third paragraph on page 550. Have students name an example of figurative language in the sentence. (*the brush was so thick and wild that it was like a jungle*) Ask what form of figurative language this is. (simile)

TEACH/MODEL

Explain that figurative language is words or phrases with meanings that are different from their literal definitions. Point out that *the brush . . . was like a jungle* is an example of a *simile*, or a comparison that says one thing is *like* another thing. Other forms of figurative language include metaphors, personification, and hyperbole. A *metaphor* compares two things by saying one thing is another. *Personification* is giving an inanimate or nonhuman object human characteristics, and *hyperbole* is an extreme exaggeration used to emphasize a point.

PRACTICE/APPLY

Have students find other examples of figurative language in the selection. (Possible responses: page 550: *thick vines grabbed at him*, personification; page 553: the riverbanks are compared to a *green wall*, metaphor; page 543: *made the river seem like a soft green tunnel*, simile)

IDEA BANK

Have students help you plan a visit to a nearby river or other wilderness area. On the field trip, encourage students to list the animals and plant life they see and to write their own story about a river.

Critical Thinking Question

What does the author mean when he says that Brian "became something other than himself that afternoon"? (Possible response: Brian was so challenged physically and so determined that he showed a side of himself that hadn't been seen before.) **CREATIVE: SPECULATING**

He kicked off the mud and began to swim. Within three strokes he knew how tired he was—his whole body felt weak and sore from the beating he'd taken in the rapids.

But he could not stop. He worked along the edge, half swimming, half pushing along with his feet in the mud.

Downriver.

He had to catch the raft.

He became something other than himself that afternoon.

When he began to swim—after he'd overcome the agony of starting and his muscles had loosened somewhat—he tried to think.

The raft would move with the current, if it did not get hung up.

Brian would also move with the current, plus he had the added speed of swimming, and he should gain rapidly.

CHALLENGE **Invite students to imagine that they can meet Brian and interview him. What will students ask? What will Brian reply? Challenge pairs of students to create and act out a short interview.**

But when he rounded that first bend and did not see the raft, and cleared the next bend two hundred yards further on and did not see the raft, worry took him.

He stopped at the side and stood as much as he could in the mud.

It was nearly a quarter of a mile to the next bend and there was no raft.

Every muscle in his body was on fire. He slipped back into the water and began swimming again, taking long, even strokes, kicking and pushing along the mud; pulling himself forward.

Another bend, and another, always reaching, and always Brian's eyes sought the still form, the thatched top of the raft.

Nothing.

The river seemed to have swallowed Derek. Altogether he rounded six shallow bends and still there was no raft, the stupid raft that had hung up on every bend when he was trying to steer it and now perversely held the center of the river somehow. There was nothing but the green wall along either side, the trees that grew higher and higher now that the rock hills were passed, until they nearly closed over the top of the river; the green wall that closed in and covered him as he slid along the water, wanting to scream, but pulling instead, always pulling, a stroke, then another stroke, until there was not a difference between him and the water, until his skin was the water and the water was him, until he *was* the river and he came to the raft.

553

Informal Assessment

SUMMARIZING/PARAPHRASING

To determine whether students can summarize or paraphrase the story events so far, ask them questions like the following:

- What are the most important events in the story so far?
- How would you retell the story in your own words?

EXPANDING VOCABULARY

CONTEXT CLUES **Have students' reread the second sentence of the last paragraph on this page, and point out the word *perversely*. Explain that *perversely* means "in a stubborn, disobedient, or difficult manner." Ask students what context clues can help them determine that meaning.** ***(hung up on every bend when he was trying to steer it, now . . . held the center of the river)***

He nearly swam past it.

Brian moved near some willows, his face down in the water, reaching with his left arm and when he raised his head he was looking at the raft.

It had somehow come through all the bends and curves, and here must have caught a slight crosscurrent. The raft had moved to the outside of a shallow curve and had glided back beneath some overhanging willows and low trees.

All that showed was the rear end of the raft—and the bottom of Derek's shoes.

"Derek!"

Brian's hand had almost brushed the raft, but had he not looked up at the exact point that he had, he would have missed it.

He grabbed the raft, pulled himself up alongside.

Derek lay still, though his body had moved, twisted sideways on the raft.

"Derek," he said again, softer.

Derek's head was still to the side, the eyes half open, but if he had been pushed underwater in the rapids, even for a moment, it might be too late.

"Derek."

He looked done, gone, dead.

Brian tried his wrist, but could feel no pulse. He watched Derek's chest but it didn't seem to move. He leaned down, put his ear against Derek's mouth, held his breath.

There.

Softly on his ear, a touch of breath—once, then again, small puffs of air.

"Derek." He was alive, still alive.

It was as if everything came loose in Brian at the same time. His body, his mind, his soul were all exhausted and he fell across Derek, asleep or unconscious, fell with his legs still in the water.

"Derek."

554

HEALTH

CPR Point out that if Brian hadn't felt Derek's breath, he may have had to use cardiopulmonary resuscitation (CPR) to revive him. CPR must be administered quickly after a victim's breathing and heartbeat have stopped. Explain that the procedure involves chest compressions and breathing into the victim's mouth. Only trained people should attempt the procedure.

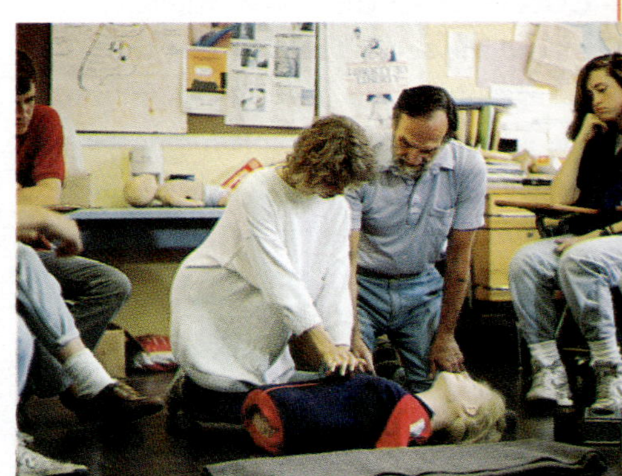

Suddenly he was paddling.

His eyes were open and he was kneeling in back of Derek and he was leaning forward with the paddle and he did not have the slightest idea of how he'd come to be there.

He had a new paddle in his hands, carved roughly from a forked branch with a piece of Derek's pantleg pulled across the fork to form the face of the paddle. Brian was moving the raft and the sun was shining down on him and it was all, everything, completely new to him.

A different world.

"I must have slept, then moved in my sleep. . . ."

The briefcase was gone—torn off in the rapids—and with it the map. Not that it mattered.

The banks were just all green and the river went ahead to the next bend. The trees hung over the top and there was nothing to see but a slot of sky and the water ahead and the endless, endless green.

Nothing to match with a map.

He could no longer think anyway. He had no idea how far they had come, how many hours or days they had been traveling or how far it still was to the trading post. He could only pull now, only pull with the paddle.

555

EXTRA SUPPORT **Point out to students that this story is told from the third-person limited point of view, so that we see things as Brian sees them. Throughout the story, the author uses quotation marks whenever Brian says something aloud, but we can also learn Brian's thoughts, which are not in quotes.**

MINILESSON

REVIEW: COMPREHENSION

Making Judgments

INFORMAL ASSESSMENT

Ask students to make a judgment about the kind of person Brian is. (Possible responses: He is brave, determined, strong, unstoppable.)

TEACH/MODEL

Explain that judgments about how characters act must be based on evidence from the selection. If there is evidence to support a judgment, it is a valid judgment. If other readers will make the same judgment based on the same evidence, it is a reliable judgment. You may want to model the thinking:

MODEL **I think that Brian is an exceptionally brave and determined young man. There is evidence in the story that backs up my judgment. For example, even though Brian is completely exhausted, he keeps paddling without stopping, through the whole day and into the night.**

PRACTICE/APPLY

Ask students to find other bits of evidence in the story that back up the judgments they have made about Brian.

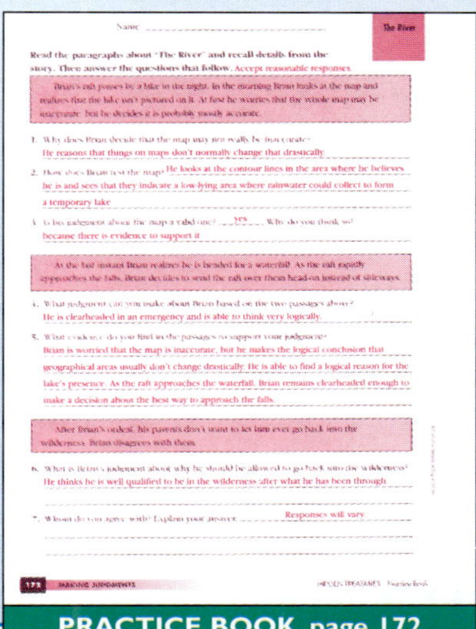

Name ______________ The River

Read the paragraphs about "The River" and recall details from the story. Then answer the questions that follow. Accept reasonable responses.

Brian's raft passes by a lake in the night. In the morning Brian looks at the map and realizes that the lake isn't pictured on it. At first he worries that the whole map may be inaccurate, but he decides it is probably mostly accurate.

1. Why does Brian decide that the map may not really be inaccurate? He reasons that things on maps don't normally change that drastically.
2. How does Brian test the map? He looks at the contour lines in the area where he believes he is and sees that they indicate a low-lying area where rainwater could collect to form a temporary lake.
3. Is his judgment about the map a valid one? yes Why do you think so? because there is evidence to support it

At the last instant Brian realizes he is headed for a waterfall! As the raft rapidly approaches the falls, Brian decides to send the raft over them head-on instead of sideways.

4. What judgment can you make about Brian based on the two passages above? He is clearheaded in an emergency and is able to think very logically.
5. What evidence do you find in the passages to support your judgment? Brian is worried that the map is inaccurate, but he makes the logical conclusion that geographical areas usually don't change drastically. He is able to find a logical reason for the lake's presence. As the raft approaches the waterfall, Brian remains clearheaded enough to make a decision about the best way to approach the falls.

After Brian's ordeal, his parents don't want to let him ever go back into the wilderness. Brian disagrees with them.

6. What is Brian's judgment about why he should be allowed to go back into the wilderness? He thinks he is well qualified to be in the wilderness after what he has been through.
7. Whom do you agree with? Explain your answer. Responses will vary.

172 MAKING JUDGMENTS [illegible] Practice Book

PRACTICE BOOK, page 172

Cooperative Reading

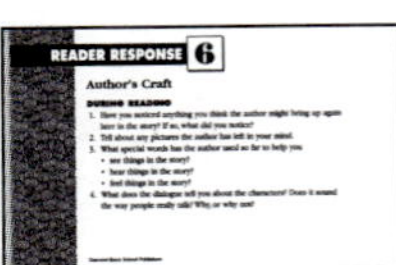
Response Card 6

After cooperative reading groups have finished reading, students should discuss any problems they had comprehending the story and address any questions they noted while reading. You may want to encourage discussion by asking questions like these:

- **What do you like about the way the author tells the story?**
- **How does the tone of the story change in the last two pages?**

He knew absolutely nothing, except the raft and the paddle and his hands, which had gone beyond bleeding now and were sores that stuck to the shaft of the crude paddle; knew nothing but the need, the numbing, crushing need to get Derek somewhere, somewhere, somewhere down the river. . . .

Food, hunger, home, distance, sleep, the agony of his body—none of it mattered anymore.

Only the reach.

The bend forward at the waist, the pull back with the arms, two on the left, two on the right.

Two left.

Two right.

Two.

Two.

Into that long day and that long night he moved the raft, so beyond thought now that even the hallucinations didn't come; nothing was there but the front of the raft, Derek, and the river.

The river.

Sometime in the morning of the next day, any day, a thousand days or eight days—he could not tell—somewhere in that morning the river widened and made a sweeping curve to the left, widened to half a mile or more, and he saw or thought he could see a building roof, a straight line in the trees that did not look natural and then he heard it, the sound of a dog barking—not a wolf or coyote, but a dog.

There was a small dock.

People had dogs that barked, and they had docks. He kept pulling, still not able to think or do anything but stroke, pulled to the edge of the river until the raft nudged against the dock, bounced, and then the paddle dropped.

556

AUTHOR'S CRAFT

Draw students' attention to the author's use of repetition on page 556. For example, Paulsen repeats *knew nothing* and *need*; he writes *somewhere, somewhere, somewhere*, and uses the word *two* six times among fourteen words. Each of these repetitions drives home the fact that the same thing is happening over and over with Brian: the same determination, the same uncertainty, the same movements.

He was done.

Above him on the bank he saw a small brown and white dog barking at him, its tail jerking with each bark, the hair of his back raised. As Brian watched, the round face of a young boy appeared next to the dog.

"Help. Help me," Brian thought he said, but heard no sound. The face of the boy disappeared and in moments two more people came, a man and woman, and they ran down to the dock and looked down at Brian and he was crying up at them, his torn hands hanging at his sides down in the water, down in the river.

The river.

"Derek. . . ."

Hands took him then, hands pulled him onto the dock; and the man jumped in the water and untied Derek and took him as well.

Hands.

Strong hands to help.

It was over.

Brian, Derek, and the raft traveled one hundred and nineteen miles down a river with an average current speed of two miles an hour, in just under sixty-three hours.

When Brian started, the raft weighed approximately two hundred pounds, but soaking up water all the way, it nearly doubled its weight by the time they reached the trading post—which was actually nothing more than a small cabin on the river where trappers could bring their furs. The post was owned and manned by a husband, wife, and one small boy, but they had a good radio and could call for help.

Derek's coma was low grade, and in truth he probably would have been all right even if Brian had not made the run—although he would have suffered significantly from dehydration. He began to come out of the coma in another week and had fully recovered within six months.

557

Student Self-Assessment

FIX-UP STRATEGY: USING PICTURE CLUES

Ask students what they can do if they have trouble visualizing scenes from the story. (Possible response: I can look at the illustrations to better understand the action in the story.)

If necessary, model using picture clues:

MODEL

I'm not sure what kind of paddle Brian is using to move down the river. I can see in the illustration on page 556 that the paddle is rough and crudely made. It makes sense that Brian has sores on his hands from holding the paddle for so long.

CHALLENGE **Brian, the hero of the story, is challenged by a treacherous river. Invite students to make a list of other challenges or obstacles a hero like Brian might face. Encourage students to choose an obstacle or challenge from their lists and write a scene featuring a hero like Brian.**

Strategic Reading

PAGES 552–558 How does Brian find Derek and the raft? (Brian looks for the raft as he swims downriver. After he rounds six bends, he finds the raft beneath overhanging willows and low trees.) STRATEGIES: SUMMARIZING/CONFIRMING PREDICTIONS

How does Brian reach the trading post? (Possible response: He paddles down the river through the night and the next day. He is hungry and exhausted, and loses his sense of time, but he keeps going until he reaches the trading post.) CRITICAL: NOTING IMPORTANT DETAILS

Returning to the Predictions/Purpose

Did you find out how Brian and Derek make it to the trading post? Encourage students to discuss whether their purposes for reading were met. STRATEGY: RETURNING TO THE PURPOSE

Appreciating the Literature

When reading, when were you most eager to find out what happens next? (Responses will vary.)

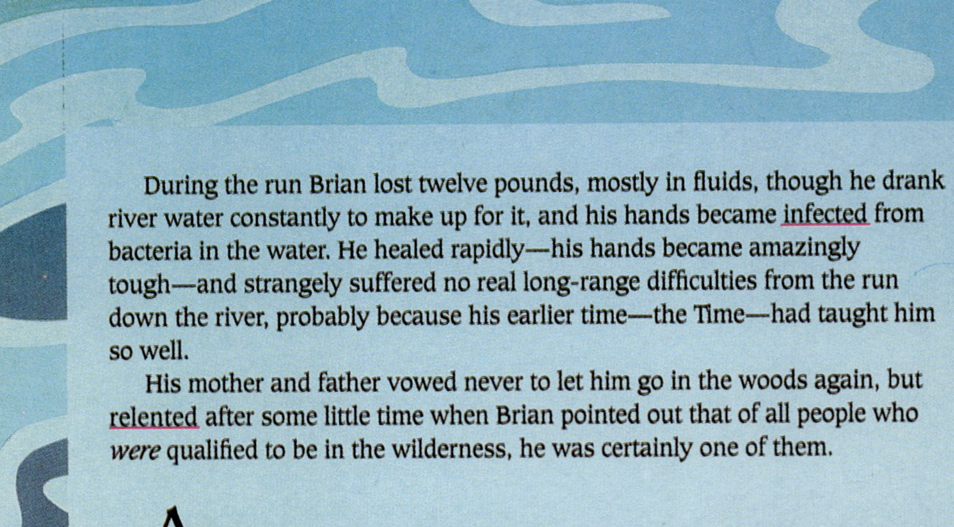

During the run Brian lost twelve pounds, mostly in fluids, though he drank river water constantly to make up for it, and his hands became infected from bacteria in the water. He healed rapidly—his hands became amazingly tough—and strangely suffered no real long-range difficulties from the run down the river, probably because his earlier time—the Time—had taught him so well.

His mother and father vowed never to let him go in the woods again, but relented after some little time when Brian pointed out that of all people who *were* qualified to be in the wilderness, he was certainly one of them.

About seven months after the incident, Brian was sitting alone at home wondering what to cook for dinner when the doorbell rang, and he opened the door to find a large truck parked in the street in front of the house.

"Brian Robeson?" the driver asked.

Brian nodded.

"Got some freight for you."

The driver went to the rear of the truck, opened it, and pulled out a sixteen-foot Kevlar canoe, with paddles taped to the thwarts. It was a beautiful canoe, light and graceful, with gently curving lines that made it look wonderfully easy to paddle.

Written in gold letters on each side of the bow were the words:
THE RAFT

"It's from a man named Derek Holtzer," the driver said, setting the canoe on the lawn. "There's a note taped inside."

He climbed back in the truck and drove away and Brian found the note.

"Next time," he read aloud, "it won't be so hard to paddle. Thanks."

GARY PAULSEN

Gary Paulsen was born in Minneapolis, Minnesota, in 1939. His father was in the army, so his family was always on the move. "The longest time I spent in one school was about five months," he remembers. "School was a nightmare and I was unbelievably shy, and terrible at sports."

One winter day he stepped into a library to get out of the cold. "The librarian walked up to me and asked me if I wanted a library card," he says. "When she handed me that card, she handed me the world. It was as though I had been dying of thirst and the librarian handed me a five-gallon bucket of water."

Paulsen has worked as a teacher, a farmer, a rancher, a truck driver, and a migrant farm worker. He was also an editor for a popular magazine. He says that working on the magazine was "the best of all possible ways to learn about writing."

Paulsen's stories are usually set in wild places and are about young people who learn more about themselves by facing the challenge of surviving in the wilderness. Besides writing, Paulsen loves dogsledding. He once entered the famous Iditarod dogsled race in Alaska. This experience was the inspiration for his book *Dogsong,* which was named a Newbery Honor Book.

559

About the Author

After students read page 559, you may wish to discuss the following questions with them:

- **What did Gary Paulsen mean when he said that when the librarian handed him a library card, she handed him the world?** (Possible responses: He meant that books opened up a new world of knowledge for him; through books he learned more about people and about life.)
- **How have Gary Paulsen's experiences influenced his writing?** (Possible response: His stories are set in the wilderness. He has spent a lot of his time working on farms and ranches and in other outdoor settings.)

Gary Paulsen suffered a heart attack after his second Iditarod race. He changed his diet and decided to give writing the same energy and attention that he had given his dogs. He describes how serious he is about writing:

> My output dramatically increased. . . . I become totally, viciously, obsessively committed to work. I still work that way, completely, all the time. I just work.

SUMMARIZING

Story Map

Have students complete the story map they began during prereading. Invite them to work with a partner to use their maps to summarize the story and to decide how well their summary reflects the story. See also *Practice Book* page 168.

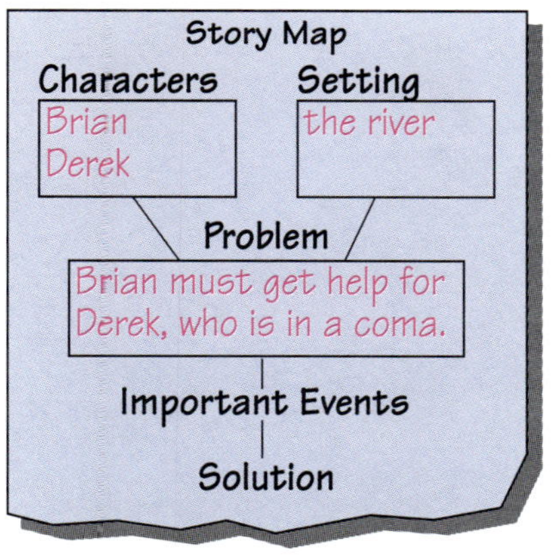

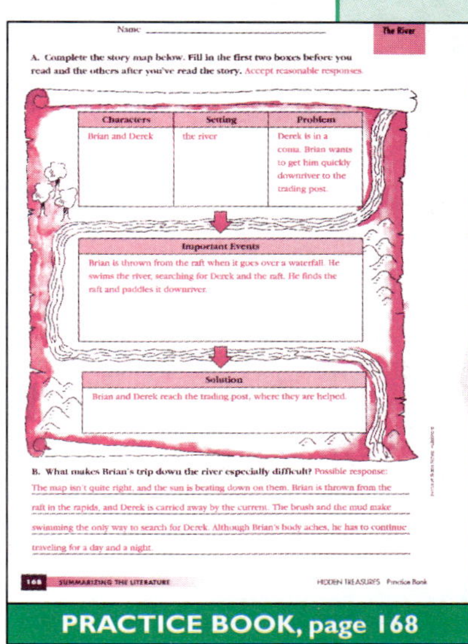

Name ______________________ The River

A. Complete the story map below. Fill in the first two boxes before you read and the others after you've read the story. Accept reasonable responses.

Characters	Setting	Problem
Brian and Derek	the river	Derek is in a coma. Brian wants to get him quickly downriver to the trading post.

Important Events

Brian is thrown from the raft when it goes over a waterfall. He swims the river, searching for Derek and the raft. He finds the raft and paddles it downriver.

Solution

Brian and Derek reach the trading post, where they are helped.

B. What makes Brian's trip down the river especially difficult? Possible response: The map isn't quite right, and the sun is beating down on them. Brian is thrown from the raft in the rapids, and Derek is carried away by the current. The brush and the mud make swimming the only way to search for Derek. Although Brian's body aches, he has to continue traveling for a day and a night.

168 SUMMARIZING THE LITERATURE HIDDEN TREASURES Practice Book

PRACTICE BOOK, page 168

ACTIVITY CHOICES

MAKE A LIST

WATER TO THE RESCUE Some students may want to work with a partner to create the list of tips. One student can display the list while the other discusses it. HEALTH/LISTENING AND SPEAKING

WRITE A REPORT

ROW, ROW, ROW YOUR BOAT Encourage students to prewrite by listing information under each category (operating, maintaining, storing, and transporting). Urge students to treat each of these topics as a separate paragraph or section of their report. PHYSICAL EDUCATION/WRITING

WRITE A POEM

TIME CAPSULE Students might enjoy illustrating their poems with the face of a watch, a calendar page, or some other timekeeping device. CRITICAL THINKING/WRITING

Response Corner

MAKE A LIST

WATER TO THE RESCUE

Brian is worried that Derek may become dehydrated. Find out more about the causes and symptoms of dehydration. Make a list of tips to help prevent dehydration, and discuss your findings with your classmates.

WRITE A REPORT

ROW, ROW, ROW YOUR BOAT

Brian knows the technique of paddling the raft like a canoe. Work with a small group to write a report about the sport of canoeing. Include information about operating, maintaining, storing, and transporting a canoe. Share your report with the rest of the class.

560

STUDENTS ACQUIRING ENGLISH Have students work on these response activities with English-proficient partners. Some students may want to write their poems about time in their first language and then work with a partner on a translation.

WRITE A POEM

TIME CAPSULE

Reread the section about *time* at the top of page 543. Do you agree with Gary Paulsen's thoughts about time? Write a poem that expresses your concept of time.

What Do You Think?

- Why are Brian and Derek on the river, and where do they end their trip?
- What would you have done about Derek if you had been in Brian's position?
- Do you think that Brian will go into the wilderness again? Explain your answer.

561

CHECKING COMPREHENSION

What Do You Think?

1. **Why are Brian and Derek on the river, and where do they end their trip?** (Possible response: They are on the river because Derek was struck by lightning and has slipped into a coma, and Brian is trying to get him help as quickly as possible. They are on the river to get to the trading post; from there, help can be called. They end their trip there.) DESCRIPTIVE RESPONSE
2. **What would you have done about Derek if you had been in Brian's position?** (Responses will vary.) PERSONAL RESPONSE
3. **Do you think that Brian will go into the wilderness again? Explain your answer.** (Possible response: Yes. In fact he tells his parents that of all people who *were* qualified to be in the wilderness, he was certainly one of them. He will probably take his new canoe on a river.) CRITICAL ANALYSIS/REFLECTING

VARYING THE ACTIVITY

To **challenge** students working on the Water to the Rescue activity, ask that they record a simple message or ad for backpackers and other adventurers about the symptoms and dangers of dehydration.

Intervention Strategies

TIPS FOR CLASSROOM MANAGEMENT

IF second-language students need additional vocabulary and during-reading strategies to understand "The River," **THEN** use *Sheltered English/ESL Manual*, pages 86–89.

IF students had difficulty understanding "The River," **THEN** complete the Rereading and Structural Analysis Strategies. See also Intervention Strategies Manual, pages 128–133.

REREADING

DETERMINING SEQUENCE Assign each student a page of the selection for rereading. Then have students take turns retelling in chronological order the portions they have reread. As students recall each part of the story, have the class fill out a sequence chart like the one below.

Sequence Chart

First ____________________

Next ____________________

Then ____________________

Finally ____________________

PERSONAL JOURNAL

Have students write a few sentences in their journals comparing and contrasting the presentation of nature in "Freedom Ride" and "The River." Ask students to tell which story gives a more vivid picture of nature and why they think so.

STRUCTURAL ANALYSIS

VERB FORMS Remind students that many common verbs have irregular past and past-participle forms. Call on volunteers to identify some irregular verbs from the first page of the selection. (Possibilities include the following: *took, was, spread, meant,* and *come*.) Ask students to give the base form of each of these verbs (*take, be, spread, mean,* and *come*).

Model the major classes of irregular verbs by writing the following verb forms on the board.

pay	give	sing	become	put	break
paid	gave	sang	became	put	broke
paid	given	sung	become	put	broken

Invite students to skim the selection, listing as many irregular verb forms as they can find. When students have finished, call on volunteers to give the principal parts of each irregular verb.

WRITING TO SUMMARIZE

Help students summarize the story by putting the phrases below in the proper chronological order.

Brian realized that .....

Derek was still alive. (4)

he had to swim after the raft. (3)

the map might be wrong. (1)

the long struggle was finally over. (5)

they were headed for a waterfall. (2)

DECODING SUPPORT
/n/kn, /r/wr

Intervention Strategies Manual pp. 132–133

ESL/TITLE I READING

Reading Trade Books

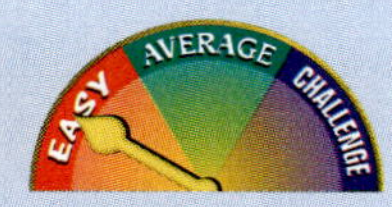

The Wreck of the Zephyr
by Chris Van Allsburg

Students will benefit from reading another book about a sailing adventure. You may wish to have students complete a Venn diagram after they read *The Wreck of the Zephyr.*

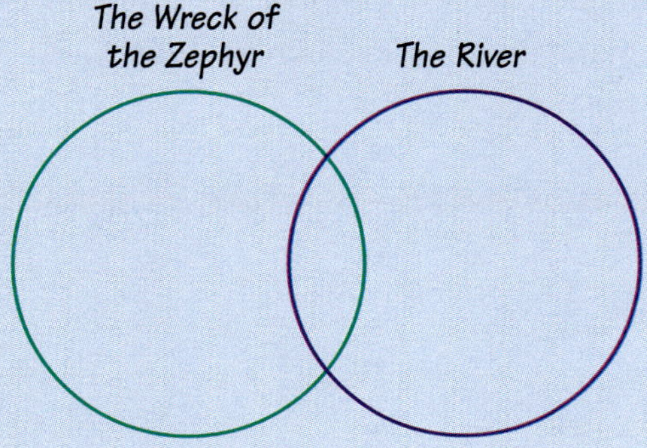

TAKE-HOME BOOK TO REINFORCE KEY WORDS

Students will read about a mentally-challenged boy in this moving story. They may want to read it when they have independent reading time in class, or they might take it home to read.

PERSONAL JOURNAL

After students have read *Jordan Waiting,* have them write in their personal journals about how the book made them feel.

See also *Intervention Strategies Manual,* page 131.

IDEA BANK

TIPS FOR CLASSROOM MANAGEMENT

IF students need practice following the sequence of events in a selection, **THEN** they should complete the Retelling activity.

IF students need to focus on strategies for reading aloud, **THEN** they should complete the Oral Language activity.

RETELLING

River Map

Have students work independently or with partners to create river maps showing what happened to Brian and Derek on their trip down the river. Encourage students to draw the river and the trading post and then annotate the map with the key events. Have students display their maps and describe story events for their classmates.

LISTENING/SPEAKING/WRITING/VIEWING

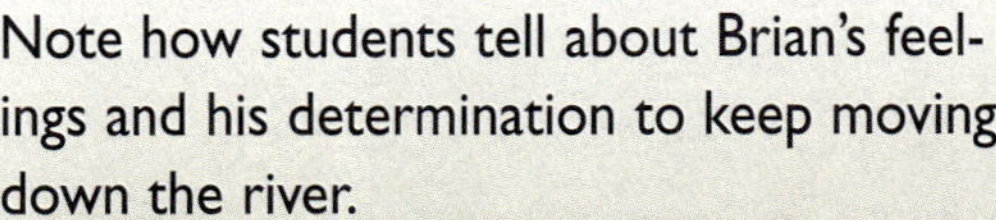

Informal Assessment

Note how students tell about Brian's feelings and his determination to keep moving down the river.

ORAL LANGUAGE

Book Review

Have students work independently to write a review of "The River." You may want to have students read a review in your local newspaper before they begin writing. Point out that a review gives an opinion about a book, and supports the opinion with details from the book. Students should read their reviews aloud to their classmates.

LISTENING/SPEAKING/READING/WRITING

TIPS FOR LISTENING AND SPEAKING

Point out that when students **read** their reviews, they should

- make frequent eye contact with their audience.
- speak clearly.
- use details from the story to support their opinions.

When students **listen** to others reading their reviews, they should

- identify the speaker's opinion.
- determine whether the speaker adequately backs up his or her opinion.
- maintain good eye contact and good posture.

VIEWING

Video/Documentary

Have students watch a documentary about rivers such as *River—Where Do You Come From?* (Learning Corporation of America). Before, during, and after students watch the video, have them fill in a K-W-L chart telling what they know, what they want to find out, and what they learned about rivers. They should also write whether watching the video helped them better understand the challenges Brian faces in "The River." **WRITING/VIEWING**

North Fork Virgin River
Zion National Park, Utah

REAL-LIFE RESOURCES

Magazine Interview

READING INTERVIEWS If Brian were a real person he might have become the subject of an exciting interview. Have students look through magazines to find quotations from people who have confronted nature as Brian did. Have students share favorite quotations and discuss how magazine interviews can be a useful source of information.

PLANNING AN INTERVIEW Discuss the steps needed to plan an interview, from selecting a good subject through writing specific questions. Suggest that students try to ask questions that begin with *why* or *how.* Point out that *yes* or *no* questions can limit a subject's response. See *Writer's Magazine* pages 84 and 85.

REAL-LIFE CHALLENGE Have students interview a friend, relative, or acquaintance with an interesting job or hobby, or who has had an exciting experience. Encourage students to use a chart to plan and take notes for the interview.

Question	Response

Students can write their interviews in the form of articles for a class magazine. **WRITING**

Amy's kind of adventure may not appeal to you. So imagine that you can go on any adventure you want. An adventure can be something as simple as hiking in the woods or visiting the zoo. What would you choose to do? In order of preference, list the adventures you'd like to take part in.

MAGAZINE PROFILE

SKYSURFER

RIDING THE CLOUDS!

Amy Baylie-Haass is scared to death of spiders and snakes. But she's not afraid to jump out of a plane and "surf"

WRITER'S MAGAZINE, pages 84–85

STUDENTS ACQUIRING ENGLISH

Students working on the Retelling activity should tell the sequence of events in their first language before they develop their maps.

EXTRA SUPPORT

Encourage some students working on the Oral Language activity to write reviews focusing on the author's style while other students focus on the story events.

WRITER'S WORKSHOP

Adventure Story

TIPS FOR CLASSROOM MANAGEMENT

IF students are familiar with the steps for writing a story, **THEN** have them begin writing, referring to the model on Transparency 55 as necessary.

IF you want a short writing activity, **THEN** adapt this lesson by having students focus on the Writer's Craft.

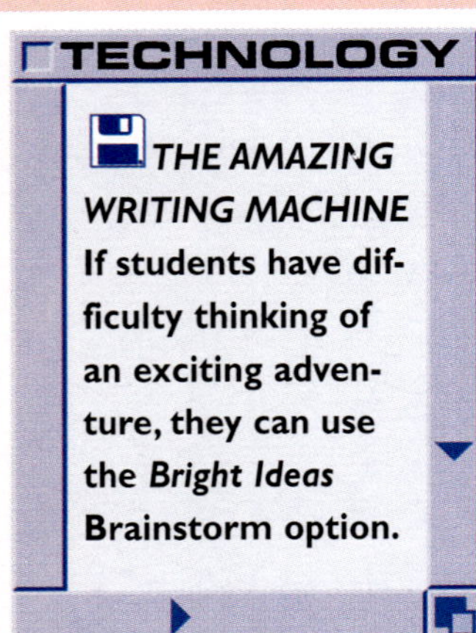

Thinking as Writers

WRITING FORM: Adventure Story
Tell students that "The River" is an adventure story because it is exciting and its main characters face high-risk challenges. Ask students to tell about other adventure stories they have read. Tell students that they are going to write their own adventure story.

Display Transparency 55 and discuss the elements of an adventure story.

TRANSPARENCY 55

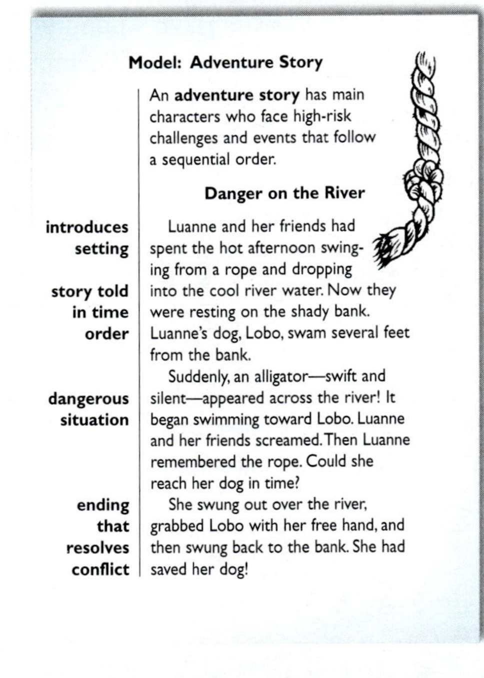

Model: Adventure Story

An **adventure story** has main characters who face high-risk challenges and events that follow a sequential order.

Danger on the River

introduces setting	Luanne and her friends had spent the hot afternoon swinging from a rope and dropping
story told in time order	into the cool river water. Now they were resting on the shady bank. Luanne's dog, Lobo, swam several feet from the bank.
dangerous situation	Suddenly, an alligator—swift and silent—appeared across the river! It began swimming toward Lobo. Luanne and her friends screamed. Then Luanne remembered the rope. Could she reach her dog in time?
ending that resolves conflict	She swung out over the river, grabbed Lobo with her free hand, and then swung back to the bank. She had saved her dog!

WRITER'S CRAFT: Sequence of Events
Explain that most events in an adventure story critically affect the events that follow. One way to recognize the sequence of events in a story is to look for signal words, such as *suddenly, then, next*, and *finally*. Point out that since adverbs tell *when*, many signal words are adverbs.

PREWRITING AND DRAFTING

Remind students that characters in adventure stories face unusual and exciting challenges. Refer to these strategies to help students begin their stories.

PREWRITING GRAPHIC ORGANIZER
Suggest that students use a page in their personal journals to record their ideas. Some students may benefit from making a chart of story elements like the one below to help them focus their thinking.

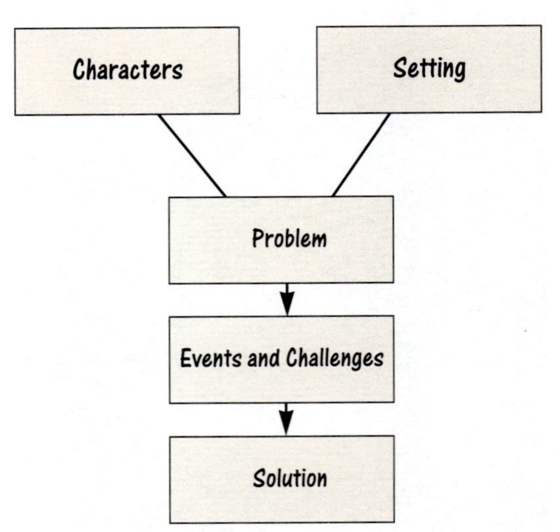

SUSTAINED SILENT WRITING Those students who have a clear idea of what they want to write may begin writing without interruption.

DURING-WRITING GRAPHIC ORGANIZER
Students who need to organize the action of the story may need to pause during writing to create a time line of the story's events.

RESPONDING AND REVISING

Suggest that students work in editing circles or with partners to help each other revise. Write this checklist on the board:

- **Does your story have a beginning, a middle, and an ending?**
- **Do events appear in a logical sequence?**
- **Have you used adverbs effectively to help describe the action in the story?**
- **Does your story show how the challenge or conflict was resolved?**

PROOFREADING

Offer the following tips as students proofread:

- Check for correct use of **adverbs**. (See Grammar Minilesson on page T1137.)
- Check for correct use of **punctuation**, including dashes to separate and emphasize phrases.
- Look for words you may have misspelled.

PUBLISHING

If you wish to have students publish their adventure stories, suggest the following options or have students choose their own.

ORAL Students may read their adventure stories aloud in small groups. Have groups comment on which part of the story was the most exciting and what the author did to create excitement.

WRITTEN Have students illustrate their stories and combine them in a class anthology, or bind them separately in specially designed covers for the classroom library. Students may also consider lending their stories to the school library for other students to enjoy.

EVALUATION BENCHMARKS: ADVENTURE STORY

An adventure story by a proficient student writer shows the following characteristics:

FORM	CRAFT	CONVENTIONS
Demonstrates understanding of the form • characters who face high-risk challenges • events ordered in logical sequence • strong ending to resolve challenge or conflict	**Uses clear and appropriate language** • adverbs used effectively • passage of time clearly indicated	**Follows conventions of grammar and usage** • adverbs used correctly • dashes, if present, used to separate and emphasize phrases

Teacher Assessment As you assess students' writing, refer to the Evaluation Benchmarks chart. For additional information, including model papers, see *Integrated Performance Assessment* Teacher's Edition.

PORTFOLIO OPPORTUNITY

Have students answer the Student Self-Assessment questions and include both their answers and their adventure stories in their portfolios.

LANGUAGE HANDBOOK

Writing to Entertain and Express, pages 40–41; Model: Realistic Fiction, pages 42–43; Adverbs, pages 27, 160–163, 220–221

Student Self-Assessment ✓

Have students answer the following questions and include the answers in their portfolios:

 What is the most exciting scene in your adventure story?

 What parts of your story might still need to be revised?

Tested Skill

GRAMMAR

Negatives

LANGUAGE HANDBOOK

Negatives, pages 163, 223

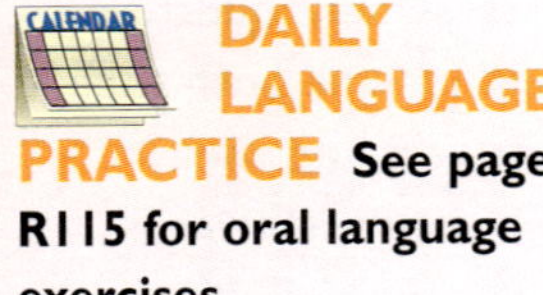

DAILY LANGUAGE PRACTICE See page R115 for oral language exercises.

Reading ↔ Writing Connection

Connect to the literature. Ask students to look back at "The River" to find some of the words that either mean or suggest "no" or "not." Write the words they find in a web on the board.

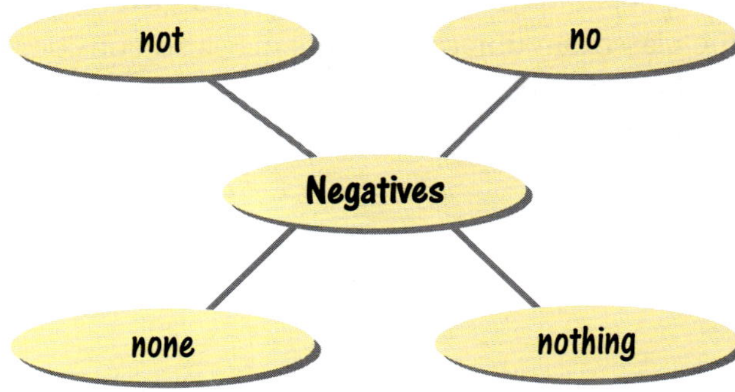

Then ask them to add similar words not found in the selection, such as *nobody, no one, never, nowhere, barely, hardly*, and *scarcely*.

Build oral language. Ask students to dictate sentences like the ones below about Brian or "The River" that contain negatives. Write students' sentences on the board, and underline the negatives.

No one could be as brave and as lucky as Brian.

Brian never gives up.

He keeps going, no matter what happens.

Ask how the underlined words are alike. (They all express the meaning "no" or "not.")

Teach/Model

Discuss using negatives. Explain that people sometimes misuse negatives by putting more than one of them into one independent clause or sentence. Write the following sentence on the board, and ask students to decide what is wrong with it:

Nobody never helped Brian.

(There are two negatives in one sentence.) Point out that this error is called a *double negative*. Then check comprehension by asking students to summarize what they have learned and correct the sentence on the board. (Nobody ever helped Brian.)

Practice/Apply

Check understanding. Write the following sentences on the board, and have students identify the negatives:

I had barely finished my lunch when it was time for dinner. (barely)

When we tried to bicycle up the mountain, we got nowhere fast. (nowhere)

Then write the following incorrect sentences on the board and ask volunteers to change them to make them correct.

He hardly never missed a day of exercise.
(He never (hardly ever) missed a day of exercise.)

Elena did not never go to that shopping mall.
(Elena did not ever go (never went) to that shopping mall.)

Not nobody knew where Martha had gone.
(Nobody knew where Martha had gone.)

Practice Activities

INTERVIEW A CHARACTER

ORAL APPLICATION Ask students to work in pairs to create an interview with Brian Robeson. Encourage students to use negatives to emphasize what Brian does not know about the map, the river, and Derek. **VISUAL/AUDITORY/KINESTHETIC**

Accentuate the Negative

WRITING APPLICATION Tell students to be on the lookout for advertisements, street signs, or common sayings that contain negative words. You may want to provide a few examples to get students started: "Don't let a headache spoil your fun," "No Parking Here to Corner," and "Never let the sun set on your anger." Students might work in pairs or in small groups. When students have gathered a number of examples, have them create attention-grabbing posters using the examples. They can design their posters to advertise a product or to give a public service message. **VISUAL/AUDITORY/KINESTHETIC**

APPLY TO WRITING

You may want students to check their adventure stories and other writing for double negatives.

USAGE TIP Use only one negative in a sentence.

STUDENTS ACQUIRING ENGLISH

Students who are native speakers of Spanish, French, and other languages may think it is perfectly normal to use double negatives. Explain that avoiding double negatives is one of the ways in which English differs from other languages.

RETEACH

See page R106 for lessons in multiple modalities.

GRAMMAR PRACTICE BOOK
pages 52–53

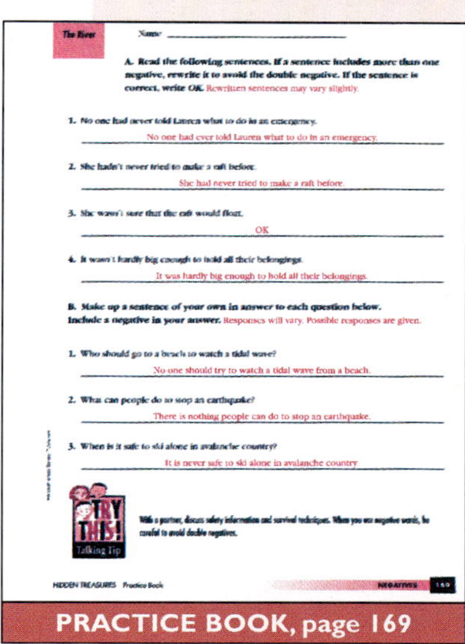
The River

Name: ______________________

A. Read the following sentences. If a sentence includes more than one negative, rewrite it to avoid the double negative. If the sentence is correct, write OK. Rewritten sentences may vary slightly.

1. No one had never told Lauren what to do in an emergency.
   No one had ever told Lauren what to do in an emergency.
2. She hadn't never tried to make a raft before.
   She had never tried to make a raft before.
3. She wasn't sure that the raft would float.
   OK
4. It wasn't hardly big enough to hold all their belongings.
   It was hardly big enough to hold all their belongings.

B. Make up a sentence of your own in answer to each question below. Include a negative in your answer. Responses will vary. Possible responses are given.

1. Who should go to a beach to watch a tidal wave?
   No one should try to watch a tidal wave from a beach.
2. What can people do to stop an earthquake?
   There is nothing people can do to stop an earthquake.
3. When is it safe to ski alone in avalanche country?
   It is never safe to ski alone in avalanche country.

TRY THIS! Talking Tip

With a partner, discuss safety information and survival techniques. When you use negative words, be careful to avoid double negatives.

HIDDEN TREASURES Practice Book — NEGATIVES 169

PRACTICE BOOK, page 169

5-DAY PLAN

Use in conjunction with Daily Language Practice.

Day 1 Complete page T1162.	**Day 4** Choose a Practice Activity or *Grammar Practice Book* pages 52–53.
Day 2 Complete a Practice Activity on page T1163.	**Day 5** Complete *Practice Book* page 169.
Day 3 Choose a Practice Activity or *Language Handbook* pages 163, 223.	

2

SPELLING

5-Day Plan

Integrated Spelling Lesson 32
student book, pages 134–137;
Teacher's Edition, pages T207–T212.

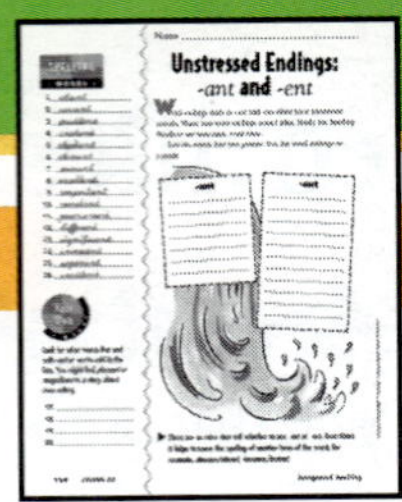

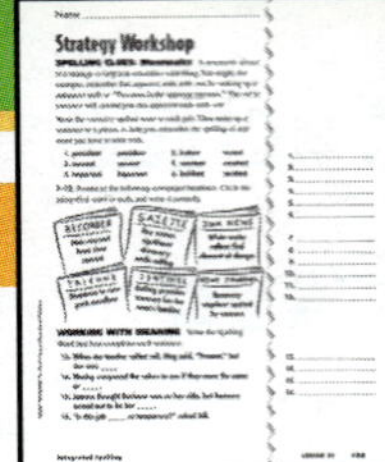

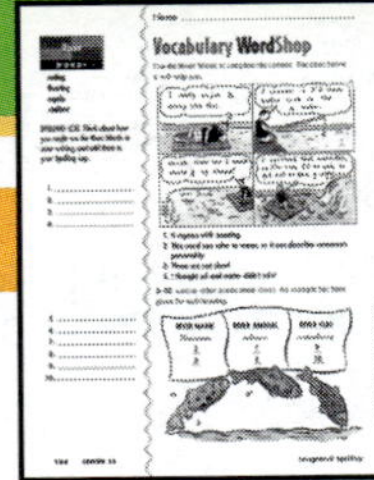

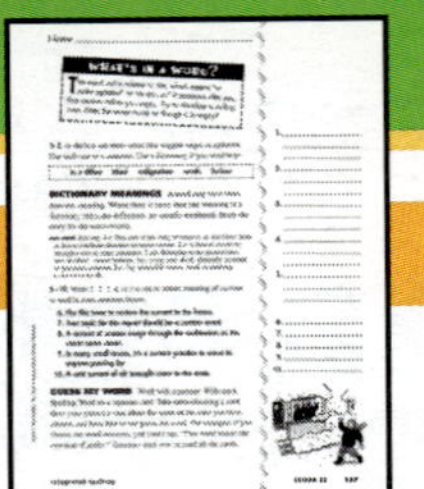

SPELLING WORDS

1. absent
2. current ★
3. president
4. instant ★
5. elephant
6. element
7. servant
8. excellent
9. important
10. constant
11. permanent ★
12. different ★
13. significant ★
14. innocent
15. opponent
16. incident ★

STUDENT'S PERSONAL WORDS

17. 19.

18. 20.

Additional story words are *apparent, moment, relent,* and *giant.*

★ Words appearing in "The River"

Unstressed Endings: *-ant* and *-ent*

Pretest

DAY 1 **Administer the pretest.** Say each word and then use it in the dictation sentence below. Help students self-check their pretests.

OPEN SORT

DAY 2 **Have students create categories.** Invite students to come up with ways to sort the Spelling Words. For example, students might sort according to number of syllables or the presence or absence of a prefix. Provide an opportunity for students to discuss their sorting methods with their classmates.

CLOSED SORT

Sort by ending. Write the headings from the following chart on the board, and have volunteers write each Spelling Word under the correct heading. Then invite students to name other words that can be placed under each heading. Ask students to add the words they name to their Student's Personal Words lists.

-ant	-ent	
instant	absent	different
elephant	current	innocent
servant	president	opponent
important	element	incident
constant	excellent	
significant	permanent	

Teach/Model

DAY 3 **Explain the generalization.** Tell students that many words end with an unstressed syllable spelled *-ant* or *-ent.* Explain that there is no rule that tells whether *-ant* or *-ent* is correct, but knowing another form of the word is helpful. For example, knowing the spelling of the words *instance* or *absence* may help them remember the spelling of the words *instant* or *absent.*

DAY 4 **Apply to writing.** Students should look for words that end in *-ant* and *-ent* in their adventure stories to be sure they are spelled correctly.

Posttest

DAY 5 **Assess students' progress.** Use the sentences below to administer the posttest.

DICTATION SENTENCES

1. Jeremy has been absent from school for a week.
2. The swimmer battled the strong current of the river.
3. Mrs. Chin is the president of the club.
4. Kris hesitated for an instant before answering.
5. Did you see the elephant at the zoo?
6. Lauren enjoys an element of suspense in a story.
7. We do not have a servant to clean that mess.
8. Keiko had excellent grades all through school.
9. An important message was delivered today.
10. Constant crying came from the sick child's room.
11. The injury left a permanent scar on his heel.
12. Did Julie get a different answer than you got?
13. The Gomezes made a significant change in their plans.
14. The prisoner said he was innocent of the crime.
15. His opponent won the game.
16. An unfortunate incident occurred at the store.

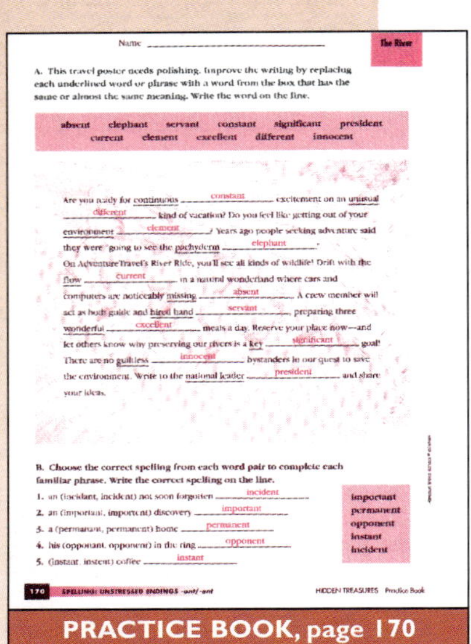

Name ____________ The River

A. This travel poster needs polishing. Improve the writing by replacing each underlined word or phrase with a word from the box that has the same or almost the same meaning. Write the word on the line.

absent elephant servant constant significant president current element excellent different innocent

Are you ready for continuous __constant__ excitement on an unusual __different__ kind of vacation? Do you feel like getting out of your environment __element__? Years ago people seeking adventure said they were "going to see the pachyderm __elephant__." On AdventureTravel's River Ride, you'll see all kinds of wildlife! Drift with the flow __current__ in a natural wonderland where cars and computers are noticeably missing __absent__. A crew member will act as both guide and hired hand __servant__ preparing three wonderful __excellent__ meals a day. Reserve your place now—and let others know why preserving our rivers is a key __significant__ goal! There are no guiltless __innocent__ bystanders in our quest to save the environment. Write to the national leader __president__ and share your ideas.

B. Choose the correct spelling from each word pair to complete each familiar phrase. Write the correct spelling on the line.

1. an (incidant, incident) not soon forgotten __incident__
2. an (importani, importent) discovery __important__
3. a (permanant, permanent) home __permanent__
4. his (opponant, opponent) in the ring __opponent__
5. (instant, instent) coffee __instant__

important permanent opponent instant incident

170 SPELLING: UNSTRESSED ENDINGS -ant/-ent HIDDEN TREASURES Practice Book

PRACTICE BOOK, page 170

VOCABULARY WORKSHOP

Reviewing Key Words

Write the Key Words on the board. Have students answer the following questions:

1. Are hallucinations real or not actually there? (not actually there)
2. Is someone infected ill or bouncing back? (ill)
3. Is someone in a coma fully awake or unconscious? (unconscious)
4. If someone relented, did he or she give in or continue? (give in)

Extending Vocabulary

FIGURATIVE LANGUAGE

Remind students that authors often use figurative language in imaginative, creative ways to make their writing more interesting and to help create vivid pictures in the reader's mind. If you taught the minilesson on figurative language on page T1145, you may remind students of other examples of figurative language used in the story. Then reread the following description of the raft from page 545 of "The River":

The raft seemed to come alive, turn into a wild, crazy animal.

Have students interpret the description in their own words. Then explain that the raft is being compared to an animal. A comparison that does not use the word *like* or *as* is called a *metaphor*. Other forms of figurative language are *simile*, *personification*, and *hyperbole*.

WRITE SENTENCES USING FIGURATIVE LANGUAGE

Have students work in small groups to come up with fresh expressions to replace common clichés. You may wish to suggest several clichés for revision, including the following: *light as a feather, hungry as a bear, mad as a hornet,* and *stubborn as a mule*.

Tested Skill

INTRODUCE: COMPREHENSION STRATEGY

Summarizing/ Paraphrasing

OBJECTIVE: To summarize and paraphrase a selection

Informal Assessment ✓

Are students able to

- ☑ summarize the important ideas of a passage?
- ☑ accurately paraphrase a passage?

Teach/Model

Return to the literature. Have students briefly tell important events in "The River." Then tell students that they have just summarized the story.

Model summarizing and paraphrasing. Explain that **paraphrasing** means retelling the selection—not just the main events—in your own words. **Summarizing** is briefly restating the main events or ideas of a selection. Read aloud the second half of page 558 to students, then model summarizing the passage:

MODEL **About seven months after the incident on the river, Brian receives a beautiful canoe and a thank-you note from Derek.**

Explain that a paraphrase of the same passage would include not only the main ideas of the passage, but also more details. Point out that you might paraphrase a passage when you want to be sure you understand all the details.

Practice/Apply

Have students demonstrate understanding. Ask students to reread page 544. Have students paraphrase the passage by restating the events in their own words. Then draw a summary chart like the one below. Ask students to help you complete the chart.

Summary Chart

Who: (Brian and Derek)

Where/When: (on the river just about noon)

Events: (The raft moves quickly down the river. Brian hears a sound.)

Problem: (The sound seems to be a waterfall.)

Work with students to summarize the passage based on information in the chart.

Practice Activities

Signs of a Good Summary

COOPERATIVE LEARNING Divide the class into groups of three or four students. One student in each group should be the Reader who prepares and then gives a summary of a selection the whole class has read previously. Two other students will serve as Checkers. They will prepare five large index cards that read *Characters, Setting, Problem, Important Events*, and *Solution*. As the Reader covers each element in his or her summary, the Checkers hold up the appropriate card. An Observer can watch the group and provide feedback. VISUAL/AUDITORY/KINESTHETIC

VENN DIAGRAM

PERFORMANCE ASSESSMENT Ask students to create a Venn diagram with one circle labeled *Paraphrase* and the other labeled *Summary*. Invite students to use the diagram to show how a summary and a paraphrase are alike and different. VISUAL

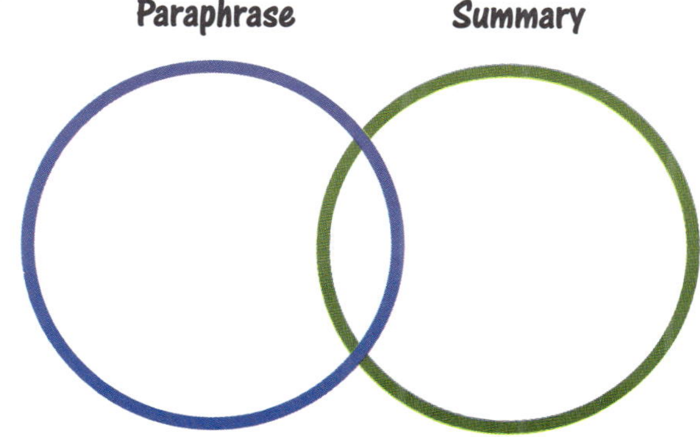

STUDENTS ACQUIRING ENGLISH

When possible, allow students to summarize a selection in their own language for other speakers of the same language.

RETEACH

See page R107 for lessons in multiple modalities.

CHALLENGE

Ask students to summarize a favorite book, television show, or movie for the class. Invite listeners to tell which books, shows, or movies they would like to read or see, based on the summaries.

Reading Trade Books TO REINFORCE SUMMARIZING/PARAPHRASING

Biography of a River: The Living Mississippi by Edith McCall. Walker, 1990. CHALLENGING

Canoeing by Donna Bailey. Steck-Vaughn, 1991. EASY

Get Out of My Face by David Masterton. Macmillan, 1991. AVERAGE

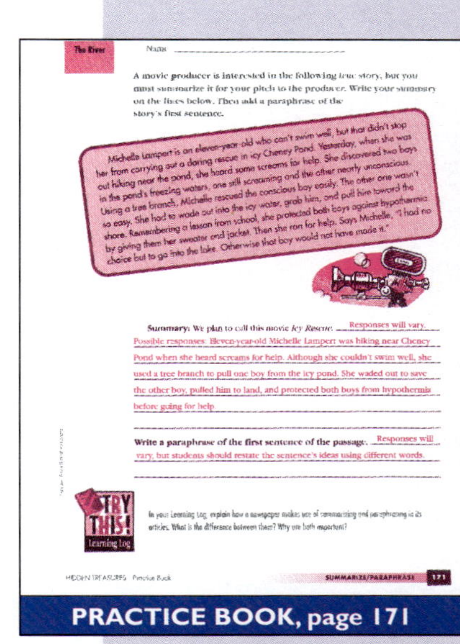

The River

Name ______

A movie producer is interested in the following true story, but you must summarize it for your pitch to the producer. Write your summary on the lines below. Then add a paraphrase of the story's first sentence.

Michelle Lampert is an eleven-year-old who can't swim well, but that didn't stop her from carrying out a daring rescue in icy Cheney Pond. Yesterday, when she was out hiking near the pond, she heard some screams for help. She discovered two boys in the pond's freezing waters, one still screaming and the other nearly unconscious. Using a tree branch, Michelle rescued the conscious boy easily. The other one wasn't so easy. She had to wade out into the icy water, grab him, and pull him toward the shore. Remembering a lesson from school, she protected both boys against hypothermia by giving them her sweater and jacket. Then she ran for help. Says Michelle, "I had no choice but to go into the lake. Otherwise that boy would not have made it."

Summary: We plan to call this movie *Icy Rescue*. Responses will vary. Possible responses: Eleven-year-old Michelle Lampert was hiking near Cheney Pond when she heard screams for help. Although she couldn't swim well, she used a tree branch to pull one boy from the icy pond. She waded out to save the other boy, pulled him to land, and protected both boys from hypothermia before going for help.

Write a paraphrase of the first sentence of the passage. Responses will vary, but students should restate the sentence's ideas using different words.

TRY THIS! Learning Log

In your Learning Log, explain how a newspaper makes use of summarizing and paraphrasing in its articles. What is the difference between them? Why are both important?

HIDDEN TREASURES Practice Book SUMMARIZE/PARAPHRASE 171

PRACTICE BOOK, page 171

Integrated Curriculum

SCIENCE

Rivers

TIPS FOR CLASSROOM MANAGEMENT

IF students are artistically inclined, **THEN** they may want to help develop the River Life Mural.

TECHNOLOGY

IMAGINATION EXPRESS, DESTINATION: TIME TRIP, USA Have students use the program's *Fact Book* to find information for their time lines.

Point out that the river in this story is both friend and enemy: a source of transportation and vital drinking water, as well as danger and disease.

SCIENCE/ART

River Life Mural

Use reference sources. A river is home to hundreds of creatures. Invite students to work as a class to research plants and animals that live in and along rivers and then make a river mural. Students can show bottom-dwellers such as catfish, middle-dwellers such as trout, surface-dwellers such as mayflies, animals that populate both the river and the shore such as frogs and ducks, and plants and birds that populate the riverbanks. Be sure students include any creatures or plants unique to rivers in their area. For example, manatees inhabit some rivers in Florida. Ask students to include sentence captions. Students might also create an inset drawing showing the microscopic contents of a drop of river water, clean or polluted. **READING/WRITING**

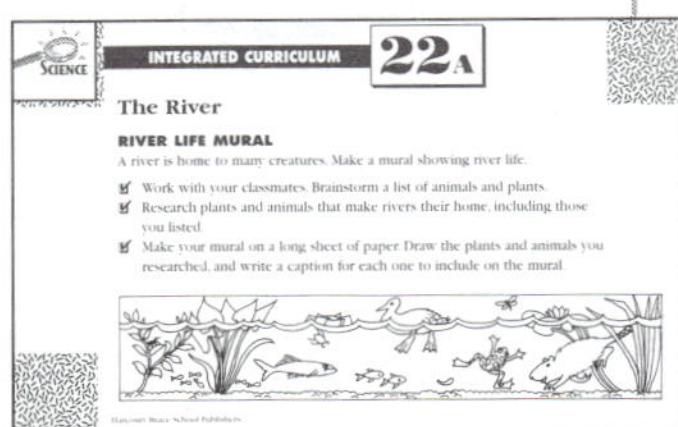
SCIENCE

INTEGRATED CURRICULUM 22A

The River

RIVER LIFE MURAL

A river is home to many creatures. Make a mural showing river life.

- Work with your classmates. Brainstorm a list of animals and plants.
- Research plants and animals that make rivers their home, including those you listed.
- Make your mural on a long sheet of paper. Draw the plants and animals you researched, and write a caption for each one to include on the mural.

Curriculum Card 22A

SOCIAL STUDIES

River of Time Line

COOPERATIVE LEARNING Students can work in small groups to learn the history of a local river or of a larger river such as the Mississippi, Hudson, Rio Grande, or Missouri. Assign the roles of Reader, Recorder, Checker, and Reporter, and ask groups to research important dates in the history of the river, such as when the first European explorers discovered it, the date of the first mills and/or settlements on it, dates of major cleanups or changes, dates of important bridges or dams, and so on. Urge groups to make a time line that stretches from the present all the way back before European colonization. Provide an opportunity for groups to share their work with the class. **LISTENING/SPEAKING/READING/WRITING**

MUSIC

River Rhythms

Invite students to locate some music that they think reflects the vitality and danger of rivers. You might want to have students listen to a recording of *River Moldau* by Bedrich Smetana or of *On the Beautiful, Blue Danube* by Johann Strauss. Encourage students to bring in their own recordings of appropriate songs and instrumentals to share with their classmates. Ask students to create their own titles for the music in order to make a better connection to "The River." **LISTENING/READING/WRITING**

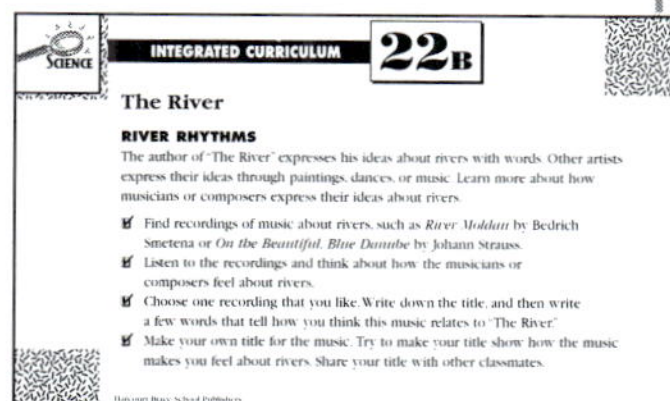
SCIENCE

INTEGRATED CURRICULUM **22B**

The River

RIVER RHYTHMS

The author of "The River" expresses his ideas about rivers with words. Other artists express their ideas through paintings, dances, or music. Learn more about how musicians or composers express their ideas about rivers.

- ☑ Find recordings of music about rivers, such as *River Moldau* by Bedrich Smetena or *On the Beautiful, Blue Danube* by Johann Strauss.
- ☑ Listen to the recordings and think about how the musicians or composers feel about rivers.
- ☑ Choose one recording that you like. Write down the title, and then write a few words that tell how you think this music relates to "The River."
- ☑ Make your own title for the music. Try to make your title show how the music makes you feel about rivers. Share your title with other classmates.

Harcourt Brace School Publishers

Curriculum Card 22B

CROSS-CURRICULAR READING

Hatchet **by Gary Paulsen. Bradbury, 1987.**
AVERAGE

Working River **by Fred Powledge. Farrar, Straus & Giroux, 1995.**
AVERAGE

MULTI-AGE CLASSROOMS

You may encourage students who have more experience visiting or exploring rivers to lead the River Life Mural activity.

Reading Trade Books

Trade Books That Connect to "The River"

The Bridge Dancers

by Carol Saller
illustrated by Gerald Talifero

When Maisie becomes injured, Callie must use all the skills their mother taught them to protect her sister. Suggest that readers describe the steps that both Callie and Brian follow to protect someone who has been injured.

Drift

by William Mayne

In this exciting adventure, Rafe and Tawena face many challenges and dangers in the North American wilderness. Suggest that readers use a Venn diagram to compare the settings of *Drift* and "The River."

The Fear Place

by Phyllis Reynolds Naylor

After reading this story about a boy who overcomes his fears during an emergency, students might want to write their own responses to the statement "Emergencies bring out the best in people."

TIPS FOR CLASSROOM MANAGEMENT

SMALL-GROUP READING Suggest that groups work together to read and act out scenes from one of the books. After reading each chapter aloud, encourage students to summarize the main events and then act them out. Ask members to switch roles for each chapter.

STUDENTS ACQUIRING ENGLISH

Some students may want to read *The Bridge Dancers* with a partner who is proficient in English and who will read aloud. Suggest that partners take time to discuss each illustration.

Paddle-to-the-Sea

by Holling Clancy Holling

A figure of a man in a canoe carved by a young Native American travels from the Nipogen country of the Great Lakes to the St. Lawrence River before finally reaching the sea. Encourage students to create simple maps to compare the journeys in this novel and "The River."

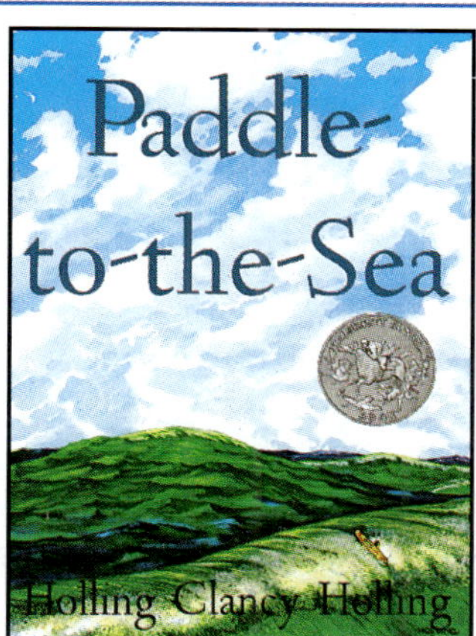

Swift Rivers

by Cornelia Meigs

Students can compare the information about river rafting in this novel with the information presented in "The River." Suggest that they create a web that includes factual details from both books.

Yukon River: An Adventure to the Gold Fields of the Klondike

by Peter Lourie

This photo-essay describes a real 460-mile canoe trip taken by two friends. After students read, encourage them to make a list of suggestions they would give to friends who were planning to take a similar trip.

EXTRA SUPPORT

Suggest that students preview *Paddle-to-the-Sea* by reading the chapter titles in the table of contents. Students can find the Great Lakes region in an atlas or on a map, and then follow Paddle's journey on the map as they read.

Trade Books

PROJECT MANAGEMENT

- PROJECT LAUNCH
- CHECKPOINT 1
- CHECKPOINT 2
- CHECKPOINT 3
- CHECKPOINT 4
- PRESENTATIONS
- ASSESSMENT

Write a Mission Statement

SELECTION CONNECTION

In "The River," Brian experiences hunger and exhaustion as he navigates a raft down an unpredictable river. Ask students to identify the mission of Brian's journey, as well as the obstacles.

PROJECT CHECKLIST

During this stage, students should

- ☑ think of their group as a wilderness team that will go on an expedition.
- ☑ brainstorm a variety of settings for their fantasy expedition and choose one.
- ☑ research the chosen setting.
- ☑ write a mission statement that describes their expedition, including its goal, type of transport, risks, and importance.

Project Card 33 can be found as a copying master on page R124.

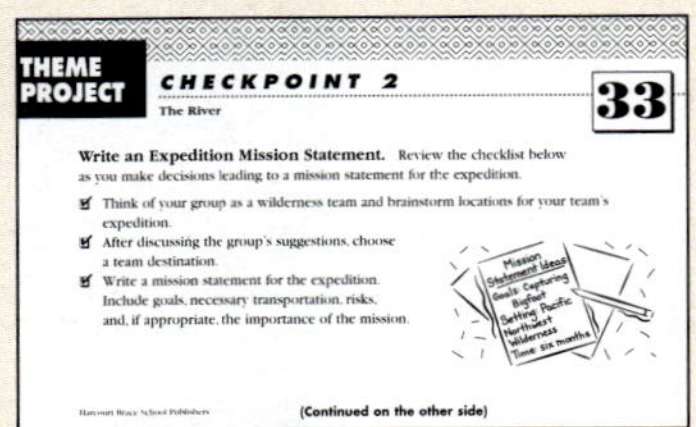

THEME PROJECT

CHECKPOINT 2

The River

33

Write an Expedition Mission Statement. Review the checklist below as you make decisions leading to a mission statement for the expedition.

- ☑ Think of your group as a wilderness team and brainstorm locations for your team's expedition.
- ☑ After discussing the group's suggestions, choose a team destination.
- ☑ Write a mission statement for the expedition. Include goals, necessary transportation, risks, and, if appropriate, the importance of the mission.

Harcourt Brace School Publishers

(Continued on the other side)

Project Card 33

RESEARCH AND PLANNING TIPS

As students prepare to write their teams' mission statements, suggest that they

- choose a Facilitator to keep the team focused and to insure that all members participate.
- go to the library in pairs, with one partner finding information while the other takes notes.
- consult a variety of resources, such as almanacs, encyclopedias, atlases, travel books, and camping guides.

Have students write about their experience in their project journals. You may wish to provide prompts such as *What appealed to your group about the setting you chose?*

Informal Assessment

During this checkpoint, students will **synthesize** information from a variety of sources to help them **predict** travel needs and obstacles and **make decisions** about their expedition. Students are thinking critically if they

- ☑ are able to use library resources to locate specific geographical information.
- ☑ are able to recognize and describe in their statements the obstacles and risks involved in the expedition.

STUDENTS ACQUIRING ENGLISH

You may wish to group these students together as an adventure team and have them use one of the *Imagination Express Destinations* to provide visual information and story support throughout the theme project.

CLASSROOM MANAGEMENT

If possible, have a large map of the world available for students to refer to as they choose a specific setting for their wilderness adventure.

ART AND LITERATURE

The Gulf Stream (1899) • Winslow Homer (1836–1910)

ABOUT THE ARTIST

Winslow Homer was born in Boston, Massachusetts, and grew up in nearby Cambridge. His active outdoor childhood and his love of nature are reflected in the subjects he returned to again and again for his paintings. As a young man, Homer earned his living as an illustrator. He gained attention for his illustrations of Civil War battles, which he depicted realistically and without heroics. After the war, Homer began to paint regularly—mainly scenes of country life. However, during a trip to England, he began to focus on the ocean as his subject of choice. Homer lived most of his adult life alone in a studio he built on the coast of Maine. He wrote of this existence in a personal letter, "The life that I have chosen gives me my full hours of enjoyment.... The Sun will not rise, or set, without my notice and thanks."

ABOUT THE PAINTING

In *The Gulf Stream* Homer portrays a dramatic scene that captures the viewer's imagination. The man has no way of controlling his boat since the mast is broken. The weather—probably the cause of the damage to the boat—still looks threatening. Sharks patrol the dark waters, and the man seems not to notice the ship that could perhaps rescue him. The dark colors of the water and sky create a sense of hopelessness and foreboding.

What problem does the man in *The Gulf Stream*, by Winslow Homer, face as he confronts nature? How would you compare his problem with that faced by the Fordreds in "Freedom Ride" or by Brian in "The River"? Notice the many colors that Homer used in painting the water. How does this use of color help to create a mood of fear and suspense?

The Gulf Stream (1899)
by Winslow Homer

Winslow Homer, a self-taught artist, began his career making drawings for magazines at a time when photographs were not widely used. Homer gained fame for his realistic drawings of Civil War battles. Later, he painted scenes from country life as well as pictures that show the force and beauty of nature. His paintings provide a visual record of life in 19th-century America.

The Metropolitan Museum of Art

562 563

Art and Literature

MAKING CONNECTIONS

Have students read and discuss the first paragraph on page 562. Lead students to see that the man in the painting, like Brian in *The River,* is struggling to survive a confrontation with the forces of nature. Some students may suggest that the man, like the Fordreds in *Freedom Ride,* may have chosen to confront nature. Discuss how the dark colors of the red-streaked water create a mood of foreboding.

EXTENDING FINE ART

Hands-On Activity Have students draw a picture showing themselves or someone else confronting nature. If students have trouble getting started, you may want to suggest situations such as being lost in a snowstorm or in a desert; surviving a flood, a tornado, or a hurricane; or experiencing an earthquake or a volcanic eruption. Encourage students to draw their pictures in a way that will cause the viewer to ask what happens next.

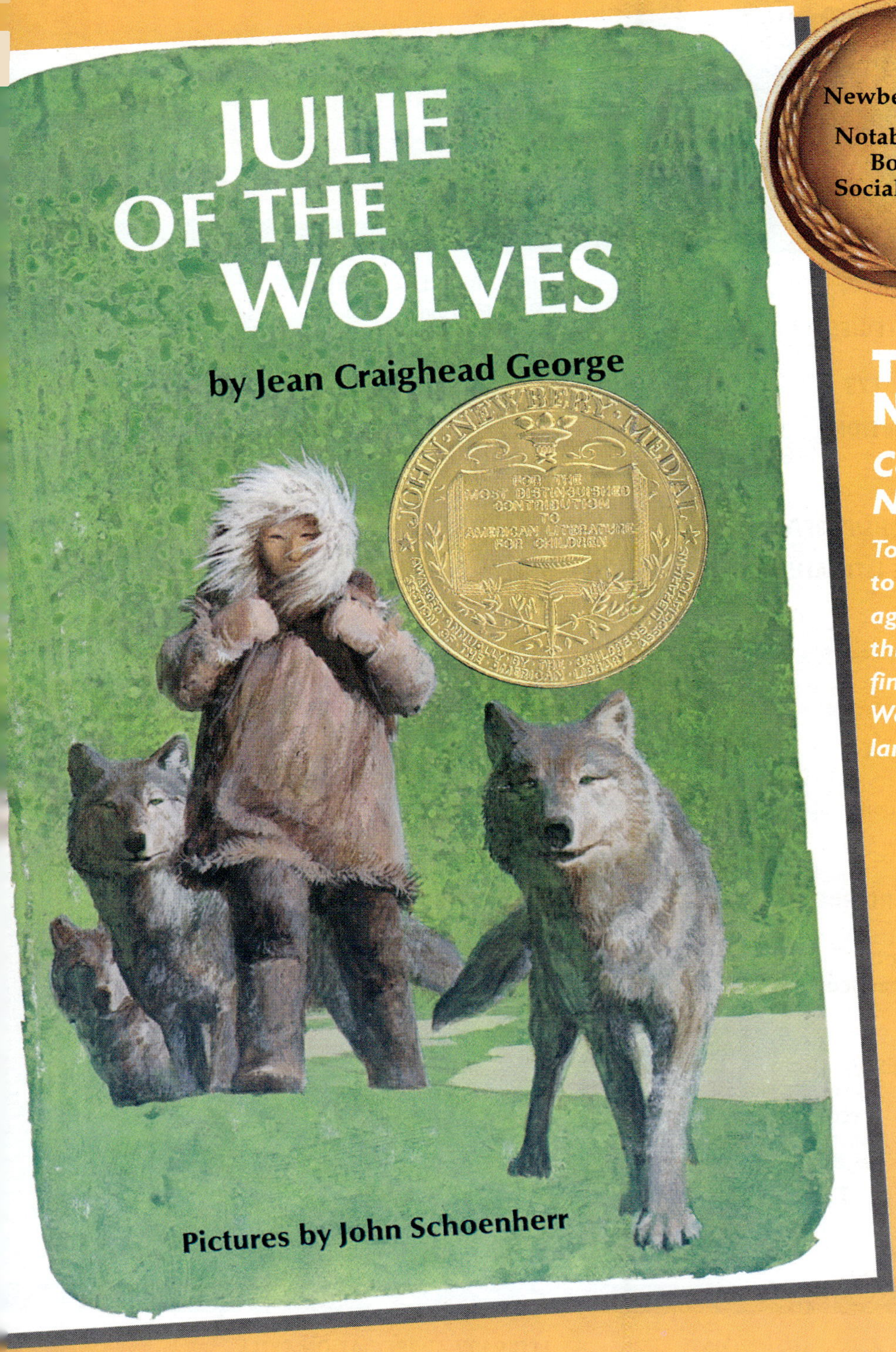

JULIE OF THE WOLVES

by Jean Craighead George

Pictures by John Schoenherr

Newbery Medal
Notable Trade Book in Social Studies

THEME: NATURE

Confronting Nature

To survive in nature means to work with it, not against it—and, as thirteen-year-old Miyax finds in "Julie of the Wolves," to speak its language.

Jean Craighead George

ABOUT THE AUTHOR

Since 1948, **JEAN CRAIGHEAD GEORGE** has shared her love of the outdoors with young people as a writer and illustrator of many award-winning novels and nonfiction works. *Julie of the Wolves* received the 1973 Newbery Medal for excellence in children's literature.

More information about Jean Craighead George and her work appears on page T1192.

SELECTION SUMMARY

Genre: Realistic Fiction

Thirteen-year-old Miyax, whose American name is Julie, is lost on Alaska's North Slope. It is summer, and the food she has brought with her is gone. Miyax camps near a pack of wolves, hoping to befriend them and share their food. At first, the pack's leader, Amaroq, ignores her, and Miyax knows that he must accept her before the other wolves will. The adult wolves go off and leave one adult behind to look after the pups. Miyax studies how they communicate and imitates them, testing her skill on two of the pups. Miyax is jubilant as she realizes they understand. When the other wolves return, Miyax bravely communicates her adoration to Amaroq and is accepted.

SUGGESTED LESSON PLANNER

▶ ***Julie of the Wolves***

PART 1 — Reading, Listening, Speaking, Viewing

Key Words
- dispelled
- vitality
- aggressively
- intimidated
- tribute

DAY 1

BUILD BACKGROUND T1178

VOCABULARY STRATEGIES T1179
Transparency 56
Practice Book p. 173

READING THE SELECTION T1180–T1193
Options for Reading T1180–T1181
Response Card 2

REVIEW PREDICTIONS/PURPOSE T1190

APPRECIATING THE LITERATURE T1190

NOTE: Students may read the selection on Day 2.

DAY 2

SUMMARIZE THE SELECTION T1191
Practice Book p. 174

◆ **RESPONSE CORNER ACTIVITIES** T1194

CHECKING COMPREHENSION T1195

End-of-Selection Test

PART 2

Writer's Workshop

DAY 1

PERSONAL NARRATIVE
Thinking as Writers T1200
Language Handbook pp. 62–63
Transparency 57

DAY 2

Prewriting T1200
Language Handbook p. 60

Grammar

DAY 1

✓ **PREPOSITIONS AND PREPOSITIONAL PHRASES**
Teach the Concept T1202
Daily Language Practice (1–2) R116

DAY 2

Daily Language Practice (3–4) R116
Practice Activity T1203

Spelling

DAY 1

ADJECTIVE SUFFIXES *-ive, -ous*

positive	*nervous*	*active*	*various*
senstive	*curious*	*negative*	*enormous*
creative	*delicious*	*effective*	*attractive*
mysterious	*furious*	*legislative*	*numerous*

Pretest/Self-Check T1204
Integrated Spelling Teacher's Edition pp. T213, T302

DAY 2

Open and Closed Sorts T1204
Integrated Spelling p. 138
Integrated Spelling Teacher's Edition p. T214

PART 3 — Skills and Strategies

DAY 1

◆ **INTEGRATED CURRICULUM**
Natural History
Science T1208
Art T1209
Music T1209
Thinkin' Things Collection 2: Toony's Tunes

DAY 2

LITERARY APPRECIATION SKILL T1206–T1207
Point of View (Introduce)
Practice Book pp. 177–178

Meeting Individual Needs

DAY 1: Use the Intervention Strategies note on T1189 to help **below-level** and **ESL students** as they read.

DAY 2: Use the Challenge note on T1190 with **above-level students.**

NOTE: An alternative lesson plan for **below-level students** appears on *Intervention Strategies Manual* pp. 134–139. A lesson for **students acquiring English** appears on *Sheltered English/ESL Manual* pp. 90–93.

DAY 3	DAY 4	DAY 5
◆ **IDEA BANK ACTIVITIES** Retelling T1198 *Response Card 6* Oral Language T1198 Rereading T1199 Real-Life Resources: Reading Postcards T1199 *Writer's Magazine* pp. 88–89 School–Home Connection 23 R143	**VOCABULARY WORKSHOP** T1205 Reviewing Key Words **READING TRADE BOOKS** T1210–T1211 *Signatures Library: Bearstone*  Signatures Library  Take-Home Book	**READING TRADE BOOKS** T1207, T1209, T1210–T1211 
Drafting T1200 *Language Handbook* pp. 23, 61 *The Amazing Writing Machine*	Responding and Revising T1201 *Language Handbook* p. 61	Proofreading and Publishing T1201 *Language Handbook* p. 61
Daily Language Practice (5–6) R116 Practice Activity T1203 *Language Handbook* pp. 164–165 *The Amazing Writing Machine*	Daily Language Practice (7–8) R116 Practice Activity T1203 *Grammar Practice Book* pp. 54–55	Daily Language Practice (9–12) R116 *Practice Book* p. 175
Discuss the Generalization T1204 *Integrated Spelling* p. 139 *Integrated Spelling Teacher's Edition* p. T215	Apply to Writing T1204 *Integrated Spelling* pp. 140–141 *Integrated Spelling Teacher's Edition* pp. T216–217	Posttest T1204 *Practice Book* p. 176 *Integrated Spelling Teacher's Edition* p. T218
STUDY SKILLS MINILESSON T1183 ✓ Reference Sources (Review) *Practice Book* p. 179 **COMPREHENSION MINILESSON** T1187 ✓ Summarizing/Paraphrasing *Practice Book* p. 180	**VOCABULARY WORKSHOP** T1205 Antonyms	**GRAMMAR MINILESSON** T1191 ✓ Negatives Theme Project Checkpoint 3 T1212 *Imagination Express, Destination: Ocean*
Use the Students Aquiring English note on T1199 to help **ESL students** with the Rereading activity.	**Below-level students** may read the *Take-Home Book: The Intruder* to help them review Key Words.	**Below-level** and **ESL students** may read the *ESL/Title I Library* book *Dream Wolf.*

✓ = Tested Skill
◆ = Optional activities used to adjust pacing throughout the lesson
Titles in *italics* are optional materials.

1 Reading and Responding

BUILDING BACKGROUND AND CONCEPTS

PRIOR KNOWLEDGE

Relate to students' lives. Ask students what they would do if they were lost and alone in the wilderness and had run out of food. Discuss with students how they might go about finding food. Have students think of the tools they would need, or would have to make, to get food to survive.

Create a Venn diagram about survival. Explain to students that "Julie of the Wolves" is about a girl who is lost on the North Slope of Alaska. Ask students how survival in the Arctic would be the same as and different from survival in a tropical rainforest. Record students' responses in a Venn diagram like the following:

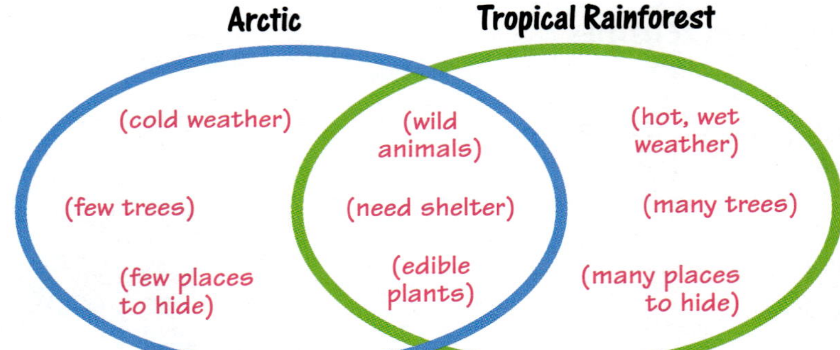

QUICKWRITE

Encourage students to write a few sentences about what they would fear most if they were lost in the Arctic. Suggest that students support their responses with reasons.

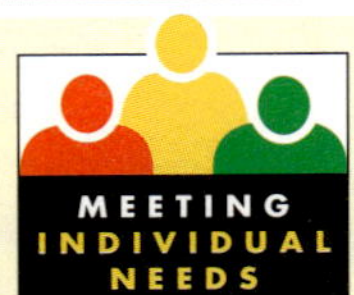

Intervention Strategies

For students who may have difficulty reading "Julie of the Wolves," support is available in *Intervention Strategies Manual* pages 134–139 and on pages T1189 and T1196–T1197 in this lesson.

STUDENTS ACQUIRING ENGLISH

See *Sheltered English/ESL Manual,* pages 90–93.

FACT FINDER — SOCIAL STUDIES

The Eskimo People

The Eskimos are a people who live in and near the Arctic. The name *Eskimo* means "eaters of raw meat," but Eskimos call themselves by words that mean "people." They are known as *Inuit* in Canada, *Inupiat* in Alaska, and *Yupik* in Alaska, Siberia, and St. Lawrence Island.

Living by the sea has provided the Eskimos with most of their clothing and food, including walruses, seals, polar bears, whales, and fish. Land inhabited by Eskimos covers five to six thousand miles, a greater straight-line distance than any other people in the world. It stretches from Asia across the North American continent to eastern Greenland. The languages of these peoples are unique and are believed not to be related to any other language in the world.

VOCABULARY STRATEGIES

KEY WORDS DEFINED

dispelled scattered or driven away; made to disappear

vitality vigor or strength of body

aggressively showing boldness and energy

intimidated made afraid

tribute something given or shown as a sign of respect or thanks

INTEGRATED SPELLING

Spelling Pretest: page T1204

Spelling Generalization: Suffixes: *-ive* and *-ous*

CONTEXT CLUES: STORY

Encourage students to use syntactic and semantic cues. Display the paragraph on Transparency 56, and ask a volunteer to read it aloud. Have students identify context clues that help them to understand the meanings of the underlined words. For example, the words *strength* and *commander* are clues to the meaning of *vitality*. Prompt students to use similar strategies to figure out the meanings of the other Key Words.

CHECK UNDERSTANDING

Have students brainstorm associations. Ask volunteers to review the meaning of each Key Word, and then have students free-associate words or phrases for each word with this question: *What do you think of when you hear the word (____)?* Keep the associations coming as quickly as possible, and encourage imaginative responses such as "chili peppers that aggressively attack my mouth." **STRATEGY: ASSOCIATIONS**

TRANSPARENCY 56

Key Words

A strong wind blew and dispelled the clouds covering the full moon. The light shone on a wolf pack that had just returned from the hunt. The catch lay at the feet of the leader, an older wolf with the strength and vitality of a commander. One of the younger wolves approached the catch hungrily. Suddenly, the leader snarled and lunged at him aggressively. The young wolf backed off quickly, clearly intimidated by the leader. Then, the wolf pack allowed the leader to begin eating the prey first as a tribute to his well-deserved position.

The winner of the kayak race showed vitality and determination.

Julie of the Wolves

Name ____

Read the wolves' speeches, using context clues to determine the meanings of the underlined words. Write a definition of each word in the space provided. Then write four sentences of your own on a separate sheet of paper, using each of the underlined words.

Why is that girl still here? Her lack of weapons has dispelled my fear that she might be a hunter.

Would she think I was acting aggressively if I crept closer, or would she see that I'm friendly?

Look how she stays a careful distance away. She seems intimidated by us.

She's coming closer! As a tribute to her courage, I will invite her to join us!

It takes a lot of vitality to keep up with our pack. I hope she won't lag behind on long hunts.

1. dispelled — driven away as if by scattering
2. intimidated — frightened; scared off
3. aggressively — in a way that warns of possible attack
4. tribute — something given to show admiration or respect
5. vitality — physical or mental energy; liveliness

TRY THIS! Writing — What animal or kind of animal do you like or respect? Write a paragraph explaining why you respect or appreciate the animal. In your explanation, use at least two of the vocabulary words.

VOCABULARY 173

PRACTICE BOOK, page 173

Prereading Strategies

PREVIEW AND PREDICT

Encourage students to preview "Julie of the Wolves" by reading the introduction and looking at the illustrations. Ask students what they think the story might be about.

Begin a story impressions chart on the board. Students may use *Practice Book* page 174. Ask a volunteer to answer the question about the introduction.

Story Impressions	
thirteen-year-old Alaska lost	without food wolf pack nearby
Group Story (Before Reading)	Story Summary (After Reading)

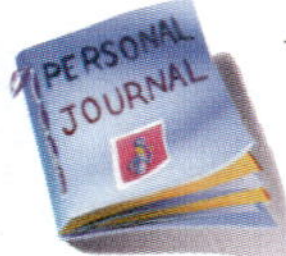

You may want to suggest that students write their predictions about the story in their personal journals.

PURPOSE

You may want to model setting a purpose:

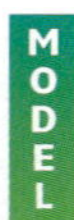

MODEL **Since the title is "Julie of the Wolves," I think Miyax will make friends with the wolves. As I read, I'll look for clues that explain how she does it.**

TIPS FOR CLASSROOM MANAGEMENT

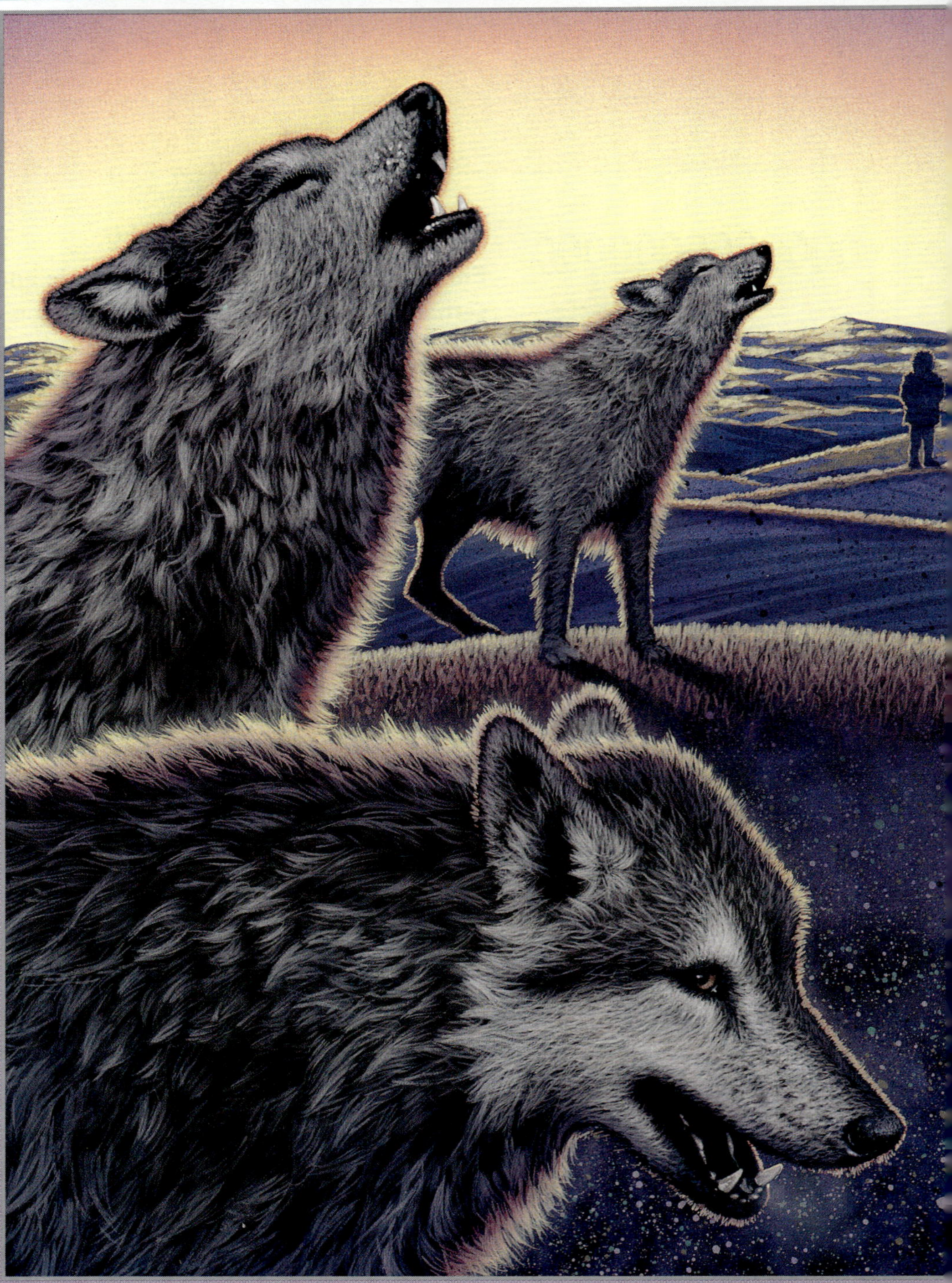

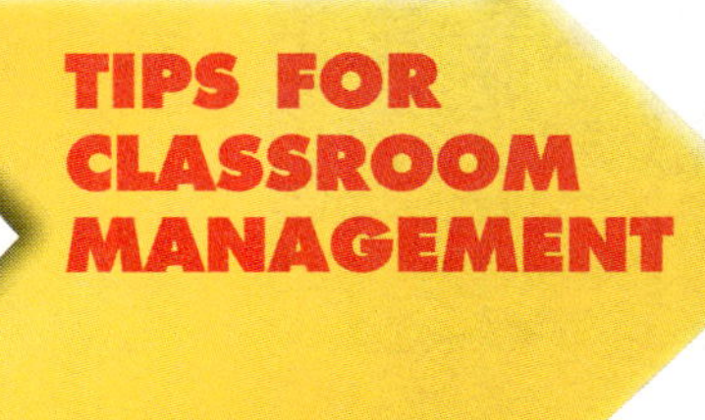

SMALL GROUP

STRATEGIC READING

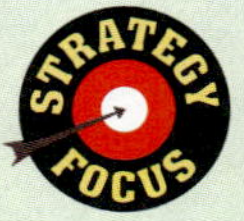

To help students understand better what they are reading, reinforce the focus strategy of **self-questioning.** Pages T1182 and T1186 offer excellent opportunities to have students model the strategy.

COOPERATIVE READING

READER RESPONSE GROUP

Small groups may use Reader Response Card 2 to focus on the **setting** of this story. Reader Response Card 2 can be found at the back of this Teacher's Edition.

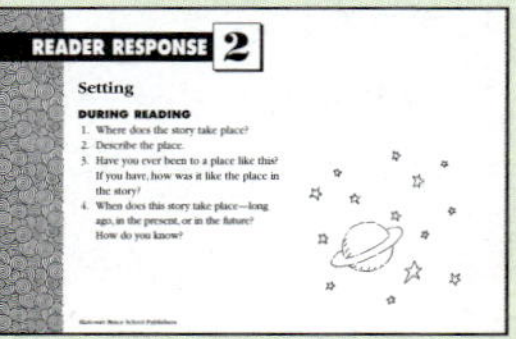

Response Card 2

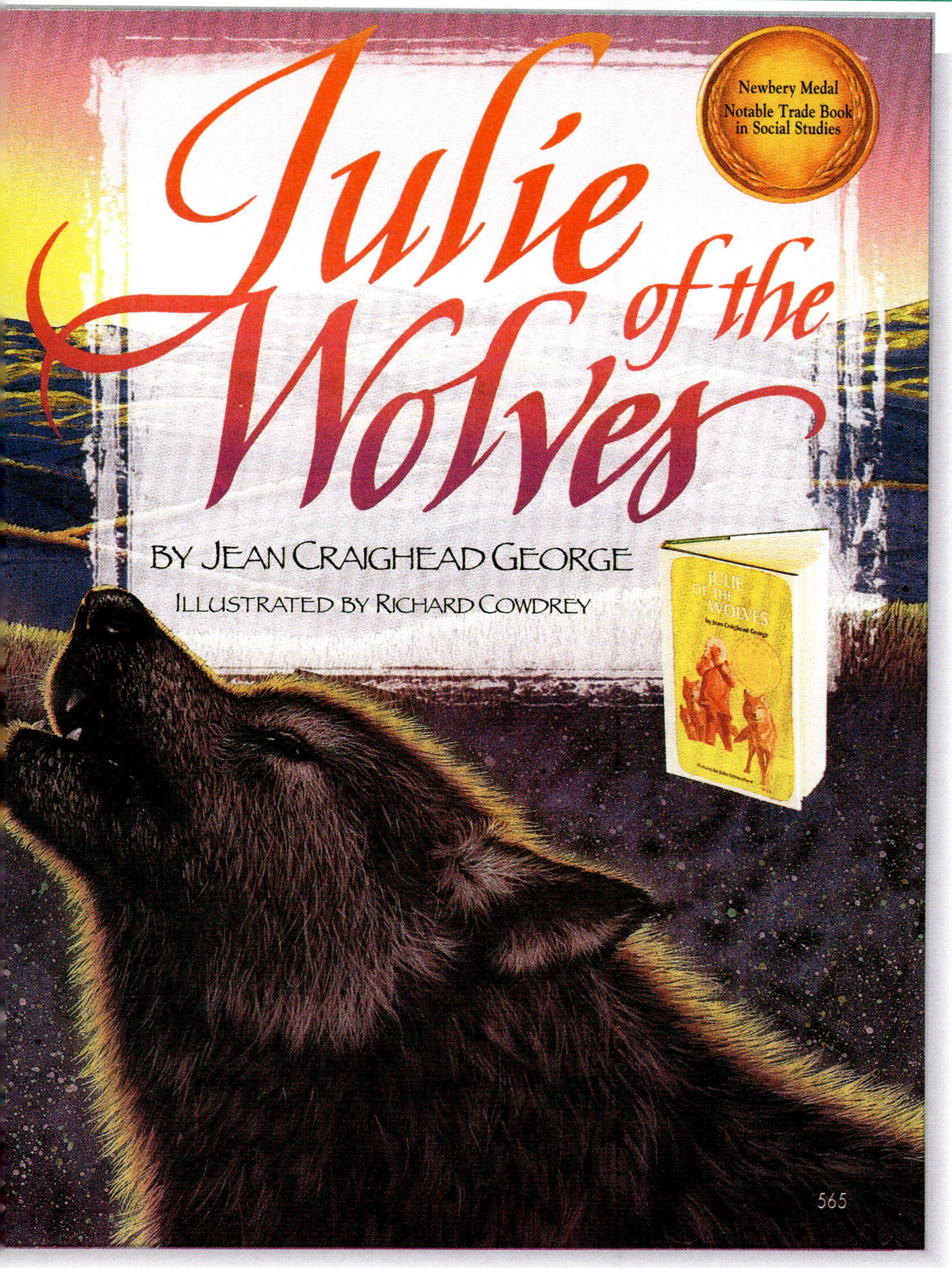

Newbery Medal
Notable Trade Book in Social Studies

Julie of the Wolves

BY JEAN CRAIGHEAD GEORGE

ILLUSTRATED BY RICHARD COWDREY

565

WHOLE CLASS

READ ALOUD

Read aloud to students through page 571. Discuss the story with students, and encourage them to revise their predictions. Then have students finish reading the story in pairs.

SILENT READING

Have students read the entire story silently. As they finish, have them summarize the story independently by completing their story maps. When all students have finished, use the story maps to begin a group discussion.

Strategic Reading

SELF-QUESTIONING

Ask students to name strategies they use during reading. Display the class-made strategy chart, and remind students about the strategy of **self-questioning**. Discuss with students how asking themselves questions about a selection might help them understand better what they are reading.

STRATEGY: SELF-QUESTIONING

PAGES 564–571

Have students read through page 571 to confirm their predictions about the story.

MIYAX, A THIRTEEN-YEAR-OLD ESKIMO GIRL, HAS LEFT HER HOME IN ALASKA AND IS HEADED FOR SAN FRANCISCO TOWARD AMY, HER PEN PAL, WHO CALLS HER JULIE. BUT SHE FINDS HERSELF LOST, WITHOUT FOOD OR A COMPASS, ON THE NORTH SLOPE OF ALASKA. SHE IS ALONE EXCEPT FOR A PACK OF ARCTIC WOLVES.

Upon discovering the wolves, she had settled down to live near them in the hope of sharing their food, until the sun set and the stars came out to guide her. She had built a house of sod, like the summer homes of the old Eskimos. Each brick had been cut with her *ulo,* the half-moon shaped woman's knife, so versatile it can trim a baby's hair, slice a tough bear, or chip an iceberg.

Her house was not well built for she had never made one before, but it was cozy inside. She had windproofed it by sealing the sod bricks with mud from the pond at her door, and she had made it beautiful by spreading her caribou ground cloth on the floor. On this she had placed her sleeping skin, a moosehide bag lined with soft white rabbit skins. Next to her bed she had built a low table of sod on which to put her clothes when she slept. To decorate the house she had made three flowers of bird feathers and stuck them in the top of the table. Then she had built a fireplace outdoors and placed her pot beside it. The pot was empty, for she had not found even a lemming to eat.

Last winter, when she had walked to school in Barrow, these mice-like rodents were so numerous they ran out from under her feet wherever she stepped. There were thousands and thousands of them until December, when they suddenly vanished. Her teacher

566

SOCIAL STUDIES

ALASKA The name *Alaska* comes from the Aleut word *Alashka*, meaning "Great Land." The state's flag, showing the North Star and the Big Dipper on a field of midnight blue, was designed by a thirteen-year-old boy, the winner of a territory-wide contest in 1927. Explaining his design, he wrote, "The blue field is for the Alaskan sky and the forget-me-not, an Alaskan flower. The North Star is for the future state of Alaska, the most northerly of the Union. The dipper is for the Great Bear—symbolizing strength."

Tested Skill

MINILESSON

REVIEW: STUDY SKILLS

Reference Sources

INFORMAL ASSESSMENT

Write the following sentence on the board:

Miyax spread the caribou ground cloth on the floor.

Ask students how they might find out what *caribou* means. (Possible response: Look in a dictionary or encyclopedia.)

TEACH/MODEL

Have students reread the second paragraph after the introduction on page 566. Then explain that students can find out more about words and topics not explained in the context of a selection by consulting reference sources. Model the thinking:

MODEL **I understand from the paragraph that *caribou* might be a kind of animal since Miyax's sleeping bag is made of animal hides and fur. If I want more information about *caribou*, I use an encyclopedia.**

PRACTICE/APPLY

Have students use reference sources to locate the area of Alaska (the North Slope) where Miyax is lost.

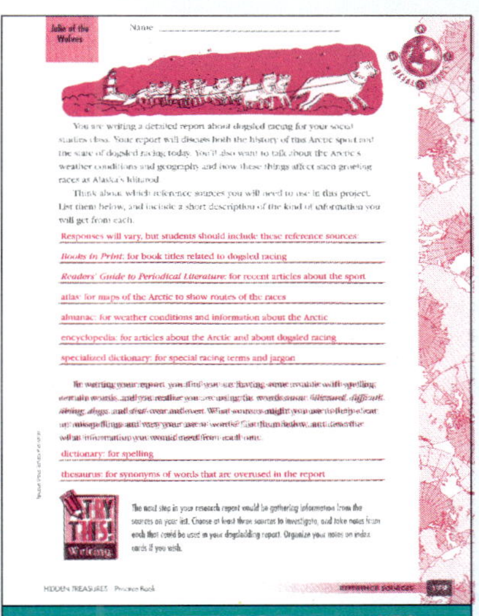
Julie of the Wolves

Name ____________

You are writing a detailed report about dogsled racing for your social studies class. Your report will discuss both the history of this Arctic sport and the state of dogsled racing today. You'll also want to talk about the Arctic's weather conditions and geography and how these things affect such grueling races as Alaska's Iditarod.

Think about which reference sources you will need to use in this project. List them below, and include a short description of the kind of information you will get from each.

Responses will vary, but students should include these reference sources:

Books in Print: for book titles related to dogsled racing

Readers' Guide to Periodical Literature: for recent articles about the sport

atlas: for maps of the Arctic to show routes of the races

almanac: for weather conditions and information about the Arctic

encyclopedia: for articles about the Arctic and about dogsled racing

specialized dictionary: for special racing terms and jargon

In writing your report, you find you are having some trouble with spelling certain words, and you realize you are using the words [illegible] over and over. What sources might you use to help clear up misspellings and vary your use of words? List them below, and describe what information you would need from each one.

dictionary: for spelling

thesaurus: for synonyms of words that are overused in the report

TRY THIS! Writing

The next step in your research report would be gathering information from the sources on your list. Choose at least three sources to investigate, and take notes from each that could be used in your dogsledding report. Organize your notes on index cards if you wish.

HIDDEN TREASURES Practice Book

PRACTICE BOOK, page 179

VIEWING

Ask students what they can learn from critically viewing the illustration on pages 566 and 567. (Possible responses: The North Slope is rugged and has some grass; it must be quite cool in summer, since Miyax wears a parka and mittens; Miyax looks fearful because she is turned away from the wolf, whereas the wolf looks brave because he is looking directly at Miyax.)

Critical Thinking Questions

1. **What do you think Miyax's father means when he says "The hour of the lemming is over for four years"? What does he mean by *hour*?** (Possible responses: There won't be a great many lemmings for another four years; *hour* may mean "time.") CRITICAL: MAKING INFERENCES

2. **How do you know that survival, even for animals, is difficult in the Arctic?** (Possible response: When there are not many lemmings, there are fewer animals that prey on them; the lemmings seem to be the major food source for many animals.) METACOGNITIVE: RECOGNIZING CAUSE-EFFECT/DRAWING CONCLUSIONS

said that the lemmings had a chemical similar to antifreeze in their blood that kept them active all winter when other little mammals were hibernating. "They eat grass and multiply all winter," Mrs. Franklin had said in her singsong voice. "When there are too many, they grow nervous at the sight of each other. Somehow this shoots too much antifreeze into their bloodstreams and it begins to poison them. They become restless, then crazy. They run in a frenzy until they die."

Of this phenomenon Miyax's father had simply said, "The hour of the lemming is over for four years."

Unfortunately for Miyax, the hour of the animals that prey on the lemmings was also over. The white fox, the snowy owl, the weasel, the jaeger, and the siskin[1] had virtually disappeared. They had no food to eat and bore few or no young. Those that lived preyed on each other. With the passing of the lemmings, however, the grasses had grown high again and the hour of the caribou was upon the land. Healthy fat caribou cows gave birth to many calves. The caribou population increased, and this in turn increased the number of wolves who prey on the caribou. The abundance of the big deer of the north did Miyax no good, for she had not brought a gun on her trip. It had never occurred to her that she would not reach Point Hope before her food ran out.

A dull pain seized her stomach. She pulled blades of grass from their sheaths and ate the sweet ends. They were not very satisfying, so she picked a handful of caribou moss, a lichen. If the deer could survive in winter on this food, why not she? She munched, decided the plant might taste better if cooked, and went to the pond for water.

As she dipped her pot in, she thought about Amaroq. Why had he bared his teeth at her? Because she was young and he knew she couldn't hurt him? No, she said to herself, it was because he was speaking to her! He had told her to lie down. She had even understood and obeyed him. He had talked to her not with his voice, but with his ears, eyes, and lips; and he had even commended her with a wag of his tail.

[1] jaeger and siskin: types of birds

568

SCIENCE

FACT FINDER

Caribou moss is also known as *reindeer moss* or *caribou candy*. It is a lichen common in the Arctic but also found as far south as the northern United States. White-tailed deer and moose also eat caribou moss, but caribou can thrive eating nothing else.

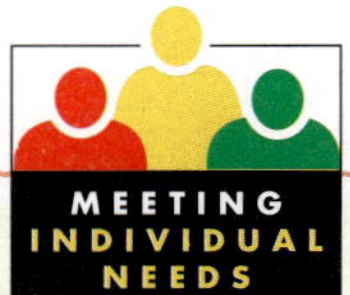

STUDENTS ACQUIRING ENGLISH Help students use context clues to figure out that Amaroq is one of the wolves.

She dropped her pot, scrambled up the frost heave and stretched out on her stomach.

"Amaroq," she called softly, "I understand what you said. Can you understand me? I'm hungry—very, very hungry. Please bring me some meat."

The great wolf did not look her way and she began to doubt her reasoning. After all, flattened ears and a tail-wag were scarcely a conversation. She dropped her forehead against the lichens and rethought what had gone between them.

"Then why did I lie down?" she asked, lifting her head and looking at Amaroq. "Why did I?" she called to the yawning wolves. Not one turned her way.

Amaroq got to his feet, and as he slowly arose he seemed to fill the sky and blot out the sun. He was enormous. He could swallow her without even chewing.

"But he won't," she reminded herself. "Wolves do not eat people. That's gussak[2] talk. Kapugen said wolves are gentle brothers."

The black puppy was looking at her and wagging his tail. Hopefully, Miyax held out a pleading hand to him. His tail wagged harder. The mother rushed to him and stood above him sternly. When he licked her cheek apologetically, she pulled back her lips from her fine white teeth. They flashed as she smiled and forgave her cub.

"But don't let it happen again," said Miyax sarcastically, mimicking her own elders. The mother walked toward Amaroq.

"I should call you Martha after my stepmother," Miyax whispered. "But you're much too beautiful. I shall call you Silver instead."

Silver moved in a halo of light, for the sun sparkled on the guard hairs that grew out over the dense underfur and she seemed to glow.

The reprimanded pup snapped at a crane fly and shook himself. Bits of lichen and grass spun off his fur. He reeled unsteadily, took a wider stance, and looked down at his sleeping sister. With a yap he jumped on her and rolled her to her feet. She whined. He barked

[2] gussak: Eskimo term for white people

569

Informal Assessment

POINT OF VIEW

To determine whether students can recognize point of view, ask them questions like the following:

- ☑ What pronouns tell you that this story is written in the third-person point of view?
- ☑ What pronouns would be used in a story written in the first person?

EXPANDING VOCABULARY

If students are not familiar with the term *frost heaves*, explain that in the Arctic the ground is permanently frozen—only the top foot or two thaw during the summer. A frost heave occurs when the top layers of soil thaw but the ground underneath is still frozen. As the top layer of soil thaws, it expands slightly, causing a raised area—a frost heave.

Strategic Reading

PAGES 564–571 **Why is it important that Miyax become accepted into the wolf pack? How is she trying to do that?** (Possible responses: She is lost and hungry, and she hopes the wolves will help her get food. She is learning to communicate with them.) STRATEGIES: SUMMARIZING/CONFIRMING PREDICTIONS

Does learning to speak wolf seem like a reasonable goal? How do you know Miyax is succeeding? (Possible response: It seemed unreasonable at first. After Miyax realized that she lay down when Amaroq "asked" her to, she began watching for other signals.) METACOGNITIVE: RECOGNIZING CHARACTERS' MOTIVATIONS

If necessary, model the strategy:

MODEL **When Miyax notices something about the wolves, I ask myself how this helps her make friends with the wolves.**

PAGES 572–575 Encourage students to revise their predictions before finishing the story.

and picked up a bone. When he was sure she was watching, he ran down the slope with it. The sister tagged after him. He stopped and she grabbed the bone, too. She pulled; he pulled; then he pulled and she yanked.

Miyax could not help laughing. The puppies played with bones like Eskimo children played with leather ropes.

"I understand *that*," she said to the pups. "That's tug-o-war. Now how do you say, 'I'm hungry'?"

Amaroq was pacing restlessly along the crest of the frost heave as if something were about to happen. His eyes shot to Silver, then to the gray wolf Miyax had named Nails. These glances seemed to be a summons, for Silver and Nails glided to him, spanked the ground with their forepaws and bit him gently under the chin. He wagged his tail furiously and took Silver's slender nose in his mouth. She crouched before him, licked his cheek and lovingly bit his lower jaw. Amaroq's tail flashed high as her mouthing charged him with vitality. He nosed her affectionately. Unlike the fox who met his mate only in the breeding season, Amaroq lived with his mate all year.

Next, Nails took Amaroq's jaw in his mouth and the leader bit the top of his nose. A third adult, a small male, came slinking up. He got down on his belly before Amaroq, rolled trembling to his back, and wriggled.

"Hello, Jello," Miyax whispered, for he reminded her of the quivering gussak dessert her mother-in-law made.

She had seen the wolves mouth Amaroq's chin twice before and so she concluded that it was a ceremony, a sort of "Hail to the Chief." He must indeed be their leader for he was clearly the wealthy wolf; that is, wealthy as she

570

CROSS-CULTURAL VIEWPOINT

The wolf pups played tug-o-war with bones the way Miyax knew Eskimo children played with leather ropes. Have students discuss other games that they play and ones they know about from other parts of the world.

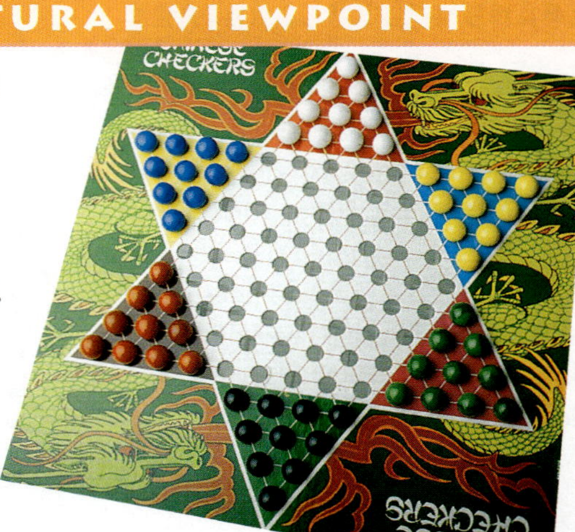

Chinese Checkers

had known the meaning of the word on Nunivak Island. There the old Eskimo hunters she had known in her childhood thought the riches of life were intelligence, fearlessness, and love. A man with these gifts was rich and was a great spirit who was admired in the same way that the gussaks admired a man with money and goods.

The three adults paid tribute to Amaroq until he was almost smothered with love; then he bayed a wild note that sounded like the wind on the frozen sea. With that the others sat around him, the puppies scattered between them. Jello hunched forward and Silver shot a fierce glance at him. Intimidated, Jello pulled his ears together and back. He drew himself down until he looked smaller than ever.

Amaroq wailed again, stretching his neck until his head was high above the others. They gazed at him affectionately and it was plain to see that he was their great spirit, a royal leader who held his group together with love and wisdom.

Any fear Miyax had of the wolves was dispelled by their affection for each other. They were friendly animals and so devoted to Amaroq that she needed only to be accepted by him to be accepted by all. She even knew how to achieve this—bite him under the chin. But how was she going to do that?

She studied the pups hoping they had a simpler way of expressing their love for him. The black puppy approached the leader, sat, then lay down and wagged his tail vigorously. He gazed up at Amaroq in pure adoration, and the royal eyes softened.

Well, that's what I'm doing! Miyax thought. She called to Amaroq. "I'm lying down gazing at you, too, but you don't look at *me* that way!"

When all the puppies were wagging his praises, Amaroq yipped, hit a high note, and crooned. As his voice rose and fell, the other adults sang out and the puppies yipped and bounced.

571

Tested Skill

MINILESSON

REVIEW: COMPREHENSION

Summarizing/ Paraphrasing

INFORMAL ASSESSMENT

Ask students what they can do to review information they've read to help them remember it. (Possible response: I can restate the most important information in my own words.)

TEACH/MODEL

Remind students that summarizing or paraphrasing is a good way to review material they want to remember. A summary tells the most important ideas; a paraphrase restates the material in their own words. If necessary, model the thinking:

MODEL **On page 571, I read a sentence that summarizes what I had read about Miyax and the wolves: *They were friendly animals and so devoted to Amaroq that she needed only to be accepted by him to be accepted by all.***

PRACTICE/APPLY

Have students paraphrase the paragraph that begins at the bottom of page 570 and ends on page 571.

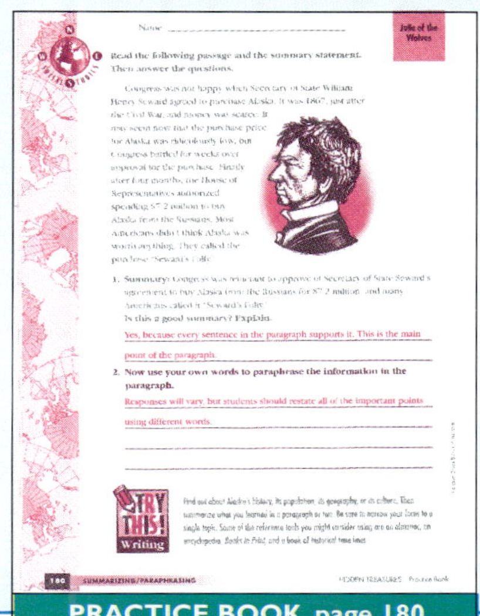
Julie of the Wolves

Read the following passage and the summary statement. Then answer the questions.

Yes, because every sentence in the paragraph supports it. This is the main point of the paragraph.

2. Now use your own words to paraphrase the information in the paragraph.

Responses will vary but students should restate all of the important points using different words.

PRACTICE BOOK, page 180

SOCIAL STUDIES CONNECTION

The North Slope stretches from the Brooks Range to the Arctic Ocean and from the Chukchi Sea to the Beaufort Sea. Encourage students to locate this area on a map and note the lack of roads or other major features that would help Miyax find her way to the coast. Then discuss how reading the map helps students to visualize the landscape and understand better the predicament Miyax is in.

Cooperative Reading

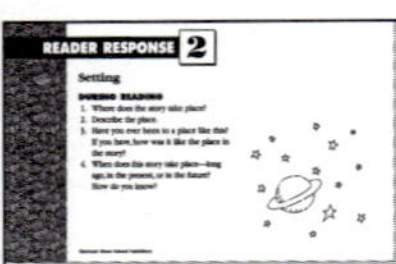
Response Card 2

Cooperative reading groups should stop and follow the during-reading suggestions on Reader Response Card 2. You might start the discussion by asking questions like these:

- **How would you describe the setting of this story?**
- **Have you ever been to a place like the one described in the story? If so, how are they alike?**

The song ended abruptly. Amaroq arose and trotted swiftly down the slope. Nails followed, and behind him ran Silver, then Jello. But Jello did not run far. Silver turned and looked him straight in the eye. She pressed her ears forward aggressively and lifted her tail. With that, Jello went back to the puppies and the three sped away like dark birds.

Miyax hunched forward on her elbows, the better to see and learn. She now knew how to be a good puppy, pay tribute to the leader, and even to be a leader by biting others on the top of the nose. She also knew how to tell Jello to baby-sit. If only she had big ears and a tail, she could lecture and talk to them all.

Flapping her hands on her head for ears, she flattened her fingers to make friends, pulled them together and back to express fear, and shot them forward to display her aggression and dominance. Then she folded her arms and studied the puppies again.

The black one greeted Jello by tackling his feet. Another jumped on his tail, and before he could discipline either, all five were upon him. He rolled and tumbled with them for almost an hour; then he ran down the slope, turned, and stopped. The pursuing pups plowed into him, tumbled, fell, and lay still. During a minute of surprised recovery there was no action. Then the black pup flashed his tail like a semaphore signal and they all jumped on Jello again.

Miyax rolled over and laughed aloud. "That's funny. They're really like kids."

When she looked back, Jello's tongue was hanging from his mouth and his sides were heaving. Four of the puppies had collapsed at his feet and were asleep. Jello flopped down, too, but the black pup still looked around. He was not the least bit tired. Miyax watched him, for there was something special about him.

He ran to the top of the den and barked. The smallest pup, whom Miyax called Sister, lifted her head, saw her favorite brother in action and, struggling to her feet, followed him devotedly. While they romped, Jello took the opportunity to rest behind a clump of

572

SOCIAL STUDIES

Students might not be familiar with the term *semaphore*. Explain that semaphore is a method of signaling with flags. The semaphore code uses two flags, whose positions represent letters and special words. Spanish-speaking students may recognize the cognate *semáforo*, which means "traffic light."

sedge, a moisture-loving plant of the tundra. But hardly was he settled before a pup tracked him to his hideout and pounced on him. Jello narrowed his eyes, pressed his ears forward, and showed his teeth.

"I know what you're saying," she called to him. "You're saying, 'lie down.'" The puppy lay down, and Miyax got on all fours and looked for the nearest pup to speak to. It was Sister.

"Ummmm," she whined, and when Sister turned around she narrowed her eyes and showed her white teeth. Obediently, Sister lay down.

"I'm talking wolf! I'm talking wolf!" Miyax clapped, and tossing her head like a pup, crawled in a happy circle. As she was coming back she saw all five puppies sitting in a row watching her, their heads cocked in curiosity. Boldly the black pup came toward her, his fat backside swinging as he trotted to the bottom of her frost heave, and barked.

"You are *very* fearless and *very* smart," she said. "Now I know why you are special. You are wealthy and the leader of the puppies. There is no doubt what you'll grow up to be. So I shall name you after my father Kapugen, and I shall call you Kapu for short."

Kapu wrinkled his brow and turned an ear to tune in more acutely on her voice.

"You don't understand, do you?"

Hardly had she spoken than his tail went up, his mouth opened slightly, and he fairly grinned.

"Ee-lie!" she gasped. "You do understand. And that scares me." She perched on her heels. Jello whined an undulating note and Kapu turned back to the den.

Miyax imitated the call to come home. Kapu looked back over his shoulder in surprise. She giggled. He wagged his tail and jumped on Jello.

She clapped her hands and settled down to watch this language of jumps and tumbles, elated that she was at last breaking the wolf

573

Student Self-Assessment

SELF-QUESTIONING

Remind students that as they read they should monitor their own comprehension by using self-questioning.

 What has happened in the story so far? Is this what I predicted might happen?

 What strategies could I use to help me clarify any part of the story that I don't understand?

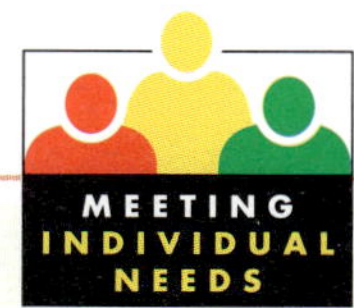

Intervention Strategies

READING AHEAD Ask students to repeat this sentence aloud or to themselves: *When I read, I sometimes read ahead if things aren't making sense.* Students should tell when and how reading ahead helped clarify any parts of the story.

Strategic Reading

PAGES 572–575 Why is it so important for Amaroq to accept Miyax? (Possible response: He is the leader of the wolf pack; Miyax needs food and if the leader accepts her, the others will too—and as one of the pack, she can share their food.) SUMMARIZING

Returning to the Predictions/Purpose

Did you find out what you wanted to know about Miyax and the wolves? Encourage students to discuss whether their purposes for reading were met.
STRATEGY: RETURNING TO THE PURPOSE

Appreciating the Literature

Which part of the story was the most interesting or exciting to you? Why? (Responses will vary.)

code. After a long time she decided they were not talking but roughhousing, and so she started home. Later she changed her mind. Roughhousing was very important to wolves. It occupied almost the entire night for the pups.

"Ee-lie, okay," she said. "I'll learn to roughhouse. Maybe then you'll accept me and feed me." She pranced, jumped, and whimpered; she growled, snarled, and rolled. But nobody came to roughhouse.

Sliding back to her camp, she heard the grass swish and looked up to see Amaroq and his hunters sweep around her frost heave and stop about five feet away. She could smell the sweet scent of their fur.

The hairs on her neck rose and her eyes widened. Amaroq's ears went forward aggressively and she remembered that wide eyes meant fear to him. It was not good to show him she was afraid. Animals attacked the fearful. She tried to narrow them, but remembered that was not right either. Narrowed eyes were mean. In desperation she recalled that Kapu had moved forward when challenged. She pranced right up to Amaroq. Her heart beat furiously as she grunt-whined the sound of the puppy begging adoringly for attention. Then she got down on her belly and gazed at him with fondness.

The great wolf backed up and avoided her eyes. She had said something wrong! Perhaps even offended him. Some slight gesture that meant nothing to her had apparently meant something to the wolf. His ears shot forward angrily and it seemed all was lost. She wanted to get up and run, but she gathered her courage and pranced closer to him. Swiftly she patted him under the chin.

The signal went off. It sped through his body and triggered emotions of love. Amaroq's ears flattened and his tail wagged in friendship. He could not react in any other way to the chin pat, for the roots of this signal lay deep in wolf history. It was inherited from generations and generations of leaders before him. As his eyes softened, the sweet odor of ambrosia arose from the gland on the top of his tail and she was drenched lightly in wolf scent. Miyax was one of the pack.

574

MEETING INDIVIDUAL NEEDS

CHALLENGE Invite students to collect the gestures Miyax learned from the wolves to make an English-Wolf Dictionary.

Tested Skill

MINILESSON

REVIEW: GRAMMAR

Negatives

INFORMAL ASSESSMENT

Ask students to identify the negative in the first full paragraph on page 574. (*nobody*) Have students suggest other ways the author could have expressed the same idea in that sentence. (Possible responses: Not one puppy came. The puppies didn't come.)

TEACH/MODEL

Have students recall other words that are negatives. (Possible responses: *never, none, nothing, nowhere*) Remind students to avoid double negatives in their speaking and writing.

PRACTICE/APPLY

Have students find other sentences on the page that contain negatives and suggest other ways the same ideas could be expressed.

SUMMARIZING

Story Impressions Chart

Have students complete the story impressions chart they began before reading. They should summarize the important events and write the solution to the problem. See *Practice Book* page 174.

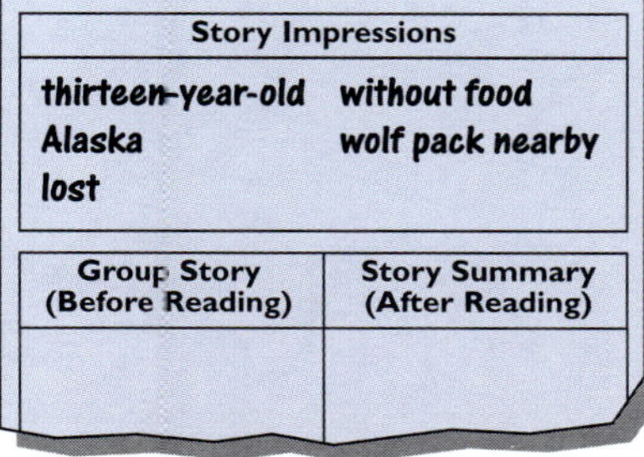

Story Impressions	
thirteen-year-old	without food
Alaska	wolf pack nearby
lost	

Group Story (Before Reading)	Story Summary (After Reading)

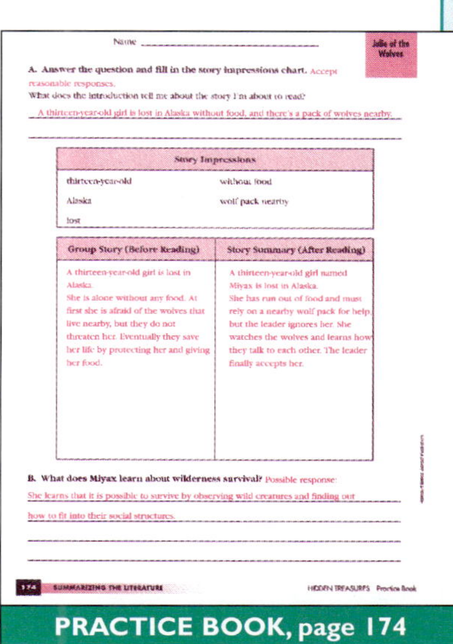

Name ______________________

Julie of the Wolves

A. Answer the question and fill in the story impressions chart. Accept reasonable responses.

What does the introduction tell me about the story I'm about to read?

A thirteen-year-old girl is lost in Alaska without food, and there's a pack of wolves nearby.

Story Impressions	
thirteen-year-old	without food
Alaska	wolf pack nearby
lost	

Group Story (Before Reading)	Story Summary (After Reading)
A thirteen-year-old girl is lost in Alaska. She is alone without any food. At first she is afraid of the wolves that live nearby, but they do not threaten her. Eventually they save her life by protecting her and giving her food.	A thirteen-year-old girl named Miyax is lost in Alaska. She has run out of food and must rely on a nearby wolf pack for help, but the leader ignores her. She watches the wolves and learns how they talk to each other. The leader finally accepts her.

B. What does Miyax learn about wilderness survival? Possible response: She learns that it is possible to survive by observing wild creatures and finding out how to fit into their social structures.

174 SUMMARIZING THE LITERATURE HIDDEN TREASURES Practice Book

PRACTICE BOOK, page 174

About the Author

After students read pages 576 and 577, you may wish to discuss the following questions with them:

- **In your opinion, how did Jean Craighead George's family influence her interest in writing books about nature?** (Possible responses: Her father influenced her because when she was very young he taught her about nature; her brothers were a big influence because they became expert falconers and even gave the author her own falcon; her mother also was an influence because she made sure her children read many books when they were growing up.)
- **If you were interviewing Jean Craighead George, what would you ask her?** (Responses will vary.)

Jean Craighead George

Many of Jean Craighead George's books involve characters who must confront nature. Here writer Ilene Cooper talks with the author about how her interest in the natural world has shaped her writing and her life.

Cooper: You come from a family that's passionate about nature, don't you?

George: When my brothers and I were very young, my father took us into the woods along the Potomac River and taught us about plants and animals. He was so excited about natural history that it just followed that we would be, too.

Cooper: So when you were twelve years old, you were already a naturalist?

George: I was out in the meadow collecting wildflowers and insects, or raising polliwogs. I loved canoeing and camping. My brothers were expert falconers and they gave me a falcon of my own.

Cooper: What did you do when you couldn't be outside?

George: We had a whole attic full of the classics, and I read my way through them. In the summer, my mother always made us read for an hour after lunch. She was smart; she got some peace and quiet, and we got an education.

Cooper: Tell me a little bit about the trip to Alaska you took, where you did the research for Julie of the Wolves.

George: I was researching an article for the *Reader's Digest* magazine, and I went up there to do a piece on friendly wolves. The scientists at the Naval Arctic Research Lab were studying the plants and animals of the region, and their study of the wolves included communication. One of the scientists showed me how to approach them.

576

Cooper: Was it a little nerve-racking at first?

George: *(laughing)* No. The wolves are like dogs. In fact, all dogs are descended from wolves.

Cooper: At what point did you think there was a book in all this?

George: Not until I got home. The article fell through, and so there I was with all that research. Besides working with the wolves, I had been out in the tundra, looking at the plant life and the wildlife, like the lemmings. I also did some study of the Eskimos. My daughter suggested that I write a book, and that's how *Julie of the Wolves* came about. The book helped put the wolf on the endangered species list.

Cooper: Do you own any dogs?

George: Yes. I have an Alaskan malamute.

Cooper: Was there anything that you learned with the wolves that you were able to translate into useful approaches for training your dog?

George: Yes, you should put your hand over the dog's muzzle. That shows them you're the leader, and they adore their leader. And be sure to look them in the eye when you give them commands. If they are not looking right at you, giving commands does no good.

Cooper: You won the Newbery Award for Julie of the Wolves. *How did you react?*

George: I thought I had taken it quite calmly, but when the neighbors came to congratulate me, I brought out dog biscuits instead of cookies, and the next morning I found I had put the book in the refrigerator!

Jean Craighead George was born in Washington, D.C., and graduated from Pennsylvania State University. Her first books were animal biographies, which she wrote with her husband and which were often based on firsthand experiences with wild creatures that became family pets. Over the years, the Georges cared for more than 100 animals. Most of these animals were returned to their natural habitat. In 1956, the Georges won the American Library Association's Aurianne Award for best nature writing for *Dipper of Copper Creek*.

Eventually, though, Jean Craighead George decided she must become a writer on her own. In 1959 she published her first novel, *My Side of the Mountain*, which was made into a movie a decade later.

Jean Craighead George has been honored in America as "our premier naturalist novelist." Her authoritative research, love of adventure, and fine writing have impressed young adults and literary critics for more than forty years.

ACTIVITY CHOICES

CALCULATE DISTANCE

MILE AFTER MILE Review the features of a map's legend with students. After they've calculated the distance, have students discuss the way they used the scale to measure it. **LISTENING AND SPEAKING**

CREATE A POSTER

SURVIVAL OF THE FITTEST Suggest that students begin their research by using the story itself as a reference source and noting the information given about the animals. Have students speculate what might happen if the animal were taken out of its natural environment. **CRITICAL THINKING**

DEMONSTRATE SIGNALS

A WAY WITH WORDS Students could relate "wolf speak" to how their own dogs or cats "get their messages across" to other animals or to their human owners. Discuss with students what *communication* really means. **LISTENING AND SPEAKING**

STUDENTS ACQUIRING ENGLISH Have students work with English-proficient partners to complete the response activities. Pre- and early-production students should be encouraged to participate in nonverbal tasks if they feel more comfortable doing so. Speech-emergent and intermediate-fluency students should be challenged to actively participate in oral language activities.

CHECKING COMPREHENSION

What Do You Think?

1. **How do you know that Miyax is resourceful and sensitive to animals? Give examples from the story.** (Possible response: She observes the wolves' behavior to learn to speak their language but doesn't demand that she be understood.) DESCRIPTIVE RESPONSE
2. **Has this selection changed your opinion of wolves? Explain why or why not.** (Responses will vary.) PERSONAL RESPONSE
3. **How do you think Miyax felt at the end of the story? Why?** (Possible responses: She felt relieved that she would get food. She felt good about having figured out how to communicate with the wolves.) REFLECTING

VARYING THE ACTIVITY

For **extra support,** provide students with an index card listing the steps involved in calculating distances using a scale of miles. Students should refer to the card before they begin the Mile After Mile activity.

Intervention Strategies

TIPS FOR CLASSROOM MANAGEMENT

IF second-language students need additional vocabulary and during-reading strategies to understand "Julie of the Wolves," **THEN** use *Sheltered English/ESL Manual*, pages 90–93.

IF students had difficulty understanding "Julie of the Wolves," **THEN** complete the Rereading and Structural Analysis Strategies. See also *Intervention Strategies Manual*, pages 134–139.

REREADING

UNDERSTANDING CHARACTERS Have each student reread from page 572 to the end of the story. If students work in pairs, encourage one student to read aloud while the other listens. Then have them answer the following questions:

- How does Miyax communicate with the wolves?
- Why do you think Miyax gives names to the wolves?
- How does Miyax show Amaroq that she is not afraid of him? How did she learn this?

PERSONAL JOURNAL

Have students write two or three sentences in their journals about a relationship they have had with a pet or a wild animal. As an alternative, students can give their opinions on communication between humans and animals. They can use information in the story to help them begin thinking about their opinions.

STRUCTURAL ANALYSIS

ADVERBS Remind students that many adverbs that tell *how* end with the suffix *-ly*. Have students carefully reread the paragraph beginning "Amaroq was pacing restlessly along the crest of the frost heave . . ." (page 570). Call on volunteers to list on the board all the adverbs in the paragraph that are formed by adding *-ly* to an adjective.

restlessly
gently
furiously
lovingly
affectionately

Point out that the letter *e* is dropped from the adjective *gentle* before the *ly* is added. Then assign each student a page of the selection. Have students list all the adverbs with the suffix *-ly* they can find.

Then invite students to take turns copying their lists on the board. As each student lists his or her adverbs, encourage the others to check to see that the lists are accurate and complete.

WRITING TO SUMMARIZE

Work with students to retell the events of "Julie of the Wolves." You may want to begin by writing on chart paper a sentence like the one at the right.

If students need help, provide practice starters such as

Hoping to share the wolves' food, Miyax had ____.

She decided that Amaroq had bared his teeth at her because he _______ .

When she flapped her hands on her head for ears, Miyax pretended that ________.

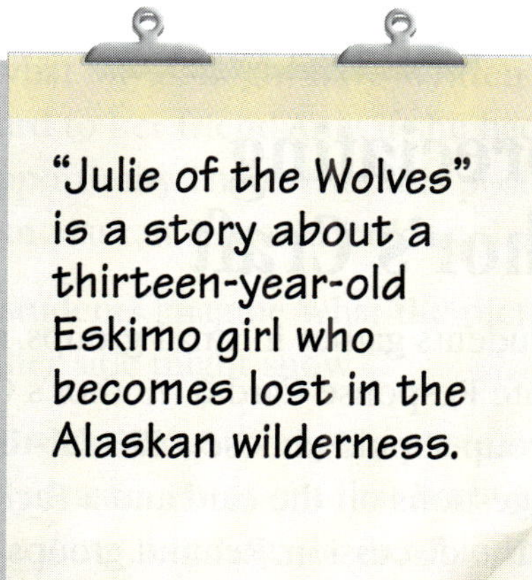

DECODING SUPPORT
/y/y; /ī/y; /ē/y, ey

Intervention Strategies Manual **pp. 138–139**

ESL/TITLE I READING

Reading Trade Books

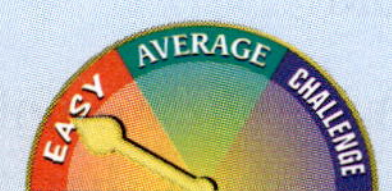

Dream Wolf

by Paul Goble

In this charming story, a friendly wolf helps two children who have become lost in the woods. Have students use a chart like the one below to compare the story with "Julie of the Wolves."

	"Julie of the Wolves"	*Dream Wolf*
Setting		
Main Characters		
Important Events		

TAKE-HOME BOOK TO REINFORCE KEY WORDS

Students will enjoy reading this humorous tale about a mischievous intruder. They may want to read it when they have independent reading time in class, or they may want to take it home to read.

PERSONAL JOURNAL

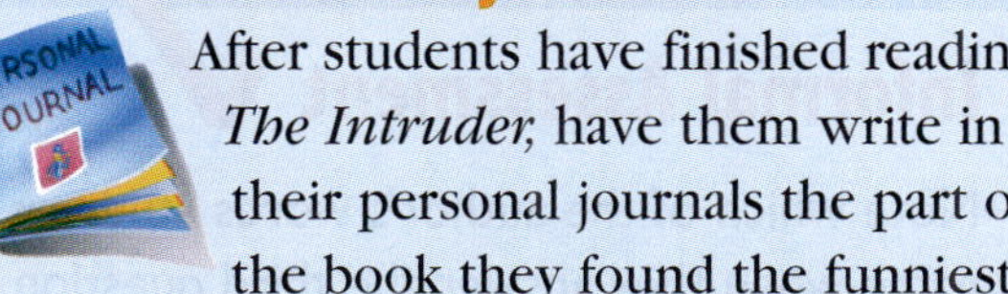

After students have finished reading *The Intruder,* have them write in their personal journals the part of the book they found the funniest.

See also *Intervention Strategies Manual,* page 137.

WRITER'S WORKSHOP

Personal Narrative

TIPS FOR CLASSROOM MANAGEMENT

IF students are familiar with the steps for writing a personal narrative, **THEN** have them begin writing, referring to the model on Transparency 57 when necessary.

IF you want a short writing activity, **THEN** adapt this lesson by having students use what they learn about the Writer's Craft to revise the ending of a personal narrative they have written earlier.

TECHNOLOGY

THE AMAZING WRITING MACHINE Have students use the program to write their personal narratives.

Thinking as Writers

WRITING FORM: Personal Narrative
Remind students that in a personal narrative a writer tells about a personal experience. Review with them the main parts of a personal narrative: an opening, descriptive details, and an ending that both summarizes and expands. Explain to students that they are going to learn how to make a personal narrative more effective.

WRITER'S CRAFT: Conclusion Explain that the conclusion of any piece of writing ties up the loose ends and summarizes the main points. The conclusion may also describe the significance of the experience. Display Transparency 57 and discuss with students how the weak ending in the draft was improved in the revision. Also remind them to use first-person pronouns such as *I*, *me*, and *my* as they write.

TRANSPARENCY 57

Draft and Revised Passages: Conclusion of Personal Narrative

draft It was really fun to play volleyball without keeping score. Maybe we can do it again at the clan picnic next year.

revision I am beginning to think that some people are just not meant to compete. These days, when I am in a competitive situation, I just pretend there is no score, grade, or judgment involved. When I simply "play for fun," everything comes easily to me.

PREWRITING AND DRAFTING

Remind students to choose a single event to write about in a personal narrative, perhaps one that involved nature. Refer to these strategies to help students begin their personal narratives.

PREWRITING GRAPHIC ORGANIZER
Have students think of a significant experience in their lives and then about what they thought and felt at the time and how the experience affected them. Students may make a chart such as the following:

Event		
What happened	How I felt	What effect it had
I learned to read a topographical map on a camping trip.	proud, happy	I felt more confident while hiking in the mountains.

SUSTAINED SILENT WRITING Those students who have a clear idea of what they want to write may begin writing without interruption.

DURING-WRITING GRAPHIC ORGANIZER
Students may need to pause during writing to create a cause-and-effect chart to help them see how events are related.

RESPONDING AND REVISING

Have students work in editing circles or with partners to help each other revise. Write this checklist on the board:

- Does your personal narrative tell about a single significant experience?
- Did you tell why the experience is significant and how it affected you?
- Did you write your narrative from the first-person point of view?
- Does your narrative have a strong conclusion?

PROOFREADING

Offer the following tips as students proofread:

- Check for correct use of **negatives**. (See Grammar Minilesson on page T1191.)
- Check for correct use of personal pronouns.
- Look for words you may have misspelled.

PUBLISHING

If you wish to have students publish their personal narratives, suggest the following options or have students choose their own methods.

ORAL Students may wish to tape-record their personal narratives for others in the class to listen to.

WRITTEN Collect the personal narratives in a class book titled "Our Unforgettable Experiences."

PORTFOLIO OPPORTUNITY

Have students answer the Student Self-Assessment questions and include both their answers and their personal narratives in their portfolios.

LANGUAGE HANDBOOK

Writing to Inform, pages 60–61; Personal Narrative, pages 62–63; Writing a Conclusion, page 23; Negatives, pages 163, 223

Student Self-Assessment ✓

Have students answer the following questions and include the answers in their portfolios:

- ☑ What did you like best about your personal narrative?
- ☑ What will you do differently the next time you write a personal narrative?

EVALUATION BENCHMARKS: PERSONAL NARRATIVE

A personal narrative by a proficient student writer shows the following characteristics:

FORM	CRAFT	CONVENTIONS
Demonstrates understanding of the form • describes a single personal experience and its significance • thoughts and feelings clearly described • strong conclusion	**Uses clear and appropriate language** • uses words that describe cause and effect • time-order words used	**Follows conventions of grammar and usage** • negatives used correctly • first-person pronouns used correctly

Teacher Assessment As you assess students' writing, refer to the Evaluation Benchmarks chart. For additional information, including model papers, see *Integrated Performance Assessment* Teacher's Edition.

Tested Skill

GRAMMAR

Prepositions and Prepositional Phrases

TECHNOLOGY

THE AMAZING WRITING MACHINE Students can enter their letters into the program and edit them on the screen.

LANGUAGE HANDBOOK Prepositions and Prepositional Phrases, pages 164–165

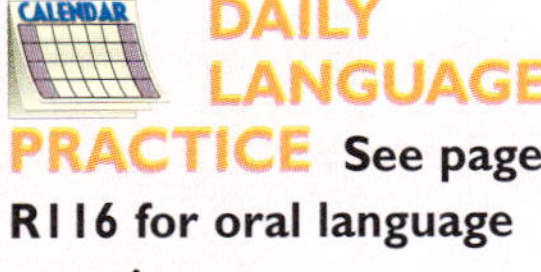

DAILY LANGUAGE PRACTICE See page R116 for oral language exercises.

Reading ↔ Writing Connection

Connect to the literature. Ask students to think about the wolves in the story and what they did. Ask students what verbs they could use to describe the wolves' actions. Record students' suggestions in a web like the one below:

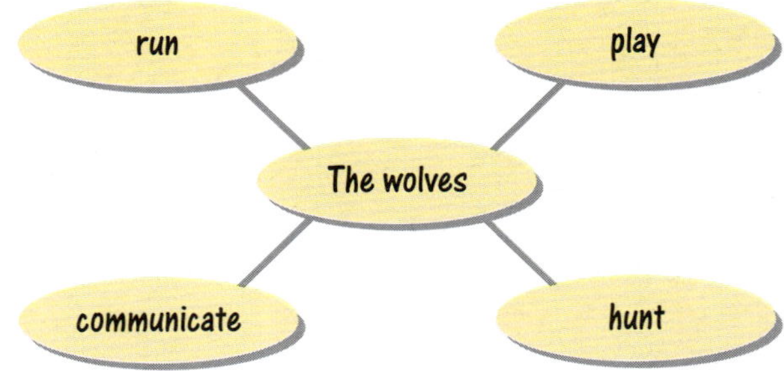

Build oral language. Have students use the words in the web to dictate sentences. Encourage them by asking questions such as *Whom do the wolves play with? Where do the wolves run?* Write students' sentences on the board, underlining the prepositional phrases in the first two sentences; for example:

The wolves run across the tundra.

The wolves play with Miyax.

Ask students how the underlined groups of words are alike. (Possible responses: They explain where the wolves' actions take place; they end with a noun or pronoun.)

Teach/Model

Use syntactic cues. Display the sentence *She is Julie of the wolves*. Ask students how the words *of the wolves* are similar to the underlined words in the sentences they wrote. (They explain something; a noun is at the end.) Explain that these groups of words are prepositional phrases. They begin with a preposition (*across, with, of*, for example) and end with a noun or pronoun, called the object of the preposition. Prepositions relate a noun or a pronoun to another word in the sentence. Help students find the relationships shown by the underlined prepositions.

Using pantomime and the relationship of two objects, help students develop lists of common prepositions that show direction (*to, from, across*), time (*before, after*), and position (*in, on, beside, under*).

Practice/Apply

Check understanding. Write the following sentences on the board, and have students identify the prepositional phrases and the objects of the prepositions.

Miyax patted him on the chin. (on the chin; chin)

She dipped the pot in the water. (in the water; water)

Practice Activities

NOTING LOCATIONS

ORAL APPLICATION Encourage pairs of students to alternate describing the location of an object in the classroom by using prepositional phrases. One student describes but does not name the object, and adds prepositional phrases to the description until his or her partner figures out what the object is. **AUDITORY**

The clock is <u>above</u> the door, <u>inside</u> the room, <u>to the right of</u> the map.

Write Letters

WRITING APPLICATION Have students brainstorm prepositional phrases Miyax might use to describe the time she spent with the wolves and how she learned to communicate with them. Then have students write letters to friends telling about Miyax's experiences and using several prepositional phrases.
AUDITORY/KINESTHETIC

They stood <u>on</u> the frost heave, <u>in front of</u> my house.

APPLY TO WRITING

You may want students to look in their writing for correct subject-verb agreement in sentences that contain prepositional phrases between the subject and the verb.

USAGE TIP Be sure to use object pronouns in prepositional phrases; for example, *between you and me, for Matthew and her.*

STUDENTS ACQUIRING ENGLISH

Demonstrate prepositions for pre- and early-production students by physically moving an object: The book is *on* the table; the pencil is *between* two books.

RETEACH

See page R108 for lessons in multiple modalities.

GRAMMAR PRACTICE BOOK
pages 54–55

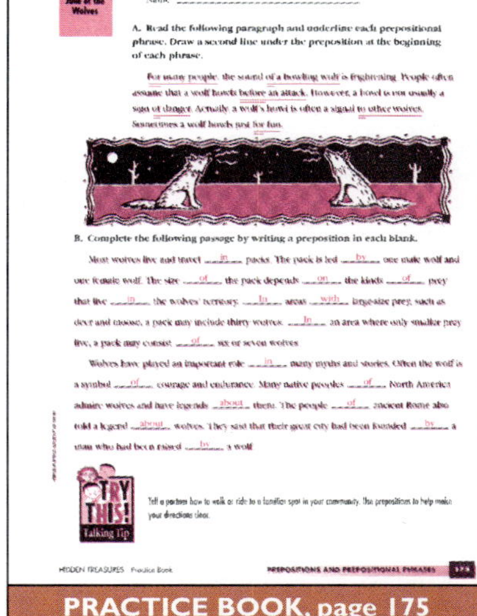

Julie of the Wolves

Name ______________________

A. Read the following paragraph and underline each prepositional phrase. Draw a second line under the preposition at the beginning of each phrase.

For many people, the sound of a howling wolf is frightening. People often assume that a wolf howls before an attack. However, a howl is not usually a sign of danger. Actually, a wolf's howl is often a signal to other wolves. Sometimes a wolf howls just for fun.

B. Complete the following passage by writing a preposition in each blank.

Most wolves live and travel __in__ packs. The pack is led __by__ one male wolf and one female wolf. The size __of__ the pack depends __on__ the kinds __of__ prey that live __in__ the wolves' territory. __In__ areas __with__ large-size prey, such as deer and moose, a pack may include thirty wolves. __In__ an area where only smaller prey live, a pack may consist __of__ six or seven wolves.

Wolves have played an important role __in__ many myths and stories. Often the wolf is a symbol __of__ courage and endurance. Many native peoples __of__ North America admire wolves and have legends __about__ them. The people __of__ ancient Rome also told a legend __about__ wolves. They said that their great city had been founded __by__ a man who had been raised __by__ a wolf.

TRY THIS! Talking Tip

Tell a partner how to walk or ride to a familiar spot in your community. Use prepositions to help make your directions clear.

HIDDEN TREASURES Practice Book — PREPOSITIONS AND PREPOSITIONAL PHRASES 175

PRACTICE BOOK, page 175

5-DAY PLAN

Use in conjunction with Daily Language Practice.

Day 1 Complete page T1202.	**Day 4** Choose a Practice Activity or *Grammar Practice Book* pages 54–55.
Day 2 Complete a Practice Activity on page T1203.	**Day 5** Complete *Practice Book* page 175.
Day 3 Choose a Practice Activity or *Language Handbook* pages 164–165.	

2

SPELLING

5-Day Plan

Integrated Spelling Lesson 33
student book, pages 138–141;
Teacher's Edition, pages T213–T218.

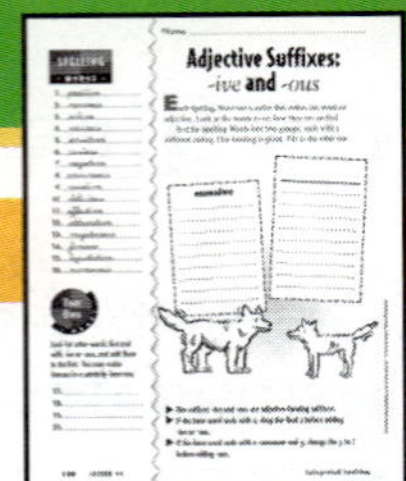

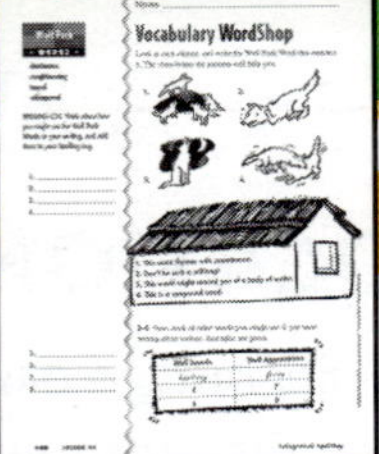
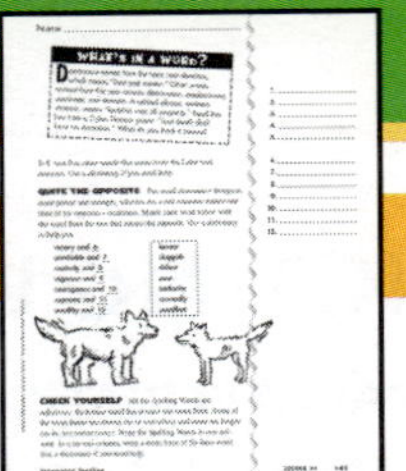

SPELLING WORDS

1. positive
2. nervous ★
3. active ★
4. various
5. sensitive
6. curious
7. negative
8. enormous ★
9. creative
10. delicious
11. effective
12. attractive
13. mysterious
14. furious ★
15. legislative
16. numerous ★

STUDENT'S PERSONAL WORDS

17. 19.
18. 20.

Additional story words are *aggressive* and *vigorous*.

★ Words appearing in "Julie of the Wolves"

PRACTICE BOOK, page 176

Adjective Suffixes *-ive, -ous*

Pretest

DAY 1 **Administer the pretest.** Say each word and then use it in the dictation sentence below. Help students self-check their pretests.

OPEN SORT

DAY 2 **Have students create categories.** Encourage students to sort the Spelling Words, using their own categories. Suggest such categories as vowel sound, degree of familiarity, or a particular spelling pattern. Ask volunteers to explain how they sorted the words.

CLOSED SORT

Sort by spelling pattern. Write the heading *massive* from the chart below on the board and have students choose a Spelling Word that ends in *-ous* as a head for the second column. Then have volunteers write each Spelling Word under the proper heading.

massive	(Possible response: nervous)
positive	various
active	curious
sensitive	enormous
negative	delicious
creative	mysterious
effective	furious
attractive	numerous
legislative	

Teach/Model

DAY 3 **Discuss the generalization.** Write on the board the words *active* and *curious* and the sentence frame *The wolf pup was* _____. Ask volunteers to complete the sentence using each word and to explain what the words do in each sentence. (describe the wolf pup) Underline the suffix in both Spelling Words and tell students that the suffixes *-ive* and *-ous* are adjective suffixes.

DAY 4 **Apply to writing.** Students should look for words with these adjective suffixes in their personal narratives or other writing to see if they are spelled correctly.

Posttest

DAY 5 **Assess students' progress.** The sentences below should be used as the posttest.

DICTATION SENTENCES

1. She was positive it would rain.
2. Rick was nervous before the game.
3. The wolf pups were active.
4. I chose various books to read.
5. Bo was sensitive to the smell and sneezed.
6. Rita was curious about the noise.
7. A negative attitude serves no purpose.
8. That pumpkin is enormous!
9. The artist was creative in her use of color.
10. Mom's spaghetti was delicious.
11. I hope the change is effective.
12. My father wore an attractive tie.
13. The costume made Carlos look mysterious.
14. The wind sounded furious.
15. One part of government is the legislative branch.
16. Numerous friends helped us move into our new house.

VOCABULARY WORKSHOP

Reviewing Key Words

Draw on the board a two-column chart like the one below. Then read aloud each of the following questions. Have students answer each question based on what they read in the story. Ask a volunteer to write the Key Word in the appropriate column. A word may be placed in both columns.

1. Who paid tribute to Amaroq—Miyax or the wolves?
2. Whose fears were dispelled—Miyax's or the wolves'?
3. Who aggressively approached Amaroq for attention—Miyax or the wolves?
4. At the beginning of the story, whose vitality was the most impressive—Miyax's or the wolves'?
5. Who intimidated the other—Miyax or the wolves?

Miyax	*The wolves*
(tribute) *(dispelled)* *(vitality)* *(intimidated)*	*(tribute)* *(aggressively)* *(vitality)*

Extending Vocabulary

ANTONYMS

Write the following sentence on the board:

The lemmings had a chemical in their blood that kept them active all winter when other little mammals were hibernating.

Ask students to identify two words in the sentence that are antonyms of one another. *(active, hibernating)* Point out how the author uses antonyms to show a direct opposition.

WRITE PAIRS OF ANTONYMS

Invite pairs of students to look through the story to find examples of antonyms and record them in a list. Students might also take turns supplying a word and challenging their partners to offer an antonym of that word. When students have several pairs of antonyms on their lists, allow them time to compare their lists with those of the rest of the class.

dark : light
sternly : apologetically
belly : back
wide : narrow
nothing : something

INTRODUCE: LITERARY APPRECIATION

Point of View

OBJECTIVE: To understand the point of view an author uses to tell a story

Informal Assessment ✓

Are students able to

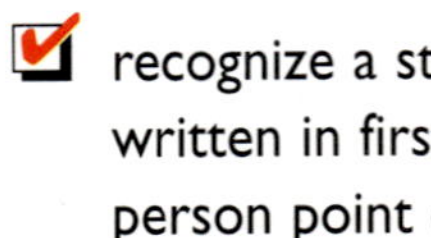

- recognize a story written in first-person point of view?
- third-person limited?

- third-person omniscient?

Teach/Model

Return to the literature. Have students name the characters in "Julie of the Wolves." (Miyax, the wolves) Then ask students to tell who the main character is and to explain how they decided that. (Miyax; the story is told from Miyax's point of view.)

Model identifying point of view. Explain that writers can narrate a story in different ways. Tell students that "Julie of the Wolves" is told from the third-person limited point of view. It is limited because the author only tells Miyax's thoughts and feelings, as if an outside observer had special insight into only Miyax's character. Model identifying point of view:

MODEL

If the narrator uses *I* or *me*, I know it is the first-person point of view. In "Julie of the Wolves," the author uses third-person pronouns. Since she only tells how Miyax feels, I know that the third-person has a limited point of view. If it were omniscient, or all-knowing, the author would also tell how the wolves felt.

Write on the board the following terms for points of view: *first-person, third-person limited,* and *third-person omniscient.* Have students look through their anthologies to find stories written from each point of view.

Practice/Apply

Have students demonstrate understanding. Have students look back at the third complete paragraph on page 574 and rewrite the passage from the first-person point of view and the third-person omniscient point of view. You may need to point out that the third-person omniscient point of view requires more changes to the original text. When students have finished, ask volunteers to share their rewrites. Have students explain how each point of view is different. Suggest that they consider why an author would choose to use a particular point of view for a story.

Demonstrate by rewriting the first sentence.

First-person point of view:

The hairs on my neck rose and my eyes widened. Amaroq's ears went forward aggressively and I remembered that wide eyes meant fear to him.

Third-person omniscient point of view:

The hairs on her neck rose and her eyes widened. Amaroq sensed her fear. He put his ears forward aggressively. Miyax remembered that wide eyes meant fear to him.

Practice Activities

What We Saw

PERFORMANCE ASSESSMENT Invite students to be omniscient writers. Using one of the illustrations in "Julie of the Wolves," have students explain what is happening from the point of view of each of the characters pictured. Remind students that they will have to "know" what both the wolves and Miyax are thinking as they rewrite that section of the story. Encourage students to compare their rewrites with those of others. VISUAL/AUDITORY

Different Points of View

COOPERATIVE LEARNING Have groups of students make a chart showing the three possible points of view, the characteristics of each, and two books or stories that are examples of each. Group members might find it easier to work with assigned roles: a Facilitator to coordinate tasks, a Recorder to keep the chart organized, and a Reporter to review the chart and present the group's examples to the rest of the class. VISUAL/AUDITORY/KINESTHETIC

STUDENTS ACQUIRING ENGLISH

Invite students to use their first language to describe a scene in first-person point of view and then in third-person limited point of view.

RETEACH

See page R109 for lessons in multiple modalities.

CHALLENGE

Have students retell one specific story event from all three points of view.

Reading Trade Books TO REINFORCE POINT OF VIEW

Arctic Hunter by Diane Hoyt-Goldsmith. Holiday House, 1992. EASY

Lost in the Barrens by Farley Mowat. Little, Brown, 1956. CHALLENGING

Snow Bound by Harry Mazer. Dell, 1975. AVERAGE

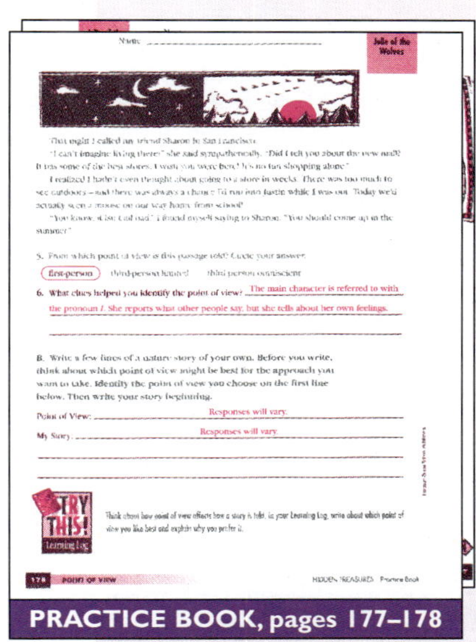

Name ______

Julie of the Wolves

That night I called my friend Sharon in San Francisco.

"I can't imagine living there!" she said sympathetically. "Did I tell you about the new mall? It has some of the best stores. I wish you were here! It's no fun shopping alone."

I realized I hadn't even thought about going to a store in weeks. There was too much to see outdoors—and there was always a chance I'd run into Justin while I was out. Today we'd actually seen a moose on our way home from school!

"You know, it isn't all bad," I found myself saying to Sharon. "You should come up in the summer."

5. From which point of view is this passage told? Circle your answer.

(first-person) third-person limited third-person omniscient

6. What clues helped you identify the point of view? The main character is referred to with the pronoun *I*. She reports what other people say, but she tells about her own feelings.

B. Write a few lines of a nature story of your own. Before you write, think about which point of view might be best for the approach you want to take. Identify the point of view you choose on the first line below. Then write your story beginning.

Point of View: Responses will vary.

My Story: Responses will vary.

TRY THIS! Learning Log — Think about how point of view affects how a story is told. In your Learning Log, write about which point of view you like best and explain why you prefer it.

178 POINT OF VIEW HIDDEN TREASURES Practice Book

PRACTICE BOOK, pages 177–178

Integrated Curriculum

SCIENCE

Natural History

"Julie of the Wolves" is filled with descriptions of the landscape and clues to the interdependence of life forms in the Arctic. Through the following activities, students will investigate these life forms.

TIPS FOR CLASSROOM MANAGEMENT

IF students are musically inclined, **THEN** they may want to participate in the Natural Sounds activity.

TECHNOLOGY

THINKIN' THINGS COLLECTION 2

Students may want to use the Toony's Tunes program after completing the Natural Sounds activity.

SCIENCE

Native Species

Use reference sources. Encourage students to compile a list of the animals Miyax was familiar with on the North Slope. While many of these animals are not native to other parts of North America, members of the same family group may be. Have students use field guides and other reference books to find out the family groups each listed animal belongs to. Students should then note any members of the same family that are native to their state or area and discuss where the habitats are likely to be. Suggest they make a chart or other display to record their comparisons. LISTENING/SPEAKING/READING/WRITING

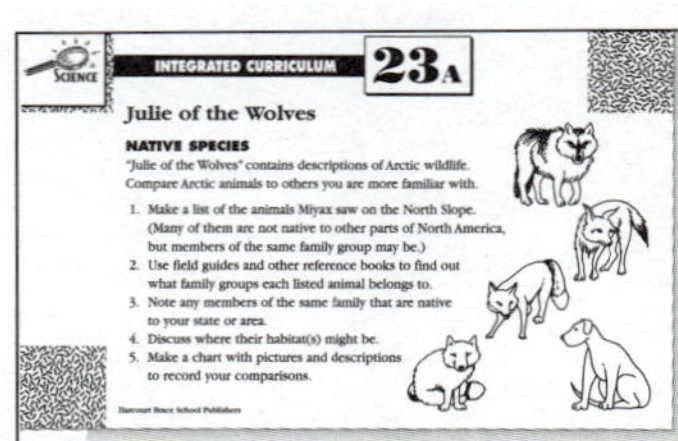
SCIENCE INTEGRATED CURRICULUM 23A

Julie of the Wolves

NATIVE SPECIES

"Julie of the Wolves" contains descriptions of Arctic wildlife. Compare Arctic animals to others you are more familiar with.

1. Make a list of the animals Miyax saw on the North Slope. (Many of them are not native to other parts of North America, but members of the same family group may be.)
2. Use field guides and other reference books to find out what family groups each listed animal belongs to.
3. Note any members of the same family that are native to your state or area.
4. Discuss where their habitat(s) might be.
5. Make a chart with pictures and descriptions to record your comparisons.

Harcourt Brace School Publishers

Curriculum Card 23A

Clockwise from above: gray wolf; coyote; domestic dog; Arctic fox; red fox

ART

Field Guides

Except for the wolves, none of the plants or animals of the North Slope were pictured in "Julie of the Wolves." Suggest that groups of students find out what these plants and animals look like and create a mural-style field guide to the North Slope. Students should take the roles of Researcher, Recorder, Fact Checker, and Artist to prepare the field guide. Have groups share their completed field guides, and keep them in the classroom library for easy reference. **LISTENING/SPEAKING/ READING**

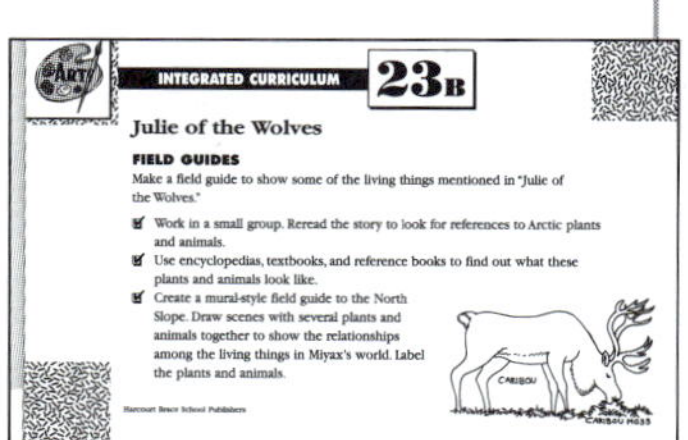
ART

INTEGRATED CURRICULUM **23B**

Julie of the Wolves

FIELD GUIDES

Make a field guide to show some of the living things mentioned in "Julie of the Wolves."

- Work in a small group. Reread the story to look for references to Arctic plants and animals.
- Use encyclopedias, textbooks, and reference books to find out what these plants and animals look like.
- Create a mural-style field guide to the North Slope. Draw scenes with several plants and animals together to show the relationships among the living things in Miyax's world. Label the plants and animals.

CARIBOU

CARIBOU MOSS

Harcourt Brace School Publishers

Curriculum Card 23B

MUSIC

Natural Sounds

Miyax listened as the wolves sang a wolf song. The songs and sounds of wolves and other animals have been recorded and used by such composers as Paul Winter, and many other composers have written works around interpretations of the sounds of nature. Have recordings of both kinds of music available for students to listen to, or challenge students to find and borrow recordings from a community library. Some students might like to close their eyes and visualize as they listen, while others might want to move about. Also, small groups of students might record sounds to create their own Nature Symphony. **LISTENING/SPEAKING**

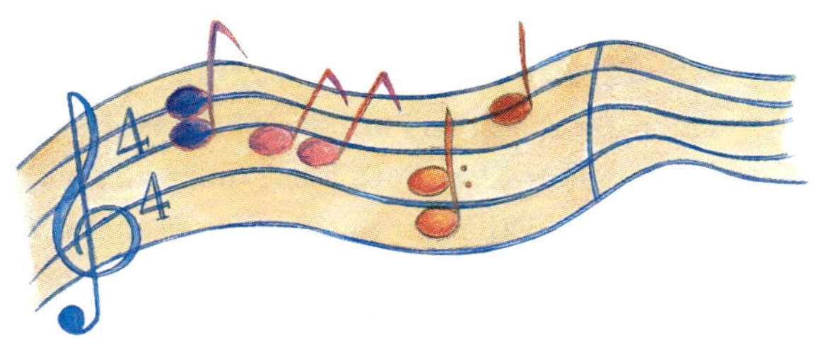

Reading Trade Books

CROSS-CURRICULAR READING

Dogsong **by Gary Paulsen. Macmillan, 1985.** **CHALLENGING**

One Day in the Alpine Tundra **by Jean Craighead George. HarperCollins, 1984.** **AVERAGE**

MULTI-AGE CLASSROOMS

Some students may choose to prepare their field guides for a younger audience. Encourage them to do so, and arrange for them to share their completed projects with younger students.

Reading Trade Books

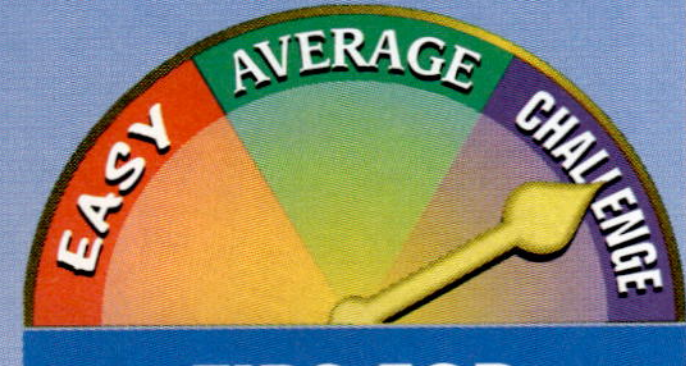

TIPS FOR CLASSROOM MANAGEMENT

INDEPENDENT READING Suggest that students who want to read *Bearstone* independently record the tale's events in a story map as they read.

For a comprehensive lesson plan, refer to the complete lesson for *Bearstone* on pages T1274–T1279.

STUDENTS ACQUIRING ENGLISH

Suggest that students prepare to read by looking up in a dictionary and writing definitions for these terms: *reservation, canyon, cliff, post, weld, ancestor, cave,* and *grizzly bear.*

Bearstone

by Will Hobbs

Signatures Library

READER'S CHALLENGE

The main characters in "Julie of the Wolves" and *Bearstone* are strongly independent. They both learn more about themselves through their adventures. What do you think they might say to each other if they met? After reading, write a conversation between Miyax and Cloyd.

READING STRATEGY: POINT OF VIEW

After students have read *Bearstone*, discuss the point of view from which the novel is told. Help students understand that although it is written in the third person, the narrator describes details from Cloyd's perspective. Ask students to imagine one scene from the novel told from a different point of view. For example, students might retell one of these scenes:

- **Cloyd's talk with the nurse from the nurse's point of view** (Chapter 1)
- **Cloyd's first dinner with Walter from Walter's point of view** (Chapter 4)

LINK TO THE THEME

After students have read *Bearstone*, suggest that they gather in small groups to discuss the novel. Groups can reflect on events from *Bearstone* and "Julie of the Wolves" to help them decide whether or not they agree with each of these statements:

- **Being alone is the best way to get to know yourself.**
- **Nature is only an obstacle if you don't understand it.**

Other Trade Books

Black Star, Bright Dawn

by Scott O'Dell

Bright Dawn is an 18-year-old Eskimo girl who races in the Iditarod, Alaska's famous dogsled race. After students read, suggest that they create character sketches to compare Bright Dawn and Miyax.

Drifting Snow: An Arctic Search

by James Houston

This adventure novel, based on historical events, describes Elizabeth Queen's search for her Inuit roots. After students read, suggest that they create a cause-and-effect chart to show how both Elizabeth and Miyax are changed by their encounters with nature.

Wolves

by R. D. Lawrence

Students who want to find out more about the wolves that Julie lives among can refer to this beautifully illustrated guide. After students read, encourage them to reflect on the animals described in "Julie of the Wolves." Discuss how accurately the author portrays these Arctic creatures.

MEETING INDIVIDUAL NEEDS

EXTRA SUPPORT

Have students read *Wolves* with a partner. Suggest that they preview the book by looking through the table of contents, the illustrations, and the index. Encourage them to create a wolf/wildlife glossary using words from the book.

Trade Books

Write a Group Story

SELECTION CONNECTION

In "Julie of the Wolves," Miyax's wilderness adventure begins when she becomes lost in Alaska. Ask students to discuss other adventure stories or films they are familiar with and the events that set their plots in motion.

PROJECT CHECKLIST

During this stage, students should

- ☑ brainstorm the kinds of supplies they will need to take with them.
- ☑ narrow the list of supplies to the ten they consider most important.
- ☑ develop a plot for their trip that includes unexpected challenges and the ways the group dealt with them.
- ☑ write a group story about their wilderness expedition.

Project Card 34 can be found as a copying master on page R125.

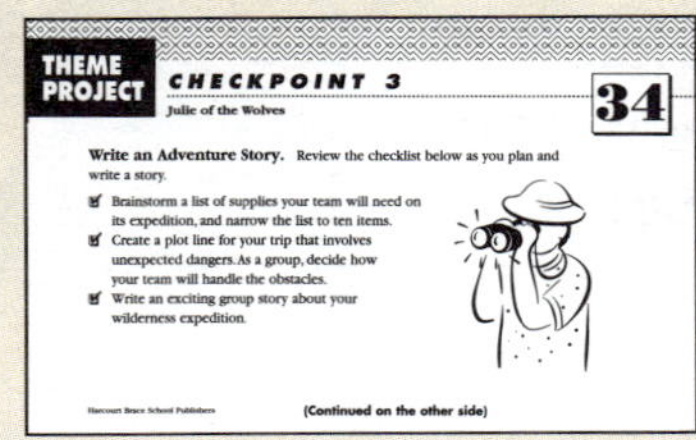

THEME PROJECT

CHECKPOINT 3

Julie of the Wolves

34

Write an Adventure Story. Review the checklist below as you plan and write a story.

- ☑ Brainstorm a list of supplies your team will need on its expedition, and narrow the list to ten items.
- ☑ Create a plot line for your trip that involves unexpected dangers. As a group, decide how your team will handle the obstacles.
- ☑ Write an exciting group story about your wilderness expedition.

Harcourt Brace School Publishers

(Continued on the other side)

Project Card 34

RESEARCH AND PLANNING TIPS

As students prepare to work on their stories, suggest that they

- consult research sources for information about camping, hunting, and hiking that they can use in their story.
- think about the adventures in the literature selections for ideas.
- brainstorm to generate useful lists such as supplies, potential hazards, and solutions to problems.

Students may wish to write in their project journals. Provide prompts such as *How did your group come up with challenging situations?*

Informal Assessment

As students complete this checkpoint, each group will **synthesize** information and use it to develop narratives for their stories. Students are thinking critically if they

- ☑ are able to work cooperatively on the list of supplies and the plot for the story.
- ☑ can infer a variety of problems that might arise on their trip.
- ☑ can identify plausible solutions for the problems.

STUDENTS ACQUIRING ENGLISH

Suggest that groups classify supplies under familiar headings *(Food, Tools, Clothing, Equipment)* to help them fit new vocabulary into familiar contexts.

TECHNOLOGY

IMAGINATION EXPRESS, DESTINATION: OCEAN

Students can use the interactive story in the program as a model and inspiration.

Jim Brandenburg

ABOUT THE AUTHOR/ PHOTOGRAPHER

JIM BRANDENBURG is an internationally renowned wildlife photographer who has been captivated with wolves and photography since he was fourteen years old. His book *To the Top of the World* has won many awards, including *School Library Journal* Best Book of 1993, ALA Best Book for Young Adults of 1994, and an Orbis Pictus Honor Book of 1993.

More information about Jim Brandenburg and his work appears on page T1243.

THEME: NATURE

Confronting Nature

Few places on earth are more difficult to survive in than the Arctic. As photographer Jim Brandenburg makes clear in "To the Top of the World," the Arctic wolf is supremely adapted to its environment and highly skilled in confronting nature.

SELECTION SUMMARY

Genre: Nonfiction

Wildlife photographer Jim Brandenburg spends a spring and summer on Ellesmere Island in Canada's Northwest Territories, photographing a pack of Arctic wolves. The wolves never appear to be bothered by his presence and regularly visit his campsite a quarter of a mile from their den. Since the sun doesn't set during the Arctic summer, Brandenburg keeps irregular hours, spending his time loitering near the den with his cameras or following the wolves in his all-terrain vehicle. He notices how the seven adults in the pack care for the six pups, and how the wolves' thick coats, superb sense of smell, acute eyesight and hearing, and highly developed system of communication enable them to survive in their harsh environment.

SUGGESTED LESSON PLANNER

▶ *To the Top of the World*

	DAY 1	DAY 2
PART 1 Reading, Listening, Speaking, Viewing **Key Words**: haughty, serene, crucial, distinctive	**BUILD BACKGROUND** T1216 **VOCABULARY STRATEGIES** T1217 *Transparency 58* *Practice Book* p. 181 **READING THE SELECTION** T1218–1243 Options for Reading T1218–T1219 *Response Card 15* **REVIEW PREDICTIONS/PURPOSE** T1242 **APPRECIATING THE LITERATURE** T1242 NOTE: Students may read the selection on Day 2.	**SUMMARIZE THE SELECTION** T1242 *Practice Book* p. 182 ◆ **RESPONSE CORNER ACTIVITIES** T1244 **CHECKING COMPREHENSION** T1245 *End-of-Selection Test* 
PART 2 Writer's Workshop	**RESEARCH REPORT** Thinking as Writers T1250 *Language Handbook* pp. 74–75 *Transparencies 59A, 59B*	Prewriting T1250 *Language Handbook* pp. 15, 60
Grammar	✓**ADJECTIVE AND ADVERB PHRASES** Teach the Concept T1252 Daily Language Practice (1–2) R117	Daily Language Practice (3–4) R117 Practice Activity T1253
Spelling	**PREFIXES:** ***pre-, per-, pro-*** *prepared, protest, professor, propeller, perfume, perhaps, progress, persuade, provided, precisely, preferred, professional, perfectly, production, protection, perceived* Pretest/Self-Check T1254 *Integrated Spelling Teacher's Edition* pp. T219, T303	Open and Closed Sorts T1254 *Integrated Spelling* p. 142 *Integrated Spelling Teacher's Edition* p. T220
PART 3 Skills and Strategies	◆ **INTEGRATED CURRICULUM** *Climate and Weather* **Science** T1258 **Social Studies** T1258 **Art** T1259  *Imagination Express, Destination: Ocean*	**STUDY SKILLS** T1256–T1257 Test-Taking Strategies (Introduce) *Transparency 60*

Use the Intervention Strategies note on page T1233 to help **below-level** and **ESL students** as they read.

Use the Students Aquiring English note on page T1253 to help **ESL students** with their writing.

NOTE: An alternative lesson plan for **below-level students** appears on *Intervention Strategies Manual* pp. 140–145. A lesson for **students acquiring English** appears on *Sheltered English/ESL Manual* pp. 94–97.

DAY 3

◆ **IDEA BANK ACTIVITIES**
Retelling T1248
Oral Language T1248
Viewing T1249
Real-Life Resources: Reading Yellow Page Ads T1249
Writer's Magazine pp. 92–93

School–Home Connection 24 R144

Drafting T1250
Language Handbook pp. 61, 164–167
The Amazing Writing Machine

Daily Language Practice (5–6) R117
Practice Activity T1253
Language Handbook pp. 166–167
The Amazing Writing Machine

Discuss the Generalization T1254
Integrated Spelling p. 143
Integrated Spelling Teacher's Edition p. T221

STUDY SKILLS MINILESSON T1221
✓ Reference Sources (Review)
Practice Book p. 186

COMPREHENSION MINILESSON T1227
✓ Summarizing/Paraphrasing (Review)
Practice Book p. 187

Above-level students may complete the Writer's Workshop independently at their own pace.

DAY 4

VOCABULARY WORKSHOP T1255
Reviewing Key Words

READING TRADE BOOKS T1260–T1261

Take-Home Book

Responding and Revising T1251
Language Handbook pp. 61, 164–167

Daily Language Practice (7–8) R117
Practice Activity T1253
Grammar Practice Book pp. 56–57

Apply to Writing T1254
Integrated Spelling pp. 144–145
Integrated Spelling Teacher's Edition pp. T222–T223

VOCABULARY WORKSHOP T1255
Specialized Vocabulary: Science Words
Practice Book p. 185

Below-level students may read the *Take-Home Book: Susan Butcher and the Iditarod* to help them review Key Words.

DAY 5

READING TRADE BOOKS T1257, T1259, T1260–T1261

Proofreading and Publishing T1251
Language Handbook p. 61

Daily Language Practice (9–12) R117
Practice Book p. 183

Posttest T1254
Practice Book p. 184
Integrated Spelling Teacher's Edition p. T224

GRAMMAR MINILESSON T1237
✓ Prepositions and Prepositional Phrases (Review)

Theme Project Checkpoint 4 T1262

Below-level and **ESL students** may read the *ESL/Title I Library* book *Long Claws*.

✓ = Tested Skill
◆ = Optional activities used to adjust pacing throughout the lesson
Titles in *italics* are optional materials.

1 Reading and Responding

BUILDING BACKGROUND AND CONCEPTS

PRIOR KNOWLEDGE

Relate to students' lives. Ask students how their lives would be different if they lived in a different climate, such as a desert, a tropical rain forest, or the Arctic. Discuss what effect climate has on people and how they live. Ask students in what kind of climate they would prefer to live, and have them support their answers with reasons.

Create a list of traits needed for survival. Have students think about the people and animals they have encountered so far in this theme. What do they all have in common? (the need to survive under difficult circumstances) Explain that encounters with nature often teach people things about themselves. Encourage students to begin a list of traits that people and animals need to survive challenging conditions.

Getting Along with Nature
People and animals need to be...
1. adaptable to changes
2. intelligent
3. creative
4. able to think quickly
5.
6.

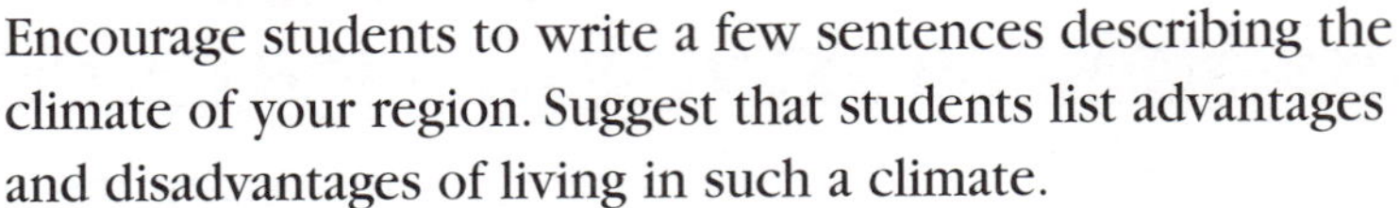

Encourage students to write a few sentences describing the climate of your region. Suggest that students list advantages and disadvantages of living in such a climate.

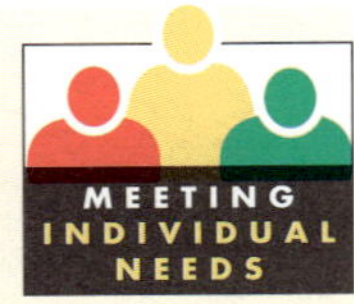

Intervention Strategies

For students who may have difficulty reading "To the Top of the World," support is available in *Intervention Strategies Manual,* pages 140–145 and on pages T1233 and T1246–T1247 in this lesson.

STUDENTS ACQUIRING ENGLISH

See *Sheltered English/ESL Manual* pages 94–97.

FACT FINDER

SOCIAL STUDIES

Ellesmere Island

Although "To the Top of the World" features wolves and the photographs show no indication of permanent human habitat, Ellesmere Island does have some human residents. There is a weather station at Eureka on the west coast and a military base at Alert in the north. An Inuit village at Grise Fiord is on the southern coast, maintaining an Inuit population that has occupied Ellesmere for over 4,300 years. More than 180 prehistoric Inuit dwelling sites have been discovered on Bache Peninsula on Ellesmere's eastern coast. Archaeological research on Skraeling Island just off Bache has uncovered links of European chain mail, pieces of oak, boat rivets, and even woven fabric, indicating early explorations by Europeans to the Arctic, probably the Norse from their settlements on Greenland.

VOCABULARY STRATEGIES

KEY WORDS DEFINED

haughty having more pride in oneself than regard for others

serene calm and peaceful; clear

crucial of the most importance

distinctive specifically characteristic

INTEGRATED SPELLING

Spelling Pretest: page T1254

Spelling Generalization: Prefixes: *pre-, per-, pro-*

CONTEXT CLUES: SENTENCES

Encourage students to use semantic and syntactic cues. Have volunteers read each sentence on Transparency 58. Model how to identify the function of *haughty* as an adjective. (It tells what kind of look—it describes a noun.) Then have students identify context clues that can help determine its meaning. (*proud, selfish*) Prompt students to use similar strategies to figure out the meanings of the other Key Words.

CHECK UNDERSTANDING

Have students write sentences. Display the Key Words and ask students to write a series of sentences or a short paragraph about other selections they've read in this theme, using as many of the Key Words as possible. Then ask volunteers to read their sentences aloud. Discuss the meaning of each Key Word as students explain how each relates to the selection(s) described. **STRATEGY: CONTEXT CLUES**

TRANSPARENCY 58

Key Words

1. Mark gave me a haughty look, proud and selfish.
2. From his serene manner, you couldn't tell that Carlos was nervous.
3. To understand the instructions, it is crucial that we read them carefully.
4. The puppy has a distinctive heart-shaped spot on her forehead.

The forest looked very serene as dawn approached.

PRACTICE BOOK, page 181

Prereading Strategies

PREVIEW AND PREDICT

Have students preview the selection by reading the introduction and quickly looking through the photographs. Ask students to recall what they know about wolves and what else they would like to know.

On the board, begin a K-W-L chart like the one below. Students may use *Practice Book* page 182. Encourage them to fill in the first two columns of the chart.

K	W	L
What I Know	What I Want to Know	What I Learned
(Wolves are smart.) (Wolves live in packs.) (One wolf is the leader.) (Wolves live in Alaska.)	(How do wolves pick a leader?) (Where else do wolves live?) (Who takes care of the wolf puppies?)	

PERSONAL JOURNAL

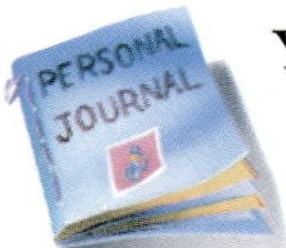

You may want to suggest that students write their predictions about the selection in their personal journals.

PURPOSE

You may want to model setting a purpose:

MODEL

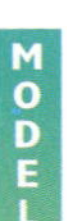

From looking at the photographs, I know that these wolves live in a harsh environment. I want to read to find out how they survive and raise their young in this place.

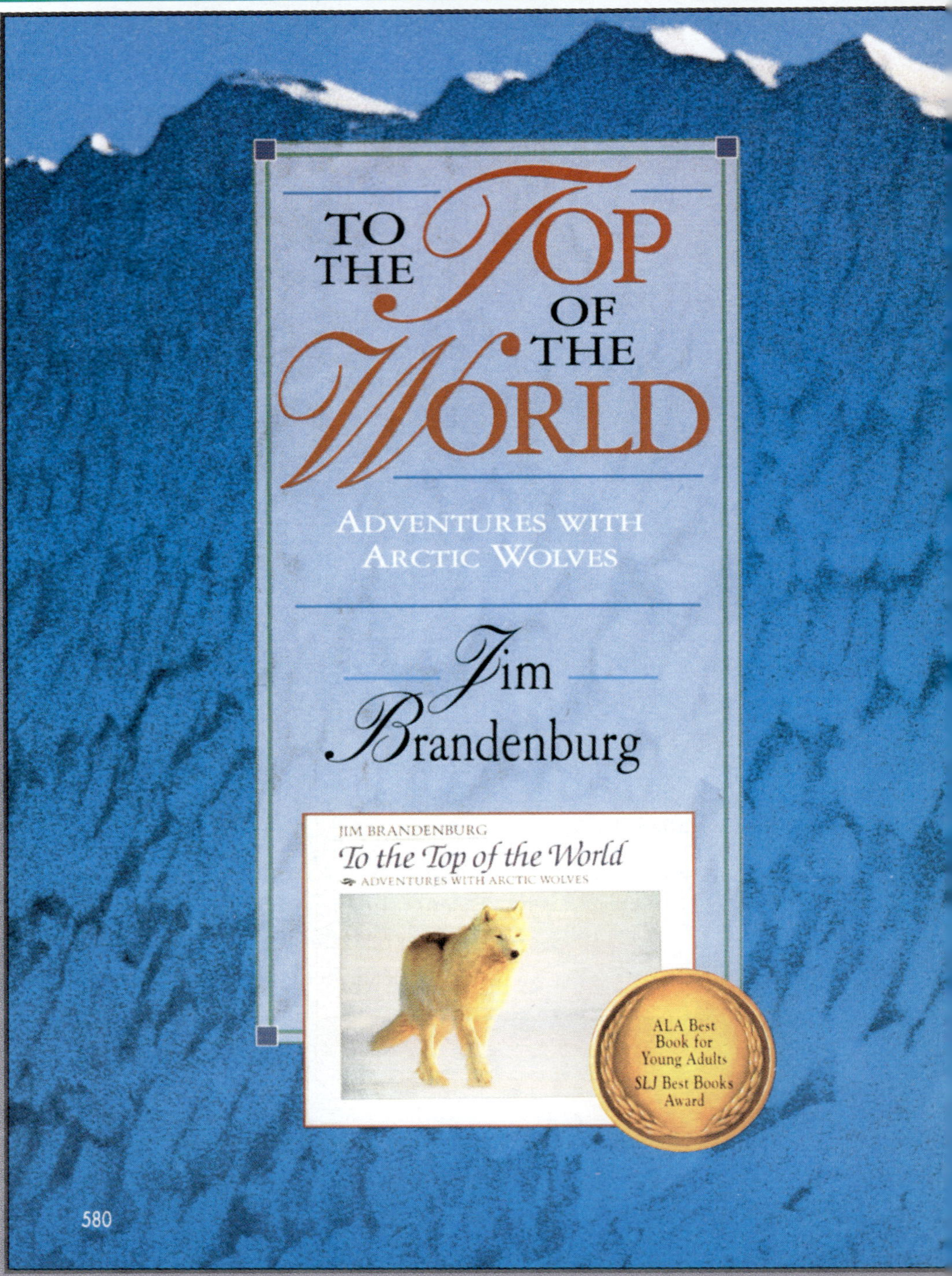

TO THE TOP OF THE WORLD
ADVENTURES WITH ARCTIC WOLVES
Jim Brandenburg
JIM BRANDENBURG
To the Top of the World
ADVENTURES WITH ARCTIC WOLVES
ALA Best Book for Young Adults
SLJ Best Books Award
580

TIPS FOR CLASSROOM MANAGEMENT

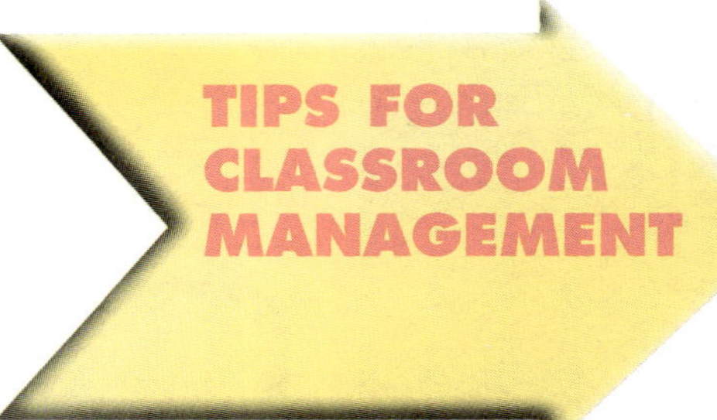

SMALL GROUP

PARTNER READING

Pair students who need extra support with more-fluent readers, and encourage them to stop frequently to review what they've read and to discuss the photographs.

COOPERATIVE READING

READER RESPONSE GROUPS Have groups of students use Reader Response Card 15 to read the selection using the Jigsaw technique. Response Card 15 can be found at the back of this Teacher's Edition.

READER RESPONSE 15
Jigsaw

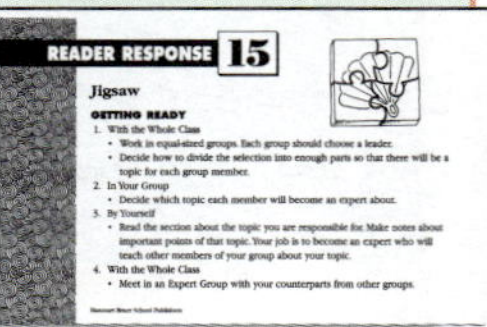

Response Card 15

Jim Brandenburg spent one special spring and summer on Ellesmere Island near the Arctic Circle in Canada. This is the story of his adventures with a pack of wild wolves and how he observed them.

581

WHOLE CLASS

STRATEGIC READING

Use the suggestions on pages T1220 and T1230 to reinforce the focus strategy of **using typographic cues.** Remind students to also refer to the class-made strategy chart for other strategies if the one they are using isn't working.

READ ALOUD

Read the first page of the selection aloud and have students revise their predictions if needed. Then have them continue reading independently, stopping to note on their K-W-L charts any new information they learn about wolves.

Strategic Reading

USING TYPOGRAPHIC CUES

Discuss the reading strategies students have used when reading a selection. Display the class-made strategy chart, and remind students that one strategy is using typographic cues. Ask students what typographic cues they found when they previewed the selection. (large capital letters, chapter or section headings) Ask students how these cues might help them better understand the material. (Possible response: The large capital letters signal a new idea, and the section headings give the main ideas of the sections.)

STRATEGY: USE TYPOGRAPHIC CUES

PAGES 580–593

Have students read through page 593 to confirm their predictions.

SCIENCE

WOLVES Dogs, coyotes, wolves, and foxes all belong to the family *Canidae*. The gray, or timber, wolf and the Arctic wolf are the same (*Canis lupus*) and have coat variations that range from almost black to nearly pure white. Arctic wolves are pale; those living in forested areas are often darker; those living in a more varied area may have variegated coats. Pups in a given litter are often very different in appearance.

Female gray timber wolf

Meeting the Family

One of my first concerns was about how much I might interfere with the lives of these wolves. Would my presence cause them to abandon their den and disappear?

During most of the year, a wolf pack roams over its entire territory, making wolf study almost impossible. But each spring, the pack stays in or near one place. The mother must take to the den to have her pups, and the behavior of the whole pack revolves around feeding their young and ensuring their safety. This phenomenon makes study easier, but it also is a uniquely sensitive time.

How could I make it clear to the pack that I meant them no harm? That I would keep my distance and simply observe?

At first, I did not set up a permanent campsite in case the pack fled and moved to another den. I approached the den cautiously, alert to any signs that my presence might be causing stress in the pack. But the wolves never appeared overly nervous or bothered.

GEOGRAPHY/MATH CONNECTION

Ellesmere Island covers about 76,000 square miles and is the tenth-largest island in the world. Have students locate the island on a map of the world and note its location relative to the Arctic Circle. Challenge students to determine how far Ellesmere Island is from the North Pole and how far it is from their own community.

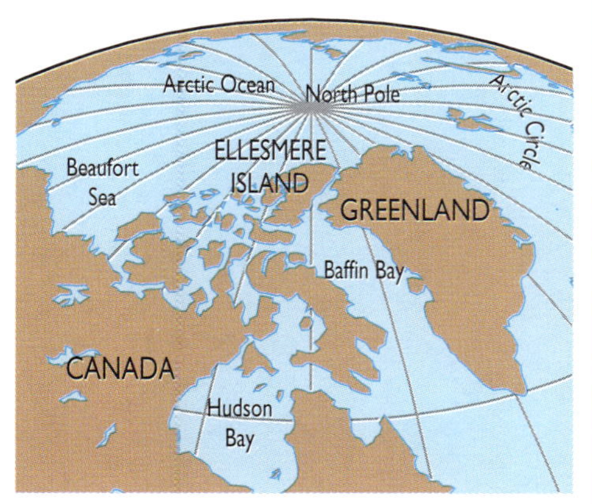

Tested Skill

MINILESSON

REVIEW: STUDY SKILLS

Reference Sources

INFORMAL ASSESSMENT

Ask students how they could find out how large Ellesmere Island is and exactly where it is located. (Use an atlas or an encyclopedia.)

TEACH/MODEL

Review reference sources with students by having them name sources they've used recently. List the sources mentioned on the board. Model how you would use different sources to locate information about topics encountered in "To the Top of the World."

MODEL

I know that an atlas contains different kinds of maps, so I know I can find the location of Ellesmere Island by consulting an atlas. Because I know that a general encyclopedia has information about many topics, I'll look there to find out the size of a wolf's territory.

PRACTICE/APPLY

Have students write five questions that can be answered only by using reference sources.

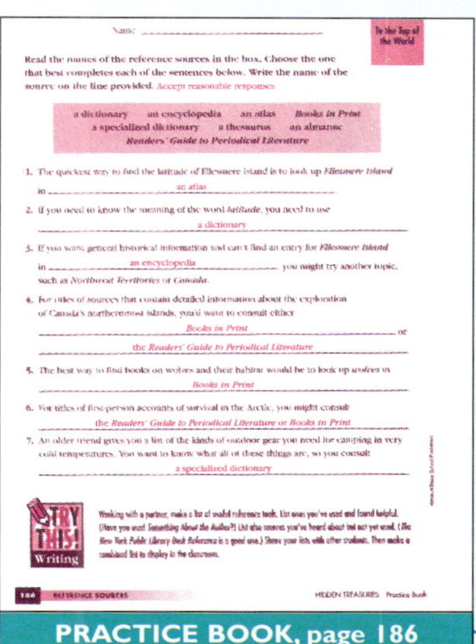

Name ______________________

To the Top of the World

Read the names of the reference sources in the box. Choose the one that best completes each of the sentences below. Write the name of the source on the line provided. Accept reasonable responses.

a dictionary an encyclopedia an atlas *Books in Print*
a specialized dictionary a thesaurus an almanac
Readers' Guide to Periodical Literature

1. The quickest way to find the latitude of Ellesmere Island is to look up *Ellesmere Island* in ___an atlas___
2. If you need to know the meaning of the word *latitude*, you need to use ___a dictionary___
3. If you want general historical information and can't find an entry for *Ellesmere Island* in ___an encyclopedia___ you might try another topic, such as *Northwest Territories* or *Canada*.
4. For titles of sources that contain detailed information about the exploration of Canada's northernmost islands, you'd want to consult either ___*Books in Print*___ or ___the *Readers' Guide to Periodical Literature*___
5. The best way to find books on wolves and their habitat would be to look up *wolves* in ___*Books in Print*___
6. For titles of first-person accounts of survival in the Arctic, you might consult ___the *Readers' Guide to Periodical Literature* or *Books in Print*___
7. An older friend gives you a list of the kinds of outdoor gear you need for camping in very cold temperatures. You want to know what all of these things are, so you consult ___a specialized dictionary___

TRY THIS! Writing

Working with a partner, make a list of useful reference tools. List ones you've used and found helpful. (Have you used *Something About the Author*?) List also sources you've heard about but not yet used. (*The New York Public Library Desk Reference* is a good one.) Share your lists with other students. Then make a combined list to display in the classroom.

186 REFERENCE SOURCES HIDDEN TREASURES Practice Book

PRACTICE BOOK, page 186

Critical Thinking Questions

1. **Jim Brandenburg doesn't see the pups until they come out of the den for the first time. How does he even know there *are* pups?** (Possible response: He knows wolf packs stay in one place only when there are pups to raise and protect.) CRITICAL: DRAWING CONCLUSIONS

2. **Do wolf pups grow quickly? How do you know?** (Possible response: Yes; they are small when Brandenburg first sees them, but he knows they'll be running with the adults by winter. Winter comes early in the Arctic.) METACOGNITIVE: NOTING IMPORTANT DETAILS/DRAWING CONCLUSIONS

The den was set high on a hill. At its opening, rocks formed a kind of porch on which the pack members spent much of their time. The den opened into the earth from an entryway just large enough to fit snugly around the mother wolf. A hungry polar bear, in other words, could not squeeze in to make a snack out of the growing pups. Inside, a clean, bug-free layer of sand covered the ground leading into a cave twenty feet deep. The rock walls provided excellent protection from the bitter cold.

Pups spend their first weeks inside the den huddled around their mother, and each other, for warmth. I was eager and impatient for my first look at them. When they finally appeared outside the den, they proved well worth the wait.

There were six puppies, cute little gray bundles of fur waddling after the adults on short, fuzzy legs and oversized paws. I guessed that they were about five weeks old. It seemed impossible that by winter they'd be running alongside their parents.

584

SOCIAL STUDIES

The Arctic is the geographic area from the North Pole south to the northern timberline. It is a dry and extremely cold area. Ellesmere Island is classified as a desert because of its low annual precipitation—less than four inches.

Above left: The pups' narrow view of the world is seen from inside the den.

Above: The rocky outcropping at the den's entrance has been carved for eons by the winds of the High Arctic.

585

GENRE

An essay expresses an individual's point of view. "To the Top of the World" is a photo essay, in which Jim Brandenburg's respect for and devotion to wolves is shown in his photographs.

SCIENCE

FACT FINDER

WOLF PUPS The gestation period for wolves is approximately nine weeks. The litter, usually of one to eleven pups, is born in a den. At birth the wolf pups weigh about one pound and are blind and deaf. They live on their mother's milk for about three weeks, after which they begin eating meat. When they are two months old, the pups leave the den permanently.

Several days later, I set up a camera about fifty yards from the den and was shooting photographs of the wriggling ball of pups. All seven adults looked in my direction, stretched, howled a few times at the sky, and took off on a hunt. I couldn't believe it! Not one adult stayed behind to bark at me and keep me away from the den. They trusted me with their precious pups. Finally, after all those frustrating years of wolf pursuit, I would be able to get close to an entire pack. And what a family it was!

The pups study the world outside their den.

586

ART CONNECTION

CAMERAS When photographing the wolves, Brandenburg relied on various cameras, including those with 600- and 300-millimeter lenses, that brought the wolves "closer" to him. He was rarely as close to the wolves as the photographs make it appear. Interested students might find out more about camera lenses and how they can shorten distances.

SCIENCE

FACT FINDER

Special hazards exist when photographing in the Arctic: The cold can cause the film to break easily if it is wound too quickly, and the photographer's breath on the viewfinder becomes an instant coating of ice.

LANGUAGE/ COMMUNICATION

FACT FINDER The nose of the wolf is such a distinctive feature that describing it is the sign for *wolf* in American Sign Language: cupping the fingertips of the right hand around the nose, palm in, then bringing the hand out as the fingers are closed.

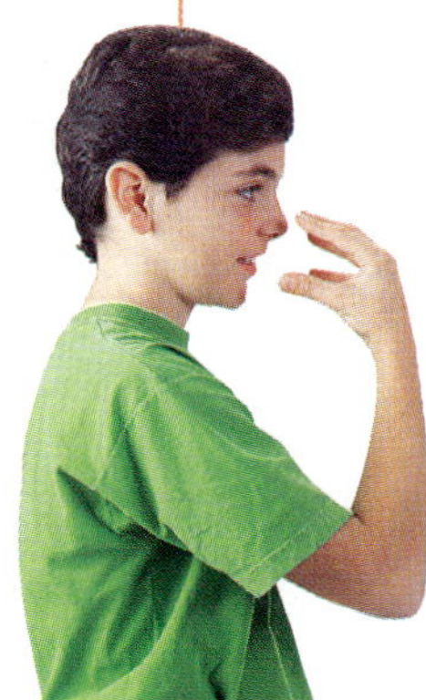

The way adult wolves are constantly caring for the young in their pack is only one of many similarities with human families. Wolves mate for life, and the whole pack functions as an extended family of aunts and uncles, brothers and sisters. They take turns baby-sitting and teaching the pups what they need to know.

Wolves have very individual personalities. Bison and musk-oxen all behave much the same within their herds. Not wolves. It probably has to do with their intelligence and gifts of perception.

At first, however, *my* perceptions were not up to the task of telling the seven wolves in this pack apart. But over the weeks of watching and listening to the wolves, I found myself more and more aware of their differences, like body scars, facial expressions, and coloring.

I also noticed that some of them behaved in dominant ways, bristling and cocky. Others were more submissive, cringing when in the presence of a "superior" and always trying to keep the peace. In other words, a hierarchy became apparent, a ranking of the wolves according to their power in relation to the others.

At the top was the alpha male, Buster. He was usually first to attack on a hunt and the first to eat after a kill. Buster's eyes were extremely expressive. Sometimes they were piercing, threatening. Other times they were amused, haughty, or quizzical. Weighing less than 100 pounds, he was not the largest of the pack. But he stood proudly on thin, long legs, taller than even the largest German shepherd.

The adult wolves are excellent caretakers of their young charges.

588

EXTRA SUPPORT **Explain that when we *perceive* something, we take in information through our senses. Wolves' "gifts of perception," as mentioned in the second paragraph, are their highly developed senses of smell, sight, and hearing.**

STUDENTS ACQUIRING ENGLISH **Use an analogy to explain *hierarchy*—for example, superintendent, principal, assistant principal, teacher, teacher aide, and so on.**

Tested Skill

MINILESSON

REVIEW: COMPREHENSION

Summarizing/ Paraphrasing

INFORMAL ASSESSMENT

Have students reread the first paragraph on page 588 and the caption at the bottom of the page. Ask students how the caption and the paragraph are alike. (Possible response: They both tell that adult wolves care for the young in the pack.)

TEACH/MODEL

Remind students that summarizing and paraphrasing material is a good way to remember what they have read. A summary tells the most important ideas; a paraphrase restates the material in the reader's own words.

PRACTICE/APPLY

Have students paraphrase the third paragraph on page 588 and summarize the fourth paragraph. Encourage students to occasionally check their understanding of what they've read by paraphrasing or summarizing the material.

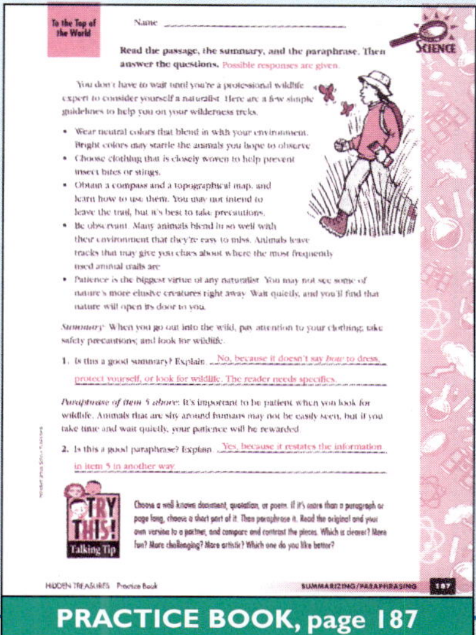

To the Top of the World

Name ______________________

SCIENCE

Read the passage, the summary, and the paraphrase. Then answer the questions. Possible responses are given.

You don't have to wait until you're a professional wildlife expert to consider yourself a naturalist. Here are a few simple guidelines to help you on your wilderness treks.

- Wear neutral colors that blend in with your environment. Bright colors may startle the animals you hope to observe.
- Choose clothing that is closely woven to help prevent insect bites or stings.
- Obtain a compass and a topographical map, and learn how to use them. You may not intend to leave the trail, but it's best to take precautions.
- Be observant. Many animals blend in so well with their environment that they're easy to miss. Animals leave tracks that may give you clues about where the most frequently used animal trails are.
- Patience is the biggest virtue of any naturalist. You may not see some of nature's more elusive creatures right away. Wait quietly, and you'll find that nature will open its door to you.

Summary: When you go out into the wild, pay attention to your clothing; take safety precautions; and look for wildlife.

1. Is this a good summary? Explain. No, because it doesn't say *how* to dress, protect yourself, or look for wildlife. The reader needs specifics.

Paraphrase of item 5 above: It's important to be patient when you look for wildlife. Animals that are shy around humans may not be easily seen, but if you take time and wait quietly, your patience will be rewarded.

2. Is this a good paraphrase? Explain. Yes, because it restates the information in item 5 in another way.

TRY THIS! Talking Tip

Choose a well-known document, quotation, or poem. If it's more than a paragraph or page long, choose a short part of it. Then paraphrase it. Read the original and your own version to a partner, and compare and contrast the pieces. Which is clearer? More fun? More challenging? More artistic? Which one do you like better?

HIDDEN TREASURES Practice Book SUMMARIZING/PARAPHRASING 187

PRACTICE BOOK, page 187

FROM THE AUTHOR

"In late April, the habitat [of Ellesmere Island] is especially surreal. The sun spins around the horizon ascending a dozen degrees at midday and dipping after midnight to confer a kind of kiss upon the ice. The sun's rays here are always diffuse and soft, imbuing the frozen landscape with the out-of-place warmth of candlelight."

—Jim Brandenburg, *White Wolf: Living with an Arctic Legend*

Cooperative Reading

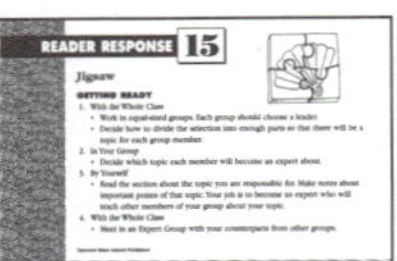
Response Card 15

Encourage students to pause here to review the notes they have taken on their topic so far. When they finish reading the selection, they will form Expert Groups to discuss specific sections.

- **What facts have you learned from your assigned text?**
- **What questions do you have that you will ask others in your Expert Group?**

MULTICULTURAL CONNECTION

Before Europeans settled the New World, the range of the wolf included most of North America. Native Americans lived closely with the wolf and respected the wolf's intelligence and hunting prowess.

QUICKWRITE

Now that students have read various facts about wolves and their behavior, suggest that they write a few sentences about which fact they find most interesting and why.

Nearly his equal was the alpha female. I called her Midback because of a trail of dark fur running down her back. She was probably the most intelligent pack member. It was also clear that she was the *least* pleased to have me around. Midback's quickness and skill made her the best hunter among the pack.

Although scientists say that only the alpha pair has pups each spring, Midback was not the mother of the pups. There is no way to know why this alpha female did not give birth, but she was the most fiercely protective "parent" the pups had. She behaved like a dominant aunt who was often jealous of the pups' mother, whom I called, simply, Mom. Midback often rivaled Mom's authority over the pups.

Scruffy

Mom quickly became one of my favorites. She was a natural mother—gentle, tolerant, and devoted to the pups. Her facial expression can only be described as sweet and serene. And for some reason she seemed to have complete trust in humans. Maybe she simply got used to having me around because she was tied to the den.

The other wolf that could most often be found with the pups was my other favorite. He was an "adolescent" wolf, probably from the previous year's litter. His position in the pack was at the opposite end from the alpha pair—the bottom. I called him Scruffy because he was always a mess. His summer coat was scraggly, with huge balls of hair hanging from virtually every part of his hide.

Mom's serene disposition makes her the most tolerant member of the pack.

591

EXPANDING VOCABULARY

Scruffy, the adolescent male wolf in the pack, was like a human teenager, caught between youth and maturity. Tell students that *adolescent* is from the Latin word *adolescere*, meaning "to grow up or toward." *Adolescent* and *adolescence*, although usually used to refer to humans, can describe anything in a developmental stage.

Strategic Reading

PAGES 580–593 What have you learned so far about wolves and how they live? (Possible response: They live in packs that are like a family. When the puppies are young, the pack's life revolves around caring for them.)

STRATEGIES: SUMMARIZING/CONFIRMING PREDICTIONS

How do the adult wolves communicate messages to the pups without harming them? (Possible response: They knock them down; they also bare their teeth and growl.)

CRITICAL: DRAWING CONCLUSIONS

USING TYPOGRAPHIC CUES

If necessary, model the strategy of using typographic cues:

MODEL **When I read the section heading "Meeting the Family" on page 583, I predicted that I would learn about the different members of the wolf pack, and I have. The heading prepared me for what I was about to read.**

PAGES 594–604
Encourage students to read the chapter heading on page 594 and predict what that chapter will be about. Then have students read the rest of the selection.

There was a kind of goofiness about Scruffy that endeared him to me, especially since he tended to follow me around a lot. He was usually left behind from a hunt, but baby-sitting was the perfect job for him because of his playfulness. It also gave him the chance to act dominantly over somebody, at least when Mom wasn't looking.

It was part of his job to play rough with the pups, knock them down hard enough to make them yelp. Though this kind of bullying may seem cruel, it is a necessary part of the pups' training. They have to learn the importance of knowing one's place in the hierarchy. This arrangement is crucial to the pack's unity and survival. Maintaining that ranking and its strict rules of behavior keeps the peace, avoids continual fights and injuries, maybe even death.

I knew less about the remaining three adults in the pack, mostly because they spent less time at the den site. Left Shoulder, a male named for a three-inch patch of missing fur on his left shoulder, was the largest, whitest wolf in the pack. Despite his size, he was submissive to the point of groveling in the presence of both Buster and Midback. The other two adults had even lower status in the pack, and I never got much of a sense of their personalities.

Many changes in the pack's membership would inevitably follow from one year to the next. But these seven adults and six pups made up the "family" as it existed one particular spring and summer on Ellesmere Island.

At times, the usually playful Scruffy must show his dominance over the pups by exposing his teeth and growling.

592

SCHOOL↔HOME CONNECTION

While the rest of the pack is off on a hunt, Scruffy is left behind to baby-sit the pups. You might want to suggest that students have a discussion about sharing responsibilities in their families.

Left Shoulder shows no sign of favoring the wounded shoulder for which he was named; the wound was probably caused by the horn or hoof of a musk-ox.

593

CROSS-CULTURAL VIEWPOINT

Wolves are not treated well in traditional myths and stories. Have students discuss how wolves are portrayed in such stories as "Red Riding Hood," "The Three Pigs," and even musically in Sergei Prokofiev's *Peter and the Wolf*. Ask students about how wolves are portrayed in stories they know from other countries.

SCIENCE

The musk ox is a large mammal that lives in the Far North and can weigh as much as 900 pounds. Both bulls and cows have horns on their foreheads and divided hooves, which they use to scrape through snow to find food.

Critical Thinking Question

What do you think Jim Brandenburg means when he says that the skull he found gave him "an unusual glimpse into the harsh lives" of the wolves? (Possible response: Up to now, he has seen the gentle side of the wolves' lifestyle. Seeing the results of a fight, and realizing the wolf had lived for a while with such a wound, shows him a more violent side.) CRITICAL: AUTHOR'S CRAFT/ APPRECIATING LANGUAGE

Living as Neighbors

While searching for an ideal campsite, I found a skull embedded in the powdery soil.

The story the skull told of the wolf's amazing survival skills intrigued me. Puncturing the lower jawbone was the tip of a musk-ox horn that had broken off, probably during combat. Bone tissue had grown thick across the point of injury, showing that he had lived for at least several months after the battle. The simple act of chewing must have been terribly painful, but his worn teeth indicated that he was very old when he died.

The discovery of this skull gave me an unusual glimpse into the harsh lives these wolves lead. It also provided a symbolic site on which to stake my own territorial claim for the spring and summer.

594

EXPANDING VOCABULARY

A *glimpse* is a brief and incomplete view of something. The word once meant "a brief flash of light." Ask students how Brandenburg's glimpse into the wolves' harsh lives was like a flash of light.

IDEA BANK

Jim Brandenburg had taken his photographs before he wrote "To the Top of the World." Students might like to start a photo or picture file that they can use for writing ideas or as ideas for independent projects.

Intervention Strategies

SUMMARIZING Ask students to repeat this sentence aloud or to themselves: *When I read, it helps me to think about what's happened so far.* Have students tell how using this strategy might help them understand the information in "To the Top of the World" up to this point.

Critical Thinking Question

Do you agree with Brandenburg when he says that animals have more feelings than we give them credit for? Explain your answer. (Responses will vary.) **CRITICAL: PERSONAL RESPONSE**

This setting was a deep valley about a quarter-mile east of the den. A pair of binoculars allowed me to keep track of the pack's activities. My presence did not seem to affect the wolves in a negative way. They made regular trips to the camp, apparently to satisfy their curiosity. My goal was to blend in, to lie low without trying to hide or trick the wolves. There was, however, one unavoidable exception to this approach. It was my means of transportation, the Suzuki all-terrain vehicle (ATV).

I used this four-wheel buggy to carry my equipment and to keep up with the free-roaming pack. It's nothing for a wolf to travel forty miles at a steady pace of six miles per hour. It would have been impossible to keep up with them on foot.

Most of my time, of course, was spent not on the ATV but loitering within camera range of the den. Since the sun was up twenty-four hours a day at this point, I didn't think—or sleep—in night-and-day patterns. Besides, the wolves did not appear to have any regular sleep patterns either. As with their diet and hunting, wolves take opportunities when and where they can; they seem to know when it makes sense to be asleep and when it makes sense to be awake.

Often I found myself staying up twenty hours or more at a stretch, fearful that if I did fall asleep, the wolves would do something never before documented and I'd miss it. I would grab my sleeping bag and telephoto lens and curl up on the hillside overlooking the den, taking catnaps and every now and then cocking an ear or raising an eyelid toward the activity across the way.

More than once I fell asleep in spite of myself, only to wake to the curious sniffing of a wolf a few yards away. It was satisfying, at these times, to know that the creatures whom I was observing were keeping a similarly watchful eye on me.

A few words here about anthropomorphism, the common practice of giving human characteristics and feelings to nonhumans. Throughout my career—even when I've felt closest to my wild subjects—I've always tried to preserve a boundary between us.

Yet, animals undoubtedly have more feelings than we give them credit for. To ignore this fact, or view their emotional range as smaller, *inferior* to ours, is just as wrong as thinking of them in strictly human terms.

I genuinely believe a magic exists in creatures as perceptive and intelligent as wolves, a magic that we may not be able to observe or measure in any scientific way.

Sometimes, during those days on Ellesmere, I would wonder how the wolves perceived me. Maybe they attributed wolflike feelings to my odd human behaviors. I wouldn't have been surprised.

596

CONVENTIONS OF LANGUAGE

ABBREVIATIONS Point out the abbreviation *ATV* in the first paragraph. Tell students that abbreviations, contractions, and acronyms are all shortened forms of words, phrases, or names. Abbreviations, such as *ATV*, use the first letter or letters of a word or phrase; a contraction, such as *I've*, leaves letters out of the middle; and acronyms, such as *scuba (self-contained underwater breathing apparatus)*, are abbreviations that have become words themselves.

Photograph © by Stephen Durst

The pack completely accepted my presence in their territory.

Exhausted from play sessions, Scruffy and the pups nap; a paw over the nose gives protection from the irritating mosquitoes.

597

Student Self-Assessment

USING TYPOGRAPHIC CUES

Remind students that they should look for typographic cues to help them comprehend what they are reading.

- Are any words written in boldface or italics that I should pay particular attention to?
- Do I see any section headings that allow me to predict what the section will be about?

SCIENCE CONNECTION

SUNLIGHT **At the North Pole, the sun doesn't set from the end of March until the end of September. Challenge students to discover how the tilt of the earth's axis creates this "land of the midnight sun." How great an area of the earth is affected? What happens at the South Pole?**

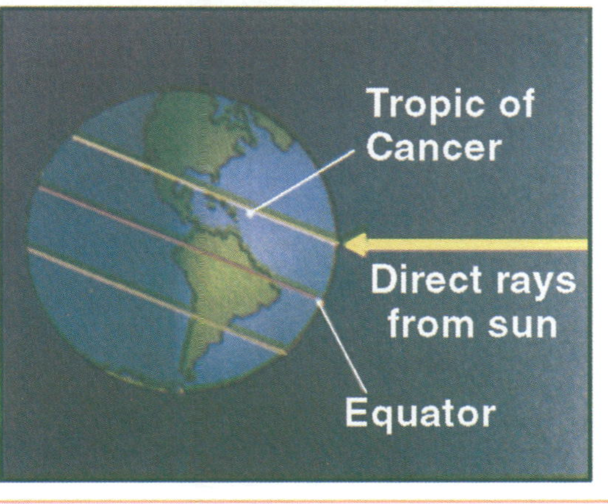

598

VIEWING

This photograph shows the pack during an Arctic blizzard. Note how thick the wolves' coats are and how their whiteness would make them difficult to pick out in a storm. We don't know how close Brandenburg actually was to the wolves, but we do know they trusted him and had no reason to be wary.

During a high Arctic winter, the sun does not appear for four months and temperatures can drop to minus seventy degrees Fahrenheit. Add fierce winds, and you have a climate that seems unsuited to any living creature. But the process of evolution produces characteristics in animals that allow them to adapt to the environment in which they live.

Adaptation

No matter how cold I felt it to be, I never observed a wolf who acted chilled. I suspect that even in the middle of the harshest winter Arctic wolves find a way to keep themselves comfortable. They probably spend much of their time in the position I saw them sleep in—curled up into tight balls with their bushy tails draped protectively over their noses. This position exposes the smallest possible amount of body surface to the cold.

Tested Skill

MINILESSON

REVIEW: GRAMMAR

Prepositions and Prepositional Phrases

INFORMAL ASSESSMENT

Ask students to read the second paragraph on page 584 and identify the prepositions. *(inside, around, for, at, outside)* Then have them identify the objects of *inside* and *at.* (den and them)

TEACH/MODEL

Ask students to name other common prepositions. (Accept reasonable responses.) Then ask how to identify the object of the preposition. (Possible response: It is the noun or pronoun that follows the preposition.) Remind students that a preposition and the words that go with it are together called a prepositional phrase. You may wish to model the thinking:

MODEL **In the second sentence, I see two words that I know are prepositions, *for* and *at.* To find the object of *for*, I look at the words that follow it and find the noun *look.* The only word following *at* is the object pronoun *them*, so I know that *them* is the object of the pronoun *at.***

PRACTICE/APPLY

Have students identify the prepositional phrases in the first sentence of the last paragraph on page 584 and name each preposition and its object or objects. *(of fur—of, fur; after the adults—after, adults; on short, fuzzy legs and oversized paws—on, legs, paws)*

SCIENCE CONNECTION

NATURAL ADAPTATIONS The Arctic wolves are perfectly adapted to their environment, but wolves do live in other places. In fact, they live in more different types of environments than any other animal except humans. To see just how the Arctic wolf has adapted, have students find out about wolves living in other parts of the world.

Critical Thinking Question

Why is it especially important for the wolves to maintain their camouflage during the winter? (Possible response: They may need to eat more during the winter and game may be harder to find. Better camouflage would help them more easily approach game undetected.) CRITICAL: MAKING INFERENCES

Minus 60 degrees Fahrenheit; the orange glow is a product of the low-hanging March sun.

600

SCIENCE

A wolf's winter coat can be as thick as three inches. Its downy undercoat is made up of short, cotton-like hairs, whereas the hairs of the outer coat are much longer. The hairs on the shoulders and back can be as long as five inches, which insures a quick runoff of snow or rain.

REAL-LIFE CONNECTION

Seasonal changes occur in humans as well as in animals. People in northern climates tend to accumulate an extra layer of fat for insulation in winter. Oddly enough, human hair tends to grow faster in the summer than in the winter. Ask students to share their experiences with seasonal changes and their effects.

Since wolves appear to prefer sleeping outside, their winter coats and "leggings" must be superbly insulated. Their legs look twice as thick in winter as they do in summer. And they even grow long hair on the bottoms of their feet, which almost hides their footpads.

As warmer weather approaches, the wolves begin to shed. At one point or another, all the wolves had great gobs of shedding undercoat trailing up to two feet behind them. All summer, I waited for the moment when all the old excess hair would be gone and the wolves would be sleek and smooth. But such a day never came. The next winter's fur started growing in before the last one's could be entirely shaken or scraped free.

This messiness doesn't mean, however, that the wolves did not care about keeping themselves clean. Maintaining their white coats of course, is necessary because it provides their camouflage during the winter. But they displayed individual differences, too, in how well-groomed they kept themselves. Left Shoulder and Scruffy represented the two extremes: The older wolf was always whiter, prettier than the rest, while Scruffy lived up to his nickname.

Buster, the alpha male, was another of the tidier individuals. This trait became evident in one of the most remarkable scenes I have ever witnessed in the animal world. Buster had turned almost black with mud in pursuit of an Arctic hare, but rather than lying down immediately to enjoy his meal, he took a long, careful swim, after which he shook himself dry—all with the dead hare clamped in his jaw. Only then did he sit down to his meal.

Another example of superb adaptation to environment is the wolf's legendary sense of smell. Some scientists have estimated that wolves can smell thousands of times better than humans can. Their snouts are always cocked in the direction of the prevailing breeze because it provides such important information about their world, especially the location of potential prey.

Buster, the alpha male, sniffs a bouquet of Arctic poppies.

NOTES

Here's a place to list ideas or activities that you would like to use the next time you teach this lesson.

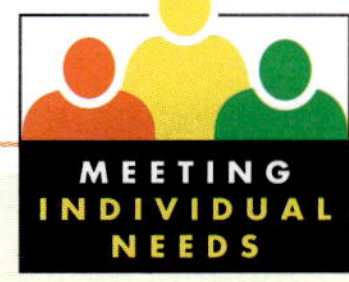

STUDENTS ACQUIRING ENGLISH **Explain that *camouflage* is like a disguise. To provide a visual clue, cut a rabbit shape out of white paper and a frog shape out of green paper. Then hold each shape up against a white background to show which animal blends in. Repeat by holding the shapes against a green background.**

Cooperative Reading

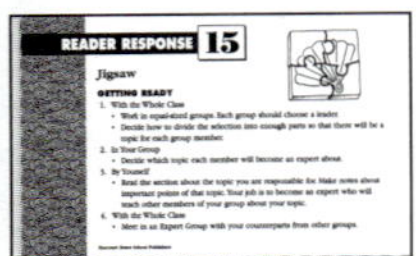

READER RESPONSE 15

Jigsaw

GETTING READY

1. With the Whole Class
   - Work in equal-sized groups. Each group should choose a leader.
   - Decide how to divide the selection into enough parts so that there will be a topic for each group member.
2. In Your Group
   - Decide which topic each member will become an expert about.
3. By Yourself
   - Read the section about the topic you are responsible for. Make notes about important points of that topic. Your job is to become an expert who will teach other members of your group about your topic.
4. With the Whole Class
   - Meet in an Expert Group with your counterparts from other groups.

Response Card 15

After Expert Groups have finished reading, they should teach the other members of their groups about their topics. Have experts summarize their information and emphasize the important points. You might encourage experts to ask questions of their group members to check whether they understand the topic.

Right: Puppies begin to practice howling very early in life; their amusing, high-pitched efforts add to the family songfest.

Below: Midback wakes up ready to hunt and howls to rouse her packmates.

SCIENCE

FACT FINDER

WOLF SOUNDS Besides howling, wolves growl, whine, and bark. Pups growl when playing, but a growl from an adult is a response to a challenge, usually over food. Whines are family noises, uttered in play, greeting, and feeding the pups. A whine is also a sign of anxiety, as when a wolf is penned. A wolf rarely barks and never barks as continually as a domestic dog. The wolf's bark is a quiet *woof* and signals a warning when the wolf is surprised.

Heavy winds, however, seem to annoy them with too much random information, and they avoid hunting altogether on such days.

On one occasion, I followed several of the wolves to a nearby beach where a dead fish had washed up on the shore. It had been dead for some time, and it smelled quite rank. The wolves took turns rolling around on the fish until they all shared in the stench. This behavior seemed odd to me, until they took off on their hunt. Evidently, they were masking their own scent so that a musk-ox or caribou could be reassured that it was only a dead fish stalking it, nothing dangerous.

The wolves' eyesight and hearing are in many ways as impressive as their sense of smell. Once it took me several minutes, *with* my binoculars, to detect an Arctic hare that Buster's eyes had been following for some time.

Their excellent senses allow these animals to do more than just locate prey efficiently. Wolves are probably one of the most social animals outside of the primates. The success of the pack depends strongly on a highly developed system of communication with neighboring packs as well as between individual pack members. Smell, vision, and hearing play crucial roles in such communication.

The most well-known form of communication wolves use is their howl. Howling begins at a very early age. Within weeks after emerging from the den, the pups cock their tiny snouts to the sky right alongside their parents.

I was often able to watch and listen to a songfest by the whole pack. Each had his or her distinctive voice and a preferred range of notes. Midback, for instance, had a high-pitched, almost whiny cry, whereas Left Shoulder would howl in the lower octaves.

A big hunt begins with a howling reveille.

603

Student Self-Assessment

FIX-UP STRATEGY: SELF-QUESTIONING

Ask students what they can do if they are baffled by the reference to the nearby beach. (Possible response: I can stop to ask myself why a beach would be mentioned.) If necessary, model using self-questioning as a fix-up strategy.

I'm confused by the reference to the beach. I ask myself where this selection takes place, and I remember that it's on an island.

SOCIAL STUDIES

FOLLOW-UP REPORT Jim Brandenburg returned to Ellesmere Island a year later and found that the pack had split up. Buster and Midback had left, presumably with some of the pups. This den site was occupied by Mom, who was the new alpha female with a litter of four, and Left Shoulder as the father and alpha male. Scruffy was still there. In another year, the den site had been abandoned altogether.

Strategic Reading

PAGES 594–604 How do the wolves survive their harsh environment? (Possible responses: They have thick coats and keen senses and live in a cooperative pack.)
STRATEGY: SUMMARIZING/CONFIRMING PREDICTIONS

Returning to the Predictions/Purpose

What new things did you learn about wolves and their lives? Encourage students to discuss whether their purposes for reading were met. STRATEGY: RETURNING TO THE PURPOSE

Appreciating the Literature

What did you find most interesting about the selection? Why? (Responses will vary.)

Whatever their preferred notes, however, one thing was certain. Every wolf avoided hitting the same note as any of its packmates. When this happened by accident, one of the voices would frantically shuffle about until discord could be achieved once again. This phenomenon apparently has evolved to suit the scattered distribution of the Arctic wolves across an unfriendly environment, not always in safe numbers. With as many different tones as possible in its howling, a pack can give the impression of greater size and can intimidate possible intruders. I know I have been fooled by a distant pack's howls, estimating its size to be double what it turns out to be when I come across its members.

Wolves howl for many reasons beyond signaling their location to other packs. When part of the pack is off hunting, they howl to those left behind, perhaps letting them know their position. Wolves also will howl after a long sleep. Such howling seems to work up the group into enthusiasm for the next hunt, much as a team of athletes will shout in unison before a big game. But whatever practical purposes the wolves' howling might serve, it also seems to be for pleasure.

604

Name ____________ To the Top of the World

A. Complete the K-W-L chart. Fill in the first two columns before you read and the third column after you've read the selection.
Responses will vary

K What I Know	W What I Want to Know	L What I Learned
Wolves are smart.	How do wolves pick a leader?	They probably pick a leader who is very smart and can dominate others.
Wolves live in Alaska.	Where else do wolves live?	Wolves roam over a large territory, but each spring they stay in or near one place. One place they live is on Ellesmere Island.
One wolf is the leader.	Who takes care of the wolf puppies?	All adults in the pack care for pups, but some baby-sit more than others.
Wolves live in packs.	How do wolves behave together?	Wolves have different personalities and show different degrees of leadership, playfulness, and sensitivity. A pack functions as a large extended family.

B. How did reading this selection change your ideas about wolves?
Possible responses: Wolves have a culture all their own. They seem caring, sensitive, fun-loving, and intelligent.

182 SUMMARIZING THE LITERATURE HIDDEN TREASURES Practice Book

PRACTICE BOOK, page 182

SUMMARIZING

K-W-L Chart

Have students summarize the selection by completing their K-W-L charts. Remind them that their completed charts should give an overview of the information in the selection that would help someone who hadn't read it know what it was about. See also *Practice Book* page 182.

K What I Know	W What I Want to Know	L What I Learned
(Wolves are smart.) (Wolves live in packs.) (One wolf is the leader.) (Wolves live in Alaska.)	(How do wolves pick a leader?) (Where else do wolves live?) (Who takes care of the wolf puppies?)	(Wolves have a hierarchy.) (Wolves live on Ellesmere Island.) (All adults in the pack care for pups.)

Jim Brandenburg

Wildlife photographer Jim Brandenburg spent twenty years looking for the perfect place to take pictures. He finally found it on Ellesmere Island, an isolated speck of land north of the Arctic Circle. What Brandenburg discovered on Ellesmere Island was so rare and unusual that no one had ever seen it before. He ended up staying on the island to take the photographs that would eventually go into his book *To the Top of the World.*

Brandenburg is considered one of the finest wildlife photographers. Because of his work on Ellesmere Island, he also became an expert on Arctic wolves.

But don't get the impression that Jim Brandenburg spent the twenty years before he found Ellesmere Island just hanging around. He stayed busy traveling to wild spots all over the world, bringing back pictures of places and animals that most people never see. More than a thousand of his photographs have been published in such magazines as *National Geographic, Life, Newsweek,* and *Smithsonian.*

605

About the Author

After students read page 605, you may wish to discuss the following questions with them:

- **What might be an advantage or disadvantage to traveling with Jim Brandenburg on assignment?** (Possible responses: One advantage would be learning about photography and seeing new places; one disadvantage might be living under harsh conditions.)
- **Why does Jim Brandenburg consider his work with wolves to be such a great achievement?** (Possible response: He holds wildlife in high regard and feels proud to have lived with the wolves while photographing them in their natural habitat.)

Jim Brandenburg worked as a photojournalist on a newspaper after graduating from the University of Minnesota, Duluth, as an art major, and soon began freelancing for *National Geographic* magazine. His assignments have taken him around the globe, to Canada, Scotland, New Zealand, Africa, China, Russia, and Alaska. Of his time spent on Ellesmere Island, he says, "This land of the midnight sun, with its perpetual sunset, is truly a photographer's paradise. But it is a paradise with a price. The air is bitter, with a windchill around minus 80 degrees Fahrenheit, and the snow is so dry and cold it squeaks like Styrofoam under your feet."

Among his distinguished honors, Brandenburg was twice named Magazine Photographer of the Year by the National Press Photographer's Association. His work shows not only an exquisite talent in a visual medium but also a deep commitment to the preservation of wildlife and the environment.

ACTIVITY CHOICES

MAKE A DIAGRAM

BARKING UP A TREE Suggest that students reread the selection as they plan their "family trees." They might want to make notes supporting the order of their hierarchy that they can use during the discussion. ART/LISTENING AND SPEAKING

DESCRIBE A WOLF

PERSONALITY PLUS As a noncompetitive alternative, have students work with partners to explain how one of the wolves would react in certain situations, such as meeting a strange wolf. LISTENING AND SPEAKING

DISCUSS HUMAN BEHAVIOR

A NEW PERSPECTIVE Groups may find that although they—as the wolves—have accepted Brandenburg, they still find him an intrusion. Some groups might want to share their perspectives with the whole class, appointing a Reporter to make the presentation. CRITICAL THINKING/LISTENING AND SPEAKING

MAKE A DIAGRAM

BARKING UP A TREE

Jim Brandenburg noted a hierarchy among the pack of wolves he studied. Make a diagram of a "family tree" of the wolves mentioned in the selection. Compare your diagram with those of your classmates. Discuss any differences.

DESCRIBE A WOLF

PERSONALITY PLUS

Play a game with a partner. Describe the personality of one of the wolves from the selection. Have your partner guess which wolf you are describing. Keep score, awarding one point for each correct guess.

606

STUDENTS ACQUIRING ENGLISH Have students play the Personality Plus game with an English-proficient partner. Suggest that students not keep individual scores, but rather that both students be awarded a point for each correct guess.

DISCUSS HUMAN BEHAVIOR

A NEW PERSPECTIVE

Suppose the selection were written from the perspective of a wolf. What might the wolf think of the presence and behavior of a human? Discuss your thoughts with a small group.

WHAT DO YOU THINK?

- What are the most important ideas you learned about wolves?
- Which wolf is your favorite? Why?
- Do you feel that the author gives the wolves human characteristics? Explain your answer.

CHECKING COMPREHENSION

What Do You Think?

1. **What are the most important ideas you learned about wolves?** (Possible response: Wolves are intelligent and perceptive animals that live in packs similar to families. They are well adapted to their environment, with keen senses and thick coats.) DESCRIPTIVE RESPONSE
2. **Which wolf is your favorite? Why?** (Responses will vary.) PERSONAL RESPONSE
3. **Do you feel that the author gives the wolves human characteristics? Explain your answer.** (Possible response: Yes, because the author gives the wolves names and describes their "personalities.") CHALLENGING THE TEXT

VARYING THE ACTIVITY

For **extra support,** allow students participating in the Personality Plus activity to mimic the behavior of the wolf they chose through pantomime rather than describing it.

Intervention Strategies

TIPS FOR CLASSROOM MANAGEMENT

IF second-language students need additional vocabulary and during-reading strategies to understand "To the Top of the World," **THEN** use *Sheltered English/ESL Manual,* pages 94–97.

IF students had difficulty understanding "To the Top of the World," **THEN** complete the Rereading and Words and Meanings Strategies. See also *Intervention Strategies Manual,* pages 140–145.

REREADING

DETERMINING MAIN IDEA Remind students that "To the Top of the World" is a piece of nonfiction writing. To read nonfiction effectively, students can use the strategy of looking for the main idea of each paragraph. By rereading paragraphs and identifying main ideas, students may better understand the selection as a whole.

Draw on the board a web like the one below:

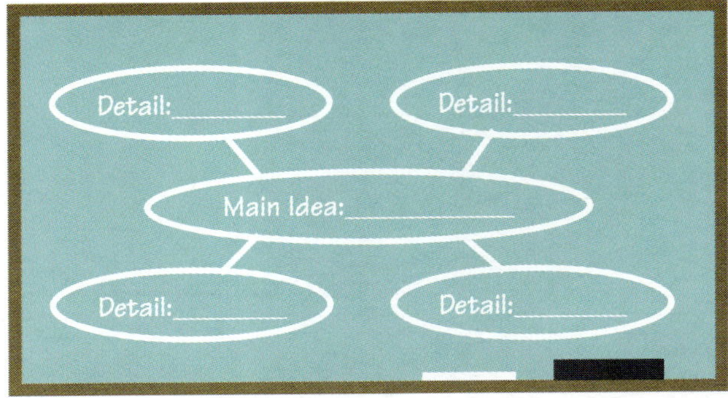

Choose paragraphs from the selection for students to reread. As each one is read aloud, have volunteers go to the board and fill in the web with suggestions from other students.

PERSONAL JOURNAL

What new information did students learn from this selection about wolves? Have them write two or three sentences in their journals about the most interesting facts they learned.

WORDS AND MEANINGS

ANTONYMS Remind students that antonyms are pairs of words with opposite or nearly opposite meanings; for example, *high* and *low, enormous* and *tiny,* or *rapid* and *sluggish.*

Practice with antonyms can help students enlarge their vocabulary and develop more confidence and comprehension in reading.

List a number of words from the selection on the board. (For example, *hungry, cute, precious, differences, threatening, serene, submissive, regular, odd,* and *emerging*) Divide students into two teams. Have team members take turns challenging their opponents to give an antonym for each word on the board.

Write a Diary Entry

Ask students to imagine that they, like Jim Brandenburg, have the assignment of spending several months studying and photographing a species of wild animal. Which species would they choose, and why? What would they hope to learn? Have students write a few sentences to identify and explain their choice as though they were recording a decision in their diaries.

ESL/Title I Reading

DECODING SUPPORT
/f/ ph, gh

Intervention Strategies Manual **pp. 144–145**

Reading Trade Books

ESL/Title I Library

Long Claws

by James Houston

Students will benefit from reading another Arctic adventure. Have students use the diagram below to contrast this fiction book with the nonfiction selection "To the Top of the World."

I know that "To the Top of the World" is nonfiction because

1.____________________

2.____________________

3.____________________

I know that *Long Claws* is fiction because

1.____________________

2.____________________

3.____________________

TAKE-HOME BOOK TO REINFORCE KEY WORDS

Students will enjoy reading a true story about Susan Butcher in this exciting nonfiction book. Students may want to read the book independently in class or take it home to read.

PERSONAL JOURNAL

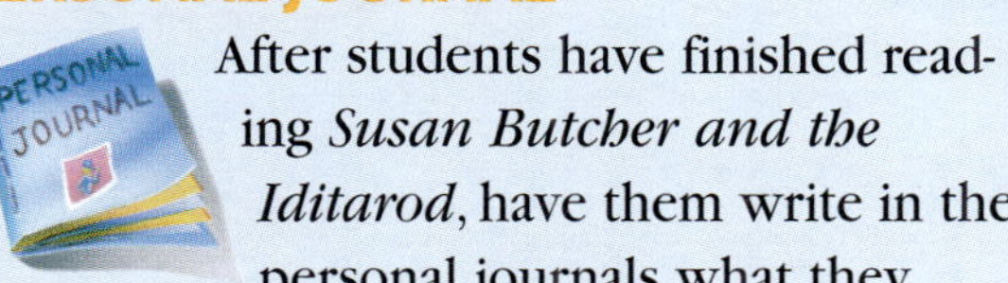

After students have finished reading *Susan Butcher and the Iditarod*, have them write in their personal journals what they learned about this unusual sport.

See also *Intervention Strategies Manual,* page 143.

IDEA BANK

TIPS FOR CLASSROOM MANAGEMENT

IF students had difficulty answering the Strategic Reading question on page T1242, **THEN** they should complete the Retelling activity.

IF students need to focus on speaking and listening strategies, **THEN** they should complete the Oral Language activity.

RETELLING

Interviewing the Experts

COOPERATIVE LEARNING Have students form an even number of small groups, and assign each group the role of Journalists or Wolf Experts. Both groups should prepare for an interview—the Journalists by writing questions to ask the Experts, and the Experts by reviewing the material to ready themselves for the Journalists. Each Expert group could focus on a specific area such as the wolves' keen sense of smell or how they care for their young. During the interview, each Journalist should ask at least one question, and each Expert should answer at least one. LISTENING/SPEAKING/READING/WRITING

Informal Assessment

Note how students use the information from the selection to ask and answer questions.

ORAL LANGUAGE

Debate an Issue

Jim Brandenburg said that the family unit was crucial to the wolves' survival. Have students discuss this statement, and then form two teams. Have each team explore opposing sides for a debate. Students can use information from the selection, from other sources, or from their own experience or beliefs. Remind them to use facts and strong evidence to back up their position. Each team should choose several members to actually debate the issue with the other team, but the entire team should help the presenters prepare. LISTENING/SPEAKING

TIPS FOR LISTENING AND SPEAKING

Remind debaters that persuasive **speakers**

- ☑ use examples or facts to support their opinions.
- ☑ speak clearly and directly to the audience.
- ☑ let teammates complete their presentation before making additional remarks.

Listeners, both in the audience and on the opposing team, should

- ☑ listen to distinguish facts from opinions.
- ☑ evaluate speakers' views to detect bias.

VIEWING

Photographs

Have students review Jim Brandenburg's photographs before focusing a discussion on them. Start the discussion by asking students how they liked the photographs overall, what information they can learn by studying the photographs, and which ones they liked best. Encourage them to explain why a particular photograph is their favorite. Then discuss how the photographs add to the selection: *How would the selection be different if it had been accompanied with drawings or paintings? Why might Brandenburg have included a particular photograph? Which is more important, the text or the photographs?*

LISTENING/SPEAKING/VIEWING

REAL-LIFE RESOURCES

Yellow Pages

READING YELLOW PAGE ADS Ask students where they might look to buy a camera to take wilderness photographs. Point out that Yellow Page advertisements contain useful information about stores. All listings include the name of an establishment, its address, and its telephone number. Write this example on the board and discuss what additional information is included:

> **Sure-Shot Camera Shop**
>
> The best prices and selection in town!
>
> - all major brands
> - repairs
> - new and used cameras
> - video cameras
> - darkroom supplies
>
> M-F 9-7 S-S 10-5
> 278 24th Street
> 555-SNAP

EVALUATING CLAIMS Have students look through local Yellow Page advertisements to find examples of factual statements and opinions. Discuss how you can use these ads to select a store or service. See *Writer's Magazine* pages 92 and 93.

REAL-LIFE CHALLENGE Have students select three Yellow Page advertisements that they feel express opinions and three ads that they feel purely express facts. Have them discuss the similarities and differences between the two sets of ads.

LISTENING/SPEAKING/CRITICAL THINKING

WHO WILL YOU CALL?

If Arctic wolves were pets, they might be taken to a pet groomer for a good wash and a brushing. How would you choose a groomer? You might look in the Yellow Pages. Many companies advertise there. First, you might look in one of the indexes to find your subject faster. Glance at the following indexes and ads from the Yellow Pages.

Pet Mobile Grooming
We Come to You!
All Breeds of Dogs and Cats!
- Custom Clips
- Supplies
- Organic Flea Dips
- Bows
Call for an Appointment 555-PETS

DOGGIEMAT!
WASH YOUR OWN DOG HERE!
Call 555-WASH Today!

Dog-Show-Perfect Grooming
All baths and clips include
- Ear and Nail Care
- Fluff Drying
- Flea Dip
Convenient People Hours
Mon.–Sat. 7 A.M. to 6 P.M.
Call for Appointment
555-DOGS
1230 Greenbriar Blvd.

WRITER'S MAGAZINE, pages 92–93

STUDENTS ACQUIRING ENGLISH

Encourage students to use selection photographs to help in formulating questions or in responding.

EXTRA SUPPORT

Write the Tips for Listening and Speaking on chart paper, and display them in the classroom. Remind students to refer to the tips while they participate in the debate.

WRITER'S WORKSHOP

Research Report

Thinking as Writers

WRITING FORM: Research Report Have students discuss how Jim Brandenburg got the information he needed to write "To the Top of the World." Explain that to write nonfiction, a writer may need to gather information about a topic in several ways:

- through reading books and magazines
- through direct observation and study
- through interviews

Display Transparencies 59A and 59B, and review with students the main parts of a research report.

TRANSPARENCIES 59A/59B

Model: Research Report—Science

A ***science report*** *relies on facts and information from several sources. The writer usually attempts to answer a question.*

How Snakes Slither

a topic that is not too broad Long ago people believed that snakes walked on their ribs. They thought that the ribs acted as if they were several pairs of legs. We know now that this is not true. How then do snakes slither?

specialized words defined and explained Along a snake's belly lie rows of overlapping scutes, or scales. Each scute is attached by muscles to a pair of the snake's ribs. When a scute is pulled back by the muscles, its edge pushes against the ground. When the scute is pushed forward by the muscles, it slides over the ground.

A snake moves the overlapping scutes on its belly in groups. With each movement, some scutes push against the ground, and others slide forward. This allows the snake to move forward in a straight line.

WRITER'S CRAFT: Appropriate Clue Words Explain that when people write to inform, they must signal the reader when they are comparing and contrasting, showing causes and effects, and presenting events in sequence. For example, ask students to find words and phrases on page 591 that signal that the author is comparing and contrasting the members of the pack. (Possible responses: *most intelligent pack member, best hunter, least pleased, most tolerant member of the pack*) Ask students to suggest clue words that signal sequence or cause-effect relationships. (Possible responses: *first, next, then; because, therefore, so*)

PREWRITING AND DRAFTING

Suggest that students choose a science-related topic that interests them. Refer to these strategies to help students begin their research reports.

PREWRITING GRAPHIC ORGANIZER Some students may benefit from using an inverted triangle to narrow their topic.

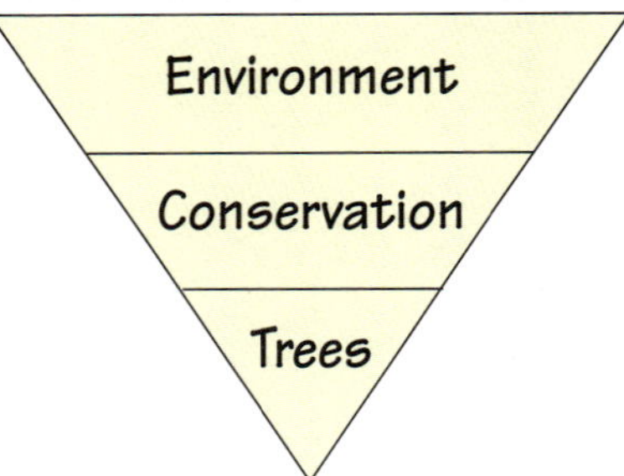

PREWRITING STRATEGY Students who are having difficulty in deciding where to find information on their topics may brainstorm appropriate reference sources with a partner.

DURING-WRITING GRAPHIC ORGANIZER Students who need to organize their information may pause during writing to make outlines.

TIPS FOR CLASSROOM MANAGEMENT

IF students are familiar with the steps for writing a research report, **THEN** have them begin writing, referring to the model on Transparencies 59A and 59B as necessary.

IF you want a short writing activity, **THEN** adapt this lesson by having students use what they learn about the Writer's Craft to revise a research report they have written earlier.

TECHNOLOGY

THE AMAZING WRITING MACHINE Have students enter their research reports using the program. They may want to examine some of the outlines in the Spin mode before they begin planning their reports.

RESPONDING AND REVISING

Have students work in editing circles or with partners to help each other revise. Write this checklist on the board:

- Does your research report have a title?
- Does your research report include an introduction and a conclusion or summary?
- Do the paragraphs present ideas that support the topic?
- Are time-order words, cause-and-effect words, and comparisons used effectively?

PROOFREADING

Offer the following tips as students proofread:

- Check for correct use of **object pronouns in prepositional phrases**. (See Grammar Minilesson on page T1237.)
- Check that **proper nouns** are capitalized.
- Look for words you may have misspelled.

PUBLISHING

If you wish to have students publish their research reports, suggest the following options or have students choose their own methods.

ORAL Students may read aloud their reports in small groups, as if narrating a TV documentary. Encourage students to speak clearly and expressively.

WRITTEN Display completed reports on the bulletin board under the heading *Recent Research.*

EVALUATION BENCHMARKS: RESEARCH REPORT

A research report by a proficient student writer shows the following characteristics:		
FORM	**CRAFT**	**CONVENTIONS**
Demonstrates understanding of the form • clearly defined introduction and conclusion • ideas that support the topic • information presented in logical order	**Uses clear and appropriate language** • time-order words, cause-and-effect words, and comparisons used effectively	**Follows conventions of grammar and usage** • pronouns used correctly in prepositional phrases • proper nouns capitalized

Teacher Assessment As you assess students' writing, refer to the Evaluation Benchmarks chart. For additional information, including model papers, see *Integrated Performance Assessment* Teacher's Edition.

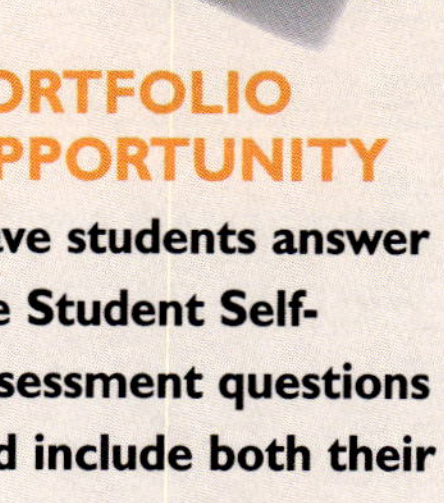

PORTFOLIO OPPORTUNITY

Have students answer the Student Self-Assessment questions and include both their answers and their research reports in their portfolios.

LANGUAGE HANDBOOK

Gathering Ideas and Information, page 15; Organizing Your Writing, pages 18–21; Writing to Inform, pages 60–61; Research Report, pages 74–77; Prepositions, Objects of the Preposition, Prepositional Phrases, pages 164–167, 224–225

Student Self-Assessment ✓

Have students answer the following questions and include the answers in their portfolios:

- What did you like best about your research report?
- What else would you like to learn about the topic of your report?

Tested Skill

GRAMMAR

Adjective and Adverb Phrases

TECHNOLOGY

THE AMAZING WRITING MACHINE Students can use the Journal feature to write their directions and the Wacky Pencil to draw an accompanying map.

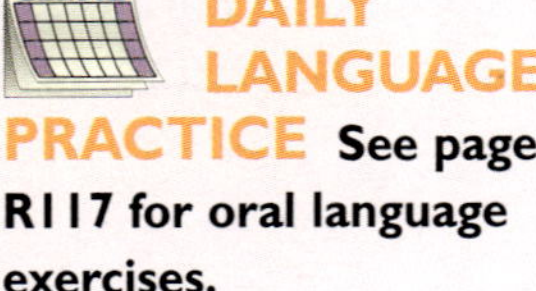

LANGUAGE HANDBOOK

Adjective Phrase, page 166; Adverb Phrase, page 167

DAILY LANGUAGE PRACTICE See page R117 for oral language exercises.

Reading ↔ Writing Connection

Connect to the literature. Write the following sentences on the board:

The wolves in this pack had white fur.

Six pups emerged from the den.

Have a volunteer read each sentence aloud. Ask students to identify and underline the prepositional phrase in each. Then have them say what each one tells. (*In this pack* tells *which* wolves; *from the den* tells *where* the pups emerged from.) Explain that prepositional phrases may tell such information as *what kind, how many*, or *which one* about a noun, and *where, when, how,* or *to what extent* about a verb, an adjective, or an adverb.

Build oral language. Remind students that a prepositional phrase consists of a preposition, its object, and all the words in between. Have students look through the selection to find examples of other prepositional phrases. Ask them to say what each example tells. Then have them make up their own sentences with prepositional phrases and say what each one tells.

Teach/Model

Discuss adjective phrases. Tell students that as they have seen, prepositional phrases can be used to describe, or modify, nouns or pronouns. Explain that prepositional phrases that modify nouns or pronouns are called **adjective phrases**. Ask a volunteer to underline the noun that the prepositional phrase *in this pack* describes. (*wolves*)

Discuss adverb phrases. Tell students that prepositional phrases can also be used to modify a verb, an adjective, or an adverb. Explain that a prepositional phrase used in this way is called an **adverb phrase**.

Ask a volunteer to underline the verb that the prepositional phrase *from the den* modifies. (*emerged*)

Practice/Apply

Check understanding. Write the following sentences on the board. Have students underline the prepositional phrase in each, identify it as an adjective or adverb phrase, and tell what word it describes:

The pups study the world outside their den. (adjective phrase—*world*)

The wolf stood on long, thin legs. (adverb phrase—*stood*)

Scruffy shows his dominance over the pups. (adjective phrase—*dominance*)

Left Shoulder howled in the lower octaves. (adverb phrase—*howled*)

Practice Activities

Coin a Phrase

ORAL APPLICATION Have students form pairs and take turns saying sentences that contain an adjective or adverb phrase. The speaker should tell whether the sentence includes an adjective or adverb phrase, and the listener should tell which word the phrase modifies. **AUDITORY**

Headlines

WRITING APPLICATION Have students look for and copy newspaper headlines containing prepositional phrases. Ask them to underline each prepositional phrase and classify it as either an adjective phrase or an adverb phrase. **VISUAL/KINESTHETIC**

The Write Direction

WRITING APPLICATION Have students write directions for getting from the classroom to another part of the school by using adjective and adverb phrases to make their explanations clear. **VISUAL/KINESTHETIC**

APPLY TO WRITING

You may want students to look for adjective and adverb phrases in their research reports or other writing to be sure they are used effectively.

USAGE TIP Place adjective and adverb phrases close to the words they modify.

MEETING INDIVIDUAL NEEDS

STUDENTS ACQUIRING ENGLISH

Provide students with sample sentences containing adjective and adverb phrases to model. Identify the phrase and what it describes in each.

RETEACH

See page R000 for lessons in multiple modalities.

GRAMMAR PRACTICE BOOK
pages 56–57

PRACTICE BOOK, page 183

Use in conjunction with Daily Language Practice.

5-DAY PLAN	
Day 1 Complete page T1252.	**Day 4** Choose a Practice Activity or *Grammar Practice Book* pages 56–57.
Day 2 Complete a Practice Activity on page T1253.	**Day 5** Complete *Practice Book* page 183.
Day 3 Choose a Practice Activity or *Language Handbook* pages 166–167.	

SPELLING

5-Day Plan

Integrated Spelling Lesson 34: student book, pages 142–145; Teacher's Edition, pages T219-T224.

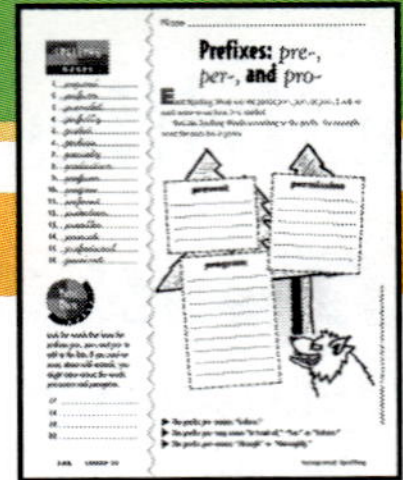
Prefixes: pre-, per-, and pro-

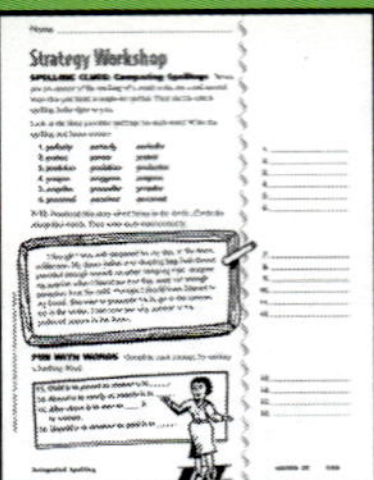
Strategy Workshop

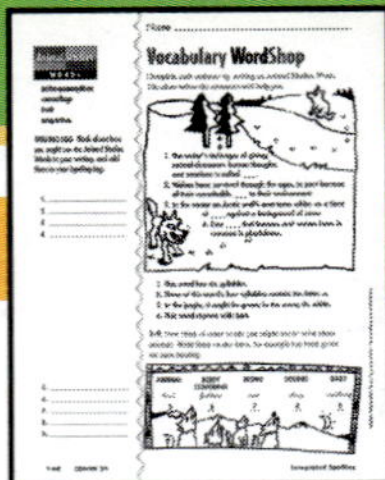
Vocabulary WordShop

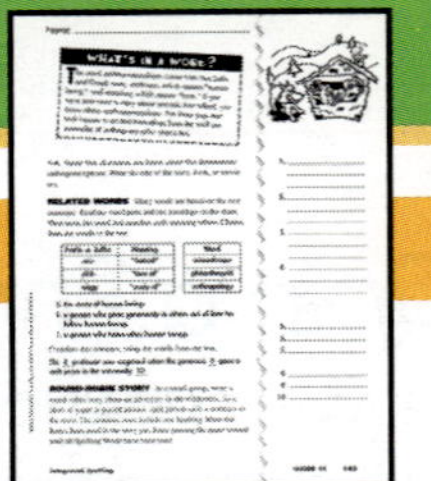

2

SPELLING WORDS

1. prepared
2. perfume
3. provided ★
4. perfectly
5. protest
6. perhaps ★
7. precisely
8. production
9. professor
10. progress
11. preferred ★
12. protection ★
13. propeller
14. persuade
15. professional
16. perceived ★

STUDENT'S PERSONAL WORDS

17.
18.
19.
20.

Additional story words are *perception, perfect, permanent, presence, prevailing, previous, process, produces,* and *protective.*

★ Words appearing in "To the Top of the World"

Prefixes: *pre-, per-,* and *pro-*

Pretest

DAY 1 **Administer the pretest.** Say each word, and then use it in the dictation sentence below. Help students self-check their pretests.

OPEN SORT

DAY 2 **Have students classify words.** Have groups of students classify the Spelling Words according to their similarities. They can sort by vowel sound, number of syllables, or some other criterion. Encourage groups to compare their lists.

CLOSED SORT

Sort by spelling pattern. Write the headings from the chart below on the board, and have volunteers write each Spelling Word under the proper heading. Ask students to name other words they know that begin with the same prefixes and to add these words to their Student's Personal Words lists.

prevent	permission	program
prepared	perfume	provided
precisely	perfectly	protest
preferred	perhaps	production
	persuade	professor
	perceived	progress
		protection
		propeller
		professional

Teach

DAY 3 **Discuss the generalization.** Tell students that one strategy they can use when spelling a word is to say the word aloud and listen to how it sounds. Then write the words *preferred, perhaps,* and *protest* on the board. Explain that words with the prefixes *pre-, per-,* and *pro-* are easy to misspell because they sound so similar. Say the words aloud, emphasizing the difference in pronunciation.

DAY 4 **Apply to writing.** Students should look for words with the prefixes *pre-, per-,* and *pro-* in their research reports or other writings to be sure they are spelled correctly.

Posttest

DAY 5 **Assess students' progress.** The sentences below should be used as the posttest.

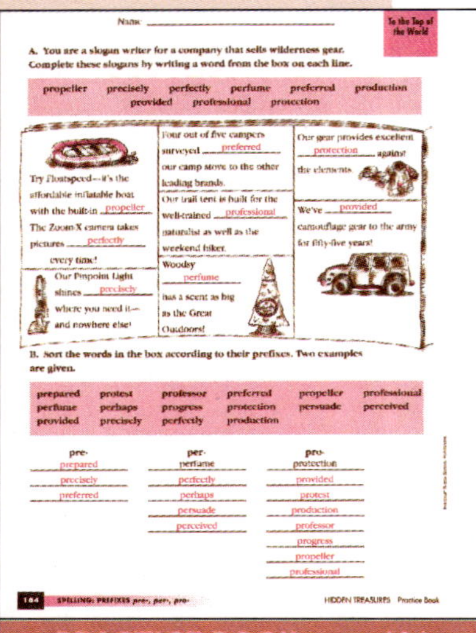
Name ______

To the Top of the World

A. You are a slogan writer for a company that sells wilderness gear. Complete these slogans by writing a word from the box on each line.

propeller precisely perfectly perfume preferred production provided professional protection

Try Floatspeed—it's the affordable inflatable boat with the built-in propeller.

The Zoom-X camera takes pictures perfectly every time!

Our Pinpoint Light shines precisely where you need it—and nowhere else!

Four out of five campers surveyed preferred our camp stove to the other leading brands.

Our trail tent is built for the well-trained professional naturalist as well as the weekend hiker.

Woodsy perfume has a scent as big as the Great Outdoors!

Our gear provides excellent protection against the elements.

We've provided camouflage gear to the army for fifty-five years!

B. Sort the words in the box according to their prefixes. Two examples are given.

prepared protest professor preferred propeller professional perfume perhaps progress protection persuade perceived provided precisely perfectly production

pre-	per-	pro-
prepared	perfume	protection
precisely	perfectly	provided
preferred	perhaps	protest
	persuade	production
	perceived	professor
		progress
		propeller
		professional

184 SPELLING: PREFIXES *pre-, per-, pro-* HIDDEN TREASURES Practice Book

PRACTICE BOOK, page 184

DICTATION SENTENCES

1. Berta is prepared for the test.
2. The perfume smelled like roses.
3. The hillside provided a good view.
4. The shoes fit perfectly.
5. We shook our heads to protest.
6. I thought perhaps they would join us.
7. The train left at precisely one o'clock.
8. The play was a fine production.
9. Dr. Digs is a college professor.
10. The patient is making steady progress.
11. Moose is a wolf's preferred meat.
12. The tree served as protection from the rain.
13. The small plane had one propeller.
14. I'll try to persuade him to come.
15. He is a professional photographer.
16. The hungry cat perceived the defenseless mouse.

VOCABULARY WORKSHOP

Reviewing Key Words

Write the Key Words on the board, and have students use them to complete the following groups of synonyms, either orally or in writing:

1. critical, necessary, *(crucial)*
2. arrogant, proud, *(haughty)*
3. calm, peaceful, *(serene)*
4. different, special, *(distinctive)*

Extending Vocabulary

SPECIALIZED VOCABULARY: SCIENCE WORDS

Tell students that many of the words Jim Brandenburg uses to describe the wolves and their behavior are commonly used words. In the context of science and the study of animal behavior, however, the words have special meanings. Discuss with students the different meanings of the noun *pack*. ("a small package of like items, such as cards"; "a container for carrying things"; "a backpack"; or "a group of wolves or dogs"). Explain that when *pack* refers to wolves, its meaning indicates that the group of wolves has a definite, organized structure.

MAKE A CHART

Have students look for other everyday words in "To the Top of the World" that have specific meanings related to animal behavior and start a chart that compares and contrasts their common and scientific uses. Encourage students to add words from their science textbooks and other reading material.

Science In and Out		
Word	Inside Science	Outside of Science
pack	a group of animals that live together with a definite organization	a group of like items such as cards a backpack

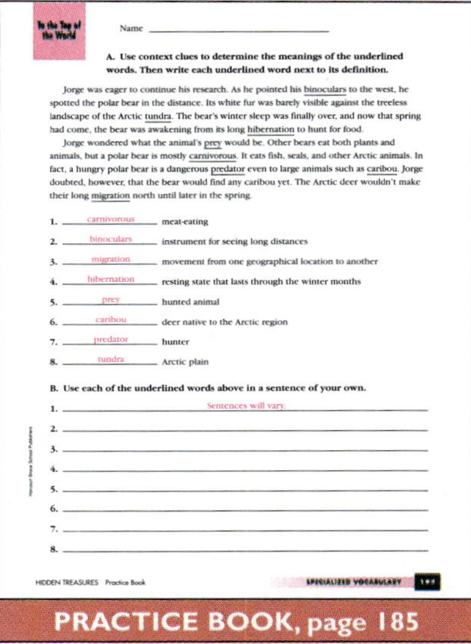

To the Top of the World

Name ____________

A. Use context clues to determine the meanings of the underlined words. Then write each underlined word next to its definition.

Jorge was eager to continue his research. As he pointed his binoculars to the west, he spotted the polar bear in the distance. Its white fur was barely visible against the treeless landscape of the Arctic tundra. The bear's winter sleep was finally over, and now that spring had come, the bear was awakening from its long hibernation to hunt for food.

Jorge wondered what the animal's prey would be. Other bears eat both plants and animals, but a polar bear is mostly carnivorous. It eats fish, seals, and other Arctic animals. In fact, a hungry polar bear is a dangerous predator even to large animals such as caribou. Jorge doubted, however, that the bear would find any caribou yet. The Arctic deer wouldn't make their long migration north until later in the spring.

1. carnivorous meat-eating
2. binoculars instrument for seeing long distances
3. migration movement from one geographical location to another
4. hibernation resting state that lasts through the winter months
5. prey hunted animal
6. caribou deer native to the Arctic region
7. predator hunter
8. tundra Arctic plain

B. Use each of the underlined words above in a sentence of your own.

1. Sentences will vary.
2. ____
3. ____
4. ____
5. ____
6. ____
7. ____
8. ____

HIDDEN TREASURES Practice Book SPECIALIZED VOCABULARY

PRACTICE BOOK, page 185

INTRODUCE: STUDY SKILLS

Test-Taking Strategies

OBJECTIVE: To learn test-taking strategies in order to improve performance on tests

Informal Assessment ✓

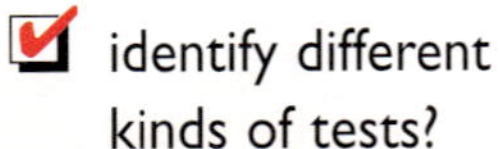

Are students able to

- ☑ identify different kinds of tests?
- ☑ identify strategies to use when taking different tests?

Teach/Model

Return to the literature. Remind students that Jim Brandenburg decided where his permanent campsite on Ellesmere Island should be by using a wait-and-see strategy. Tell students that knowing what strategies to use for different kinds of tests can influence the outcome—just as Brandenburg's strategy did. (The wolves did not seem to mind his presence.)

Model identifying kinds of tests. Explain that there are different strategies for taking different kinds of tests and that knowing which strategy to use in a given situation will help them improve their test performances. Model identifying kinds of tests:

MODEL

When I first get a test, I look to see how the questions are worded: Do they ask for a written answer? Are they true-false? Are there several answer choices that I select from? I also check how many questions there are and how much time I have so I can pace myself and not spend too much time on a single question.

Practice/Apply

Have students demonstrate understanding. Display Transparency 60, and have volunteers read each strategy aloud. Discuss the purpose of each strategy and what kind (or kinds) of tests it would be useful for.

TRANSPARENCY 60

Test-Taking Strategies

1. Find and use key words in the question.
2. Eliminate wrong or silly answers immediately.
3. Check back to the paragraph or story.
4. If a question has a word you don't know, use the words you do know to figure out its meaning.
5. Read the test questions and answer choices first, and then skim the text selection for the right answer.
6. Recognize and use the signal question words *who, what, when, where, why, how,* and *which (one).*
7. Read the question, write down the answer you think is right, and compare it with the answers given.

Have students work in small groups and take turns answering questions, such as: *Suppose you had ten questions to answer in thirty minutes. What is the most time you should spend on each question?* (three minutes); *Which questions should you work on first?* (the easiest ones)

Practice Activities

Public Service Announcements

COOPERATIVE LEARNING Have students work in pairs or small groups to write and produce a public service announcement about taking tests. Suggest that each group choose a different form for their presentation, such as a radio or television spot, a poster, a straightforward presentation, or a funny song. Allow students to refer to the test-taking advice on Transparency 60. When they're ready, have students share their public service announcements with the rest of the class. VISUAL/AUDITORY/KINESTHETIC

Taking Tests

PERFORMANCE ASSESSMENT Have students work in small groups to come up with two true-false and two multiple-choice test items based on the selection. When they are finished, suggest that groups exchange papers and take each other's tests. Afterward, they can discuss which test-taking strategies they used. VISUAL/AUDITORY/KINESTHETIC

STUDENTS ACQUIRING ENGLISH

Have students discuss which strategies they will use before taking their next test.

RETEACH

See page R111 for lessons in multiple modalities.

CHALLENGE

Encourage students to use the strategies on the next test they take in another subject. Afterward, discuss with them the strategies they used and how they helped.

Reading Trade Books TO REINFORCE TEST-TAKING STRATEGIES

How to Be School Smart: Secrets of Successful Schoolwork by Elizabeth James and Carol Barkin. Lothrop, Lee & Shepard, 1988. EASY

Making the Grades: How You Can Achieve Greater Success with Less Stress in School and Beyond by Frederick Hageman. Rising Crescent, 1995. CHALLENGING

School Power: Strategies for Succeeding in School by Jeanne M. Schumm and Marguerite Radencich. Free Spirit, 1992. AVERAGE

Integrated Curriculum

SCIENCE

Climate and Weather

Once, most people were as directly exposed to climate and weather patterns as the wolves are in "To the Top of the World." Today our survival depends little on watching the weather, unless a natural disaster strikes.

TIPS FOR CLASSROOM MANAGEMENT

IF students are artistically inclined, **THEN** they may want to participate in the A Change in Scene activity.

TECHNOLOGY

IMAGINATION EXPRESS, DESTINATION: OCEAN
Students can use the program to create weather and wind direction graphs or to create a climate report.

SCIENCE

Local Patterns

COOPERATIVE LEARNING Have students set up a weather station and monitor the weather each day for a month or more. They can chart the temperature at the beginning and end of the school day, the daily amount of precipitation, and the wind direction by using a compass and a flag on a flagpole or a simple string on a post in an open area. Students can report brief daily descriptions of weather conditions, such as "overcast" or "sunny, hot, and humid." Have students take turns acting as Recorders. A Reporting Team could analyze the month's results and report their findings to the class. **LISTENING/SPEAKING/READING/WRITING**

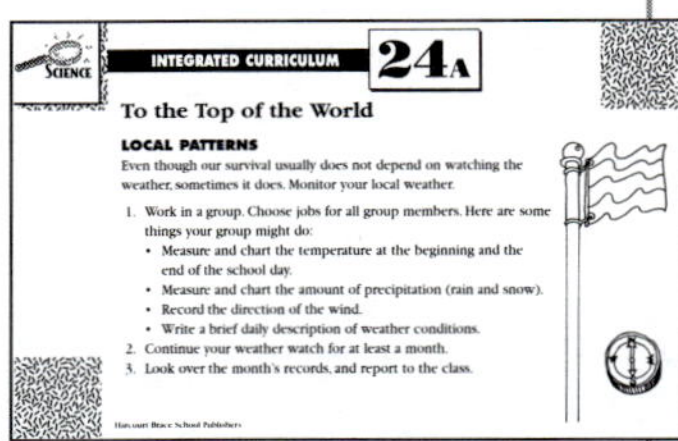
INTEGRATED CURRICULUM 24A
To the Top of the World
LOCAL PATTERNS

Curriculum Card 24A

SOCIAL STUDIES

Different Climates

Use reference sources. Have students use an encyclopedia to find out the difference between *climate* and *weather*. Then invite students to work in pairs or small groups to investigate the climate of some place in the world. Students can use a variety of reference sources to describe how climate influences the kinds of clothing that people wear and the kinds of foods they grow and eat. Students can also find out how climate affects the types of homes people live in, the kinds of transportation they use, and the kinds of plants and animals that live in that area. Invite students to present a climate report to share their findings with the rest of the class. **LISTENING/SPEAKING/READING/WRITING**

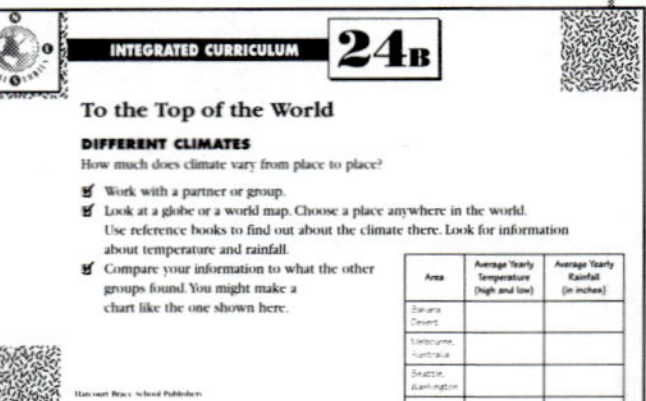
INTEGRATED CURRICULUM 24B
To the Top of the World
DIFFERENT CLIMATES

Curriculum Card 24B

ART

A Change in Scene

Remind students of the photograph showing the wolves in a storm so thick there was no background scenery (pages 598–599). Challenge students to create two drawings or paintings of the same image—one on a clear day, the other during a snowstorm, rainstorm, or in the fog—to compare how weather affects what we see and how things appear. Before they begin, have students review the photographs in "To the Top of the World" and photographs in other books that were taken during different kinds of weather.

Encourage artists to share their finished works with the class and describe how they achieved the differences.

LISTENING/SPEAKING

Reading Trade Books

CROSS-CURRICULAR READING

Arctic Summer **by Downs Matthews. Simon & Schuster, 1993.** **AVERAGE**

Tundra: The Arctic Land **by Bruce Hiscock. Macmillan, 1986.** **EASY**

MULTI-AGE CLASSROOMS

You may wish to group students of different ages and ability levels to complete various activities.

Reading Trade Books

Trade Books That Connect to "To the Top of the World"

The Call of the Wolves

by Jim Murphy
illustrated by Mark Alan Weatherby

This nonfiction book describes the social life of a pack of wolves. After students read, encourage them to compare these wolves with the pack that Jim Brandenburg observed in "To the Top of the World."

My Life with the Chimpanzees

by Jane Goodall

Students can evaluate strategies for observing wildlife by comparing Goodall's methods for getting to know a group of chimpanzees with Brandenburg's experiences with wolves. Encourage students to create step-by-step lists that show each researcher's methods.

Wildlife Rescue: The Work of Dr. Kathleen Ramsay

by Jennifer Owings Dewey

After reading about Dr. Ramsay's efforts to save endangered wildlife, students might want to write letters to local or national politicians presenting their opinions about wildlife conservation programs. Encourage them to use facts from their reading to support their opinions.

TIPS FOR CLASSROOM MANAGEMENT

SMALL-GROUP READING Suggest that groups of three students work together to read one of the nonfiction books. Assign these roles to group members: Reader, Recorder, and Summarizer. Students might take turns looking up unfamiliar terms in a dictionary. Readers might change roles after each chapter.

STUDENTS REQUIRING EXTRA SUPPORT

Suggest that partners work together to read *My Life with the Chimpanzees.* To set a goal for reading, suggest that students read to find similarities between chimpanzees and wolves.

The Wolfling

by Sterling North
illustrated by John Schoenherr

This novel tells about a 19th-century boy who befriends a wolf. He also meets Thure Kumlien, who was a Swedish-American naturalist. After students read, suggest that they consider whether Kumlien would enjoy reading "To the Top of the World." Ask students to write a review of the selection from Kumlien's point of view.

Wolves

by Seymour Simon

Students can compare the information about wolves presented in this book with the facts in "To the Top of the World." After students read, ask them to list ten words that best describe Arctic wolves. Encourage students to compare their lists.

A World Full of Animals: The Roger Caras Story

by Roger Caras

This autobiography describes how Caras was inspired to become a naturalist. Since Caras stresses the small but vital ways in which everyone can be a naturalist, students might respond by making a list of three things they will do to support or find out more about our environment.

CHALLENGE

Have students locate another book that ties to the Confronting Nature theme and reflects the message of "To the Top of the World." Allow each student to decide how to share with the class what they read. Interested students might also prepare speeches, posters, or other projects to share with students from other classes.

Trade Books

THEME PROJECT CHECKPOINT 4

Tape-Record "Travelogues"

SELECTION CONNECTION

Jim Brandenburg's photography in "To the Top of the World" provides a look at what life is like in the Arctic. Ask students to describe the challenges—and advantages—of creating a "travelogue" in audio form, without visual support.

PROJECT CHECKLIST

During this stage, students should

 assign expedition roles for teammates.
 brainstorm sound effects that could heighten interest.
 develop two different endings.
- tape-record their travelogues

Project Card 35 can be found as a copying master on page R126.

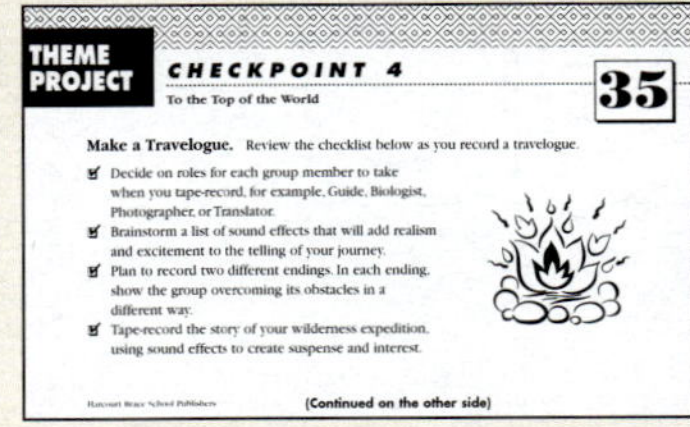

THEME PROJECT

CHECKPOINT 4

To the Top of the World

35

Make a Travelogue. Review the checklist below as you record a travelogue.

- Decide on roles for each group member to take when you tape-record, for example, Guide, Biologist, Photographer, or Translator.
- Brainstorm a list of sound effects that will add realism and excitement to the telling of your journey.
- Plan to record two different endings. In each ending, show the group overcoming its obstacles in a different way.
- Tape-record the story of your wilderness expedition, using sound effects to create suspense and interest.

Harcourt Brace School Publishers (Continued on the other side)

Project Card 35

RESEARCH AND PLANNING TIPS

As students develop their travelogues, suggest that they

- discuss a procedure to assign roles.
- use different group members to develop each outcome.
- sufficiently rehearse travelogues before recording them.

Have students write about their experience in their project journals. Ask them to describe how they resolved group conflicts about how to meet the challenges of the expedition.

Informal Assessment

As students complete this checkpoint, they will **evaluate** the effectiveness of various sound effects and develop two endings for a storyline. Students are thinking critically if they

 are able to select appropriate sound effects for the recordings.
 are able to develop two plausible outcomes for the plot complications.

MEETING INDIVIDUAL NEEDS

STUDENTS ACQUIRING ENGLISH

To provide positive reinforcement of students' bilingual abilities, suggest that groups assign these students the role of the expedition's translator.

MULTIPLE INTELLIGENCES

Encourage students with musical/rhythmic intelligence to contribute to the creation of sound effects.

TECHNOLOGY

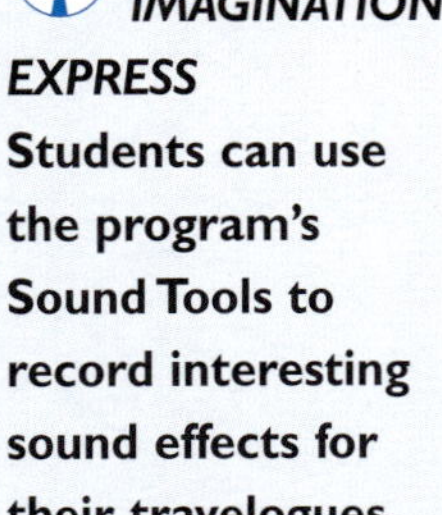

IMAGINATION EXPRESS

Students can use the program's Sound Tools to record interesting sound effects for their travelogues.

THEME WRAP-UP

Some of the people in this theme choose to confront nature; others have no choice but to survive as best they can. Do you think that you would have taken the risks that the people in these selections did? Explain your answer.

If Miyax had the opportunity to share some of her knowledge about wolves with author Jim Brandenburg, what do you think she would tell him?

ACTIVITY CORNER

Picture yourself confronting nature either in one of the settings in this theme or in a setting of your own. Tape record a radio message you would send out to rescuers giving details of your situation and telling what you are doing to survive it.

608

THEME 6 Wrap-Up

1. **Some of the people in this theme choose to confront nature; others have no choice but to survive as best they can. Do you think that you would have taken the risks that the people in these selections did? Explain your answer.** (Responses will vary.) CRITICAL: SYNTHESIZING

2. **If Miyax had the opportunity to share some of her knowledge about wolves with author Jim Brandenburg, what do you think she would tell him?** (Possible response: She might have helped him tell the wolves apart in the beginning and given him details that explain how wolves communicate.) CRITICAL: IDENTIFYING WITH CHARACTERS/ SPECULATING

ACTIVITY CORNER Suggest that students begin by making notes about their situation and how it came about. Some might even find it helpful to draw a picture illustrating the situation or to write a journal entry describing it. Scout handbooks are good resources for information about surviving in the wilderness.

THEME PROJECT PRESENTATIONS

Options

ADVENTURERS' FORUM

- Turn the classroom into an adventurers' club by having groups play their tapes to the class to share their exploits.
- Following each presentation, invite the class to vote on the ending they prefer and then to discuss why they chose it.
- Encourage other groups to suggest alternate endings and different solutions to problems and to make general comments on the tape recordings.

ADVENTURE SERIAL

- Invite students to think of a title for the collection of travelogues, such as *Journey to the Unknown.*
- Offer the tapes to the school as an adventure series that classes can hear over the PA system.
- Each week, schedule a different segment of the series to be played over the PA system. If the series is popular, encourage ambitious groups to create more wilderness expedition adventures.

SCHOOL↔HOME CONNECTION

Have students plan a Wilderness Party to play their tapes and explain their projects to family members and friends. Students can make invitations for their guests, using the adults' first language if possible.

Community Connections

Discovering that their fantasy expeditions have genuine entertainment value, students will want to share their product with the community in a positive way. A prime audience could be patients in hospitals and residents of nursing homes. The following suggestions are ways for students to reach out and make the connection happen:

- Have students compile a mailing list of institutions to which they would like to offer tapes.
- Have each group write a synopsis of its travelogue.
- Compose a cover letter to be included with the synopses, and mail them to each institution's librarian or director.
- Arrange for groups to visit and interact with people who have enjoyed listening to the tapes at the institutions.

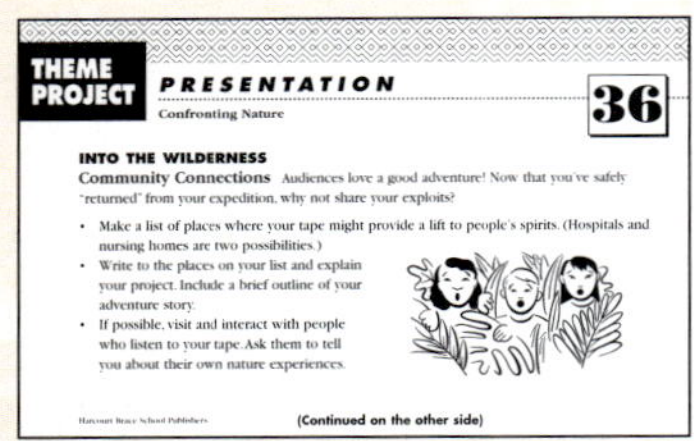
THEME PROJECT
PRESENTATION
Confronting Nature
36

INTO THE WILDERNESS

Community Connections Audiences love a good adventure! Now that you've safely "returned" from your expedition, why not share your exploits?

- Make a list of places where your tape might provide a lift to people's spirits. (Hospitals and nursing homes are two possibilities.)
- Write to the places on your list and explain your project. Include a brief outline of your adventure story.
- If possible, visit and interact with people who listen to your tape. Ask them to tell you about their own nature experiences.

Harcourt Brace School Publishers (Continued on the other side)

Project Card 36

Project Card 36 can be found as a copying master on page R127.

THEME PROJECT ASSESSMENT

SELF-ASSESSMENT

To assess students' perception of their own performance during this project, ask them to respond to the following questions orally or in writing:

- Did you actively participate in all phases of the theme project? Explain.
- Describe some of the work you did. What did you enjoy most?
- What did you learn about nature that you didn't already know?

Students may also complete the Student-Assessment Checklist on page T216 in the Teacher's Edition, Volume 1.

PEER ASSESSMENT

To assess their group's effectiveness in working cooperatively during this project, ask students to respond to the following questions orally or in writing:

- How did your group try to make sure everyone had an opportunity to express opinions and ideas about the fantasy expedition?
- Were you surprised by anyone's personal experiences? Explain.

Students may also complete the Peer-Assessment Checklist on page T408 in the Teacher's Edition, Volume 1.

RUBRIC

Performance Goals	Observable Characteristics		
	3	2	1
LAUNCH Consensus on an expedition destination	• listens fully to others and offers many useful suggestions	• listens respectfully to others but gives limited input	• does not listen to others or offers little input
CHECKPOINT 1 Nature journal entries	• observes a wide range of wildlife	• observes some wildlife	• observes little or no wildlife
CHECKPOINT 2 Mission statement	• thoughtfully discusses mission statement	• gives adequate input on mission statement	• offers few or no ideas about mission statement
CHECKPOINT 3 Group story	• suggests many appropriate supplies • identifies problems and imaginative solutions	• suggests some appropriate supplies • identifies some problems and solutions	• suggests few or inappropriate supplies • contributes few or no problems or solutions
CHECKPOINT 4 Travelogue	• suggests and helps create a number of sound effects • imaginatively creates different outcomes for story	• suggests and helps create some sound effects • helps write outcomes	• suggests no or inappropriate sound effects • has difficulty with alternative outcomes
PRESENTATIONS Overall project	• creative and well-organized • strongly motivated • completed on time	• reasonably creative and organized • reasonably motivated • completed in reasonable time	• uncreative and somewhat disorganized • may hinder group efforts • completed late or not at all

Break Time

THE RHYTHM OF THE TIDES

Natural sounds, such as the rhythm of ocean surf, can have a soothing effect. Musicians and recording technicians have created soundtracks for people who are stressed or busy—people who are living out of touch with nature. In music stores or at the library, you will find all sorts of environmental sounds—from odes of the ocean to roarings from the rain forest.

Pick some music that will take you on a vacation anywhere. Follow these tips:

1. Find a quiet, comfortable place where you are not likely to be disturbed. Use headphones to help eliminate outside noise.
2. Sit or lie comfortably. Turn on the music. As you start to listen, breathe deeply and let yourself relax.
3. Use your imagination to visualize the scene that the music suggests to you. Relax and enjoy the view!

APPLES, APPLES, APPLES

Make apple activities a part of your nature study. Apples (always available and versatile) offer connections to science, art, language arts, and math. Here's just a taste:

- Use apples to hone students' observation skills. Have students describe shape, color, texture, smell, and taste, and then compare their observations.
- Combine art and science activities by making apple-head dolls. To make heads, have students peel apples, dip them in a mixture of lemon juice and salt, and hang the apples by the stems. Students observe the dehydration process (over a period of about two weeks) as the apples dry. Suggest that students use pipe cleaners as bodies, and dress the dolls in tissue paper.
- Other activities to explore include reading about apples in literature, discovering the nutrition content of apples, learning about how apples grow, and making a cookbook full of apple recipes.

The Lure of the Sea

Do your students want to know more about traveling the seas? Whet their appetites with some of these facts:

- Scientists don't know how old the oceans are, but they believe oceans did not exist during the first stage of the earth's growth. Some scientists believe oceans began as clouds of vapor that turned into water as the forming earth cooled.
- Much of the earth was covered by oceans at one time in the past, but scientists do not know which land was covered by water and which part of the ocean bottom used to be land.
- Waves in water are caused by an up-and-down movement of water particles. As the bottom of a wave strikes the ocean floor near the beach, the water slows from friction but the top of the wave keeps going, thus "breaking" on the shore.
- The movement of water with the tides is a source of energy. Some people have experimented with harnessing that energy and converting it into electric power.

Close creature Encounters

It has probably happened to you—a child arrives at school with an injured baby bird (or a baby squirrel or rabbit) in a shoe box. Too often, the animal soon dies.

You and your students may someday help save a wild creature's life by taking these measures.

- If you find an injured animal or bird, call a veterinarian or the nearest branch of the Audubon Society or the local animal control office.

Children may find it hard to give up their "find," but they can usually be persuaded if they know that the animal's life is at stake.

- Don't assume that baby animals found alone are abandoned; some species leave their young for long periods.

- Never try to feed an injured animal unless you have been advised how to do so by a professional.

Reading Trade Books
Signatures Library

Life in the Oceans

by Norbert Wu

THEME: NATURE

Confronting Nature

This eye-opening book draws attention to a part of nature that is often overlooked. By considering the animals and plants that live throughout the ocean, students can begin to form their own opinions about the dangers of changing these environments. The ocean can be a dangerous part of nature to confront; but it also needs our protection.

SUMMARY Genre: Nonfiction

This vividly illustrated guide introduces readers to the animals and environments that exist under the surface of the ocean. Readers can gather information from the straightforward text, specific captions, and detailed photographs.

This guide is divided into five main sections. "The Open Ocean" describes many creatures that live in the upper region of the ocean and introduces the concept of the food chain. "Coral Reefs" and "The Kelp Forest" describe the animals and plants that make up these remarkable ecosystems.

"The Deep Ocean" brings readers to the lower reaches of the ocean. These areas have only recently been explored by people, using submersibles and robot cameras. Finally, "The Future" provides a groundwork for students to consider important problems facing oceans today.

ABOUT THE AUTHOR

Norbert Wu is a writer, photographer, and cinematographer whose work has appeared in many magazines, including *National Geographic* and *Omni.* His journeys in search of ocean life have taken him from the Arctic to the Pacific Oceans. His other books include *Beneath the Waves* and *Fish Faces*.

Building Background and Concepts

PRIOR KNOWLEDGE

Describing the Ocean Have students complete a chart categorizing the information they already know about the ocean environment. Encourage volunteers to write words and phrases in the chart and explain their contributions.

OCEANS

ANIMALS	PLANTS	PEOPLE	PROBLEMS
fish sharks whales jellyfish	seaweed	divers sailors treasure hunters	oil spills pollution global warming

STUDENTS ACQUIRING ENGLISH

Instead of writing context sentences, students might benefit from writing simple definition sentences. Suggest that partners work together to write brief, clear definitions of each concept term.

Developing Concept Vocabulary

Students can extend their exploration of words used to describe the ocean by writing a context sentence for each term below. Suggest that students look up the definition of the word and then write a sentence that makes the meaning clear by using context clues.

SPELLING GENERALIZATION

Words with double consonants
Integrated Spelling Lesson 35

Word	Context Sentence
scuba	You need to be a scuba diver in order to explore under water.
trenches	Underwater trenches might look like deep canyons if they were above water.
vastness	The vastness of an ocean makes it impossible to see the whole thing at once.
nutrients	Some sea creatures get all of the nutrients they need by eating plants.
abyss	The abyss was so deep and dark that the diver was afraid to dive into it.

OTHER VOCABULARY IDEAS

AN OCEAN OF WORDS

Create a large classroom board on which students can place cutouts describing interesting words from *Life in the Oceans.* The display might be made of blue cardboard. Suggest that students cut out representative shapes, such as starfish and sharks.

SEA GLOSSARY

Have students collect terms for a miniature dictionary about oceans and ocean life. Encourage them to write each term on a separate card to make alphabetizing easier when all words have been collected. Remind students to include correct spellings, definitions, example sentences, and guide words.

Coral Reefs/Deep Sea Anglerfish

RESPONSE

Celebrating *Life in the Oceans*

FISHY FUNNIES

COMIC BOOK Have students work together to create a nonfiction comic book that will introduce readers to the wide variety of plants and animals that live in the oceans. Encourage students to follow these steps:

- First, make a list of topics you want to illustrate.
- Then choose an organization that makes sense.
- Next, distribute the tasks among researchers, artists, writers, and letterers.
- Create a rough draft before you work on the final version.

Share your comic books with students in your class and in other grades. **READING/WRITING**

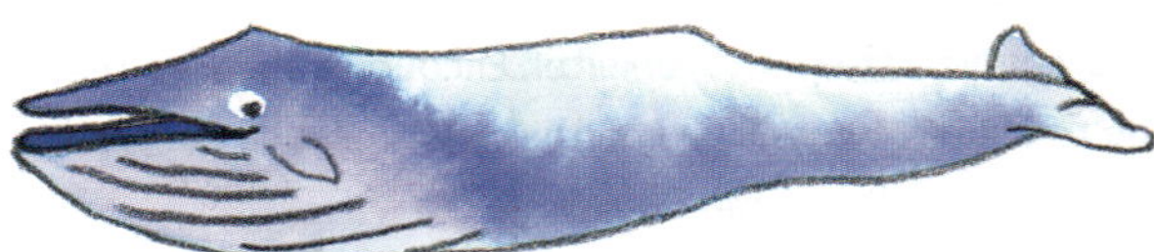

The blue whale can grow almost 100 feet long. But don't worry, it has no teeth!

Stamps Out Sea Lions

DESIGN PROPOSAL Many countries issue commemorative stamps. Ask students to design a set of stamps that commemorate life in the oceans and write a proposal explaining why they think that this is a good idea for a set of stamps. Encourage students to study examples of commemorative stamps in reference sources. Teams might work together to decide on a common theme, such as coral reefs, and then work separately to design individual stamps for the set. Allow students to share their work with the class. **READING/WRITING/VIEWING**

AT LAST AN ATLAS

STUDY SKILLS: USING AN ATLAS Encourage students to use an atlas to find locations mentioned in the text, such as the following:

- the South Pacific
- the Pacific Coast of California
- the southern tip of Florida
- the southern coasts of New Zealand, Australia, and South Africa

After they are familiar with the organization of maps in the atlas, students can play "geography hide-and-seek" by thinking of a location mentioned in the text. Other students ask "yes" or "no" questions based on maps in the atlas to try to find the secret location. **READING/VIEWING**

ACTIVITIES

Signs of Support

PETITION After reading *Life in the Oceans*, many students will be inspired to find out how they can help to protect our ocean ecosystems. Encourage students to contact conservation organizations and identify steps citizens can take. Students can work together to create a class, school, or community petition supporting specific legislation or governmental support for conservation issues. Students can work together to draft a petition, keeping in mind these points:

- Petitions should be short. People usually do not have time to read a long petition.
- Language needs to be very clear, precise, and expressive. Make sure that significant points are stressed.
- The petition should call for specific action. A general plea will not be as effective as a specific demand.

After collecting signatures, students can send copies of the petition to local, state, or national representatives. Share results as a class. **READING/WRITING/LISTENING/SPEAKING**

You Asked For It

SCIENCE Ask each student to write a question about the environments described in *Life in the Oceans.* For example, students might ask:

- How do fish breathe underwater?
- Why are sponges classified as animals instead of plants?
- How are kelp forests and rain forests similar? How are they different?

After students write their questions on separate pieces of paper, place the questions in a box and have each student pick one. They can then write an information paragraph that answers the question. Students might publish questions and answers in a science column of a class or school newspaper. **READING/WRITING**

Life in My Neighborhood

SCHOOL-HOME CONNECTION Suggest that readers take photographs of animals and plants in their community to create a local sequel to *Life in the Oceans.* If students do not have access to cameras, encourage them to draw pictures or use photographs from newspapers and magazines. Remind students to choose a logical organization to help present their information clearly. **WRITING/VIEWING**

Reading Trade Books

Signatures Library

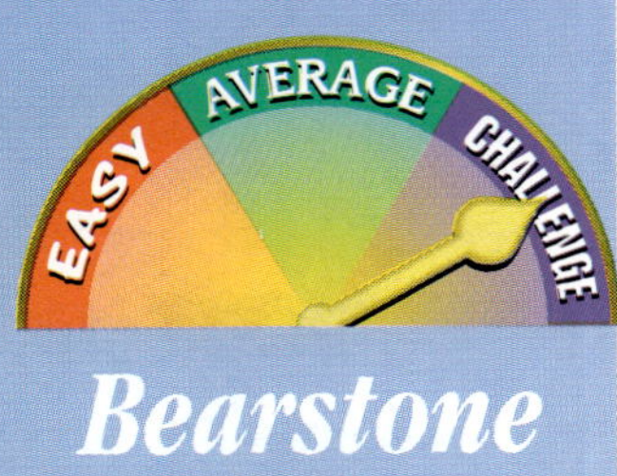

Bearstone

by Will Hobbs

THEME: NATURE

Confronting Nature

Cloyd faces many challenges in the natural world. His rash behavior often leads him into dangerous situations. He hurts his leg badly when he becomes caught in a hailstorm. When he ignores signs of mud, his horse falls and becomes mired. As Cloyd matures, he makes fewer mistakes, showing that his maturity will help him confront challenges in the future.

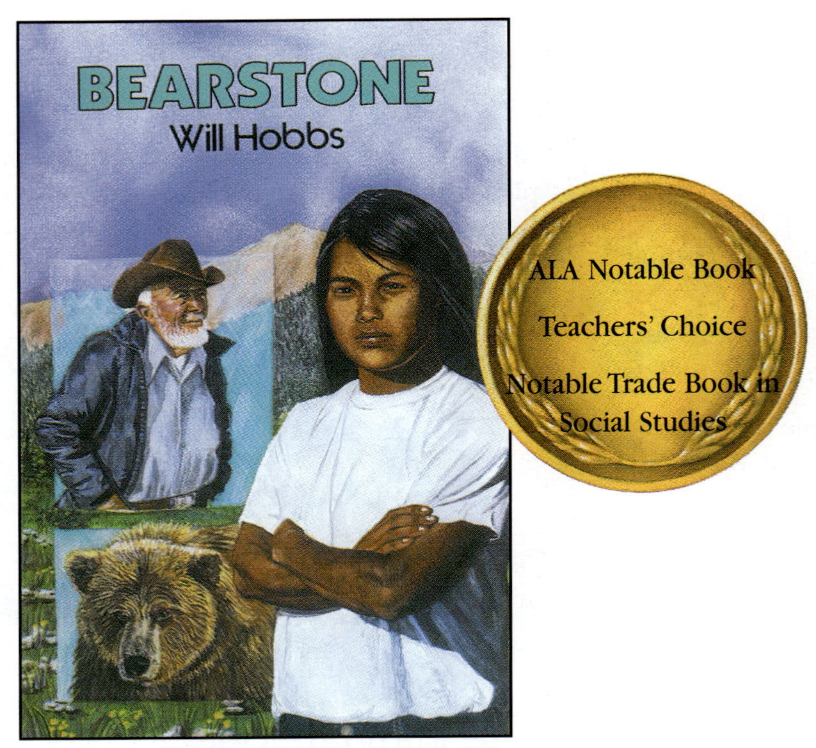

SUMMARY Genre: Realistic Fiction

Cloyd, a Native American boy, has had a difficult childhood. Without parents or schooling, he has spent four years almost alone and wild in the canyons of Utah. As the novel begins, he is sent to Colorado to live for the summer with Walter Landis, an elderly rancher who has also lived alone for many years.

At first, Cloyd resists Walter's friendship, but the man's kindness and caring start to break through to him. Then Rusty, a bear hunter, visits. Cloyd feels insulted by the man and takes revenge against Walter by cutting down his peach orchard.

Cloyd is sent away, but soon decides to return to Walter, who accepts him back. The bond that has grown between them strengthens as they search for gold in an abandoned mine. Over time, Cloyd learns to fight his own anger and hostility. At the end of the novel, Cloyd is given permission to return to his tribe, but instead returns to Walter, who is now ill and needs his help.

ABOUT THE AUTHOR

Will Hobbs has written several novels that celebrate his love of nature. One source of ideas for *Bearstone* was "a friend's gold mine. My friend, who was the starting point for the old man in the story, was always talking about reopening his mine. I thought his chances were slim in real life; why not have a go at making it happen in a story?"

Building Background and Concepts

PRIOR KNOWLEDGE

Describing Nature Have students locate photographs or maps of Colorado, or use the cover of *Bearstone,* to brainstorm words that might be used to describe the landscape of the novel. Encourage volunteers to add words and phrases to a word tree.

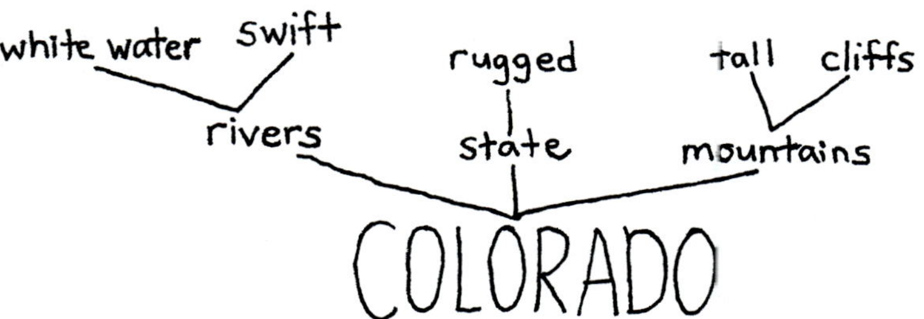

STUDENTS ACQUIRING ENGLISH

Using photographs from encyclopedia sources on Colorado will help students visualize concept vocabulary. Encourage partners to work together to describe each photograph.

SPELLING GENERALIZATION

Words with double consonants

Integrated Spelling Lesson 35

Developing Concept Vocabulary

Have students develop concept vocabulary by creating a word definition map for each term below. Maps should include a quick sketch of the landscape feature being described.

mesa canyon orchard peak summit

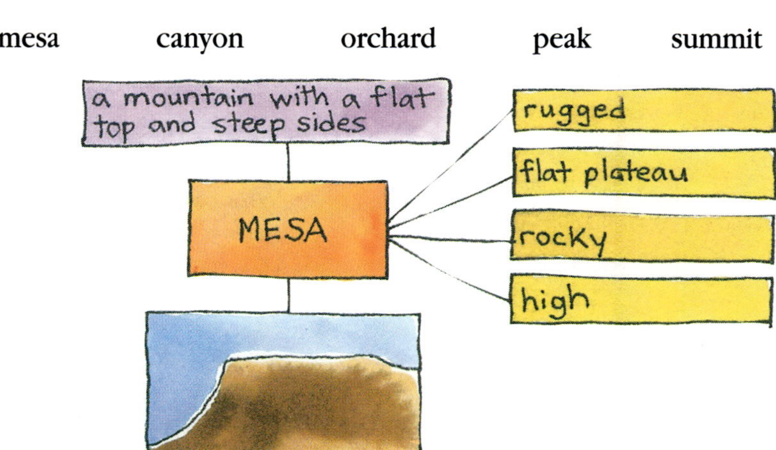

OTHER VOCABULARY IDEAS

KEY WORD STORIES

Have students collect interesting or unfamiliar words in their personal journals as they read. When they have collected five terms, suggest that they take a break to write a paragraph or story that includes all five words.

Max used a posthole digger to begin building a fence. He would put a juniper post into each hole.

ILLUSTRATED FLASH CARDS

Have students select important story words and create illustrated flash cards to help them remember each term. On the front of a card, students can draw an illustration for the term; on the back they can write the term and its definition.

post: a piece of wood set upright to support or mark something

OPTIONS FOR

FLEXIBLE GROUPING

TIPS FOR CLASSROOM MANAGEMENT

IF some students are highly proficient readers **THEN** you may want to have them participate in whole-class activities and then read ahead independently

IF some students have experience with natural sights of the American Southwest **THEN** you may want to have these students act as group leaders to guide small group activities

	SMALL GROUPS	WHOLE CLASS	INDEPENDENT
PREVIEW AND PREDICT	Encourage students to make a **prediction chart** after previewing the book by looking at the front and back jacket. We Predict | What Actually Happens Students can use Reader Response Card 15, Jigsaw, to help them conduct group discussions.	Tell students that this novel takes place in Colorado. Have students locate the state on a map and **discuss** what natural challenges characters might face in that location. COLORADO	Suggest that students begin a **reader's journal** for this book by taking 6 pieces of paper and folding them once. Suggest that they use one page of the journal to write notes about each chapter. Reading Bearstone by Joseph McGill
CHAPTERS 1-3	Have students begin a **word web** around the term *bearstone*. Encourage them to add to the web as they find out more about what the stone means to Cloyd. Native American; carved; turquoise; What It Looks Like; BEARSTONE; What It Represents; age; wisdom; nature	Have students create a **story map** that shows the events that took place before the novel begins. Encourage volunteers to suggest events; then work as a class to place them in chronological order. Cloyd causes trouble among his tribe. → He is sent to live in a group home. → He is sent to live with Walter Landis.	Encourage readers to **quickwrite** their feelings about the conflicts established in the novel so far. They can answer these questions: • What conflict does Cloyd face? • How does his personality influence his situation? QUICKWRITE
CHAPTERS 4-8	Have students make a **list of advice** that they might give to Walter about how to deal with Cloyd.	Have students begin a **character chart** to analyze the characters of Cloyd and Walter. Volunteers can add words and phrases to the chart as they summarize events from this section.	Readers can **create sketches or illustrations** for important scenes from this section. Allow them to display their artwork in the class. Have viewers determine which scenes are shown.

	Cloyd	Walter
personality		
appearance		
habits		
strengths		

READING

FLEXIBLE GROUPING

	SMALL GROUPS	WHOLE CLASS	INDEPENDENT
CHAPTERS 9-13	Students can develop **critical thinking** skills by thinking about Walter's decision to take Cloyd back after he destroys the peach orchard. • Why do you think Walter decides to forgive Cloyd? • Do you think Walter makes the right choice?	Students can use **cause and effect diagrams** to analyze important events in this section. These charts can also help readers understand character motivations. Cause → Event → Effect	Have students imagine that Cloyd and Walter kept personal journals. Have them write one entry from each character's **point of view**. Both entries might describe the same story event.
CHAPTERS 14-17	If students began a prediction chart earlier, they can now add what has happened so far. If students did not create a chart, ask them to **evaluate their expectations** by asking themselves "Is this what I thought would happen?" Encourage students to make new predictions.	Have students **analyze the symbol** of the bearstone in a class discussion. Ask: • What does the bearstone represent to Cloyd? • Why are bears important to Cloyd? • How do some of the other characters view bears?	Suggest that students **create imaginary maps** showing the route Cloyd and Walter travel to Walter's mine. Encourage them to annotate maps with specific story events.
CHAPTERS 18-22	Suggest that group members **retell** the events that lead up to Cloyd's decision to go back to live with Walter. Students can use Reader Response Card 15, Jigsaw, to help them conduct group discussions.	Have students use a **comparison chart** to list the ways that Cloyd changes during the novel. Focus discussion on new abilities and strengths that Cloyd develops.	Have students put themselves in Cloyd's place and think about his final decision. Suggest that they write **lists of reasons** that show how he made his choice.

PERSONAL RESPONSE 

- **Do you think that this novel is believable? Why or why not?**
- **Would you like to see a movie based on this novel?** 

RESPONSE

Celebrating *Bearstone*

MY ICON

UNDERSTANDING SYMBOLS Cloyd chooses the bearstone as a personal charm, or amulet. After discussing why this carved bear is so important to Cloyd, students can design their own amulets. Encourage them to draw a sketch of one item that they feel represents something of personal importance. Then ask them to write a paragraph describing the amulet.

If possible, students can create their amulets using clay, wood, or other suitable materials. Prepare a classroom display to house these items. Encourage viewers to think about what values are emphasized by each amulet. **WRITING/VIEWING**

Book Blurbs

COMPREHENSION: SUMMARIZE Have students write summaries of *Bearstone* for a Book Chat column in their school newspaper. Remind them that this is a special purpose for a summary. Talk about

- how much of the plot the summary should reveal.
- which characters should be mentioned.
- which events should be left out of the summary so that readers can be surprised.

After students have written summaries, have them read aloud for the class. Listeners can decide which summary strikes the best balance between describing what the book is like and giving away too much detail. **READING/WRITING**

STAYING ALIVE

HOW-TO GUIDE Readers can prepare survival guides that provide hints and advice for people traveling into the wilderness. Encourage them to begin by considering the difficult situations that Cloyd gets into and suggesting strategies that he could have used to avoid these problems. Then have students work together to decide what other survival tips they should include and what organization would make sense for their guides. Students should consult an expert or reference sources to make sure that all of their advice is helpful and safe. **READING/WRITING**

ACTIVITIES

Colorado, Here I Come

ITINERARY Have students plan a *Bearstone* tour in which they will visit locations that inspired the novel. Students can use maps, travel guides, encyclopedias, and other sources to find specific places they will visit or stay in. As they plan their itineraries, students should think about

- how they will be traveling (bus, bicycle, car, etc.).
- how long they will stay in each location.
- where they will be sleeping (camping out, hotels, motels, etc.).

Students can describe their trips to the class using visual aids to make the route clear. Interested students might also estimate a travel budget. READING/WRITING/VIEWING

Monday: Arrive at Rio Grande Reservation.
Tuesday: Climb Rio Grande Pyramid with guide.
Wednesday: Travel by bus to Ute Mountain Indian Reservation.

What Do You Know About the Utes?

SOCIAL STUDIES Students can use reference sources to find out more about the Ute Indians. Encourage teams to work together to create reports about this tribe's culture, history, and present situation. Students might also be interested in finding out about other Native American tribes and how they live today. Students can share their information by collecting articles and illustrations to create a class book. READING/WRITING/VIEWING

Older and Wiser?

SCHOOL-HOME CONNECTION Cloyd learns many valuable lessons while he lives with Walter. When he accepts Walter's advice and friendship, he starts to benefit from the rancher's wisdom, too. Encourage students to interview someone from another generation. Encourage them to write a list of questions that they would like answered, but remind them to ask follow-up questions in order to get more thorough responses. If possible, students can tape-record their interviews and play back sections for the class. READING/WRITING/LISTENING/SPEAKING/VIEWING

Notes on the Theme

ABOUT THE STUDENT ANTHOLOGY

Reading Trade Books

Signatures Library

Other Theme-Related Books

FAVORITE ACTIVITIES

Your own ideas for customizing the theme:

MATERIALS:

STEPS:

MATERIALS:

STEPS:

MATERIALS:

STEPS:

Notes on the Theme

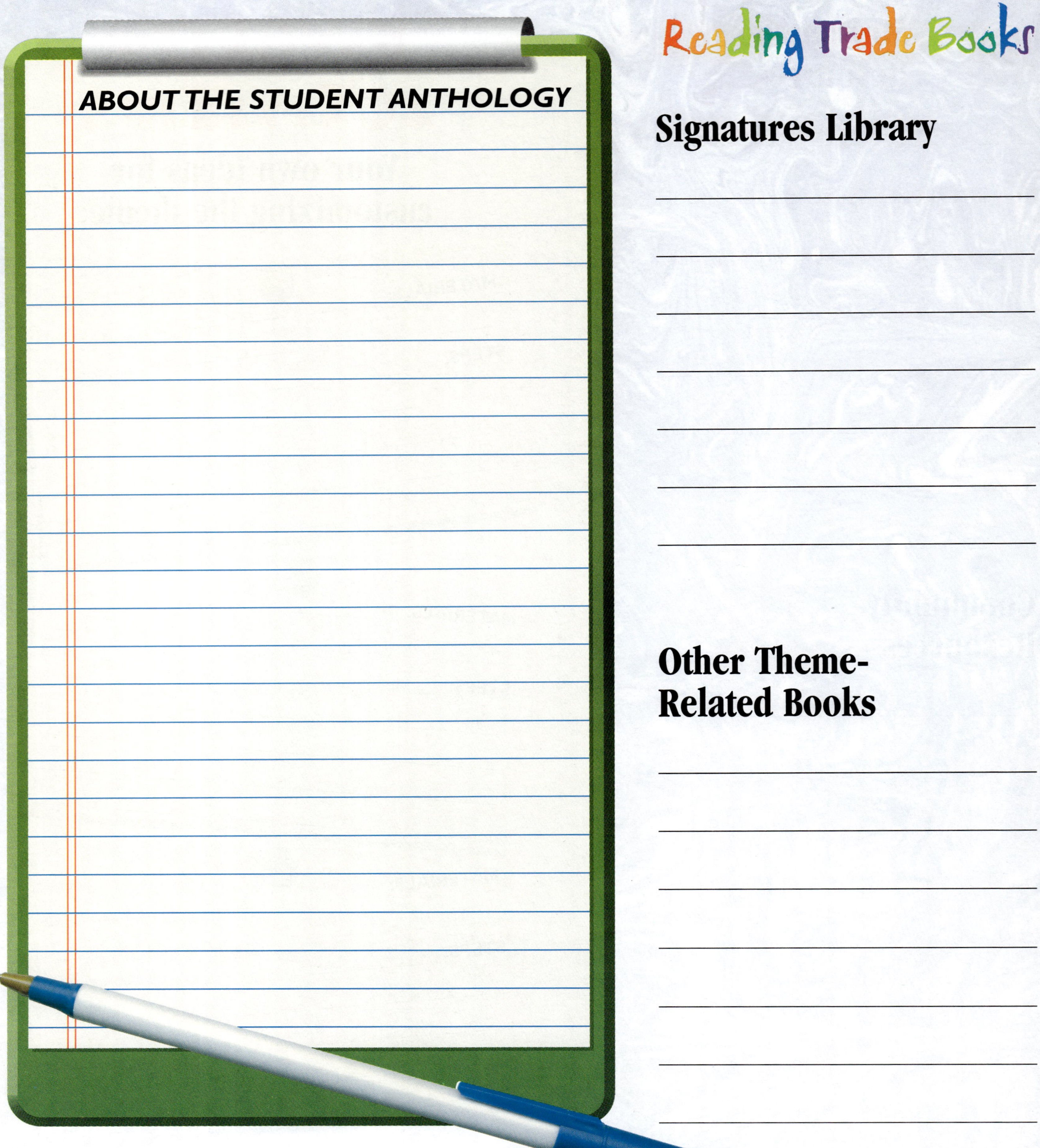

Reading Trade Books

Signatures Library

Other Theme-Related Books

Multimedia Resources

Community Resources

FAVORITE ACTIVITIES

Your own ideas for customizing the theme:

MATERIAL S:

STEPS:

MATERIALS:

STEPS:

MATERIALS:

STEPS:

End-of-Theme Assessment Tools

IF you want to measure a student's mastery of reading and language skills and strategies, **THEN** administer the multiple-choice diagnostic **Skills Assessment.**	**IF** you want information about a student's ability to apply thinking skills in a global and holistic manner, **THEN** administer the **Holistic Reading Assessment.**	**IF** you want a comprehensive view of a student's reading and writing development skills, **THEN** administer the **Integrated Performance Assessment.**

Your Name ______________________ Date ______________

Partner's Name ______________________

Writing Form/Title of Work ______________________

Complete items 1. and 2. with your classmate.

1. The purpose for writing this work is
   - ❏ to describe
   - ❏ to entertain
   - ❏ to inform
   - ❏ to persuade
   - ❏ other purpose

2. The audience for this work is
   - ❏ a friend
   - ❏ the writer
   - ❏ our classmates
   - ❏ a teacher
   - ❏ a family member
   - ❏ other

Finish the rest of the page by yourself.

3. Use this checklist to respond to your classmate's writing.

This writing selection:	**Well Done**	**Needs Work**	**Comments or Suggestions**
met its purpose			
captured and kept my attention			
had an interesting and effective beginning and ending			
was well-organized, clear, and made sense			
had enough details			
used a good choice of words			
was proofread for usage errors, spelling, and punctuation			

4. Tell what you liked best about your classmate's writing selection.

"Critical Friends" Checklist

Resources

Theme 4

Tested Skill

RETEACH: GRAMMAR

Comparing with Adjectives

OBJECTIVES: To understand that adjectives can be used to compare nouns; to use the comparative and superlative forms of adjectives correctly

Focus

Share the following information with students:

> **The *comparative form* of an adjective is used to compare two things. The *superlative form* of an adjective is used to compare three or more things. With most one-syllable adjectives and some two-syllable adjectives, the comparative is formed by adding *-er* and the superlative is formed by adding *-est*. With other two-syllable adjectives and adjectives with three or more syllables, *more* is used to form the comparative and *most* is used to form the superlative.**

Choose a Teaching Model

VISUAL/SPATIAL MODEL Draw three stick figures of different heights on the board.

Write *tall, taller,* and *tallest* under the appropriate stick figures. Then ask volunteers to add details to the stick figures, such as facial expressions and clothing. Invite students to brainstorm more words that can describe the stick figures, and add each one, with its comparative and superlative forms, to the chart. Include examples of comparative and superlative adjectives formed by adding *-er* and *-est* and those formed with *more* and *most* (for example: *happy, happier, happiest; slender, more slender, most slender; warm, warmer, warmest*). Then follow the suggestions in **Summarize/Reinforce.**

AUDITORY MODEL Draw the three stick figures from the Visual/Spatial Model on the board, and describe them for students as *tall, taller,* and *tallest*. Add details to the stick figures, such as facial expressions and clothing. Ask students to suggest other adjectives that could describe the stick figures. Repeat the adjectives they suggest and their comparative and superlative forms. Encourage students to include examples of comparative and superlative adjectives formed by adding *-er* and *-est* and those formed with *more* and *most* (for example: *happy, happier, happiest; slender, more slender, most slender; warm, warmer, warmest*). Then follow the suggestions in **Summarize/ Reinforce.**

KINESTHETIC/TACTILE MODEL Have students create their own versions of the stick figures shown in the Visual/Spatial Model. Help students identify the figures as *tall, taller,* and *tallest,* and have them write each form under the appropriate figure. Have students add details to the figures, such as facial expressions and clothing. Then discuss other adjectives that could be used to describe the stick figures and name the form of the adjective that would be appropriate for each stick figure. Invite students to write some of the adjectives under the appropriate figures. Encourage students to include adjectives that compare by adding *more* and *most*. Then follow the suggestions in **Summarize/Reinforce.**

Summarize/Reinforce

Have students summarize what they have learned. (The comparative form of an adjective is used to compare two things. The superlative form is used to compare three or more things. With most one-syllable adjectives and some two-syllable adjectives, the comparative is formed by adding *-er* and the superlative is formed by adding *-est*. With other two-syllable adjectives and adjectives with three or more syllables, *more* is used to form the comparative and *most* is used to form the superlative.) Reinforce the lesson by having students compose sentences comparing two or three things in the classroom. Remind them to use the comparative form to compare two items and the superlative form to compare three or more items.

Structural Analysis

OBJECTIVE: To analyze words containing Greek and Latin roots, prefixes, and suffixes

Focus

Share the following information with students:

Even the best readers sometimes encounter words that are unfamiliar to them. By using context clues along with what they know about the meanings of prefixes, suffixes, and Greek and Latin roots, readers can often figure out the meanings of unfamiliar words.

Choose a Teaching Model

VISUAL/SPATIAL MODEL Display this chart and the sentences that follow on the board.

Word Part	Origin and Meaning
ad-	prefix meaning "to"
anti-	prefix meaning "against"
mon	from Latin root for "advise, warn"
path	from Greek root for "feeling"
pre-	prefix meaning "before"
sym-	prefix meaning "with"
–tion	from Latin; suffix meaning "process or action of"

The crowd was sympathetic toward Hippomenes.
Atalanta herself felt no antipathy toward him.
She admonished him to give up the race.
She had no premonition that he would win.

Have students read the sentences and review the chart independently. Then ask volunteers to underline the word in each sentence that contains word parts listed in the chart. *(sympathetic, antipathy, admonished, premonition)* Have students use the information in the chart to help them write definitions for the underlined words. Ask volunteers to share their definitions and explain how they used the word parts and context to figure out word meaning. Then follow the suggestions in **Summarize/Reinforce.**

AUDITORY MODEL Display the chart from the Visual/Spatial Model and review it with students. Then ask them to listen carefully as you read the sentences aloud. After you have read each sentence, have a volunteer identify the word in the sentence that contains word parts listed on the chart. Have students explain what they think the word means and discuss how the information on the chart and context helped them figure out the meaning. Then follow the suggestions in **Summarize/Reinforce.**

KINESTHETIC MODEL Distribute copies of the chart from the Visual/Spatial Model. Display the sentences on the board and read each one aloud. After you have read a sentence, underline the target word and invite students to look for context clues that help them figure out the word's meaning. Then ask students to locate the word parts that make up the word and point to them on their charts. Ask a volunteer to tell the meaning of the underlined word and explain how he or she figured it out. Then use the suggestions in **Summarize/Reinforce.**

Summarize/Reinforce

Have students summarize what they learned. (Readers can often use the meanings of Greek and Latin roots, prefixes, and suffixes, along with context clues, to help them determine the meanings of unfamiliar words.) To reinforce the lesson, have students think of other words that have the word parts presented on the chart. Remind students to use the strategies in this lesson when they encounter unfamiliar words in their reading.

Daily Language Practice

Use Daily Language Practice as a quick and easy way to help students sharpen their proofreading skills as they check two or more sentences each day for errors in grammar, usage, mechanics, and spelling.

Daily Language Practice . . .

- is a set of proofreading exercises, one set for each major lesson in *Hidden Treasures.*
- provides practice and reinforcement of language skills presented in each lesson.
- reinforces spelling and vocabulary in the context of sentences.

How to Use Daily Language Practice

1. Each day, write two exercises on the board or on a transparency for students to proofread and correct. Corrected exercises are shown.
2. Have students correct the exercises and explain why each correction is needed.

SENTENCES OF THE DAY

PROOFREADER'S MARKS

≡	Capitalize.		Replace something.
⊙	Add a period.		Transpose.
^	Add a comma.		Spell correctly.
	Add quotation marks.		Indent paragraph.
	Cut something.	/	Make a lowercase letter.

Daily Language Practice

Atalanta's Race

Comparing with adjectives; kinds of adjectives; spelling

1. Ariadne was one of the most cleverest maidens in Crete.

1. Ariadne was one of the cleverest (most clever) maidens in Crete.

2. Her grandfather was a immortel god named Helios.

2. Her grandfather was an immortal god named Helios.

3. One day, a strangir arrived in Crete with the most amazingest goal.

3. One day, a stranger arrived in Crete with the most amazing goal.

4. He planned too slay the most cruelest monster in Crete, the Minotaur.

4. He planned to slay the cruelest monster in Crete, the Minotaur.

5. Ariadne soon bestowed her love on the greek heroe, called Theseus.

5. Ariadne soon bestowed her love on the Greek hero, called Theseus.

6. She had never scene a more bolder man.

6. She had never seen a bolder man.

7. The Minotaur was a half-human, half-bull creature, who lived in a emmpty maze.

7. The Minotaur was a half-human, half-bull creature who lived in an empty maze.

8. Theseus new that he was smartest than the monster.

8. Theseus knew that he was smarter than the monster.

9. Ariadne helped Theseus figyure an way out of the maze.

9. Ariadne helped Theseus figure a way out of the maze.

10. The clamor of the fighting was, the most scariest sound Ariadne had ever heard.

10. The clamor of the fighting was the scariest sound Ariadne had ever heard.

11. After killing the beast, Theseus used Ariadne's string to excape. She implored him to let her travell with his ship, and he happily agreed

11. After killing the beast, Theseus used Ariadne's string to escape. She implored him to let her travel with his ship, and he happily agreed.

12. According to won legend, Theseus later abandoned Ariadne on a island. A more kinder tale says that they became separated by mistake.

12. According to one legend, Theseus later abandoned Ariadne on an island. A kinder tale says that they became separated by mistake.

Key Words are underlined. Spelling Words are printed in red.

Daily Language Practice

Joan Benoit Samuelson

Action and linking verbs; comparing with adjectives; spelling

1. Rae prepares, for her appearence in today's marathon.

1. Rae prepares for her appearance in today's marathon.

2. She are most capable than she has ever been.

2. She is more capable than she has ever been.

3. A marathon is, a race over a distence of 26 miles.

3. A marathon is a race over a distance of 26 miles.

4. Because it is more longer than most races, endurance are a key factor.

4. Because it is longer than most races, endurance is a key factor.

5. Rae understand the importence of good pacing.

5. Rae understands the importance of good pacing.

6. She establish her dominance early by take a fifty-second lead.

6. She establishes her dominance early by taking a fifty-second lead.

7. The runners experiances the rigors of the difficult coarse.

7. The runners experience the rigors of the difficult course.

8. Most runners say the final 6 miles is the most hardest.

8. Most runners say the final 6 miles are the hardest.

9. To complete the race, you need, to push your performence to the brink.

9. To complete the race, you need to push your performance to the brink.

10. The audiance are at the finish line, cheering wildly.

10. The audience is at the finish line, cheering wildly.

11. Rae clears her mind of any incidental worries. She focuses on only the most effectivest strategies. The more harder she concentrates, the more faster she runs.

11. Rae clears her mind of any incidental worries. She focuses on only the most effective strategies. The harder she concentrates, the faster she runs.

12. She cross the line a moment ahead of the next runner. The differance between their times is lesser than one-tenth of one second. Rae are the winner in a hard-fought race.

12. She crosses the line a moment ahead of the next runner. The difference between their times is less than one-tenth of one second. Rae is the winner in a hard-fought race.

Key Words are underlined. Spelling Words are printed in red.

Daily Language Practice

City: A Story of Roman Planning and Construction

Main and helping verbs; action and linking verbs; spelling

1. Our roads is similer to ancient Roman streets.

1. Our roads are similar to ancient Roman streets.

2. The majorety of them are builded above layers of rock.

2. The majority of them are built above layers of rock.

3. Engineers have develop efficient new road design's.

3. Engineers have developed efficient new road designs.

4. Residents has asked the governmant for a new bridge over the illinois river.

4. Residents have asked the government for a new bridge over the Illinois River.

5. The project have been under discusion for many years.

5. The project has been under discussion for many years.

6. Experts has to determine if we have the abilety to pay for the bridge.

6. Experts have to determine if we have the ability to pay for the bridge.

7. The old bridges pier's consist of stone, just like those of a roman bridge.

7. The old bridge's piers consisted of stone, just like those of a Roman bridge.

8. New plans calls for the developmant of a steal and concrete bridge.

8. New plans call for the development of a steel and concrete bridge.

9. All bridges has the function of connectting two places.

9. All bridges have the function of connecting two places.

10. The communety board will be voting next weak.

10. The community board will be voting next week.

11. The proposal is been debated on Friday night. Everyone is encourage to attend. You has to know the facts before you can make an educated choice.

11. The proposal is being debated on Friday night. Everyone is encouraged to attend. You have to know the facts before you can make an educated choice.

12. Mayor Finn have recommended a special partnershipp. The city will provide half the money fore the project. Businesses is being asked to contribute the rest.

12. Mayor Finn has recommended a special partnership. The city will provide half the money for the project. Businesses are being asked to contribute the rest.

Key Words are underlined. Spelling Words are printed in red.

Daily Language Practice

The Secrets of Vesuvius

Transitive and intransitive verbs; objects; main and helping verbs; spelling

1. I has just visited a dig site with my grandmother, who is a archaeologists.

1. I have just visited a dig site with my grandmother, who is an archaeologist.

2. Her coments taught I a lot about life in ancient rome.

2. Her comments taught me a lot about life in ancient Rome.

3. The bilding she is excavates collapsed in about A.D. 22.

3. The building she is excavating collapsed in about A.D. 22.

4. A comittee of experts created guidelines about how the work should been done.

4. A committee of experts created guidelines about how the work should be done.

5. They has founded some fossils of extinct animals, to.

5. They have found some fossils of extinct animals, too.

6. The area look like a connstruction site, accept nothing is being built.

6. The area looks like a construction site, except nothing is being built.

7. Our visit made we feel overwhelmed buy a sense of history.

7. Our visit made us feel overwhelmed by a sense of history.

8. Grandma conttinued her work after I left.

8. Grandma continued her work after I left.

9. A good archaeologist is alway studies intricate details.

9. A good archaeologist is always studying intricate details.

10. Diggers constantly search for clews from the passed.

10. Diggers constantly search for clues from the past.

11. Yesterday, Grandma found a broken peace of clay pot. That one little piece of clay can tells a lot about the past. Even though it looks insignificant, I almost feel awe when I think about them.

11. Yesterday, Grandma found a broken piece of clay pot. That one little piece of clay can tell a lot about the past. Even though it looks insignificant, I almost feel awe when I think about it.

12. The trip gave we some wonderful surprises. Visiting the dig was a way to comunicate with the past. We is still listening to what it has to say.

12. The trip gave us some wonderful surprises. Visiting the dig was a way to communicate with the past. We are still listening to what it has to say.

Key Words are underlined. Spelling Words are printed in red.

READER RESPONSE 9

WRITING IN YOUR PERSONAL JOURNAL

Sometimes, the members of your Literature Circle may want to write your responses to the selection and then discuss what each of you has written. Here are some things to write about. Choose one.

1. Think of at least three things that the story reminds you of in another story or in your own lives. Tell about them.
2. Copy in your personal journal an important paragraph, sentence, or word from the selection. Explain why it is important to you.
3. What influenced you most as you read: the setting, one of the characters, or the plot of the story? Write about it.

Harcourt Brace School Publishers

FOLD

READER RESPONSE 9

Literature Circle

ORGANIZING A LITERATURE CIRCLE

The members of your group

- may want to read the selection independently.
- may want to read the selection together to discuss certain parts during reading.
- should decide how many pages to read and what to discuss.

DURING AND AFTER READING

Your group members can

- discuss your reactions to the selection.
- ask questions about parts you did not understand.

Here are some sentence starters to help your Literature Circle begin a discussion. Choose one.

1. My first reaction to the selection was...
2. I loved the way the author...
3. I didn't like the part...
4. The part I remember most is...

Harcourt Brace School Publishers

READER RESPONSE 14

Hot Seat

GETTING READY

1. Work with a group. Make a list of the characters in the story. Each group member should choose one of the main characters to think about.
2. As you read or reread the story, write some questions to help you think about the character's point of view. Here are some suggestions:
   - How does my character act and feel?
   - Why does my character act and feel as he or she does?
   - What relationships does my character have with other story characters?
   - What problems does my character face? How does he or she solve them?

Questions	Notes
How does my character act and feel? Why does my character act and feel as he or she does? What relationships does my character have with other story characters? What problems does my character face? How does he or she solve them?	She is angry with her friend.

Harcourt Brace School Publishers

FOLD

READER RESPONSE 14

AFTER READING

1. Each member of the group should remind the others which character he or she chose.
2. Each character should take a turn in the Hot Seat while the other members of your group ask questions to "get to know" him or her. You may want to ask the character to explain why he or she acted in a certain way.
3. After each member of your group has been in the Hot Seat, try holding conversations among groups of characters.

Harcourt Brace School Publishers

Harcourt Brace School Publishers

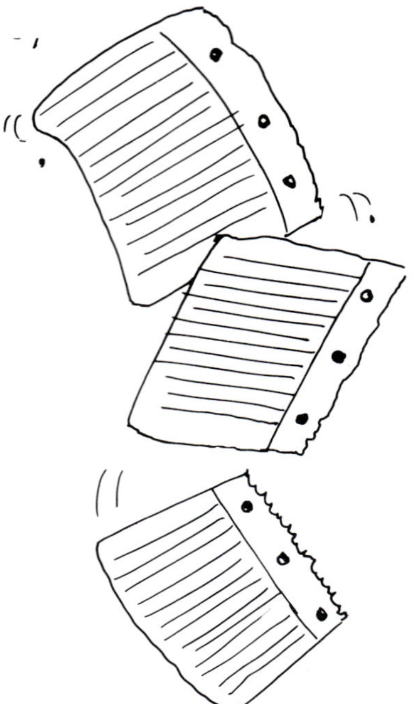

AFTER READING

6. Read the rest of the story. Repeat steps 2–5.
7. Discuss the story. Use the questions and answers on your paper to help you.

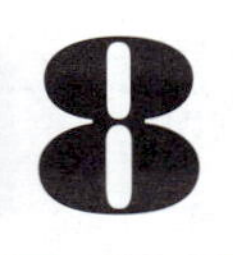

FOLD

READER RESPONSE 8

Written Conversation

DURING READING

1. Work with a partner. Silently read the pages your teacher suggests.
2. On a sheet of paper, write a comment about something you didn't understand or something you would like your partner's opinion about.
3. Pass your paper to your partner.
4. Write the answer to your partner's question. Then add a new question to the paper.
5. Pass the paper back to your partner. Answer the new question your partner wrote.

Harcourt Brace School Publishers

FOLD

READER RESPONSE 

Text Sets

Text sets are things that you read that have the same topic, theme, or genre (nonfiction, fiction, poetry, biography), are written by the same author, or are illustrated by the same illustrator. Text sets include:

- selections in your reading anthology,
- articles found in magazines, newspapers, encyclopedias, or other reference sources, and
- books.

To compare texts, use **one** of these ideas.

COMPARING TEXT SETS

1. Have everyone in your group read *all* of the selections. After everyone has read the selections, use some of these questions for discussion.
   - What are the similarities in the way these stories were written?
   - What information did you find presented in more than one of the texts?

READER RESPONSE 12

2. Have each group member read one of the selections that have the same theme, are by the same author, or are the same genre (nonfiction, fiction, poetry, biography).
   - Each group member should share what he or she has read.
   - Everyone should discuss the similarities and differences in the selections.
   - At the end of the discussion, the group may want to brainstorm how to present the comparisons.

SHOW YOUR GROUP'S COMPARISONS

- Create a comparison chart to display your findings.
- Write a drama or a Readers Theatre that fits the text set.
- Make a game showing the comparisons.
- Create a mural and display it in your classroom.

Harcourt Brace School Publishers

TIPS FOR RESOLVING CONTRADICTIONS

- Gather all the information your group has for each community change that you have contradictory stories about.
- Sort the information according to which story it supports.
- Evaluate the evidence for each conflicting story.
- Decide which information comes from the most reliable source.

FOLD

CHECKPOINT 3

22

City: A Story of Roman Planning and Construction

Resolve Conflicting Facts. Review the checklist below as you resolve contradictions and review your chart.

- ☑ Review your chart to find conflicting stories or ideas about the history of the community.
- ☑ Do extra research and interview more people who can give new information about the contradictions.
- ☑ If you can, visit places in the community that have changed.
- ☑ Resolve the conflicts and revise your chart.

Harcourt Brace School Publishers

(Continued on the other side)

TIPS FOR WRITING YOUR REPORT

- Assign one group member the role of Recorder. The Recorder will write the final copy of your report.
- Have a few group members act as Checkers to proofread the report and check its facts against research notes.
- Choose one person to be a Facilitator to help the group stay focused.
- Let one person act as Encourager to help the group complete hard tasks without getting discouraged.

FOLD

THEME PROJECT

CHECKPOINT 4

The Secrets of Vesuvius

23

Write a Group Report. The following checklist will help you monitor your progress as you organize your findings into a report.

- ☑ Assign a role, such as Recorder, Checker, or Facilitator, to each group member.
- ☑ Talk about how to organize the information in your report.
- ☑ Assign responsibilities to each person in the group for a part of the written report.
- ☑ Use the group's research to write about changes in the community and create a final report.

(Continued on the other side)

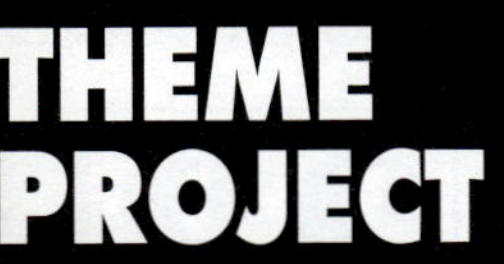

PRESENTATION

Turning Points

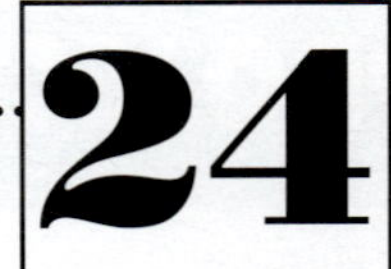

FOLD

HISTORICAL CHANGES

Community Connections Now that you know how your community has changed over the years, it's time to share your information. Your projects may unite community members and encourage others to share their own memories.

- Turn your reports into museum displays by mounting the pages on poster boards. Illustrate report pages with drawings or photographs.
- If you can borrow historical objects or clothing, add them to your display.
- Invite community members to your museum opening.

Harcourt Brace School Publishers

(Continued on the other side)

- Use your interviews to write an oral history of your community. Whenever possible, use your interview subjects' actual words.
- From your library research, add background details for your readers.
- Bind the pages together. Distribute copies to the people you interviewed and to interested organizations, such as the local historical society.

OR

- Make a character who can comment on your community's history. For example your character might be a hundred-year-old resident.
- Create stories your character might tell about the community changes you've researched, and role-play an interview for other classes.

Harcourt Brace School Publishers

Harcourt Brace School Publishers

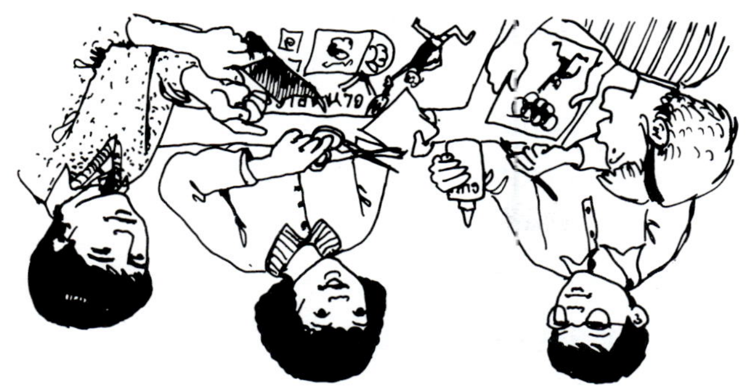

INTEGRATED CURRICULUM

13B

Atalanta's Race

OLYMPIC COLLAGE

When the Olympic Games first began, their purpose was to encourage "a sound mind in a sound body." In the modern world, they also promote friendship among nations. Make a collage that shows what the Olympic Games stand for.

1. Choose group members to be Materials Managers, Researchers, and Reporters.
2. Decide what big ideas the group wants to show. Then decide how you will represent those ideas in pictures. Look for pictures in magazines and newspapers, or draw your own.
3. The Reporters can present and explain your collage to the class.

FOLD

INTEGRATED CURRICULUM

13A

Atalanta's Race

OLYMPICS THROUGH TIME

The Olympic Games were first held in ancient Greece about twenty-seven centuries ago. Create a time line that illustrates the history of the Olympics.

- ☑ Work in a group. Make your time line on tagboard or construction paper.
- ☑ Use the three dates shown here to begin your time line.
- ☑ Use an encyclopedia to find other important events and dates to add to the time line.
- ☑ Record your findings on the time line.

Harcourt Brace School Publishers

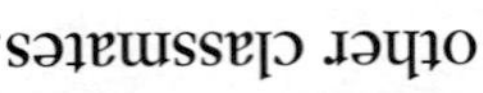
Harcourt Brace School Publishers

INTEGRATED CURRICULUM 14B

Joan Benoit Samuelson

EATING SMART

Eating pasta (a food rich in carbohydrates) before a marathon is an example of "carbo-loading." Find out why athletes carbo-load and how carbohydrates help them perform well.

- ☑ Work with a partner. Look in a health or science textbook for information about how the body uses carbohydrates.
- ☑ Speak with your physical education teacher or local coaches and athletes. Ask about eating carbohydrates before competing. Also ask their advice on other eating habits or diets for athletes.
- ☑ Take notes about what you learn, and share them with other classmates.

FOLD

INTEGRATED CURRICULUM 14A

Joan Benoit Samuelson

MARATHON MILES

Joan Benoit has done many remarkable things in her life, including setting records in the 1983 Boston Marathon and in the 1984 Olympic Games. Find out how long those records stood.

- ☑ Use an almanac or other reference book. Look for information about the Boston Marathon and the Olympics.
- ☑ Locate Benoit's records for both events. Then look in later years for women's times faster than Benoit's.
- ☑ Find other statistics about the Boston Marathon, the New York Marathon, the marathoners themselves, or the marathon events for both men and women in the Olympics. Create a map showing marathon routes. Present your information to classmates.

Harcourt Brace School Publishers

INTEGRATED CURRICULUM

City: A Story of Roman Planning and Construction

RISE TO THE OCCASION

Bread was an important food for the residents of Verbonia. Work with a partner to conduct an experiment with yeast. Write your predictions and results in your Personal Journal.

Step 1: Pour one cup of warm water into a zip-top plastic bag.

Step 2: Add one package of yeast and two teaspoons of sugar to the bag of water. Seal the bag.

Step 3: Mix the ingredients by kneading the bag.

Step 4: Wait 30 to 40 minutes, and observe what happens.

Compare the results to your predictions.

Harcourt Brace School Publishers

FOLD

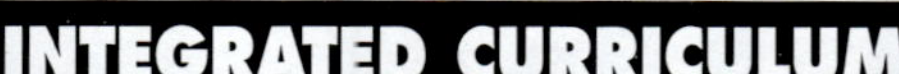

INTEGRATED CURRICULUM

15A

City: A Story of Roman Planning and Construction

RUINS OF ANCIENT ROME

The remains of structures designed by ancient architects and engineers still exist in Rome today. Investigate one of the structures, such as the Colosseum or the Pantheon, and present your findings to other classmates.

1. Use reference books to research your structure.
2. Write a report that includes when and why the structure was built.
3. Make a drawing or a scale model of the structure, using foam board or a cardboard box.
4. Display your work. Vote on the ruins you would most like to visit.

Harcourt Brace School Publishers

Harcourt Brace School Publishers

INTEGRATED CURRICULUM

16B

The Secrets of Vesuvius

SKELETON KEYS

Work with classmates to make a chart, collage, or diagram that tells how bones can reveal secrets for archaeologists.

1. By reading "The Secrets of Vesuvius" or doing research in reference sources, find out what scientists can learn from bones.
2. Decide what type of display will work best. Plan your chart, collage, or diagram.
3. Work together to complete the display and create a title for it.

FOLD

INTEGRATED CURRICULUM

16A

The Secrets of Vesuvius

MAKE A DIORAMA

You've learned about Roman villas in "The Secrets of Vesuvius" and in "City: A Story of Roman Planning and Construction." Make a diorama of a Roman villa.

1. Work with a partner or a small group. Look through both selections to find pictures of and information about villas.
2. Think about the floor plans of these homes. Consider the following:
   - the number and position of windows
   - the sizes of rooms
   - other architectural details such as doors, and decorative features such as mosaics
3. Make your diorama, using materials provided by your teacher. Show as many features as possible. Share your diorama with other classmates.

Harcourt Brace School Publishers

Model: Descriptive Paragraph

*A **descriptive paragraph** appeals to the reader's senses of sight, hearing, smell, touch, and taste. In a few words, it paints a picture of a subject.*

topic sentence	Big Lake is prettiest just before sunset. The waves lap gently on the shoreline, and loons call eerily
vivid verbs	across the water. A breeze carries the spicy scent of pine trees. The
sensory details	sky fades at the edges, turning first light blue, then lilac, then pink, and then orange. Streaky clouds are reflected on the lake. Bass and pickerel dance just below the shimmering surface, sometimes rising up to capture a mosquito. Everything is calm.

Model: Rhymed Poem

Poetry *can express a mood or paint a picture with just a few words. Poetry is usually written in rhythmic lines rather than in sentences. In a rhymed poem, syllable sounds are repeated at the ends of paired lines. For example, the following poem follows a rhyme scheme, or pattern, of a/b/a/b: the first and third lines rhyme, and the second and fourth lines rhyme.*

a pattern	A sleeping fawn,
of rhythm	A single crow—
and rhyme	Above, the dawn.
	Still night below.

Model: Unrhymed Poem

In unrhymed poetry, rhythm, figurative language, and imagery express a mood.

imagery	The quiet night
strengthened	Gentle breathing of branches.
by rhythm	The sun creeps
	Glinting edges of hilltops.
	A crow calls
	Shrill salute to the morning.

Scale-Model Drawing

introduction Your assignment is to draw a scale model of your classroom. You will need a yardstick, white paper, a pencil, an eraser, a ruler, a calculator, and scrap paper.

body First, measure your classroom with the yardstick. Next, determine a scale for your drawing, such as 1 inch = 1 foot.

Next, calculate the scale measurements of the room and write them down on the scrap paper. Then, sketch the room on the white paper. Don't forget to include the scale you used.

conclusion Finally, add drawings of furniture and other objects to your scale model. Someone who has never been in your classroom should be able to tell what it looks like from your drawing.

Writing Models

Model: Research Report Outline

Lengthy informative writing, such as a ***research report****, may be organized by using an outline. An outline uses Roman numerals for main topics, capital letters for subtopics, and Arabic numerals for details.*

Jacob Riis

main topics

I. Early life
  A. Born in Denmark in 1849
  B. Moved to New York City

never an A without a B; never a 1 without a 2

II. Reform work
  A. Police reporter
    1. Firsthand look at poverty
    2. Firsthand look at crime
  B. Crusader supported by Theodore Roosevelt
    1. An improved water supply
    2. Changes in child labor laws
    3. Renovation of slums
III. Major works
  A. How the Other Half Lives (1890)
  B. The Making of an American (1901)
    1. Autobiography
    2. Description of his crusades

Additional Reading
Hidden Treasures

The following list is a compilation of the Reading Trade Books selected for the lesson plans.

THEME: TURNING POINTS

***Ancient Greece* by Rowena Loverance. Viking Penguin, 1993. AVERAGE**
With its eye-catching illustrations, this nonfiction book provides an attractive survey of the history and culture of the ancient Greek civilization. *Notable Trade Book in Social Studies*

***Ancient Rome* by Simon James. Dorling Kindersley, 1990. AVERAGE**
Each page of this informative book is packed with text and photographs, providing a worthwhile examination of life in the Roman Empire.

***Bonnie Blair: Golden Streak* by Cathy Breitenbucher. Lerner, 1994. AVERAGE**
This is the biography of speed skater Bonnie Blair, the only American woman to have won gold medals in three consecutive Olympics.

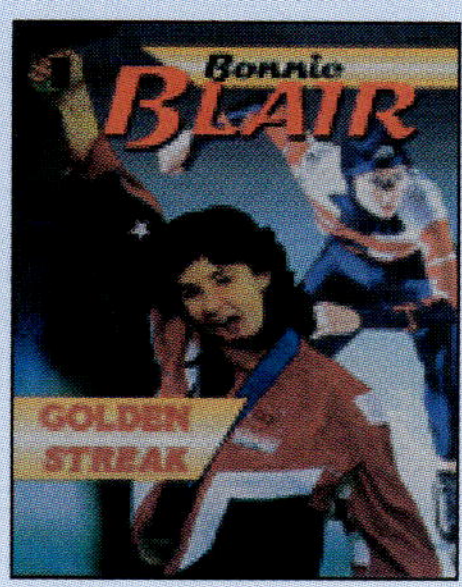

***Bridge to Terabithia* by Katherine Paterson. HarperCollins, 1977. CHALLENGING**
Jess has been sure all summer that he'd be the school's fastest runner. Then he's beaten by the new girl, Leslie—and to his surprise they embark on a friendship that changes his life. *Newbery Medal*

***Cathedral: The Story of Its Construction* by David Macaulay. Houghton Mifflin, 1973. AVERAGE**
Text and black-and-white drawings clearly describe the intricate step-by-step process of building a Gothic cathedral in medieval Europe. *Caldecott Honor;* New York Times *Best Illustrated Book*

***The Children of Odin: The Book of Northern Myths* by Padraic Colum. Macmillan, 1984. CHALLENGING**
The gods and goddesses of the Norse sagas are brought to life in this vivid retelling by a celebrated author.

***The Children's Homer: The Adventures of Odysseus and the Tale of Troy* retold by Padraic Colum. Macmillan, 1982. CHALLENGING**
First published in 1918, this adaptation of Homer's classic tales provides a compelling introduction to the Greek epics.

***Coubertin's Olympics: How the Games Began* by David Kristy. Lerner, 1995. AVERAGE**
Coubertin's crusade to bring athletes of all nations together in competition resulted in the modern-day Olympic games.

***D'Aulaires' Book of Greek Myths* by Ingri and Edgar P. D'Aulaire. Doubleday, 1980. EASY**
From Athena to Zeus, this classic collection introduces young readers to the great myths with easy-to-follow text and striking illustrations.

Digging to the Past: Excavations in Ancient Lands **by W. John Hackwell. Scribner's, 1986. CHALLENGING**
This brief introduction to the goals and methods of archaeological digs focuses on the Middle East.

Digging Up the Past: The Story of an Archaeological Adventure **by Carollyn James. Franklin Watts, 1990. CHALLENGING**
The science of archaeology is used to determine how people lived on a nineteenth-century farm.

Digging Up Tyrannosaurus Rex **by John R. Horner and Don Lessem. Crown, 1992. EASY**
Photographs, illustrations, and diagrams are included in this story of the discovery and excavation of the world's only complete Tyrannosaurus fossil. *Outstanding Science Trade Book*

The Dragon in the Cliff: A Novel Based on the Life of Mary Anning **by Sheila Cole. Lothrop, Lee & Shepard, 1991. AVERAGE**
This historical novel about a nineteenth-century paleontologist is based on the true story of Mary Anning, who in 1811 found the first complete skeleton of an icthyosaur. *Outstanding Science Trade Book; Notable Trade Book in Social Studies*

Favorite Greek Myths **retold by Mary Pope Osborne. Scholastic, 1989. EASY**
Twelve tales from Greek mythology are gracefully retold and beautifully illustrated. *Notable Trade Book in Social Studies*

Florence Griffith Joyner: Dazzling Olympian **by Nathan Aaseng. Lerner, 1989. AVERAGE**
The career of America's "Flo Jo," crowned by her successful quest for Olympic gold in 1988, makes for inspiring reading.

The Greeks and Troy **by Deborah Tyler. Macmillan, 1993. AVERAGE**
Was there really a ten-year siege of a city called Troy, or did the Greek poet Homer create a fictional war epic? You weigh the evidence.

In Lane Three, Alex Archer **by Tessa Duder. Bantam, 1991. AVERAGE**
Alex, a medal-winning swimmer, faces some doubts about her athletic career as she trains for the Olympics. *IRA Children's Book Award*

Jackie Joyner-Kersee **by Neil Cohen. Little, Brown, 1992. AVERAGE**
This is the inspiring story of the woman whose dedication and hard work earned her two gold medals in the 1988 Olympics.

Jim Thorpe: Olympic Champion **by Guernsey Van Riper, Jr. Aladdin, 1986. EASY**
This easy-to-read biography re-creates scenes from Thorpe's early life and shows why this gifted Native American was considered by many to be the world's greatest all-around athlete.

The Kingfisher Book of the Ancient World: From the Ice Age to the Fall of Rome **by Hazel Mary Martell. Kingfisher, 1995. AVERAGE**
This visual encyclopedia of ancient history provides a wealth of information about our distant past.

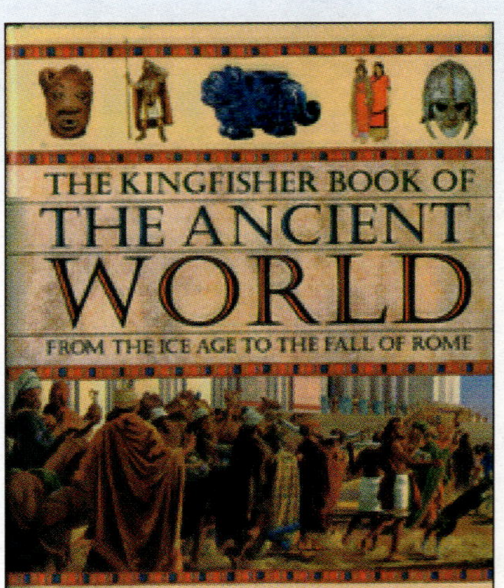

The Macmillan Book of Greek Gods and Heroes **by Alice Low. Macmillan, 1985. AVERAGE**
This book introduces a number of the most popular Greek myths, including the legend of Odysseus. *Notable Trade Book in Social Studies*

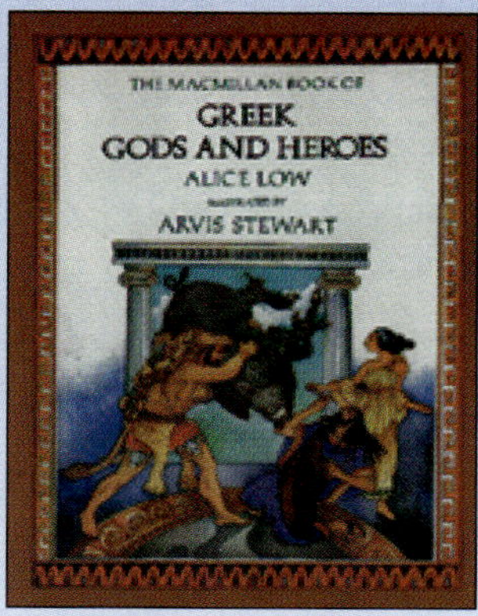

Maniac Magee **by Jerry Spinelli. Little, Brown, 1990. AVERAGE**
Jerry Magee's athletic ability makes him a legend in the town of Two Mills in this modern-day tall tale.

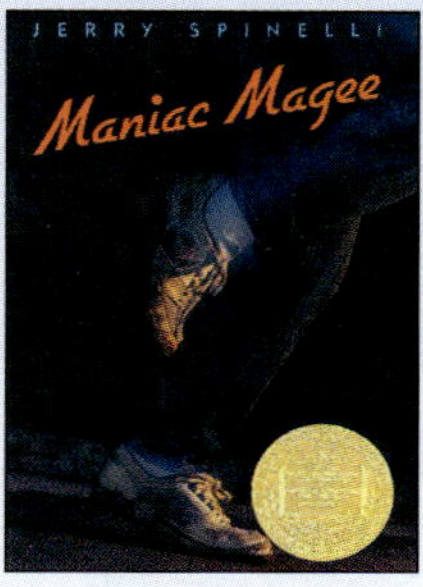

Myths and Legends from Around the World **by Sandy Shepherd. Macmillan, 1995. AVERAGE**
Glowing illustrations grace this collection of more than fifty stories from around the world.

The Nutrition-Fitness Link: How Diet Can Help Your Body and Mind **by Charles A. Salter. Millbrook, 1993. AVERAGE**
Athletes will be particularly interested in the author's discussion of carbo-loading and other aspects of nutrition related to sports.

Peak Performance: Sports, Science, and the Body in Action **by Emily Isberg. Simon & Schuster, 1989. AVERAGE**
Using the case histories of real-life athletes, both amateur and professional, this book explores the myriad ways that technology has changed the world of sports training and injury rehabilitation.

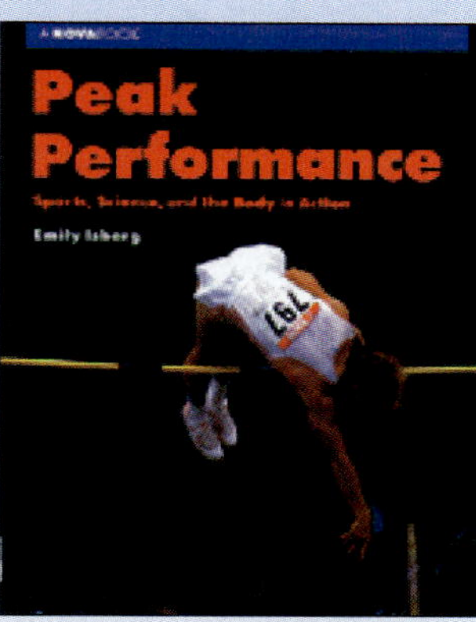

Pompeii **by Peter Connolly. Oxford University Press, 1990. AVERAGE**
The everyday life of Pompeii's people is described in this nonfiction book.

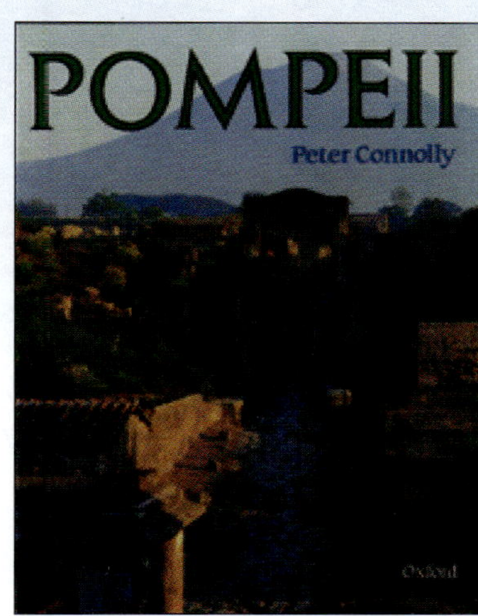

The Roman Empire and the Dark Ages **by Giovanni Casilli. Peter Bedrick, 1985. CHALLENGING**
Both Roman and medieval times are described and illustrated with drawings, maps, and diagrams.

Roman Places **by Sarah Howarth. Millbrook, 1993. AVERAGE**
All facets of life in ancient Rome are described in this book, including villa life, city buildings, and social customs.

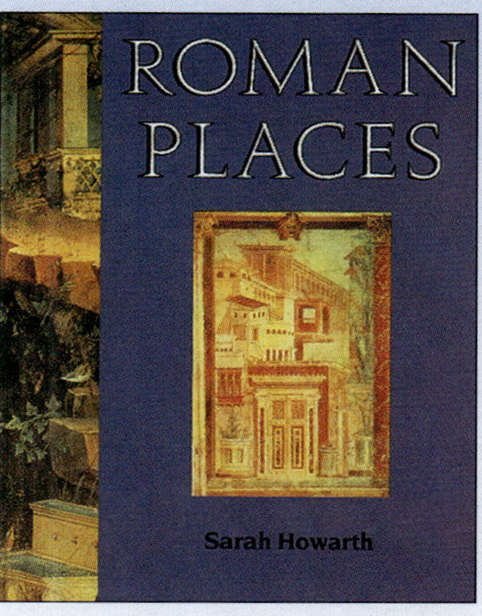

A Roman Villa **by Jacqueline Morley. Peter Bedrick, 1992. AVERAGE**
Much can be learned about ancient Roman culture in this book describing life at a single Roman home in the country.

The Romans **by Pamela Odijk. Macmillan, 1989. AVERAGE**
The oversized format of this nonfiction book provides space for large illustrations to accompany the informative text.

The Romans: Life in the Empire **by Charles Guittard and Annie-Claude Martin. Millbrook, 1992. AVERAGE**
How did the Roman Empire come into being? How did its people live, work, and play? Find out in this detailed history.

The Romans and Pompeii **by Philip Steele. Macmillan, 1994. AVERAGE**
Illustrated with photographs of Pompeii's ruins and with art from the period, the expository text describes the eruption of Mount Vesuvius and the excavations of Pompeii by archaeologists.

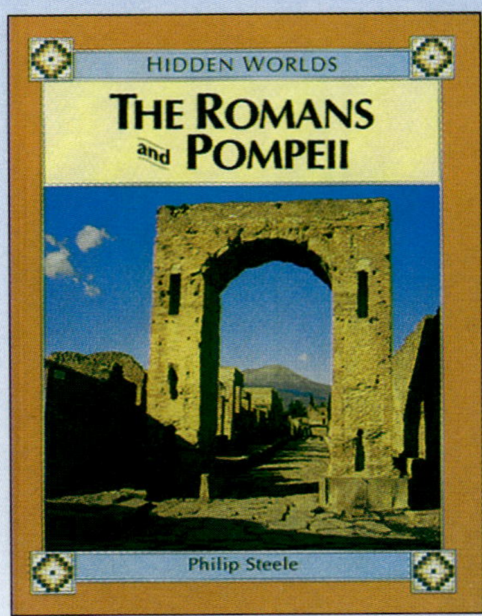

The Shark Callers **by Eric Campbell. Harcourt Brace, 1994. CHALLENGING**
Though Andy and Kaleku have never met, their fates become unknowingly linked in the wake of a disastrous volcanic eruption in Papua New Guinea.

Ship **by David Macaulay. Houghton Mifflin, 1993. CHALLENGING**
Join underwater archaeologists as they search for lost caravels, the wooden ships of exploration from the fifteenth century. *Teachers' Choice; Parents' Choice*

The Summer Olympics **by Caroline Arnold. Franklin Watts, 1991. EASY**
Photos and text tell the story of the summer Olympics, including highlights of past Olympic events.

SUNK! Exploring Underwater Archaeology. **Runestone, 1994. AVERAGE**
The special problems of underwater archaeological work are discussed and its techniques are illustrated in this informative work.

Surtsey: The Newest Place on Earth **by Kathryn Lasky. Hyperion, 1994. AVERAGE**
Illustrated with spectacular photographs, this book describes the recent emergence of the island of Surtsey off the coast of Iceland. *ALA Notable Book; Outstanding Science Trade Book; Notable Trade Book for the Language Arts*

Volcano & Earthquake **by Susanna Van Rose. Knopf, 1992. EASY**
In this book, the author provides a strongly visual introduction to two fascinating—and terrifying—natural phenomena.

Volcanoes **by Seymour Simon. William Morrow, 1988. EASY**
The photo-essay format provides dramatic images of the volcanoes described by the author. *Outstanding Science Trade Book*

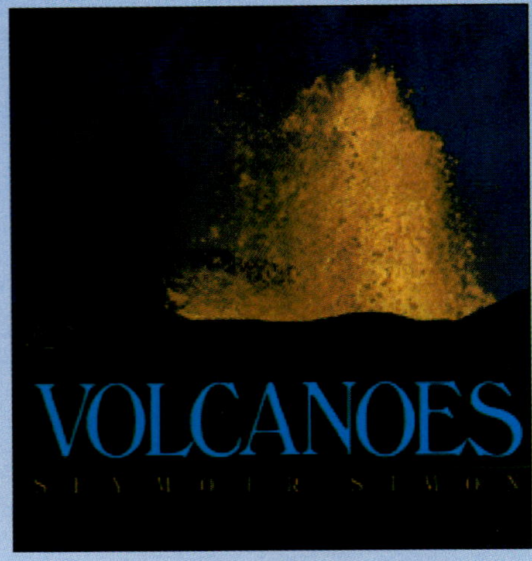

The Way Things Work **by David Macaulay. Houghton Mifflin, 1988. AVERAGE**
Through drawings and text, Macaulay attempts to demystify both the simple and complex technologies of modern life.

What Do We Know About the Romans? **by Mike Corbishley. Peter Bedrick, 1992. EASY**
Each chapter in this illustrated survey answers a specific question about Roman life, such as *What did Romans wear?* and *What was life like in the Roman army?*

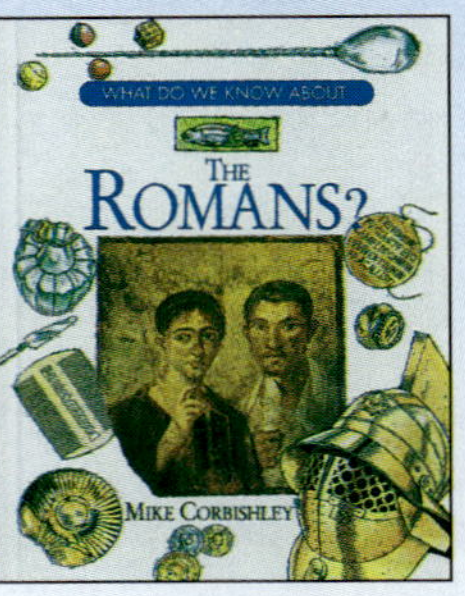

Winners and Losers **by Stephen Hoffius. Simon & Schuster, 1993. CHALLENGING**
The competition between Curt and Daryl does not end at the race's finish line, and both athletes learn lessons about winning and losing. *Notable Trade Book in Social Studies*

SCHOOL ↔ HOME CONNECTION

ATALANTA'S NEXT RACE

Here are Atalanta and Hippomenes five years later, married, and getting ready to race again. Why are they racing? What do you suppose is going through their minds? Fill in their thought balloons. Then write a sequel to "Atalanta's Race," and call it "Atalanta's Next Race."

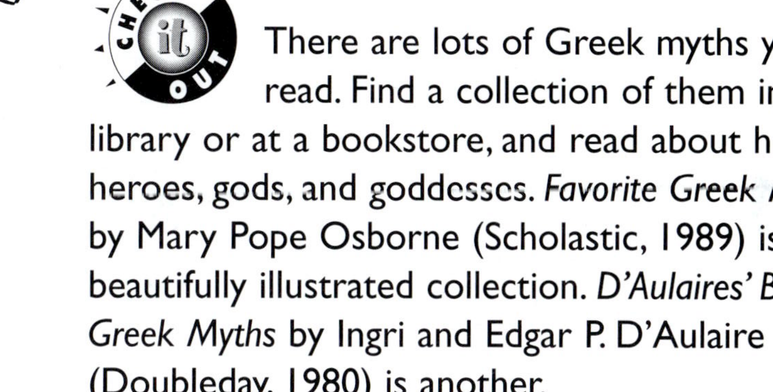

CHECK it OUT There are lots of Greek myths you can read. Find a collection of them in the library or at a bookstore, and read about human heroes, gods, and goddesses. *Favorite Greek Myths* by Mary Pope Osborne (Scholastic, 1989) is one beautifully illustrated collection. *D'Aulaires' Book of Greek Myths* by Ingri and Edgar P. D'Aulaire (Doubleday, 1980) is another.

FOR THE FAMILY ALBUM

Make illustrated versions of the myth "Atalanta's Race" and your myth "Atalanta's Next Race" to add to your family's library of favorite stories.

MY FAVORITE ATHLETE

SCHOOL ↔ HOME CONNECTION

Who's your favorite athlete? What makes this athlete "the best" in your view?

Create a profile of your favorite athlete to share with your family and your classmates. Model your profile on a magazine feature. You could write about the person. You could find a lot of pictures of him or her and write captions for them, or you could draw your own pictures. The idea is to share what you know about the person and to tell what makes him or her extra-special.

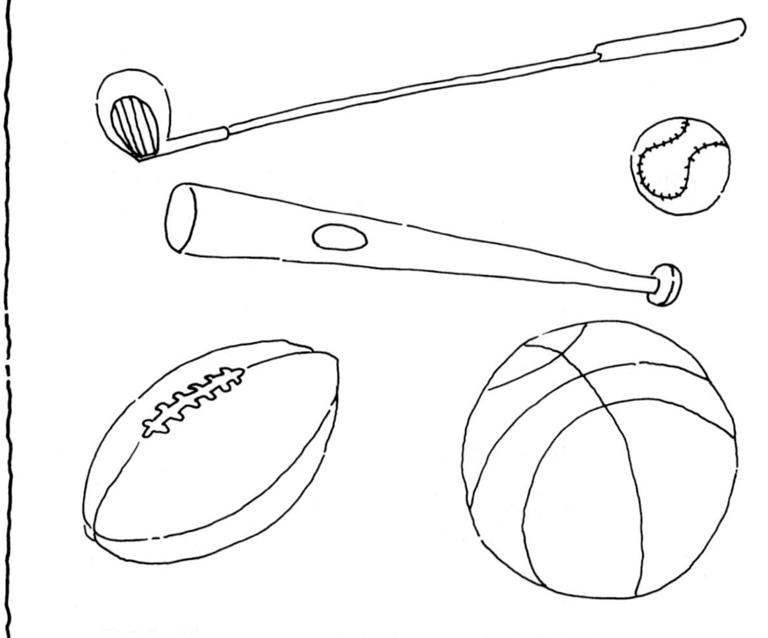

CHECK it OUT You may want to read books about other Olympic athletes. Check out these books at a library or bookstore: *Bonnie Blair: Golden Streak* by Cathy Breitenbucher (Lerner, 1994); *Florence Griffith Joyner: Dazzling Olympian* by Nathan Aaseng (Lerner, 1989); and *Jim Thorpe: Olympic Champion* by Guernsey Van Riper, Jr. (Aladdin, 1986).

Get everyone in your family to write about or tell about a favorite athlete—from the present or from the past. Younger brothers and sisters may want to tell about their favorite athletes by drawing pictures.

AT HOME IN ROME

SCHOOL ↔ HOME CONNECTION

1. This floor plan shows the home of a Roman family. Use what you learned from reading "City: A Story of Roman Planning and Construction" to place the following labels in the correct places on the floor plan: *front door, impluvium, bedroom, kitchen, garden or peristyle, atrium,* and *family shrine*. If you wish, add other details and information to the plan. Then think of or make up a Roman family name and write "Home of the __________ Family" beneath the floor plan.
2. Use the back of this paper to explain how a Roman home was different from homes today.
3. Share your "At Home in Rome" floor plan with a family member.

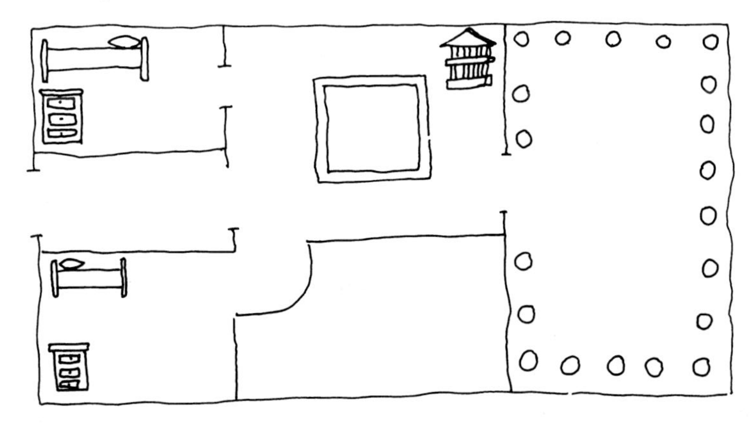

CHECK it OUT

David Macaulay is the author of several other books about the way things are built and the way things work. Next time you're in a library or bookstore, check out some of these titles: *The Way Things Work* (Houghton Mifflin, 1988); *Cathedral: The Story of Its Construction* (Houghton Mifflin, 1973); and *Ship* (Houghton Mifflin, 1993).

FOR THE FAMILY ALBUM

Create a floor plan of the home you or a relative lives in, or a home you might like to live in. Label parts of the home to show what is special or unique about it. Then give your floor plan a title, such as "Our Family's Home."

Harcourt Brace School Publishers

Nine Secrets of Vesuvius

SCHOOL ↔ HOME CONNECTION

1. The bones and objects Dr. Bisel found in Herculaneum told a lot about the people of the town and their times. Fill in the grid by drawing and labeling nine objects or remains that Dr. Bisel found.
2. Use the back of this paper to write a sentence telling what information each object or type of skeletal remain revealed to Dr. Bisel.
3. Tell a family member that you know nine secrets of Vesuvius. Then share your pictures, labels, and sentences.

CHECK it OUT Check your local library or bookstore for the following books about archaeology: *Digging to the Past: Excavations in Ancient Lands* by W. John Hackwell (Scribner's, 1986) and *Digging Up Tyrannosaurus Rex* by John R. Horner and Don Lessem (Crown, 1992).

FOR THE FAMILY ALBUM

Copy the shape of the grid onto another sheet of paper. Think about objects that would reveal a lot about your family and your way of life to archaeologists of the future. Draw nine objects, label them, and write a sentence about each one, telling what it shows.

Graph-a-Book

Dear Family Members,
As a book is read at home, have the student graph his or her response. The student should write the title of the book and the author's name on the numbered line and then color the corresponding bar on the graph to evaluate the book. Ask the student to give a reason for his or her rating.

Book Titles and Authors' Names

1. ______________________________
2. ______________________________
3. ______________________________
4. ______________________________
5. ______________________________
6. ______________________________

Graph

	Would Not Recommend	OK	Good	GREAT!
Book 1				
Book 2				
Book 3				
Book 4				
Book 5				
Book 6				

Please return the graph to school when completed. Thank you.

Signature ______________________________

Duplicate the page and send it home with students to be completed with family members.

Dear Family,

Book Corner

Special Announcements

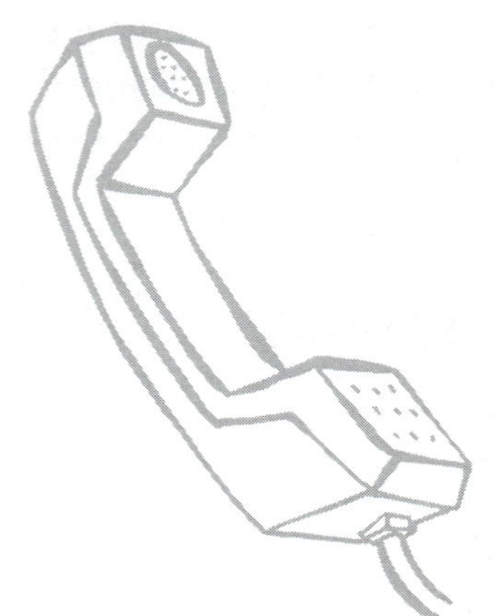

Something to Try at Home

We have been very busy lately!

Spotlight on . . .

From Your Child . . .

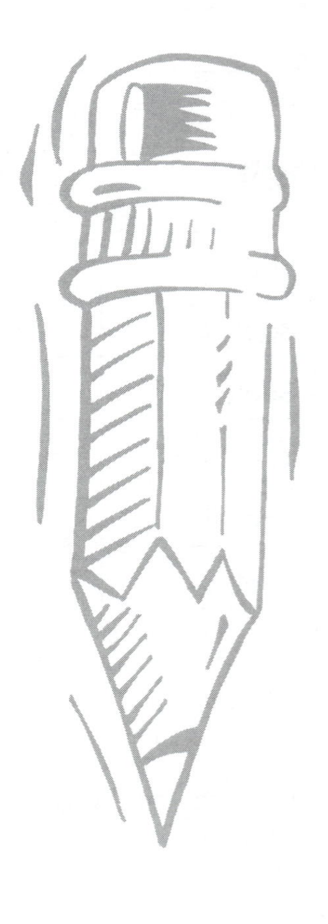

Harcourt Brace School Publishers

Complete the newsletter with news items from your class. Duplicate the page, and send it home to family members.

Create Your Own School-to-Home Newsletter

Insert your school name or newsletter title to head your newsletter.

Personal note to parents

from the desk of...

Too Good to Miss

List of recommended books for reading

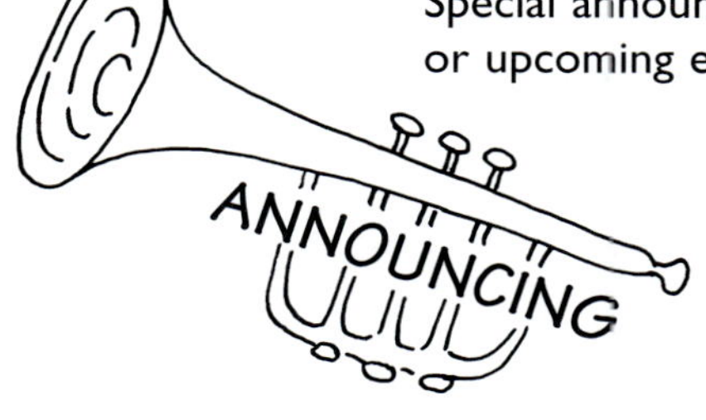

Special announcements or upcoming events

Current events from the classroom, school, or community

Reminder of upcoming meetings, conferences, or field trips

Focus on a certain subject area, or parent self-help information

Classroom projects

Call for volunteers or materials

Future goals or study themes

STAR STUDENT REPORTERS

Student column

Use any of these clip-art graphics to create a classroom newsletter to send home.

Harcourt Brace School Publishers

because: ______________________________

____

____

____

____

____

Signed: ______________________________

Harcourt Brace School Publishers

Resources

Theme 5

Tested Skill

RETEACH: GRAMMAR

Predicate Nominatives and Adjectives

OBJECTIVES: To understand that a predicate nominative renames the subject and that a predicate adjective describes the subject; to use predicate nominatives and predicate adjectives effectively

Focus

Share the following information with students:

A noun or pronoun that follows a linking verb and renames the subject is called a *predicate nominative*.

An adjective that follows a linking verb and describes the subject is called a *predicate adjective*.

Choose a Teaching Model

VISUAL/SPATIAL MODEL Review common linking verbs *(be, appear, become, feel, look, smell, seem, taste)* with students. Then have them look at the picture *Philip IV on Horseback* on page 440 and imagine what either the horse or the king is thinking. Ask them to use linking verbs to describe what the two are experiencing or what they are. To get students started, you may want to write the following sentences on the board under the point-of-view headings:

Horse	King
My rider is the king.	This horse seems excited.

Write the sentences they suggest and have volunteers underline the subject of each sentence as well as the predicate nominative if it has one. Predicate adjectives could be circled and connected to the subject with an arrow. Be sure students understand that predicate nominatives are nouns that rename; predicate adjectives describe. Follow the suggestions given in **Summarize/Reinforce.**

AUDITORY MODEL Review common linking verbs with students. Have them look at the picture on page 440 and ask *Who is the rider?* (Philp IV) Restate their answer as *The rider is Philip IV.* Repeat the sentence and point out that you used a linking verb to help rename the rider. Ask a volunteer to identify the linking verb *(is)* and the words you used to rename *(Philip IV)*. Ask if it is a noun or an adjective. (noun) Then ask what a noun that follows a linking verb and renames the subject is. (predicate nominative) Provide other sentences about the picture, such as the following, and help students identify the predicate adjectives and predicate nominatives.

The king's armor is sparkling. (predicate adjective)
His horse appears powerful. (predicate adjective)
This painting is a masterpiece. (predicate nominative)

Encourage students to suggest other sentences about the painting before following the suggestions in **Summarize/Reinforce.**

VERBAL/LINGUISTIC MODEL Review the common linking verbs with students. Then have them look at the picture *Philip IV on Horseback* on page 440 and think of nouns and adjectives they could use to describe the horse, the rider, or the painting as a whole. Write their suggestions on the board. Then have students use those words with linking verbs to create sentences about the subjects of the painting. Write the sentences they suggest on the board and have students identify the predicate nominatives and adjectives. Then follow the suggestions in **Summarize/Reinforce.**

Summarize/Reinforce

Check students' understanding of predicate nominatives and predicate adjectives by asking them to summarize what they have learned. (A predicate nominative is a noun or pronoun that follows a linking verb and renames the subject. A predicate adjective is an adjective that follows a linking verb and describes the subject.) To reinforce the lesson, have students work with a partner to write a description of something by "renaming" it or telling what it is like. After they have written their description, partners could identify and label the predicate nominatives and predicate adjectives.

Main Idea and Details

OBJECTIVE: To identify a main idea and its supporting details

Focus

Share the following information with students:

The main idea of a paragraph, passage, or selection is the most important point the author is trying to make. Details are given to support the main idea. When an author doesn't state the main idea directly, readers can use the details to infer what that main idea is.

Choose a Teaching Model

VERBAL/LINGUISTIC MODEL Have students look at the last three paragraphs on page 439. Explain that the author states that Velázquez is recognized as a great artist. Ask students to read the passage and look for details that support that idea. Write their suggestions on the board. Then have students review the passage again. Ask, *What other details does the author give about Velázquez?* (Possible responses: He died at 61; his devotion to art brought him compassion and understanding; he was popular with kings and commoners.) Help students make another inference about Velázquez based on these details. Then have students look at all the details about Velázquez and create one main idea about the passage. (Possible response: The great artist Velázquez was a popular and happy man.) Then follow the suggestions in **Summarize/Reinforce.**

LOGICAL/MATHEMATICAL MODEL Have students reread page 439. Suggest that they look for details the author gives to introduce us to Velázquez. When students have finished reading, have them categorize details in a chart like the one below:

Velázquez as an Artist	Velázquez as a Person
paintings showed reality paintings showed dreams dedicated to truth in art	was compassionate was understanding became popular with everyone

Have students combine the two sets of details and create a main idea for the passage. (The great artist Velázquez was a popular and happy man.) Then follow the suggestions in **Summarize/Reinforce.**

KINESTHETIC/TACTILE MODEL Provide each student with several slips of paper. On one slip, have them write *Main Idea: The great artist Velázquez was a popular and happy man.* Then tell students to read page 439 and write details the author gives about Velázquez on individual slips of paper. After students read, have them group together the slips that have details that support the given main idea. Then follow the suggestions in **Summarize/Reinforce.**

Summarize/Reinforce

Ask students to summarize what they have learned about identifying main ideas and details. (The main idea is the most important point the author is trying to make in a passage. Details support the main idea. When an author doesn't state the main idea directly, readers can use the details to infer what that main idea is.) To reinforce the lesson, have students identify the main idea and details in their science texts or in a recently read magazine article. Remind them that identifying main ideas and details will help them understand and remember the things they read.

Simple Tenses

OBJECTIVE: **To understand that the tense of a verb shows time and that the simple tenses are past, present, and future**

Focus

Share the following information with students:

> **The *tense* of a verb shows when the action happens. The simple verb tenses are *past, present,* and *future.* The present tense tells about action that is happening now or that continues to happen. If the subject of a sentence is singular, form the present tense of most verbs by adding *-s* or *-es.* The past tense shows action that took place in the past. Form the past tense for most verbs by adding *-ed.* The future tense shows action that will happen in the future. Use the helping verb *will* with the main verb to form the future tense.**

Choose a Teaching Model

VISUAL/SPATIAL MODEL Write the following sentences on the board:

I never dreamed of being free so soon.
I will stay with you, Mistress.
I thank you.

For each sentence, have a student underline the verb or verb phrase and tell when the action it describes takes place. Have other students identify the verb as past, present, or future and circle the clues that helped them know the tense. Ask them to point out how the past and future tenses are formed (past: by adding *-ed* to the main verb; future: by using the helping verb *will* with the main verb). Then remind students that Lolis spoke these sentences after her Mistress had written the letter releasing her from slavery. Encourage students to suggest responses Mistress might have made. Write the responses on the board and ask other students to identify the tense of each verb and the clues that helped them know. Then follow the suggestions in **Summarize/Reinforce.**

LOGICAL/MATHEMATICAL MODEL Write the sentences in the Visual/Spatial Model on the board. Have students rearrange the sentences so they are in the order in which the action described would occur (I dreamed ..., I thank ..., I will stay ...). Have volunteers identify the tense of each verb and explain what clues helped them know what the tense is. Ask students how the past and future tenses are formed (past: by adding *-ed* to the main verb; future: by using the helping verb *will* with the main verb). Remind students that Lolis spoke these sentences after Mistress had written the letter of manumission. Have three volunteers each choose a different tense and write a response Mistress might have made on the board. Then follow the suggestions in **Summarize/Reinforce.**

VERBAL/LINGUISTIC MODEL Write the sentences in the Visual/Spatial Model on the board. Remind students that Lolis spoke these sentences after Mistress had written her letter of manumission. Ask volunteers to read the sentences aloud with feeling, as if they were Lolis. Have other students identify the verb or verb phrase and tell when the action takes place. Then have the students tell whether the verb is in the present, past, or future tense. If the verb is the past or future tense, have the student explain how the tense was formed. Then follow the suggestions in **Summarize/Reinforce.**

Summarize/Reinforce

Ask students to summarize what they have learned. (The *tense* of a verb shows when the action happens. The *present tense* tells about action that is happening now or that continues to happen. If the subject of a sentence is singular, form the present tense of most verbs by adding *-s* or *-es.* The *past tense* shows action that took place in the past and is formed for most verbs by adding *-ed.* The *future tense* shows action that will happen in the future and is formed by using the helping verb *will* with the main verb.) To reinforce the lesson, have students write past, present, and future sentences about classroom occurrences.

Tested Skill

Context Clues/Multiple-Meaning Words

OBJECTIVE: To use context clues to determine the meanings of multiple-meaning words

Focus

Share the following information with students:

> **When you come across a word that has more than one meaning, look for *context clues* in the surrounding words, phrases, and sentences to help you figure out which meaning makes sense. Knowing how to use context clues to determine the right meaning of a multiple-meaning word will help you better understand what you read.**

Choose a Teaching Model

VISUAL/SPATIAL MODEL Write the words *letter* and *hand* on the board and ask students what they picture in their minds as they read each word. Use their images to create several definitions for each word. (Possible answers may include: *Letter*—a letter of the alphabet; a note written to someone. *Hand*—to give an object to someone else; the end part of the arm; to help someone; clapping; the indicators on a clock). Then write the following sentence on the board:

Mistress wrote the letter and put it into Lolis' hand.

Have students read the sentence silently, then describe what they picture happening. Have them determine which meanings *letter* and *hand* have in that sentence and identify the context clues that helped them know. Then have students write sentences using the other meanings for *letter* and *hand*. After volunteers have read their sentences aloud, follow the suggestions in **Summarize/Reinforce.**

AUDITORY MODEL Write the words *letter* and *hand* on the board and have students recall different meanings they know for each word. (See the Visual/Spatial Model for possible answers.) Then read the following sentence aloud:

Mistress wrote the letter and put it into Lolis' hand.

Have students determine which meanings *letter* and *hand* have in the sentence. Ask them what context clues helped them know that. Then orally give students sentences using another meaning for *letter* and *hand*, and ask volunteers to tell the correct meaning and identify any helpful context clues. Have volunteers use different meanings for the two words in sentences. Then follow the suggestions in **Summarize/Reinforce.**

KINESTHETIC/TACTILE MODEL Give each student several slips of paper. Write the words *letter* and *hand* on the board and discuss with students the different meanings each word has. (See the Visual/Spatial Model for possible answers.) Have students write each meaning on a separate slip of paper. Read the following sentence aloud:

Mistress wrote the letter and put it into Lolis' hand.

Then as you read the sentence again, have students hold up their slips that have the definitions for *letter* and *hand* as they are used in the sentence. Ask volunteers to read their definitions aloud and explain which context clues helped them know the correct meanings. Have volunteers write sentences using other meanings for *letter* and *hand* on the board, and have other volunteers underline the context clues in each sentence that helped them figure out the word's meaning. Then follow the suggestions in **Summarize/Reinforce.**

Summarize/Reinforce

Have students summarize what they have learned. (The surrounding words, phrases, and sentences can contain helpful clues to determining which meaning of a multiple-meaning word is intended.) To reinforce the lesson, have students look for words with more than one meaning in material they have read recently for another subject. Remind students to be on the lookout for multiple-meaning words and to use the strategies from this lesson as they read to help them know what those words mean.

Daily Language Practice

Use Daily Language Practice as a quick and easy way to help students sharpen their proofreading skills as they check two or more sentences each day for errors in grammar, usage, mechanics, and spelling.

Daily Language Practice . . .

- **is a set of proofreading exercises, one set for each major lesson in *Hidden Treasures.***
- **provides practice and reinforcement of language skills presented in each lesson.**
- **reinforces spelling and vocabulary in the context of sentences.**

How to Use Daily Language Practice

1. **Each day, write two exercises on the board or on a transparency for students to proofread and correct. Corrected exercises are shown.**
2. **Have students correct the exercises and explain why each correction is needed.**

SENTENCES OF THE DAY

❷

PROOFREADER'S MARKS

≡	Capitalize.	⌃—	Replace something.
⊙	Add a period.	∿	Transpose.
⌃,	Add a comma.	◯	Spell correctly.
‟ ”	Add quotation marks.	¶	Indent paragraph.
↗	Cut something.	/	Make a lowercase letter.

Daily Language Practice

The Art of Velázquez

Predicate nominatives and adjectives; transitive and intransitive verbs; objects; spelling

1. Velázquez is me sister's favorite artest.

1. Velázquez is my sister's favorite artist.

2. She admires his' devotion to precizion.

2. She admires his devotion to precision.

3. His artworks are both historik and beautifully.

3. His artworks are both historic and beautiful.

4. The peopel in his pictures seem really.

4. The people in his pictures seem real.

5. We compaired two portraits that Velázquez paintid.

5. We compared two portraits that Velázquez painted.

6. A painter who is always striving is probly a good workers.

6. A painter who is always striving is probably a good worker.

7. An appointed court artist worked for the royal familly.

7. An appointed court artist worked for the royal family.

8. His teacher gave lessens about how to paint presisely.

8. His teacher gave lessons about how to paint precisely.

9. Precice observation is an important tools for any artist.

9. Precise observation is an important tool for any artist.

10. A quickly painted canvas can seem inaccurately and clumsily.

10. A quickly painted canvas can seem inaccurate and clumsy.

11. A portrait is a painted piture of some one. The portrait painter and the subject may not have equall roles, but both people are necessarily.

11. A portrait is a painted picture of someone. The portrait painter and the subject may not have equal roles, but both people are necessary.

12. This portrait of me is successfully. You can cents, a strong bond between the painter and I. The cool colors are sign of harmony and relaxation.

12. This portrait of me is successful. You can sense a strong bond between the painter and me. The cool colors are signs of harmony and relaxation.

Key Words are underlined. Spelling Words are printed in red.

Daily Language Practice

I, Juan de Pareja

Simple tenses; predicate nominatives and adjectives; spelling

1. It was aparent that the two painters are good friends.

1. It was apparent that the two painters were good friends.

2. As contemporaries, they shared back grounds and often agree.

2. As contemporaries, they shared backgrounds and often agreed.

3. Their asociation was lengthily and rewardingly.

3. Their association was lengthy and rewarding.

4. They worked tagether on many projects, but each do his own paintings as well.

4. They worked together on many projects, but each did his own paintings as well.

5. For several years, the asistant works even when the master was indisposed.

5. For several years, the assistant worked even when the master was indisposed.

6. Collaborating helpt each painter identified his virtues.

6. Collaborating helped each painter identify his virtues.

7. You can see each painter's aproach when you looked at the work of both of them.

7. You can see each painter's approach when you look at the work of both of them.

8. The radiant glow in her eyes are a difficult things to paint.

8. The radiant glow in her eyes is a difficult thing to paint.

9. When he studies carefully, his pictures were more acurate.

9. When he studied carefully, his pictures were more accurate.

10. His intentions are usualy obviously in the final picture.

10. His intentions are usually obvious in the final picture.

11. If you apreciate art, you probably liked going to art museums. They are good place to analyze different artistic styles.

11. If you appreciate art, you probably like going to art museums. They are good places to analyze different artistic styles.

12. Study how the painter use the paint itself. Look at the textures on the canvas. Some paint layers are very thinly. Others were almost an inch thick!

12. Study how the painter used the paint itself. Look at the textures on the canvas. Some paint layers are very thin. Others are almost an inch thick!

Key Words are underlined. Spelling Words are printed in red.

Daily Language Practice

Two Women Photographers

Perfect tenses; simple tenses; spelling

1. Photography can be an innexpensive hobby if you were careful.

1. Photography can be an inexpensive hobby if you are careful.

2. Many legendary photographers has snapped photos of people in action.

2. Many legendary photographers have snapped photos of people in action.

3. It have always been inpolite to take someone's picture without asking first.

3. It has always been impolite to take someone's picture without asking first.

4. My neice smiled spontaneously and I snap a picture.

4. My niece smiled spontaneously, and I snapped a picture.

5. Ann Bronsen have always wants to be a photographer.

5. Ann Bronsen has always wanted to be a photographer.

6. She took encredible photos when she is in mexico.

6. She took incredible photos when she was in Mexico.

7. She has becomes a avid fan of Flor Garduño's work.

7. She has become an avid fan of Flor Garduño's work.

8. By the end of last year, Ann has started an almost inpossible task.

8. By the end of last year, Ann had started an almost impossible task.

9. Her idea were to take innformal pictures of evry human pose imaginable.

9. Her idea was to take informal pictures of every human pose imaginable.

10. Thousands of negatives has been collected allready.

10. Thousands of negatives have been collected already.

11. Such a monumental project will not happens quickly. Ann hopes that she will has finished by the time she is in college. Luckily, Ann is rarely inpatient.

11. Such a monumental project will not happen quickly. Ann hopes that she will have finished by the time she is in college. Luckily, Ann is rarely impatient.

12. Over the past few months, Ann's project will have been developing rapidly. When she is finished, she will collects her photos in a book. Then she will has a permanent record of her work.

12. Over the past few months, Ann's project has been developing rapidly. When she is finished, she will collect her photos in a book. Then she will have a permanent record of her work.

Key Words are underlined. Spelling Words are printed in red.

Daily Language Practice

The Will and the Way

Regular and irregular verbs; perfect tenses; spelling

1. A highway sine shown the way to are town's new baseball stadium.

1. A highway sign shows the way to our town's new baseball stadium.

2. The stadium have been finished for too years now.

2. The stadium has been finished for two years now.

3. The seats has been slightly revized since the stadium first opend.

3. The seats have been slightly revised since the stadium first opened.

4. After an intensive studie, the city chosed a plan.

4. After an intensive study, the city chose a plan.

5. The stadium were disigned by a prestigious firm.

5. The stadium was designed by a prestigious firm.

6. The architect's avoidid trendy ideas that might become dated quick.

6. The architects avoided trendy ideas that might become dated quickly.

7. The vizitors received a supervized tour of the stadium.

7. The visitors received a supervised tour of the stadium.

8. At the first game, our principal catched a base ball.

8. At the first game, our principal caught a baseball.

9. All game's from the new stadium has been televized.

9. All games from the new stadium have been televised.

10. Our State governor gived a speech on opening day.

10. Our state governor gave a speech on opening day.

11. The architect's vizion has been fully realized. A sparkling new stadium rised up in less than two years. Hard work, careful planning and good ideas have bringed new pride to local sports.

11. The architect's vision has been fully realized. A sparkling new stadium rose up in less than two years. Hard work, careful planning, and good ideas have brought new pride to local sports.

12. A good designer relys on restraint to create popular and functional buildings. Some architects have maked the mistake of trying to be too trendy. A good architect realizes that buildings has to last for a long time.

12. A good designer relies on restraint to create popular and functional buildings. Some architects have made the mistake of trying to be too trendy. A good architect realizes that buildings have to last for a long time.

Key Words are underlined. Spelling Words are printed in red.

FOLD

READER RESPONSE 5

Author's Viewpoint

DURING READING

1. What do you know about the author?
2. What is the author trying to tell you? How do you know?
3. Can you tell what kinds of things (people, places, behavior, feelings) the author likes? If so, how do you know?

READER RESPONSE 5

AFTER READING

4. Do you agree with the author? Why, or why not?
5. What did the author have to know in order to write this article or story?
6. What else could the author have said to support his or her opinion?

FOLD

READER RESPONSE 13

Grand Conversation

GETTING STARTED

1. Work in a group. Decide whether you will read the selection together or on your own.
2. Preview the selection together. Look at pictures, titles, and subtitles. Look for things you might want to talk about later.
3. Discuss what you already know.
   - You might talk about other books by the same author.
   - You might talk about the setting.
   - You might talk about what you already know about the topic.

   Then set a purpose for reading.
4. Read the selection.
   - If the selection is fiction, think about the characters, the setting, the problem, the events, and the solution.

READER RESPONSE 13

AFTER READING

1. Begin a discussion. Choose a leader to keep the discussion going.
2. Make a list of questions to help you get started or to use when group members run out of ideas. The questions listed here are just suggestions.

IF YOU RUN OUT OF IDEAS

- What did you like or dislike about the selection?
- Did the selection make you want to keep reading?
- Did this selection relate to your own life?
- What part was the most interesting or exciting to you?
- What would you say to the author of this selection if you had a chance to meet him or her?

READER RESPONSE 6

AFTER READING

5. What is your favorite word, line, or paragraph in the story? Why is it your favorite?
6. What do you like about the way the author has written the story?
7. Would you like to read something else by this author? Why, or why not?
8. What was the most important thing you learned from the dialogue in this story?

Harcourt Brace School Publishers

FOLD

READER RESPONSE 6

Author's Craft

DURING READING

1. Have you noticed anything you think the author might bring up again later in the story? If so, what did you notice?
2. Tell about any pictures the author has left in your mind.
3. What special words has the author used so far to help you
   - see things in the story?
   - hear things in the story?
   - feel things in the story?
4. What does the dialogue tell you about the characters? Does it sound the way people really talk? Why, or why not?

Harcourt Brace School Publishers

FOLD

READER RESPONSE

Critics Circle

As a member of a Critics Circle, you are going to be comparing two or more selections or articles. Here's what to do.

WHEN READING FICTION

1. The members of your group should preview the selection that you are going to read to decide what it's about.
2. Before your group members read the selection, each of you should find another book or selection or a story in your reading anthology that you have read that has the same topic or theme.
3. With your group members, decide when you should read the new selection in your reading anthology and when you will discuss it.
4. After reading, bring with you to your discussion group the book, selection, or story that you want to compare.

WHEN READING NONFICTION

1. The members of your group should preview the selection that you are going to read to decide what it's about.
2. Before your group members read the selection, find a book or a magazine, newspaper, or encyclopedia article that you have read that gives information about the same topic.
3. After reading the selection in your reading anthology, bring your book or article to your discussion group.
4. Talk about how the information in the selection and the information in your book or article is the same or different.

DISCUSSION QUESTIONS

Your group members may want to use one of these questions to talk about the materials you have read:

1. How is the information alike?
2. How is the information different?
3. Did one of the reading materials offer more or better information? Which one?

FOLD

READER RESPONSE 7

Responding Freely

DURING READING

1. Work with a partner. Look over the story, and decide whether you will read it silently or aloud.
2. Think about the way the story is organized. Decide with your partner how often you will stop to discuss it.
3. Each time you stop, tell what you think, and listen to what your partner says. Discuss things you like or dislike, things you do not understand, or what has happened or what might happen next.
4. Stop and discuss each section until you finish the story.

Harcourt Brace School Publishers

AFTER READING

5. Talk about the whole story.
   - You might talk about your favorite part of the story.
   - You might discuss the author's writing.
   - You might discuss whether what you thought would happen really did happen.

Harcourt Brace School Publishers

WRITING IN YOUR PERSONAL JOURNAL

Sometimes, the members of your Literature Circle may want to write your responses to the selection and then discuss what each of you has written. Here are some things to write about. Choose one.

1. Think of at least three things that the story reminds you of in another story or in your own lives. Tell about them.
2. Copy in your personal journal an important paragraph, sentence, or word from the selection. Explain why it is important to you.
3. What influenced you most as you read: the setting, one of the characters, or the plot of the story? Write about it.

Harcourt Brace School Publishers

READER RESPONSE 9

Literature Circle

ORGANIZING A LITERATURE CIRCLE

The members of your group

- may want to read the selection independently.
- may want to read the selection together to discuss certain parts during reading.
- should decide how many pages to read and what to discuss.

DURING AND AFTER READING

Your group members can

- discuss your reactions to the selection.
- ask questions about parts you did not understand.

Here are some sentence starters to help your Literature Circle begin a discussion. Choose one.

1. My first reaction to the selection was...
2. I loved the way the author...
3. I didn't like the part...
4. The part I remember most is...

Harcourt Brace School Publishers

Harcourt Brace School Publishers

TIPS FOR WORKING IN A GROUP

- When you brainstorm, the goal is to list as many ideas as possible even if they seem disorganized or strange. You can revise the list later.
- Listen carefully and respectfully to all ideas that are suggested.
- If the brainstorming stalls, think about the launch activities the class did and about art mentioned in literature you've read.

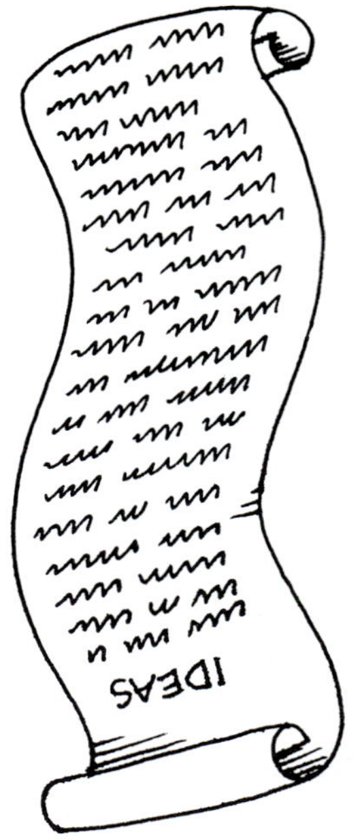

FOLD

THEME PROJECT

LAUNCH 25

Masterpieces

ART IN THE COMMUNITY

Make a List of Types of Art. Work with a group of students who are interested in learning about art events and artists in the community.

GETTING STARTED

- As a group, brainstorm as many types of art as you can.
- Begin by listing artforms that entertain you or just make you feel good.
- For more ideas, think about the works of famous artists through history, and add to your list examples of each type of art you discuss.

TYPE OF ART	EXAMPLES
Recordings	soundtrack to The Wizard of Oz
Paintings	anything by Georgia O'Keeffe
Movies	Star Wars Trilogy

Harcourt Brace School Publishers

(Continued on the other side)

TIPS FOR RESEARCHING ART EVENTS

- As you do your research, write down on index cards the name, address, and phone number of each art organization, as well as the dates of the events or exhibits being presented at each one.
- To find out more about the artists whose work you'll visit, use library resources and ask the librarian for help.
- As you plan visits, feel free to split into subgroups, or join students from other groups who are interested in the same exhibits you are.
- Work cooperatively to try to make sure everyone in your group has an opportunity to observe art in the community.

Harcourt Brace School Publishers

FOLD

THEME PROJECT

CHECKPOINT 1

The Art of Velázquez

26

Research Art Opportunities. Review the checklist below to investigate art experiences available in your community.

- ☑ Go to the library and look through art directories, newspapers, and magazines to find upcoming art exhibits in the community.
- ☑ Contact the Chamber of Commerce, local museums, art schools, colleges, and galleries for additional information.
- ☑ Decide who will visit each event, and make travel arrangements.
- ☑ If you can't visit art exhibits out of school, prepare questions to ask invited speakers about art, or arrange to view art objects in your classroom.

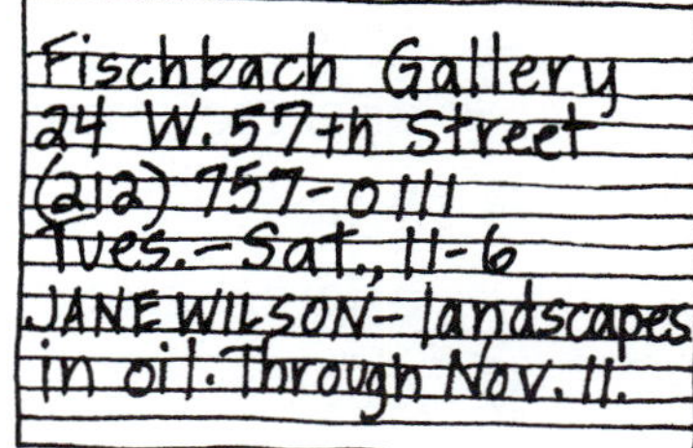

Harcourt Brace School Publishers

(Continued on the other side)

Harcourt Brace School Publishers

TIPS FOR WRITING AN ART REVIEW

- Find a partner who saw the same artwork. Compare notes and ideas about the art experience.
- Look at art reviews in newspapers and magazines to see how they're organized and what kinds of information they include.
- Look through your notes and sketches as you think about the artwork. Support your opinions about the artwork with concrete examples of your observations.

FOLD

THEME PROJECT

CHECKPOINT 2

I, Juan de Pareja

27

Write Reviews of Art Experiences. Review the checklist below as you observe art in the community and write art reviews.

- ☑ Visit the art shows, exhibits, or performances you've selected, listen to guest speakers, or view in-class art displays.
- ☑ As you look at the art, write down your thoughts and feelings or sketch your favorite works in an art journal.
- ☑ When you return to class, be prepared to talk with your original group about your experiences.
- ☑ Choose one of the art shows or artists to focus on as you write a review.

Harcourt Brace School Publishers

(Continued on the other side)

Model: Business Letter

A ***business letter*** *is more formal than a friendly letter. It may be sent to inform, to persuade, or to request information.*

heading

40 Terrace Rd.
Fremont, CA 94539
May 28, 199–

inside address

Mr. Peter Decker
Decker Industries
717 Decker Court
Carmel, IN 46032

greeting

Dear Mr. Decker:

body

We are studying environmental issues at school, and I have learned that your company is on the cutting edge of recycling technology. Please send a catalog or a brochure about your recycled products to the address above. Thank you.

closing

Sincerely,

signature

Cal Ventura

return address

Cal Ventura
40 Terrace Rd.
Fremont, CA 94539

mailing address

Mr. Peter Decker
Decker Industries
717 Decker Court
Carmel, IN 46032

Additional Reading
Hidden Treasures

The following list is a compilation of the Reading Trade Books selected for the lesson plans.

THEME: MASTERPIECES

Amazing Buildings **by Philip Wilkinson. Dorling Kindersley, 1993. EASY**
Twenty famous buildings from around the world are discussed in this book, which includes photographs, floorplans, and cutaway diagrams.

The American Eye: Eleven Artists of the Twentieth Century **by Jan Greenberg and Sandra Jordan. Delacorte, 1995. AVERAGE**
From the abstract sculptures of Isamu Noguchi to Warhol's soup cans, the works described here cover a range of styles and media.

The Apprentice **by Pilar Molina Llorente. Translated by Robin Longshaw. Farrar, Straus & Giroux, 1989. AVERAGE**
Arduino feels lucky to be Maestro di Flori's apprentice, but when he stumbles upon the Maestro's secret Arduino must make a decision that could risk his painting career. *ALA Notable Book*

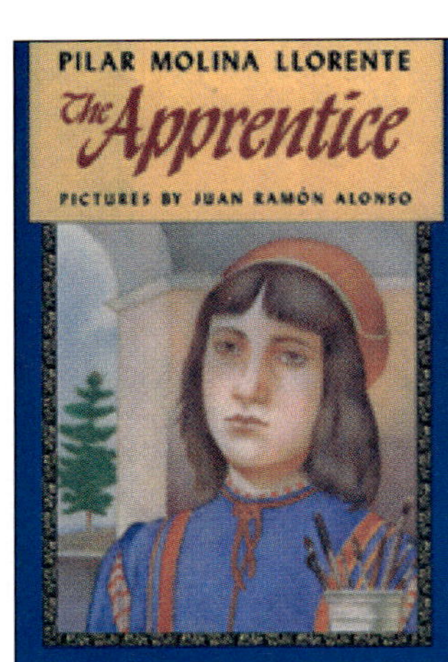

AS: A Surfeit of Similes **by Norton Juster. William Morrow, 1989. EASY**
A simile is defined by many rhyming examples. *Children's Choice; Parents' Choice*

Boy of the Painted Cave **by Justin Denzel. G. P. Putnam's Sons, 1988. EASY**
A boy in Cro-Magnon times longs to be a cave artist.

Cameras **by Ian Graham. Franklin Watts, 1991. AVERAGE**
The author describes different types of cameras, a camera's different parts, and such topics as film and special effects.

Children of Promise: African-American Literature and Art for Young People **edited by Charles Sullivan. Harry N. Abrams, 1991. CHALLENGING**
African-American history and culture are celebrated in this collection of poems, folk songs, and literary excerpts. Well-chosen historical photographs and art reproductions accompany the literature. *ALA Best Book for Young Adults*

The Cuckoo Clock **by Mary Stolz. Godine, 1986. EASY**
An apprentice helps his aging master, Ula, make one last cuckoo clock. It promises to be the most remarkable of his creations.

Cutters, Carvers, and the Cathedral **by George Ancona. Lothrop, Lee & Shepard, 1995. EASY**
This photo essay describes a program to restore one of New York's historic cathedrals using apprentices and artisans from all over the world.

Don Quixote and Sancho Panza **by Miguel de Cervantes. Adapted by Margaret Hodges. Scribner's, 1992. CHALLENGING**
This lively retelling of the classic tale of Don Quixote focuses on the often hilarious misadventures of the Don and his "squire," Sancho.

Dorothea Lange **by Robyn Montana Turner. Little, Brown, 1994. AVERAGE**
This biography describes the struggles of the famous photographer and how her stunning black-and-white photographs stirred the nation to action during the Great Depression. *Notable Trade Book in Social Studies*

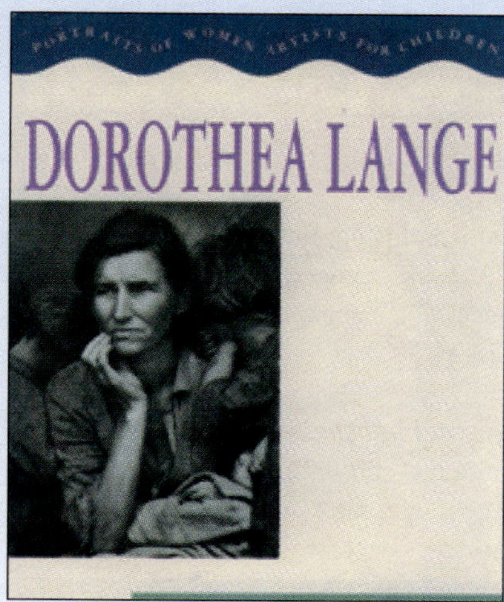

El Güero **by Elizabeth Borton de Treviño. Farrar, Straus & Giroux, 1989. CHALLENGING**
When his father is jailed under false charges, a young Mexican boy must travel a great distance to seek help. *Notable Trade Book in Social Studies*

Georgia O'Keeffe **by Robyn Montana Turner. Little, Brown, 1991. AVERAGE**
The life of this fiercely original artist is described. The text is enhanced by large color reproductions of her work. *Teachers' Choice; Notable Trade Book in Social Studies*

Hold Fast to Dreams **by Andrea Davis Pinkney. William Morrow, 1995. AVERAGE**
Dierdre likes to look at life through her camera's viewfinder. Everything seems to go out of focus, though, when she moves to a new town.

Home **edited by Michael J. Rosen. HarperCollins, 1992. AVERAGE**
Thirty famous authors and illustrators of books for young people express how they feel about home in this collaboration whose proceeds go to benefit the homeless. *Notable Trade Book in Social Studies*

Jace the Ace **by Joanne Rocklin. Macmillan, 1990. EASY**
Jason has dreams of becoming a famous photojournalist, but his habit of making up stories about his life gets him into trouble.

Jacques-Henri Lartigue: Boy with a Camera **by John Cech. Four Winds, 1994. EASY**
Lartigue's boyhood photographs have a freshness and humor that hint at the success he would one day find as one of France's most famous photographers.

Julia Morgan: Architect of Dreams **by Ginger Wadsworth. Lerner, 1990. AVERAGE**
In almost fifty years of productive work, this remarkable architect designed almost 700 buildings. *Notable Trade Book in Social Studies*

Kids at Work: Lewis Hine and the Crusade Against Child Labor **by Russell Freedman. Clarion, 1994. AVERAGE**
Hine used his powerful photographs to portray the evils of child labor in the early 1900s, and his work led to important legal reforms. *ALA Notable Book; SLJ Best Books; Notable Trade Book in Social Studies*

Leona **by Elizabeth Borton de Treviño. Farrar, Straus & Giroux, 1994. CHALLENGING**
This work of historical fiction recounts the true story of Leona Vicario, a courageous young woman who helped the Mexican rebels obtain their independence from Spain.

Leonardo da Vinci: Artist, Inventor, and Scientist of the Renaissance **by Francesca Romei. Peter Bedrick, 1994. CHALLENGING**
Da Vinci's genius spanned the arts and sciences, and his work in both areas testifies to the power of the imagination.

Looking at Paintings: Dogs **by Peggy Roalf. Hyperion, 1993. AVERAGE**
Man's best friend has been a favorite subject of artists from many cultures and eras.

Looking at Photographs: People **by Jacques Lowe. Chronicle, 1994. AVERAGE**
Using the work of a number of famous photographers, the author vividly demonstrates that photographs can capture human personality and drama.

Mary Cassatt **by Robyn Montana Turner. Little, Brown, 1992. AVERAGE**
Read about the life of a woman who became one of America's best-loved painters at a time when few women painted professionally. *Notable Trade Book in Social Studies*

Maya Lin: Architect and Artist **by Mary Malone. Enslow, 1995. AVERAGE**
This is a biography of the remarkable young architect who designed the Vietnam Veterans Memorial.

Monet **by Antony Mason. Barron's, 1994. AVERAGE**
Interesting facts about the famous Impressionist painter's life are interspersed with full-color reproductions of his work in this attractive book.

My First Photography Book: A Life-Size Guide to Taking Creative Photographs and Making Exciting Projects with Your Prints **by Dave King. Dorling Kindersley, 1994. AVERAGE**
Shutterbugs will find plenty of advice about beginning photography projects in this book.

Natural Wonders: Stories Science Photos Tell **by Vicki Cobb. Lothrop, Lee & Shepard, 1990. AVERAGE**
Often beautiful as well as informative, the photographs in this collection capture a variety of natural phenomena which are explained in clear, easy-to-read text.

Pablo Picasso **by Ernest Raboff. HarperCollins, 1987. AVERAGE**
This is a biography of the visionary artist responsible for creating the artistic style of Cubism.

Paint and Painting. **Scholastic, 1994. EASY**
This book examines artists' materials and techniques in a unique "interactive" design. *Teachers' Choice*

Painting: Behind the Scenes **by Andrew Pekarik. Hyperion, 1992. EASY**
Works by famous artists are used to illustrate basic art concepts.

Perspective **by Alison Cole. Dorling Kindersley, 1992. AVERAGE**
Gorgeous illustrations accompany this highly detailed study of the development of perspective in art over four centuries.

Rembrandt **by Ernest Raboff. HarperCollins, 1987. AVERAGE**
This examination of the life and work of the Dutch master includes many full-color reproductions of his work.

Roy Lichtenstein: The Artist at Work **by Lou Ann Walker. Dutton, 1994. AVERAGE**
Lichtenstein's fun, fresh approach to painting made groundbreaking art out of such everyday things as comic strips.

***A Short Walk Around the Pyramids and Through the World of Art* by Philip M. Isaacson. Knopf, 1993. CHALLENGING**

What makes a work of art? The author provides some insights on his tour of the art world, from ancient times to today. *ALA Notable; SLJ Best Books; Notable Trade Book in Social Studies*

***Starting Home: The Story of Horace Pippin, Painter* by Mary E. Lyons. Scribner's, 1993. AVERAGE**

Folk artist Horace Pippin taught himself to paint, and his simple style remains a unique contribution to the history of African-American art. *ALA Notable Book*

***Take a Look: An Introduction to the Experience of Art* by Rosemary Davidson. Viking Penguin, 1993. CHALLENGING**

Lively, informal text makes this a thoroughly entertaining introduction to art styles and concepts. *Teachers' Choice*

***Talking with Artists* by Pat Cummings. Bradbury, 1992. CHALLENGING**

In these interviews, fourteen children's book illustrators talk about their lives and their work. *ALA Notable Book; Children's Choice; Teachers' Choice*

***Vincent Van Gogh* by Ernest Raboff. HarperCollins, 1988. AVERAGE**

Van Gogh's brilliant use of brushwork and vivid colors made his work utterly unique, but he was unknown in his own lifetime.

***Walking the Log: Memories of a Southern Childhood* by Bessie Nickens. Rizzoli, 1995. EASY**

African American artist Bessie Nickens describes her rural childhood and accompanies the text with her distinctive artwork.

***A Weekend with Velázquez* by Florian Rodari. Translated by Ann K. Beneduce. Rizzoli, 1993. EASY**

This informal "visit" with the Spanish master reveals a great deal about his life and work.

***Western Art: 1600-1800* by Christopher McHugh. Thomson Learning, 1995. AVERAGE**

The eventful years between 1600 and 1800 are the subject of this study, which presents many full-color reproductions of the period's artwork with accompanying explanations.

***The Young Artist* by Thomas Locker. Dial, 1989. EASY**

When Adrian realizes that his subjects want portraits of themselves not as they are, but as they would *like* to be, he finds himself in the middle of a dilemma.

As I See Myself

School ↔ Home Connection

1. Many famous artists have painted self-portraits. These show how the artist viewed himself or herself. How do you view yourself? Use the space provided to draw a self-portrait. Your portrait can be realistic, or it can be abstract. Use any medium you wish: pencil, crayon, pen and ink, colored marker, and so on.
2. Share your self-portrait with a family member.

Harcourt Brace School Publishers

Check It Out

Did you enjoy reading about Diego Velázquez and his paintings? If so, you may want to check out some of these books about other artists the next time you visit the library: *Leonardo da Vinci: Artist, Inventor, and Scientist of the Renaissance* by Francesca Romei (Peter Bedrick, 1994); *Georgia O'Keeffe* by Robyn Montana Turner (Little, Brown, 1991); and *Rembrandt* by Ernest Raboff (HarperCollins, 1987).

For the Family Album

Does your family have a photograph album that shows family members of the present and past? Sit down with your family and go through the album. Talk about what the pictures show about life long ago, in more recent times, and today.

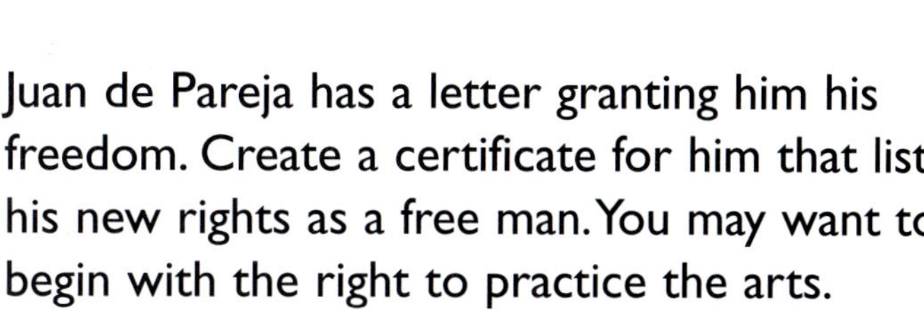

SCHOOL ↔ HOME CONNECTION

1. Juan de Pareja has a letter granting him his freedom. Create a certificate for him that lists his new rights as a free man. You may want to begin with the right to practice the arts.
2. On the back, write a brief explanation of why you think Juan would especially value or enjoy those rights.
3. Share your certificate and explanation with a family member.

A CERTIFICATE OF RIGHTS

CHECK it OUT If you visit the library soon, check out some of the following books about people who fought for their own freedom or the freedom of others: *The Apprentice* by Pilar Molina Llorente (Farrar, Straus & Giroux, 1989); *El Güero* by Elizabeth Borton de Treviño (Farrar, Straus & Giroux, 1989); and *Kids at Work: Lewis Hines and the Crusade Against Child Labor* by Russell Freedman (Clarion, 1994).

FOR THE FAMILY ALBUM

Along with rights go responsibilities to prevent those rights from being abused. For example, along with the right to privacy in your own room goes the responsibility for keeping it clean. Talk with family members about the rights you have or would like to have. Discuss the responsibilities that accompany those rights. Work with family members to make a list of rights you might be given if you accept certain responsibilities.

SCHOOL ↔ HOME CONNECTION

1. A photograph tells a story that the photographer sees. Photographs may tell a very different story to a viewer.
2. What stories do you see in the photographs taken by Margaret Bourke-White and Flor Garduño? Choose a photograph from the selections and write a caption that tells the story you see. What's happening in the picture? What is the person thinking? Where is he or she going? Why?
3. Remember that five different viewers of one photograph may see five different stories in it.

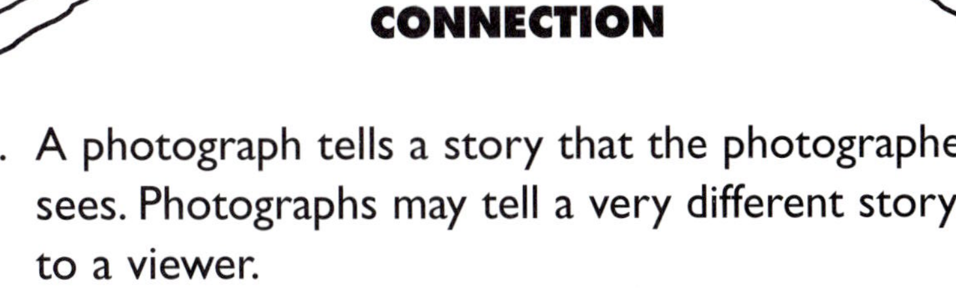

Harcourt Brace School Publishers

THE STORY BEHIND THE PICTURE

If you would like to find out more about photography, you might look for these books: *Cameras* by Ian Graham (Franklin Watts, 1991); *Jacques-Henri Lartigue: Boy with a Camera* by John Cech (Four Winds, 1994); and *Looking at Photographs: People* by Jacques Lowe (Chronicle, 1994).

FOR THE FAMILY ALBUM

What are the stories behind photos in your family's album? Gather some photographs together and talk with family members about what they remember about that picture or about that day. Do you remember most what the picture shows, or what it doesn't? Ask the person who took the picture to recall his or her point of view when taking it. Compare that to the point of view of the picture's subject(s) and to those who were there but were not pictured.

MY DREAM HOUSE

SCHOOL ↔ HOME CONNECTION

1. Architects often design "dream houses," either for themselves or for their clients. What would your dream house look like? In the space provided, draw the house you would like to live in. You may draw a picture of the house from the outside or draw a complete floor plan.
2. On the back, describe the special features your house has.
3. Share your dream house with a family member.

Harcourt Brace School Publishers

CHECK it OUT If you plan a library visit soon, you may want to check out the following books about creative people who had the will and found the way to succeed: *The American Eye: Eleven Artists of the Twentieth Century* by Jan Greenberg and Sandra Jordan (Delacorte, 1995); *Dorothea Lange* by Robyn Montana Turner (Little, Brown, 1994); and *Maya Lin: Architect and Artist* by Mary Malone (Enslow, 1995).

FOR THE FAMILY ALBUM

The house of your dreams may not be the house other family members dream of. Talk about the features family members would like to have in a house. Work with them to create a plan for a house all of you would like to live in.

Harcourt Brace School Publishers

Resources

Theme 6

Tested Skill

RETEACH: GRAMMAR

Adverbs

OBJECTIVE: To understand that an adverb modifies, or describes, a verb, an adjective, or another adverb

Focus

Share the following information with students:

> **An adverb is a word that describes a verb, an adjective, or another adverb. It explains *how, when, where,* or *to what extent.* Many adverbs end with *-ly.***

Choose a Teaching Model

INTERPERSONAL MODEL Write the following sentences on the board:

Liz wanted to build something, so Pete showed her what to do.
She began working on the cupboards.
She got tangled up with curves and angles.
She asked for help.
Pete explained.

Have students read the sentences on the board and think about how Liz Fordred might have used adverbs to help others understand her experience. After students have read all the sentences, help them add adverbs to each sentence by asking questions such as these: *To what extend did Liz want to build?* (Possible responses: really, very much) *How did she begin working?* (enthusiastically) *Where were the cupboards?* (below) *To what extent did she get tangled?* (absolutely) *When did she ask for help?* (soon) *When or to what extent did Pete explain?* (once again) Discuss with students how the adverbs help explain what happened, and how they help others know what Liz experienced. Then follow the suggestions in **Summarize/Reinforce.**

AUDITORY MODEL Read all the sentences from the Interpersonal Model aloud and have students think about ways Liz Fordred might have used adverbs to describe her experience building the boat.

Then, as you read each sentence again, pause and ask questions such as the ones below to help students add adverbs to the sentences. Ask volunteers to suggest appropriate adverbs and repeat the sentence with the adverb added.

To what extent did Liz want to build? (really)
How did she begin working? (enthusiastically)
Where were the cupboards? (below)
To what extent did she get tangled? (absolutely)
When did she ask for help? (soon)
When or to what extent did Pete explain? (once again)

Discuss how the added adverbs change Liz's description. Then following the suggestions in **Summarize/Reinforce.**

VERBAL/LINGUISTIC MODEL Write the sentences from the Interpersonal Model on the board. Ask students to read the sentences to themselves and think of what adverbs Liz Fordred might have included to help readers understand her experience. After they have read the sentences through, read each sentence aloud and help them brainstorm for appropriate adverbs by asking questions such as those given for the Auditory Model. Write students' suggestions on the board. Then have students rewrite the sentences, choosing adverbs from the board. Ask volunteers to read their sentences aloud. Discuss how the added adverbs change Liz's description. Then follow the suggestions in **Summarize/Reinforce.**

Summarize/Reinforce

Have students summarize what they have learned about adverbs. (An adverb is a word that describes a verb, an adjective, or another adverb. It explains *how, when, where,* or *to what extent.* Many adverbs end with *-ly.*) To reinforce the lesson, have students add different adverbs to the sentence *Pete explained.* to answer the questions *How?, When?, Where?,* and *To what extent?*

Reference Sources

OBJECTIVE: To identify and use reference sources

Focus

Share the following information with students:

> **Knowing which reference source to consult allows readers to find specific information they need. Commonly-used reference sources include these: dictionary, specialized dictionaries, thesaurus, encyclopedia, almanac, atlas, *Readers' Guide to Periodical Literature,* and *Books in Print.* Some information can be found in more than one reference source.**

Choose a Teaching Model

KINESTHETIC/MOTOR MODEL Display examples of various reference sources. Arrange students in small groups and give each group one of the reference sources. Have each group write a description of what information the source contains and two questions, on separate slips of paper, that could be answered by consulting the source. Have each group read its description and one of the questions its source could answer. Then display the reference sources together and distribute the second questions that the groups wrote. Have each group explain how it would approach finding the answer to the question and which reference source it would use. Follow the suggestions in **Summarize/Reinforce.**

VISUAL/SPATIAL MODEL List the various reference sources on the board. Help students describe the kind of information they would find in each source. Ask volunteers to choose one source and explain how they would use it. Then write the following list on the board:

South Africa	***Kon Tiki***
foredeck	**rainfall in Rhodesia (Zimbabwe)**
restrictions	**current ocean voyages**

Have students copy the list on a separate sheet of paper. Then ask them to write, next to each entry, one or more reference sources they would use to find information about that topic. After volunteers have shared responses with the class, follow the suggestions in **Summarize/Reinforce.**

AUDITORY MODEL List the various reference sources on the board, and discuss with students the kind of information found in each. Then pose questions that begin *Where can I look to find out about* _______ *?* and insert a topic listed in the Visual/Spatial Model. Ask students who answer the questions to explain why they would choose the reference source(s) they suggested. Follow the suggestions in **Summarize/Reinforce.**

Summarize/Reinforce

Have students summarize the importance of knowing which reference source to use. (Knowing which reference source to consult allows readers to find specific information they need.) To reinforce the lesson, have students use one of the sources to find more information about oceans. Remind students that good readers consult reference sources often—even when reading for pleasure.

Negatives

OBJECTIVES: To understand that negatives mean "no"; to use negatives in sentences and phrases correctly

Focus

Share the following information with students:

> **Negatives are words that mean "no." Commonly used negatives include *no, not, never, none, nowhere, nothing, nobody, no one, neither, hardly, scarcely,* and *barely.* Avoid using a double negative, or two negative words, when only one in necessary.**

Choose a Teaching Model

VISUAL/SPATIAL MODEL Write the following sentences on the board without the words in brackets:

The barking sound was [not] a wolf.
Brian could [not] easily speak to the boy.
The trading post was [nothing] more than a small cabin.
Brian's hands suffered [no] long-range damage.

Ask students to read the sentences. Discuss with them that each sentence is based on "The River," and each is a false statement. Help them determine that each needs a negative to become true. Have students brainstorm together possible negatives but write their own lists. Ask a volunteer to tell which negative he or she would use in the first sentence and to rewrite the sentence on the board. (The barking sound was not a wolf.) You may want to rewrite the sentence *The barking sound was not no wolf* and point out the incorrect double negative. Have students add a negative from their list to rewrite each of the remaining sentences. Discuss the sentences volunteers share, and then follow the suggestions in **Summarize/Reinforce.**

AUDITORY MODEL Have students recall the part of "The River" where Brian finally gets the raft to the trading post, including what he saw and how he felt. Then read the sentences from the Visual/Spatial Model aloud. Explain that each is a false statement based on Brian's experience and each sentence needs a negative to be true. Have students brainstorm a list of negatives. Then, as you reread the sentences one at a time, have students repeat the sentence and suggest ways a negative could be used to make the sentence true. Add a double negative to one or two sentences—for example: *The barking sound was not no wolf. Brian's hands didn't suffer no long-range damage.* Ask students to identify the double negative and restate the sentence correctly. Then follow the suggestions in **Summarize/Reinforce.**

KINESTHETIC/MOTOR MODEL Write the sentences from the Visual/Spatial Model on sentence strips. Have several blank index cards or short strips of paper available. Help students recall the part of "The River" where Brian arrives at the trading post, including what he saw and how he felt. Then display the sentence strips and explain that each sentence is a false statement based on Brian's experience and needs a negative to be true. Have students brainstorm together for negatives and write each one on a card. Read each sentence with students and ask them which negatives could be used to make the sentence true. Have a volunteer cut the sentence strip and insert an appropriate negative. After completing all four sentences, show students a sentence with a double negative and explain why only one is needed. Then follow the suggestions in **Summarize/Reinforce.**

Summarize/Reinforce

Have students summarize what they have learned about using negatives. (Negatives are words that mean "no." Avoid using a double negative if only one is necessary.) Reinforce the lesson by having students work in pairs, writing sentences about what they see going on in the classroom for their partner to rewrite, adding appropriate negatives. Remind students to watch out for double negatives in their own writing.

Tested Skill

Summarizing/Paraphrasing

OBJECTIVE: To summarize and paraphrase a selection

Focus

Share the following information with students:

> **When you *summarize* a selection, you state the main events or ideas as briefly as possible. You can use the author's words or your own. When you *paraphrase,* you retell the whole story, not just the main events, in your own words. A paraphrase usually contains more details than a summary does. Both summarizing and paraphrasing can help you understand and remember the selections you read.**

Choose a Teaching Model

LOGICAL/MATHEMATICAL MODEL Tell students that although summarizing and paraphrasing are a little different, they both recount a flow of information or a series of events. Have students reread the end of "The River," starting with the paragraph on page 558 that begins *About seven months,* and note the order in which events happened. After students have finished reading, discuss what happened, listing the main events on the board.

1. Brian was at home.
2. A delivery person came to the door.
3. He set a canoe on the lawn.
4. The driver drove away.
5. Brian read the note from Derek attached to the canoe.

Then have students refer to the list as they write their own summary of the passage. Ask volunteers to share their summaries with the group. Discuss how their paragraphs would be different if they had paraphrased the passage. Then follow the suggestions in **Summarize/Reinforce.**

VERBAL/LINGUISTIC MODEL Have students reread the end of "The River," starting with the paragraph on page 558 that begins *About seven months.* As they read, suggest that they think of the points they need to remember to explain this part of the story to someone else. What words could they use to simply explain how the story ends? After students have finished reading, write the points they suggest on the board. (See the Logical/Mathematical Model for a possible list.) Then have students use the list as they write their own summaries of the passage. Ask volunteers to share their summaries with the group, explaining how they might have written their paragraph differently if it were a paraphrase. Then follow the suggestions in **Summarize/Reinforce.**

INTERPERSONAL MODEL Have students recall books they have read that they have wanted to tell someone else about, and then remind them that summarizing or paraphrasing can help them do that. Ask students to reread the end of "The River," starting with the paragraph on page 558 that begins *About seven months,* and think about the points they would remember to help someone else understand how the story ends. List their suggestions on the board. (See the Logical/Mathematical Model for a possible list.) Then have volunteers paraphrase the passage aloud to the class, putting into their own words how the story ends without changing the author's meaning. Discuss with students how a summary would be different. Then follow the suggestions in **Summarize/Reinforce.**

Summarize/Reinforce

Have students summarize the difference between a summary and a paraphrase. (A summary states the main ideas or events of a selection. It often contains the author's own words. A paraphrase is a retelling of the selection in your own words and often contains details that a summary would not.) To reinforce the lesson, have students review a magazine article they have read recently and write a summary or a paraphrase of it. Remind them that summarizing or paraphrasing the material they read will help them understand and remember it.

Prepositions and Prepositional Phrases

OBJECTIVES: To understand that a preposition shows the relationship of a noun or a pronoun to another word in the sentence; to understand that the noun or the pronoun that follows a preposition is the object of that preposition; to understand that a prepositional phrase is made up of a preposition, its object, and all the words in between

Focus

Share the following information with students:

Prepositions help show the relationship between a noun or a pronoun and another word in a sentence. Commonly used prepositions are *around, at, behind, by, for, from, in, into, of, on, over, to, under,* and *with.* A prepositional phrase is a group of words that begins with a preposition and ends with a noun or a pronoun, which is the object of the preposition, and includes all the words in between.

Choosing a Teaching Model

AUDITORY MODEL Use the following sentences as examples:

Miyax looked at the wolves.
She put the flowers in her pot.
Miyax sealed her house with mud from the pond.

Help students recall some commonly used prepositions. Then have them listen for a prepositional phrase as you read the first example sentence aloud. Remind students that a preposition signals the beginning of a prepositional phrase; a noun or pronoun is at the end of the phrase. Read aloud the first sentence about Miyax. Ask a volunteer to identify the prepositional phrase, the preposition at the beginning and its object. Tell students that *at the wolves* explains what Miyax looked at. Read the second and third sentences one at a time. Help students identify and analyze the prepositional phrase or phrases in each. Have them suggest other sentences that contain prepositional phrases before following the suggestions in **Summarize/Reinforce.**

VISUAL/SPATIAL MODEL Help students recall some commonly used prepositions, and write their suggestions on the board. Then have students recall the story "Julie of the Wolves." Ask volunteers to describe how they remember the setting and how Julie (as Miyax) got to know the wolves. Have them describe what the terrain looked like, how Miyax and the wolves moved around it, and where they lived in relationship to each other. Encourage students to refer to the list of prepositions to help them imagine the scene. Ask volunteers to write sentences on the board about what they picture and underline any prepositional phrases. Help students analyze each prepositional phrase, identifying the whole phrase as well as the preposition and its object. Ask what the phrase helps explain. Then follow the suggestions in **Summarize/Reinforce.**

KINESTHETIC/MOTOR MODEL Help students recall some commonly used prepositions, and write their suggestions on the board. Then choose one preposition and ask two volunteers to stand in a way that uses that preposition. The two students, for instance, stand *beside* each other. Have students write a sentence that explains the relationship of the two students. (For example, *Marc is standing beside María.*) Then have the students identify the prepositional phrase in their sentence, the preposition, and its object. Have several volunteers—singly or in pairs—choose prepositions from the list to demonstrate for others to write sentences about. Help students analyze each prepositional phrase and determine what it explains or describes. Then follow the suggestions in **Summarize/Reinforce.**

Summarize/Reinforce

Have students summarize what they have learned about prepositions and prepositional phrases. (A preposition shows the relationship between a noun or pronoun and another word in the sentence. A prepositional phrase is a group of words that begins with a preposition and ends with a noun or pronoun.) To reinforce the lesson, have students write a description of where they are sitting in the classroom relative to other students, to windows or the door, or to some other reference points. Have them identify the prepositional phrases they use. Remind them that prepositional phrases are useful in explaining relationships between objects and ideas.

Point of View

OBJECTIVE: To understand the point of view an author uses to tell a story

Focus

Share the following information with students:

> **The *point of view* is the position an author uses to tell a story. For a *first-person* point of view, the story is told from the position—or through the eyes—of a narrator who uses the pronouns *I* and *me*. A story with a *third-person* point of view is told from the position of an outside observer. It is either *limited*, with the narrator telling only one character's thoughts and feelings, or *omniscient*, with all the characters' thoughts and feelings revealed. A story told from a third-person point of view uses third-person pronouns *(he, him, she, her, they, them)*.**

Choose a Teaching Model

VISUAL/SPATIAL MODEL Use the following passages as examples.

- the first three paragraphs on page 452 of "I, Juan de Pareja" (first person)
- page 540 of "The River" (third-person limited)
- page 236 of "Number the Stars" (third-person omniscient)

After students have read each passage silently, discuss its point of view with them. Have students point out the words that help them know from what position the story is told. Ask students to explain how the passage would be different if it were written from a different point of view. Write a sentence from each passage on the board for students to rewrite. After reviewing the four passages, follow the suggestions in **Summarize/Reinforce.**

INTRAPERSONAL MODEL Use the passages provided for the Visual/Spatial Model as examples. Have students read each passage silently. As they read, encourage them to imagine themselves as the narrator of the story. Ask *What is your vantage point, your point of view? Do you know the thoughts and feelings of all the characters? Do you know just what you, the observer-narrator, see? Or do you really understand what is happening to just one character?* Discuss the point of view of each passage with students, asking them how they know what it is. Then ask them to reread the passage, imagining themselves observing and narrating from a different point of view. Have volunteers share their views with the class. Then follow the suggestions in **Summarize/Reinforce.**

AUDITORY MODEL Use the passages provided for the Visual/Spatial Model as examples. Ask a volunteer to read each passage aloud. Discuss the point of view expressed in the passage with students, asking them to explain how they know from what point of view the story is told. Then have students listen carefully as you reread the passage. Encourage them to think about how the passage would be different if told from another point of view is limited, the thought or feelings of only one retell one passage to the rest of the group. Then follow the suggestions in **Summarize/Reinforce.**

Summarize/Reinforce

Check students' understanding of point of view by having them summarize how the three points of view differ. (A story told from a first-person point of view uses the pronouns *I* and *me*. It is told through the eyes of one person, the narrator. Stories with a third-person point of view use third-person pronouns. If the point of view is limited, the thoughts or feelings of only one character are revealed. If the narrator watches and tells all the characters' thoughts and feelings, the point of view is third-person omniscient.) To reinforce the lesson, have students find other examples of each point of view. Encourage them to always identify the point of view of the stories they read.

Adjective and Adverb Phrases

OBJECTIVES: To recognize adjective and adverb phrases; to use adjective and adverb phrases effectively

Focus

Share the following information with students:

> **A *prepositional phrase* is made up of a preposition, its object, and all words in between. When a prepositional phrase describes a noun, it is called an *adjective phrase.* When a prepositional phrase describes a verb, it is an *adverb phrase.***

Choose a Teaching Model

VISUAL/SPATIAL MODEL Write the sentences below on the board, leaving space between them.

The pack of wolves roams.
The pack travels.
Each spring the pack stays.
The behavior ensures the pups' safety.

Ask a volunteer to read the first sentence and underline the prepositional phrase. Have students identify the preposition *(of)* and its object *(wolves)*. Help students identify the phrase as an adjective phrase because it modifies *pack.* Then have students read the second sentence and describe what they visualize when you ask *Where does the pack travel?* (Possible responses: "around its territory," "across the snow," "over long distances") Have students incorporate their responses into the sentence—*The pack travels around its territory*. Write the sentence on the board, and have students identify the prepositional phrase as an adverb phrase and explain how they know. (It describes the verb *travels.*) Follow the same procedure with the third and fourth sentences: Ask *Where do you see the pack staying?* to generate adverb phrases for the third sentence, and *Whose behavior ensures the pups' safety?* to generate adjective phrases for the fourth sentence. Then follow the suggestions in **Summarize/Reinforce.**

VERBAL/LINGUISTIC MODEL Write the sentences from the Visual/Spatial Model on the board. Have students read the first sentence and identify the prepositional phrase as an adjective phrase describing *pack.* Ask students to name other common prepositions. Write them on the board. Then ask students to identify the noun and verb in the second sentence. Have volunteers suggest a prepositional phrase using one of the prepositions from the list that describes either *pack* or *travels*. To get them started, ask *Where does the pack travel?* or *Which pack travels?* Incorporate a phrase in the sentence, and have students identify it as an adjective or an adverb phrase and explain why. Follow the same procedure with the third and fourth sentences before following the suggestions in **Summarize/Reinforce.**

KINESTHETIC/MOTOR MODEL Write the four example sentences from the Visual/Spatial Model on the board and the phrases *of the wolves, in one place, around its territory* on sentence strips. Display the strips near the sentences. Have students read the first sentence and identify the prepositional phrase as an adjective phrase describing *pack.* Have volunteers read the three remaining sentences on the board and match them with phrases, taking the strips and placing them where they belong in the sentences. (For the last sentence, students can place the phrase *of the wolves* after the word *behavior.*) Be sure students identify the phrase inserted as either an adjective or an adverb phrase and explain how they know. You may want to ask them to suggest other prepositional phrases they could use in the sentences before following the suggestions in **Summarize/Reinforce.**

Summarize/Reinforce

Have students summarize what they have learned about adjective and adverb phrases. (An adverb phrase is a prepositional phrase that describes a verb. An adjective phrase describes a noun.) To reinforce the lesson, have students work in pairs, each writing three sentences containing adjective or adverb phrases for his or her partner to identify. Remind students to place a prepositional phrase as close as possible to the word it describes.

Test-Taking Strategies

OBJECTIVE: To learn test-taking strategies in order to improve performance on tests

Focus

Share the following information with students:

> **Different test-taking strategies work best on different kinds of tests. Knowing which strategy to use can help you answer questions and solve test problems. Using test-taking strategies will help you improve your test scores.**

Choose a Teaching Model

VERBAL/LINGUISTIC MODEL Write the following strategies on the board:

1. Read the instructions carefully.
2. Identify signal and key words in the question.
3. Eliminate wrong answer choices.
4. Reread the item to check your answer.
5. Pace yourself; do the easy questions first.

Have students recall and name a few of the kinds of tests they have taken. (Possible responses: true-false, multiple choice, matching, vocabulary with context clues, essay) Then discuss each strategy point with students, making sure they understand which kind of test they could use the strategy on and how it would help them approach a test question. Remind them that different strategies work best for different tests. Provide students with an old test and have them orally walk through the taking of it. Guide them as needed by asking questions based on the strategies, such as: *What is the first thing you'd do when starting a test? How long should you spend on each question? What key/signal words might help you answer the first question?* Then follow the suggestions in **Summarize/Reinforce.**

AUDITORY MODEL Discuss with students the kinds of test questions they have encountered on recent tests. Then write the strategies from the Verbal/Linguistic Model on the board. Ask a volunteer to read each strategy aloud, and discuss it with students. Remind students that different strategies work best for different tests, and help them recall a test they have taken that they could have applied each strategy to. Have students orally walk through the taking of an old test, employing appropriate strategies. Then follow the suggestions in **Summarize/Reinforce.**

LOGICAL/MATHEMATICAL MODEL Write the strategies from the Verbal/Linguistic Model on the board, but in random order without the numbers. Provide students with copies of an old test. Have them identify what kind of test questions are on it, then recall other kinds of tests they have taken. Walk students through the taking of the sample test by identifying the steps they would follow if they were actually taking it. Point out the strategies on the board, and have students identify those appropriate to the sample test. Review the strategies with students and encourage them to put the strategies in a logical order to create their own test-taking checklist. Then follow the suggestions in **Summarize/Reinforce.**

Summarize/Reinforce

Check students' understanding by having them summarize why and how approaching a test strategically could help them improve their test scores. (Different test-taking strategies work best on different kinds of tests. Choose the strategies that make sense for the test you are taking. They can help you answer questions and solve test problems.) Reinforce the lesson by reminding students how they might use strategies when taking an upcoming test in another discipline or by reviewing the strategies again as they prepare for taking a test in the future. Remind students that these strategies can be used for tests in all their classes and that they should always ask a teacher, not another student, if they have a question about a test.

Daily Language Practice

Use Daily Language Practice as a quick and easy way to help students sharpen their proofreading skills as they check two or more sentences each day for errors in grammar, usage, mechanics, and spelling.

Daily Language Practice . . .

- is a set of proofreading exercises, one set for each major lesson in *Hidden Treasures.*
- provides practice and reinforcement of language skills presented in each lesson.
- reinforces spelling and vocabulary in the context of sentences.

How to Use Daily Language Practice

1. Each day, write two exercises on the board or on a transparency for students to proofread and correct. Corrected exercises are shown.
2. Have students correct the exercises and explain why each correction is needed.

SENTENCES OF THE DAY

❷

PROOFREADER'S MARKS

≡	Capitalize.	⌃—	Replace something.
⊙	Add a period.	∽	Transpose.
⁁	Add a comma.	⬭	Spell correctly.
❛❛ ❜❜	Add quotation marks.	¶	Indent paragraph.
⤴	Cut something.	/	Make a lowercase letter.

Daily Language Practice

Freedom Ride

Adverbs; regular and irregular verbs; spelling

1. After the accident, Nat reefused to give up hope.

1. After the accident, Nat refused to give up hope.

2. His life was quick throwed into turmoil.

2. His life was quickly thrown into turmoil.

3. Ecksperts cautious advised him about his new restrictions.

3. Experts cautiously advised him about his new restrictions.

4. Nat's new wheel chair comed last week.

4. Nat's new wheelchair came last week.

5. He could hardely contain his exsitement.

5. He could hardly contain his excitement.

6. The new chair rided much more smoother than the first.

6. The new chair rode much more smoothly than the first.

7. He will esxplore the hole neighborhood in his new wheelchair.

7. He will explore the whole neighborhood in his new wheelchair.

8. Because the chair is excellent made, it run very good.

8. Because the chair is excellently made, it runs very well.

9. It have helped Nat reegain his independence.

9. It has helped Nat regain his independence.

10. Now he goes easy from class to class at scool.

10. Now he goes easily from class to class at school.

11. Nat triys to reemain totaly alert when he is riding outside. Even a short lapse of attention could be extreme dangerous.

11. Nat tries to remain totally alert when he is riding outside. Even a short lapse of attention could be extremely dangerous.

12. Some people thinks that he is incompetent to drive a car, but they is wrong. He can drive as safe as anyone. All his car's controls have been clever adapted to be hand-operated.

12. Some people think that he is incompetent to drive a car, but they are wrong. He can drive as safely as anyone. All his car's controls have been cleverly adapted to be hand-operated.

Key Words are underlined. Spelling Words are printed in red.

Daily Language Practice

The River

Negatives; adverbs; spelling

1. Jan and Selene hadn't never been kayaking before.

1. Jan and Selene had never (hadn't ever) been kayaking before.

2. There first trip was going to be a significent challenge.

2. Their first trip was going to be a significant challenge.

3. They had never seen nothing like the rushing river.

3. They had never (hadn't ever) seen anything like the rushing river.

4. "This is an excellant opportunity," Jan said confident.

4. "This is an excellent opportunity," Jan said confidently.

5. Their trip began calm and without no single unfortunate incidant.

5. Their trip began calmly and without a single unfortunate incident.

6. Sudden, a tremendous storm broke loud.

6. Suddenly, a tremendous storm broke loudly.

7. After being struck by a falling branch, Selene couldn't hardly move.

7. After being struck by a falling branch, Selene could hardly move.

8. Jan worryd that Selene might go into a coma at any instent.

8. Jan worried that Selene might go into a coma at any instant.

9. The rain final relented, but Selene could not see very good.

9. The rain finally relented, but Selene could not see very well.

10. She thought she saw a elephent and a monkey, but she new they must be an hallucination.

10. She thought she saw an elephant and a monkey, but she knew they must be hallucinations.

11. No one had told them nothing about how to kayak in a storm. They had to teach themselves quick. Paddling in fast water was much differant from rowing in a calm stream.

11. No one had told them anything about how to kayak in a storm. They had to teach themselves quickly. Paddling in fast water was much different from rowing in a calm stream.

12. By dusk they had made it safely to their destination. They weren't hardly even tired. They're trip had been exciting and thrilling. Selene felt fine and said that she couldn't not wait to try it again.

12. By dusk they had made it safely to their destination. They were hardly even tired. Their trip had been exciting and thrilling. Selene felt fine and said that she couldn't wait to try it again.

Key Words are underlined. Spelling Words are printed in red.

Daily Language Practice

Julie of the Wolves

Prepositions and prepositional phrases; negatives; spelling

1. Rez was not never intimidated by the idea. Of dog sled racing.

1. Rez was not (never) intimidated by the idea of dog sled racing.

2. His positave attitude helped him prepare For each race.

2. His positive attitude helped him prepare for each race.

3. No one had never seen a more confident team leader.

3. No one had ever seen a more confident team leader.

4. Riding, behind his team, of dogs dispelled any of his nervus thoughts.

4. Riding behind his team of dogs dispelled any of his nervous thoughts.

5. Rez's faverite path ran parallel to a mountin range.

5. Rez's favorite path ran parallel to a mountain range.

6. He admired the dogs enormus vitality.

6. He admired the dogs' enormous vitality.

7. In a close, race, Rez drove his team aggressively.

7. In a close race, Rez drove his team aggressively.

8. A good leader knows effectave strategies for win.

8. A good leader knows effective strategies for winning.

9. It isn't hardly easy to control a team, of strong dogs.

9. It isn't (is hardly) easy to control a team of strong dogs.

10. One dog, Kabu, is very curius and is allways nosing around.

10. One dog, Kabu, is very curious and is always nosing around.

11. Rez always gives his dogs a reward. He also puts their pictures. In his scrapbook. It is a simple tribute to the wonderful dogs who have raced, with him.

11. Rez always gives his dogs a reward. He also puts their pictures in his scrapbook. It is a simple tribute to the wonderful dogs who have raced with him.

12. Rez is a good captain because he is sensiteve to his dogs. He knows when they are to tired to go on. He also knows when they can keep going. Him and his dogs understand each other. Without any words.

12. Rez is a good captain because he is sensitive to his dogs. He knows when they are too tired to go on. He also knows when they can keep going. He and his dogs understand each other without any words.

Key Words are underlined. Spelling Words are printed in red.

Daily Language Practice

To the Top of the World

Adjective and adverb phrases; prepositions and prepositional phrases; spelling

1. Dr. Parsing studies the distinctive habbits, of the lion.

1. Dr. Parsing studies the <u>distinctive</u> habits of the lion.

2. She precisly records her observations; in her journal.

2. She precisely records her observations in her journal.

3. She followed a pride of lions, at Kruger National Park, in south Africa.

3. She followed a pride of lions at Kruger National Park in South Africa.

4. Her prefessional goal is to find out how lion's communicate With each other.

4. Her professional goal is to find out how lions communicate with each other.

5. Patience and persistence are crucial to her sucess.

5. Patience and persistence are <u>crucial</u> to her success.

6. The prefessor and her student's watch the lions. From special tents.

6. The professor and her students watch the lions from special tents.

7. They call one Lion Snoots for his haughty ways.

7. They call one lion Snoots for his <u>haughty</u> ways.

8. Prehaps the favorite member, of the pride is a serene lioness they call Peace.

8. Perhaps the favorite member of the pride is a <u>serene</u> lioness they call Peace.

9. The pride often divides; into small groups for hunt.

9. The pride often divides into small groups to hunt.

10. The lion's live under the pertection of the goverment.

10. The lions live under the protection of the government.

11. After only two months the team has made great pragress in gaining the lions' trust. Using vans, they can now approach, within 20 feet of the animals.

11. After only two months, the team has made great progress in gaining the lions' trust. Using vans, they can now approach within 20 feet of the animals.

12. Dr Parsing had to peresuade a University to fund her research. She hopes that her work will increase our understanding; of animal intelligence.

12. Dr. Parsing had to persuade a university to fund her research. She hopes that her work will increase our understanding of animal intelligence.

Key Words are underlined. Spelling Words are printed in red.

READER RESPONSE 

AFTER READING

5. Talk about the whole story.
   - You might talk about your favorite part of the story.
   - You might discuss the author's writing.
   - You might discuss whether what you thought would happen really did happen.

Harcourt Brace School Publishers

FOLD

READER RESPONSE 

Responding Freely

DURING READING

1. Work with a partner. Look over the story, and decide whether you will read it silently or aloud.
2. Think about the way the story is organized. Decide with your partner how often you will stop to discuss it.
3. Each time you stop, tell what you think, and listen to what your partner says. Discuss things you like or dislike, things you do not understand, or what has happened or what might happen next.
4. Stop and discuss each section until you finish the story.

Harcourt Brace School Publishers

READER RESPONSE 

Author's Craft

DURING READING

1. Have you noticed anything you think the author might bring up again later in the story? If so, what did you notice?
2. Tell about any pictures the author has left in your mind.
3. What special words has the author used so far to help you
   - see things in the story?
   - hear things in the story?
   - feel things in the story?
4. What does the dialogue tell you about the characters? Does it sound the way people really talk? Why, or why not?

Harcourt Brace School Publishers

FOLD

AFTER READING

5. What is your favorite word, line, or paragraph in the story? Why is it your favorite?
6. What do you like about the way the author has written the story?
7. Would you like to read something else by this author? Why, or why not?
8. What was the most important thing you learned from the dialogue in this story?

Harcourt Brace School Publishers

RESEARCH AND PLANNING TIPS

- Find a way to assign team roles that everyone agrees on.
- Form subgroups to create different endings for the story.
- Practice your story until everyone feels ready for the recording. Listen to the audiotape and rerecord parts of it, if necessary.

FOLD

THEME PROJECT

CHECKPOINT 4

To the Top of the World

35

Make a Travelogue. Review the checklist below as you record a travelogue.

- ☑ Decide on roles for each group member to take when you tape-record, for example, Guide, Biologist, Photographer, or Translator.
- ☑ Brainstorm a list of sound effects that will add realism and excitement to the telling of your journey.
- ☑ Plan to record two different endings. In each ending, show the group overcoming its obstacles in a different way.
- ☑ Tape-record the story of your wilderness expedition, using sound effects to create suspense and interest.

(Continued on the other side)

THEME PROJECT

PRESENTATION

Confronting Nature

INTO THE WILDERNESS

Community Connections Audiences love a good adventure! Now that you've safely "returned" from your expedition, why not share your exploits?

- Make a list of places where your tape might provide a lift to people's spirits. (Hospitals and nursing homes are two possibilities.)
- Write to the places on your list and explain your project. Include a brief outline of your adventure story.
- If possible, visit and interact with people who listen to your tape. Ask them to tell you about their own nature experiences.

(Continued on the other side)

FOLD

PRESENTATION IDEAS

- Hold a classroom adventurers' forum to share groups' stories.
- After listening to each group's tape, discuss what you liked most about it.
- Choose the ending you preferred for each story—or suggest a different one.

OR

- Create a schoolwide "adventure series" by arranging to play your tapes over the school PA system for other classes to enjoy.
- If the series is popular, join with interested students to create new adventures.

INTEGRATED CURRICULUM **21A**

Freedom Ride

SALISBURY, RHODESIA—HARARE, ZIMBABWE

When Liz and Pete Fordred were building their boat, they were living in Salisbury, Rhodesia. Today, this place is called Harare, Zimbabwe. Find out more about Zimbabwe.

1. Use an encyclopedia to learn the answers to these questions:
   - Whom was Rhodesia named for? What did that person do?
   - Why was the capital of Rhodesia called Salisbury?
   - When and why was the name of the country changed?
   - Why was the name *Zimbabwe* chosen for the country?
   - Why was the name *Harare* chosen for the capital city?
2. Get together with classmates to check your answers. Discuss other facts about Zimbabwe that you learned during your research.

FOLD

INTEGRATED CURRICULUM

Freedom Ride

DISCOVERING COLONIAL AFRICA

Zimbabwe was once a British colony. Investigate other African countries that were once colonies.

1. Work in a group. Use an encyclopedia or social studies textbook to research colonial and modern Africa.
2. Make a map of contemporary Africa that shows the names of each country and its borders. Be sure the map is large enough to be displayed for other classmates.
3. Using tracing paper, create an overlay of the map. Add the borders and the names of the colonies that existed in 1914. A Reporter from the group can present the two maps to other classmates.

INTEGRATED CURRICULUM

The River

RIVER LIFE MURAL

A river is home to many creatures. Make a mural showing river life.

- Work with your classmates. Brainstorm a list of animals and plants.
- Research plants and animals that make rivers their home, including those you listed.
- Make your mural on a long sheet of paper. Draw the plants and animals you researched, and write a caption for each one to include on the mural.

Harcourt Brace School Publishers

FOLD

INTEGRATED CURRICULUM

The River

RIVER RHYTHMS

The author of "The River" expresses his ideas about rivers with words. Other artists express their ideas through paintings, dances, or music. Learn more about how musicians or composers express their ideas about rivers.

- Find recordings of music about rivers, such as *River Moldau* by Bedrich Smetena or *On the Beautiful, Blue Danube* by Johann Strauss.
- Listen to the recordings and think about how the musicians or composers feel about rivers.
- Choose one recording that you like. Write down the title, and then write a few words that tell how you think this music relates to "The River."
- Make your own title for the music. Try to make your title show how the music makes you feel about rivers. Share your title with other classmates.

Harcourt Brace School Publishers

INTEGRATED CURRICULUM 23B

Julie of the Wolves

FIELD GUIDES

Make a field guide to show some of the living things mentioned in "Julie of the Wolves."

- Work in a small group. Reread the story to look for references to Arctic plants and animals.
- Use encyclopedias, textbooks, and reference books to find out what these plants and animals look like.
- Create a mural-style field guide to the North Slope. Draw scenes with several plants and animals together to show the relationships among the living things in Miyax's world. Label the plants and animals.

FOLD

SCIENCE INTEGRATED CURRICULUM 23A

Julie of the Wolves

NATIVE SPECIES

"Julie of the Wolves" contains descriptions of Arctic wildlife. Compare Arctic animals to others you are more familiar with.

1. Make a list of the animals Miyax saw on the North Slope. (Many of them are not native to other parts of North America, but members of the same family group may be.)
2. Use field guides and other reference books to find out what family groups each listed animal belongs to.
3. Note any members of the same family that are native to your state or area.
4. Discuss where their habitat(s) might be.
5. Make a chart with pictures and descriptions to record your comparisons.

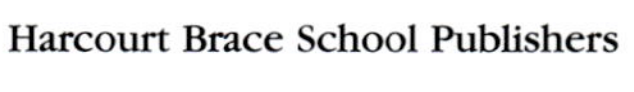

Area	Average Yearly Temperature (high and low)	Average Yearly Rainfall (in inches)
Sahara Desert		
Melbourne, Australia		
Seattle, Washington		

☑ Compare your information to what the other groups found. You might make a chart like the one shown here.

☑ Look at a globe or a world map. Choose a place anywhere in the world. Use reference books to find out about the climate there. Look for information about temperature and rainfall.

☑ Work with a partner or group.

How much does climate vary from place to place?

DIFFERENT CLIMATES

To the Top of the World

INTEGRATED CURRICULUM

To the Top of the World

LOCAL PATTERNS

Even though our survival usually does not depend on watching the weather, sometimes it does. Monitor your local weather.

1. Work in a group. Choose jobs for all group members. Here are some things your group might do:
   - Measure and chart the temperature at the beginning and the end of the school day.
   - Measure and chart the amount of precipitation (rain and snow).
   - Record the direction of the wind.
   - Write a brief daily description of weather conditions.
2. Continue your weather watch for at least a month.
3. Look over the month's records, and report to the class.

Writing Models

Model: News Story

*A **news story** contains a headline, a lead, and a body. It gives information about a current event, an issue, or a person.*

headline	**Sanchez Seeks Presidency of School Board**
lead telling *who, what, where, when,* and *why*	Maria Sanchez, a local business executive, is running for president of the school board in Duane County this year because she wants to make the board more responsive to the needs of students and their taxpaying parents.
body telling *how*	Sanchez, who grew up in Duane County and attended its public schools, says she wants to help students realize their full potential. She wants the board to focus on keeping potential dropouts in school and on spending tax dollars where they can do the most good. "Head Start and Students in Business are examples of two successful programs I would continue to support," Sanchez says. "Let's fund programs that work." Sanchez would like to change the way board meetings are run. If elected, she would encourage students to participate as nonvoting members of the board. Sanchez believes she can accomplish most of these changes within the first six months if she is elected.

Model: Adventure Story

An **adventure story** has main characters who face high-risk challenges and events that follow a sequential order.

Danger on the River

introduces setting	Luanne and her friends had spent the hot afternoon swinging from a rope and dropping
story told in time order	into the cool river water. Now they were resting on the shady bank. Luanne's dog, Lobo, swam several feet from the bank.
dangerous situation	Suddenly, an alligator—swift and silent—appeared across the river! It began swimming toward Lobo. Luanne and her friends screamed. Then Luanne remembered the rope. Could she reach her dog in time?
ending that resolves conflict	She swung out over the river, grabbed Lobo with her free hand, and then swung back to the bank. She had saved her dog!

Draft and Revised Passages: Conclusion of Personal Narrative

draft

It was really fun to play volleyball without keeping score. Maybe we can do it again at the clan picnic next year.

revision

I am beginning to think that some people are just not meant to compete. These days, when I am in a competitive situation, I just pretend there is no score, grade, or judgment involved. When I simply "play for fun," everything comes easily to me.

Model: Research Report—Science

*A **science report** relies on facts and information from several sources. The writer usually attempts to answer a question.*

How Snakes Slither

a topic that is not too broad

Long ago people believed that snakes walked on their ribs. They thought that the ribs acted as if they were several pairs of legs. We know now that this is not true. How then do snakes slither?

specialized words defined and explained

Along a snake's belly lie rows of overlapping scutes, or scales. Each scute is attached by muscles to a pair of the snake's ribs. When a scute is pulled back by the muscles, its edge pushes against the ground. When the scute is pushed forward by the muscles, it slides over the ground.

A snake moves the overlapping scutes on its belly in groups. With each movement, some scutes push against the ground, and others slide forward. This allows the snake to move forward in a straight line.

In another common method of movement, the snake flexes its muscles to produce a series of waves down the length of its body. The curves of the body push against the ground, moving the snake forward.

supporting details

A few desert snakes use a strange form of movement called sidewinding. The snake arches the front of its body upward and throws its head to one side. It then pulls its body across and throws its head to the other side. Because sand gives the snake little to push against, sidewinding works better than other forms of movement would.

summarizing statement

Describing in detail the way snakes move makes their movements sound jerky. In fact, their movements are very smooth and efficient. Undulating muscles and overlapping scutes move snakes forward steadily at an average speed of about two miles per hour.

Additional Reading
Hidden Treasures

The following list is a compilation of the Reading Trade Books selected for the lesson plans.

THEME: CONFRONTING NATURE

***Acorn Pancakes, Dandelion Salad, and 38 Other Wild Recipes* by Jean Craighead George. HarperCollins, 1995. AVERAGE**
Nature offers a wide variety of edible plants, as the author demonstrates in this attractively illustrated recipe book.

***African Landscapes* by Warren J. Halliburton. Macmillan, 1993. EASY**
Take a geographical tour through Africa, from its tropical jungles to its waterless desert areas.

***Arctic Hunter* by Diane Hoyt-Goldsmith. Holiday House, 1992. EASY**
This photo essay about an Inupiat boy at a summer fishing camp north of the Arctic Circle tells how his family maintains traditions in today's world. *Notable Trade Book in Social Studies*

***Arctic Summer* by Downs Matthews. Simon & Schuster, 1993. AVERAGE**
Perhaps the shortest of all seasons, the Arctic summer is a brief time for many kinds of wildlife to flourish.

***Biography of a River: The Living Mississippi* by Edith McCall. Walker, 1990. CHALLENGING**
The story of this mighty American river is told with emphasis on the role it has played in American history.

***Black Star, Bright Dawn* by Scott O'Dell. Houghton Mifflin, 1988. AVERAGE**
Bright Dawn, an Eskimo girl, enters the 1,000-mile Iditarod dogsled race. *Notable Trade Book in Social Studies*

***The Bridge Dancers* by Carol Saller. Carolrhoda, 1991. EASY**
Ma sie must help her sister cope with an injury until their mother returns from a journey beyond the mountain where they live.

***The Call of the Wolves* by Jim Murphy. Scholastic, 1989. EASY**
To survive, a wounded wolf must make a desperate journey. *Outstanding Science Trade Book*

***Canoeing* by Donna Bailey. Steck-Vaughn, 1991. EASY**
Basic techniques and safety tips are provided in this introduction to the sport.

***Dogsong* by Gary Paulsen. Bradbury, 1985. CHALLENGING**
A boy travels alone into the wilderness of Alaska by dogsled and faces the dangers of land and climate. *Newbery Honor; ALA Notable Book; SLJ Best Books*

***Drift* by William Mayne. Dell, 1990. AVERAGE**
When Rafe and Tawena become trapped on an ice floe, they must use their wits to stay alive.

***Drifting Snow: An Arctic Search* by James Houston. McElderry, 1992. CHALLENGING**
A fourteen-year-old Inuit girl searches for her identity. *Outstanding Science Trade Book*

***Everyday Things and How They Work* by Steve Parker. Kingfisher Books, 1991. AVERAGE**
In simple, concise language, this book explains how useful but ordinary items work, such as light bulbs, microwave ovens, and telecommunication networks.

***The Fear Place* by Phyllis Reynolds Naylor. Atheneum, 1994. AVERAGE**
When Doug and his brother Gordon are left alone on a camping trip, Doug finds reserves of courage within himself that he didn't realize he had.

Get Out of My Face **by David Masterton. Macmillan, 1991. AVERAGE**
Step-siblings learn to get along after a near-disaster.

Hatchet **by Gary Paulsen. Bradbury, 1985. AVERAGE**
The plane Brian is traveling in goes down in the wilderness. With no supplies or transportation, how can he find his way back to civilization? *Newbery Honor; ALA Notable Book; Notable Trade Book in Social Studies*

How to Be School Smart: Secrets of Successful Schoolwork **by Elizabeth James and Carol Barkin. Lothrop, Lee & Shepard, 1988. EASY**
Study techniques and tips on report writing are introduced.

How to Write a Great School Report **by Elizabeth James and Carol Barkin. William Morrow, 1993. EASY**
In this helpful resource, students will find information on research and note-taking techniques.

Jodie's Journey **by Colin Thiele. HarperCollins, 1990. AVERAGE**
After winning a jumping championship riding her beloved horse, Monarch, Jodie faces far more challenging hurdles. She learns that she has a crippling disease and will never ride Monarch again.

Julie **by Jean Craighead George. HarperCollins, 1994. AVERAGE**
In this sequel to *Julie of the Wolves,* Julie returns to live with her father but finds many things have changed during the time she was away. *Outstanding Science Trade Book; Notable Trade Book in Social Studies*

Lost in the Barrens **by Farley Mowat. Little, Brown, 1956. CHALLENGING**
Awasin and his friend Jamie become lost while hunting for caribou and must find a way to survive in the wilderness until they can find their way home.

Making the Grades: How You Can Achieve Greater Success with Less Stress in School and Beyond **by Frederick Hageman. Rising Crescent, 1995. CHALLENGING**
These tips can help any student make better use of study time and improve test-taking skills.

My Life with the Chimpanzees **by Jane Goodall. Silver Burdett, 1993. EASY**
Read this fascinating autobiography of this famous naturalist, who has devoted her life to studying primates in their natural habitat.

My Side of the Mountain **by Jean Craighead George. Dutton, 1988. AVERAGE**
Sam Gribley goes to the woods and lives off the land. With a tree as his home and a falcon as his companion, Sam relies on his own ingenuity to survive.

One Day in the Alpine Tundra **by Jean Craighead George. HarperCollins, 1984. AVERAGE**
This fast-paced narrative makes a highly readable introduction to the fascinating ecosystem of the Alpine Tundra. *Notable Trade Book in Social Studies*

On the Far Side of the Mountain **by Jean Craighead George. Puffin, 1990. AVERAGE**
Sam and his sister Alice have made a comfortable home for themselves in the wilderness, but one day Alice is missing—and it's up to Sam to find her.

Paddle-to-the-Sea **by Holling C. Holling. Houghton Mifflin, 1980. EASY**
When a boy sets a toy wooden canoe adrift in Lake Superior, the small vessel begins a journey that takes it down some of North America's greatest waterways. *Caldecott Honor; Lewis Carroll Shelf Award*

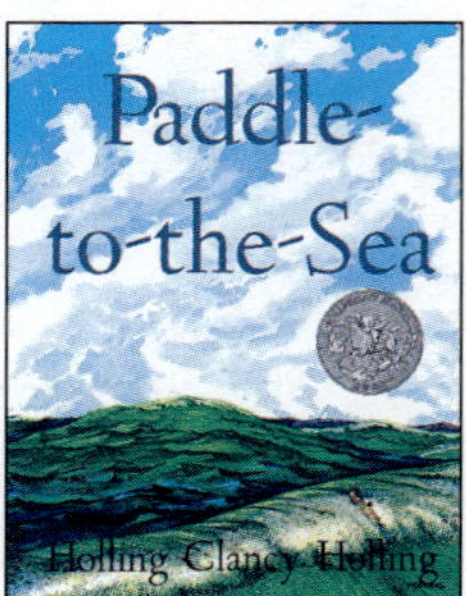

Research to Write **by Maity Schrecengost. Highsmith, 1994. AVERAGE**
Writing a research report requires careful documentation of facts. This reference book shows how it can be done.

Sand & Fog: Adventures in Southern Africa **by Jim Brandenburg. Walker, 1994. AVERAGE**
Brandenburg treks across the African landscape to capture stunning photographs of a wide variety of animals. *Outstanding Science Trade Book*

School Power: Strategies for Succeeding in School **by Jeanne M. Schumm and Marguerite Radencich. Free Spirit, 1992. AVERAGE**
This book is full of tips to improve study skills and make studying more fun.

Second Ascent: The Story of Hugh Herr **by Alison Osius. Dell, 1993. CHALLENGING**
This is the true story of a young climber's recovery from a disabling accident, and his courageous quest to once again conquer the world's most challenging peaks.

Snow Bound **by Harry Mazer. Dell, 1975. AVERAGE**
Two stranded teenagers realize they will have to overlook their disagreements and cooperate in order to survive.

Swift Rivers **by Cornelia Meigs. Walker, 1994. CHALLENGING**
Hoping to make enough money to give him a start in life, Chris agrees to drive a load of logs to market by rafting down the dangerous rapids of the Mississippi.

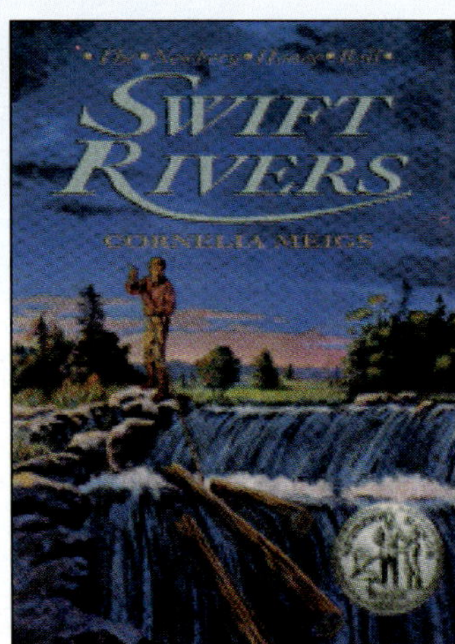

To the Top of the World **by Jim Brandenburg. Walker, 1993. AVERAGE**
The author-photographer lived with a wolf pack for a number of weeks to collect photographs and take notes for this remarkable portrait of life in a wolf pack.

Tundra: The Arctic Land **by Bruce Hiscock. Macmillan, 1986. EASY**
This book describes the geography of the tundra as well as the animals, plants, birds, and people who have adapted to life on these Arctic plains. *Outstanding Science Trade Book*

The Voyage of the Frog **by Gary Paulsen. Orchard, 1989. EASY**
A boy sailing California's coast must discover his inner strength and use it to successfully complete his solo voyage. *ALA Notable Book; SLJ Best Books*

Wildlife Rescue: The Work of Dr. Kathleen Ramsay **by Jennifer Owings Dewey. Boyds Mills Press, 1994. AVERAGE**
This photo essay captures the day-to-day struggles of a veterinarian as she works to save injured animals and return them to the wild. *SLJ Best Books; Orbis Pictus Award*

The Wolfling **by Sterling North. Scholastic, 1989. AVERAGE**
A boy raises a wolf pup with the help of his friend, the respected naturalist Thure Kumlien.

Wolves **by R. D. Lawrence. Little, Brown, 1990. EASY**
Beautiful photographs complement this engrossing study of an often-misunderstood animal.

Wolves **by Seymour Simon. HarperCollins, 1993. EASY**
The author discusses wolf behavior in easy-to-read text.

Working River **by Fred Powledge. Farrar, Straus & Giroux, 1995. AVERAGE**

By focusing on the ecological concerns of one river, the Patuxent, the author urges that we support conservation efforts for all rivers.

A World Full of Animals: The Roger Caras Story **by Roger Caras. Chronicle, 1994. CHALLENGING**

Roger Caras has dedicated his life to saving all kinds of animals. In this entertaining book, he discusses his life as a naturalist.

The Wreck of the Zanzibar **by Michael Morpurgo. Viking Penguin, 1995. AVERAGE**

When Michael's great-aunt dies, she leaves him a diary, and inside it he finds the answer to a decades-old mystery.

Yukon River: An Adventure to the Gold Fields of the Klondike **by Peter Lourie. Boyds Mills Press, 1992. AVERAGE**

The author takes a 260-mile canoe trip, following the route used by prospectors who flocked to the Yukon during the Gold Rush.

Zimbabwe: A Treasure of Africa **by Al Stark. Macmillan, 1986. AVERAGE**

This history of Zimbabwe describes the wildlife and cultural heritage of this African nation.

SCHOOL ↔ HOME CONNECTION

Before you can build a boat, you need to know what your boat will be like. You need a plan. Your plan can be a drawing or an actual model of what the boat will look like.

Imagine that you, like Liz and Pete Fordred, want to build a boat that's uniquely designed for your own needs. Think about what it will look like and what special features it will have. Then make drawings or a model of the boat that could guide you if you were to actually build it.

DESIGN YOUR OWN BOAT

CHECK it OUT

The following books will help you share other people's experiences at sea: *The Voyage of the Frog* by Gary Paulsen (Orchard, 1989) and *The Wreck of the* Zanzibar by Michael Morpurgo (Viking, 1995).

FOR THE FAMILY ALBUM

Liz and Pete Fordred built a boat because they wanted to travel. Most people are intrigued by the idea of traveling and have places they'd like to visit. Talk about traveling with your family members, and get them to tell where they would like to go if they could travel anywhere. Don't overlook the possibility of undersea or space travel!

Harcourt Brace School Publishers

LIFE RAFT

SCHOOL ↔ HOME CONNECTION

1. To survive on a river, or to survive in life, a person needs certain abilities, skills, and character traits. Use the raft to show the skills, abilities, and character traits or qualities Brian demonstrated while on the river. Write just one skill, ability, or quality on each log of the raft.
2. Use the back of this paper to write a paragraph summing up Brian's talents. Tell how he used his qualities and abilities to help Derek and himself survive.
3. Share Brian's life raft with a family member. Explain what it shows about Brian.

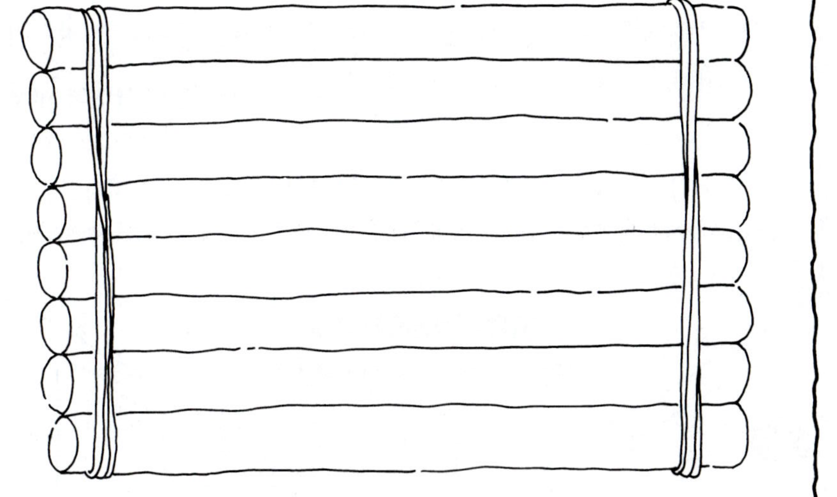

CHECK it OUT

If you want to read more books by Gary Paulsen, check your local library or bookstore for *Dogsong* (Macmillan, 1985) and *Hatchet* (Bradbury, 1987).

FOR THE FAMILY ALBUM

Talk with family members about all the talents, abilities, and qualities that help you and your family meet challenges in daily life. On a separate sheet of paper, make a life raft like the one shown. Use it to tell what keeps your family afloat!

MY VIEW OF MIYAX

SCHOOL ↔ HOME CONNECTION

As Eskimos draw a picture or carve a sculpture of a person or an animal, they watch to see whether the material they are using helps them reveal the essence of their subject. They try to capture their subject's true qualities.

In your view, what is Miyax's true essence, or most outstanding quality?

Draw a picture of Miyax that captures her essence or that shows what is outstanding about her. Share your drawing with members of your family as you tell them her story.

CHECK it OUT Check out other books by Jean Craighead George at your library. *One Day in the Alpine Tundra* (HarperCollins, 1984) is one example of her nonfiction writing, and *On the Far Side of the Mountain* (Puffin, 1991) is a sequel to her award-winning novel *My Side of the Mountain* (Dutton, 1959).

FOR THE FAMILY ALBUM

Talk with your family about the outstanding individual characteristics each of you possesses. Who is observant? Who sees the humor in things? Who is most active or most serene? How would you describe these things in a simple Eskimo carving or drawing?

HERE'S TO THE WOLF!

SCHOOL ↔ HOME CONNECTION

Some people believe that wolves are mean and dangerous and that all wolves are bad wolves.

- What do you think?
- How do you feel about wolves?
- What things about wolves do you think are important for others to know?

Design a poster about wolves. Use the chart below to organize your thoughts. Try to show something about wolves' behavior or their lives that you admire. You might even campaign for preserving the Arctic wolves' native environment!

What I think about wolves:	
What I admire most about them:	
How I might try to help them:	

CHECK it OUT

Look for the book *To the Top of the World* in a library or bookstore. Read the rest of the wolves' story. Look for other books about wolves, too, such as *Wolves* by Seymour Simon (HarperCollins, 1993) and *Wolf Pack: Tracking Wolves in the Wild* by Sylvia A. Johnson (Lerner, 1985).

FOR THE FAMILY ALBUM

Photographing wolves where they live was a lifelong dream for Jim Brandenburg. "Adopt" a favorite animal with your family and talk about why you like that animal. Together, find out as much as you can about the animal. If it is native to a distant place, imagine that you could make a photography expedition to study it. Plan how you would get there and how long it would take.

GRAPH-A-BOOK

Dear Family Members,
As a book is read at home, have the student graph his or her response. The student should write the title of the book and the author's name on the numbered line and then color the corresponding bar on the graph to evaluate the book. Ask the student to give a reason for his or her rating.

Book Titles and Authors' Names

1. ______________________________
2. ______________________________
3. ______________________________
4. ______________________________
5. ______________________________
6. ______________________________

Graph

Book 1				
Book 2				
Book 3				
Book 4				
Book 5				
Book 6				
	Would Not Recommend	OK	Good	GREAT!

Please return the graph to school when completed. Thank you.

Signature ______________________________

Duplicate the page and send it home with students to be completed with family members.

NEWS FROM:

Dear Family,

Special Announcements

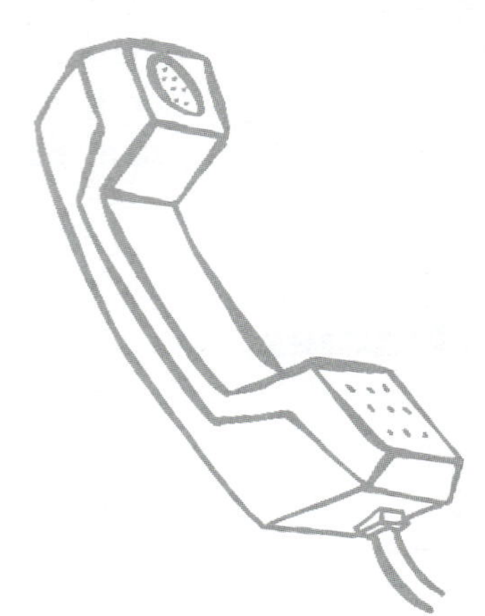

Spotlight on . . .

Something to Try at Home

From Your Child . . .

Book Corner

We have been very busy lately!

Harcourt Brace School Publishers

Complete the newsletter with news items from your class. Duplicate the page, and send it home to family members.

CREATE YOUR OWN SCHOOL-TO-HOME NEWSLETTER

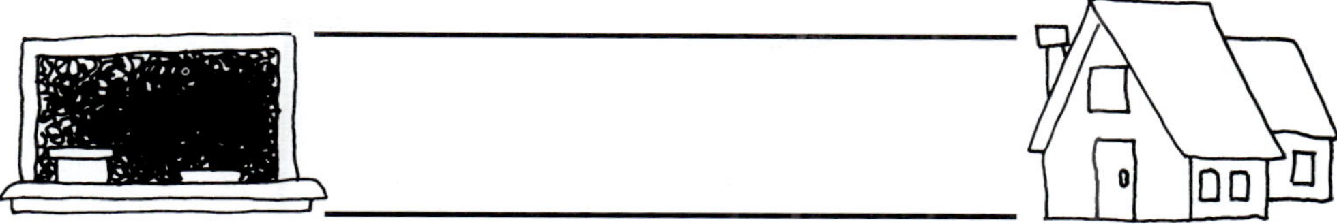

Insert your school name or newsletter title to head your newsletter.

Personal note to parents

from the desk of...

Too Good to Miss

List of recommended books for reading

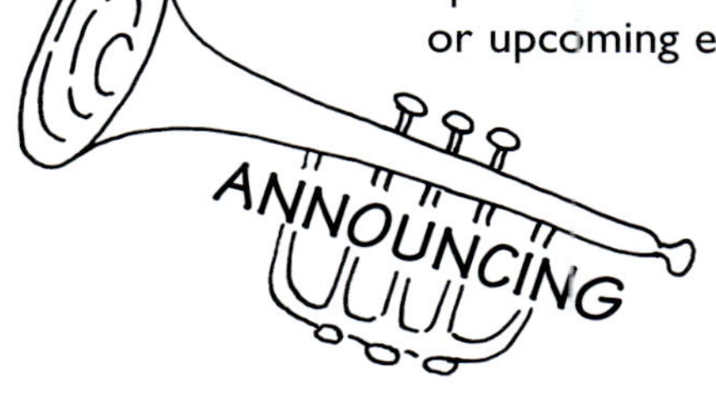

Special announcements or upcoming events

Current events from the classroom, school, or community

Focus on a certain subject area, or parent self-help information

Reminder of upcoming meetings, conferences, or field trips

Classroom projects

Call for volunteers or materials

Future goals or study themes

STAR STUDENT REPORTERS

Student column

Harcourt Brace School Publishers

Use any of these clip-art graphics to create a classroom newsletter to send home.

AWARD
To:
For:
By:
On this day of:
EXCELLENCE
Harcourt Brace School Publishers

Harcourt Brace School Publishers

Additional Resources

Introducing the Glossary

Explain to students that a glossary is often included in a book so that readers can look up words used in the book. You may want to model looking up one or more words, pointing out how you rely on alphabetical order and the guide words at the top of the Glossary pages to help you locate an entry. Then demonstrate how to use the Pronunciation Key on page 611 to determine the correct pronunciation of the word.

As students look over the Glossary, you may want to point out that illustrations accompany some definitions, such as those of archaeologist *and* caress *on pages 612 and 613. Point out that an expanded explanation of some words, such as* brink, *may be presented in the margin.*

You may wish to have students look up several words in the Glossary, identifying the correct page and the guide words. Have them tell which words are accompanied by illustrations or additional information in the margin.

Glossary

WHAT IS A GLOSSARY?

A glossary is like a small dictionary at the back of a book. It lists some of the words used in the book, along with their pronunciations, their meanings, and other useful information. If you come across a word you don't know as you are reading, you can look up the word in this glossary.

Using the Glossary

Like a dictionary, this glossary lists words in alphabetical order. To find a word, look it up by its first letter or letters.

To save time, use the **guide words** at the top of each page. These show you the first and last words on the page. Look at the guide words to see if your word falls between them alphabetically.

Here is an example of a glossary entry:

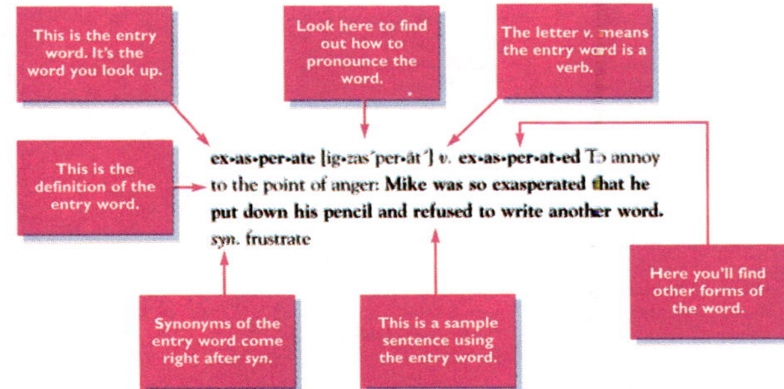

ex•as•per•ate [ig•zas′per•āt′] *v.* **ex•as•per•at•ed** To annoy to the point of anger: **Mike was so exasperated that he put down his pencil and refused to write another word.** *syn.* frustrate

ETYMOLOGY

Etymology is the study or history of how words are developed. Words often have interesting backgrounds that can help you remember what they mean. Look in the margins of the glossary to find the etymologies of certain words.

Here is an example of an etymology:

archaeologist This word is made up of two Greek words: *archaios*, which means "ancient or old" and *logia*, which means "knowledge." The *-ist* was added to show that it was talking about a person, giving the meaning "ancient-knowledge person."

PRONUNCIATION

The pronunciation shows the important sounds of a word by giving a respelling within brackets; for example, [dis•pel′]. It will help you say the word correctly.

Below is the **pronunciation key**. It explains what the symbols in a respelling mean. A short **pronunciation key** appears on every other page of the glossary.

- • separates words into syllables
- ′ indicates heavier stress on a syllable
- ′ indicates light stress on a syllable

PRONUNCIATION KEY*

a	add, map	m	move, seem	u	up, done
ā	ace, rate	n	nice, tin	û(r)	burn, term
â(r)	care, air	ng	ring, song	yo͞o	fuse, few
ä	palm, father	o	odd, hot	v	vain, eve
b	bat, rub	ō	open, so	w	win, away
ch	check, catch	ô	order, jaw	y	yet, yearn
d	dog, rod	oi	oil, boy	z	zest, muse
e	end, pet	ou	pout, now	zh	vision, pleasure
ē	equal, tree	o͝o	took, full	ə	the schwa, an
f	fit, half	o͞o	pool, food		unstressed vowel
g	go, log	p	pit, stop		representing the
h	hope, hate	r	run, poor		sound spelled
i	it, give	s	see, pass		a in *above*
ī	ice, write	sh	sure, rush		e in *sicken*
j	joy, ledge	t	talk, sit		i in *possible*
k	cool, take	th	thin, both		o in *melon*
l	look, rule	th	this, bathe		u in *circus*

Abbreviations: *adj.* adjective, *adv.* adverb, *conj.* conjunction, *interj.* interjection, *n.* noun, *prep.* preposition, *pron.* pronoun, *syn.* synonym, *v.* verb.

archaeologists

awe In Old Norse, *agi* simply meant "fear." Today the word *awe* expands on "fear" to include "respect" and "wonder."

brink This word is related to the word *break*. The Middle English word *brink* meant "the shore" or "the edge of the land." The shore is where the end of the land breaks off.

A

a•brupt [ə•brupt′] *adj.* Rude in speech and manner: **My aunt will not shop in that store because the clerks are *abrupt* and unfriendly.**

a•dorn [ə•dôrn′] *v.* **a•dorned, a•dorn•ing** To decorate: **The house was *adorned* with flowers and balloons for the party.**

ag•gres•sive•ly [ə•gres′iv•lē] *adv.* In a way that shows readiness to attack or fight: **The seagull *aggressively* chased the other birds away from the bread crumbs.**

an•tag•o•nism [an•tag′ə•niz′əm] *n.* Opposition to each other: ***Antagonism* had existed for years between the two countries.**

ap•point [ə•point′] *v.* **ap•point•ed, ap•point•ing** To select for a job: **Mrs. Ro was *appointed* spokesperson for the Parent-Teacher Association.**

ar•chae•ol•o•gist [är′kē•ol′ə•jist] *n.* A person who studies past times and cultures, usually by examining ancient artifacts: **The *archaeologists* were very excited when they discovered the lost city.**

av•id [av′id] *adj.* Enthusiastic: **My father is an *avid* golfer who plays every weekend, even when it rains.**

awe [ô] *n.* A feeling of wonder, fear, and respect: **Yoshihiro was in *awe* of his grandfather.**

B

bel•lig•er•ent•ly [bə•lij′ər•ənt•lē] *adv.* In an argumentative or challenging manner: **The wrestlers *belligerently* took their positions on the mat.**

be•stow [bi•stō′] *v.* **be•stowed, be•stow•ing** To give as a gift: **The king *bestowed* land and gold on his loyal soldiers.**

bi•zarre [bi•zär′] *adj.* Odd or unusual: **We were puzzled by the stranger's *bizarre* behavior.** *syns.* strange, weird

bond [bond] *n.* A force that holds things together: **The *bond* between true friends cannot be broken.**

brink [bringk] *n.* The point before something happens: **Scientists are on the *brink* of finding a cure for that disease.**

C

ca•pa•ble [kā′pə•bəl] *adj.* Having the ability or skill for a task: **We were amazed that he was *capable* of doing so much work in so little time.**

car•cass [kär′kəs] *n.* The dead body of an animal: **The vultures picked at the rabbit *carcass* by the roadside.**

ca•ress [kə•res′] *v.* **ca•ressed, ca•ress•ing** To stroke lovingly and gently: **Dottie *caressed* the soft fur on the puppy's back.**

cas•u•al•ly [kazh′o͞o•əl•ē] *adv.* Done offhandedly or without thinking: **Their family dressed too *casually* for the wedding.** *syn.* informally

chant [chant] *n.* A simple, rhythmic melody sung or shouted: **The monks joined together to sing *chants* after their evening meal.**

cir•cum•stance [sûr′kəm•stans′] *n.* The condition surrounding an event or situation: **The *circumstances* of the accident still are not clear.**

clam•or [klam′ər] *n.* A loud and ongoing noise: **The *clamor* from the construction was so loud that Ellen had to cover her ears.** *syn.* racket

col•lapse [kə•laps′] *v.* **col•lapsed, col•laps•ing** To give way or fall in: **The floor *collapsed* under the weight of the machinery.**

co•ma [kō′mə] *n.* A lasting unconsciousness caused by injury or illness: **The family was overjoyed when little Eddie came out of his *coma*.**

con•sist [kən•sist′] *v.* **con•sist•ed, con•sist•ing** To be made up of: **The software package *consisted* of two disks, a manual, and a hint book.**

con•tem•po•rar•y [kən•tem′pə•rer′ē] *n.* A person who lives at the same time as another: **My *contemporaries* and I like the same kind of music.**

cor•dial•ly [kôr′•jəl•ē] *adv.* With friendliness and sincerity: **Smiling with delight, Mr. Cortez greeted his guests *cordially*.** *syns.* warmly, heartily

crev•ice [krev′is] *n.* A narrow opening or split in a rock or in the ground: **The *crevice* in the rock was caused by an earthquake.**

cru•cial [kro͞o′shəl] *adj.* Extremely important: **The energy supply was *crucial* to the space station.** *syn.* essential

caressed

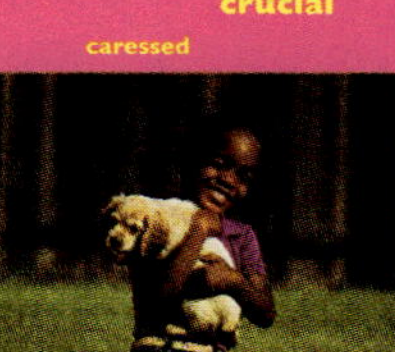

crevice

a	add	o͝o	took
ā	ace	o͞o	pool
â	care	u	up
ä	palm	û	burn
e	end	yo͞o	fuse
ē	equal	oi	oil
i	it	ou	pout
ī	ice	ng	ring
o	odd	th	thin
ō	open	th	this
ô	order	zh	vision

ə = a in *above*, e in *sicken*, i in *possible*, o in *melon*, u in *circus*

curtsy

curtsy This word comes from the Latin *cort*, from which we also get the word *court*. In medieval times, the politeness practiced in the king's court was called *courtesy*, and one of the things women did there was *curtsy*.

curtsy

debris

curt•sy [kûrt′sē] *n.* A bow made by women by bending the knees and lowering the head and shoulders as a sign of respect: **Dinah made a deep *curtsy* before the queen.**

D

de•bris [də•brē′ *or* dā•brē′] *n.* Scattered leftover pieces: **The workers cleaned up the *debris* left from the repairs to the wall.** *syn.* rubble

de•vo•tion [di•vō′shən] *n.* The act of giving oneself completely to: **No one questioned her complete *devotion* to environmental issues.** *syn.* dedication

di•ag•nos•tic [dī′əg•nos′tik] *adj.* Having to do with analyzing or evaluating a condition or situation: **The *diagnostic* exam helped the school determine which grade the new student belonged in.**

dis•card [dis•kärd′] *v.* **dis•card•ed, dis•card•ing** To throw away or get rid of: **Sasha *discarded* the expired coupons.**

dis•dain•ful•ly [dis•dān′fəl•lē] *adv.* In a scornful or disgusted manner: **Claudia *disdainfully* looked at the old dress her sister had given her.**

dis•pel [dis•pel′] *v.* **dis•pelled, dis•pel•ling** To drive away: **Max's mother *dispelled* his worries about the trip by telling him about the wonderful things he would see.**

dis•tinc•tive [dis•tingk′tiv] *adj.* Easy to tell apart; standing out: **His *distinctive* laugh could be heard clear across the room.**

dis•tract [dis•trakt′] *v.* **dis•tract•ed, dis•tract•ing** To take one's attention away from something: **The music *distracted* Jason while he was doing his homework.**

dom•i•nance [dom′ə•nəns] *n.* Power, influence, or authority: **He defeated his enemies one by one until his *dominance* over the entire land was complete.**

du•bi•ous [d(y)ōō′bē•əs] *adj.* Not sure or certain; having doubt: **Tai Wong was *dubious* about leaving without permission.**

614

E

ef•fi•cient [i•fish′ənt] *adj.* Working well with little waste: **The most *efficient* light bulb gives off the least heat.**

em•bark [im•bärk′] *v.* **em•barked, em•bark•ing** To start a project: **The city *embarked* on building a new bridge as soon as the floodwaters went down.**

ex•as•per•ate [ig•zas′pə•rāt′] *v.* **ex•as•per•at•ed, ex•as•per•at•ing** To annoy to the point of anger: **Mike was so *exasperated* that he put down his pencil and refused to write another word.** *syn.* frustrate

ex•ca•va•tion [eks′•kə•vā′shən] *n.* The digging up and uncovering of something: **Mila is working on an *excavation* of dinosaur bones in Montana this summer.**

ex•tinct [ik•stingkt′] *adj.* No longer living or active; often used to refer to a species: **The whooping crane is in danger of becoming *extinct*.**

F

fas•ci•na•tion [fas′ə•nā′shən] *n.* Great interest: **Li-Yuan's *fascination* with the building of models led to a career in architecture.**

for•bid•ding [fər•bid′ing] *adj.* Unfriendly and frightening: **The desert at noontime was *forbidding* and hot.**

frag•ile [fraj′əl] *adj.* Easily broken: **The sign next to the pottery display said, "*Fragile*—handle with care."** *syn.* delicate

fran•ti•cal•ly [fran′tik•lē] *adv.* In a wild and nervous way, full of fear or worry: **When the horses felt the earthquake, they *frantically* started running.**

func•tion [fungk′shən] *n.* The purpose something serves; use: **The *function* of this saw is to cut wood.**

fu•tile [fyōō′təl] *adj.* Useless; not effective: **It was *futile* to try to stop the floodwaters.**

futile

excavation

frantically The Greek word *phren* referred to the mind, and *phrenitikos* was "a disease of the mind" in which someone was acting without thinking.

a	add	o͝o	took
ā	ace	o͞o	pool
â	care	u	up
ä	palm	û	burn
e	end	yo͞o	fuse
ē	equal	oi	oil
i	it	ou	pout
ī	ice	ng	ring
o	odd	th	thin
ō	open	t͟h	this
ô	order	zh	vision

ə = a in *above*, e in *sicken*, i in *possible*, o in *melon*, u in *circus*

615

hallucination

H

hal•lu•ci•na•tion [hə•lōō′sə•nā′shən] *n.* Something one sees that is not really there: **The intense heat caused the hikers to experience *hallucinations*.**

harsh [härsh] *adj.* Rough: **The strong winds and rain made the journey a *harsh* one.**

haugh•ty [hô′tē] *adj.* Thinking of oneself as being better than, or superior to, others: **Because of her *haughty* ways she had few friends.** *syn.* arrogant

head•land [hed′lənd] *n.* A high point of land that overlooks water, such as a cliff: **Sean stood on the *headland* and watched the ships sail away.**

hos•tile [hos′təl] *adj.* Opposing; unfriendly: **The *hostile* nations fought for many years.**

hu•mil•i•ty [hyōō•mil′ə•tē] *n.* The quality of not being proud: **After Susan won the spelling bee, people were surprised at her *humility*.**

headland

I

im•mor•tal [i•môr′təl] *adj.* Living forever; never dying: **Mr. Garcia recited the poet's *immortal* words.**

im•plore [im•plôr′] *v.* **im•plored, im•plor•ing** To beg: **The students were *imploring* the teacher to have a party on the last day of school.**

in•ci•den•tal [in′sə•den′təl] *adj.* Related but of little importance: **Frank just wanted to compete; winning was *incidental*.** *syn.* minor

in•ci•sive [in•sī′siv] *adj.* Sharp and direct: **May's *incisive* wit kept everyone at the table laughing through the entire meal.**

in•com•pe•tent [in•kom′pə•tənt] *adj.* Without ability or skill: **The boss fired the lazy and *incompetent* worker.**

in•crim•i•nate [in•krim′ə•nāt′] *v.* To show to be guilty: **The fingerprints at the scene of the crime may *incriminate* the suspect.**

in•dis•posed [in′dis•pōzd′] *adj.* Not feeling well: **Mrs. Clark was *indisposed* and could not receive visitors.** *syns.* sick, ill

616

in•fect [in•fekt′] *v.* **in•fect•ed, in•fect•ing** To make ill by spreading germs or viruses: **Janice stayed home so no one would become *infected* with her cold.**

in•ten•sive [in•ten′siv] *adj.* Done with energy and concentration: **Pablo made an *intensive* effort to score the winning goal.**

in•ten•tion [in•ten′shən] *n.* Plan or purpose: **Our *intention* is to learn some Chinese phrases before our trip to China.**

in•ter•val [in′tər•vəl] *n.* The distance between two points: **A football field is marked in *intervals* of ten yards.**

in•tim•i•date [in•tim′ə•dāt′] *v.* **in•tim•i•dat•ed, in•tim•i•dat•ing** To frighten: **The little poodle was *intimidated* by the big German shepherd.**

in•tri•cate [in′tri•kit] *adj.* Containing many detailed parts: **The patchwork quilt had a very *intricate* design.**

K

ken•nel [ken′əl] *n.* A place where people house and raise dogs: **Serena bought her puppy from a *kennel*.**

L

lair [lâr] *n.* The home of a wild animal: **My dad told us not to walk near the cave because it might be a bear's *lair*.**

lapse [laps] *n.* A slip or fall, as from a better to a worse condition: **A *lapse* in concentration caused Marcus to miss a good move in the chess game.**

leg•en•dar•y [lej′ən•der′ē] *adj.* Very well known: **Houdini was *legendary* for his escape act.** *syn.* famous

M

mas•sive [mas′iv] *adj.* Very large; gigantic: **Loc and his family were amazed at the sight of the *massive* volcano.**

mis•chie•vous•ly [mis′chi•vəs•lē] *adv.* In a teasing or naughty way: **Cary *mischievously* hid her father's slippers under the sofa.**

mis•hap [mis′hap] *n.* Something that goes wrong: **After his *mishap*, Lee's parents didn't let him help paint anymore.** *syn.* accident

mishap

kennel

lair

a	add	o͝o	took
ā	ace	o͞o	pool
â	care	u	up
ä	palm	û	burn
e	end	yo͞o	fuse
ē	equal	oi	oil
i	it	ou	pout
ī	ice	ng	ring
o	odd	th	thin
ō	open	t͟h	this
ô	order	zh	vision

ə = a in *above*, e in *sicken*, i in *possible*, o in *melon*, u in *circus*

617

monumental

optimism The Latin word *optimus* meant "the best." Then the French expanded its meaning to "a person who thinks the best about everything."

pose

mon•u•men•tal [mon′yə•men′təl] *adj.* Great and important; like a monument: **The statue was *monumental* and impossible to ignore.** *syn.* impressive

N

no•mad•ic [nō•mad′ik] *adj.* Moving from place to place; not settled: **Many *nomadic* people live in tents.**

oc•cu•pa•tion [ok′yə•pā′shən] *n.* The taking and holding of land by military force: **During the *occupation*, there was little freedom.**

om•i•nous•ly [om′ə•nəs•lē] *adv.* In a way that points to something bad or frightening: **The clouds gathered *ominously* before the storm.**

op•ti•mism [op′•tə•miz′əm] *n.* The habit or ability of seeing the good side of things: **In spite of the problems, Greg never lost his *optimism*.**

o•ver•whelm [ō′vər•(h)welm′] *v.* **o•ver•whelmed, o•ver•whelm•ing** To overcome completely: **The avalanche was sudden, and soon the skiers were *overwhelmed* by the wave of snow.**

plun•der [plun′dər] *v.* **plun•dered, plun•der•ing** To steal things by force: **The police caught the robbers *plundering* the village.**

poised [poizd] *adj.* Ready to move or act: **Knees slightly bent and bat *poised*, Hugo waited for the pitcher to release the ball.**

pose [pōz] *v.* **posed, pos•ing** To sit or stand in a position for a picture: **The photographer would like Uncle Albert to *pose* behind Aunt Jenny.**

pre•cise•ly [pri•sīs′lē] *adv.* Exactly: **Thomas hit the ball *precisely* into the corner to win the tennis match.**

prej•u•dice [prej′ŏŏ•dis] *n.* An unfair opinion formed without examining the available facts: **Some of the doctors had *prejudices* against the new medicine.**

618

pres•tig•ious [pres•tē′jəs *or* pres•tij′əs] *adj.* Honored and valued: **The Nobel Prize is one of the most *prestigious* awards.**

pri•or•i•ty [prī•ôr′ə•tē] *n.* Something that is first in order of importance: **Finishing your homework has *priority* over watching television.**

quiv•er [kwiv′ər] *v.* **quiv•ered, quiv•er•ing** To make a slight trembling motion; vibrate: **Pete's knees *quivered* a little when he got up to give his speech.**

ra•di•ant•ly [rā′dē•ənt•lē] *adv.* Brilliantly; in a bright or glowing way: **Jamal smiled *radiantly* as he stepped up to receive first prize.**

re•lent [ri•lent′] *v.* **re•lent•ed, re•lent•ing** To become less severe and more gentle and cooperative: **The children finished their homework, so their parents *relented* and let them watch the video.**

rel•ic [rel′ik] *n.* Something remaining from a past culture or time period: **The *relics* from the lost city were displayed in the museum.** *syn.* artifact

res•i•dent [rez′ə•dənt] *n.* A person who lives in a certain place; not a visitor: **The *residents* of this neighborhood want a new park and cleaner streets.**

re•straint [ri•strānt′] *n.* The act of holding back: **The interior designer used *restraint* when decorating the room.**

re•stric•tion [ri•strik′shən] *n.* A limit: **The doctor gave her two *restrictions*: no fat and no sugar.**

re•trieve [ri•trēv′] *v.* **re•trieved, re•triev•ing** To get something back: **Mohammed *retrieved* the keys he had dropped into the swimming pool.**

re•vive [ri•vīv′] *v.* **re•vived, re•viv•ing** To bring back to consciousness: **The doctors *revived* the young girl who had almost drowned in the lake.**

ric•o•chet [rik′ə•shā′] *v.* To bounce off a surface: **Be careful if you play golf near trees, because a ball can hit a tree and *ricochet*.**

ricochet

relic This word comes from the Latin word *relinquere*, meaning "to leave behind." In English it slowly developed two meanings. One of them is *relic*, and the other was "a widow," or a woman who was "left behind" after her husband's death. The second meaning is not used today.

ricochet

a	add	ŏŏ	took
ā	ace	ōō	pool
â	care	u	up
ä	palm	û	burn
e	end	yōō	fuse
ē	equal	oi	oil
i	it	ou	pout
ī	ice	ng	ring
o	odd	th	thin
ō	open	*th*	this
ô	order	zh	vision

ə = a in *above*, e in *sicken*, i in *possible*, o in *melon*, u in *circus*

619

rigor

spontaneously The Latin word *sponte* originally meant "my will" or "a promise." Later the meaning became "of my own free will," or "something I do willingly." So, this word describes something you do on impulse, because you want to do it.

swerved

terminal

rig•or [rig′ər] *n.* Difficulty and discomfort; challenge: **Only a few people are able to handle the *rigors* of climbing Mt. Everest.**

scape•goat [skāp′gōt′] *n.* A person, group, or animal made to bear the blame for the errors of others: **There will be no *scapegoat* in this group because we are all to blame for missing the bus.**

se•rene [si•rēn′] *adj.* Peaceful; tranquil; unruffled: **The *serene* mood was shattered when a motorcycle roared past.**

slay [slā] *v.* **slew, slain, slay•ing** To kill violently: **More than three hundred people were *slain* in the battle that day.** *syn.* slaughter

spon•ta•ne•ous•ly [spon•tā′nē•əs•lē] *adv.* Naturally and without planning: **The winner of the contest *spontaneously* hugged the announcer.**

strive [strīv] *v.* **strove, stiv•en [striv′ən], striv•ing** To make a strong effort: **Wendy was *striving* to make her science project the best she had ever presented.**

sum•mon [sum′ən] *v.* **sum•moned, sum•mon•ing** To order to come: **The hotel clerk will *summon* a bellhop to help you with your suitcase.**

swerve [swûrv] *v.* **swerved, swerv•ing** To turn suddenly to one side: **Manisha had to *swerve* off the road to avoid hitting the deer.**

ter•mi•nal [tûr′mə•nəl] *n.* A bus, airplane, or train station at the end of a route: **Sylvia was to wait at the *terminal* for her Uncle Paul to pick her up.**

trend•y [tren′dē] *adj.* Of the latest fashion; popular for only a short time: **Barb wanted to buy those *trendy* new shoes, but they were very expensive.**

trib•ute [trib′yōōt] *n.* Respect and admiration: **The city paid *tribute* to the fireman who rescued the family from the burning house.**

tur•moil [tûr′moil] *n.* A condition of great confusion: **After the terrible hurricane, the town was in *turmoil*.**

620

un•eas•i•ness [un•ē′zē•nəs] *n.* A feeling that there will be trouble: **The house was too quiet, and Sergio could not shake his *uneasiness* about being home alone.** *syn.* worry

un•wav•er•ing [un•wā′və•ring] *adj.* Not faltering or failing: **No matter what trouble the boy got into, his mother's love was *unwavering*.** *syn.* continuous

vast [vast] *adj.* Very large in size or area: **The *vast* forest covered thousands of acres.** *syn.* huge

vir•tue [vûr′chōō] *n.* A good quality or feature: **Honesty and hard work are admirable *virtues*.**

vi•tal•i•ty [vī•tal′ə•tē] *n.* Energy: **Their *vitality* returned after they had had a short rest.**

whim•per [(h)wim′pər] *n.* Soft and broken crying or sobbing: **The puppy's *whimpers* caught the attention of its mother.**

whimper

vast The Latin word *vastus* originally meant that something was "empty," like a desert. Because deserts are usually very large, over the years the meaning of this word changed to "huge."

virtue The ancient Romans used the word *virtus* to mean "a man's strength." Later this word represented "courage" and other good qualities of both men and women.

a	add	ŏŏ	took
ā	ace	ōō	pool
â	care	u	up
ä	palm	û	burn
e	end	yōō	fuse
ē	equal	oi	oil
i	it	ou	pout
ī	ice	ng	ring
o	odd	th	thin
ō	open	*th*	this
ô	order	zh	vision

ə = a in *above*, e in *sicken*, i in *possible*, o in *melon*, u in *circus*

621

Using the Index of Titles and Authors

Explain to students that an index is often found at the back of a book and usually consists of an alphabetical listing of topics covered in that particular book. Tell students that sometimes books have special kinds of indexes, such as the Index of Titles and Authors at the back of their anthologies.

When looking at the first page of the Index, page 622, you may want to point out that all the entries are in alphabetical order and that authors are listed with last names first. Ask students how they can tell at a glance which entries are selection titles and which are authors' names. Then call attention to the references to page numbers in red type. You may want to select several index entries and have students predict what they will find when they turn to the page or pages listed.

INDEX OF
Titles and Authors

Page numbers in color refer to biographical information.

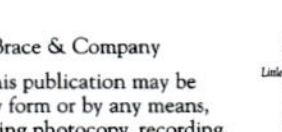

Requests for permission to make copies of any part of the work should be mailed to: Permissions Department, Harcourt Brace & Company, 6277 Sea Harbor Drive, Orlando, Florida 32887-6777.

HARCOURT BRACE and Quill Design is a registered trademark of Harcourt Brace & Company.

Printed in the United States of America

Acknowledgments

For permission to reprint copyrighted material, grateful acknowledgment is made to the following sources:

Editors of the Antioch Review: "On Watching the Construction of a Skyscraper" by Burton Raffel. Text copyright © 1960 by the Antioch Review, Inc. Originally published in the *Antioch Review*, Winter 1960.

Avon Books: Cover illustration by Patricia Mulvihill from *Beardance* by Will Hobbs. Illustration copyright © 1989 by Patricia Mulvihill.

Bantam Doubleday Dell Books for Young Readers: From *Last Summer with Maizon* by Jacqueline Woodson, cover illustration by Leo and Diane Dillon. Text copyright © 1990 by Jacqueline Woodson; illustration copyright © 1990 by Leo and Diane Dillon.

Blackbirch Press, Inc.: Cover photograph from *Wilma Rudolph: Olympic Gold!* by Wayne Coffey. © 1993 by Blackbirch Press, Inc.

Bradbury Press, an Affiliate of Macmillan, Inc.: Cover photograph by Lyn Topinka from *Volcano: The Eruption and Healing of Mt. St. Helens* by Patricia Lauber. Photograph courtesy of United States Department of the Interior, U.S. Geological Survey, David A. Johnston Cascades Volcano Observatory, Vancouver, Washington.

George Braziller, Inc.: "Fear" from *Dismantling the Silence* by Charles Simic. Text copyright © 1971 by Charles Simic.

Curtis Brown Ltd.: From "Elizabeth Borton de Treviño" in PAUSES: *Autobiographical Reflections of 101 Creators of Children's Books* by Lee Bennett Hopkins. Text copyright © 1995 by Lee Bennett Hopkins. Published by HarperCollins Publishers.

Richard Curtis Associates: "Freedom Ride" by Liz Fordred with Susie Blackmun.

Joan Daves Agency, on behalf of The Heirs to the Estate of Martin Luther King, Jr.: From "I Have a Dream" speech by Martin Luther King, Jr. Text copyright 1963 by Martin Luther King, Jr.; text copyright renewed 1991 by Coretta Scott King.

Delacorte Press, a division of Bantam Doubleday Dell Publishing Group, Inc.: From *The River* by Gary Paulsen, cover illustration by Neil Waldman. Text copyright © 1991 by Gary Paulsen; illustration copyright © 1991 by Neil Waldman. Cover illustration by Robert Hunt from *Cat Running* by Zilpha Keatley Snyder. Illustration copyright © 1994 by Robert Hunt.

Dell Books, a division of Bantam Doubleday Dell Publishing Group, Inc.: From *Where the Red Fern Grows* by Wilson Rawls, cover illustration by Robert McGinnis. Text copyright © 1961 by Sophie S. Rawls, Trustee, or successor Trustee(s) of the Rawls Trust, dated July 21, 1991; text copyright © 1961 by The Curtis Publishing Company; illustration copyright © 1989 by Robert McGinnis.

Dial Books for Young Readers, a division of Penguin Books USA Inc.: Cover illustration by E. B. Lewis from *The Baby Grand, The Moon in July, & Me* by Joyce Annette Barnes. Illustration © 1994 by E. B. Lewis.

Peter B. G. Duffy: Photograph of Liz and Peter Fordred by Peter B. G. Duffy from "Freedom Ride" by Liz Fordred with Susie Blackmun.

Dutton Children's Books, a division of Penguin Books USA Inc.: From "Four Generals" in *Shen of the Sea: Chinese Stories for Children* by Arthur Bowie Chrisman, cover illustration by Else Hasselriis. Copyright 1925 by E.P. Dutton, renewed 1953 by Arthur Bowie Chrisman.

Farrar, Straus & Giroux, Inc.: Cover photograph by Johnny Johnson from *Making Sense: Animal Perception and Communication* by Bruce Brooks. Photograph © by Johnny Johnson/Animals Animals. From *I, Juan de Pareja* by Elizabeth Borton de Treviño. Text and cover illustration copyright © 1965 by Elizabeth Borton de Treviño.

James Cross Giblin: "The Great Wall of China" from *Walls: Defenses Throughout History* by James Cross Giblin. Text copyright © 1984 by James Cross Giblin.

Greenwillow Books, a division of William Morrow & Company, Inc.: Cover illustration by Frank Modell from *Journal of a Teenage Genius* by Helen V. Griffith. Copyright © 1987 by Helen V. Griffith.

Harcourt Brace & Company: Cover illustration by Leo and Diane Dillon from *Aïda* by Leontyne Price. Illustration copyright © 1990 by Leo and Diane Dillon. "Photograph" from *Something Permanent* by Cynthia Rylant. Text copyright © 1994 by Cynthia Rylant. "The Challenge" from *Local News* by Gary Soto. Text copyright © 1993 by Gary Soto. Cover illustration by Goro Sasaki from *Pacific Crossing* by Gary Soto. Copyright © 1992 by Gary Soto.

HarperCollins Publishers: From *Julie of the Wolves* by Jean Craighead George, cover illustration by John Schoenherr. Text copyright ©1972 by Jean Craighead George; illustration copyright ©1972 by John Schoenherr. Cover illustration by Carl Burger from *Old Yeller* by Fred Gipson. Copyright © 1956 by Fred Gipson. Cover illustration by Stephen Fieser from *The Silk Route* by John S. Major. Illustration copyright © 1995 by Stephen Fieser.

Holiday House, Inc.: Cover photograph from *The Wright Brothers: How They Invented the Airplane* by Russell Freedman. Photograph courtesy of The Smithsonian Institution.

Houghton Mifflin Company: "A Song of Greatness" from *The Children Sing in the Far West* by Mary Austin. Text copyright 1928 by Mary Austin; text © renewed 1956 by Kenneth M. Chapman and Mary C. Wheelwright. From *Number the Stars* by Lois Lowry. Text and cover photograph copyright © 1989 by Lois Lowry. From *City* by David Macaulay. Copyright © 1974 by David Macaulay. From *Island of the Blue Dolphins* by Scott O'Dell, cover illustration by Ted Lewin. Text copyright © 1960 by Scott O'Dell, renewed 1988 by Scott O'Dell; illustration copyright © 1990 by Ted Lewin. Cover illustration by Troy Howell from *Apple Is My Sign* by Mary Riskind. Illustration © 1981 by Troy Howell.

Karen E. Hudson: From *The Will and the Way: Paul R. Williams, Architect* by Karen E. Hudson. Text copyright © 1994 by Karen E. Hudson.

Hyperion Books for Children: Cover illustration by Jeff Mangiat from *Stranded* by Ben Mikaelsen. Illustration copyright © 1995 by Jeff Mangiat. Cover illustration by Joe Burleson from *Climb or Die* by Edward Myers. Illustration copyright © 1994 by Joe Burleson.

Intellectual Properties Management, Atlanta, Georgia, as Manager for the King Estate: License to reprint image/likeness of Martin Luther King, Jr.

Kids Discover: From "The Pyramids of Egypt" in *Kids Discover: Pyramids*. Text © 1993 by Kids Discover. From *Kids Discover: Ancient Greece*. Text © 1994 by Kids Discover.

Alfred A. Knopf, Inc.: "On Hearing a Flute at Night from the Wall of Shou-Hsiang" by Li Yi from *The Jade Mountain*, translated by Witter Bynner. Text copyright 1929, renewed 1957 by Alfred A. Knopf, Inc. "City" from *Collected Poems* by Langston Hughes. Text copyright © 1994 by the Estate of Langston Hughes. Cover photographs from *Round Buildings, Square Buildings, & Buildings That Wiggle Like a Fish* by Philip M. Isaacson. Copyright © 1988 by Philip M. Isaacson.

Deborah Nourse Lattimore: Cover illustration by Deborah Nourse Lattimore from *Detectives in Togas* by Henry Winterfeld.

Lerner Publications Company, Minneapolis, MN: From *Great Summer Olympic Moments* by Nate Aaseng. Text copyright © 1990 by Lerner Publications Company. From *The Vietnamese in America* by Paul Rutledge. Text copyright 1973 by Lerner Publications.

Little, Brown & Company: Cover illustration from *Walls: Defenses Throughout History* by James Cross Giblin. Cover photographs from *It's Our World, Too! Stories of Young People Who Are Making a Difference* by Phillip Hoose. Copyright © 1993 by Phillip Hoose. "Joan Benoit Samuelson" from *Champions: Stories of Ten Remarkable Athletes* by Bill Littlefield, illustrated by Bernie Fuchs. Text copyright © 1993 by Bill Littlefield; illustrations copyright © 1993 by Bernie Fuchs. Cover photograph from *Life in the Oceans* by Norbert Wu. Copyright © 1991 by Tern Enterprise, Inc.

Lodestar Books, an affiliate of Dutton Children's Books, a division of Penguin Books USA Inc.: Cover photographs by David Hautzig from *The Other Side: How Kids Live in a California Latino Neighborhood* by Kathleen Krull. Photographs copyright © 1994 by David Hautzig.

Lothrop, Lee & Shepard Books, a division of William Morrow & Company, Inc.: From *Hello, My Name Is Scrambled Eggs* by Jamie Gilson, cover illustration by John Wallner. Text copyright © 1985 by Jamie Gilson; illustration copyright © 1985 by John Wallner.

LRN Company: From *Diego Rodríguez de Silva y Velásquez* (Retitled: "The Art of Velásquez") by Ernest Raboff. Published by HarperCollins Publishers.

The Madison Press Limited: Cover photographs from *Into the Mummy's Tomb* by Nicholas Reeves. Photographs courtesy of The Robert Harding Picture Library and Lehnert and Landrock.

Alan Mazzetti: Cover illustration by Alan Mazzetti from *Taking Sides* by Gary Soto.

Margaret K. McElderry Books, an imprint of Simon & Schuster: "Volcano" from *A Tree Place and Other Poems* by Constance Levy. Text copyright © 1994 by Constance Kling Levy. Cover illustration by Kinuko Craft from *A Jar of Dreams* by Yoshiko Uchida. Copyright © 1981 by Yoshiko Uchida.

Morrow Junior Books, a division of William Morrow & Company, Inc.: Cover illustration by Derek James from *Tales of a Dead King* by Walter Dean Myers. Copyright © 1983 by Walter Dean Myers. From *The Star Fisher* by Laurence Yep, cover illustration by David Wiesner. Text copyright © 1991 by Laurence Yep; illustration copyright © 1991 by David Wiesner.

National Council of Teachers of English: "Foreign Student" by Barbara B. Robinson from *English Journal*, May 1976. Text copyright 1976 by The National Council of Teachers of English.

New Directions Publishing Corporation: "View from the Cliffs" by Tu Mu from *One Hundred More Poems from the Chinese* by Kenneth Rexroth. Text copyright © 1970 by Kenneth Rexroth.

Oxford University Press: "Hieroglyphics" from *Oxford Children's Encyclopedia*, Vol 3. © 1991 by Oxford University Press.

Puffin Books, a division of Penguin Books USA Inc.: From *The Golden Goblet* by Eloise Jarvis McGraw, cover illustration by Maureen Hyde. Text copyright © 1961, renewed © 1989 by Eloise Jarvis McGraw; illustration copyright © 1989 by Viking Penguin.

Random House, Inc.: "Passports to Understanding" from *Wouldn't Take Nothing For My Journey Now* by Maya Angelou. Text copyright © 1993 by Maya Angelou. Cover illustration by Jules Feiffer from *The Phantom Tollbooth* by Norton Juster. Illustration copyright © 1961, 1989 by Jules Feiffer.

Marian Reiner, on behalf of Lilian Moore: "Until I Saw the Sea" from *I Feel the Same Way* by Lilian Moore. Text copyright © 1967 by Lilian Moore; text © renewed 1995 by Lilian Moore.

Dominic C. H. Rieu, Executor of the Estate of E. V. Rieu: "The Paint Box" from *The Flattered Fish and Other Poems* by E. V. Rieu. Text copyright © 1962 by E. V. Rieu. Published by Methuen, London, 1962.

Rizzoli International Publications, Inc.: Cover from *The Will and the Way: Paul R. Williams, Architect* by Karen E. Hudson. Illustration copyright © 1994 by Rizzoli International Publications, Inc.; photograph copyright © 1994 by The Paul R. Williams Collection.

Scholastic Inc.: Cover illustration from *The Lost Wreck of the Isis* by Robert D. Ballard. Copyright © 1990 by The Madison Press Limited. From *The Secrets of Vesuvius* by Sara C. Bisel. Copyright © 1990 by Sara C. Bisel and Family and The Madison Press Limited.

The Rod Serling Trust: "The Monsters Are Due on Maple Street" by Rod Serling. Text © 1960 by Rod Serling; text © 1988 by Carolyn Serling, Jodi Serling and Anne Serling.

Sniffen Court Books: From *Behind the Sealed Door: The Discovery of the Tomb and Treasures of Tutankhamun* by Irene and Laurence Swinburne. Text copyright © 1977 by Sniffen Court Books.

Troll Associates: Cover illustration by Richard Hook from *Growing Up in Ancient China* by Ken Teague. © 1994 by Eagle Books.

University Press of New England: "The Inner Tube" from *A Summer Life* by Gary Soto. Text copyright © 1990 by University Press of New England.

Walker and Company, 435 Hudson Street, New York, NY 10014: From *To the Top of the World* by Jim Brandenburg. Copyright © 1993 by Jim Brandenburg.

Albert Whitman & Company: From *Five Women Photographers* (Retitled: "Two Women Photographers") by Sylvia Wolf. Text copyright © 1994 by Sylvia Wolf.

Photo Credits

Key: (t) top, (b) bottom, (c) center, (l) left, (r) right.

Tim Kelly/Black Star/Harcourt Brace & Company, 43; Courtesy of MacIntosh & Otis, 107; Tom Sobolik/Black Star/Harcourt Brace & Company, 186; Dale Higgins/Harcourt Brace & Company, 315; Courtesy of Houghton Mifflin, 396; Courtesy of Farrar, Straus & Giroux, 465; Warren Faubel/Black Star/Harcourt Brace & Company, 507; Alinari/Art Resource, NY, 422 (t); Ancient Art & Architecture, 430-431, ;Ancient Art and Architecture Collection, 363, (r); Art Resource, NY, 423; David Austen/TSW, 121, (r); The Bettmann Archive, 340; Jonathan Blair/Woodfin Camp & Associates, 404-405, 407, 415, 418, 426 (t) ; Borromeo/Art Resource, NY, 121 (b); Margaret Bourke-White, Syracuse University Library, 475, Time Warner, 476-480; Jim Brandenburg, 580-607; Bridgeman/Art Resource, NY, 127, (br); Geoffrey Clifford/The Stock Market, 119, 128, (t); Original Art by Phil Colprit/Wood Ronsaville Harlin, Inc., 365, (b); Comstock, 184; Dennis Cox/ChinaStock, 176-177, 190-190; Culver Pictures, Inc., 365 (cl); William Curtsinger/Photo Researchers, Inc., 366 (b); Timothy Eagan/Woodfin Camp & Associates, 185; Thomas Eakins, The National Gallery of Art, Washington, D.C., Gift of Mr. and Mrs. Cornelius Vanderbilt Whitney, 70-71; Foto Marburg/Art Resource, NY, 364, (ct); Donald A. Frey/Institute of Nautical Archaeology, 367 (l); © Flor Garduno, 482-486; Giraudon/Art Resource, NY, 120-121, 362 (cl), 364, (c); The Granger Collection, 362 (lt), 362 (bl), 364(cb & b), 365 (tl), 365 (tr), 367 (b, the Schliemans); Farrell Grehan/Photo Researchers, Inc, 364, (rl); Robert Harding Picture Library, 152-153; © Adriano Heitmann, 472 (r), 491; Michael Holford, 361(b), 351(tr) ; Winslow Homer, The Metropolitan Museum of Art, Catherine Lorillard Wolfe, Collection, Wolfe Fund, 1906, 56-563; Courtesy of Karen E. Hudson, 492-504, 506, 510-511 (l, b, & r); Hulton-Deutsch Collection, 367, (b); Michael Jacobs/Woodfin Camp & Associates, 123, (t, c, & b, inset), 128, (b), 129, (b); J. Kerth/Leo de Wys, 367 (tr); Hiroji Kubota/Magnum, 182-183 ; Jacob Lawrence, The National Museum of American Art, washington, D.C., Art Resource, NY, 260-261; Erich Lessing/Art Resource, NY, 118, 120, 122, 124, (bl), 360 (l), 360-361 (c), 362, (br); LIFE Magazine © Time Warner, 472 (l), 490; Painting by Ken Marshall, Courtesy of Madison Press Books, 402-403, 408-409; O. Louis Mazzatenta © National Geographic Society, 405 (inset), 416-417, 421, 422 (b), 424-425, 426-427(b & r); Will & Deni McIntyre/Photo Researchers, Inc., 366, (l); George Munday/Leo de Wye, 358; NASA, 179; Katsushuika Oi, Museum of Fine Arts, Boston, Courtesy of William Sturgis Bigelow Collection, 470-471, ; Georgia O'Keefe, Columbus Muiseum of Art, Howard Fund II, 368-369; Courtesy of Oxford University Press, 126-127; John M. Roberts/The Stock Market, 186; Scala/Art Resource, NY, 120 (l), 122, 124-125, 359, 362, (tr & cr), 366 (c), 414; SEF/Art Resource, NY, 367 (tl); Julius Shulman, 505, 510-511 (c); SuperStock, 118, 129 (l), 124; Jean-Marc Truchet/TSW, 181; UPI/The Bettmann Archive, 351; Diego Velasquez Scala/Art Resource, NY, 439-443 , 448 (b), 449 (c),Staatliche Museen zu Berlin-PreuBischer Kulturbesitz Gemaldegalese, 444,449 (l), Christie's, London/SuperStock, 445, 449 (r), Erich Lessing/Art Resource, NY, 446, 448 (t) Luis Villota/The Stock Market, 123; Original art by Williams, Wood Ronsaville Harlin, Inc., 361-363;

Illustration Credits

Kazuhiko Sano, Cover Art; Rocco Baviera, 108-109; Alaiyo Bradshaw, 46-69; Deborah Chabrian, 294-315, 318-319; Richard Cowdrey, 564-579; David Diaz, 466-467; Chris Duke, 400-401; Rick Farrell, 172-173, 450-465, 468-469; Bernie Fuchs, 342-357; Jack Graham, 90-95; Darrin Johnston, 338-341; Hui Han Liu, 204-223, 226-227; Lori Lohstoeter, 96-107, 110-111; Roberta Ludlow, 228-251, 258-259; David Macaulay, 370-397; John Nickle, 262-287, 292-293; Guy Porfirio, 254-257; Edward Potthast, 534-535; Mike Reed, 72-89; Mark Reidy, 538-561; Oren Sherman, 130-147, 150-151; Peter Siu, 188-189; Heidi Stevens, 154-171, 174-175; Cynthia Torp, 290-291; David Wilgus, 326-337, Larry Winborg, 22-45

Handwriting

Manuscript Alphabet

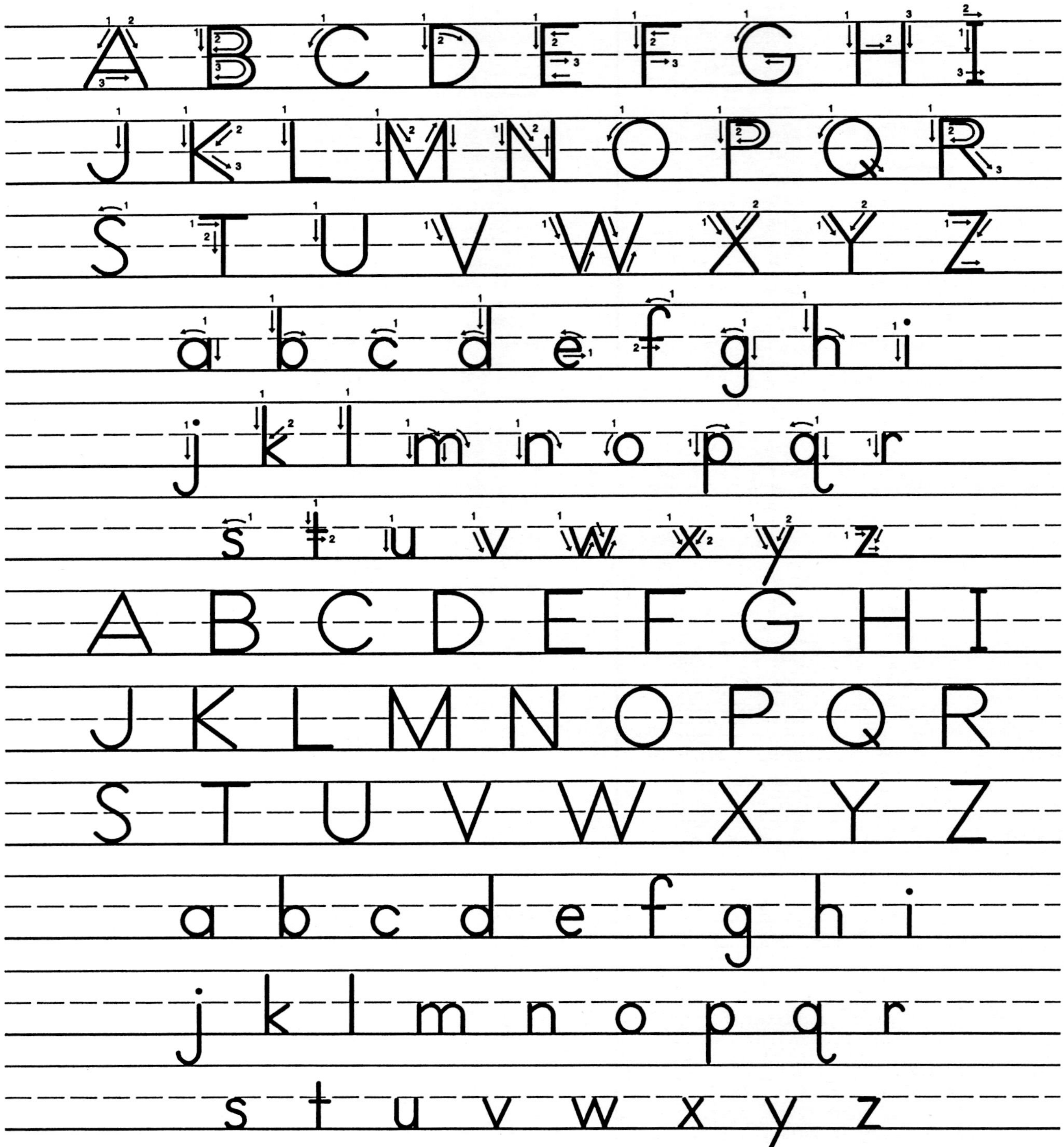

Harcourt Brace School Publishers

Handwriting

Cursive Alphabet

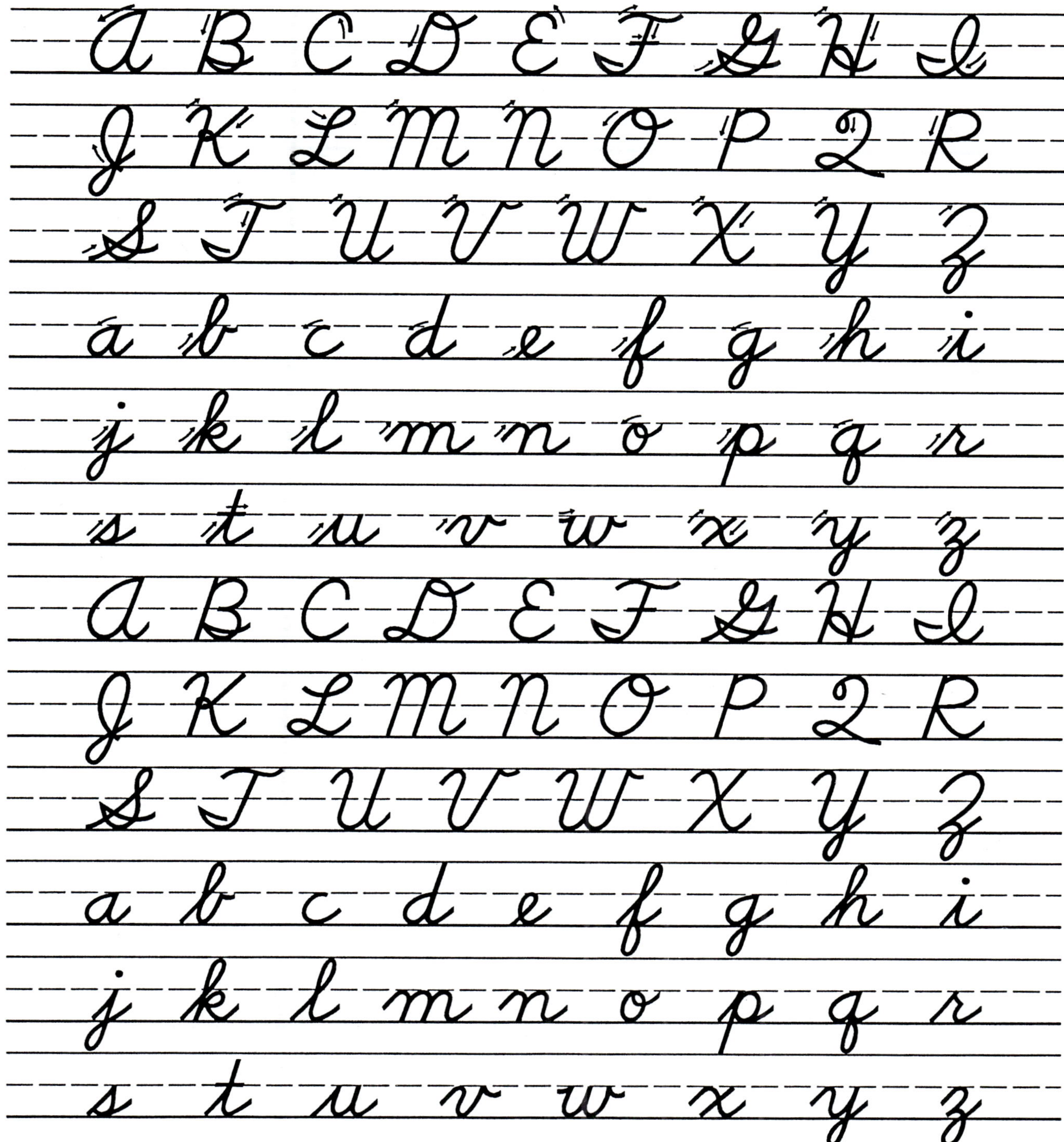

Harcourt Brace School Publishers

Prediction Chart

What I Predict Will Happen	What Actually Happened

Knowledge Chart

Prior Knowledge About ______	New Knowledge About ______
1.	1.
2.	2.
3.	3.
4.	4.
5.	5.
6.	6.
7.	7.

Predict-o-gram

Setting	Characters	Problem	Events	Solution

Story Map

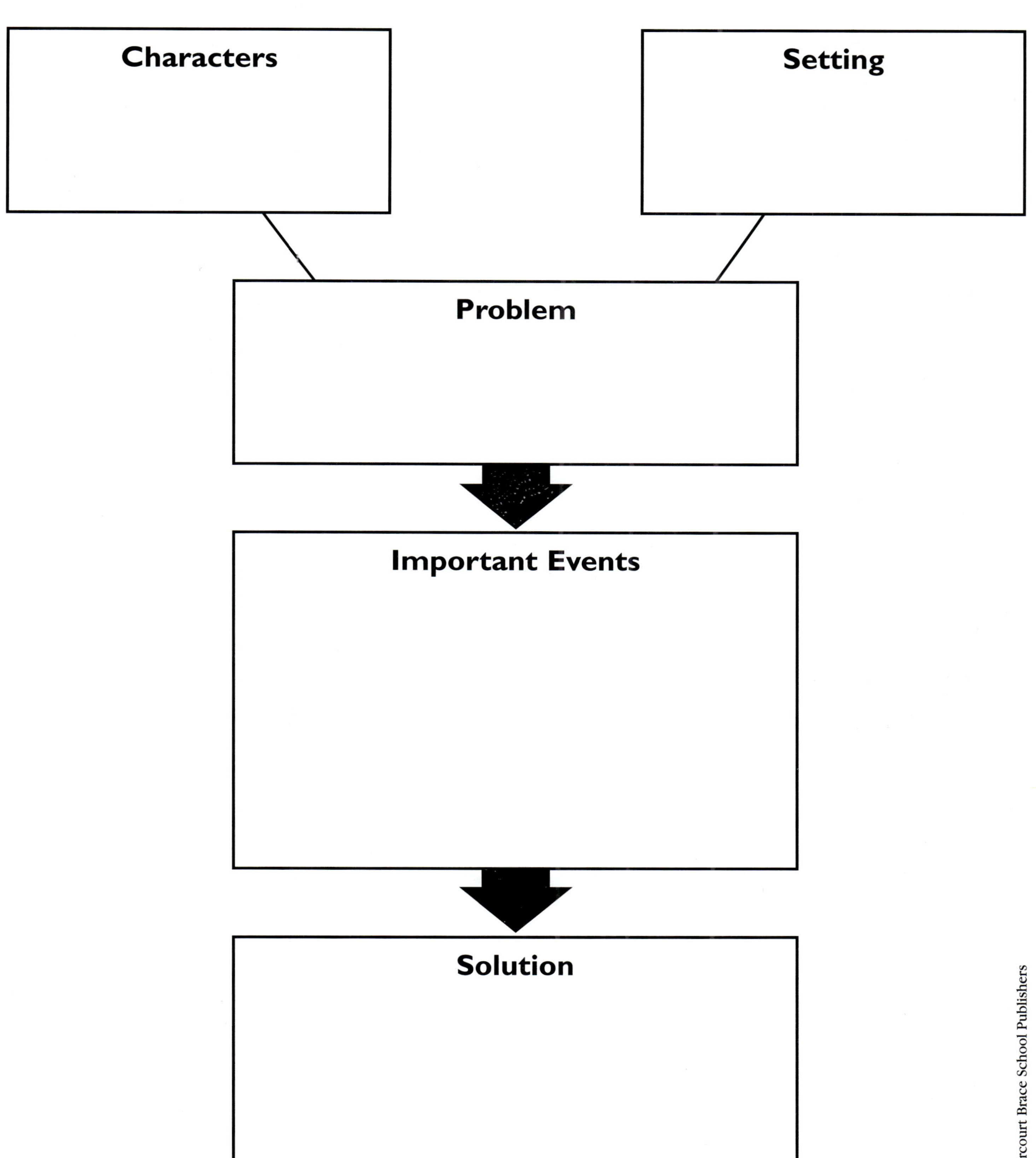

K–W–L Chart

What I Know	What I Want to Know	What I Learned

Organizing Ideas

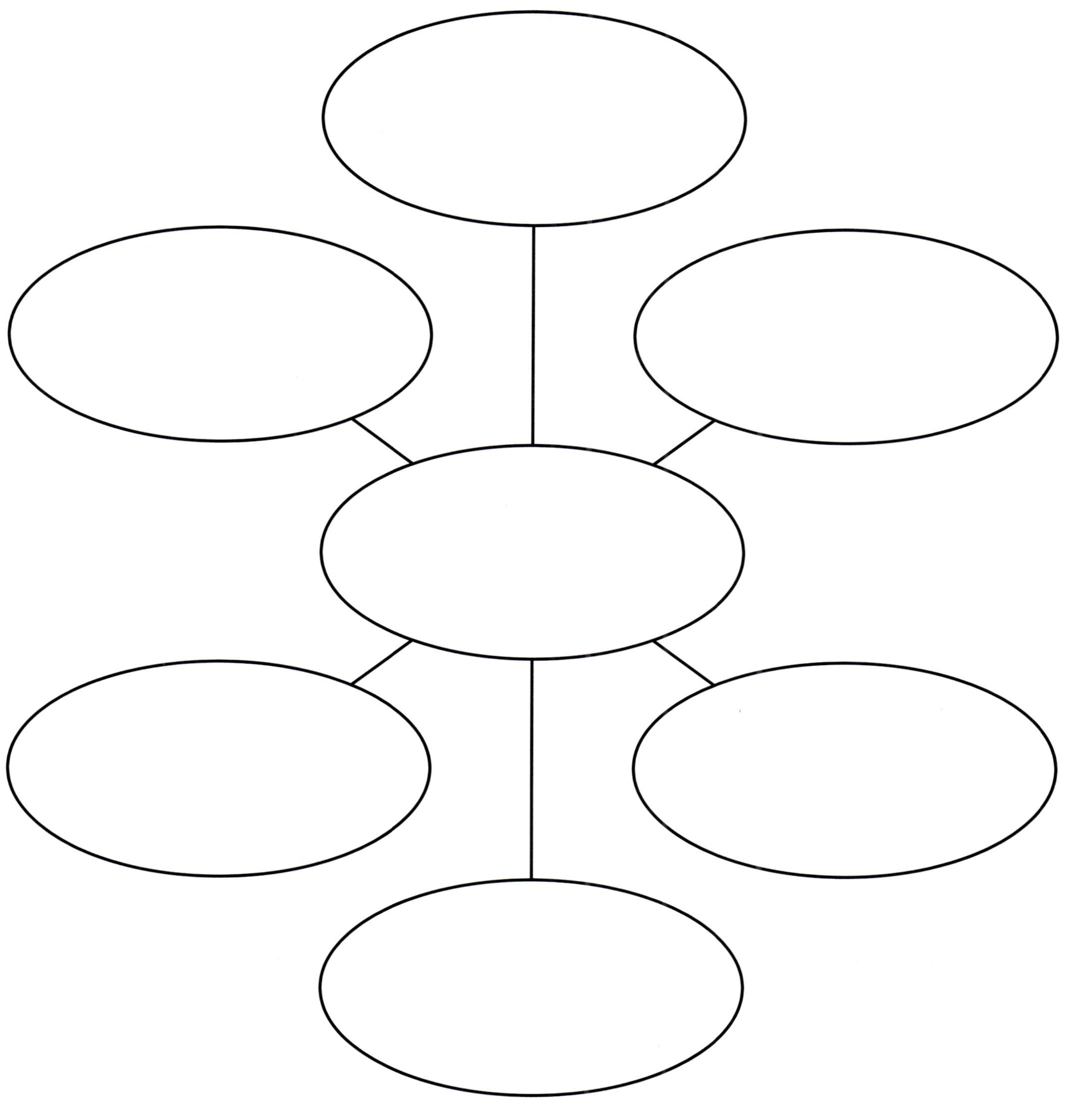

VIDEOCASSETTES
FOR USE WITH
SIGNATURES, Grade 6

The pages that follow are intended to help classroom teachers effectively integrate videocassettes into instruction in SIGNATURES. Some of the videocassettes listed within this correlation are dramatizations or animations of literature in the Student Anthologies of SIGNATURES. Others are videos of additional thematically related literature, while still others build background for understanding and appreciating literature and themes in SIGNATURES.

Each page of the correlation consists of three columns. The first identifies a theme within Grade 6. The second column provides a related videocassette title. The third identifies the publisher or distributor from whom the videocassette is available.

This correlation was produced by Harcourt Brace School Publishers as a service to teachers using SIGNATURES. The videocassettes listed within this correlation are neither published nor distributed by Harcourt Brace School Publishers. The names, addresses, and telephone numbers of videocassette publishers or distributors appear on the final page of the correlation with a listing of the videocassettes available from the publisher or distributor.

Grade 6

THEME	TITLE	PUBLISHER/DISTRIBUTOR
1 Meeting Challenges	*Where the Red Fern Grows*	Permabound
	Sounder	Paramount
	Island of the Blue Dolphins	Knowledge Unlimited
2 Ancient Civilizations	*The Treasures of Tutankhamen*	Guidance Associates
	Mainland China with Laura McKenzie	Republic Pictures Home Video
	The Silk Road Pack Collector's Gift Box	Central Park Media
3 Celebrating Differences	*The Diary of Anne Frank*	Schlessinger Video Production
	Chinese Americans	Schlessinger Video Production
4 Turning Points	*World of Ancient Rome*	United Learning Inc.
	Great Cities of the Ancient World Series: Rome and Pompeii	Schlessinger Video Production
	In the Shadow of Vesuvius	National Geographic
5 Masterpieces	*Black Americans: Artists, Entertainers, and More*	Spoken Arts
6 Confronting Nature	*Kon-Tiki*	Voyager Company
	River—Where Do You Come From?	Learning Corporation of America

VIDEOCASSETTE DISTRIBUTORS

Addresses and Phone Numbers

Central Park Media
250 W. 57 Street
Suite 317
New York, NY 10107
1-800-833-7456
FAX(212)977-8709

- *The Silk Road Pack Collector's Gift Box*

Guidance Associates
90 S. Bedford Road
Mount Kisco, NY 10549
1-800-431-1242
FAX(914)666-0172

- *The Treasures of Tutankhamen*

Knowledge Unlimited
P.O. Box 52
Madison, WI 53701-0052
1-800-356-2303
FAX(608)831-1570

- *Island of the Blue Dolphins*

Learning Corporation of America
1440 S. Sepulveda
Los Angeles, CA 91602
(310)444-8166
FAX(310)444-8460

- *River—Where Do You Come From?*

National Geographic Society
1145 17 Street N.W.
Washington, D.C. 20036
1-800-368-2728
FAX(202)828-6640

- *In the Shadow of Vesuvius*

Paramount
5555 Melrose Avenue
Los Angeles, CA 90038
(213)956-5000

- *Sounder*

Perma Bound Books
Vandalia Road
Jacksonville, IL 62650
1-800-637-6581
FAX(217)245-2105

- *Where the Red Fern Grows*

Republic Pictures Home Video
5700 Wilshire Blvd.
Los Angeles, CA 90036
(213)965-6950
FAX(213)965-6949

- *Mainland China with Laura McKenzie*

Schlessinger Video Productions
P.O. Box 1110 Dept. SVP-2
Bala Cynwyd, PA 19004
1-800-843-3620

- *Chinese Americans*
- *The Diary of Anne Frank*
- *Great Cities of the Ancient World Series: Rome and Pompeii*

Spoken Arts
801 94th Avenue North
St. Petersburg, FL 33702
1-800-326-4090
FAX(813)578-3110

- *Black Americans: Artists, Entertainers, and More*

United Learning, Inc.
6633 W. Howard Street
Niles, IL 60714
1-800-424-0362
FAX(708)647-0918

- *The World of Ancient Rome*

Voyager Company
424 35th Avenue
Seattle, WA 98122
1-206-323-1112
FAX(206)329-2416

- *Kon-Tiki*

INTEGRATED TECHNOLOGY COMPONENTS

FOR USE WITH SIGNATURES, Grade 6

This page focuses on technology resources that are integrated components of SIGNATURES. These components, all available from Harcourt Brace School Publishers, may be used with SIGNATURES or are referenced at appropriate points of use within teaching plans to enhance, extend, and enliven instruction.

The Amazing Writing Machine, Harcourt Brace School Edition, is a rich, creative desktop publishing program that encourages students to write and illustrate their own SIGNATURES-related stories, letters, journals, essays, and poems.

Imagination Express, School Version, is a series of six CD-ROM programs that go a marvelous step beyond electronic books, enabling students to be not consumers, but creators of their own multimedia books and reports directly related to themes in SIGNATURES. The following destinations are cited in various themes: ***Castle, Neighborhood, Ocean, Pyramids, and Time Trip, USA.***

Thinkin' Things, School Versions, consists of three leveled collections of delightful activities that help students develop the logical reasoning and critical thinking skills necessary for successful problem solving in their daily lives. ***Thinkin' Things, Collections 2*** and ***3*** are cited in various themes.

Assessment Workshop: Scoring Student Writing offers a software resource for teacher training to support holistic scoring of student writing. It is available in **Primary, Intermediate,** and **Middle School** Levels.

Computer Management System provides a technology aid for scoring and recording theme reading skills.

Benchmarks

These benchmark statements represent a continuum of learning. The highlighted column describes observable behaviors most of your students should exhibit by the end of the school year.

LISTENING

Listens to a variety of texts
Listens for a purpose
Listens for enjoyment
Listens to and follows directions
Recalls main idea, details, and facts after listening
Asks for repetition, restatement, or clarification
Listens and responds to peers in small groups
Participates in cooperative groups
Listens to others' opinions and points of view
Listens to pros and cons of an argument

Listens to a variety of texts
Listens for a purpose
Listens for enjoyment
Listens to and follows directions
Recalls main idea, details, and facts after listening
Asks for repetition, restatement, or clarification
Listens and responds to peers in small groups
Participates in cooperative groups
Listens to others' opinions and points of view
Listens to pros and cons of an argument

Listens to a variety of texts
Listens for a purpose
Listens for enjoyment
Listens to and follows directions
Recalls main idea, details, and facts after listening
Asks for repetition, restatement, or, clarification
Listens and responds to peers in small groups
Participates in cooperative groups
Listens to others' opinions and points of view
Listens to pros and cons of an argument

SPEAKING

Discusses or retells a variety of texts
Participates in storytelling, retelling, rhyme, and song
Participates in group activities
Uses talk to clarify or explain ideas or experiences
Reads orally with expression
Gives oral reports
Presents a point of view to an audience

Discusses or retells a variety of texts
Participates in storytelling, retelling, rhyme, and song
Participates in group activities
Uses talk to clarify or explain ideas or experiences
Reads orally with expression
Gives oral reports
Presents a point of view to an audience

Discusses or retells a variety of texts
Participates in storytelling, retelling, rhyme, and song
Participates in group activities
Uses talk to clarify or explain ideas or experiences
Varies tone, pitch, and pace of speech for effect in speaking and oral reading
Gives oral reports
Presents a point of view to an audience
Participates in public speaking and debate

VIEWING

Discusses work of various illustrators and illustration styles
Uses pictures to get meaning from or to support text
Predicts from visuals
Uses illustrations for details
Uses visuals to follow directions
Views critically

Discusses work of various illustrators and illustration styles
Uses pictures to get meaning from or to support text
Predicts from visuals
Uses illustrations for information or details
Uses visuals to follow directions
Views critically

Discusses work of various illustrators and illustration styles
Uses illustrations to get meaning from or to support text
Predicts from visuals
Uses illustrations for information or details
Uses visuals to follow directions
Views critically
Infers and evaluates the narrative connection between two pieces of viewed text

Student ______________ Teacher ______________ Grade ________

Listening, Speaking, and Viewing Checklist

	Date	Date	Date	Date	Date	Date
LISTENING						
Listens to a variety of texts						
Listens for a purpose						
Listens for enjoyment						
Listens to and follows directions						
Recalls main idea, details, and facts after listening						
Asks for repetition, restatement, or clarification						
Listens and responds to peers in small groups						
Participates in cooperative groups						
Listens to others' opinions and points of view						
Listens to pros and cons of an argument						
SPEAKING						
Discusses or retells a variety of texts						
Participates in group activities						
Uses talk to clarify or explain ideas or experiences						
Varies tone, pitch, and pace of speech for effect in speaking and oral reading						
Gives oral reports						
Presents a point of view to an audience						
Participates in public speaking and debate						
VIEWING						
Discusses work of various illustrators and illustration styles						
Predicts from visuals						
Uses illustrations for information or details						
Uses visuals to follow directions						
Views critically						
Infers and evaluates the narrative connection between two pieces of viewed text						

Comments:

Key:

N – Not Observed
O – Observed Occasionally
R – Observed Regularly

Benchmarks

These benchmark statements represent a continuum of learning. The highlighted column describes observable behaviors most of your students should exhibit by the end of the school year.

WRITING: CONTENT AND ORGANIZATION

Writes for a purpose and an audience
Writes a sentence that elaborates another sentence
Joins related sentences into paragraphs and uses paragraphs to organize information and ideas
Stays on topic and sequences ideas
Includes introduction, development, closing in writing
Uses supporting ideas to develop topic and specific details to support ideas
Uses appropriate word choice
Uses concepts of order and time in writing
Uses descriptive language
Uses transitional words and phrases

Writes for a purpose and an audience
Writes a sentence that elaborates another sentence
Joins related sentences into paragraphs and uses paragraphs to organize information and ideas
Writes several paragraphs focused on a single topic
Includes introduction, development, closing in writing
Uses supporting ideas to develop topic and specific details to support ideas
Uses a range of vocabulary appropriate to purpose and audience
Uses concepts of order and time in writing
Uses descriptive language
Uses transitional words and phrases
Uses a range of writing styles appropriate to purpose and audience

Writes for a purpose and an audience
Writes a sentence that elaborates another sentence
Joins related sentences into paragraphs and uses paragraphs to organize information and ideas
Writes several paragraphs focused on a single topic
Includes introduction, development, closing in writing
Uses supporting ideas to develop topic and specific details to support ideas
Uses a range of vocabulary appropriate to purpose and audience
Uses multiple characters and episodes
Uses concepts of order and time in writing
Uses concrete images, vivid descriptions, and figurative language
Uses transitional words and phrases
Uses a range of writing styles appropriate to purpose and audience

WRITING: CONVENTIONS AND MECHANICS

Uses appropriate spacing and directionality
Recognizes and produces simple, compound, and complex sentences
Uses punctuation correctly
Uses capitalization correctly
Makes few errors in usage

Uses appropriate spacing and directionality
Recognizes and produces simple, compound, and complex sentences
Uses punctuation correctly
Uses capitalization correctly
Makes few errors in usage
Writes correct possessive and pronoun forms
Uses a range of grammatical structures and forms

Uses appropriate spacing and directionality
Recognizes and produces simple, compound, and complex sentences
Uses punctuation correctly
Uses capitalization correctly
Makes few errors in usage
Writes correct possessive and pronoun forms
Uses a range of grammatical structures and forms

WRITING: SPELLING

Applies spelling generalizations
Uses conventional spelling

Applies spelling generalizations
Uses conventional spelling

Applies spelling generalizations
Uses conventional spelling

Student ______________________ Teacher ______________________ Grade ____________

Writing Checklist

	Date	Date	Date	Date	Date	Date
CONTENT AND ORGANIZATION						
Writes for a purpose and an audience						
Writes a sentence that elaborates another sentence						
Joins related sentences into paragraphs and uses paragraphs to organize information and ideas						
Writes several paragraphs focused on a single topic						
Includes introduction, development, closing in writing						
Uses supporting ideas to develop topic and specific details to support ideas						
Uses a range of vocabulary appropriate to purpose and audience						
Uses concepts of order and time in writing						
Uses multiple characters and episodes						
Uses descriptive and figurative language						
Uses transitional words and phrases						
Uses a range of writing styles appropriate to purpose and audience						
CONVENTIONS AND MECHANICS						
Uses appropriate spacing and directionality						
Recognizes and produces simple, compound, and complex sentences						
Uses punctuation correctly						
Uses capitalization correctly						
Makes few errors in usage						
Writes correct possessive and pronoun forms						
Uses a range of grammatical structures and forms						
SPELLING						
Applies spelling generalizations						
Uses conventional spelling						

Comments:

Key:

N – Not Observed
O – Observed Occasionally
R – Observed Regularly

Scope and Sequence

GRADE/LEVEL	K/1	1–1	1–2	1–3	1–4	1–5	2	3	4	5	6
THINKING											
Observing											
Brainstorming											
Classifying and Categorizing											
Comparing and Contrasting											
Visualizing											
Evaluating											
Synthesizing											
Analyzing											
EMERGENT LITERACY											
Phonemic Awareness											
Print Awareness											
Concept of Letter, Word, Sentence											
STRATEGIC READING											
Active Reading Strategies											
Read Fiction (Narrative Text)											
Read Nonfiction (Expository Text; Text Structure)											
Analyze Details											
Synthesize Ideas/Information											
Make Inferences											
Decoding Strategy: Use phonemic/structural analysis plus context to unlock pronunciation											
Vocabulary Strategy: Use phonetic/structural/contextual clues to determine meanings											
Use Self-Assessment Strategies											
COMPREHENSION											
Cause-Effect							●	●	●	●	●
Classify/Categorize											
Compare and Contrast								●	●	●	●
Draw Conclusions							●	●	●	●	●
Fact-Fantasy/Nonfact											
Author's Purpose										●	●
Author's Viewpoint										●	●
Fact-Opinion								●	●	●	●
Main Idea (Global Meaning)/Details						●	●	●	●	●	●
Make Generalizations											
Make Judgments											
Make Predictions					●		●	●	●	●	●
Paraphrase								●	●	●	●
Referents											
Sequence				●			●	●	●	●	●
Summarize								●	●	●	●
VOCABULARY											
High-frequency Words											
Key Words/Selection Vocabulary	●	●	●	●	●	●	●	●	●	●	●
Vocabulary Strategy: Use phonetic/structural/contextual clues to determine meanings											
Synonyms/Antonyms											
Multiple-Meaning Words										●	
Homophones/Homographs											
Context Clues								●	●	●	●
Analogies											
Connotation/Denotation											
Glossary											
Dictionary (for Word Meaning)											
DECODING											
Phonics											
Initial/Medial/Final Consonants	●	●	●	●							
Phonograms and Word Patterns											
Short Vowels/Long Vowels		●	●	●	●	●	●				
Consonant Clusters/Digraphs (Initial/Final)			●	●	●	●					
R-Controlled Vowels							●				
Vowel Diphthongs/Vowel Digraphs/Variant Vowels							●				
Schwa											
Decoding Strategy: Use phonetic/structural analysis plus context to unlock pronunciation											
Decoding Strategy: Use graphophonic, semantic, and syntactic cues to decode or identify words											
Decoding Strategy: Use visual and graphophonic cues to decode long (multisyllabic) words											

Shaded Area **Modeling / Instruction / Application** ● **Tested**

Testing options include Skills Assessment, Holistic Reading Assessment, and Integrated Performance Assessment. For a complete scope and sequence of the kindergarten program, see the Teacher's Edition for that level.

GRADE/LEVEL	K/1	1–1	1–2	1–3	1–4	1–5	2	3	4	5	6
Structural Analysis											
Inflected Forms (Nouns; Verbs With and Without Spelling Changes)		●			●	●	●				
Possessives, Comparatives, Superlatives											
Contractions			●	●							
Compound Words											
Syllables and Syllabication											
Suffixes/Prefixes							●	●	●	●	●
Greek and Latin Roots									●	●	●
Spelling Patterns											
STUDY SKILLS											
Locate Sources of Information											
Use the Library (Parts of, Card Catalog, Computerized Card Catalog, Call Numbers, Database Searching Strategies, *Books in Print, Readers' Guide to Periodical Literature*)											
Alphabet/Alphabetical Order					●		●				
Skimming/Scanning											
Select Appropriate Resources											
Use Sources of Information											
Book Parts											
Graphic Aids (Maps, Charts, Graphs, Tables/Schedules, Diagrams, Time Lines Calendars)											
Compare Information from More Than One Source											
Use Reference Sources (Glossary/Dictionary, Thesaurus, Specialized Dictionary, Atlas/Globe, Encyclopedia, Almanac, Telephone Directory, Newspaper, Electronic and Audiovisual Media, *Books in Print, Reader's Guide to Periodical Literature*)								●	●	●	●
Organizing Information: Outlining, Note-Taking, Mapping, Webbing, Clustering, Classifying, Highlighting											
Study Strategies (K-W-L, SQ3R, How to Study)											
Content-Area Reading											
Adjust Method/Rate of Reading											
Test-Taking Strategies											
Follow Directions											
Forms/Applications											
LITERARY APPRECIATION											
Select Books for Individual Needs and Interests											
Read Full-length Books											
Literary Elements											
Plot Development											
Plot									●	●	●
Conflict (Internal/External)											
Climax											
Theme										●	●
Character (Emotions, Development, Traits)									●	●	●
Setting									●	●	●
Mood/Tone											
Point of View											
Narration											
Dialogue											
Author's Craft/Technique											
Figurative Language											
Characterization											
Imagery											
Humor											
Sound Devices (Rhythm/Rhyme/Alliteration/Onomatopoeia)											
Idiom, Slang, Dialect, Colloquialism											
Formal/Informal Language											
Literary Forms/Genre											
Fiction											
Realistic Fiction											
Historical Fiction											
Mystery											
Fantasy											
Science Fiction											
Full-length Book											
Riddle, Word Play, Pun											
Drama/Play											
Novel											
Short Story											
Pourquoi Tales											
Poetry/Song											

Shaded Area **Modeling / Instruction / Application** ● **Tested**

Testing options include Skills Assessment, Holistic Reading Assessment, and Integrated Performance Assessment. For a complete scope and sequence of the kindergarten program, see the Teacher's Edition for that level.

GRADE/LEVEL	K/1	1–1	1–2	1–3	1–4	1–5	2	3	4	5	6
Folklore (Folktale, Fairy Tale, Fable, Myth, Tall Tale, Legend, Nursery Rhyme)											
Nonfiction											
Biography/Autobiography											
Journal/Diary/Letters											
Essay											
Informational Article											
How-to Article											
Encyclopedia Article											
Magazine Article											
Newspaper Article/Feature											
Interview											
Speech											
Photo Essay											
Predictable and Patterned Text											
Personal Narrative											
MULTICULTURALISM											
Respond to Literature Representing Our Pluralistic Culture											
View Concepts/Issues from Diverse Perspectives											
Understand the Concept That All Groups Have Contributed to Society											
Acquire Attitudes/Skills/Knowledge to Interact Successfully with Members of Diverse Groups											
Recognize the Universality of Literary Themes Across Cultures and Languages											
LANGUAGE											
Composition											
Writing Process (Prewriting, Drafting, Revising, Proofreading, Publishing)											
Writer's Craft											
Capturing Reader's Interest											
Identifying Audience and Purpose							●	●	●	●	●
Using Appropriate Language							●	●	●	●	●
Writing Approaches											
Collaborative Writing											
Shared Writing											
Timed Writing											
Writing to Prompts							●	●	●	●	●
Responding to Essay Questions											
Forms of Writing											
Expository Writing (Compare/Contrast, Explanation, Directions, Speech, How-to, Friendly/Business Letters, News Story, Essay, Report)							●	●	●	●	●
Narrative Writing (Stories, Paragraphs, Personal Narrative, Personal Journal, Play, Poetry)							●	●	●	●	●
Descriptive Writing (Titles, Captions, Ad, Poster, Paragraphs, Stories, Poetry)							●	●	●	●	●
Persuasive Writing (Paragraph/s, Essay, Letter)								●	●	●	●
Cross-Curricular Writing											
Everyday Writing (Journals, Messages, Forms, Note-Taking, Summaries)											
Skills of Revision											
Correcting Sentence Fragments/Run-ons								●	●	●	●
Sentence Combining									●	●	●
Adding/Deleting/Rearranging Information											
Choosing Words Effectively (Exact/Precise Words, Vivid Words, Trite/Overused Words, Clichés)								●	●	●	●
Elaborating (Details, Examples, Dialogue, Quotations)								●	●	●	●
Unity and Coherence							●	●	●	●	●
Varying Sentence Structure, Word Order, and Sentence Length								●	●	●	●
Grammar											
Sentences											
Types (Declarative, Interrogative, Exclamatory, Imperative)							●	●	●	●	●
Structure (Simple, Compound, Complex)									●	●	●
Parts (Subjects/Predicates: Complete, Simple, Compound; Clauses: Independent, Subordinate; Phrases)								●	●	●	●
Complements (Direct/Indirect Objects; Predicate Nominatives/Adjectives)											●
Word Order							●				
Nouns (Singular, Plural, Common, Proper, Possessive, Collective, Abstract, Concrete; Abbreviations)							●	●	●	●	●
Verbs (Action, Helping, Linking, Transitive, Intransitive, Regular, Irregular)							●	●	●	●	●
Verb Tenses (Present, Past, Future; Present, Past, and Future Perfect)							●	●	●	●	●
Participles; Infinitives											
Adjectives (Common, Proper; Articles; Comparison)								●	●	●	●
Adverbs (Place, Time, Manner, Degree)								●	●	●	●
Pronouns (Subject, Object, Possessive, Reflexive, Demonstrative)							●	●	●	●	●
Prepositions; Prepositional Phrases										●	●
Conjunctions										●	●

Shaded Area **Modeling / Instruction / Application** ● **Tested**

Testing options include Skills Assessment, Holistic Reading Assessment, and Integrated Performance Assessment. For a complete scope and sequence of the kindergarten program, see the Teacher's Edition for that level.

GRADE/LEVEL	K/1	1–1	1–2	1–3	1–4	1–5	2	3	4	5	6
Usage											
Nouns (Abbreviations, Plural Forms, Appositives)				■	■	■	■ ●	■ ●	■ ●	■ ●	■ ●
Verbs (Subject-Verb Agreement)						■	■ ●	■ ●	■ ●	■ ●	■ ●
Adjectives (Articles; Positive, Comparative, Superlative)						■	■	■ ●	■ ●	■ ●	■ ●
Adverbs (Positive, Comparative, Superlative)									■ ●	■ ●	■ ●
Pronouns (Antecedents; Subject, Object, Possessive, and Reflexive Forms)					■	■	■ ●	■ ●	■ ●	■ ●	■ ●
Troublesome words								■	■	■	■
Mechanics											
Capitalization	■	■	■	■	■	■	■	■	■	■	■
Punctuation	■	■	■	■	■	■	■	■	■	■	■
Listening											
Participate in Cooperative Groups	■	■	■	■	■	■	■	■	■	■	■
Participate in Reader Response Groups			■	■	■	■	■	■	■	■	■
Receive Directions/Gain Information/Enhance Appreciation of Language	■	■	■	■	■	■	■	■	■	■	■
Respond to a Speaker by Retelling What Was Heard, Asking Questions, and/or Contributing Information	■	■	■	■	■	■	■	■	■	■	■
Analyze/Evaluate Intent and Content of Speaker's Message							■	■	■	■	■
Note Details	■	■	■	■	■	■	■	■	■	■	■
Visualize	■	■	■	■	■	■	■	■	■	■	■
Determine Problem/Solution	■	■	■	■	■	■	■	■	■	■	■
Make Justifiable Inferences	■	■	■	■	■	■	■	■	■	■	■
Identify Supporting Details	■	■	■	■	■	■	■	■	■	■	■
Recognize Persuasion								■	■	■	■
Identify Mood/Tone								■	■	■	■
Recognize Bias/Prejudice/Propaganda/Emotional Appeals										■	■
Speaking											
Participate in Cooperative Groups	■	■	■	■	■	■	■	■	■	■	■
Identify Audience/Purpose		■	■	■	■	■	■	■	■	■	■
Use a Variety of Words to Convey Meaning	■	■	■	■	■	■	■	■	■	■	■
Describe Personal Ideas, Feelings, Expressions, and Events	■	■	■	■	■	■	■	■	■	■	■
Retell Orally/Summarize Stories	■	■	■	■	■	■	■	■	■	■	■
Entertain Others with Stories, Poems, Dramatic Activities	■	■	■	■	■	■	■	■	■	■	■
Give Directions				■	■	■	■	■	■	■	■
Share Information	■	■	■	■	■	■	■	■	■	■	■
Compare/Contrast							■	■	■	■	■
Persuade Others							■	■	■	■	■
Develop Skill in Using the Conventions of English	■	■	■	■	■	■	■	■	■	■	■
Recite Rhyme, Chants, Poems	■	■	■	■	■	■	■				
Participate in Choral and Echo Reading	■	■	■	■	■	■	■	■	■	■	■
Read Orally	■	■	■	■	■	■	■	■	■	■	■
Present Oral Reports							■	■	■	■	■
Read Fluently with Expression, Phrasing, and Intonation		■	■	■	■	■	■	■	■	■	■
Conduct Interviews or Surveys								■	■	■	■
Viewing											
Appreciate/Interpret Artists' Techniques				■	■	■	■	■	■	■	■
View Information	■	■	■	■	■	■	■	■	■	■	■
View Critically	■	■	■	■	■	■	■	■	■	■	■
Compare Visual Materials	■	■	■	■	■	■	■	■	■	■	■
Compare Visual and Written Versions of the Same Materials										■	■
Handwriting											
Letter Forms (Manuscript, Cursive)	■	■	■	■	■	■	■	■	■	■	■
Elements	■	■	■	■	■	■	■	■	■		
Common Errors	■	■	■	■	■	■	■	■	■		
Integrated Spelling											
Sound-Letter Relationship (Consonants, Vowels, Schwa, Double Letters, Stress and Accents)		■	■	■	■	■	■	■	■	■	■
Word Structure (Plural Nouns/Inflected Verbs and Adjectives With and Without Spelling Changes, Prefixes, Suffixes, Greek and Latin Roots, Abbreviations, Contractions, Possessives, Compound Words)							■	■	■	■	■
Word Analysis (Syllable/Letter Patterns, Pronunciation and Stress, Phonograms, Rhyming Words, Related Words, Word Origins)					■	■	■	■	■	■	■
Study Methods and Strategies (Rhyming Words, Pronunciation, Word Shapes, Placeholders, Dictionary, Related Words, Mnemonic Devices, Proofreading)					■	■	■	■	■	■	■
Apply Spelling Generalizations					■ ●	■ ●	■ ●	■ ●	■ ●	■ ●	■ ●
Apply Spelling Strategies					■	■	■	■	■	■	■
Master Frequently Misspelled Words					■	■	■	■	■	■	■
Personal Spelling Lists								■	■	■	■

Shaded Area (■) **Modeling / Instruction / Application** ● **Tested**

Testing options include Skills Assessment, Holistic Reading Assessment, and Integrated Performance Assessment.
For a complete scope and sequence of the kindergarten program, see the Teacher's Edition for that level.

Reviewers

TEACHERS, ADMINISTRATORS, AND READING SPECIALISTS

Pamela Atkins
Teacher
Artesia Intermediate School
Artesia, New Mexico

Darlene A. Beamon
Teacher
Liberty School
Springfield, Massachusetts

Kay L. Bollinger
Teacher
Coolbaugh Elementary
Tobyhanna, Pennsylvania

Joanne Boston
Supervisor of Reading
School District of the City of York
York, Pennsylvania

Margaret Burley
Teacher
Miller School
Pittsburgh, Pennsylvania

Linda Chick
Teacher
Paloma Elementary
San Marcos, California

Patricia L. DeJagger
Coordinator for Curriculum Differentiation
Rochester Community Schools
Rochester, Michigan

Carla B. Ford, Ph.D.
Coordinator, Office of Early Learning Years
City of Baltimore Department of Education
Baltimore, Maryland

James R. Gambardella
Administrator
Providence School Department
Providence, Rhode Island

Susan L. Guy
Teacher
Joslyn Elementary
Omaha, Nebraska

Catherine Hill
Elementary Education Consultant
New Mexico Department of Education
Santa Fe, New Mexico

Jacque Huffman
Teacher
Eastside Elementary
Clinton, Mississippi

Jody Irola-Pishione
Teacher
Susan B. Anthony Elementary
Fresno, California

Cynthia Ko
Teacher
Glenview Elementary
Oakland, California

Beverly Lynch
Director of Communication Arts
N.Y.C. Board of Education, District 20
Brooklyn, New York

Karen A. McGee
Reading Coordinator
Bullis Curriculum & Instruction Center
Reno, Nevada

Susan M. Middleton
Librarian
La Jolla Country Day School
La Jolla, California

Cynthia R. Muse
Teacher
Patterson School
Philadelphia, Pennsylvania

Lisbé P. Page
Teacher
Wacona Elementary
Waycross, Georgia

Ruby B. Pannoni
Supervisor of Language Arts
Boyertown Area School District
Boyertown, Pennsylvania

Dr. Anne M. Primavera
Coordinator of Language Arts
Brentwood Union Free School District
Brentwood, New York

Barbara Schweiger
Supervisor, Reading Services
Omaha Public School
Omaha, Nebraska

Barbara Singleton
Curriculum Coordinator
Harrison County School District
Gulfport, Mississippi

Denise Sontag
Reading Coordinator
Community School District 27
Ozone Park, New York

Kathy Stehr
Director of Curriculum
Chandler Unified School District
Chandler, Arizona

Karen Whitworth–Thompson
Teacher
Forest Street School
Orange, New Jersey

JoAnn Yerkes
Principal
St. Columba Elementary
Chicago, Illinois

Lillian Yoshimura
Teacher
Prisk Elementary
Long Beach, California

Linda Zankowsky
Principal
Townsend Elementary
Townsend, Delaware

PARENTS

Tracy Clark
Benicia, California

Sharon Dominguez
Hazel Crest, Illinois

James Dorsett
Los Angeles, California

Karen Fultz
Chicago, Illinois

Kari Kruger
Santa Barbara, California

Diana Lukenbill
Boise, Idaho

Susan Monken
Solana Beach, California

Amy Sather
Santa Rosa, California

Kaylene T. White
Spanish Fort, Alabama

KINDERGARTEN REVIEWERS

Dara Lothi-Phaisith
Des Moines, Iowa

Shannon Applegate
Solana Vista Elementary
Solana Vista, CA

Eleanor Skolnick
P.S. 131Q
Jamaica, NY

SPANISH REVIEWERS

Eduardo Nunez
Citrus Grove Elementary School
Miami, FL

Martha Estrella
Cesar Chavez Elementary School
San Francisco, CA

Sylvia Hernandez
Bilingual Coordinator
Sheridan Street Elementary School
Los Angeles, CA

Index

This index includes references to both volumes of the Teacher's Edition *for grade 6 of* Signatures. *Page numbers for this level are in blue. The index is divided into six color-coded sections, as shown below.*

KEY

6-1 *Hidden Treasurers*

6-2 *Hidden Treasurers*

✓= Tested

Skills and Strategies

Reading

Comprehension

KEY
✓ = Tested   Blue = Pages in this volume

Skills and Strategies

Literary Appreciation

Phonics/Decoding

Reading Activities

KEY
✓ = Tested Blue = Pages in this volume

Reading Strategies

Index

Real-Life Reading

Study Skills

Skills and Strategies

KEY
✓ = Tested   Blue = Pages in this volume

Vocabulary

Thinking

Skills and Strategies

KEY
✓ = Tested   Blue = Pages in this volume

Index

Skills and Strategies

Writing and Language

Composition

Forms of Writing

KEY
✓ = Tested Blue = Pages in this volume

Skills and Strategies

Grammar

Skills and Strategies

Handwriting

Listening

KEY
✓ = Tested Blue = Pages in this volume

Mechanics

Oral Language Development

See *Listening* and *Speaking*.

Speaking

Skills and Strategies

Spelling

Usage

KEY
✓ = Tested   Blue = Pages in this volume

Skills and Strategies

Viewing

Assessment

Formal Assessment

Informal Assessment

Classroom Management

Connections

Flexible Grouping

KEY

✓ = Tested   Blue = Pages in this volume

Intervention Strategies

ESL/Title I Reading

ESL Title I Library

Strategies

Classroom Management

KEY
✓ = Tested   Blue = Pages in this volume

Students Acquiring English

Pacing

Scope and Sequence

Theme Projects

Integrated Curriculum

Centers

Content Areas

Art

Activities

Integrated Curriculum

KEY
✓ = Tested   Blue = Pages in this volume

Index

Integrated Curriculum

Discussion

Fact Finders

Theme Projects

Content-Area Reading

Nonfiction Selections

KEY
✓ = Tested Blue = Pages in this volume

Integrated Curriculum Focus Topics

Multiculturalism

Technology

CD-ROM

Floppy Disk

Internet

Video/Audio

Technology

Literature

Literary Forms/Genre

KEY

✓ = Tested Blue = Pages in this volume

Literature

Index

Responding to Literature

Literature

Selection Information

Artists

Authors/Poets

Author/Illustrator

Author/Photographer

Illustrators

KEY
✓ = Tested   Blue = Pages in this volume

Themes

Trade Books

permission to reprint copyrighted material, grateful acknowledgment is made to the following sources:

rry N. Abrams, Inc., New York: Cover illustration from *Children of Promise: African-American Literature d Art for Young People,* edited by Charles Sullivan. Copyright © 1991 by Charles Sullivan.

addin Books, Ltd., 28 Percy Street, London: Cover photograph from *How It Works: Cameras* by Ian Graham. 1990 Aladdin Books Ltd.

theneum Books for Young Readers, an imprint of Simon & Schuster: Cover illustration from *Digging to the ist: Excavations in Ancient Lands* by W. John Hackwell. Copyright © 1986 by W. John Hackwell. Cover lustration from *TUNDRA: The Arctic Land* by Bruce Hiscock. Copyright © 1986 by Bruce Hiscock. Cover lustration by Stephen Marchesi from *Don Quixote and Sancho Panza,* adapted by Margaret Hodges. lustration copyright © 1992 by Stephen Marchesi. Cover illustration from *Get Out of My Face* by David asterton. Copyright © 1991 by David Stuart Masterton. Cover illustration by Tudor Humphries from *Myths nd Legends from Around the World* by Sandy Shepherd. Copyright © 1994 by Marshall Editions evelopments Ltd

antam Books, a division of the Bantam Doubleday Dell Publishing Group, Inc.: Cover illustration from *'Aulaires' Book of Greek Myths* by Ingri and Edgar Parin D'Aulaire. Copyright © 1962 by Ingri and Edgar arin D'Aulaire. Cover illustration by Ben Stahl from *In Lane Three, Alex Archer* by Tessa Duder. Illustration opyright © 1991 by Ben Stahl.

arron's Educational Series, Inc.: Cover illustration from *Monet: Famous Artists* by Antony Mason. © 1994 y Aladdin Books Ltd.

ter Bedrick Books, Inc., 2112 Broadway, New York, NY 10023: Cover illustration from *History of Everyday hings: The Roman Empire and the Dark Ages* by Giovanni Caselli. © 1981 by Giovanni Caselli. Published in e USA and Canada by Peter Bedrick Books, Inc. Cover illustration from *What Do We Know About the omans?* by Mike Corbishley. Illustration © 1991 by Macdonald Young Books. Published in the USA and Canada Peter Bedrick Books, Inc. Cover illustration from *Inside Story Series: A Roman Villa* by Jacqueline Morley d John James. © 1992 by The Salariya Book Co. Ltd. Published in the USA and Canada by Peter Bedrick Books. over by Sergio and Andrea Ricciardi from *Leonardo da Vinci: Artist, Inventor, and Scientist of the naissance* by Francesca Romei. © 1994 by Donati-Giudici Associati. Published in the USA and Canada by ter Bedrick Books, Inc.

roline House, Boyds Mills Press, Inc.: Cover photograph by Don MacCarter from *Wildlife Rescue: The Work Dr. Kathleen Ramsay* by Jennifer Owings Dewey. Photograph copyright © 1994 by Don MacCarter. Cover otograph from *Yukon River: An Adventure to the Gold Fields of the Klondike* by Peter Lourie. Photograph pyright © 1992 by Peter Lourie.

rolrhoda Books, Inc., Minneapolis, MN: Cover photographs from *Bonnie Blair: Golden Streak* by Cathy itenbucher. Copyright © 1994 by Lerner Publications Company. Cover illustration by Gerald Talifero from *Bridge Dancers* by Carol Saller. Illustration copyright © 1991 by Carolrhoda Books, Inc.

ronicle Books, San Francisco, CA: Cover photograph from *A World Full of Animals: The Roger Caras Story* Roger Caras. Photograph copyright © 1993 by Capital Cities/ABC, Inc. Cover photograph from *Looking at otographs: People* by Jacques Lowe. © 1993 by Jacques Lowe.

arion Books, a Houghton Mifflin Company imprint: Cover photograph by Lewis Hines from *Kids at Work* Russell Freedman.

own Publishers, Inc.: Cover illustration from *Digging Up Tyrannosaurus Rex* by John R. Horner & Don ssem. Copyright © 1992 by John R. Horner & Don Lessem.

mbert Davis: Cover illustration by Lambert Davis from *The Shark Callers* by Eric Campbell. Illustration pyright © 1994 by Lambert Davis.

lacorte Press, a division of Bantam Doubleday Dell Publishing Group, Inc.: Cover illustration from *The merican Eye: Eleven Artists of the Twentieth Century* by Jan Greenberg and Sandra Jordan. Copyright © 1995 Jan Greenberg and Sandra Jordan. Cover illustration from *Snow Bound* by Harry Mazer. Copyright © 1973 Harry Mazer.

ll Books a division of Bantam Doubleday Dell: Cover illustration from *Drift* by William Mayne. Copyright 1985 by William Mayne.

al Books, a division of Penguin Books USA Inc.: Cover illustration from *The Young Artist* by Thomas Locker. pyright © 1989 by Thomas Locker

llon Press, an imprint of Silver Burdett Press, Simon & Schuster, Elementary: Cover photograph by Ric hy from *Zimbabwe: A Treasure of Africa* by Al Stark. © 1986 by Dillon Press, Inc

tton Childrens Books, a division of Penguin Books USA Inc.: Cover illustration by John Schoenherr from *e Wolfling* by Sterling North. Illustration copyright © 1969 by E.P. Dutton & Co., Inc.

slow Publishers, Inc.: Cover photograph from *Maya Lin: Architect and Artist* by Mary Malone. Copyright 1995 by Mary Malone. Photograph courtesy of AP/Wide World Photos.

rrar, Straus & Giroux, Inc.: Cover illustration by Juan Ramón Alonso from *The Apprentice* by Pilar Molina rente. Illustration copyright © 1989 by Juan Ramón Alonso. Cover photograph from *Working River* by d Powledge. Copyright © 1995 by Fred Powledge.

e Spirit Publishing, Inc., Minneapolis, MN (800) 735-7323: Cover illustration from *School Power: Strategies Succeeding in School* by Jeanne Shay Schumm, Ph.D. and Marguerite Radencich, Ph.D. Copyright © 1992 by nne Shay Schumm and Marguerite C. Radencich.

llimard Jeunesse: Cover illustration from *Paint and Painting.* Copyright © 1993 by Éditions Gallimard nesse; English translation copyright © by Scholastic Inc

vid R. Godine, Publisher, Inc.: Cover illustration by Pamela Johnson from *The Cuckoo Clock* by Mary Stolz. stration copyright © 1987 by Pamela Johnson

rperCollins Publishers: Cover illustration by Walter Gaffney-Kessell from *One Day in the Alpine Tundra* by n Craighead George. Illustration copyright © 1984 by Walter Gaffney-Kessell. Cover illustration by Michael as from *Bridge to Terabithia* by Katherine Paterson. Illustration copyright © 1987 by Michael Deas. Cover stration by Leo and Diane Dillon from *Home* by Michael J. Rosen. Illustration © 1992 by Leo and Diane on. Cover photograph by Joe McDonald from *Wolves* by Seymour Simon. Photograph © 1992 by Joe Donald. Cover photograph by Carole Palmer from *Maniac Magee* by Jerry Spinelli. Photograph copyright 992 by HarperCollins Publishers. Cover illustration by Nela McPheeters from *Jodie's Journey* by in Thiele. Illustration copyright © 1990 by Nela McPheeters.

bsmith Press LLC: Cover illustration by Stan Serkosky from *Research to Write* by Maity Schrecengost. pyright © 1994 by S. Maitland Schrecengost.

Holiday House, Inc.: Cover photograph by Lawrence Migdale from *Arctic Hunter* by Diane Hoyt-Goldsmith. Photograph copyright © 1992 by Lawrence Migdale.

Houghton Mifflin Company: Cover illustration from *Paddle-to-the-Sea* by Holling Clancy Holling. Copyright © 1941 by Holling Clancy Holling; copyright © renewed 1969 by Holling Clancy Holling. Cover illustration from *Black Star, Bright Dawn* by Scott O'Dell. Copyright © 1988 by Scott O'Dell.

Hyperion Books for Children: Cover photograph by Sigurgeir Jónasson from *Surtsey: The Newest Place on Earth* by Kathryn Lasky. Photograph copyright © 1992 by Sigurgeir Jónasson. Cover illustration by David Hockney from *Painting: Behind the Scenes* by Andrew Pekarik. Illustration © 1986 by David Hockney. Cover illustration from *Looking at Paintings: Dogs* by Peggy Roalf.

Dorling Kindersley Limited, London: Cover illustration from *Perspective* by Alison Cole. Copyright © 1992 by Dorling Kindersley Limited. Cover photograph from *Ancient Rome* by Simon James. Copyright © 1990 by Dorling Kindersley Limited. Published in the United States by Alfred A. Knopf, Inc., 1990. Cover photograph from *My First Photography Book* by Dave King. Copyright © 1994 by Dorling Kindersley Limited. Cover photographs from *Volcano & Earthquake* by Susanna Van Rose. Copyright © 1992 by Dorling Kindersley Limited. Published in the United States by Alfred A. Knopf, Inc., 1992. Cover illustration by Paolo Donati and Studio Illibill from *Amazing Buildings* by Philip Wilkinson. Copyright © 1993 by Dorling Kindersley Limited.

Alfred A. Knopf, Inc.: Cover photograph from *A Short Walk Around the Pyramids & Through the World of Art* by Philip M. Isaacson. Copyright © 1993 by Philip M. Isaacson.

Larousse PLC: Cover illustration from *The Kingfisher Book of the Ancient World: From the Ice Age to the Fall of Rome* by Hazel Mary Martell. Copyright © 1995 by Larousse plc. Published by Kingfisher. Cover illustration by Peter Bull and Ian Moores from *Tell Me About Everyday Things and How They Work,* edited by Jackie Goff. Copyright © 1991 by Grisewood & Dempsey Ltd. Published by Kingfisher Books Ltd.

Lerner Publications Company, Minneapolis, MN: Cover photograph by David Madison from *Florence Griffith Joyner: Dazzling Olympian* by Nathan Aaseng. Copyright © 1989 by Lerner Publications Company. Cover illustration from *Coubertin's Olympics: How the Games Began* by Davida Kristy. Illustration copyright © 1994 by Eric Peterson. Photograph courtesy of the International Olympic Committee Archives. Cover photograph from *Julia Morgan: Architect of Dreams* by Ginger Wadsworth. Copyright © 1990 by Ginger Wadsworth.

Little, Brown and Company: Cover photograph by Tony Duffy/Allsport USA from *Jackie Joyner-Kersee* by Neil Cohen. Copyright © 1992 by The Time Inc. Magazine Company. Cover photograph from *Wolves* by R. D. Lawrence. Copyright © 1990 by R. D. Lawrence. Cover illustration by Charles Geer from *Lost in the Barrens* by Farley Mowat. Copyright © 1956 by Farley Mowat. Cover illustration from *Georgia O'Keeffe* by Robyn Montana Turner. Copyright © 1991 by Robyn Montana Turner. Cover photograph from *Dorothea Lange (Portraits of Women Artists for Children)* by Robyn Montana Turner. Copyright © 1994 by Robyn Montana Turner. Cover illustration from *Mary Cassatt* by Robyn Montana Turner. Copyright © 1992 by Robyn Montana Turner.

Lodestar Books, an affiliate of Dutton Children's Books, a division of Penguin Books USA Inc.: Cover photograph by Michael Abramson, illustration by Roy Lichtenstein from *Roy Lichtenstein: The Artist at Work* by Lou Ann Walker. Photograph copyright © 1994 by Michael Abramson; illustration copyright © by Roy Lichtenstein

Lothrop, Lee & Shepard Books, a division of William Morrow & Company, Inc.: Cover photograph from *Cutters, Carvers & the Cathedral* by George Ancona. Copyright © 1995 by George Ancona. Cover photograph from *Natural Wonders: Stories Science Photos Tell* by Vicki Cobb. Copyright © 1990 by Vicki Cobb. Photograph courtesy of NASA. Cover illustration by T. C. Farrow from *The Dragon in the Cliff* by Sheila Cole. Illustration copyright © 1991 by T. C. Farrow. Cover illustration by Roy Doty from *How to Be School Smart* by Elizabeth James and Carol Barkin. Illustration copyright © 1988 by Roy Doty. Cover illustration from *How to Write a Great School Report* by Elizabeth James and Carol Barkin. Copyright © 1983 by Elizabeth James and Carol Barkin.

Macmillan Publishing Company: Cover illustration by Diane deGroat from *Jace the Ace* by Joanne Rocklin. Illustration copyright © 1990 by Diane deGroat

Stephen Marchesi: Cover illustration from *The Fear Place* by Phyllis Reynolds Naylor. Illustration copyright © 1994 by Stephen Marchesi.

Margaret K. McElderry Books, an imprint of Simon & Schuster: Cover illustration from *Drifting Snow: An Arctic Search* by James Houston. Copyright © 1992 by James Houston.

The Millbrook Press, Inc.: Cover illustration by Annie-Claude Martin from *The Romans: Life in the Empire* by Charles Guittard. Copyright © 1991 by Editions Nathan, Paris. Cover illustration from *Roman Places* by Sarah Howarth. Illustration courtesy of The Bridgeman Art Library. Cover photograph from *The Nutrition-Fitness Link* by Charles A. Salter. Photograph courtesy of Doug Demsey/White Light.

Morrow Junior Books, a division of William Morrow & Company, Inc: Cover illustration by David Small from *AS: A Surfeit of Similes* by Norton Juster. Illustration copyright © 1989 by David Small. Cover illustration from *Hold Fast to Dreams* by Andrea Davis Pinkney. Copyright © 1995 by Andrea Davis Pinkney. Cover photograph from *Volcanoes* by Seymour Simon. Copyright © 1988 by Seymour Simon.

Orchard Books, New York: Cover illustration by Neil Waldman from *The Voyage of the Frog* by Gary Paulsen. Illustration copyright © 1989 by Neil Waldman.

Oxford University Press: Cover photograph from *Pompeii* by Peter Connolly. © 1979, 1990 by Peter Connolly. Photograph courtesy of Werner Forman Archive, London.

Philomel Books: Cover illustration from *Boy of the Painted Cave* by Justin Denzel.

Rising Crescent Publishing: Cover from *Making the Grades* by Frederick Hageman. Copyright © 1995 by Frederick Hageman

Rizzoli International Publications, Inc., New York: Cover illustration from *Walking the Log: Memories of a Southern Childhood* by Bessie Nickens. Copyright © 1994 by Bessie Nickens. Cover illustration from *A Weekend with Velázquez* by Florian Rodari, translated by Ann Keay Beneduce. Copyright © 1992 by Editions d'Art Albert Skira S.A., Geneva; English edition copyright © 1993 by Rizzoli International Publications, Inc.

Runestone Press, a division of Lerner Publications Company, Minneapolis, MN: Cover illustration from *Sunk! Exploring Underwater Archaeology* by Runestone Press, Geography Department. Copyright © 1994 by Runestone Press, a division of Lerner Publications Company

Scholastic Inc.: Cover illustration by Mark Alan Weatherby from *The Call of the Wolves* by Jim Murphy. Illustration copyright © 1989 by Mark Alan Weatherby. Cover illustration by Troy Howell from *Favorite Greek Myths* by Mary Pope Osborne. Illustration copyright © 1989 by Troy Howell.

Simon & Schuster Books for Young Readers, a division of Simon & Schuster: Cover photograph from *Jacques-Henri Lartigue: Boy with a Camera* by John Cech. Photograph copyright © 1994 by L'Association des Amis de

Jacques-Henri Lartigue. Cover illustration from *Talking with Artists* by Pat Cummings. Copyright © 1992 by Pat Cummings. Cover photograph by Baron Hugo van Lawick from *My Life with the Chimpanzees* by Jane Goodall. Photograph copyright © by National Geographic Society. Cover photograph by George Rodger from *African Landscapes* by Warren J. Halliburton, edited by Kathilyn Solomon Probosz. Copyright © 1993 by Crestwood House, Macmillan Publishing Company. Cover illustration from *Winners and Losers* by Stephen Hoffius. Copyright © 1993 by Stephen Hoffius. Cover photograph from *Peak Performance: Sports, Science, and the Body in Action* by Emily Isberg. Copyright © 1989 by Emily Isberg and WGBH Educational Foundation. Cover illustration by Arvis Stewart from *The Macmillan Book of Greek Gods and Heroes* by Alice Low. Copyright © 1985 by Macmillan Publishing Company, a division of Macmillan, Inc. Cover photograph by Dan Guravich from *Arctic Summer* by Downs Matthews. Photograph copyright © 1993 by Dan Guravich. Cover illustration by Neil Waldman from *Dogsong* by Gary Paulsen. Copyright © 1985 by Bradbury Press. Cover illustration from *Jim Thorpe: Olympic Champion* by Guernsey Van Riper, Jr. Copyright © 1956, 1961, 1983 by the Bobbs-Merrill Company, Inc.

Stackpole Books: Cover photograph by S. Peter Lewis from *Second Ascent: The Story of Hugh Herr* by Alison Osius. Copyright © 1991 by Stackpole Books.

Steck-Vaughn Company: Cover photograph by All Sport (Simon Bruty) from *Canoeing* by Donna Bailey. Copyright 1991 by Steck-Vaughn Company.

Viking Penguin, a division of Penguin Books USA Inc.: Cover illustration from *Take a Look* by Rosemary Davidson. Cover illustration by Bill Le Fever from *Ancient Greece* by Rowena Loverance and Tim Wood. Illustration copyright © 1992 by Reed International Books Ltd., on behalf of Hamlyn Children's Books.

Neil Waldman: Cover illustration by Neil Waldman from *Hatchet* by Gary Paulsen. Illustration copyright © 1987 by Bradbury Press.

Walker and Company, 435 Hudson Street, New York, NY 10014: Cover illustration from *Biography of a River: The Living Mississippi* by Edith McCall. Copyright © 1990 by Edith McCall. Cover illustration from *Swift Rivers* by Cornelia Meigs. Copyright 1932, 1937 by Cornelia Meigs; copyright renewed © 1964 by Cornelia Meigs.

Franklin Watts, Inc.: Cover photographs from *The Summer Olympics* by Caroline Arnold. Photographs courtesy of UPI/Bettmann Newsphotos, Inc. Cover illustration by S. D. Schindler from *Digging Up the Past: The Story of an Archaeological Adventure* by Carollyn James. Illustration copyright © 1990 by S. D. Schindler.

Wayland Publishers Ltd., Hove, England: Cover illustration from *Western Art 1600-1800* by Christopher McHugh. Illustration courtesy of Glasgow Art Gallery and Museum, Scotland.

Zoë Books Limited: Cover photograph by C. M. Dixon from *The Romans and Pompeii* by Philip Steele. Copyright © 1994 by Zoë Books Limited. Cover photograph from *The Greeks and Troy* by Deborah Tyler. Copyright © 1993 by Zoë Books Limited. Photograph courtesy of Ancient Art & Architecture Collection. Published in the United States by Dillon Press, an imprint of Silver Burdett Press, Simon & Schuster Elementary.

PHOTO CREDITS

Lesson 1: T17(tr & bl), Patti Murray/Earth Scenes;T19(l), Courtesy of Bacon Publishing, Idaho;T19(r),Tim Kelly/Black Star/Harcourt Brace & Co.;T33, Bill Beatty/Earth Scenes;T34, Gerard Lacz/Animals Animals;T48, Ellen Senisi/Harcourt Brace & Co.;T49, Jeanne White/Photo Researchers, Inc.;T55, Francis Clark Westfield/Harcourt Brace & Co.;T59, Stephanie Hollyman/Gamma Liaison;T61(t&b) Francis Clark Westfield/Harcourt Brace & Co.

Lesson 2: T65(tr & bl), Bie Bostrom/Harcourt Brace & Co.;T67(r),Tom Sobolik/Black Star/Harcourt Brace & Co.; T69, Steve Chenn/West Light;T71, Francis Clark Westfield/Harcourt Brace & Co.;T78, Bill Ross/West Light;T82, SuperStock;T84, Herbert Lange/West Light;T96, Robert Brenn/PhotoEdit;T97, Ellen Senisi/Harcourt Brace & Co.; T99, Francis Clark Westfield/Harcourt Brace & Co.;T106, Bie Bostrom/Harcourt Brace & Co.;T107, Francis Clark Westfield/Harcourt Brace & Co.

Lesson 3: T115, Dale Higgins/Harcourt Brace & Co.;T116, SuperStock;T116(ball) Bie Bostrom/Harcourt Brace & Co.; T119,Tony Freeman/PhotoEdit;T125, SuperStock;T131, Adrienne T. Gibson/Animals Animals;T139, Ellen Senisi/Harcourt Brace & Co.;T141, Skjold Photographs;T149, Francis Clark Westfield/Harcourt Brace & Co.

Lesson 4: T163, Courtesy of Little, Brown Publishers;T165, Breck P. Kent/Animals Animals;T167, Francis Clark Westfield/Harcourt Brace & Co.;T169, Emil Muench/Photo Researchers, Inc.;T171, J. Cooke/Animals Animals; T173, Donald Specker/Earth Scenes;T187, David Young-Wolff/PhotoEdit;T191, Uniphoto;T194, Chromosohm/Joe Sohm/Photo Researchers, Inc.

Lesson 5: T233(tr & tl), Ken Bennett/Black Star/Harcourt Brace & Co.;T234, Mary Evans Picture Library/Photo Researchers, Inc.;T235, Jonathan Blair/Woodfin Camp & Assoc.;T238, Dallas & John Heaton/West Light;T239, Uniphoto;T240, Art Resource, NY;T242, Erich Lessing/Art Resource, NY;T250, Francis Clark Westfield/ Harcourt Brace & Co.;T251, Scala/Art Resource, NY;T253, Francis Clark Westfield/Harcourt Brace & Co.;T254, SuperStock;T255(l), Francis Clark Westfield/Harcourt Brace & Co.;T255(r), Jacana/Photo Researchers, Inc.;T259, Francis Clark Westfield/Harcourt Brace & Co.;T260(l), Scala/Art Resource, NY;T260(tr), Uniphoto;T260(br), Bettmann

Lesson 6: T269, Billy E. Barnes/PhotoEdit;T276, Giraudon/Art Resource, NY;T281, Scala/Art Resource, NY;T282, Valley of the Kings, Thebes, Egypt/Kurt Scholz/ SuperStock;T294, Victoria Bowen/Harcourt Brace & Co.;T295, Giraudon/Art Resource, NY;T297, Victoria Bowen/Harcourt Brace & Co.;T299, Francis Clark Westfield/ Harcourt Brace & Co.;T301, Laurent Van Der Stockt/Gamma Liaison;T303, NASA/Mark Marten/Science Source/Photo Researchers, Inc.;T304(l), Dallas & John Heaton/West Light;T304(r), Uniphoto;T305(t), Silvio Fiove/SuperStock;T305(b), Bridgeman/Art Resource, NY

Lesson 7: T314, Manfred Gottschalk/West Light;T315, SuperStock;T319, Phil Borden/PhotoEdit;T326, Gian Berto Vanni/Art Resource;T328, Archive Photos;T340, Bie Bostrom/Harcourt Brace & Co.;T341(tl & bl), SuperStock;T343, Frank Siteman/Uniphoto;T345, Rafael Macia/Photo Researchers, Inc.;T350(tr & br), SuperStock

Lesson 8: T357, Tom Sobolik/Black Star/Harcourt Brace & Co.;T358, The Granger Collection, New York;T359, SuperStock;T367, The Granger Collection, New York;T379, Francis Clark Westfield/Harcourt Brace & Co.;T381, ©1987 Lawrence Migdale;T385, Larry Mayer/Liaison International;T387(l), Francis Clark Westfield/Harcourt Brace & Co.;T387(r), Mary Kale Denny/PhotoEdit

Lesson 9: T426, The Granger Collection, New York;T429, Envision;T433(l), ©1995 Matthew Gilson;T433(r), Dale Higgins/Harcourt Brace & Co.;T435, Francis Clark Westfield/Harcourt Brace & Co.;T439, Bie Bostrom/ Harcourt Brace & Co.;T441, Tony Sica/Gamma Liaison;T442, Skjold Photographs;T443, Harcourt Brace & Co.;T448, Stan Pantvoic/Photo Researchers, Inc.;T462, Francis Clark Westfield/Harcourt Brace & Co.;T463, Francis Clark Westfield/Harcourt Brace & Co.;T465, Ellen Senisi/Harcourt Brace & Co.;T466, Bie Bostrom/ Harcourt Brace & Co.;T467, Francis Clark Westfield/Harcourt Brace & Co.;T472, Bie Bostrom/Harcourt Brace & C T473(bl), Bie Bostrom/Harcourt Brace & Co.;T473(br), Victoria Bowen/Harcourt Brace & Co.

Lesson 10: T479, Rick Friedman/Black Star/Harcourt Brace & Co.;T481, Archive Photos;T485, Bettmann;T486 SuperStock;T488, Uniphoto;T491, The Granger Collection, New York;T496, Bill Aron/PhotoEdit;T510; Bettman T517, Bettmann;T521(l), Ellen Senisi/Harcourt Brace & Co.,T521(r), Francis Clark Westfield/Harcourt Brace & Co.; T527, Francis Clark Westfield/Harcourt, Brace & Co.

Lesson 11: T535, Gabi Rona/Motion Picture & Television;T536, SuperStock;T537, Uniphoto;T542, Uniphoto; T544, Archive Photos;T548, John Sanford/Science Photo Library/Photo Researchers, Inc.;T549, Archive Photos; T557, Larry Mulvehill/Photo Researchers, Inc.;T572, Ellen Senisi/Harcourt Brace & Co.;T573, Ellen Senisi/ Harcourt Brace & Co.;T575 Francis Clark Westfield/Harcourt Brace & Co.;T581, Francis Clark Westfield/ Harcourt Brace & Co.

Lesson 12: T589(tl & tr), Dale Higgins/Harcourt Brace & Co.;T590, The Granger Collection, New York;T593, Ellen Senisi/Photosynthesis;T595, Felicia Martinez/PhotoEdit;T596, Archive Photos;T600, Ken Cole/Animals Animals;T601, SuperStock;T602, Ellen Senisi/Harcourt Brace & Co.;T605, Elena Rooraid/PhotoEdit;T606, SuperStock;T608, Alan Oddie/PhotoEdit;T610, Victoria Bowen/Harcourt Brace & Co.;T612, John Neubauer/ PhotoEdit;T623, Skjold Photographs;T629(l), Richard Shiell/Animals Animals;T629(r), Bie Bostrom/ Harcourt Brace & Co.;T630, David Young Wolff/PhotoEdit;T631, Francis Clark Westfield/Harcourt Brace & Co.

Lesson 13: T665, Nancy Pierce/Black Star/Harcourt Brace & Co.;T666, Spectrum Colour Library/West Light; T673, Scala/Art Resource, NY;T676, Joan Meisel;T683, Francis Clark Westfield/Harcourt Brace & Co.;T689(l), Stuart Westmorland/Photo Researchers, Inc.;T689(r), Uniphoto;T691, Jerry Wachter/Photo Researchers, Inc.; T692, Victoria Bowen/Harcourt Brace & Co.;T693, Victoria Bowen/Harcourt Brace & Co.

Lesson 14: T705, Ellise Fuchs;T706, Bob Daemmrich/Uniphoto;T707, Bruce Waters/Uniphoto;T709, Michael Newman/PhotoEdit;T717, Bettmann Newsphotos;T718, Australian Picture Library/John Carnemolla/West Ligh T723, B. Daemmrich/Uniphoto;T726, Victoria Bowen/Harcourt Brace & Co.,T727, Ellen Senisi/Harcourt Brace & Co.; T729, Francis Clark Westfield/Harcourt Brace & Co.;T733, Ralph Starkweather/West Light;T737, Ellen Senisi/ Harcourt Brace & Co.

Lesson 15: T755, Bie Bostrom/Harcourt Brace & Co.;T758, Erich Lessing/PhotoEdit;T759, SuperStock;T765, SuperStock;T768, Scala/Art Resource, NY;T772, Bie Bostrom/Harcourt Brace & Co.;T775, Bie Bostrom/ Harcourt Brace & Co.;T786, Bie Bostrom/Harcourt Brace & CO.;T789, The Granger Collection, New York;T79 Francis Clark Westfield/Harcourt Brace & Co.;T791, Francis Clark Westfield/Harcourt Brace & Co.;T794, Franc Clark Westfield/Harcourt Brace & Co.;T797, Susan Lapides;T799, Francis Clark Westfield/Harcourt Brace & Co T803(l), Robert & Eunice Pearcy/Earth Scenes;T803(r), Chromosohm/Sohm/Photo Researchers, Inc.;T804(bl, & cr), SuperStock;T805, Bie Bostrom, Harcourt Brace & Co.

Lesson 16: T812, SuperStock;T813, The Granger Collection, New York;T817, SuperStock;T818, SuperStock; T819, Anna E. Zuckerman/PhotoEdit;T825, U.S. Geological Survey/Science Photo Library/Photo Researchers, Inc.;T827, Mike Andrews/Earth Scenes;T831, Scala/Art Resource, NY;T835, Stan Goldberg/SuperStock;T836, James Stevenson/Photo Researchers, Inc.;T846, Ellen Senisi/Harcourt Brace & Co.;T851(bl & tl), Francis Clark Westfield/Harcourt Brace & Co.;T851(r), Philippe Brylak/Gamma Liaison;T855, Francis Clark Westfield/ Harcourt Brace & Co.;T856(br & tr), Breck P. Kent/Earth Scenes;T857(l), Jean-Claude Aunos/Gamma Liaison; T857(r), Charlie Ott/Photo Researchers, Inc.

Lesson 17: T894, Erich Lessing/Art Resource, NY;T898, Kul Bhatia/Photo Researchers, Inc.;T899, SuperStock T901, Courtesy of The International Side Saddle Organization;T904, Mike Yamashita/West Light;T907, Francis Clark Westfield/Harcourt Brace & Co.;T911, Francis Clark Westfield/Harcourt Brace & Co.;T913, Ellen Senisi/ Harcourt Brace & Co.;T914, Scala/Art Resource, NY;T917, SuperStock;T920(l), Erich Lessing/Art Resource, NY T920(r), Michael Newman/PhotoEdit

Lesson 18: T927, Courtesy of Farrar Straus & Giroux;T928, The Bettmann Archive;T933, Tony Freeman/ PhotoEdit;T935, Scala/Art Resource, NY;T940, Lawrence Migdale/Photo Researchers, Inc.;T952, Museo del Prado, Madrid, Spain/A.K.G., Berlin/SuperStock;T953, Francis Clark Westfield/Harcourt Brace & Co.;T955, Ellen Senisi/Photosynthesis

Lesson 19: T969(tr & bl), Bie Bostrom/Harcourt Brace & Co.;T971, Larry Evans/Black Star/Harcourt Brace & Co.; T972(t), Bettmann Archive;T972(b), SuperStock;T975, Ellen Senisi/Harcourt Brace & Co.;T983, SuperStock; T984, Ulrike Welsch/Photo Researchers, Inc.;T987, Bie Bostrom/Harcourt Brace & Co.;T996, Ellen Senisi/ Harcourt Brace & Co.;T997, Marja Paraskevas/Harcourt Brace & Co.;T999, ©1987 Lawrence Migdale;T1001, Ellen Senisi/Harcourt Brace & Co.;T1006(tl), Mehau Kulyk/Science Photo Library/Photo Researchers, Inc.; T1006(tr), Doug Plummer/Photo Researchers, Inc.;T1006(bc), Larry Mulvehill/Photo Researchers, Inc.;T1007, Francis Clark Westfield/Harcourt Brace & Co.

Lesson 20: T1011, Bie Bostrom/Harcourt Brace & Co.;T1013, Warren Faubel/Black Star/Harcourt Brace & Co T1014, Courtesy Marc Schurer;T1020, Tony Freeman/ PhotoEdit;T1029, UPI/Bettmann;T1038, Francis Clark Westfield/Harcourt Brace & Co.;T1039, Courtesy Karen Hudson;T1041, Ellen Senisi/Photosynthesis;T1048, Llewellyn/ Uniphoto;T1049(l), CC Lockwood/Earth Scenes;T1049(r), Bill Ross/West Light

Lesson 21: T1088, Amy Etra/PhotoEdit;T1093, UPI/Bettmann;T1095, B. Daemmrich/The Image Works;T1102, National Portrait Gallery, London/SuperStock;T1113, UPI/Bettmann

Lesson 22: T1129, Larry Mayer/Black Star/Harcourt Brace & Co.;T1130, Joseph Nettis/Photo Researchers, Inc T1139, Pat & Tom Leeson/Photo Researchers, Inc.;T1145, Kenneth Murray/Photo Researchers, Inc.;T1148, Richard Hutchings/Photo Researchers, Inc.;T1154, Francis Clark Westfield/Harcourt Brace & Co.;T1159, Renee Lynn/Photo Researchers, Inc.;T1161, Ellen Senisi/Photosynthesis;T1163(l), Francis Clark Westfield/ Harcourt Brace & Co.;T1163(r), Courtesy of Jeff Place

Lesson 23: T1177, Courtesy of Ellan Young Photography/HarperCollins;T1178, David Young-Wolff/PhotoEdit; T1181, Tony Freeman/PhotoEdit;T1184, SuperStock;T1186, Tony Freeman/PhotoEdit;T1198, Francis Clark Westfield/Harcourt Brace & Co.;T1199, Thomas Kitchin/Tom Stack & Assoc.;T1201, ©1987 Lawrence Migdale T1207, SuperStock;T1208(tl), Uniphoto;T1208(bl & bc)), Joe McDonald/Animals Animals;T1208(tc), Len Rue Jr./Animals Animals;T1208(r), SuperStock

Lesson 24: T1217, Uniphoto;T1219, Barbara von Hoffmann/Tom Stack & Assoc.;T1220, Robert Winslow/Tom Stack & Assoc.;T1225, Victoria Bowen/Harcourt Brace & Co.;T1229, John Shaw/Tom Stack & Assoc.;T1231, Thomas Kitchin/Tom Stack & Assoc.;T1233, Bob Daemmrich/Uniphoto;T1237, Jim Brandenburg/Minden Pictures;T1239, W. Perry Conway/Tom Stack & Assoc.;T1240, Gerald & Buff Corsi/Tom Stack & Assoc.;T1248 Francis Clark Westfield/Harcourt Brace & Co.;T1249, Francis Clark Westfield/ Harcourt Brace & Co.;T1251, ©1991 Lawrence Migdale;T1252, Thomas Kitchin/Tom Stack & Assoc.;T1258(l), SuperStock;T1258(r), Boisvieux/Explorer/Photo Researchers, Inc.